# The Quotable Woman

# The Quotable Woman

## 1800-On

compiled and edited by

## Elaine Partnow

Anchor Books
Anchor Press/Doubleday
GARDEN CITY, NEW YORK
1978

Anchor Books Edition: 1978
This book was originally published in hardcover by Corwin Books.

ISBN: 0-385-14520-9
Library of Congress Catalog Card Number 78-7765

*This book is dedicated
in memoriam
to my mother
Jeanette Bernstein Partnow
1912–1973
who gifted me with the joy of reading*

# Contents

# Permissions and Acknowledgments

The following have given their permission for inclusion of extracts from the works named; this permission is gratefully acknowledged.

Bantam Books, Inc. From *The Feminist Papers: From Adams to de Beauvoir*. Edited and with Introductory Essays by Alice S. Rossi. Copyright © 1973 by Alice S. Rossi. Published by Columbia University Press and Bantam Books, Inc. Reprinted by permission of Bantam Books, Inc.

Bouquet Music, United Artists Music, Mediarts, Inc. From *On My Way to Where* by Dory Previn. Copyright © 1971. Saturday Review Press. Used by permission.

Broadside Series Press. From *Prophets for a New Day* by Margaret Walker. Copyright © 1970. Used by permission.

Curtis Brown, Ltd. From "A Ballad of Anthologies" by Phyllis McGinley. Published in the *Saturday Evening Post*, December 20, 1941. Reprinted by permission of Curtis Brown, Ltd. Copyright © 1941 by Phyllis McGinley.

Cleveland Press. From *Collected Poems* by Dilys Laing. Copyright © 1967 by David Laing. Used by permission of Cleveland Press and Western Reserve University.

Thomas Y. Crowell Company, Inc. Reprinted from *Poems From the Hebrew* by Robert Mezey. Copyright © 1773 by Robert Mezey. With permission of Thomas Y. Crowell Co., Inc.

Dodd, Mead & Company. From *India's Love Lyrics* by Laurence Hope. Copyright © 1922. Used by permission.

Doubleday & Company, Inc. From *Poems* by Barbara Guest. Copyright © 1962 by Doubleday & Co., Inc. Reprinted by permission of Doubleday & Company, Inc.

Dramatists Play Service, Inc. From *Slam the Door Softly* by Clare Boothe Luce. Copyright © 1970. Used by permission.

Farrar, Straus & Giroux, Inc. From *My Mother's House* by Colette, translated by Una Vicenzo Troubridge and Enid McLeod. Copyright © 1953 by Farrar, Straus and Young, Inc. Reprinted with the permission of Farrar, Straus & Giroux, Inc.

From *Play It As It Lays* by Joan Didion. Copyright © 1970 by Joan Didion. Reprinted with the permission of Farrar, Straus & Giroux, Inc.

Grove Press, Inc. From *A Taste of Honey* by Shelagh Delaney. Reprinted by permission of Grove Press, Inc. Copyright © 1959 by Theatre Workshop (Pioneer Theatres, Ltd.).

Harcourt Brace Jovanovich, Inc. From *A Room of One's Own* by Virginia Woolf. Copyright © 1929 by Harcourt Brace Jovanovich, Inc.; copyright © 1957 by Leonard Woolf. Reprinted by permission of the publisher.

From *The World of Gwendolyn Brooks* (1971) by Gwendolyn Brooks: "We Real Cool" copyright © 1959 by Gwendolyn Brooks; "Pete at the Zoo," copyright © 1960 by Gwendolyn Brooks; and about 46 lines of poetry, copyright © 1971 by Gwendolyn Brooks Blakely; by permission of Harper & Row, Publishers, Inc.

From *Collected Poems*. Copyright 1917, 1920, 1921, 1922, 1923, 1931, 1934, 1940, 1945, 1948, 1950, 1951, 1958, 1962 by Edna St. Vincent Millay and Norma Millay Ellis.

Excerpts from *Elizabeth Cady Stanton: As Revealed in Her Letters, Diary and Reminiscences*, edited by Theodore Stanton and Harriot Stanton Blatch. By permission of Harper & Row, Publishers, Inc.

Excerpts from *Ariel* by Sylvia Plath. Copyright © 1965 by Ted Hughes. By permission of Harper & Row, Publishers, Inc.

From *Pilgrim at Tinker Creek* by Annie Dillard. Copyright © 1974 by Annie Dillard. Used by permission.

Hereford Music. From "Laid Off," "Get Off Me Baby," "Started Out Fine" by Holly Near. Copyright © 1973. Used by permission.

Houghton Mifflin Company. From *Silent Spring* by Rachel Carson. Copyright © 1962 by Rachel L. Carson. Reprinted by permission of Houghton Mifflin Company.

From *The Complete Poetical Works of Amy Lowell*. Copyright © 1955 by Houghton Mifflin Company. Reprinted by permission of Houghton Mifflin Company.

Indiana University Press. From *Poems 1930–1960* by Josephine Miles. Copyright © 1960 by

Josephine Miles. Used by permission of Macmillan Company and Indiana University Press.

From *Selected Poems of Gabriela Mistral*, translated by Langston Hughes. Copyright © 1957. Used by permission.

International Creative Management. From *Waterlily Fire* and *The Speed of Darkness* by Muriel Rukeyser. Copyright © 1962, 1968 by Muriel Rukeyser. Used by permission.

Irving Music, Inc. From "I Am Woman," words by Helen Reddy, music by Ray Burton. Copyright © 1971, 1972, Irving Music, Inc., and Buggerlugs Music Co. (BMI). All rights reserved. Used by permission.

Alfred A. Knopf, Inc. From *Collected Poems of Elinor Wylie* by Elinor Wylie. Copyright © 1932 by Alfred A. Knopf, Inc., and renewed 1960 by Edwina C. Rubenstein. Reprinted by permission of the publisher.

From *The Woman's Eye* by Anne Tucker. Copyright © 1973. Used by permission.

Little, Brown and Company. *Four Plays* by Enid Bagnold. Copyright © 1964 by Enid Bagnold. By permission of Little, Brown and Co. in association with the Atlantic Monthly Press.

Liveright Publishing Corporation. From *My Life* by Isadora Duncan. By permission of Liveright Publishing Corporation. Copyright © 1927 by Boni & Liveright, Inc. Copyright renewed 1955 by Liveright Publishing Corporation.

Macmillan, Inc. The Vera Brittain quotations from *Poems of the War and After* are included with the permission of her literary executors, Sir George Catlin and Paul Berry.

Reprinted with permission of Macmillan Publishing Co., Inc., from *Collected Poems* by Marianne Moore. Copyright © 1935 by Marianne Moore, renewed 1963 by Marianne Moore and T. S. Eliot. Reprinted with permission of Macmillan Publishing Co., Inc., from *Collected Poems* by Marianne Moore. Copyright © 1941 by Marianne Moore, renewed 1969 by Marianne Moore. Reprinted with permission of Macmillan Publishing Co., Inc., from *Collected Poems* by Marianne Moore. Copyright © 1944 by Marianne Moore, renewed 1972 by Marianne Moore.

Edward B. Marks Music Corporation. From "God Bless the Child" by Billie Holiday. © Copyright: Edward B. Marks Music Corporation. Used by Permission.

McClelland & Stewart Ltd. From *Over the Hills of Home* by Lillian Leveridge. Reprinted by permission of the Canadian Publishers, McClelland & Stewart, Ltd., Toronto.

William Morris Agency, Inc. From *Funnyhouse of a Negro* by Adrienne Kennedy. Reprinted by permission of William Morris Agency, Inc. Copyright © 1969 by Adrienne Kennedy.

William Morrow & Co., Inc. From *Black Feeling, Black Talk, Black Judgement* by Nikki Giovanni. Reprinted by permission of William Morrow & Company, Inc. Copyright © 1968, 1970 by Nikki Giovanni.

Ms. Magazine. From 1972, 1973, 1974, 1975 issues. Copyright © *Ms.* Magazine. Reprinted with permission.

New York Urban Coalition, Inc. Poster copy by Corita Kent. Used by permission.

Reprinted from *Eleanor: The Years Alone* by Joseph P. Lash. By permission of W. W. Norton & Company, Inc. Copyright © 1972 by Joseph P. Lash.

Reprinted from *The Feminine Mystique* by Betty Friedan. By permission of W. W. Norton & Company, Inc. Copyright © 1974, 1963 by Betty Friedan.

Reprinted from *Snapshots of A Daughter-in-Law, Poems, 1954, 1962*, by Adrienne Rich. By permission of W. W. Norton & Company, Inc. Copyright © 1956, 1957, 1958, 1959, 1960, 1961, 1962, 1963, 1967 by Adrienne Rich Conrad.

Reprinted from *The Will to Change, Poems, 1968–1970*, by Adrienne Rich. By permission of W. W. Norton & Company, Inc. Copyright © 1971 by W. W. Norton & Company, Inc.

Random House, Inc. From *Sisterhood Is Powerful* edited by Robin Morgan, from the Introduction by Robin Morgan. Copyright © 1970 by Robin Morgan. Used by permission. From same book, "Does the Law Oppress Women?" by Diane Schulder. Used by author's permission. From the same book, "Women and the Welfare System" by Carol Glassman. Used by author's permission. From *Monster: Poems of Robin Morgan* by Robin Morgan. Copyright © 1970 by Robin Morgan. Reprinted by permission of Random House, Inc.

From *Toys in the Attic* by Lillian Hellman. Copyright © 1959 by Lillian Hellman. Used by permission.

From *Over Twenty-One* by Ruth Gordon. Copyright © 1943 by Ruth Gordon. Used by permission.

From *The Chalk Garden* by Enid Bagnold. Copyright © 1953 by Enid Bagnold. Used by permission.

From *A Raisin in the Sun* by Lorraine Hansberry. Copyright © 1958 by Lorraine Hansberry. Used by permission.

From *The Women* by Clare Boothe Luce. Copyright © 1936 by Clare Boothe Luce. Used by permission.

It was simply not possible to contact all living contributors (or their representatives) quoted in these pages in order to request permission to be included in this work. This was done only with the more extensive excerpts from individual sources. But acknowledgments—and deepest thanks—are given to every woman quoted and to all the publishers, periodicals, and other sources without whose talent, commitment, and very existence this book could not have been compiled.

## BOOK PUBLISHERS

Abbey • Worthington, Robin, *Thinking About Marriage* (1971).

Abelard-Schuman • Leek, Sybil, *The Magic Within You* (1971).

Academic • Mullick, Dhiren, *Indira Speaks* (1972).

Ace • Le Guin, Ursula, *The Left Hand of Darkness* (1969).

Albatross • Sayers, Dorothy, *Busman's Honeymoon* (1947).

Aldine • Reeves, Nancy G., *Womankind Beyond the Stereotypes* (1971).

Allen & Unwin • Bingham, Madeleine, *Scotland Under Mary Stuart* (1971). Brittain, Vera, *The Rebel Passion* (1964); *The Envoy Extraordinary* (1965). Hurst, Florence J., *From Pinafores to Politics* (1924).

Alston Rivers • Lathbury, Eva, *Mrs. Meyer's Pupil* (1907).

Anchor • Aidoo, Ama Ata, *No Sweetness Here* (1970). Parker, Gail Thain, *The Oven Birds: American Women on Womanhood, 1820–1920* (1972).

Angus & Robertson • Bhatia, Krishnan, *Indira* (1974).

Appleton-Century-Crofts • Bacon, Josephine, *Truth o' Women* (1923). Barnes, Gilbert Hobbs, and Dumond, Dwight L., eds., *Letters of Theodore Dwight Weld, Antoinette Grimké Weld, and Sarah Grimké, 1822–1844*, Vols. I and II (1934). De Wolfe, Elsie, *The House in Good Taste* (1920). Gale, Zona, *Miss Lulu Bett* (1920);

*The Biography of Blade* (1924). Gilman, Charlotte Perkins, *The Living of Charlotte Perkins Gilman* (1935). Wharton, Edith, *A Backward Glance* (1934).

Arbor House • Calisher, Hortense, *Queenie* (1971); *Herself* (1972).

Armitage • Stewart, Virginia, ed., *Modern Dance* (1935).

Arno • Husted, Eda, *The Life and Work of Susan B. Anthony*, Vol. II (1969). New York Times, eds., *Women: Their Changing Roles*.

Asia • Naidu, Sarojini, *The Feather of the Dawn* (1927, 1961).

Atheneum • Gordon, Ruth, *Myself Among Others* (1970). LeShan, Eda, *The Conspiracy Against Childhood* (1967). Peterson, Virgilia, *A Matter of Life and Death* (1961). Sitwell, Edith, *Taken Care Of* (1965).

Avon • Corliss, Richard, *The Hollywood Screenwriters* (1972). Keyes, Frances Parkinson, *The Great Tradition* (1939). Meacock, Norma, *Thinking Girl* (1968).

Bantam • Cookson, Catherine, *The Fifteen Streets* (1973). Dillard, Annie, *Pilgrim at Tinker Creek* (1945). Dreifus, *Woman's Fate* (1973). Nin, Anaïs, *A Spy in the House of Love* (1968).

Barnes • Robyns, Gwen, *Light of a Star* (1968).

Basic • Ravitch, Diane, *The Great School Wars* (1974).

Beacon • Daly, Mary, *Beyond God the Father* (1973). Roepke, Gabriela, *A White Butterfly* (1960). Zassenhaus, Hiltgunt, *Walls: Resisting the Third Reich—One Woman's Story* (1974).

Being • *1976 Appointment Book and Calendar of Saints* (1975).

R. Bemporad • Castellani, Maria, *Italian Women, Past and Present* (1937).

Black Sparrow • Haas, Robert Bartlett, ed., *Reflections on the Atomic Bomb* (1973).

Bleecker Street • Miller, Isobel, *A Place for Us* (1969).

Blue Heron • Le Sueur, Meridel, *Crusaders* (1955).

Bobbs-Merrill • Barker, Myrtie, *I Am Only One* (1963). Haggerty, Joan, *Daughters of the Moon* (1971). Josephson, Hannah, *Jeannette Rankin: First Lady in Congress* (1974). Rand, Ayn, *The Fountainhead* (1943). Thomas, Audrey, *Songs My Mother Taught Me* (1973).

Boosey & Hawkes • Lehmann, Lotte, *More Than Singing* (1945).

Brandt & Brandt • Kerr, Jean, *Mary, Mary* (1960).

Braziller • Frame, Janet, *Faces in the Water* (1961).

Brentano • Sanger, Margaret, *Woman and the New Race* (1920). Montgomery, Roselle Mercier, *Ulysses Return and Other Poems* (1925).

Brice • Johstone, Wilhelmina Kemp, *Bahamian Jottings* (1973).

Broadside • Lorde, Audre, *From a Land Where Other People Live* (1973).

Bruce • Maynard, Theodore, *Too Small a World* (1945).

Theodore Brun • Buck, Pearl, *The Bondsmaid* (1949).

Burke • Franks, A. H., ed., *Pavlova: A Biography* (1956).

Burt • Speare, Dorothy, *Dancers in the Dark* (1922). Wood, Ellen Price, *East Lynne* (1902).

Butterworth • Asquith, Margot, *Autobiography* (1920). Melba, Nellie, *Melodies and Memories* (1925).

Jonathan Cape • Chambers, Jessie, *D. H. Lawrence: A Personal Record* (1935). Hall, Radclyffe, *A Saturday Life* (1930); *The Master of the House* (1932). O'Brien, Edna, *August Is a Wicked Month* (1965). Origo, Iris, *War in Val d'Orcia* (1947); *A Measure of Love* (1957). Ptaschkina, Nellie (Jacques Povolotsky, ed.), *The Diary of Nellie Ptaschkina*. Suyin, Han, *A Many-Splendoured Thing* (1952); *The Mountain Is Young* (1958); *Winter Love* (1962).

Cassell • Asquith, Margot, *Octavia* (1928). Stoddard, Elizabeth, *Two Men* (1888).

Caxton • Rand, Ayn, *Anthem* (1961).

Chapman • Leverson, Ada, *The Twelfth Hour* (1951).

Charlton • Gilman, Charlotte Perkins, *The Home* (1910).

Charterhouse • Shain, Merle, *Some Men Are More Perfect Than Others* (1973).

Chatto & Windus • Allingham, Margery, *The Tiger in the Smoke* (1952).

Chilton • Beals, Carleton, *Cyclone Carry* (1962).

Arthur H. Clark • Hebard, Gracy Raymond, *Washakie* (1930); *The Pathbreakers from River to Ocean* (1932).

Clarke, Unwin • Carr, Emily, *Hundreds and Thousands* (1966).

Collins • Stassinopoulos, Arianna, *The Female Woman* (1974).

Cornell University • Benedict, Ruth, *Thai Culture and Behavior* (1952).

Covici, Friede • Anderson, Margaret, *My Thirty Years' War* (1930).

Coward, McCann & Geoghegan • Bender, Marilyn, *The Beautiful People* (1967). Decter, Midge, *The Liberated Woman and Other Americans* (1971); *The New Chastity and Other Arguments Against Women's Liberation* (1971); *Liberal Parents/Radical Children* (1975). Goudge, Elizabeth, *Green Dolphin Street* (1944); *The Child from the Sea* (1970); Loud, Pat, and Johnson, Nora, *A Woman's Story* (1974). Miller, Alice Duer, *The White Cliffs* (1940). Rosen, Marjorie, *Popcorn Venus* (1973). Sargeant, Winthrop, *Divas: Impressions of Six Opera Superstars* (1973).

Cowdy • Janis, Elsie, *Poems Now and Then* (1927).

Crowell • Eliot, George, *George Eliot's Life as Related in Her Letters* (1900). Jordan, June,

*New Life, New Room* (1975). Lessing, Doris, *The Habit of Loving* (1957). Stoddard, Hope, *Famous American Women* (1970).

Crown • Smith, Ella, *Starring Miss Barbara Stanwyck* (1974).

Current • Rukeyser, Muriel, *The Life of Poetry* (1949).

Andrew Dakers • Brittain, Vera, *Lady into Woman* (1953).

Davis • Allingham, Margery, *The Villa Marie Celeste* (1960).

John Day • Buck, Pearl, *The Good Earth* (1931); *Sons* (1932); *First Wife and Other Stories* (1933); *A House Divided* (1935); *This Proud Heart* (1938); *The Patriot* (1939); *American Unity and Asia* (1942); *What America Means to Me* (1942); *China, Past and Present* (1972); *The Goddess Abides* (1972). Perkins, Frances, *People at Work* (1934). Sand, George, *Intimate Journal* (1929).

Delacorte • Babitz, Eve, *Eve's Hollywood* (1972). Sheehy, Gail, *Hustling* (1973).

Dell • Hollander, Xaviera (with Robin Moore and Yvonne Dunleavy), *The Happy Hooker* (1972). Leduc, Violette, *Therese and Isabelle* (1968). Olsen, Tillie, *Tell Me a Riddle* (1960).

J. M. Dent • Schiaparelli, Elsa, *Shocking Life* (1954).

Andre Deutsch • Sheridan, Clare, *To the Four Winds* (1955).

Diablo • Minott, Rodney G., *The Sinking of the Lollipop* (1968).

Dial • Baez, Joan, *Daybreak* (1966). Bowen, Elizabeth, *The Hotel* (1928). Painter, Charlotte, *Confession from the Malaga Madhouse* (1971). Rossner, Judith, *Nine Months in the Life of an Old Maid* (1969).

Discus • Ross, Lillian, *Picture* (1969). Ross, Susan C., *The Rights of Women* (1973).

Dodd, Mead • Baldwin, Faith, *Alimony* (1928). Bowen, Marjorie, *General Crack* (1928). Campbell, Mrs. Patrick, *My Life and Some Letters* (1922). Christie, Agatha, *Witness for the Prosecution* (1924); *Endless Night* (1967). Curtiss, Ursula Reilly, *The Wasp* (1963). Eliot, George, *Adam Bede* (1947); *Silas Marner* (1948). Hinkle, Beatrice, *Recreating the Individual* (1949). James, Alice (Leon Edel, ed.), *The Diary of Alice James* (1964). Kenny, Elizabeth, and Ostenso, Martha, *And They Shall Walk* (1943). Newton, Frances, *Light Like the Sun* (1937). Ostenso, Martha, *Wild Geese* (1925); *The Mad Carews* (1927); *O, River, Remember!* (1943). Roe, Anne, *The Making of a Scientist* (1952). Skinner, Cornelia Otis, *Dithers and Jitters* (1937); *Bottoms Up!* (1955); and Kimbrough, Emily, *Our Hearts Were Young and Gay* (1942). Trevisan, Anna F., *Easter Eve* (1946); *In the Valley of the Shadow* (1946).

Doubleday • Ace, Goodman, *The Fine Art of Hypochondria* (1966). Allingham, Margery, *The Oaken Heart* (1941). Antoine-Dariaux, Geneviève, *The Fall Collection* (1973). Asquith, Margot, *My Impressions of America* (1922). Astor, Nancy, *My Two Countries (1923)*. Barreno, Maria Isabel; Velho da Costa, Maria Fatima; and Horta, Maria Theresa, *New Portuguese Letters* (1972). Baum, Vicki, *And Life Goes On* (1932). Bibesco, Elizabeth, *Balloons* (1922). Boyle, Kay, *The Underground Woman* (1974). Brown, Rosellen, *Street Games* (1975). Caldwell, Taylor, *The Sound of Thunder* (1957); *The Late Clara Beame* (1963); *Great Lion of God* (1970); *Captains and the Kings* (1972). Chase, Ilka, *I Love Miss Tilli Bean* (1946); *Free Admission* (1948). Chesler, Phyllis, *Women and Madness* (1972). Chicago, Judy, *Through the Flower: My Struggle as a Woman Artist* (1975). Choate, Anne Hyde, and Ferris, Helen, eds., *Juliette Low and the Girl Scouts* (1928). Curie, Eve, *Journey Among Warriors* (1943). Diller, Phyllis, *Phyllis Diller's Housekeeping Hints* (1966). Du Maurier, Daphne, *Mary Anne* (1954); *Don't Look Now* (1970). Eliot, George, *Romola* (1922). Fallaci, Oriana, *Nothing, and So Be It* (1972). Ferber, Edna, *So Big* (1924); *Show Boat* (1926); *Giant* (1952). Frank, Anne, *The Diary of a Young Girl* (1952). Gale, Zona, *The Book Man* (1925). Glasgow, Ellen, *The Sheltered Life* (1932). Goldman, Emma, *My Disillusionment in Russia* (1923). Hale, Nancy, *Mary Cassatt: A Biography of the Great American Painter* (1975). Hobson, Laura Z., *Consenting Adult* (1975). Hopper, Hedda, *From Under My Hat* (1952). Hurst, Fannie, *Anatomy of Me* (1958). Inagaki, Etsu, *A Daughter of the Samurai* (1925); *Sugimoto* (1931). Kaufman, Sue, *Falling Bodies* (1974). Keller, Helen, *The Story of My Life* (1954); *The Open Door* (1957). Kennedy, Rose Fitzgerald, *Times to Remember* (1974). Kerr, Jean, *The Snake Has All the Lines* (1960); *Poor Richard* (1963); *Finishing Touches* (1973). Lagerlöf, Selma, *From a Swedish Homestead* (1926); *The Diary of Selma Lagerlöf* (1936). Lawrence, Gertrude, *A Star Danced* (1945). Lillie, Beatrice, *Every Other Inch a Lady* (1972). Loos, Anita, *A Mouse Is Born* (1950). Mannes, Marya, *They* (1968); *Out of My Time* (1971). Marion, Frances, *Westward the Dream* (1948). Millett, Kate, *Sexual Politics* (1970). Monroe, Anne Shannon, *Singing in the Rain* (1926). Mortimer, Penelope, *Long Distance* (1974). Norris, Kathleen, *Noon* (1924); *Bread in Two Roses* (1936). O'Neill, Rose, *Garda* (1929). Orczy, Baroness, *The Scarlet Pimpernell* (1905). Piercy, Marge, *Small Changes* (1973). Porter, Sylvia, *Sylvia Porter's Money Book* (1975). Rinehart, Mary Roberts, *Kings, Queens, and Pawns* (1915); *The Works of Mary Roberts Rinehart* (1920); *My Story* (1931, 1943). Rochefort, Christiane, *Les*

*Stances à Sophie* (1970). Rukeyser, Muriel, *Beast in View* (1944). Rule, Jane, *Lesbian Images* (1975). Sackville-West, Vita, *The Edwardians* (1958). Sheppard, Dick, *Elizabeth* (1974). Vanderbilt, Amy, *New Complete of Etiquette* (1963). Walters, Barbara, *How to Talk with Anybody About Practically Anything* (1970). Wells, Carolyn, *In the Onyx Lobby* (1920); *The Book of Humorous Verse* (1936). West, Rebecca, *Ending in Earnest* (1931); *The Harsh Voice* (1937).

Dramatists' Play Service • Christie, Agatha, *Towards Zero* (1957). Resnik, Muriel, *Any Wednesday* (1966).

Duckworth • Sitwell, Edith, *Collected Poems* (1930); *Facade and Other Poems: 1920–1935* (1950).

Duell, Sloan & Pearce • Gilpin, Laura, *The Rio Grande* (1949). Kramer, Jane, *Off Washington Square* (1963).

Duffield • Cooper, Courtney Ryley, *Annie Oakley: Woman at Arms* (1927).

Dutton • Adler, Renata, *Toward a Radical Middle* (1971). Bashkirtseff, Marie, *The Journal of a Young Artist* (1884). Dostoevsky, Anna (S. S. Koteliansky, ed.), *Reminiscences of Madame Dostoevsky* (1926). Fairless, Michael, *The Complete Works of Michael Fairless* (1932). Gaskell, Elizabeth, *Cranford* (1965). Howard, Jane, *A Different Woman* (1973). Jesus, Caroline Maria de, *Child of the Dark: The Diary of Caroline Maria de Jesus* (1962). Maurois, André, *The Life of Sir Alexander Fleming* (1959). Norris, Kathleen, *Home* (1928). Pell, Eve, *Maximum Security Letters* (1972). Pless, Daisy, *Daisy, Princess of Pless* (1923); *Better Left Unsaid* (1931); *What I Left Unsaid* (1936). Sagan, Françoise, *A Certain Smile* (1956). Underhill, Evelyn, *Mysticism* (1930). Webb, Mary G., *Precious Bane* (1946).

Echo Park Evangelistic Association • McPherson, Aimee Semple, *This Is That* (1923).

Eisenach • Diehl, Guida, *The German Woman and National Socialism* (1933).

Eugenics • Stopes, Marie, *Married Love* (1918).

M. Evans • Drexler, Rosalyn, *The Cosmopolitan Girl* (1975). Hayes, Helen (with Lewis Funke), *A Gift of Joy* (1965); (with Sandford Dody), *On Reflection* (1968).

Eyre & Spottiswood • Asquith, Margot, *The Autobiography of Margot Asquith* (1922). Compton-Burnett, Ivy, *A House and Its Head* (1935).

Fabian Society • Webb, Beatrice Potter, *Socialism and National Minimum* (1909); *Health of Working Girls* (1917).

Fantasy House • *Fifty Short Science Fiction Tales* (1952).

Farrar, Straus & Giroux • Colette, *Cheri* (1951); *The Last of Cheri* (1951); *Gigi* (1952); *Sido* (1953); *The Cat* (1955); *Creatures Great and Small* (1957); *Music-Hall Sidelights* (1957);

*The Blue Lantern* (1963). Didion, Joan, *Slouching Towards Bethlehem* (1968). Harris, Eleanor, *The Real Story of Lucille Ball* (1954). Jackson, Shirley, *Life Among the Savages* (1953); *The Bird's Nest* (1954); *Raising Demons* (1956); (Stanley Edgar Hyman, ed.), *The Magic of Shirley Jackson* (1966). Kramer, Jane, *Honor to the Bride* (1973). Leduc, Violette, *La Bâtarde* (1965); *Mad in Pursuit* (1971). Le Gallienne, Eva, *The Mystic in the Theatre* (1965). Macaulay, Rose, *The Towers of Trebizond* (1956). Mann, Erika, *The Lights Go Down* (1940); *The Last Year of Thomas Mann* (1958). McCarthy, Mary, *On the Contrary* (1961). McCormick, Anne O'Hare (Marion Turner Sheehan, ed.), *Vatican Journal, 1921–1954* (1957). O'Connor, Flannery, *Wise Blood* (1949); *The Violent Bear It Away* (1955, 1960); *Mystery and Manners* (1961); *Everything That Rises Must Converse* (1965). Paley, Grace, *Enormous Changes at the Last Minute* (1974). Sachs, Nelly, *The Seeker and Other Poems* (1970). Sanger, Margaret, *My Fight for Birth Control* (1931). Sontag, Susan, *The Benefactor* (1963); *Death Kit* (1967); *Styles of Radical Will* (1969). Widdemer, Margaret, *Hill Garden* (1936). Yourcenar, Marguerite, *Memoirs of Hadrian* (1954); *Coup de Grâce* (1957).

Fawcett • Berg, Stephen, and Marks, S. J., *About Women* (1973).

G. Feltrinelli • Maraini, Dacia, *Crudelta all'Aria Aperia* (1966).

Feminist • Davis, Rebecca Harding, *Life in the Iron Mills* (1972).

Four Seas • Hardin, Charlotte, *Coins and Medals* (1921). Stein, Gertrude, *Sacred Emily* (1922).

Four Winds • McGovern, Ann, *The Secret Soldier* (1975).

Free Press • Komarovsky, Mirra, *Common Frontiers of the Social Sciences* (1957).

Samuel French • Aguirre Isidora, *Express for Santiago* (1960). Christie, Agatha, *The Hollow* (1952); *Spider's Web* (1956). Kummer, Clare, *Good Gracious, Annabelle* (1916); *Rollo's Wild Oat* (1922); *Her Master's Voice* (1933). Loos, Anita, *Happy Birthday* (1947). Nichols, Anne, *Abie's Irish Rose* (1922).

Friendship • Buck, Pearl, *The Young Revolutionist* (1932).

Funk & Wagnalls • Dix, Dorothy, *Her Book* (1926). Post, Emily, *Etiquette* (1922, 1945); *Children Are People* (1940, 1947).

Gallimard • Weil, Simone, *La Condition Ouvrière* (1951); *La Source Grecque* (1952).

Garden City • Moore, Grace, *You're Only Human Once* (1946).

Glide • Martin, Del, and Lyon, Phyllis, *Lesbian/Woman* (1972).

Victor Gollancz • Baker, Corothy, *Cassandra at the Wedding* (1962). Compton-Burnett, Ivy,

*Elders and Betters* (1944); *Two Worlds and Their Ways* (1949); *A Heritage and Its History* (1959); *The Mighty and Their Fall* (1961). Gordimer, Nadine, *The Late Bourgeois World* (1966). Head, Bessie, *Maru* (1971). Mitford, Jessica, *Sons and Rebels* (1960). Ocampo, Victoria, *338171TE—Lawrence of Arabia* (1947, 1963). Pethick-Lawrence, Emmeline, *My Part in a Changing World* (1938). Sprigge, Elizabeth, *The Life of Ivy Compton-Burnett* (1973). Syrkin, Marie, *Golda Meir: Woman with a Cause* (1964). Tolstoy, Sophie, *A Diary of Tolstoy's Wife, 1860–1891* (1928). Ware, Porter W., and Lockard, Thaddeus C., Jr., eds., *The Lost Letters of Jenny Lind* (1966).

Grasset • Lenéru, Marie, *Journal* (1945).

Grosset & Dunlap • Alcott, Louisa May, *An Old-Fashioned Girl* (1911); *Jack and Jill* (1928); *Jo's Boys* (1949). Ferber, Edna, *Cimarron* (1929); *Saratoga Trunk* (1941). Mailer, Norman, *Marilyn* (1973). Montgomery, Lucy M., *Ann of Green Gables* (1908); *Anne's House of Dreams* (1917); Porter, Eleanor H., *Pollyanna* (1913). Sewell, Anna, *Black Beauty* (1945). Spyri, Johanna, *Heidi* (1945). Woollcott, Alexander, *While Rome Burns* (1934).

Grossman • Deming, Barbara, *We Cannot Live Without Our Lives* (1974). Strouse, Jean, ed., *Women and Analysis: Dialogues on Psychoanalytic Views of Femininity* (1974).

Grune & Stratton • Deutsch, Helene, *The Psychology of Women*, Vol. I (1944).

Halcyon House • Johson, Osa, *Four Years in Paradise* (1944).

Hamish Hamilton • Mitford, Nancy, *The Pursuits of Love* (1945).

Harcourt Brace Jovanovich • Austin, Hary H., *The American Rhythm* (1923). Bailey, Pearl, *The Raw Pearl* (1968); *Pearl's Kitchen* (1973). Barnes, Djuna, *Nightwood* (1937). Beard, Mary Ritter, *A Short History of the American Labor Movement* (1920). Bracken, Peg, *The I Hate to Cook Book* (1960). Craigin, Elizabeth, *Either Is Love* (1937, 1963). Davis, Adele, *Let's Eat Right to Keep Fit* (1954). Delmar, Viña, *The Becker Scandal* (1968); *A Time Remembered* (1968). Drew, Elizabeth, *The Modern Novel* (1926). Fisher, Dorothy Canfield, *The Bent Twig* (1915); *Her Son's Wife* (1926); *The Deepening Stream* (1930); *Bonfire* (1933); *Seasoned Timber* (1939). Fox, Mary Virginia, *Lady for the Defense* (1975). Glasgow, Ellen, *In This Our Life* (1941). Hays, Elinor R., *Morning Star* (1961); *Those Extraordinary Blackwells* (1967). Howard, Maureen, *Bridgeport Bus* (1966). Kelley, Edith Summers, *Weeds* (1923). Lanchester, Elsa, *Charles Laughton and I* (1938). Lindbergh, Anne Morrow, *North to the Orient* (1935); *The Wave of the Future* (1940); *The Steep Ascent* (1944); *Hour of Gold, Hour of Lead* (1973); *Locked Rooms and Open Doors: Diaries of Anne Morrow Lindbergh, 1933–1935* (1974). McCarthy, Mary, *The Group* (1954); *Vietnam* (1967); *Hanoi* (1968); *Birds of America* (1971). Meyer, Agnes E., *Journey Through Chaos* (1943). Morris, Jan, *Conundrum* (1974). Nin, Anaïs, *Diary of Anaïs Nin*, Vols. I–V (1966–1974). O'Connor, Flannery, *A Good Man Is Hard to Find* (1955). Origo, Iris, *Images and Shadows* (1970). Porter, Katherine Anne, *Flowering Judas and Other Stories* (1930); *Old Mortality* (1936); *Noon Wine* (1937); *Pale Horse, Pale Rider* (1939). Roarke, Constance, *The Trumpets of Jubilee* (1927); *American Humor* (1931). Roy, Gabrielle, *The Cashier* (1955). Sayers, Dorothy L., *The Third Omnibus of Crime* (1935). Scudder, Janet, *Modeling My Life* (1925); Struther, Jan, *Mrs. Miniver* (1940). Walker, Alice, *In Love and Trouble: Stories of Black Women* (1973). Welty, Eudora, *A Curtain of Green and Other Stories* (1936); *The Wide Net and Other Stories* (1943); *The Golden Apples* (1949); *The Ponder Heart* (1954). West, Jessamyn, *The Friendly Persuasion* (1945); *Love, Death, and the Ladies' Drill Team* (1955); *To See the Dream* (1956); *South of the Angels* (1960); *Hide and Seek* (1973). Widdemer, Margaret, *The Boardwalk* (1920). Winn, Mary Day, *Adam's Rib* (1931). Woolf, Virginia, *Monday or Tuesday* (1921); *The Common Reader* (1925); *Second Common Reader* (1932); *Three Guineas* (1938); *The Moment and Other Essays* (1952); (Leonard Woolf, ed.), *A Writer's Diary* (1954).

Harper & Row • Akins, Zoë, *The Hills Grow Smaller* (1937). Allilueva, Svetlana, *Twenty Letters to a Friend* (1967); *Only One Year* (1969). Bankhead, Tallulah, *Tallulah* (1952). Banning, Margaret Culkin, *Letters to Susan* (1936). Bowen, Marjorie, *Mignonette* (1948). Breuer, Bessie, *The Actress* (1955). Brooks, Gwendolyn, *The World of Gwendolyn Brooks* (1971). Chiang Kai-shek, Madame, *This Is Our China* (1940); *China Shall Rise Again* (1941). Chisholm, Shirley, *The Good Fight* (1973). Coulson, Thomas, *Mata Hari* (1930). Daly, Mary, *The Church and the Second Sex* (1968). Dash, Joan, *A Life of One's Own* (1973). Day, Dorothy, *The Long Loneliness* (1952); *Loaves and Fishes* (1963). Emshwiller, Carol, *Joy in Our Cause* (1974). Fraser, Kathleen, *What I Want* (1975). Gelb, Barbara and Arthur, *O'Neill* (1960). Gibson, Althea, *I Always Wanted to Be Somebody* (1958). Hurst, Fanny, *Imitation of Life* (1932). Janeway, Elizabeth, *Accident* (1964). Jhabvala, Ruth Prawer, *Travelers* (1973). Lee, Gypsy Rose, *Gypsy* (1957). Leech, Margaret, *Reveille in Washington* (1941); *In the Days of McKinley* (1959). Lilienthal, David E., *The Journals of David E. Lilienthal*, Vols. I and IV (1964, 1967). Millay, Edna St. Vincent (Allen R. Macdougall, ed.), *Letters of Edna*

*St. Vincent Millay* (1952). Mitford, Nancy, *Noblesse Oblige* (1956). Moses, Grandma (Aotto Kallir, ed.), *My Life's History* (1952). Plath, Sylvia, *The Bell Jar* (1971); *Crossing the Water* (1971). Riding, Laura, *The Telling* (1975). Roosevelt, Eleanor, *This Is My Story* (1937); *My Own Story* (1958); *The Autobiography of Eleanor Roosevelt* (1961); *Tomorrow Is Now* (1963). Sackville-West, Vita, *Country Notes* (1940). Sayers, Dorothy L., *Unnatural Death* (1955); *Clouds of Witness* (1956); *The Unpleasantness at the Bellona Club* (1956); *Gaudy Night* (1960). Smith, Betty, *A Tree Grows in Brooklyn* (1943); *Maggie-Now* (1958). Toklas, Alice B., *The Alice B. Toklas Cook Book* (1954). Wilder, Laura Ingalls, *Little House in the Big Woods* (1932). Winwar, Frances, *Wingless Victory* (1956). Wolff, Charlotte, *Love Between Women* (1972).
Harrap • St. Denis, Ruth, *An Unfinished Life* (1939).
Harvill • Graham, Virginia, *Say Please* (1949).
Hart-Davis • Cooper, Diana, *The Rainbow Comes and Goes* (1958); *Trumpets from the Steep* (1960).
Harvard University • Vendler, Helen, ed., *The Poetry of George Herbert* (1975).
Hawthorne • Davis, Bette (with Whitney Stine), *Mother Goddamn* (1974).. Jackson, Mahalia (with Evan McLoud Wylie), *Movin' on Up* (1966). Lawrenson, Helen, *Latins Are Still Lousy Lovers* (1968).
Hearst International • Pankhurst, Emmeline, *My Own Story* (1914).
James H. Heineman • Parturier, Françoise, *Open Letter to Men* (1968). Summerskill, Edith, *A Woman's World* (1967).
William Heinemann • Bingham, Charlotte, *Lucinda* (1966). Lawrence, Frieda (E. W. Tedlock, ed.), *The Memoirs and Correspondence* (1961). De Wolfe, Elsie, *Recipes for Successful Dining* (1934).
Hill & Wang • Giovanni, Nikki, *Sing a Soft Black Song* (1971). Jacoby, Susan, *Inside Soviet Schools* (1974).
Historical Association of London • Cam, Helen, *Historical Novel* (1961).
P. B. Hoeber • Todd, Mabel Elsworth, *The Thinking Body* (1937).
Hogarth • Harrison, Jane, *Reminiscences of a Student's Life* (1925). Macaulay, Rose, *Catchwords and Claptrap* (1926). Sackville-West, Vita, *Passenger to Teheran* (1926); *Twelve Days* (1928); *All Passion Spent* (1931); *Solitude* (1938). Stopes, Marie C., *Joy and Verity* (1952). Woolf, Virginia, *A Room of One's Own* (1931).
Holt, Rinehart & Winston • Adler, Polly, *A House Is Not a Home* (1953). Bainbridge, John, *Garbo* (1955). Baldwin, Faith, *Medical Center* (1938). Baldwin, Monica, *I Leap Over the Wall* (1950).

Crist, Judith, *The Private Eye, the Cowboy, and the Very Naked Lady* (1968). Gorbanevskaya, Natalya, *Red Square at Noon* (1972). Green, Hannah, *I Never Promised You a Rose Garden* (1964). Haskell, Molly, *From Reverence to Rape* (1973). Johnson, Lady Bird, *A White House Diary* (1970). Jong, Erica, *Fruits and Vegetables* (1971); *Fear of Flying* (1973); *Half-Lives* (1973). Kerr, Sophie, *The Man Who Knew the Date* (1951). King, Coretta Scott, *My Life with Martin Luther King, Jr.* (1969). Livingstone, Belle, *Belle Out of Order* (1959). Montessori, Maria, *The Absorbent Mind* (1967). Morrison, Toni, *The Bluest Eye* (1970). Sitwell, Edith, *Poetry and Criticism* (1959). Stead, Christina, *Dark Places of the Heart* (1966). Wagman, Fredrica, *Magic Man, Magic Man* (1975).
Home & Van Thal • Gingold, Hermione, *The World Is Square* (1945).
Johns Hopkins • Langer, Susanne K., *Mind: An Essay on Human Feelings*, Vol. I (1967).
Horizon • Anderson, Margaret, *The Fiery Fountains* (1969). Lamont, Corliss, ed., *The Trial of Elizabeth Gurley Flynn by the American Civil Liberties Union* (1968). Richardson, Dorothy, *Pilgrimage*, Vols. II and IV (1935).
Houghton Mifflin • Axline, Virginia, *Dibs: In Search of Self* (1965). Ayscough, Florence, and Lowell, Amy, *Fir-Flower Tablets* (1921). Benedict, Ruth, *Patterns of Culture* (1934); *The Chrysanthemum and the Sword* (1946). Carson, Rachel, *The Edge of the Sea* (1955). Chesnut, Mary Boykin, *Diary from Dixie* (1949). Chisholm, Shirley, *Unbought and Unbossed* (1970). Foley, Martha, and Burnett, David, *The Best American Short Stories of 1969* (1969). Forbes, Esther, *Paul Revere* (1942). Gallant, Mavis, *Green Water, Green Sky* (1959). Giroud, Françoise, *I Give You My Word* (1974). Hale, Lucretia Peabody, *The Peterkin Papers* (1959). Johnson, Osa, *Bride in the Solomons* (1944). Lavin, Mary, *Happiness and Other Stories* (1970). Lowell, Amy, *A Dome of Many-Coloured Glass* (1912); *Legends* (1921); *A Critical Fable* (1922). McCullers, Carson, *The Heart Is a Lonely Hunter* (1940); *Reflections in a Golden Eye* (1941); *The Members of the Wedding* (1946); *The Ballad of the Sad Cafe* (1951). Mead, Margaret, *An Anthropologist at Work: Writings of Ruth Benedict* (1951). Peabody, Josephine, *Collected Poems of Josephine Peabody* (1927). Repplier, Agnes, *To Think of Tea!* (1932); *In Pursuit of Laughter* (1936). Seton, Anya, *Green Darkness* (1972). Sexton, Anne, *To Bedlam and Partway Back* (1960); *Live or Die* (1966); *The Death Notebooks* (1974); *The Awful Rowing Toward God* (1975). Skinner, Cornelia Otis, *The Ape in Me* (1959); *Elegant Wits and Grand Horizontals* (1962). Stevenson, Egbert, ed., *Poems of Ameri-*

*can History* (1922). Turnbull, Agnes Sligh, *The Golden Journey* (1955); *The Flowering* (1972). Yglesias, Helen, *How She Died* (1972).

Hutchinson of London • Bowen, Marjorie, *World's Wonder* (1937). Cam, Helen, *England Before Elizabeth* (1950). Cartland, Barbara, *The Isthmus Years* (1942). Duffy, Maureen, *The Microcosm* (1966). Lejeune, Caroline, *Thank You for Having Me* (1964). Mortimer, Penelope, *The Pumpkin Eater* (1962). O'Brien, Edna, *The Country Girls* (1960). Pankhurst, Sylvia, *The Home Front* (1932).

Illinois State Historical Society • Turner, Justin G., ed., *The Mary Lincoln Letters to Mrs. Felician Slataper* (1956).

Inner City • Richards, Beah, *A Black Woman Speaks and Other Poems* (1974).

Insel-Verlag • Schneider, Edouard, *Erinnerungen, Betrachtungen und Briefe* (1926).

International • Figner, Vera, *Memoirs of a Revolutionist* (1927). Flynn, Elizabeth Gurley, *The Rebel Girl* (1955); *The Alderson Story* (1963). Ibarruri, Dolores, *Speeches and Articles, 1936–1938* (1938). Le Sueur, Meridel, *Salute to Spring* (1940).

Ives Washburn • Fleming, Joan, *The Chill and the Kill* (1964).

Herbert Jenkins • Bowen, Marjorie, *My Tattered Loving* (1937).

Jero • *Death House Letters of Ethel and Julius Rosenberg* (1953).

Michael Joseph • Fallaci, Oriana, *Penelope at War* (1966). Mortimer, Penelope, *Daddy's Gone A-Hunting* (1958). Sackville-West, Vita, *In Your Garden Again* (1953); *No Signposts in the Sea* (1961).

Knopf • Arnow, Harriette, *The Kentucky Trace* (1974). Ashton-Warner, Sylvia, *Three* (1970). Beauvoir, Simone de, *The Second Sex* (1953). Bengis, Ingrid, *Combat in the Erogenous Zone* (1973). Bowen, Elizabeth, *The Little Girls* (1963); *Eva Trout* (1968). Cather, Willa, *Youth and the Bright Medusa* (1920); *The Professor's House* (1925); *Death Comes for the Archbishop* (1927); *Shadows on the Rock* (1931); *Lucy Grayheart* (1935); *On Writing* (1949). Child, Julia, *Julia Child's Kitchen* (1975). Devlin, Bernadette, *The Price of My Soul* (1969). Dodge, Mabel, *Lorenzo in Taos* (1932). Drabble, Margaret, *The Needle's Eye* (1972); *The Realms of Gold* (1975). Duffy, Maureen, *Wounds* (1969); *Love Child* (1971). Ephron, Nora, *Crazy Salad: Some Things About Women* (1975). Grau, Shirley Ann, *The Keepers of the House* (1964); *The Condor Passes* (1971); *The Wind Shifting West* (1973). Godwin, Gail, *The Odd Woman* (1974). Goldman, Emma, *Living My Life* (1931). Hazzard, Shirley, *The Evening of the Holiday* (1965); *People in Glass Houses* (1967). Heilbrun, Carolyn, *Toward a Recognition of Androgyny* (1973). Johnson, Diane, *The*

*Shadow Knows* (1974). Katkov, Norman, *The Fabulous Fanny* (1952). Kemble, Fanny (John Scott, ed.), *Journal of a Residence on a Georgian Plantation, 1838–1839* (1961). Laurence, Margaret, *A Jest of God*—later known as *Rachel, Rachel* (1966). Lessing, Doris, *The Summer Before Dark* (1973). Lewis, Edith, *Willa Cather Living* (1953). Luce, Clare Boothe, *Europe in the Spring* (1940). Mackenzie, Midge, ed., *Shoulder to Shoulder* (1975). Mansfield, Katherine, *Bliss and Other Stories* (1927); (John Middleton Murry, ed.), *Journal of Katherine Mansfield* (1927); *The Short Stories of Katherine Mansfield* (1937). McCormick, Anne O'Hare, *The Hammer and Scythe* (1927). Mitford, Jessica, *Kind and Unusual Punishment* (1973). Morrison, Toni, *Sula* (1974). Nathan, George Jean, *The Theatre in the Fifties* (1953). O'Brien, Edna, *The Love Object* (1962); *A Scandalous Woman and Other Stories* (1974). Ozick, Cynthia, *The Pagan Rabbi and Other Stories* (1971). Randal, Vera, *The Inner Room* (1964). Scott-Maxwell, Florida, *The Measure of My Days* (1972). Shulman, Alix Kates, *Memoirs of an Ex-Prom Queen* (1972). Spark, Muriel, *Collected Stories: I* (1968). Suckow, Ruth, *Country People* (1924); *The Odyssey of a Nice Girl* (1925); *Children and Other People* (1931). Turner, Justin G., ed., *Mary Todd Lincoln: Her Life and Letters* (1972), Viva, *The Baby* (1975).

Fritzes Kungl • Lagerlöf, Selma, *The Story of Gösta Berling* (1891).

Lalibela House • Pankhurst, Sylvia, *Ethiopia* (1955).

Lancer • Holiday, Billie, *Lady Sings the Blues* (1956).

John Lane • Naidu, Sorojini, *The Bird of Time* (1912); *The Golden Threshold* (1890, 1916); *The Broken Wing* (1916). Sackville-West, Vita, *Poems of West and East* (1917).

Links • Johnston, Jill, *Gullible's Travels* (1974).

Lippincott • Gingold, Hermione, *Sirens Should Be Seen and Not Heard* (1963). Giovanni, Nikki, and Baldwin, James, *A Dialogue* (1973). Hungerford, Margaret, *Molly Dawn* (1870). Hurston, Zora Neale, *Their Eyes Were Watching God* (1937). Johnson, Osa, *I Married Adventure* (1940). Karmel, Marjorie, *Thank You, Dr. Lamaze* (1959). Lee, Harper, *To Kill a Mockingbird* (1960). Nichols, Ruth, *Wings for Life* (1957). Schultz, Gladys Denny, *Jenny Lind: The Swedish Nightingale* (1962). Spark, Muriel, *Memento Mori* (1959); *The Prime of Miss Jean Brodie* (1961).

Literary Guild of America • *Works in Progress* (1972).

Little, Brown • Allingham, Margery, *The Gallantrys* (1943). De Mille, Agnes, *Dance to the Piper* (1952). Dressler, Marie, *My Own Story* (1934). Farmer, Fannie, *The Boston Cooking-*

*School Cookbook* (1896). FitzGerald, Frances, *Fire in the Lake* (1972). Haedrich, Marcel, *Coco Chanel: Her Life, Her Secrets* (1971). Hale, Nancy, *The Life in the Studio* (1969). Hazzard, Shirley, *The Bay of Noon* (1970). Head, Edith (with Jean Kesner Ardmore), *The Dress Doctor* (1959). Hellman, Lillian, *An Unfinished Woman* (1969). Howard, Maureen, *Before My Time* (1974). Hulme, Kathryn, *The Wild Place* (1953); *The Nun's Story* (1956); *Annie's Captain* (1961). Kael, Pauline, *Kiss Kiss Bang Bang* (1968); *Going Steady* (1970). Knopf, Olga, *The Art of Being a Woman* (1932); *Women on Their Own* (1935). Komarovsky, Mirra, *Women in the World* (1953). Macaulay, Rose, *The World of My Wilderness* (1950). Maxwell, Elsa, *R.S.V.P.* (1954); *How to Do It* (1957). Meyer, Agnes E., *Out of These Roots* (1953). Porter, Katherine Anne, *Ship of Fools* (1962). Rascoe, Judith, *Yours and Mine* (1973). Richards, Laura Elizabeth Howe, *Tirra Lirra* (1955). Suyin, Han, *Destination Chungking* (1942); *And the Rain My Drink* (1956). Smith, Dodie, *I Capture the Castle* (1948). Thurber, James, *The Years with Ross* (1959).

Liveright • Akins, Zoë, *Déclassé* (1923); *Daddy's Gone A-Hunting* (1923); *Greatness* (1923). Duncan, Isadora, *My Life* (1955). Harrison, Barbara Grizzuti, *Unlearning the Lie: Sexism in School* (1973). LaFollette, Suzanne, *Concerning Women* (1926). Macaulay, Rose, *Told by an Idiot* (1923). Marbury, Elizabeth, *My Crystal Ball* (1923). Parker, Dorothy, *Enough Rope* (1926). Stein, Gertrude, *Q.E.D. and Other Early Writings* (1971). Stevens, Doris, *Jailed for Freedom* (1920). Toklas, Alice B. (Ed Burns, ed.), *Playing on Alone: Letters of Alice B. Toklas* (1973).

Longmans, Green • Beard, Mary Ritter, *Understanding Women* (1931). Gibbons, Stella, *Conference at Cold Comfort Farm* (1949). Webb, Beatrice Potter, *My Apprenticeship* (1926).

MacBride • Dressler, Marie, *The Life Story of an Ugly Duckling* (1924).

McCall • Alexander, Shana, *The Feminine Eye* (1970). Shenker, Israel and Mary, eds., *As Good as Golda* (1970).

McClelland & Stewart • Moodie, Susanna, *Roughing It in the Bush* (1923).

MacGibbon & Kee • Lessing, Doris, *The Four-Gated City* (1969).

McGraw-Hill • Adler, Freda, *Sisters in Crime: The Rise of the New Female* (1975). Bogan, Louise, *A Poet's Alphabet* (1970). Dayan, Yael, *Death Had Two Sons* (1967); *Israel Journal: June, 1967* (1967). Greer, Germaine, *The Female Eunuch* (1971). Lessing, Doris, *The Golden Notebook* (1965). Loos, Anita, *No Mother to Guide Me* (1961). Marshall, Catherine, *A Man Called Peter* (1951); *Christy* (1967).

Munro, Alice, *Something I've Been Meaning to Tell You* (1974). Rossner, Judith, *Any Minute I Can Split* (1972). Vehanen, Kosti, *Marian Anderson: A Portrait* (1941).

McKay • Ballard, Bettina, *In My Fashion* (1960). Bird, Caroline, *Born Female* (1968); *The Case Against College* (1975). Colette, *For a Flower Album* (1959). Kilgallen, Dorothy, *Girl Around the World* (1936).

Macmillan • Addams, Jane, *Newer Ideals of Peace* (1927); *Twenty Years at Hull House* (1968). Arnow, Harriette, *The Dollmaker* (1954). Beard, Mary Ritter, *Women as a Force in History* (1946). Beard, Miriam, *Realism in Romantic Japan* (1930). Bowen, Louise de Koven, *Growing Up with a City* (1926). Brittain, Vera, *England's Hour* (1941); *On Being an Author* (1948); *Born* (1949). Dane, Clemence, *Naboth's Vineyard* (1925). Fromberg, Susan Schaeffer, *Falling* (1973). Froug, William, *The Screenwriter Looks at the Screenwriter* (1972). Gildersleeve, Virginia, *Many a Good Crusade* (1954). Hagen, Uta, *Respect for Acting* (1973). Lawton, Mary, *Schumann-Heink: The Last of the Titans* (1935). Lowell, Amy, *Men, Women, and Ghosts* (1916); *Tendencies in Modern American Poetry* (1917); *Can Grande's Castle* (1918); *Pictures of the Floating World* (1919). Marion, Francis, *Off with Their Heads* (1972). Martin, Martha, *O Rugged Land of Gold* (1952). McBride, Mary Margaret, *America for Me* (1941). Mew, Charlotte, *Collected Poems* (1953). Meyer, Agnes E., *Education for a New Morality* (1957). Mitchell, David, *The Fighting Pankhursts* (1967). Moss, Howard, ed., *The Poet's Story* (1974). Mitchell, Margaret, *Gone with the Wind* (1936). O'Neill, Moira, *Songs of the Glens of Antrim* (1922). Tarbell, Ida, *In Lincoln's Chair* (1920). Tuchman, Barbara, *The Guns of August* (1962); *Stilwell and the American Experience in China* (1970); *Notes from China* (1972). Turnbull, Agnes Sligh, *The Rolling Years* (1936).

Mama's • Boucher, Sandy, *Assaults and Rituals* (1975).

Manor • Baum, Vicki, *Grand Hotel* (1931).

Elisabeth Marton • Owens, Rochelle, *The Karl Marx Play* (1971). Terry, Megan, *The Magic Realist* (1968).

Messner • Keyes, Frances Parkinson, *Blue Camellia* (1957).

Methuen • Delaney, Shelagh, *Sweetly Sings the Donkey* (1963). Macaulay, Rose, *A Casual Commentary* (1925).

Meyer • Patterson, Ada, *Maude Adams: A Biography* (1907).

Modern Age • Mann, Erika, *School for Barbarians* (1938).

Modern Library • Schreiner, Olive, *The Story of an African Farm* (1927). Woolf, Virginia, *To the Lighthouse* (1937).

A. Mondadori • Nardi, Piero, *Vita di Arrigo Boito* (1942).

Morrow • Caine, Lynn, *Widow* (1974). Dixon, Jeane (with Rene Noorbergen), *My Life and Prophecies* (1969). Firestone, Shulamith, *The Dialectics of Sex* (1970). Gerson, Noel, *Because I Loved Him* (1971). Mead, Margaret, *Coming of Age in Samoa* (1928); *Sex and Temperament in Three Primitive Societies* (1935); *From the South Seas* (1939); *Male and Female* (1948); *Blackberry Winter: My Earlier Years* (1972). Renault, Mary, *North Face* (1948).

Mouton • Snow, Helen Foster, *Women in Modern China* (1967).

Frederick Muller • Fields, Gracie, *Sing as We Go* (1960).

John Murray • Chapman-Huston, Marjorie Desmond, *The Lost Historian* (1936). Pless, Daisy, *From My Private Diary* (1931).

Nash • Barrett, Rona, *Miss Rona* (1974).

Eveleigh Nash • Meyer, Arthur, *Forty Years of Parisian Society* (1912).

National Council for the Unmarried Mother and Her Child • Jeger, Lena, *Illegitimate Children and Their Parents* (1951).

National Education Association • Clarenbach, Kathryn, *Sex Role Stereotyping in the Schools* (1973).

New American Library • Cade, Toni, ed., *The Black Woman* (1970). Colette, *Gigi and Selected Writings* (1973). Giffin, Frederick C., ed., *Woman as Revolutionary* (1973). Lessing, Doris, *A Proper Marriage* (1964). Ozick, Cynthia, *Trust* (1966). Rand, Ayn, *The Virtue of Selfishness* (1964); *The New Left: The Anti-Industrial Revolution* (1970). Tanner, Leslie B., ed., *Voices from Women's Liberation* (1970). Viorst, Judith, *It's Hard to Be Hip Over Thirty* (1968).

New Century • Flynn, Elizabeth Gurley, *Labor's Own: William Z. Foster* (1949).

New Directions • Levertov, Denise, *O Taste and See* (1963); *The Sorrow Dance* (1966). Rukeyser, Muriel, *Selected Poems* (1955).

New Light • Alexander, Mithrapuram K., *Indira Gandhi* (1968).

Nistri • Antonia-Traversi, C., *Eleanora Duse* (1926).

Noonday • Bogan, Louise, *Collected Poems, 1923–1953* (1953); *Selected Criticism* (1955).

Northwestern University • Spolin, Viola, *Improvisation for the Theater* (1963).

Norton • Cosman, Carol, ed., *The Other Voices: An Anthology of Modern and Contemporary Poetry by Women in Transition* (1975). Deutsch, Helene, *Confrontations with Myself* (1973). Drew, Elizabeth, *Poetry: A Modern Guide to Its Understanding and Enjoyment* (1959); *The Literature of Gossip* (1964). Fuller, Margaret, *Woman in the Nineteenth Century* (1971). Hamilton, Edith, *The Greek Way* (1930); *The*

*Roman Way* (1932); *Three Greek Plays* (1937); *Witness to the Truth* (1948). Higham, Charles, *Kate: The Life of Katharine Hepburn* (1975). Horney, Karen, *Self-Analysis* (1942); *Our Inner Conflicts* (1945). MacLaine, Shirley, *Don't Fall Off the Mountain* (1970); *You Can Get There from Here* (1975). Rich, Adrienne, *Necessities of Life* (1966); *Leaflets* (1969); *Poems: Selected and New, 1950–1974* (1975). Riding, Laura, *Selected Poems: In Five Sets* (1975). Roosevelt, Eleanor, *It Seems to Me* (1954). Sarton, May, *The Small Room* (1961); *Mrs. Stevens Hears the Mermaids Singing* (1965); *Journal of a Solitude* (1973). Sanger, Margaret, *An Autobiography* (1938). Sayer, Anne, *Rosalind Franklin and DNA* (1973). Seton, Cynthia Propper, *The Sea Change of Angela Lewes* (1971); *The Half-Sisters* (1974). Smith, Lillian, *Killers of the Dream* (rev. ed., 1961). Strong Maurice F., ed., *Who Speaks for Earth?* (1973). Trachtenberg, Inge, *So Slow the Dawning* (1973). Ward, Barbara, *The Rich Nations and the Poor Nations* (1962).

Notre Dame/Fides • Montessori, Maria, *The Secret of Childhood* (1966).

Obolensky • Didion, Joan, *Run River* (1963).

Olympia • Solanis, Valerie, *SCUM Manifesto* (1968).

Owen • Ono, Yoko, *Grapefruit* (1970).

Oxford University • Carson, Rachel, *The Sea Around Us* (1951). Origo, Iris, *Leopardi* (1935). Weil, Simone, *Selected Essays, 1934–1953* (1962); (Richard Rees, ed.), *On Science, Necessity, and the Love of God* (1968); (Richard Rees, ed.), *First and Late Notebooks* (1970).

Paetel • Ebner von Eschenbach, Marie, *Aphorism* (1903).

Pantheon • Head, Bessie, *A Question of Power* (1973). Lerner, Gerda, ed., *Black Women in White America* (1972). Lindbergh, Anne Morrow, *The Unicorn and Other Poems* (1948); *Gift from the Sea* (1955). Renault, Mary, *The King Must Die* (1958); *The Bull from the Sea* (1962).

Panther • Figes, Eva, *Patriarchical Attitudes* (1972).

Penguin • Field, Joanna, *A Life of One's Own* (1934). Goulianos, Joan, ed., *By a Woman Writt* (1974). Millar, Susanna, *The Psychology of Play* (1968). Trevelyan, Raleigh, ed., *Italian Writing Today* (1967).

Penn • Wells, Carolyn, *The Meaning of Thanksgiving Day* (1922).

Philosophical Library • Beauvoir, Simone de, *The Ethics of Ambiguity* (1948).

Phoenix • Lejeune, Caroline, *Chestnuts in Her Lap* (1947).

Pocket Books • Brown, Helen Gurley, *Sex and the Single Girl* (1963). Hall, Radclyffe, *The Well of Loneliness* (1950).

Prentice-Hall • *An Anthology of Spanish Ameri-*

can *Literature* (1968). Devi, Indra, *Renew Your Life Through Yoga* (1963). Kaufman, Bel, *Up the Down Staircase* (1964). Leek, Sybil, *Diary of a Witch* (1968). Martin, Ralph G., *The Life of Lady Randolph Churchill: The Dramatic Years, 1895–1921*, Vol. II (1971).

Public Affairs • Beard, Mary Ritter, *The Force of Women in Japanese History* (1963).

Putnam • Beauvoir, Simone de, *Les Belles Images* (1968); *The Coming of Age* (1972); *All Said and Done* (1974). Bibesco, Elizabeth, *The Fir and the Palm* (1924). Davis, Bette, *The Lonely Life* (1962). Davis, Elizabeth Gould, *The First Sex* (1971). Earheart, Amelia, *Twenty Hours, Forty Minutes: Our Flight in the Friendship* (1928). Gaskell, Elizabeth, *Mary Barton* (1972). Gregory, Lady, *Aristotle Bellows* (1921); *The Jester* (1923); *The Story Brought by Brigit* (1924). Harris, Janet, *The Prime of Ms. America* (1975). Herbert, Marie, *The Snow People* (1973). Key, Ellen, *The Century of the Child* (1909); *The Renaissance of Motherhood* (1914); *War, Peace, and the Future* (1916). Kiernan, Thomas, *Jane: An Intimate Biography of Jane Fonda* (1973). Kinsolving, Sally, *Many Waters* (1942). McBride, Mary Margaret, *A Long Way from Missouri* (1959). Parent, Gail, *Sheila Levine Is Dead and Living in New York* (1972). Suyin, Han, *The Cripple Tree* (1965). Weintraub, Joseph, ed., *The Wit and Wisdom of Mae West* (1967).

Random House • Adler, Roberta, *A Year in the Dark* (1967). Angelou, Maya, *I Know Why the Caged Bird Sings* (1969); *Give Me a Cool Drink of Water 'fore I Diiie* (1974); *Gather Together in My Name* (1974). Bernikow, Louise, ed., *The World Split Open* (1974). Bingham, Charlotte, *Coronet Among the Weeds* (1963). Buck, Pearl, *Children for Adoption* (1964). Clark, Eleanor, *Baldur's Gate* (1955). Davis, Angela, *An Autobiography* (1974). Dinesen, Isak, *Out of Africa* (1938). Fletcher, Lucille, *The Girl in Cabin B54* (1968). Gallant, Mavis, *My Heart Is Broken* (1964); *A Fairly Good Time* (1970); *The Pegnitz Junction* (1973). Gould, Lois, *Such Good Friends* (1970); *Necessary Objects* (1972). Hardwick, Elizabeth, *Seduction and Betrayal: Women in Literature* (1974). Hawkes, Jacquetta, *A Land* (1952). Hellman, Lillian, *The Little Foxes* (1939); *Watch on the Rhine* (1941). Hobson, Laura Z., *The First Papers* (1964). Howe, Louise Kapp, ed., *The White Majority* (1970). Jacobs, Jane, *The Death and Life of Great American Cities* (1961); *The Economy of Cities* (1969). Jones, Gayl, *Corregidora* (1975). Katz, Naomi, and Milton, Nancy, eds., *Fragment from a Lost Diary and Other Stories* (1973). Kaufman, Sue, *Diary of a Mad Housewife* (1967). Lennart, Isobel, *Funny Girl* (1964). LeShan, Eda J., *How to Survive Parenthood* (1965). Mitford,

Nancy, *Love in a Cold Climate* (1949). Owens, Rochelle, *Futz and What Came After* (1968). Painter, Charlotte, and Moffat, Mary Jane, eds., *Revelations: Diaries of Women* (1974). Rand, Ayn, *Atlas Shrugged* (1957); *We the Living* (1959); *For the New Intellectual* (1961). Robinson, Jill, *Bed/Time/Story* (1975). Robinson, Mabel, *Bright Island* (1937). Rukeyser, Muriel, *The Speed of Darkness* (1968); *Breaking Open* (1973). Schneir, Muriel, ed., *Feminism: The Essential Writings* (1972). Stein, Gertrude, *Four Saints in Three Acts* (1934); *The Geographical History of America* (1936). Tracy, Honor, *The Butterflies of the Province* (1970). Welty, Eudora, *The Optimist's Daughter* (1969). Wilhelm, Gale, *We Too Are Drifting* (1975).

Ransdall • Terrell, Mary Church, *A Colored Woman in a White World* (1940).

Regnery • Kollwitz, Käthe (Hans, Kollwitz, ed.), *Diaries and Letters* (1955). Montessori, Maria, *The Child in the Family* (1970).

Reilly & Lee • Turnbull, Margaret, *Alabaster Lamps* (1925); *The Left Lady* (1926).

Reynal • Roy, Gabrielle, *The Tin Flute* (1947).

Riverside • Barnes, Margaret Ayer, *Years of Grace* (1930); *Westward Passage* (1931).

Routledge • Russell, Dora, *The Right to Be Happy* (1927). Sand, George, *The Letters of George Sand* (1930). Weil, Simone, *The Need for Roots* (1952); (Elisabeth Chase Geissbuhler, ed.), *Intimations of Christianity* (1957); *Oppression and Liberty* (1958).

Saturday Review • Gornick, Vivian, *In Search of Ali-Mahmoud: An American Woman in Egypt* (1973). Ziegler, Mel, ed., *Bella!* (1972).

Schocken • Senesh, Hannah, *Hannah Senesh: Her Life and Diary* (1966).

Scribner's • Caldwell, Taylor, *Dynasty of Death* (1938); *This Side of Innocence* (1946). Davis, Dorothy Salisbury, *Old Sinners Never Die* (1959); *Black Sheep Among White Lamb* (1963); *The Little Brothers* (1973). Gerould, Katherine F., *Modes and Morals* (1920; *Conquistadors* (1923). Hunter, Kristin, *The Landlord* (1969). Hurston, Zora Neale, *Seraph on the Swanee* (1948). Mead, Margaret, ed., *American Women: The Report on the President's Commission on the Status of Women* (1965). Miller, Helen Hill, *Sicily and the Western Colonies of Greece* (1965). Le Guin, Ursula K., *The Lathe of Heaven* (1971). Leslie, Anita, *Lady Randolph Churchill* (1970). Nemser, Cindy, *Art Talk* (1975). Rawlings, Marjorie Kinnan, *South Moon Under* (1933); *The Yearling* (1938); *The Sojourner* (1953). Robinson, Corinne Roosevelt, *The Call of Brotherhood and Other Poems* (1912); *My Brother Theodore Roosevelt* (1921); *Out of Nymph* (1930). Wharton, Edith, *Ethan Frome* (1911);

*Xingu and Other Stories* (1926); *The Descent of Man* (1932); *The House of Mirth* (1933).

Secker & Warburg · Carswell, Catherine, *The Savage Pilgrimage* (1932). Colette, *The Tender Shoot and Other Stories* (1958); *Break of Day* (1961). Gilliatt, Penelope, *A State of Change* (1967).

Sedgwick & Jackson · Fleming, Marjory, *Journal* (1934). Harrison, Jane, *Alpha and Omega* (1915).

Thomas Seltzer · Scott, Evelyn, *Escapade* (1923).

Seven Woods · Schaeffer, Susan Fromberg, *The Witch and the Weather Report* (1972).

Seymour · Key, Ellen, *The Morality of Woman and Other Essays* (1911).

Simon & Schuster · Ashton-Warner, Sylvia, *Teacher* (1963); *Myself* (1967). Brownmiller, Susan, *Against Our Will: Men, Women, and Rape* (1975). Edwards, Anne, *Judy Garland* (1974). Garden, Mary, and Biancolli, Louis, *Mary Garden's Story* (1951). Halsey, Margaret, *With Malice Toward Some* (1939); *The Folks at Home* (1952). Head, Bessie, *When Rain Clouds Gather* (1968). Hobson, Laura Z., *Gentlemen's Agreement* (1946). Howe, Louise Kapp, ed., *The Future of the Family* (1972). Johnston, Jill, *Lesbian Nation: The Feminist Solution* (1973). Lessing, Doris, *Martha Quest* (1964); *Particularly Cats* (1967). Miller, Alice Duer, *Forsaking All Others* (1931). Mitford, Jessica, *The American Way of Death* (1963). Morgan, Edward P., ed., *This I Believe* (1953). Quinn, Sally, *We're Going to Make You a Star* (1975). Roiphe, Anne Richardson, *Up the Sandbox!* (1970); *Long Division* (1972). Rossner, Judith, *Looking for Mr. Goodbar* (1975). Rubinstein, Helena, *My Life for Beauty* (1961). Stead, Christine, *The Man Who Loved Children* (1940). Wakoski, Diane, *The Motorcycle Betrayal Poems* (1971).

Small, Maynard · Glaspell, Susan, *Suppressed Desires* (1914); *Bernice* (1919); *Inheritors* (1921).

Smith & Haas · Bowen, Marjorie, *Moss Rose* (1935). Dinesen, Isak, *Seven Gothic Tales* (1934).

Stein & Day · Abbott, Sidney, and Love, Barbara J., *Sappho Was a Right-On Woman* (1972). Albertson, Chris, *Bessie* (1972). Howar, Barbara, *Laughing All the Way* (1973). Morgan, Elaine, *The Descent of Woman* (1972). Nelson, Paula, *The Joy of Money* (1975). Perry, Eleanor, *The Swimmer*—screenplay (1967). Restout, Denise, *Landowska on Music* (1964).

Lyle Stuart · Wolfe, Don, ed., *American Scene: New Voices* (1963).

Sun Dial · Baker, Dorothy, *Young Man with a Horn* (1944); *Trio* (1945).

Suomen Teatterilitto · Manner, Eeva-Liisa, *Snow in May* (1966).

Swallow · Nin, Anaïs, *Under a Glass Bell* (1948); *Winter of Artifice* (1948).

Taplinger · Goodman, Linda, *Sun Signs* (1968).

Tarcher · Edwards, Marie, and Hoover, Eleanor, *The Challenge of Being Single* (1975).

Theosophical · Besant, Annie Wood, *Wake Up, India: A Plea for Social Reform* (1913).

Theta Arts · Eustis, Morton, *Players at Work* (1937).

Time-Life · Bishop, Elizabeth, *Brazil* (1962). *This Fabulous Century: 1930–1940* and *1950–1960* (1969, 1970).

Turret · Plath, Sylvia, *Three Women* (1968).

University of California · Epstein, Cynthia Fuchs, *Woman's Place* (1971). Miles, Josephine, *Poetry and Change* (1974). Moore, Marianne, *The Ewing Lectures* (1958).

University of Chicago · Putnam, Emily James, *The Lady* (1970). Wells, Ida B. (Alfreda M. Duster, ed.), *The Autobiography of Ida B. Wells* (1970).

University of Oklahoma · Stevens, David H. ed., *Ten Talents in the American Theater* (1957).

University of Pittsburgh · Kaufman, Shirley, *The Floor Keeps Turning* (1970).

University (Cambridge) · Hazeltine, H. D., Lapsley, G., and Winfield, P. H., *Selected Essays of F. W. Maitland* (1936).

T. Fisher Unwin · Stanton, Elizabeth Cady, *Eighty Years and More* (1898). Strachy, Ray, *Frances Willard: Her Life and Work* (1912). Troubridge, Lady, *The Millionaire* (1907).

Vanguard · Markova, Alicia, *Giselle and I* (1960). Oates, Joyce Carol, *Upon the Sweeping Flood and Other Stories* (1965); *A Garden of Earthly Delights* (1966); *Them* (1969); *The Wheel of Love and Other Stories* (1970); *Do with Me What You Will* (1973). Sitwell, Edith, *Collected Poems of Edith Sitwell* (1954).

Van Nostrand · Brownell, Baker, *Art and the Worth-While* (1929).

Viking · Arendt, Hannah, *Between Past and Future* (1961); *Eichmann in Jerusalem* (1963); *On Revolution* (1963). Benedict, Ruth, *Race: Science and Politics* (1945). Gilliatt, Penelope, *Sunday Bloody Sunday* (1972). Gordimer, Nadine, *Not for Publication and Other Stories* (1965); *The Conservationist* (1975). Guest, Barbara, *Moscow Mansions* (1975). Hacker, Marilyn, *Presentation Piece* (1974). Hochman, Sandra, *Love Letters from Asia* (1967). Hurnscot, Loran, *A Prison, a Paradise*, Vol. II (1959). Lawrence, Frieda, *Not I, But the Wind* (1934). Loos, Anita, *A Girl Like I* (1966); *Kiss Hollywood Good-by* (1974). Mannes, Marya, *Message from a Stranger* (1948). Mariia, Grand Duchess of Russia (H. J. Ferris, ed.), *Education of a Princess* (1930). McGinley, Phyllis, *The Province of the Heart* (1959); *Saint-Watching* (1969). Moore, Marianne, *A Marianne Moore Reader* (1961). Murdoch, Iris, *The Flight from the Enchanter* (1955); *The Bell* (1958); *A Severed Head* (1961); *The Uni-*

*corn* (1963); *The Nice and the Good* (1968); *The Sacred and the Profane* (1974). Parker, Dorothy, *The Portable Dorothy Parker* (1944). Perkins, Frances, *The Roosevelt I Knew* (1946). Primrose, George, *They All Sang* (1934). Silver, Joan, and Gottlieb, Linda, *Limbo* (1972). Spark, Muriel, *The Hothouse by the East River* (1973). Warner, Sylvia Townsend, *Opus* (1931); *The Cat's Cradle-Book* (1940); *Swans on an Autumn River* (1966). Werfel, Alma Mahler, *Gustav Mahler* (1946). West, Jessamyn, *Black Lamb and Grey Falcon* (1941); *The Quaker Reader* (1962).

Vintage • Laurel, Alicia Bay, *Living on the Earth* (1971). Shulman, Alix Kates, ed., *Red Emma Speaks: Selected Writings and Speeches by Emma Goldman* (1972). Stein, Gertrude, *Everybody's Autobiography* (1973).

Washington • Ashman, Charles, and Engelmayer, Sheldon, *Martha: The Mouth That Roared* (1973).

Weidenfield & Nicholson • Maraini, Dacia, *The Holiday* (1966). Nicolson, Nigel, *Portrait of a Marriage* (1973).

Whitney Museum of Modern Art • Goodrich, Lloyd, and Bly, Doris, *Georgia O'Keeffe* (1970).

Windmill • Saunders, Edith, *Lourdes* (1940).

Winston • Sinclair, Upton Beall, ed., *The Cry for Justice* (1915).

Wollstonecraft • Alexander, Shana, *State-by-State Guide to Women's Legal Rights* (1975). Billings, Victoria, *The Womansbook* (1974).

Workers Library • Flynn, Elizabeth Gurley, *Debs, Haywood, Ruthenberg* (1939).

World • Beauvoir, Simone de, *All Men Are Mortal* (1955); *Memoirs of a Dutiful Daughter* (1959). Dayan, Yael, *New Face in the Mirror* (1959); *Envy the Frightened* (1960). Fadiman, Clifton, *Party of One* (1955). Rieux, M. Virginie des, *Le Satyre* (1967). Smith, Lillian, *The Journey* (1954).

The Writer • Mirrielees, Edith Ronald, *Story Writing* (1947).

Yale University • Stein, Gertrude, *Alphabets and Birthdays* (1957). West, Rebecca, *The Court and the Castle* (1957).

## MAGAZINES

*AFTRA Magazine, American Film Magazine, American Journal of Orthopsychiatry, American Journal of Psychotherapy, American Mercury, American Scholar, American Sociological Review, Arts Weekly, Asia, Atlantic Monthly, The Black Scholar, Branching Out, Broadside, Cahiers du Cinema, Cahiers du Sud, Canadian Forum, The Center Magazine, College English, Commentary, Coronet, Dancemagazine, Ebony, Ellery Queen's Mystery Magazine, Esquire, Everybody's Magazine, Forbes, Foreign Affairs, Fortune, Freedomways, Good Housekeeping, Hadassah, Harper's Bazaar, Harper's, Holiday, Infinity, Israel Magazine, Journal of the American Psychoanalytical Association, Journal of Negro History, Journal of Neuropsychiatry, Journal of Southern History, Ladies' Home Journal, Liberty, Life, Leviathan, Look, Nadenoiselle, McCall's, Metropolitan Magazine, Monthly Review, Motive Magazine, Movie Digest, Ms., The Nation, Natural History, Negro Digest, New Left Review, New Orleans, Newsweek, New Woman, New York Review of Books, The New Yorker, North American Review, Nouveaux Cahiers, Nova, Onyx, Oui, Paris Review, People, Pictorial Review, The. Progressive, Psychoanalytic Quarterly, Psychology Today, Quote, Ramparts, Reader's Digest, Redbook, The Reporter, Retirement Living, Rolling Stone, Saturday Evening Post, Saturday Review, Science, Scientific American, Scribner's Magazine, Signature, South Dakota Review, Southern Voices, Spare Rib, Survey Graphic, Theatre Arts, Time, U.S. News & World Report, Viva, Vogue, Voices, Westways, Who, Womanspace, Women: A Journal of Liberation, Women and Film, Writer's Digest.*

## NEWSPAPERS

*Afro-American, Birmingham* (England) *Post, The Christian Science Monitor, L'Europeo, Le Gaulois, El Grito del Norte, London Daily Chronicle, London Times, Los Angeles Herald-Examiner, Los Angeles Times, Louisiana Weekly, Le Matin, New York Call, New York Herald-Tribune, New York Journal-American, New York Mirror, New York Post, The New York Times, New York World-Telegram, The Observer, Pittsburgh Courier, PM, San Francisco Chronicle* and *Examiner, Shanghai Evening Post, Village Voice, The Washington Post.*

## MISCELLANEOUS

American Unitarian Association, Baldwin School (Bryn Mawr, Pennsylvania), CBS-TV ("60 Minutes"), Conservation in Action, Creative Management Associates, English Association, Foreign Language Press, Graph Communications Consultants, Information Documentation on the Concillar Church, Intellectual Co-operative, William Morris Agency, Museum of Modern Art, National Organization for Women (NOW), Phoenix Films, Bernard Quaritch.

## REFERENCE SOURCES

In addition to the books and periodicals from which quotations were taken, another group of works was consulted to obtain biographical and bibliographical information. The author wishes to express her indebtedness to the following reference works, catalogs, and indices for the invaluable aid they provided in compiling this book.

*The Academic Who's Who*, 1973–1974
*American Architects Directory*, 1970
*American Authors and Books*
*The American Heritage Dictionary*, 1969, 1970
*American Men and Women of Science: Behavioral and Social Sciences*, 12th ed.
*American Psychological Association Directory*, 1974
*Bartlett's Familiar Quotations* (several editions)
*The Biographical Encyclopedia and Who's Who of the American Theater*, 1966
*Biography Index*, Vols. 1–9 and Sept. 1973–Aug. 1975
*Books in Print* (several editions)
Brown University Library Catalog of American Poetry and Plays
*Chamber's Biographical Dictionary*, 1969
*The Columbia Encyclopedia*, 3rd ed., 1963
*Contemporary Authors*, Vols. 1–56
*Current Biography*, 1940–1975
*Cumulative Book Index* (several editions)
*Dictionary of American Biography*, Vols. 1–10, 1933
*Dictionary of American Scholars*
*Dictionary of Authors*
*Dictionary of National Biography*, Vols. 1–22 and 1901–1960
*Dictionary of North American Authors*
*Encyclopedia Britannica*, 1953
*Encyclopedia of American Biography*, 1974
*The Great Quotations*, 1967
*The Home Book of Quotations*

*Index to Literary Biographies*, Vols. 1 & 2, 1975
*Index to Women*, 1970
*International Directory of Psychologists*, 1966
*Leaders in Education*
Los Angeles Public Library Catalog
*National Cyclopedia of American Biography*
*National Faculty Directory*, Vols. 1 & 2, 1975
National Union Catalog
*New York Times Obituary Index*
*The Oxford Dictionary of Quotations*, 2nd ed., 1955
*The Penguin Book of Modern Quotations*
*Readers' Guide to Periodical Literature*
*Roget's International Thesaurus*, 3rd ed., 1962
Southern California Answering Network
UCLA Card Catalog
USC Card Catalog
*Webster's American Biographies*, 1974
*Webster's Biographical Dictionary*, 1972
*Webster's New Twentieth Century Dictionary*, 2nd ed., unabridged, 1971
*Webster's New World Thesaurus*, 1974
*Who Was Who in America*, 1607–1973
*Who's Who*, 1897–1975
*Who's Who in America*, 38th ed.
*Who's Who in American Education*
*Who's Who in American Politics*, 4th ed.
*Who's Who in American Women*, 1974–1975
*Who's Who in France*, 12th ed.
*Who's Who in Germany*, 5th ed.
*Who's Who in Government*, 2nd ed.
*Who's Who in the Theatre*, 15th ed.
*Who's Who in the World*, 1974
*World Book Encyclopedia*, 1972
*Writer's Dictionary*

# Introduction

What makes anyone quotable? To have been at some time in the public eye, to have had wit, a way with words, been able to make a cogent observation in few words, to have hit hard in wrath or fervor! The choice of such quotations is probably determined both by the prestige of the quoted person and by the intrinsic worth of the quotation itself.

The case of *The Quotable Woman* is something else. It bears witness to an exhaustive study of the thought of women in virtually every walk of life and in most of communicative society, selected and distilled; but the selection is not made on the basis of exterior criteria of relative values nor according to the preferences of the author of the book, Elaine Partnow. Her inclusiveness takes us chronologically from Catharine Esther Beecher, born in 1800 to Denise M. Boudrot, 1952, and in diversity from Mme. Chiang Kai-Shek to Amelia Earhart, from Margaret Mead to Golda Meir, from Zsa Zsa Gabor to Simone de Beauvoir.

What Ms. Partnow has achieved over and above the standard guidelines of a *Bartlett's* kind of volume is to make the quotations representative of the *total* woman—at least that is the impression she conveys to me relative to the women I recognize and know in her list. I found only one important woman absent from her roster: Nathalie Sarraute, the French novelist who in her quiet way has revolutionized the modern novel, and who does not get involved in women's movements. No grandiose statements have come from her direction, yet in her book of critical writings, entitled *Era of Suspicion*, she has provided our time with a label that may become as memorable as W. H. Auden's "age of anxiety" which characterized an earlier period.

Ms. Partnow's international optic has included most other women of note by giving the reader telling excerpts from their writings and communications; the space allotted to each and the length of the passage are determined, as far as I can judge, by the pertinence and strength of the remarks. There are perhaps too many movie stars—but that is the circle she is closest to, and if I do not find enough scholars and educators that is my own professional bias. All anthologies bear the imprint of the collector, and out of this one Ms. Partnow emerges with a great deal of good sense, a great deal of faith in women's wisdom, and approval of their positive thinking. Many of the current women's liberation leaders are represented but not to the exclusion of those of another age. We read with pleasure Emma Goldman's comprehension of what real liberation is: "true emancipation begins neither at the polls nor in courts. It begins in woman's soul," in *Tragedy of Women's Emancipation*. We are encouraged by Helen Gahagan Douglas' conviction: "I know the force women can exert in directing the course of events." We wish *that* time would come sooner than it has!

The reader will realize, indeed, how many substantial women had distinguished careers as writers, artists, and publicists before the fanfare about the "new" woman. Hopefully, the availability of this volume will encourage speechwriters to look for words of wisdom to quote from famous women as they do from men. As a matter of fact, one of the greatest disadvantages that women have suffered in gaining entry into the mainstream of public life, intellectually and socially, beyond the limits of quotas and tokenism, has been their inability to penetrate the consciousness and frame of reference of the central intelligence of society.

*The Quotable Woman* should henceforth find its place next to *Webster's Dictionary* on executive desks of thinkers, writers, movers, and shakers.

Beginning with a cursory reading, quickly you become absorbed, and as you read on and on, and follow the passage of the years, you realize that women's concerns follow closely those of men, that interests are not determined by sex but by the human condition. According to Ms. Partnow's meticulous analytical subject index, the most numerous of quotable reflections concern the self, life, love, marriage, children, death, war, and God. Ms. Partnow has allowed the poets among the women to speak in verse. She has wisely avoided aphorisms, and when she extracts from speeches and essays she deftly averts fragmentation; she succeeds in providing the reader with a clear-cut unity of thoughts. She also whets the appetite and is apt to send us to library shelves for further reading from the women quoted.

Let us hope that preachers, commencement speakers, and political speech writers, along with government agencies and groups searching for women executives, college presidents, etc., will have resource to this valuable guide to the mind and heart of the modern woman, and that as a reference book it may turn into *the portable woman*.

—Anna Balakian

Anna Balakian is Professor of French and Comparative Literature at New York University, author of four books on surrealism and symbolism, and of over a hundred essays on modern literature, and is currently President of the American Comparative Literature Association.

# Preface

There is some controversy over the very concept of anthology and abridgment. In her anthology *The Feminist Papers*, Alice Rossi says, "Abridgment of any published book or essay is an assault, a cutting or pruning by one mind of the work of another." A flip of the coin and we find Louise Imogen Guiney's opinion that "quotations . . . from the great old authors are an act of filial reverence," expressed in an article she wrote for *Scribner's*. Since the coin will probably land on its edge, perhaps one should go along with Elizabeth Janeway, who wrote in *The Writer's Book*: "As long as mixed grills and combination salads are popular, anthologies will undoubtedly continue in favor."

And so they have. One of the most popular forms of anthology have been books of quotations. In January of 1974 the idea for *The Quotable Woman* crystallized in my mind's eye—not as a feminist book, nor a book of feminists; not as a "woman's book," nor a book for women only—but a book of women, by women, for everyone.

For more than a hundred years now women have been "les frondeuses" for abolition, children's rights, unionism, and more. From their first embryonic struggles for suffrage to today's fight for the Equal Rights Amendment, woman's impact on society has been felt in all its spheres—the arts, politics, theater, literature; they've even altered the structure of the family. Yet, despite their impact, there has not been one single encyclopedic volume from which we could cull the contemplations, insights, and instructions of the daring women who have braved these good fights—at no uncertain risks, if not always of their lives, certainly of their reputations. Not one dusty offering have we from the patriarchal archives of our nation's libraries.

The staggering dearth of women in so many well-known books of quotations prompted me to compile the chart shown on the next page.

A few of the greats were there—Dickinson, Stein, Woolf—along with a few obscure poets who wrote of hearts and flowers, but that was it! Where were the great female revolutionaries, educators, and artists? The adventurers, the feminists, the Third World women? I was appalled—and determined to accomplish what I'd set out to do.

My ground rules for choosing the contributors were based on reputation, remarkability, quotability, and availability of their work. Also, the attempt was made to be as representative of as many professions and nations as possible, though writers and poets, American and English, do predominate.

| BOOK | TOTAL CONTRIBUTORS | PERCENTAGE OF WOMEN | TOTAL QUOTES | PERCENTAGE OF WOMEN |
|---|---|---|---|---|
| Bartlett's Familiar Quotations | 2,000 | 7½ % | 117,000 | ½ % |
| The Oxford Book of Quotations | 1,500 | 8½ | 40,000 | 1 |
| The New Dictionary of Thoughts | 1,800 | 10 | 20,000 | 2½ |
| Home Book of Quotations* | | 10 | | 5½ |
| Contemporary Quotations* | | 16 | | |
| Best Quotations for All Occasions* | | 5 | | ¾ |

* Random samples.

I used many standard guides to create my bibliography—the *Encyclopedia Britannica*, reputable anthologies—and many off-beat guides as well: small presses, feminist bibliographies, *Rolling Stone*.† I estimate having made use of some 3500 books and innumerable periodicals.

The quotations were chosen for various reasons—some for their lyricism, some for their uniqueness and piquancy, some because they were revelatory of the author's character, some because they were memorable and pertinent. Considered were infamous quotations, celebrated quotations, inventive quotations, and always, always usable quotations. A conscious effort was maintained to be as objective and eclectic as possible.

If usability was one of the criteria used in selecting the quotations, it was the only criterion used in compiling the Subject Index. Breaking from the tradition of indexing quotations by key words or phrases, I have attempted to synthesize the meaning of each quotation into one or more classifications.

If "Graceless, Pointless, Feckless and Aimless waited their turn to be milked" (from *Conference at Cold Comfort Farm* by Stella Gibbons) is indexed as "graceless" it gives little help to a reader who wants to illustrate a point. Indexing of this nature may amount to little more than a gargantuan vestigial organ. The same is true of the "by subject" method of indexing in which, for example, George Eliot's "An ass may bray a good while before he shakes the stars down" will be

† A comprehensive list, alphabetized by publisher, of the majority of works used in compiling this book may be found in the front of the book on pages xi through xxii. Additionally, a list of all reference works used in my research can be found on page xxiii.

placed under the heading of "fool." Somewhat helpful, yes, but not nearly so much as indexing it under "braggart" and "egotist."

I like an index that is practical and usable, one that tells the reader what the quotation is *about*. Of course, there are shortcomings to this type of index. The reader searching for that favorite old quotation whose author is forgotten must try to duplicate my thinking processes to find "Graceless and Pointless . . ." classified under "cows" (of necessity) as well as under "passivity," the point of the phrase. One might object—no, no "idleness" is more to the point. I can only ask the reader to use her/his imagination and/or thesaurus, as I did. To have indexed all possible synonymous meanings as well as multiple meanings would have produced an elephantine index. Still, most quotations are classified under at least two different subjects, and some under three or four.

This Subject Index is not meant, however, to categorically pigeonhole the thoughts expressed in the quotations—simply to serve as a guide. There is a not so subtle philosophical difference in this approach which ironically makes the index both more arbitrary and more useful while implying—with some justification— that the key word/phrase method tends to serve the book, not the reader.

It seemed propitious to present the contributors chronologically, to project a sense of history and give the reader a perspective on where women in general have been and where they are going. It offers insight into changes in ideas, language (original spellings and idiosyncrasies of speech have been maintained), the use of newly gained freedoms—even in the popularity of first names. Thus, the chronological order is one more useful tool.

The frustration of tracking down biographical data on "lost" women was at times maddening. Scores of letters were sent to women in care of publishers, agents, and various organizations. Information was sought in the biographies of a contributor's husband, son, brother, or great-grandnephew. Years of birth were most elusive. Occasionally, when faced with a missing chink in the biographical or bibliographical armor, I included the woman or quotation anyway. Rather than lose fine contributors and good quotations to be true to form, I chose to be true to the women.

Through all this sleuthing I have come to feel that the public regards women in past and current history very much like fine character actors—we recognize them but do not know their names; we need them but do not pay them homage; we make demands on them but do not document their contributions. I hope that the quotations garnered here will counteract some of those lapses, that they will stimulate reading and study, that they will help retrieve "lost" women and help "found" women get some of their own back.

The most difficult part of an impossible task was, simply, to stop. This is—and probably always will be—an unfinished work. For every woman included, five, ten, twenty more could be added. Among those most frequently missing are non-English speaking women. The highly prolific Marie von Ebner-Eschenbach, for example, is sorely underrepresented because so few English translations of her works could be found. I even had difficulty finding translations of George Sand! But at least these women are represented—there were dozens more I wanted to include, but I could find nothing by them available in English. Helplessly, I was forced to eliminate one woman after another.

Many talented and deserving women whose works were collaborations with male partners also had to be ignored. And several distinguished scientists and mathematicians were left out because, though the women were/are memorable, I could find nothing "quotable"—at least nothing most of us could understand. And quotability is the principal measure for inclusion in *The Quotable Woman.*

As this is a book of learning and sharing,there is a section for Readers' Notes at the back of the book, where the reader should feel free to enter her/his own favorite quotations or comments.

With sharing in mind, I'd like to take some space to thank the people who contributed to the making of this book:

To the women who worked as my assistants and co-workers, who went beyond the tasks asked of them, working golden time for grey wages: Janine Watson, Paula Gray, Krista Michaels, Hazel Medina and, most especially, Georgia Griggs, my right—and left—hand;

To the one who saw me through it all, and held me up a good part of the time: Turner Browne, my friend and consort, if you will;

To family, friends, and associates who supported me and advised me: Al and Sylvia Partnow, Judith and Herb Hyman, Susan and Barry Partnow-Ganapol, Alejandro Grattan, Aniko Klein, Stanley Corwin, Marcy Posner, Beth Sue Rose, and all the staff at Corwin Books, Bob Garfield, Beverly Iser, Annett H. Welles, Gilda Cohen, Michele Kort, Robin Pearl, Ann and Burt Witkovsky, and Connell Cowan;

To the librarians and information service of the Los Angeles City Public Library's Main Branch, and to the Graduate Reserve Desk and general facilities of UCLA's Research Library;

To all of them—a hearty and keenly felt thanks.

But most of all I am indebted to the women who made this book possible—the contributors. Thank you, sisters.

Elaine Partnow
Los Angeles
April, 1977

# How to Use This Book

The women quoted are presented in chronological order according to the year of their birth, beginning with the year 1800, and alphabetically within each year. Each has been given a contributor number; these numbers appear in the headings for each page in the Quotations section, and are used in the Biographical and Subject Indices rather than page numbers.

Firm birth and/or death dates are not known for every woman. When it was possible to make an accurate guess, a date followed by a question mark is given. If this was not possible, the women were given "flourished" decade dates (e.g., fl. 1850s), meaning that as near as can be figured they were most active in a certain decade. Such women are grouped together at the beginning of that decade's entries. If it is not known when a woman died but it is probable that she is no longer living, there is a question mark instead of a death date. Women who are presumably still alive and active but for whom, despite all efforts, no birth date could be found are grouped together at the end of the Quotations section, following a "Contemporary/No Date" subhead.

The quotations for each woman are presented chronologically according to the copyright date or publication date of the source. If the source was published after a woman's death, it is followed by a "p" (e.g.,1973p), indicating that it is posthumous. If only an approximate year of publication is known, the date is preceded by "c" for circa (e.g., c.1943). Parenthetical dates within a source indicate the time at which the quotation was originally spoken or written, whereas dates appearing in quotation marks indicate chapter or section titles in the sources.

In some cases no date could be found for a quotation (especially true for some poems and essays); these quotations follow the dated sources, separated from them by three asterisks across the column, and are listed alphabetically, by the first word of each new quotation.

When possible, the location of the quotation within the source is given—that is, the part, chapter, act, scene, etc. If, however, a quote was derived from somewhere other than the source itself—for example, from a book review—and the precise location is not known, it precedes those quotations that are more specifically designated. Of course, many books have no chapter or part numbers or headings, and so locations cannot be specified for these.

Abbreviations used in source citations are: Vol.—volume; Pt.—part; Bk.—book; Ch.—chapter; St.—stanza; Sec.—section; No.—number; Sc.—scene; l.—line; c.—circa; p.—posthumous; ed.—editor.

When a quotation was taken from a book, article, or any work by a writer other than our contributor, it is indicated by the words quoted in followed by the source and its author. In the instance of anthological works "quoted in" is not used, but editors are indicated.

Quote marks around a quotation indicate that it is dialogue spoken by a character in a work of fiction. Except for exchanges of dialogue, original paragraphing is not indicated.

For information concerning the Biographical and Subject Indices, see notes preceding each index.

I would venture to guess that Anon,
who wrote so many poems without signing
them, was often a woman.

—*Virginia Woolf*

American women are not the only people
in the world who manage to lose track
of themselves, but we do seem to
mislay the past in a singularly
absent-minded fashion.

—*Elizabeth Janeway*

The signals of the century
Proclaim the things that are to be—
The rise of woman to her place,
The coming of a nobler race.

—*Angela Morgan*

# The Quotations

## 1. Catharine Esther Beecher
### (1800–1878)

1 Woman's great mission is to train immature, weak, and ignorant creatures to obey the laws of God; the physical, the intellectual, the social, and the moral—first in the family, then in the school, then in the neighborhood, then in the nation, then in the world. . . .
> "An Address to the Christian Women of America," *Woman Suffrage and Women's Professions* 1871

2 To open avenues to political place and power for all classes of women would cause [the] humble labors of the family and school to be still more undervalued and shunned. Ibid.

3 . . . as if *reasoning* were *any kind* of writing or talking which tends to convince people that some doctrine or measure is true and right. Ibid.

4 How many young hearts have revealed the fact that what they had been trained to imagine the highest earthly felicity was but the beginning of care, disappointment, and sorrow, and often led to the extremity of mental and physical suffering.
> Ibid., "Statistics of Female Health"

5 The delicate and infirm go for sympathy, not to the well and buoyant, but to those who have suffered like themselves. Ibid.

## 2. Julia Crawford
### (1800–1885)

1 Kathleen Mavourneen! The grey dawn is breaking
The horn of the hunter is heard
on the hill.
> "Kathleen Mavourneen," St. 1
> 1835

2 Oh! Hast thou forgotten how soon we must sever?
Oh! Hast thou forgotten this day we must part?
It may be for years, and it may be for ever;
Then why art thou silent, thou voice of my heart?
> Ibid.

## 3. Frederika Bremer
### (1801–1865)

1 Thou mayest own the world, with health
And unslumbering powers;
Industry alone is wealth,
What we do is ours.
> "Home" 1885

## 4. Jane Welsh Carlyle
### (1801–1866)

1 He [Thomas Carlyle] has his talents, his vast and cultivated mind, his vivid imagination, his independence of soul and his high-souled principles of honour. But then—ah, these Buts! Saint Preux never kicked the fireirons, nor made puddings in his tea cup.
> Letter to Friend (July, 1821), *Letters and Memorials* 1883p

2 If they had said the sun and the moon was gone out of the heavens, it could not have struck me with the idea of a more awful and dreary blank in the creation than the words: Byron is dead.
> Ibid., Letter to Thomas Carlyle (1824)

3 . . . the only thing that makes one place more attractive to me than another is the quantity of *heart* I find in it. . . .
> Ibid., Letter (1829)

4 Medical men all over the world having merely entered into a tacit agreement to call all sorts of maladies people are liable to, in cold weather, by one name; so that one sort of treatment may serve for all, and their practice thereby be greatly simplified.
> Ibid., Letter to John Welsh (March 4, 1837)

5 Some new neighbors, that came a month or two ago, brought with them an accumulation of all the things to be guarded against in a London neighborhood, viz., a pianofort, a lap-dog, and a parrot. Ibid., Letter to Thomas Carlyle's Mother (May 6, 1839)

3

6 . . . I can see that the Lady has a genius for ruling, whilst I have a genius for *not being ruled.*
Ibid., Letter to Thomas Carlyle (1845)

7 It is sad and wrong to be so dependent for the life of my life on any human being as I am on you; that I cannot by any force of logic cure myself at this date, when it has become second nature. If I have to lead another life in any of the planets, I shall take precious good care not to hang myself round any man's neck, either as a locket or a millstone.     Ibid. (1850)

8 Never does one feel oneself so utterly helpless as in trying to speak comfort for great bereavement. I will not try it. Time is the only comforter for the loss of a mother.
Ibid. (December 27, 1853)

9 If peace and quietness be not in one's own power, one can always give oneself at least bodily fatigue—no such bad *succe daneum**
after all.        Ibid., Journal Entry
(October 23, 1855)

10 When one has been threatened with a great injustice, one accepts a smaller as a favour.
Ibid. (November 21, 1855)

11 All that senseless singing of *Te Deum* before the battle has begun!     Ibid., Letter

12 It's [society] like seasickness: one thinks at the time one will never risk it again, and then the impression wears off and one thinks perhaps one's constitution has changed and that this time it will be more bearable.      Ibid.

* * *

13 Of all God's creatures, Man alone is poor.
"To a Swallow Building
Under Our Eaves"

## 5. Lydia M. Child
### (1802–1880)

1 In most nations the path of antiquity is shrouded in darkness, rendered more visible by the wild, fantastic light of fable; but with us, the vista of time is luminous to its remotest point.     *Hobomok*, Ch. 1    *1824*

2 The old men gazed on them in their loveliness, and turned away with that deep and painful sigh, which the gladness of childhood, and the transient beauty of youth, are so apt to awaken in the bosom of the aged.     Ibid., Ch. 8

* Substitution.

3 "The fact is, passengers to heaven are in haste, and will walk one way or the other. If a man doubts of his way, Satan is always ready at hand to help him to a new set of opinions at every stage. . . ."      Ibid., Ch. 13

4 England may as well dam up the waters from the Nile with bulrushes as to fetter the step of Freedom, more proud and firm in this youthful land. . . .     *The Rebels*, Ch. 4    *1825*

5 I sometimes think the gods have united human beings by some mysterious principle, like the according notes of music. Or is it as Plato has supposed, that souls originally one have been divided, and each seeks the half it lost?
*Philothea: A Romance*, Ch. 1    *1836*

6 Every human being has, like Socrates, an attendant spirit; and wise are they who obey its signals. If it does not always tell us what to do, it always cautions us what not to do.
Ibid., Ch. 6

7 No music is so pleasant to my ears as that word —father. Zoroaster tells us that children are a bridge joining this earth to a heavenly paradise, filled with fresh springs and blooming gardens. Blessed indeed is the man who hears many gentle voices call him father!    Ibid., Ch. 19

8 Now twilight lets her curtain down
And pins it with a star.
Obituary for MacDonald Clark
*1842*

9 Whoso does not see that genuine life is a battle and a march has poorly read his origin and his destiny.     *Letters from New York*, Vol. I
*1852*

10 It is right noble to fight with wickedness and wrong; the mistake is in supposing that spiritual evil can be overcome by physical means.
Ibid.

11 Not in vain is Ireland pouring itself all over the earth. . . . The Irish, with their glowing hearts and reverent credulity, are needed in this cold age of intellect and skepticism.
Ibid., No. 33 (December 8, 1842)

12 None speaks of the bravery, the might, or the intellect of Jesus; but the devil is always imagined as being of acute intellect, political cunning, and the fiercest courage.     Ibid.

13 But now I have lost the power of looking merely on the surface. Everything seems to me to come from the Infinite, to be filled with the Infinite, to be tending toward the Infinite.
Ibid.

14 The more women become rational companions, partners in business and in thought, as well as in affection and amusement, the more highly will men appreciate *home*—that blessed work, which opens to the human heart the most perfect glimpse of Heaven, and helps to carry it thither, as on an angel's wings.
Ibid., No. 34 (January, 1843)

15 Spiritual bloom and elasticity are . . . injured by modes of life untrue to nature.
Ibid., Vol. II, No. 31
(December 31, 1844)

16 Use is the highest law of our being, and it cannot be disobeyed with impunity.        Ibid.

17 So he began to be very thoughtful about every action of his life; and if he felt uneasy about anything he was tempted to do, he said to himself, "This is the inward light, showing me that the thing is wrong. I will not do it." Pursuing this course, he became careful not to do anything which did not bring peace to his soul; and as the soul can never be peaceful when it disobeys God, he was continually travelling toward Zion while he strove to follow this inward light in his soul; and the more humbly he tried to follow it, the clearer the light became.
"William Boen," *The Freedmen's Book*
*1865*

18 But men never violate the laws of God without suffering the consequences, sooner or later.
Ibid., "Toussaint L'Ouverture"

19 There are not many people who are conscientious about being kind in their relations with human beings; and therefore it is not surprising that still fewer should be considerate about humanity to animals. . . . The fact is, reasonable and kind treatment will generally produce a great and beneficial change in vicious animals as well as in vicious men.
Ibid., "Kindness to Animals"

20 Ah, my friend, that is the only true church organization, when heads and hearts unite in working for the welfare of the human race!
Letter to Theodore Weld        *1880*

* * *

21 Genius hath electric power
Which earth can never tame.
"Marius Amid the Ruins of Carthage"

22 Over the river and through the wood,
To grandfather's house we'll go.
"Thanksgiving Day," St. 1

## 6. Dorothea Dix
(1802–1887)

1 The present state of insane persons, confined within this commonwealth, in cages, closets, cellars, stalls, pens! Chained, naked, beaten with rods, and lashed into obedience.
*Memorial to the Legislature of*
*Massachusetts        1843*

2 I think even lying on my bed I can still do something.        Attributed        *July 17, 1887*

3 In a world where there is so much to be done, I felt strongly impressed that there must be something for me to do.
*Letters from New York*, Vol. II
(1852), Lydia Maria Child, ed.
*December 31, 1944p*

* * *

4 I have myself seen more than nine thousand idiots, epileptics and insane in the United States . . . bound with galling chains, bowed beneath fetters, lacerated with ropes, scourged with rods.
First Petition to Congress

## 7. Letitia Landon
(1802–1838)

* * *

1 As beautiful as woman's blush—
As evanescent too.
"Apple Blossoms"

2 Childhood, whose very happiness is love.
"Erinna"

3 Few, save the poor, feel for the poor.
"The Poor"

4 I loved him too as woman loves—
Reckless of sorrow, sin or scorn.
"The Indian Bride"

5 We might have been—These are but common words,
And yet they make the sum of life's bewailing.
"Three Extracts from the
Diary of a Week"

6 Were it not better to forget
Than but remember and regret?
"Despondency"

## 8. Harriet Martineau
### (1802–1876)

1 If a test of civilisation be sought, none can be so sure as the condition of that half of society over which the other half has power—from the exercises of the right of the strongest.
"Women," *Society in America*, Vol. III
*1837*

2 . . . there is no country in the world where there is so much boasting of the "chivalrous" treatment she enjoys. . . . In short, indulgence is given her as a substitute for justice. Ibid.

3 There is a profusion of some things being taught which are supposed necessary because everybody learns them. . . . But what is given is, for the most part, passively received; and what is obtained is, chiefly, by means of the memory. Ibid.

4 Religion is a temper, not a pursuit. Ibid.

5 . . . the sum and substance of female education in America, as in England, is training women to consider marriage as the sole object in life, and to pretend that they do not think so. Ibid.

6 . . . fidelity to conscience is inconsistent with retiring modesty. If it be so, let the modesty succumb. It can be only a false modesty which can be thus endangered. Ibid.

7 Persecution for opinion, punishment for all manifestations of intellectual and moral strength, are still as common as women who have opinions and who manifest strength. . . . Ibid.

8 If there is any country on earth where the course of true love may be expected to run smooth, it is America. Ibid., "Marriage"

9 Marriage . . . is still the imperfect institution it must remain while women continue to be ill-educated, passive, and subservient. . . . Ibid.

10 . . . the early marriages of silly children . . . where . . . every woman is married before she well knows how serious a matter human life is. Ibid.

11 In no country, I believe, are the marriage laws so iniquitous as in England, and the conjugal relation, in consequence, so impaired. Ibid.

12 . . . nobody, I believe, defends the arrangement by which . . . divorce is obtainable only by the very rich. The barbarism of granting that as a privilege. . . ! Ibid.

13 Retribution is known to impend over violations of conjugal duty. Ibid.

14 It is clear that the sole business which legislation has with marriage is with the arrangements of property; to guard the reciprocal rights of the children of the marriage and the community. There is no further pretence for the interference of the law, in any way. Ibid.

15 I have no sympathy for those who, under any pressure of circumstances, sacrifice their heart's-love for legal prostitution. Ibid.

16 Any one must see at a glance that if men and women marry those whom they do not love, they must love those whom they do not marry. Ibid.

17 Laws and customs may be creative of vice; and should be therefore perpetually under process of observation and correction: but laws and customs cannot be creative of virtue: they may encourage and help to preserve it; but they cannot originate it. Ibid.

18 For my own part, I had rather suffer any inconvenience from having to work occasionally in chambers and kitchen . . . than witness the subservience in which the menial class is held in Europe. Ibid., "Occupation"

19 Readers are plentiful: thinkers are rare. Ibid.

20 They are better educated by Providence than by men. Ibid.

21 Their charity is overflowing, if it were but more enlightened. . . . Ibid.

22 . . . but is it not the fact that religion emanates from the nature, from the moral state of the individual? Is it not therefore true that unless the nature be completely exercised, the moral state harmonised, the religion cannot be healthy? Ibid.

23 During the present interval between the feudal age and the coming time, when life and its occupations will be freely thrown open to women as to men, the condition of the female working classes is such that if its sufferings were but made known, emotions of horror and shame would tremble through the whole of society. Ibid.

24 What office is there which involves more responsibility, which requires more qualifications, and which ought, therefore, to be more honourable, than that of teaching? Ibid.

25 The progression or emancipation of any class usually, if not always, takes place through the efforts of individuals of that class. . . . Ibid.

26 . . . is it to be understood that the principles of the Declaration of Independence bear no relation to half of the human race? Ibid.

27 . . . I declare that if we are to look for a hell upon earth, it is where polygamy exists: and that, as polygamy runs riot in Egypt, Egypt is the lowest depth of this hell.

"The Harem," *Eastern Life: Present and Past*     *1848*

28 Everywhere they [Egyptian women] pitied us European women heartily. . . . They think us strangely neglected in being left so free, and boast of their spy system and imprisonment as tokens of the value in which they are held.

Ibid.

29 I am sure that no traveler seeing things through author spectacles can see them as they are. . . .

*Harriet Martineau's Autobiography,* Vol. I     *1877p*

30 . . . in the history of human affections . . . the least satisfying is the fraternal. Brothers are to sisters what sisters can never be to brothers as objects of engrossing and devoted affection.

Ibid.

31 I am in truth very thankful for not having married at all.     Ibid.

32 The veneration in which I hold domestic life has always shown me that that life was not for those whose self respect had been early broken down, or had never grown.     Ibid.

33 The older I have grown, the more serious and irremediable have seemed to me the evils and disadvantages of married life as it exists among us at this time.     Ibid.

## 9. Marjory Fleming
### (1803–1811)

1 but gently said Marjory
go into another room and
think what a great crime
you are committing
letting your temper
git the better of you

*Diary of Marjory Fleming*, St. 1 (1811)
*1934p*

2 the most Devilish thing is 8 times 8
and 7 times 7 it is what nature itselfe
cant endure. . . .

Ibid.

3     love is a very
papithatick thing as well as
troubelsom and tiresome. . . .

Ibid.

4 To Day I pronounced a
word which should never
come out of a ladys lips it was
that I called John a Impu-
dent Bitch. . . .

Ibid., St. 3

5 Sentiment is what I am not acquainted with.
Ibid.

6 I confess that I have been
more like a little young
Devil then a creature. . . .

Ibid.

## 10. Marie Lovell
### (1803–1877)

1 PARTHENIA.   Clear be mine eyes, and thou, my soul, be steel!

*Ingomar, the Barbarian,* Act I    *1896p*

2 INGOMAR.   Freedom is hunting, feeding, danger;
that, that is freedom—that it is which makes
the veins to swell, the breast to heave and glow.
Aye, that is freedom,—that is pleasure—life!

Ibid., Act II

3 INGOMAR.   —This slavery
that gives thee freedom, brings along with it
so rich a treasure of consoling joy,
liberty shall be poor and worthless by its side.

Ibid., Act V

## 11. Maria McIntosh
### (1803–1878)

1 Beneficent Nature, how often does the heart of man, crushed beneath the weight of his sins or his sorrows, rise in reproach against thine unchanged serenity!    *Two Lives*, Ch. 1
*1846*

2 "Now, Jessie, there is some beauty and some goodness in every thing God has made, and he who has a pure conscience is like one looking into a clear stream; he sees it all; while him who has a bad conscience, all things look as you say they did in the muddy stream—black and ugly."    "Jessie Graham," *Aunt Kitty's Tales*    *1847*

3 ". . . there is selfishness in our hearts as long as we live; but while you watch over yourself, and pray earnestly to God against it, He will give you power always to act generously—to subdue your selfish feelings."

Ibid., "Florence Arnott"

4 To the inhabitants of the Southern States, not only the New Englander, but everyone who dwelt north of the Potomac was a Yankee—a name which was with him a synonym of meanness, avarice and low cunning—while the native of the Northern States regarded his southern fellow-citizens as an indolent and prodigal race, in comparison with himself but half civilized, and far better acquainted with the sword and the pistol than with any more useful instrument.      *The Lofty and the Lowly*, Ch. 1

*1852*

5 Why is it that the young, ingenuous soul shrinks so from the disclosure of its first, earnest views of the relations in which it stands to God and man—to its Creator and its fellow-creatures?

Ibid., Ch. 16

6 ". . . it is only death which is hopeless. . . ."

Ibid., Ch. 19

## 12. Susanna Moodie

(1803–1885)

1 I had heard and read much of savages, and have since seen, during my long residence in the bush, somewhat of uncivilized life, but the Indian is one of Nature's gentlemen—he never says or does a rude or vulgar thing. The vicious, uneducated barbarians, who form the surplus of overpopulace European countries, are far behind the wild man in delicacy of feeling or natural courtesy.      *Roughing It in the Bush*,

Ch. 1    *1852*

2 A nose, kind sir! Sure, Mother Nature,
With all her freaks, ne'er formed this feature.
If such were mine, I'd try and trade it,
And swear the gods had never made it.

Ibid., "Old Satan and Tom Wilson's
Nose," Ch. 6

3 I have a great dislike to removing, which involves a necessary loss, and is apt to give to the emigrant roving and unsettled habits.

Ibid., Ch. 12

4 But hunger's good sauce.      Ibid.

5 "I have no wish for a second husband. I had enough of the first. I like to have my own way —to lie down mistress, and get up master."

Ibid.

6 The pure beauty of the Canadian water, the somber but august grandeur of the vast forest that hemmed us in on every side and shut us out from the rest of the world, soon cast a magic spell upon our spirits, and we began to feel charmed with the freedom and solitude around us.      Ibid., Ch. 13

7 When hands are tightly clasped, 'mid struggling sighs
And streaming tears, those whisper'd accents rise,
  Leaving to God the objects of our care
In that short, simple, comprehensive prayer—
ADIEU!

Ibid., Ch. 25

8 I have given you a faithful picture of a life in the backwoods of Canada. . . . To the poor, industrious working man it presents many advantages; to the poor gentleman, *none*! The former works hard, puts up with coarse, scanty fare, and submits, with a good grace, to hardships that would kill a domesticated animal at home. Thus he becomes independent. . . . The gentleman can neither work so hard, live so coarsely, nor endure so many privations as his poorer but more fortunate neighbor.    Ibid.

9 Ah, Hope! what would life be, stripped of thy encouraging smiles, that teach us to look behind the dark clouds of to-day, for the golden beams that are to gild the morrow.

*Life in the Clearing*, Ch. 1    *1853*

10 To wean a fellow-creature from the indulgence of a gross sensual propensity, as I said before, we must first convince the mind: the reform must commence there. Merely withdrawing the means of gratification, and treating a rational being like a child, will never achieve a great moral conquest.      Ibid., Ch. 2

11      This is my tale of woe; and if thou wilt
Be warn'd by me, this sparkling cup resign;
A serpent lurks within the ruby wine,
  Guileful and strong as him who erst betray'd
The world's first parents in their bowers of joy.

Ibid., "The Drunkard's Return"

12 The want of education and moral training is the only *real* barrier that exists between the different classes of men. Nature, reason, and Christianity recognize no other. Pride may say Nay; but Pride was always a liar, and a great hater of the truth.      Ibid., Ch. 3

13 What a wonderful faculty is memory!—the most mysterious and inexplicable in the great riddle of life; that plastic tablet on which the Almighty registers with unerring fidelity the records of being, making it the depository of all our words, thoughts, and deeds—this faithful witness against us for good or evil. . . .

Ibid., Ch. 15

14 Large parties given to very young children, which are so common in this country [Canada], are very pernicious in the way in which they generally operate upon youthful minds. They foster the passions of vanity and envy, and produce a love of dress and display which is very repulsive in the character of a child.
*Ibid.*, Ch. 19

15 The emigrant's hope of bettering his condition, and securing a sufficient competence to support his family, to free himself from the slighting remarks too often hurled at the poor gentleman by the practical people of the world, which is always galling to a proud man, but doubly so when he knows that the want of wealth constitutes the sole difference between him and the more favoured offspring of the same parent stock. "Canada: A Contrast" *1871*

## 13. Sarah Power Whitman
### (1803–1878)
\* \* \*

1 And evening trails her robes of gold
Through the dim halls of the night.
"Summer's Call"

2 Raven from the dim dominions
On the Night's Plutonian shore,
Oft I hear thy dusky pinions
Wave and flutter round my door.
"The Raven"

3 Star of resplendent front! Thy glorious eye
Shines on me still from out yon clouded sky.
"Arcturus (To Edgar Allen Poe)"

## 14. Delphine de Girardin
### (1804–1855)

1 Business is other people's money.
*Marguerite*, Vol. II *1852*

## 15. George Sand
### (1804–1876)

1 She is Choice at odds with Necessity; she is Love blindly butting its head against all the obstacles set in its path by civilization.
*Indiana*, Preface *1832*

2 "I know that I am a slave, and you are my lord. The law of this country has made you my master. You can bind my body, tie my hands, govern my actions: you are the strongest, and

society adds to your power; but with my will, sir, you can do nothing. God alone can restrain it and curb it. Seek then a law, a dungeon, an instrument of torture, by which you can hold it, it is as if you wished to grasp the air, and seize vacancy." *Ibid.*

3 She did not love her husband, for the very reason that love had been imposed upon her as a duty, and that to resist all forms of moral constraint had become, with her, a second nature, a principle of behavior, a law of conscience. . . . *Ibid.*

4 "How shall I free myself from this marble envelope which grips me round the knees, and holds me as totally imprisoned as a corpse by its tomb?" *Lelia*, Vol. I *1833*

5 "Where love is absent there can be no woman."
*Ibid.*

6 I had forgotten how to be young, and Nature had forgotten to awaken me. My dreams had moved too much in the world of sublimity, and I could no longer descend to the grosser level of fleshly appetites. A complete divorce had come about, though I did not realize it, between body and spirit. *Ibid.*, Vol. II

7 What led to my loving him for so long . . . was a feverish irritation which took possession of my faculties as a result of never achieving personal satisfaction. *Ibid.*

8 Desire, in my case, was an ardour of the spirit which paralysed the power of the senses even before they had been awakened, a savage ecstasy which took possession of my brain, and became exclusively concentrated there. *Ibid.*

9 Having let my longings float away towards the land of dreams, I ended by following them in a fancy, seizing them on the wing and imperiously demanding of them, if not happiness at least the ephemeral emotion of a few days. . . . *Ibid.*

10 As things are, they [women] are ill-used. They are forced to live a life of imbecility, and are blamed for doing so. If they are ignorant, they are despised, if learned, mocked. In love they are reduced to the status of courtesans. As wives they are treated more as servants than as companions. Men do not love them: they make use of them, they exploit them, and expect, in that way, to make them subject to the law of fidelity.
"La Fauvette du Docteur," *Almanach du Mois* November, 1844

11 "And yet," plied [sic] my friend, "nature has not changed. The night is still unsullied, the stars still twinkle, and the wild thyme smells as sweetly now as it did then. . . . We may be afflicted and unhappy, but no one can take from

us the sweet delight which is nature's gift to those who love her and her poetry."
*La Petite Fadette*, Preface          *1848*

12 Oh God! protect those who will the good, cast down those who intend evil. . . . Destroy the blind rule of the scribes and pharisees, and open a way for the traveller who seeks Thy holy places.          *Souvenirs de 1848*          *1848*

13 No one makes a revolution by himself; and there are some revolutions, especially in the arts, which humanity, accomplishes without quite knowing how, because it is everybody who takes them in hand.
*The Haunted Pool*, Preface          *1851*

14 Art is not a study of positive reality, it is the seeking for ideal truth. . . .          Ibid., Ch. 1

15 It is sad, no doubt, to exhaust one's strength and one's days in cleaving the bosom of this jealous earth, which compels us to wring from it the treasures of its fertility, when a bit of the blackest and coarsest bread is, at the end of the day's work, the sole recompense and the sole profit attaching to so arduous a toil.
Ibid., Ch. 2

16 He who draws noble delights from the sentiments of poetry is a true poet, though he has never written a line in all his life.          Ibid.

17 I see upon their [peasants'] noble brows the seal of the Lord, for they were born kings of the earth far more truly than those who possess it only from having bought it.          Ibid.

18 "One never knows how much a family may grow; and when a hive is too full, and it is necessary to form a new swarm, each one thinks of carrying away his own honey."
Ibid., Ch. 4

19 "Parents . . . sacrifice all the time of youth, which is the best, to forseeing what will happen to one at the age when one is no longer good for anything, and when it makes little difference whether one ends in one way or another."
Ibid., Ch. 13

20 "Thus far my daughter has understood very clearly that the best part of her life would be that which she spent in allowing herself to be courted, and she did not feel in haste to become the servant of one man, when she can command several. Therefore, so long as the game pleases her, she can amuse herself; but if you pleasure her better than the game, the game can cease."
Ibid.

21 For everything, alas! is disappearing. During even my own lifetime there has been more progress in the ideas and customs of my village than had been seen during centuries before the Revolution.          Ibid., Appendix

22 It is extraordinary how music sends one back into memories of the past—and it is the same with smells.          *Story of My Life*, Vol. I
*1856*

23 . . . since it always happens that one gives form and substance to the dangers upon which one broods to excess, the dread of the possibility became an accurate forecast of the future.
Ibid.

24 My heart once captured [by religion], I deliberately and, with a sort of frantic joy, showed reason the door. I accepted everything, I believed everything, without a struggle, without any consciousness of suffering, without regret, and without false shame. How could I blush for what I had learned to adore?
Ibid., Vol. III

25 Marriage is the ultimate goal of love. When love ceases, or is absent from the beginning, all that remains is sacrifice. . . . All very well for those who understand sacrifice . . . there is probably no middle way between the strength of the great-hearted, and that convenient negative attitude in which the poor-spirited find refuge—or, rather, there is a middle way, and its name is despair.          Ibid., Vol. IV

26 I regard as mortal sin not only the lying evidence of the senses in matters of love, but also the illusion which the senses seek to create where love is not whole or complete. One must love, say I, with all of one's self—or live a life of utter chastity.          Ibid.

27 The whole secret of the study of nature lies in learning how to use one's eyes. . . .
*Nouvelles Lettres d'un Voyageur*
*1869*

28 Classification is Ariadne's clue through the labyrinth of nature.          Ibid.

29 "I hated the pride of men of rank, and thought that I should be sufficiently avenged for their disdain if my genius raised me above them. Dreams and illusions all! My strength has not equalled my mad ambition. I have remained obscure; I have done worse—I have touched success, and allowed it to escape me. I thought myself great, and I was cast down to the dust; I imagined that I was almost sublime, and I was condemned to be ridiculous. Fate took me —me and my audacious dreams—and crushed me as if I had been a reed. I am a most wretched man!"          "The Marquise"          *1869*

30 The beauty that addresses itself to the eyes is only the spell of the moment; the eye of the body is not always that of the soul.
*Handsome Lawrence*, Ch. 1 *1872*

31 A man is not a wall, whose stones are crushed upon the road; or a pipe, whose fragments are thrown away at a street corner. The fragments of an intellect are always good. Ibid., Ch. 2

32 Be prudent, and if you hear . . . some insult or some threat . . . have the appearance of not hearing it. Ibid.

33 Consciousness lies in the consciousness we have of it, and by no means in the way the future keeps its promises. Ibid., Ch. 3

34 Universal suffrage, that is to say the expression of the will of all, whether for good or ill, is a necessary safety-valve. Without it, you will get merely successive outbreaks of civil violence. This wonderful guarantee of security is there to our hands. It is the best social counterweight so far discovered. *Impressions et Souvenirs* *1873*

35 There is only one happiness in life, to love and be loved. . . . Letter to Lina Calamatta (March 31, 1862), *Correspondence*, Vol. IV *1883p*

36 The constant winds of petty appetite dissipate the power of response.
Ibid., Letter to Flaubert (November 30, 1866)

37 One is happy as a result of one's own efforts, once one knows the necessary ingredients of happiness—simple tastes, a certain degree of courage, self denial to a point, love of work, and, above all, a clear conscience. Happiness is no vague dream, of that I now feel certain.
Ibid., Vol. V

38 Faith is an excitement and an enthusiasm: it is a condition of intellectual magnificence to which we must cling as to a treasure, and not squander on our way through life in the small coin of empty words, or in exact and priggish argument. . . . Ibid., Letter to Des Planches (May 25, 1866)

39 One wastes so much time, one is so prodigal of life, at twenty! Our days of winter count for double. That is the compensation of the old.
Ibid., Letter to Joseph Dessauer (July 5, 1868)

40 I have had my belly full of great men (forgive the expression). I quite like to read about them in the pages of Plutarch, where they don't outrage my humanity. Let us see them carved in marble or cast in bronze, and hear no more

about them. In real life they are nasty creatures, persecuters, temperamental, despotic, bitter and suspicious. *Correspondence*, Vol. II *1895p*

41 Liszt said to me today that God alone deserves to be loved. It may be true, but when one has loved a man it is very different to love God.
*Intimate Journal* (1834) *1926p*

42 I realize that when one no longer loves, one no longer loves. Ibid.

43 The capacity for passion is both cruel and divine. The sufferings of love should ennoble, not degrade. Pride is of some use here.
Ibid.

44 But if these people of the future are better than we are, they will, perhaps, look back at us with feelings of pity and tenderness for struggling souls who once divined a little of what the future would bring. Ibid.

45 What sort of life do *you* lead, my fine men and women in the street? What has become of your eyes, your ears, your memories? You call me a cynic because I see and remember, and because I would blush to owe to blindness that sham kindliness which makes you at once fools and knaves. . . . Ibid.

46 Can one ever really sum one's self up? Does one ever truly know oneself? Is one ever a *person*? I can no longer feel any certainty in these matters. I have the feeling now that one changes from day to day, and that after a few years have passed one has completely altered. Examine myself as I may, I can no longer find the slightest trace of the anxious, agitated individual of those years, so discontented with herself, so out of patience with others. Ibid.

47 He is unaware that any man who is adored as a god is deceived, mocked and flattered.
Ibid. (June 13, 1837)

48 Immodest creature, you do not want a woman who will accept your faults, you want one who pretends that you are faultless—one who will caress the hand that strikes her and kiss the lips that lie to her. Ibid.

49 Stupid men—you who believe in laws which punish murder by murder and who express vengeance in calumny and defamation!
Ibid.

50 In spite of occasional moods of disgust, in spite of periods of laziness and exhaustion which break in upon my work, in spite of the more than modest way in which I live, I know that I have found fulfillment. I have an object in life, a task, a—let me be frank and say a

passion. The trade of authorship is a violent, and indestructible obsession.

Letter to Jules Boucoiran (March 4, 1831), *The Letters of George Sand* 1930p

51 Search as I may for the remedies to sore injustice, endless misery, and the incurable passions which trouble the union of the sexes, I can see *no* remedy but the power of breaking and reforming the marriage bond.

Ibid., Letter to Abbe de Lamennais (c. 1836–1837)

52 Whether it be by the law, whether by generally recognised morality, whether by opinion or by prejudice the fact remains that woman having given herself to man is either enchained or considered a culprit. Ibid., Letter to Mlle. Leroyer de Chantepie

53 For me Communism is the ideal which all progressive societies must set as their goal. It is a religion which will be a living reality centuries from now. Quoted in *Women: A Journal of Liberation* Fall, 1970p

54 No religion can be built on force. Ibid.

* * *

55 Education will in time be the same for men and women, but it will be in the female heart par excellence, as it always has been, that love and devotion, patience and pity, will find their true home. On woman falls the duty, in a world of brute passions, of preserving the virtues of charity and the Christian spirit. . . . When women cease to play that role, life will be the loser. *Impressions Littéraires*

56 Men do not wish to be shown for what they are, nor to be made to laugh at the masks they have assumed. If you are no longer capable of love, then you must lie, or draw a veil so close about you that no eye can penetrate it. You must treat your heart as ageing libertines treat their bodies—hide it beneath the disguise of paint and subterfuge. *Sketches and Hints*

57 She prided herself on being educated, erudite and eccentric. She had read a little of everything, even of politics and philosophy, and it was curious to hear her bringing out as her own, for the delectation of the ignorant, things that she had read that same morning in a book, or had heard the night before from the lips of some serious-minded man of her acquaintance. "Horace"

58 The old woman I shall become will be quite different from the woman I am now. Another *I* is beginning, and so far I have not had to complain of her. *Isadora*, Vol. II

## 16. Sarah Fowler Adams
### (1805–1848)
* * *

1 And joys and tears alike are sent
To give the soul fit nourishment.
As comes to me or cloud or sun,
Father! thy will, not mine, be done.
"He Sendeth Sun, He Sendeth Shower"

2 Once have a priest for enemy, goodbye
To peace.
*Vivia Perpetua*, Act III, Sc. 2

3 Though like the wanderer,
the sun gone down,
Darkness be over me,
my rest a stone;
Yet in my dreams I'd be
Nearer, my God, to Thee,
Nearer to Thee.
"Nearer, My God, to Thee," St. 2

## 17. Jeanne-Françoise Deroin
### (1805–1894)

1 Because the revolutionary tempest, in overturning at the same time the throne and the scaffold, in breaking the chain of the black slave, forgot to break the chain of the most oppressed of all—of Woman, the pariah of humanity. . . .
Letter from Prison of St. Lazare (Paris, June 15, 1851), Written with Pauline Roland; Quoted in *History of Woman Suffrage*, Vol. I, by Elizabeth Cady Stanton, Susan B. Anthony, and Mathilda Gage 1881

2 We have, moreover, the profound conviction that only by the power of association based on solidarity—by the union of the working classes of both sexes to organize labor—can be acquired, completely and pacifically, the civil and political equality of women, and the social right for all. Ibid.

## 18. Angelina Grimké
### (1805–1879)

1 I know you do not make the laws, but I also know that *you are the wives and mothers, the sisters and daughters of those who do.* . . .
"Appeal to the Christian Women of the South," *The Anti-Slavery Examiner* September, 1836

2 I have not placed reading before praying because I regard it more important, but because, in order to pray aright, we must understand what we are praying for. . . . *Ibid.*

3 . . . when the books and papers of the Anti-Slavery Society were thrown out of the windows of their office, one individual laid hold of the Bible and was about tossing it out to the ground, when another reminded him that it was the Bible he had in his hand. *"O! 'tis all one,"* he replied, and out went the sacred volume, along with the rest. We thank him for the acknowledgment. *Ibid.*

4 It is through the tongue, the pen, and the press that truth is principally propagated. *Ibid.*

5 So precious a talent as intellect never was given to be wrapt in a napkin and buried in the earth. *Ibid.*

6 . . . we are commanded to love God with *all our minds*, as well as with all our hearts, and we commit a great sin if we *forbid or prevent* that cultivation of the mind in others which would enable them to perform this duty. *Ibid.*

7 What was the conduct of Shadrach, Meshach and Abednego? . . . Did these men *do right in disobeying the law* of their sovereign? Let their miraculous deliverance from the burning fiery furnace answer. . . . *Ibid.*

8 Duty is ours and events are God's. *Ibid.*

9 If a law commands me to *sin I will break it*; if it calls me to *suffer*, I will let it take its course *unresistingly*. The doctrine of blind obedience and unqualified submission to any human power, whether civil or ecclesiastical, is the doctrine of despotism, and ought to have no place 'mong Republicans and Christians. *Ibid.*

10 Slavery always has, and always will, produce insurrections wherever it exists, because it is a violation of the natural order of things, and no human power can much longer perpetuate it. . . . *Ibid.*

11 . . . there is something in the heart of man which *will bend under moral suasion*. There is a swift witness for truth in his bosom, which *will respond to truth* when it is uttered with calmness and dignity. *Ibid.*

12 Our fathers waged a bloody conflict with England, because *they* were taxed without being represented. . . . *They* were not willing to be governed by laws which *they* had no voice in making; but this is the way in which women are governed in this Republic.

> Letter No. 11, *Letters to Catherine Beecher*, Isaac Knapp, ed. *1836*

13. I am not afraid to trust my sisters—not I. *Ibid.*

14 Human beings have *rights*, because they are *moral* beings: the rights of *all* men grow out of their moral nature; and as all men have the same moral nature, they have essentially the same rights. *Ibid., Letter No. 12*

15 When human beings are regarded as *moral* beings, *sex*, instead of being enthroned upon the summit, administrating upon rights and responsibilities, sinks into insignificance and nothingness. . . . *Ibid.*

16 Hitherto, instead of being a help meet to man, in the highest, noblest sense of the term, as a companion, a co-worker, an equal; she has been a mere appendage of his being, an instrument of his convenience and pleasure, the pretty toy with which he whiled away his leisure moments, or the pet animal whom he humored into playfulness and submission. *Ibid.*

17 I recognize no rights but *human* rights—I know nothing of men's rights and women's rights; for in Christ Jesus there is neither male nor female. It is my solemn conviction that, until this principal of equality is recognized and embodied in practice, the church can do nothing effectual for the permanent reformation of the world. *Ibid.*

18 Ought God to be *all in all* to us on *earth*? I thought so, and am frightened to find He is not, that is, I feel something else is necessary to my happiness. I laid awake thinking why it was that my heart longed and panted and reached after you as it does. Why my Savior and my God is not enough to *satisfy* me. Am I sinning, am I ungrateful, *am I an* IDOLATOR? I trust I am not, and yet—but I cannot tell how I feel. I am a mystery to myself.

> Letter to Theodore Dwight Weld (February, 1838), *Letters of Theodore Dwight Weld, Angelina Grimké Weld, and Sarah Grimké, 1822–1844*, Vol. II, Gilbert Hobbs Barnes and Dwight L. Dumond, eds. *1934p*

19 . . . thou art blind to the danger of marrying a woman who feels and acts out the principle of equal rights. . . . *Ibid.*

## 19. Elizabeth Barrett Browning
(1806–1861)

1 Eve is a twofold mystery. . . .
"The Poet's Vow," Pt. I, St. 1, *The
Seraphim and Other Poems*      1838

2          Is it thus,
Ambition, idol of the intellect?
Shall we drink aconite,* alone to use
Thy golden bowl? and sleep ourselves to death—
To dream thy visions about life?
Ibid., "The Student," 1. 56

3 O earth the thundercleft, windshaken, where
The louder voice of "blood and blood" doth
rise,
Hast thou an altar for this sacrifice?
Ibid., "The Seraphim," Pt. I, 1. 288

4          But since he had
The genius to be loved, why, let him have
The justice to be honored in his grave.
"Crowned and Buried," St. 27,
*Athenoeum*     July 4, 1840

5 And lips say "God be pitiful,"
Who ne'er said "God be praised."
"The Cry of the Human," St. 1,
*Graham's American Magazine*     1842

6 And I smiled to think God's greatness flowed
around our incompleteness—
Round our restlessness, His rest.
"Rhyme of the Duchess May," St. 11,
*Poems of 1844*     1844

7 Do ye hear the children weeping, O my
brothers,
Ere the sorrow comes with the years?
Ibid., "The Cry of the Children," St. 1

8 But the child's sob in the silence curses deeper
Than the strong man in his wrath.
Ibid., St. 13

9 Experience, like a pale musician, holds
A dulcimer of patience in his hand. . . .
Ibid., "Perplexed Music"

10 I tell you, hopeless grief is passionless. . . .
Ibid., "Grief"

11 Our Euripides, the human,
With his droppings of warm tears,
And his touches of things common
Till they rose to touch the spheres!
Ibid., "Wine of Cyprus, St. 12

12 Poets ever fail in reading their own verses to
their worth.
Ibid., "Lady Geraldine's Courtship,"
St. 42

* Poisonous plant.

13 Then we talked—oh, how we talked! her voice
so cadenced in the talking,
Made another singing—of the soul! a music
without bars. . . .
Ibid., St. 45

14          behold me! I am worthy
Of thy loving, for I love thee!
Ibid., St. 79

15 Therefore to this dog will I,
Tenderly not scornfully,
Render praise and favor. . . .
Ibid., "To Flush, My Dog," St. 14

16 There Shakespeare, on whose forehead climb
The crowns o' the world: O eyes sublime
With tears and laughters for all time!
Ibid., "A Vision of Poets," 1. 298

17 Life treads on life, and heart on heart;
We press too close in church and mart
To keep a dream or grave apart. . . .
Ibid., Conclusion, 1. 820

18 "Knowledge by suffering entereth
And Life is perfected by death."
Ibid., 1. 929

19 Thou large-brained woman and large-hearted
man. . . .
Ibid., "To George Sand, A Desire"

20 "Yes," I answered you last night;
"No," this morning, sir, I say:
Colors seen by candle-light
Will not look the same by day.
Ibid., "The Lady's 'Yes,' " St. 1

21 By thunders of white silence, overthrown. . . .
"Hiram Powers' Greek Slave,"
*Poems of 1850*     1850

22 "Guess now who holds thee?"—"Death," I said.
But there,
The silver answer rang,—"Not Death, but
Love."
Sonnets from the Portuguese, I
1850

23 Go from me. Yet I feel that I shall stand
Henceforward in thy shadow.
Ibid., VI

24          What I do
And what I dream includes thee, as the wine
Must taste of its own grapes.
Ibid.

25 If thou must love me, let it be for nought
Except for love's sake only.
Ibid., XIV

26 Say thou dost love me, love me, love me—toll
   The silver iterance!—only minding, Dear,
   To love me also in silence, with thy soul.
   *Ibid.*, XXI

27 God only, who made us rich, can make us poor.
   *Ibid.*, XXIV

28 Because God's gifts put man's best dreams to
   shame.
   *Ibid.*, XXVI

29 How do I love thee? Let me count the ways.
   I love thee to the depth and breadth and height
   My soul can reach. . . .
   *Ibid.*, XLIII

30 I love thee with a love I seemed to lose
   With my lost saints,—I love thee with the
   breath,
   Smiles, tears, of all my life!—and, if God
   choose,
   I shall but love thee better after death.
   *Ibid.*

31    Women know
   The way to rear up children (to be just),
   They know a simple, merry, tender knack
   Of tying sashes, fitting baby-shoes,
   And stringing pretty words that make no
   sense. . . .
   *Aurora Leigh*, Bk. I, 1. 47    *1857*

32    Life, struck sharp on death,
   Makes awful lightning.
   *Ibid.*, 1. 210

33    the beautiful seems right
   By force of Beauty, and the feeble wrong
   Because of weakness.
   *Ibid.*, 1. 753

34 Whoever loves true life, will love true love.
   *Ibid.*, 1. 1066

35    Men do not think
   Of sons and daughters, when they fall in
   love. . . .
   *Ibid.*, Bk II, 1. 608

36    If I married him,
   I should not dare to call my soul my own
   Which so he had bought and paid for. . . .
   *Ibid.*, 1. 785

37 God answers sharp and sudden some prayers,
   And thrusts the thing we have prayed for in
   our face,
   A gauntlet with a gift in 't.—Every wish
   Is like a prayer, with God.
   *Ibid.*, 1. 952

38 How many desolate creatures on the earth
   Have learnt the simple dues of fellowship
   And social comfort, in a hospital. . . .
   *Ibid.*, Bk. III, 1. 1122

39    For poets (bear the word),
   Half-poets even, are still whole democrats. . . .
   *Ibid.*, Bk. IV, 1. 413

40 A little sunburnt by the glare of life. . . .
   *Ibid.*, 1. 1140

41    Measure not the work
   Until the day's out and the labor done. . . .
   *Ibid.*, Bk. V, 1. 76

42 Men get opinions as boys learn to spell,
   By reiteration chiefly. . . .
   *Ibid.*, Bk. VI, 1. 6

43 Since when was genius found respectable?
   *Ibid.*, 1. 275

44    Earth's crammed with heaven,
   And every common bush afire with God;
   But only he who sees, takes off his shoes—
   The rest sit round it and pluck blackberries. . . .
   *Ibid.*, Bk. VII, 1. 820

45 (Sweet cousin, walls must get the weather stain
   Before they grow the ivy!)
   *Ibid.*, Bk. VIII, 1. 694

46    Genuine government
   Is but the expression of a nation, good
   Or less good—even as all society,
   Howe'er unequal, monstrous, crazed and cursed,
   Is but the expression of men's single lives,
   The loud sum of the silent units.
   *Ibid.*, 1. 867

47 Alas, this Italy has too long swept
   Heroic ashes up for hour-glass sand. . . .
   *Casa Guidi Windows*, Pt. I, 1. 187
   *1851*

48    If we tried
   To sink the past beneath our feet, be sure
   The future would not stand.
   *Ibid.*, 1. 416.

49    But "Live the People," who remained and
   must,
   The unrenounced and unrenounceable.
   Long live the people! How they lived! and
   boiled
   And bubbled in the cauldron of the street. . . .
   *Ibid.*, Pt. II, 1. 115

50    That tree of liberty, whose fruit is doubted,
   Because the roots are not of nature's granting!
   A tree of good and evil: none, without it,
   Grow gods; alas and, with it, men are wanting!

   O holy knowledge, holy liberty,
   O holy rights of nations! If I speak
   These bitter things against the jugglery
   Of days that in your names proved blind and
   weak,
   It is that tears are bitter.
   *Ibid.*, 1. 179

51 "What monster have we here?
A great Deed at this hour of day?
A great just Deed—and not for pay?
Absurd,—or insincere."
"A Tale of Villafrance," St. 4,
*Athenoeum* *September 24, 1859*

52 For civilization perfected
Is fully developed Christianity.
"Italy and the World," St. 11,
*Poems Before Congress* *1860*

53 The thinkers stood aside
To let the nation act.
Ibid., "Napoleon III in Italy," St. 3

54 And each man stands with his face in the light
Of his own drawn sword,
Ready to do what a hero can.
Ibid., St. 8

55 The world goes whispering to its own,
"This anguish pierces to the bone;"
And tender friends go sighing round,
"What love can ever cure this wound?"
My days go on, my days go on.
"De Profundis," St. 5, *Last Poems*
*1862*

56 Grief may be joy misunderstood;
Only the Good discerns the good.
Ibid., St. 21

57 We walked too straight for fortune's end,
We loved too true to keep a friend;
At last we're tired, my heart and I.
Ibid., "My Heart and I," St. 9

## 20. Maria Weston Chapman
### (1806–1885)

1 As *wives* and *mothers*, as *sisters* and *daughters*,
we are deeply responsible for the influence we
have on the human race. We are bound to exert
it; we are bound to urge man to cease to do
evil, and learn to do well. We are bound to
urge them to regain, defend and preserve inviolate the rights of all, especially those whom
they have most deeply wronged.
Address, Boston Female
Anti-Slavery Society, *Liberator*
*August 13, 1836*

2 Let us rise in the moral power of womanhood;
and give utterance to the voice of outraged
mercy, and insulted justice, and eternal truth,
and mighty love and holy freedom. . . .
Ibid.

3 Grudge no expense—yield to no opposition—
forget fatigue—till, by the strength of prayer
and sacrifice, the spirit of love shall have overcome sectional jealousy, political rivalry, prejudice against color, cowardly concession of principle, wicked compromise with sin, devotion to
gain, and spiritual despotism. . . . Ibid.

4 My disgust was unutterable . . . at the stupid
schemes by which selfish men were then, as
now, trying to make capital for themselves out
of the sacred cause of human rights. . . . Hear
them clamorously and meanly taking advantage of ignorance, for the promotion of self-
interest. Address, "How Can I Help to
Abolish Slavery," New York *1855*

5 In a republican land the power behind the
throne is *the* power. Ibid.

6 Don't drag the engine, like an ignoramus, but
bring wood and water and flame, like an engineer. Ibid.

7 Slavery can only be abolished by raising the
character of the people who compose the nation;
and *that* can be done only by showing them a
higher one. Ibid.

8 We may draw good out of evil; we must not do
evil, that good may come. Ibid.

## 21. Juliette Drouet
### (1806–1883)

1 I love you [Victor Hugo] *because* I love you,
because it would be impossible for me not to
love you. I love you without question, without
calculation, without **reason good or bad**, faithfully, with all my heart and soul, and every
faculty. *Letters to Victor Hugo* (1833)
*1915p*

2 It is wicked of me to torment you, yet I cannot
help myself. My offence goes by the name of
"jealousy." Ibid. (1834)

3 If I were a clever woman, my gorgeous bird, I
could describe to you how you unite in yourself
the beauties of form, plumage, and song!
Ibid. (1835)

4 Love exalts as much as glory does.
Ibid. (January 21, 1838)

5 There are no wrinkles in the heart, and you will
see my face only in the reflection of your
attachment, eh, Victor, my beloved?
Ibid. (November 19, 1841)

6 In my opinion, infidelity does not consist in action only; I consider it already accomplished by the sole fact of desire.

Ibid. (April 4, 1847)

7 I come to fetch my heart where I left it, that is to say in yours.

Ibid. (December 14, 1881)

## 22. Mary Ann Dwight
### (1806–1858)

1 Janus was invoked at the commencement of most actions; even in the worship of the other gods the voterie began by offering wine and incense to Janus. The first month in the year was named from him; and under the title of Matutinus he was regarded as the opener of the day.    "Janus," *Grecian and Roman*    *1849*

## 23. Flora Hastings
### (1806–1839)
\* \* \*

1 Grieve not that I die young. Is it not well
To pass away ere life hath lost its brightness?
"Swan Song"

## 24. Nomura Motoni
### (1806–1867)

1 The whistle of the samurai's arrow is changing today to the thunder of cannon.
Untitled Poem    *1855*

2 This is a world that cages all warblers with a beautiful voice.
Untitled Poem    *1861*

3 Many are the victims of the waves that rush in, then out of the beach.
Untitled Poem    *1861*

4 The song of the warbler, joyful at his release, has drawn forth the cry of many other birds.
Untitled Poem    *1863*

## 25. Julia Pardoe
### (1806–1862)

1 Raising his truncheon above his head, he broke it in the centre, and throwing the pieces among the crowd, exclaimed in a loud voice, "Le roi est mort!" Then seizing another staff, he flourished it in the air as he shouted, "Vive le Roi!"
*Life of Louis XIV*, Vol. III    *1947*

\* \* \*

2 The heart is a free and fetterless thing—
A wave of the ocean, a bird on the wing.
"The Captive Greek Girl"

## 26. Elizabeth Oakes Smith
### (1806–1893)
\* \* \*

1 Faith is the subtle chain
Which binds us to the infinite.
"Faith"

2 My friends, do we realize for what purpose we are convened? Do we fully understand that we aim at nothing less than an entire subversion of the present order of society, a dissolution of the whole existing social compact?    Speech

3 Yes, this is life, and everywhere we meet,
Not victor crowns, but wailings of defeat.
"The Unattained"

## 27. Lady Dufferin
### (1807–1867)

1 The poor make no new friends.
"Lament of the Irish Emigrant"
*1894p*

2 They say there's bread and work for all,
And the sun shines always there:
But I'll not forget old Ireland,
Were it fifty times as fair.

Ibid.

## 28. Frances Dana Gage
### (1808–1884)
\* \* \*

1 The home we first knew on this beautiful earth,
The friends of our childhood, the place of our birth,
In the heart's inner chamber sung always will be,
As the shell ever sings of its home in the sea.
"Home"

17

## 29. Caroline Sheridan Norton

### (1808–1877)

1 God made all pleasures innocent.
*The Lady of LaGaraye, Pt. I*     1862

2 Until I truly loved, I was alone.
Ibid., Pt. II

3 They serve God well, who serve his creatures.
Ibid., Conclusion

      *   *   *

4 A soldier of the legion lay dying in Algiers—
There was a lack of woman's nursing,
There was dearth of woman's tears.
"Bingen on the Rhine," St. 1

5 O Friend, I fear the lightest heart makes sometimes heaviest mourning.
Ibid.

6       . . . (for ere the moon be risen
My body will be out of pain—my soul be out
of prison). . . .
Ibid.

7 I do not love thee!—no! I do not love thee!
And yet when thou art absent I am sad.
"I Do Not Love Thee"

8 Love not! Love not! Ye hapless sons of clay;
Hope's gayest wreaths are made of earthly
flowers—
Things that are made to fade and fall away,
Ere they have blossomed for a few short years.
"Love Not"

9 My beautiful, my beautiful! That standest
meekly by,
With thy proudly-arched and glossy neck,
and dark and fiery eye!
"The Arab's Farewell to His Steed"

10 The stranger hath thy bridle-rein, thy master
hath his gold;—
Fleet limbed and beautiful, farewell; thou'rt
sold, my steed, thou'rt sold.
Ibid.

## 30. Fanny Kemble

### (1809–1893)

1 . . . children are made of eyes and ears, and
nothing, however minute, escapes their microscopic observation. *Journal of a Residence
on a Georgian Plantation in 1838–1839,*
John Scott, ed.     *1961p*

2 Just in proportion as I have found the slaves
on this plantation intellectual and advanced
beyond the general brutish level of the majority, I have observed this pathetic expression
of countenance in them, a mixture of sadness
and fear, the involuntary exhibition of the two
feelings, which I suppose must be the predominant experience of their whole lives, regret
and apprehension. . . .     Ibid.

3 For the last four years of my life that preceded
my marriage I literally coined money, and
never until this moment, I think, did I reflect
on the great means of good, to myself and
others, that I so gladly agreed to give up forever
for a maintenance by the unpaid labor of
slaves—people toiling . . . unpaid.    Ibid.

4 This is no place for me, since I was not born
among slaves, and cannot bear to live among
them.     Ibid.

      *   *   *

5 A sacred burden is this life ye bear;
Look on it; lift it; bear it solemnly;
Fail not for sorrow; falter not for sin;
But onward, upward, till the goal ye win.
"Lines to the Young Gentlemen
Graduates at Lenox Academy,
Massachusetts"

6 Better trust all and be deceived,
And weep that trust, and that deceiving,
Than doubt one heart that, if believed,
Had blessed one's life with true believing.
"Faith"

7 Maids must be wives and mothers, to fulfill
The entire and holiest end of woman's being.
"Woman's Heart"

8 Nature lay frozen dead,—and still and slow,
A winding sheet fell o'er her body fair,
Flakey and soft, from his wide wings of snow.
"Winter"

9 What shall I do with all the days and hours
That must be counted ere I see thy face?
How shall I charm the interval that lowers
Between this time and that sweet time of
grace?
"Absence"

## 31. Margaret Fuller

### (1810–1850)

1 . . . not a few believe, and men themselves
have expressed the opinion, that the time is
come when Euridice is to call for an Orpheus,
rather than Orpheus for Euridice; that the idea
of man, however imperfectly brought out, has
been far more so than that of woman, and that

an improvement in the daughters will best aid the reformation of the sons of this age.
"The Great Lawsuit. Man Versus Men. Woman Versus Women," *The Dial* *July, 1843*

2   "You are not the head of your wife. God has given her a mind of her own."
"I am the head and she is the heart."
"God grant you play true to one another then."       Ibid.

3 And knowing that there exists, in the world of men, a tone of feeling towards women as towards slaves, such as is expressed in the common phrase, "Tell that to women and children." . . .       Ibid.

4 The female Greek, of our day, is as much in the street as the male, to cry, What news?       Ibid.

5 For human beings are not so constituted, that they can live without expansion; and if they do not get it one way, must another, or perish.       Ibid.

6 If the negro be a soul, if the woman be a soul, apparelled in flesh, to one master only are they accountable.       Ibid.

7 In every-day life the feelings of the many are stained with vanity. Each wishes to be lord in a little world, to be superior at least over one; and he does not feel strong enough to retain a lifelong ascendant over a strong nature. Only a Brutus would rejoice in a Portia. . . .       Ibid.

8 Two persons love in one another the future good which they aid one another to unfold.       Ibid.

9 Plants of great vigor will almost always struggle into blossom, despite impediments. But there should be encouragement, and a free genial atmosphere for those of more timid sort, fair play for each in its own kind.       Ibid.

10 The well-instructed moon flies not from her orbit to seize on the glories of her partner.       Ibid.

11 George Sand smokes, wears male attire, wishes to be addressed as Mon frère; perhaps, if she found those who were as brothers indeed, she would not care whether she were a brother or sister.       Ibid.

12 Harmony exists in difference no less than in likeness, if only the same key-note govern both parts.       Ibid.

13 It has been seen that as the loss of no bond ought to destroy a human being, so ought the missing of none to hinder him from growing.       Ibid.

14 The especial genius of women I believe to be electrical in movement, intuitive in function, spiritual in tendency.       Ibid.

15 Male and female represent the two sides of the great radical dualism. But, in fact, they are perpetually passing into one another. Fluid hardens to solid, solid rushes to fluid. There is no wholly masculine man, no purely feminine woman.       Ibid.

16 Nature provides exceptions to every rule.       Ibid.

17 Union is only possible to those who are units. To be fit for relations in time, souls, whether of man or woman, must be able to do without them in the spirit.       Ibid.

18 It is a vulgar error that love, *a* love, to woman is her whole existence; she is also born for Truth and Love in their universal energy.       Ibid.

19 What I mean by the Muse is that unimpeded clearness of the intuitive powers, which a perfectly truthful adherence to every admonition of the higher instinct would bring to a finely organized human being.
*Woman in the 19th Century*     *1845*

20 It should be remarked that, as the principle of liberty is better understood, and more nobly interpreted, a broader protest is made in behalf of women. As men become aware that few [of them] have had a fair chance, they are inclined to say that no women have had a fair chance.       Ibid.

21 What woman needs is not as a woman to act or rule, but as a nature to grow, as an intellect to discern, as a soul to live freely and unimpeded, to unfold such powers as were given her when we left our common home.       Ibid.

22 If any individual live too much in relations, so that he becomes a stranger to the resources of his own nature, he falls, after a while, into a distraction, or imbecility, from which he can only be cured by a time of isolation, which gives the renovating fountains time to rise up. With a society it is the same.       Ibid.

23 It does not follow because many books are written by persons born in America that there exists an American literature. . . . Before such

can exist, an original idea must animate this nation and fresh currents of life must call into life fresh thoughts along its shores.
Quoted in the *New York Tribune* 1846

24 Truth is the nursing mother of genius. Ibid.

25 . . . the public must learn how to cherish the nobler and rarer plants, and to plant the aloe, able to wait a hundred years for its bloom, or its garden will contain, presently, nothing but potatoes and pot-herbs. Ibid.

26 Essays, entitled critical, are epistles addressed to the public, through which the mind of the recluse relieves itself of its impressions.
"A Short Essay on Critics," *Art, Literature and the Drama* 1858p

27 The critic is the historian who records the order of creation. In vain for the maker, who knows without learning it, but not in vain for the mind of his race. Ibid.

28 POET. Yes, that is always the way. You understand me, who never have the arrogance to pretend that I understand myself.
Ibid., "A Dialogue"

29 It is not because the touch of genius has roused genius to production, but because the admiration of genius has made talent ambitious, that the harvest is still so abundant.
Ibid., "The Modern Drama"

30 'Tis, indeed, hard to believe that the drama, once invented, should cease to be a habitual and healthy expression of the mind. . . . But . . . no form of art will succeed with him to whom it is the object of deliberate choice. It must grow from his nature. . . . Ibid.

31 . . . there are two modes of criticism. One which . . . crushes to earth without mercy all the humble buds of Phantasy, all the plants that, though green and fruitful, are also a prey to insects or have suffered by drouth. It weeds well the garden, and cannot believe the weed in its native soil may be a pretty, graceful plant. There is another mode which enters into the natural history of every thing that breathes and lives, which believes no impulse to be entirely in vain, which scrutinizes circumstances, motive and object before it condemns, and believes there is a beauty in natural form, if its law and purpose be understood.
Ibid., "Poets of the People"

32 The lives of the musicians are imperfectly written for this obvious reason. The soul of the great musician can only be expressed in music.

. . . We must read them in their works; this, true of artists in every department, is especially so of the high priestesses of sound.
Ibid., "Lives of the Great Composers"

33 We cannot have expression till there is something to be expressed.
Ibid., "American Literature"

34 This was one of the rye-bread days, all dull and damp without.
Diary Entry, *Life of Margaret Fuller-Ossoli*, Ch. 7, Thomas Wentworth Higginson, ed. 1884p

35 For precocity some great price is always demanded sooner or later in life.
Ibid., Ch. 18

36 Genius will live and thrive without training, but it does not the less reward the watering-pot and pruning-knife. Ibid.

37 It is so true that a woman may be in love with a woman, and a man with a man. It is pleasant to be sure of it, because it is undoubtedly the same love that we shall feel when we are angels, when we ascend to the only fit place for the Mignons, where *sie fragen nicht nach Mann und Weib.*
Quoted in *Margaret Fuller, Whetstone of Genius* by Mason Wade 1940p

38 I myself am more divine than any I see.
Letter to Emerson (March 1, 1838), *The Feminist Papers*, Alice Rossi, ed. 1973p

39 . . . men are called on from a very early period to reproduce all that they learn. . . . But women learn without any attempt to reproduce. Their only reproduction is for purposes of display.
Ibid., Lecture, "Conversations" (1839)

40 Beware of over-great pleasure in being popular or even beloved.
Ibid., Letter to Her Brother, Arthur (December 20, 1840)

41 What a difference it makes to come home to a child! Ibid., Letter to Friends (1849)

42 They [the Irish] are looked upon with contempt for their want of aptitude in learning new things; their ready and ingenious lying; their eye-service. These are the faults of an oppressed race, which must require the aid of better circumstances through two or three generations to eradicate. . . . Ibid., Untitled Essay

43 Ye cannot believe it, men; but the only reason why women ever assume what is more appropriate to you is because you prevent them from finding out what is fit for themselves. Were they free . . . to develop the strength and beauty of women, they would never wish to be men.        Ibid.

## 32. Elizabeth Gaskell
### (1810–1865)

1 A man . . . is *so* in the way in the house!
       *Cranford*, Ch. 1     *1853*

2 Bombazine would have shown a deeper sense of her loss.        Ibid.

3 There, economy was always "elegant," and money-spending always "vulgar" and ostentatious—a sort of sour grapeism, which made us very peaceful and satisfied.        Ibid.

4 Correspondence, which bears much the same relation to personal intercourse that the books of dried plants I sometimes see ("Hortus Siccus," I think they call the thing) do to the living and fresh flowers in the lanes and meadows. . . .        Ibid., Ch. 3

5 One gives people in grief their own way.
       Ibid., Ch. 6

6 A little credulity helps one on through life very smoothly.        Ibid., Ch. 11

7 I'll not listen to reason. . . . Reason always means what someone else has got to say.
       Ibid., Ch. 14

8 What's the use of watching? A watched pot never boils.    *Mary Barton*, Ch. 31    *1932p*

## 33. Ernestine Rose
### (1810–1892)

1 Oh, she [Frances Wright] had her reward!— that reward of which no enemies could deprive her, which no slanders could make less precious —the eternal reward of knowing that she had done her duty; the reward springing from the consciousness of right, of endeavoring to benefit unborn generations.
       Convention Speech, "Petitions Were Circulated" (1860), Quoted in *History of Woman Suffrage*, Vol. I, by Elizabeth Cady Stanton, Susan B. Anthony, and Mathilda Gage     *1881*

## 34. Fanny Fern
### (1811–1872)
* * *

1 The way to a man's heart is through his stomach.        "Willis Parton"

## 35. Frances Sargent Osgood
### (1811–1850)
* * *

1 Work—for some good, be it ever so slowly;
Cherish some flower, be it ever so lowly;
Labor!—all labor is noble and holy!
   Let thy great deeds be thy prayer to thy god!
       "Laborare Est Orare," St. 6

## 36. Harriet Beecher Stowe
### (1811–1896)

1 "Well, I've got just as much conscience as any man in business can afford to keep—just a little, you know, to swear by as 't were. . . ."
       *Uncle Tom's Cabin*, Ch. 1    *1852*

2 So long as the law considers all these human beings, with beating hearts and living affections, only as so many *things* belonging to the master—so long as the failure, or misfortune, or imprudence, or death of the kindest owner, may cause them any day to exchange a life of kind protection and indulgence for one of hopeless misery and toil—so long it is impossible to make anything beautiful or desirable in the best-regulated administration of slavery.
       Ibid.

3 "I b'lieve in religion, and one of these days, when I've got matters tight and snug, I calculate to 'tend to my soul, and them are matters: and so what's the use of doin' any more wickedness than's re'lly necessary?—it don't seem to me it's 'tall prudent."    Ibid., Ch. 8

4 "Treat 'em like dogs, and you'll have dogs' works and dogs' actions. Treat 'em like men, and you'll have men's works."
       Ibid., Ch. 11

5 If ever Africa shall show an elevated and cultivated race—and come it must, some time, her turn to figure in the great drama of human improvement—life will awake there with a gorgeousness and splendour of which our cold western tribes faintly have conceived.
       Ibid., Ch. 16

6    "Who was your mother?"
     "Never had none!" said the child, with an-
other grin.
     "Never had any mother? What do you mean?
Where were you born?"
     "Never was born!" persisted Topsy. . . .
     "Do you know who made you?"
     "Nobody, as I knows on," said the child with
a short laugh. . . "I 'spect I grow'd. Don't think
nobody never made me."          Ibid., Ch. 20

7    "Cause I's wicked—I is. I's mighty wicked, any
how. I can't help it."          Ibid.

8    Whipping and abuse are like laudanum: You
have to double the dose as the sensibilities
decline.          Ibid.

9    For how imperiously, how coolly, in disregard
of all one's feelings, does the hard, cold, un-
interesting course of daily reality move on!
          Ibid., Ch. 28

10   "Knows all that, Mas'r St. Clare; Mas'r's been
too good: but, Mas'r, I'd rather have poor
clothes, poor house, poor everything, and have
'em *mine*, than have the best, and have 'em
any man's else! I had so, Mas'r; I think it's
natur, Mas'r!"          Ibid.

11   Who can speak the blessedness of that first day
of freedom? Is not the *sense* of liberty a higher
and finer one than any of the five? To move,
speak, and breathe, go out and come in, unwatched and free from danger! Who can speak
the blessings of that rest which comes down on
the free man's pillow, under laws which ensure
to him the rights that God has given to man?
          Ibid., Ch. 37

12   No one is so thoroughly superstitious as the
godless man.          Ibid., Ch. 39

13   The longest day must have its close—the
gloomiest night will wear on to a morning. An
eternal, inexorable lapse of moments is ever
hurrying the day of the evil to an eternal night,
and the night of the just to an eternal day.
          Ibid., Ch. 40

14   "They wanted us all to be like snow-flakes, and
all that. And they were quite high, telling they
wouldn't marry this, and they wouldn't marry
that, till, at last, I made them a courtesy, and
said, 'Gentlemen, we ladies are infinitely obliged
to you, but *we* don't intend to marry people
that read naughty books, either. Of course, you
know, "snow-flakes don't like soot!" ' "
          *Dred*, Ch. 1          *1856*

15   "Ah, Miss Nina, we mustn't 'spect more of
folks than dere is in them."
     "Expect? I don't expect."

     "Well, bless you, honey, bless you, honey,
when you knows what folks *is*, don't let's worry.
Ye can't fill a quart cup out of a thimble,
honey, no way you can fix it. Dere's just where
'tis."          Ibid., Ch. 6

16   "They breed like rabbits! What God Almighty
makes such people for, I don't know! I suppose
He does. But there's these poor miserable trash
have children like sixty; and there's folks living in splendid houses, dying for children, and
can't have any. If they manage one or two,
the scarlet-fever or whooping cough makes off
with 'em. Lord bless me, things go on in a
terrible mixed-up way in this world."
          Ibid., Ch. 17

17   "Oh, I think," said Clayton, "the African race
evidently are made to excel in that department
which lies between the sensuousness and the
intellectual—what we call the elegant arts.
These require rich and abundant animal nature,
such as they possess; and if ever they become
highly civilised, they will excel in music, dancing and elocution."          Ibid., Ch. 29

18   He declared that the gold made in it [slavery]
was distilled from human blood, from mother's
tears, from the agonies and dying groans of
gasping, suffocating men and women, and that
it would sear and blister the soul of him that
touched it; in short, he talked as whole-souled,
impractical fellows are apt to talk about what
respectable people sometimes do. Nobody had
ever instructed him that a slave-ship, with a
procession of expectant sharks in its wake, is a
missionary institution, by which closely-packed
heathen are brought over to enjoy the light of
the Gospel.          *The Minister's Wooing*, Ch. 1
          *1859*

19   So we go, so little knowing what we touch and
what touches us as we talk! We drop our
common piece of news, "Mr. So-and-so is dead,
Miss Such-a-one is married, such a ship has
sailed," and lo, on our right hand or on our
left, some heart has sunk under the news
silently—gone down in the great ocean of Fate,
without even a bubble rising to tell its drowning
pang. And this—God help us!—is what we call
living!          Ibid., Ch. 4

20   And ever and anon came on the still air the
soft eternal pulsations of the distant sea—sound
mournfulest, most mysterious, of all the harp-
ings of Nature. It was the sea—the deep,
eternal sea—the treacherous, soft, dreadful,
inexplicable sea. . . .          Ibid., Ch. 5

21   There are some people who receive from Nature
as a gift a sort of graceful facility of sympathy,
by which they incline to take on, for the time

being, the sentiments and opinions of those with whom they converse, as the chameleon was fabled to change its hue with every surrounding. Such are often supposed to be willfully acting a part, as exerting themselves to flatter and deceive, when in fact they are only framed so sensitive to the sphere of mental emanation which surrounds others that it would require an exertion not in some measure to harmonize with it. In approaching others in conversation, they are like a musician who joins a performer on an instrument—it is impossible for them to strike a discord; their very nature urges them to bring into play faculties according in vibration with those another is exerting. Ibid., Ch. 16

22 All systems [of thought] that deal with the infinite are, besides, exposed to danger from small, unsuspected admixtures of human error, which become deadly when carried to such vast results. The smallest speck of earth's dust, in the focus of an infinite lens, appears magnified among the heavenly orbs as a frightful monster. Ibid., Ch. 23

23 Slavery, it is true, was to some extent introduced into New England, but it never suited the genius of the people, never struck deep root, or spread so as to choke the good seed of self-helpfulness. . . . People, having once felt the thorough neatness and beauty of execution which came of free, educated, and thoughtful labor, could not tolerate the clumsiness of slavery. "The Lady Who Does Her Own Work," *Atlantic Monthly* 1864

24 Everyone confesses in the abstract that exertion which brings out all the powers of body and mind is the best thing for us all; but practically most people do all they can to get rid of it, and as a general rule nobody does much more than circumstances drive them to do. Ibid.

25 . . . these remarkable women of olden times are like the ancient painted glass—the art of making them is lost; my mother was less than her mother, and I am less than my mother. Ibid.

26 They come here feeling that this is somehow a land of liberty, and with very dim and confused notions of what liberty is. Ibid.

27 The great danger of all this, and of the evils that come from it, is that society by and by will turn as blindly against female intelligent culture as it now advocates it, and, having worked disproportionately one way, will work disproportionately in the opposite direction. Ibid., "Servants"

28 . . . women are the real architects of society. Ibid., "Dress, or Who Makes the Fashions"

29 One would like to be grand and heroic, if one could; but if not, why try at all? One wants to be *very* something, *very* great, *very* heroic; or if not that, then at least very stylish and very fashionable. It is this everlasting mediocrity that bores me. Ibid.

30 Many a humble soul will be amazed to find that the seed it sowed in weakness, in the dust of daily life, has blossomed into immortal flowers under the eye of the Lord. Ibid., "The Cathedral"

31 What makes saintliness in my view, as distinguished from ordinary goodness, is a certain quality of magnanimity and greatness of soul that brings life within the circle of the heroic. Ibid.

32 . . . she never saw her hero, and so never married. Ibid.

33 In a good old age, Death, the friend, came and opened the door of this mortal state, and a great soul, that had served a long apprenticeship to little things, went forth into the joy of its Lord; a life of self-sacrifice and self-abnegation passed into a life of endless rest. Ibid.

34 The pain of the discipline is short, but the glory of the fruition is eternal. Ibid.

35 "Take us the foxes, the little foxes, that spoil the vines: for our vines have tender grapes." . . . "Little Foxes," by which I mean those unsuspected, unwatched, insignificant *little* causes that nibble away domestic happiness, and make home less than so noble an institution should be. . . . The reason for this in general is that home is a place not only of strong affections, but of entire unreserve; it is life's undress rehearsal, its backroom, its dressing room, from which we go forth to more careful and guarded intercourse, leaving behind us much *debris* of cast-off and everyday clothing. *Little Foxes*, Ch. 1 1865

36 Irritability is, more than most unlovely states, a sin of the flesh. . . . It is a state of nervous torture; and the attacks which the wretched victim makes on others are as much a result of disease as the snapping and biting of a patient convulsed with hydrophobia. Ibid., Ch. 2

37 I am speaking now of the highest duty we owe our friends, the noblest, the most sacred—that of keeping their own nobleness, goodness, pure and incorrupt. . . . If we *let* our friend become

cold and selfish and exacting without a remonstrance, we are no true lover, no true friend.
Ibid., Ch. 3

38 Wrath and bitterness speak themselves and go with their own force; love is shame-faced, looks shyly out of the window, lingers long at the doorlatch. Ibid.

39 The bitterest tears shed over graves are for words left unsaid and deeds left undone.
Ibid.

40 . . . the obstinancy of cleverness and reason is nothing to the obstinancy of folly and inanity.
Ibid., Ch. 4

41 A little reflection will enable any person to detect in himself that *setness in trifles* which is the result of the unwatched instinct of self-will and to establish over himself a jealous guardianship. Ibid.

42 Now, if the principle of toleration were once admitted into classical education—if it were admitted that the great object is to read and enjoy a language, and the stress of the teaching were placed on the few things absolutely essential to this result, if the tortoise were allowed time to creep, and the bird permitted to fly, and the fish to swim, towards the enchanted and divine sources of Helicon—all might in their own way arrive there, and rejoice in its flowers, its beauty, and its coolness.
Ibid., Ch. 5

43 Every human being has some handle by which he may be lifted, some groove in which he was meant to run; and the great work of life, as far as our relations with each other are concerned, is to lift each one by his own proper handle, and run each one in his own proper groove. Ibid.

44 "For my part," said my wife, "I think one of the greatest destroyers of domestic peace is Discourtesy. People neglect, with their nearest friends, those refinements and civilities which they practice with strangers." Ibid., Ch. 6

45 Yet there are persons who keep the requirements of life strained up always at concert pitch and are thus worn out, and made miserable all their days by the grating of a perpetual discord.
Ibid., Ch. 7

46 It lies around us like a cloud,
A world we do not see;
Yet the sweet closing of an eye
May bring us there to be.
"The Other World," St. 1    *1867*

47 One must be very much of a woman for whom a man can sacrifice the deepest purpose of his life without awaking to regret it.
*Old Town Folks*, Ch. 2    *1869*

48 The burning of rebellious thoughts in the little breast, of internal hatred and opposition, could not long go on without slight whiffs of external smoke, such as mark the course of subterranean fire. Ibid., Ch. 11

49 These words dropped into my childish mind as if you should accidentally drop a ring into a deep well. I did not think of them much at the time, but there came a day in my life when the ring was fished up out of the well, good as new.
Ibid., Ch. 25

50 All men are lovers of sunshine and spring gales, but they are no one's in particular; and he who seeks to hold them to one heart finds his mistake. Ibid., Ch. 36

51 All my life my desire to visit the beautiful places of this earth has been so intense, that I cannot but hope that after my death I shall be permitted to go and look at them.
"Household Papers and Stories,"
*The Writings of Harriet Beecher Stowe*,
Vol. III    *1896*

52 . . . talent, especially in a woman, creates a zest for variety that the deepest passion cannot entirely supply. A monotonous life, even in the bosom of content, dismays a mind so constituted.
Quoted in *The Trumpets of Jubilee*
by Constance Roarke    *1927p*

## 37. Sarah Boyle
### (1812–1869)
* * *
1 Here I come creeping, creeping everywhere. . . .
"The Voice of Grass"

## 38. Sarah Ellis
### (1812–1872)
1 To act the part of a true friend requires more conscientious feeling than to fill with credit and complacency any other station or capacity in social life. *Pictures of Private Life*, Ch. 4
*1834*

## 39. Ann Preston
### (1813–1872)

1 Wherever it is proper to introduce women as patients, there also it is in accordance with the instinct of truest womanhood for women to appear as physicians and students.

> Quoted in *The Liberated Woman's Appointment Calendar*, Lynn Sherr and Jurate Kazickas, eds.      *1975p*

## 40. Ellen Wood
### (1813–1887)

1 Years ago, by dint of looking things steady in the face, and by economizing, he might have retrieved his position; but he had done what most people do in such cases—put off the evil day *sine die*, and gone on increasing his enormous list of debts. The hour of exposure and ruin was now advancing fast.

> *East Lynne* (novel), Ch. 1      *1861*

2 Petty ills try the temper worse than great ones.

> Ibid., Ch. 16

3 When folks act childishly, they must be treated as children.      Ibid., Ch. 37

4 Nothing but stabs; nothing but stabs! Was her punishment ever to end?      Ibid., Ch. 40

5 LEVISON. But there are moments when our hearts' dearest feelings break through the conventionalities of life, and betray themselves in spite of our sober judgment.

> *East Lynne* (play), Act II, Sc. 1
> *1862*

6 ARCHIBALD. A woman may almost as well love herself as suffer herself to love unsought.

> Ibid.

7 LEVISON. All strategems are fair in love and war.      Ibid., Act III, Sc. 2

8 "Afflictions are of two kinds—as I class them. The one we bring upon ourselves, through our own misconduct; the other is laid upon us by God for our real advantage. Yes, my boys, we receive many blessings in disguise. Trouble of this sort will only serve to draw out your manly energies, to make you engage vigorously in the business of life, to strengthen your self-dependence and your trust in God."

> *The Channings*, Vol. I, Ch. 3      *1862*

9 Things often seem to go by the rule of contrary.

> Ibid., Ch. 8

10 One thing is certain: that natures are not all formed to *feel* in a like degree. While the shock of some great trouble, whether anticipated or falling unexpectedly, as the case may happen, is passed over lightly by one man—hardly seen when it comes; to another it is as a terrible agony, shattering the spirit for the time, leaving its marks until death.

> *Our Children*      *1876*

11 Life has become to the most of us one swift, headlong race—a continuous fight in which there is so much to do that the half of it has to be left undone. . . . It is not so much what we have done amiss, as what we have left undone, that will trouble us, looking back.      Ibid.

12 We are truly indefatigable in providing for the needs of the body, but we starve the soul.

> *About Ourselves*, Ch. 1      *1883*

## 41. Anne Botta
### (1815–1891)
### * * *

1 The honey-bee that wanders all day long . . .
Seeks not alone the rose's glowing breast,
The lily's dainty cup, the violet's lips,
But from all rank and noxious weed he sips
The single drop of sweetness closely pressed
Within the poison chalice.

> "The Lesson of the Bee"

## 42. Julia Margaret Cameron
### (1815–1879)

1 I longed to arrest all beauty that came before me, and at length the longing has been satisfied.

> *Annals of My Glass House*      *1874*

## 43. Eliza Farnham
### (1815–1864)

1 The ultimate aim of the human mind, in all its efforts, is to become acquainted with Truth.

> *Woman and Her Era*, Pt. I, Ch. 1
> *1864*

2 Our own theological Church, as we know, has scorned and vilified the body till it has seemed almost a reproach and a shame to have one, yet at the same time has credited it with power to drag the soul to perdition.      Ibid.

3 Again the human face is the organic seat of beauty. . . . It is the register of value in development, a record of Experience, whose legitimate office is to perfect the life, a legible language to those who will study it, of the majestic mistress, the soul. . . .                Ibid.

4 Each of the Arts whose office it is to refine, purify, adorn, embellish and grace life is under the patronage of a Muse, no god being found worthy to preside over them.
                Ibid., Pt. II, Ch. 1

## 44. Elizabeth Phelps
### (1815–1852)

1 She found out there was no doctor for her like Dr. "Have-To."        "What Sent One Husband to California," *The Tell-Tale* 1853p

2 "You gentlemen," said she, "have such odd ideas of *house-cleaning!* You imagine you can do it up just as you buy and sell—so much labor for so much money. Now, the fact is, the simple labor is the easiest part of it. It is the getting ready for labor—contriving, planning, arranging—that is so wearisome."
                Ibid., "The Old Leather Portfolio"

3 Put in *your* oar, and share the sweat of the brow with which you must both start up the stream. You will richly enjoy the rest, when you reach the harbor.        Ibid., "First Trials of a Young Physician"

## 45. Elizabeth Cady Stanton
### (1815–1902)

1 . . . we still wonder at the stolid incapacity of all men to understand that woman feels the invidious distinctions of sex exactly as the black man does those of color, or the white man the more transient distinctions of wealth, family, position, place, and power; that she feels as keenly as man the injustice of disfranchisement.        *History of Woman Suffrage,* Vol. I, with Susan B. Anthony and Mathilda Gage        *1881*

2 . . . the impassable gulf that lies between riches and poverty.        Ibid.

3 It is impossible for one class to appreciate the wrongs of another.        Ibid.

4 And here is the secret of the infinite sadness of women of genius; . . . [she] must ever be surprised and aggravated with his assumptions of leadership and superiority, a superiority she never concedes, an authority she utterly repudiates.        Ibid.

5 In a republic where all are declared equal an ostracised class of half of the people, on the ground of a distinction founded in nature, is an anomalous position, as harassing to its victims as it is unjust, and as contradictory as it is unsafe to the fundamental principles of a free government.        Ibid.

6 But standing alone we learned our power; we repudiated man's counsels forevermore; and solemnly vowed that there should never be another season of silence until we had the same rights everywhere on this green earth, as man.        Ibid.

7 But when at last woman stands on an even platform with man, his acknowledged equal everywhere, with the same freedom to express herself in the religion and government of the country, then, and not until then, . . . will he be able to legislate as wisely and generously for her as for himself.        Ibid.

8 The prolonged slavery of women is the darkest page in human history.        Ibid.

9 But if a chivalrous desire to protect woman has always been the mainspring of man's dominion over her, it should have prompted him to place in her hands the same weapons of defense he has found to be most effective against wrong and oppression.        Ibid.

10 . . . woman's discontent increases in exact proportion to her development.        Ibid.

11 Like all disfranchised classes, they began by asking to have certain wrongs redressed, and not by asserting their own right to make laws for themselves.        Ibid.

12 It requires philosophy and heroism to rise above the opinion of the wise men of all nations and races. . . .        Ibid.

13 The creeds of all nations make obedience to man the corner-stone of her religious charter.        Ibid.

14 Though woman needs the protection of one man against his whole sex, in pioneer life, in threading her way through a lonely forest, on the highway, or in the streets of the metropolis on a dark night, she sometimes needs, too, the protection of all men against this one.        Ibid.

15 The ignorance and indifference of the majority of women, as to their status as citizens of a republic, is not remarkable, for history shows that the masses of all oppressed classes, in the most degraded conditions, have been stolid and apathetic until partial success had crowned the faith and enthusiasm of the few.     Ibid.

16 Sex pervades all nature, yet the male and female tree and vine and shrub rejoice in the same sunshine and shade. The earth and air are free to all the fruits and flowers, yet each absorbs what best ensures its growth.     Ibid.

17 Wherever the skilled hands and cultured brain of women have made the battle of life easier for man, he has readily pardoned her sound judgment and proper self-assertion.     Ibid.

18 Conceding to women wisdom and goodness, as they are not strictly masculine virtues, and substituting moral power for physical force, we have the necessary elements of government for most of life's emergencies.     Ibid.

19 The queens in history compare favorably with the kings.     Ibid.

20 . . . there is no force in the plea, that "if women vote they must fight." Moreover, war is not the normal state of the human family in its higher development, but merely a feature of barbarism lasting on through the transition of the race, from the savage to the scholar.     Ibid.

21 The virtue of patriotism is subordinant in most souls to individual and family aggrandizement.     Ibid.

22 A mind always in contact with children and servants, whose aspirations and ambitions rise no higher than the roof that shelters it, is necessarily dwarfed in its proportions.     Ibid.

23 Womanhood is the great fact in her life; wifehood and motherhood are but incidental relations.     Ibid.

24 But the love of offspring . . . tender and beautiful as it is, can not as a sentiment rank with conjugal love.     Ibid.

25 Two pure souls fused into one by an impassioned love—friends, counselors—a mutual support and inspiration to each other amid life's struggles, must know the highest human happiness;—this is marriage; and this is the only corner-stone of an enduring home.     Ibid.

26 They who give the world a true philosophy, a grand poem, a beautiful painting or statue, or can tell the story of every wandering star . . . have lived to a holier purpose than they whose children are of the flesh alone, into whose minds they have breathed no clear perceptions of great principles, no moral aspiration, no spiritual life.     Ibid.

27 . . . the woman is uniformly sacrificed to the wife and mother.     Ibid.

28 The more complete the despotism, the more smoothly all things move on the surface.     Ibid.

29 As the most ignorant minds cling with the greatest tenacity to the dogmas and traditions of their faith, a reform that involves an attack on that stronghold can only be carried by the education of another generation. Hence the self-assertion, the antagonism, the rebellion of women, so much deplored in England and the United States, is the hope of our higher civilization.     Ibid.

30 Modern inventions have banished the spinning-wheel, and the same law of progress makes the woman of to-day a different woman from her grandmother.     Ibid.

31 *Declaration of Sentiments:* . . . We hold these truths to be self-evident: that all men and women are created equal. . . .     Ibid.

32 *Declaration of Sentiments:* Now, in view of this entire disfranchisement of half the people of this country, through social and religious degradation—in view of the unjust laws above mentioned, and because women do feel themselves aggrieved, oppressed, and fraudulently deprived of their most sacred rights, we insist that they have immediate admission to all the rights and privileges which belong to them as citizens of the United States.     Ibid.

33 *Declaration of Sentiments: Resolved,* That such laws as conflict, in any way, with the true and substantial happiness of women, are contrary to the great precept of nature and of no validity, for this is "superior in obligation to any other."     Ibid.

34 *Declaration of Sentiments: Resolved,* That all laws which prevent women from occupying such a station in society as her conscience shall dictate, or which place her in a position inferior to that of man, are contrary to the great precept of nature, and therefore of no force or authority.     Ibid.

35 *Declaration of Sentiments: Resolved,* That the same amount of virtue, delicacy, and refinement of behavior that is required of woman in the social station, should also be required of man, and the same transgressions should be visited with equal severity on both man and woman.     Ibid.

36 *Declaration of Sentiments: Resolved, therefore,* That, being invested by the Creator with the same capabilities, and the same consciousness of responsibility for their exercises, it is demonstrably the right and duty of woman, equally with man, to promote every righteous cause by every righteous means . . . and this being a self-evident truth growing out of the divinely implanted principles of human nature, any custom or authority adverse to it, whether modern or wearing the hoary sanction of antiquity, is to be regarded as a self-evident falsehood, and at war with mankind. Ibid.

37 She [Susan B. Anthony] supplied the facts and statistics, I the philosophy and rhetoric, and together we have made arguments that have stood unshaken by the storms of thirty long years. Ibid.

38 The tyrant, Custom, has been summoned before the bar of Common-Sense. His majesty no longer awes the multitude—his sceptre is broken—his crown is trampled in the dust—the sentence of death is pronounced upon him.
Ibid., Speech, New York State
Legislature (1854)

39 You who have read the history of nations, from Moses down to our last election, where have you ever seen one class looking after the interests of another? Ibid. (1860)

40 Reformers can be as bigoted and sectarian and as ready to malign each other, as the Church in its darkest periods has been to persecute its dissenters.
Ibid., "The Kansas Campaign of 1867"

41 There never was a more hopeful interest concentrated in the legislation of any single State, than when Kansas submitted the two propositions to her people to take the words "white" and "male" from her Constitution. Ibid.

42 . . . mothers of the race, the most important actors in the grand drama of human progress. . . . Ibid.

43 Having gleefully chased butterflies in our young days on our way to school, we thought it might be as well to chase them in our old age on the way to heaven.
Ibid., "The Newport Convention"

44 The *ennui* and utter vacuity of a life of mere pleasure is fast urging fashionable women to something better. . . . Ibid.

45 . . . they had souls large enough to feel the wrongs of others. . . .
Ibid., "Seneca Falls Convention"

46 The Bible teaches that woman brought sin and death into the world, that she precipitated the fall of the race, that she was arraigned before the judgment seat of Heaven, tried, condemned and sentenced. Marriage for her was to be a condition of bondage, maternity a period of suffering and anguish, and in silence and subjection, she was to play the role of a dependent on man's bounty for all her material wants. . . .
*The Woman's Bible,* Pt. I 1895

47 If the Bible teaches the equality of women, why does the church refuse to ordain women to preach the gospel, to fill the offices of deacons and elders, and to administer the Sacraments . . . ? Ibid.

48 Why is it more ridiculous to arraign ecclesiastics for their false teaching and acts of injustice to women, than members of Congress and the House of Commons? Ibid.

49 Come, come, my conservative friend, wipe the dew off your spectacles, and see that the world is moving. Ibid.

50 For so far-reaching and momentous a reform as her complete independence, an entire revolution in all existing institutions is inevitable.
Ibid.

51 Reformers who are always compromising, have not yet grasped the idea that truth is the only safe ground to stand upon. Ibid.

52 So long as tens of thousands of Bibles are printed every year, and circulated over the whole habitable globe, and the masses in all English-speaking nations revere it as the word of God, it is vain to belittle its influence.
Ibid.

53 The Bible cannot be accepted or rejected as a whole, its teachings are varied and its lessons differ widely from each other. Ibid.

54 The Bible and Church have been the greatest stumbling blocks in the way of woman's emancipation. Quoted in *Free Thought Magazine*
*September, 1896*

55 The whole tone of Church teaching in regard to women is, to the last degree, contemptuous and degrading. Ibid. *November, 1896*

56 The memory of my own suffering has prevented me from ever shadowing one young soul with the superstitutions of the Christian religion. *Eighty Years and More* 1898

57 It is a proud moment in a woman's life to reign supreme within four walls, to be the one to whom all questions of domestic pleasure and economy are referred. Ibid.

58 Though motherhood is the most important of all the professions—requiring more knowledge than any other department in human affairs—there was no attention given to preparation for this office.          Ibid., Rev. Ed.          *1902*

59 . . . I had . . . as little faith in the popular theories in regard to babies as on any other subject. I saw them, on all sides, ill half the time, pale and peevish, dying early, having no joy in life. . . . Everyone seemed to think these inflictions were a part of the eternal plan—that Providence had a kind of Pandora's box, from which he scattered these venerable diseases most liberally among those whom he especially loved.          Ibid.

60 The life and well-being of the race seemed to hang on the slender thread of such traditions as were handed down by ignorant mothers and nurses.          Ibid.

61 Besides the obstinacy of the nurse, I had the ignorance of the physicians to contend with.          Ibid.

62 They smiled at each other, and one said, "Well, after all, a mother's instinct is better than a man's reason." "Thank you, gentlemen, there was no instinct about it. I did some hard thinking. . . ."          Ibid.

63 So closely interwoven have been our lives, our purposes, and experiences that, separated, we have a feeling of incompleteness—united, such strength of self-assertion that no ordinary obstacles, differences, or dangers ever appear to us insurmountable.          Ibid.

64 I am at a boiling point! If I do not find some day the use of my tongue on this question I shall die of an intellectual repression, a woman's rights convulsion.
          *Elizabeth Cady Stanton*, Vol. II,
          Theodore Stanton and Harriot
          Stanton Blatch, eds.          *1922p*

65 Dear me, how much cruel bondage of mind and suffering of body poor woman will escape when she takes the liberty of being her own physician of both body and soul!          Ibid.

66 I never felt more keenly the degradation of my sex. To think that all in me of which my father would have felt a proper pride had I been a man, is deeply mortifying to him because I am a woman.          Ibid.

67 I think if women would indulge more freely in vituperation, they would enjoy ten times the health they do. It seems to me they are suffering from repression.          Ibid.

68 . . . one of the best gifts of the gods came to me in the form of a good, faithful housekeeper.          Ibid.

69 Last evening we spoke of the propriety of women being called by the names which are used to designate their sex, and not by those assigned to males. . . . I have very serious objections, dear Rebecca, to being called Henry. There is a great deal in a name. . . . The custom of calling women Mrs. John This and Mrs. Tom That, and colored men Sambo and Zip Coon, is founded on the principle that white men are lords of all. I cannot acknowledge this principle as just; therefore, I cannot bear the name of another.
          Ibid., Letter to Rebecca R. Eyster
          (May 1, 1847)

70 Man in his lust has regulated long enough this whole question of sexual intercourse. Now let the mother of mankind, whose prerogative it is to set bounds to his indulgence, rouse up and give this whole matter a thorough, fearless examination.
          Ibid., Letter to Susan B. Anthony
          (1853)

71 Women's degradation is in man's idea of his sexual rights.          Ibid. (1860)

72 I shall not grow conservative with age.          Ibid.

73 I have no sympathy with the old idea that children owe such immense gratitude to their parents that they can never fulfill their obligations to them. I think the obligation is all on the other side. Parents can never do too much for their children to repay them for the injustice of having brought them into the world, unless they have insured them high moral and intellectual gifts, fine physical health, and enough money and education to render life something more than one ceaseless struggle for necessities.          Ibid., Diary Entry (1880)

74 I have come to the conclusion that the first great work to be accomplished for women is to revolutionize the dogma that sex is a crime, marriage a defilement and maternity a bane.          Ibid. (1881)

75 I have been into many of the ancient cathedrals—grand, wonderful, mysterious. But I always leave them with a feeling of indignation because of the generations of human beings who have struggled in poverty to build these altars to the unknown god.          Ibid. (1882)

76 I am weary seeing our laboring classes so wretchedly housed, fed, and clothed, while thousands of dollars are wasted every year over

unsightly statues. If these great men must have outdoor memorials let them be in the form of handsome blocks of buildings for the poor.
Ibid. (1886)

77 Our trouble is not our womanhood, but the artificial trammels of custom under false conditions. We are, as a sex, infinitely superior to men, and if we were free and developed, healthy in body and mind, as we should be under natural conditions, our motherhood would be our glory. That function gives women such wisdom and power as no male ever can possess. When women can support themselves, have their entry to all the trades and professions, with a house of their own over their heads and a bank account, they will own their bodies and be dictators in the social realm.
Ibid. (1890)

78 I asked them why . . . one read in the synagogue service every week the "I thank thee, O lord, that I was not born a woman." ". . . It is not meant in an unfriendly spirit, and it is not intended to degrade or humiliate women." "But it does, nevertheless. Suppose the service read, 'I thank thee, O Lord, that I was not born a jackass.' Could that be twisted in any way into a compliment to the jackass?"
Ibid. (1895)

79 Men as a general rule have very little reverence for trees. Ibid. (1900)

80 In a word, I am always busy, which is perhaps the chief reason why I am always well.
Ibid.

81 The growth of the mind should mean as much in citizenship as the growth of the body; perhaps even more. Ibid. (1902)

82 I do not know whether the world is quite willing or ready to discuss the question of marriage. . . . I feel, as never before, that this whole question of women's rights turns on the pivot of the marriage relation, and, mark my word, sooner or later it will be the topic for discussion. I would not hurry it on, nor would I avoid it.
Letter to Susan B. Anthony (1853), Feminism, Miriam Schneir, ed.
1972p

83 We who like the children of Israel have been wandering in the wilderness of prejudice and ridicule for forty years feel a peculiar tenderness for the young women on whose shoulders we are about to leave our burdens.
Ibid., Speech, International Council of Women (1888)

84 Thus far women have been the mere echoes of men. Our laws and constitutions, our creeds and codes, and the customs of social life are all of masculine origin. The true woman is as yet a dream of the future. Ibid.

85 No matter how much women prefer to lean, to be protected and supported, nor how much men desire to have them do so, they must make the voyage of life alone, and for safety in an emergency, they must know something of the laws of navigation.
Ibid., Speech, "Solitude of Self," House Judiciary Committee (1892)

## 46. Harriet Tubman
### (1815?–1913)

1 When I found I had crossed dat *line*, I looked at my hands to see if I was de same pusson. There was such a glory ober ebery ting; de sun came like gold through the trees, and ober the fields, and I felt like I was in Heaben.
Quoted in *Scenes in the Life of Harriet Tubman* by Sarah H. Bradford    *1869*

2 I had crossed the line. I was *free*; but there was no one to welcome me to the land of freedom. I was a stranger in a strange land; and my home, after all, was down in Maryland; because my father, my mother, my brothers, and sisters, and friends were there. But I was free, and *they* should be free. I would make a home in the North and bring them there, God helping me. Ibid.

3 Don't you think we colored people are entitled to some credit for that exploit, under the lead of the brave Colonel Montgomery? We weakened the rebels somewhat on the Combahee River, by taking and bringing away *seven hundred and fifty-six* head of their most valuable live stock, known up in your region as "contrabands," and this, too, without the loss of a single life on our part, though we had good reason to believe that a number of rebels bit the dust. Of these seven hundred and fifty-six contrabands, nearly or quite all the ablebodied men have joined the colored regiments here. . . . Ibid., Article in the *Boston Commonwealth* (June 30, 1863)

4 I tink dar's many a slaveholder'll git to Heaven. Dey don't know no better. Dey acts up to de light dey hab. You take dat sweet little child— 'pears more like an angel dan anyting else— take her down dere, let her nebber know nothing 'bout niggers but they was made to be

whipped, an' she'll grow up to use the whip on 'em jus' like de rest. No, Missus, it's because dey don't know no better.      Ibid.

5 I had reasoned this out in my mind, there was two things I had a right to, liberty and death. If I could not have one, I would have the other, for no man should take me alive.
> Quoted in "Lost Women: Harriet Tubman—The Moses of her People" by Marcy Galen, *Ms. August, 1973p*

## 47. Charlotte Brontë
### (1816–1855)

1 Life, believe, is not a dream
  So dark as sages say;
Oft a little morning rain
  Foretells a pleasant day.
> "Life," St. 1      *1846*

2 The human heart has hidden treasures,
  In secret kept, in silence sealed;—
The thoughts, the hopes, the dreams, the
    pleasures,
Whose charms were broken if revealed.
> "Evening Solace," St. 1      *1846*

3 Conventionality is not morality. Self-righteousness is not religion. To attack the first is not to assail the last. To pluck the mask from the face of the Pharisee is not to lift an impious hand to the Crown of Thorns.
> *Jane Eyre*, Preface      *1847*

4 Vain favour! coming, like most other favours long deferred and often wished for, too late!
> Ibid., Ch. 3

5 Something of vengeance I had tasted for the first time; as aromatic wine it seemed, on swallowing, warm and racy: its after-flavour, metallic and corroding, gave me a sensation as if I had been poisoned.      Ibid., Ch. 4

6 It is in vain to say human beings ought to be satisfied with tranquillity: they must have action; and they will make it if they cannot find it. Millions are condemned to a stiller doom than mine, and millions are in silent revolt against their lot. Nobody knows how many rebellions besides political rebellions ferment in the masses of life which people earth.
> Ibid., Ch. 12

7 My help had been needed and claimed; I had given it: I was pleased to have done something; trivial, transitory though the deed was, it was yet an active thing, and I was weary of an existence all passive.      Ibid.

8 . . . if you are cast in a different mould to the majority, it is no merit of yours: Nature did it.
> Ibid., Ch. 14

9 Little girl, a memory without blot or contamination must be an exquisite treasure—an inexhaustible source of pure refreshment: is it not?      Ibid.

10 "Dread remorse when you are tempted to err, Miss Eyre: remorse is the poison of life."
> Ibid.

11 "I grant an ugly *woman* is a blot on the fair face of creation; but as to the *gentlemen*, let them be solicitous to possess only strength and valour: let their motto be:—Hunt, shoot, and fight: the rest is not worth a fillip."
> Ibid., Ch. 17

12 "Reason sits firm and holds the reins, and she will not let the feelings burst away and hurry her to wild chasms. The passions may rage furiously, like true heathens, as they are; and the desires may imagine all sorts of vain things, but judgment shall still have the last word in every argument, and the casting vote in every decision."      Ibid., Ch. 19

13 ". . . as much good-will may be conveyed in one hearty word as in many."    Ibid., Ch. 21

14 "You had no right to be born; for you make no use of life. Instead of living for, in, and with yourself, as a reasonable being ought, you seek only to fasten your feebleness on some other person's strength. . . ."      Ibid.

15 Feeling without judgment is a washy draught indeed; but judgment untempered by feeling is too bitter and husky a morsel for human deglutition [sic].      Ibid.

16 "Laws and principles are not for the times when there is no temptation: they are for such moments as this, when body and soul rise in mutiny against their rigour; stringent are they; inviolate they shall be. If at my individual convenience I might break them, what would be their worth?"      Ibid., Ch. 28

17 The soul, fortunately, has an interpreter—often an unconscious, but still a truthful interpreter—in the eye.      Ibid.

18 "I hold that the more arid and unreclaimed the soil where the Christian labourer's task of tillage is appointed him—the scantier the meed his toil brings—the higher the honour."
> Ibid., Ch. 30

19 One does not jump, and spring, and shout hur-rah! at hearing one has got a fortune, one begins to consider responsibilities, and to pon-der business. . . .       *Ibid.*, Ch. 33

20 Reader, I married him.       *Ibid.*, Ch. 38

21 Prejudices, it is well known, are most difficult to eradicate from the heart whose soil has never been loosened or fertilized by education; they grow there, firm as weeds among stones.       *Ibid.*

22 An abundant shower of curates has fallen upon the north of England.       *Shirley*, Ch. 1
      *1849*

23 Give him rope enough and he will hang him-self.       *Ibid.*, Ch. 3

24 Look twice before you leap.       *Ibid.*, Ch. 9

25 Like March, having come in like a lion, he purposed to go out like a lamb.       *Ibid.*, Ch. 15

26 . . . nothing moved her [Emily Brontë] more than any insinuation that the faithfulness and clemency, the long-suffering and loving-kindness which are esteemed virtues in the daughters of Eve, become foibles in the sons of Adam. She held that mercy & forgiveness are the divinest attributes of the Great Being who made both man and woman, and that what clothes the Godhead in glory, can disgrace no form of feeble humanity.       Preface to *Wuthering Heights* by Emily Brontë       *1850*

27 But this I know; the writer who possesses the creative gift owns something of which he is not always master—something that at times strangely wills and works for itself. . . . If the result be attractive, the World will praise you, who little deserve praise; if it be repulsive, the same World will blame you, who almost as little deserve blame.       *Ibid.*

28 Alfred and I intended to be married in this way almost from the first; we never meant to be spliced in the hum-drum way of other people.       *Villete*, Ch. 42       *1853*

## 48. Frances Brown
### (1816–1864)
\* \* \*

1 Oh! those blessed times of old! with their chivalry and state;
I love to read their chronicles, which such brave deeds relate. . . .
      "Oh! The Pleasant Days of Old," St. 7

## 49. Charlotte Saunders Cushman
### (1816–1876)

1 To me it seems as if when God conceived the world, that was Poetry; He formed it, and that was Sculpture; He colored it, and that was Painting; He peopled it with living beings, and that was the grand, divine, eternal Drama.
      Quoted in *Charlotte Cushman* by Emma Stebbins       *1879p*

2 Art is an absolute mistress; she will not be coquetted with or slighted; she requires the most entire self-devotion, and she repays with grand triumphs.       *Ibid.*, Ch. 10
      \* \* \*

3 There is a God! the sky his presence snares,
His hand upheaves the billows in their mirth,
Destroys the mighty, yet the humble spares
And with contentment crowns the thought of worth.
      "There Is a God"

## 50. Ellen Sturgis Hooper
### (1816–1841)
\* \* \*

1 I slept, and dreamed that life was Beauty;
I woke, and found that life was Duty.
      "Beauty and Duty"

2 The straightest path perhaps which may be sought,
Lies through the great highway men call "I ought."
      "The Straight Road"

## 51. Eliza "Mother" Stewart
### (1816–1908)

1 No power on earth or above the bottomless pit has such influence to terrorize and make cow-ards of men as the liquor power. Satan could not have fallen on a more potent instrument with which to thrall the world. Alcohol is king!       *Memories of the Crusade*, Ch. 1
      *1888*

2 But you must know the class of sweet women—who are always so happy to declare "they have all the rights they want"; "they are perfectly willing to let their husbands vote for them"—are and always have been numerous, though it is an occasion for thankfulness that they are becoming less so.       *Ibid.*, Ch. 7

## 52. Jane Montgomery Campbell

(1817–1879)

\* \* \*

1 We plough the fields and scatter
The good seed on the land,
But it is fed and watered
By God's Almighty hand.
"We Plough the Fields,"<br>*Garland of Songs*

2 He paints the wayside flower,
He lights the evening star.
Ibid.

## 53. Mrs. Cecil Frances Alexander

(1818–1895)

\* \* \*

1 Jesus calls us, o'er the tumult
Of our life's wild, restless sea.
"Jesus Calls Us"

2 The rich man at his castle,
The poor man at his gate,
God made them, high or lowly,
And ordered their estate.
"All Things Bright"

3 All things bright and beautiful,
All creatures great and small,
All things wise and wonderful,
The Lord God made them all.
Ibid.

## 54. Amelia Jenks Bloomer

(1818–1894)

1 Another cannot make fit to eat without wine or brandy. A third must have brandy on her apple dumplings, and a fourth comes out boldly and says she likes to drink once in a while herself too well. What flimsy excuses these! brandy and apple dumplings forsooth! That lady must be a wretched cook indeed who cannot make apple dumplings, mince pie or cake palatable without the addition of poisonous substances.
*Water Bucket* *1842*

2 Like the beautiful flower from which it derives its name, we shall strive to make *The Lily* [a newspaper] the emblem of "sweetness and purity"; and may heaven smile on our attempt to advocate the great cause of Temperance reform!
*The Lily* *January 1, 1849*

3 Man represents us, legislates for us, and now holds himself accountable for us! How kind in him, and what a weight is lifted from us! We shall no longer be answerable to the laws of God or man, no longer be subject to punishment for breaking them, no longer be responsible for any of our doings.
Ibid. *March, 1850*

4 Ah, how steadily do they who are guilty shrink from reproof! Ibid. *April, 1853*

5 The costume of women should be suited to her wants and necessities. It should conduce at once to her health, comfort, and usefulness; and, while it should not fail also to conduce to her personal adornment, it should make that end of secondary importance.
Letter to Charlotte A. Joy<br>*June 3, 1857*

## 55. Emily Brontë

(1818–1848)

1 Faithful, indeed, is the spirit that remembers
After such years of change and suffering!
"Remembrance" *1846*

2 Once drinking deep of that divinest anguish,
How could I seek the empty world again?
Ibid.

3 I'll walk where my own nature would be leading—
It vexes me to choose another guide. . . .
"Often Rebuked" *1846*

4 Love is like the wild rose-briar;
Friendship like the holly-tree.
The holly is dark when the rose-briar blooms,
But which will bloom most constantly?
"Love and Friendship" *1846*

5 No coward soul is mine,
No trembler in the world's storm-troubled sphere:
I see Heaven's glories shine,
And faith shines equally, arming me from fear.
"Last Lines" *1846*

6 Vain are the thousand creeds
That move men's hearts: unutterably vain. . . .
Ibid.

7 Though earth and man were gone,
And suns and universes ceased to be,
And Thou wert left alone,
Every existence would exist in Thee.
Ibid.

8 There is not room for Death.
Ibid.

9 Oh! dreadful is the check—intense the agony—
When the ear begins to hear, and the eye
begins to see;
When the pulse begins to throb, the brain to
think again;
The soul to feel the flesh, and the flesh to feel
the chain.
"The Prisoner"     1846

10 Sleep not, dream not; this bright day
Will not, cannot, last for aye;
Bliss like thine is bought by years
Dark with torment and with tears.
"Sleep Not," St. 1     1846

11 "Wretched inmates!" I ejaculated, mentally,
"you deserve perpetual isolation from your species for your churlish inhospitality."
Wuthering Heights, Ch. 2     1847

12 "I am now quite cured of seeking pleasure in
society, be it country or town. A sensible man
ought to find sufficient company in himself."
Ibid., Ch. 3

13 "Proud people breed sad sorrows for themselves."     Ibid., Ch. 7

14 "A good heart will help you to a bonny face,
my lad . . . and a bad one will turn the bonni-
est into something worse than ugly."     Ibid.

15 "A person who has not done one half his day's
work by ten o'clock, runs a chance of leaving
the other half undone."     Ibid.

16 "My love for Linton is like the foliage in the
woods: time will change it, I'm well aware, as
winter changes the trees. My love for Heathcliff resembles the eternal rocks beneath: a
source of little visible delight, but necessary.
Nelly, I am Heathcliff!"     Ibid., Ch. 9

17 "The tyrant grinds down his slaves and they
don't turn against him; they crush those beneath them."     Ibid., Ch. 11

18 "Having levelled my palace, don't erect a hovel
and complacently admire your own charity in
giving me that for a home."     Ibid.

19 Any relic of the dead is precious, if they were
valued living.     Ibid., Ch. 13

20 "And we'll see if one tree won't grow as
crooked as another with the same wind to twist
it!"     Ibid., Ch. 17

21 Good things lost amid a wilderness of weeds,
to be sure, whose rankness far over-topped
their neglected growth; yet, notwithstanding,
evidence of a wealthy soil, that might yield
luxuriant crops under other and favourable
circumstances.     Ibid., Ch. 18

22 I lingered round them [tombstones], under that
benign sky: watched the moths fluttering
among the heath and harebells; listened to the
soft wind breathing through the grass; and wondered how anyone could ever imagine unquiet
slumbers for the sleepers in that quiet earth.
Ibid., Conclusion

## 56. Emily Collins
(1818?–1879?)

1 . . . from the earliest dawn of reason I pined
for that freedom of thought and action that was
then denied to all womankind. I revolted in
spirit against the customs of society and the
laws of the State that crushed my aspirations
and debarred me from the pursuit of almost
every object worthy of an intelligent, rational
mind.
"Reminiscences of Emily Collins,"
Quoted in History of Woman Suffrage,
Vol. I, by Elizabeth Cady Stanton,
Susan B. Anthony, and Mathilda Gage
1881p

2 It is ever thus; where Theology enchains the
soul, the Tyrant enslaves the body.     Ibid.

3 Every argument for the emancipation of the
colored man was equally one for that of
women; and I was surprised that all Abolition-
ists did not see the similarity in the condition of
the two classes.     Ibid.

4 We breathe a freer, if not a purer, atmosphere
here among the mountains than do the dwellers
in cities,—have more indeed, are less subject
to the despotism of fashion, and are less absorbed with dress and amusements.
Ibid., Letter to Sarah C. Owen
(October 23, 1848)

5 Moral Reform and Temperance Societies may
be multiplied ad infinitum, but they have about
the same effect upon the evils they seek to cure
as clipping the top of a hedge would have toward extirpating it.     Ibid.

6 People are more willing to be convinced by the
calm perusal of an argument than in a personal
discussion.     Ibid.

7 From press, and pulpit, and platform, she was
taught that "to be unknown was her highest
praise," that "dependence was her best protection," and "her weakness her sweetest
charm."     Ibid.

## 57. Eliza Cook

(1818–1889)

\*   \*   \*

1 Better build schoolrooms for "the boy,"
   Than cells and gibbets for "the man."
               "A Song for the Ragged Schools,"
                             St. 12

2 Hunger is bitter, but the worst
   Of human pangs, the most accursed
   Of Want's fell scorpions, is thirst.
                           "Melaia"

3 I love it—I love it, and who shall dare
   To chide me for loving that old Arm-chair?
                "The Old Arm-Chair"

4 Let Reason become your employer,
   And your body be ruled by your soul.
                "Where There's a Will
                   There's a Way," St. 3

5 Oh! much may be done by defying
   The ghosts of Despair and Dismay;
   And much may be gained by relying
   On "Where there's a will there's a way."
                       Ibid., St. 4

6 Oh! better, then, to die and give
   The grave its kindred dust,
   Than live to see Time's bitter change
   In those we love and trust.
                  "Time's Changes"

7 Oh, how cruelly sweet are the echoes that start
   When Memory plays an old tune on the heart!
                "Old Dobbin," St. 16,
                   *The Journal*, Vol. IV

8 On what strange stuff Ambition feeds!
                  "Thomas Hood"

9 Spring, Spring, beautiful Spring.
                       "Spring"

10 There's a star in the West\* that shall never go
     down
   Till the Records of Valour decay,
   We must worship its light though it is not our
     own,
   For liberty burst in its ray.
             "There's a Star in the West"

11 Though language forms the preacher,
   'Tis "good works" make the man.
                  "Good Works"

12 'Tis a glorious charter, deny it who can,
   That's birthed in the words, "I'm an Englishman."
                 "An Englishman"

\* Referring to George Washington.

13 'Tis well to give honour and glory to Age,
   With its lessons of wisdom and truth;
   Yet who would not go back to the fanciful page,
   And the fairytale read but in youth?
                     "Stanzas"

14 Who would not rather trust and be deceived?
                     "Love On"

15 Whom do we dub as Gentleman? The
   Knave, the fool, the brute—
   If they but own full tithe of gold, and
   Wear a courtly suit.
           "Nature's Gentleman," St. 1

16 Why should we strive, with cynic frown,
   To knock their fairy castles down?
            "Oh! Dear to Memory"

## 58. Mary A. E. Green

(1818?–1895)

1 Of all the royal daughters of England who, by
the weight of personal character, or the influence of advantageous circumstances, had exercised a permanent bearing on its destiny, few
have occupied so prominent a place as Elizabeth, queen of bohemia, the high-minded but
ill-fated daughter of James I.
        *Elizabeth, Queen of Bohemia*, Ch. 1
                                1855

## 59. Mary Elizabeth Hewitt

(1818–?)

1 A sumptuous dwelling the rich man hath.
   And dainty is his repast;
   But remember that luxury's prodigal hand
   Keeps the furnace of toil in blast.
            "A Plea for the Rich Man,"
                *Poems*, St. 3     1853

2 Ah me! poor heart! that love like thine
   Should seek with dreams to be content!

   With dreams—and what is life, alas!
   But of the visions that we see?
   Shadows of love, and hope, that pass
   To mock us, like my dream of thee.
       Ibid., "Leonora Thinking of Tasso,"
                       Sts. 4–5

3 And I shall hear thy song resound,
   Till from his shackles man shall bound
   And shout exultant, "LIBERTY!"
       Ibid., "The Songs of Our Land," St. 12

4 Then hail! thou noble conquerer!
   That, when tyranny oppressed,
   Hewed for our fathers from the wild
   A land wherein to rest.
       Ibid., "The Axe of the Settler," St. 5

## 60. Mary Todd Lincoln

(1818–1882)

1 The change from this gloomy earth, to be forever reunited to my idolized husband & my darling Willie, would be happiness indeed!
>Letter to Mrs. Slataper (September 29, 1868), *The Mary Lincoln Letters,* Justin G. Turner, ed.    *1956p*

2 I am convinced, the longer I live, that life & its blessings are not so entirely unjustly distributed [as] when we are suffering greatly, we are inclined to suppose. My home for so many years was so rich in love and happiness; now I am so lonely and isolated—whilst others live on in a careless lukewarm state—not appearing to fill Longfellow's measure: "Into each life, some rain must fall."    Ibid.

3 Beautiful, glorious Scotland, has spoilt me for every other country!
>Ibid. (August 21, 1869)

4 My feelings & hopes are all so sanguine that in this dull world of reality 'tis best to dispell our delusive daydreams as soon as possible.
>Letter to Mercy Levering (July 23, 1840), *Mary Todd Lincoln: Her Life and Letters,* Justin G. Turner, ed.    *1972p*

5 My evil genius Procrastination has whispered me to tarry 'til a more convenient season. . . .
>Ibid. (June, 1841)

6 Clouds and darkness surround us, yet Heaven is just, & the day of triumph will *surely* come, when justice & truth will be vindicated. Our wrongs will be made right, & we will once more, taste the blessings of freedom, of which the degraded rebels, would deprive us.
>Ibid., Letter to James Gordon Bennett (October 25, 1861)

## 61. Maria Mitchell

(1818–1889)

1 Why can not a man act himself, be himself, and think for himself? It seems to me that naturalness alone is power; that a borrowed word is weaker than our own weakness, however small we may be.
>Diary Entry (1867), *Maria Mitchell, Life, Letters, and Journals,* Phebe Mitchell Kendall, ed.    *1896p*

2 We travel to learn; and I have never been in any country where they did not do something better than we do it, think some thoughts better than we think, catch some inspiration from heights above our own.    Ibid. (July, 1873)

3 This ignorance of the masses leads to a misconception in two ways; the little that a scientist can do, they do not understand—they suppose him to be god-like in his capacity, and they do not see results; they overrate him and they underrate him—they underrate his work.
>Ibid. (1874)

4 For women there are, undoubtedly, great difficulties in the path, but so much the more to overcome. First, no woman should say, "I am but a woman!" But a woman! what more can you ask to be?
>Ibid., Address to Students (1874)

5 The whole system is demoralizing and foolish. Girls study for prizes and not for learning, when "honors" are at the end. The unscholarly motive is wearying. If they studied for sound learning, the cheer which would come with every day's gain would be health-preserving.
>Ibid. (March 13, 1882)

6 . . . to-day I am ready to say, "Give no scholarships at all." I find a helping-hand lifts the girl as crutches do; she learns to like the help which is not self-help. If a girl has the public school, and wants enough to learn, she will learn. It is hard, but she was born to hardness—she cannot dodge it. Labor is her inheritance.
>Ibid. (February 10, 1887)

7 Health of body is not only an accompaniment of health of mind, but is the cause; the converse may be true—that health of mind causes health of body; but we all know that intellectual cheer and vivacity act upon the mind. If the gymnastic exercise helps the mind, the concert or the theatre improves the health of the body.    Ibid.

8 . . . I do think, as a general rule, that teachers talk too much! A book is a very good institution! To read a book, to think it over, and to write out notes is a useful exercise; a book which will not repay some hard thought is not worth publishing.    Ibid. (July, 1887)

9 Every formula which expresses a law of nature is a hymn of praise to God.
>Inscription on Bust in the Hall of Fame    *1905p*

## 62. Elizabeth Prentiss

(1818–1878)

\* \* \*

1        Sleep, baby, sleep!
Thy father's watching the sheep,
Thy mother's shaking the dreamland tree,
And down drops a little dream for thee.
>Sleep, baby, sleep.

"Cradle Song"

## 63. Lucy Stone

(1818–1893)

1 I know not what you believe of God, but I believe He gave yearnings and longings to be filled, and that He did not mean all our time should be devoted to feeding and clothing the body.      Speech, "Disappointment Is the Lot of Women" (October 17–18, 1855), Quoted in *History of Woman Suffrage,* Vol. I, by Elizabeth Cady Stanton, Susan B. Anthony, and Mathilda Gage
*1881*

2 In education, in marriage, in religion, in everything, disappointment is the lot of women. It shall be the business of my life to deepen this disappointment in every woman's heart until she bows down to it no longer.      Ibid.

3 The widening of woman's sphere is to improve her lot. Let us do it, and if the world scoff, let it scoff—if it sneer, let it sneer. . . .
Ibid.

4 We want rights. The flour-merchant, the house-builder, and the postman charge us no less on account of our sex; but when we endeavor to earn money to pay all these, then, indeed, we find the difference.      Ibid.

5 I expect some new phases of life this summer, and shall try to get the honey from each moment.      Quoted in *Antoinette Brown Blackwell: Biographical Sketch* by Sarah Gilson     *1909p*

6 Because I know that I shall suffer, shall I, for this, like Lot's wife, turn back? No, mother, if in this hour of the world's need I should refuse to lend my aid, however small it may be, I should have no right to think myself a Christian, and I should forever despise Lucy Stone. If, while I hear the wild shriek of the slave mother robbed of her little ones, or the muffled groan of the daughter spoiled of her virtue, I do not open my mouth for the dumb, am I not guilty?
Letter to Her Mother (c.1847), Quoted in *Morning Star,* Pt. II, Ch. 6, by Elinor Rice Hays     *1961p*

7 I was a woman before I was an abolitionist. I must speak for the women.     Ibid. (c. 1848)

8 The privations I have learned to endure, and the isolation, I scarcely regret; while the certainties that I am *living usefully* brings a deep and *abiding* happiness.     Ibid., Letter to Henry Blackwell     (c.1849)

9 "We, the people of the United States." Which "We, the people"? The women were not included.     Ibid., Speech, *New York Tribune* (April, 1853)

10 My heart aches to love somebody that shall be all its own . . . [but] I shall not be married ever. I have not yet seen the person whom I have the slightest wish to marry, and if I had, it will take longer than my lifetime for the obstacles to be removed which are in the way of a married woman having any being of her own.     Ibid., Ch. 9, Letter to Nette Brown (1853)

11 Our victory is sure to come, and I can endure anything but recreancy to principle.
Ibid., Pt. III, Ch. 19

12 I think God rarely gives to one man, or one set of men, more than *one* great moral victory to win.     Ibid. (c.1867)

## 64. George Eliot

(1819–1880)

1 Any coward can fight a battle when he's sure of winning; but give me the man who has pluck to fight when he's sure of losing. That's my way, sir; and there are many victories worse than a defeat.     *Janet's Repentance,* Ch. 6
*1857*

2 Opposition may become sweet to a man, when he has christened it persecution.     Ibid., Ch. 8

3 In every parting scene there is an image of death.     "Amos Barton," *Scenes of Clerical Life*     *1858*

4 Animals are such agreeable friends—they ask no questions, they pass no criticisms.
Ibid., "Mr. Gilfi's Love Story"

5 It's but little good you'll do a-watering the last year's crop.     *Adam Bede,* Ch. 18
*1859*

6 It was a pity he couldna be hatched o'er again, an' hatched different.     Ibid.

7 A patronizing disposition always has its meaner side.     Ibid., Ch. 28

8 Our deeds determine us, as much as we determine our deeds.     Ibid., Ch. 29

9 It's them as take advantage that get advantage i' this world.     Ibid., Ch. 32

10 A maggot must be born i' the rotten cheese to like it.     Ibid.

11 He was like a cock, who thought the sun had risen to hear him crow.      *Ibid.*, Ch. 33

12 We hand folks over to God's mercy, and show none ourselves.      *Ibid.*, Ch. 42

13 I'm not denyin' the women are foolish: God Almighty made 'em to match the men.      *Ibid.*, Ch. 43

14 I'm not one o' those as can see the cat 'i the dairy an' wonder what she's come after.      *Ibid.*, Ch. 52

15 Anger and jealousy can no more bear to lose sight of their objects than love.      *The Mill on the Floss,* Bk. I, Ch. 10     *1860*

16 The law's made to take care o' raskills.      *Ibid.*, Bk. III, Ch. 4

17 I've never any pity for conceited people, because I think they carry their comfort about them.      *Ibid.*, Bk. V, Ch. 4

18 In their death they were not divided.     *Ibid.*

19 The happiest women, like the happiest nations, have no history.      *Ibid.*, Bk. VI, Ch. 3

20 I should like to know what is the proper function of women, if it is not to make reasons for husbands to stay at home, and still stronger reasons for bachelors to go out.      *Ibid.*, Ch. 6

21 Jealousy is never satisfied with anything short of an omniscience that would detect the subtlest fault of the heart.      *Ibid.*, Ch. 10

22 We are not apt to fear for the fearless, when we are companions in their danger.      *Ibid.*, Bk. VII, Ch. 5

23 Nothing is so good as it seems beforehand.      *Silas Marner*, Ch. 18     *1861*

24 There is a mercy which is weakness, and even treason against the common good.      *Romola*     *1863*

25 Marriage must be a relation either of sympathy or of conquest.      *Ibid.*, Ch. 48

26 An ass may bray a good while before he shakes the stars down.      *Ibid.*, Ch. 50

27 There are glances of hatred that stab, and raise no cry of murder.    *Felix Holt, the Radical,* Introduction     *1866*

28 In all private quarrels the duller nature is triumphant by reason of dullness.      *Ibid.*, Ch. 9

29 The beginning of compunction is the beginning of a new life.      *Ibid.*, Ch. 13

30 In our springtime every day has its hidden growth in the mind, as it has in the earth when the little folded blades are getting ready to pierce the ground.      *Ibid.*, Ch. 18

31 One way of getting an idea of our fellow-countrymen's miseries is to go and look at their pleasures.      *Ibid.*, Ch. 28

32 But is it what we love, or how we love, That makes true good?      "The Spanish Gypsy," Bk. I     *1868*

33 'Tis what I love determines how I love.      *Ibid.*

34 Death is the king of this world: 'tis his park Where he breeds life to feed him. Cries of pain Are music for his banquet.      *Ibid.*, Bk. II

35 Best friend, my well-spring in the wilderness!      *Ibid.*, Bk. III

36 Kisses honeyed by oblivion. . . .      *Ibid.*

37     What if my words Were meant for deeds?      *Ibid.*

38 Our words have wings, but fly not where we would.      *Ibid.*

39     Women know no perfect love: Loving the strong, they can forsake the strong; Man clings because the being whom he loves Is weak and needs him.      *Ibid.*

40 Prophecy is the most gratuitous form of error.      *Middlemarch*, Ch. 10     *1871–1872*

41 If we had keen vision of all that is ordinary in human life, it would be like hearing the grass grow or the squirrel's heart beat, and we should die of that roar which is the other side of silence.      *Ibid.*, Ch. 22

42 What loneliness is more lonely than distrust?      *Ibid.*, Ch. 44

43 Our deeds still travel with us from afar, And what we have been makes us what we are.      *Ibid.*, Ch. 70

44 Truth has rough flavors if we bite it through.      *Armgart*, Sc. 2     *1871*

45 . . . a woman's heart must be of such a size and no larger, else it must be pressed small, like Chinese feet. . . .      *Daniel Deronda*     *1876*

46 Gossip is a sort of smoke that comes from the dirty tobacco-pipes of those who diffuse it; it proves nothing but the bad taste of the smoker.       Ibid.

47 The Jews are among the aristocracy of every land; if a literature is called rich in the possession of a few classic tragedies, what shall we say to a national tragedy lasting for fifteen hundred years, in which the poets and actors were also the heroes.       Ibid.

48 A difference of taste in jokes is a great strain on the affections.       Ibid., Bk. II, Ch. 15

49 Men's men: gentle or simple, they're much of a muchness.       Ibid., Bk. IV, Ch. 31

50 Friendships begin with liking or gratitude— roots that can be pulled up.       Ibid., Ch. 32

51 The reward of one duty is the power to fulfill another.       Ibid., Bk. VI, Ch. 46

52 Blessed is the man who, having nothing to say, abstains from giving wordy evidence of the fact.
*The Impressions of Theophrastus Such*, Ch. 4     1879

53 One may prefer fresh eggs, though laid by a fowl of the meanest understanding, but why fresh sermons?       Ibid., "Looking Backward"

54 Life is too precious to be spent in this weaving and unweaving of false impressions, and it is better to live quietly under some degree of misrepresentation than to attempt to remove it by the uncertain process of letter-writing.
Letter to Mrs. Peter Taylor (June 8, 1856), *George Eliot's Life as Related in Her Letters and Journals*     1900p

55 Few women, I fear, have had such reason as I have to think the long sad years of youth were worth living for the sake of middle age.
Ibid. (December 31, 1857)

56 The years seem to rush by now, and I think of death as a fast approaching end of a journey— double and treble reason for loving as well as working while it is day.
Ibid., Letter to Miss Sara Hennell (November 22, 1861)

57 I have the conviction that excessive literary production is a social offence.
Ibid., Letter to Alexander Main (September 11, 1871)

58 I like not only to be loved, but also to be told that I am loved. I am not sure that you are of the same kind. But the realm of silence is large enough beyond the grave. This is the world of literature and speech, and I shall take leave to tell you that you are very dear.
Ibid., Letter to Mrs. Burne-Jones (May 11, 1875)

59 To fear the examination of any proposition appears to me an intellectual and moral palsy that will ever hinder the firm grasping of any substance whatever.
*The George Eliot Letters*     1954p

\* \* \*

60 Oh may I join the choir invisible
Of those immortal dead who live again
In minds made better by their presence.
"Oh May I Join the Choir Invisible,"
*Poems*

61      May I reach
That purest heaven, be to other souls
The cup of strength in some great agony.
      Ibid.

62       'Tis God gives skill,
But not without men's hands: He could not make
Antonio Stradivari's violins
Without Antonio.
Ibid., "Stradivarius," 1. 140

## 65. Julia Ward Howe
### (1819–1910)

1 Mine eyes have seen the glory
Of the coming of the Lord
He is trampling out the vintage
Where the grapes of wrath are stored.
He hath loosed the fateful lightning
Of His terrible, swift sword;
His truth is marching on!
"Battle Hymn of the Republic"
*1862*

2 In the beauty of the lilies
Christ was born across the sea,
With a glory in His bosom
That transfigures you and me:
As He died to make men holy,
Let us die to make men free;
His truth is marching on!
      Ibid.

\* \* \*

3 O Land, the measure of our prayers,
Hope of the world in grief and wrong!
      "Our Country"

4 'Twas red with the blood of freemen and white with the fear of the foe;
And the stars that fit in their courses 'gainst tyrants its symbols know.
      "The Flag"

## 66. Harriet Sewall

(1819–1889)

\* \* \*

1 Why thus longing, thus forever sighing
For the far-off, unattain'd, and dim,
While the beautiful all round thee lying
Offers up its low, perpetual hymn?
"Why Thus Longing?"

## 67. Queen Victoria

(1819–1901)

1 We are not interested in the possibilities of defeat.
Letter to A. J. Balfour
1899

2 We are not amused.
*Notebooks of a Spinster Lady*    1900

3 I sat between the King and Queen. We left supper soon. My health was drunk. I then danced one more quadrille with Lord Paget. . . . I was *very* much amused.
Journal Entry (June 16, 1833), *The Girlhood of Queen Victoria*, Vol. I, Viscount Esher, ed.    1912p

4 . . . I *too well* know its truth, from experience, that whenever any poor Gipsies are encamped anywhere and crimes and robberies &c. occur, it is invariably laid to their account, which is shocking; and if they are always looked upon as vagabonds, how *can* they become good people?    Ibid. (December 29, 1836)

5 *Russia* having *failed*, she *must see* that she *cannot* again *attempt* a similar *coup d'état.* One of the first conditions should therefore be to bring about a reconciliation. . . . Russia has gravely compromised herself. . . . She will therefore be more easily worked upon, for she cannot avow such monstrous conduct.
Letter to Marquis of Salisbury (August 25, 1886), *The Letters of Queen Victoria*, Vol. I, George Earle Buckle, ed.    1930p

6 The Queen is most anxious to see the Government strengthened and supported, and she *does* think that want of firmness in the leader of the House of Commons is most detrimental to it.
Ibid. (June 27, 1890)

7 . . . now let me entreat you seriously not to do this, not to let your feelings (very natural and usual ones) of momentary irritation and discomfort be seen by others; don't (as you so often did and do) let every little feeling be read in your face and seen in your manner, pray don't give way to irritability before your

ladies. All this I say with the love and affection I bear you—as I know what you have to contend with—and struggle against.
Letter to Princess Royal (September 27, 1858), *Dearest Child*, Roger Fulford, ed.    1964p

\* \* \*

8 He [Mr. Gladstone] speaks to Me as if I was a public meeting.
Quoted in *Collections and Recollections* by G. W. E. Russell

## 68. Susan Warner

(1819–1885)

1 One chapter a day was all we took. We searched that carefully, and noted down with miser eagerness everything which seemed to us to have an important bearing upon any point in our scheme. . . . But by dint of this practice we ourselves grew daily in the power of judging; and not only that, but the skill and the power of seeing, too; till by the time we were half through the Bible, we were just fit to begin again at the beginning. And so we did. . . .    *The Law and the Testimony*, Foreword    1853

2 Many a bit we passed in our ignorance, in the days when we could see no metal but what glittered on the surface; and many a good time we went back again, long afterward, and broke our rejected lump with great exultation to find it fat with the riches of the mind.    Ibid.

3 "There is a world there, Winthrop—another sort of world—where people know something; where other things are to be done than running plow furrows; where men may distinguish themselves!—where men may read and write; and do something great; and grow to be something besides what nature made them!—I want to be in that world."
*The Hills of the Shatemuc*, Ch. 1    1856

4 "Did it ever happen to you to want anything you could not have, Miss Elizabeth?"
"No—never," said Elizabeth slowly.
"You have a lesson to learn yet."
"I hope I sha'n't learn it," said Elizabeth.
"It must be learned," said Mrs. Landholm gently. "Life would not be life without it. It is not a bad lesson either."    Ibid., Ch. 10

5 "The back is fitted to the burden, they say; and I always *did* pray that if I had work to do, I might be able to do it; and I always was, somehow."    *What She Could*, Ch. 3    1870

6　"And I, Maria—am I not somebody?" her aunt asked.

"Well, we're all *somebody*, of course, in one sense. Of course we're not *nobody*."

"I am not so sure what you think about it," said Mrs. Candy. "I think that in your language, who isn't somebody, is nobody."

Ibid., Ch. 7

7　"He who serves God with what costs him nothing, will do very little service, you may depend on it."　　　　Ibid., Ch. 11

8　"Why should not a woman be as brave as a man, and as strong—in one way?"

"I suppose, because she is not as strong in the other way."　　*The House in Town*, Ch. 1
1871

## 69.　Amelia C. Welby

### (1819–1852)

\* \* \*

1　As the dew to the blossom, the bud to the bee,
As the scent to the rose, are those memories to me.

"Pulpit Eloquence"

2　Ten thousand stars were in the sky,
Ten thousand on the sea.

"Twilight at Sea," St. 4

## 70.　Susan B. Anthony

### (1820–1906)

1　Men their rights and nothing more; women their rights and nothing less.

Motto, *The Revolution*　　1868

2　. . . gentlemen. . . . Do you not see that so long as society says a woman is incompetent to be a lawyer, minister or doctor, but has ample ability to be a teacher, that every man of you who chooses this profession tacitly acknowledges that he has no more brains than a woman?　　Speech, State Convention of
Schoolteachers, *History of
Woman Suffrage*, Vol. I, with
Elizabeth Cady Stanton and
Mathilda Gage　　1881

3　Of all the old prejudices that cling to the hem of the woman's garments and persistently impede her progress, none holds faster than this. The idea that she owes service to a man instead of to herself, and that it is her highest duty to aid his development rather than her own, will be the last to die.

"The Status of Women, Past, Present
and Future," *The Arena
May, 1897*

4　While in most states the divorce laws are the same for men and women, they never can bear equally upon both while all the property earned during marriage belongs wholly to the husband.

Ibid.

5　Suffrage is the pivotal right. . . .

Ibid.

6　. . . there never will be complete equality until women themselves help to make laws and elect lawmakers.　　Ibid.

7　. . . who can measure the advantages that would result if the magnificent abilities of [women] . . . could be devoted to the needs of government, society, home, instead of being consumed in the struggle to obtain their birthright of individual freedom?　　Ibid.

8　. . . the day will come when men will recognize woman as his peer, not only at the fireside, but in the councils of the nation. Then, and not until then, will there be the perfect comradeship, the ideal union between the sexes that shall result in the highest development of the race.　　Ibid.

9　As when the slaves who got their freedom had to take it over or under or through the unjust forms of the law, precisely so now must women take it to get their right to a voice in this government. . . .

Courtroom Speech (June 18, 1873),
Quoted in *Jailed for Freedom*
by Doris Stevens　　1920p

10　. . . and I shall earnestly and persistently continue to urge all women to the practical recognition of the old Revolutionary maxim, "Resistance to tyranny is obedience to God."

Ibid.

11　Those of you who have the talent to do honor to poor womanhood, have all given yourself over to baby-making. . . .

Quoted in *Elizabeth Cady Stanton,*
Vol. II, Theodore Stanton and Harriot Stanton Blatch, eds.　　1922p

12　So, for the love of me and for the saving of the reputation of womanhood, I beg you, with one baby on your knee and another at your feet, and four boys whistling, buzzing, halooing "Ma, Ma," set yourself about the work.

Ibid.

13　And yet, in the schoolroom more than any other place, does the difference of sex, if there is any, need to be forgotten.　　Ibid.

14　The rank and file are not philosophers, they are not educated to think for themselves, but simply to accept, unquestioned, whatever comes. Speech, "Woman Wants Bread, Not the Ballot!," *The Life and Work of Susan B. Anthony*, Vol. II, Ida Husted, ed. *1969p*

15 . . . just so long as there is a degraded class of labor in the market, it always will be used by the capitalists to checkmate and undermine the superior classes. *Ibid.*

16 Failure is impossible.
Quoted by Carrie Chapman Catt in Her Speech "Is Woman Suffrage Progressing?" (1911), *Feminism*, Miriam Schneir, ed. *1972p*

17 The fact is, women are in chains, and their servitude is all the more debasing because they do not realize it. O to compel them to see and feel and to give them the courage and the conscience to speak and act for their own freedom, though they face the scorn and contempt of all the world for doing it!
Quoted in *The Liberated Woman's Appointment Calendar*, Lynn Sherr and Jurate Kazickas, eds. *1975p*

## 71. Urania Locke Bailey
(1820–1882)

\* \* \*

1 I want to be an angel,
And with the angels stand
A crown upon my forehead,
A harp within my hand.
"I Want to Be an Angel," St. 1

## 72. Alice Cary
(1820–1871)

\* \* \*

1 For the human heart is the mirror
Of the things that are near and far;
Like the wave that reflects in its bosom
The flower and the distant star.
"The Time to Be"

2 How many lives we live in one,
And how much less than one, in all!
"Life's Mysteries"

3 Kiss me, though you make believe;
Kiss me, though I almost know
You are kissing to deceive.
"Make Believe"

4 Three little bugs in a basket,
And hardly room for two.
"Three Bugs"

5 True worth is in *being*, not *seeming*—
In doing, each day that goes by,
Some little good—not in dreaming
Of great things to do by and by.
"Nobility," St. 1

6 We cannot bake bargains for blisses,
Nor catch them like fishes in nets;
And sometimes the thing our life misses
Helps more than the thing which it gets.
*Ibid.*, St. 4

7 Women and men in the crowd meet and mingle,
Yet with itself every soul standeth single. . . .
"Life," St. 2

8 Work, and your house shall be duly fed:
Work, and rest shall be won;
I hold that a man had better be dead
Than alive when his work is done.
"Work"

## 73. Lucretia Peabody Hale
(1820–1900)

1 It was one of the first of the spring days—one of the days that seemed to be promise and fulfillment in one. They are only of promise; for the east wind shuts them in, behind and before. But behind the east wind is hidden the summer, and in these early spring days we feel a little of its breath, its warmth, and its languor. The invitation it gives to come out from winter activities and winter confinements, into its soft lassitude, and all its offers of freedom. *The Struggle for Life*, Ch. 4 *1867*

2 All the years before, she had lived in a roving, aimless way, and the old love of change came up often to assert its power. Often came back the old longing to live where she would not be bound to anybody—where she might be free, even if she were only free to starve. *Ibid.*, Ch. 18

3 It is so hard to melt away the influences of an early life, to counteract all the lessons of the first ten years, to tear up the weeds that are early planted. There are evil inheritances to be struggled with, childish prejudices and fancies banished. *Ibid.*, Ch. 33

4 They say that the lady from Philadelphia, who is staying in town, is very wise. Suppose I go and ask her what is best to be done?
*The Peterkin Papers*
(c.1870), Ch. 1 *1924p*

## 74. Jean Ingelow
(1820–1897)

\* \* \*

1 A sweeter woman ne'er drew breath
Than my sonne's wife Elizabeth.
"The High Tide on the Coast of
Lincolnshire"

2 O Land where all the men are stones,
Or all the stones are men.
"A Land That Living Warmth
Disowns"

3 There's no dew left on the daisies and clover,
There's no rain left in heaven:
I've said my "seven times" over and over,
Seven times one are seven.
"Seven Times One," St. 1,
*Songs of Seven*

4 You Moon! Have you done something wrong
in heaven,
That God has hidden your face?
Ibid., St. 4

## 75. Jenny Lind
(1820–1887)

1 The [unfortunate] experience has passed over
my soul like a beneficent storm which has
broken through the hard shell of my being and
freed many little green shoots to find their way
to the sun. And I see quite clearly how infinitely much there is for me to do with my life.
I have only one prayer, that I may be able to
show a pure soul to God. . . . I am glad and
grateful from morning to night! I do not feel
lonely or bored, and my only complaint is that
the days fly by too quickly. I have a brightness
in my soul, which strains toward Heaven. I
am like a bird!
Quoted in *Jenny Lind: The Swedish
Nightingale* by Gladys Denny Shultz
*1962p*

2 I have appeared twice in *Norma*; and was called
so many times before the curtain that I was
quite exhausted. Bah! I don't like it. Everything
should be done in moderation; otherwise it is
not pleasing.
Letter (April 27, 1846), *The Lost
Letters of Jenny Lind*, W. Porter Ware
and Thaddeus C. Lockard, Jr., eds.
*1966p*

3 I have often wished for the blessing of motherhood, for it would have given me a much-
needed focal point for my affections. With it,
and through the varied experiences that accom-

pany it, I could perhaps have achieved something better than that which I have attained up
to now.
Ibid., Letter (July 11, 1849)

4 My voice is still the same, and this makes me
beside myself with joy! Oh, *mon Dieu*, when I
think what I might be able to do with it!
Ibid., Letter (January 10, 1855)

## 76. Mary Livermore
(1820?–1905)

1 For humanity has moved forward to an era
when wrong and slavery are being displaced,
and reason and justice are being recognized as
the rule of life. . . . The age looks steadily to
the redressing of wrong, to the righting of
every form of error and injustice; and a tireless
and prying philanthropy, which is almost
omniscient, is one of the most hopeful characteristics of the time. *What Shall We Do with
Our Daughters?*, Ch. 1 *1883*

2 Other books have been written by men physicians. . . . One would suppose in reading them
that women possess but one class of physical
organs, and that these are always diseased. Such
teaching is pestiferous, and tends to cause and
perpetuate the very evils it professes to remedy.
Ibid., Ch. 2

3 Almost every one of the great religions of the
world has made special provision for them,
and the woman who has preferred a celibate to
a domestic life has been able to occupy a position of honor and usefulness. Ibid., Ch. 7

4 Above the titles of wife and mother, which,
although dear, are transitory and accidental,
there is the title human being, which precedes
and out-ranks every other. Ibid.

## 77. Princess Mathilde
(1820–1904)

1 But I think him lost for ever for any kind of
locomotion. Nowadays it is only his mind that
travels; his body stays behind on the bank.
Quoted in *Revue Bleu
August 6, 1863*

2 He knew that his conversation had the power
to fascinate, and he used it like a prodigal man
who knew he had an everlasting fortune. . . .
Quoted in *Le Moniteur Universelle
October 15, 1869*

3 I was born in exile—civically dead. . . .
"Souvenirs des Années d'Exile,"
*La Revue des Deux Mondes
December 15, 1927p*

## 78. Florence Nightingale
### (1820–1910)

1 But when you have done away with all that pain and suffering, which in patients are the symptoms, not of their disease, but of the absence of one or all of the essentials to the success of Nature's reparative processes, we shall then know what are the symptoms of, and the sufferings inseparable from, the disease.

， *Notes on Nursing* 1859

2 No *man*, not even a doctor, ever gives any other definition of what a nurse should be than this—"devoted and obedient." This definition would do just as well for a porter. It might even do for a horse. It would not do for a policeman.

*Ibid.*

3 Merely looking at the sick is not observing.

*Ibid.*

4 It may seem a strange thing to begin a book with:—This Book is not for any one who has time to read it—but the meaning of it is: this reading is good only as a preparation for work. If it is not to inspire life and work, it is bad. Just as the end of food is to enable us to live and work, and not to live and eat, so the end of most reading perhaps, but certainly of mystical reading, is not to read but to work.

*Mysticism*, Preface 1873

5 For what is Mysticism? Is it not the attempt to draw near to God, not by rites or ceremonies, but by inward disposition? Is it not merely a hard word for "The Kingdom of Heaven is within"? Heaven is neither a place nor a time.

*Ibid.*

6 So I never lose an opportunity of urging a practical beginning, however small, for it is wonderful how often in such matters the mustard-seed germinates and roots itself.

"Health Missionaries for Rural India,"
*India* December, 1896

7 Nothing ever laughs or plays [in Egypt]. Everything is grown up and grown old.

Quoted in *The Life of Florence Nightingale* by Sir Edward Cook 1913p

8 I stand at the altar of the murdered men, and, while I live, I fight their cause.

*Ibid.*, Private Note (1856)

9 Asceticism is the trifling of an enthusiast with his power, a puerile coquetting with his selfishness or his vanity, in the absence of any sufficiently great object to employ the first or overcome the last.

*Ibid.*, Letter to Dr. Sutherland (1857)

10 I can stand out the war with any man.

Quoted in *The World Book Encyclopedia* 1972p

## 79. Margaret Preston
### (1820–1897)

1 Pain is no longer pain when it is past.

"Nature's Lesson" *c.1875*

2 'Tis the motive exalts the action;
'Tis the doing, and not the deed.

"The First Proclamation of Miles Standish" *c.1875*

3 Whoso lives the holiest life
Is fittest far to die.

"Ready" *c.1875*

## 80. Anna Sewell
### (1820–1878)

1 "I never yet could make out why men are so fond of this sport; they often hurt themselves, often spoil good horses, and tear up the fields, and all for a hare, or a fox, or a stag, that they could get more easily some other way; but we are only horses, and don't know."

*Black Beauty*, Pt. I, Ch. 2 1877

2 . . . he said that cruelty was the Devil's own trademark, and if we saw anyone who took pleasure in cruelty we might know whom he belonged to, for the Devil was a murderer from the beginning, and a tormentor to the end.

*Ibid.*, Ch. 13

3 I am never afraid of what I know.

*Ibid.*, Pt. II, Ch. 29

4 I said, "I have heard people talk about war as if it was a very fine thing."
"Ah!" said he, "I should think they never saw it. No doubt it is very fine when there is no enemy, when it is just exercise and parade, and sham fight. Yes, it is very fine then; but when thousands of good, brave men and horses are killed or crippled for life, it has a very different look."

*Ibid.*, Pt. III, Ch. 34

5 "My doctrine is this, that *if we see cruelty or wrong that we have the power to stop, and do nothing, we make ourselves sharers in the guilt.*"

*Ibid.*, Ch. 38

6 "Is it not better," she said, "to lead a good fashion than to follow a bad one?"

*Ibid.*, Pt. IV, Ch. 46

## 81. Anna Bartlett Warner

(1820–1915)

\* \* \*

1 Daffy-down-dilly came up in the cold. . . .
"Daffy-Down-Dilly"

2 Jesus loves me, this I know
For the Bible tells me so.

"Jesus Loves Me"

## 82. Clara Barton

(1821–1912)

1 It is wise statesmanship which suggests that in time of peace we must prepare for war, and it is no less a wise benevolence that makes preparation in the hour of peace for assuaging the ills that are sure to accompany war.
*The Red Cross,* Ch. 1    *1898*

2 An institution or reform movement that is not selfish, must originate in the recognition of some evil that is adding to the sum of human suffering, or diminishing the sum of happiness. I suppose it is a philanthropic movement to try to reverse the process.    Ibid.

## 83. Elizabeth Blackwell

(1821–1910)

1 Social intercourse—a very limited thing in a half civilized country, becomes in our centers of civilization a great power. . . .
*Medicine as a Profession for Women,*
with Emily Blackwell    *1860*

2 . . . every advance in social progress removes us more and more from the guidance of instinct, obliging us to depend upon reason for the assurance that our habits are really agreeable to the laws of health, and compelling us to guard against the sacrifice of our physical or moral nature while pursuing the ends of civilization.    Ibid.

3 Our school education ignores, in a thousand ways, the rules of healthy development. . . .
Ibid.

4 . . . health has its science as well as disease. . . .
Ibid.

5 As teachers, then, to diffuse among women the physiological and sanitary knowledge which they need, we found the first work for women physicians.    Ibid.

6 . . . the church, with its usual sagacity in availing itself of all talents, opens the attractive prospect of active occupation, personal standing and authority, social respect, and the companionship of intelligent co-workers, both men and women—the feeling of belonging to the world, in fact, instead of a crippled and isolated life. For though it is common to speak of the sisters as renouncing the world, the fact is that the members of these sisterhoods have a far more active participation in the interests of life than most of them had before.    Ibid.

7 Medicine is so broad a field, so closely interwoven with general interests, dealing as it does with all ages, sexes, and classes, and yet of so personal a character in its individual applications, that it must be regarded as one of those great departments of work in which the cooperation of men and women is needed to fulfill all its requirements.    Ibid.

8 How often homes, which should be the source of moral and physical health and truth, are centers of selfishness or frivolity!    Ibid.

9 For what is done or learned by one class of women becomes, by virtue of their common womanhood, the property of all women.
Ibid.

10 This failure to recognize the equivalent value of internal with external structure has led to such a crude fallacy as a comparison of the penis with such a vestige as the clitoris, whilst failing to recognize that vast amount of erectile tissue, mostly internal, in the female, which is the direct seat of sexual spasm.
*The Human Element in Sex*    *1894*

11 . . . the total deprivation of it [sex] produces irritability.    Ibid.

12 I must have something to engross my thoughts, some object in life which will fill this vacuum and prevent this sad wearing away of the heart.
*Pioneer Work for Women*    *1914p*

13 . . . I, who so love a hermit life for a good part of the day, find myself living in public, and almost losing my identity.    Ibid.

14 Do you think I care about medicine? Nay, verily, it's just to kill the devil, whom I hate so heartily—that's the fact, mother.
Letter to Mother, Quoted in
*Those Extraordinary Blackwells*
by Elinor R. Hays    *1967p*

## 84. Mary Baker Eddy

(1821–1910)

1 The prayer that reforms the sinner and heals the sick is an absolute faith that all things are possible to God—a spiritual understanding of Him, an unselfish love.
*Science and Health, with Key
to the Scriptures*    *1875*

2 The highest prayer is not one of faith merely; it is demonstration. Such prayer heals sickness, and must destroy sin and death.     Ibid.

3 Christian Science explains all cause and effect as mental, not physical.     Ibid.

4 Disease can carry its ill-effects no farther than mortal minds map out the way.     Ibid.

5 If materialistic knowledge is power, it is not wisdom. It is but a blind force.     Ibid.

6 Sin makes its own hell, and goodness its own heaven.     Ibid.

7 We classify disease as error, which nothing but Truth or Mind can heal, and this Mind must be divine, not human.     Ibid.

8 Jesus of Nazareth was the most scientific man that ever trod the globe. He plunged beneath the material surface of things, and found the spiritual cause.     Ibid.

9 The basis of all health, sinlessness, and immortality is the great fact that God is the only Mind; and this Mind must be not merely believed, but it must be understood.     Ibid.

10 You conquer error by denying its verity.     Ibid.

11 Stand porter at the door of thought. Admitting only such conclusions as you wish realized in bodily results, you will control yourself harmoniously.     Ibid.

12 Disease is an image of thought externalized.     Ibid.

13 Sin brought death, and death will disappear with the disappearance of sin.     Ibid.

14 Health is not a condition of matter, but of Mind; nor can the material senses bear reliable testimony on the subject of health.     Ibid.

15 You command the situation if you understand that mortal existence is a state of self-deception and not the truth of being.     Ibid.

16 God is incorporeal, divine, supreme, infinite Mind, Spirit, Soul, Principle, Life, Truth, Love.     Ibid.

17 Spirit is the real and eternal; matter is the unreal and temporal.     Ibid.

18 Truth is immortal; error is mortal.     Ibid.

19 Sickness, sin and death, being inharmonious, do not originate with God, nor belong to his government.     Ibid.

20 Then comes the question, how do drugs, hygiene and animal magnetism heal? It may be affirmed that they do not heal, but only relieve suffering temporarily, exchanging one disease for another.     Ibid.

21 God is Mind, and God is infinite; hence all is Mind.     Ibid.

22 Disease is an expression of so-called mortal mind. It is fear made manifest on the body.     Ibid.

23 Divine love always has met and always will meet every human need.     Ibid.

24 I would no more quarrel with a man because of his religion than I would because of his art.     *Miscellaneous Writings*     *1883–1896*

25 How would you define Christian Science? As the law of God, the law of good, interpreting and demonstrating the divine Principle and rule of universal harmony.     *Rudimental Divine Science*    *1891*

26 To live and let live, without clamor for distinction or recognition; to wait on Divine Love; to write truth first on the tablet of one's own heart, this is the sanity and perfection of living, and my human ideal.     *Message to Mother Church*    *1902*

27 To live so as to keep human consciousness in constant relation with the Divine, the spiritual and the eternal, is to individualize infinite power; and this is Christian Science.     *The First Church of Christ, Scientist and Miscellany*    *1906*

\ * * *

28 It matters not what be thy lot,
    So Love doth guide;
For storm or shine, pure peace is Thine
    What'er betide.
              "Satisfied," St. 1

29 My prayer, some daily good to do
    To Thine, for Thee—
An offering of pure Love, whereto
    God leadeth me.
        "O'er Waiting Harp-Strings of the Mind," St. 7

# 85. Frances P. Cobbe
## (1822–1904)

1 The time comes to every dog when it ceases to care for people merely for biscuits or bones, or even for caresses, and walks out of doors. When a dog *really* loves, it prefers the person who gives it nothing, and perhaps is too ill ever to take it out for exercise, to all the liberal cooks and active dog-boys in the world.
        *The Confessions of a Lost Dog*    *1867*

2 I could discern clearly, even at that early age, the essential difference between people who are *kind* to dogs and people who really *love* them.
Ibid.

3 Then the Sorcerer Science entered, and where e'er he waved his wand
Fresh wonders and fresh mysteries rose on every hand.
"The Pageant of Time,"
St. 1
(December, 1859),
*Rest in the Lord*    1887

4 Is it to mock a world of woe
The soft winds laugh, the clear streams flow?
Is it a proof of wrath Divine
That the earth is gilt by the bright sunshine?
*"A Vale of Tears"?* Does not each sense
Proclaim a good Omnipotence?
Ibid., "A Vale of Tears," Sts. 6–7

5 . . . I must avow that the halo which has gathered round Jesus Christ obscures Him to my eyes.     *Life of Frances Power Cobbe,*
Vol. II, Ch. 15    1894

## 86. Caroline Dall
(1822–1912)

1 A solution of an old mystery must bring justification and proof to every assertion.
*The Romance of the Association,*
Preface    1875

2 I have seen no Hindu who seemed to me prepared intellectually and morally for the freedom he would find in American society; nor are Americans prepared for the air of innocence and exaltation worn by very undeserving Orientals.     *The Life of Doctor Anandabai Joshee*
1888

3 It is not learning, intellect, subtlety, or imagination that is wanting in the average Hindu; it is purity, faith, and honesty.     Ibid.

4 Why is it that human hearts are so dead to the heroic?     *Barbara Fritchie,* Pt. I    1892

5 It was the glorious function of [John Greenleaf] Whittier to lift us nearer to the Infinite Spirit, to keep us intent upon our immortal destiny, and to fill us with that love of Beauty which is the love of God.     Ibid., "L'Envoi"

## 87. Julia Carney
(1823–1908)

1 Little drops of water, Little grains of sand,
Make the mighty ocean, And the pleasant land.
So the little minutes, Humble tho' they be,
Make the mighty ages Of Eternity!
"Little Things," St. 1    1845

2 Little deeds of kindness, little words of love,
Help to make earth happy, like the heaven above.
Ibid., St. 4

## 88. Mary Bokin Chesnut
(1823–1886)

1 "You know how women sell themselves and are sold in marriage, from queens downwards, eh? You know what the Bible says about slaves, and marriage. Poor women, poor slaves."
*Diary from Dixie* (March 4, 1861)
*1949p*

2 I think this journal will be disadvantageous for me, for I spend my time now like a spider spinning my own entrails, instead of reading as my habit was in all spare moments.
Ibid. (March 14, 1861)

3 Women—wives and mothers—are the same everywhere.     Ibid. (July 24, 1861)

4 You see, Mrs. Stowe did not hit the sorest spot. She makes Legree a bachelor.
Ibid. (August 27, 1861)

5 . . . those soul-stirring Negro camp-meeting hymns. To me this is the saddest of all earthly music, weird and depressing beyond my power to describe.     Ibid. (October 13, 1861)

6 They live in nice New England homes, clean, sweet-smelling, shut up in libraries, writing books which ease their hearts of their bitterness against us. What self-denial they do practice is to tell John Brown to come down here and cut our throats in Christ's name.
Ibid. (November 28, 1861)

7 I say we are no better than our judges in the North, and no worse. We are human beings of the nineteenth century and slavery has to go of course.     Ibid.

8 I hate slavery. I even hate the harsh authority I see parents think it is their duty to exercise toward their children.     Ibid.

9 Conscription has waked the Rip Van Winkles. To fight and to be made to fight are different things.     Ibid. (March 19, 1862)

10 Does anybody wonder so many women die. Grief and constant anxiety kill nearly as many women as men die on the battlefield.
Ibid. (June 9, 1862)

11 "Hysterical grief never moves me. It annoys me. You think yourself a miracle of sensibility; but self-control is what you need. That is all that separates you from those you look down upon as unfeeling."
Ibid. (December 7, 1863)

12 Is the sea drying up? It is going up into mist
and coming down on us in this water spout,
the rain. It raineth every day, and the weather
represents our tearful despair on a large scale.
                 *Ibid.* (March 5, 1865)

13 We are scattered, stunned, the remnant of heart
left alive in us filled with brotherly hate. We
sit and wait until the drunken tailor [President
Andrew Johnson] who rules the United States
issues a proclamation and defines our anomalous position.          *Ibid.* (May 16, 1865)

## 89. Caroline Mason

### (1823–1890)

1 Do they miss me at home—do they miss me?
'Twould be an assurance most dear,
To know that this moment some loved one
Were saying, "I wish he were here."
          "Do They Miss Me at Home," St. 1
                          *1850*

\* \* \*

2 . . . like a story well-nigh told,
Will seem my life—when I am old.
           "When I Am Old," St. 1

3 Ere I am old, O! Let me give
My life to learning how to live.
                 *Ibid.*, St. 8

4 His grave a nation's heart shall be,
His monument a people free!
          "President Lincoln's Grave"

## 90. Elizabeth Stoddard

### (1823–1902)

1 A woman despises a man for loving her, unless
she returns his love.
         *Two Men*, Ch. 32     *1888*

## 91. Phoebe Cary

### (1824–1871?)

\* \* \*

1 And though hard be the task,
"Keep a stiff upper lip."
         "Keep a Stiff Upper Lip"

2 And wouldn't it be nicer
For you to smile than pout,
And so make sunshine in the house
When there is none without?
              "Suppose," St. 2

3 And isn't it, my boy or girl,
The wisest, bravest plan,
Whatever comes, or doesn't come,
To do the best you can?
                 *Ibid.*, St. 5

4        Charley Church, was a preacher who
         praught,
Though his enemies called him a screecher who
         scraught.
                    "The Lovers"

5 For of all the hard things to bear and grin,
The hardest is being taken in.
                 "Kate Ketchem"

6 Give plenty of what is given to you,
And listen to pity's call;
Don't think the little you give is great
And the much you get is small.
       "A Legend of the Northland," I, St. 8

7 I think true love is never blind
But rather brings an added light,
An inner vision quick to find
The beauties hid from common sight.
                 "True Love," St. 1

8 Sometimes, I think, the things we see
Are shadows of the things to be;
That what we plan we build. . . .
         "Dreams and Realities," St. 7

9 There's many a battle fought daily
The world knows nothing about.
              "Our Heroes," St. 2

10 Be steadfast, my boy, when you're tempted,
To do what you know to be right.
Stand firm by the colors of manhood,
And you will o'ercome in the fight.
                 *Ibid.*, St. 3

11 Thou hast battled for the right
With many a brave and trenchant word
And shown us how the pen may fight
A mightier battle than the sword.
        "John Greenleaf Whittier"

## 92. Julia Kavanagh

### (1824–1877)

1 Most children are aristocratic. . . .
         *Daisy Burns*, Vol. I     *1853*

2 Alas! why has the plain truth the power of
offending so many people. . . .     *Ibid.*, Ch. 4

3 It is the culprit who must seek the glance of
the judge, and not the judge that must look at
the culprit.          *Nathalie*, Ch. 1     *1872*

4 A beauty must regret the past; a noble-born and impoverished lady cannot look with favour on a new order of things. *Adele*, Ch. 2
1872

## 93. Adeline Dutton Whitney
### (1824–1906)
* * *

1 I bow me to the thwarting gale:
I know when that is overpast,
Among the peaceful harvest days
An Indian Summer comes at last.
"Equinoctial," St. 6

## 94. Mrs. Alexander
### (1825–1902)

1 ". . . it is impossible to rely on the prudence or common sense of any man. . . ."
*Ralph Wilton's Weird*, Ch. 1 1875

2 "There's nothing more mischievous than moping along and getting into the blue devils!—nothing more likely to drive a man to suicide or matrimony, or some infernal entanglement even worse!" Ibid., Ch. 6

## 95. Antoinette Brown Blackwell
### (1825–1921)

1 Mr. Darwin . . . has failed to hold definitely before his mind the principle that the difference of sex, whatever it may consist in, must itself be subject to natural selection and to evolution.
*The Sexes Throughout Nature*
1875

2 . . . the sexes in each species of beings . . . are always true equivalents—equals but not identicals. . . . Ibid.

3 Any positive thinker is compelled to see everything in the light of his own convictions. Ibid.

4 It is difficult to perceive what self-adjusting forces, in the organic world, have developed men everywhere the superiors of women, males characteristically the superiors of females. Ibid.

5 I do not underrate the charge of presumption which must attach to any woman who will attempt to controvert the great masters of science and scientific inference. But there is no alternative! Ibid.

6 All insect mothers act with the utmost wisdom and good faith, and with a beautiful instinctive love towards a posterity which they are directly never to caress or nurture. . . . These tiny creatures work with the skill of carpenters and masons, and often with a prudence and forethought which is even more than human; for they never suffer personal ease or advantage to prevent their making proper provision for their young. Ibid.

7 If woman's sole responsibility is of the domestic type, one class will be crushed by it, and the other throw it off as a badge of poverty. The poor man's motto, "Women's work is never done," leads inevitably to its antithesis—ladies' work is never begun. Ibid.

8 Woman's share of duties must involve direct nutrition, man's indirect nutrition. She should be able to bear and nourish their young children, at a cost of energy equal to the amount expended by him as household provider. Beyond this, if human justice is to supplement Nature's provisions, all family duties must be shared equitably, in person or by proxy.
Ibid.

9 Work, alternated with needful rest, is the salvation of man or woman. Ibid.

10 Nature is just enough; but men and women must comprehend and accept her suggestions.
Ibid.

11 Every nursing mother, in the midst of her little dependent brood, has far more right to whine, sulk, or scold, as temperament dictates, because beefsteak and coffee are not prepared for her and exactly to her taste, than any man ever had or ever can have during the present stage of human evolution. Ibid.

12 The interests of their children *must not be sacrificed* by her over-exhaustion, even though she were willing and eager for the sacrifice of herself. Ibid.

13 A woman finds the natural lay of the land almost unconsciously; and not feeling it incumbent on her to be guide and philosopher to any successor, she takes little pains to mark the route by which she is making her ascent.
Ibid.

14 The brain is not, and cannot be, the sole or complete organ of thought and feeling. Ibid.

15 Conventionality has indeed curtailed feminine force by hindering healthful and varied activity. . . . Ibid.

16 Women's thoughts are impelled by their feelings. Hence the sharp-sightedness, the direct

instinct, the quick perceptions; hence also their warmer prejudices and more unbalanced judgments. . . . In this the child is like the woman.
Ibid.

17 The immediate sensation or perception seems also to be the impelling power of the savage and of all animal instincts. Call it automatic activity if you will; yet the incident force is real feeling, is perception, is intelligence. . . .
Ibid.

18 The law of grab is the primal law of infancy.
Ibid.

19 That she is not his peer in all intellectual and moral capabilities, cannot at least be very well provided until she is allowed an equally untrammelled opportunity to test her own strength.
Ibid.

20 There is a broader, not a higher, life outside, which she is impelled to enter, taking some share also in its responsibilities.
Ibid.

21 If Evolution, as applied to sex, teaches any one lesson plainer than another, it is the lesson that the monogamic marriage is the basis of all progress.
Ibid.

22 No theory of unfitness, no form of conventionality, can have the right to suppress any excellence which Nature has seen fit to evolve.
Ibid.

23 It had seemed to both Lucy Stone and myself in our student days that marriage would be a hindrance to our public work.
Quoted in *Antoinette Brown Blackwell: Biographical Sketch* by Sarah Gibson
*1909*

24 . . . you asked me one day if it seemed like giving up much for your sake. Only leave me free, as free as you are and everyone ought to be, and it is giving up nothing.
Ibid.

## 96. Julia Dorr
### (1825–1913)
* * *

1 And the stately lilies stand
  Fair in the silvery light,
Like saintly vestals, pale in prayer.
"A Red Rose"

2 April's rare capricious loveliness.
"November"

3 Come, blessed Darkness, come and bring thy balm
For eyes grown weary of the garish day!

Come with thy soft, slow steps, thy garments grey,
Thy veiling shadows, bearing in thy palm
The poppy-seeds of slumber, deep and calm.
"Darkness"

4 Grass grows at last above all graves.
"Grass-Grown"

5 O beautiful, royal Rose,
  O Rose, so fair and sweet!
Queen of the garden art thou,
  And I—the Clay at thy feet.
"The Clay to the Rose"

6 O golden Silence, bid our souls be still,
And on the foolish fretting of our care
Lay thy soft touch of healing unaware!
"Silence"

7 Stars will blossom in the darkness,
  Violets bloom beneath the snow.
"For a Silver Wedding"

8 What dost thou bring me, O fair To-day,
That comest o'er the mountains with swift feet?
"To-day"

9 Who soweth good seed shall surely reap;
The year grows rich as it groweth old,
And life's latest sands are its sands of gold!
"To the 'Bouquet Club' "

## 97. Henrietta Heathorn
### (1825–1915)

1 Be not afraid, ye waiting hearts that weep,
For God still giveth His belovèd sleep,
And if an endless sleep He wills—so best.*
"Browning's Funeral"    *1889*

* * *

2 To all the gossip that I hear
I'll give no faith; to what I see
But only half, for it is clear
All that led up is dark to me.
  Learn me the larger life to live,
  To comprehend is to forgive.
"Tout Comprendre, C'est Tout Pardonner"

## 98. Adelaide Proctor
### (1825–1864)

1 Dreams grow holy put in action.
"Philip and Mildred," *The Poems of Adelaide Proctor*    *1869p*

* Epitaph on T. H. Huxley's tombstone.

2 Half my life is full of sorrow,
　Half of joy, still fresh and new;
　One of these lives is a fancy,
　　But the other one is true.
　　　　　　　Ibid., "Dream-Life"

3 Now Time has fled—the world is strange,
　Something there is of pain and change;
　My books lie closed upon the shelf;
　I miss the old heart in myself.
　　　　　　　Ibid., "A Student"

4 One by one the sands are flowing,
　　One by one the moments fall;
　Some are coming, some are going;
　　Do not strive to grasp them all.
　　　　　　　Ibid., "One by One," St. 1

5　　　Only heaven
　Means crowned, not conquered, when it says
　　"Forgiven."
　　　　　　　Ibid., "A Legend of Provence"

6 One dark cloud can hide the sunlight;
　Loose one string, the pearls are scattered;
　Think one thought, a soul may perish;
　Say one word, a heart may break.
　　　　　　　Ibid., "Phillip and Mildred"

7 But I struck one chord of music,
　Like the sound of a great Amen.
　　　　　　　Ibid., "A Lost Chord," St. 2

8 See how time makes all grief decay.
　　　　　　　Ibid., "Life in Death"

9 O, there are Voices of the Past,
　　Links of a broken chain,
　Wings that can bear me back to Times
　　Which cannot come again. . . .
　　　　　　　Ibid., "Voices of the Past"

10 Joy is like restless day; Peace divine
　　Like quiet night. . . .
　　　　　　　Ibid., "Per Pacem ad Lucem"

11 I know too well the poison and the sting
　　Of things too sweet.
　　　　　　　Ibid.

12 Tell her that the lesson taught her
　Far outweighs the pain.
　　　　　　　Ibid., "Friend Sorrow"

13 Rise! for the day is passing
　And you lie dreaming on. . . .
　　　　　　　Ibid., "Now," St. 1

14 The Past and the Future are nothing,
　In the face of the stern To-day.
　　　　　　　Ibid.

## 99. Harriet Robinson
### (1825–1911)

1 What if she did hunger and thirst after knowledge? She could do nothing with it even if she could get it. So she made a *fetish* of some male relative, and gave him the mental food for which she herself was starving; and devoted all her energies towards helping him to become what she felt, under better conditions, she herself might have been. It was enough in those early days to be the *mother* or *sister* of somebody. "Early Factory Labor in New England,"
　　　　*Massachusetts in the Woman Suffrage
　　　　　　　　Movement　　1883*

2 In those days there was no need of advocating the doctrine of the proper relation between employer and employed. *Help was too valuable to be ill-treated. . . .*　　　　Ibid.

3 Skilled labor teaches something not to be found in books or in colleges.　　　　Ibid.

## 100. Emily Blackwell
### (1826–1911)

Co-author of *Medicine as a Professions for Women* with Elizabeth Blackwell. See 83:1–9.

## 101. Dinah Mulock Craik
### (1826–1887)

1 . . . a Brownie is a curious creature. . . .
　　　*The Adventures of a Brownie　　1872*

2 Altogether, his conscience pricked him a good deal; and when people's consciences prick them, sometimes they get angry with other people, which is very silly, and only makes matters worse.　　　　Ibid.

3 Now, I have nothing to say against uncles in general. They are usually very excellent people, and very convenient to little boys and girls.
　　　*The Little Lame Prince, Ch. 2　　1875*

4 There is much that we do not know, and cannot understand—we big folks, no more than you little ones.　　　　Ibid., Ch. 6

5 It seemed as if she had given these treasures and left him alone—to use them, or lose them, apply them, or misapply them, according to his own choice. That is all we can do with children, when they grow into big children, old enough to distinguish between right and wrong, and too old to be forced to do either.
　　　　　　　Ibid., Ch. 7

6 "You are a child. Accept the fact. Be humble—
be teachable. Lean upon the wisdom of others
till you have gained your own."
*Ibid.*, Ch. 10

7 "One cannot make oneself, but one can sometimes help a little in the making of somebody
else. It is well."          *Ibid.*

8 Friend, what years could us divide?
"A Christmas Blessing," *Thirty Years
1881*

9 Those rooks, dear, from morning till night,
They seem to do nothing but quarrel and fight,
And wrangle and jangle, and plunder.
*Ibid.*, "The Blackbird and the Rooks"

10 And when I lie in the green kirkyard,
With mould upon my breast,
Say not that she did well—or ill,
Only "she did her best."
"Obituary"     *1887*

*   *   *

11 Never was owl more blind than a lover.
*Magnus and Morna*

12 A secret at home is like rocks under tide.
*Ibid.*, Sc. 2

13 Silence is sweeter than speech.
*Ibid.*, Sc. 3

14 Wedlock's a lane where there is no turning.
*Ibid.*

15 Autumn to winter, winter into spring,
Spring into summer, summer into fall,—
So rolls the changing year, and so we change;
Motion so swift, we know not that we move.
"Immutable"

16 Duty's a slave that keeps the keys,
But Love the master goes in and out
Of his goodly chambers with song and shout,
Just as he pleases—just as he pleases.
"Plighted"

17 Faith needs her daily bread.
*Fortune's Marriage*, Ch. 10

18 Forgotten? No, we never do forget:
We let the years go by; wash them clean with
tears,
Leave them to bleach out in the open day,
Or lock them careful by, like dead friends'
clothes,
Till we shall dare unfold them without pain,—
But we forget not, never can forget.
"A Flower of a Day"

19 God rest ye, little children; let nothing you
afright,
For Jesus Christ, your Saviour, was born this
happy night;

Along the hills of Galilee the white blocks
sleeping lay,
When Christ, the child of Nazareth, was born
on Christmas day.
"Christmas Carol," St. 2

20 Hour after hour that passionless bright face
Climbs up the desolate blue.
"Moon-Struck"

21        Immortality
Alone could teach this mortal how to die.
"Looking Death in the Face"

22 Keep what is worth keeping—
And with the breath of kindness
Blow the rest away.
"Friendship"

23 Life bears love's cross, death brings love's
crown.
"Lettice"

24 Lo! all life this truth declares,
Laborare est orare;
And the whole earth rings with prayers.
"Labour Is Prayer," St. 4

25 Love that asketh love again
Finds the barter nought but pain;
Love that giveth in full store
Aye receives as much, and more.
"Love That Asketh Love Again"

26 Oh my son's my son till he gets him a wife,
But my daughter's my daughter all her life.
"Young and Old"

27 O the green things growing, the green things
growing,
The faint sweet smell of the green things
growing!
"Green Things Growing"

28 Pierce with thy trill the dark,
Like a glittering music spark.
"A Rhyme About Birds"

29 Sing away, ay, sing away,
Merry little bird
Always gayest of the gay,
Though a woodland roundelay
You ne'er sung nor heard;
Though your life from youth to age
Passes in a narrow cage.
"The Canary in His Cage"

30 Sweet April-time—O cruel April-time!
"April"

31 There never was night that had no morn.
"The Golden Gate"

32 Tomorrow is, ah, whose?
"Between Two Worlds"

## 102. Mathilda Gage
### (1826–1898)

Co-author of *History of Woman Suffrage*, Vols.
I and II, with Elizabeth Cady Stanton and
Susan B. Anthony. See 45:1–37.

## 103. Lucy Larcom
### (1826–1893)

\* \* \*

1 Breathe thy balm upon the lonely,
　Gentle Sleep!
　　　　　　　　　　　　　"Sleep Song"

2 Each red stripe has blazoned forth
　Gospels writ in blood;
　Every star has sung the birth
　Of some deathless good.
　　　　　　　　　　　　　"The Flag"

3 He who plants a tree
　Plants a hope.
　　　　　　　　　　　"Plant a Tree," St. 1

4 Canst thou prophesy, thou little tree,
　What the glory of thy boughs shall be?
　　　　　　　　　　　　　　Ibid.

5 I do not own an inch of land,
　But all I see is mine.
　　　　　　　　　　　"A Strip of Blue"

6 If the world seems cold to you,
　Kindle fires to warm it!
　　　　　　　　　　　"Three Old Saws"

7 If the world's a wilderness,
　Go, build houses in it!
　　　　　　　　　　　　　　Ibid.

8 June falls asleep upon her bier of flowers.
　　　　　　　　　　　"Death of June"

9 Oh, her heart's adrift, with one
　On an endless voyage gone!
　　Night and morning
　Hannah's at the window binding shoes.
　　　　　"Hannah Binding Shoes," St. 2

10 The land is dearer for the sea,
　The ocean for the shore.
　　　　　　　　　　"On the Beach," St. 11

11 There is light in shadow and shadow in light,
　And black in the blue of the sky.
　　　　　　　　"Black in Blue Sky," St. 2

## 104. Dorothy Nevill
### (1826–1913)

1 It seems to be that, had the educational authorities attempted to keep alive these local industries by encouraging the children under their
charge not to abandon them, they would have
been doing much more good than by teaching
smatterings of many totally useless subjects,
which, imperfectly understood and soon forgotten, have but served to convert the English rus-
tic into a somewhat dissatisfied imitation of the
Londoner, whilst thoroughly stamping out that
local character and individuality which was
such an admirable feature of old-time country
life.　　*The Reminiscences of Lady Dorothy*
　　　　　　　　　　　*Nevill*, Ch. 3　　*1907*

2 Society to-day and Society as I formerly knew
it are two entirely different things; indeed, it
may be questioned whether Society, as the word
used to be understood, now exists at all. . . .
Now all is changed, and wealth has usurped
the place formerly held by wit and learning.
The question is not now asked, "Is So-and-so
clever?" but, instead, "Is So-and-so rich?"
　　　　　　　　　　　　　Ibid., Ch. 8

3 It is, I think, a good deal owing to the pre-
ponderance of the commercial element in Society that conversation has sunk to its present
dull level of conventional chatter. The commercial class has always mistrusted verbal brilliancy
and wit, deeming such qualities, perhaps with
some justice, frivolous and unprofitable.
　　　　　　　　　　　　　　　Ibid.

4 The French I think are improved, not so
childish—how refined their manners and talk
and how dirty their habits—morality and decency they know nothing of, but yet with
benefit we might exchange a little of our morality for some of their cooking virtues. . . .
　　　　Letter to a Friend (1871), *The Life*
　　　　*and Letters of Lady Dorothy Nevill*,
　　　　Ralph Nevill, ed.　　*1919p*

## 105. Jane Francesca Wilde
### (1826–1896)

\* \* \*

1 Weary men, what reap ye?—"Golden corn for
　the stranger."
　What sow ye?—"Human corpses that await
　for the Avenger."
　Fainting forms, all hunger-stricken, what see
　you in the offing?
　"Stately ships to bear our food away amid the
　stranger's scoffing."
　There's a proud array of soldiers—what do
　they round your door?
　"They guard our master's granaries from the
　thin hands of the poor."
　　　　　　　"Ballad on the Irish Famine"

## 106. Ethel Lynn Beers
### (1827–1879)

1 All quiet along the Potomac to-night,
  No sound save the rush of the river,
  While soft falls the dew on the face of the
    dead,
  The picket's off duty forever.
          "The Picket Guard," St. 6 (1861),
            *All Quiet Along the Potomac and
                Other Poems    1879*

\* \* \*

2 Art thou a pen, whose task shall be
  To drown in ink
  What writers think?
  Oh, wisely write,
  That pages white
  Be not the worse for ink and thee.
                        "The Gold Nugget"

3 Oh, Mother! Laugh your merry note,
  Be gay and glad, but don't forget
  From baby's eyes look out a soul
    That claims a home in Eden yet.
                        "Weighing the Baby"

4 Only a mother's heart can be
  Patient enough for such as he.
                        "Which Shall It Be"

## 107. Rose Terry Cooke
### (1827–1892)
\* \* \*

1 Darlings of the forest!
    Blossoming alone
  When Earth's grief is sorest
    For her jewels gone. . . .
                        "Trailing Arbutus"

2 Yet courage, soul! nor hold thy strength in vain,
  In hope o'er come the steeps God set for thee,
  For past the Alpine summits of great pain
  Lieth thine Italy.
                        "Beyond," St. 4

## 108. Ellen Howarth
### (1827–1899)
\* \* \*

1 Where is the heart that doth not keep,
    Within its inmost core,
  Some fond remembrance hidden deep,
    Of days that are no more?
                " 'Tis But a Little Faded Flower"

2 Who hath not saved some trifling thing
    More prized than jewels rare,
  A faded flower, a broken ring,
    A tress of golden hair.
                                Ibid.

3 I may not to the world impart
    The secret of its power,
  But treasured in my inmost heart
    I keep my faded flower.
                                Ibid.

## 109. Johanna Spyri
### (1827–1901)

1 "You mischievous child!" she cried, in great
  excitement. "What are you thinking of? Why
  have you taken everything off? What does it
  mean?"
    "I do not need them," replied the child, and
  did not look sorry for what she had done.
                        *Heidi,* Ch. 1    1885

2 "Oh, I wish that God had not given me what
  I prayed for! It was not so good as I thought."
                        Ibid., Ch. 11

3 "One must wait," she said after a while, "and
  must always think that soon the good God will
  bring something to make one happier; that
  something will come out of the trouble, but I
  must keep perfectly quiet, and not run away."
                        Ibid., Ch. 17

4 "If your A B C is not learned to-day,
  Go to be punished to-morrow, I say."
                        Ibid., Ch. 19

5 "Anger has overpowered him, and driven him
  to a revenge which was rather a stupid one, I
  must acknowledge, but anger makes us all
  stupid."                Ibid., Ch. 23

## 110. Elizabeth Charles
### (1828–1896)

1 To know how to say what others only know
  how to think is what makes men poets or
  sages; and to dare to say what others only
  dare to think makes men martyrs or reformers
  —or both.        *Chronicle of the Schönberg-
                        Cotta Family    1863*

## 111. Mary Jane Holmes
### (1828–1907)

1 ". . . but needn't tell me that prayers made up
  is as good as them as isn't. . . ."
                *The Cameron Pride,* Ch. 1    1867

2 "Keep yourself unspotted from the world," Morris had said, and she repeated it to herself asking "how shall I do that? how can one be good and fashionable too?"    Ibid., Ch. 19

3 "If the body you bring back has my George's heart within it, I shall love you just the same as I do now. . . ."    *Rose Mather*, Ch. 3
*1868*

## 112. Margaret Oliphant
### (1828–1897)

1 The first thing which I can record concerning myself is, that I was born. . . . These are wonderful words. This life, to which neither time nor eternity can bring diminution—this everlasting living soul, *began*. My mind loses itself in these depths.    *Memoirs and Resolutions of Adam Graeme, of Mossgray*
Vol. I, Bk. I,
Ch. 1    *1852*

2 "I am perfectly safe—nobody can possibly be safer than such a woman as I am, in poverty and middle age," said this strange acquaintance. "It is an immunity that women don't often prize, Mr. Vincent, but it is very valuable in its way."    *Salem Chapel*, Ch. 9    *1863*

3 ". . . the world does not care, though our hearts are breaking; it keeps its own time."
Ibid., Ch. 18

4 "There ain't a worm but will turn when he's trod upon. . . ."    *The Perpetual Curate*,
Vol. II, Ch. 20
*1864*

5 It, the thirteenth century, possessed few of the virtues of civilization, had little time for thought and none for speculation, and was marked by all the rudeness of manners and morals, indifference to human life and callousness to suffering which are almost inseparable from continuous and oft-repeated wars.
*Francis of Assisi*, Introduction
*1871*

6 She was not clever; you might have said she had no mind at all; but so wise and right and tender a heart, that it was as good as genius.
*A Little Pilgrim*, Ch. 1    *1882*

7 "And we who were the workers began to contend one against another to satisfy the gnawings of the rage that were in our hearts. For we had deceived ourselves, thinking once more that all would be well; while all the time nothing was changed."    Ibid., Ch. 2

8 "One does not want to hear one's thoughts; most of them are not worth hearing."
Ibid., Ch. 3

9   "I am afraid; I am afraid!" I cried.
"And I too am afraid; but it is better to suffer more and to escape than to suffer less and to remain."    Ibid.

10 It *was* a bore to go out into those aimless assemblies where not to go was a social mistake, yet to go was weariness of the flesh and spirit.    *A Country Gentleman and His Family*, Vol. III, Ch. 5    *1886*

11 "A girl who has been talked about is always at a disadvantage. She had much better keep quite quiet until the story has all died away."
Ibid., Ch. 12

12 In the history of men and of commonwealth there is a slow progression, which, however faint, however deferred, yet gradually goes on, leaving one generation always a trifle better than that which preceded it, with some scrap of new possession, some right assured, some small inheritance gained.
*The Literary History of England*,
Introduction    *1889*

13 There are many variations in degree of the greatest human gifts, but they are few in kind.
*Royal Edinburgh*, Pt. IV,
Ch. 3    *1890*

14 The highest ideal [in the fifteenth century] was that of war, war no doubt sometimes for good ends, to redress wrongs, to avenge injury, to make crooked things straight—but yet always war, implying a state of affairs in which the last thing that men thought of was the Golden Rule, and the highest attainment to be looked for was the position of a protector, doer of justice, deliverer of the oppressed.
*Jeanne d'Arc*, Ch. 1    *1896*

15 It is not necessary to be a good man in order to divine what in certain circumstances a good and pure spirit will do.    Ibid., Ch. 17

\*   \*   \*

16 Imagination is the first faculty wanting in those that do harm to their kind.    "Innocent"

## 113. Elizabeth Doten
### (1829–?)

1 God of the granite and the rose,
Soul of the sparrow and the bee,
The mighty tide of being flows
  Through countless channels, Lord, from
    Thee.

"Reconciliation"   *c.1870*

## 114. Edna Dean Proctor

(1829–1923)

\* \* \*

1   Into Thy hands, O Lord,
Into Thy hands I give my soul.
"Columbus Dying"

2   Now God avenges the life he gladly gave,
Freedom reigns to-day!
"John Brown"

3    O there are tears for him,\*
O there are cheers for him—
Liberty's champion, Cid of the West.
"Cid of the West"

4   The fasts are done; the Aves said;
The moon has filled her horn,
And in the solemn night I watch
Before the Easter morn.
"Easter Morning"

## 115. Charlotte Barnard

(1830–1869)

1   I cannot sing the old songs,
Or dream those dreams again.
"I Cannot Sing the Old Songs"
c.1860

2   Take back the freedom thou cravest,
Leaving the fetters to me.
"Take Back the Heart"    c.1860

## 116. Helen Olcott Bell

(1830–1918)

1   To a woman, the consciousness of being well-dressed gives a sense of tranquility which religion fails to bestow.
Letters and Social Aims:
R. W. Emerson    1876

## 117. Emily Dickinson

(1830–1886)

1   Angels—twice descending
Reimbursed my store—
Burglar! Banker!—Father!
I am poor once more.
No. 49, St. 2    c.1858

2   I never lost as much but twice,
And that was in the sod.
Twice have I stood a beggar
Before the door of God.
Ibid.

\* Referring to Theodore Roosevelt.

3   Surgeons must be very careful
When they take the knife!
Underneath their fine incisions
Stirs the Culprit—Life!
No. 108    c.1859

4   Here a star, and there a star,
Some lose their way!
Here a mist, and there a mist,
Afterwards—Day!
No. 113    c.1859

5   For each ecstatic instant
We must an anguish pay
In keen and quivering ratio
To the ecstasy. . . .
No. 125, St. 1    c.1859

6   There are days when Birds come back—
A very few—a Bird or two—
To take a backward look.

There are days when skies resume
The old—old sophistries of June—
A blue and gold mistake.
No. 130, Sts. 1–2    c.1859

7   Besides the Autumn poets sing
A few prosaic days
A little this side of the snow
And that side of the Haze. . . .
No. 131, St. 1    1859

8   Just lost when I was saved!
No. 160, St. 1    1860

9   Inebriate of Air—am I—
And Debauchee of Dew—
Reeling through endless summer days—
From inns of Molten Blue.
No. 214, St. 2    1860

10   "Hope" is the thing with feathers
That perches in the soul
And sings the tune without the words
And never stops—at all. . . .
No. 254, St. 1    1861

11   There's a certain Slant of light,
Winter Afternoons—
That oppresses, like the Heft
Of Cathedral Tunes. . . .
No. 258, St. 1    1861

12   I'm nobody, Who are you?
Are you—Nobody,—too?
No. 288, St. 1    1861

13   How dreary—to be—Somebody!
How public—like a Frog—
To tell one's name—the livelong June—
To an admiring Bog!
Ibid., St. 2

14 I tasted—careless—then—
   I did not know the Wine
   Came once a World—Did you?
                      No. 296, St. 3    *1861*

15 The Soul selects its own Society—
   Then—shuts the Door.
                      No. 303, St. 1    *1862*

16 I'll tell you how the Sun rose—
   A Ribbon at a time. . . .
                   No. 318    *1862*

17 Some keep the Sabbath going to Church—
   I keep it, staying at Home—
   With a boblink for a Chorister—
   And an Orchard, for a Dome. . . .
                      No. 324, St. 1    *1862*

18 After great pain, a formal feeling comes.
                No. 341, St. 1    *1862*

19 Of Course—I prayed—
   And did God Care?
                   No. 376    *1862*

20 Except Thyself may be
   Thine Enemy—
   Captivity is Consciousness—
   So's Liberty.
                   No. 384, St. 4    *1862*

21 This is my letter to the World
   That never wrote to Me. . . .
                No. 441, St. 1    *1862*

22 I died for Beauty—but was scarce
   Adjusted in the Tomb
   When One who died for Truth, was lain
   In an adjoining Room. . . .
                No. 449, St. 1    *1862*

23 I reckon—when I count at all—
   First—Poets—Then the Sun—
   Then Summer—Then the Heaven of God—
   And then—the List is done. . . .
                No. 569, St. 1    *1862*

24 Afraid! Of whom am I afraid?
   Not Death—for who is He?
   The Porter of my Father's Lodge
   As much abasheth me!
                No. 608, St. 1    *1862*

25 The Brain—is wider than the Sky—
   For—put them side by side—
   The one the other will contain
   With ease—and You—beside.
                No. 632, St. 1    *1862*

26 I cannot live with You—
   It would be Life—
   And Life is over there—
   Behind the Shelf.
                No. 640, St. 1    *1862*

27 Pain—has an Element of Blank—
   It cannot recollect
   When it begun—or if there were
   A time when it was not. . . .
                No. 650, St. 1    *1862*

28 I dwell in Possibility—
   A fairer House than Prose—
   More numerous of Windows—
   Superior—for Doors.
                No. 657, St. 1    *1862*

29 The Soul unto itself
   Is an imperial friend—
   Or the most agonizing Spy—
   An Enemy—could send. . . .
                No. 683, St. 1    *1862*

30 God gave a Loaf to every Bird—
   But just a Crumb—to Me. . . .
                No. 791, St. 1    *1863*

31 Truth—is as old as God—
   His Twin identity
   And will endure as long as He
   A Co-Eternity. . . .
                No. 836, St. 1    *1864*

32 Love—is anterior to Life—
   Posterior—to Death—
   Initial of Creation, and
   The Exponent of Earth.
                No. 917    *1864*

33 'Twas my one Glory—
   Let it be
   Remembered
   I was owned of Thee. . . .
                No. 1028    *1865*

34 Not to discover weakness is
   The Artifice of strength. . . .
                No. 1054, St. 1    *1865*

35 The Sweeping up the Heart,
   And putting Love away. . . .
                No. 1078, St. 2    *1866*

36 Truth is such a rare thing, it is delightful to
   tell it.           Letter to Thomas Wentworth
                Higginson    *August, 1870*

37 A word is dead
   When it is said,
   Some say.
   I say it just
   Begins to live
   That day.
                No. 1212    *1872*

38 Not with a Club, the Heart is broken
   Nor with a Stone—
   A Whip so small you could not see it
   I've known
   To lash the Magic Creature
   Till it fell.
                No. 1304, St. 1    *1874*

39 That short—potential stir
That each can make but once.
No. 1307, St. 1    *1874*

40 A little Madness in the Spring
Is wholesome even for the King.
No. 1333    *1875*

41 Bees are Black, with Gilt Surcingles—
Buccaneers of Buzz.
No. 1405, St. 1    *1877*

42 Success is counted sweetest
By those who ne'er succeed.
"Success," *Poems*, V    *1891p*

43 The distant strains of triumph
Break agonized and clear.
Ibid.

44 The pedigree of honey
Does not concern the bee
A clover, anytime, to him
Is aristocracy.
Ibid., "The Bee"

45 His labor is a chant
His idleness a tune;
Oh, for a bee's experience
Of clovers and of noon!
Ibid.

46 So, instead of getting to Heaven at last—
I'm going, all along.
Ibid., VI, "A Service of Song," St. 3

47 Much madness is divinist sense
To a discerning eye;
Much sense the starkest madness.
Ibid., XI

*    *    *

48 Because I could not stop for Death,
He kindly stopped for me.
"Because I Could Not Stop for Death"

49 Faith is a fine invention
For gentlemen who see;
But microscopes are prudent
In an emergency.
"Faith"

50    Great Spirit, give to me
A heaven not so large as yours
But large enough for me.
"A Prayer"

51 I believe the love of God may be taught not to
seem like bears.
"In Protest Over Severe Religious
Ideas of Ancestors"

52 If I can stop one heart from breaking,
I shall not live in vain;
If I can ease one life the aching,
Or cool one pain,

Or help one fainting robin
Into his nest again,
I shall not live in vain.
"Life"

53 Parting is all we know of heaven,
And all we need of hell.
"Parting"

## 118. Marie Ebner von Eschenbach
### (1830–1916)

1 "Good heavens!" said he, "if it be our clothes
alone which fit us for society, how highly we
should esteem those who make them."
*The Two Countesses*    *1893*

2 HE. You apparently occupy yourself but little
with reading?

I. Just enough to do penance for my sins, and
to keep up my English.    Ibid.

3 He says a learned woman is the greatest of all
calamities.    Ibid.

4 "Everyone plays at the game for a time, my
dear Paula, because it is the correct thing to
do. . . . But thinking persons cannot hide from
themselves the consciousness of the hollowness
of it all, and then they turn to the realities of
life, often bitterly to repent of their wasted
years."    Ibid.

5 "Nothing is too strong to express the humiliation of knowing the being one looks up to—
or rather one should look up to—to be a non-
entity, or the hypocrisy of seeming to defer to
him one knows to be one's inferior."    Ibid.

6 Accident is veiled necessity.
*Aphorism*    *1905*

7 Fear not those who argue but those who dodge.
Ibid.

8 Conquer, but don't triumph.
Ibid.

9 To be content with little is hard, to be content
with much, impossible.    Ibid.

10 No one is so eager to gain new experience as
he who doesn't know how to make use of the
old ones.    Ibid.

11 If there is a faith that can move mountains, it
is faith in your own power.    Ibid.

12 He who believes in freedom of the will has
never loved and never hated.    Ibid.

13 Whenever two good people argue over principles, they are both right.    Ibid.

14 Imaginary evils are incurable.    Ibid.

15 Many think they have a kind heart who only have weak nerves.    Ibid.

16 We don't believe in rheumatism and true love until after the first attack.    Ibid.

17 We are so vain that we even care for the opinion of those we don't care for.    Ibid.

18 Privilege is the greatest enemy of right.    Ibid.

19 As far as your self-control goes, as far goes your freedom.    Ibid.

20 Even a stopped clock is right twice a day.    Ibid.

21 Those whom we support hold us up in life.    Ibid.

22 Only the thinking man lives his life, the thoughtless man's life passes him by.    Ibid.

23 You can stay young as long as you can learn, acquire new habits and suffer contradiction.    Ibid.

24 In youth we learn; in age we understand.    Ibid.

25 Oh, say not foreign war! A war is never foreign.
Quoted in *War, Peace, and the Future* by Ellen Key    *1916*

## 119. Helen Fiske Hunt Jackson
### (1830–1885)

1 There is nothing so skillful in its own defence as imperious pride.    *Ramona,* Ch. 13
   *1884*

2 Wounded vanity knows when it is mortally hurt; and limps off the field, piteous, all disguises thrown away. But pride carries its banner to the last.    Ibid.

3 There cannot be found in the animal kingdom a bat, or any other creature, so blind in its own range of circumstance and connection, as the greater majority of human beings are in the bosoms of their families.    Ibid.

4 That indescribable expression peculiar to people who hope they have not been asleep, but know they have.    Ibid., Ch. 14

5 Words are less needful to sorrow than to joy.    Ibid., Ch. 17

6 My body, eh. Friend Death, how now?
   Why all this tedious pomp of writ?
Thou hast reclaimed it sure and slow
   For half a century, bit by bit.
     "Habeas Corpus," St. 1    *1885*

\* \* \*

7 And newest friend is oldest friend in this:
That, waiting him, we longest grieved to miss
One thing we sought.
     "My New Friend"

8 Bee to the blossom, moth to the flame;
Each to his passion; what's in a name?
     "Vanity of Vanities"

9 But all lost things are in the angels' keeping. . . .      "At Last," St. 6

10 Father, I scarcely dare to pray,
   So clear I see, now it is done,
How I have wasted half my day,
   And left my work but just begun.
     "A Last Prayer"

11 Find me the men on earth who care
   Enough for faith or creed today
To seek a barren wilderness
   For simple liberty to pray.
     "The Pilgrim Forefathers," St. 5

12 Great loves, to the last, have pulses red;
All great loves that have ever died dropped dead.
     "Dropped Dead"

13 Love has a tide!
     "Tides"

14 Oh, write of me, not "Died in bitter pains,"
But "Emigrated to another star!"
     "Emigravit"

15 O suns and skies and clouds of June,
   And flowers of June together,
Ye cannot rival for one hour
   October's bright blue weather.
     "October's Bright Blue
     Weather," St. 1

16 O Sweet delusive Noon,
   Which the morning climbs to find,
O moment sped too soon,
   And morning left behind.
     "Noon," *Verses*

17 She said: "The daisy but deceives;
   'He loves me not,' 'He loves me well,'
One story no two daisies tell."
Ah foolish heart, which waits and grieves
   Under the daisy's mocking spell.
     "The Sign of the Daisy"

18  The mighty are brought low by many a thing
Too small to name. Beneath the daisy's disk
Lies hid the pebble for the fatal sling.
"Danger"

19  We sail, at sunrise, daily, "outward bound."
"Outward Bound"

20  When love is at its best, one loves
So much that he cannot forget.
"Two Truths"

21  Who longest waits of all most surely wins.
"The Victory of Patience"

## 120.  Mother Jones
### (1830–1930)

1  Sometimes I'm in Washington, then in Pennsylvania, Arizona, Texas, Alabama, Colorado, Minnesota. My address is like my shoes. It travels with me. I abide where there is a fight against wrong.          Congressional Hearing, Quoted in *The Rebel Girl*, Pt. II, by Elizabeth Gurley Flynn          *1955p*

\* \* \*

2  Pray for the dead and fight like hell for the living.          Motto

## 121.  Belva Lockwood
### (1830–1917)

1  I do not believe in sex distinction in literature, law, politics, or trade—or that modesty and virtue are more becoming to women than to men, but wish we had more of it everywhere.
Quoted in *Lady for the Defense*, Pt. II, Ch. 8, by Mary Virginia Fox          *1975p*

2  I know we can't abolish prejudice through laws, but we can set up guidelines for our actions by legislation. If women are given equal pay for Civil Service jobs, maybe other employers will do the same.
Ibid., Pt. III, Ch. 11

3  I have been told that there is no precedent for admitting a woman to practice in the Supreme Court of the United States. The glory of each generation is to make its own precedents. As there was none for Eve in the Garden of Eden, so there need be none for her daughters on entering the colleges, the church, or the courts.
Ibid., Ch. 13

4  If nations could only depend upon fair and impartial judgments in a world court of law, they would abandon the senseless, savage practice of war.          Ibid., Ch. 15

5  No one can claim to be called Christian who gives money for the building of warships and arsenals.     Ibid., Address at Westminster Hall, London (c.1886)

## 122.  Louise Michel
### (1830–1905)

1  In rebellion alone, woman is at ease, stamping out both prejudices and sufferings; all intellectual women will sooner or later rise in rebellion.          Attributed     *1890*

## 123.  Christina Rossetti
### (1830–1894)

1  Why strive for love when love is o'er. . . .
"Hearts' Chill Between," St. 2
*September 22, 1847*

2  When I am dead, my dearest,
Sing no sad songs for me;
Plant thou no roses at my head,
Nor shady cypress tree.
Be the green grass above me
With showers and dew drops wet:
And if thou wilt, remember,
And if thou wilt, forget.
"Song," St. 1
*December 12, 1848*

3  To-day is still the same as yesterday,
To-morrow also even as one of them;
And there is nothing new under the sun. . . .
"One Certainty"
*June 2, 1849*

4  O dream house sweet, too sweet, too bittersweet,
Whose wakening should have been in Paradise,
Where souls brimfull of love abide and meet;
Where thirsting longing eyes
Watch the slow door
That opening, letting in, lets out no more.
"Echo," St. 2
*December 18, 1854*

5  My friends had failed one by one,
Middle-aged, young, and old,
Till the ghosts were warmer to me
Than my friends that had grown cold.
"A Chilly Night," St. 2
*February 11, 1856*

6  We, one, must part in two:
Verily death is this:
I must die.
"Wife to Husband," St. 5
*June 8, 1861*

7 Too late for love, too late for joy,
   Too late, too late!
You loitered on the road too long,
   You trifled at the gate. . . .
          "The Prince's Progress," St. 1
               *November 11, 1861*

8 "Does the road wind up-hill all the way?"
"Yes, to the very end."
"Will the day's journey take the whole long
   day?"
"From morn to night, my friend."
          "Up-Hill," St. 1    *1861*

9 "May not the darkness hide it from my face?"
"You cannot miss that inn."
                    **Ibid.**

10 My heart is like a singing bird.
          "A Birthday," St. 1   *1861*

11   Because the birth of my life
Is come, my love is come to me.
                Ibid., St. 2

12 All earth's full rivers cannot fill
The sea, that drinking thirsteth still.
     "By the Sea," *Goblin Market*   *1862*

13 Darkness more clear than noonday holdeth her,
Silence more musical than any song.
              Ibid., "Rest"

14 For there is no friend like a sister
   In calm or stormy weather;
To cheer one on the tedious way,
To fetch one if one goes astray,
To lift one if one totters down,
To strengthen whilst one stands.
        Ibid., "Goblin Market"

15 One day in the country
Is worth a month in town.
            Ibid., "Summer"

16 Remember me when I am gone away,
Gone far away into the silent land.
           Ibid., "Remember"

17 Better by far that you should forget and smile
Than that you should remember and be sad.
        Ibid. (July 25, 1849)

18 I might show facts as plain as day:
But, since your eyes are blind, you'd say,
   "Where? What?" and turn away.
          "A Sketch," St. 3
             *August 15, 1864*

19 "I ate his life as a banquet,
   I drank his life as new wine,
   I've fattened upon his leanness,
Mine to flourish and his to pine."
        "Cannot Sweeten," St. 7
             *March 8, 1866*

20 "For the nobility have blood, if you please,
and the literary beggars are welcome to all the
brains they've got" (the Doctor smiled, Allen
winced visibly); "but you'll find it's us city men
who've got backbone, and backbone's the best
to wear. . . ."
          *Commonplace, A Tale of*
          *Today*, Ch. 6    *1870*

21 So gradually it came to pass that, from looking
back together, they took also to looking forward together.          Ibid., Ch. 17

22 Glow-worms that gleam but yield no warmth
in gleaming. . . .
        "Till To-morrow," St. 2   *c.1882*

23 If thou canst dive, bring up pearls. If thou
canst not dive, collect amber.
        *The Face of the Deep,*
        Prefatory Note    *1892*

24 Multitude no less than Unity characterizes various types of God the Holy Spirit.
                Ibid., Ch. 1

25 Rapture and rest, desire and satisfaction, perfection and progress, may seem to clash to-day:
to-morrow the paradoxes of earth may re-
appear as the demonstrations of heaven.
                Ibid., Ch. 4

26 Well spake that soldier who being asked what
he would do if he became too weak to cling to
Christ, answered, "Then I will pray Him to
cling to me."          Ibid., Ch. 16
              *    *    *

27 Hope is like a harebell trembling from its
birth. . . .
        "Hope Is Like a Harebell"

28 No wonder that his soul was sad,
When not one penny piece he had.
                "Johnny"

29 Snow had fallen, snow on snow,
   Snow on snow,
In the bleak mid-winter,
   Long ago.
               "Mid-Winter"

30 Who has seen the wind?
   Neither you nor I:
But when the trees bow down their heads,
   The wind is passing by.
      "Who Has Seen the Wind?," St. 2

## 124. Amelia Barr

### (1831–1919)

1 But what do we know of the heart nearest to
our own? What do we know of our own heart?

Some ancestor who sailed with Offa, or who fought with the Ironsides, or protested with the Covenanters, or legislated with the Puritans, may, at this very hour, be influencing us, in a way of which we never speak, and in which no other soul intermeddles.

*Jan Vedder's Wife*, Ch. 1 *1885*

2 ". . . for still I see that forethought spares afterthought and after-sorrow."

Ibid., Ch. 5

3 "There is no corner too quiet, or too far away, for a woman to make sorrow in it."

Ibid., Ch. 9

4 " 'Is she not handsome, virtuous, rich, amiable?' they asked. 'What hath she done to thee?' The Roman husband pointed to his sandal. 'Is it not new, is it not handsome and well made? But none of you can tell where it pinches me.' That old Roman and I are brothers. Everyone praises 'my good wife, my rich wife, my handsome wife,' but for all that, the matrimonial shoe pinches me."

Ibid.

5 "Let me tell thee, time is a very precious gift of God; so precious that He only gives it to us moment by moment. He would not have thee waste it."

Ibid., Ch. 11

6 "It is a sin to be merciful to the wicked, it is that; and the kindness done to them is unblessed, and brings forth sin and trouble."

Ibid.

7 "It is little men know of women; their smiles and their tears alike are seldom what they seem."

Ibid.

8 That is the great mistake about the affections. It is not the rise and fall of empires, the birth and death of kings, or the marching of armies that move them most. When they answer from their depths, it is to the domestic joys and tragedies of life.

Ibid., Ch. 14

9 It is only in sorrow bad weather masters us; in joy we face the storm and defy it.

Ibid.

10 But the lover's power is the poet's power. He can make love from all the common strings with which this world is strung.

*The Belle of Bolling Green,* Ch. 3 *1904*

11 The fate of love is that it always seems too little or too much.

Ibid., Ch. 5

12 Now jealousy is only good when she torments herself. . . .

Ibid.

13 "When men make themselves into brutes it is just to treat them like brutes."

Ibid., Ch. 8

14 I entered this incarnation on March-the-twenty-ninth, A.D. 1831, at the ancient town of Ulverston, Lancashire, England. My soul came with me. This is not always the case. Every observing mother of a large family knows that the period of spiritual possession varies. . . . I brought my soul with me—an eager soul, impatient for the loves and joys, the struggles and triumphs of the dear, unforgotten world.

*All the Days of My Life,* Ch. 1 *1913*

15 With renunciation life begins.

Ibid., Ch. 9

16 The great difference between voyages rests not with the ships, but with the people you meet on them.

Ibid., Ch. 11

17 For moral and spiritual gifts are bought and not given. We pay for them in some manner, or we go empty away. It is *every day duty* that tells on life. Spiritual favors are not always to be looked for, and not always to be relied on.

Ibid., Ch. 19

18 What we call death was to him only emigration, and I care not where he now tarries. He is doing God's will, and more alive than ever he was on earth.

Ibid., Ch. 23

19 Old age is the verdict of life.

Ibid., Ch. 26

20 Whatever the scientists may say, if we take the supernatural out of life, we leave only the unnatural.

Ibid.

## 125. Elena Petrovna Blavatsky
### (1831–1891)

1 We live in an age of prejudice, dissimulation and paradox, wherein, like dry leaves caught in a whirlpool, some of us are tossed helpless, hither and thither, ever struggling between our honest convictions and fear of that cruelest of tyrants—PUBLIC OPINION.

"A Paradoxical World," *Lucifer February, 1889*

2 For fourteen years our Theosophical Society has been before the public. Born with the threefold object of infusing a little more mutual brotherly feeling in mankind; of investigating the mysteries of nature from the Spiritual and Psychic aspect. . . . If it did not do all the good that a richer Society might, it certainly did no harm.

Ibid., "On Pseudo-Theosophy" *March, 1889*

3 We must prepare and study truth under every aspect, endeavoring to ignore nothing, if we do not wish to fall into the abyss of the unknown when the hour shall strike.

Quoted in *La Revue Theosophique*
*March 21, 1889*

4 Just back from under the far-reaching shadow of the Eighth Wonder of the World—the gigantic iron carrot that goes by the name of the Eiffel Tower. Child of its country, wondrous in its size, useless in its object, as shaky and vacillating as the republican soil upon which it is built, it has not one single moral feature of its seven ancestors, not one trait of atavism to boast of.

"The Eighth Wonder," *Lucifer*
*October, 1891*

5 This idea of passing one's whole life in moral idleness, and having one's hardest work and duty done by another—whether God or man—is most revolting to us, as it is most degrading to human dignity. *The Key to Theosophy*,
Sec. 5     *1893*

6 And so the only reality in our conception is the hour of man's *post mortem* life, when, disembodied—during the period of that. pilgrim-, age which we call "the cycle of re-births"—he stands face to face with truth and not the mirages of his transitory earthly existences.

Ibid., Sec. 9

7 It is the worst of crimes and dire in its results. . . . Voluntary death would be an abandonment of our present post and of the duties incumbent on us, as well as an attempt to shirk karmic responsibilities, and thus involve the creation of new Karma.     Ibid., Sec. 12

8 For in this age of crass and illogical materialism, the Esoteric Philosophy [theosophy] alone is calculated to withstand the repeated attacks on all and everything man holds most dear and sacred in his inner spiritual life.

*The Secret Doctrine*, Introduction
(1893)     *1918p*

9 If there were such a thing as a void, a vacuum in Nature, one ought to find it produced, according to a physical law, in the minds of helpless admirers of the "lights" of Science, who pass their time in mutually destroying their teachings.     Ibid., Sec. 17

## 126. Isabel Burton
### (1831–1896)

1 Without any cant, does not Providence provide wonderfully for us?     *Arabia Egypt India*,
Ch. 15     *1879*

2 Like most outsiders, I cannot see the difficulty of settling the Eastern Question (*malé pereat!*), but I thoroughly see the danger of leaving it, as at present, half settled.     Ibid., Ch. 20

3 I have no leisure to think of style or of polish, or to select the best language, the best English —no time to shine as an authoress. I must just think aloud, so as not to keep the public waiting.     *The Life of Captain Sir Richard F.*
*Burton*, Foreword     *1898p*

## 127. Rebecca Harding Davis
### (1831–1910)

1 The idiosyncrasy of this town is smoke. It rolls solemnly in slow folds from the great chimneys of the iron-foundries, and settles down in black, slimy pools on the muddy streets. Smoke on the wharves, smoke on the dingy boats, on the yellow river—clinging in a coating of greasy soot to the house-front, the two faded poplars, the faces of the passers-by.

"Life in the Iron Mills," *Atlantic
Monthly*     *April, 1861*

2 You, Egoist, or Pantheist, or Arminian, busy in making straight paths for your feet on the hills, do not see it clearly—this terrible question which men here have gone mad and died trying to answer. I dare not put this secret into words. I told you it was dumb. These men, going by with drunken faces and brains full of unawakened power, do not ask it of Society or of God. Their lives ask it; their deaths ask it.

Ibid.

3 There are moments when a passing cloud, the sun glinting on the purple thistles, a kindly smile, a child's face, will rouse him to a passion of pain—when his nature starts up with a mad cry of rage against God, man, whoever it is that has forced·this vile, slimy life upon him.

Ibid.

4 Be just—not like man's law, which seizes on one isolated fact, but like God's judging angel, whose clear, sad eye saw all the countless cankering days of this man's life. . . .     Ibid.

5 He was . . . a man who sucked the essence out of a science or philosophy in an indifferent, gentlemanly way; who took Kant, Novalis, Humboldt, for what they were worth in his own scale; accepting all, despising nothing, in heaven, earth, or hell, but one-idea'd men; with a temper yielding and brilliant as summer water, until his Self was touched, when it was ice, though brilliant still. Such men are not rare in the States.     Ibid.

6 "I tell you, there's something wrong that no talk of *'Liberté'* or *'Egalité'* will do away. If I had the making of men, these men who do the lowest part of the world's work should be machines—nothing more—hands. It would be kindness. God help them! What are taste, reason, to creatures who must live such lives as that?"                                    Ibid.

7 "Reform is born of need, not pity. No vital movement of the people has worked down, for good or evil; fermented, instead, carried up the heaving, cloggy mass."                          Ibid.

8 Something is lost in the passage of every soul from one eternity to the other—something pure and beautiful, which might have been and was not: a hope, a talent, a love, over which the soul mourns, like Esau deprived of his birthright.                                      Ibid.

9 Every child was taught from his cradle that money was Mammon, the chief agent of the flesh and the devil. As he grew up it was his duty as a Christian and a gentleman to appear to despise filthy lucre, whatever his secret opinion of it might be.    *Bits of Gossip*, Ch. 1
                                                1904

10 Nowhere in this country, from sea to sea, does nature comfort us with such assurance of plenty, such rich and tranquil beauty as in those unsung, unpainted hills of Pennsylvania.
                                      Ibid., Ch. 4

11 North and South were equally confident that God was on their side, and appealed incessantly to Him.                            Ibid., Ch. 5

12 We don't look into these unpleasant details of our great struggle [the Civil War]. We all prefer to think that every man who wore the blue or gray was a Philip Sidney at heart. These are sordid facts that I have dragged up. But—they are facts. And because we have hidden them our young people have come to look upon war as a kind of beneficent deity, which not only adds to the national honor but uplifts a nation and develops patriotism and courage. That is all true. But it is only fair, too, to let them know that the garments of the deity are filthy and that some of her influences debase and befoul a people.                          Ibid.

13 But while the light burning within may have been divine, the outer case of the lamp was assuredly cheap enough. [Walt] Whitman was, from first to last, a boorish, awkward *poseur*.
                                      Ibid., Ch. 8

## 128. Henrietta Dobree
### (1831–1894)
\* \* \*

1 Safely, safely, gather'd in,
Far from sorrow, far from sin.
                          "Child's Hymn Book"

## 129. Amelia Edwards
### (1831–1892)
\* \* \*

1 The Queen has lands and gold, Mother
   The Queen has lands and gold,
While you are forced to your empty breast
   A skeleton Babe to hold. . . .
            "Give Me Three Grains of Corn,
                          Mother," St. 4

2 What has poor Ireland done, Mother,
   What has poor Ireland done,
That the world looks on, and sees us starve,
   Perishing one by one?
                          Ibid., St. 5

3 There are rich and proud men there, Mother,
   With wondrous wealth to view
And the bread they fling to their dogs tonight
   Would give life to me and you.
                          Ibid., St. 6

## 130. Nora Perry
### (1831–1896)
\* \* \*

1 But not alone with the silken snare
Did she catch her lovely floating hair,
For, tying her bonnet under her chin,
She tied a young man's heart within.
                          "The Love-Knot," St. 1

2 Some day, some day of days, threading the street
   With idle, headless pace,
   Unlooking for such grace,
   I shall behold your face!
Some day, some day of days, thus may we meet.
                          "Some Day of Days"

3 What silences we keep, year after year,
With those who are most near to us,
   And dear!
                          "Too Late," St. 1

4 Who knows the thoughts of a child?
                          "Who Knows?," St. 1

## 131. Elizabeth Chase Akers

(1832–1911)

1 Backward, turn backward, O Time, in your
flight,
Make me a child again, just for to-night!
"Rock Me to Sleep, Mother"
*1860*

2 I have grown weary of dust and decay—
Weary of flinging my soul-wealth away;—
Weary of sowing for others to reap;
Rock me to sleep, Mother—rock me to sleep!
Ibid., St. 2

\* \* \*

3 Blush, happy maiden, when you feel
The lips that press love's glowing seal.
But as the slow years darker roll,
Grown wiser, the experienced soul
Will own as dearer far than they
The lips which kiss the tears away.
"Kisses"

4 Carve not upon a stone when I am dead
The praises which remorseful mourners give
To women's graves—a tardy recompense—
But speak them while I live.
"Till Death," St. 6

5 Though we be sick and tired and faint and
worn,—
Lo, all things can be borne!
"Endurance," St. 5

6 Unremembered and afar
I watched you as I watched a star,
Through darkness struggling into view,
I loved you better than you knew.
"Left Behind," St. 5

## 132. Louisa May Alcott

(1832–1888)

1 A little kingdom I possess,
Where thought and feelings dwell;
And very hard the task I find
Of governing it well.
"My Kingdom," St. 1 *c.1845*

2 I do not ask for any crown
But that which all may win;
Nor try to conquer any world
Except the one within.
Ibid., St. 4

3 Above man's aims his nature rose.
The wisdom of a just content
Made one small spot a continent,
And turned to poetry life's prose.
"Thoreau's Flute," St. 2, *Atlantic
Monthly* September, 1863

4 "Energy is more attractive than beauty in a
man." *Behind a Mask*, Ch. 2 *1866*

5 "You *are* master here, but not of me, or my
actions, and you have no right to expect obedience or respect, for you inspire neither."
Ibid., Ch. 4

6 ". . . rivalry adds so much to the charms of
one's conquests." Ibid., Ch. 7

7 "Christmas won't be Christmas without any
presents." *Little Women*, Pt. I *1868*

8 "I shall have to toil and moil all my days, with
only little bits of fun now and then, and get
old and ugly and sour, because I'm poor, and
can't enjoy my life as other girls do. It's a
shame!" Ibid.

9 "You have a good many little gifts and virtues,
but there is no need of parading them, for
conceit spoils the finest genius. There is not
much danger that real talent or goodness will
be overlooked long, and the great charm of all
power is modesty." Ibid.

10 ". . . It seems as if I could do anything when
I'm in a passion. I get so savage I could hurt
anyone and enjoy it. I'm afraid I *shall* do
something dreadful some day, and spoil my
life, and make everybody hate me. O Mother,
help me. . . ." Ibid.

11 "Housekeeping ain't no joke." Ibid.

12 "November is the most disagreeable month in
the whole year." Ibid.

13 "People don't have fortunes left them . . . nowadays; men have to work, and women to marry
for money. It's a dreadfully unjust world. . . ."
Ibid.

14 . . . love is a great beautifier. Ibid.

15 It takes people a long time to learn the difference between talent and genius, especially ambitious young men and women. Ibid., Pt. II

16 . . . she was one of those happily created beings who please without effort, make friends
everywhere, and take life so gracefully and
easily that less fortunate souls are tempted to
believe that such are born under a lucky star.
Ibid.

17 "My lady" . . . had yet to learn that money
cannot buy refinement of nature, that rank does
not always confer nobility, and that true breeding makes itself felt in spite of external drawbacks. Ibid.

18 ". . . It's a great comfort to have an artistic sister." Ibid.

19 ". . . elegance has a bad effect upon my constitution. . . ." Ibid.

20 . . . she had a womanly instinct that clothes possess an influence more powerful over many than the worth of character or the magic of manners. Ibid.

21 ". . . girls are so queer you never know what they mean. They say No when they mean Yes, and drive a man out of his wits for the fun of it. . . ." Ibid.

22 . . . public opinion is a giant which has frightened stouter-hearted Jacks on bigger beanstalks than hers. Ibid.

23 ". . . I don't believe I shall ever marry. I'm happy as I am, and love my liberty too well to be in any hurry to give it up for any mortal man." Ibid.

24 ". . . Oh dear! How can girls like to have lovers and refuse them? I think it's dreadful." Ibid.

25 "Rome took all the vanity out of me; for after seeing the wonders there, I felt too insignificant to live, and gave up all my foolish hopes in despair." Ibid.

26 ". . . talent isn't genius, and no amount of energy can make it so. I want to be great, or nothing. I won't be a commonplace dauber, so I don't intend to try any more." Ibid.

27 "It takes two flints to make a fire." Ibid.

28 ". . . love is the only thing that we can carry with us when we go, and it makes the end so easy." Ibid.

29 . . . when women are the advisers, the lords of creation don't take the advice till they have persuaded themselves that it is just what they intended to do; then they act upon it, and if it succeeds, they give the weaker vessel half the credit of it; if it fails, they generously give her the whole. Ibid.

30 . . . when a man has a great sorrow, he should be indulged in all sorts of vagaries till he has lived it down. Ibid.

31 ". . . I'm not afraid of storms, for I'm learning how to sail my ship." Ibid.

32 ". . . What *do* girls do who haven't any mothers to help them through their troubles?" Ibid.

33 "Help one another, is part of the religion of our sisterhood, Fan." *An Old-Fashioned Girl* 1869

34 ". . . women have been called queens for a long time, but the kingdom given them isn't worth ruling." Ibid.

35 I believe that it is as much a right and duty for women to do something with their lives as for men and we are not going to be satisfied with such frivolous parts as you give us. *Rose in Bloom* 1876

36 "[Molly] remained a merry spinster all her days, one of the independent, brave and busy creatures of whom there is such need in the world to help take care of other people's wives and children, and to do the many useful jobs that married folk have no time for." *Jack and Jill* 1880

37 "[I'm] very glad and grateful that my profession will make me a useful, happy and independent spinster." *Jo's Boys* 1886

38 Now I am beginning to live a little, and feel less like a sick oyster at low tide. *Louisa May Alcott: Her Life, Letters, and Journals*, Edna D. Cheney, ed. *1889p*

39 My definition [of a philosopher] is of a man up in a balloon, with his family and friends holding the ropes which confine him to the earth and trying to haul him down. Ibid.

40 Resolved to take Fate by the throat and shake a living out of her. Ibid., Ch. 3

41 Father asked us what was God's noblest work. Anna said *men*, but I said *babies*. Men are often bad; babies never are. Ibid., Early Diary Kept at Fruitlands (1843)

42 I had a pleasant time with my mind, for it was happy. Ibid.

43 I have at last got the little room I have wanted so long, and am very happy about it. It does me good to be alone. . . . Ibid. (1846)

44 Philosophers sit in their sylvan hall
And talk of the duties of man,
Of Chaos and Cosmos, Hegel and Kant,
With the Oversoul well in the van;
All on their hobbies they amble away
And a terrible dust they make;
Disciples devout both gaze and adore,
As daily they listen and bake.
"Philosophers" (1845), *Alcott and the Concord School of Philosophy*, Florence Whiting Brown, ed. *1926p*

## 133. Mary Walker

(1832–1919)

1 If men were really what they profess to be
they would not compel women to dress so that
the facilities for vice would always be so easy.
Quoted in *Saturday Review*          *1935p*

## 134. Mary Woolsey

(1832–1864)

\* \* \*

1 I lay me down to sleep with little thought or
care
Whether my waking find me here, or there.
"Rest"

## 135. Gail Hamilton

(1833–1896)

1 Whatever an author puts between the two
covers of his book is public property; whatever
of himself he does not put there is his private
property, as much as if he had never written a
word.          *Country Living and Country
Thinking*, Preface          *1862*

2 Every person is responsible for all the good
within the scope of his abilities, and for no
more, and none can tell whose sphere is the
largest.          Ibid., "Men and Women"

\* \* \*

3 What's virtue in man can't be virtue in a cat.
"Both Sides"

## 136. Julia Harris May

(1833–1912)

\* \* \*

1          If we could know
Which of us, darling, would be the first to go,
Who would be first to breast the swelling tide
And step alone upon the other side—
If we could know!
"If We Could Know"

## 137. Emily Miller

(1833–1913)

\* \* \*

1 I love to hear the story
Which angel voices tell.
"I Love to Hear," *The Little Corporal*

2 Then sing, young hearts that are full of cheer,
With never a thought of sorrow;
The old goes out, but the glad young year
Comes merrily in tomorrow.
"New Year Song"

## 138. Julia Woodruff

(1833–1909)

1 Out of the strain of the Doing,
Into the race of the Done.
"Harvest Home," *Sunday at Home
May, 1910p*

## 139. Sabine Baring-Gould

(1834–1924)

\* \* \*

1 Now the day is over,
Night is drawing nigh,
Shadows of the evening
Steal across the sky.
"Now the Day Is Over"

2 Onward, Christian soldiers,
Marching as to war,
With the Cross of Jesus
Going on before.
"Onward Christian Soldiers"

3 Through the night of doubt and sorrow,
Onward goes the pilgrim band,
Singing songs of expectation,
Marching to the Promised Land.
"Through the Night of
Doubt and Sorrow"

## 140. Katherine Hankey

(1834–1911)

\* \* \*

1 Tell me the old, old story
Of unseen things above,
Of Jesus and His glory
Of Jesus and His love.

Hymn

## 141. Harriet Kimball

(1834–1917)

\* \* \*

1 A very rapturing of white;
A wedlock of silence and light:
White, white as the wonder undefiled
Of Eve just wakened in Paradise.
"White Azaleas"

## 142. Josephine Pollard

(1834–1892)

\* \* \*

1 Though he had Eden to live in,
Man cannot be happy alone.
"We Cannot Be Happy Alone," St. 5

## 143. Ellen Palmer Allerton

(1835–1893)

\* \* \*

1 Beautiful faces are those that wear
Whole-souled honesty printed there.
"Beautiful Things"

## 144. Mary Bradley

(1835–1898)

\* \* \*

1 Of all the flowers that come and go
The whole twelve months together,
This little purple pansy brings
Thoughts of the sweetest, saddest things.
"Heartsease"

## 145. Augusta Evans

(1835–1909)

1 Money is everything in this world to some
people, and more than the next to other poor
souls.                Beulah, Ch. 2    1859

2 Can the feeling that you are independent and
doing your duty, satisfy the longing for other
idyls? Oh! Duty is an icy shadow. It will freeze
you. It cannot fill the heart's sanctuary.
Ibid., Ch. 13

3 Oh, has the foul atmosphere of foreign lands
extinguished *all* your self respect? Do you come
back sordid and sycophantic, and the slave of
opinions you would once have utterly detested?
Ibid., Ch. 18

4 Human genius has accomplished a vast deal for
man's temporal existence. . . . But . . . what
has it affected for philosophy, that great burden
which constantly recalls the fabled labors of
Sisyphus and the Danaides? Since the rising of
Bethlehem's star, in the cloudy sky of polythe-
ism, what has human genius discovered of God,
eternity, destiny?           Ibid., Ch. 41

5 Fortuitous circumstances constitute the moulds
that shape the majority of human lives, and

the hasty impress of an accident is too often
regarded as the relentless decree of all or-
daining fate. . . .
Until Death Us Do Part, Ch. 1
1869

## 146. Ellen Gates

(1835–1920)

\* \* \*

1 Sleep sweet within this quiet room,
O thou! who'er thou art;
And let no mournful yesterday,
Disturb thy peaceful heart.
"Sleep Sweet"

## 147. Louise Moulton

(1835–1908)

\* \* \*

1 Bend low, O dusky night,
And give my spirit rest,
Hold me deep to your breast,
And put old cares to flight.
"Tonight"

2 Give me back the lost delight
That once my soul possessed,
When love was loveliest.
Ibid.

3 The month it was the month of May,
And all along the pleasant way,
The morning birds were mad with glee,
And all the flowers sprang up to see. . . .
"The Secret of Arcady"

4 This life is a fleeting breath. . . .
"When I Wander Away with Death"

## 148. Harriet Spofford

(1835–1921)

\* \* \*

1 Beauty vanishes like a vapor,
Preach the men of musty morals.
"Evanescence"

2 Something to live for came to the place,
Something to die for maybe,
Something to give even sorrow a grace,
And yet it was only a baby!
"Only"

3 The awful phantom of the hungry poor.
"A Winter's Night"

## 149. Celia Thaxter

(1835–1894)

\* \* \*

1 Across the narrow beach we flit,
One little sandpiper and I.
"The Sandpiper," St. 1

2 Look to the East, where up the lucid sky
The morning climbs! The day shall yet be
fair.
"Faith"

3 Sad soul, take comfort, nor forget
That sunrise never failed us yet.
"The Sunrise Never Failed Us Yet,"
St. 4

## 150. Mary Frances Butts

(1836–1902)

\* \* \*

1 Build a little fence of trust
Around today;
Fill the space with loving work,
And therein stay.
"Trust"

## 151. Frances Ridley Havergal

(1836–1879)

\* \* \*

1 Doubt indulged soon becomes doubt realized.
"The Imagination of the Thoughts of
the Heart," *Royal Bounty*

2 Love understands love; it needs no talk.
"Loving Allegiance," *Royal
Commandments*

3 Silence is no certain token
That no secret grief is there;
Sorrow which is never spoken
Is the heaviest load to bear.
"Misunderstood," St. 15

## 152. Marietta Holley

(1836?–1926)

1 Yes, this world is a curious place, very, and
holler, holler as a drum. Lots of times the
ground seems to lay smooth and serene under
your rockin' chair, when all the time a earthquake may be on the very p'int of bustin' it
open and swollerin' you up—chair and all.
"Josiah Allen Gits a Stray," *My
Wayward Pardner; or My Trials
with Josiah, America, the Widow
Bump, and Etcetery* 1880

2 We are blind creeters, the fur-seein'est of us;
weak creeters, when we think we are the strong-
mindedest. Now, when we hear of a crime, it
is easy to say that the one who committed that
wrong stepped flat off from goodness into sin,
and should be hung. It is so awful easy and
sort of satisfactory to condemn other folks'es
faults that we don't stop to think that it may
be that evil was fell into through the weakness
and blindness of a mistake.
Ibid., "Kitty Smith and Caleb Cobb"

3 And then when we read of some noble, splendid act of generosity, our souls burn within us,
and it is easy to say, the one who did that
glorious deed should be throned and crowned
with honor—not thinkin' how, mebby, un-
beknown to us, that act was the costly and
glitterin' varnish coverin' up a whited sepulchre.
That deed was restin' on self-seekin', ambitious
littleness. Ibid.

4 But I am a-eppisodin', and a-eppisodin' to a
length and depth almost onprecedented and
onheard on—and to resoom and go on.
*Samantha at the World's Fair*, Ch. 4
1893

5 And I sez, "Children and trees have to be
tackled young, Josiah, to bend their wills the
way you want 'em to go."
*Around the World with Josiah Allen's
Wife*, Ch. 18 1899

## 153. Jane Ellice Hopkins

(1836–1904)

1 Gift, like genius, I often think only means an
infinite capacity for taking pains.
*Work Amongst Working Men*
1870

## 154. Mary Elizabeth Braddon

(1837–1915)

1 ". . . it is easy to starve, but it is difficult to
stoop." *Lady Audley's Secret*, Ch. 23
1862

2 "Let any man make a calculation of his existence, subtracting the hours in which he has
been *thoroughly* happy—really and entirely at
his ease, without one *arrièr pensée* to mar his
enjoyment—without the most infinitesimal cloud
to overshadow the brightness of his horizon.
Let him do this, and surely he will laugh in
utter bitterness of soul when he sets down the
sum of his felicity, and discovers the pitiful
smallness of the amount." Ibid., Ch. 25

3 There can be no reconciliation where there is no open warfare. There must be a battle, a brave boisterous battle, with pennants waving and cannon roaring, before there can be peaceful treaties and enthusiastic shaking of hands.
　　　　　　　　　　　　　　　　*Ibid.*, Ch. 32

4 She was no longer innocent, and the pleasure we take in art and loveliness, being an innocent pleasure, had passed beyond her reach.
　　　　　　　　　　　　　　　　*Ibid.*

5 "Do you think that there will not come a day in which my meerschaums will be foul, and the French novels more than usually stupid, and life altogether such a dismal monotony that I shall want to get rid of it somehow or other?"
　　　　　　　　　　　　　　　　*Ibid.*, Ch. 41

6 "A priest can achieve great victories with an army of women at his command. How are our churches beautified, our sick tended, our poor fed, our children taught and cared for and civilised? Do you think the masculine element goes for much in these things? No, Westray; women are the Church's strong rock. As they were the last at the foot of the cross, so they have become the first at the altar."
　　　　　　　　*Hostages to Fortune*, Vol. I, Ch. 1
　　　　　　　　　　　　　　　　1875

7 "Progress is a grand word," he said at last, "but how few they are who have the elements of progress in their nature! To go up like a rocket and come down like a stick seems the natural tendency of human genius."
　　　　　　　　　　　　　　　　*Ibid.*, Ch. 3

8 Life, which he had thought worn out and done with, save as a mere mechanical process, seems to have begun afresh for him—life and youth and happiness all renewed together like a second birth.　　　*Ibid.*, Vol. II, Ch. 5

9 "After all, what the world says of a man never yet made his finger ache. But how many a heartache the slave of opinion gives himself!"
　　　　　　　　　　　　　　*Ibid.*, Vol. III, Ch. 2

10 Paris is a mighty schoolmaster, a grand enlightener of the provincial intellect.
　　　　　　　　*The Cloven Foot*, Ch. 4　　1879

11 He had lived for himself alone, and had sinned for his own pleasure; and if his life within the last decade had been comparatively pure and harmless, it was because the bitter apples of the Dead Sea could tempt him no longer by their outward beauty.
　　　　　　　*Dead-Sea Fruit*, Vol. II, Ch. 1
　　　　　　　　　　　　　　　　1868

12 "I do not think the stage, as it is at present constituted, offers a brilliant prospect for any woman. Of course there are exceptional circumstances, and there is exceptional talent; but, unhappily, exceptional talent does not always win its reward unless favoured by exceptional circumstances."　　　*Ibid.*, Ch. 4

13 "Are there not, indeed, brief pauses of mental intoxication, in which the spirit releases itself from its dull mortal bondage, and floats starward on the wings of inspiration?"
　　　　　　　　　　　　　　　　*Ibid.*, Ch. 9

14 "I think that most wearisome institution, the honeymoon, must have been inaugurated by some sworn foe to matrimony, some vile misogynist, who took to himself a wife in order to discover, by experience, the best mode of rendering married life a martyrdom."
　　　　　　　　　　　　　　　　*Ibid.*

15 "My life was one long yawn—and if I still lived, it was only because I knew not what purgatory a perpetual *ennui* might await me on Acheron's further shore."　　　*Ibid.*

16 Flatterers fawned upon him, intimate acquaintances hung fondly upon him, reminding him pathetically that they knew him twenty years ago, when he hadn't a sixpence, as if that knowledge of bygone adversity were a merit and a claim.　　　　　　*Ibid.*, Ch. 14

17 The brother had strange views of life and duty, and a beautiful young woman, essentially worldly and modern, could hardly be expected to get on well with a young man whose master and guide was St. Francis of Assisi.
　　　　　　　*The White House*, Ch. 1　　1906

18 "A London house without visitors is so triste."
　　　　　　　　　　　　　　　　*Ibid.*, Ch. 6

19 He had compelled her to think of the sons of toil as she had never thought before, this world outside the world of Skepton, the lower-grade labour, the unskilled, uncertain, casual work; a life in which thrift would seem impossible, since there was nothing to save, cleanliness and decency impracticable and drunken oblivion the only possible relief.
　　　　　　　　　　　　　　　　*Ibid.*, Ch. 15

20 "I have heard that Africa is irresistible, that the man who has once been there, most of all who has lived there for years, must go back. The mountains and the lakes call him."
　　　　　　　　　　　　　　　　*Ibid.*

21 It may be that Miranda had enjoyed too much of the roses and the lilies of life, and that a girlhood of such absolute indulgence was hardly

the best preparation for the battle which has to come in the lives of women—whatever their temporal advantages—the battle of the heart, or of the brain, the fight with fate, or the fight with man.
*Miranda*, Book I, Ch. 2    *1913*

22 "I hope they won't uglify the house," sighed Lady Laura. "People generally do when they try to improve a sweet, picturesque old place."
Ibid., Book II, Ch. 1

23 "Love is life, love is the lamp that lights the universe: without that light this goodly frame, the earth, is a barren promontory and man the quintessence of dust."    Ibid., Ch. 9

24 Be happy! What a cruel mockery that advice may sometimes sound in the patient's ear! How impossible to obey!    Ibid., Book III, Ch. 13
\* \* \*

25 When once estrangement has arisen between those who truly love each other, everything seems to widen the breach.
*Run to Earth*, Ch. 8

26 "I'm an old stager, ma'am, and have seen a good deal of life, and I have generally found that people who are ready to promise so much before-hand, are apt not to give anything when their work has been done."    Ibid., Ch. 15

## 155. Jeanne Detourbey
(1837–1908)

1 Is it necessary to have read Spinoza in order to make out a laundry list?
Quoted in *Forty Years of Parisian Society* by Arthur Meyer    *1912p*

2 Of course, fortune has its part in human affairs, but conduct is really much more important.    Ibid.

3 So I cannot bear to be told that So-and-so is lucky. Too often the phrase is a covert attack upon the man; for what does it amount to in plain speech but that he is an idiot with nothing but his luck to recommend him?    Ibid.

## 156. Mary Mapes Dodge
(1838?–1905)

1 Should this simple narrative . . . cause even one heart to feel a deeper trust in God's goodness and love, or aid any in weaving a life, wherein, through knots and entanglements, the golden thread shall never be tarnished or

broken, the prayer with which it was begun and ended will have been answered.
*Hans Brinker or The Silver Skates,*
Preface    *1865*

2 . . . in Holland ice is generally an all-winter affair.    Ibid.

3 I'm as true a Protestant, in sooth, as any fine lady that walks into church, but it's not wrong to turn sometimes to the good St. Nicholas.
Ibid.

4 To her mind, the poor peasant-girl Gretel was not a human being, a God-created creature like herself—she was only something that meant poverty, rags and dirt.    Ibid.

5 This kind of work is apt to summon Vertigo, of whom good Hans Andersen writes—the same who hurls daring young hunters from the mountains, or spins them from the sharpest heights of the glaciers, or catches them as they tread the stepping-stones of the mountain torrent.    Ibid., "Jacob Poot Changes the Plan"

6 What a dreadful thing it must be to have a dull father. . . .    Ibid., "Boys and Girls"

7 Ten years dropped from a man's life are no small loss; ten years of manhood, of household happiness and care; ten years of honest labor, of conscious enjoyment of sunshine and outdoor beauty; ten years of grateful life—one day looking forward to all this; the next, waking to find them passed, and a blank.
Ibid., "The Father's Return"

8 . . . the dame was filled with delightful anxieties caused by the unreasonable demands of ten thousand guilders' worth of new wants that had sprung up like mushrooms in a single night.
Ibid., "A Discovery"

9 "It is an ugly business, boy, this surgery," said the doctor, still frowning at Hans, "it requires great patience, self-denial and perseverance."
Ibid., "Broad Sunshine"

10 How faithfully those glancing eyes shall yet seek for the jewels that lie hidden in rocky schoolbooks!    Ibid.

11 "Modern ways are quite alarming,"
Grandma says, "but boys were charming"
(Girls and boys she means, of course) "long ago."
"The Minuet," St. 3    *1879*
\* \* \*

12 All things ready with a will,
April's coming up the Hill.
"Now the Noisy Winds Are Still"

13 Life is a mystery as deep as ever death can be;
Yet oh, how dear it is to us, this life we live
and see!
"The Two Mysteries," St. 3

14 But I believe that God is overhead;
And as life is to the living, so death is to the
dead.
Ibid., St. 5

15 She wants from me, my lady Earth,
Smiles and waits and sighs.
"How the Rain Comes"

## 157. Kate Field
### (1838–1896)
* * *

1 They talk about a woman's sphere,
As though it had a limit.
There's not a place in earth or heaven,
There's not a task to mankind given . . .
Without a woman in it.
"Woman's Spirit"

## 158. Lydia Kamekeha Liliuokalani
### (1838–1917)

1 The Hawaiian people have been from time immemorial lovers of poetry and music, and have
been apt in improvising historic poems, songs
of love, and chants of worship, so that praises
of the living or wails over the dead were with
them but the natural expression of their feelings.          *Hawaii's Story*, Ch. 5     1898

2 Oh, honest Americans, as Christians hear me
for my down-trodden people! Their form of
government is as dear to them as yours is
precious to you. Quite as warmly as you love
your country, so they love theirs. With all your
goodly possessions, covering a territory so immense that there yet remains parts unexplored,
possessing islands that, although near at hand,
had to be neutral ground in time of war, do not
covet the little vineyard of Naboth's, so far
from your shores, lest the punishment of Ahab
fall upon you, if not in your day, in that of
your children, for "be not deceived, God is not
mocked."                    Ibid., Ch. 57
* * *

3 Farewell to thee, farewell to thee,
Thou charming one who dwells among the
bowers,
One fond embrace before I now depart
Until we meet again.
"Aloha Oe"

## 159. Margaret Sangster
### (1838–1912)
* * *

1 And hearts have broken from harsh words
spoken
That sorrow can ne'er set right.
"Our Own," St. 1

2 We have careful thought from the stranger,
And smiles from the sometime guest;
But oft from "our own" the bitter tone,
Though we love our own the best.
Ibid., St. 3

3 And it isn't the thing you do, dear,
It's the thing you leave undone
Which gives you a bit of a heartache
At the setting of the sun.
"The Sin of Omission"

4 Never yet was a springtime
When the buds forgot to blow.
"Awakening"

5 Not always the fanciest cake that's there
Is the best to eat!
"French Pastry," St. 3

6 Out of the chill and the shadow,
Into the thrill and the shine;
Out of the dearth and the famine,
Into the fullness divine.
"Going Home"

7 Prophet and priest he stood
In the storm of embattled years;
The broken chain was his heart's refrain,
And the peace that is balm for tears.
"John Greenleaf Whittier"

## 160. Victoria Claflin Woodhull
### (1838–1927)

1 I have an inalienable constitutional and natural
right to love whom I may, to love as long or
as short a period as I can, to change that love
every day if I please!
Article in *Woodhull and Claflin's
Weekly*     November 20, 1871

2 A Vanderbilt may sit in his office and manipu-
late stocks or declare dividends by which in a
few years he amasses fifty million dollars from
the industries of the country, and he is one of
the remarkable men of the age. But if a poor,
half-starved child should take a loaf of bread
from his cupboard to appease her hunger, she
would be sent to the tombs.
Campaign Speech     1872

3 The wife who submits to sexual intercourse against her wishes or desires, virtually commits suicide; while the husband who compels it, commits murder. . . .     Speech, "The Elixir of Life," American Association of Spiritualists (1873), Chicago, *Feminism,* Miriam Schneir, ed.     *1972p*

4 It is a fact terrible to contemplate, yet it is nevertheless true, and ought to be pressed upon the world for its recognition: that fully one-half of all women seldom or never experience any pleasure whatever in the sexual act. Now this is an impeachment of nature, a disgrace to our civilization.       *Ibid.*

## 161. Mary Clemmer

### (1839–1884)

\* \* \*

1 A shining isle in a stormy sea,
  We seek it ever with smiles and sighs;
To-day is sad. In the bland To-be,
  Serene and lovely To-morrow lies.
          "To-morrow"

2 I lie amid the Goldenrod,
I love to see it lean and nod.
          "Goldenrod"

3 The Indian Summer, the dead Summer's soul.
          "Presence"

4 To serve thy generation, this thy fate:
"Written in water," swiftly fades thy name;
But he who loves his kind does, first or late,
A work too great for fame.
          "The Journalist"

5 Only a newspaper! Quick read, quick lost,
Who sums the treasure that it carries hence?
Torn, trampled under feet, who counts thy cost,
Star-eyed intelligence?
          *Ibid.*

## 162. Ouida

### (1839–1908)

1 . . . with peaches and women, it's only the side next the sun that's tempting.
          *Strathmore*    *1865*

2 What is it that love does to a woman? Without it she only sleeps; with it alone, she lives.
      *Wisdom, Wit and Pathos*    *1884*

3 To vice, innocence must always seem only a superior kind of chicanery.
      *Ibid.,* "Two Little Wooden Shoes" (1874)

4 Fame has only the span of a day, they say. But to live in the hearts of the people—that is worth something.     *Ibid.,* "Signa" (1875)

5 The song that we hear with our ears is only the song that is sung in our hearts.
          *Ibid.,* "Ariadne" (1877)

6 Petty laws breed great crimes.
          *Ibid.,* "Pipistrello" (1880)

7 Take hope from the heart of man, and you make him a beast of prey.
       *Ibid.,* "A Village Commune" (1881)

8 She knew how to be "so naughty and so nice" in the way that society in London likes and never punishes.     *Ibid.,* "Moths"

9 A cruel story runs on wheels, and every hand oils the wheels as they run.     *Ibid.*

\* \* \*

10 Christianity has ever been the enemy of human love.     "The Failure of Christianity"

11 Christianity has made of death a terror which was unknown to the gay calmness of the Pagan.
          *Ibid.*

## 163. Frances Willard

### (1839–1898)

1 Geology teaches that death was in the world before sin, which is contrary to the Bible. But it is nowhere stated in the Bible that sin was the cause of the death of any save man: he only has sinned. Any other idea is a superstition and without foundation.
    Quoted in *Frances Willard: Her Life and Work,* Ch. 2, by Ray Strachey *1912p*

2 Here's a recipe for the abolishment of the Blues which is worth a dozen medical nostrums:
  Take one spoonful of Pleasant memories.
  Take two spoonfuls of Endeavours for the Happiness of others.
  Take two spoonfuls of Forgetfulness of Sorrow.
  Mix well with half a pint of Cheerfulness.
  Take a portion every hour of the day.
      *Ibid.,* Journal Entry (c.1860)

3 Germany is the purgatory of women and dogs.
      *Ibid,* Journal Entry (November 30, 1868), Ch. 5

4 The world is wide, and I will not waste my life in friction when it could be turned into momentum.     *Ibid.,* Ch. 6

5 Recognising that our cause is, and will be, combated by mighty, determined, and relentless forces, we will, trusting in Him who is the Prince of Peace, meet argument with argument, misjudgment with patience, denunciations with kindness, and all our difficulties and dangers with prayer.          Ibid., Ch. 7

6 Everything is not in the temperance movement, but the temperance movement should be in everything.          Ibid., Ch. 11

## 164. Mary Branch
### (1840–1922)

\* \* \*

1 So, I think, God hides some souls away,
Sweetly to surprise us, the last day.
          "The Petrified Fern"

## 165. Elizabeth York Case
### (1840?–1911)

\* \* \*

1 There is no unbelief;
Whoever plants a seed beneath the sod
And waits to see it push away the clod,
    He trusts in God.
          "There Is No Unbelief"

## 166. Harriet King
### (1840–1920)

\* \* \*

1 Measure thy life by loss instead of gain,
Not by the wine drunk, but by the wine poured forth.
          "The Disciples"

## 167. Helena Modjeska
### (1840–1910)

1 Alas! it was not my destiny to die for my country, as was my cherished dream, but instead of becoming the heroine I had to be satisfied with acting heroines, exchanging the armor for tinsel, and the weapon for words.
          *Memories and Impressions*, Pt. I, Ch. 1
          *1910*

2 It is never right to be more Catholic than the Pope.          Ibid., Ch. 25

3 . . . the word "great" is not sufficient anymore, if you do not add to it, "Genius!" In Europe the word "genius" is only applied to

the greatest of the world, but here [in America] it has become an everyday occurrence.
          Ibid., Pt. III, Ch. 51

4 It seems to me that there are only two schools, one of good acting, the other of bad acting.
          Ibid.

5 We foreigners, born outside of the magic pale of the Anglo-Saxon race, place Shakespeare upon a much higher pedestal. We claim that, before being English, he was human, and that his creations are not bound either by local or ethnological limits, but belong to humanity in general.          Ibid.

## 168. Marilla Ricker
### (1840–1920)

1 The only thing that ever came back from the grave that we know of was a lie.
          *The Philistine*, Vol. XXV
          *c.1901*

2 He [Thomas Paine] was as democratic as nature, as impartial as sun and rain.          Ibid.

## 169. Katharine Walker
### (1840–1916)

1 However divinity schools may refuse to "skip" in unison, and may butt and butter each other about the doctrine and origin of human depravity, all will join devoutly in the credo, I believe in the total depravity of inanimate things.          "The Total Depravity of Inanimate
          Things," *Atlantic Monthly*
          *September, 1864*

2 The elusiveness of soap, the knottiness of strings, the transitory nature of buttons, the inclination of suspenders to twist and of hooks to forsake their lawful eyes, and cleave only unto the hairs of their hapless owner's head.
          Ibid.

## 170. Elizabeth Wordsworth
### (1840–1932)

1 If all the good people were clever,
And all the clever people were good,
The world would be nicer than ever
We thought that it possibly could.

But somehow, 'tis seldom or never
The two hit it off as they should;
The good are so harsh to the clever,
The clever so rude to the good.
          "The Good and the Clever,"
          *St. Christopher and Other Poems*
          *1890*

## 171. Mary Wood Allen
### (1841–1908)

1 Woman embroiders man's life—Embroider is
to beautify—The embroidery of cleanliness—
Of a smile—Of gentle words.
*What a Young Girl Ought to Know,*
Summary    *1897*

## 172. Mathilde Blind
### (1841–1896)
\* \* \*

1 Children mothered by the saint . . .
Blossoms of humanity!
Poor soiled blossoms in the dust!
"The St.-Children's Dance"

2 The dead abide with us. Though stark and
cold,
Earth seems to grip them, they are with us
still:
They have forged our chains of being of good
or ill,
And their invisible hands these hands yet hold.
"The Dead"

3 The moon returns, and the spring; birds warble,
trees burst into leaf,
But love once gone, goes forever, and all that
endures is the grief.
"Love Trilogy," No. 3

## 173. Sarah Knowles Bolton
### (1841–1916)
\* \* \*

1          He alone is great
Who by a life heroic conquers fate.
"The Inevitable"

## 174. Mary Lathbury
### (1841–1913)

1 Day is dying in the west;
Heaven is touching earth with rest.
"Day Is Dying in the West," St. 1
*1877*
\* \* \*

2 Children of yesterday,
Heirs of tomorrow,
What are you weaving?
Labor and sorrow?
"Song of Hope," St. 1

## 175. Kate Brownlee Sherwood
### (1841–1914)

1 One heart, one hope, one destiny, one flag from
sea to sea.
"Albert Sidney Johnstone,"
*Dream of the Ages    1893*

## 176. Sarah Sadie Williams
### (1841–1868)
\* \* \*

1 Is it so, O Christ in heaven, that the highest
suffer most,
That the strongest wander farthest, and more
hopelessly are lost,
That the mark of rank in nature is capacity for
pain,
That the anguish of the singer makes the sweetness of the strain?
"Is It So, O Christ in Heaven?"

## 177. Mary Elizabeth Brown
### (1842–1917)
\* \* \*

1 I'll go where you want me to go, dear Lord,
O'er mountain, or plain, or sea;
I'll say what you want me to say, dear Lord,
I'll be what you want me to be.
"I'll Go Where You Want Me to Go"

## 178. Ina Coolbrith
### (1842–1928)
\* \* \*

1 He walks with God upon the hills!
And sees, each morn, the world arise
New-bathed in light of paradise.
"The Poet"

## 179. May Riley Smith
### (1842–1927)

1 How these little hands remind us,
As in snowy grace they lie,
Not to scatter thorns—but roses—
For our reaping by and by.
"If We Knew," St. 3    *1867*

2 Strange we never prize the music
Till the sweet-voiced bird has flown. . . .
Ibid., St. 4

3 Let us gather up the sunbeams
   Lying all around our path;
   Let us keep the wheat and roses,
   Casting out the thorns and chaff.
                              Ibid., St. 6

4 God's plan, like lilies pure and white, unfold.
   We must not tear the close-shut leaves apart.
   Time will reveal the calyxes of gold.
         "Sometime," *Sometime and Other*
                           *Poems*     *1892*

* * *

5 My life's a pool which can only hold
   One star and a glimpse of blue.
         "My Life Is a Bowl," St. 2

## 180.  Sarah Doudney
### (1843–1926)

1 Oh, the wasted hours of life
   That have drifted by!
   Oh, the good that might have been,
   Lost without a sigh.
         "The Lesson of the Water-Mill"
                                    *1864*

2 "No," said Faith sternly, "we don't want this
   girl to be hanged; we wish her to spend a useful life, full of repentance and good deeds."
         *Faith Harrowby; or, The Smuggler's*
                   *Cave*, Ch. 4     *1871*

3 "Ah, how good God is to me! He has not suffered me to be tried and tempted! Had I been
   in her place I might have done just the same."
                                        Ibid.

4 "There are no such things as mermaids," exclaimed Frank, her schoolboy brother; "and if
   there are, their company wouldn't suit you,
   Ada. How do you suppose you would get on
   under the sea, with no circulating library, no
   dressmakers and milliners, and knick knacks
   and fal-lals?"                Ibid., Ch. 19

5 We love thee well, but Jesus loves thee best.
         "The Christian's Good-Night     *1892*

* * *

6 But the waiting time, my brothers,
   Is the hardest time of all.
         "The Hardest Time of All,"
                   *Psalms of Life*

7 Take the sweetness of a gift unsought,
   And for the pansies send me back a thought.
                                   "Pansies"

## 181.  Violet Fane
### (1843–1905)

* * *

1 Ah, "All things come to those who wait,"
   (I say these words to make me glad),
   But something answers soft and sad,
   "They come, but often come too late."
         "Tout Vient à Qui Sait Attendre"

2 Let me arise and open the gate,
   To breathe the wild warm air of the heath,
   And to let in Love, and to let out Hate,
   And anger at living and scorn of Fate,
   To let in Life, and to let out Death.
                                 "Reverie"

3 Nothing is right and nothing is just;
   We sow in ashes and reap in dust.
                                    Ibid.

## 182.  Anna Hamilton
### (1843–1875)

* * *

1 This learned I from the shadow of a tree,
   That to and fro did sway against a wall,
   Our shadow selves, our influence, may fall
   Where we ourselves can never be.
                               "Influence"

## 183.  Caroline Le Row
### (1843–?)

* * *

1 But I will write of him who fights
   And vanquishes his sins,
   Who struggles on through weary years
   Against himself and wins.
                           "True Heroism"

## 184.  Isabella Stephenson
### (1843–1890)

* * *

1 Holy Father, in Thy mercy,
   Hear our anxious prayer,
   Keep our loved ones, now far absent,
   'Neath thy care.
         "Holy Father, in Thy Mercy"

## 185.  Bertha von Suttner
### (1843–1914)

1 After the verb "To Love," "To Help" is the
   most beautiful verb in the world!
         "Epigram," *Ground Arms*     *1892*

## 186. Carmen Sylva

(1843–1916)

1 Life was a radiant maiden, the daughter of the Sun, endowed with all the charm and grace, all the power and happiness, which only such a mother could give to her child.
"The Child of the Sun," *Pilgrim Sorrow* 1884

2 But Truth was not in love, neither was it in renunciation, for I murmured and knew not why I should renounce. Ibid., "A Life"

3 Surely he could never have borne such a life, and must have died of misery, save for one only consolation. Every man must have some such, be it only a dog, a flower, or a spider. Ovid had a snake, a tiny, bewitching snake. . . .
"The Serpent Isle," *Legends from River and Mountain* 1896

4 Complaints were heard no longer, for dull despair had reduced all men to silence; and when the starving people tore one another to pieces, no one even told of it.
Ibid., "Rîul Doamnei"

5 " 'Tis the ignorant who boast. . . ."
Ibid., "The Nixies' Cleft"

6 . . . he hesitated to pluck the fruit, for fear it should leave a bitter taste behind.
Ibid., "A Doubting Lover"

7 "It seems to me," said a young man who, sitting by the fire in deep study over a roll of paper, had not yet spoken, "that in these tales of yours, only those came to harm who themselves sought after money, greedily, and merely for their own use. But methinks, after all, the best and safest way of getting wealth is to work for it. I, too, hope to find a pot of gold in the earth, but not by your manner of seeking it."
Ibid., "Seekers After Gold"

8 "Ill could I resign myself to dwell forever shut in between four walls. I must be free, free to roam where I please, like the birds in the woodlands." "Carma, the Harp-Girl," *Real Queen's Fairy Tales* 1901

9 "One cannot help those who will not help themselves, so we felt it would be quite useless for us to come again."
Ibid., "The Little People"

10 There was another thing that did not exist in these islands; that was money. The swans would never have permitted anything so low and degrading to enter their domain. Gold they tolerated, but merely for ornamentation, where it could light up some dull surface. But to traffic with money, and to bargain, and to barter—that was unheard of. Ibid., "The Swan Lake"

11 "Our work was only play, we never knew what it was to feel fatigue; and as for loving others, since it has been granted to us to see how all things are, and have been, and must ever be, how should any feeling but love and infinite compassion fill our hearts for all who live?"
Ibid.

12 The pangs
Are hushed, for life is wild no more with strife,
Nor breathless uphill work, nor heavy with
The brewing tempests, which have torn away
So much, that nothing more remains to fear.
"A Friend," St. 3, *Sweet Hours* 1904

13 Our life is seldom open,
For love and fear have shut it.
Ibid., "Out of the Deep," St. 2

14 Great Solitude
Hath one thousand voices and a flood of light,
Be not afraid, enter the Sanctuary,
Thou wilt be taken by the hand and led
To Life's own fountain, never-ending Thought!
Ibid., "Solitude"

15 Ye not dare tell
Your heart what it has suffered, dare not look
Into the past again, for fear of turning
To stone, for white lipped fear of waking from
Its sleep that heart to make it throb again,
Like millstones.
Ibid., "Rest"

## 187. St. Bernadette

(1844–1879)

1 I fear only bad Catholics.
Quoted in *Lourdes* by Edith Sanders 1940p

## 188. Sarah Bernhardt

(1844–1923)

1 Cloister existence is one of unbroken sameness for all. . . . The rumor of the outside world dies away at the heavy cloister gate.
*Memories of My Life*, Ch. 3 1907

2 For the theatre one needs long arms; it is better to have them too long than too short. An *artiste* with short arms can never, never make a fine gesture. Ibid., Ch. 6

3 Those who know the joys and miseries of celebrity . . . know. . . . It is a sort of octopus with innumerable tentacles. It throws out its clammy arms on the right and on the left, in front and behind, and gathers into its thousand little inhaling organs all the gossip and slander and praise afloat to spit out again at the public when it is vomiting its black gall.

> Ibid., Ch. 22

## 189. Madeline Bridges

### (1844–1920)

\* \* \*

1 Then give to the world the best you have,
And the best will come back to you.

> "Life's Mirror," St. 1

2 And a smile that is sweet will surely find
A smile that is just as sweet.

> Ibid., St. 3

3 When Psyche's friend becomes her lover,
How sweetly these conditions blend!
But, oh, what anguish to discover
Her lover has become—her friend!

> "Friend and Lover"

## 190. Bertha Buxton

### (1844–1881)

1 After all, the eleventh commandment (thou shalt not be found out) is the only one that is virtually impossible to keep in these days.

> *Jenny of the Princes*, Ch. 3
> 1879

## 191. Mary Cassatt

### (1844–1926)

1 I am independent! I can live alone and I love to work. Sometimes it made him [Degas] furious that he could not find a chink in my armor, and there would be months when we just could not see each other, and then something I painted would bring us together again. . . .

> Quoted in *Sixteen to Sixty, Memoirs of a Collector* by Louisine W.
> Havemeyer    *1930p*

2 A woman artist must be . . . capable of making the primary sacrifices.

> Quoted in "Mary Cassatt" by Forbes
> Watson, *Arts Weekly*   *1932p*

3 You know how hard it is to inaugurate anything like independent action among French artists, and we are carrying on a despairing fight and need all our forces, as every year there are new deserters. . . .

> Letter to J. Alden Weir, Paris
> (March 10, 1878), Quoted in
> *Mary Cassatt: A Biography
> of the Great American Painter*
> by Nancy Hale    *1975p*

4 The occasion [World's Colombian Exposition, Women's Building mural, 1893] is one of rejoicing, a great national fête. . . . I reserved all the seriousness for the execution, for the drawing and painting.

> Ibid., Letter to Mrs. Potter Palmer
> (October 11, 1892)

5 Yet in spite of the total disregard of the dictionary of manners, he [Cézanne] shows a politeness toward us which no other man here would have shown. . . . Cézanne is one of the most liberal artists I have ever seen. He prefaces every remark with *Pour moi* it is so and so, but he grants that everyone may be as honest and as true to nature from their convictions; he doesn't believe that everyone should see alike.    Ibid., Letter to Mrs. Stillman

> (1894)

6 Why do people so love to wander? I think the civilized parts of the World will suffice for me in the future.

> Ibid., Letter to Louisine Havemeyer
> (February 11, 1911)

## 192. Elizabeth Stuart Phelps

### (1844–1911)

1 Who originated that most exquisite of inquisitions, the condolence system?

> *The Gates Ajar*, Ch. 2    *1869*

2 That a girl could possibly be pretty with straight hair, had never once entered her mind. All the little girls in story-books had curls. Whoever heard of the straight-haired maiden that made wreaths of the rosebuds, or saw the fairies, or married the Prince?

> *Gypsy Breynton*, Ch. 1    *1876*

3 "There are several disadvantages in being a girl, my dear, as you will find out, occasionally," said Tom, with a lordly air.

> Ibid., Ch. 4

4 I must say distinctly that, though after the act of dying I departed from the surface of the earth, and reached the confines of a different locality, I cannot yet instruct another *where* this place may be.

> *Beyond the Gates*, Ch. 3    *1883*

5 The meaning of liberty broke upon me like a sunburst. Freedom was in and of itself the highest law. Had I thought that death was to mean release from personal obedience? Lo, death itself was but the elevation of moral claims, from lower to higher.          Ibid.

6 I mean that the *soul of a sense* is a more exquisite thing than what we may call the body of the sense, as developed to earthly consciousness.          Ibid., Ch. 11

7 The great law of denial belongs to the powerful forces of life, whether the case be one of coolish baked beans, or an unrequited affection.
          *A Singular Life*, Ch, 1          *1896*

## 193. Margaret Sidney

(1844–1924)

1 The little old kitchen had quieted down from the bustle and confusion of mid-day; and now, with its afternoon manners on, presented a holiday aspect, that as the principal room in the brown house, it was eminently proper it should have.
          "A Home View," *Five Little Peppers and How They Grew*          *1881*

2 "And you're very impertinent, too," said Miss Jerusha; "a good child *never* is impertinent."
          Ibid., "New Friends"

3 . . . "we've got to do something 'cause we've begun. . . ."          Ibid., "Getting a Christmas for the Little Ones"

4 "It's better'n a Christmas," they told their mother, "to get ready for it!"          Ibid.

5 . . . "it can't be Christmas all the time."
          Ibid., "Christmas Bells"

6 "Corners are for little folks; but when people who know better, do wrong, there aren't any corners they *can* creep into, or they'd get into them pretty quick!"
          Ibid., "Which Treats of a Good Many Matters"

7 "You're just the splendidest, *goodest* mamsie in all the world. And I'm a hateful cross old bear, so I am!"          Ibid., "Polly's Dismal Morning"

## 194. Arabella Smith

(1844–1916)

\* \* \*

1 Oh, friends! I pray to-night,
Keep not your roses for my dead, cold brow
The way is lonely, let me feel them now.
          "If I Should Die To-Night"

## 195. Sophie Tolstoy

(1844–1919)

1 One can't live on love alone; and I am so stupid that I can do nothing but think of him.
          *A Diary of Tolstoy's Wife, 1860–1891*
          (November 13, 1862)          *1928p*

2 Of course I am idle, but I am not idle by nature; I simply haven't yet discovered what I can do here. . . .
          Ibid. (November 23, 1862)

3 I am a source of satisfaction to him, a nurse, a piece of furniture, a *woman*—nothing more.
          Ibid. (November 13, 1863)

4 As for me, I both *can* and *want* to do everything, but after a while I begin to realize there is nothing to want, and that I can't do anything beyond eating, drinking, sleeping, nursing the children, and caring for them and my husband. After all, this *is* happiness, yet why do I grow sad and weep, as I did yesterday?
          Ibid. (February 25, 1865)

5 The thing to do is *not* to love, to be clever and sly, and to hide all one's bad points. . . .
          Ibid. (September 12, 1865)

6 I want nothing but his love and sympathy, and he won't give it me; and all my pride is trampled in the mud; I am nothing but a miserable crushed worm, whom no one wants, whom no one loves, a useless creature with morning sickness, and a big belly, two rotten teeth, and a bad temper, a battered sense of dignity, and a love which nobody wants and which nearly drives me insane.          Ibid.

7 It makes me laugh to read over this diary. It's so full of contradictions, and one would think I was such an unhappy woman. Yet is there a happier woman than I?
          Ibid. (July 31, 1868)

8 How deep is the unconscious hatred of even one's nearest people, and how great their selfishness.          Ibid. (October 25, 1886)

9 He would like to destroy his old diaries and to appear before his children and the public only in his patriarchal robes. His vanity is immense!
          Ibid. (December 17, 1890)

10 It is sad that my emotional dependence on the man I love should have killed so much of my energy and ability; there was certainly once a great deal of energy in me.
          Ibid. (December 31, 1890)

## 196. Tennessee Claflin
### (1845–1923)

1 If the disenfranchised woman should still be compelled to remain the servile, docile, meekly-acquiescent, self-immolated and self-abnegative wife, there would be no difficulty about the voting. At the ballot-box is not where the shoe pinches. . . . It is at home where the husband . . . is the supreme ruler, that the little difficulty arises; he will not surrender this absolute power unless he is compelled.

> "Constitutional Equality, a Right of Women"    *1871*

2 A *free* man is a noble being; a *free* woman is a contemptible being. . . . In other terms, the use of this one word, in its two-fold application to men and to women, reveals the unconscious but ever present conviction in the public mind that men tend, of course, heavenward in their natures and development, and that women tend just as naturally hellward.

> Article in *Woodhull and Claflin's Weekly*    *1871*

3 The revolt against any oppression usually goes to an opposite extreme for a time; and that is right and necessary.    Ibid.

4 The world enslaves our sex by the mere fear of an epithet; and as long as it can throw any vile term at us, before which we cower, it can maintain our enslavement.    Ibid.

5 He or she who would be free must defy the enemy, and must be *ultra* enough to exhaust the possibilities of the enemy's assault; and it will not be until women can contemplate and accept unconcernedly whatsoever imputation an ignorant, bitter, lying and persecuting world may heap on them that they will be really free.

> Ibid.

6 When people had slaves, they expected that their pigs, chickens, corn and everything lying loose about the plantation would be stolen. But the planters began by stealing the liberty of their slaves, by stealing their labor, by stealing, in fact, all they had; and the natural result was that the slaves stole back all they could.

> Ibid., "Which Is to Blame?"    *1872*

## 197. Susan Coolidge
### (1845–1905)
\* \* \*

1 "A commonplace life," we say and we sigh;
But why would we sigh as we say?
The commonplace sun in the commonplace sky
Makes up the commonplace day.

> "Commonplace"

2 And God, who studies each commonplace soul,
Out of commonplace things makes His beauty whole.

> Ibid.

3 Men die, but sorrow never dies;
The crowding years divide in vain,
And the wide world is knit with ties
Of common brotherhood in pain.

> "The Cradle Tomb in Westminster Abbey"

4 New morn has come
And with the morn the punctual tide again.

> "Floodtide"

5 Slow buds the pink dawn like a rose
From out night's gray and cloudy sheath;
Softly and still it grows and grows,
Petal by petal, leaf by leaf.

> "The Morning Comes Before the Sun"

6 Yesterday's errors let yesterday cover.

> "New Every Morning"

## 198. Emily Hickey
### (1845–1924)
\* \* \*

1 Beloved, it is morn!
A redder berry on the thorn,
A deeper yellow on the corn,
For this good day new-born!
Pray, Sweet, for me
That I may be
Faithful to God and thee.

> "Beloved, It Is Morn"

2 Strive we, and do, lest by-and-by we sit
In that blind life to which all other fate
Is cause for envy. . . .

> "Michael Villiers, Idealist"

## 199. Margaret Janvier
### (1845–1913)
\* \* \*

1 You needn't try to comfort me—
I tell you my dolly is dead!
There's no use in saying she isn't, with
A crack like that in her head.

> "The Dead Doll," St. 1

## 200. Katharine Bradley
### (1846–1914)

* * *

1 Come, mete out my loneliness, O wind,
For I would know
How far the living who must stay behind
Are from the dead who go.
"Mete Out My Loneliness," with
Edith Cooper

2 Sweet and of their nature vacant are the days
I spend—
Quiet as a plough laid by at the furrow's end.
"Old Age," with Edith Cooper

3 The enchanting miracles of change.
"Renewal," with Edith Cooper

## 201. Anna Dostoevsky
### (1846–1918)

1 From a timid, shy girl I had become a woman
of resolute character, who could not longer be
frightened by the struggle with troubles.
*Dostoevsky Portrayed by His Wife*
(c.1871)     *1926p*

2 It seems to me that he has never loved, that he
has only imagined that he has loved, that there
has been no real love on his part. I even think
that he is incapable of love; he is too much
occupied with other thoughts and ideas to become strongly attached to anyone earthly.
Ibid. (1887)

## 202. Anna Green
### (1846–1935)

* * *

1 Hath the spirit of all beauty
Kissed you in the path of duty?
"On the Threshold"

## 203. Princess Kazu-no-miya
### (1846–1877)

1 Please understand the heart of one who leaves
as the water in the streams; never to return again.     Untitled Poem     *1861*

2 I wear the magnificent dress of brocade and
damask in vain, now that you are not here
to admire it.
Untitled Poem     *1866*

3 I would cross the river with you, if there were
no barrier to stop me.
Untitled Poem     *1866*

## 204. Carry Nation
### (1846–1911)

1 The women and children of Barber County are
calling to you men for bread, for clothes, and
education. . . . [Instead] men in Medicine Lodge
and other towns of Barber County are selling
whiskey. . . . No wonder the women want the
ballot.     Quoted in *Cyclone Carry*
by Carleton Beals     *1962p*

2 Who hath sorrow? Who hath woe?
They who do not answer no;
They whose feet to sin incline,
While they tarry at the wine.
Ibid., Ch. 12

3 A woman is stripped of everything by them
[saloons]. Her husband is torn from her; she is
robbed of her sons, her home, her food, and
her virtue; and then they strip her clothes off
and hang her up bare in these dens of robbery
and murder. Truly does the saloon make a
woman bare of all things!
Ibid. (c.1893), Ch. 14

4 You have put me in here [jail] a cub, but I
will come out roaring like a lion, and I will
make all hell howl!     Ibid. (c.1901)

## 205. Annie Wood Besant
### (1847–1933)

1 There is no birthright in the white skin that it
shall say that wherever it goes, to any nation,
amongst any people, there the people of the
country shall give way before it, and those to
whom the land belongs shall bow down and
become its servants. . . .
*Wake Up, India: A Plea for
Social Reform*     *1913*

2 For I believe that the colour bar and all it implies are largely due to thoughtlessness, to silly
pride, to the pride of race, which has grown
mad in a country where there is no public
opinion to check it.     Ibid.

3 . . . when there shall be no differences save by
merit of character, by merit of ability, by merit
of service to the country. Those are the true
tests of the value of any man or woman, white
or coloured; those who can serve best, those
who help most, those who sacrifice most, those
are the people who will be loved in life and
honoured in death, when all questions of colour
are swept away and when in a free country free
citizens shall meet on equal grounds.     Ibid.

## 206. Mary Catherwood
### (1847–1901)

1 They [the Chippewa] were a people ruled only by persuasive eloquence moving on the surface of their passion. . . .
*The White Islander*, Pt. I    *1893*

2 He reveled in this swimming of the wilderness. He had capacities for woodcraft. It gave freedom to a repressed and manly part of him, and in the darkness of the buried path he breathed largely.      Ibid., Pt. II

3 Two may talk together under the same roof for many years, yet never really meet; and two others at first speech are old friends.
"Marianson," *Mackinac and Lake Stories*    *1899*

4 Though in those days of the young century a man might become anything; for the West was before him, an empire, and woodcraft was better than learning.
Ibid., "The Black Feather"

5 She might struggle like a fly in a web. He wrapped her around and around with beautiful sentences.      Ibid., "The King of Beaver"

6 "O God, since Thou hast shut me up in this world, I will do the best I can, without fear or favor. When my task is done, let me out!"
Ibid.

7 The world of city-maddened people who swarmed to this lake for their annual immersion in nature. . . .
Ibid., "The Cursed Patois"

## 207. Alice Meynell
### (1847–1922)
\*   \*   \*

1     And when you go
There's loneliness in loneliness.
"Song"

2 A voice peals in this end of night
A phrase of notes resembling stars,
Single and spiritual notes of light.
"A Thrush Before Dawn"

3 Dear Laws, be wings to me!
The feather merely floats, O be it heard
Through weight of life—the skylark's gravity—
That I am not a feather, but a bird!
"The Laws of Verse"

4 Flocks of the memories of the day draw near
The dovecote doors of sleep.
"At Night"

5 I come from nothing: but from where
come the undying thoughts I bear?
"The Modern Poet, or a
Song of Derivations"

6 I shall not hold my little peace; for me
There is no peace but one.
"The Poet to the Birds"

7 My heart shall be thy garden.
"The Garden"

8 New every year,
New born and newly dear,
He comes with tidings and a song,
The ages long, the ages long.
"Unto Us a Son Is Given"

9 O Spring! I know thee.
"In Early Spring"

10 She walks—the lady of my delight—
A shepherdess of sheep
Her flocks are thoughts.
"The Shepherdess," St. 1

11 The sense of humour has other things to do than to make itself conspicuous in the act of laughter.
"Laughter"

12 With the first dream that comes with the first sleep
I run, I run, I am gathered to thy heart.
"Renouncement"

## 208. Julia A. Moore
### (1847–1920)
\*   \*   \*

1 And now, kind friends, what I have wrote
I hope you will pass over,
And not critjcize as some have done
Hitherto herebefore.
"To My Friends and Critics"

2 Leave off the agony, leave off style,
Unless you've got money by us all the while.
"Leave Off the Agony in Style"

## 209. Annie Rankin Annan
### (1848–1925)
\*   \*   \*

1 A dandelion in his verse,
Like the first gold in childhood's purse.
"Dandelions"

## 210. Alice James
(1848–1892)

1 It is so comic to hear oneself called old, even at ninety I suppose!      Letter to William James (June 14, 1889), *The Diary of Alice James,* Leon Edel, ed.     *1964p*

2 . . . the immutable law that however great we may seem to our own consciousness no human being would exchange his for ours. . . .
     Ibid. (July 7, 1889)

3 Ah! Those strange people who have the courage to be unhappy! *Are* they unhappy, by-the-way?
     Ibid.

4 How sick one gets of being "good," how much I should respect myself if I could burst out and make every one wretched for twenty-four hours; embody selfishness. . . .
     Ibid. (December 11, 1889)

5 It is an immense loss to have all robust and sustaining expletives refined away from one! At . . . moments of trial refinement is a feeble reed to lean upon.
     Ibid. (December 12, 1889)

6 . . . who would ever give up the reality of dreams for relative knowledge?     Ibid.

7 Every hour I live I become an intenser devotee to common-sense!     Ibid. (June 16, 1890)

8 I suppose one has a greater sense of intellectual degradation after an interview with a doctor than from any human experience.
     Ibid. (September 27, 1890)

9 Having it to look forward to for a while seems to double the value of the event. . . .
     Ibid. (June 1, 1891)

10 The grief is all for K. and H.,* who will *see* it all [her death], whilst I shall only feel it. . . .
     Ibid.

11 The difficulty about all this dying is that you can't tell a fellow anything about it, so where does the fun come in?
     Ibid. (December 11, 1891)

12 . . . I feel sure that it can't be possible but what the bewildered little hammer that keeps me going will very shortly see the decency of ending his distracted career; . . . physical pain however great ends in itself and falls away like dry husks from the mind, whilst moral discords and nervous horrors sear the soul.
     Ibid. (March 4, 1892)

* K. is Katharine Loring Peabody, her companion and nurse; H. is Henry James, her brother.

13 Notwithstanding the poverty of my outside experience, I have always had a significance for myself, and every chance to stumble along my straight and narrow little path, and to worship at the feet of my Deity, and what more can a human soul ask for?     Ibid. (1892)

## 211. Catherine Liddell
(1848–?)

\* \* \*

1 "Isn't this Joseph's son?"—ah, it is He; Joseph the carpenter—same trade as me.
     "Jesus the Carpenter"

## 212. Ellen Terry
(1848–1928)

1 Imagination! imagination! I put it first years ago, when I was asked what qualities I thought necessary for success upon the stage. And I am still of the same opinion. Imagination, industry, and intelligence—"the three I's"—are all indispensable to the actress, but of these three the greatest is, without any doubt, imagination.
     *The Story of My Life*, Ch. 2 *1908*

2 Some people are "tone-deaf," and they find it physically impossible to observe the law of contrasts. But even a physical deficiency can be overcome by that faculty for taking infinite pains which may not be genius but is certainly a good substitute for it.     Ibid., Ch. 4

3 What is a diary as a rule? A document useful to the person who keeps it, dull to the contemporary who reads it, invaluable to the student, centuries afterwards, who treasures it!
     Ibid., Ch. 14

4 Wonderful women! Have you ever thought how much we all, and women especially, owe to Shakespeare for his vindication of women in these fearless, high-spirited, resolute and intelligent heroines?
     "The Triumphant Women," Lecture (1911), *Four Lectures on Shakespeare* *1932p*

## 213. Frances Burnett
(1849–1924)

1 "Are you a 'publican, Mary?" "Sorra a bit," sez I; "I'm the bist o' dimmycrats!" An' he looks up at me wid a look that ud go to yer heart, an' sez he: "Mary," sez he, "the country

will go to ruin." An' nivver a day since thin has he let go by widout argyin' wid me to change me polytics.
> *Little Lord Fauntleroy*, Ch. 1    *1888*

2 It is astonishing how short a time it takes for very wonderful things to happen.
> *Ibid.*, Ch. 14

## 214. Sarah Orne Jewett
### (1849–1909)

1 A harbor, even if it is a little harbor, is a good thing. . . . It takes something from the world and has something to give in return.
> "River Driftwood," *Country By-Ways*    *1886*

2 This was one of those perfect New England days in late summer where the spirit of autumn takes a first stealthy flight, like a spy, through the ripening country-side, and, with feigned sympathy for those who droop with August heat, puts her cool cloak of bracing air about leaf and flower and human shoulders.
> "The Courting of Sister Wisby," *Atlantic Monthly*    *1887*

3 "Now I'm a believer, and I try to live a Christian life, but I'd as soon hear a surveyor's book read out, figgers an' all, as try to get any simple truth out o' most sermons."    *Ibid.*

4 The thing that teases the mind over and over for years, and at last gets itself put down rightly on paper—whether little or great, it belongs to Literature.
> Letter to Willa Cather in Preface, *The Country of the Pointed Firs and Other Stories*    *1896*

5 Wrecked on the lee shore of age.
> *Ibid.*, Ch. 7

6 Tact is after all a kind of mind reading.
> *Ibid.*, Ch. 10

7 "Yes'm, old friends is always best, 'less you can catch a new one that's fit to make an old one out of."    *Ibid.*, Ch. 12

8 "T'ain't worthwhile to wear a day all out before it comes."    *Ibid.*, Ch. 16

9 The road was new to me, as roads always are, going back.    *Ibid.*, Ch. 19

10 So we die before our own eyes; so we see some chapters of our lives come to their natural end.    *Ibid.*

11 God bless them all who die at sea!
If they must sleep in restless waves,
God make them dream they are ashore,
With grass above their graves.
> "The Gloucester Mother," St. 3    *1908*

\* \* \*

12 A lean sorrow is hardest to bear.
> *Life of Nancy*

## 215. Ellen Key
### (1849–1926)

1 Poverty hinders suitable marriages.
> *The Century of the Child*, Ch. 1    *1909*

2 . . . the emancipation of women is practically the greatest egoistic movement of the nineteenth century, and the most intense affirmation of the right of the self that history has yet seen. . . .    *Ibid.*, Ch. 2

3 According to my method of thinking, and that of many others, not woman but the mother is the most precious possession of the nation, so precious that society advances its highest well-being when it protects the functions of the mother.    *Ibid.*

4 All philanthropy—no age has seen more of it than our own—is only a savoury fumigation burning at the mouth of a sewer. This incense offering makes the air more endurable to passersby, but it does not hinder the infection in the sewer from spreading.    *Ibid.*

5 For success in training children the first condition is to become as a child oneself, but this means no assumed childishness, no condescending baby-talk that the child immediately sees through and deeply abhors. What it does mean is to be as entirely and simply taken up with the child as the child himself is absorbed by his life.    *Ibid.*, Ch. 3

6 At every step the child should be allowed to meet the real experiences of life; the thorns should never be plucked from his roses.
> *Ibid.*

7 Nothing would more effectively further the development of education than for all flogging pedagogues to learn to educate with the head instead of with the hand.    *Ibid.*

8 Anyone who would attempt the task of felling a virgin forest with a penknife would probably feel the same paralysis of despair that the reformer feels when confronted with existing school systems.    *Ibid.*, Ch. 5

9 I wrote in the sand [at age ten], "God is dead." In doing so I thought, If there is a God, He will kill me now with a thunderbolt. But since the sun continued to shine, the question was answered for the time being; but it soon turned up again.     *Ibid., Ch. 7*

10 Corporal punishment is as humiliating for him who gives it as for him who receives it; it is ineffective besides. Neither shame nor physical pain have any other effect than a hardening one. . . .     *Ibid., Ch. 8*

11 A destroyed home life, an idiotic school system, premature work in the factory, stupefying life in the streets, these are what the great city gives to the children of the under classes. It is more astonishing that the better instincts of human nature generally are victorious in the lower class than the fact that this result is occasionally reversed.     *Ibid.*

12 Love is moral even without legal marriage, but marriage is immoral without love.
    "The Morality of Woman," *The Morality of Woman and Other Essays*　*1911*

13 Purity is the new-fallen snow which can be melted or sullied; chastity is steel tempered in the fire by white heat.     *Ibid.*

14 . . . everything which is exchanged between husband and wife in their life together can only be the free gift of love, can never be demanded by one or the other as a right. Man will understand that when one can no longer continue the life of love then this life must cease; that all vows binding forever the life of feeling are a violence of one's personality, since one cannot be held accountable for the transformation of one's feeling.     *Ibid.*

15 After some generations . . . we shall see marriages such as even now not a few are seen, in which not observation of a duty but liberty itself is the pledge that assures fidelity.
    *Ibid.*

16 My ideal picture of the woman of the future, and when one paints an ideal one does not need to limit one's imagination, is that she will be a being of profound contrasts which have attained harmony. She will appear as a great multiplicity and a complete unity; a rich plentitude and a perfect simplicity; a thoroughly educated creature of culture and an original spontaneous nature; a strongly marked human individuality and a complete manifestation of most profound womanliness.
    *Ibid., "The Woman of the Future"*

17 Conventionality is the tacit agreement to set appearance before reality, form before content, subordination before principle.
    *Ibid., "The Conventional Woman"*

18 The discovery that each personality is a new world—which in Shakespeare found its Columbus, a Columbus after whom new mariners immediately undertook new conquests—this discovery of literature has as yet only partially penetrated the universal consciousness, as a truth of experience.     *Ibid.*

19 For outside the field of immutable laws, children ought not to be constrained nor coerced against their nature and their disposition, against their healthy egoism and against their especial taste.     *Ibid.*

20 The educator must above all understand how to wait; to reckon all effects in the light of the future, not of the present.     *Ibid.*

21 The destruction of the personality is the great evil of the time.     *Ibid.*

22 Instead of defending "free love," which is a much-abused term capable of many interpretations, we ought to strive for the freedom of love; for while the former has come to imply freedom of any sort of love, the latter must only mean freedom for a feeling which is worthy the name of love. This feeling, it may be hoped, will gradually win for itself the same freedom in life as it already possesses in poetry.     *Spreading Liberty and the Great Libertarians*　*1913*

23 Such conceptions as knightly honour or warrior pride, business integrity or artistic conscience, indicate a few of those unwritten laws [of convention] which proffer sufficient evidence that man in his sphere, to a greater extent perhaps than woman in hers, has been a maker of convention, objectionable and otherwise.
    *The Renaissance of Motherhood, Pt. I, Ch. 1*　*1914*

24 The home was a closed sphere touched only at its edge by the world's evolution.     *Ibid.*

25 Woman, however, as the bearer and guardian of the new lives, has everywhere greater respect for life than man, who for centuries, as hunter and warrior, learned that the taking of lives may be not only allowed, but honourable.
    *Ibid., Ch. 2*

26 No emancipation must make women indifferent to sexual self-control and motherly devotion, from which some of the highest life values we possess on this earth have sprung.
    *Ibid., Ch. 4*

27 . . . the child craves of the mother, the work craves of its creator: the vision, the waiting, the hope, the pure will, the faith, and the love; the power to suffer, the desire to sacrifice, the ecstasy of devotion. Thus, man also has his "motherliness," a compound of feelings corresponding to those with which the woman enriches the race, oftener than the work, but which in woman, as in man, constitutes the productive mental process without which neither new works nor new generations turn out well. Ibid., Pt. II, Ch. 1

28 . . . art, that great undogmatized church. . . . Ibid.

29 Motherhood has . . . for many women ceased to be the sweet secret dream of the maiden, the glad hope of the wife, the deep regret of the ageing woman who has not had this yearning satisfied. Ibid., Ch. 3

30 The socially pernicious, racially wasteful, and soul-withering consequences of the working of mothers outside the home must cease. And this can only come to pass, either through the programme of institutional upbringing, or through the intimated renaissance of the home. Ibid., Pt. III, Ch. 2

31 The belief that we some day shall be able to prevent war is to me one with the belief in the possibility of making humanity really human.
War, Peace, and the Future,
Preface    1916

32 But the havoc wrought by war, which one compares with the havoc wrought by nature, is not an unavoidable fate before which man stands helpless. The natural forces which are the causes of war are human passions which it lies in our power to change. Ibid., Ch. 1

33 Formerly, a nation that broke the peace did not trouble to try and prove to the world that it was done solely from higher motives. . . . Now war has a bad conscience. Now every nation assures us that it is bleeding for a human cause, the fate of which hangs in the balance of its victory. All now declare themselves to be fighting for right, against might, the very thing that the pacifists urged. No nation will admit that it was solely to insure its own safety and to increase its power that it declared war. No nation dares to admit the guilt of blood before the world. Ibid.

34 Everything, everything in war is barbaric. . . . But the worst barbarity of war is that it forces men collectively to commit acts against which individually they would revolt with their whole being. Ibid., Ch. 6

35 Every State that relies on its war-preparedness for its power, honour, and glory must look upon its mothers with the same eyes as the first Napoleon, of whom someone had said that "he looked as if he wished to rive new war material out of the wombs of the mothers." Ibid., Ch. 9

36 Only calm thinking will lead one to the root of war. The peace movement that has only appealed to the emotions has never put the axe to the root of the problem. This movement, which was started in America and England, presupposed that Christianity is already realized. Ibid., Ch. 10

37 . . . feelings of sympathy and admiration are the indispensable mortar that holds the stones of international justice together.
Ibid., Ch. 16

## 216.  Marie La Coste

### (1849–1936)

\*   \*   \*

1 Into a ward of the whitewashed walls
Where the dead and dying lay—
Wounded by bayonets, shells, and balls—
Somebody's darling was borne one day.
"Somebody's Darling," St. 1

2 Tenderly bury the fair young dead,
Pausing to drop on his grave a tear;
Carve on the wooden slab at his head,
"Somebody's darling lies buried here!"
Ibid., St. 5

## 217.  Emma Lazarus

### (1849–1887)

1 Give me your tired, your poor,
Your huddled masses yearning to breathe free,
The wretched refuse of your teeming shore,
Send these, the homeless, tempest-tossed to me,
I lift my lamp beside the golden door!
"The New Colossus"    c.1886

2 Here at our sea-washed, sunset gates shall stand
A mighty woman with a torch, whose flame
Is the imprisoned lightning, and her name
Mother of exiles.
Ibid.

\*   \*   \*

3 His cup is gall, his meat is tears,
His passion lasts a million years.
"Crowing of the Red Cock"

4 Still on Israel's head forlorn,
Every nation heaps its scorn.
"The World's Justice"

## 218. Pauline Roland

(fl. 1850s)

Co-author with Jeanne-Françoise Deroine. See 17:1–2.

## 219. Frances Xavier Cabrini

(1850–1917)

1 But don't think that my Institute can be confined to one city or to one diocese. The whole world is not wide enough for me.

> Quoted by Bishop Gelmini in *Too Small a World* by Theodore Maynard, Pt. I, Ch. 3    *1945p*

2 To become perfect, all you have to do is to obey perfectly. When you renounce your personal inclinations you accept a mortification counter-signed with the cross of Christ.

> Ibid., Ch. 3

3 God commands, the sea obeys. If also in religion every Sister would obey her superior—with perfect submission, that is, without relying on her own judgment—what peace, what paradisal sweetness would be hers.

> Ibid., Diary (1889), Pt. II, Ch. 7

4 I want all of you to take on wings and fly swiftly to repose in that blessed peace possessed by a soul that is all for God.    Ibid.

5 Love is not loved, my daughters! Love is not loved! And how can we remain cold, indifferent and almost without heart at this thought? . . . If we do not burn with love, we do not deserve the title which ennobles us, elevates us, makes us great, and even a portent to the angels in heaven.    Ibid., Diary (1891)

## 220. Emma Carleton

(1850–1925)

\* \* \*

1 Reputation is a bubble which a man bursts when he tries to blow it for himself.

> *The Philistine*, Vol. XI, No. 82

## 221. Florence Earle Coates

(1850–1927)

\* \* \*

1 Age, out of heart, impatient, sighed:—
"I ask what will the *Future* be?"
Youth laughed contentedly, and cried:—
"The future leave to me!"

> "Youth and Age"

2 Ah me! the Prison House of Pain!—what lessons there are bought!—
Lessons of a sublimer strain than any elsewhere taught.

> "The House of Pain"

3 Columbus! Other title needs he none.

> "Columbus"

4 Death—Life's servitor and friend—the guide
That safely ferries us from shore to shore!

> "Sleep"

5 Fear is the fire that melts Icarian wings.

> "The Unconquered Air"

6 He turned with such a smile to face disaster
That he sublimed defeat.

> "The Hero"

7 I love, and the world is mine!

> "The World Is Mine"

8 Though his beginnings be but poor and low,
Thank God a man can grow!

> "Per Aspera"

9 The soul hath need of prophet and redeemer:
Her outstretched wings against her prisoning bars,
She waits for truth; and truth is with the dreamer,—
Persistent as the myriad light of stars!

> "Dream the Great Dream"

## 222. Geneviève

(1850–?)

1 The feminine chest was not made for hanging orders on.

> Quoted in *Pomp and Circumstance* by E. de Gramont    *1929*

## 223. Margaret Collier Graham

(1850–1910)

1 . . . it's no more 'n fair to be civil to a man when you're gettin' the best of 'im; but I hain't.

> "The Withrow Water Right," *Stories of the Foot-hills*    *1875*

2 "Harvest's a poor time fer wishin'; it's more prof'table 'long about seedin'-time. . . ."

> Ibid., "Idy"

3 The mind of the most logical thinker goes so easily from one point to another that it is not hard to mistake motion for progress.

> *Gifts and Givers*    *1906*

4 People need joy quite as much as clothing. Some of them need it far more.    Ibid.

5 We are all held in place by the pressure of the crowd around us. We must all lean upon others. Let us see that we lean gracefully and freely and acknowledge their support. Ibid.

6 Conscience, as I understand it, is the impulse to do right because it is right, regardless of personal ends, and has nothing whatever to do with the ability to distinguish between right and wrong. "A Matter of Conscience," *Do They Really Respect Us? and Other Essays* 1911p

7 If any good results to a man from believing a lie, it certainly comes from the honesty of his belief. Ibid., "Some Immortal Fallacy"

## 224. Jane Harrison

### (1850–1928)

1 Youth and Crabbed Age stand broadly for the two opposite poles of human living, poles equally essential to any real vitality, but always contrasted. Youth stands for rationalism, for the intellect and its concomitants, egotism and individualism. Crabbed Age stands for tradition, for the instincts and emotions, with their concomitant altruism. . . . The whole art of living is a delicate balance between the two tendencies. Virtues and vices are but convenient analytic labels attached to particular forms of the two tendencies. "Crabbed Age and Youth," *Alpha and Omega* 1915

2 Any association of men begets a force, which is not the sum of the forces of its individual members; and this new force, this group-begotten potency, is more real, more living, than any orthodox divinity. Moreover, each group-god is necessarily a Unanimistic force. For better for worse it unites, not divides. Ibid., "Unanimism and Conversion"

3 To be meek, patient, tactful, modest, honourable, brave, is not to be either manly or womanly; it is to be humane, to have social virtue. To be womanly is one thing, and one only; it is to be sensitive to man, to be highly endowed with the sex instinct; to be manly is to be sensitive to woman. Ibid., "Homo Sum"

4 Your thoughts are—for what they are worth—self-begotten by some process of parthenogenesis. But there comes often to me, almost always, a moment when alone I cannot bring them to birth, when, if companionship is denied, they die unborn. Ibid., "Scientlae Sacra Fames"

5 A child's mind is, indeed, throughout the best clue to understanding of savage magic. A young and vital child knows no limit to his own will, and it is the only reality to him. It is not that he wants at the outset to fight other wills, but that they simply do not exist for him. Like the artist, he goes forth to the work of creation, gloriously alone. Ibid., "Darwinism and Religion"

6 Whenever at an accusation blind rage burns up within us, the reason is that some arrow has pierced the joints of our harness. Behind our shining armour of righteous indignation lurks a convicted and only half-repentant sinner . . . [and] we may be almost sure some sharp and bitter grain of truth lurks within it, and the wound is best probed. Ibid., "Epilogue on the War"

7 Here was a big constructive imagination; here was a mere doctor laying bare the origins of Greek drama as no classical scholar had ever done, teaching the anthropologist what was really meant by his *totem and taboo*, probing the mysteries of sin, of sanctity, of sacrament—a man who, because he understood, purged the human spirit from fear. I have no confidence in psycho-analysis as a method of therapeutics . . . but I am equally sure that for generations almost every branch of human knowledge will be enriched and illumined by the imagination of Freud. "Conclusion," *Reminiscences of a Student's Life* 1925

8 I have elsewhere tried to show that Art is not the handmaid of Religion, but that Art in some sense springs out of Religion, and that between them is a connecting link, a bridge, and that bridge is Ritual. Ibid.

9 If I think of Death at all it is merely as a negation of life, a close, a last and necessary chord. What I dread is disease, that is, bad, disordered life, not Death, and disease, so far, I have escaped. I have no hope whatever of personal immortality, no desire even for a future life. My consciousness began in a very humble fashion with my body; with my body, very quietly, I hope it will end. Ibid.

10 Marriage, for a woman at least, hampers the two things that made life to me glorious—friendship and learning. Ibid.

11 Old age, believe me, is a good and pleasant thing. It is true you are gently shouldered off the stage, but then you are given such a comfortable front stall as spectator. . . . Ibid.

## 225. Laura Howe Richards
### (1850–1943)

1 "And the storm went on. It roared, it bellowed, and it screeched: it thumped and it ker-whalloped. The great seas would come bunt agin the rocks, as if they were bound to go right through to Jersey City, which they used to say was the end of the world."
*Captain January*, Ch. 2      *1890*

2 "A cap'n on a quarterdeck's a good thing; but a cap'n on a pint o' rock, out to sea in a northeast gale, might just as well be a fo'c'sle hand and done with it."      Ibid.

3 "There's times when a man has strength given to him, seemin'ly, over and above human strength. 'Twas like as if the Lord ketched holt and helped me: maybe he did, seein' what 'twas I was doing. Maybe he did!"      Ibid.

4 Be you clown or be you King,
Still your singing is the thing.
"Dedication," *Tirra Lirra*      *1890*

5 Every little wave has its nightcap on.
Ibid., "Song for Hal," Refrain

6 Great is truth and shall prevail,
Therefore must we weep and wail.
Ibid., "The Mameluke and the Hospodar," St. 4

7 Once there was an elephant
Who tried to use the telephant—
No! No! I mean an elephone
Who tried to use the telephone.
Ibid., "Eletelephony," St. 1

8 Ponsonby Perks,
He fought with Turks,
Performing many wonderful works.
Ibid., "Nonsense Verses," St. 2

9 "Mighty poor country up that way. Some say the Rome folks don't see any garden-truck from year's end to year's end, and that if you ask a Rome girl to cook you up a mess of string beans, she takes the store beans and runs 'em on a string, and boils 'em that way. . . ."      *Narcissa*, Pt. II      *1892*

## 226. Rose Hartwick Thorpe
### (1850–1939)

1 And her face so sweet and pleading, yet with sorrow pale and worn,
Touched his heart with sudden pity—lit his eye with misty light;
"Go, your lover lives!" said Cromwell; "Curfew shall not ring tonight!"
"Curfew Shall Not Ring Tonight"      *1866*

## 227. Nellie Cashman
### (1851–1925)

1 When I saw something that needed doing, I did it.      Interview, *Daily British Colonist*      *1898*

## 228. Kate Chopin
### (1851–1904)

1 In entering upon their new life they decided to be governed by no precedential methods. Marriage was to be a form, that while fixing legally their relation to each other, was in no wise to touch the individuality of either; that was to be preserved intact. Each was to remain a free integral of humanity, responsible to no dominating exactness of so-called marriage laws. And the element that was to make possible such a union was trust in each other's love, honor, courtesy, tempered by the reserving clause of readiness to meet the consequences of reciprocal liberty.
"A Point at Issue!"      *1889*

2 The mother-women seemed to prevail that summer at Grand Isle. It was easy to know them, fluttering about with extended, protecting wings when any harm, real or imaginary, threatened their precious brood. They were women who idolized their children, worshipped their husbands, and esteemed it a holy privilege to efface themselves as individuals and grow wings as ministering angels.
*The Awakening*, Ch. 4      *1889*

3 A certain light was beginning to dawn dimly within her—the light which, showing the way, forbids it. . . . But the beginning of things, of a world especially, is necessarily vague, tangled, chaotic, and exceedingly disturbing. How few of us ever emerge from such beginning! How many souls perish in its tumult!
Ibid., Ch. 6

4 The voice of the sea speaks to the soul. The touch of the sea is sensuous, enfolding the body in its soft, close embrace.      Ibid.

5 "Pirate gold isn't a thing to be hoarded or utilized. It is something to squander and throw to the four winds, for the fun of seeing the golden specks fly."      Ibid., Ch. 12

6 The past was nothing to her; offered no lesson which she was willing to heed. The future was a mystery which she never attempted to penetrate. The present alone was significant. . . .
Ibid., Ch. 15

7 "The way to become rich is to make money, my dear Edna, not to save it. . . ."
Ibid., Ch. 18

8 It sometimes entered Mr. Pontellier's mind to wonder if his wife were not growing a little unbalanced mentally. He could see plainly that she was not herself. That is, he could not see that she was becoming herself and daily casting aside that fictitious self which we assume like a garment with which to appear before the world.
Ibid., Ch. 19

9 . . . "a wedding is one of the most lamentable spectacles on earth."          Ibid., Ch. 22

10 Alcée Arobin's manner was so genuine that it often deceived even himself.   ·   Ibid., Ch. 25

11 ". . . when I left her today, she put her arms around me and felt my shoulder blades, to see if my wings were strong, she said. 'The bird that would soar above the level plain of tradition and prejudice must have strong wings. It is a sad spectacle to see the weaklings bruised, exhausted, fluttering back to earth.' "
Ibid., Ch. 27

12 "There are some people who leave impressions not so lasting as the imprint of an oar upon the water."          Ibid., Ch. 34

13 "The years that are gone seem like dreams—if one might go on sleeping and dreaming—but to wake up and find—oh! well! perhaps it is better to wake up after all, even to suffer, rather than to remain a dupe to illusions all one's life."          Ibid., Ch. 38

14 The children appeared before her like antagonists who had overcome her; who had overpowered and sought to drag her into the soul's slavery for the rest of her days.
Ibid., Ch. 39

15 Only the birds had seen, and she could count on their discretion.          "A Shameful Affair"
1891

16 There would be no one to live for her during these coming years; she would live for herself. There would be no powerful will bending hers in that blind persistence with which men and women believe they have a right to impose a private will upon a fellow-creature.
"The Story of an Hour"          1894

17 What could love, the unsolved mystery, count for in face of this possession of self-assertion which she suddenly recognized as the strongest impulse of her being!          Ibid.

18 "I don't hate him," Athenaise answered. . . . "It's jus' being married that I detes' an' despise."          "Athenaise"          1895

## 229. Anna Garlin Spencer
### (1851–1931)

1 The failure of woman to produce genius of the first rank in most of the supreme forms of human effort has been used to block the way of all women of talent and ambition for intellectual achievement in a manner that would be amusingly absurd were it not so monstrously unjust and socially harmful.
*Woman's Share in Social Culture*
1912

2 The whole course of evolution in industry, and in the achievements of higher education and exceptional talent, has shown man's invariable tendency to shut women out when their activities have reached a highly specialized period of growth.          Ibid.

3 And when her biographer says of an Italian woman poet, "during some years her Muse was intermitted," we do not wonder at the fact when he casually mentions her ten children.
Ibid.

4 It is not alone the fact that women have generally had to spend most of their strength in caring for others that has handicapped them in individual effort; but also that they have almost universally had to care wholly for themselves.
Ibid.

5 A successful woman preacher was once asked "what special obstacles have you met as a woman in the ministry?" "Not one," she answered, "except the lack of a minister's wife."
Ibid.

## 230. Mary Augusta Ward
### (1851–1920)

1 "Propinquity does it"—as Mrs. Thornburgh is always reminding us.
*Robert Elsmer*, Bk. I, Ch. 2          1888

2 "Every man is bound to leave a story better than he found it."          Ibid., Ch. 3

3 One may as well preach a respectable mythology as anything else.          Ibid., Ch. 5

4 In my youth people talked about Ruskin; now they talk about drains.          Ibid., Bk. II, Ch. 12

5 This Laodicean* cant of tolerance.          Ibid.

6 "Put down enthusiasm." . . . The Church of England in a nutshell.          Ibid., Ch. 16

* Lukewarm.

7 Conviction is the Conscience of the Mind.
Ibid., Bk. IV, Ch. 26

8 All things change, creeds and philosophies and outward system—but God remains!
Ibid., Ch. 27

9 Truth has never been, can never be, contained in any one creed.     Ibid., Bk. VI, Ch. 38

## 231. Mary A. Barr
### (1852–?)
### * * *

1 I sing the Poppy! The frail snowy weed!
    The flower of Mercy! That within its heart
Doth keep "a drop serene" of human need,
A drowsy balm of every bitter smart.
For happy hours the rose will idly blow
The Poppy hath a charm of pain and woe.
"White Poppies"

## 232. Martha Jane Burke
### (1852–1903)

1 During the month of June I acted as a pony express rider carrying the U.S. mail between Deadwood and Custer, a distance of fifty miles. . . . It was considered the most dangerous route in the Hills, but as my reputation as a rider and quick shot was well known, I was molested very little, for the toll gatherers looked on me as being a good fellow, and they knew that I never missed my mark.
*Life and Adventures of Calamity Jane*    *1896*

2 There are thousands of Sioux in this valley. I am not afraid of them. They think I am a crazy woman and never molest me. . . . I guess I am the only human being they are afraid of.
Letter to Daughter (September 28, 1877), Quoted in *Calamity Was the Name for Jane* by Glenn Clairmonte *1959p*

3 I Jane Hickok Burke better known as Calamity Jane of my own free will and being of sound mind do this day June 3, 1903 make this confession. I have lied about my past life. . . . People got snoopy so I told them lies to hear their tongues wag. The women are all snakes and none of them I can call friends.
Ibid., Document to James O'Neill (June 3, 1903)

## 233. Vera Figner
### (1852–1942)

1 Generally speaking, there was in her [Sofia Perovskaya] nature both feminine gentleness and masculine severity. Tender, tender as a mother with the working people, she was exacting and severe toward her comrades and fellow-workers, while towards her political enemies, the government, she could be merciless. . . .
*Memoirs of a Revolutionist*    *1927*

## 234. Mary Wilkins Freeman
### (1852–1930)

1 . . . it took her a long time to prepare her tea; but when ready it was set forth with as much grace as if she had been a veritable guest to her own self.    *A New England Nun*    *1891*

2 Louisa's feet had turned into a path . . . so straight and unswerving that it could only meet a check at her grave, and so narrow that there was no room for anyone at her side.    Ibid.

3 She gazed ahead through a long reach of future days strung together like pearls in a rosary, every one like the others, and all smooth and flawless and innocent, and her heart went up in thankfulness.    Ibid.

## 235. Gertrude Kasebier
### (1852–1934)

1 . . . from the first days of dawning individuality, I have longed unceasingly to make pictures of people . . . to make likenesses that are biographies, to bring out in each photograph the essential personality that is variously called temperament, soul, humanity.
Quoted in *The Woman's Eye* by Anne Tucker    *1973p*

## 236. Lily Langtry
### (1853–1929)

1 The sentimentalist ages far more quickly than the person who loves his work and enjoys new challenges.
Quoted in the *New York Sun*    *1906*

2 Anyone who limits his vision to his memories of yesterday is already dead.
Quoted in *Because I Loved Him* by Noel B. Gerson    *1971p*

## 237. Mary Lease

(1853–1933)

1 What you Kansas farmers ought to do is to raise less corn and raise more hell.
Political Speech     *1890*

## 238. Sofia Perovskaya

(1853–1881)

1 . . . my lot is not at all such a dark one. I have lived as my convictions have prompted me; I could not do otherwise; therefore I await what is in store for me with a clear conscience.
Letter to Her Mother,
*Woman as Revolutionary,*
Fred C. Giffin, ed.     *1973p*

## 239. Emilie Poulsson

(1853–1939)

\* \* \*

1 Books are keys to wisdom's treasure;
Books are gates to lands of pleasure;
Books are paths that upward lead;
Books are friends. Come, let us read.
Inscription in Children's Reading Room, Hopkington, Massachusetts

## 240. Jennie Jerome Churchill

(1854–1921)

1 The best society does not necessarily mean the "smart set."    Quoted in the *New York World*
*October 13, 1908*

2 Of all nationalities, Americans are the best in adapting themselves. With them, to see is to know—and to know is to conquer.    Ibid.

3 You may be a princess or the richest woman in the world, but you cannot be more than a lady. . . .     Ibid.

4 It is so tempting to try the most difficult thing possible.    Quoted in the *Daily Chronicle*
(London)     *July 8, 1909*

5 BASIL. But remember, a man ends by hating the woman who he thinks has found him out.
*His Borrowed Plumes*     *1909*

6 ALMA. I rather suspect her of being in love with him.

MARTIN. Her own husband? Monstrous! What a selfish woman!     Ibid.

7 All natures are in nature.     Ibid.

8 What is love without passion?—A garden without flowers, a hat without feathers, tobogganing without snow.     Ibid.

9 Italians love—sun, sin and spaghetti.     Ibid.

10 We don't elope nowadays, and we don't divorce, except out of kindness.    *The Bill*   *1913*

11 Your castle in Spain has no foundations, that is why it is so easily built. . . .
"Mars and Cupid," *Pearson's*
*September, 1915*

12 . . . we owe something to extravagance, for thrift and adventure seldom go hand in hand. . . .
Ibid., "Extravagance"
*October, 1915*

13 Treat your friends as you do your pictures, and place them in their best light.
"Friendship," *Small Talk on Big Subjects*     *1916*

14 There is no such thing as a moral dress. . . . It's people who are moral or immoral. . . .
Quoted in the *Daily Chronicle*
(London)    *February 16, 1921*

15 It's a wise virgin who looks after her own lamp.    Quoted in *Bystander*   *July 6, 1921*

16 But I suppose experience of life will in time teach you that tact is a very essential ingredient in all things.    Letter to Winston Churchill (October 4, 1895), Quoted in *Jennie*, Vol. II, by Ralph G. Martin     *1971p*

17 Life is not always what one wants it to be, but to make the best of it as it is, is the only way of being happy. . . .
Ibid., Letter to Lord Kitchener
(November 27, 1896)

18 You seem to have no real purpose in life and won't realize at the age of twenty-two that for a man life means work, and hard work if you mean to succeed. . . .
Ibid., Letter to Winston Churchill
(February 26, 1897)

19 . . . be modest. . . . One must be tempted to talk of oneself . . . *but resist.* Let them *drag* things out.    Ibid. (November 4, 1897)

20 If we can alleviate sufferings and at the same time comfort the many aching and anxious hearts at home, shall we not be fulfilling our greatest mission in life? These are "Women's Rights" in the best sense of the word. We need no others.    Ibid., Speech, First Meeting of General Committee for Hospital Ship
(November 18, 1899)

21 One is forever throwing away substance for
shadows.　　　　Ibid., Letter to Her Sister,
Leonie Leslie (July 24, 1914)

## 241. Eva March Tappan
### (1854–1930)

* * *

1 We drove the Indians out of the land,
But a dire revenge those Redmen planned,
For they fastened a name to every nook,
And every boy with a spelling book
Will have to toil till his hair turns gray
Before he can spell them the proper way.
"On the Cape," St. 1

## 242. Edith Thomas
### (1854–1925)

1 How on the moment all changes!
Quietude midmost the throng,
Peace amid tumult, and dissonance
Charmed into vespertine song!

Dew on the dust of the noontime,
Spring at the dead of the year,
Freedom discerned out of bondage,
Grace in condition austere!
"Optimi Consiliarii Mortui, XXXIV,"
Sts. 1–2, *The Inverted Torch*　　1890

2 When the wind through the trees makes a path
for the moon!
Praise June!
"Praise June," *In Sunshine Land*
1894

3 Sweet, sweet, you've no reason
To hurry away;
Stay so, sweet Season,
Stay, oh stay!
Ibid., "Stay So, Sweet Season," St. 1

4 They troop to their work in the gray of the
morning,
Each with a shovel swung over his
shoulder . . .
You have cut down their wages without any
warning—
Angry? Well, let their wrath smolder!
"Their Argument," St. 2,
*The Guest at the Gate*
1909

5 And Heaven gave me strivings blind
By Justice to be schooled,
And purpose branded in the mind,
To rule not, nor be ruled. . . .
Ibid., "Of the Middle World," St. 2

* * *

6 The God of Music dwelleth out of doors.
"The God of Music"

## 243. Mary Dow Brine
### (1855?–1925?)

1 She's somebody's mother, boys, you know,
For all she's aged, and poor, and slow.
"Somebody's Mother," St. 15,
*Harper's Weekly*　　　March 2, 1878

## 244. Margaret Wolfe Hungerford
### (1855?–1897)

1 Beauty is in the eye of the beholder.
*Molly Bawn*　　1878

## 245. Alice Freeman Palmer
### (1855–1902)

* * *

1 Exquisite child of the air.
"The Butterfly"

## 246. Olive Schreiner
### (1855–1920)

1 An ox at the roadside, when it is dying of
hunger and thirst, does not lie down; it walks
up and down—up and down, seeking it knows
not what;—but it does not lie down.
*From Man to Man*, Ch. 1　　1876

2 "Nothing can ever alter, nothing can ever
change, our happiness, that springs from such
deep love. Death itself will be but going home
to the Father's house to be made perfect there
in that which made us loved and loving here."
He looked up at her. "For those who love as
we love, there is no parting, and no death,
only eternal union."　　　　Ibid., Ch. 4

3 "There are some men," said Lyndall, "whom
you never can believe were babies at all; and
others you never see without thinking how
very nice they must have looked when they
wore socks and pink sashes."
*The Story of an African Farm*,
"Lyndall"　　1883

4 They are called finishing-schools and the name
tells accurately what they are. They finish
everything. . . .　　　　　　　　　Ibid.

5 I have seen some souls so compressed that they
would have fitted into a small thimble, and
found room to move there—wide room.
Ibid.

6 . . . how hard it is to make your thoughts look
anything but imbecile fools when you paint
them with ink on paper.　　　　Ibid.

7 "It is delightful to be a woman; but every man thanks the Lord devoutly that he isn't one."
Ibid.

8 "But this one thought stands, never goes—if I might but be one of those born in the future; then, perhaps, to be born a woman will not be to be born branded." Ibid.

9 "Wisdom never kicks at the iron walls it can't bring down." Ibid.

10 "Everything has two sides—the outside that is ridiculous, and the inside that is solemn."
Ibid.

11 "Look at this little chin of mine, Waldo, with the dimple in it. It is but a small part of my person; but though I had a knowledge of all things under the sun, and the wisdom to use it, and the deep loving heart of an angel, it would not stead me through life like this little chin. I can win money with it, I can win love; I can win power with it, I can win fame."
Ibid.

12 "The less a woman has in her head the better she is for climbing." Ibid.

13 "We fit our sphere as a Chinese woman's fits her shoe, exactly as though God had made both; and yet He knows nothing of either."
Ibid.

14 "We were equals once when we lay newborn babes on our nurse's knees. We shall be equals again when they tie up our jaws for the last sleep." Ibid.

15 "If the bird *does* like its cage, and *does* like its sugar, and will not leave it, why keep the door so very carefully shut?" Ibid.

16 "The surest sign of fitness is success."
Ibid.

17 "*We* bear the world, and we make it. . . . There was never a great man who had not a great mother—it is hardly an exaggeration."
Ibid.

18 "By every inch we grow in intellectual height our love strikes down its roots deeper, and spreads out its arms wider." Ibid.

19 ". . . when love is no more bought or sold, when it is not a means of making bread, when each woman's life is filled with earnest, individual labor—then love will come to her. . . . Then, but not now. . . ." Ibid.

20 ". . . till I have been delivered I can deliver no one." Ibid.

21 "Men are like the earth and we are the moon; we turn always one side to them, and they think there is no other, because they don't see it— but there is." Ibid.

22 All day, where the sunlight played on the sea-shore, Life sat.
"The Lost Joy," *Dreams*    1892

23 And he said, "I take it, ages ago the Aegis-of-Dominion-of-Muscular-Force found her, and when she stooped low to give suck to her young, and her back was broad, he put his burden of subjection on to it, and tied it on with the broad band of Inevitable Necessity. Then she looked at the earth and the sky, and knew there was no hope for her; and she lay down on the sand with the burden she could not loosen. Ever since she has lain here, and the ages have come, and the ages have gone, but the band of Inevitable Necessity has not been cut." Ibid., "Three Dreams in a Desert"

24 I said to God, "What are they doing?"
God said, "Making pitfalls into which their fellows may sink."
I said to God, "Why do they do it?"
God said, "Because each thinks that when his brother falls he will rise."
Ibid., "Across My Bed"

25 "There are only two things that are absolute realities, love and knowledge, and you can't escape them." "The Buddhist Priest's Wife,"
*Stories, Dreams, and Allegories*
*1892*

26 "I suppose the most absolutely delicious thing in life is to feel a thing needs you, and to give at the moment it needs. Things that don't need you, you must love from a distance." Ibid.

27 "No woman has the right to marry a man if she has to bend herself out of shape for him. She might wish to, but she could never be to him with all her passionate endeavor what the other woman could be to him without trying. Character will dominate over all and will come out at last." Ibid.

28 "There is nothing ridiculous in love."
Ibid.

29 There are artists who, loving their work, when they have finished it, put it aside for years, that, after the lapse of time, returning to it and reviewing it from the standpoint of distance, they may judge of it in a manner which was not possible while the passion of creation and the link of unbroken emotion bound them to it. What the artist does intentionally, life often does for us fortuitously in other relationships.
*Thoughts on South Africa*, Ch. 1
*1892*

30 If Nature here wishes to make a mountain, she runs a range for five hundred miles; if a plain, she levels eighty; if a rock, she tilts five thousand feet of strata on end; our skies are higher and more intensely blue; our waves larger than others; our rivers fiercer. There is nothing measured, small nor petty in South Africa.        Ibid.

31 Slavery may, perhaps, be best compared to the infantile disease of measles; a complaint which so commonly attacks the young of humanity in their infancy, and when gone through at that period leaves behind it so few fatal marks; but which when it normally attacks the fully developed adult becomes one of the most virulent and toxic of diseases, often permanently poisoning the constitution where it does not end in death.        Ibid.

32 St. Francis of Assissi preached to the little fishes: we eat them. But the man who eats fish can hardly be blamed, seeing that the eating of fishes is all but universal among the human race!—if only he does not pretend that while he eats them he preaches to them!        Ibid., Ch. 4

33 The modern woman stands with the prospect of shrinking fields of labour on every hand. She is brought face-to-face with two possibilities. Either, on the one hand, she may remain quiescent and, as her old fields of labour fall from her, seek no new: in which case . . . she is bound to become more or less parasitic, as vast bodies of women in our wealthier and even our middle classes have already become. . . . On the other hand, woman may determine not to remain quiescent. As her old fields of labour slip from her under the inevitable changes of modern life, she may determine to find labour in the new and to obtain that training which, whether in the world of handicraft or the mental field of toil, increasingly all-important in our modern world, shall fit her to take as large a share in the labours of her race in the future as in the past.        Ibid.

34 "Yes, the life of the individual is short, but the life of the nation is long; and it is longer, and stronger, more vigorous and more knit, if it grows slowly and spontaneously than if formed by violence or fraud. The individual cannot afford to wait but the nation can and must wait for true unity, which can only come as the result of internal growth and the union of its atoms, and in no other way whatsoever."        Ibid., Ch. 8

35 I know there will be spring; as surely as the birds know it when they see above the snow two tiny, quivering green leaves. Spring cannot fail us.     "The Woman's Rose"    *1893*

36 The greatest nations, like the greatest individuals, have often been the poorest; and with wealth comes often what is more terrible than poverty—corruption.
       *An English South African's View*
       *of the Situation*    *c.1899*

37 I suppose there is no man who to-day loves his country who has not perceived that in the life of the nation, as in the life of the individual, the hour of external success may be the hour of irrevocable failure, and that the hour of death, whether to nations or individuals, is often the hour of immortality.        Ibid.

38 We have in us the blood of a womanhood that was never bought and never sold; that wore no veil and had no foot bound; whose realized ideal of marriage was sexual companionship and an equality in duty and labor.
       *Woman and Labor*    *1911*

39 We demand that . . . in this new world we also shall have our share of honored and socially useful human toil, our full half of the labor of the Children of Woman. We demand nothing more than this, and will take nothing less.        Ibid.

40 We have always borne part of the weight of war, and the major part. . . . Men have made boomerangs, bows, swords, or guns with which to destroy one another; we have made the men who destroyed and were destroyed! . . . *We pay the first cost on all human life.*
       Ibid., Ch. 4
       *   *   *

41 And it came to pass that after a time the artist was forgotten, but the work lived.
       *The Artist's Secret*

## 247. Ella Wheeler Wilcox
### (1855–1919)

1 Laugh and the world laughs with you;
   Weep, and you weep alone;
For the sad old earth must borrow its mirth,
   But has trouble enough of its own.
       "Solitude," St. 1, *New York Sun*
       *February 25, 1883*
       *   *   *

2 And the life that is worth the honor of earth,
   Is the one that resists desire.
       "Worth While"

3 'Tis easy enough to be pleasant,
   When life flows along like a song;
But the man worth while is the one who will smile
   When everything goes dead wrong.
       Ibid.

4      Apart
Must dwell those angels known as Peace and
     Love,
For only death can reconcile the two.
                 "Peace and Love"

5 A weed is but an unloved flower!
                  "The Weed," St. 1

6 But with every deed you are sowing a seed,
Though the harvest you may not see.
             "You Never Can Tell," St. 2

7 Distrust that man who tells you to distrust.
                     "Distrust"

8 For why should I fan, or feed with fuel,
A love that showed me but blank despair?
So my hold was firm, and my grasp was cruel—
I meant to strangle it then and there!
                "Ad Finem," St. 2

9 Give us that grand word "woman" once again,
And let's have done with "lady"; one's a term
Full of fine force, strong, beautiful, and firm,
Fit for the noblest use of tongue or pen;
And one's a word for lackeys.
                     "Woman"

10 I love your lips when they're wet with wine
And red with a wicked desire.
                  "I Love You," St. 1

11 Not from me the cold calm kiss
Of a virgin's bloodless love.
                    Ibid., St. 2

12 I think of death as some delightful journey
That I shall take when all my tasks are done.
                   "The Journey"

13 It ever has been since time began,
And ever will be, till time lose breath,
That love is a mood—no more—to man,
And love to a woman is life or death.
                   "Blind," St. 1

14 Let there be many windows to your soul,
That all the glory of the world
May beautify it.
                  "Progress," St. 1

15      Tear away
The blinds of superstition; let the light
Pour through fair windows broad as Truth itself
And high as God.
                     Ibid.

16 Sweep up the debris from decaying faiths;
Sweep down the cobwebs of worn-out beliefs,
And throw your soul open to the light
Of Reason and Knowledge.
                     Ibid., St. 2

17 Love lights more fires than hate extinguishes,
And men grow better as the world grows old.
                     "Optimism"

18 Talk happiness. The world is sad enough
Without your woe. No path is wholly rough.
                     Ibid., St. 1

19 No one will ever grieve because your lips are
dumb.
                     Ibid.

20 No! The two kinds of people on earth that I
mean
Are the people who lift and the people who
lean.
             "To Lift or to Lean"

21 O man bowed down with labor,
O woman young yet old,
O heart oppressed in the toiler's breast
And crushed by the power of gold—
Keep on with your weary battle against tri-
     umphant might;
No question is ever settled until it is settled
right.
           "Settle the Question Right"

22 One ship drives east and another drives west
With the selfsame winds that blow.
'Tis the set of sails and not the gales
Which tells us the way to go.
               "Winds of Fate," St. 1

23 The days grow shorter, the nights grow longer;
The headstones thicken along the way;
And life grows sadder, but love grows stronger
For those who walk with us day by day.
                "Growing Old," St. 1

24 The splendid discontent of God
With chaos, made the world.
And from the discontent of man
     The world's best progress springs.
                   "Discontent"

25 We flatter those we scarcely know,
We please the fleeting guest,
And deal full many a thoughtless blow
To those who love us best.
               "Life's Scars," St. 3

26 Whatever is—is best.
            "Whatever Is—Is Best"

27      Why, even death stands still,
And waits an hour sometimes for such a will.
                   "Will," St. 2

28 Why, half the gossip under the sun,
If you trace it back, you will find begun
In that wretched House of They.
                   "They Say"

## 248. Elisabeth Marbury
### (1856–1933)

1 I began to realize that the world was divided into three groups: wasters, mollusks, and builders.    *My Crystal Ball,* Ch. 1    *1923*

2 "Ah, daughter," said Mother, "where there is room in the heart, there is always room on the hearth."      Ibid.

3 I began to realize the woefulness of ignorance. Things of unimportance fell into their proper places. I was inoculated with beauty and my feet became shod with a sense of its value. . . .      Ibid., Ch. 3

4 Throughout my life, I have always found that events which seemed at the time disastrous ultimately developed into positive blessings. In fact, I have never known one instance when this has not proved to be the case.      Ibid., Ch. 5

5 The praise of injudicious friends frequently fosters bad mannerisms.    Ibid., Ch. 6

\* \* \*

6 A caress is better than a career.      "Careers for Women"

7 No influence so quickly converts a radical into a reactionary as does his election to power.      Ibid.

8 The richer your friends, the more they will cost you.      Ibid.

## 249. Lizette Reese
### (1856–1935)

\* \* \*

1 A book may be a flower that blows;
A road to a far town;
A roof, a well, a tower;
A book
May be a staff, a crook.      "Books"

2 Creeds grow so thick along the way,
Their boughs hide God.      "Doubt"

3 Fame is a bugle call
Blown past a crumbling wall.      "Taps"

4 Glad that I live am I;
That the sky is blue;
Glad for the country lanes,
And the fall of dew.      "A Little Song of Life," St. 1

5 Oh, far, far, far,
As any spire or star,
Beyond the cloistered wall!
Oh, high, high, high,
A heart-throb in the sky—
Then not at all!      "The Lark"

6 The old faiths light their candles all about,
But burly Truth comes by and puts them out.      "Truth"

7 We that are twain by day, at night are one.
A dream can bring me to your arms once more.      "Compensation"

8 When I consider life and its few years—
A wisp of fog betwixt us and the sun;
A call to battle, and the battle done
Ere the last echo dies within our ears,
I wonder at the idleness of tears.      "Tears"

## 250. Kate Douglas Wiggin
### (1856–1923)

1 Women never hit what they aim at: but if they just shut their eyes and shoot in the air they generally find themselves in the bull's eye.    *New Chronicles of Rebecca*    *1907*

\* \* \*

2 My heart is open wide tonight
For stranger, kith or kin.
I would not bar a single door
Where love might enter in.      "The Romance of a Christmas Card"

## 251. Ada Alden
### (1857–1936)

\* \* \*

1 Can this be Italy, or but a dream
Emerging from the broken waves of sleep? . . .
This world of beauty, color, and perfume,
Hoary with age, yet of unaging bloom.      "Above Salerno"

2 The years shall right the balance tilted wrong,
The years shall set upon his\* brows a star.      "Ave"

## 252. Gertrude Atherton
### (1857–1948)

1 We love the lie that saves their pride, but never an unflattering truth.    *The Conqueror,* Bk. III, Ch. 6    *1902*

\* Referring to Woodrow Wilson.

2 To put a tempting face aside when duty demands every faculty . . . is a lesson which takes most men longest to learn.      Ibid.

3 The perfect friendship of two men is the deepest and highest sentiment of which the finite mind is capable; women miss the best in life.      Ibid., Ch. 12

4 No matter how hard a man may labor, some woman is always in the background of his mind. She is the one reward of virtue.
     Ibid., Bk. IV, Ch. 3

## 253. Alice Brown
### (1857–1948)

\*   \*   \*

1 And led by silence more majestical
Than clash of conquering arms, He comes! He comes!
And strikes out flame from the adoring hills.
     "Sunrise on Mansfield Mountain"

2 Praise not the critic, lest he think
You crave the shelter of his ink.
     "The Critic"

3 Take with thee, too, our bond of gratitude
That in a cynic and a tattle age
Thou didst consent to write; in missal script,
Thy name on the poor players' slandered page,
And teach the lords of empty birth a king may walk the stage.
     "Edwin Booth"

4 Yet thou, O banqueter on worms,
Who wilt not let corruption pass!—
Dost search out mildew, mould and stain,
Beneath a magnifying-glass.
     "The Slanderer"

## 254. Mary Lee Demarest
### (1857–1888)

\*   \*   \*

1 Like a bairn to his mither, a wee birdie to its nest,
I wud fain be ganging nod unto my Saviour's breast;
For he gathers in his bosom witless, worthless lambs like me,
An' he carries them himsel' to his ain countree.
     "My Ain Countree"

## 255. Fannie Farmer
### (1857–1915)

1 Progress in civilization has been accompanied by progress in cookery.
     *The Boston Cooking-School Cookbook*, Ch. 2    1896

2 I certainly feel that the time is not far distant when a knowledge of the principles of diet will be an essential part of one's education. Then mankind will eat to live, be able to do better mental and physical work, and disease will be less frequent.
     Ibid., Preface to the First Edition

3 . . . France, that land to which we ever look for gastronomic delights. . . .
     *Chafing Dish Possibilities*, Ch. 1
     1898

## 256. Minna Irving
### (1857–1940)

\*   \*   \*

1 A nation thrills, a nation bleeds,
A nation follows where it leads,
And every man is proud to yield
His life upon a crimson field
For Betsy's battle flag.
     "Betsy's Battle Flag"

2 He's cheerful in weather so bitterly cold
It freezes your bones to the marrow;
I'll admit he's a beggar, a gangster, a bum,
But I take off my hat to the sparrow.
     "The Sparrow"

3 I used to climb the garret stairs
On a rainy day and lift the lid
And loose the fragrance of olden times
That under the faded finery hid.
     "The Wedding Gift," St. 2

4 The flowery frocks and the ancient trunk,
And Grandmother Granger, too, are dust,
But something precious and sweet and rare
Survives the havoc of moth and rust.
     Ibid., St. 6

## 257. Edna Lyall
### (1857–1903)

1 Two is company, three is trumpery, as the proverb says.      *Wayfaring Men*, Ch. 24
     1897

## 258. Agnes Mary Robinson
### (1857–1944)

\*   \*   \*

1 When I was young the twilight seemed too long.
     "Twilight"

2 You hail from dream-land, Dragon-fly?
A stranger hither? So am I.
     "To a Dragonfly"

## 259. Ida Tarbell

(1857–1944)

1 The first and most imperative necessity in war is money, for money means everything else— men, guns, ammunition.
*The Tariff in Our Times*, Ch. 1
*1906*

2 There is no man more dangerous, in a position of power, than he who refuses to accept as a working truth the idea that all a man does should make for rightness and soundness, that even the fixing of a tariff rate must be moral.
Ibid., Ch. 12

3 Sacredness of human life! The world has never believed it! It has been with life that we settled our quarrels, won wives, gold and land, defended ideas, imposed religions. We have held that a death toll was a necessary part of every human achievement, whether sport, war, or industry. A moment's rage over the horror of it, and we have sunk into indifference.
*New Ideals in Business*, Ch. 3
*1914*

4 Those who talk of the mine, the mill, the factory as if they were inherently inhuman and horrible are those who never have known the miner, the weaver, or the steel or iron worker.
Ibid., Ch. 7

5 There is no more effective medicine to apply to feverish public sentiment than figures. To be sure, they must be properly prepared, must cover the case, not confine themselves to a quarter of it, and they must be gathered for their own sake, not for the sake of a theory. Such preparation we get in a national census.
*The Ways of Woman*, Ch. 1    *1914*

6 They did not understand it [culture] to be ripeness and sureness of mind, it was not taste, discrimination, judgment; it was an acquisition— something which came with diplomas and degrees and only with them.    Ibid., Ch. 5

7 A mind which really lays hold of a subject is not easily detached from it.    Ibid.

8 A mind truly cultivated never feels that the intellectual process is complete until it can reproduce in some media the thing which it has absorbed.    Ibid.

9 "Yes, sir; he was what I call a *godly* man. Fact is, I never knew anybody I felt so sure would walk straight into Heaven, everybody welcomin' him, nobody fussin' or fumin' about his bein' let in, as Abraham Lincoln."
*In Lincoln's Chair*    *1920*

10 "It takes God a long time to work out His will with men like us, Billy, bad men, stupid men, selfish men. But even if we're beat, there's a gain. There are more men who see clear now how hard it is for people to rule themselves, more people to determine government by the people shan't perish from the earth, more people willin' to admit that you can't have peace when you've got a thing like slavery goin' on. That something, that's goin' to help when the next struggle comes."    Ibid.

## 260. Martha Thomas

(1857–1935)

1 Women are one-half of the world but until a century ago . . . it was a man's world. The laws were man's laws, the government a man's government, the country a man's country. . . . The man's world must become a man's and a woman's world. Why are we afraid? It is the next step forward on the path to the sunrise, and the sun is rising over a new heaven and a new earth.    Address, North American Woman Suffrage Association, Buffalo, New York    *October, 1908*

## 261. Clara Zetkin

(1857–1933)

1 . . . women must remain in industry despite all narrow-minded caterwauling; in fact the circle of their industrial activity must become broader and more secure daily. . . .
*The Question of Women Workers and Women at the Present Time*
*1889*

2 The organization and enlightenment of working women, the struggle to attain their economic and political equal rights is not only desirable for the socialist movement. It is and will become more and more a life-and-death question for it. . . .    Ibid.

3 The beginnings of the class-conscious organized proletarian woman's movement in Germany are indissolubly bound up with the coming into being and maturing of the socialist conception of society in the proletariat. . . .
*Zur Geschichte der proletarischen Frauenbewegung Deutschlands*
*1928*

4 The position of women could only be improved through the improvement of workers, that is, through abolition of the wage system.    Ibid.

5 . . . as the liberation of the proletariat is possible only through the abolition of the capitalist productive relation, so too the emancipation of woman is possible only through doing away with private property.      Ibid.

6 All roads led to Rome. Every truly Marxist analysis of an important part of the ideological superstructure of society, of an outstanding social phenomenon, had to lead to an analysis of bourgeois society and its foundation, private property. It should lead to the conclusion that "Carthage must be destroyed."
> "My Recollections of Lenin" (1925),
> Quoted in *The Emancipation of*
> *Women*      *1966p*

## 262. Dorothy Gurney

(1858–1932)

\* \* \*

1 The kiss of sun for pardon,
  The song of the birds for mirth—
One is nearer God's Heart in a garden
Than anywhere else on earth.
> "The Lord God Planted a Garden,"
> St. 3

## 263. Selma Lagerlöf

(1858–1940)

1 There were no accusers; there could be no judge.      *The Story of Gösta Berling,*
Introduction, Ch. 1      *1891*

2 Burdensome are the ways men have to follow here on earth. They lead through deserts, and through marshes, and over mountains. Why is so much sorrow allowed to go on without interruption, until it loses itself in the desert or sinks in the bog, or is killed in the mountains? Where are the little flower-pickers, where are the little princesses of the fairy tale about whose feet roses grow; where are they who should strew flowers on the weary path?
> Ibid., Pt. II, Ch. 2

3 There was nothing to do but to rest after the endless journey she had made. But that she could never do. She began to weep because she would never reach her journey's end. Her whole life long she would travel, travel, travel, and never reach the end of her journey.
> *The Miracles of Anti-Christ,*
> Bk. I, Ch. 7      *1899*

4 Does it always end so with a woman? When they build their palaces they are never finished. Women can do nothing that has permanence.
> Ibid., Bk. II, Ch. 2

5 It is a strange thing to come home. While yet on the journey, you cannot at all realize how strange it will be.      Ibid., Bk. III, Ch. 3

6 Just fancy what an effect his violin could have! It made people quite forget themselves. It was a great power to have at his disposal. Any moment he liked he could take possession of his kingdom.
> "The Story of a Country House,"
> Ch. 1, *From a Swedish Homestead*
> *1901*

7 In that region of terror, in that great desert, there had at any rate grown one flower that had comforted him with fragrance and beauty, and now he felt that love would dwell with him forever. The wildflower of the desert had been transplanted into the garden of life, and had taken root and grown and thriven, and when he felt this he knew he was saved; he knew that the darkness had found its master.
> Ibid., Ch. 6

8 The fair sun is like a mother whose son is about to set out for a far-off land, and who, in the hour of the leave-taking, cannot take her eyes from the beloved.
> Ibid., "Astrid," Ch. 3

9 There is nothing so terrible as perjury. There is something uncanny and awful about that sin. There is no mercy or condonation for it.
> "The Girl from the Marsh Croft,"
> *The Girl from the Marsh Croft*
> *1911*

10 "When I see a stream like this in the wilderness," he thought, "I am reminded of my own life. As persistent as this stream have I been in forcing my way past all that has obstructed my path. Father has been my rock ahead, and Mother tried to hold me back and bury me between moss-tufts, but I stole past both of them and got out in the world. Hey-ho, hi, hi!"
> Ibid., "The Musician"

11 Thinking is never so easy as when one follows a plow up a furrow and down a furrow.
> *Jerusalem*, Bk. I, Ch. 1      *1915*

12 "The ways of Providence cannot be reasoned out by the finite mind," he mused. "I cannot fathom them, yet seeking to know them is the most satisfying thing in all the world."
> Ibid., Bk. II

13 "It has been said, as you know," Hellgum went on, "that if somebody strikes us on one cheek we must turn the other cheek also, and that we should not resist evil, and other things of the same sort; all of which none of us can live up to. Why, people would rob you of your

house and home, they'd steal your potatoes and carry off your grain, if you fail to protect what was yours."      Ibid.

14 Could I ever be happy again now that I knew there was so much evil in the world?
*The Diary of Selma Lagerlöf*
(March 24, 1872)     *1936*

15 To be sure, I believe in the power of the dead, but I also know that Selma Otillia Lovisa Lagerlöf is inclined to imagine things that are utterly impossible.    Ibid. (March 26, 1872)

## 264. Edith Nesbit

(1858–1924)

\*   \*   \*

1 Little brown brother, oh! little brown brother,
Are you awake in the dark?
"Baby Seed Song"

2 The chestnut's proud, and the lilac's pretty,
The poplar's gentle and tall,
But the plane tree's kind to the poor dull city—
I love him best of all!
"Child's Song in Spring"

## 265. Emmeline Pankhurst

(1858–1928)

1 It is time that the women took their place in Imperial politics.
Quoted in *The Standard* (London)
*October 5, 1911*

2 Those men and women are fortunate who are born at a time when a great struggle for human freedom is in progress.
*My Own Story*     *1914*

3 I was transfixed with horror, and over me there swept the sudden conviction that hanging was a mistake—worse, a crime. It was my awakening to one of the most terrible facts of life—that justice and judgment lie often a world apart.      Ibid.

4 . . . if civilisation is to advance at all in the future, it must be through the help of women, women freed of their political shackles, women with full power to work their will in society. It was rapidly becoming clear to my mind that men regarded women as a servant class in the community, and that women were going to remain in the servant class until they lifted themselves out of it.      Ibid.

5 Women had always fought for men, and for their children. Now they were ready to fight for their own human rights. Our militant movement was established.      Ibid.

6 "I have never felt a prouder woman than I did one night when a police constable said to me, after one of these demonstrations, 'Had this been a man's demonstration, there would have been bloodshed long ago.' Well, my lord, there has not been any bloodshed except on the part of the women themselves—these so-called militant women. Violence has been done to us, and I who stand before you in this dock have lost a dear sister in the course of this agitation."
Ibid.

7 . . . I was sadly aware that we were but approaching a far goal. The end, though certain, was still distant. Patience and still more patience, faith and still more faith, well, we had called upon these souls' help before and it was certain that they would not fail us at this greatest crisis of all.      Ibid.

8 . . . I said [to the prison doctor]: "I will not be examined by you because your intention is not to help me as a patient, but merely to ascertain how much longer it will be possible to keep me alive in prison. I am not prepared to assist you or the government in any such way. I am not prepared to relieve you of any responsibility in this matter."      Ibid.

9 Why is it that men's blood-shedding militancy is applauded and women's symbolic militancy punished with a prison-cell and the forcible feeding horror? It means simply this, that men's double standard of sexual morals, whereby the victims of their lust are counted as outcasts while the men themselves escape all social censure, really applies to morals in all departments of life. Men make the moral code and they expect women to accept it.
Ibid.

10 It always seems to me when the anti-suffrage members of the Government criticize militancy in women that it is very like beasts of prey reproaching the gentler animals who turn in desperate resistance when at the point of death.
Ibid., Speech, "I Incite This Meeting
to Rebellion" (October 17, 1912)

11 There is something that governments care far more for than human life, and that is the security of property, and so it is through property that we shall strike the enemy.     Ibid.

12 One thing is essential to an army, and that thing is made up of a two-fold requirement. In an army you need unity of purpose. In an army you also need unity of policy.     Ibid.

13 How different the reasoning is that men adopt when they are discussing the cases of men and those of women. *Ibid.*, Speech, "When Civil War Is Waged by Women" (November 13, 1913)

14 You have to make more noise than anybody else, you have to make yourself more obtrusive than anybody else, you have to fill all the papers more than anybody else, in fact you have to be there all the time and see that they do not snow you under, if you are really going to get your reform realized. *Ibid.*

15 Some of the guards—I think men who had never known what it was to earn a living, who knew nothing of the difficulties of a man's life, let alone the difficulties of a woman's life— came out, and they said: "Why did you break our windows? We have done nothing." She said: "It is because you have done nothing I have broken your windows." *Ibid.*

16 We are driven to this. We are determined to go on with the agitation. We are in honour bound to do so until we win. Just as it was the duty of our forefathers to do it for you, it is our duty to make this world a better place for women. Speech (1908), Quoted in *The Fighting Pankhursts* by David Mitchell *1967p*

17 I am what you call a hooligan! *Ibid.*, Speech (1909)

18 I have no sense of guilt. I look upon myself as a prisoner of war. I am under no moral obligation to conform to, or in any way accept, the sentence imposed upon me. *Ibid.*, Speech to the Court (April, 1913)

19 Our sons and daughters must be trained in national service, taught to give as well as to receive. *Ibid.*, Speech, British Columbia (May, 1920)

20 Help us to educate the people of the Dominion to the necessity of a single standard of morals— that of the highest. Teach your children reverence for the marriage vow of men and women. Instill into their minds the belief in purity of body, mind and soul. *Ibid.*, Speech, Federated Women's Institutes, Ottawa (March, 1924)

21 I don't think they [women] have done badly, considering that it is so hard not to get wrapped up in the mere struggle for existence. Of course we expected a great deal from our enfranchisement. But so did men when they fought for theirs. It is the only way—to keep fighting, to believe that the miracle is going to happen. *Ibid.*, Press Conference (1926)

22 We have taken this action, because as women . . . we realize that the condition of our sex is so deplorable that it is our duty even to break the law in order to call attention to the reasons why we do so. Speech to the Court (October 21, 1908), *Shoulder to Shoulder*, Midge Mackenzie, ed. *1975p*

23 Over one thousand women have gone to prison in the course of this agitation, have suffered their imprisonment, have come out of prison injured in health, weakened in body, but not in spirit. . . . I ask you . . . if you are prepared to go on doing that kind of thing indefinitely, because that is what is going to happen. There is absolutely no doubt about it. . . . We are women, rightly or wrongly convinced that this is the only way in which we can win power to alter what for us are intolerable conditions, absolutely intolerable conditions. From the moment I leave this court I shall deliberately refuse to eat food—I shall join the women who are already in Holloway [Women's Prison] on the hunger strike. I shall come out of prison, dead or alive, at the earliest possible moment; and once again, as soon as I am physically fit I shall enter into this fight again. Life is very dear to all of us. I am not seeking, as was said by the Home Secretary, to commit suicide. I do not want to commit suicide. I want to see the women of this country enfranchised, and I want to live until that is done. *Ibid.*, Speech to the Court (April 2, 1913)

24 In time of war the rules of peace must be set aside and we must put ourselves without delay upon a war basis, let the women stand shoulder to shoulder with the men to win the common victory which we all desire. *Ibid.*, Speech, London Pavilion (October 5, 1915)

25 Better that we should die fighting than be outraged and dishonoured. . . . Better to die than to live in slavery. *Ibid.*, Speech, Army and Navy Hall, Petrograd (August, 1917)

26 What we want to proclaim to this meeting is that we want the bill, the whole bill, and nothing but the bill. . . . We want the vote so that we may serve our country better. We want the vote so that we shall be more faithful and more true to our allies. We want the vote so that we may help to maintain the cause of Christian civilisation for which we entered this war. We want the vote so that in future such wars if possible may be averted. *Ibid.*, Speech, Queen's Hall (April 23, 1917)

## 266. Agnes Repplier

(1858–1950)

1 . . . but the children of to-day are favored beyond their knowledge and certainly far beyond their deserts.

> "Children, Past and Present,"
> *Books and Men*    1888

2 And what universal politeness has been fostered by the terror that superstition breeds, what delicate euphemisms containing the very soul of courtesy!

> Ibid., "On the Benefits of Superstition"

3 Again, in the stress of modern life, how little room is left for that most comfortable vanity which whispers in our ears that failures are not faults! Now we are taught from infancy that we must rise or fall upon our own merits; that vigilance wins success, and incapacity means ruin.      Ibid.

4 A happy commonplaceness is now acknowledged to be, next to brevity of life, man's best inheritance; but in the days when all the virtues and vices were flaunted in gala costume, people were hardly prepared for that fine simplicity which has grown to be the crucial test of art.

> Ibid., "The Decay of Sentiment"

5 So if the masterpieces of the present, the triumphs of learned verbs and realistic prose, fail to lift their readers out of themselves, like the masterpieces of the past, the fault must be our own.      Ibid.

6 There is nothing in the world so enjoyable as a thorough-going monomania. . . .      Ibid.

7 We are tethered to our kind, and may as well join hands in the struggle.      Ibid.

8 But self-satisfaction, if as buoyant as gas, has an ugly trick of collapsing when full blown, and facts are stony things that refuse to melt away in the sunshine of a smile.

> Ibid., "Some Aspects of Pessimism"

9 It is a humiliating fact that, notwithstanding our avaricious greed for novelties, we are forced, when sincere, to confess that *"les anciens ont tout dit,"* and that it is probable the contending schools of thought have always held the same relative positions they do now: Optimism glittering in the front ranks as a deservedly popular favorite; pessimism speaking with a still, persistent voice to those who, unluckily for themselves, have the leisure and the intelligence to attend.      Ibid.

10 The pessimist, however—be it recorded to his credit—is seldom an agitating individual. His creed breeds indifference to others, and he does not trouble himself to thrust his views upon the unconvinced.      Ibid.

11 Memory cheats us no less than hope by hazing over those things that we would fain forget; but who that has plodded on to middle age would take back upon his shoulders ten of the vanished years, with their mingled pleasures and pains? Who would return to the youth he is forever pretending to regret?      Ibid.

12 The great masterpieces of humor, which have kept men young by laughter, are being tried in the courts of an orthodox morality, and found lamentably wanting; or else, by way of giving them another chance, they are being subjected to the *peine forte et dure* of modern analysis, and are revealing hideous and melancholy meanings in the process.

> "A Plea for Humor," *Points of View*
> 1891

13 Whatever has "wit enough to keep it sweet" defies corruption and outlasts all time; but the wit must be of that outward and visible order which needs no introduction or demonstration at our hands.      Ibid.

14 Sensuality, too, which used to show itself coarse, smiling, unmasked, and unmistakable, is now serious, analytic, and so burdened with a sense of its responsibility that it passes muster half the time as a new type of asceticism.

> Ibid., "Fiction in the Pulpit"

15 Amusement is merely one side of pleasure, but a very excellent side, against which, in truth, I have no evil word to urge. The gods forbid such base and savorless ingratitude!

> Ibid., "Pleasure: A Heresy"

16 A villain must be a thing of power, handled with delicacy and grace. He must be wicked enough to excite our aversion, strong enough to arouse our fear, human enough to awaken some transient gleam of sympathy. We must triumph in his downfall, yet not barbarously nor with contempt, and the close of his career must be in harmony with all its previous development.      "A Short Defence of Villains,"

> *Essays in Miniature*    1892

17 We have but the memories of past good cheer, we have but the echoes of departed laughter. In vain we look and listen for the mirth that has died away. In vain we seek to question the gray ghosts of old-time revelers.

> Ibid., "Humors of Gastronomy"

18 Philadelphians are every whit as mediocre as their neighbours, but they seldom encourage each other in mediocrity by giving it a more agreeable name.
>*Philadelphia: The Place and the People*, Introduction    *1898*

19 It is hard for us who live in an age of careless and cheerful tolerance to understand the precise inconveniences attending religious persecution.    Ibid., Ch. 1

20 Necessity knows no Sunday. . . .
>Ibid., Ch. 18

21 We have reached a point of idle curiosity which forces into print every pitiful scrap of correspondence which has lain sacred—or forgotten —in the bottoms of old desks, and every five minutes chat with people of distinction.
>"Memoirs and Biographies," *Counsel Upon the Reading of Books*    *1900*

22 Anyone, however, who has had dealings with dates knows that they are worse than elusive, they are perverse. Events do not happen at the right time, nor in their proper sequence. That sense of harmony with place and season which is so strong in the historian—if he be a readable historian—is lamentably lacking in history, which takes no pains to verify its most convincing statements.
>*To Think of Tea!*, Ch. 1    *1932*

23 It has been well said that tea is suggestive of a thousand wants, from which spring the decencies and luxuries of civilization.    Ibid., Ch. 2

24 The English do not strain their tea in the fervid fashion we [Americans] do. They like to see a few leaves dawdling about the cup. They like to know what they are drinking.
>Ibid., Ch. 13

25 No man pursues what he has at hand. No man recognizes the need of pursuit until that which he desires has escaped him.
>*In Pursuit of Laughter*, Ch. 1    *1936*

26 People who cannot recognize a palpable absurdity are very much in the way of civilization.
>Ibid., Ch. 9

27 It is not depravity that afflicts the human race so much as a general lack of intelligence.
>Ibid.

28 The worst in life, we are told, is compatible with the best in art. So too the worst in life is compatible with the best in humour.    Ibid.

29 Wit is a pleasure-giving thing, largely because it eludes reason; but in the apprehension of an absurdity through the working of the comic spirit there is a foundation of reason, and an impetus to human companionship.    Ibid.

30 Humour brings insight and tolerance. Irony brings a deeper and less friendly understanding.
>Ibid.

31 On the preservation of the Comic Spirit depends in some measure the ultimate triumph of civilization. Science may carry us to Mars, but it will leave the earth peopled as ever by the inept.    Ibid.

## 267. Beatrice Potter Webb
### (1858–1943)

1 The underlying principle of the industrial revolution—the creed of universal competition— the firm faith that every man free to follow his own self-interest would contribute most effectually to the common weal, with the converse proposition that each man should suffer the full consequence of his own actions—this simple and powerful idea was enabling a rising middle class to break up and destroy those restraints on personal freedom, those monopolies for private gain, with which a Parliament of landowners had shackled the enterprise and weighted the energies of the nation.
>*The Cooperative Movement in Great Britain*, Ch. 1    *1891*

2 For the committee-man or officer who accepts a bribe or neglects his duty must be fully aware that he is not simply an indifferently honest man, like many of his fellows in private trade, but the deliberate betrayer of the means of salvation to thousands of his fellow-countrymen of this and all future generations.
>Ibid., Ch. 7

3 The hand-to-mouth existence of the casual labourer . . . the restlessness or mortal weariness arising from lack of nourishment, tempered by idleness, or intensified by physical exhaustion, do not permit the development, in the individual or the class, of the qualities of democratic association and democratic self-government.    Ibid., Ch. 8

4 The caprices of fashion, the vagaries of personal vanity and over-indulged appetites can find no satisfaction in an organization of industry based on the supply of rational and persistent wants.    Ibid.

5 But evidence drawn empirically from facts, though it may justify the action of the practical man, is not scientifically conclusive.
>"The Economics of Factory Legislation," *Socialism and National Minimum*    *1909*

6 All along the line, physically, mentally, morally, alcohol is a weakening and deadening force, and it is worth a great deal to save women and girls from its influence.
                    *Health of Working Girls*, Ch. 10
                                            *1917*

7 The inevitability of gradualness.
                    Presidential Address, British Labour
                    Party Congress       *1923*

8 Beneath the surface of our daily life, in the personal history of many of us, there runs a continuous controversy between an Ego that affirms and an Ego that denies. On the course of this controversy depends the attainment of inner harmony and consistent conduct in private and public affairs.          *My Apprenticeship,*
                    Introduction       *1926*

9 Religion is love; in no case is it logic.
                                        Ibid., Ch. 2

10 For any detailed description of the complexity of human nature, of the variety and mixture in human motive, of the insurgence of instinct in the garb of reason, of the multifarious play of the social environment on the individual ego and of the individual ego on the social environment, I had to turn to novelists and poets. . . .
                                        Ibid., Ch. 3

11 . . . if I had been a man, self-respect, family pressure and the public opinion of my class would have pushed me into a money-making profession; as a mere woman I could carve out a career of disinterested research.
                                        Ibid., Ch. 8

12 . . . what we had to do was . . . to make medical treatment not a favour granted to those in desperate need but to compel all sick persons to submit to it . . . to treat illness, in fact, as a public nuisance to be suppressed in the interests of the community.
                    Quoted by Anne Fremantle in
                    *Woman as Revolutionary,*
                    Fred C. Giffin, ed.       *1973p*


## 268.  Eva Rose York

### (1858–1925?)

\* \* \*

1 I shall not pass this way again;
    Then let me now relieve some pain,
    Remove some barrier from the road,
    Or brighten some one's heavy load.
            "I Shall Not Pass This Way Again,"
                                        St. 2

2 . . . I have drunk the cup of bliss
    Remembering not that those there be
    Who drink the dregs of misery.
                                        Ibid., St. 3


## 269.  Katherine Lee Bates

### (1859–1929)

1 O beautiful for spacious skies,
    For amber waves of grain,
    For purple mountain majesties
        Above the fruited plain!
    America! America!
        God shed His grace on thee
    And crown thy good with brotherhood
        From sea to shining sea!
            "America the Beautiful," St. 1
                                        *1893*

2 O beautiful for patriot dream
    That sees beyond the years.
    Thine alabaster cities gleam
        Undimmed by human tears!
                                        Ibid., St. 4

\* \* \*

3 Dawn love is silver,
    Wait for the west:
    Old love is gold love—
    Old love is best.
                    "For a Golden Wedding"

4 Nay, brother of the sod,
    What part hast thou in God?
    What spirit art thou of?
    It answers, "Love."
                                        "Laddie"

5 Spirit long shaping for sublime endeavor,
    A sword of God, the gleaming metal came
    From stern Scotch ancestry, where whatsoever
    Was true, was pure, was noble, won acclaim.
                                "Woodrow Wilson"


## 270.  Louise de Koven Bowen

### (1859–1953)

1 I hated myself because I smelt of onions and meat, and I seriously considered suicide in the cistern which supplied the house.
                    *Growing Up with a City*, Ch. 1
                                        *1926*

2 By the time I made my entry into society I was ignorant in everything and accomplished in nothing.                                 Ibid.

3 It is always a real satisfaction to know that politics has not yet dominated the Juvenile Court of Cook County; that we still have these judges who are incorruptible and devoted to their work.                          Ibid., Ch. 4

## 271. Carrie Chapman Catt
### (1859–1947)

1 The sacrifice of suffering, of doubt, of obloquy, which has been endured by the pioneers in the woman movement will never be fully known or understood. . . .
> Speech, "For the Sake of Liberty" (February 8–14, 1900), Quoted in *History of Woman Suffrage*, Vol. IV, by Susan B. Anthony and Ida Husted
> 1902

2 There are two kinds of restrictions upon human liberty—the restraint of law and that of custom. No written law has ever been more binding than unwritten custom supported by popular opinion.
> Ibid.

3 Once, this movement represented the scattered and disconnected protests of individual women. . . . Happily those days are past; and out of that incoherent and seemingly futile agitation, which extended over many centuries, there has emerged a present-day movement possessing a clear understanding and a definite, positive purpose.
> Speech, "Is Woman Suffrage Progressing?," Stockholm   1911

4 The Government evidently nurses a forlorn hope that by delay it may tire out the workers and destroy the force of the campaign.
> Ibid.

5 When a just cause reaches its flood-tide, as ours has done in that country, whatever stands in the way must fall before its overwhelming power.
> Ibid.

6 There they swell that horrid, unspeakably unclean peril of civilisation, prostitution—augmented by the White Slave Traffic and by the machinations of the male parasites who live upon the earnings of women of vice. . . . We must be merciful, for they are the natural and inevitable consequence of centuries of false reasoning concerning woman's place in the world. . . . Upon these women we have no right to turn our backs. Their wrongs are our wrongs. Their existence is part of our problem. They have been created by the very injustice against which we protest.
> Ibid.

## 272. Helen Gray Cone
### (1859–1934)

1 A song of hate is a song of Hell;
Some there be who sing it well.
> "Chant of Love for England"
> 1945p

2 Bind higher, grind higher, burn higher with fire,
Cast her ashes into the sea,—
She shall escape, she shall aspire,
She shall arise to make men free.
> Ibid.

\*   \*   \*

3 Peerless, fearless, an army's flower!
Sterner soldiers the world never saw,
Marching lightly, that summer hour,
To death and failure and fame forever.
> "Greencastle Jenny," St. 4

4 Upon a showery night and still,
Without a second of warning,
A trooper band surprised the hill,
And held it in the morning.
We were not waked by bugle notes,
No cheer our dreams invaded,
And yet at dawn their yellow coats
On the green slopes paraded.
> "The Dandelions"

## 273. Eleanora Duse
### (1859–1924)

1 Before passing my lips each word seemed to have coursed through the ardor of my blood. There wasn't a fiber in me that did not add its notes to the harmony. Ah, grace—the state of grace!
> Quoted in *Il Fuoco* by D'Annunzio
> 1900

2 I know nothing, nothing! I have everything to learn. Twelve years ago, when I left the theatre, I did so with no regrets. I was tired of living for others; I wanted to live for myself and learn and learn!
> Quoted in *Errinerungen, Betrachtungen und Brief* by Edouard Schneider
> 1921

3 I did not use paint. I made myself up morally.
> Quoted by Louis Schneider in
> *Le Gaulois*   July 27, 1922

4 I'm only a little Italian actress. Nobody would understand me abroad. Let me first perfect myself in my art which I dearly love, and don't try to lead me astray.
> Quoted in *Le Matin*
> April 12, 1924

5 Do you think one can speak about art? It would be like trying to explain love. There are many ways of loving and there are as many kinds of art. There is the love that elevates and leads to good—there is the love that absorbs all one's will, all one's strength and intelligence.

In my opinion this is the truest love—but it is certainly fatal. . . . So is it with art. . . .
Quoted in *Eleanora Duse* by C. Antonia-Traversi    *1926p*

6 You never told me that life is vulgar, you—alone—sadly agreed with me that life is grievous.    Ibid.

7 Oh, art, that consumes my life! But what resource! I could not bear to live if I did not have it.    Quoted in *Signorelli* by Olga Resnevic (1884)    *1938p*

8 Work means so many things! So many! Among other things Work also means Freedom. . . . Without it even the miracle of love is only a cruel deception.
Quoted in *Vita de Arrigo Boito* by Piero Nardi    *1942p*

9 The strongest is the loneliest and the loneliest is the strongest.    Ibid.

10 When moral sensibility alone is in question, I am won; but as soon as doctrinal intransigence and a purely ecclesiastical point of view enter in, I rebel.
Quoted in *The Mystic in the Theatre* by Eva Le Gallienne    *1965p*

## 274. Lady Gregory

(1859?–1932)

1 CHRISTIE. It's a grand thing to be able to take up your money in your hand and to think no more of it when it slips away from you than you would of a trout that would slip back into the stream.    *Twenty Five*    *1903*

2 MRS. TARPEY. Business, is it? What business would the people here have but to be minding one another's business?
*Spreading the News*    *1905*

3 MRS. DELANE. I'm not one that blames the police. Sure, they have their own bread to earn like every other one. And indeed it is often they will let a thing pass.    *Hyacinth Halvey*    *1906*

4 MRS. DONOHOE. There is many a thing in the sea is not decent, but cockles is fit to put before the Lord!    *The Workhouse Ward*    *1908*

5 HAZEL. To have no power of revenge after death! My strength to go nourish weeds and grass!    *Coats*    *1910*

6 MRS. BRODERICK. A splendid shot he was; the thing he did not see he'd hit it the same as the thing he'd see.    *The Full Moon*    *1910*

7 DARBY. I am maybe getting your meaning wrong, your tongue being a little hard and sharp because you are Englified, but I am without new learnments and so I speak flat.
*The Bogiemen*    *1912*

8 O'MALLEY. Well, there's no one at all, they do be saying, but is deserving of some punishment from the very minute of his birth. . . . Sure it is allotted to every Christian to meet with his share of trouble.
*Shanwalla*, Act II    *1915*

9 1st POLICEMAN. There's nothing in the world more ignorant than to give any belief to ghosts. I am walking the world these twenty years, and never met anything worse than myself!
Ibid., Act III

10 GIANT. Fru, Fa, Fashog! I smell the smell of a melodious lying Irishman!
*The Golden Apple*, Act I, Sc. 4    *1916*

11 GIANT. One person to know it, and you to know him to know it, is the same as if it was known to all the world.
Ibid., Act II, Sc. 2

12 MOTHER. Them that have too much of it [learning] are seven times crosser than them that never saw a book.
*Aristotle Bellows*, Act I    *1921*

13 CELIA. It is better to be tied to any thorny bush than to be with a cross man.    Ibid.

14 JESTER. There's more learning than is taught in books.    *The Jester*, Act I    *1923*

15 OGRE. I'll take no charity! What I get I'll earn by taking it. I would feel no pleasure it being given to me, any more than a huntsman would take pleasure being made a present of a dead fox, in place of getting a run across country after it.    Ibid., Act II, Sc. 1

16 JOEL. That's the way of it! All the generations looking for him, and praying for him. We wanted him, and we got him, and what we did with him was to kill him. And that is the way it will be ever and always, so long as leaves grow upon the trees!
*The Story Brought by Brigit*, Act III    *1924*

## 275. Florence Kelley

(1859–1932)

1 . . . the utter unimportance of children compared with products in the minds of the people. . . .
"My Philadelphia," *The Survey Graphic* *October 1, 1926*

## 276. Nora Archibald Smith

(1859–1934)

\* \* \*

1 They'd knock on a tree and would timidly say
To the spirit that might be within there that
day:
"Fairy fair, Fairy fair, wish thou me well;
'Gainst evil witcheries weave me a spell!"
"Knocking on Wood," St. 3

## 277. Mary Gardiner Brainard

(fl. 1860s)

\* \* \*

1 I would rather walk with God in the dark than
go alone in the light.
"Not Knowing," St. 1

2 And what looks dark in the distance may
brighten as I draw near.
Ibid., St. 2

## 278. Jane Addams

(1860–1935)

1 The new growth in the plant swelling against
the sheath, which at the same time imprisons
and protects it, must still be the truest type of
progress. "Filial Relations," *Democracy and
Social Ethics　　1907*

2 The colleges have long been full of the best
ethical teaching. . . . But while the teaching
has included an ever-broadening range of obligation and has insisted upon the recognition of
the claims of human brotherhood, the training
has been singularly individualistic; it has fostered ambitions for personal distinction, and
has trained the faculties almost exclusively in
the direction of intellectual accumulation.
Ibid.

3 In our pity for Lear, we fail to analyze his
character. . . . His paternal expression was
one of domination and indulgence, without the
perception of the needs of his children, without
any anticipation of their entrance into a wider
life, or any belief that they could have a worthy
life apart from him. Ibid.

4 Doubtless the clashes and jars which we feel
most keenly are those which occur when two
standards of morals, both honestly held and
believed in, are brought sharply together.
Ibid.

5 A city is in many respects a great business
corporation, but in other respects it is enlarged
housekeeping. . . . May we not say that city
housekeeping has failed partly because women,
the traditional housekeepers, have not been
consulted as to its multiform activities?
"Utilization of Women in City
Government," *Newer Ideals of
Peace　　1907*

6 Old-fashioned ways which no longer apply to
changed conditions are a snare in which the
feet of women have always become readily
entangled. Ibid.

7 . . . the administration of the household has
suffered because it has become unnaturally isolated from the rest of the community. Ibid.

8 Unless our conception of patriotism is progressive, it cannot hope to embody the real affection and the real interest of the nation. Ibid.

9 Private beneficence is totally inadequate to deal
with the vast numbers of the city's disinherited.
*Twenty Years at Hull House　　1910*

10 Perhaps I may record here my protest against
the efforts, so often made, to shield children
and young people from all that has to do with
death and sorrow, to give them a good time at
all hazards on the assumption that the ills of
life will come soon enough. Young people themselves often resent this attitude on the part of
their elders; they feel set aside and belittled as
if they were denied the common human experiences. Ibid.

11 We were often distressed by the children of
immigrant parents who were ashamed of the
pit whence they were digged, who repudiated
the language and customs of their elders, and
counted themselves successful [when] they were
able to ignore the past. Ibid.

12 In his own way each man must struggle, lest
the moral law become a far-off abstraction
utterly separated from his active life. Ibid.

13 You do not know what life means when all the
difficulties are removed! I am simply smothered
and sickened with advantages. It is like eating
a sweet dessert the first thing in the morning.
Ibid.

14 Only in time of fear is government thrown
back to its primitive and sole function of self-
defense and the many interests of which it is
the guardian become subordinated to that.
"Women, War and Suffrage," *Survey
November 6, 1915*

15 Each exponent in this long effort to place law above force was called a dreamer and a coward, but each did his utmost to express clearly the truth that was in him, and beyond that human effort cannot go.      Ibid.

16 . . . the fruitful processes of cooperation in the great experiment of living together in a world become conscious of itself.      Ibid.

17 Civilization is a method of living, an attitude of equal respect for all men.
Speech, Honolulu     *1933*

## 279. Marie Konstantinovna Bashkirtseff

(1860–1884)

1 Ah, when one thinks what a miserable creature man is! Every other animal can, at his will, wear on his face the expression he pleases. He is not obligated to smile if he has a mind to weep. When he does not wish to see his fellows he does not see them. While man is the slave of everything and everybody!
*The Journal of a Young Artist*
(May 6, 1873)    *1884*

2 To say that my grief will be eternal would be ridiculous—nothing is eternal.
Ibid. (October 17, 1873)

3 Let us love dogs; let us love only dogs! Men and cats are unworthy creatures. . . .
Ibid. (July 16, 1874)

4 In the studio all distinctions disappear. One has neither name nor family; one is no longer the daughter of one's mother, one is one's self—an individual—and one has before one art, and nothing else. One feels so happy, so free, so proud.     Ibid. (October 5, 1877)

5 . . . I write down everything, everything, everything. Otherwise why should I write?
Ibid. (May 1, 1884)

6 If I had been born a man, I would have conquered Europe. As I was born a woman, I exhausted my energy in tirades against fate, and in eccentricities.    Ibid. (June 25, 1884)

7 For my own part I think love—-impossible—to one who looks at human nature through a microscope, as I do. They who see only what they wish to see in those around them are very fortunate.     Ibid. (August 1, 1884)

## 280. Ellen Thorneycroft Fowler

(1860–1929)

\* \* \*

1 Though outwardly a gloomy shroud,
The inner half of every cloud
   Is bright and shining:
I therefore turn my clouds about
And always wear them inside out
   To show the lining.
"Wisdom of Folly"

## 281. Charlotte Perkins Gilman

(1860–1935)

1 "Your exercise depends on your strength, my dear," said he, "and your food somewhat on your appetite; but air you can absorb all the time."     "The Yellow Wall-Paper,"
*New England Magazine*    *1891*

2 I used to lie awake as a child and get more entertainment and terror out of blank walls and plain furniture than most children could find in a toy-store.     Ibid.

3 I do not want to be a fly,
I want to be a worm!
"A Conservative,"
*In This Our World*    *1893*

4 From the day laborer to the millionaire, the wife's worn dress or flashing jewels, her low roof or her lordly one, her weary feet or her rich equipage—these speak of the economic ability of the husband.
*Women and Economics*, Ch. 1
*1898*

5 Grateful return for happiness conferred is not the method of exchange in a partnership. The comfort a man takes with his wife is not in the nature of a business partnership, nor are her frugality and industry.     Ibid.

6 The labor of women in the house, certainly, enables men to produce more wealth than they otherwise could; and in this way women are economic factors in society. But so are horses.     Ibid.

7 The women who do the most work get the least money, and the women who have the most money do the least work.     Ibid.

8 It is not motherhood that keeps the housewife on her feet from dawn till dark; it is house service, not child service.     Ibid.

9 . . . with her overcharged sensibility, her prominent modesty, her "eternal feminity"—the female genus homo is undeniably over-sexed.
Ibid.

10 Boys and girls are expected, also, to behave differently to each other, and to people in general—a behavior to be briefly described in two words. To the boy we say, "Do"; to the girl, "Don't." Ibid.

11 The transient trade we think evil. The bargain for life we think good. Ibid., Ch. 4

12 To be surrounded by beautiful things has much influence upon the human creature: to make beautiful things has more. Ibid.

13 Specialization and organization are the basis of human progress. Ibid.

14 Where young boys plan for what they will achieve and attain, young girls plan for whom they will achieve and attain. Ibid., Ch. 5

15 Marriage is the woman's proper sphere, her divinely ordered place, her natural end. It is what she is born for, what she is trained for, what she is exhibited for. It is, moreover, her means of honorable livelihood and advancement. *But*—she must not even look as if she wanted it! Ibid.

16 Legitimate sex-competition brings out all that is best in man. Ibid., Ch. 6

17 It is not for nothing that a man's best friends sigh when he marries, especially if he is a man of genius. Ibid.

18 The world is quite right. It does not have to be consistent. Ibid.

19 We have built into the constitution of the human race the habit and desire of taking, as divorced from its natural precursor and concomitant of making. Ibid.

20 As the priestess of the temple of consumption, as the limitless demander of things to use up, her economic influence is reactionary and injurious. Ibid.

21 The sexuo-economic relationship . . . sexualizes our industrial relationship and commercializes our sex-relation. Ibid.

22 The female segregated to the uses of sex alone naturally deteriorates in racial development.
Ibid., Ch. 9

23 When we see great men and women, we give credit to their mothers. When we see inferior men and women—and that is a common circumstance—no one presumes to the question of the motherhood which has produced them.
Ibid.

24 The human mother does less for her young, both absently and proportionately, than any kind of mother on earth. . . . The necessary knowledge of the world, so indispensable to every human being, she cannot give, because she does not possess it. Ibid.

25 "To bear and rear the majestic race to which they can never fully belong! To live vicariously forever, through their sons, the daughters being only another vicarious link! What a supreme and magnificent martyrdom!" Ibid.

26 Maternal instinct, merely as an instinct, is unworthy of our superstitious reverence.
Ibid.

27 A family unity which is only bound together with a table-cloth is of questionable value.
Ibid., Ch. 11

28 The child learns more of the virtues needed in modern life—of fairness, of justice, of comradeship, of collective interest and action—in a common school than can be taught in the most perfect family circle. Ibid., Ch. 13

29 Work the object of which is merely to serve one's self is the lowest. Work the object of which is merely to serve one's family is the next lowest. Work the object of which is to serve more and more people, in widening range . . . is social service in the fullest sense, and the highest form of service we can reach.
Ibid.

30 A baby who spent certain hours of every day among other babies, being cared for because he was a baby and not because he was "my baby," would grow to have a very different opinion of himself from that which is forced upon each new soul that comes among us by the ceaseless adoration of his own immediate family. Ibid.

31 . . . while we flatter ourselves that things remain the same, they are changing under our very eyes from year to year, from day to day.
Ibid.

32 You cannot teach every mother to be a good school educator or a good college educator. Why should you expect every mother to be a good nursery educator? Ibid.

33 The mother as a social servant instead of a home servant will not lack in true mother duty. . . . From her work, loved and honored though it is, she will return to the home life, the child life, with an eager, ceaseless pleasure, cleansed of all the fret and fraction and weariness that so mar it now. Ibid.

34 Allegiance and long labor due my lord—
 Allegiance in an idleness abhorred—
 I am the squaw—the slave—the harem
 beauty—
 I serve and serve, the handmaid of the world.
    "Two Callings," *The Home,*
    Introduction, Pt. I   *1910*

35 So when the great word "Mother!" rang once
 more,
 I saw at last its meaning and its place;
 Not the blind passion of the brooding past,
 But Mother—the World's Mother—come at
 last,
 To love as she had never loved before—
 To feed and guard and teach the human race.
    Ibid., Pt. II

36 Habits of thought persist through the centuries;
 and while a healthy brain may reject the doctrine it no longer believes, it will continue to
 feel the same sentiments formerly associated
 with that doctrine.    Ibid., Ch. 3

37 The original necessity for the ceaseless presence
 of the woman to maintain that altar fire—and
 it was an altar fire in very truth at one period—
 has passed with the means of prompt ignition;
 the matchbox has freed the housewife from
 that incessant service, but the *feeling* that
 women should stay at home is with us yet.
    Ibid.

38 Noticed, studied, commented on, and incessantly interfered with; forced into miserable
 self-consciousness by this unremitting glare;
 our little ones grow up permanently injured in
 character by this lack of one of humanity's most
 precious rights—privacy.    Ibid.

39 Let us revere, let us worship, but erect and
 open-eyed, the highest, not the lowest; the
 future, not the past!    Ibid.

40 It will be a great thing for the human soul
 when it finally stops worshiping backwards.
    Ibid.

41 You may observe mother instinct at its height
 in a fond hen sitting on china eggs—instinct,
 but no brains.    Ibid.

42 Eternity is not something that begins after you
 are dead. It is going on all the time. We are
 in it now.
    Quoted in *The Forerunner Magazine*
    *1909–1916*

43 How many a useless stone we find
 Swallowed in that capacious blind
 Faith-swollen gullet, our ancestral mind.
    Ibid.

44 There was a time when Patience ceased to be
 a virtue. It was long ago.    Ibid.

45 Human life consists in mutual service. No
 grief, pain, misfortune, or "broken heart," is
 excuse for cutting off one's life while any power
 of service remains. But when all usefulness is
 over, when one is assured of an unavoidable
 and imminent death, it is the simplest of human
 rights to choose a quick and easy death in
 place of a slow and horrible one.
    Suicide Note   *August 17, 1935*

46 If love, devotion to duty, sublime self-sacrifice,
 were enough in child-culture, mothers would
 achieve better results; but there is another
 requisite too often lacking—knowledge.
    *The Living of Charlotte Perkins*
    *Gilman*   *1935p*

47 One may have a brain specialized in its grasp
 of ethics, as well as of mechanics, mathematics
 or music.    Ibid.

48 It is told that Buddha, going out to look on
 life, was greatly daunted by death. "They all
 eat one another!" he cried, and called it evil.
 This process I examined, changed the verb,
 said, "They all feed one another," and called
 it good.    Ibid.

49 Death? Why this fuss about death. Use your
 imagination, try to visualize a world *without*
 death! . . . Death is the essential condition of
 life, not an evil.    Ibid.

50 However, one cannot put a quart in a pint cup.
    Ibid.

51 The first duty of a human being is to assume
 the right functional relationship to society—
 more briefly, to find your real job, and do it.
    Ibid.

52 . . . love grows by service.    Ibid.

53 We are told to hitch our wagons to a star, but
 why pick on Betelgeuse?*    Ibid.

54 . . . New York . . . that unnatural city where
 every one is an exile, none more so than the
 American.    Ibid.

55 Socialism, long misrepresented and misunderstood under the violent propaganda of Marx-
 ism, has been fairly obliterated in the public
 mind by the Jewish-Russian nightmare, Bol-
 shevism.    Ibid.

56 But reason has no power against feeling, and
 feeling older than history is no light matter.
    Ibid.

* Largest star in the galaxy.

57 It is no wonder we behave badly, we are literally ignorant of the laws of ethics, which is the simplest of sciences, the most necessary, the most constantly needed.     *Ibid.*

58 There is no female mind. The brain is not an organ of sex. As well speak of a female liver.
Quoted in *The Liberated Woman's Appointment Calendar*, Lynn Sherr and Jurate Kazickas, eds.     *1975p*

* * *

59 A concept is stronger than a fact.
"Human Work"

60 To swallow and follow, whether old doctrine or new propaganda, is a weakness still dominating the human mind.     *Ibid.*

61 Cried this pretentious ape one day,
"I'm going to be a Man!
And stand upright, and hunt, and fight,
And conquer all I can."
"Similar Cases"

62 Cried all, "Before such things can come,
You idiotic child,
*You must alter Human Nature!*"
And they all sat back and smiled.
    *Ibid.*

63 I ran against a Prejudice.
That quite cut off the view.
"An Obstacle," St. 1

64 The people people have for friends
Your common sense appall,
But the people people marry
Are the queerest folks of all.
"Queer People"

65 There's a whining at the threshold—
There's a scratching at the floor—
To work! To work! In heaven's name!
The wolf is at the door!
"The Wolf at the Door," St. 6

66 We are the wisest, strongest race:
Long may our praise be sung—
The only animal alive
That lives upon its young!
"Child Labor"

## 282. Amy Leslie
### (1860–1939)

1 Those who make the most memorable racket are of two classes—wary diplomats looking for the best of a business proposition and irresponsible parrots who croak and yell and chatter simply because exclamation points and interrogatories swim through the misty Chicago air.
*Amy Leslie at the Fair*     *1893*

2 No animal is so inexhaustible as an excited infant.     *Ibid.*

3 When these marvels of art and architecture begin to crumble the hearts of nations will stand still. Now the city blooms apace like a great white rose perfuming the clouds and smiling out upon the waters, but it is to fade! It is to die and that is one of its most exquisite enchantments.     *Ibid.*

4 As a singer you're a great dancer.
Quoted by George Primrose in *They All Sang* by E. W. Marks     *1934*

## 283. Juliette Low
### (1860–1927)

1 To put yourself in another's place requires real imagination, but by so doing each Girl Scout will be able to live among others happily.
Letter to Girl Scouts of America (October 31, 1923),* *Juliette Low and the Girl Scouts*, Anne Hyde Choate and Helen Ferris, eds.     *1928p*

2 I am like the old woman who lived in the shoe! And now the shoe has become too small for the many children and we must have a building that will be large enough for us all.
*Ibid.* (October 31, 1924)*

3 I hope that during the coming year we shall all remember the rules of this Girl Scouting game of ours. They are: To play fair. To play in your place. To play for your side and not for yourself. And as for the score, the best thing in a game is the fun and not the result. . . .     *Ibid.*

## 284. Harriet Monroe
### (1860–1936)

1 Great ages of art come only when a widespread creative impulse meets an equally widespread impulse of sympathy. . . . The people must grant a hearing to the best poets they have else they will never have better.
Quoted in "Harriet Monroe," *Famous American Women* by Hope Stoddard     *1970p*

2 . . . poetry, "The Cinderella of the Arts."
*Ibid.*

3 Poetry has been left to herself and blamed for inefficiency, a process as unreasonable as blaming the desert for barrenness.     *Ibid.*

* Ms. Low's birthday.

4 . . . poetry might become the fashion—a real danger, because the poets need an audience not fitful and superficial, but loyal and sincere.
*Ibid.*

### .285. Grandma Moses
(1860–1961)

1 I don't advise any one to take it [painting] up as a business proposition, unless they really have talent, and are crippled so as to deprive them of physical labor, Then with help they might make a living, But with taxes and income tax there is little money in that kind of art for the ordinary artis [sic] But I will say that I have did remarkable for one of my years, and experience, As for publicity, that Im [sic] too old to care for now. . . .
"How Do I Paint?," *The New York Times* May 11, 1947

2 What a strange thing is memory, and hope; one looks backward, the other forward. The one is of today, the other is the Tomorrow. Memory is history recorded in our brain, memory is a painter, it paints pictures of the past and of the day. *Grandma Moses, My Life's History*, Ch. 1, Aotto Kallir, ed. *1947*

3 If I didn't start painting, I would have raised chickens. *Ibid., Ch. 3*

### 286. Annie Oakley
(1860–1926)

1 I can shoot as well as you [her husband]. I think I should be able to go on and trade shot for shot with you. You take one shot while I hold the object for you, and then I take the next one, you acting as object holder for me.
Quoted in *Annie Oakley: Woman at Arms*, Ch. 4, by Courtney Ryley Cooper *1927p*

2 The contents of his [Sitting Bull's] pockets were often emptied into the hands of small, ragged little boys, nor could he understand how so much wealth should go brushing by, unmindful of the poor. *Ibid., Ch. 7*

### 287. Minna Antrim
(1861–?)

1 Satan will be obliged to extend his courtyard, since men insist upon furnishing him with such quantities of paving material.
*Naked Truth and Veiled Allusions* 1902

2 Doing all we can to promote our friend's happiness is better than to continually drink to his prosperity. *Ibid.*

3 A homely face and no figure have aided many women heavenward. *Ibid.*

4 Smart society is a body of autocrats in deadly warfare against plutocrats. *Ibid.*

5 Gratitude is the rosemary of the heart.
*Ibid.*

6 Illusion is the dust the devil throws in the eyes of the foolish. *Ibid.*

7 Somnolence in society is a crime; better chatter like a magpie than blink like an owl. *Ibid.*

8 Being pertinently impertinent and properly improper has often won an impecunious man social prestige. *Ibid.*

9 A fool bolts pleasure, then complains of moral indigestion. *Ibid.*

10 Man forgives woman anything save the wit to outwit him. *Ibid.*

11 Experience has no text books nor proxies. She demands that her pupils answer her roll-call personally. *Ibid.*

12 Satiety is a mongrel that barks at the heels of plenty. *Ibid.*

13 Politeness is a guilt-edged investment that seldom misses a dividend. *Ibid.*

14 To be loved is to be fortunate, but to be hated is to achieve distinction. *Ibid.*

15 Sympatica is the touchstone that leads to talent's highest altitude. *Ibid.*

16 To know one's self is wisdom, but to know one's neighbor is genius. *Ibid.*

17 Between condolence and consolation there flows an ocean of tears. *Ibid.*

18 Saying smart things achieves eclat, but doing them wins substance. *Ibid.*

19 Man is kind only to be cruel; woman cruel only to be kind. *Ibid.*

20 Smiles are the soul's kisses. . . . *Ibid.*

21 The "Green-Eyed Monster" causes much woe, but the absence of this ugly serpent argues the presence of a corpse whose name is Eros.
*Ibid.*

22 To control a man a woman must first control herself. *Ibid.*

23 Many women plume themselves upon their impregnable virtue, who have never met *the* man.
*Ibid.*

24 Experience is a good teacher, but she sends in terrific bills.
*Ibid.*

25 Golden fetters hurt as cruelly as iron ones.
*Ibid.*

## 288. Mary Byron
### (1861–?)
* * *

1 On gossamer nights when the moon is low,
  And stars in the mist are hiding,
Over the hill where the foxgloves grow
  You may see the fairies riding.
*"The Fairy Thrall"*

## 289. Mary Coleridge
### (1861–1907)

1 The fruits of the tree of knowledge are various; he must be strong indeed who can digest all of them.
*Gathered Leaves from the Prose of Mary E. Coleridge*    1910p

2 Solitude affects some people like wine; they must not take too much of it, for it flies to the head.
*Ibid.*

* * *

3 Into the land of dreams I long to go.
  Bid me forget!
*"Mandragora"*

4 Where is delight? and what are pleasures now?—
Moths that a garment fret.
*Ibid.*

5 Mother of God! No lady thou:
Common woman of common earth!
*"Our Lady"*

6 We were young, we were merry, we were very, very wise,
  And the door stood open at our feast,
When there passed us a woman with the West in her eyes,
  And a man with his back to the East.
*"Unwelcome"*

## 290. Clemence Dane
### (1861–1965)

1 SYDNEY. It's extraordinary to me—whenever you middle-aged people want to excuse yourselves for anything you've done that you know you oughtn't have done, you say it was the war.
*A Bill of Divorcement*, Act I
1921

2 HILARY. I was a dead man. You know what the dead do in heaven? They sit on their golden chairs and sicken for home.
*Ibid.*

3 MARGARET. It's the things I might have said that fester.
*Ibid.*, Act II

4 DR. ALLIOT. That young, young generation found out, out of their own unhappiness, the war taught them, what peace couldn't teach us —that when conditions are evil it is not your duty to submit—that when conditions are evil, your duty, in spite of protests, in spite of sentiment, your duty, though you trample on the bodies of your nearest and dearest to do it, though you bleed your own heart white, your duty is to see that those conditions are changed. If your laws forbid you, you must change your laws. If your church forbids you, you must change your church. And if your God forbids you, why then, you must change your God.
*Ibid.*

5 ZEDEKIAH. How else should I treat an idol but tread on it?
*Naboth's Vineyard*, Act I, Sc. 1
1925

6 JEZEBEL. How often must I stoop to hold you up?
*Ibid.*, Sc. 2

7 JEZEBEL. Toss back the ball! Shall I flinch because a heavy hand flings it? At least it is a friend's hand.
*Ibid.*

8 JEZEBEL. What is it to sit on a throne? Weariness! But to shift the dolls that sit there, that's a game, Jehu, for a man or a woman! Let me teach you my game!
*Ibid.*, Act II, Sc. 1

9 I think of our century as a sixty-year-old housewife in love with modern ideas.
Speech, "Approach to Drama,"
London    1961

10 I suppose there is not one of us here who has not, at some time or other, evoked the good in which we believe to take our part, to speak for us, to put our case to the invisible evil (if it is evil) that thwarts and destroys our efforts toward happiness. . . .
*Ibid.*

## 291. Dorothy Dix
### (1861–1951)

1 It is only the women whose eyes have been washed clear with tears who get the broad vision that makes them little sisters to all the world.
*Dorothy Dix, Her Book*,
Introduction    1926

2 I have learned in the great University of Hard Knocks a philosophy that no woman who has had an easy life ever acquires. I have learned to live each day as it comes, and not to borrow trouble by dreading tomorrow. It is the dark menace of the future that makes cowards of us.                                                      Ibid.

3 Now one of the great reasons why so many husbands and wives make shipwreck of their lives together is because a man is always seeking for happiness, while a woman is on a perpetual still hunt for trouble.          Ibid., Ch. 1

4 So many persons think divorce a panacea for every ill, who find out, when they try it, that the remedy is worse than the disease.
                                              Ibid., Ch. 13

5 Confession is always weakness. The grave soul keeps its own secrets, and takes its own punishment in silence.                      Ibid., Ch. 20

6 In reality, the mother who rears her children up to be monsters of selfishness has no right to expect appreciation and gratitude from them because she has done them as ill a turn as one human being can do another. She has warped their characters.                      Ibid., Ch. 44

7 Extravagance. The price of indulging yourself in your youth in the things you cannot afford is poverty and dependence in your old age.
                                              Ibid., Ch. 53

8 Women have changed in their relationship to men, but men stand pat just where Adam did when it comes to dealing with women.
                                              Ibid., Ch. 59

9 For in all the world there are no people so piteous and forlorn as those who are forced to eat the bitter bread of dependency in their old age, and find how steep are the stairs of another man's house. Wherever they go they know themselves unwelcome. Wherever they are, they feel themselves a burden. There is no humiliation of the spirit they are not forced to endure. Their hearts are scarred all over with the stabs from cruel and callous speeches.
                                              Ibid., Ch. 69
                        *   *   *
10 Nobody wants to kiss when they are hungry.
                                              News Item

11 The reason that husbands and wives do not understand each other is because they belong to different sexes.                              Ibid.

## 292. Frances Greville
### (1861–1938)

1 Love and Misery proverbially go together. There is a popular notion . . . that a lover could not get along without a little misery. . . .
                Quoted in the *Anglo-Saxon Review*
                                              *June, 1900*

## 293. Louise Imogen Guiney
### (1861–1920)

1 To be Anonymous is better than to be Alexander. Cowley said it engagingly, in his little essay on *Obscurity: "Bene qui latuit, bene vixit*; he lives well that has lain well hidden." The pleasantest condition of life is in incognito.
                "On the Delights of an Incognito,"
                                *Patrins      1897*

2 A certain sesquipedalianism* is natural to Americans: witness our press editorials, our Fourth of July orations, and the public messages of all our Presidents since Lincoln.
                Quoted in *Scribner's Magazine*
                                        *January, 1911*

3 Quotations (such as have point and lack triteness) from the great old authors are an act of filial reverence on the part of the quoter, and a blessing to a public grown superficial and external.                                      Ibid.
                        *   *   *
4 A short life in the saddle, Lord!
   Not long life by the fire.
                        "The Knight Errant," St. 2

5 He has done with roofs and men,
   Open, Time, and let him pass.
                                "Ballad of Kenelm"

6 High above hate I dwell,
   O storms! Farewell.
                                    "The Sanctuary"

7 The fears of what may come to pass,
      I cast them all away,
   Among the clover scented grass,
      Among the new-mown hay.
                        "A Song from Sylvan," St. 2

8 The fool who redeemed us once of our folly,
   And the smiter that healed us, our right John Brown!
                        "John Brown: A Paradox"

9 To fear not sensible failure,
      Nor covet the game at all,
   But fighting, fighting, fighting,
      Die, driven against the wall.
                                        "The Kings"

* Use of long words.

## 294. Gracy Hebard
### (1861-1936)

1 These indians [Shoshones] believe also that God pulled out the upper teeth of the elk because the elk were meant to be eaten by the indians, and not the indians by the elk.
*Washakie    1930*

2 The buffaloes were the original engineers, as they followed the lay of the land and the run of the water. These buffalo paths became indian trails, which always pointed out the easiest way across the mountain barriers. The white man followed in these footpaths. The iron trail finished the road.
*The Pathbreakers from River to Ocean*, Ch. 9    *1932*

3 While we are enjoying the luxuries of this new era of the great west let us not forget to honor those who endured hardships and privations, encountered dangers and peril; yes, even gave up their lives to make these things possible. . . . It is all a story that has never had its equal in the world's history. The great American desert is no more.    *Ibid.*

## 295. Katharine Tynan Hinkson
### (1861-1931)
\* \* \*

1 Good is an orchard. . . .
*"Of an Orchard"*

2 O you poor folk in cities,
A thousand, thousand pities!
Heaping the fairy gold that withers and dies;
One field in the June weather
Is worth all the gold ye gather,
One field in June weather—one Paradise.
*"June Song"*

3 The dear Lord God, of His glories weary—
Christ our Lord had the heart of a boy—
Made Him birds in a moment merry,
Bade them soar and sing for His joy.
*"The Making of Birds"*

4 To me the wonderful charge was given,
I, even a little ass, did go
Bearing the very weight of heaven;
So I crept cat-foot, sure and slow.
*"The Ass Speaks"*

## 296. Alice Hubbard
### (1861-1915)

1 [Thomas] Paine was a Quaker by birth and a friend by nature. The world was his home,

mankind were his friends, to do good was his religion.
*An American Bible,*
Introduction    *1911*

## 297. Jessie Brown Pounds
### (1861-?)

1 Somewhere, Somewhere, Beautiful Isle of Somewhere,
Land of the true, where we live anew,
Beautiful Isle of Somewhere.
*"Beautiful Isle of Somewhere"*
*1901*

## 298. Corinne Roosevelt Robinson
### (1861-1933)

1 Serene amid the clamor and the strife
She bore the lily of a blameless life!
*"To F.W.," The Call of Brotherhood and Other Poems    1912*

2 Stretch out your hand and take the world's wide gift
Of Joy and Beauty.
*Ibid.*, "Stretch Out Your Hand"

3 Though Love be deeper, Friendship is more wide. . . .
*Ibid.*, "Friendship"

4 Is life worth living?
Aye, with the best of us,
Heights of us, depths of us,—
Life is the test of us!
*"Life, A Question," One Woman to Another    1914*

5 Nothing is as difficult as to achieve results in this world if one is filled full of great tolerance and the milk of human kindness. The person who achieves must generally be a one-ideaed individual, concentrated entirely on that one idea, and ruthless in his aspect toward other men and other ideas.
*My Brother Theodore Roosevelt*, Ch. 1
*1921*

6          Spirit of the air,
And of the seas, and of the fragrant earth,
I thank thee that thou didst attend my birth
To dower me with wonder. . . .
*"The Gift of Wonder,"*
*Out of Nymph    1930*

7 Thy love was like a royal accolade. . . .
*Ibid.*, "Afterward"

## 299. Ernestine Schumann-Heink
(1861–1936)

1 One can never either hear or see himself, and there is a need—if one would make real progress in art—for constant criticism.
> Quoted in *Schumann-Heink, the Last of the Titans* by Mary Lawton
> *1935*

2 This shall be my parting word—know what you want to do—then do it. Make straight for your goal and go undefeated in spirit to the end.
> Ibid.

## 300. Carrie Jacobs Bond
(1862–1946)

1 When God made up this world of ours,
   He made it long and wide,
And meant that it should shelter all,
   And none should be denied.
> "Friends," St. 1, *Little Stories in Verse*    *1905*

2 Kind words smooth all the "Paths o' Life"
   And smiles make burdens light,
And uncomplainin' friends can make
   A daytime out o' night.
> Ibid., "The Path o' Life," St. 11

3 And we find at the end of a perfect day,
   The soul of a friend we've made.
> "A Perfect Day," St. 2    *1926*

## 301. Edith Cooper
(1862–1913)

Co-author with Katharine Bradley. See 200:1–3.

## 302. Ella Higginson
(1862–1940)

\*   \*   \*

1 Forgive you?—Oh, of course, dear,
   A dozen times a week!
We women were created
   Forgiveness but to speak.
> "Wearing Out Love," St. 1

2 One leaf is for hope, and one is for faith,
   And one is for love, you know,
And God put another in for luck.
> "Four-Leaf Clover," St. 2

## 303. Ada Leverson
(1862–1933)

1 Absurdly improbable things happen in real life as well as in weak literature.
> *The Twelfth Hour*    *1907*

## 304. Ts'ai-t'ien Chang
(1862–1945)

1 ". . . I wanted to study and not to marry. My brother and Mao Tse-tung also hated marriage and declared they would never marry. . . ."
> Quoted in *Women in Modern China* by Helen Foster Snow    *1967p*

## 305. Ida B. Wells
(1862–1931)

1 Let the Afro-American depend on no party, but on himself for his salvation. Let him continue to education, character, and above all, put money in his purse. When he has a dollar in his pocket and many more in the bank, he can move from injustice and oppression and no one to say him nay. When he has money, and plenty of it, parties and races will become his servants.
> "Iola's Southern Field,"
> *The New York Age*
> *November 11, 1892*

2 The first excuse given to the civilized world for the murder of unoffending Negroes was the necessity of the white man to repress and stamp out "race riots." . . . It was always a remarkable feature in these insurrections and riots that only Negroes were killed during the rioting, and that all the white men escaped unharmed.
> *A Red Record*    *1895*

3 True chivalry respects all womanhood, and no one who reads the record, as it is written in the faces of the million mulattoes in the South, will for a minute conceive that the southern white man had a very chivalrous regard for the honor due the women of his race or respect for the womanhood which circumstances placed in his power. . . . Virtue knows no color lines, and the chivalry which depends upon complexion of skin and texture of hair can command no honest respect.
> Ibid.

4 I felt that one had better die fighting against injustice than to die like a dog or a rat in a trap. I had already determined to sell my life as dearly as possible if attacked. I felt if I could take one lyncher with me, this would even up the score a little bit.
> *The Autobiography of Ida B. Wells,*
> Alfreda M. Duster, ed.    *1970p*

## 306. Edith Wharton
### (1862–1937)

1 . . . he had been drawn to her by the unperturbed gaiety which kept her fresh and elastic at an age when most women's activities are growing either slack or febrile.
"The Other Two," Ch. 1,
*The Descent of Man* 1904

2 A New York divorce is in itself a diploma of virtue. . . . Ibid.

3 People shook their heads over him, however, and one grudging friend, to whom he affirmed that he took the step with his eyes open, replied oracularly: "Yes—and with your ears shut." Ibid.

4 "It feels uncommonly queer to have enough cash to pay one's bills. I'd have sold my soul for it a few years ago!" Ibid., Ch. 3

5 A man would rather think that his wife has been brutalized by her first husband than that the process has been reversed. Ibid.

6 "I don't know as I think a man is entitled to rights he hasn't known how to hold on to. . . ." Ibid., Ch. 4

7 Her pliancy was beginning to sicken him. Had she really no will of her own . . . ? She was "as easy as an old shoe"—a shoe that too many feet had worn. Ibid.

8 He had fancied that a woman can shed her past like a man. Ibid.

9 If he paid for each day's comfort with the small change of his illusions, he grew daily to value the comfort more and set less store upon the coin. Ibid.

10 She keeps on being queenly in her own room with the door shut. *The House of Mirth* 1905

11 When she spoke it was only to complain, and to complain of things not in his power to remedy; and to check a tendency to impatient retort he had first formed the habit of not answering her, and finally of thinking of other things while she talked.
*Ethan Frome*, Ch. 4 1911

12 Almost everybody in the neighborhood had "troubles," frankly localized and specified; but only the chosen had "complications." To have them was in itself a distinction, though it was also, in most cases, a death-warrant. People struggled on for years with "troubles," but they almost always succumbed to "complications." Ibid., Ch. 7

13 . . . they seemed to come suddenly upon happiness as if they had surprised a butterfly in the winter woods. . . . Ibid., Ch. 9

14 "Oh, what good'll writing do? I want to put my hand out and touch you. I want to do for you and care for you. I want to be there when you're sick and when you're lonesome." Ibid.

15 Mrs. Ballinger is one of the ladies who pursue Culture in bands, as though it were dangerous to meet it alone.
"Xingu," *Xingu and Other Stories* 1916

16 To [Henry] James's intimates, however, these elaborate hesitancies, far from being an obstacle, were like a cobweb bridge flung from his mind to theirs, an invisible passage over which one knew that slur-footed ironies, veiled jokes, tiptoe malices, were stealing to explode a huge laugh at one's feet.
*A Backward Glance*, Ch. 8 1934
* * *

17 My little old dog:
A heart-beat at my feet.
"A Lyrical Epigram"

18 There are two ways of spreading light: to be
The candle or the mirror that receives it.
"Vesalius in Zante"

## 307. Annie Jump Cannon
### (1863–1941)

1 . . . a life spent in the routine of science need not destroy the attractive human element of a woman's nature. Quoted in *Science*
*June 30, 1911*

## 308. Elaine Goodale
### (1863–1953)

1 We feel our savage kind,—
And thus alone with conscious meaning wear
The Indian's moccasin.
"Moccasin Flower," *In Berkshire with the Wild Flowers* 1879
* * *

2 Bronzed and molded by wind and sun,
Maddening, gladdening everyone
With a gypsy beauty full and fine,—
A health to the crimson columbine!
"Columbine"

3 Nature lies disheveled, pale,
With her feverish lips apart,—
Day by day the pulses fail,
Nearer to her bounding heart.
"Goldenrod"

## 309. Mary Church Terrell
### (1863–1954)

1 Lynching is the aftermath of slavery. The white men who shoot negroes to death and flay them alive, and the white women who apply flaming torches to their oil-soaked bodies today, are the sons and daughters of women who had but little, if any, compassion on the race when it was enslaved.
"Lynching from a Negro's Point of View," *North American Review*
*June, 1904*

2 The whole country seems tired of hearing about the black man's woes. The wrongs of the Irish, of the Armenians, of the Roumanian and Russian Jews, of the exiles of Russia and of every other oppressed people upon the face of the globe, can arouse sympathy and fire the indignation of the American public, while they seem to be all but indifferent to the murderous assaults upon the negroes in the South.
Ibid.

3 As a colored woman I might enter Washington any night, a stranger in a strange land, and walk miles without finding a place to lay my head. . . . The colored man alone is thrust out of the hotels of the national capital like a leper.
"What It Means to Be Colored in the Capital of the United States" (1907),
*A Colored Woman in a White World*
*1940*

4 It is impossible for any white person in the United States, no matter how sympathetic and broad, to realize what life would mean to him if his incentive to effort were suddenly snatched away. To the lack of incentive to effort, which is the awful shadow under which we live, may be traced the wreck and ruin of scores of colored youth. And surely no where in the world do oppression and persecution based solely on the color of the skin appear more hateful and hideous than in the capital of the United States, because the chasm between the principles upon which this Government was founded, in which it still professes to believe, and those which are daily practiced under the protection of the flag, yawn so wide and deep.
Ibid.

5 Please stop using the word "Negro." . . . We are the only human beings in the world with fifty-seven variety of complexions who are classed together as a single racial unit. Therefore, we are really truly colored people, and that is the only name in the English language which accurately describes us.
Ibid., Letter to the Editor,
*The Washington Post*
*May 14, 1949*

6 Some of our group say they will continue to classify us as Negroes, until an individual referred to as such will be proud of that name. But that is a case of wishful thinking and nothing else.
Ibid.

## 310. Margot Asquith
### (1864–1945)

1 Riches are overestimated in the Old Testament: the good and successful man received too many animals, wives, apes, she-goats and peacocks.
*The Autobiography of Margot Asquith*, Vols. I and II
*1920–1922*

2 To marry a man out of pity is folly; and, if you think you are going to influence the kind of fellow who has "never had a chance, poor devil," you are profoundly mistaken. One can only influence the strong characters in life, not the weak; and it is the height of vanity to suppose that you can make an honest man of anyone.
Ibid., Ch. 6

3 There are big men, men of intellect, men of talent and men of action; but the great man is difficult to find, and it needs—apart from discernment—a certain graveness to find him. The Almighty is a wonderful handicapper: He will not give us everything.
Ibid., Ch. 7

4 The first element of greatness is fundamental humbleness (this should not be confused with servility); the second is freedom from self; the third is intrepid courage, which, taken in its widest interpretation, generally goes with truth; and the fourth—the power to love—although I have put it last, is the rarest.
Ibid.

5 Rich men's houses are seldom beautiful, rarely comfortable, and never original. It is a constant source of surprise to people of moderate means to observe how little a big fortune contributes to Beauty.
Ibid., Ch. 17

6 Haunted from my early youth by the transitoriness and pathos of life, I was aware that it was not enough to say, "I am doing no harm," I ought to be testing myself daily, and asking what I was really achieving.
*My Impressions of America*, Ch. 4
*1922*

7 Journalism over here [in America] is not only an obsession but a drawback that cannot be overrated. Politicians are frightened of the press, and in the same way as bull-fighting has a brutalising effect upon Spain (of which she is unconscious), headlines of murder, rape, and rubbish, excite and demoralise the American public.
Ibid., Ch. 10

8 It is always dangerous to generalise, but the American people, while infinitely generous, are a hard and strong race and, but for the few cemeteries I have seen, I am inclined to think they never die.　　*Ibid.*, Ch. 14

9 The ingrained idea that, because there is no king and they despise titles, the Americans are a free people is pathetically untrue. . . . There is a perpetual interference with personal liberty over there that would not be tolerated in England for a week.　　*Ibid.*, Ch. 17

10 . . . her one idea was to exercise a moderating influence; and without knowing it she would in a subtle and disparaging manner check the enthusiasm, dim the glow, and cramp the extravagance of everyone round her.
　　*Octavia*, Ch. 1　　1928

11 "Women are like horses, and should never be ridden on the curb."　　*Ibid.*, Ch. 9

12 She wanted to *give* life; to warm the blood and kindle the hope of drab and cautious people. You could not make others live unless you had life yourself.　　*Ibid.*, Ch. 12

13 She was not an individual when she was with him, she was an audience—an audience that only came in at the end. When people clapped, was it the last sentence, or the whole speech they were applauding? Or was it merely relief that the speech was over?　　*Ibid.*

14 Life was cruel, demanding wisdom from the young before they had the chance of acquiring it! Innocence was admired, ignorance despised: yet, in their effects, they had a dangerous resemblance.　　*Ibid.*, Ch. 22

## 311. Elinor Glyn
### (1864–1943)

1 Marriage is the aim and end of all sensible girls, because it is the meaning of life.
　　"Letters to Caroline,"
　　*Harper's Bazaar*
　　*September, 1913*

## 312. Margaret P. Sherwood
### (1864–1955)
* * *

1 Whisper some kindly word, to bless
A wistful soul who understands
That life is but one long caress
Of gentle words and gentle hands.
　　"In Memoriam—Leo: A Yellow Cat"

## 313. Wenonah Stevens Abbott
### (1865–1950)
* * *

1 To-day the journey is ended,
　I have worked out the mandates of fate;
Naked, alone, undefended,
　I knock at the Uttermost Gate.
　　"A Soul's Soliloquy"

## 314. Evangeline Booth
### (1865–1950)
* * *

1 Drink has drained more blood,
Hung more crepe,
Sold more houses,
Plunged more people into bankruptcy,
Armed more villains,
Slain more children,
Snapped more wedding rings,
Defiled more innocence,
Blinded more eyes,
Twisted more limbs,
Dethroned more reason,
Wrecked more manhood,
Dishonored more womanhood,
Broken more hearts,
Blasted more lives,
Driven more to suicide, and
Dug more graves than any other poisoned
Scourge that ever swept its death-
Dealing waves across the world.
　　"Good Housekeeping"

## 315. Mrs. Patrick Campbell
### (1865–1940)

1 I believe I was impatient with unintelligent people from the moment I was born: a tragedy —for I am myself three-parts a fool.
　　*My Life and Some Letters*, Ch. 2
　　*1922*

2 I remember a certain dinner party given for me by a well-known Jewish financier, and being asked by him at table in an earnest, curious voice, what I kept in a small locket I wore on a chain round my neck. Everyone stopped talking and listened for my answer. I replied gravely, "One hair of a Jew's moustache."
　　*Ibid.*, Ch. 6

3 To be made to hold his [George Bernard Shaw's] tongue is the greatest insult you can offer him—though he might be ready with a poker to make you hold yours.
　　*Ibid.*, Ch. 16

4 . . . there can be a fundamental gulf of grace-lessness in a human heart which neither our love nor our courage can bridge.
Ibid., Ch. 19

5 Wedlock—the deep, deep peace of the double bed after the hurly-burly of the chaise-longue.
Quoted in *Jennie* (1914), Vol. II,
by Ralph G. Martin     *1971p*

## 316. Edith Louisa Cavell
(1865–1915)

1 I realize that patriotism is not enough. I must have no hatred or bitterness towards anyone.
Last Words, Quoted in
*The Times* (London)
*October 23, 1915p*

## 317. Elsie De Wolfe
(1865–1950)

1 It is the personality of the mistress that the home expresses. Men are forever guests in our homes, no matter how much happiness they may find there.
*The House in Good Taste*, Ch. 1
*1920*

2 What a joyous thing is color! How influenced we all are by it, even if we are unconscious of how our sense of restfulness has been brought about.
Ibid., Ch. 6

3 It does not matter whether one paints a picture, writes a poem, or carves a statue, simplicity is the mark of a master-hand. Don't run away with the idea that it is easy to cook simply. It requires a long apprenticeship.
"Why I Wrote This Book," *Recipes
for Successful Dining*     *1934*

## 318. Minnie Fiske
(1865–1932)

1 You must make your own blunders, must cheer-fully accept your own mistakes as part of the scheme of things. You must not allow yourself to be advised, cautioned, influenced, persuaded this way and that.     Letter to Alexander
Woollcott (1908), Quoted in *Mrs. Fiske*
by Alexander Woollcott     *1917*

2 Among the most disheartening and dangerous of . . . advisors, you will often find those closest to you, your dearest friends, members of your own family, perhaps, loving, anxious, and knowing nothing whatever. . . .     Ibid.

3 "Bosh! do not talk to me about the repertory idea. It is an outworn, needless, impossible, *harmful* scheme. . . . This, my friend, is an age of specialization, and in such an age the repertory theatre is an anachronism, a ludicrous anachronism."     Ibid., Ch. 1

4 But there are times when the actor is an artist far greater and more creative than his ma-terial. . . .     Ibid., Ch. 5

5 The essence of acting is the conveyance of truth through the medium of the actor's mind and person. The science of acting deals with the perfecting of that medium. The great actors are the luminous ones. They are the great con-ductors of the stage.     Ibid.

## 319. Yvette Guilbert
(1865–1944)

1 Try to make a woman who does badly on the stage understand that she might do better in trade, or in any other occupation. She will never believe you. It seems impossible to her to make linen garments or millinery, but very sim-ple to enact the dandy on the stage.
*La Vedette*     *1902*

2 Caper without cease, and caper again. . . . You are gaiety, which passes away.     Ibid.

3 All women are alike. All demand stimulation for their sense. . . . These ladies of society also feel the need of language strong enough to stimulate them. . . . Licentiousness takes them all in the same manner.     Ibid.

4 One cannot remain the same. Art is a mirror which should show many reflections, and the artist should not always show the same face, or the face becomes a mask.     Ibid.

## 320. Laurence Hope
(1865–1904)

1 For this is wisdom: to love, to live,
To take what Fate, or the Gods, may give.
"The Teak Forest,"
*India's Love Lyrics*     *1922*

2 Speed passion's ebb as you greet its flow—
To have, to hold, and in time let go!
Ibid.

3 Less than the dust beneath thy chariot wheel,
Less than the weed that grows beside thy door,
Less than the rust that never stained thy sword,
Less than the need thou hast in life of me,
Even less am I.
Ibid., "Less Than the Dust," St. 1

4 Pale hands I loved beside the Shalimar,
Where are you now? Who lies beneath your
spell?
> Ibid., "Kashmiri Song," St. 1

\*   \*   \*

5 Men should be judged, not by their tint of skin,
The Gods they serve, the Vintage that they
drink,
Nor by the way they fight, or love, or sin,
But by the quality of thought they think.
> "Men Should Be Judged"

6 Often devotion to virtue arises from sated
desire.
> "I Arise and Go Down to the River,"
> St. 6

7 Yet I, this little while ere I go hence,
Love very lightly now, in self-defence.
> "Verse by Taj Mahomed"

8 Your work was waste? Maybe your share
Lay in the hour you laughed and kissed;
Who knows but that your son shall wear
The laurels that his father missed?
> "The Masters"

## 321. Anandabai Joshee
### (1865–1887)

1 Holes are bored through the lower part of the
left nostril for the nose-ring, and all around
the edge of the ear for jewels. This may appear
barbarous to the foreign eye; to us it is a
beauty! Everything changes with the clime.
> Letter to Mrs. Carpenter (1880),
> Quoted in *The Life of Anandabai
> Joshee* by Caroline H. Dall   *1888p*

2 Your American widows may have difficulties
and inconveniences to struggle with, but
weighed in the scale against ours, all of them
put together are but as a particle against a
mountain.     Ibid.

3 When I think over the sufferings of women in
India in all ages, I am impatient to see the
Western light dawn as the harbinger of eman-
cipation.     Ibid.

4 Had there been no difficulties and no thorns in
the way, then man would have been in his
primitive state and no progress made in civilisation and mental culture.
> Ibid., Letter to Her Aunt
> (August 27, 1881)

5 . . . I regard irreligious people as pioneers. If
there had been no priesthood the world would
have advanced ten thousand times better than
it has now.     Ibid.

## 322. Nellie Melba
### (1865?–1931)

1 The first rule in opera is the first rule in life:
see to everything yourself.
> *Melodies and Memories*    1925

2 Music is not written in red, white and blue. It
is written in the heart's blood of the composer.
> Ibid.

3 One of the drawbacks of Fame is that one can
never escape from it.     Ibid.

## 323. Baroness Orczy
### (1865–1947)

1 A surging, seething, murmuring crowd of beings that are human only in name, for to the
eye and ear they seem naught but savage creatures, animated by vile passions and by the
lust of vengeance and of hate.
> *The Scarlet Pimpernel*, Ch. 1    *1905*

2 Marguerite St. Just was from principle and by
conviction a republican—equality of birth was
her motto—inequality of fortune was in her
eyes a mere untoward accident, but the only
inequality she admitted was that of talent.
"Money and titles may be hereditary," she
would say, "but brains are not. . . ."
> Ibid., Ch. 6

3 "I sometimes wish you had not so many lofty
virtues. . . . I assure you little sins are far
less dangerous and uncomfortable. But you
*will* be prudent?" she added earnestly.
> Ibid., Ch. 7

4 "We seek him here, we see him there,
Those Frenchies seek him everywhere.
Is he in heaven?—Is he in hell?
That damned elusive Pimpernel?"
> Ibid., Ch. 12

5 It is only when we are very happy that we can
bear to gaze merrily upon the vast and limitless expanse of water, rolling on and on with
such persistent, irritating monotony, to the
accompaniment of our thoughts, whether grave
or gay. When they are gay, the waves echo
their gaiety; but when they are sad, then every
breaker, as it rolls, seems to bring additional
sadness, and to speak to us of hopelessness and
of the pettiness of all our joys.
> Ibid., Ch. 21

6 The weariest nights, the longest days, sooner
or later must perforce come to an end.
> Ibid., Ch. 22

7 An apology? Bah! Disgusting! cowardly! beneath the dignity of any gentleman, however wrong he might be.
*I Will Repay*, Prologue     1906

8 "To love is to feel one being in the world at one with us, our equal in sin as well as in virtue. To love, for us men, is to clasp one woman with our arms, feeling that she lives and breathes just as we do, suffers as we do, thinks with us, loves with us, and, above all, sins with us. Your mock saint who stands in a niche is not a woman if she have not suffered, still less a woman if she have not sinned. Fall at the feet of your idol as you wish, but drag her down to your level after that—the only level she should ever reach, that of your heart."
Ibid., Ch. 7

9 "We are not masters of our heart, Messire."
*Leatherface*, Bk. I, Ch. 3     1918

10 "But a wife! . . . What matters what she thinks and feels? if she be cold or loving, gentle or shrewish, sensitive to a kind word or callous to cruelty? A wife! . . . Well! so long as no other man hath ever kissed her lips—for that would hurt masculine vanity and wound the pride of possession!"     Ibid.

11 This, mayhap, was not logic, but it was something more potent, more real than logic—the soft insinuating voice of Sentiment. . . .
Ibid., Bk. II, Ch. 5

12 A blind, unreasoning rage, an irresistible thirst for revenge: a black hatred of all those placed in authority; of all those who were rich, who were independent or influential, filled André Vallon's young soul to the exclusion of every other thought and every other aspiration.
*A Child of the Revolution,*
Bk. II, Ch. 5     1932

13 "My dear, since the beginning of all times, men have perpetrated horrors against one another. It is the devil in them, but the devil would have no power over men if God did not allow it. Could He not, if He so willed, quell this revolution with His Word? Must we not rather bow to His will and try to realize that something great, something good, something, at any rate, that is in accordance with the great scheme of the universe must in the end come out of all this sorrow?"
Ibid., Bk. III, Ch. 31

## 324. Emily James Putnam
### (1865–1944)

1 But the typical lady everywhere tends to the feudal habit of mind. In contemporary society she is an archaism, and can hardly understand herself unless she knows her own history.
*The Lady*, Introduction     1910

2 Sentimentally the lady has established herself as the criterion of a community's civilisation. . . . When it is flatly put to her that she cannot become a human being and yet retain her privileges as a non-combatant, she often enough decides for etiquette.     Ibid.

3 Maternity is on the face of it an unsocial experience. The selfishness that a woman has learned to stifle or to dissemble where she alone is concerned, blooms freely and unashamed on behalf of her offspring.     Ibid.

4 Until changing economic conditions made the thing actually happen, struggling early society would hardly have guessed that woman's road to gentility would lie through doing nothing at all.     Ibid.

## 325. Louisa Thomas
### (1865–?)
* * *

1 Charm is the measure of attraction's power
To chain the fleeting fancy of the hour.
"What Is Charm?," St. 1

## 326. Mary A. Arnim
### (1866–?)

1 A marriage, she found, with someone of a different breed is fruitful of small rubs. . . .
*Mr. Skeffington*, Ch. 1     1940

2 Life was certainly a queer business—so brief, yet such a lot of it; so substantial, yet in a few years, which behaved like minutes, all scattered and anyhow.     Ibid.

3 She had been dragged in the most humiliating of all dusts, the dust reserved for older women who let themselves be approached, on amorous lines, by boys. . . . It had all been pure vanity, all just a wish, in these waning days of hers, still to feel power, still to have the assurance of her beauty and its effects.     Ibid., Ch. 3

4 . . . without it [love], without, anyhow, the capacity for it, people didn't seem to be much good. Dry as bones, cold as stones, they seemed to become, when love was done; inhuman, indifferent, self-absorbed, numb.     Ibid., Ch. 5

5 Strange that the vanity which accompanies beauty—excusable, perhaps, when there is such great beauty, or at any rate understandable—should persist after the beauty was gone.
Ibid., Ch. 6

6 How could one live, while such things were going on? How could one endure consciousness, except by giving oneself up wholly and forever to helping, and comforting, and at last, at last, perhaps healing? Ibid., Ch. 11

## 327. Martha Dickinson Bianchi
### (1866–1943)
### * * *

1 Deeper than chords that search the soul and die,
Mocking to ashes color's hot array,—
Closer than touch,—within our hearts they lie—
The words we do not say.
"The Words We Do Not Say"

## 328. Voltairine de Cleyre
### (1866–1912)

1 I had never seen a book or heard a word to help me in my loneliness.
"The Making of an Anarchist," *The Selected Works of Voltairine de Cleyre 1914p*

2 And Now, Humanity, I turn to you;
I consecrate my service to the world!
Ibid., "The Burial of My Past Self" (1885)

3 [Anarchism] . . . not only the denial of authority, not only a new economy, but a revision of the principles of morality. It means . . . self-responsibility, not leader-worship.
Ibid. (c.1887)

4 Consider the soul reflected on the advertising page. . . . Commercial man has set his image therein; let him regard himself when he gets time. Ibid.

5 [Language] . . . this great instrument which men have jointly built . . . every word the mystic embodiment of a thousand years of vanished passion, hope, desire, thought. Ibid.

6 Do I repent? Yes, I do; but wait till I tell you of what I repent and why. I repent that I ever believed a man could be anything but a living lie! Ibid., "Betrayed"

7 I die, as I have lived, a free spirit, an Anarchist, owing no allegiance to rulers, heavenly or earthly. . . . If my comrades wish to do aught for my memory, let them print my poems.
Ibid., Journal (1912)

## 329. Annie Johnson Flint
### (1866–1932)
### * * *

1 Have you come to the Red Sea place in your life
Where, in spite of all you can do,
There is no way out, there is no way back,
There is no other way but through?
"At the Place of the Sea," St. 1

2 The thrones are rocking to their fall—
It is the twilight of the Kings!
"The Twilight of the Kings"

## 330. Dora Read Goodale
### (1866–1915)
### * * *

1 The earth and sky, the day and night
Are melted in her depth of blue.
"Blue Violets"

2 The modest, lowly violet
In leaves of tender green inset,
So rich she cannot hide from view,
But covers all the bank with blue.
"Spring Scatters Far and Wide"

## 331. Eleanor Prescott Hammond
### (1866–1933)

1 Prone on my back I greet arriving day,
A day no different than the one just o'er;
When I will be, to practically say,
Considerably like I have been before.
Why then get up? Why wash, why eat, why pray?
—Oh, leave me lay!
"Oh, Leave Me Lay,"
*Atlantic Monthly*
*August, 1922*

## 332. Beatrix Potter
### (1866–1943)

1 Once upon a time there were four little Rabbits, and their names were—Flopsy, Mopsy, Cottontail, and Peter. *The Tale of Peter Rabbit 1904*

2 The water was all slippy-sloppy in the larder and the back passage. But Mr. Jeremy liked getting his feet wet; nobody ever scolded him, and he never caught a cold.
*The Tale of Mr. Jeremy Fisher 1906*

## 333. Annie Sullivan
### (1866–1936)

1 I have thought about it a great deal, and the more I think the more certain I am that obedience is the gateway through which knowledge, yes, and love, too, enter the mind of the child.      Letter (March 11, 1887),
Quoted in *The Story of My Life* by Helen Keller    *1903*

2 My heart is singing for joy this morning. A miracle has happened! The light of understanding has shone upon my little pupil's mind, and behold, all things are changed!
Ibid. (March 20, 1887)

3 I am beginning to suspect all elaborate and special systems of education. They seem to me to be built upon the supposition that every child is a kind of idiot who must be taught to think.      Ibid. (May 8, 1887)

4 It is a rare privilege to watch the birth, growth, and first feeble struggles of a living mind. . . .
Ibid. (May 22, 1887)

5 It's queer how ready people always are with advice in any real or imaginary emergency, and no matter how many times experience has shown them to be wrong, they continue to set forth their opinions, as if they had received them from the Almighty!
Ibid. (June 12, 1887)

6 It's a great mistake, I think, to put children off with falsehoods and nonsense, when their growing powers of observation and discrimination excite in them a desire to know about things.
Ibid. (August 28, 1887)

7 . . . people seldom see the halting and painful steps by which the most insignificant success is achieved.      Ibid. (October 30, 1887)

8 She likes stories that make her cry—I think we all do, it's so nice to feel sad when you've nothing particular to be sad about.
Ibid. (December 12, 1887)

9 I see no sense in "faking" conversation for the sake of teaching language. It's stupid and deadening to pupil and teacher. Talk should be natural and have for its object an exchange of ideas.      Ibid. (January 1, 1888)

10 The truth is not wonderful enough to suit the newspapers; so they enlarge upon it and invent ridiculous embellishments.
Ibid. (March 4, 1888)

11 Why, it is as easy to teach the name of an idea, if it is clearly formulated in the child's mind, as to teach the name of an object.
Ibid. (May 15, 1888)

12 Language grows out of life, out of its needs and experiences. . . . *Language* and *knowledge* are indissolubly connected; they are interdependent. Good work in language presupposes and depends on a real knowledge of things.
Ibid., Speech, American Association to Promote the Teaching of Speech to the Deaf (July, 1894)

13 I never taught language for the PURPOSE of teaching it; but invariably used language as a medium for the communication of *thought*; thus the learning of language was *coincident* with the acquisition of knowledge.    Ibid.

## 334. Pearl Craigie
### (1867–1906)

1 To love is to know the sacrifices which eternity exacts from life.
*Schools of Saints*, Ch. 25    *1897*

2 Women may be whole oceans deeper than we are, but they are also a whole paradise better. She may have got us out of Eden, but as a compensation she makes the earth very pleasant.      *The Ambassador*, Act III
*1898*

3 A false success made by the good humor of outside influences is always peaceful; a real success made by the qualities of the thing itself is always a declaration of war.
*The Dream and the Business*    *1906*

## 335. Marie Curie
### (1867–1934)

1 Men of moral and intellectual distinction could scarcely agree to teach in schools where an alien attitude was forced upon them.
*Pierre Curie*    *1923*

2 All my life through, the new sights of Nature made me rejoice like a child.      Ibid.

3 . . . I was taught that the way of progress is neither swift nor easy. . . .      Ibid.

4 You cannot hope to build a better world without improving the individuals. To that end each of us must work for his own improvement, and at the same time share a general responsibility for all humanity, our particular duty being to aid those to whom we think we can be most useful.      Ibid.

5 One never notices what has been done; one can only see what remains to be done. . . .
Ibid., Letter to Her Brother (March 18, 1894)

6 Indeed, if the mentality of the scholars of the various countries, as revealed by the recent war, often appears to be on a lower level than that of the less cultured masses, it is because there is a danger inherent in all power that is not disciplined and directed toward the higher aims which alone are worthy of it.
"Intellectual Co-operation,"
*Memorandum* (magazine)
*June 16, 1926*

7 After all, science is essentially international, and it is only through lack of the historical sense that national qualities have been attributed to it.      Ibid.

8 I have no dress except the one I wear every day. If you are going to be kind enough to give me one,* please let it be practical and dark so that I can put it on afterwards to go to the laboratory.
Letter to a Friend (1849), Quoted in
"She Did Not Know How to Be Famous,"
*Party of One* by Clifton Fadiman
*1955p*

## 336. Edith Hamilton

### (1867–1963)

1 The fundamental fact about the Greek was that he had to use his mind. The ancient priests had said, "Thus far and no farther. We set the limits of thought." The Greeks said, "All things are to be examined and called into question. There are no limits set on thought."
*The Greek Way*      *1930*

2 The anthropologists are busy, indeed, and ready to transport us back into the savage forest where all human things, the Greek things, too, have their beginnings; but the seed never explains the flower.      Ibid., Ch. 1

3 The Greeks were the first intellectualists. In a world where the irrational had played the chief role, they came forward as the protagonists of the mind.      Ibid.

4 Mind and spirit together make up that which separates us from the rest of the animal world, that which enables a man to know the truth and that which enables him to die for the truth.      Ibid.

5 The spirit has not essentially anything to do with what is outside of itself. It is mind that keeps hold of reality.      Ibid., Ch. 3

* A wedding gown.

6 The English method [of poetry] is to fill the mind with beauty; the Greek method was to set the mind to work.      Ibid., Ch. 4

7 None but a poet can write a tragedy. For tragedy is nothing less than pain transmuted into exaltation by the alchemy of poetry, and if poetry is true knowledge and the great poet's guides safe to follow, this transmutation has arresting implications.      Ibid., Ch. 11

8 A people's literature is the great textbook for real knowledge of them. The writings of the day show the quality of the people as no historical reconstruction can.
*The Roman Way*, Preface      *1932*

9 Theories that go counter to the facts of human nature are foredoomed.      Ibid., Ch. 1

10 A good-humored crowd, those people who filled the Roman theatre in its first days of popularity, easily appealed to by any sentimental interest, eager to have the wicked punished—but not too severely—and the good live happily after. No occasions wanted for intellectual exertion, no wit for deft malice; fun such as could be passably enjoyed, broad with a flavor of obscenity. Most marked characteristic of all, a love of mediocrity, a complete satisfaction with the average. The people who applauded these plays wanted nothing bigger than their own small selves. They were democratic.
     Ibid., Ch. 2

11 There are few efforts more conducive to humility than that of the translator trying to communicate an incommunicable beauty. Yet, unless we do try, something unique and never surpassed will cease to exist except in the libraries of a few inquisitive book lovers.
*Three Greek Plays*, Introduction
*1937*

12 Christ must be rediscovered perpetually.
*Witness to the Truth*, Ch. 1      *1948*

13 "Bless me," he [Socrates] said, looking around the market where all an Athenian wanted lay piled in glowing profusion, "what a lot of things there are a man can do without."      Ibid.

14 So Socrates loved the truth and so he made it live. He brought it down into the homes and hearts of men because he showed it to them in himself, the spirit of truth manifest in the only way that can be, in the flesh.      Ibid.

15 A life can be more lasting than systems of thought.      Ibid., Ch. 2

16 The power of Christianity, the power of all religion, is sustained by that strange capacity we call faith, a word very commonly used and very commonly misunderstood. Ages of faith and of unbelief are always said to mark the course of history.     Ibid., Ch. 9

17 But it is not hard work which is dreary; it is superficial work. That is always boring in the long run, and it has always seemed strange to me that in our endless discussions about education so little stress is ever laid on the pleasure of becoming an educated person, the enormous interest it adds to life. To be able to be caught up into the world of thought—that is to be educated.     Quoted in the *Bryn Mawr School Bulletin*    1959

## 337. Käthe Kollwitz
### (1867–1945)

1 No longer diverted by other emotions, I work the way a cow grazes.
*Diaries and Letters* (April, 1910),
Hans Kollwitz, ed.     *1955p*

2 Sensuality is burgeoning. . . . I feel at once grave, ill at ease and happy as I watch our children—our *children*—growing to meet the greatest of instincts. May it have mercy on them!     Ibid. (May 5, 1910)

3 For the last third of life there remains only work. It alone is always stimulating, rejuvenating, exciting and satisfying.
Ibid. (January 1, 1912)

4 Where do all the women who have watched so carefully over the lives of their beloved ones get the heroism to send them to face the cannon?     Ibid. (August 27, 1914)

5 The grave mood that comes over one when one knows: there is war, and one cannot hold on to any illusions any more. Nothing is real but the fruitfulness of this state, which we almost grow used to.
Ibid. (September 30, 1914)

6 I do not want to die . . . until I have faithfully made the most of my talent and cultivated the seed that was placed in me until the last small twig has grown.
Ibid. (February 15, 1915)

7 Culture arises only when the individual fulfills his cycle of obligations.     Ibid.

8 When we married, we took a leap in the dark. . . . There were grave contradictions in my own

feelings. In the end I acted on this impulse: jump in—you'll manage to swim.
Ibid. (1916)

9 Men without joy seem like corpses.
Ibid. (September 19, 1918)

10 Age remains age, that is, it pains, torments and subdues. When others see my scant achievements, they speak of a happy old age. I doubt that there is such a thing as a happy old age.
Ibid. (January 1, 1932)

11 I am afraid of dying—but being dead, oh yes, that to me is often an appealing prospect.
Ibid. (December, 1941)

12 Although my leaning toward the male sex was dominant, I also felt frequently drawn toward my own sex—an inclination which I could not correctly interpret until much later on. As a matter of fact I believe that bisexuality is almost a necessary factor in artistic production; at any rate, the tinge of masculinity within me helped me in my work.     Ibid. (1942)

## 338. Emmeline Pethick-Lawrence
### (1867–?)

1 Under the flagstones of the pavements in London lie the dormant seeds of life—ready to spring into blossom if the opportunity should ever occur. And under our cruel and repressive financial and economic system lie dormant human energy and joy that are ready to burst into flower. So far as a drop may be compared to the ocean, we witnessed in many individual cases that releasing of the spirit that is possible when the conditions of life afford some modicum of dignity and of leisure.
*My Part in a Changing World*, Ch. 7
*1938*

2 I find in many writers of the present day a persistent inclination to refer to the suffrage movement as inspired by enmity towards men. So far as my own experience goes, during the six years with which I was connected with the campaign no effort was spared to instruct the public that we had no enemy except a Government that was false to its professions. We refused to have any quarrel even with the police who, acting under their orders, did us violence, or the prison officials and doctors who became the agents of torture in prison because their livelihood depended upon their obedience.
Ibid., Ch. 19

3 A change of heart is the essence of all other change and it is brought about by a re-education of the mind.     Ibid., Ch. 23

## 339. Laura Ingalls Wilder
### (1867–1957)

1 But they didn't believe that Santa Claus could, really, have given any of them nothing but a switch. That happened to some children, but it couldn't happen to them. It was so hard to be good all the time, every day, for a whole year.
*Little House in the Big Woods*, Ch. 4 *1932*

2 "Did little girls have to be as good as that?" Laura asked, and Ma said: "It was harder for little girls. Because they had to behave like little ladies all the time, not only on Sundays. Little girls could never slide downhill, like boys. Little girls had to sit in the house and stitch on samplers." Ibid., Ch. 5

3 "That machine's a great invention!" he said. "Other folks can stick to old-fashioned ways if they want to, but I'm all for progress. It's a great age we're living in." Ibid., Ch. 12

## 340. Mary Hunter Austin
### (1868–1934)

1 When a woman ceases to alter the fashion of her hair, you guess that she has passed the crisis of her experience.
*The Land of Little Rain*   *1903*

2 Life set itself to new processions of seed-time and harvest, the skin newly tuned to seasonal variations, the very blood humming to new altitudes. The rhythm of walking, always a recognizable background for our thoughts, altered from the militaristic stride to the job of the wide unrutted earth.
*The American Rhythm*   *1923*

\* \* \*

3 Oh, the Shepards in Judea!
Do you think the shepards know
How the whole round world is brightened
In the ruddy Christmas glow?
"The Shepards in Judea"

4 Never was it printed on a page,
Never was it spoken, never heard.
"Whisper of the Wind"

5 What need has he of clocks who knows
When highest peaks are gilt and rose
Day has begun?
"Clocks and Calendars," St. 1

## 341. Guida Diehl
### (1868–?)

1 Never did Hitler promise to the masses in his rousing speeches any material advantage what-

ever. On the contrary he pleaded with them to turn aside from every form of advantage-seeking and serve the great thought: Honor, Freedom, Fatherland!
*The German Woman and National Socialism*   *1933*

2 We long to see Men and Heroes who scorn fate. . . . Call us to every service, even to weapons!
Ibid.

## 342. Maude Glasgow
### (1868–1955)

1 When new-born humanity was learning to stand upright, it depended much on its mother and stood close to her protecting side. Then women were goddesses, they conducted divine worship, woman's voice was heard in council, she was loved and revered and genealogies were reckoned through her.
*The Subjection of Women and the Traditions of Men*   *1940*

2 As the race grew older, rationality flourished at the expense of moral sense. Ibid.

## 343. Agnes Lee
### (1868–1939)

\* \* \*

1 Bed is the boon for me!
It's well to bake and sweep,
But hear the word of old Lizette:
It's better than all to sleep.
"Old Lizette on Sleep," St. 1

2 But I'll not venture in the drift
Out of this bright security,
Till enough footsteps come and go
To make a path for me.
"Convention"

3 Oh, mine was rosy as a bough
Blooming with roses, sent, somehow,
To bloom for me!
His balmy fingers left a thrill
Deep in my breast that warms me still.
"Motherhood," St. 5

## 344. Caroline "La Belle" Otero
### (1868–1965)

1 . . . Paco took care of me; protected me; taught me to dance and sing, and was my lover. It was the first time in over two years that I knew where I was going to sleep every night, and the first time in my life that I knew there would

be something for me to eat when I woke up. Then Paco fell in love with me; wanted me to marry him, and spoiled everything.

> Quoted in the *Pittsburgh Leader*
> *April 11, 1904*

2 There are two things in Spain which are not found elsewhere—flowers, lovely flowers in such abundance, and bull fights. I love both.

> Quoted in the *New York World*
> *May 10, 1908*

## 345. Eleanor H. Porter

### (1868–1920)

1   "Oh, yes, the game was to just find something about everything to be glad about—not matter what 'twas," rejoined Pollyanna earnestly. "And we began right then—on the crutches."

"Well, goodness me! I can't see anythin' ter be glad about—gettin' a pair of crutches when you wanted a doll!" . . .

"Goosey! Why, just be glad because you *don't—need—'em*! . . ."    *Pollyanna*, Ch. 5
> *1912*

2   "Oh, but Aunt Polly, Aunt Polly, you haven't left me any time at all just to—to live."

"To live, child! What do you mean? As if you weren't living all the time!"

"Oh, of course I'd be *breathing* all the time I was doing those things, Aunt Polly, but I wouldn't be living. You breathe all the time you're sleep, but you aren't living. I mean *living*—doing the things you want to do. . . . That's what I call living, Aunt Polly. Just breathing isn't living!"    Ibid., Ch. 7

3   ". . . he said, too, that he wouldn't *stay* a minister a minute if 'twasn't for the rejoicing texts. . . . Of course the Bible didn't name 'em that. But it's all those that begin 'Be glad in the Lord,' or 'Rejoice greatly,' or 'Shout for joy,' and all that, you know—such a lot of 'em. Once, when father felt specially bad, he counted 'em. There were eight hundred of 'em."

> Ibid., Ch. 22

4   "What men and women need is encouragement. Their natural resisting powers should be strengthened, not weakened. . . . Instead of always harping on a man's faults, tell him of his virtues. Try to pull him out of his rut of bad habits. Hold up to him his better self, his *real* self that can dare and do and win out! . . . The influence of a beautiful, helpful, hopeful character is contagious, and may revolutionize a whole town. . . . People radiate what

is in their minds and in their hearts. If a man feels kindly and obliging, his neighbors will feel that way, too, before long. But if he scolds and scowls and criticizes—his neighbors will return scowl for scowl, and add interest!"

> Ibid.

## 346. Margaret Fairless Barber

### (1869–1901)

1   . . . Earth, my Mother, whom I love.

> *The Roadmender*, Vol. I,
> Dedication    *1900*

2 The people who make no roads are ruled out from intellectual participation in the world's brotherhood.    Ibid., Ch. 5

3 Necessity can set me helpless on my back, but she cannot keep me there; nor can four walls limit my vision.    Ibid., Vol. II, Ch. 6

4 Revelation is always measured by capacity.

> Ibid., Vol. III, Ch. 3

5 To look backward for a while is to refresh the eye, to restore it, and to render it the more fit for its prime function of looking forward.

> Ibid.

6 This place is peace and would be silent peace were it not for an Eisteddfod of small birds outvying each other with an eagerness which cannot wait until the last candidate has finished.

> Letter (May 19, 1900), *The Complete*
> *Works of Michael Fairless*    *1932p*

7 "In my Father's house are many mansions," and I suppose we are stripped of something in each till at last we can do without the Tree of Life and the candle and the sun and the protecting gates, in the innermost mansion which is the Beatific Vision.    Ibid.

8 Having first insulted you and then calmed you with poetry, I can sleep the sleep of drugs and justice.    Ibid. (May 30, 1900)

## 347. Elsa Barker

### (1869–1954)

1 They never fail who light
Their lamp of faith at the unwavering flame
Burnt for the altar service of the Race
Since the beginning.
> "The Frozen Grail"    *1910*

## 348. Olive Dargan

(1869–1968)

\* \* \*

1 Be a God, your spirit cried;
Tread with feet that burn the dew;
Dress with clouds your locks of pride;
Be a child, God said to you.
"To William Blake"

2 The mountains lie in curves so tender
I want to lay my arm about them
As God does.    "Twilight"

## 349. Anna Bunston De Bary

(1869–?)

\* \* \*

1 Close to the sod there can be seen
A thought of God in white and green.
"The Snowdrop"

## 350. Emma Goldman

(1869–1940)

1 The motto should not be: Forgive one another;
rather, Understand one another.
"The Tragedy of Women's Emancipation," *Anarchism and
Other Essays    1911*

2 Merely external emancipation has made of the
modern woman an artificial being. . . . Now,
woman is confronted with the necessity of
emancipating herself from emancipation, if she
really desires to be free.    Ibid.

3 Corruption of politics has nothing to do with
the morals, or the laxity of morals, of various
political personalities. Its cause is altogether a
material one.    Ibid.

4 Politics is the reflex of the business and industrial world. . . .    Ibid.

5 There is no hope even that woman, with her
right to vote, will ever purify politics.    Ibid.

6 As to the great mass of working girls and
women, how much independence is gained if
the narrowness and lack of freedom of the
home is exchanged for the narrowness and lack
of freedom of the factory, sweatshop, department store, or office?    Ibid.

7 Every movement that aims at the destruction of
existing institutions and the replacement thereof
with something more advanced, more perfect,
has followers who in theory stand for the most
radical ideas, but who, nevertheless, in their
every-day practice, are like the average Philistine, feigning respectability and clamoring for
the good opinion of their opponents.    Ibid.

8 True, the movement for women's rights has
broken many old fetters, but it has also forged
new ones.    Ibid.

9 . . . the higher mental development of woman,
the less possible it is for her to meet a congenial mate who will see in her, not only sex,
but also the human being, the friend, the com-
rade and strong individuality, who cannot and
ought not lose a single trait of her character.
Ibid.

10 And yet we find many emancipated women who
prefer marriage, with all its deficiencies, to the
narrowness of an unmarried life; narrow and
unendurable because of the chains of moral
and social prejudice that cramp and bind her
nature.    Ibid.

11 These internal tyrants [conscience] . . . these
busybodies, moral detectives, jailers of the human spirit, what will they say?    Ibid.

12 If love does not know how to give and take
without restrictions, it is not love, but a transaction that never fails to lay stress on a plus
and a minus.    Ibid.

13 Salvation lies in an energetic march onward
towards a brighter and clearer future.    Ibid.

14 . . . true emancipation begins neither at the
polls nor in courts. It begins in woman's soul.
Ibid.

15 . . . the most vital right is the right to love
and be loved.    Ibid.

16 A true conception of the relationship of the
sexes . . . knows of but one great thing: to
give of one's self boundlessly, in order to find
one's self richer, deeper, better.    Ibid.

17 It is significant that whenever the public mind
is to be diverted from a great social wrong, a
crusade is inaugurated against indecency, gambling, saloons, etc.
Ibid., "The Traffic in Women"

18 Whether our reformers admit it or not, the
economic and social inferiority of women is
responsible for prostitution.    Ibid.

19 As to a thorough eradication of prostitution,
nothing can accomplish that save a complete
transvaluation of all accepted values—especially the moral ones—coupled with the abolition of industrial slavery.    Ibid.

20 Those who sit in a glass house do wrong to
throw stones about them; besides, the American
glass house is rather thin, it will break easily,
and the interior is anything but a gainly sight.
Ibid.

21 Marriage is primarily an economic arrangement, an insurance pact. . . . Its returns are insignificantly small compared with the investments. In taking out an insurance policy one pays for it in dollars and cents, always at liberty to discontinue payments. If, however, woman's premium is a husband, she pays for it with her name, her privacy, her self-respect, her very life, "until death doth part." . . . Man, too, pays his toll. . . .
Ibid., "Marriage and Love"

22 The important and only God of practical American life: Can the man make a living? Can he support a wife? That is the only thing that justifies marriage.     Ibid.

23 Yet, if motherhood be of free choice, of love, of ecstasy, of defiant passion, does it not place a crown of thorns upon an innocent head and carve in letters of blood the hideous epithet, Bastard?     Ibid.

24 Love, the strongest and deepest element in all life, the harbinger of hope, of joy, of ecstasy; love, the defier of all laws, of all conventions; love, the freest, the most powerful moulder of human destiny; how can such an all-compelling force be synonymous with that poor little State and Church-begotten weed, marriage?     Ibid.

25 Man has bought brains, but all the millions in the world have failed to buy love. Man has subdued bodies, but all the power on earth has been unable to subdue love. Man has conquered whole nations but all his armies could not conquer love. Man has chained and fettered the spirit, but he has been utterly helpless before love. High on a throne, with all the splendor and pomp his gold can command, man is yet poor and desolate, if love passes him by. And if it stays, the poorest hovel is radiant with warmth, with life and color. Thus love has the magic power to make of a beggar a king. Yes, love is free; it can dwell in no other atmosphere. In freedom it gives itself unreservedly, abundantly, completely.     Ibid.

26 Capitalism . . . has . . . grown into a huge insatiable monster.
"The Social Aspects of Birth Control,"
*Mother Earth*     *April, 1916*

27 And through its destructive machinery, militarism, capitalism proclaims, "Send your sons on to me, I will drill and discipline them until all humanity has been ground out of them; until they become automatons ready to shoot and kill at the behest of their masters." Capitalism cannot do without militarism and since the masses of people furnish the material to be destroyed in the trenches and on the battlefield, capitalism must have a large race.
    Ibid.

28 . . . the soldier's business is to take life. For that he is paid by the State, eulogized by political charlatans and upheld by public hysteria. But woman's function is to give life, yet neither the State nor politicians nor public opinion have ever made the slightest provision in return for the life woman has given.
    Ibid.

29 No, it is not because woman is lacking in responsibility, but because she has too much of the latter that she demands to know how to prevent conception.     Ibid.

30 After all, that is what laws are for, to be made and unmade.     Ibid.

31 But even judges sometimes progress.     Ibid.

32 I may be arrested, I may be tried and thrown into jail, but I never will be silent. . . .
    Ibid.

33 . . . the government will . . . go on in the highly democratic method of conscripting American manhood for European slaughter.
"Address to the Jury,"
*Mother Earth*     *July, 1917*

34 . . . all wars are wars among thieves who are too cowardly to fight and who therefore induce the young manhood of the whole world to do the fighting for them.     Ibid.

35 . . . always and forever we have stood up against war, because we say that the war going on in the world is for the further enslavement of the people, for the further placing of them under the yoke of a military tyranny. . . .
    Ibid.

36 The conscientious objector, rightly or wrongly —that is a thing which you will have to argue with him—does not believe in war . . . because he insists that, belonging to the people whence he has come and to whom he owes his life, it is his place to stand on the side of the people, for the people and by the people and not on the side of the governing classes. . . .     Ibid.

37 . . . the tree of Russian liberty is watered with the blood of Russian martyrs.     Ibid.

38 . . . no great idea in its beginning can ever be within the law. How can it be within the law? The law is stationary. The law is fixed. The law is a chariot wheel which binds us all regardless of conditions or place or time.     Ibid.

39 But progress is ever changing, progress is ever renewing, progress has nothing to do with fixity. Ibid.

40 . . . democracy must first be safe for America before it can be safe for the world. Ibid.

41 Anarchy stands for the liberation of the human mind from the dominion of religion; the liberation of the human body from the dominion of property; liberation from the shackles and restraints of government. Anarchism 1917

42 . . . the experience of Russia, more than any theories, has demonstrated that all government, whatever its forms or pretenses, is a dead weight that paralyzes the free spirit and activities of the masses.
My Disillusionment in Russia 1923

43 The ultimate end of all revolutionary social change is to establish the sanctity of human life, the dignity of man, the right of every human being to liberty and well-being.
My Further Disillusionment in Russia 1924

44 No revolution ever succeeds as a factor of liberation unless the means used to further it be identified in spirit and tendency with the purpose to be achieved. Ibid.

45 Anarchy asserts the possibility of organization without discipline, fear or punishment, and without the pressure of property.
Living My Life 1931

46 Revolution is but thought carried into action.
Quoted in The Feminist Papers,
Alice Rossi, ed. 1973p

47 There's never been a good government.
Quoted by Katherine Anne Porter in
the Los Angeles Times
July 7, 1974p

## 351. Corra May Harris
(1869–1935)

1 The deadly monotony of Christian country life where there are no beggars to feed, no drunkards to credit, which are among the moral duties of Christians in cities, leads as naturally to the outvent of what Methodists call "revivals" as did the backslidings of the people in those days. A Circuit Rider's Wife, Ch. 3 1910

2 This is the wonderful thing about the pure in heart—they do see God. Ibid., Ch. 6

3 After you are dead it doesn't matter if you were not successful in a business way. No one has yet had the courage to memorialize his wealth on his tombstone. A dollar mark would not look well there. Ibid., Ch. 11

4 So long as a man attends to his business the public does not count his drinks. When he fails they notice if he takes even a glass of root beer.
Eve's Second Husband, Ch. 6
1910

5 Adam was a man who could believe any statement he could evolve out of his ambitious imagination easier than he could believe the literal facts of his life. Ibid., Ch. 7

6 "The world smacks most of us out of shape so soon." Ibid., Ch. 14

7 A woman would rather visit her own grave than the place where she has been young and beautiful after she is aged and ugly. Ibid.

## 352. Else Lasker-Schuler
(1869–1945)

1 We shall rest from love like two rare beasts
In the high reeds behind this world.
"A Love Song" (c.1902),
The Other Voices,
Carol Cosman, ed. 1975p

## 353. Charlotte Mew
(1869–1928)

1 . . . Oh! my God! the down,
The soft young down of her, the brown,
The brown of her. . . .
"The Farmer's Bride,"
Collected Poems 1916

2 When us was wed she turned afraid
Of love and me and all things human;
Like the shut of a winter's day.
Ibid.

## 354. Jessie Rittenhouse
(1869–1948)

* * *

1 I worked for a menial's hire,
Only to learn, dismayed,
That any wage I had asked of life,
Life would have paid.
"My Wage"

2 My debt to you, Beloved,
   Is one I cannot pay
In any coin of any realm
   On any reckoning day.
"Debt"

## 355. Carolyn Wells

### (1869–1942)

1 Total is a book. We find it
   Just a little past its prime;
And departing leaves behind it
   Footprints on the sands of time.
"Four," St. 3, At the Sign of the<br>Sphinx   1896

2 There was a young man of St. Kitts
Who was very much troubled with fits;
   The eclipse of the moon
   Threw him into a swoon,
When he tumbled and broke into bits.
"Limericks," No. 3, The Book of<br>Humorous Verse   1920

3 A Tutor who tooted the flute
Tried to teach two young tutors to toot;
   Said the two to the Tutor,
   "Is it harder to toot, or
To tutor two tutors to toot?"
Ibid., No. 6

4 "Women are all right, in their place—which,
by the way, is not necessarily in the home—
but a family feud, of all things, calls for masculine management and skill."
In the Onyx Lobby, Ch. 1<br>1920

5   "I'll bet Sherlock Holmes could find a lot of
data just by going over the floor with a lens."
  "He could in a story book—and do you know
why? Because the clews and things, in a story,
are all put there for him by the property man.
Like a salted mine. But in real life, there's
nothing doing of that sort."    Ibid., Ch. 5

6 The earth has rolled around again and harvest
   time is here,
The glory of the seasons and the crown of all
   the years.
"The Meaning of Thanksgiving Day"<br>1922

*   *   *

7 A canner can can
   Anything that he can,
But a canner can't can a can, can he?
"The Canner"

8 But Woman is rare beyond compare,
   The poets tell us so;
How little they know of Woman
   Who only Women know!
"Woman"

9 I love the Christmas-tide, and yet;
   I notice this, each year I live;
I always like the gifts I get,
   But how I love the gifts I give!
"A Thought"

10 The books we think we ought to read are poky,
   dull, and dry;
The books that we would like to read we are
   ashamed to buy;
The books that people talk about we never can
   recall;
And the books that people give us, oh, they're
   the worst of all.
"On Books"

11 When Venus said "Spell no for me,"
"N-O," Dan Cupid wrote with glee,
   And smiled at his success:
"Ah, child," said Venus, laughing low,
"We women do not spell it so,
   We spell it Y-E-S."
"The Spelling Lesson"

## 356. Elizabeth Botume

### (fl. 1870s)

1 It was not an unusual thing to meet a woman
coming from the fields, where she had been
hoeing cotton, with a small bucket or cup on
her head, and a hoe over her shoulder, contentedly smoking a pipe and briskly knitting as
she strode along. I have seen, added to all these,
a baby strapped to her back.
First Days Amongst the<br>Contrabands   1893

## 357. Mrs. Edmund Craster

### (fl. 1870s)

1 The Centipede was happy quite,
Until the Toad in fun
Said, "Pray which leg goes after which?"
And worked her mind to such a pitch,
She lay distracted in a ditch
Considering how to run.
"Pinafore Poems," Cassell's Weekly<br>1871

## 358. Clara Dolliver
### (fl. 1870s)

1 No merry frolics after tea,
No baby in the house.
"No Baby in the House,"
*No Baby in the House and Other*
*Stories for Children*    1868

## 359. Mary Pyper
### (fl. 1870s)
* * *

1 I sat me down; 'twas autumn eve,
And I with sadness wept;
I laid me down at night, and then
'Twas winter, and I slept.
"Epitaph: A Life"

## 360. Sarah Ann Sewell
### (fl. 1870s)

1 It is a man's place to rule, and a woman's to
yield. He must be held up as the head of the
house, and it is her duty to bend so unmur-
muringly to his wishes, that the rest of the
household will follow her example, and treat
him with the due respect his sex demands.
*Woman and the Times We Live In*
*1869*

## 361. Sharlot Mabridth Hall
### (1870–1943)

1 I stayed not, I could not linger; patient, resist-
less, alone,
I hewed the trail of my destiny deep in the
hindering stone.
"Song of the Colorado," *Cactus Pine*
*1910*

## 362. Florence Hurst Harriman
### (1870–1967)

1 Next to entertaining or impressive talk, a thor-
oughgoing silence manages to intrigue most
people.    *From Pinafores to Politics*, Ch. 4
*1924*

## 363. Grace Hibbard
### (1870?–1911)
* * *

1 "An Honest Lawyer"—book just out—
What can the author have to say?
Reprint perhaps of ancient tome—
A work of fiction anyway.
"Books Received"

## 364. Mary Johnston
### (1870–1936)

1 "I am weary of swords and courts and kings.
Let us go into the garden and watch the
minister's bees."
*To Have and to Hold*, Ch. 9    1899

## 365. Marie Lloyd
### (1870–1922)
* * *

1 A little of what you fancy does you good.
Song

2 I'm one of the ruins that Cromwell knocked
about a bit.
Ibid.

## 366. Rosa Luxemburg
### (1870–1919)

1 . . . profits are springing, like weeds, from the
fields of the dead.
*The Crisis in the German*
*Social Democracy*    1919

2 Shamed, dishonored, wading in blood and dripping with filth, thus capitalist society stands.
Ibid.

3 Self-criticism, cruel, unsparing criticism that
goes to the very root of the evil, is life and
breath for the proletarian movement.    Ibid.

4 It is a foolish delusion to believe that we need
only live through the war, as a rabbit hides
under the bush to await the end of a thunder-
storm, to trot merrily off in his old accustomed
gait when all is over.    Ibid.

5 If the proletariat learns *from* this war and *in*
this war to exert itself, to cast off its serfdom
to the ruling classes, to become the lord of its
own destiny, the shame and misery will not
have been in vain.    Ibid.

6 . . . we will be victorious if we have not forgotten how to learn.    Ibid.

7 Passive fatalism can never be the role of a
revolutionary party. . . .    Ibid.

8 Victory or defeat? It is the slogan of all-power-
ful militarism in every belligerent nation. . . .
And yet, what can victory bring to the proletariat?    Ibid.

9 Reduced to its objective historic significance,
the present world war as a whole is a competitive struggle of a fully developed capitalism for
world supremacy, for the exploitation of the
last remnant of noncapitalistic world zones.
Ibid.

10 The high stage of world-industrial development in capitalistic production finds expression in the extraordinary technical development and destructiveness of the instruments of war. . . .
                     Ibid.

11 This madness will not stop, and this bloody nightmare of hell will not cease until the workers . . . will drown the bestial chorus of war agitators and the hoarse cry of capitalist hyenas with the mighty cry of labor, "Proletarians of all countries, unite!"     Ibid.

12 Freedom for supporters of the government only, for the members of one party only—no matter how big its membership may be—is no freedom at all. Freedom is always freedom for the man who thinks differently.
     Quoted in *Die Russische Revolution*
     by Paul Froelich     *1940p*

13 Without general elections, without freedom of the press, freedom of speech, freedom of assembly, without the free battle of opinions, life in every public institution withers away, becomes a caricature of itself, and bureaucracy rises as the only deciding factor.     Ibid.

\*   \*   \*

14 I hope to die at my post; on the street, or in prison.     Letter to Sonia Liebnecht

## 367. Lucia Clark Markham

(1870–?)

\*   \*   \*

1 To-night from deeps of loneliness I wake in wistful wonder
To a sudden sense of brightness, an immanence of blue.
                   "Bluebells"

## 368. Maria Montessori

(1870–1952)

1 A single fact lies at the source of all deviations, viz., that the child has been prevented from fulfilling the original pattern of his development at the formative age. . . .
     *The Secret of Childhood*     *1939*

2 . . . in nature nothing creates itself and nothing destroys itself.     Ibid.

3 The babies . . . sought to render themselves independent of adults in all the actions which they could manage on their own, manifesting clearly the desire not to be helped, except in cases of absolute necessity. And they were seen to be tranquil, absorbed and concentrating on their work, acquiring a surprising calm and serenity.    *The Child in the Family*    *1956p*

4 . . . humanity is still far from that stage of maturity needed for the realization of its aspirations, for the construction, that is, of a harmonious and peaceful society and the elimination of wars. Men are not yet ready to shape their own destinies, to control and direct world events, of which—instead—they become the victims.    *The Absorbent Mind*    *1967p*

5 And if education is always to be conceived along the same antiquated lines of a mere transmission of knowledge, there is little to be hoped from it in the bettering of man's future. For what is the use of transmitting knowledge if the individual's total development lags behind?     Ibid.

6 If help and salvation are to come, they can only come from the children, for the children are the makers of men.     Ibid.

7 The greatness of the human personality begins at the hour of birth. From this almost mystic affirmation there comes what may seem a strange conclusion: that education must start from birth.     Ibid.

8 The only language men ever speak perfectly is the one they learn in babyhood, when no one can teach them anything!     Ibid.

9 And so we discovered that education is not something which the teacher does, but that it is a natural process which develops spontaneously in the human being.     Ibid.

10 We teachers can only help the work going on, as servants wait upon a master.     Ibid.

11 How strange it is to observe that in times like ours, when war has achieved a destructiveness without parallel . . . future plans for unity are made, which means not only that love exists, but that its power is fundamental.     Ibid.

12 Love and the hope of it are not things one can learn; they are a part of life's heritage.     Ibid.

13 The child endures all things.     Ibid.

14 The Absorbent Mind welcomes everything, puts its hope in everything, accepts poverty equally with wealth, adopts any religion and the prejudices and habits of its countrymen, incarnating all in itself.     Ibid.

15 Strange, is it not, that among all the wonders man has worked, and the discoveries he has made, there is only one field to which he has paid no attention; it is that of the miracle that God has worked from the first: the miracle of children.     Ibid.

## 369. Alice Caldwell Rice
### (1870–1942)

1 Life is made up of desires that seem big and vital one minute, and little and absurd the next. I guess we get what's best for us in the end.
*A Romance of Billy-Goat Hill,*
Ch. 2     1912

2 To him work appeared a wholly artificial and abnormal action, self-imposed and unnecessary. The stage of life presented so many opportunities for him to exercise his histrionic ability, that the idea of settling down to a routine of labor seemed a waste of talent.
Ibid., Ch. 6

3 The arbitrary division of one's life into weeks and days and hours seemed, on the whole, useless. There was but one day for the men, and that was pay day, and one for the women, and that was rent day. As for the children, every day was theirs, just as it should be in every corner of the world.     Ibid., Ch. 15

4 "Fer my part I can't see it's to any woman's credit to look nice when she's got the right kind of a switch and a good set of false teeth. It's the woman that keeps her good looks without none of them luxuries that orter be praised."     *Calvary Alley,* Ch. 2     1918

5 When one has a famishing thirst for happiness, one is apt to gulp down diversions wherever they are offered. The necessity of draining the dregs of life before the wine is savored does not cultivate a discriminating taste.
Ibid., Ch. 14

## 370. Helena Rubinstein
### (1870–1965)

1 I have always felt that a woman has the right to treat the subject of her age with ambiguity until, perhaps, she passes into the realm of over ninety. Then it is better she be candid with herself and with the world.
*My Life for Beauty,* Pt. I, Ch. 1
1966p

2 There are no ugly women, only lazy ones.
Ibid., Pt. II, Ch. 1

3 But what parent can tell when some such fragmentary gift of knowledge or wisdom will enrich her children's lives? Or how a small seed of information passed from one generation to another may generate a new science, a new industry—a seed which neither the giver nor the receiver can truly evaluate at the time.
Ibid., Ch. 10

## 371. Maud Younger
### (1870–1936)

1 We have so many ideas about things we have never tried.     "New York, May 6, 1907,"
*McClure's Magazine*     1907

2 It is not pleasant to have a stranger doubt your respectability.     Ibid.

3 "See here. How am I ever going to get experience if everyone tells me that I must have it before I begin?"     Ibid.

4 I did not know the working classes were so united. There is more affection and loyalty toward one another than among other people. Perhaps this is because the working people feel that there is a class struggle, and the leisure class does not know it yet.
Ibid., "New York, May 15"

5 "Then why don't all girls belong to unions?" I asked, feeling very much an outsider; but she of the gents' neckwear replied: "Well, there's some that thinks it ain't fashionable; there's some that thinks it ain't no use; and there's some that never thinks at all."
Ibid., "New York, June 8"

6 A trade unionist—of course I am. First, last, and all the time. How else to strike at the roots of the evils undermining the moral and physical health of women? How else grapple with the complex problems of employment, overemployment, and underemployment alike, resulting in discouraged, undernourished bodies, too tired to resist the onslaughts of disease and crime?
Speech, Quoted in *Ms.*
*January, 1973p*

## 372. Emily Carr
### (1871–1945)

1 I wonder why we are always sort of ashamed of our best parts and try to hide them. We don't mind ridicule of our "sillinesses" but of our "sobers," oh! Indians are the same and even dogs.     *Hundreds and Thousands*
(November 23, 1930)     1966p

2 You come into the world alone and you go out of the world alone yet it seems to me you are more alone while living than even going and coming.     Ibid. (July 16, 1933)

3 Oh, the glory of growth, silent, mighty, persistent, inevitable! To awaken, to open up like a flower to the light of a fuller consciousness! Ibid. (October 17, 1933)

4 It is not all bad, this getting old, ripening. After the fruit has got its growth it should juice up and mellow. God forbid I should live long enough to ferment and rot and fall to the ground in a squash.　　Ibid. (December 12, 1933)

5 B-a-a-a-, old sheep, bleating for fellows. Don't you know better by now?
　　　　　　Ibid. (April 6, 1934)

6 Twenty can't be expected to tolerate sixty in all things, and sixty gets bored stiff with twenty's eternal love affairs.　　Ibid. (August 12, 1934)

7 It is wonderful to feel the grandness of Canada in the raw, not because she is Canada but because she is something sublime that you were born into, some great rugged power that you are a part of.　　Ibid. (April 16, 1937)

8 I am not half as patient with old women now that I am one.　　Ibid. (March 6, 1940)

9 Everything holds its breath except spring. She bursts through as strong as ever.
　　　　　　Ibid. (March 7, 1941)

## 373. Maxine Elliott
(1871–1940)

1 Beauty, what is that? There are phalanxes of beauty in every comic show. Beauty neither buys food nor keeps up a home.
　　　　　　News Item　　1908

## 374. Margaret Witter Fuller
(1871–1954)

\* \* \*

1 I am immortal! I know it! I feel it!
Hope floods my heart with delight!
Running on air, mad with life, dizzy, reeling,
Upward I mount—faith is sight, life is feeling,
Hope is the day-star of might!
　　　　　　"Dryad Song"

2 It was thy kiss, Love, that made me immortal.
　　　　　　Ibid.

## 375. Pamela Glenconner
(1871–1928)

1 Giving presents is a talent; to know what a person wants, to know when and how to get it, to give it lovingly and well. Unless a character possesses this talent there is no moment more

annihilating to ease than that in which a present is received and given.
　　　　　　*Edward Wyndhan Tennant:*
　　　　　　*A Memoir*, Ch. 5　　1919

\* \* \*

2 Bitter are the tears of a child:
　　Sweeten them.
Deep are the thoughts of a child:
　　Quiet them.
Sharp is the grief of a child:
　　Take it from him.
Soft is the heart of a child:
　　Do not harden it.
　　　　　　"A Child"

## 376. Agnes C. Laut
(1871–1936)

1 They had reached the fine point where it is better for the weak to die trying to overthrow strength, than to live under the iron heel of brute oppression.
　　　　　　*Vikings of the Pacific*, Ch. 4
　　　　　　1905

2 Countless hopes and fears must have animated at the breasts of the Frenchmen.\* It is so with every venture that is based on the unknown. The very fact that possibilities *are* unknown gives scope to unbridled fancy and the wildest hopes; gives scope, too, when the pendulum swings the other way to deepest distrust.
　　　　　　*The Conquest of the Great Northwest,*
　　　　　　Ch. 7　　1908

3 The ultimate umpire of all things in life is—Fact.　　Ibid., Ch. 20

4 Canada's prosperity is literally overflowing from a cornucopia of superabundant plenty. Will her Constitution, wrested from political and civil strife; will her moral stamina, bred from the heroism of an heroic past, stand the strain, the tremendous strain of the new conditions? . . . Above all, will she stand the strain, the tremendous strain, of prosperity, and the corruption that is attendant on prosperity? *Quien sabe?*
　　　　　　*Canada, the Empire of the North,*
　　　　　　Ch. 16　　1909

5 Yet when you come to trace when and where national consciousness awakened, it is like following a river back from the ocean to its mountain springs. . . . You can guess the eternal striving, the forward rush and the throwback that have carved a way through the

\* Radisson and Groseillers' voyage in 1668 to Hudson Bay.

solid rock; but until you have followed the river to its source and tried to stem its current you can not know.

> *The Canadian Commonwealth,*
> Ch. 1     *1915*

## 377. Florence Sabin

### (1871–1953)

1 The prohibition law, written for weaklings and derelicts, has divided the nation, like Gaul, into three parts—wets, drys and hypocrites.

> Speech     *February 9, 1931*

## 378. Maude Adams

### (1872–1953)

1 If I smashed the traditions it was because I knew no traditions.

> Quoted in *Maude Adams: A Biography*
> by Ada Patterson     *1907*

2 Genius is the talent for seeing things straight. It is seeing things in a straight line without any bend or break or aberration of sight, seeing them as they are, without any warping of vision. Flawless mental sight! That is genius.

> *Ibid.*

## 379. Mary Reynolds Aldis

### (1872–1949)

\* \* \*

1 They flush joyously like a cheek under a lover's kiss;
They bleed cruelly like a dagger-wound in the breast;
They flame up madly of their little hour,
Knowing they must die.

> "Barberries"

## 380. Eva Gore-Booth

### (1872–1926)

\* \* \*

1 The little waves of Breffney go stumbling through my soul.

> "The Little Waves of Breffney,"
> *Poems*

## 381. Mildred Howells

### (1872–1966)

\* \* \*

1 And so it criticized each flower,
This supercilious seed;
Until it woke one summer hour,
And found itself a weed.

> "The Different Seed," St. 5

2 Oh, tell me how my garden grows,
Where I no more may take delight,
And if some dream of me it knows,
Who dream of it by day and night.

> "Oh, Tell Me How My Garden
> Grows," St. 5

## 382. Aleksandra Kollontai

### (1872–1952)

1 In place of the indissoluble marriage based on the servitude of women, we shall see rise the free union, fortified by the love and the mutual respect of the two members of the workers' state, equal in their rights and in their obligations. In place of the individual and egotistic family, there will arise a great universal family of workers, in which all the workers, men and women, will be, above all, workers, comrades. . . .

> *Communism and the Family*
> *1918*

2 The "upper" elements may divert the masses from the straight road of history which leads toward communism only when the masses are mute, obedient, and when they passively and credulously follow their leaders.

> *The Workers' Opposition in Russia*
> *c.1921*

3 . . . beginning with the appointment of a sovereign for the state and ending with a sovereign director for the factory. This is the supreme wisdom of bourgeois thought.

> *Ibid.*

4 . . . the middle class with their hostility toward communism, and with their predilections toward the immutable customs of the past, with resentments and fears toward revolutionary acts—these are the elements that bring decay into our Soviet institutions, breeding there an atmosphere altogether repugnant to the working class.

> *Ibid.*

5 It is well known to every Marxian that reconstruction of industry and development of creative forces of a country depend on two factors: on the development of technique, and the efficient organization of labor by means of increasing productivity and finding new incentives to work.

> *Ibid.*

6 Bureaucracy, as it is, is a direct negation of mass self-activity. . . . Ibid.

7 Fear of criticism and freedom of thought by combining together with bureaucracy quite often produce ridiculous forms. Ibid.

8 The practice of [political] appointments rejects completely the principle of collective work; it breeds irresponsibility. Ibid.


## 383. Julia Morgan
### (1872–1957)

1 I don't think you understand just what my work has been here. The decorative part was all done by a New York firm. My work was structural [on the rebuilding of the Fairmont Hotel following the 1906 earthquake].
Quoted in the *San Francisco Call*
*1907*

2 The building should speak for itself.
Quoted in "Some Examples of the Work of Julia Morgan" by Walter T. Steilberg, *Architect and Engineer*
*November, 1918*

3 Never turn down a job because you think it's too small, you don't know where it can lead. Ibid.


## 384. Grace Seton-Thompson
### (1872–1959)

1 . . . the outfit I got together for my first [hunting] trip appalled that good man, my husband, while the number of things I had to learn appalled me. *A Woman Tenderfoot*, Ch. 1
*1900*

2 I know what it means to be a miner and a cowboy, and have risked my life when need be, *but*, best of all, I have felt the charm of the glorious freedom, the quick rushing blood, the bounding motion, of the wild life, the joy of the living and of the doing, of the mountain and the plain; I have learned to know and feel some, at least, of the secrets of the Wild Ones. Ibid., Ch. 18

3 Courage! Speed the day of world perfection. Straining from the Wheel of Things, Let us break the bonds of lost direction! Godward! Borne on Freedom's wings!
"The Wheel of Life," St. 6,
*The Singing Traveler* *1947*

4 My Mother is everywhere . . .
In the perfume of a rose,
The eyes of a tiger,
The pages of a book,
The food that we partake,
The whistling wind of the desert,
The blazing gems of sunset,
The crystal light of full moon,
The opal veils of sunrise.
Ibid., "Hindu Chant," St. 4

5 Beckon, dreams of passion, luring snare!
Your guileful bed of satin-white
Calls to lustful ease.
Ibid., "Opium Poppy," St. 2

6 If I must suffer more re-birth
Upon the weary plain of earth,
Grant that my rest be deep,
And happy be my sleep
Until the turning Wheel of Life
Wakes me to Illusion's strife.
Ibid., "Goddess of Mercy," St. 1

7 Butterflies and birds fly over me unconcerned . . .
The forest accepts me.
Ibid., "Forest," St. 4

8 What is an eye?
A strange device,
A bit of film and nerve, the first camera obscura,
A wonder steeped in mystery . . .
Recording scenes and filing prints in cabinets of the brain?
Ibid., "Windows of the Soul," St. 1

9 Many times I have looked into the eyes of wild animals
And we have parted friends.
What did they see, and recognize,
Shining through the windows of a human soul?
Ibid., St. 9


## 385. Leonora Speyer
### (1872–1956)

1 I'll sing, "Here lies, here lies, here lies—"
Ah, rust in peace below!
Passers will wonder at my words,
But your dark dust will know.
"I'll Be Your Epitaph,"
*Fiddler's Farewell* *1926*

2 Poor patch-work of the heart,
This healing love with love;
Binding the wound to wound,
The smart to smart!
Ibid., "Therapy," St. 3

3 Love has a hundred gentle ends.
    Ibid., "Two Passionate Ones Part,"
    St. 5

4 Houses are like the hearts of men,
    I think;
    They must have life within,
    (This is their meat and drink),
    They must have fires and friends and kin,
    Love for the day and night,
    Children in strong young laps:
    Then they live—then!
    Ibid., "Abrigada," St. 10

5 You gave me wings to fly;
    Then took away the sky.
    Ibid., Introduction, Pt. V

6 Let me declare
    That music never dies;
    That music never dies.
    Ibid., "Fiddler's Farewell," St. 13

7 . . . no amount of study will contrive a talent,
    that being God's affair; but having the gift,
    "through Grace," as John Masefield says, it
    must be developed, the art must be learned.
    "On the Teaching of Poetry,"
    The Saturday Review of Literature
    1946

8 There is not much stitching and unstitching in
    some of the hasty and cocksure writing of
    today.                                          Ibid.

9 . . . to be exact has naught to do with pedantry
    or dogma. . . .                                 Ibid.

10 I believe in anthologies, although I know they
    offer only a glimpse.                           Ibid.

11 . . . I quote a good deal in my talks. . . . I do
    like to call upon my radiant cloud of witnesses
    to back me up, saying the thing I would say,
    and saying it so much more eloquently.
    Ibid.

12 I do not think that too severe comment is
    good teaching.                                  Ibid.

*   *   *

13 Sky, be my depth;
    Wind, be my width and my height;
    World, my heart's span:
    Loneliness, wings for my flight!
    "Measure Me, Sky"

14 Thunder crumples the sky,
    Lightning tears at it.
    "The Squall"

## 386. Willa Cather
(1873–1947)

1 No one can build his security upon the noble-
    ness of another person.
    Alexander's Bridge, Ch. 8     1912

2 There are only two or three human stories, and
    they go on repeating themselves as fiercely as
    if they had never happened before.
    O Pioneers!, Pt. II, Ch. 4     1913

3 The history of every country begins in the
    heart of a man or woman.                        Ibid.

4 I like trees because they seem more resigned
    to the way they have to live than other things
    do.                                     Ibid., Ch. 8

5 "There was certainly no kindly Providence that
    directed one's life; and one's parents did not
    in the least care what became of one, so long
    as one did not misbehave and endanger their
    comfort. One's life was at the mercy of blind
    chance. She had better take it in her own hands
    and lose everything than meekly draw the
    plough under the rod of parental guidance.
    She had seen it when she was at home last
    summer—the hostility of comfortable, self-
    satisfied people towards serious effort."
    The Song of the Lark     1915

6 We all like people who do things, even if we
    only see their faces on a cigar-box lid.
    Ibid.

7 "I tell you there is such a thing as creative
    hate!"                                  Ibid., Pt. I

8 Artistic growth is, more than it is anything
    else, a refining of the sense of truthfulness. The
    stupid believe that to be truthful is easy; only
    the artist, the great artist, knows how difficult
    it is.                             Ibid., Pt. VI, Ch. 11

9 "Oh, better I like to work out of doors than in
    the house. . . . I not care that your grandmother
    says it makes me like a man. I like to be like
    a man."                         My Antonia     1918

10 That is happiness; to be dissolved into some-
    thing completely great.
    Ibid., Bk. I, Ch. 2, Epitaph

11 Winter lies too long in country towns; hangs on
    until it is stale and shabby, old and sullen.
    Ibid., Bk. II, Ch. 7

12 Old men are like that, you know. It makes
    them feel important to think they are in love
    with somebody.          Ibid., Bk. III, Ch. 4

13 This was a lie, but Paul was quite accustomed to lying; found it, indeed, indispensable for overcoming friction.
> "Paul's Case," *Youth and the Bright Medusa*     1920

14 It was not that symphonies, as such, meant anything in particular to Paul, but the first sigh of the instruments seemed to free some hilarious spirit within him; something that struggled there like the Genius [sic] in the bottle found by the Arab fisherman.     Ibid.

15 It was a highly respectable street, where all the houses were exactly alike, and where business men of moderate means begot and reared large families of children, all of whom went to sabbath-school and learned the shorter catechism, and were interested in arithmetic; all of whom were as exactly alike as their homes, and of a piece with the monotony in which they lived.     Ibid.

16 Perhaps it was because, in Paul's world, the natural nearly always wore the guise of ugliness, that a certain element of artificiality seemed to him necessary in beauty.     Ibid.

17 He . . . knew now, more than ever, that money was everything, the wall that stood between all he loathed and all he wanted.     Ibid.

18 It was a losing game in the end, it seemed, this revolt against the homilies by which the world is run.     Ibid.

19 Art, it seems to me, should simplify. That, indeed, is very nearly the whole of the higher artistic process; finding what conventions of form and what details one can do without and yet preserve the spirit of the whole. . . .
> *On the Art of Fiction*     1920

20 There was this to be said for Nat Wheeler, that he liked every sort of human creature; he liked good people and honest people, and he liked rascals and hypocrites almost to the point of loving them.     *One of Ours*, Bk. I, Ch. 1     1922

21 The dead might as well try to speak to the living as the old to the young.
> Ibid., Bk. II, Ch. 6

22 The sun was like a great visiting presence that stimulated and took its due from all animal energy. When it flung wide its cloak and stepped down over the edge of the fields at evening, it left behind it a spent and exhausted world.     Ibid.

23 Yes, inside of people who walked and worked in the broad sun, there were captives dwelling in darkness,—never seen from birth to death.
> Ibid., Bk. III, Ch. 2

24 He was still burning with the first ardour of the enlisted man. He believed that he was going abroad with an expeditionary force that would make war without rage, with uncompromising generosity and chivalry.     Ibid., Ch. 10

25 "When I'm in normal health, I'm a Presbyterian, but just now I feel that even the wicked get worse than they deserve."
> Ibid., Bk. IV, Ch. 9

26 They were mortal, but they were unconquerable.     Ibid., Bk. V, Ch. 18

27 Theoretically he knew that life is possible, maybe even pleasant, without joy, without passionate griefs. But it had never occurred to him that he might have to live like that.
> *The Professor's House*     1925

28 That irregular and intimate quality of things made entirely by the human hand.
> *Death Comes for the Archbishop,* Bk. I, Ch. 3     1927

29 The miracles of the church seem to me to rest not so much upon faces or voices or healing power coming suddenly near to us from afar off, but upon our perceptions being made finer, so that for a moment our eyes can see and our ears can hear what is there about us always.     Ibid., Ch. 4

30 The universal human yearning for something permanent, enduring, without shadow of change.     Ibid., Bk. III, Ch. 3

31 CECILE. Do you think it wrong for a girl to know Latin?

PIERRE. Not if she can cook a hare or a partridge as well as Mademoiselle Auclaire! She may read all the Latin she pleases.
> *Shadows on the Rock*     1931

32 Only solitary men know the full joys of friendship. Others have their family; but to a solitary and an exile his friends are everything.
> Ibid., Bk. III, Ch. 5

33 There are all those early memories; one cannot get another set; one has only those.
> Ibid., Bk. IV, Ch. 2

34 One made a climate within a climate; One made the days—the complexion, the special flavor, the special happiness of each day as it passed; one made life.     Ibid., Ch. 3

35 Sometimes a neighbor whom we have disliked a lifetime for his arrogance and conceit lets fall a single commonplace remark that shows us another side, another man, really; a man uncertain, and puzzled, and in the dark like ourselves.     Ibid., Epilogue

36 "Nothing really matters but living—accomplishments are the ornaments of life, they come second."    *Lucy Gayheart*    1935

37 The revolt against individuals naturally calls artists severely to account, because the artist is of all men the most individual: those who were not have long been forgotten. The condition every art requires is, not so much freedom from restriction, as freedom from adulteration and from the intrusion of foreign matter, considerations and purposes which have nothing to do with spontaneous invention.
*On Writing*    1949p

38 Religion and art spring from the same root and are close kin. Economics and art are strangers.
Ibid.

* * *

39 Incapable of compromises,
Unable to forgive or spare,
The strange awarding of the prizes
He had no fortitude to bear.
"A Likeness"

40 So blind is life, so long at last is sleep,
And none but love to bid us laugh or weep.
"Evening Song"

41 Oh, this is the joy of the rose:
That it blows,
And goes.
"In Rose-Time"

42 Where are the loves that we have loved before
When once we are alone, and shut the door?
"L'Envoi"

## 387. Colette
### (1873–1954)

1 All those beautiful sentiments I've uttered have made me feel genuinely upset.
"The Journey"    1905

2 I look like a discouraged beetle battered by the rains of a spring night. I look like a molting bird. I look like a governess in distress. I look —Good Lord, I look like an actress on tour, and that speaks for itself.
"On Tour," *Music Hall Sidelights*
1913

3 How can one help shivering with delight when one's hot fingers close around the stem of a live flower, cool from the shade and stiff with new-born vigor!    Ibid.

4 Nothing ages a woman like living in the country.    Ibid.

5 We don't feel at ease here: we are surrounded by too much beauty.    Ibid.

6 A bed, a nice fresh bed, with smoothly drawn sheets and a hot-water bottle at the end of it, soft to the feet like a live animal's tummy.
Ibid., "Arrival and Rehearsal"

7 Happy in our obtuse way, devoid of intuition or foresight, we give no thought to the future, to misfortune, to old age. . . .    Ibid.

8 Privation prevents all thought, substitutes for any other mental image that of a hot, sweet-smelling dish, and reduces hope to the shape of a rounded loaf set in rays of glory.
Ibid., "A Bad Morning"

9 Our goal, though difficult to attain, is not inaccessible. Words, as we cease to feel their urgency, become detached from us, like graceless chips from a precious gem. Invested with a subtler task than those who speak classical verse or exchange witticisms in lively prose, we are eager to banish from our mute dialogues the earthbound word, the one obstacle between us and silence—perfect, limpid, rhythmic silence —proud to give expression to every emotion and every feeling, and accepting no other support, no other restraint than that of music alone.    Ibid.

10 "My dear sir, *they* don't debate. Each of them merely issues an ultimatum, and in what a tone! It all goes to show what extraordinary people they are, each more unequivocal than the other."    "The Old Lady and the Bear"
1914

11 I hate guests who complain of the cooking and leave bits and pieces all over the place and cream-cheese sticking to the mirrors.
*Cheri*    1920

12 Years of close familiarity rendered silence congenial. . . .    Ibid.

13 Life is nothing but a series of crosses for us mothers.    Ibid.

14 . . . they had become mistrustful, self-indulgent, and cut off from the world, as women are who have lived only for love.    Ibid.

15 . . . her smile was like a rainbow after a sudden storm.    Ibid.

16 Give me a dozen such heart-breaks, if that would help me to lose a couple of pounds.
Ibid.

17 Life as a child and then as a girl had taught her patience, hope, silence; and given her a prisoner's proficiency in handling these virtues as weapons.    Ibid.

18 You aren't frightened when a door slams, though it may make you jump. It's a snake creeping under it that's frightening.      Ibid.

19 . . . the sudden desire to look beautiful made her straighten her back. "Beautiful? For whom? Why, for myself, of course."      Ibid.

20 The divorce will be gayer than the wedding.      Ibid.

21 Let's go out and buy playing-cards, good wine, bridge-scorers, knitting needles—all the paraphernalia to fill a gaping void, all that's required to disguise that monster, an old woman.      Ibid.

22 That lovely voice; how I should weep for joy if I could hear it now!
      "Where Are the Children,"
      *My Mother's House*   1922

23 If there be a place of waiting after this life, then surely she who so often waited for us has not ceased to tremble for those two who are yet alive.      Ibid.

24 "Where, oh where are the children . . . ?"
      Ibid.

25 "What a nuisance! Why should one have to eat? And what shall we eat this evening?"
      Ibid., "Jealousy"

26 Blushing beneath the strands of her graying hair, her chin trembling with resentment, this little elderly lady is charming when she defends herself without so much as a smile against the accusations of a jealous sexagenarian. Nor does he smile either as he goes on to accuse her now of "gallivanting." But I can still smile at their quarrels because I am only fifteen and have not yet divined the ferocity of love beneath his old man's eyebrows, or the blushes of adolescence upon her fading cheeks.      Ibid.

27 "What are you thinking about, Bel-Gazou?"
   "Nothing, Mother."
   An excellent answer. The same that I invariably gave when I was her age.
      Ibid., "The Priest on the Wall"

28 It is not a bad thing that children should occasionally, and politely, put parents in their place.
      Ibid.

29 I know that to her faithful nurse, my Bel-Gazou is alternately the center of the universe, a consummate masterpiece, a possessed monster from whom the devil must hourly be exorcised, a champion runner, a dizzy abyss of perversity, a *dear little one*, and a baby rabbit. But who will tell me how my daughter appears to herself?      Ibid.

30 What's come over our daughters that they don't like essence of violet any more?
      Ibid., "My Mother and Illness"

31 It's pretty hard to retain the characteristics of one's sex after a certain age.      Ibid.

32 You'll understand later that one keeps on forgetting old age up to the very brink of the grave.      Ibid.

33 Imagine killing all those young flowers for the sake of an old woman.      Ibid.

34 . . . she has lost her torturer, her tormentor, the daily poison, the lack of which may well kill her.      Ibid.

35 Those love children always suffer because their mothers have crushed them under their stays trying to hide them, more's the pity. Yet after all, a lovely unrepentant creature, big with child, is not such an outrageous sight.      Ibid.

36 But at my age there's only one virtue: not to make people unhappy.      Ibid.

37 . . . great joys must be controlled.
      Ibid., "The Seamstress"

38 But it would seem that with this needleplay she has discovered the perfect means of adventuring, stitch by stitch, point by point, along a road of risks and temptations.      Ibid.

39 Oh, for those young embroiderers of bygone days, sitting on a hard little stool in the shelter of their mother's ample skirts! Maternal authority kept them there for years and years, never rising except to change the skein of silk or to elope with a stranger.      Ibid.

40 . . . the telephone shone as brightly as a weapon kept polished by daily use. . . .
      *The Last of Cheri*   1926

41 I love my past. I love my present. I'm not ashamed of what I've had, and I'm not sad because I have it no longer.      Ibid.

42 If one wished to be perfectly sincere, one would have to admit there are two kinds of love— well-fed and ill-fed. The rest is pure fiction.
      Ibid.

43 Whenever I feel myself inferior to everything about me, threatened by my own mediocrity, frightened by the discovery that a muscle is losing its strength, a desire its power, or a pain the keen edge of its bite, I can still hold up my head and say to myself: . . . "Let me not forget that I am the daughter of a woman who bent her head, trembling, between the blades of a cactus, her wrinkled face full of ecstasy over the promise of a flower, a woman who

herself never ceased to flower, untiringly, during three quarters of a century."

*Break of Day      1928*

44 A second place [setting]. . . . If I say that it is to be taken away for good, no pernicious blast will blow suddenly from the horizon to make my hair stand on end and alter the direction of my life as once it did. If that plate is removed from my table, I shall still eat with appetite.        Ibid.

45 I instinctively like to acquire and store up what promises to outlast me.        Ibid.

46 My true friends have always given me that supreme proof of devotion, a spontaneous aversion for the man I loved.        Ibid.

47 For to dream and then to return to reality only means that our qualms suffer a change of place and significance.        Ibid.

48 I have suffered, oh yes, certainly I learned how to suffer. But is suffering so very serious? I have come to doubt it. It may be quite childish, a sort of undignified pastime—I'm referring to the kind of suffering a man inflicts on a woman or a woman on a man. It's extremely painful. I agree that it's hardly bearable. But I very much fear that this sort of pain deserves no consideration at all.        Ibid.

49 "Love is not a sentiment worthy of respect."        Ibid.

50 O Man, my former loves, how one gains and learns in your company!        Ibid.

51 . . . that wild, unknown being, the child, who is both bottomless pit and impregnable fortress. . . .        "Look!"      *1929*

52 I have not forgotten how I used to take a child every year to the sea, as to a maternal element better fitted than I to teach, ripen, and perfect the mind and body that I had merely rough-hewn.        Ibid.

53 I am seized with the itch to possess the secrets of a being who has vanished forever. . . .        "The Savages," *Sido*      *1929*

54 He was such an inoffensive little boy, she could find no fault with him, except his tendency to disappear.        Ibid.

55 "You don't like them? Then what was it you wanted?"
Rashly he confessed: "I wanted to ask for them."        Ibid.

56 When ordinary parents produce exceptional children they are often so dazzled by them that they push them into careers that they consider

superior, even if it takes some lusty kicks on their behinds to achieve this result.        Ibid.

57 He finds him again without difficulty, slips into the light and nimble little body that he never leaves long, and roams through a century of the mind, where all is to the measure and liking of one who for sixty years has triumphantly remained a child.        Ibid.

58 The age we call awkward and the growing pains it inflicts on young bodies exact occasional sacrifices.        Ibid.

59 She [the cat] hasn't had her full ration of kisses-on-the-lips today. She had the quarter-to-twelve one in the Bois, she had the two o'clock one after coffee, she had the half-past-six one in the garden, but she's missed tonight's.        *The Cat      1933*

60 This life's idiotic: we're seeing far too much of each other and yet we never see each other properly.        Ibid.

61 He shut his eyes while Saha [the cat] kept vigil, watching all the invisible signs that hover over sleeping human beings when the light is put out.        Ibid.

62 He loved his dreams and cultivated them.        Ibid.

63 . . . that provisional tomb where the living exile sighs, weeps, fights, and succumbs, and from which he rises, remembering nothing, with the day.        Ibid.

64 "She never misses an opportunity to shrink away from anything that can be tasted or touched or smelled."        "Armande"      *1944*

65 "All women are monkeys. They're interested only in our absurdities and our love affairs and our illnesses."        Ibid.

66 He wondered why sexual shyness, which excites the desire of dissolute women, arouses the contempt of decent ones.        Ibid.

67 . . . love made him gloomy, jealous, self-conscious, unable to break down an obstacle between the two of them that perhaps did not exist.        Ibid.

68 "Drawers are one thing, decorum is another. . . ."        *Gigi      1944*

69 "If you didn't find *me* discouraging, then you'd find something else."        Ibid.

70 . . . she drew no advantage other than the close relationship of Gaston Lachaille and the pleasure to be derived from watching a rich man enjoying the comforts of the poor. . . .        Ibid.

71 "She's smart enough to keep herself to herself." Ibid.

72 "If only her brain worked as well as her jaws!" Ibid.

73 . . . pessimists have good appetites. Ibid.

74 "Call your mother, Gigi! Liane d'Exelmans has committed suicide."
The child replied with a long drawn-out "Oooh!" and asked, "Is she dead?"
"Of course not. She knows how to do things." Ibid.

75 "You must always start by refusing to give an interview to anybody. Then later you can fill the front page." Ibid.

76 "The telephone is of real use only to important businessmen or to women who have something to hide." Ibid.

77 "Instead of marrying 'at once,' it sometimes happens that we marry 'at last.' " Ibid.

78 "Boredom helps one to make decisions." Ibid.

79 "Explain yourself without gestures. The moment you gesticulate you look common." Ibid.

80 "A pretty little collection of weaknesses and a terror of spiders are indispensable stock-in-trade with men." Ibid.

81 "They forgive us—oh, for many things, but not for the absence in us of their own failings." Ibid.

82 "All that's in the past. All that's over and done with."
"Of course, Tonton, until it begins again." Ibid.

83 . . . he was always ready to part with twenty francs or even a "banknote," so much so that he died poor, in the arms of his unsuspected honesty.
"The Photographer's Missus" *1944*

84 "Oh, you know, when it comes to pearls, it's very seldom there isn't some shady story behind them." Ibid.

85 "In our part of the world, as you well know, they say raw meat is for cats and the English." Ibid.

86 "Don't be too nice to me. When anyone's too nice to me, I don't know what I'm doing—I boil over like a soup." Ibid.

87 The unexpected sound of sobbing is demoralizing. Ibid.

88 On this narrow planet, we have only the choice between two unknown worlds. Ibid.

89 In the matter of furnishing, I find a certain absence of ugliness far worse than ugliness. Ibid.

90 Like so many saviors, heavenly or earthly, the angel tended to overdo her part. Ibid.

91 Sorrow, fear, physical pain, excessive heat and excessive cold, I can still guarantee to stand up to all these with decent courage. But I abdicate in the face of boredom, which turns me into a wretched and, if necessary, ferocious creature. Ibid.

92 It is easy to relate what is of no importance. Ibid.

93 "Such a happy woman, why exactly, that's what I would have been if, here and there, in my trivial little life, I'd had something great. What do I call great? I've no idea, madame, because I've never had it!" Ibid.

94 "But once I had set out, I was already far on my way." Ibid.

95 "Madame, people very seldom die because they lost someone. I believe they die more often because they haven't had someone." Ibid.

96 A mouth is not always a mouth, but a bit is always a bit, and it matters little what it bridles. "The Sick Child" *1944*

97 Exhausted under the burden of universal kindness, he shut his eyes. . . . Ibid.

98 . . . the majesty that illness confers on children whom it strikes down. . . . Ibid.

99 [There are] two forms of luxury: fastidiousness and pain. Ibid.

100 . . . one word escaped, crisp and lively, and made a beeline for Jean, the word "crisis." Sometimes it entered ceremoniously, like a lady dressed up to give away prizes, with an *h* behind its ear and a *y* tucked into its bodice: Chrysis, Chrysis Salutari. Ibid.

101 The confused murmur of his nights began to rise, expected but not familiar. Ibid.

102 A boiled egg raised its little lid and revealed its buttercup yolk. Ibid.

103 Slightly intoxicated with the power to work marvels, he called up his boom companions of the cruel but privileged hours: the visible sounds; the tangible images; the breathable seas; the nourishing, navigable air; the wings that mocked feet; the laughing suns. Ibid.

104 A time comes when one is forced to concentrate on living. A time comes when one has to renounce dying in full flight.     Ibid.

105 My only remaining property is . . . a living beast, the fire . . . like all other beasts, it likes to have its belly scratched from underneath.     "The Blue Lantern"    1949

106 How pleasant a companion, the fire is
To the prisoner, during the long winter evenings!
Very near me a benevolent spirit warms itself
Who drinks or smokes or sings an old tune. . . .     Ibid.

107 A line of verse need not necessarily be beautiful for it to remain in the depths of our memory and occupy maliciously the place overrun by certain condemnable but unerasable melodies.     Ibid.

108 . . . writing leads only to writing.     Ibid.

109 The more the wonders of the visible world become inaccessible, the more intensely do its curiosities affect us.
    "Orchid," *For a Flower*    1949

## 388. Mary Elizabeth Crouse
### (1873–?)
* * *

1 How often do the clinging hands, though weak,
Clasp round strong hearts that otherwise would break.
    "Strength of Weakness"

## 389. Marie Dressler
### (1873–1934)

1 Fate cast me to play the role of an ugly duckling with no promise of swanning. Therefore, I sat down when a mere child—fully realizing just how *utterly* "mere" I was—and figured out my life early. Most people do it, but they do it too late. At any rate, from the beginning I have played my life as a comedy rather than the tragedy many would have made of it.    *The Life Story of an Ugly Duckling,* Ch. 1    1924

2 . . . poor had no terror for me! It was pie for me! My whole life had been a fight!
    Ibid., Ch. 5

3 I was born serious and I have earned my bread making other people laugh.
    *My Own Story,* Ch. 1    1934p

4 It is well enough to be interested in one's profession, but to restrict one's leisure to association with the members of one's own guild, so to speak, is to be doomed to artificiality and eventually to sterility. In order to represent life on the stage, we must rub elbows with life, live ourselves.     Ibid., Ch. 3

5 Love is not getting, but giving. It is sacrifice. And sacrifice is glorious! I have no patience with women who measure and weigh their love like a country doctor dispensing capsules. If a man is worth loving at all, he is worth loving generously, even recklessly.     Ibid., Ch. 7

6 There is a vast difference between success at twenty-five and success at sixty. At sixty, nobody envies you. Instead, everybody rejoices generously, sincerely, in your good fortune.     Ibid., Ch. 17

7 By the time we hit fifty, we have learned our hardest lessons. We have found out that only a few things are really important. We have learned to take life seriously, but never ourselves.     Ibid.

## 390. Nellie McClung
### (1873–1951)

1 When they felt tired, they called it laziness and felt disgraced, and thus they had spent their days, working, working from the grey dawn, until the darkness came again, and all for what? When in after years these girls, broken in health and in spirits, slipped away to premature graves, or, worse still, settled into chronic invalidism, of what avail was the memory of the cows they milked, the mats they hooked, the number of pounds of butter they made.
    *Sowing Seeds in Danny*    1908

2 "While we are side by side" the violins sang, glad, triumphant, that old story that runs like a thread of gold through all life's patterns; that old song, old yet ever new, deathless, unchangeable, which maketh the poor man rich and without which the richest becomes poor!
    Ibid.

## 391. Virginia Taylor McCormick
### (1873–1957)
* * *

1 Not any leaf from any book
Can give what Pan, in going, took.
    "Regret from Pan"

2 Now she is dead she greets Christ with a nod,—
(He was a carpenter)—*but she knows God.*
    "The Snob"

## 392. Elizabeth Reeve Morrow

(1873–1955)

* * *

1 My friend and I have built a wall
Between us thick and wide:
The stones of it are laid in scorn
And plastered high with pride.
"Wall," St. 1

2 There is no lover like an island shore
For lingering embrace;
No tryst so faithful as the turning tide
At its accustomed place.
"Islands," St. 1

## 393. Daisy, Princess of Pless

(1873–?)

1 My parents, with hearts full of tender love, did nothing whatever to prepare me for life and its ordeals. . . . Without a rudder or chart, I was at the mercy of any winds that blew close enough to reach me. Either of my parents would have done anything in the world for me —except tell me the truth.
*Daisy, Princess of Pless*, Ch. 1
*1923*

2 How seldom people find their happiness on a darkened stage; they must turn up all the limelights to find it.     Entry (August 16, 1903),
*From My Private Diary*     *1926*

3 No theatre is prosperous, or a play complete, unless there is a bedroom scene in the second act. . . .     Ibid. (April 28, 1904)

4 It is no use having illusions about life. Life, as we live it, *is* commonplace unless one chooses to renounce the world, and live out of it, and therefore be different from others.     Ibid.

5 The souls we have loved here, we may love and meet again because we have once loved them; but our intercourse with them will not be tainted with the remembrance of this heartbreaking little world; we shall not recognize them in their personal limitations.
Ibid. (February 13, 1907)

6 I was always frank by nature and cannot understand the absurd reticences which many people seem to consider so necessary.
*Better Left Unsaid*, Ch. 1     *1931*

7 The Irish sit by a peat fire; the English by a coal one. That is the unbridgeable difference between the two peoples: We prefer the glamorous, the quick, the pungent; they the lasting and substantial.
*What I Left Unsaid*, Ch. 1     *1936*

8 For each of us, after middle-age, the world is always emptying.     Ibid., Ch. 3

## 394. Emily Post

(1873–1960)

1 Considering manners even in their superficial aspect, no one—unless he be a recluse who comes in contact with no other human being— can fail to reap the advantage of a proper, courteous and likeable approach, or fail to be handicapped by an improper, offensive and resented one.     *Etiquette*, Ch. 1     *1922*

2 Ideal conversation must be an exchange of thought, and not, as many of those who worry most about their shortcomings believe, an eloquent exhibition of wit or oratory.
Ibid., Ch. 6

3 . . . to do *exactly as your neighbors* do is the only sensible rule.     Ibid., Ch. 33

4 To the old saying that man built the house but woman made of it a "home" might be added the modern supplement that woman accepted cooking as a chore but man has made of it a recreation.     Ibid., Ch. 34

5 Far more important than any mere dictum of etiquette is the fundamental code of honor, without strict observance of which no man, no matter how "polished," can be considered a gentleman. The honor of a gentleman demands the inviolability of his word, and the incorruptibility of his principles. He is the descendant of the knight, the crusader; he is the defender of the defenseless and the champion of justice —or he is not a gentleman.     Ibid., Ch. 48

6 To tell a lie in cowardice, to tell a lie for gain, or to avoid deserved punishment—are all the blackest of black lies. On the other hand, to teach him to try his best to avoid the truth— even to press it when necessary toward the outer edge of the rainbow—for a reason of kindness, or of mercy, is far closer to the heart of truth than to repeat something accurately and mercilessly that will cruelly hurt the feelings of someone.
*Children Are People*, Ch. 11     *1940*

7 The natural impulses of every thoroughbred include his sense of honor; his love of fair play and courage; his dislike of pretense and of cheapness.     Ibid., Ch. 30

## 395. Dorothy Miller Richardson
### (1873–1957)

1 "There; how d'ye like that, eh? A liberal education in twelve volumes, with an index."
*Pilgrimage*, Vol. II, Ch. 24    *1938*

2 . . . women stopped being people and went off into hideous processes.    Ibid.

3 If there was a trick, there must be a trickster.
Ibid.

4 It will all go on as long as women are stupid enough to go on bringing men into the world. . . .    Ibid.

5 They invent a legend to put the blame for the existence of humanity on women and, if she wants to stop it, they talk about the wonders of civilizations and the sacred responsibilities of motherhood. They can't have it both ways.
Ibid.

6 No future life could heal the degradation of having been a woman. Religion in the world had nothing but insults for women.    Ibid.

7 *Coercion.* The unpardonable crime.
Ibid., Vol. IV, Ch. 9

8 In and out of every year of his ascent her life had been woven, and was now a kind of compendium for him of it all, one of his supports, one of those who through having known the beginnings, through representing them every time she appeared, brought to him a realization of his achievements.    Ibid.

9 . . . she saw how very slight, how restricted and perpetually baffled must always be the communication between him and anything that bore the name of woman. Saw the price each one had paid with whom he had been intimate either in love or friendship, in being obliged to shut off . . . three-fourths of their being.
Ibid.

10 "Women carry all the domesticity they need about with them. That is why they can get along alone so much better than men."    Ibid.

11 "Religious people in general are in some way unsatisfactory. Not fully alive. Exclusive. Irreligious people are unsatisfactory in another way. Defiant."    Ibid.

12 . . . men want recognition of their work, to help them to believe in themselves.    Ibid.

13 With the familiar clothes, something of his essential self seemed to have departed.    Ibid.

## 396. Margaret Baillie Saunders
### (1873–1949?)

1 I've often known people more shocked because you are not bankrupt than because you are.
*A Shepherd of Kensington*    *1907*

2 One's old acquaintances sometimes come upon one like ghosts—and most people hate ghosts.
Ibid.

3 Very few men care to have the obvious pointed out to them by a woman.    Ibid.

## 397. Janet Scudder
### (1873–1940)

1 I don't believe artists should be subjected to experiences that harden the sensibilities; without sensibility no fine work can ever be done.
*Modeling My Life*, Ch. 2    *1925*

2 Someone has said that even criticism is better than silence. I don't agree to this. Criticism can be very harmful unless it comes from a master; and in spite of the fact that we have hundreds of critics these days, it is one of the most difficult of professions.    Ibid.

## 398. Edith Franklin Wyatt
### (1873–1958)

1 Every true poem is a lone fount, of whose refreshment the traveler himself must drink, if he is to quench his thirst for poetry.
"Modern Poetry," *Art and the Worth-While*, Baker Brownell, ed.
*1929*

2 Our criticism is always devoting itself to . . . watching the sticks and straws on the surface of the current, without interest, apparently, in the natural force of the stream, the style and turn of the whole composition, its communicative social imagination.    Ibid.

## 399. Ch'iu Chin
### (1874–1907)

1 We'll follow Joan of Arc—
With our own hands our land we shall regain!
"Ch'iu Chin—A Woman Revolutionary," Quoted in *Women of China* by Fan Wen-Lan    *1956p*

2 "We want to unite our two hundred million sisters into a solid whole, so that they can call to each other. Our journal will act as the mouthpiece for our women. It is meant to help our sisters by giving their life a deeper meaning and hope and to advance rapidly towards a bright, new society. We Chin women should because the vanguard in rousing the people to welcome enlightenment." Ibid. (1905)

## 400. Isabel La Howe Conant
### (1874–?)
* * *
1 He who loves an old house
Never loves in vain.
"Old House," St. 1

## 401. Olive Custance
### (1874–1944)
* * *
1 Spirit of Twilight, through your folded wings
I catch a glimpse of your averted face,
And rapturous on a sudden, my soul sings
"Is not this common earth a holy place?"
"Twilight"

## 402. Zona Gale
### (1874–1938)
1 They were all dimly aware that something was escaping them, some inheritance of joy which they had meant to share. How was it they were not sharing it? *Birth*, Ch. 1 *1918*

2 Loving, like prayer, is a power as well as a process. It's curative. It is creative.
Ibid., Ch. 3

3 DWIGHT. Energy—it's the driving power of the nation. *Miss Lulu Bett*, Act I, Sc. 1
*1920*

4 NINIAN. Education: I ain't never had it and I ain't never missed it. Ibid., Sc. 2

5 DWIGHT. I tell you of all history the most beautiful product is the family tie. Of it are born family consideration. . . .
Ibid., Act II, Sc. 2

6 He faced the blind wall of human loneliness. He was as one who, expecting to be born, is still-born, and becomes aware not of the cradle, but of eternity. "The Biography of Blade,"
*Century Magazine* *1924*

7 Always he had wanted to tell somebody about his life, but when he had tried, his confidante had looked at him.
"Evening," *The Book Man* *1925*

8 But the romance, the true interpretation of any habit, of any convention, lies in this faint inner significance for which few have memory or attention. "Modern Prose," *Art and the Worth-While*, Baker Brownell, ed.
*1929*

9 The unexpressed, then, is always of greater value than the expressed. Ibid.
* * *
10 He was integrated into life,
He was a member of life,
He was harmonized, orchestrated, identified
with the program of being.
"Walt Whitman"

## 403. Theodosia Garrison
### (1874–1944)
* * *
1 At first cock-crow the ghosts must go
Back to their quiet graves below.
"The Neighbors"

2 I have known laughter—therefore I
May sorrow with you far more tenderly
Than those who never guess how sad a thing
Seems merriment to one heart's suffering.
"Knowledge"

3 I never crossed your threshold with a grief
But that I went without it.
"The Closed Door," St. 1

4 The hardest habit of all to break
Is the terrible habit of happiness.
"The Lake"

5 The kindliest thing God ever made,
His hand of very healing laid
Upon a fevered world, is shade.
"The Shade," St. 1

6 When the red wrath perisheth, when the dulled swords fail,
These three who have walked with death—these shall prevail.
Hell bade all its millions rise; Paradise sends three:
Pity, and self-sacrifice, and charity.
"This Shall Prevail"

## 404. Ellen Glasgow

(1874–1945)

1 And the spring passed into Nicholas also. The wonderful renewal of surrounding life thrilled through the repression of his nature. With the flowing of the sap the blood flowed more freely in his veins. New possibilities were revealed to him; new emotions urged him into fresh endeavours. All his powerful, unspent youth spurred on to manhood.

*The Voice of the People,*
Bk. II, Ch. 3   *1900*

2 With a sudden shout Nicholas voiced the glorification of toil—of honest work well done. He felt with the force of a revelation that to throw up the clods of earth manfully is as beneficent as to revolutionise the world. It was not the matter of the work, but the mind that went into it, that counted—and the man who was not content to do small things well would leave great things undone.   Ibid., Ch. 4

3 "A farmer's got to be born, same as a fool. You can't make a corn pone out of flour dough by the twistin' of it."   Ibid.

4 "What a man marries for's hard to tell," she returned; "an' what a woman marries for's past findin' out."   Ibid., Bk. III, Ch. 1

5 "I ain't never seen no head so level that it could bear the lettin' in of politics. It makes a fool of a man and a worse fool of a fool. The government's like a mule, it's slow and it's sure; it's slow to turn, and it's sure to turn the way you don't want it."   Ibid., Ch. 2

6 "I d'clare if it don't beat all—one minute we're thar an' the next we're here. It's a movin' world we live in, ain't that so, Mum?"

*The Deliverance,* Bk. I, Ch. 1
*1904*

7 "Maria has been so long at her high-and-mighty boarding-school," he said, "that I reckon her head's as full of fancies as a cheese is of maggots."   Ibid., Ch. 3

8 "I haven't much opinion of words. . . . They're apt to set fire to a dry tongue, that's what I say."   Ibid., Bk. II, Ch. 4

9 "I hate lies, I have had so many of them, and I shall speak the truth hereafter, no matter what comes of it. Anything is better than a long, wearing falsehood, or than those hideous little shams that we were always afraid to touch for fear they would melt and show us our own nakedness."   Ibid., Bk. IV, Ch. 2

10 I wondered why anyone so rich and so beautiful should ever be unhappy—for I had been schooled by poverty to believe that money is the first essential of happiness—and yet her unhappiness was as evident as her beauty, or the luxury that enveloped her.

"The Past," *Good Housekeeping*
*1920*

11 "For once we were natural. . . . And it was a relief, even to the women, especially to the women, when the savage hunger broke through the thin crust we call civilization. It was a relief to us all, no doubt, to be able to think murder and call it idealism. But the war wasn't the worst thing," he concluded grimly. "The worst thing is this sense of having lost our way in the universe. The worst thing is that the war has made peace seem so futile. It is just as if the bottom had dropped out of idealism. . . ."

*They Stooped to Folly,*
Pt. I, Ch. 1   *1929*

12 "Oh, but it feels so nice to be hard! If I had known how nice it felt, I should have been hard all my life."   Ibid., Ch. 12

13 After all, you can't expect men not to judge by appearances.   *The Sheltered Life*   *1932*

14 Shadows are not enough.   Ibid.

15 Women like to sit down with trouble as if it were knitting.   Ibid.

16 No idea is so antiquated that it was not once modern. No idea is so modern that it will not someday be antiquated.

Address, Modern Language
Association   *1936*

17 To seize the flying thought before it escapes us is our only touch with reality.   Ibid.

18 "Grandpa says we've got everything to make us happy but happiness."   *In This Our Life,*
Pt. I, Ch. 1   *1941*

19 "Heaven knows, I'm not a snob, and I realize it's the fashion nowadays to climb down and not up; but all the radicals you see in the newspapers look so untidy, and I'm afraid when he gets middle-aged he will never want to brush his hair or wash his face."   Ibid., Ch. 9

20 "I don't like human nature, but I do like human beings."   Ibid., Pt. II, Ch. 1

21 "We didn't talk so much about happiness in my day. When it came, we were grateful for it, and, I suppose, a little went farther than it does nowadays. We may have been all wrong in our ideas, but we were brought up to think other things more important than happiness."

Ibid., Ch. 10

22 No matter how vital experience might be while you lived it, no sooner was it ended and dead than it became as lifeless as the piles of dry dust in a school history book.
Ibid., Pt. III, Ch. 9

23 Tilling the fertile soil of man's vanity.
*A Certain Measure* 1943

## 405. Beatrice Hinkle
### (1874–1953)

1 Fundamentally the male artist approximates more to the psychology of woman, who, biologically speaking, is a purely creative being and whose personality has been as mysterious and unfathomable to the man as the artist has been to the average person.
"The Psychology of the Artist,"
*Recreating the Individual* 1923

2 . . . woman is a being dominated by the creative urge and . . . no understanding of her as an individual can be gained unless the significance and effects of that great fact can be grasped. Ibid.

3 . . . the artist has always been and still is a being somewhat apart from the rest of humanity. Ibid.

4 When one looks back over human existence, however, it is very evident that all culture has developed through an *initial resistance against adaptation to the reality in which man finds himself.* Ibid.

5 The mystics are the only ones who have gained a glimpse into what is possible. . . . Ibid.

6 The amount which cannot be harnessed and domesticated, but insists on its own form of activity rather than one which is offered ready made, is the energy used for the creation of art. Ibid.

7 The creator does not create only for the pleasure of creating but . . . he also desires to subdue other minds. Ibid.

8 The attitude and reactions of artists toward their art children reveal an attitude similar to that which mothers in general possess toward their children. There is the same sensitivity to any criticism, the same possessive pride, the same devotion and love, with the accompanying anxiety and distress concerning them. Ibid.

## 406. Bettina von Hutten
### (1874–1957)

1 A good many women are good tempered simply because it saves the wrinkles coming too soon. *The Halo* 1907

2 Everybody in the world ought to be sorry for everybody else. We all have our little private hell. Ibid.

## 407. Yamamuro Kieko
### (1874–1915)

1 . . . I realize that were I a man, I would be at the battlefront fighting amidst bullets and explosives, instead of sitting serenely at my desk.
Untitled Essay 1895

## 408. Amy Lowell
### (1874–1925)

1 Time! Joyless emblem of the greed
Of millions, robber of the best
Which earth can give. . . .
"New York at Night," *A Dome of
Many-Coloured Glass* 1912

2     Brave idolatry
Which can conceive a hero! No deceit,
No knowledge taught by unrelenting years,
Can quench this fierce, untamable desire.
Ibid., "Hero-Worship"

3 Every castle of the air
Sleeps in the fine black grains, and there
Are seeds for every romance, or light
Whiff of a dream for a summer night.
"Sword Blades and Poppy Seeds,"
*Sword Blades and Poppy Seeds*
1914

4 Visions for those too tired to sleep.
These seeds cast a film over eyes which weep.
Ibid., St. 3

5 All books are either dreams or swords,
You can cut, or you can drug, with words.
Ibid.

6 Happiness, to some, elation;
Is, to others, mere stagnation.
Ibid., "Happiness"

7 Marshalled like soldiers in gay company,
The tulips stand arrayed. Here infantry
Wheels out into the sunlight.
Ibid., "A Tulip Garden"

8 My God, but you keep me starved! You write
"No Entrance Here," over all the doors. . . .
Hating bonds as you do, why should I be
denied the rights of love if I leave you free?
Ibid., "The Basket," III

9 My words are little jars
For you to take and put upon a shelf.
Ibid., "Gift"

10 Also the scent from them fills the room
With sweetness of flowers and crushed grass.
*Ibid.*

11 You are beautiful and faded,
Like an old opera tune
Played upon a harpsichord.
*Ibid.,* "A Lady," St. 1

12 I too am a rare
Pattern. As I wander down
The garden paths.
"Patterns," *Men, Women, and
Ghosts* 1916

13 A pattern called a war.
Christ! What are patterns for?
*Ibid.,* St. 7

14 The cost runs into millions, but a woman must
have something to console herself for a
broken heart.
*Ibid.,* "Malmaison," V

15 Art is the desire of a man to express himself,
to record the reactions of his personality to
the world he lives in.
*Tendencies in Modern American
Poetry* 1917

16 Youth condemns; maturity condones. *Ibid.*

17 All Naples prates of this and that, and runs
about its little business, shouting, bawling,
incessantly calling its wares.
"Sea-Blue and Blood-Red," II,
*Can Grande's Castle* 1918

18 Let the key-guns be mounted, make a brave
show of waging war, and pry off the lid
of Pandora's box once more.
*Ibid.,* "Guns as Keys: And the
Great Gate Swings," Pt. I

19 A wise man,
Watching the stars pass across the sky,
Remarked:
In the upper air the fireflies move more slowly.
"Meditation," *Picture of the
Floating World* 1919

20 Moon!
Moon!
I am prone before you.
Pity me,
And drench me in loneliness.
*Ibid.,* "On a Certain Critic"

21 If failure, then another long beginning.
Why hope,
Why think that Spring must bring relenting.
"A Legend of Porcelain," St. 25,
*Legends* 1921

22 "The sun weaves the seasons," thought Many
Swans, "I have been under and over the
warp of the world. . . ."
*Ibid.,* "Many Swans"

23 There are few things so futile, and few so
amusing,
As a peaceful and purposeless sort of perusing
Of old random jottings set down in a blank-
book
You've unearthed from a drawer as you looked
for your bank-book. . . .
"A Critical Fable," St. 1,
*A Critical Fable* 1922

24 A man must be sacrificed now and again
To provide for the next generation of men.
*Ibid.,* St. 2

25 I am sorry myself to be forced to distort a
Fine line unduly, and if I or my thought err
I am willing to own it without the least *hauteur.*
*Ibid.,* St. 9

26 And the sight of a white church above thin
trees in a city square
Amazes my eyes as though it were the
Parthenon.
"Meeting-House Hill,"
*What's O'Clock* 1925

27 And what are we?
We, the people without a race,
Without a language;
Of all races, and of none;
Of all tongues, and one imposed;
Of all traditions and all pasts,
With no tradition and no past.
A patchwork and an altar-piece. . . .
*Ibid.,* "The Congressional
Liberty," St. 1

28 Heart-leaves of lilac all over New England,
Roots of lilac under all the soil of New
England,
Lilac in me because I am New England.
*Ibid.,* "Lilacs," St. 4

29 I went a-riding, a-riding,
Over a great long plain.
And the plain went a-sliding, a-sliding
Away from my bridle-rein.
*Ibid.,* "Texas," St. 1

30 Love is a game—yes?
I think it is a drowning. . . .
*Ibid.,* "Twenty-four Hokku on a
Modern Theme," XIX

31 Sappho would speak, I think, quite openly,
And Mrs. Browning guard a careful silence,
But Emily would set doors ajar and slam them
And love you for your speed of observation.
*Ibid.,* "The Sisters," St. 2

\* \* \*

32 Finally, most of us [imagist poets] believe that
concentration is the very essence of poetry.
"Imagist Poetry"

33 For books are more than books, they are the
life
The very heart and core of ages past,
The reason why men lived and worked and
died,
The essence and quintessence of their lives.
Untitled Poem, *The Boston
Athenoeum*

### 409. Dorothy Reed Mendenhall
(1874–1964)

1 My early life had been fed with dreams and a
deep feeling that if I waited, did my part and
was patient, love would come to me and with
it such a family life as fiction depicted and
romance built up. It seems to me that I have
always been waiting for something better—
sometimes to see the best I had snatched from
me.      Quoted in "Dorothy Mendenhall:
'Childbirth Is Not a Disease' "
by Gena Corea, *Ms.*    *April, 1974p*

2 When hurry in the attendant meets fear in the
mother, the combination . . . militates against
safe and sane obstetrics.       Ibid.

### 410. Alice Duer Miller
(1874–1942)

1 And now too late, we see these things are one:
That art is sacrifice and self-control,
And who loves beauty must be stern of soul.
"An American to France,"
*Welcome Home*    1928

2 When a woman like that whom I've seen so
much
All of a sudden drops out of touch,
Is always busy and never can
Spare you a moment, it means a Man.
"Forsaking All Others,"
*Forsaking All Others*    1931

3      Frenchmen, when
The ultimate menace comes, will die for France
Logically as they lived.
Ibid., XXI

4 Good manners are the technique of expressing
consideration for the feelings of others.
"I Like American Manners,"
*Saturday Evening Post
August 13, 1932*

5 The white cliffs of Dover, I saw rising steeply
Out of the sea that once made her [England]
secure.
"The White Cliffs," St. 1,
*The White Cliffs*    1940

6      I am American bred,
I have seen much to hate here—much to
forgive,
But in a world where England is finished
and dead,
I do not wish to live.
Ibid., St. 52

### 411. Lucy Montgomery
(1874–1942)

1 "Isn't it splendid to think of all the things there
are to find out about? It just makes me feel
glad to be alive—it's such an interesting world.
It wouldn't be half so interesting if we knew
all about everything, would it? There'd be no
scope for imagination then, would there?"
*Anne of Green Gables*, Ch. 2
*1908*

2 "There's such a lot of different Annes in me. I
sometimes think that is why I'm such a troublesome person. If I was just one Anne it would
be ever so much more comfortable, but then
it wouldn't be half so interesting."
Ibid., Ch. 20

3 "As for Horace Baxter, he was in financial
difficulties a year ago last summer, and he
prayed to the Lord for help; and when his wife
died and he got her life insurance he said he
believed it was the answer to his prayer.
Wasn't that like a man?"
*Anne's House of Dreams*, Ch. 15
*1917*

4 "When a man is alone he's mighty apt to be
with the devil—if he ain't with God. He has to
choose which company he'll keep, I reckon."
Ibid.

5 The point of good writing is knowing when to
stop.      Ibid., Ch. 24

### 412. Roselle Mercier Montgomery
(1874–1933)

1 I would always be with the thick of life,
Threading its mazes, sharing its strife;
Yet—somehow, singing!
"Somehow, Singing,"
*Ulysses Returns*    1925

2 Never a ship sails out of the bay
  But carries my heart as a stowaway.
               Ibid., "The Stowaway"

3 Put by, O waiting ones, put by your weaving,
  Unlike Ulysses, love is unreturning.
               Ibid., "Counsel"

4 . . . to that they know, their dearest never
  guess!
               Ibid., "Penelope Speaks"

5 The fates are not quite obdurate.
  They have a grim, sardonic way
  Of granting men who supplicate
  The things they wanted—yesterday!
    "The Fates," *Many Devices*    *1929*

\* \* \*

6 Companioned years have made them
  comprehend
  The comradeship that lies beyond a kiss.
          "For a Wedding Anniversary"

## 413. Angela Morgan
### (1874?–1957)
\* \* \*

1 A courage mightier than the sun—
  You rose and fought and, fighting, won!
              "Know Thyself"

2 God, when you thought of a pine tree,
  How did you think of a star?
         "God, the Artist," St. 1

3 I will hew great windows for my soul.
               "Room"

4 Lad, you took the world's soul,
  Thrilled it by your daring,
  Lifted the uncaring
  And made them joyous men.
             "Lindbergh"

5 O thrilling age,
  O willing age!
             "Today," St. 1

6 The signals of the century
  Proclaims the things that are to be—
  The rise of woman to her place,
  The coming of a nobler race.
            Ibid., St. 3

7 To be alive in such an age—
  To live in it,
  To give to it!
            Ibid., St. 4

8 Praised be the gods that made my spirit mad;
  Kept me aflame and raw to beauty's touch.
            "June Rapture"

9 Work!
  Thank God for the swing of it,
  For the clamoring, hammering ring of it,
  Passion of labor daily hurled
  On the mighty anvils of the world.
      "Work: A Song of Triumph"

## 414. Rose O'Neill
### (1874–1944)

1 Remember, men of guns and rhymes,
  And kings who kill so fast,
  That men you kill too many times
  May be too dead at last.
      "When the Dead Men Die,"
      *The Master's Mistress*    *1922*

2 "My face is a caricature of her, and her soul
  is a caricature of mine. In fact, she has no soul.
  She is my substance. She robbed me of substance in the womb. That's why I named her
  Narcissa. . . . She grew her beauty on me like
  a flower on a dunghill. She is my material. I
  am her soul. We are that perilous pair."
         *Garda,* Ch. 1    *1929*

3 "When we are in bed, or floating in water, is
  the only time when we are really out of pain.
  In every other situation there is always some
  stress."    Ibid., Ch. 5

4 Her mind was as spry as a humming bird, but
  its beak was not so long for the inward flower
  of things. Still, she had always been looked
  upon as a wit; and when a creature is witty
  enough, he will occasionally say something
  that smacks of the profound.    Ibid., Ch. 11

5 They lose least who have least to lose.    Ibid.

6 It was not her way to invent obstacles, that
  blood-thinning process of the sickly imaginative.    Ibid., Ch. 15

## 415. Josephine Preston Peabody
### (1874–1922)
\* \* \*

1 That you should follow our poor humanhood,
  Only because you would!
            "To a Dog"

2     . . . The elements rehearse
  Man's urgent utterance, and his words traverse
  The spacious heav'ns like homing birds.
           "Wireless"

3 The little Road says, Go;
  The little House says, Stay;
  And oh, it's bonny here at home,
  But I must go away.
        "The House and the Road"

## 416. Gertrude Stein
### (1874–1946)

1 Honesty is a selfish virtue. Yes, I am honest enough. "Adele," *Q.E.D.*, Bk. I *1903*

2 I simply contend that the middle-class ideal which demands that people be affectionate, respectable, honest and content, that they avoid excitements and cultivate serenity is the ideal that appeals to me, it is in short the ideal of affectionate family life, of honorable business methods. *Ibid.*

3 "You are so afraid of losing your moral sense that you are not willing to take it through anything more dangerous than a mud-puddle." *Ibid.*

4 "I never wanted to be a hero, but on the other hand I am not anxious to cultivate cowardice." *Ibid.*

5 "I could undertake to be an efficient pupil if it were possible to find an efficient teacher." *Ibid.*

6 One must either accept some theory or else believe one's instinct or follow the world's opinion. *Ibid.*, "Helen," Bk. III

7 I am writing for myself and strangers. This is the only way that I can do it.
*The Making of Americans*
*1906–1908*

8 "Rose is a rose is a rose is a rose."
"Sacred Emily" *1913*

9 I suppose I pose I expose, I repose, I close the door when the sun shines so, I close the door when the wind is so strong and the dust is not there. . . . "Mildred's Thoughts" *1922*

10 You are all a lost generation.
Letter to Ernest Hemingway *1926*

11 Pigeons on the grass alas.
*Four Saints in Three Acts* *1927*

12 Before the flowers of friendship faded friendship faded.
*Before the Flowers of Friendship*
*Faded Friendship Faded* *1931*

13 Remarks are not literature.
*The Autobiography of*
*Alice B. Toklas* *1933*

14 She always says she dislikes the abnormal, it is so obvious. She says the normal is so much more simply complicated and interesting. *Ibid.*

15 America is my country and Paris is my hometown. And it is as it has come to be. After all anybody is as their air and land is. Anybody is as the sky is low or high, the air heavy or clear and anybody is as there is wind or no wind there. It is that which makes them and the arts they make and the work they do and the way they eat and the way they drink and the way they learn and everything. And so I am an American and I have lived half my life in Paris, not the half that made me but the half in which I made what I made.
"An American and France" *1936*

16 In the United States there is more space where nobody is than where anybody is. That is what makes America what it is.
*The Geographical History of*
*America* *1936*

17 Everybody knows if you are too careful you are so occupied in being careful that you are sure to stumble over something.
*Everybody's Autobiography*, Ch. 1
*1937*

18 . . . native always means people who belong somewhere else, because they had once belonged somewhere. That shows that the white race does not really think they belong anywhere because they think of everybody else as native. *Ibid.*

19 . . . one never discusses anything with anybody who can understand one discusses things with people who cannot understand. . . . *Ibid.*

20 . . . if anything is a surprise then there is not much difference between older or younger because the only thing that does make anybody older is that they cannot be surprised.
*Ibid.*, Ch. 2

21 . . . money . . . is really the difference between men and animals, most of the things men feel animals feel and vice versa, but animals do not know about money, money is purely a human conception and that is very important to know very very important. *Ibid.*

22 A distraction is to avoid the consciousness of the passage of time. *Ibid.*

23 . . . considering how dangerous everything is nothing is really very frightening. *Ibid.*

24 . . . what is the use of thinking if after all there is to be organization. *Ibid.*

25 More great Americans were failures than they were successes. They mostly spent their lives in not having a buyer for what they had for sale. *Ibid.*

26 It is funny the two things most men are proudest of is the thing that any man can do and doing does in the same way, that is being drunk and being the father of their son.
*Ibid.*

27 It takes a lot of time to be a genius, you have to sit around so much doing nothing, really doing nothing.
*Ibid.*

28 . . . understanding is a very dull occupation.
*Ibid.*

29 I am also fond of saying that a war of fighting is like a dance because it is all going forward and back, and that is what everybody likes they like that forward and back movement, that is the reason that revolutions and Utopias are discouraging they are up and down and not forward and back.
*Ibid., Ch. 3*

30 The minute you or anybody else knows what you are you are not it, you are what you or anybody else knows you are and as everything in living is made up of finding out what you are it is extraordinarily difficult really not to know what you are and yet to be that thing.
*Ibid.*

31 Too few is as many as too many.
*Ibid.*

32 America is not old enough yet to get young again.
*Ibid.*

33 I am always ready to sign anything a bank tells me to sign but anything else fills me with suspicion.
*Ibid.*

34 Counting is the religion of this generation it is its hope and its salvation.
*Ibid.*

35 I understand you undertake to overthrow my undertaking.
*Ibid.*

36 . . . I do want to get rich but I never want to do what there is to do to get rich.
*Ibid.*

37 That is natural enough when nobody has had fathers they begin to long for them and then when everybody has had fathers they begin to long to do without them.
*Ibid.*

38 If things happen all the time you are never nervous it is when they are not happening that you are nervous.
*Ibid., Ch. 4*

39 In America if they do not do it right away they do not do it at all in France they very often seem not to be going to do it at all but if it has ever really been proposed at all sometimes it really is done.
*Ibid.*

40 The only thing that anybody can understand is mechanics and that is what makes everybody feel that they are something when they talk

about it. About every other thing nobody is of the same opinion nobody means the same thing by what they say as the other one means and only the one who is talking thinks he means what he is saying even though he knows very well that that is not what he is saying.
*Ibid.*

41 . . . what is the use of being a little boy if you are going to grow up to be a man.
*Ibid.*

42 . . . it is a peaceful thing to be one succeeding.
*Ibid.*

43 She was thinking about it she was thinking about life. She knew it was just like that through and through.
She never did not want to leave it.
She did not want to stop thinking about it thinking about life, so that is what she was thinking about.
*"Ida"     1941*

44 Nothing has happened today except kindness. . . .
*"A Diary," Alphabets and Birthdays*
*1957p*

45 A diary means yes indeed. . . .
*Ibid.*

46 What is the answer? (I was silent.) In that case, what is the question?
Quoted in *What Is Remembered*
by Alice B. Toklas     *1963p*

47 You know very well that it is not necessary to explain to an intelligent person—one only explains to a stupid one.
Quoted in *Playing on Alone: Letters*
*of Alice B. Toklas,* Ed Burns, ed.
*1973p*

48 And how do you look backward. By looking forward. And what do they see. As they look forward. They see what they had to do before they could look backward. And there we have it all.
"Thoughts on an American
Contemporary Feeling" (1932),
*Reflection on the Atomic Bomb,*
Vol. I     *1973p*

49 Everybody gets so much information all day long that they lose their common sense.
Ibid., Untitled Essay (1946)

## 417. Etsu Inagaki Sugimoto
(1874?–1950)

1 A careless or perturbed state of mind always betrays itself in the intricate shadings of ideographs, for each one requires absolute steadiness and accuracy of touch. Thus, in careful

guidance of the hand were we children taught to hold the mind in leash.

*A Daughter of the Samurai*, Ch. 2
*1925*

2 "Look in the mirror every day," she said, "for if scars of selfishness or pride are in the heart, they will grow into the lines of the face. Watch closely. Be strong like the pine, yield in gentle obedience like the swaying bamboo, and yet, like the fragrant plum blossoming beneath the snow, never lose the gentle perseverance of loyal womanhood."      Ibid., Ch. 6

## 418. Mary McLeod Bethune

(1875–1955)

1 If our people are to fight their way up out of bondage we must arm them with the sword and the shield and the buckler of pride. . . .

"Clarifying Our Vision with the Facts,"
*Journal of Negro History*
*January, 1938*

2 Mr. Lincoln had told our race we were free, but mentally we were still enslaved.

"Faith That Moved a Dump Heap,"
*Who, The Magazine About People*
*June, 1941*

3 "For God so loved the world, that He gave His only begotten Son, that whosoever believeth in Him should not perish, but have everlasting life." With these words the scales fell from my eyes and the light came flooding in. My sense of inferiority, my fear of handicaps, dropped away. "Whosoever," it said. No Jew nor Gentile, no Catholic nor Protestant, no black nor white; just "whosoever." It meant that I, a humble Negro girl, had just as much chance as anybody in the sight and love of God. These words stored up a battery of faith and confidence and determination in my heart, which has not failed me to this day. . . .      Ibid.

4 I never stop to plan. I take things step by step. For thirty-five years we [Bethune-Cookman College] have never had to close our doors for lack of food or fuel, although often we had to live from day to day. . . .      Ibid.

5 For I am my mother's daughter, and the drums of Africa still beat in my heart. They will not let me rest while there is a single Negro boy or girl without a chance to prove his worth.      Ibid.

6 I do feel, in my dreamings and yearnings, so undiscovered by those who are able to help me. . . . The burden is so heavy just now, the task is so great, that speedy reinforcement is needed.

My mind is over-taxed. Brave and courageous as I am I feel that creeping on of that inevitable thing, a breakdown, if I cannot get some immediate relief. I need somebody to come and get me.

Letter to George R. Arthur
(November 1, 1930), *Black Women
in White America*, Gerda Lerner, ed.
*1972p*

7 The true worth of a race must be measured by the character of its womanhood. . . .

Ibid., Address, "A Century of
Progress of Negro Women,"
Chicago Women's Federation
(June 3, 1933)

## 419. Anna Hempstead Branch

(1875–1937)

1 His screaming stallions maned with whistling wind.

"Nimrod Wars with the Angels"
*1910*

     * * *

2 God wove a web of loveliness,
Of clouds and stars and birds,
But made not anything at all
So beautiful as words.

"Songs for My Mother:
Her Words," St. 5

3 If there is no God for thee
Then there is no God for me.

"To a Dog"

4 Oh, grieve not, ladies, if at night
Ye wake to feel your beauty going.
It was a web of frail delight,
Inconstant as an April snowing.

"Grieve Not, Ladies," St. 1

5 Order is a lovely thing;
On disarray it lays its wing,
Teaching simplicity to sing.

"The Monk in the Kitchen"

## 420. Abbie Farwell Brown

(1875–1927)

     * * *

1 No matter what my birth may be,
No matter where my lot is cast,
I am the heir in equity
Of all the precious past.

"The Heritage," St. 1

2 They named their rocky farmlands,
Their hamlets by the sea,
For the mother-towns that bred them
In racial loyalty.

"Names," St. 7

## 421. Louise Driscoll
(1875–1957)

* * *

1 Power and gold and fame denied,
Love laughs glad in the paths aside.
"The Highway"

2 Some men die early and are spared much care,
Some suddenly, escaping worse than death;
But he is fortunate who happens where
He can exult and die in the same breath.
"The Good Hour"

3 There you will find what
Every man needs,
Wild religion
Without any creeds.
"Spring Market," St. 5

4 When youth is spent, a penny at a fair,
The old men tell of the bargains there.
There was this and that for a price and a wage,
But when they came away they had all bought
age.
"Bargain"

## 422. Elie Faure
(1875–1937)

* * *

1 The stamping out of the artist is one of the
blind goals of every civilization. When a civilization becomes so standardized that the individual can no longer make an imprint on it,
then that civilization is dying. The "mass mind"
has taken over and another set of national
glories is heading for history's scrap heap.
Quoted in *Forbes Magazine*

## 423. Minnie Haskins
(1875–1957)

1 And I said to the man who stood at the gate of
the year:
"Give me a light that I may tread safely into
the Unknown."
And he replied: "Go out into the darkness and
put your hand
Into the hand of God. That shall be to you
better than light
And safer than a known way."
"The Desert"        1908

## 424. Helen Huntington
(1875?–1950)

* * *

1 With the bitter past I will deck to-morrow.
"The Wayfarer"

## 425. Marie Lenéru
(1875–1940)

1 To be deaf is perhaps not to hear, but certainly it is this: to hold your tongue. Whatever
spontaneous feelings may move you, to resist
the impulse to communicate them, to remember
that *your* world, your moment, are not other
people's to hold your tongue . . . a *haute
école* of self-control, of nonspontaneousness,
of solitude and indifference.        *Journal*
*1945p*

2 Books, books, these are the only things that
have come to my aid! In the end, it makes one
terribly arrogant, always to do without one's
equals!        Ibid.

3 One *sees* intelligence far more than one hears
it. People do not always say transcendental
things, but if they are *capable* of saying them,
it is always visible.        Ibid.

4 Isolation has led me to reflection, reflection to
doubt, doubt to a more sincere and intelligent
love of God.        Ibid. (1896)

5 I will never abdicate. I shall always want
everything. To accept my life I must prefer it.
Ibid. (1898)

6 I have discovered that in an intellectual society
individual intelligence is no more frequent than
anywhere else, and its absence is more tedious,
for not to speak in a superior manner of
superior subjects is both boring and ridiculous.
Ibid.

7 If I were honest, I would admit that money is
one half of happiness; it makes it so much
more attractive!        Ibid.

8 To succeed is nothing, it's an accident. But to
feel no doubts about oneself is something very
different: it is character.        Ibid.

## 426. Belle Livingstone
(1875–1957)

1 That winter two things happened which made
me see that the world, the flesh, and the devil
were going to be more powerful influences in
my life after all than the chapel bell. First, I
tasted champagne; second, the theatre.
*Belle Out of Order*        1959p

2 Like Moses, I wasn't born. I was found.
Ibid., Pt. I, Ch. 1

3 Odd how the erotic appeal has swung away
from legs; today a smart girl takes her legs for
granted and gets herself a good sweater.
Ibid., Ch. 2

4 The courtesan, alas, is gone, extinct as the American buffalo. . . . Anyone can become a mistress; one has to be born a courtesan.
Ibid.

5 Much has been written about the beauty, the stillness, the terror of the desert but little about its flies.      Ibid., Ch. 5

6 Oddly enough, a gambler never entertains the thought of loss. He can't afford to. No one who has never gambled can possibly understand the projects, plans, dreams a gambler can create on the turn of a card or the chance of a horse going to the post.      Ibid., Ch. 9

7 . . . I had swallowed the sugar-coated pill of Rabelaisian philosophy—that life is its own justification and we need not live depriving ourselves of anything.      Ibid., Pt. II, Ch. 1

8 It is a truism that most people take their adventures vicariously.      Ibid., Epilogue

## 427. Vilda Sauvage Owens
(1875–1950)

\* \* \*

1 If ever I have time for things that matter,
If ever I have the smallest chance,
I'm going to live in
Little Broom Gardens,
Moat-by-the-Castle,
Nettlecombe, Hants.
"If Ever I Have Time for Things
That Matter," St. 1

## 428. Anne Goodwin Winslow
(1875–?)

\* \* \*

1 And how can curses make him yours
When kisses could not make him so?
"The Beaten Path"

## 429. Josephine Dodge Bacon
(1876–1961)

1 "Girls, it isn't likely that we'll win, *but we can give 'em something to beat!*"
"The Emotions of a Sub-Guard,"
*Smith College Stories*    1900

2 Life in all its phases possessed for him unsounded depths of entertainment, and in the intervals of uncontrolled laughter at the acts and words of his astonished elders he gave way

to frequent subtle smiles resulting from subjectively humorous experiences unguessed by the world at large.
*The Memoirs of a Baby*, Ch. 2
1904

3 You musn't say anything that won't be perfectly true when he's grown up, you see. It's learning two sets of things that makes a child distrust you.      Ibid., Ch. 6

4 You mark my words, Toots, if you ever hear a darn-fool thing to-day, you can make up your mind some woman said it that writes books. . . . It ought to be a crime for any woman to have children that writes books.
*The Biography of a Boy*, Ch. 2
1910

5 Starved once and forever,
By a cruel love.
I lost my life—
The public gained it.
*Truth o' Women*, Ch. 15    1923

6 I do not see how there can be any real respect,
Or any real privacy such as women love,
When you marry a man.
A man makes trouble.
Ibid., Ch. 20

7 To you in reality dead,
Dragging your bodies after you,
Persistently vital,
I say this:
Death will come. Be patient.
Ibid., Ch. 42

## 430. Mary Ritter Beard
(1876–1958)

1 The prosecution of modern wars rests completely upon the operation of labor in mines, mills and factories, so that labor fights there just as truly as the soldiers do in the trenches.
*A Short History of the American
Labor Movement*, Ch. 1    1920

2 The trade agreement has become a rather distinct feature of the American labor movement. It does not represent any revolutionary tendency in industry. It is based on the idea that labor shall accept the capitalist system of production and makes terms of peace with it.
Ibid., Ch. 9

3 Viewed narrowly, all life is universal hunger and an expression of energy associated with it.
*Understanding Women,*
Ch. 1    1931

4 In their quest for rights they [women] have naturally placed emphasis on their wrongs, rather than their achievements and possessions, and have retold history as a story of their long Martyrdom.      Ibid.

5 Unless one's philosophy is all-inclusive, nothing can be understood.      Ibid., Ch. 4

6 In matters pertaining to the care of life there has been no marked gain over Greek and Roman antiquity.      Ibid., Ch. 5

7 In other words, those who sit at the feast will continue to enjoy themselves even though the veil that separates them from the world of toiling reality below has been lifted by mass revolts and critics.      Ibid., Ch. 6

8 The emphasis in Communism, if its ideal is realized, will be on woman as a worker, and the opportunities for a life of leisure, patronage, noblesse oblige, religious service and idle curiosity will vanish.      Ibid.

9 If this analysis of history is approximately sound and if the future like the past is to be crowded with changes and exigencies, then it is difficult to believe that the feminism of the passing generation, already hardened into dogma and tradition, represents the completed form of woman's relations to work, interests and society.      Ibid.

10 The dogma of woman's complete historical subjection to men must be rated as one of the most fantastic myths ever created by the human mind.      *Woman as a Force in History*    *1946*

11 . . . history has been conceived—and with high justification in the records—as the human struggle for civilization against barbarism in different ages and places, from the beginning of human societies.      Ibid., Ch. 12

12 Beneath the surface of civilian interests and capitalistic enterprises smoldered embers of the world's war spirit—humanity's traditional flare —now to be enflamed by new instruments for fighting and the associated aspiration for world trade and world power.
     *The Force of Women in Japanese History*, Ch. 9    *1963p*

## 431. Anne Bronaugh
### (1876–1961)

\*   \*   \*

1 Life is patchwork—here and there,
Scraps of pleasure and despair
Join together, hit or miss.
     "Patchwork"

## 432. Sarah Norcliffe Cleghorn
### (1876–1959)

1 The golf links lie so near the mill
   That almost every day
The laboring children can look out
   And watch the men at play.
     "The Conning Tower,"
     *New York Tribune*
     *January 1, 1915*

2 Since more than half my hopes came true
   And more than half my fears
Are but the pleasant laughing-stock
   Of these my middle years . . .
Shall I not bless the middle years?
Not I for youth repine
While warmly round me cluster lives
   More dear to me than mine.
     "Contented at Forty"    *1916*

3 Come, Captain Age,
With your great sea-chest full of treasure!
Under the yellow and wrinkled tarpaulin
Disclose the carved ivory
And the sandalwood inlaid with pearl:
Riches of wisdom and years.
     "Come, Captain Age,"
     *Three Score*    *1936*

\*   \*   \*

4 "The unfit die—the fit both live and thrive."
Alas, who say so? They who do survive.
     "The Survival of the Fittest"

## 433. Mata Hari
### (1876–1917)

1 The dance is a poem of which each movement is a word.    *Scrapbook*    *1905*

2 The [military] officer is a being apart, a kind of artist breathing the grand air in the brilliant profession of arms, in a uniform that is always seductive. . . . To me the officer is a separate race.      *Life*    *1906*

3 I firmly believe that the only means of living in beauty consists in avoiding the thousand and one daily annoyances which interfere with an existence in the full ideal. That is why I cannot tolerate European things, not even the religion.      Quoted in *Mata Hari* (1917), by Major Thomas Coulson, O.B.E.    *1930p*

## 434. Norah M. Holland
(1876–1925)

\* \* \*

1 Life has given me of its best—
Laughter and weeping, labour and rest,
Little of gold, but lots of fun;
Shall I then sigh that all is done?

"Life"

## 435. Sally Kinsolving
(1876–?)

1 Ships, young ships,
I do not wonder men see you as women—
You in the white length of your loveliness
Reclining on the sea!

"Ships," *Many Waters*    1942

## 436. Mary Sinton Leitch
(1876–1954)

\* \* \*

1 And deaf, he sings of nightingales
Or, blind, he sings of stars.

"The Poet"

2 He who loves the ocean
And the ways of ships
May taste beside a mountain pool
Brine on his lips.

"He Who Loves the Ocean"

3 They would not be the great, were not the cause
They love so great that it must needs be lost.

"Pity the Great"

4 While far below men crawl in clay and cold,
Sublimely I shall stand alone with God.

"The Summit, Mt. Everest"

## 437. Grace Fallow Norton
(1876–1926)

\* \* \*

1 I have loved many, the more and the few—
I have loved many that I might love you.

"Song of the Sum of All"

2 Take me upon thy breast,
O River of Rest.
Draw me down to thy side,
Slow-moving tide.

"O Sleep"

## 438. Mary Roberts Rinehart
(1876–1958)

1 There is something magnificent, a contagion of
enthusiasm, in the sight of a great volunteer
army. The North and the South knew the thrill
during our own great war. Conscription may
form a great and admirable machine, but it
differs from the trained army of volunteers as
a body differs from a soul. But it costs a country heavy in griefs, does a volunteer army; for
the flower of the country goes.

*Kings, Queens, and Pawns,*
Introduction    *1915*

2 War is a thing of fearful and curious anomalies.
. . . It has shown that government by men only
is not an appeal to reason, but an appeal to
arms; that on women, without a voice to protest, must fall the burden. It is easier to die
than to send a son to death. It has shown that
a single hatred may infect a world, but it has
shown that mercy too may spread among nations. That love is greater than cannon, greater
than hate, greater than vengeance; that it triumphs over wrath, as good triumphs over evil.

Ibid., Ch. 37

3 What was I to do? You may say what you
like—a lot of married women get into things
they never meant to simply because they are
kind-hearted and hate to be called quitters.

"Affinities," *Affinities and Other
Stories*    *1920*

4 "You're a perfect child, a stubborn child! Your
mind's in pigtails, like your hair."

Ibid., "The Family Friend"

5 "Nurses in hospitals are there to carry out the
doctor's orders. Not to think or to say what
they think unless they are asked."

"Twenty-Two," *Love Stories
1920*

6 The great God endows His children variously.
To some He gives intellect—and they move the
earth. To some He allots heart—and the beating pulse of humanity is theirs. But to some He
gives only a soul, without intelligence—and
these, who never grow up, but remain always
His children, are God's fools, kindly, elemental,
simple, as if from His palette the Artist of all
had taken one colour instead of many.

Ibid., "God's Fool"

7 Men deceive themselves; they look back on the
children who were once themselves, and attempt
to reconstruct them. But they can no longer
think like the child, and against the unpleasant
and the horrid the mind has set up the defensive
machinery of forgetfulness.

*My Story,* Ch. 1    *1931*

8 But it is interesting to see how the Socialist becomes the conservative when given power; Mussolini, Briand, Masaryk, all considered radicals at one time. Or is it that our own ideas change, and that we are after all moving slowly toward greater justice?    *Ibid., Ch. 40*

9 Will we never learn? Is our cupidity greater than our patriotism? And is our generosity greater than our common sense?
       *My Story*, Ch. 19, Rev. Ed.    *1948*

## 439. Helen Rowland
### (1876–1950)

1 Woman: the peg on which the wit hangs his jest, the preacher his text, the cynic his grouch, and the sinner his justification.
       *Reflections of a Bachelor Girl*
       *1903*

2 When you see what some girls marry, you realize how they must hate to work for a living.    *Ibid.*

3 Love, the quest; marriage, the conquest; divorce, the inquest.    *Ibid.*

4 Marriage: a souvenir of love.    *Ibid.*

5 The follies which a man regrets most in his life are those which he didn't commit when he had the opportunity.    *Ibid.*

6 It takes a woman twenty years to make a man of her son, and another woman twenty minutes to make a fool of him.    *Ibid.*

7 To a woman the first kiss is the end of the beginning; to a man it is the beginning of the end.    *Ibid.*

8 One man's folly is another man's wife.    *Ibid.*

9 Never trust a husband too far, nor a bachelor too near.    *The Rubaiyat of a Bachelor*
       *1915*

10 A husband is what is left of the lover after the nerve has been extracted.    *Ibid.*

11 Better a lively old epigram than a deadly new one.    "The World in Epigram,"
       *The Book of Diversion,*
       F. P. Adams, D. Taylor,
       J. Bechdolt, eds.    *1925*

12 The woman who appeals to a man's vanity may stimulate him; the woman who appeals to his heart may attract him; but it's the woman who appeals to his imagination who *gets* him.
       *Ibid., "Personally Speaking"*

13 A man may talk inspiringly to a woman about love in the abstract—but the look in his eyes is always perfectly concrete.    *Ibid.*

14 Nothing annoys a man as to hear a woman promising to love him "forever" when he merely wanted her to love him for a few weeks.    *Ibid.*

15 A bachelor has to have an inspiration for making love to a woman—a married man needs only an excuse.    *Ibid.*

16 At twenty, a man feels awfully aged and blasé; at thirty, almost senile; at forty, "not so old"; and at fifty, positively skittish.    *Ibid.*

17 Courtship is a republic; marriage, a monarchy; divorce, a soviet.    *Ibid.*

18 Alas, why will a man spend months trying to hand over his liberty to a woman—and the rest of his life trying to get it back again?
       *Ibid.*

19 Honeymoons are the beginning of wisdom—but the beginning of wisdom is the end of romance.
       *Ibid.*

20 The same woman may be a goddess to a boy, a temptation to a married man, and a "menace" to a bachelor.    *Ibid.*

21 The honeymoon is not actually over until we cease to stifle our sighs and begin to stifle our yawns.    *Ibid.*

22 True love says, "Love me—or I suffer!" Infatuation says, "Love me—or I'll make *you* suffer!"    *Ibid.*

23 The feminine vanity-case is the grave of masculine illusions.    *Ibid.*

24 Marriage is the only thing that affords a woman the pleasure of company and the perfect sensation of solitude at the same time.    *Ibid.*

25 A man always mistakes a woman's clinging devotion for weakness, until he discovers that it requires the strength of Samson, the patience of Job, and the finesse of Solomon to untwine it.    *Ibid.*

## 440. Helen L. Sumner
### (1876–1933)

1 The story of women's work in gainful employments is a story of constant changes or shiftings of work and workshop, accompanied by long hours, low wages, insanitary conditions, overwork, and the want on the part of the

woman of training, skill, and vital interest in her work.

> Senate Report, *History of Women in Industry in the United States*, Vol. IX
> 1911

2 . . . the history of women's work in this country shows that legislation has been the only force which has improved the working conditions of any large number of women wage-earners.      Ibid.

## 441. Katharine Anthony

### (1877–1965)

1 For mothers who must earn, there is indeed no leisure time problem. The long hours of earning are increased by the hours of domestic labor, until no slightest margin for relaxation or change of thought remains.

> *Mothers Who Must Earn*, Ch. 6
> 1914

2 Personal ambitions and disappointments, personal desire and weaknesses, personal shrewdness or slackness play their part in these narrow homes as they do in more spacious ones.

> Ibid., Ch. 8

3 Beyond all superficial differences and incidental forms, the vision of the emancipated woman wears the same features, whether she be hailed as *frau, fru,* or *woman.* The disfranchisement of a whole sex, a condition which has existed throughout the civilized world until a comparatively recent date, has bred in half the population an unconscious internationalism. The man without a country was a tragic exception; the woman without a country was the accepted rule.

> *Feminism in Germany and
> Scandinavia*, Ch. 1    1915

4 The cult of "arms and the man" must reckon with a newer cult, that of "schools and the woman." Schools, which exalt brains above brawn, and women, who exalt life-giving above life-taking, are the natural allies of the present era.      Ibid., Ch. 2

5 The struggle for self-consciousness is the essence of the feminist movement. Slowly but inevitably, the soul of a sex is emerging from the dim chamber of instinct and feeling into the strong sunshine of reason and will.

> Ibid., Ch. 9

6 There can be no doubt as to who began the literary war between the sexes. Also there is no comparison between the severity and harsh-

ness of the tone of criticism in the opposing camps. If we search the polemic writings of the most militant feminists, we can nowhere find expressions which compare in venom and ruthlessness with the woman-eating sentiments of certain medieval "saints" and modern "philosophers."      Ibid.

7 The generosity of childless people toward the children of near relatives and favorite friends strikes one as mere justice and propriety, after all, and such voluntary acts of evening-up between one generation and the next are not at all uncommon among the families and classes who can afford to be kind.

> *The Endowment of Motherhood*,
> Preface    1920

8 Principles are a dangerous form of social dynamite. . . .      Ibid., Introduction

9 Foremost among the barriers to equality is the system which ignores the mother's service to Society in making a home and rearing children. The mother is still the unchartered servant of the future, who receives from her husband, at *his* discretion, a share in *his* wages.    Ibid.

10 To the biographer all lives bar none are dramatic constructions.

> "Writing Biography," *The Writer's
> Book*, Helen Hull, ed.    1950

11 . . . people . . . seem to think that life began with the achievement of personal independence.      Ibid.

12 The lovers of romance can go elsewhere for satisfaction but where can the lovers of truth turn if not to history?      Ibid.

13 Persons who are born too soon or born too late seldom achieve the eminence of those who are born at the right time.      Ibid.

## 442. Grace Noll Crowell

### (1877–1965?)

1 I am one ever journeying toward the "light that never was on land or sea," and yet ever beckons one onward and upward to the glory ahead.    Quoted in *Grace Noll Crowell*,
> Foreword, by Beatrice Plumb
> 1938

\* \* \*

2 God wrote His loveliest poem on the day He made the first tall silver poplar tree.

> "Silver Poplars," St. 1

3 The woman who can move about a house,
Whether it be a mansion or a camp,
And deftly lay a fire, and spread a cloth,
And light a lamp,
And by the magic of a quick touch give
The look of home wherever she may be—
Such a woman always will seem great
And beautiful to me.
> "The Home Makers," St. 1

4 Home may be near,
Home may be far—
But it is anywhere love
And a few plain household treasures are.
> Ibid.

## 443. Isabelle Eberhardt
### (1877–1904)

1 For those who know the value and the exquisite taste of solitary freedom (for one is only free when alone), the act of leaving is the bravest and most beautiful of all.
> Journal Entry, Quoted in *The Destiny
> of Isabelle Eberhardt* by Cecily
> Mackworth     *1975p*

2 In the staid costume of a European girl I would never have seen anything. The world would have been closed to me, for . . . external life seems to have been made for man, not for woman.
> Ibid.

3 I love to dive into the bath of street life, the waves of the crowd flowing over me, to impregnate myself with the fluids of the people.
> Ibid.

4 Death does not frighten me, but dying obscurely and above all uselessly does.    Ibid.

## 444. Rose Fyleman
### (1877–1957)

* * *

1 The Fairies have never a penny to spend,
They haven't a thing put by,
But theirs is the dower of bird and of flower,
And theirs are the earth and the sky.
> "The Fairies Have Never a Penny to
> Spend," St. 1

2 There are fairies at the bottom of our garden.
> "The Fairies," St. 1

3 The queen—now can you guess who that could be
(She's a little girl by day, but at night she
. steals away)?
Well—it's me!
> Ibid., St. 3

## 445. Mary Garden
### (1877?–1967)

1 That was my first real flutter. I am sure Mr. Smith never knew, for he never paid the slightest attention to me except as a pupil. But *I* knew—I was in such a state of excitement every time I came back for a lesson; but my Mr. Smith never noticed it and to the end was as correct as a metronome, and as cold.
> *Mary Garden's Story*, Ch. 1,
> with Louis Biancolli    *1951*

2 I have never been nervous in all my life and I have no patience with people who are. If you know what you're going to do, you have no reason to be nervous. And I knew what I was going to do.      Ibid., Ch. 3

3 If I ever had complete charge of an opera house, the chances are I wouldn't get anybody to sing for me. I would be very emphatic about some things. I would never have a curtain call. I would never allow an encore. I would never permit a claque. There would be only art in my theatre.    Ibid., Ch. 11

4 I used my voice to color my roles. Salomé was blood red. Melissande was ice, melting ice. . . .
> Ibid., Ch. 21

## 446. Virginia Gildersleeve
### (1877–1965)

1 Medicine is a profession which naturally appeals deeply to women, as they are instinctively concerned with conserving life.
> "The Advancement of Women,"
> *Many a Good Crusade*    *1954*

2 The delicate first moment of dawn, before its mystery is invaded by the clatter of daily living, the bright hour of sunset before it is quenched in darkness, the last days of health unbroken, the last year of man's assurance that his civilization moves "ever upward and onward"— these are the moments, hours, days, years that have for us a poignant significance.
> Ibid., "The Turning of the Tide"

3 I well know from my own experience how essential it is for the survival of our democracy that scholars and teachers should have freedom of the mind to pursue truth "with clear eyes unafraid." Now our witchhunters are trying to drive students and teachers into conformity with a rigid concept of Americanism defined by ignorant and irresponsible politicians. If we do not check this movement, we shall become a totalitarian state like the Fascist

and Communist models and our colleges and universities will produce frightened rabbits instead of scholars with free minds.

    *Ibid.,* "The Inescapable Desert"

## 447. Mathilda von Kemnitz
### (1877–?)

1 Since the fundamental principle of eroticism imperiously governs every human life, since the manner of the first erotic happiness determines in a far-reaching manner the laws of the individual's eroticism throughout his entire life, the majority of men have become entirely incapable of concentrating their erotic will consistently on one human being; therefore, they have become incapable of monogamy.

    *The Triumph of the Immortal Will*
    *1932*

2 The man experiences the highest unfolding of his creative powers not through asceticism but through sexual happiness.     *Ibid.*

## 448. Marian Le Sueur
### (1877–1954)

1 The American destiny is what our fathers dreamed, a land of the free, and the home of the brave; but only the brave can be free. Science has made the dream of today's reality for all the earth if we have the courage and vision to build it. American Democracy must furnish the engineers of world plenty—the builders of world peace and freedom.

    Quoted in *Crusaders* by
    Meridel Le Sueur     *1955p*

## 449. Anne Shannon Monroe
### (1877–1942)

1 I have never been much cheered by the "stenciled smile," the false front, the pretending that there was no trouble when trouble stalked, that there was no death when Death laid his cold hand upon one dearer to us than life: but I have been tremendously cheered by the *brave* front; the imagination that could travel past the trouble and see that there were still joys in the world. . . .     *Singing in the Rain,*
    Ch. 1     *1926*

2 For loneliness is but cutting adrift from our moorings and floating out to the open sea; an opportunity for finding ourselves, our *real* selves, what we are about, where we are heading during our little time on this beautiful earth.     *Ibid.,* Ch. 6

3 "Don't get hung up on a snag in the stream, my dear. Snags alone are not so dangerous—it's the debris that clings to them that makes the trouble. Pull yourself loose and go on."

    *Ibid.,* Ch. 13

## 450. Maude Royden
### (1877–1956)

1 The belief that the personality of men and women are of equal dignity in the sight of God is necessary to a right moral standard.

    *The Church and Woman*     *c.1920*

## 451. Rosika Schwimmer
### (1877–1948)

1 I am no uncompromising pacifist. . . . I have no sense of nationalism, only a cosmic consciousness of belonging to the human family.

    Court Testimony, Citizenship
    Hearings     *1928*

2 Women's rights, men's rights—human rights—all are threatened by the ever-present spectre of war so destructive now of human material and moral values as to render victory indistinguishable from defeat.

    Speech, Centennial Celebration of
    Seneca Falls Convention of
    Women's Rights     *July, 1948*

3 We who successfully freed half of the human race without violence must now undertake with equal devotion, perseverance and intelligence the supreme act of human statesmanship involved in the creation of institutions of government on a world scale.     *Ibid.*

4 Women's function of homemaker, we once dreamed, would extend into politics and economics our highest creative and conserving instincts. Let us go back to the task of building that safe, decent and wholesome home for the entire human family to which we once pledged ourselves.     *Ibid.*

## 452. Laura Simmons
### (1877–1949)

* * *

1 The face within that passport book
Will rise to haunt you yet.

    "Your Passport Picture"

## 453. Alice B. Toklas
(1877–1967)

1 What is sauce for the goose may be sauce for the gander, but is not necessarily sauce for the chicken, the duck, the turkey or the guinea hen.
*The Alice B. Toklas Cook Book*
*1954*

2 She quoted a friend who used to say any advice is good as long as it is strong enough.
Letter to Carl Van Vechten
(September 3, 1946),
*Staying On Alone*, Ed Burns, ed.
*1973p*

3 I am staying on here alone now.
Ibid., Letter to Julian Beck
(September 8, 1946)

4 Now I ask you what is the impulse that comes from the possession of even the kindest heart compared to real faith in God and a hereafter. Without it one just plods on. . . .
Ibid., Letter to Fania Marinoff Van
Vechten (February 21, 1948)

5 Austerity has gone so far that the population has become submissive through lack of physical resistance.
Ibid., Letter to Donald Gallup
(October 12, 1948)

6 . . . he [Basket, a dog] has filled the corners of the room and the minutes and me so sweetly these last years.
Ibid., Letter to Thornton Wilder
(April 5, 1949)

7 Well, I've gotten to the end of the subject— of the page—of your patience and my time.
Ibid., Letter to Elizabeth Hansen
(July 19, 1949)

8 The young men of today seem mostly to be interested in the manner rather than the matter.
Ibid., Letter to Mark Lutz
(August 16, 1951)

9 I love Spain and things Spanish and Picasso!
Ibid., Letter to Louise Taylor
(August 16, 1951)

10 Haven't you learned yet· that it isn't age but lack of experience that makes us fall off ladders or have radiators fall on us.
Ibid., Letter to Princess Dilkusha de
Rohan (March 5, 1955)

11 . . . the past is not gone—nor is Gertrude.
Ibid., Letter to Samuel Steward
(August 7, 1958)

12 Dawn comes slowly but dusk is rapid.
Ibid., Letter to Virginia Knapik
(August 9, 1960)

## 454. Elizabeth Arden
(1878–1966)

1 Nothing that costs only a dollar is worth having. Quoted in "In Cosmetics the Old Mystique Is No Longer Enough" by Eleanore Carruth, *Fortune* October, 1973p

## 455. Florence Ayscough
(1878–1942)

1 Ideals determine government, and government determines social life, and social life, with all that the term connotes, is the essence of every literature. *Fir-Flower Tablets*, Introduction *1921*

## 456. Amelia Burr
(1878–1940?)

1 Because I have loved life, I shall have no sorrow to die.
"A Song of Living," St. 3,
*Life and Living* *1916*

2 Spring comes laughing down the valley
All in white, from the snow
Where the winter's armies rally
Loth to go.
Ibid., "New Life"

\* \* \*

3 But I have certainty enough,
For I am sure of you.
"Certainty Enough"

4 Swift and sure go the lonely feet,
 And the single eye sees cold and true,
And the road that has room and to spare for
 one
May be sorely narrow for two.
"To Lovers"

## 457. Grace H. Conkling
(1878–1958)

\* \* \*

1 I have an understanding with the hills.
"After Sunset"

2 Invisible beauty has a world so brief
A flower can say it or a shaken leaf,
But few may ever snare it in a song.
Ibid.

3 I wonder if it *is* a bird
That sings within the hidden tree,
Or some shy angel calling me
To follow far away?
"Nightingale"

4 Mountains are good to look upon
But do not look too long.
They are made of granite. They will break your
　　heart.
　　　　　　　　　　　　　　"Mountains"

5 Over the stones to lull and leap
Herding the bubbles like white sheep;
The claims of worry to deny,
And whisper sorrow into sleep.
　　　　　　　　　"The Whole Duty of
　　　　　　　　　　Berkshire Brooks"

6 To build the trout a crystal stair.
　　　　　　　　　　　　　　Ibid.

7 The forest looks the way
Nightingales sound.
　　　　　　　　　"Frost on a Window"

## 458.  Adelaide Crapsey

### (1878–1914)

\* \* \*

1 If I'd as much money as I could tell,
I never would cry my songs to sell.
　　　　　　　　　　"Vendor's Song"

2 Is it as plainly in our living shown,
By slant and twist, which way the wind hath
　　blown?
　　　　　"On Seeing Weather-Beaten Trees"

3 These be
Three silent things:
The falling snow . . . the hour
Before the dawn . . . the mouth of one
Just dead.
　　　　　　　　　　"Cinquain: Triad"

4 Wouldst thou find my ashes? Look
In the pages of my book;
And, as this thy hands doth turn,
Know here is my funeral urn.
　　　　　　　　　"The Immortal Residue"

## 459.  Isadora Duncan

### (1878–1927)

1 America has all that Russia has not. Russia has
things America has not. Why will America not
reach out a hand to Russia, as I have given my
hand?　　　　Curtain Speech, Symphony Hall,
　　　　　　　　　　Boston　　*1922*

2 You were once wild here. Don't let them tame
you!　　　　　　　　　　Ibid.

3 All Puritan vulgarity centers in Boston. The
Back Bay conservatives are impoverished by
custom and taboo. They are the lifeless and
sterile of this country.　　　Interview, Boston
　　　　　　　　　　　　　　　*1922*

4 . . . [I] would rather live in Russia on black
bread and vodka than in the United States at
the best hotels. America knows nothing of food,
love or art.　　Interview Aboard Ship　　*1922*

5 So that ends my first experience with matrimony, which I always thought a highly overrated performance.
　　　　　　　Interview, *The New York Times*
　　　　　　　　　　　　　　*1923*

6 . . . the artist is the only lover, he alone has
the pure vision of beauty, and love is the
vision of the soul when it is permitted to gaze
upon immortal beauty. . . .　　　*My Life*
　　　　　　　　　　　　　　*1927*

7 I have discovered the dance. I have discovered
the art which has been lost for two thousand
years.　　　　　　　　　　Ibid.

8 . . . when I listened to music the rays and
vibrations of the music streamed to this one
fount of light within me—there they reflected
themselves in Spiritual Vision, not the brain's
mirror, but the soul's, and from the vision I
could express them in Dance. . . .　　　Ibid.

9 . . . I believe, as a wage-earning woman, that
if I make the great sacrifice of strength and
health and even risk my life, to have a child, I
should certainly not do so if, on some future
occasion, the man can say that the child belongs to him by law and he will take it from
me and I shall see it only three times a year!
　　　　　　　　　　　　　　Ibid.

10 Any intelligent woman who reads the marriage
contract, and then goes into it, deserves all the
consequences.　　　　　　　Ibid.

11 With what a price we pay for the glory of
motherhood. . . .　　　　　　Ibid.

12 It is unheard of, uncivilized barbarism that any
woman should still be forced to bear such
monstrous torture. It should be remedied. It
should be stopped. It is simply absurd that with
our modern science painless childbirth does not
exist as a matter of course. . . . I tremble with
indignation when I think of . . . the unspeakable
egotism and blindness of men of science who
permit such atrocities when they can be
remedied. . . .　　　　　　　Ibid.

13 . . . now that I had discovered that Love might
be a pastime as well as a tragedy, I gave myself to it with pagan innocence. Men seemed
so hungry for Beauty, hungry for that love
which refreshes and inspires without fear or
responsibility.　　　　　　　Ibid.

14 . . . if you have a body in which you are born to a certain amount of pain . . . why should you not, when the occasion presents, draw from this same body the maximum of pleasure?
                                                    Ibid.

15 No composer has yet caught this rhythm of America—it is too mighty for the ears of most.
                                                    Ibid.

16 And this dance will have nothing in it of the inane coquetry of the ballet, or the sensual convulsion of the Negro. It will be clean.
                                                    Ibid.

17 The real American type can never be a ballet dancer. The legs are too long, the body too supple and the spirit too free for this school of affected grace and toe walking.        Ibid.

18 . . . let [them] come forth with great strides, leaps and bounds, with lifted forehead and far-spread arms, to dance the language of our Pioneers, the Fortitude of our heroes, the Justice, Kindness, Purity of our statesmen, and all the inspired love and tenderness of our Mothers.
                                                    Ibid.

19 She [Eleanora Duse] never said, "Cease to grieve" but she grieved with me.        Ibid.

20 The whole world is absolutely brought up on lies. We are fed nothing but lies. It begins with lies and half our lives we live with lies.
                            "Memoirs" (1924), *This Quarter*
                                            *Autumn, 1929p*

21 Art is not necessary at all. All that is necessary to make this world a better place to live in is to love—to love as Christ loved, as Buddha loved.                            Ibid.

22 Lenin was God, as Christ was God, because God is love and Christ and Lenin were all love.
                                                    Ibid.

23 So long as little children are allowed to suffer, there is no true love in this world.        Ibid.

24 People do not live nowadays—they get about ten percent out of life.        Ibid.

## 460. Edith Ronald Mirrielees
### (1878–1962)

1 In the thinking out of most stories, the thing the story is about, as apart from merely what happens in it, is of the utmost importance. For a story is not the sum of its happenings.
                            "The Substance of the Story,"
                                    *Story Writing*        1947

2 Incident piled on incident no more makes life than brick piled on brick makes a house.
                                                    Ibid.

3 . . . belief that persistence is all and is bound to be rewarded has no . . . foundation. . . .
                                                    Ibid.

4 Experience shows that exceptions are as true as rules.                                    Ibid.

## 461. Ethel Watts Mumford
### (1878–1940)

1 There was a young lady named Julie,
Who was terribly fond of patchouli;
    She used bottles seven,
    'Til smelt up to heaven,
Which made all the angels unruly.
                "Lavishness," *The Limerick Up to
                                Date Book*        1903

2 There was a young person of Tottenhem,
Whose manners, good Lord! she'd forgotten 'em.
                        Ibid., "Good Manners"

3 There was a young lady from Skye,
With a shape like a capital I;
    She said, "It's too bad!
    But then I can pad,"
Which shows you that figures can lie.
                    Ibid., "Appearances Deceitful"

4 There was a young damsel named Nell,
Who considered herself quite a belle.
    She sat on the sand,
    And held her own hand,
And never got on to the swell.
                        Ibid., "Self-Sufficiency"

5 Said a Rooster, "I'd have you all know
I am nearly the whole of the show;
    Why, the Sun every morn
    Gets up with the dawn
For the purpose of hearing me crow!"
                    Ibid., "Know Your Own Worth"

## 462. Bertha Runkle
### (1878–1958)
* * *
1 We own the right of roaming, and the world is wide.
                        "Songs of the Sons of Esau"

## 463. Nancy Astor
(1879–1964)

1 I can conceive of nothing worse than a man-governed world—except a woman-governed world.
"America," *My Two Countries*, Ch. 1
*1923*

2 Mercifully, we have no political past; we have all the mistakes of one-sex legislation, with its appalling failures, to guide us. We should know what to avoid. It is no use blaming the men—we made them what they are—and now it is up to us to try and make ourselves—the makers of men—a little more responsible.     Ibid.

3 In passing, also, I would like to say that the first time Adam had a chance he laid the blame on woman. . . .     Ibid.

4 I believe that the safest and surest way to get out of war is to join some sort of league of nations. That misrepresented and much despised League has already prevented three small wars, it has registered over one hundred treaties, has repatriated nearly four hundred thousand prisoners—not a bad record for only a half a league.     Ibid., Ch. 2

5 The most practical thing in the world is common sense and common humanity.
Ibid., Ch. 7

6 Real education should educate us out of self into something far finer—into a selflessness which links us with all humanity. Political education should do the same.     Ibid.

7 A fool without fear is sometimes wiser than an angel with fear.     Ibid., Ch. 8

8 My vigor, vitality and cheek repel me. I am the kind of woman I would run from.
News Item     *1955*

## 464. Ethel Barrymore
(1879–1959)

1 That's all there is, there isn't any more.
Curtain Speech After Performance of
*Sunday*     *1904*

2 For an actress to be a success she must have the face of Venus, the brains of Minerva, the grace of Terpsichore, the memory of Macaulay, the figure of Juno, and the hide of a rhinoceros.
Quoted in *The Theatre in the Fifties*
by George Jean Nathan     *1953*

## 465. Catherine Carswell
(1879–1946)

1 . . . it wasn't a woman who betrayed Jesus with a kiss.     *The Savage Pilgrimage*
*1932*

## 466. Mabel Dodge
(1879–1962)

1 . . . she [Frieda Lawrence] had to see life from the sex center, she endorsed or repudiated experience from that angle. She was the mother of orgasm and of the vast, lively mystery of the flesh. But no more.     *Lorenzo in Taos*
*1932*

2 The womb behind the womb—the significant, extended and transformed power that succeeds primary sex, that he [D. H. Lawrence] was ready, long since, to receive from woman.
Ibid.

3 The groping, suffering, tragic soul of man was so much filthiness to that healthy creature.
Ibid.

4 . . . I knew instinctively that the strongest, surest way to the soul is through the flesh.
Ibid.

## 467. Dorothy Canfield Fisher
(1879–1958)

1 "He divides us all into two kinds: the ones that get what they want by taking it away from other people—those are the dolichocophalic blonds—though I believe it doesn't refer to the color of their hair. The other kind are the white folks, the unpredatory ones who have scruples, and get pushed to the wall for their pains."     *The Bent Twig*, Bk. I, Ch. 5
*1915*

2 No European could have conceived how literally it was true that the birth or wealth or social position of a child made no difference in the estimation of his mates. There were no exceptions to the custom of considering the individual on his own merits.     Ibid., Ch. 7

3 "I am thinking that I am being present at a spectacle which cynics say is impossible, the spectacle of a woman delighting—and with most obvious sincerity—in the beauty of another."     Ibid., Bk. III, Ch. 23

4 A mother is not a person to lean on but a person to making leaning unnecessary.
*Her Son's Wife*     *1926*

5 This was a nighttime memory, one of those that never come to you at all in daylight, but when you get about so far asleep, start to unroll themselves in the dark.
*The Deepening Stream*, Pt. I, Ch. 2
1930

6 "Father sticks to it that anything that promises to pay too much can't help being risky. He always says he doesn't advise people against taking risks. . . . 'What is life but one long risk?' . . . You know how father talks."
Ibid., Pt. II, Ch. 1

7 "I've seen children before who'd had too great a fright. They are always imbeciles. . . ." There had been long periods in her youth when she too had crept into a corner and turned her face away from what life seemed to be.
Ibid., Pt. III, Ch. 11

8 The skull of life suddenly showed through its smile.     *Bonfire*     1933

9 Freedom is not worth fighting for if it means no more than license for everyone to get as much as he can for himself. And freedom *is* worth fighting for. Because it does mean more than unrestricted grabbing. He saw in imagination those young faces looking up at him attentively, and told them, "Laugh in the faces of the Fascist priests who chant the new Black Mass, when they tell you boys and girls that democratic government means nothing but license for the money-getters."
*Seasoned Timber*     1939

## 468. Katherine Gerould
### (1879-1944)

1 There are only three things worth while—fighting, drinking, and making love.
"The Tortoise," *Vain Oblations*
1914

2 The commonest field may be chosen by opposing generals to be decisive; and in a day history is born where before only the quiet wheat has sprung.     Ibid., "The Case of Paramore"

3 You don't care about this State: you want to put it into white petticoats and see it across a muddy street.
"The Knights' Move," *Atlantic Monthly*
1917

4 . . . I have always, privately and humbly, thought it a pity that so good a word [as culture] should go out of the best vocabularies; for when you lose an abstract term, you are very apt to lose the thing it stands for.
"The Extirpation of Culture,"
*Modes and Morals*     1920

5 . . . it is one thing to sow your wild oats in talk, and quite another to live by your own kaleidoscopic paradoxes. The people who frowned on the manifestations of "temperament" were merely those logical creatures who believed that if you expressed your opinions regardless of other people's feelings, you probably meant what you said. They did not know the pathology of epigram, the basic truth of which is that word-intoxicated people express an opinion long before they dream of holding it.     Ibid., "Tabu and Temperament"

6 We were a plutocracy; which means that so long as a man had the house and the drinks, you asked no questions. The same rule holds—allowing for their dizzier sense of figures—in New York and Chicago.
"French Eva," *Scribner's Magazine*
1920

7 Politics, which, the planet over, are the fly in the amber, the worm in the bud, the rift in the loot, had, with great suddenness, deprived Wharton Cameron of a job.
*Conquistador*, Ch. 1     1923

8 Codes cohabit easily until it comes to women. Then jungle and steppe, delta and forest, proceed to argue their differences.     Ibid., Ch. 5

## 469. Wanda Landowska
### (1879-1959)

1 Music of the past has become a distant and vague country where everything is totally different from our surroundings, our life, our art, our impressions, and our concepts.
"Music of the Past" (1905),
*Landowska on Music*,
Denise Resout, ed.     1964p

2 Obviously the good lady [melody] has a tough constitution. The more attempts made against her, the more she blooms with health and rotundity. It is interesting to note that all those accused of being her murderers are becoming, in turn, her benefactors and her saviors.
Ibid., "Why Does Modern Music Lack Melody?" (February 9, 1913)

3 In this obstinate race after the original—while avoiding thoroughly that which has already been said and taking refuge on an island that we thought was uninhabited—do we not risk running into a good old acquaintance who has just been dropped? . . . Is it really indispensable to believe with such seriousness that every little change will, at last, bring the definitive salvation? If it gives us a thrill, it is already delightful enough; and if this thrill reminds us of the dear caresses of old, it is all for the best!
Ibid., Book Review (1923)

4 To embrace an epoch in all its splendor and truth, to understand the fluctuations of taste, one needs perspective.
Ibid., Letter (September 8, 1948)

5 But I cannot help it if, having never stopped working, I have learned a great deal, especially about this divine freedom that is to music the air without which it would die. What would you say of a scientist or of a painter who, like stagnant water, would stop his experimentation and remain still?
Ibid., Letter to a Former Pupil (1950)

6 The most beautiful thing in the world is, precisely, the conjunction of learning and inspiration. Oh, the passion for research and the joy of discovery!
Ibid.

## 470.　Frieda Lawrence
### (1879–1956)

1 Everything he met had the newness of a creation, just that moment come into being.
*Not I, But the Wind . . .*　　　*1934*

2 In spite of his age and strong passions he [D. H. Lawrence] had never let himself go. Sex was suppressed in him with ferocity. He had suppressed it so much, put it away so entirely, that now, married, it overwhelmed him.
*Frieda Lawrence: The Memoirs and Correspondence*, E. W. Tedlock, ed.
*1961p*

3 He loved me absolutely, that's why he hates me absolutely. . . .
Ibid., Letter to Edward Garnett (c.1914)

4 . . . he hated me for being miserable, not a moment of misery did he put up with; he denied all the suffering and suffered all the more. . . .
Ibid.

5 But it was nice to feel him at the back of her days, solid and firm her rock of ages. He bored her a bit occasionally.
Ibid., Letter (1938 or 1939)

## 471.　Lilian Leveridge
### (1879–1953)

1 Brother, little brother, your childhood is passing by,
And the dawn of a noble purpose I see in your thoughtful eye.
"A Cry from the Canadian Hills,"
St. 6, *Over the Hills of Home*
*1918*

2 Laddie! Laddie! Laddie! "Somewhere in France" you sleep,
Somewhere 'neath alien flowers and alien winds that weep,
Bravely you marched to battle, nobly your life laid down,
You unto death were faithful, laddie; yours is the victor's crown.
Ibid., St. 9

3 Over the hills of home, laddie, over the hills of home.
Ibid.

## 472.　Sarojini Naidu
### (1879–1949)

1 *To-day* it is spring!
"Ecstasy," *The Golden Threshold*
*1890*

2 What hope shall we gather, what dreams shall we sow?
Where the wind calls our wandering footsteps we go.
No love bids us tarry, no joy bids us wait;
The voice of the wind is the voice of our fate.
Ibid., "Wandering Singers," St. 3

3 And spirits of Truth were the birds that sang,
And spirits of Love were the stars that glowed,
And spirits of Peace were the streams that flowed
In that magical wood in the land of sleep.
Ibid., "Song of a Dream," St. 1

4 O Bird of Time on your fruitful bough
What are the songs you sing?
"The Bird of Time," St. 1
*The Bird of Time*　　　*1912*

5 Shall hope prevail where clamorous hate is rife,
Shall sweet love prosper or high dreams find place
Amid the tumult of reverberant strife.
Ibid., "At Twilight," St. 2

6 What do you know in your blithe, brief season
Of dreams deferred and a heart grown old?
Ibid., "A Song in Spring," St. 2

7 The Indian woman of to-day is once more awake and profoundly alive to her splendid destiny as the guardian and interpreter of the Triune Vision of national life—the Vision of Love, the Vision of Faith, the Vision of Patriotism.
*The Broken Wing*, Foreword
*1916*

8 Can ye measure the grief of the tears I weep
Or compass the woe of the watch I keep?
Ibid., "The Gift of India," St. 3

9 Thy changing kings and kingdoms pass away
The gorgeous legends of a bygone day,
But thou dost still immutably remain
Unbroken symbol of proud history, unageing
    priestess of old mysteries
Before whose shrine the spells of Death are
    vain.
> Ibid., "Imperial Delhi," St. 2

10 Two gifts for our portion
We ask thee, O Fate,
A maiden to cherish,
A kinsman to hate.
> "A Song of the Khyber Pass," St. 2,
> *The Feather of the Dawn*    1927

11 What, O my heart, though tomorrow be tragic,
Today is inwoven of rapture and magic.
> Ibid., "Spring in Kashmir," St. 9

## 473. Alma Mahler Werfel
### (1879–1964)

1 Mahler, ascetic though he was, had a lurid
reputation. In fact, he was a child and women
were his dread. It was only because I was a
stupid, inexperienced girl that I took him off
his guard.     "First Meeting," *Gustav Mahler*
> 1946

2 From the moment of his spiritual triumph, too,
he looked down on me and did not recover his
love for me until I had broken his tyranny.
Sometimes he played the part of a schoolmaster, relentlessly strict and unjust. He soured
my enjoyment of life and made it an abomina-
tion. That is, he tried to. Money—rubbish!
Clothes—rubbish! Beauty—rubbish! Traveling
—rubbish! Only the spirit was to count. I know
today that he was afraid of my youth and
beauty. He wanted to make them safe for himself by simply taking from me any atom of life
in which he himself played no part. I was a
young thing he had desired and whose education he now took in hand.
> Ibid., "Marriage and Life Together"

3 I can never forget his dying hours and the
greatness of his face as death drew nearer. His
battle for the eternal values, his elevation above
trivial things and his unflinching devotion to
truth are an example of the saintly life.
> Ibid., "The End"

## 474. Beth Slater Whitson
### (1879–1930)

1 Meet me in Dreamland, sweet dreamy Dream-
land,
There let my dreams come true.
> "Meet Me To-Night in Dreamland"
> *1909*

## 475. Alice Williams Brotherton
### (fl. 1880s–1930)

* * *

1 Books we must have though we lack bread.
> "Ballade of Poor Bookworms"

2 Heap high the board with plenteous cheer, and
gather to the feast,
And toast the sturdy Pilgrim band whose courage never ceased.
> "The First Thanksgiving Day"

## 476. Ophelia Guyon Browning
### (fl. 1880s)

1 She knows Omnipotence has heard her prayer
And cries, "It shall be done—sometime, somewhere."
> "Pray Without Ceasing,"
> *Singing with Grace*    1882

## 477. Mrs. E. T. Corbett
### (fl. 1880s)

1 Ef you want to be sick of your life,
Jest come and change places with me a
spell—for I'm an inventor's wife.
> *The Inventor's Wife*    1883

## 478. Ellen M. Hutchinson
### (fl. 1880s–1933)

* * *

1 They are all in the lily-bed, cuddled close
together—
Purple, yellow-cap, and baby-blue;
How they ever got there you must ask the April
weather,
The morning and the evening winds, the sunshine and the dew.
> "Vagrant Pansies"

## 479. Meta Orred
### (fl. 1880s)

1 In the gloaming, O, my darling!
When the lights are dim and low,
And the quiet shadows falling
Softly come and softly go.
> "In the Gloaming"    1890

## 480. Helen Keller
### (1880–1968)

1 . . . we could never learn to be brave and
patient, if there were only joy in the world.
> Quoted in the *Atlantic Monthly*
> *May, 1890*

2 Literature is my Utopia. Here I am not disenfranchised. No barrier of the senses shuts me out from the sweet, gracious discourse of my book friends. They talk to me without embarrassment or awkwardness.
*The Story of My Life*    1903

3 There is no king who has not had a slave among his ancestors, and no slave who has not had a king among his.    Ibid., Ch. 1

4 . . . I find that fact and fancy look alike across the years that link the past with the present.
Ibid.

5 There is nothing more beautiful, I think, than the evanescent fleeting images and sentiments presented by a language one is just becoming familiar with—ideas that flit across the mental sky, shaped and tinted by capricious fancy.
Ibid., Ch. 16

6 I hung about the dangerous frontier of "guess," avoiding with infinite trouble to myself and others the broad valley of reason.
Ibid., Ch. 17

7 Everything had its wonders, even darkness and silence, and I learn, whatever state I may be in, therein to be content.    Ibid., Ch. 22

8 . . . a people's peace—a peace without victory, a peace without conquests or indemnities.
Ibid.

9 . . . militarism . . . is one of the chief bulwarks of capitalism, and the day that militarism is undermined, capitalism will fail.    Ibid.

10 Now I feel as if I should succeed in doing something in mathematics, although I cannot see why it is so very important. . . . The knowledge doesn't make life any sweeter or happier, does it?
Ibid., Pt. II, Letter to Laurence Hutton

11 Now, however, I see the folly of attempting to hitch one's wagon to a star with a harness that does not belong to it.
Ibid., Letter to Charles T. Copeland

12 "I never fight," she replied, "except against difficulties."    Ibid., Pt. III

13 Toleration . . . is the greatest gift of the mind; it requires the same effort of the brain that it takes to balance oneself on a bicycle.    Ibid.

14 I know that daisies and pansies come from seeds which have been put in the ground; but children do not grow out of the ground. I am sure. I have never seen a plant child. . . .
Ibid., Quoted in Annie Sullivan's Report of 1891

15 One can never consent to creep when one feels an impulse to soar.    Ibid., Speech, Mt. Airy

16 Every industry, every process, is wrought by a hand, or by a superhand—a machine whose mighty arm and cunning fingers the human hand invents and wields.
"The Hand of the World," *American Magazine* *December, 1912*

17 Study the hand, and you shall find in it the true picture of man, the story of human growth, the measure of the world's greatness and weakness.    Ibid.

18 . . . as the eagle was killed by the arrow winged with his own feather, so the hand of the world is wounded by its own skill.    Ibid.

19 Rebuffed, but always persevering; self-reproached, but ever regaining faith; undaunted, tenacious, the heart of man labors toward immeasurably distant goals.    Ibid.

20 How reconcile this world of fact with the bright world of my imagining? My darkness has been filled with the light of intelligence, and behold, the outer day-light world was stumbling and groping in social blindness.
Quoted in *The Cry for Justice*, Upton Sinclair, ed.    1915

21 Let us start a world-encircling revolt, a revolt which shall make a junk heap out of the civilization of Kaisers and Kings and all the things that make of man a brute and of God a monster.    Speech, New York City *December 19, 1915*

22 The burden of war always falls heaviest on the toilers.    "Menace of the Militarist Program," *New York Call*    *December 20, 1915*

23 The only moral virtue of war is that it compels the capitalist system to look itself in the face and admit it is a fraud. It compels the present society to admit that it has no morals it will not sacrifice for gain.    Ibid.

24 I look upon the whole world as my fatherland, and every war has to me a horror of a family-feud. I look upon true patriotism as the brotherhood of man and the service of all to all.
Ibid.

25 The few who profit by the labor of the masses want to organize the workers into an army which will protect the interests of the capitalists.
Speech, New York City *December, 1916*

26 Security is mostly a superstition. It does not exist in nature, nor do the children of men as a whole experience it. Avoiding danger is no safer in the long run than outright exposure. Life is either a daring adventure, or nothing.
*The Open Door*    1957

## 481. Sophie Kerr
### (1880–1965)

1 Freud and his three slaves, Inhibition, Complex and Libido. "The Age of Innocence," *Saturady Evening Post* *April 9, 1932*

2 The longing to produce great inspirations didn't produce anything but more longing.
*The Man Who Knew the Date*, Ch. 1 *1951*

3 If peace, he thought (as he had often thought before), only had the music and pageantry of war, there'd be no more wars.
*Ibid.*, Ch. 8

## 482. Edith Lewis
### (1880?–1955?)

1 . . . it is not in any form of biographical writing, but in art alone, that the deepest truth about human beings is to be found.
*Willa Cather Living* *1953*

## 483. Kathleen Norris
### (1880–1966)

1 "If you have children, you never have anything else!" *Mother*, Ch. 2 *1911*

2 We cooked, cleaned, laboured, worried, planned, we wept and laughed, we groaned and we sang—but we never despaired. All this was but a passing phase; "we will certainly laugh at this someday," we all said buoyantly, laughing even then. *Noon*, Ch. 1 *1924*

3 And so came middle-age, for I have discovered that middle-age is not a question of years. It is that moment in life when one realizes that one has exchanged, by a series of subtle shifts and substitutes, the vague and vaporous dreams of youth for the definite and tangible realization.
*Ibid.*, Ch. 3

4 Never in the history of the big round world has anything like us occurred. A country without caste, without serfs, peons or slaves, without banishment or exile or whipping post, without starvation and oppression! *Home* *1928*

5 Home ought to be our clearinghouse, the place from which we go forth lessoned and disciplined, and ready for life. *Ibid.*

6 When they were going to be flagrantly, brutally selfish, how men did love to talk of being fair!
*Bread into Roses*, Ch. 2 *1936*

7 The bright panorama was only a panorama, that was the trouble. Under its undeniable joy and excitements . . . there was a strange emptiness, a feeling that somehow reality was escaping her, that the business of being amused was altogether too successful. Life wasn't, after all, only amusement—or was it? *Ibid.*, Ch. 11

8 But somehow one never had time to stop and savor the taste of life as the stream of it flowed by. It would be good to find some quiet inlet where the waters were still enough for reflection, where one might sense the joy of the moment, rather than plan breathlessly for a dozen mingled treats in the future. *Ibid.*

9 "There seems to be so much more winter than we need this year." *Ibid.*, Ch. 14

## 484. Christabel Pankhurst
### (1880–1958)

1 We are not ashamed of what we have done, because, when you have a great cause to fight for, the moment of greatest humiliation is the moment when the spirit is proudest. The women we do pity, the women we think unwomanly, the women for whom we have almost contempt, if our hearts could let us have that feeling, are the women who can stand aside, who take no part in this battle—and perhaps even more, the women who know what the right path is and will not tread it, who are selling the liberty of other women in order to win the smiles and favour of the dominant sex.
Speech, Albert Hall, London
*March 19, 1908*

2 We are here to claim our rights as women, not only to be free, but to fight for freedom. It is our privilege, as well as our pride and our joy, to take some part in this militant movement, which, as we believe, means the regeneration of all humanity. Nothing but contempt is due to those people who ask us to submit to unmerited oppression. We shall not do it.
Speech *March 23, 1911*

3 What we suffragettes aspire to be when we are enfranchised is ambassadors of freedom to women in other parts of the world, who are not so free as we are.
Speech, "America and the War,"
Carnegie Hall, New York
*October 25, 1915*

4 Some people are tempted to say that all war is wrong, and that both sides to every war must be in the wrong. I challenge that statement and deny it utterly, absolutely, and with all the power I have at my disposal. All wars are not wrong. Was your war against a British Government wrong? As an Englishwoman, I say that when you fought us for the principle of freedom, for the right of self-government, you did right. I am glad you fought us and I am glad you beat us. Ibid.

5 I have known passion that strengthens one for endurance, shakes one with its mighty force, makes humans god-like, fills them with creative force. The passion of my life has been for the freeing of women, not only for reasons political and economic.
"Confessions of Christabel: Why I Never Married," *Weekly Dispatch* (London) *April, 1921*

6 Never lose your temper with the Press or the public is a major rule of political life.
*Unshackled* 1959p

7 The spirit of the movement was wonderful. It was joyous and grave at the same time. Self seemed to be laid down as the women joined us. Loyalty, the greatest of the virtues, was the keynote of the movement—first to the cause, then to those who were leading, and member to member. Courage came next, not simply physical courage, though so much of that was present, but still more the moral courage to endure ridicule and misunderstandings and harsh criticism and ostracism. There was a touch of the "impersonal" in the movement that made for its strength and dignity. Humour characterized it, too, in that our militant women were like the British soldier who knows how to joke and smile amid his fighting and trials. Ibid.

8 I go about with the Bible in one hand and a newspaper in the other. The two go well together, for the concentrated study of the newspapers is a Christian's duty as this Age draws to its close. Speech, Albert Hall, London (September, 1926), Quoted in *The Fighting Pankhursts* by David Mitchell 1967p

9 We are suffering today from a greed for knowledge of evil. Moral disease and sin is rampant. Groups here and there are striving to keep us from slipping back into barbarism. But nothing can save us but divine intervention. . . .
Ibid., Speech, California (1930)

# 485. Jeannette Rankin
(1880–    )

1 As a woman I can't go to war, and I refuse to send anyone else.
Quoted in *Jeannette Rankin: First Lady in Congress*, Prologue (c.1941), by Hannah Josephson *1974*

2 You take people as far as they will go, not as far as you would like them to go. Ibid.

3 The individual woman is required . . . a thousand times a day to choose either to accept her appointed role and thereby rescue her good disposition out of the wreckage of her self-respect, or else follow an independent line of behavior and rescue her self-respect out of the wreckage of her good disposition. Ibid., Ch. 3

4 Establish democracy at home, based on human rights as superior to property rights. . . .
Ibid., Ch. 6

5 You can no more win a war than you can win an earthquake. Ibid., Ch. 8

# 486. Ruth St. Denis
(1880–1968)

1 I used to say that if a person wanted to keep alive, in distinction to merely existing, he should change his occupation every ten years. . . . Our individuality is based upon something much vaster than a circumscribed profession. We should be in a position to bring our intelligence to any challenging objective and be at no disadvantage. *Ruth St. Denis: An Unfinished Life*, Ch. 3 *1939*

2 I am a child of nature. Too much civilization and a touch of luxury have only depressed me. I must find a way to live more simply.
Ibid., Ch. 6

3 I want to dance always, to be good and not evil, and when it is all over not to have the feeling that I might have done better. Ibid.

4 The human tragedy of artists must, at some time, bring itself to the attention of all earnest thinkers and seekers after truth. That something is terribly wrong with the whole round of artists' lives must be apparent to anyone who take the trouble to observe it. Ibid., Ch. 15

5 We were a Poet* and a Dancer; and we became lovers. And let it be said of us that Beauty was our god whom we worshipped in

* Referring to her husband, Ted Shawn.

rites of such pure loveliness that he became my Emperor and I became Moon to his Imperial Sun. Poems, like shy white birds, rose from our union: records of the strange drama of our love.　　　　　　　　　　　　　Ibid.

## 487. Marie Carmichael Stopes
### (1880–1958)

1 The surface freedom of our women has not materially altered the pristine purity of a girl of our northern race.　　*Married Love*　　*1918*

2 Each heart knows instinctively that it is only a mate who can give full comprehension of all the potential greatness in the soul, and have tender laughter for all the childlike wonder that lingers so enchantingly even in the white-haired.　　　　　　　　　　Ibid., Ch. 1

3 An impersonal and scientific knowledge of the structure of our bodies is the surest safeguard against prurient curiosity and lascivious gloating.　　　　　　　　　　　　Ibid., Ch. 5

4 . . . each coming together of man and wife, even if they have been mated for many years, should be a fresh adventure; each winning should necessitate a fresh wooing.
　　　　　　　　　　　　　　Ibid., Ch. 10

5 So deeply are we woven I can lend
You outwardly to other hands who clutch
Small corners of your heart, greedy that such
Resplendence should its rays to darkness send.
　　　　　　　"You," St. 2, *Joy and Verity*
　　　　　　　　　　　　　　　　　*1952*

6 London, scarred mistress of proud Freedom's heart,
The love we bear you has no counterpart.
　　　　　　　　　　　　Ibid., "London"

7 We are not much in sympathy with the typical hustling American business man, but we have often felt compunction for him, seeing him nervous and harassed, sleeplessly, anxiously hunting dollars and all but overshadowed by his over-dressed, extravagant and idle wife, who sometimes insists that her spiritual development necessitates that she shall have no children. Such husbands and wives are also found in this country; they are a growing produce of the upper reaches of the capitalist system. Yet such wives imagine that they are upholding women's emancipation.
　　　　　Article in *Dreadnought* (c.1919),
　　　　　Quoted in *The Fighting Pankhursts*
　　　　　by David Mitchell　　*1967p*

## 488. Nancy Byrd Turner
### (1880–1954?)
\* \* \*

1 Burn, wood, burn—
　Wood that once was a tree, and knew
Blossom and sheaf, and the Spring's return,
　Nest, and singing, and rain, and dew—
Burn, wood, burn!
　　　　　　　　　　　　"Flame Song"

2 Death is only an old door
Set in a garden wall.
　　　　　　　　　"Death Is a Door"

3 Men climb tall hills to suffer and die.
　　　　　　　　　　　　　　"Hills"

## 489. Margaret Widdemer
### (1880–　　)

1 I have shut my little sister in from light and life
(For a rose, for a ribbon, for a wreath across my hair),
I have made her restless feet still until the night,
Locked from sweets of summer and from wild spring air.
　　　　"The Factories," St. 1　　*c.1916*

2 The old road to Paradise
Easy it is missed!
　　　"The Old Road to Paradise," St. 2
　　　　　　　　　　　　　　　　*1919*

3 To grown people a girl of fifteen and a half is a child still; to herself she is very old and very real; more real, perhaps, than ever before or after. . . .　　　　　　　"The Changeling,"
　　　　　　　　*The Boardwalk*　　*1920*

4 She was poor, and she was broken. But the young are improvident—not having yet learned how hard to come by money is and of how little account are other things.
　　　　　　　Ibid., "The Congregation"

5 No one had told them that Age was a place
Where you sat with a curious mask on your face.
　　　　"Old Ladies," St. 6, *Hill Garden*
　　　　　　　　　　　　　　　　*1936*

6 "It only was gifts that I let them take.
　I never gave dreams away."
　　　　Ibid., "Spendthrift Nancy," St. 3
　　　　　　　　　　　　\* \* \*

7 And all that you are sorry for is what you haven't done.
　　　　　　　　　　　"De Senectute"

8 I am the Dark Cavalier; I am the Last Lover:
My arms shall welcome you when other arms
are tired.
"The Dark Cavalier"

9 Love and grief and motherhood,
Fame and mirth and scorn—
These are all shall befall
Any woman born.
"A Cyprian Woman"

## 490. Mary Antin
(1881–1949)

1 "So at last I was going to America! Really,
really going, at last! The boundaries burst. The
arch of heaven soared. A million suns shone
out of every star. The winds rushed into outer
space, roaring in my ears, 'America! America!' "
*The Promised Land* 1912

## 491. Mary Breckinridge
(1881–1965)

1 To meet the needs of the frontierman's child,
you must begin before he is born and carry him
through the hazards of childbirth. This means
that the nurses who serve him must be mid-
wives. . . . Even after his birth, the young child
is not an isolated individual. His care not only
means the care of the mother before, during
and after his birth, but the care of his whole
family as well. . . . Health teaching must also
be on a family basis—in the homes.
Quoted in "Birth Control Gains in the
Mountains of Kentucky" by Kenneth
Reich, *Los Angeles Times*
*May 9, 1975p*

## 492. Grace Stone Coates
(1881–?)
\* \* \*

1 Now, no doubt, my friend and I
Will proceed to lie and lie
To ourselves, till we begin
To act the truth and call it sin.
"As It Is"

## 493. Alice Corbin
(1881–1949)
\* \* \*

1 Then welcome Age and fear not sorrow;
Today's no better than tomorrow.
"Two Voices"

2 I know we grow more lovely
Growing wise.
Ibid.

## 494. Rose Macaulay
(1881–1958)

1 "You, you see, have seemed equally happy for
a time, equally unhappy after a time, in all the
creeds or no-creeds. And equally good, my
dear. I suppose I may say that I believe in
none of them, or believe in all. In any case, it
matters very little."
*Told by an Idiot*, Pt. I, Ch. 14
*1923*

2 Decades have a delusive edge to them. They are
not, of course, really periods at all, except as
any other ten years would be. But we, looking
at them, are caught by the different name each
bears, and give them different attributes, and
tie labels on them, as if they were flowers in a
border.
Ibid., Pt. II, Ch. 1

3 Sleeping in a bed—it is, apparently, of immense
importance. Against those who sleep, from
choice or necessity, elsewhere society feels
righteously hostile. It is not done. It is dis-
orderly, anarchical.
"Beds and 'Omes," *A Casual*
*Commentary* 1925

4 Does conduct rank with food, wine, and
weather as a department of life in which goodness is almost universally admired?
Ibid., "A Platonic Affection"

5 Cranks live by theory, not by pure desire. They
want votes, peace, nuts, liberty, and spinning-
looms not because they love these things, as a
child loves jam, but because they think they
ought to have them. That is one element which
makes the crank.
Ibid., "Cranks"

6 Yet, because prolonged anarchy is impossible
to man's law-bound nature, as to that of the
universe which bore him, each attempt at it
defeats itself. . . .
*Catchwords and Claptrap* 1926

7 . . . he desired to exaggerate. And here we
have what may be called a primary human
need, which should be placed by psychologists
with the desire for nourishment, for safety, for
sense-gratifications, and for appreciation, as one
of the elemental lusts of man.
Ibid.

8 In our attacks on conduct we mislike, we wave
the corpses of women and children about us like
banners as we charge.
Ibid.

9 "The century of the common man": ominous
phrase, that he and his friends like to turn on
their tongues with relishing distaste; lacking
this bogy, this sense of there being massed
against them a Philistine, vocal army terrible
with slogans, illiterate cries, and destructive

leveling aims, the young gentlemen would have been less happy, less themselves.
*The World My Wilderness*, Ch. 2
*1950*

10 . . . the desire not to work; indeed, I share it to the full. As to one's country, why should one feel any more interest in its welfare than in that of any other countries? And as to the family, I have never understood how that fits in with the other ideals—or, indeed, why it should be an ideal at all. A group of closely related persons living under one roof; it is a convenience, often a necessity, sometimes a pleasure, sometimes the reverse; but who first exalted it as admirable, an almost religious ideal?
Ibid., Ch. 20

11 "Take my camel, dear," said my aunt Dot, as she climbed down from this animal on her return from High Mass.
*The Towers of Trebizond*, Ch. 1
*1956*

## 495. Anna Pavlova
### (1881–1931)

1 . . . although one may fail to find happiness in theatrical life, one never wishes to give it up after having once tasted its fruits. To enter the School of the Imperial Ballet is to enter a convent whence frivolity is banned, and where merciless discipline reigns.
"Pages of My Life," *Pavlova: A Biography*, A. H. Franks, ed.
*1956p*

2 As is the case in all branches of art, success depends in a very large measure upon individual initiative and exertion, and cannot be achieved except by dint of hard work. Even after having reached perfection, a ballerina may never indulge in idleness.
Ibid.

3 To tend, unfailingly, unflinchingly, towards a goal, is the secret of success. But success? What exactly is success? For me it is to be found not in applause, but in the satisfaction of feeling that one is realising one's ideal. When a small child . . . I thought that success spelled happiness. I was wrong. Happiness is like a butterfly which appears and delights us for one brief moment, but soon flits away.
Ibid.

## 496. Mary Heaton Vorse
### (1881–1966)

1 "Some folks is born in the world feeling it and knowing it in their hearts that creation don't

stop where the sight of the eyes stop, and the thinner the veil is the better, and something in them sickens when the veil gets too thick."
"The Other Room," *McCall's* *1919*

2 He had seized the one loophole that life had given her and had infused her relentless courage into another's veins.
"The Wallow of the Sea," *Harper's*
*1921*

## 497. Mary Webb
### (1881–1927)

1 The past is only the present become invisible and mute; and because it is invisible and mute, its memoried glances and its murmurs are infinitely precious. We are tomorrow's past.
*Precious Bane*, Foreword *1924*

2 It made me gladsome to be getting some education, it being like a big window opening.
Ibid., Bk. I, Ch. 5

3 Saddle your dreams afore you ride 'em.
Ibid., Ch. 6

4 If you stop to be kind, you must swerve often from your path.
Ibid., Bk. II, Ch. 3

5 It's the folks that depend on us for this and for the other that we most do miss.
Ibid., Bk. IV, Ch. 4

## 498. Marie Bonaparte
### (1882–1962)

1 The residue of virility in the woman's [sexual] organism is utilized by nature in order to eroticize her: otherwise the functioning of the maternal apparatus would wholly submerge her in the painful tasks of reproduction and motherhood.
"Passivity, Masochism, and Femininity" (1934), *International Journal of Psycho-Analysis*, Vol. 16 *1935*

2 On the one hand, then, in the reproduction functions proper—menstruation, defloration, pregnancy and parturition—woman is biologically doomed to suffer. Nature seems to have no hesitation in administering to her strong doses of pain, and she can do nothing but submit passively to the regimen prescribed. On the other hand, as regards sexual attraction, which is necessary for the act of impregnation, and as regards the erotic pleasure experienced during the act itself, the woman may be on equal footing with the man.
Ibid.

3 Now every living organism dreads invasion from without, and this is a dread bound up with life itself and governed by the biological law of self-preservation. Moreover . . . little girls . . . bear imprinted on their minds from earliest childhood the terrifying vision of a sexual attack by a man upon a woman, which they believe to be the cause of the [menstrual] bleeding. It follows therefore that, in spite of the instinct, which urges them forward, they draw back from the feminine erotic function itself, although of all the reproductive functions of woman this is the only one which should really be free from suffering and purely pleasurable. *Ibid.*

## 499. Charlotte Brown
### (1882–1961)

1 . . . I propose the raising of dollars to $500,000 as an endowment. . . . This seems tremendous, I know, for me to undertake but folks don't seem to pay much attention nowadays to anything that's small and a fund like this places a sort of permanence to the thing.
> Letter to Mr. and Mrs. Galen Stone
> (June 19, 1920), *Black Women
> in White America*, Gerda Lerner, ed.
> *1972p*

2 A few of us must be sacrificed perhaps in order to get a step further.
> Ibid., Letter to F. P. Hobgood, Jr.
> (October 19, 1921)

3 Now that things are turning and many are opening their eyes to what I've tried to do and desiring to have a share in the same, the question in my heart and mind, and God only knows how it hurts, is just what are they going to ask me to submit to as a negro woman to get their interest for there are some men who occupy high places who feel that no negro woman whether she be cook, criminal or principal of a school should ever be addressed as *Mrs.*    Ibid., Letter Fragment

4 As a part of my argument for education for Negroes I used the incident as illustration that most white people looked upon every Negro, regardless of his appearance, modulated tones that reflected some culture and training, as a servant. . . .
> Ibid., Autobiographical Sketch

## 500. Susan Glaspell
### (1882–1948)

1 HENRIETTA. It is through suppression that hells are formed in us.
> *Suppressed Desires*, Sc. 1    *1914*

2 MABEL. I think it's perfectly wonderful! Why, if it wasn't for psychoanalysis you'd never find out how wonderful your own mind is!
> Ibid., Sc. 2

3 "We live close together and we live far apart. We all go through the same things—it's all just a different kind of the same thing!"
> "A Jury of Her Peers," *Every Week
> 1917*

4 FATHER. But in a world that won't have visions —why not study Sanscrit while such a world is being made over—into another such world.
> *Bernice*, Act I    *1919*

5 Those who were neither mourning nor rejoicing were being kept awake by mourners or rejoicers. All the while, diluted whiskey that could be bought on the quiet was in use for the deadening or the heightening of emotion.
> "Government Goat," *The Pictorial
> Review    1919*

6 GRANDMOTHER. That's the worst of a war—you have to go on hearing about it so long.
> *Inheritors*, Act I    *1921*

7 GRANDMOTHER. Seems nothing draws men together like killing other men.    *Ibid.*

8 HOLDEN. And I think a society which permits things to go on which I can prove go on in our federal prisons had better stop and take a fresh look at itself. To stand for that and then talk of democracy and idealism—oh, it shows no mentality, for one thing.
> Ibid., Act II, Sc. 2

9 A new town was only the same town in a different place. . . .
> "His Smile," *The Pictorial Review
> 1921*

## 501. Emma Jung
### (1882–1955)

1 Neither arrogance nor presumption drives us to the audacity of wanting to be like God—that is, like man; we are not like Eve of old, lured by the beauty of the fruit of the tree of knowledge, nor does the snake encourage us to enjoy it. No, there has come to us something like a command; we are confronted with the necessity of biting into this apple, whether we think it good to eat or not, confronted with the fact that the paradise of naturalness and unconsciousness, in which many of us would only too gladly tarry, is gone forever.
> "On the Nature of Animus" (1931),
> *Animus and Anima    1957p*

2 The real thinking of woman . . . is preeminently practical and applied. It is something we describe as sound common sense, and is usually directed to what is close at hand and personal. . . . In general, it can be said that feminine mentality manifests an undeveloped, childlike, or primitive character; instead of the thirst for knowledge, curiosity; instead of judgment, prejudice; instead of thinking, imagination or dreaming; instead of will, wishing. Where a man takes up objective problems, a woman contents herself with solving riddles; where he battles for knowledge and understanding, she contents herself with faith or superstition, or else she makes assumptions.
Ibid.

3 Very frequently, feminine activity also expresses itself in what is largely a retrospectively oriented pondering over what we ought to have done differently in life, and how we ought to have done it; or, as if under compulsion, we make up strings of causal connections. We like to call this thinking; though, on the contrary, it is a form of mental activity that is strangely pointless and unproductive, a form that really leads only to self-torture.     Ibid.

4 And now we come to the 'magic of words. A word, also, just like an idea, a thought, has the effect of reality upon undifferentiated minds. Our Biblical myth of creation, for instance, where the world grows out of the spoken word of the Creator, is an expression of this.
Ibid.

5 For by her unconsciousness, woman exerts a magical influence on man, a charm that lends her power over him. Because she feels this power instinctively and does not wish to lose it, she often resists to the utmost the process of becoming conscious. . . . Many men take pleasure in woman's unconsciousness. They are bent on opposing her development of greater consciousness in every possible way, because it seems to them uncomfortable and unnecessary.
Ibid.

6 Learning to cherish and emphasize feminine values is the primary condition of our holding our own against the masculine principle. . . .
Ibid.

## 502.  Winifred Letts
### (1882–?)

1 Age after age the children give
Their lives that Herod still may live.
"The Children's Ghosts,"<br>
Hallow-e'en, and Poems of War<br>
1916

2 God rest you, happy gentlemen,
  Who laid your good lives down,
Who took the khaki and the gun
  Instead of cap and gown.
"The Spires of Oxford," St. 4,<br>
The Spires of Oxford and<br>
Other Poems     1917

* * *

3 I do be thinking God must laugh
The time he makes a boy,
All element the creatures are,
And divilment and joy.
"Boys"

4 That God once loved a garden
We learn in Holy writ.
And seeing gardens in the spring
I well can credit it.
"Stephen's Green," St. 1

## 503.  Anne O'Hare McCormick
### (1882?–1954)

1 Whoever goes to Russia discovers Russia.
The Hammer and the Scythe, Ch. 1<br>
1927

2 The peasant wanders; he is still a nomad, a creature of pilgrimages and excursions, harnessed to rather than rooted in the soil.
Ibid., Ch. 6

3 There is no place where you can see more human nature in a few hours than in a session of the Parliament of Italy, and no place where you are more impressed by the unchanging tradition of the Catholic Church than at a consistory at the Vatican.
"A Papal Consistory and a Political<br>
Debut" (July 24, 1921), Vatican<br>
Journal, 1921–1954, Marion<br>
Turner Sheehan, ed.     1957p

4 A new Italy demands a new Rome.
Ibid., "A New Rome Arises to Rival<br>
the Old" (January 16, 1927)

5 One little angry, brooding man [Hitler] has put the whole world on wartime. A man who could never keep step with anybody has forced millions of free and intelligent human beings to keep the time he sets.
Ibid., "Reflections in Time of War"<br>
(April 4, 1942)

6 For what is the naked issue of the most universal war in history but the right of man to be himself?
Ibid., "Where the Christmas Lights<br>
Are Out" (December 25, 1943)

## 504. Sylvia Pankhurst

(1882–1960)

1 English is the most modern of the great languages, the most widely spoken, and the most international. . . . Its swiftness and transparent accuracy of expression, and especially the fact that it has shed most of the old grammatical forms which time has rendered useless and scarcely intelligible, have made English a model, pointing the way which must be followed in building the Interlanguage. . . .
*Delphos*, Ch. 5     *1926*

2 The Interlanguage will provide a means by which the thoughts and emotions of mankind, as expressed in language, may achieve a world-comprehension, which is to-day possible only in music. There is work here for our teachers and students, our pacifists, and our sociologists. Let them rally to the standard of Interlanguage— to perfect it, and to advance it.     Ibid., Ch. 7

3 We do not make beams from the hollow, decaying trunk of the fallen oak. We use the upsoaring tree in the full vigour of its sap.
Quoted in the *Evening Standard*
(London)     *March 5, 1930*

4 Hourly the War drew nearer; threat followed threat; ultimatum, ultimatum. My mind shrank from the menace sweeping down on us, as children's do from belief in death and misfortune, vainly clinging to the fancy that great disasters only happen to other people.
*The Home Front*, Ch. 1     *1932*

5 The machinery of succour might be preparing; but the people were hungry.     Ibid., Ch. 2

6 I could not give my name to aid the slaughter in this war, fought on both sides for grossly material ends, which did not justify the sacrifice of a single mother's son. Clearly I must continue to oppose it, and expose it, to all whom I could reach with voice or pen.
Ibid., Ch. 25

7 Racked with pain, prostrate with headache, at times I might be, yet within me was a rage at this merciless War, this squalor of poverty! Oh! that all the wealth and effort the nation was squandering might be to rebuild these slums, to restore these faded women, these starved and stunted children.     Ibid., Ch. 58

8 The cause of Ethiopia cannot be divorced from the cause of international justice, which is permanent and is not to be determined by ephemeral military victories. . . . *New Times* is opposed to the conception of dictatorship. It understands that Fascism destroys all personal liberty and is in fundamental opposition to all forms of intellectual and moral progress.
Quoted in the *New Times &*
*Ethiopia News*     *May 5, 1936*

9 My belief in the growth and permanence of democracy is undimmed. I know that the people will cast off the new dictatorships as they did the old. I believe as firmly as in my youth that humanity will surmount the era of poverty and war. Life will be happier and more beautiful for all. I believe in the GOLDEN AGE.
Essay in *Myself When Young*,
Margot Asquith, ed.     *1938*

10 The discerning traveler who records what appears to the citizens of a country [to be] commonplace performs a service to posterity.
*Ethiopia*, Preface     *1955*

11 I am proud to call myself a Bolshevist.
Article in *Dreadnought* (1918),
Quoted in *The Fighting Pankhursts*
by David Mitchell     *1967p*

12 We have only one life in this world. Can't we see the revolution in our time? Can't we live in it and enjoy it? I want to see the beginning. I want to see something done. When are you going to begin? If the police came here tonight and killed some of us, I think it would do a great deal of good!
Ibid., Speech, "Hands Off Russia"
Rally, London (January, 1919)

13 . . . but all my experience showed that it was useless trying to palliate an impossible system. It is a *wrong* system and has got to be smashed. I would give my life to smash it. You cannot frighten me with any sentence you may impose. . . . You will not stop this agitation. The words that are being written in my paper [*Dreadnought*] will be as common as daily bread.     Ibid., Courtroom Speech
(October 28, 1919)

14 I have gone to war too. . . . I am going to fight capitalism even if it kills me. It is wrong that people like you should be comfortable and well fed while all around you people are starving.     Ibid. (January, 1921)

15 Love and freedom are vital to the creation and upbringing of a child. I do not advise anyone to rush into either legal or free marriage without love, sympathy, understanding, friendship and frankness. These are essentials, and having these, no legal forms are necessary. Indifference, hostility and compulsion are the factors to be feared, and the influences that lead to sorrow for the individual and danger to the progress of the race.
Ibid., Article in *News of the World*
(April, 1928)

16 Socialism is the greatest thing in life for me. You will never crush it out of me or kill it. I am only one of thousands or millions. Socialists make it possible to practise what you say in church, that we should love our neighbours as ourselves. If you work against socialism, you are standing with reaction against life, standing with the dead past against the coming civilization.      *Ibid.*, Pt. II, Ch. 4

17 The emancipation of today displays itself mainly in cigarettes and shorts. There is even a reaction from the ideal of an intellectual and emancipated womanhood, for which the pioneers toiled and suffered, to be seen in painted lips and nails, and the return of trailing skirts and other absurdities of dress which betoken the slave-woman's intelligent companionship.      *Ibid.*, Pt. V, Ch. 3

## 505. Frances Perkins
### (1882–1965)

1 In America, public opinion is the leader.      *People at Work*, Sec. I    1934

2 But with the slow menace of a glacier, depression came on. No one had any measure of its progress; no one had any plan for stopping it. Everyone tried to get out of its way.      *Ibid.*, Sec. IV

3 To one who believes that really good industrial conditions are the hope for a machine civilization, nothing is more heartening than to watch conference methods and education replacing police methods.      *Ibid.*, Sec. VIII

4 The quality of his [F. D. Roosevelt] being one with the people, of having no artificial or natural barriers between him and them, made it possible for him to be a leader without ever being or thinking of being a dictator.      *The Roosevelt I Knew*, Ch. 7    1946

5 He [F. D. Roosevelt] didn't like concentrated responsibility. Agreement with other people who he thought were good, right-minded, and trying to do the right thing by the world was almost as necessary to him as air to breathe.      *Ibid.*, Ch. 12

## 506. Mabel Ulrich
### (1882?–?)

1 A man, it seems, may be intellectually in complete sympathy with a woman's aims. But only about ten percent of him is his intellect—the other ninety his emotions.      "A Doctor's Diary, 1904–1932," *Scribner's Magazine*    June, 1933

2 It can't be so easy being the husband of a "modern" woman. She is everything his mother wasn't—and nothing she was.      *Ibid.*

3 But, oh, what a woman I should be if an able young man would consecrate his life to me as secretaries and technicians do to their men employers.      *Ibid.*

4 Verily what bishops are to the English, bankers are to Americans.      *Ibid.*

## 507. Virginia Verona
### (1882– )

1 I blame the unions, first, last and all the time. The nation has gotten to the place where unskilled labor is getting paid more than skilled. The unions have gone too far. They rule this country, and they have no compassion, no mercy for people, not even other union members.      Quoted in "Fighting for Her—and Our—Rights" by Ursula Vils, *Los Angeles Times* *January 5, 1975*

2 People are too easygoing. The American people will not stand up for their rights. They'll be violent, of course, but they will not stand up for their rights.      *Ibid.*

## 508. Virginia Woolf
### (1882–1941)

1 "Doesn't one always think of the past, in a garden with men and women lying under the trees? Aren't they one's past, all that remains of it, those men and women, those ghosts lying under the trees . . . one's happiness, one's reality?"      *Kew Gardens*    1919

2 Desiring truth, awaiting it, laboriously distilling a few words, for ever desiring . . . truth.      "Monday or Tuesday," *Monday or Tuesday*    1921

3 Life's what you see in people's eyes; life's what they learn, and having learnt it, never, though they seek to hide it, cease to be aware of what? That life's like that, it seems.      *Ibid.*, "An Unwritten Novel"

4 We all know—the *Times* knows—but we pretend we don't.      *Ibid.*

5 The eyes of others our prisons; their thoughts our cages.      *Ibid.*

6 But when the self speaks to the self, who is speaking?—the entombed soul, the spirit driven in, in, in to the central catacomb; the self that took the veil and left the world—a coward perhaps, yet somehow beautiful, as it flits with its lantern restlessly up and down the dark corridors. *Ibid.*

7 Life's bare as a bone. *Ibid.*

8 I too sit passive on a gilt chair, only turning the earth above a buried memory, as we all do, for there are signs, if I'm not mistaken, that we're all recalling something, furtively seeking something. *Ibid.*, "The String Quartet"

9 How lovely goodness is in those who, stepping lightly, go smiling through the world! *Ibid.*

10 The older one grows the more one likes indecency. *Ibid.*

11 In people's eyes, in the swing, tramp, and trudge; in the bellow and uproar; the carriages, motor cars, omnibuses, vans, sandwich men shuffling and swinging; brass bands; barrel organs; in the triumph and the jingle and the strange high singing of some aeroplane overhead was what she loved; life; London; this moment in June. *Mrs. Dalloway* 1925

12 The word-coining genius, as if thought plunged into a sea of words and came up dripping. "An Elizabethan Play," *The Common Reader* 1925

13 Those comfortably padded lunatic asylums which are known, euphemistically, as the stately homes of England. *Ibid.*, "Lady Dorothy Nevill"

14 Trivial personalities decomposing in the eternity of print. *Ibid.*, "The Modern Essay"

15 The beauty of the world has two edges, one of laughter, one of anguish, cutting the heart asunder. *A Room of One's Own* 1929

16 If truth is not to be found on the shelves of the British Museum, where, I asked myself, picking up a notebook and a pencil, is truth? *Ibid.*, Ch. 2

17 How shall I ever find the grains of truth embedded in all this mass of paper? *Ibid.*

18 Why are women . . . so much more interesting to men than men are to women? *Ibid.*

19 Yet it is in our idleness, in our dreams, that the submerged truth sometimes comes to the top. *Ibid.*

20 When an arguer argues dispassionately he thinks only of the argument. *Ibid.*

21 Without self-confidence we are as babes in the cradle. And how can we generate this imponderable quality, which is yet so invaluable, most quickly? By thinking that other people are inferior to oneself. *Ibid.*

22 Women have served all these centuries as looking-glasses possessing the magic and delicious power of reflecting the figure of man at twice its natural size. *Ibid.*

23 Indeed, I thought, slipping the silver into my purse, it is remarkable, remembering the bitterness of those days, what a change of temper a fixed income will bring about. *Ibid.*

24 Great bodies of people are never responsible for what they do. *Ibid.*

25 . . . for fiction, imaginative work that is, is not dropped like a pebble upon the ground, as science may be; fiction is like a spider's web, attached ever so lightly perhaps, but still attached to life at all four corners. *Ibid.*, Ch. 3

26 . . . women have burnt like beacons in all the works of all the poets from the beginning of time. *Ibid.*

27 When, however, one reads of a witch being ducked, of a woman possessed by devils, of a wise woman selling herbs, or even a very remarkable man who had a mother, then I think we are on the track of a lost novelist, a suppressed poet . . . indeed, I would venture to guess that Anon, who wrote so many poems without signing them, was often a woman. *Ibid.*

28 Chastity . . . has, even now, a relative importance in a woman's life, and has so wrapped itself round with nerves and instincts that to cut it free and bring it to the light of day demands courage of the rarest. *Ibid.*

29 For surely it is time that the effect of discouragement upon the mind of the artist should be measured, as I have seen a dairy company measure the effect of ordinary milk and Grade A milk upon the body of the rat. *Ibid.*

30 The history of men's opposition to women's emancipation is more interesting perhaps than the story of that emancipation itself. *Ibid.*

31 Literature is strewn with the wreckage of men who have minded beyond reason the opinions of others. *Ibid.*

32 . . . the mind of an artist, in order to achieve the prodigious effort of freeing whole and entire the work that is in him, must be incandescent. . . . There must be no obstacle in it, no foreign matter unconsumed. *Ibid.*

33 . . . virility has now become self-conscious.
Ibid., Ch. 6

34 . . . it is fatal for anyone who writes to think of their sex. It is fatal to be a man or woman pure and simple; one must be woman-manly or man-womanly. Ibid.

35 . . . anything written with . . . conscious bias is doomed to death. Ibid.

36 Everybody looked overdressed or badly dressed —some, indeed, looked positively dirty beside him. His clothes seemed to melt into each other with the perfection of their cut and the quiet harmony of their color. Without a single point of emphasis everything was distinguished. . . . He was the personification of freshness and cleanliness and order.
"Beau Brummell," *The Second Common Reader*    1932

37 And then he said very cutting things about other people. They were not exactly witty; they were certainly not profound; but they were so skillful, so adroit—they had a twist in them which made them slip into the mind and stay there when more important phrases were forgotten.
Ibid.

38 To enjoy freedom, if the platitude is pardonable, we have of course to control ourselves. We must not squander our powers, helplessly and ignorantly, squirting half the house in order to water a single rose-bush; we must train them, exactly and powerfully, here on the very spot.
Ibid., "How Should One Read a Book?"

39 I have sometimes dreamt, at least, that when the Day of Judgment dawns and the great conquerors and lawyers and statesmen come to receive their rewards—their crowns, their laurels, their names carved indelibly upon imperishable marble—the Almighty will turn to Peter and will say, not without a certain envy when he sees us coming with our books under our arms, "Look, these need no reward. They have nothing to give them here. They have loved reading." Ibid.

40 But what have I done with my life? thought Mrs. Ramsay, taking her place at the head of the table, and looking at all the plates making white circles on it. *To the Lighthouse* 1937

41 She took up once more her old painting position with the dim eyes and the absent-minded manner, subduing all her impressions as a woman, to something more general; becoming once more under the power of that vision which she had been clearly once and must now grope for among hedges and houses and children—her picture. Ibid.

42 If people are highly successful in their professions they lose their senses. Sight goes. They have no time to look at pictures. Sound goes. They have no time to listen to music. Speech goes. They have no time for conversation. They lose their sense of proportion—the relations between one thing and another. Humanity goes. . . . *Three Guineas* 1938

43 How can we enter the professions and yet remain civilized human beings? Ibid.

44 To make ideas effective, we must be able to fire them off. We must put them into action. . . . "I will not cease from mental fight," Blake wrote. Mental fight means thinking against the current, not with it. The current flows fast and furious. It issues a spate of words from the loudspeakers and the politicians. Every day they tell us that we are a free people fighting to defend freedom. That is the current that has whirled the young airman up into the sky and keeps him circulating there among the clouds. Down here, with a roof to cover us and a gas mask handy, it is our business to puncture gas bags and discover the seeds of truth.
Article in the *New Republic* October 21, 1940

45 Surely it was time someone invented a new plot, or that the author came out from the bushes. *Between the Acts* 1941

46 If you do not tell the truth about yourself you cannot tell it about other people.
*The Moment and Other Essays* 1952p

47 It is worth mentioning, for future reference, that the creative power which bubbles so pleasantly in beginning a new book quiets down after a time, and one goes on more steadily. Doubts creep in. Then one becomes resigned. Determination not to give in, and the sense of an impending shape keep one at it more than anything. *A Writer's Diary* (May 11, 1919), Leonard Woolf, ed. 1954p

48 Why is life so tragic; so like a little strip of pavement over an abyss. I look down; I feel giddy; I wonder how I am ever to walk to the end. Ibid. (October 25, 1920)

49 But as I said, I must face the despicable vanity which is at the root of all this niggling and haggling. Ibid. (April 8, 1921)

50 I get such a sense of tingling and vitality from an evening's talk like that; one's angularities and obscurities are smoothed and lit.
Ibid. (October 27, 1928)

51 How physical the sense of triumph and relief is!
Ibid. (February 7, 1931)

52 Odd how the creative power at once brings the whole universe to order.

Ibid. (July 27, 1934)

53 I mark Henry James' sentence: observe perpetually. Observe the oncome of age. Observe greed. Observe my own despondency. By that means it becomes serviceable.

Ibid. (March 8, 1941)

54 Occupation is essential.       Ibid.

## 509. Dorothy Brett

(1883–?)

1 She [Mabel Dodge] had an insatiable appetite for tasting life in all its aspects. She tasted and spat it out.

"My Long and Beautiful Journey,"
*South Dakota Review*
*Summer, 1967*

## 510. Nannie Helen Burroughs

(1883–1961)

1 In fact, America will destroy herself and revert to barbarism if she continues to cultivate the things of the flesh and neglect the higher virtues. The Negro must not, therefore, contribute to her doom, but must ransom her. Furthermore it will profit the Negro nothing to enter into ungodly competition for material possessions when he has gifts of greater value.

"With All They Getting,"
*The Southern Workman*
*July, 1927*

2 When the Negro learns what manner of man he is spiritually, he will wake up all over. He will stop playing white even on the stage. He will rise in the majesty of his own soul. He will glorify the beauty of his own brown skin. He will stop thinking white and go to thinking straight and living right. He will realize that wrong-reaching, wrong-bleaching and wrong-mixing have "most nigh ruin't him" and he will redeem his body and rescue his soul from the bondage of that death. . . .       Ibid.

3 The aim of the National Training School is to give a training of head, hand and heart and develop a definite and active social interest in the spiritual and moral forces that make the human welfare. . . .     Quoted in "That's Nannie Burroughs' Job, And She Does It" by Floyd Calvin, *Pittsburgh Courier*
*June 8, 1929*

4 Chloroform your "Uncle Toms." The Negro must unload the leeches and parasitic leaders who are absolutely eating the life out of the struggling, desiring mass of people. Negroes like that went out of style seventy years ago. They are relics and good for museums.

Article in *The Louisiana Weekly*
*December 23, 1933*

5 Don't wait for deliverers. . . . I like that quotation, "Moses, my servant, is dead. Therefore, arise and go over Jordan." There are no deliverers. They're all dead. We must arise and go over Jordan. We can take the promised land.

Ibid.

6 This nation openly endorses, tolerates and legalizes the very abuses against which she originally waged a bloody revolution. A colored boy, a nickel penknife and a screaming woman were no more the cause of the Harlem uprising in 1935 than was a shipload of tea in the Boston harbor, in 1773, the cause of the Revolutionary War.     "Declaration of 1776 Is Cause of Harlem Riot," *The Afro-American*
*April 13, 1935*

7 The framers of the Declaration of Independence prophesied that uprisings would occur "in the course of human events," if people are denied those inalienable rights to which the "laws of nature and of nature's God entitle them." Reread their prophecy. . . . If that's Red, then the writers of the Declaration of Independence were very Red. They told Americans not to stand injustice after "patient sufferance."

Ibid.

8 We specialize in the wholly impossible.

Motto, National Training School for
Girls, Washington, D.C. (c.1909),
*Black Women in White America,*
Gerda Lerner, ed.     *1972p*

## 511. Coco Chanel

(1883–1971)

1 There goes a woman who knows all the things that can be taught and none of the things that cannot be taught.

Quoted in *Coco Chanel, Her Life, Her Secrets* by Marcel Haedrich    *1971*

2 Youth is something very new: twenty years ago no one mentioned it.       Ibid.

3 A fashion for the young? That is a pleonasm: there is no fashion for the old.     Ibid.

4 Great loves too must be endured.     Ibid.

5 You see, that's what fame is: solitude.
Ibid.

6 My friends, there are no friends. Ibid.

7 Since everything is in our heads, we had better not lose them. Ibid.

8 Legend is the consecration of fame. Ibid.

9 I am no longer what I was. I will remain what I have become. Ibid.

10 Silence is the cruelty of the provincial. Ibid.

11 "Where should one use perfume?" a young woman asked. "Wherever one wants to be kissed," I said. Ibid.

12 Love? For whom? An old man? How horrible. A young man? How shameful. Ibid.

13 Elegance does not consist in putting on a new dress. Ibid.

14 I am doing an optimistic collection because things are going badly. Ibid.

15 Fashion is architecture: it is a matter of proportions. Ibid.

16 Nothing is ugly as long as it is alive. Ibid.

17 In order to be irreplaceable one must always be different. Ibid.

## 512. Imogen Cunningham
### (1883–1976)

1 People who are living aren't famous—they're just infamous. Quoted in *Never Give Up*, a Film by Ann Hershey 1975

2 One thing about being born without beauty—you don't look for it. Ibid.

## 513. Elsa Maxwell
### (1883–1963)

1 Fade little searchlight, fade forever.
Please go without a fuss,
For you don't interfere
With the Zeppelins, dear,
But you do interfere with us.
"Shine Little Searchlight" 1912

2 I married the world—the world is my husband. That is why I'm so young. No sex. Sex is the most tiring thing in the world.
"I Married the World," *This Fabulous Century: 1930–1940* 1940

3 First I want a woman guest to be beautiful. Second, I want her to be beautifully dressed. Third, I demand animation and vivacity. Fourth, not too many brains. Brains are always awkward at a gay and festive party.
Interview, *New York Mirror* 1938

4 Most rich people are the poorest people I know. *R.S.V.P.*, Ch. 1 1954

5 Giving parties is a trivial avocation, but it pays the dues for my union card in humanity.
Ibid., Ch. 16

6 Intolerance of mediocrity has been the main prop of my independence. . . . Ibid.

7 Yet "old friends" always seemed a contradiction to me. Age cannot wither nor custom stale the infinite variety of friends who, as long as you know them, remain as vibrant and stimulating as the day you first met them. Ibid.

8 I have lived by my wits all my life and I thank the Lord they are still in one, whole piece. I don't need glasses, Benzedrine or a psychiatrist. Ibid.

9 Anatomize the character of a successful hostess and the knife will lay bare the fact that she owes her position to one of three things: either she is liked, or she is feared, or she is important. *How to Do It*, Ch. 3 1957

## 514. Frances Newman
### (1883?–1928)

1 . . . she did not understand how her father could have reached such age and such eminence without learning that all mothers are as infallible as any pope and more righteous than any saint. *The Hard-Boiled Virgin* 1926

2 Katherine Faraday's mother had heard in her cradle that a nation which could prefer a Lincoln to a Breckenridge was unlikely to return to the conviction that elegance is the greatest of human virtues, and she had even heard delicate suggestions that a god who could look down unmoved on the triumph of a Grant over a Lee could hardly expect to be acquitted of increasingly Democratic sympathies. Ibid.

3 For the first time, she realised that conversation might have been entirely satisfactory if women had been allowed to admit they understood the limited number of subjects men were interested in, and she was so excited by her idea that she almost committed the social crime of allowing a conversation to pause. Ibid.

4 And while she wondered at all the things civilization can teach a woman to endure, she was able to take Mrs. Abbott's departing hand, and to watch Mrs. Abbott walk out of a door into the temporary silence civilization would require of her until she found another acquaintance on whom her conversation could pour as if she were emerging from a year and a day of solitary confinement.
*Dead Lovers Are Faithful Lovers*
*1928*

5 But she was disturbed when her mind astonished something which she did not think was her mind, and which she called herself.
Ibid.

## 515. Mabel Louise Robinson
### (1883?–1962)

1 "Can't you have sense?"
Thankful, [the girl] hurried him on. "Not if I can have anything else."
*Bright Island*, Pt. I     *1937*

2 We have thought that because children are young they are silly. We have forgotten the blind stirrings, the reaching outward of our own youth.
"Writing for the Younger Generation,"
*The Writer's Book*,
Helen Hull, ed.     *1950*

3 What if the truth does make them sad, what if it haunts them? Better be saddened than dead.
Ibid.

4 If this generation, like those before it, repeats the blunders of the past, we might possibly be to some degree at fault.
Ibid.

5 From the dog's point of view his master is an elongated and abnormally cunning dog.
Quoted in *The New York Times Magazine*    *May 14, 1967p*

## 516. Margaret Sanger
### (1883–1966)

1 Women of the working class, especially wage workers, should not have more than two children at most. The average working man can support no more and the average working woman can take care of no more in decent fashion.    *Family Limitations*    *1917*

2 A mutual and satisfied sexual act is of great benefit to the average woman, the magnetism of it is health giving. When it is not desired on the part of the woman and she has no response,

*it should not take place.* This is an act of prostitution and is degrading to the woman's finer sensibility, all the marriage certificates on earth to the contrary notwithstanding.    Ibid.

3 The problem of birth control has arisen directly from the effort of the feminine spirit to free itself from bondage.
*Women and the New Race*    *1920*

4 A free race cannot be born of slave mothers.
Ibid.

5 Women are too much inclined to follow in the footsteps of men, to try to think as men think, to try to solve the general problems of life as men solve them. . . . The woman is not needed to do man's work. She is not needed to think man's thoughts. . . . Her mission is not to enhance the masculine spirit, but to express the feminine; hers is not to preserve a man-made world, but to create a human world by the infusion of the feminine element into all of its activities.    Ibid.

6 Woman must not accept; she must challenge. She must not be awed by that which has been built up around her; she must reverence that woman in her which struggles for expression.
Ibid.

7 She goes through the vale of death alone, each time a babe is born.    Ibid.

8 Diplomats make it their business to conceal the facts. . . .    Ibid.

9 Behind all war has been the pressure of population . . . let countries become overpopulated and war is inevitable. It follows as daylight follows the sunrise. . . .    Ibid.

10 . . . behind all the slogans and shibboleths coined out of the ideals of the peoples for the uses of imperialism, women must and will see the iron hand of that same imperialism, condemning women to breed and men to die for the will of the rulers.    Ibid.

11 Upon women the burden and the horrors of war are heaviest. . . . When she sees what lies behind the glory and the horror, the boasting and the burden, and gets the vision, the human perspective, she will end war. She will kill war by the simple process of starving it to death. For she will refuse longer to produce the human food upon which the monster feeds.    Ibid.

12 When we voice, then, the necessity of setting the feminine spirit utterly and absolutely free, thought turns naturally not to rights of the woman, nor indeed of the mother, but to the rights of the child—of all children in the world.    Ibid.

13 When motherhood becomes the fruit of a deep yearning, not the result of ignorance or accident, its children will become the foundation of a new race. Ibid.

14 Like begets like. We gather perfect fruit from perfect trees. . . . Abused soil brings forth stunted growths. Ibid.

15 Custom controls the sexual impulse as it controls no other.
Interview, *American Mercury* 1924

16 The menace of another pregnancy hung like a sword over the head of every poor woman. . . .
"Awakening and Revolt,"
*My Fight for Birth Control* 1931

17 "Yes, yes—I know, Doctor," said the patient with trembling voice, "but," and she hesitated as if it took all of her courage to say it, "*what* can I do to prevent getting that way again?"
"Oh ho!" laughed the doctor good naturedly. "You want your cake while you eat it too, do you? Well, it can't be done. . . . I'll tell you the only sure thing to do. Tell Jake to sleep on the roof!" Ibid.

18 I seemed chained hand and foot, and longed for an earthquake or a volcano to shake the world out of its lethargy into facing these monstrous atrocities. Ibid.

19 Awaken the womanhood of America to free the motherhood of the world! Ibid.

20 . . . there was not a darkened tenement, hovel, or flat but was brightened by the knowledge that motherhood could be voluntary; that children need not be born into the world unless they are wanted and have a place provided for them. Ibid., "A Public Nuisance"

21 . . . we were dispossessed by the law as a "public nuisance." In Holland the clinics were called "public utilities." Ibid.

22 . . . I wondered, and asked myself *what* had gone out of the race. Something had gone from them which silenced them, made them impotent to defend their rights. Ibid.

23 I was resolved to seek out the root of the evil, to do something to change the destiny of mothers whose miseries were as vast as the sky. *An Autobiography* 1938

## 517. Florida Scott-Maxwell
### (1883– )

1 Age puzzles me. I thought it was a quiet time. My seventies were interesting and fairly serene, but my eighties are passionate. I grow more intense as I age. *The Measure of My Days* 1972

2 No matter how old a mother is she watches her middle-aged children for signs of improvement. Ibid.

3 If a grandmother wants to put her foot down, the only safe place to do it these days is in a note book. Ibid.

4 Age is a desert of time—hours, days, weeks, years perhaps—with little to do. So one has ample time to face everything one has had, been, done; gather them all in: the things that came from outside, and those from inside. We have time at last to make them truly ours. Ibid.

5 You need only claim the events of your life to make yourself yours. Ibid.

6 Is there any stab as deep as wondering where and how much you failed those you loved? Ibid.

7 I wonder why love is so often equated with joy when it is everything else as well. Devastation, balm, obsession, granting and receiving excessive value, and losing it again. It is recognition, often of what you are not but might be. It sears and it heals. It is beyond pity and above law. It can seem like truth. Ibid.

8 I have made others suffer, and if there are more lives to be lived, I believe I ought to do penance for the suffering I have caused. I should experience what I have made others experience. It belongs to me, and I should learn it. Ibid.

9 Is life a pregnancy? That would make death a birth. Ibid.

10 Order, cleanliness, seemliness make a structure that is half support, half ritual, and—if it does not create it—maintains decency. Ibid.

## 518. Marguerite Wilkinson
### (1883–1928)
\* \* \*

1 God bless pawnbrokers!
They are quiet men.
"Pawnbrokers"

2 My father got me strong and straight and slim
And I give thanks to him.
My mother bore me glad and sound and sweet,
I kiss her feet!
"The End"

## 519. Laura Benét

(1884–      )

\* \* \*

1 Lost in the spiral of his conscience, he
Detachedly takes rest.
"The Snail"

2 No voice awoke. Dwelling sedate, apart
Only the thrush, the thrush that never spoke,
Sang from her bursting heart.
"The Thrush"

## 520. Helene Deutsch

(1884–      )

1 They have an extraordinary need of support
when engaged in any *activity directed outward,*
but are absolutely independent in such feeling
and thinking as related to their inner life, that
is to say, in their *activity directed inward.*
Their capacity for identification is not an expression of inner poverty but of inner wealth.
*The Psychology of Women,* Vol. I
*1944–1945*

2 All observations point to the fact that the intellectual woman is masculinized; in her, warm,
intuitive knowledge has yielded to cold unproductive thinking.                          Ibid.

3 After all, the ultimate goal of all research is
not objectivity, but truth.                 Ibid.

4 It is interesting to note that in every phase of
life feminine masochism finds some form of
expression.                          Ibid., Ch. 1

5 The very fact that the youthful soul feels
insecure strengthens its active aspiration to
master its insecurity.                 Ibid., Ch. 2

6 . . . adolescence is the period of the decisive
last battle fought before maturity. The ego
must achieve independence, the old emotional
ties must be cast off, and new ones created.
Ibid.

7 It is no exaggeration to say that among all
living creatures, only man, because of his pre-
hensile appendages, is capable of rape in the
full meaning of this term—that is, sexual possession of the female against her will.
Ibid., Ch. 6

8 The vagina—a completely passive, receptive
organ—awaits an active agent to become a
functioning excitable organ.           Ibid.

9 The embattled gates to equal rights indeed
opened up for modern women, but I sometimes think to myself: "That is not what I
meant by freedom—it is only 'social progress.' "
*Confrontations with Myself,* Ch. 1
*1973*

10 She [Rosa Luxembourg] was too great to be
considered "only a woman," even by her
enemies.                          Ibid., Ch. 7

11 Psychoanalysis was my last and most deeply
experienced revolution; and Freud, who was
rightly considered a conservative on social and
political issues, became for me the greatest
revolutionary of the century.       Ibid., Ch. 10

## 521. Caroline Giltinan

(1884–      )

\* \* \*

1 Betrayer of the Master,
He sways against the sky,
A black and broken body,
Iscariot—or I?
"Identity"

2 Let me keep my eyes on yours;
I dare not look away
Fearing again to see your feet
Cloven and of clay.
"Disillusioned"

## 522. Texas Guinan

(1884–1933)

1 Fifty million Frenchmen can't be wrong.
Quoted in the
*New York World-Telegram*
*March 21, 1931*

\* \* \*

2 I've been married once on the level, and twice
in America.                          Nightclub Act

3 Success has killed more men than bullets.
Ibid.

## 523. Rose Henniker Heaton

(1884–?)

\* \* \*

1 She left no little things behind
Excepting loving thoughts and kind.
"The Perfect Guest"

## 524. Fanny Heaslip Lea

### (1884–1955)

\*   \*   \*

1 It's odd to think we might have been
Sun, moon and stars unto each other—
Only, I turned down one little street
As you went up another.

"Fate," St. 5

## 525. Alice Roosevelt Longworth

### (1884– )

1 He [Coolidge] looks as if he had been weaned
on a pickle.     *Crowded Hours*    1934

2 Were it not for Czolgosz [the assassin of President McKinley], we'd all be back in our brownstone-front houses. That's where we'd be. And I would have married for money and been divorced for good cause.

Quoted by Jean Vanden Heuvel in the
*Saturday Evening Post*
*December 4, 1965*

3 I have a simple philosophy. Fill what's empty. Empty what's full. And scratch where it itches.

Quoted in *The Best* by Peter Russell
and Leonard Ross    1974

## 526. Adela Pankhurst

### (1884?–?)

1 We have no religious doctrine to preach, only a morality that is big enough to include all religions and that should give offence to none.

Quoted in *The Fighting Pankhursts*
by David Mitchell    1967

2 We do not want strong leaders in Parliament, but servants who will carry out the dictates of the industrial bodies.

Ibid., Article in *The Socialist*

3 Profits and prostitution—upon these empires are built and kingdoms stand. . . .

Ibid., "Communism and Social
Purity," *Dreadnought*, London
(February, 1921)

4 Their [politicians'] most outstanding characteristic, I should say, would be their inability to manage anything properly. What industry have they ever promoted but the gambling industry? What have they ever produced but strife and deficits? What resolve have they shown but a determination to grab for themselves, their friends and supporters whatever is available to grab?    Ibid., Speech (c.1929)

5 Capital and labour in alliance will require neither government control nor political interference, and the vast network of government which is impoverishing us today will become useless and will shrivel up and die away.

Ibid.

## 527. Ruth Mason Rice

### (1884–1927)

1 An oval, placid woman who assuaged men's
lives;
Her comely hands wrought forth a century
Of oval, placid women who engaged, as wives,
In broideries and tea.

"Queen Victoria," *Afterward*    1927

2 But now—a loaf's an easy thing;
Made quickly by a blind machine;
And still—I find me hungering
For fare—unseen.

Ibid., "Daily Bread"

3 Your people build—to gain the firmaments;
They dig—to reach the sunken heart of hell;
They question every answer Life presents;
For they are sons of Lucifer—who fell.
Where are you going, multitude of feet?

Ibid., "New York"

## 528. Eleanor Roosevelt

### (1884–1962)

1 No one can make you feel inferior without your
consent.     *This Is My Story*    1937

2 A democratic form of government, a democratic way of life, presupposes free public education over a long period; it presupposes also an education for personal responsibility that too often is neglected.

"Let Us Have Faith in Democracy,"
*Land Policy Review*, Department of
Agriculture    *January, 1942*

3 I think if the people of this country can be reached with the truth, their judgment will be in favor of the many, as against the privileged few.    Quoted in the *Ladies' Home Journal*
*May, 1942*

4 Perhaps in His wisdom the Almighty is trying to show us that a leader may chart the way, may point out the road to lasting peace, but that many leaders and many peoples must do the building.    "My Day" Newspaper Column
*April 16, 1945*

5 Perhaps nature is our best assurance of immortality.    Ibid.    *April 24, 1945*

6 We must be willing to learn the lesson that cooperation may imply compromise, but if it brings a world advance it is a gain for each individual nation. Ibid. *January 21, 1946*

7 I am sorry that Governments in all parts of the world have not seen fit to send more women as delegates, alternates or advisors to the Assembly [U.N.]. I think it is in these positions that the women of every nation should work to see that equality exists. Ibid. *January 28, 1946*

8 None of us has lived up to the teachings of Christ. Ibid. *February 14, 1946*

9 It is not fair to ask of others what you are not willing to do yourself. Ibid. *June 15, 1946*

10 If I do not run for office, I am not beholden to my Party. What I give, I give freely and I am too old to want to be curtailed in any way in the expression of my own thinking. "Why I Do Not Choose to Run," *Look July 9, 1946*

11 . . . a trait no other nation seems to possess in quite the same degree that we do—namely, a feeling of almost childish injury and resentment unless the world as a whole recognizes how innocent we are of anything but the most generous and harmless intentions. "My Day" Newspaper Column *November 11, 1946*

12 It is very difficult to have a free, fair and honest press anywhere in the world. In the first place, as a rule, papers are largely supported by advertising, and that immediately gives the advertisers a certain hold over the medium which they use. *If You Ask Me 1946*

13 It is not that you set the individual apart from society but that you recognize in any society that the individual must have rights that are guarded. Quoted in *The New York Times February 4, 1947*

14 I used to tell my husband that, if he could make *me* understand something, it would be clear to all the other people in the country. "My Day" Newspaper Column *February 12, 1947*

15 The economy of Communism is an economy which grows in an atmosphere of misery and want. Ibid. *March 15, 1947*

16 Franklin had a good way of simplifying things. He made people feel that he had a real understanding of things and they felt they had about the same understanding. Interview in *PM April 6, 1947*

17 . . . I deplore . . . the attitude of self-righteous governments. . . . Our own Government's position has never gone beyond pious hopes and unctuous words. "My Day" Newspaper Column *April 26, 1947*

18 Justice cannot be for one side alone, but must be for both. . . . Ibid. *October 15, 1947*

19 . . . certain rights can never be granted to the government, but must be kept in the hands of the people. Quoted in *The New York Times May 3, 1948*

20 A society in which everyone works is not necessarily a free society and may indeed be a slave society; on the other hand, a society in which there is widespread economic insecurity can turn freedom into a barren and vapid right for millions of people. Speech, "The Struggle for Human Rights," Paris *September 27, 1948*

21 We must preserve our right to think and differ. . . . The day I'm afraid to sit down with people I do not know because five years from now someone will say five of those people were Communists and therefore you are a Communist—that will be a bad day. Speech, Americans for Democratic Action *April 2, 1950*

22 My own feeling is that the Near East, India and many of the Asiatic people have a profound distrust of white people. This is understandable since the white people they have known intimately in the past have been the colonial nations and in the case of the United States, our businessmen. . . . Report to President Truman *1950*

23 For it isn't enough to talk about peace. One must believe in it. And it isn't enough to believe in it. One must work at it. Broadcast, Voice of America *November 11, 1951*

24 I believe that it is a great mistake not to stand up for people, even when you differ with them, if you feel that they are trying to do things that will help our country. Quoted in *The Nation June 7, 1952*

25 There is a small articulate minority in this country which advocates changing our national symbol which is the eagle to that of the ostrich and withdrawing from the United Nations. Speech, Democratic National Convention *July 23, 1952*

26 Too often the great decisions are originated and given form in bodies made up wholly of men, or so completely dominated by them that whatever of special value women have to offer is shunted aside without expression.
Speech, United Nations
*December, 1952*

27 Go down and answer up if you can. . . . It's not easy.          Quoted in the *New York Post*
*May 13, 1953*

28 You have to accept whatever comes and the only important thing is that you meet it with courage and with the best that you have to give.
Essay in *This I Believe*,
Edward P. Morgan, ed.      *1953*

29 Life has got to be lived—that's all there is to it. At 70, I would say the advantage is that you take life more calmly. You know that "this, too, shall pass!"
Quoted in *The New York Times*
*October 8, 1954*

30 As for accomplishments, I just did what I had to do as things came along.          Ibid.

31 I would like . . . to see us take hold of ourselves, look at ourselves and cease being afraid.
Ibid.      *October 12, 1954*

32 A mature person is one who does not think only in absolutes, who is able to be objective even when deeply stirred emotionally, who has learned that there is both good and bad in all people and in all things, and who walks humbly and deals charitably with the circumstances of life, knowing that in this world no one is all-knowing and therefore all of us need both love and charity.      *It Seems to Me*      *1954*

33 The only hope for a really free press is for the public to recognize that the press *should* not express the point of view of the owners and the writers but be factual; whereas the editorials *must* express the opinions of owners and writers.          Ibid.

34 Our party may be the oldest democratic party, but our party must live as a young party, and it must have a young leadership.
Speech, Democratic National
Convention      *August 13, 1956*

35 Could we have the vision of doing away in this great country with poverty? . . . what can make us not only the nation that has some of the richest people in the world, but the nation where there are no people that have to live at a substandard level. That would be one of the very best arguments against Communism that we could possibly have.          Ibid.

36 I have always felt that anyone who wanted an election so much that they would use those* methods did not have the character that I really admired in public life.
"Meet the Press," NBC-TV
*September 16, 1956*

37 . . . you always admire what you really don't understand.          Ibid.

38 I have a great objection to seeing anyone, particularly anyone whom I care about, lose his self-control.
"My Day" Newspaper Column
*February 3, 1958*

39 When the Tammany Hall boss bossed the convention it meant the defeat of the democratic process.      Quoted in the *New York Post*
*November 5, 1958*

40 Where, after all, do universal human rights begin? In small places, close to home—so close and so small that they cannot be seen on any maps of the world. Yet they *are* the world of the individual persons; the neighborhood he lives in; the school or college he attends; the factory, farm or office where he works. Such are the places where every man, woman and child seeks equal justice, equal opportunity, equal dignity without discrimination. Unless these rights have meaning there, they have little meaning anywhere. Without concerned citizen action to uphold them close to home, we shall look in vain for progress in the larger world.          Speech, "The Great Question,"
United Nations      *1958*

41 You can't move so fast that you try to change the mores faster than people can accept it. That doesn't mean you do nothing, but it means that you do the things that need to be done according to priority.      *On My Own*
*1958*

42 We cannot exist as a little island of well-being in a world where two-thirds of the people go to bed hungry every night. I want unity but above everything else, I want a party that will fight for the things that we know to be right at home and abroad.
Speech, Democratic Fund-Raising
Dinner      *December 8, 1959*

43 We have to face the fact that either all of us are going to die together or we are going to learn to live together and if we are to live together we have to talk.
Quoted by A. David Gurewitsch in
*The New York Times*
*October 15, 1960*

* Referring to Richard Nixon's smear campaign against Helen Gahagan Douglas.

44 Everybody wants something.
Interview with Maureen Corr     *1960*

45 You gain strength, courage, and confidence by every experience in which you really stop to look fear in the face.
"You Learn by Living"     *1960*

46 You must do the thing you think you cannot do.     Ibid.

47 . . . I could not, at any age, be content to take my place in a corner by the fireside and simply look on. Life was meant to be lived. Curiosity must be kept alive. The fatal thing is the rejection. One must never, for whatever reason, turn his back on life.
Quoted by Emma Bugbee in the
*New York Herald Tribune*
*October 11, 1961*

48 Both the President and his wife can never give way to apprehension even though they are probably more aware than most citizens of the dangers which may surround us. If the country is to be confident, they must be confident.
"My Day" Newspaper Column
*May 29, 1962*

49 You get well but is it really worth it?
Ibid.     *August 14, 1962*

50 They [Israelis] are still dreamers, but they make their dreams come true. . . .
Quoted by Ruth G. Michaels in
*Hadassah*     *December, 1962*

51 This I know. This I believe with all my heart. If we want a free and peaceful world, if we want to make the deserts bloom and man grow to greater dignity as a human being—*we can do it!*     *Tomorrow Is Now*     *1963*

52 . . . when you know to laugh and when to look upon things as too absurd to take seriously, the other person is ashamed to carry through even if he was serious about it.
Letter to Harry S. Truman
(May 14, 1945), Quoted in
*Eleanor: The Years Alone*
by Joseph P. Lash     *1972p*

53 So—against odds, the women inch forward, but I'm rather old to be carrying on this fight!
Ibid., Letter to Joseph P. Lash
(February 13, 1946)

54 Not all Jewish people want a nation and a national home. . . .
Ibid., Letter to Miss Siegel
(September 5, 1946)

55 . . . we do not always like what is good for us in this world.     Ibid., Letter to Miss Binn
(October 24, 1947)

56 . . . perhaps man's spirit, his striving, is indestructible. It is set back but it does not die and so there is a reason why each one of us should do our best in our own small corner. Do you think I'm too optimistic?
Ibid., Letter to A. David Gurewitsch
(December 18, 1947)

57 I cannot believe that war is the best solution. No one won the last war, and no one will win the next war.
Ibid., Letter to Harry S. Truman
(March 22, 1948)

58 The President [Harry S. Truman] is so easily fooled in spite of his good intentions.
Ibid., Letter to Joseph P. Lash
(November 5, 1948)

59 Our real battlefield today is Asia and our real battle is the one between democracy and communism. . . . We have to prove to the world and particularly to downtrodden areas of the world which are the natural prey to the principles of communist economics that democracy really brings about happier and better conditions for the people as a whole.
Ibid., Memo to Harry S. Truman
(December 28, 1948)

60 Spiritual leadership should remain spiritual leadership and the temporal power should not become too important in any Church.
Ibid., Letter to Cardinal Francis
Spellman (July 23, 1949)

61 . . . there is no complete unanimity here on what course should be followed any more than at home but fear is unanimous!
Ibid., Letter to Trude Lash
(June 18, 1950)

62 We need our heroes*. . . .
Ibid., Letter to Joseph Lash
(January 21, 1952)

63 The Jews in their own country are doing marvels and should, once the refugee problem is settled, help all the Arab countries.
Ibid., Letter to Maude Gray
(March 5, 1952)

64 Television has completely revolutionized what should go on at a convention.
Ibid., Letter to Frank E. McKinney
(July 13, 1952)

65 It isn't within my hands to resign or not to resign. Each of us does that automatically. . . .
Ibid., Letter to Bernard Baruch
(November 18, 1952)

---

* Referring to General Dwight D. Eisenhower.

66 . . . I have spent many years of my life in opposition and I rather like the role.    Ibid.

67 It is always hard to tell people that it is the causes of war which bring about such things as Hiroshima, and that we must try to eliminate these causes because if there is another Pearl Harbor there will be undoubtedly another Hiroshima.
Ibid., Letter to John Golden
(June 12, 1953)

68 I believe that it is essential to our leadership in the world and to the development of true democracy in our country to have no discrimination in our country whatsoever. This is most important in the schools of our country.
Ibid., Letter to Richard Bolling
(January 20, 1956)

69 I doubt if Eisenhower can stand a second term and I doubt if the country can stand Nixon as President.    Ibid., Letter to Lord Elibank
(January 20, 1956)

70 Mr. Dulles has just frightened most of our allies to death with a statement that there is an art in actually threatening war and coming to the brink but retreating from the brink.
Ibid., Letter to Gus Ranis
(January 23, 1956)

71 They [Russians] love to keep you waiting . . . but they hate you to deviate from a plan you once make!
Ibid., Letter to Joseph and Trude Lash
(September 20, 1957)

72 It seems to me . . . we have reached a place where it is not a question of "can we live in the same world and cooperate" but "we must live in the same world and learn to cooperate."
Ibid., Letter to Queen Juliana of the
Netherlands (February 14, 1958)

73 When you cease to make a contribution you begin to die.    Ibid., Letter to Mr. Horne
(February 19, 1960)

74 I cannot, of course, ever feel safe . . . because with Mr. Nixon I always have the feeling that he will pull some trick at the last minute.
Ibid., Letter to John F. Kennedy
(August 27, 1960)

75 To say he [John F. Kennedy] would not make mistakes would be silly. Anyone would make mistakes with the problems that lie ahead of us.
Ibid., Letter to Peter Kamitchis
(October 21, 1960)

76 . . . on the whole, life is rather difficult for both the children and their parents in the "fish bowl" that lies before you.
Ibid., Letter to Jacqueline Kennedy
(December 1, 1960)

77 You seem to think that everyone can save money if they have the character to do it. As a matter of fact, there are innumerable people who have a wide choice between saving and giving their children the best possible opportunities. The decision is usually in favor of the children.
Ibid., Letter to Franklin Roosevelt III
(January 15, 1962)

78 . . . I must reluctantly admit that I am not quite as I was. . . .
Ibid., Letter to Tom Stix
(May 10, 1962)

79 I'm so glad I never *feel* important, it does complicate life.    Ibid., Ch. 2

## 529. Sara Teasdale
### (1884–1933)

1 Let it be forgotten for ever and ever,
Time is a kind friend, he will make us old.
"Let It Be Forgotten," St. 1    *1921*

\* \* \*

2 I shall not let a sorrow die
Until I find the heart of it,
Nor let a wordless joy go by
Until it talks to me a bit.
"Servitors"

3 Joy was a flame in me
Too steady to destroy.
"The Answer"

4 I found more joy in sorrow
Than you could find in joy.
Ibid.

5 My soul is a broken field
Ploughed by pain.
"The Broken Field"

6 No one worth possessing
Can be quite possessed.
"Advice to a Girl"

7 O beauty, are you not enough?
Why am I crying after love?
"Spring Night"

8 Of my own spirit let me be
In sole though feeble mastery.
"Mastery"

9 One by one, like leaves from a tree,
All my faiths have forsaken me.
"Leaves"

10 Spend all you have for loveliness.
"Barter"

11 Strephon's kiss was lost in jest,
Robin's lost in play,
But the kiss in Colin's eyes
Haunts me night and day.
"The Look," St. 2

12 Then, like an old-time orator
Impressively he rose;
"I make the most of all that comes
And the least of all that goes."
"The Philosopher," St. 4

13 When I am dead and over me bright April
Shakes out her rain-drenched hair,
Though you should lean above me broken-
hearted,
I shall not care.
"I Shall Not Care," St. 1

14 When I can look Life in the eyes,
Grown calm and very coldly wise,
Life will have given me the Truth,
And taken in exchange—my youth.
"Wisdom"

## 530. Sophie Tucker
(1884–1966)

1 Success in show business depends on your abil-
ity to make and keep friends.
*Some of These Days*, with
Dorothy Giles, Ch. 4    *1945*

2 From birth to age eighteen, a girl needs good
parents. From eighteen to thirty-five, she needs
good looks. From thirty-five to fifty-five, she
needs a good personality. From fifty-five on,
she needs good cash.    Attributed    *1953*

3 Keep breathing.    Anniversary Speech
*January 13, 1964*

## 531. Sophie Tunnell
(1884–?)
* * *

1 Fear is a slinking cat I find
Beneath the lilacs of my mind.
"Fear"

## 532. Anna Wickham
(1884–1947)

1 I desire Virtue, though I love her not—
I have no faith in her when she is got:
I fear that she will bind and make me slave
And send me songless to the sullen grave.
"Self-Analysis," St. 3,
*The Contemplative Quarry*    *1915*

2 When I am sick, then I believe in law.
Ibid., St. 4

3 'Tis folly to my dawning, thrifty thought
That I must run, who in the end am caught.
Ibid., "The Contemplative Quarry"

4 I smother in the house in the valley below,
Let me out to the night, let me go, let me go!
"Divorce," *The World Split Open*,
Louise Bernikow, ed.    *1974p*
* * *

5 Alas! For all the pretty women who marry dull
men,
Go into the suburbs and never come out again.
"Meditation at Kew"

6 Because of the body's hunger we are born,
And by contriving hunger are we fed;
Because of hunger is our work well done,
And so our songs well sung, and things well
said.
"Sehnsucht"

7 Desire and longing are the whips of God.
Ibid.

8 But the true male never yet walked
Who liked to listen when his mate talked.
"The Affinity"

9 I have to thank God I'm a woman,
For in these ordered days a woman only
Is free to be very hungry, very lonely.
Ibid.

10 If I had peace to sit and sing,
Then I could make a lovely thing. . . .
"The Singer"

11 I have been so misused by chaste men with
one wife
That I would live with satyrs all my life.
"Ship Near Shoals"

12 Oh, give me a woman of my race
As well controlled as I,
And let us sit by the fire,
Patient till we die!
"The Tired Man"

13 Think how poor Mother Eve was brought
To being as God's afterthought.
"To Men"

## 533. Helen M. Cam

### (1885–1968)

1 We must not read either law or history backwards.        Introduction to *Selected Essays of F. W. Maitland*, H. D. Hazeltine, G. Gapsley, P. H. Winfield, eds.
*1936*

2 The authority of a statute made in Parliament is universally recognized as superior to that of any other legislative act.
*England Before Elizabeth*, Ch. 12
*1950*

3 Feudalism, for all its insistence on priority and place, had proved inadequate for the needs of government, however much its traditions of deference and responsibility might linger in the English social system.        Ibid.

4 If civilisation is the art of living together with people not entirely like oneself, the first step in civilisation is not so much the invention of material tools as the regularisation of social habits. As soon as you begin to say "We always do things this way" the foundations are laid. "Custom is before all law." As soon as you begin to say "We have always done things this way—perhaps *that* might be a better way," conscious law-making is beginning. As soon as you begin to say "*We* do things this way *they* do things that way—what is to be done about it?" men are beginning to feel towards justice, that resides between the endless jar of right and wrong.
Lecture, "Law as It Looks to a Historian," Gurton College
*February 18, 1956*

5 Law offers a guiding thread to us . . . one of purpose—and a purpose infinitely worthwhile, for in the long view it is more important that human beings should learn to get on with each other than that they should be more comfortable materially and safer physically.        Ibid.

6 Historical fiction is not only a respectable literary form: it is a standing reminder of the fact that history is about human beings.
*Historical Novel        1961*

7 What the rule of law means for Englishmen, what due process of law means to Americans, is inseparably bound up with our traditional notions of Magna Carta. Whether all that has been read into the document is historically or legally sound, is not of the first importance; every historian knows that belief itself is a historical fact, and that legend and myth cannot be left out of account in tracing the sequence of cause and effect.
Lecture, "Magna Carta—Event or Document?," Old Hall of Lincoln's Inn        *July 7, 1967*

## 534. Gladys Cromwell

### (1885–1919)

\* \* \*

1 Sorrow can wait,
For there is magic in the calm estate
Of grief; lo, where the dust complies
Wisdom lies.
"Folded Power"

## 535. Isak Dinesen

### (1885–1962)

1 "What is man, when you come to think upon him, but a minutely set, ingenious machine for turning, with infinite artfulness, the red wine of Shiraz into urine?"        *Seven Gothic Tales*
*1934*

2 Woman. I understand the word itself, in that sense, has gone out of the language. Where we talk of woman . . . you talk of women, and all the difference lies therein. . . .
Ibid., "The Old Chevalier"

3 I do not know if you remember the tale of the girl who saves the ship under mutiny by sitting on the powder barrel with her lighted torch . . . and all the time knowing that it is empty? This has seemed to me a charming image of the women of my time. There they were, keeping the world in order . . . by sitting on the mystery of life, and knowing themselves that there was no mystery.        Ibid.

4 "If only I could so live and so serve the world that after me there should never again be birds in cages. . . ."
Ibid., "The Deluge at Norderney"

5 I have seen a herd of elephants traveling through dense native forest . . . pacing along as if they had an appointment at the end of the world.        *Out of Africa*, Pt. I, Ch. 1        *1938*

6 The giraffe, in their queer, inimitable, vegetating gracefulness, as if it were not a herd of animals but a family of rare, long-stemmed, speckled gigantic flowers slowly advancing.
Ibid.

7 If I knew a song of Africa—I thought of the giraffe, and the African new moon lying on her back, of the plows in the fields, and the sweaty faces of the coffee-pickers—does Africa know a song for me?        Ibid., Ch. 4

8 I have before seen other countries, in the same manner, give themselves to you when you are about to leave them.        Ibid., Pt. V, Ch. 1

9 "But the trouble is not as you think now, that we have put up obstacles too high for you to jump, and how could we possibly do that, you great leaper? It is that we have put up no obstacles at all. The great strength is in you, Lulu, and the obstacles are within you as well, and the thing is, that the fullness of time has not yet come." Ibid.

10 The true aristocracy and the true proletariat of the world are both in understanding with tragedy. To them it is the fundamental principle of God, and the key, the minor key, to existence. They differ in this way from the bourgeoisie of all classes, who deny tragedy, who will not tolerate it, and to whom the word tragedy means in itself unpleasantness." Ibid.

11 "All Natives are masters in the art of the pause, and thereby give perspective to a discussion." Ibid.

12 When Africans speak of the personality of God, they speak like the Arabian Nights or the last chapters of the Book of Job; it is . . . the infinite power of imagination with which they are impressed. Ibid.

13 She was like a man who has been given an elephant gun and asked to shoot little birds.
*Winter's Tales* 1942

14 But she was badly hurt and disappointed because the world was not a much greater place . . . and because nothing more colossal, more like the dramas of the stage, took place in it. Ibid.

## 536. Malvina Hoffman
(1885–1966)

1 My true center of work was not commissions. It was an enormous capacity for falling in love with everything around me. . . .
Quoted in "Malvina Hoffman,"
*Famous American Women*
by Hope Stoddard 1970p

2 . . . at heart we are really working for the angels. . . . What counts is the lasting integrity of the artist and the enduring quality of his work. Ibid.

## 537. Karen Horney
(1885–1952)

1 Psychoanalysis is the creation of a male genius, and almost all those who have developed his ideas have been men. It is only right and reasonable that they should evolve more easily a masculine psychology and understand more of the development of men than of women.
"The Flight from Womanhood,"
*Feminine Psychology* 1926

2 Like all sciences and all valuations, the psychology of women has hitherto been considered only from the point of view of men. Ibid.

3 Is not the tremendous strength in men of the impulse to creative work in every field precisely due to their feeling of playing a relatively small part in the creation of living beings, which constantly impels them to an overcompensation in achievement? Ibid.

4 It seems to me impossible to judge to how great a degree the unconscious motives for the flight from womanhood are reinforced by the actual social subordination of women. Ibid.

5 . . . it is necessary not to be too easily satisfied with ready-at-hand explanations for a disturbance. *Self-Analysis* 1942

6 . . . concern should drive us into action and not into a depression. Ibid.

7 But miracles occur in psychoanalysis as seldom as anywhere else. Ibid.

8 . . . a person who feels helplessly caught in his neurotic entanglements tends to hope against hope for a miracle. Ibid.

9 Fortunately [psycho]analysis is not the only way to resolve inner conflicts. Life itself still remains a very effective therapist.
*Our Inner Conflicts* 1945

## 538. Frances Parkinson Keyes
(1885–1970)

1 Women were cats, all of them, unless they were fools, and there was no way of getting even with them, ever, except by walking off with the men they wanted. . . .
*The Great Tradition*, Pt. I, Ch. 3
1939

2 "I can't see that the Nazis are any different from the Communists, except that they're cleaner and better looking and better drilled. They're both stirring up trouble, they're both bent on destruction and despotism, they're both ready to go to any lengths to gain their ends!"
Ibid., Pt. V, Ch. 15

3 Folks with their wits about them knew that advertisements were just a pack of lies—you had only to look at the claims of patent medicines! *Blue Camellia*, Pt. I, Ch. 3 1957

4 "Well, it's a good thing to trust in Providence. But I believe the Almighty likes a little cooperation now and again."
*Ibid., Pt. III, Ch. 10*

5 ". . . young folks, them, don' never think 'bout nothin' only spend, spend, spend money, instead of save, save, save money, like us used to do, us. It's education, or either it's clothes, or either it's something else, as long as somebody got to spend, spend, spend. Boys is plenny bad, I got to admit, yes, but girls is even worser."
*Ibid., Pt. V, Ch. 22*

## 539. Marie Laurencin
### (1885–1956)

1 Why should I paint dead fish, onions and beer glasses? Girls are so much prettier.
*Quoted in Time    June 18, 1956p*

## 540. Ettie Lee
### (1885–1974)

1 Every child has a right to a good home.
*Quoted in the Los Angeles Times*
*April 27, 1974p*

## 541. Aline Triplett Michaelis
### (1885–?)

\* \* \*

1 Alone, yet never lonely,
Serene, beyond mischance,
The world was his, his only,
When Lindbergh flew to France.
*"Lindbergh"*

## 542. Constance Roarke
### (1885–1941)

1 Ardent and tired and overwrought, in that sensitive state where the imagination grows fluid, where inner and outer motives coalesce. . . .
*The Trumpets of Jubilee   1927*

2 An emotional man may possess no humor, but a humorous man usually has deep pockets of emotion, sometimes tucked away or forgotten.
*American Humor, Ch. 1   1931*

3 Comic resilience swept through them in waves, transcending the past, transcending terror, with a sense of comedy, itself a wild emotion.
*Ibid., Ch. 2*

4 It is a mistake to look for the social critic—even Manqué—in Mark Twain. In a sense the whole American comic tradition had been that of social criticism: but this had been instinctive and incomplete, and so it proved to be in Mark Twain. . . . He was primarily a *raconteur*. . . . He was never the conscious artist, always the improvisor.
*Ibid., Ch. 7*

5 In comedy, reconcilement with life comes at the point when to the tragic sense only an inalienable difference or dissension with life appears.
*Ibid., Ch. 8*

6 Humor has been a fashioning instrument in America, cleaving its way through the national life, holding tenaciously to the spread elements of that life. Its mode has often been swift and coarse and ruthless, beyond art and beyond established civilization. It has engaged in warfare against the established heritage, against the bonds of pioneer existence. Its objective—the unconscious objective of a disunited people—has seemed to be that of creating fresh bonds, a new unity, the semblance of a society and the rounded completion of an American type.
*Ibid., Ch. 9*

## 543. Marjorie Allen Seiffert
### (1885–1968)

1 For to your heart
Beauty is a burned-out torch,
And Faith, a blind pigeon,
Friendship, a curious Persian myth,
And love, blank emptiness,
Bearing no significance
Nor any reality.

Only Weariness is yours. . . .
*"Singalese Love Song, II," Sts. 2–3,*
*A Woman of Thirty   1919*

2 And when I search your soul until
I see too deeply and divine
That you can never love me—Still
I hold you fast for you are mine!
*Ibid., "Possession," St. 3*

3 Sorrow stands in a wide place,
Blind—blind—
Beauty and joy are petals blown
Across her granite face,
They cannot find sight or sentience in stone.

Yesterday's beauty and joy lie deep
In sorrow's heart, asleep.
*Ibid., "Sorrow"*

4 Spring raged outside, but ghostly in my bed
  A dead self lay and knew itself for dead.
      "A Full Storm," *The King with Three*
          *Faces and Other Poems*   1929

5 "Pay as you enter!" is written on heaven's door.
  The beggar may go in velvet or in tatters,
  Hell's rubbish heap is the unpaid bills he
    scatters,
  And love is worth what it cost you, nothing
    more.
      Ibid., "The Horse-Leech's Daughter"

6 We are damned with the knowledge of good
    and evil: they,
  Whose new estate is freedom, suffer worse
  And find life empty, trivial and boring,
  A sort of game that every one must play,
  And no one knows the rules, and no one's
    scoring,
  And nothing's at stake, for youth has lost its
    purse.
      Ibid., "Youth Visits Our Inferno"

         \*   \*   \*

7 Lust is the oldest lion of them all.
          "An Italian Chest"

## 544. Clare Sheridan

### (1885–?)

1 At the end of her days, she became superbly
squaw-like, and would sit impassively for hours,
staring into the fire, her head shrouded in a
shawl. A figure of great moral fortitude and
self-oblation was gradually fading out.
      *To the Four Winds*   1955

## 545. Bess Truman

### (1885– )

1 I deplore any action which denies artistic talent
an opportunity to express itself because of
prejudice against race origin.
      Quoted by Helen Weigel Brown in
          *Liberty*   June 9, 1945

## 546. Elinor Wylie

### (1885–1928)

1 Avoid the reeking herd,
  Shun the polluted flock,
  Live like that stoic bird
    The eagle of the rock.
      "The Eagle and the Mole," St. 1
      (1921), *Collected Poems*   1932p

2 If you would keep your soul
    From spotted sight and sound,
  Live like the velvet mole,
    Go burrow underground.
          Ibid., St. 5

3 I was, being human, born alone;
  I am, being woman, hard beset;
  I live by squeezing from a stone
    The little nourishment I get.

  In masks outrageous and austere
  The years go by in single file;
  But none has merited my fear,
  And none has quite escaped my smile.
      Ibid., "Let No Charitable Hope,"
          Sts. 2–3 (1923)

4   Honeyed words like bees,
  Gilded and sticky, with a little sting.
      Ibid., "Pretty Words"

5 I love smooth words, like gold-enameled fish
  Which circle slowly with a silken swish. . . .
          Ibid.

6 If any has a stone to throw
  It is not I, ever or now.
      Ibid., "The Pebble"

7 I've played the traitor over and over;
  I'm a good hater but a bad lover.
      Ibid., "Peregrine"

8 The worst and best are both inclined
  To snap like vixens at the truth;
  But, O, beware the middle mind
  That purrs and never shows a tooth!
      Ibid., "Nonsense Rhyme," St. 2

## 547. Zoë Akins

### (1886–1958)

1 LADY HELEN. To accuse is so easy that it is
infamous to do so where proof is impossible!
      *Déclassé*, Act I   1919

2 LADY HELEN. My life is like water that has
gone over the dam and turned no mill wheels.
Here I am, not happy, but not unhappy, as my
days run on to the sea, idly—but not too
swiftly—for I love living.       Ibid.

3 LADY HELEN. Englishmen are like that. They
love life more and value it less than any other
people in the world.     Ibid., Act II

4 SOLOMON. Like a fool I thought I was the
arbiter of her destiny; and all the time Fate
had happier plans for her.   Ibid., Act III

5 EDITH. . . . there's a great strangeness about love. . . . Yes, I'm very sure that love is the strangest thing in the world—much stranger than death—or—or just life.
*Daddy's Gone A-Hunting*, Act I
1921

6 OSCAR. But you've got a wife. It's all right to tell a wife the brutal truth, but you've got to go sort of easy with your lady-love.
*Ibid.*, Act II

7 MRS. DAHLGREN. Shutting one's eyes is an art, my dear. I suppose there's no use trying to make you see that—but that's the only way one *can* stay married.    *Ibid.*

8 EDITH. This world is a very unsafe place. It's all shifting sands, Ned. Shifting sands and changing winds.    *Ibid.*, Act III

9 TILLERTON. "To him that hath it shall be given—" She hath . . . that's all. That's greatness.

PRESCOTT. One sort of greatness, maybe.

TILLERTON. Even the great can have only their own sort of greatness.

PRESCOTT. And it's often only that they're great sponges. . . .

TILLERTON. Often, yes, or great roses for whose blooming the trees have been pruned and stripped. But they make the beauty of the world and that's enough.    *Greatness*, Act I
1922

10 CANAVA. The success-haters. . . . That's what I call them—the people who have never got what they want and turned sour on everybody who has. The world's full of them. . . . As soon as you've made good they begin to watch for you to fail. . . .    *Ibid.*

11 TILLERTON. And I wonder if peace is enough for any man. . . .    *Ibid.*, Act II

12 RAYMOND. No one can ever help loving anyone.
*Ibid.*, Act III

13 SENTONI. My cousin Cleofante does not believe in inspiration. She shuns the false energy of all stimulants, even those of criticism and sympathy, when she sets herself to a task. What she does, she does alone—unencouraged, unadvised, unmoved. She has a man's broad and vital technique, and a man's ability for thinking straight and far. For years I have watched her work—coldly, intelligently, solely with the power of her brain—achieving effects that are in no way miracles, but are matters of technique and deliberation.
*The Portrait of Tiero*    1924

14 CLEOFANTE. Work alone qualifies us for life, Sentoni. It is much more exquisite to be blown from the tree as a flower than to be shaken down as a shriveled and bitter fruit.    *Ibid.*

15 And they shall know that in the ordering
Of every world to come the law shall read
That he who dares be lawless wears the wing

Of bird and prophet and his light shall lead
On through the darkness to eventual light,
To undiscovered wealth, to newer need. . . .
"The Anarchist, III," *The Hills Grow
Smaller*, Sts. 15–16    1937

16 Mine was a love so exquisite that I
Rather than watch it wither chose to die:
So dress my grave, O friend, with no poor flower
Which in your quiet garden blooms an hour!
*Ibid.*, "Epitaph"

17 And have we lost the right
To look on a blooming bough
Without remembering how
Once with high promising
We were a part of spring—
We who are now the dead
Leaves of other years strewn where flowers spread?
*Ibid.*, "Jazz Nocturne," St. 3

18 I know not where I go; I scarcely feel
The menacing fatigue about my feet,
The skies that scourge, the distances that cheat,
the constant wounds that neither hurt nor heal.
*Ibid.*, "Lethargy," St. 2

19 Indifferent to all the fun of chance
I watched black spiders of inertia spin
The far-flung web which I was strangling in.
*Ibid.*, "Indifference," St. 1

20 In all my locked-up songs
No one but you belongs.
*Ibid.*, "To H.R.," St. 1

## 548. Margaret Ayer Barnes
(1886–1967)

1 There they were. Opinions. Jane bumped into them, tangible obstacles in her path, things to be recognized, and accepted or evaded, as the exigencies of the situation demanded.
*Years of Grace*, Pt. I, Ch. 1    1930

2 "Curious, isn't it," he went on airily, "that 'talking with the right people' means something so very different from 'talking with the right person'?"    *Ibid.*, Pt. III, Ch. 1

3 Childless women, Olivia reflected, slipped gracefully into middle age. There was no one particular awkward moment when they climbed up on the shelf.     *Westward Passage*, Ch. 1
                                                      *1931*

4 "There's nothing half so real in life as the things you've done," she whispered. "Inexorably, unalterably *done*."        Ibid., Ch. 4

5 Sentiment, crystallized, grows into sentimentality. It lost all spontaneity, which was the essence of feeling. It was dated—old-fashioned.
            "Prelude," *Within This Present*
                                                      *1933*

6 "Character comes before scholarship. . . ."
                                        Ibid., Pt. I, Ch. 1

## 549.  Frances Darwin Cornford
### (1886–?)
\* \* \*

1 O fat white woman whom nobody loves,
  Why do you walk through the fields in gloves?
            "To a Fat Lady Seen from the Train"

2 Magnificently unprepared
  For the long littleness of life.
                                        "Rupert Brooke"

## 550.  Hilda Doolittle
### (1886–1961)
\* \* \*

1 Egypt had maimed us,
  offered dream for life,
  an opiate for a kiss,
  and death for both.
                                                "Egypt"

## 551.  Florence Kiper Frank
### (1886?–?)

1 The canny among the publishers know that an enormous popular appetite for the insulting of the famous must be gratified, and the modern biographer emerges from the editorial conference a sadist and a wiser man.
            *Morrow's Almanac*     *1929*
\* \* \*

2 Pooh-Men!
  We are done with them now,
  Who had need of them then,—
  I and you!
                                                "Baby"

## 552.  Hazel Hall
### (1886–1924)
\* \* \*

1 *I am the dance of youth, and life is fair!*
  Footfall, footfall;
  *I am a dream, divinely unaware!*
  Footfall, footfall;
  *I am the burden of an old despair!*
  Footfall.
                                            "Footsteps"

## 553.  Radclyffe Hall
### (1886–1943)

1 Acknowledge us, o God, before the whole world. Give us also the right to our existence.
            *The Well of Loneliness*   *1928*

2 "You're neither unnatural, nor abominable, nor mad; you're as much a part of what people call nature as anyone else; only you're unexplained as yet—you've not got your niche in creation."                                  Ibid.

3 But the intuition of those who stand midway between the two sexes is so ruthless, so poignant, so accurate, so deadly as to be in the nature of an added scourge.                   Ibid.

4 They had sought among the ruins of a dead civilization for the beauty they missed subconsciously in their own.
            *A Saturday Life*, Ch. 1     *1930*

5 But when told that to appear naked in a drawing-room might be considered somewhat odd, since it was no longer the custom, she had argued that our bodies were very unimportant, only there so that people might perceive us. "We couldn't see each other without them, you know," she had said, smiling up at her mother.                             Ibid.

6 At a time of great strain and unhappiness a comparatively insignificant event may discover the chink in our armour; an event connected, as likely as not, with an equally insignificant person. . . .       *The Master of the House*,
                                        Ch. 25     *1932*

7 Cry out until the world shook with her cries: "You shall not take him, I care nothing for honour. I care only for the child that my womb has held, that my pain has brought forth, that my breasts have nourished. I care nothing for your wars. He was born of love; shall the blossom of love be destroyed by your hatreds? I care nothing. . . ."         Ibid., Ch. 41

## 554. Elizabeth Kenny
### (1886–1952)

1 . . . panic plays no part in the training of a nurse. *And They Shall Walk*, with Martha Ostenso 1943

2 . . . it is easier to recount grievances and slights than it is to set down a broad redress of such grievances and slights. The reason is that one fears to be thought of as an arrant braggart. Ibid.

3 The record of one's life must needs prove more interesting to him who writes it than to him who reads what has been written. Ibid., Foreword

4 O sleep, O gentle sleep, I thought gratefully, Nature's gentle nurse! Ibid., Ch. 2

5 Fortunately, perhaps, I was completely ignorant of the orthodox theory of the disease [poliomyelitis]. Ibid.

6 He looked at the book, took my name, and consulted his records. Then he informed me that I had been lost at sea and was dead. Under the circumstances, he could not possibly give me any money. . . . Even the fact that he was dealing with someone who had been dead for several days failed to awaken the slightest interest in his official heart. Ibid., Ch. 3

7 I was wholly unprepared for the extraordinary attitude of the medical world in its readiness to condemn anything that smacked of reform or that ran contrary to approved methods of practice. Ibid., Ch. 6

8 Some minds remain open long enough for the truth not only to enter but to pass on through by way of a ready exit without pausing anywhere along the route. Ibid.

9 My mother used to say, "He who angers you, conquers you!" But my mother was a saint. Ibid., Ch. 7

10 His response was remarkable for its irrelevance, if for nothing else. Ibid.

11 A measure of victory has been won, and honors have been bestowed in token thereof. But honors fade or are forgotten, and monuments crumble into dust. It is the battle itself that matters—and the battle must go on. Ibid., Ch. 14

## 555. Frances Marion
### (1886–1973)

1 The thought had taken root in his imagination and grown as a tree grows from a tiny seed until it crowded out all other thoughts in his mind. *Westward the Dream*, Pt. I, Ch. 1 1948

2 The land around San Juan Capistrano is the pocket where the Creator keeps all his treasures. Anything will grow there, from wheat and beans to citrus fruit. Ibid., Ch. 3

3 "Do we really know anybody? Who does not wear one face to hide another?" Ibid., Ch. 10

4 What a strange pattern the shuttle of life can weave. . . . Ibid., Pt. II, Ch. 14

5 This is not dead land, it is only thirsty land. Ibid., Ch. 22

6 "A coin, Mr. Fox, can only fall heads or tails, and I'll gamble on heads, they last longer." *Off with Their Heads* 1972

7 I shall refrain from mentioning to our southern neighbors that San Franciscans look upon the City of the Queen of the Angels as California's floating kidney transplanted from the Middle West. Ibid., "1914 Through 1924"

8 Promises that you make to yourself are often like the Japanese plum tree—they bear no fruit. Ibid.

9 We have a little catch phrase in our family which somehow fits almost everyone in the movie colony: "Spare no expense to make everything as economical as possible." Ibid.

10 One thing you learned when you wrote for the movies: all nationalities were sensitive except Americans. The Arabs were always to be pictured as a sweet, friendly people. So were the Greeks, the Dutch, Turks, Laps, Eskimoes, and so on down the line. Everyone was honest and virtuous, except Americans. You could make them the most sinister villains and never hear a word of protest from Washington, Chicago, Kalamazoo, or all points south. But should you describe a villain belonging to any country but America, you found yourself spread-eagled between the Board of Censors and the diplomatic service of some foreign power. Ibid., "1925 Through 1928"

## 556. Mary Wigman

(1886–1973)

1 Strong and convincing art has never arisen from theories.    "The New German Dance," *Modern Dance*, Virginia Stewart, ed.    *1935*

2 Art is communication spoken by man for humanity in a language raised above the everyday happening.    Ibid.

3 During the process of artistic creation, man descends into the primordial elements of life. He reverts to himself to become lost in something greater than himself, in the immediate, indivisible essence of life.    Ibid.

## 557. Anzia Yezierska

(1886–1970)

1 "If you have no luck in this world, then it's better not to live."    "The Fat of the Land," *The Century*    *1919*

2 "The world is a wheel always turning," philosophized Mrs. Pelz. "Those who were high go down low, and those who've been low go up higher."    Ibid.

## 558. Ruth Benedict

(1887–1948)

1 No man ever looks at the world with pristine eyes. He sees it edited by a definite set of customs and institutions and ways of thinking.    *Patterns of Culture*, Ch. 1    *1934*

2 War is, we have been forced to admit, even in the face of its huge place in our own civilization, an asocial trait.    Ibid.

3 If we justify war, it is because all peoples always justify the traits of which they find themselves possessed, not because war will bear an objective examination of its merits.    Ibid.

4 Racism is the new Calvinism which asserts that one group has the stigmata of superiority and the other has those of inferiority. . . . For racism is an *ism* to which everyone in the world today is exposed; for or against, we must take sides. And the history of the future will differ according to the decision which we make.    *Race: Science and Politics*, Ch. 1    *1940*

5 "Hybrid vigor" has been shown in studies of American Indian-White mixture, stature in the half-breeds being greater than that of either race contributing to the cross. Mixed bloods also show over and over again evidence of increased fertility. . . . Nature apparently does not condemn the half-caste to physiological inferiority. The rule for the breeding of good human stock is that both parents be of good physique and good mental ability.    Ibid., Ch. 4

6 Racism in its nationalistic phase, therefore, has been a politician's plaything. . . . It is a dangerous plaything, a sword which can be turned in any direction to condemn the enemy of the moment.    Ibid., Ch. 7

7 But the Thai have an indestructible conviction that existence is good, and they have characteristically placed the promised rewards of Buddhism in this life rather [than] in the life to come.    *Thai Culture and Behavior*, Pt. II, Ch. 5    *1943*

8 Everybody repeats the proverbial maxim: "In this world everything changes except good deeds and bad deeds; these follow you as the shadow follows the body."    Ibid.

9 The Japanese are, to the highest degree, both aggressive and unaggressive, both militaristic and aesthetic, both insolent and polite, rigid and adaptable, submissive and resentful of being pushed around, loyal and treacherous, brave and timid, conservative and hospitable to new ways.    *The Chrysanthemum and the Sword*, Ch. 1    *1946*

10 Love, kindness, generosity, which we value just in proportion as they are given without strings attached, necessarily must have their strings in Japan. And every such act received makes one a debtor.    Ibid., Ch. 5

11 A man's indebtedness . . . is not virtue; his repayment is. Virtue begins when he dedicates himself actively to the job of gratitude.    Ibid., Ch. 6

12 I have always used the world of make-believe with a certain desperation.    Quoted in *An Anthropologist at Work* by Margaret Mead    *1951p*

13 . . . the passionate belief in the superior worthwhileness of our children. It is stored up in us as a great battery charged by the accumulated instincts of uncounted generations.    Ibid.

14 Life was a labyrinth of petty turns and there
was no Ariadne who held the clue.
Ibid. (October, 1912)

15 So much of the trouble is because I am a
woman.                                    Ibid.

16 If we are not to have the chance to fulfill our
one potentiality—the power of loving—why
were we not born men? At least we could have
had an occupation then.                   Ibid.

17 The trouble is not that we are never happy—
it is that happiness is so episodical.     Ibid.

18 We turn in our sleep and groan because we
are parasites—we women—because we produce
nothing, say nothing, find our whole world in
the love of a man.—For shame! We are become
the veriest Philistines—in this matter of
woman's sphere. I suppose it is too soon to
expect us to achieve perspective on the problem
of women's rights. . . .                   Ibid.

19 We hurt each other badly, for words are
clumsy things, and he is inexorable. But, at any
rate, he does not baby me, and honesty helps
even when it is cruel.
Ibid. (Christmas, 1916)

20 I long to speak out the intense inspiration that
comes to me from the lives of strong women.
Ibid. (January, 1917)

21 . . . it is my necessary breath of life to understand and expression is the only justification of
life that I can feel without prodding.
Ibid. (October, 1920)

22 . . . work even when I'm satisfied with it is
never my child I love nor my servant I've
brought to heel. It's always busy work I do
with my left hand, and part of me watches
grudging the wastes of a lifetime.
Ibid. (June 9, 1934)

## 559. Jessie Chambers

(1887–1944)

1 So instead of a release and deliverance from
bondage, the bondage was glorified and made
absolute. His [D. H. Lawrence's] mother conquered indeed, but the vanquished one was her
son.     *D. H. Lawrence: A Personal Record*
*1935*

## 560. Elizabeth Drew

(1887–1965)

1 But though personality is a skin that no writer
can slip, whatever he may write about: though

it is a shadow which walks inexorably by his
side, so also is the age he lives in.
"The Novel and the Age,"
*The Modern Novel     1926*

2 The world is not run by thought, nor by
imagination, but by opinion. . . .
Ibid., "Sex Simplexes and Complexes"

3 Sown in space like one among a handful of
seeds in a suburban garden, the earth exists; a
revolving, tepid sphere, whose every rotation
brings it relentlessly nearer to the moon's dim,
white, rotten desolation. Dwelling in this spinning island of terror, under immutable sentence
of death, is Man, who, whether we regard him
with the Psalmist as a little lower than the
angels, or as "an ape, reft of his tail and grown
rusty at climbing"; whether we see him shouting exultantly that he is the captain of his soul,
or meeting his fate with all the lumbering discomfort of a cow being hustled into a railway
truck, remains yet the ultimate mystery.
Ibid., "The New Psychology"

4 The test of literature is, I suppose, whether we
ourselves live more intensely for the reading
of it. . . .     Ibid., "Is There a 'Feminine'
Fiction?"

5 In spite of equal education and equal opportunity, the *scope* of woman remains still smaller
than the scope of man. . . . Just as it is still
in her close personal relationships that woman
most naturally uses her human genius and her
artistry in life, so it is still in the portrayal of
those relationships that she perfects her most
characteristic genius in writing.         Ibid.

6 How poetry comes to the poet is a mystery.
Quoted in "On the Teaching of
Poetry" by Leonora Speyer,
*The Saturday Review of
Literature     1946*

7 We read poetry because the poets, like ourselves, have been haunted by the inescapable
tyranny of time and death; have suffered the
pain of loss, and the more wearing, continuous
pain of frustration and failure; and have had
moods of unlooked-for release and peace. They
have known and watched in themselves and
others. . . . Sympathy and empathy, feeling
with and feeling into, are the bases for his
search for the true embodiment in words of his
perception, great or small.
*Poetry: A Modern Guide to Its
Understanding and Enjoyment,*
Pt. II, Ch. 7     *1959*

8 The pain of loss, moreover, however agonizing,
however haunting in memory, quiets imper-
ceptibly into acceptance as the currents of

active living and of fresh emotions flow over it. Worse, perhaps, than the sufferings of grief are the torments that man endures from the conflicts within his own being.　　Ibid., Ch. 9

9 Propaganda has a bad name, but its root meaning is simply to disseminate through a medium, and all writing therefore is propaganda for *something*. It's a seeding of the self in the consciousness of others.　　Ibid., Ch. 10

10 The torment of human frustration, whatever its immediate cause, is the knowledge that the self is in prison, its vital force and "mangled mind" leaking away in lonely, wasteful self-conflict.
　　Ibid., Ch. 13

11 But it is true that the inspired scribbler always has the gift for gossip in our common usage too; he or she can always inspire the commonplace with an uncommon flavor, and transform trivialities by some original grace or sympathy or humor or affection.
　　"The Literature of Gossip,"
　　*The Literature of Gossip*　　1964

12 How frail and ephemeral too is the material substance of letters, which makes their very survival so hazardous. Print has a permanence of its own, though it may not be much worth preserving, but a letter! Conveyed by uncertain transportation, over which the sender has no control; committed to a single individual who may be careless or inappreciative; left to the mercy of future generations, of families maybe anxious to suppress the past, of the accidents of removals and house-cleanings, or of mere ignorance. How often it has been by the veriest chance that they survived at all.　　Ibid.

## 561. Edna Ferber
### (1887–1968)

1 Roast Beef, Medium, is not only a food. It is a philosophy. Seated at Life's Dining Table, with the menu of Morals before you, your eye wanders a bit over the entrées, the hors d'oeuvres, and the things *à la* though you know that Roast Beef, Medium, is safe and sane, and sure.
　　*Roast Beef, Medium*, Foreword　　1911

2 From supper to bedtime is twice as long as from breakfast to supper.　　Ibid., Ch. 1

3 "Music! That's my gift. And I varied it. Why? Because the public won't take a fat man seriously. When he sits down at the piano they begin to howl for Italian rag."　　Ibid., Ch. 2

4 "There's certain things always go hand-in-hand in your mind. You can't think of one without

the other. Now, Lillian Russell and cold cream is one; and new potatoes and brown crocks is another."　　Ibid., Ch. 5

5 Even in her childhood she extracted from life double enjoyment that comes usually only to the creative mind. "Now I am doing this. Now I am doing that," she told herself while she was doing it. Looking on while she participated.
　　*So Big*, Ch. 1　　1924

6 "There are only two kinds of people in the world that really count. One kind's wheat and the other kind's emeralds."　　Ibid.

7 But young love thrives on colour, warmth, beauty. It becomes prosaic and inarticulate when forced to begin its day at four in the morning . . . and to end that day at nine, numb and sodden with weariness, after seventeen hours of physical labour.　　Ibid., Ch. 8

8 "Woman's work! Housework's the hardest work in the world. That's why men won't do it."
　　Ibid.

9 "But 'most any place is Baghdad if you don't know what will happen in it."　　Ibid., Ch. 10

10 "Any piece of furniture, I don't care how beautiful it is, has got to be lived with, kicked about, and rubbed down, and mistreated by servants, and repolished, and knocked around and dusted and sat on or slept in or eaten off of before it develops its real character," Salina said. "A good deal like human beings."
　　Ibid., Ch. 15

11 But his gifts were many, and not the least of them was the trick of appearing sartorially and tonsorially flawless when dishevelment and a stubble were inevitable in any other male.
　　*Show Boat*, Ch. 1　　1926

12 . . . the Negroes whose black faces dotted the boards of the Southern wharves as thickly as grace notes sprinkle a bar of lively music.
　　Ibid., Ch. 2

13 They . . . never exchanged civilities. This state of affairs lent spice to an existence that might otherwise have proved too placid for comfort. The bickering acted as a safety valve.
　　Ibid., Ch. 5

14 "Don't you believe 'em when they say that what you don't know won't hurt you. Biggest lie ever was. See it all and go your own way and nothing'll hurt you. If what you see ain't pretty, what's the odds! See it anyway. Then next time you don't have to look."
　　Ibid., Ch. 13

15 Faro was not a game with Ravenal—it was for him at once his profession, his science, his drug, his drink, his mistress. He had, unhappily, as was so often the case with your confirmed gambler, no other vice.       *Ibid.*

16 There was about her—or them—nothing of genius, of greatness, of the divine fire. But the dramatic critics of the younger school who were too late to have seen past genius in its hey-day and for whom the theatrical genius of their day was yet to come, viewed her performance and waxed hysterical, mistaking talent and intelligence and hard work and ambition for something more rare.    Ibid., Ch. 19

17 Wasn't marriage, like life, unstimulating and unprofitable and somewhat empty when too well ordered and protected and guarded. Wasn't it finer, more splendid, more nourishing, when it was, like life itself, a mixture of the sordid and the magnificent; of mud and stars; of earth and flowers; of love and hate and laughter and tears and ugliness and beauty and hurt?       *Ibid.*

18 It had no definite expression. It was not in their bearing; it could not be said to look out from the dead, black, Indian eye, nor was it anywhere about the immobile, parchment face. Yet somewhere black implacable resentment smoldered in the heart of this dying race.     *Cimarron,* Ch. 3    *1929*

19 "The difference in America is that the women have always gone along. When you read the history of France you're peeking through a bedroom keyhole. The history of England is a joust. The womenfolks were always Elaineish and anemic, it seems. . . . But here in this land, Sabra, my girl, the women, they've been the real hewers of wood and drawers of water. You'll want to remember that."     *Ibid.*

20 "The gaudiest star-spangled cosmic joke that ever was played on a double-dealing government burst into fireworks today when, with a roar that could be heard for miles around, thousands of barrels of oil shot into the air on the miserable desert land known as the Osage Indian reservation and occupied by those duped and wretched—!"    Ibid., Ch. 20

21 "If American politics are too dirty for women to take part in, there's something wrong with American politics."    Ibid., Ch. 23

22 "I am not belittling the brave pioneer men, but the sunbonnet as well as the sombrero has helped to settle this glorious land of ours."     *Ibid.*

23 The goat's business is none of the sheep's concern.    *Saratoga Trunk,* Ch. 2   *1941*

24 Adventurers, both. . . . They were like two people who, searching for buried treasure, are caught in a quicksand. Every struggle to extricate themselves only made them sink deeper.    Ibid., Ch. 6

25 "Men often marry their mothers. . . ."    *Ibid.*

26 "You lose in the end unless you know how the wheel is fixed or can fix it yourself."    Ibid., Ch. 14

27 "Most people don't know how to have a good time, any more than spoiled children. I show them. I spend their money for them, and they're grateful for it. I've got nothing to lose, because I live by my wits. They can't take that away from me."    *Ibid.*

28 It was part of the Texas ritual. We're rich as son-of-a-bitch stew but look how homely we are, just as plain-folksy as Grandpappy back in 1836. We know about champagne and caviar but we talk hog and hominy.    *Giant,* Ch. 2   *1952*

29 But undeniably there was about these three young women an aura, a glow, a dash of what used to be called diablerie that served as handily as beauty and sometimes handier. These exhilarating qualities wore well, too, for they lasted the girls their lifetime, which beauty frequently fails to do.    Ibid., Ch. 5

30 "Texas air is so rich you can nourish off it like it was food."    Ibid., Ch. 9

31 A woman can look both moral and exciting— if she also looks as if it was quite a struggle.    Quoted in *Reader's Digest*   *December, 1954*

## 562. Helen Hoyt

(1887–?)

\* \*＊\*

1 My heart led me past and took me away; And yet it was my heart that wanted to stay.    "In the Park"

## 563. Agnes Meyer

(1887–1970?)

1 When you travel through the wheat fields of Kansas for a day and a night and see endless herds grazing on the pastureland, when you have spent weeks visiting factory after factory in city after city producing at top speed, when

you have seen the tireless effort, the intelligent application of management and labor and their ever-increasing co-operation, you realize that there are enough resources, actual and potential, enough brains and good will in this country to turn the whole world into a paradise.
"Juvenile Delinquency and Child Labor," *Washington Post* *March 14, 1943*

2 What the Nation must realize is that the home, when both parents work, is non-existent. Once we have honestly faced that fact, we must act accordingly. Ibid., "Living Conditions of the Woolworker" *April 10, 1943*

3 We have forgotten that democracy must live as it thinks and think as it lives.
*Journey Through Chaos*, Introduction *1943*

4 An orderly existence creates primarily an unconscious relation to the silent progression of the days, seasons, and the music of the spheres.
*Out of These Roots* *1953*

5 Fortunate are the people whose roots are deep.
Ibid., Ch. 1

6 In pursuit of an educational program to suit the bright and the not-so-bright we have watered down a rigid training for the elite until we now have an educational diet in many of our public high schools that nourishes neither the classes nor the masses. Ibid., Ch. 2

7 Let us hope that in the process of integration in our society, which fortunately is now well underway, the Negro will not allow the American steam roller of conformity to destroy his creative gifts. Ibid., Ch. 8

8 The children are always the chief victims of social chaos. Ibid., Ch. 13

9 Science was the method used in the struggle by which mankind has passed from habit, routine, and caprice, from efforts to use nature magically, to intellectual self-control.
Lecture, "Democracy and Clericalism" *May 21, 1954*

10 Christianity must now rise above the limitations of orthodoxy just as the free world must rise above the limitations of nationalism if we are not to pull the civilized world down around our ears. Ibid.

11 There is a need for heroism in American life today. *Education for a New Morality*, Ch. 1 *1957*

12 We Americans must now throw off our childishness and parochialism and create a new idea of man acceptable to thinking people the world over. Ibid.

13 From the nineteenth-century view of science as a god, the twentieth century has begun to see it as a devil. It behooves us now to understand that science is neither one nor the other.
Ibid., Ch. 3

14 We can never achieve absolute truth but we can live hopefully by a system of calculated probabilities. The law of probability gives to natural and human sciences—to human experience as a whole—the unity of life we seek.
Ibid., Ch. 3

15 We are immoral in America today precisely because our existing institutions do not perform their function of abolishing our inherited dualism between thought and action, between our American ideals and what we do about them. Let us bear in mind that idealism when separated from empirical methods and experimental utilization in concrete social situations is vague, semantic mouthing. . . .
Ibid., Ch. 16

16 It certainly must have been a relief for the women of the country to realize that one could be a woman and a lady and yet be thoroughly political. Letter to Eleanor Roosevelt (July 25, 1952), Quoted in *Eleanor: The Years Alone* by Joseph P. Lash *1972p*

# 564. Marianne Moore
## (1887–1972)

1 The monkeys
winked too much and were afraid of
snakes. The zebras, supreme in
their abnormality; the elephants, with
their fog-colored skin
and strictly practical appendages
were there.
"The Monkeys" *1921*

2 I, too, dislike it: there are things that are important beyond all this fiddle.
"Poetry," *Collected Poems* *1935*

3 There is a great amount of poetry in unconscious fastidiousness.
Ibid., "Critics and Connoisseurs"

4 I wonder what Adam and Eve
think of it by this time.
Ibid., "Marriage"

5 My father used to say,
"Superior people never make long visits,"
Have to be shown Longfellow's grave
or the glass flowers at Harvard.
Ibid., "Silence"

6 The deepest feeling always shows itself in
silence;
not in silence, but restraint. . . .
Ibid.

7    What is our innocence,
what is our guilt? All are
naked, none is safe.
"What Are Years?," St. 1,
Collected Poems    1941

8 . . . satisfaction is a lowly
thing, how pure a thing is joy.
Ibid., St. 3

9 Denunciations do not affect
the culprit; nor blows, but it
is torture to him not to be spoken to.
Ibid., "Spenser's Ireland," St. 1

10 I am troubled, I'm dissatisfied, I'm Irish.
Ibid.

11    Among animals, one has a sense of humor.
Humor saves a few steps, it saves years.
Ibid., "The Pangolin," St. 1

12    As contagion
of sickness makes sickness,
contagion of trust can make trust.
"In Distrust of Merits," St. 2,
Collected Poems    1944

13 . . . "When a man is prey to anger,
he is moved by outside things; when he holds
his ground in patience patience
patience, that is action or
beauty."
Ibid., St. 6

14 . . . The world's an orphan's home. . . .
Ibid., St. 7

15 Beauty is everlasting
And dust is for a time.
Ibid.

16 Three foremost aids to persuasion which occur
to me are humility, concentration, and gusto.
Speech, "Humility, Concentration,
and Gusto," Grolier Club
December 21, 1948

17 [The] whirlwind fife-and-drum of the storm
bends the salt
marsh grass, disturbs stars in the sky and the
star on the steeple; it is a privilege to see so
much confusion.
"The Steeple-Jack,"
Collected Poems    1951

18 One must be as clear as one's natural reticence
allows one to be.
Quoted in "Reading Contemporary
Poetry" by Louise Bogan,
College English    February, 1953

19 Verbal felicity is the fruit of art and diligence
and refusing to be false.    Ibid.

20 Since writing is not only an art but a trade
embodying principles attested by experience, we
would do well not to forget that it is an expedient for making oneself understood and that
what is said should at least have the air of
having meant something to the person who
wrote it—as is the case with Gertrude Stein
and James Joyce.
Lecture, "Idiosyncrasy and Technique,"
Oxford University    June, 1956

21    O to be a dragon
a symbol of the power of Heaven—of
silkworm
size or immense; at times invisible.
Felicitous phenomenon!
"O to Be a Dragon"    1959

22 To wear the arctic fox
you have to kill it.
"The Arctic Fox (Or Goat)"    1959

23 Camels are snobbish
and sheep, unintelligent;
water buffaloes, neurasthenic—
even murderous.
Reindeer seem over-serious.
Ibid.

## 565. Georgia O'Keeffe
(1887–   )

1 Those hills! They go on and on—it was like
looking at two miles of gray elephants.
Quoted in Time
October 12, 1970

2 I grew up pretty much as everybody else grows
up, and one day . . . [in 1916] found myself
saying to myself—I can't live where I want to—
I can't go where I want to—I can't do what I
want to—I can't even say what I want to—
School and things that painters have taught me
even keep me from painting as I want to. I
decided I was a very stupid fool not to at
least paint as I wanted to and say what I
wanted to when I painted as that seemed to be
the only thing I could do that didn't concern
anybody but myself—that was nobody's business but my own. . . .
Quoted in Georgia O'Keeffe by Lloyd
Goodrich and Doris Bry    1970

3 . . . nobody sees a flower—really—it is so small—we haven't time—and to see takes time like to have a friend takes time. If I could paint the flower exactly as I see it no one would see what I see because I would paint it small like the flower is small. So I said to myself— I'll paint what I see—what the flower is to me but I'll paint it big and they will be surprised into taking time to look at it—I will make even busy New Yorkers take time to see what I see of flowers. . . . Well, I made you take time to look at what I saw and when you took time to really notice my flower you hung all your own associations with flowers on my flower and you write about my flower as if I think and see what you think and see of the flower—and I don't.      Ibid. (c.1939)

4 This is the only place that I really belonged [the Texas panhandle], that I really felt at home. This is my country—terrible winds and wonderful emptiness.
> Quoted in "Flowers, Bones, and the Blue" by Alfred Frankenstein (c. 1919), *San Francisco Examiner & Chronicle*      March 14, 1971

5 . . . that Blue [of the sky] . . . will always be there as it is now after all man's destruction is finished.      Ibid.

6 I don't very much enjoy looking at paintings in general. I know too much about them. I take them apart.
> Quoted in "An Artist of Her Own School" by Alexander Fried, *San Francisco Examiner & Chronicle*      March 16, 1971

7 The desert is the last place you can see all around you. The light out here makes everything close, and it is never, never the same. Sometimes the light hits the mountains from behind and front at the same time, and it gives them the look of Japanese prints, you know, distances in layers.
> Quoted in "A Visit with Georgia O'Keeffe" by Beth Coffelt, *San Francisco Examiner & Chronicle*      April 11, 1971

## 566. Edith Sitwell

### (1887–1964)

1 Every one hundred years or so it becomes necessary for a change to take place in the body of poetry. . . . A fresh movement appears and produces a few great men, and once more the force and vigour die from the results of age; the movement is carried on by weak and worthless imitators, and a change becomes necessary again.      *Poetry and Criticism*      1926

2 Still falls the Rain—
Dark as the world of man, black as our loss—
Blind as the nineteen hundred and forty nails
Upon the Cross.
> "Still Falls the Rain"    1940

3 Daisy and Lily
Lazy and silly. . . .
> "Facade" (1922), *Facade and Other Poems 1920–1935*    1950

4 But a word stung him like a mosquito. . . .
> Ibid., "I do like to be beside the Seaside" (1922)

5 The air still seems to reverberate with the wooden sound of numskulls being soundly hit.
> "Dylan Thomas," *Atlantic Monthly*    February, 1954

6 He had full eyes . . . giving at first the impression of being unseeing, but seeing all, looking over immeasurable distances.      Ibid.

7 Alas, that he who caught and sang the sun in flight, yet was the sun's brother, and never grieved it on its way, should have left us with no good-by, good night.      Ibid.

8 After the first death, there is no other. . . .
> Ibid.

9 I'm not the man to baulk at a low smell,
I'm not the man to insist on asphodel.
This sounds like a He-fellow, don't you think?
It sounds like that. I belch, I bawl, I drink.
> "One-Way Song," *Collected Poems*    1954

10 Jane, Jane
Tall as a crane,
The morning light creaks down again.
> Ibid., "Aubade"

11 My poems are hymns of praise to the glory of life.
> Ibid., "Some Notes on My Poetry"

12    A lady asked me why, on most occasions, I wore black. "Are you in mourning?"
"Yes."
"For whom are you in mourning?"
"For the world."
> *Taken Care Of*, Ch. 1    1965p

13 . . . I have never, in all my life, been so odious as to regard myself as "superior" to any living being, human or animal. I just walked alone— as I have always walked alone.
> Ibid., Ch. 2

14 By the time I was eleven years old, I had been taught that nature, far from abhorring a Vacuum, positively adores it.
                 Ibid., Ch. 3

15 I have lived through the shattering of two civilizations, have seen two Pandora's boxes opened. One contained horror, the other emptiness. . . . In both the new worlds hatched in those Pandora's boxes, mud and flies had taken over the spirit.          Ibid., Ch. 7

16 At last the day drifted into a long lacquered afternoon.               Ibid., Ch. 13

17 We stand on one leg and put our heads under our arms, and when the blood rushes into our heads we are in the full state of Awareness and the Cosmos is just round the corner, and we rush to it and rebound right into the Fourth Dimension. . . .             Ibid.

18 MR. MUGGLEBY LION. I hate to disturb you, but I have just finished a *Little Sonnet,* that I *must* read to you.

HIERATIC WOMAN (coldly). It can't be a *Little* Sonnet, Mr. Muggleby Lion. Sonnets are all of the same size.              Ibid.

19 Rhythm is one of the principal translators between dream and reality. Rhythm might be described, as to the world of sound, what light is to the world of sight. It shares and gives new meaning. Rhythm was described by Schopenhauer as melody deprived of its pitch.
                 Ibid., Ch. 14

20 Eccentricity is *not,* as dull people would have us believe, a form of madness. It is often a kind of innocent pride, and the man of genius and the aristocrat are frequently regarded as eccentrics because genius and aristocrat are entirely unafraid of and uninfluenced by the opinions and vagaries of the crowd.
                 Ibid., Ch. 15

21 A pompous woman of his acquaintance, complaining that the head-waiter of a restaurant had not shown her and her husband immediately to a table, said, "We had to tell him who we were." Gerald [Lord Berners], interested, enquired, "And who were you?"    Ibid.

22 Vulgarity is, in reality, nothing but a modern, chic, pert descendant of the goddess Dullness.
                 Ibid., Ch. 19

23 I do not know how to address you. I cannot call you a goose, as geese saved the capitol of Rome, and no amount of cackling on your part would awaken anybody! Nor can I call you an ass, since Balaam's constant companion saw an angel, and recognised it.       Ibid., Ch. 22

24 . . . the heartless stupidity of those who have never known a great and terrifying poverty.
                 Ibid.

25 When we think of cruelty, we must try to remember the stupidity, the envy, the frustration from which it has arisen.      Ibid.

26 Winter is the time for comfort, for good food and warmth, for the touch of a friendly hand and for a talk beside the fire: it is the time for home.               Ibid., Ch. 22

27 Then all will be over, bar the shouting and the worms.                  Ibid.

\*   \*   \*

28 Remember only this of our hopeless love
That never till time is done
Will the fire of the heart and the fire of the mind be one.
                 "Heart and Mind"

29 Under great yellow flags and banners of the ancient Cold
Began the huge migrations
From some primeval disaster in the heart of Man.
                 "The Shadow of Cain"

## 567. Anna Akhmatova
### (1888?–1966)

1 What hangs in the balance is nowise in doubt;
We know the event and we brave what we know;
Our clocks are all striking the hour of courage.
           "Courage"      1942

2    O great language we love:
It is you, Russian tongue, we must save, and we swear
We will give you unstained to the sons of our sons;
You shall live on our lips, and we promise you—never
A prison shall know you, but you shall be free Forever.
                 Ibid.

## 568. Vicki Baum
### (1888–1960)

1 Fame always brings loneliness. Success is as ice cold and lonely as the north pole.
           *Grand Hotel*      1931

2 A woman who is loved always has success.
                 Ibid.

3 Marriage always demands the greatest understanding of the art of insincerity possible between two human beings. *And Life Goes On* *1932*

4 Pity is the deadliest feeling that can be offered to a woman. Ibid.

5 To be a Jew is a destiny. Ibid.

## 569. Marjorie Bowen
### (1888–1952)

1 "But will it last?"
"What a ridiculous question," returned the colonel blandly. "Will you, or I, or anything last? Flesh is grass, my dear Count."
*General Crack*, Ch. 1 *1928*

2 Useless for one who did not believe in Heaven to renounce the World: that would be to fall into a void. Ibid., Ch. 10

3 "If you live in the world you must live on the world's terms." Ibid.

4 "I thought," sighed the young man, "that you might tell me the secret of peace."
"How can I tell you that? It's like talking to a general who wants to know how to set various troops in order. If you have not the power of authority, no one can give it to you. If you can't command your own soul, how can I give you enlightenment how to do so?" Ibid.

5 "Why do I concern myself with all these passions, that to me are withered as the last leaf on a dead tree?" Ibid., Ch. 35

6 "What is the most dangerous possession in the world, Mr. Falkland?"
"No use at riddles," replied the young man cautiously.
Dobree picked up the speaking-tube.
"Someone else's secret," he remarked. . . .
*The Shadow on Mockways*, Ch. 2 *1932*

7 "If I continue to drink I shall soon be like these—how long would it take? It has not really got hold of me yet. I could stop it if I wanted. Sometimes I take nothing for days together—yes, if it were worth while and something else offered, I could stop. But it is not worth while and nothing else offers."
*Moss Rose* *1935*

8 . . . she was cured of love as she was cured of drunkenness. Indulgence had soon brought her to a point of nausea; she had never given anyone tenderness or affection, and the recollection of dead passions that had ended in disgust or rage was like the recollection of the stench of decay. Ibid.

9 "It is more difficult, my lord, to rule the King's favourites than for the favourites to rule the King." *My Tattered Loving*, Ch. 1 *1937*

10 Meanwhile, he continued to search for a brisk and subtle poison, for it seemed to him that one who could make the discovery of such a weapon as this would be more powerful than the greatest of kings. Ibid., Ch. 2

11 But it had not needed much of a turn of fortune's wheel for the Frenchman to have been the quack counting up his illicit gains and the Englishman to have been the courtly physician to whom all the great ones ran for help in their distresses. Ibid.

12 As civilisation advanced, people began to discover that more was to be gained by flattery than by force—and that flattery had a larger purchasing power than coin of the realm.
"The Art of Flattery," *World's Wonder* *1937*

13 Flattery is so necessary to all of us that we flatter one another just to be flattered in return. . . . Ibid.

14 "Leave well alone, my dear Miss Lawne."
"But perhaps we are leaving evil alone," replied the lady, smiling.
"In that case, also, have nothing to do with it." *Mignonette*, Ch. 1 *1948*

15 "Rich and free," Barbara repeated to herself. It was hard to accept the meaning of the words. There was no one to thwart her, to scold her, to warn her, to advise her; there was only Mr. Bompast who had no authority over her and whose dry prudence would be ignored. She could not even be checked if she did anything eccentric. Ibid.

16 Custom reclaimed her. . . . So, insidiously, her middle-class respectability hemmed in Barbara Lawne. . . . Only in her dreams did she explore wild and darkling landscapes. . . .
Ibid., Ch. 2

\* \* \*

17 Even a fool can deceive a man—if he be a bigger fool than himself.
"The Glen o' Weeping"

## 570. Aline Murray Kilmer
### (1888–1941)

\* \* \*

1 For there is only sorrow in my heart;
There is no room for fear.
But how I wish I were afraid again,
My dear, my dear.
"I Shall Not Be Afraid"

2 I'm sorry you are wiser,
  I'm sorry you are taller;
  I liked you better foolish,
  And I liked you better smaller.
  "For the Birth of a Middle-Aged
  Child," St. 1

3 I cannot see myself as I once was;
  I would not see myself as I am now.
  "To Aphrodite: With a Mirror"

4 I sing of little loves that glow
  Like tapers shining in the rain,
  Of little loves that break themselves
  Like moths against the window-pane.
  "Prelude"

5 Things have a terrible permanence
  When people die.
  "Things," St. 6

6 When people inquire I always just state,
  "I have four nice children, and hope to have
  eight."
  "Ambition"

## 571. Olga Knopf
(1888–    )

1 . . . the sexes are living, we might say, in a
  vast communal neurosis; a highly contagious
  neurosis which parents pass on to their children
  and men and women pass on to each other.
  *The Art of Being a Woman*    1932

2 The art of being a woman can never consist of
  being a bad imitation of a man.    Ibid.

3 The outer limitations to woman's progress are
  caused by the fact we are living in a man's
  culture.    *Women on Their Own*    1935

## 572. Clare Kummer
(1888–1948)

1 ETHEL. Did you sell your verses to Binder?

  JENNINGS. No—he seemed to think they were
  indecent and when I explained to him that they
  weren't he lost interest in them—so that's all.
  *Good Gracious, Annabelle*, Act I
  1916

2 STEIN. It's the public. You can't count on it.
  Give 'em something good and they'll go to see
  something bad. Give 'em something bad and
  they don't like that either.
  *Rollo's Wild Oat*, Act I, Sc. 1
  1922

3 STEIN. Pictures are a great business. You take
  a picture and you got something.

  MRS. PARK-GALES. Yes, but what?

  STEIN. You get all through with the actors and
  there they are playing for you every night. If
  they are sick or dead, it don't make any difference. They are working just the same.

  LUCAS. Anything to make us work for nothing!
  Ibid., Sc. 2

4 AUNT MIN. He should have started worrying
  before he had things to worry about.
  *Her Master's Voice*, Act I    1933

5 QUEENA. Don't you know when people are in
  love they don't think? Merciful heavens!

  AUNT MIN. Well, they ought to. I don't know
  of any time when it's more important for them
  to think. In love! In foolishness!
  Ibid., Act II

\* \* \*

6 Oh, there was a woman-hater hated women all
  he could,
  And he built himself a bungle in a dingle in
  the wood;
  Here he lived and said of ladies things I do not
  think he should,
  "If they're good they're not good-looking; if
  good-looking, they're not good."
  "In the Dingle-Dongle Bell"

## 573. Lotte Lehmann
(1888–1976)

1 But to me the actual sound of the words is all-
  important; I feel always that the words complete the music and must never be swallowed
  up in it. The music is the shining path over
  which the poet travels to bring his song to the
  world.    "The Singing Actor," *Players at
  Work*, Morton Eustis, ed.    1937

2 I have never understood the star who enjoys
  playing with a mediocre cast in order to shine
  out the more brilliantly himself, for the essence
  of any fine dramatic or operatic production is
  harmonious integration of all performances.
  Ibid.

3 Imitation is, and can only be, the enemy of
  artistry. Everything which breathes the breath
  of life is changeable. . . . Only from life itself
  may life be born.    *More Than Singing*,
  Introduction    1945

4 That fine God-given instrument—the voice—must be capable of responding with the greatest subtlety to every shade of each emotion. But it must be subordinate, it must only be the foundation, the soil from which flowers true art.      Ibid.

5 Do not become paralyzed and enchained by the set patterns which have been woven of old. No, build from your own youthful feeling, your own groping thought and your own flowering perception—and help to further that beauty which has grown from the roots of tradition. . . .      Ibid.

6 . . . if your soul can soar above technique and float in the lofty regions of creative art, you have fulfilled your mission as a singer. For what mission can be greater than that of giving to the world hours of exaltation in which it may forget the misery of the present, the cares of everyday life and lose itself in the eternally pure world of harmony. . . .      Ibid.

## 574. Katherine Mansfield

(1888–1923)

1 How idiotic civilization is! Why be given a body if you have to keep it shut up in a case like a rare, rare fiddle?
"Bliss," *Bliss and Other Stories*
1920

2 ". . . Why! Why! Why is the middle-class so stodgy—so utterly without a sense of humour!"      Ibid.

3 . . . roses are the only flowers that impress people at garden-parties; the only flowers that everybody is certain of knowing.
"The Garden Party"      1922

4 Hundreds, yes, literally hundreds, had come out in a single night; the green bushes bowed down as though they had been visited by archangels.      Ibid.

5 Fancy cream puffs so soon after breakfast. The very idea made one shudder. All the same, two minutes later Jose and Laura were licking their fingers with that absorbed inward look that only comes from whipped cream.      Ibid.

6 "If you're going to stop a band playing every time someone has an accident, you'll lead a very strenuous life."      Ibid.

7 There lay a young man, fast asleep—sleeping so soundly, so deeply, that he was far, far away from them both. Oh, so remote, so peaceful. He was dreaming. Never wake him up again.      Ibid.

8 Although over six years had passed away, the boss never thought of the boy except as lying unchanged, unblemished in his uniform, asleep for ever.      "The Fly," *The Dove's Nest*
1923

9 How on earth could he have slaved, denied himself, kept going all those years without the promise for ever before him of the boy's stepping into his shoes carrying on where he left off?      Ibid.

10 It is as though God opened his hand and let you dance on it a little, and then shut it . . . so tight that you could not even cry.
*The Journal of Katherine Mansfield*
(February, 1914)      1927p

11 Oh, the times when she had walked upside down on the ceiling . . . floated on a lake of light . . . !      Ibid. (December 31, 1918)

12 There is no limit to human suffering. When one thinks "Now I have touched the bottom of the sea—now I can go no deeper," one goes deeper. . . . Suffering is boundless, is eternity. One pang is eternal torment. Physical suffering is—child's play.      Ibid. (December 19, 1920)

13 Everything in life that we really accept undergoes a change. So suffering must become Love. That is the mystery.      Ibid.

14 As in the physical world, so in the spiritual world, pain does not last forever.      Ibid.

15 "Do you know what individuality is?"
"No."
"Consciousness of will. To be conscious that you have a will and can act."
Yes, it is. It's a glorious saying.
     Ibid. (September 30, 1922)

16 Nearly all my improved health is pretence—acting. What does it amount to? . . . I am an absolutely helpless invalid. What is my life? It is the existence of a parasite.
     Ibid. (October 14, 1922)

17 Risk! Risk anything! Care no more for the opinions of others, for those voices. Do the hardest thing on earth for you. Act for yourself. Face the truth.      Ibid.

18 By health I mean the power to live a full, adult, living, breathing life in close contact with . . . the earth and the wonders thereof—the sea—the sun.      Ibid.

19 To be wildly enthusiastic, or deadly serious—both are wrong. Both pass. One must keep ever present a sense of humor.
     Ibid. (October 17, 1922)

20 Now perhaps you understand what "indifference" means. It is to learn not to mind, and not to show your mind. *Ibid.*

21 *Important.* When we can begin to take our failures nonseriously, it means we are ceasing to be afraid of them. It is of immense importance to learn to laugh at ourselves.
*Ibid.* (October, 1922)

22 Whenever I prepare for a journey I prepare as though for death. Should I never return, all is in order. This is what life has taught me.
*Ibid.* (1922)

23 I want, by understanding myself, to understand others. I want to be all that I am capable of becoming. . . . This all sounds very strenuous and serious. But now that I have wrestled with it, it's no longer so. I feel happy—deep down. *All is well.* *Ibid.*

24 I feel like a fly who has been dropped into the milk-jug and fished out again, but is still too milky and drowned to start cleaning up yet.
*Katherine Mansfield's Letters to John Middleton Murry, 1913–1922*
*1951p*

## 575.  Carlotta Monterey O'Neill
### (1888–1970)

1 To understand his [Eugene O'Neill's] work you must understand the man, for the work and the man are one. Quoted in *O'Neill* by Arthur and Barbara Gelb　*1960*

2 He got a racing car, a Bugatti, and when he was very nervous and tired he would go out in it and drive ninety-five miles an hour and come back looking nineteen years old and perfectly relaxed. *Ibid.*, Ch. 4

3 O'Neill was a tough mick, and never loved a woman who walked. He loved only his work. But he had respect for me. I had an independent income, and I told him I'd marry him if he would let me pay half of all the household expenses. . . . He said he needed a home. "I want a home properly run," he told me. And that is what I did for him, I saw to it that he was able to work. *Ibid.*

4 I had to work like a dog. I was Gene's secretary, I was his nurse. His health was always bad. I did everything. He wrote the plays, but I did everything else. I loved it. It was a privilege to live with him, because he was mentally stimulating. My God, how many women have husbands who are very stimulating? *Ibid.*

## 576.  Agnes Sligh Turnbull
### (1888–　　)

1 "Now ain't that funny! I thought it was you, an' you thought it was me; an' begob, it's *nayther* of us!" *The Rolling Years,*
Bk. I, Ch. 6　*1936*

2 "The older I get, Jeannie, the more I wonder whether a life shouldn't perhaps be like a river—flowing along in the channel God gave it. Not too many radical deflections."
*Ibid.*, Bk. II, Ch. 1

3 "That's it! The long look ahead. Doesn't it change things, though? Staking neck or nothing on a life to come! Keeps us from being too fussy over affairs here, I guess." *Ibid.*, Ch. 4

4 "There is still vitality under the winter snow, even though to the casual eye it seems to be dead." *Ibid.*

5 "It's the trail of the old Puritan over us. We assume that the only natural course of events is the wrath of God and the miseries of this life. We're afraid to believe that the Creator might sometimes actually wish us well!"
*Ibid.*

6 "The trouble with the average human being is that he never goes on mountain journeys. He stops at the first way station and refuses to believe there is country beyond."
*Ibid.*, Ch. 5

7 "You must learn to drink the cup of life as it comes, Connie, without stirring it up from the bottom. That's where the bitter dregs are!"
*Ibid.*

8 "Wasn't it [religion] invented by man for a kind of solace? It's as though he said, 'I'll make me a nice comfortable garment to shut out the heat and the cold'; and then it ends by becoming a straitjacket." *Ibid.*, Ch. 6

9 "I don't know that I care so much about going far," he said at last; "but I should like to go *deep* where I go." *Ibid.*, Epilogue

10 "You can put city polish *on* a man, but by golly, it seems you can't ever rub it off him."
*The Golden Journey*, Ch. 2　*1955*

11 "The idea of perfection always gives one a chance to talk without knowing facts."
*Ibid.*, Ch. 4

12 "The older you get the more you realize that gray isn't such a bad color. And in politics you work with it or you don't work at all."
*Ibid.*, Ch. 7

13 There would seem to be a law operating in human experience by which the mind once suddenly aware of a verity for the first time immediately invents it again.    Ibid., Ch. 10

14 Oh, the utter unpredictability of a quarrel! How inflammable words were to ignite each other until the blaze of them scorched and seared.    Ibid.

15 "Do you know that the tendrils of graft and corruption have become mighty interlacing roots so that even men who would like to be honest are tripped and trapped by them?"    Ibid., Ch. 11

16 Defeat in itself was part and parcel of the great gambling game of politics. A man who could not accept it and try again was not of the stuff of which leaders are made.    Ibid., Ch. 12

17 . . . she *was* a widow, that strange feminine entity who had once been endowed with a dual personality and was now only half of what she had been.    *The Flowering*, Ch. 1    1972

18 "Dogs' lives are too short. Their only fault, really."    Ibid., Ch. 2

19 "If you keep things long enough, some fool or other will come along an' buy 'em."    Ibid., Ch. 3

20 Girls! Girls! Girls!
With platted hair an' mebbe curls
Singin' in a *chorus*!
Lord have mercy o'er us.    Ibid., Ch. 4

## 577. Mary Day Winn
### (1888–1965)

1 Sex is the tabasco sauce which an adolescent national palate sprinkles on every course in the menu.    *Adam's Rib*    1931

2 In the argot of the sub-deb, "U.S.A." has long ago lost its patriotic meaning. It now stands for "Universal Sex Appeal."    Ibid.

## 578. Enid Bagnold
### (1889– )

1 "She keeps 'er brains in 'er 'eart. An' that's where they ought ter be. An' a man or woman who does that's one in a million an' 'as got my backing."    *National Velvet*    1935

2 "Things come suitable to the time. Childbirth. An' bein' in love. An' death. You can't know 'em till you come to them. No use guessing an' dreading."    Ibid.

3 "There's men . . . as can see things in people. There's men . . . as can choose a horse, an' that horse'll win. It's not the look of the horse, no, nor of the child, nor of the woman. It's the thing *we* can see. . . .    Ibid.

4 "*You're all faith.* An' that's the kind of power that dumb animal can understand."    Ibid.

5 "What's the use of £7000 to me? . . . I shouldn't know what to do with it. What'd I do? It would give me the itch."    Ibid.

6 "This living in the middle of fame's upsetting. It's been like them sweepstakes you read of break up the home."    Ibid.

7 "Love don't seem dainty on a fat woman."    Ibid.

8 LAUREL. She says true devotion is only to be got when a man is worked to death and has no rival.    *The Chalk Garden*, Act I    1953

9 MAITLAND. Madame loves the unusual! It's a middle-class failing—she says—to run away from the unusual.    Ibid.

10 MRS. ST. MAUGHAM. You can't fit false teeth to a woman of character. As one gets older and older, the appearance becomes such a bore.    Ibid.

11 MRS. ST. MAUGHAM. Life without a room to oneself is a barbarity.    Ibid.

12 MRS. ST. MAUGHAM. Privilege and power make selfish people—but gay ones.    Ibid.

13 MAITLAND. Praise is the only thing that brings to life again a man that's been destroyed.    Ibid.

14 MRS. ST. MAUGHAM. Love can be had any day! Success is far harder.    Ibid.

15 MADRIGAL. Truth doesn't ring true in a court of law.    Ibid., Act II

16 JUDGE. Judges don't age. Time decorates them.    Ibid.

17 OLIVIA. The thoughts of a *daughter* are a kind of memorial.    Ibid., Act III

18 SHE. But it's dishonest to make friends with the next generation.    *The Chinese Prime Minister*, Act I, Sc. 1    1964

19 SHE. And that's the real truth about people! They are not types. They aren't mothers-in-law and daughters-in-law! They are creatures ardently engaged on themselves!     Ibid.

20 ALICE. Oh—a girl's looks are *agony!*     Ibid.

21 SHE. Yes, I was kind. But kindness is so fugitive. It comes like a gust into the heart. And blows out again.     Ibid.

22 SHE. I want to get *out!* (*Picking up and shaking the engagement book.*) *Out* of this book—with its procession—moving me on!     Ibid.

23 SHE. It was charming of God! I never expected it! . . . That as beauty vanishes the eyes grow dimmer.     Ibid., Act II

24 SHE. If you fight an old battle—where are the witnesses! And the evidence—obliterated!     Ibid.

25 SIR GREGORY. Marriage. The beginning and the end are wonderful. But the middle part is hell.     Ibid.

26 ALICE. It must be pleasant to reach that age when one can go to the lavatory without explanation.     Ibid.

27 BENT. So few people achieve the final end. *Most* are caught napping.     Ibid., Act III

28 SHE. We were so different that when two rooms separated us for half an hour—we met again as strangers.     Ibid.

29 SHE. The using-up of grandmothers is not for me. It was pre-Christian! Now only the Latins and the natives do it! . . . I *had* my babies—it was like love! But I won't do things twice!     Ibid.

30 SHE. And if I die in ten years—or ten minutes —you can't measure Time! In ten minutes everything can be felt! In four minutes you can be born! Or live. In two minutes God may be understood! And what one woman grasps— all men may get nearer to.     Ibid.

31 SHE. I have always been a punctual woman. I have never glanced at the sea as I drove to the station. If God had been stoking the engine I wouldn't have seen Him!     Ibid.

## 579.  Mildred Cram

### (1889–?)

1 Publicity tripped upon the heels of publicity. "Billy," *Harper's Bazaar*     1924

2 He was capitalized, consolidated, incorporated, copyrighted, limited. protected, insured, and all rights reserved, including the Scandinavian.     Ibid.

3 "I am vulgar, my friend! I mix tears with idiocy. I put the grotesque into love. I tickle sluggish minds. My recipe is a mixture of legend and pep, pantomime and beauty, artifice and art."     Ibid.

## 580.  Fannie Hurst

### (1889–1968)

1 It's hard for a young girl to have patience for old age sitting and chewing all day over the past.     "Get Ready the Wreaths," *Cosmopolitan*     1917

2 It is doubtful if in all its hothouse garden of women the Hotel Bon Ton boasted a broken finger-nail or that little brash place along the forefinger that tattles so of potato peeling or asparagus scraping.     "She Walks in Beauty," *Cosmopolitan*     1921

3 "I always say he wore himself out with conscientiousness."     Ibid.

4 To housekeep, one had to plan ahead and carry items of motley nature around in the mind and at the same time preside, as mother had, at table, just as if everything, from the liver and bacon, to the succotash, to the French toast and strawberry jam, had not been matters of forethought and speculation.     *Imitation of Life*, Ch. 2     1932

5 He had always said of himself that people first tasted the command in his voice and then came nibbling at his products.     Ibid., Ch. 14

6 "I know it, and when I knows a thing wid my knowin', I knows it."     Ibid., Ch. 33

7 "Honey-chile, it will shore seem a funny world up dar widout washin'. If de Lawd's robes only needed launderin', I'd do his tucks de way He's never seen 'em done."     Ibid., Ch. 36

8 Papa lived so separately within himself that I retreated to Mama, who wore herself on the outside. Everything about her hung in view like peasant adobe houses with green peppers and little shrines, drying diapers and cooking utensils on the facade.     *Anatomy of Me*, Bk. I     1958

9 This anatomy of me is serving the double purpose of revealing me to myself.     Ibid., Bk. III

## 581. Elsie Janis
### (1889–1956)

1 When I think of the hundreds of things I
  might be,
  I get down on my knees and thank God that
  I'm me.
            "Compensation," *Poems Now and
                        Then    c.1927*

2 Why do we do it?
  Oh, Hell! What's the use?
  Why battle with the universe?
  Why not declare a truce?
                        Ibid., "Why?"

3 Up and down the burning sidewalks
  Praying ever for a job,
  In my heart a curse for mankind,
  In my pocket not a bob.
                  Ibid., "The Actor's Lament"

4 It was Mother who fought. Fought! To keep
  me up to par! To make me study and improve.
  Fought! To keep my name in the large type
  she believed I merited. Fought for heat in
  trains to protect my health. Fought to make
  ends meet, when each week she had finished
  sending money to the many dependents that
  automatically arrived on the high heels of
  success. Invincible! best describes her.
        *So Far, So Good!*, Pt. I    1931

5 I realize, at least, that I have never been really
  virtuous, I have only been egotistical.
                        Ibid., Pt. VI

6 Life is marvelous! There is no death! It's a
  pity, everything that goes up must come down.
                                    Ibid.

## 582. Dorothy McCall
### (1889–    )

1 One cannot have wisdom without living life.
            Quoted in the *Los Angeles Times
                        March 14, 1974*

2 Lawmakers and employers should not be allowed to continue their shameful practice of
  punishing still-producing and competent people
  merely because of age.            Ibid.

3 Technology dominates us all, diminishing our
  freedom.                    Ibid.

## 583. Gabriela Mistral
### (1889–1957)

1 A son, a son, a son! I wanted a son of yours
  and mine, in those distant days of burning bliss
  when my bones would tremble at your least
  murmur
  and my brow would glow with a radiant mist.
                "Poem of the Son," St. 1,
                        *Desolacion    1922*

2 he kissed me and now I am someone else;
  someone
  else in the pulse that repeats the pulse of my
  own veins and in the breath that mingles with
  my
  breath. Now my belly is as noble as my heart.
                Ibid., "He Kissed Me," St. 1

3       When he shall roam free on the
  highways, even though he is far away from me,
  the wind that
  lashes him will tear at my flesh, and his cry
  will be in my
  throat, too. My grief and my smile begin in
  your face, my
  son.
                Ibid., "Eternal Grief," St. 2

4 Blushing, full of confusion, I talked with her
  about my
  worries and the fear in my body. I fell on her
  breast,
  and all over again I became a little girl sobbing
  in her
  arms at the terror of life.
                Ibid., "Mother," St. 2

5 I have a true happiness
  and a happiness betrayed,
  the one like a rose,
  the other like a thorn.
                "Richness," *Tala    1938*

6 I love the things I never had
  along with those I have no more.
                Ibid., "Things," St. 1

## 584. Julia Seton
### (1889–?)

1 Dancing is a universal instinct—zoölogic, a
  biologic impulse, found in animals as well as
  in man.    "Why Dance?," *The Rhythm of the
                        Redman    1930*

2 In its natural, primitive form, dancing is vigorous muscular action to vent emotion. Originally, it was the natural expression of the basic impulses of a simple form of life. Triumph, defeat, war, love, hate, desire, propitiation of the gods—all were danced by the hero or the tribe to the rhythm of beaten drums.

> Ibid., "Dance in the Animal World"

3 I have listened by a thousand fires as the Buffalo Wind blew through our lives. . . . And so would come a flood of revelation, an unceasing flow of inspiration such as could not be courted. Many a time have I sat by the embers, in motionless silence for hours, while the words came in unhesitating rhythm of passionate life—for we did not measure our life together with a shallow cup. Each time we dipped, we brought up the chalice brimming full and running over.

> By a Thousand Fires, Prologue
> 1967

4 But life has taught me that it knows better plans than we can imagine, so that I try to submerge my own desires, apt to be too insistent, into a calm willingness to accept what comes, and to make the most of it, then wait again. I have discovered that there is a Pattern, larger and more beautiful than our short vision can weave. . . .

> Ibid., Epilogue

## 585.  Mary E. Buell

### (fl. 1890s)

\* \* \*

1 Something made of nothing, tasting very sweet,
A most delicious compound, with ingredients complete;
But if, as on occasion, the heart and mind are sour,
It has no great significance, and loses half its power.

> "The Kiss"

## 586.  Harriet L. Childe-Pemberton

### (fl. 1890s)

1 As I allays say to my brother,
If it isn't one thing it's the tother.

> "Geese: A Dialogue," Dead Letters and Other Narrative and Dramatic Pieces    1896

2 MURIEL. In fact you expect me to submit to your unreasonableness because you haven't the courage to be honest. How like a man!

> Ibid., "The Deuce of Clubs"

3 MRS. CATERMOLE MACFADIE. No one will deny that things that are wrong frequently have their roots in things that are right; therefore, things that are right are things that are wrong. We are nothing if not logical; and when you have once become a member of the Sour Grape Club, of the Ishmaelites Club, and of the Clean-Sweepers League, you will understand these matters with a more enlightened apprehension.

> Ibid.

4 Whenever any one tells me that he or she has a headache, has business letters to write,—doesn't want to be disturbed,—I take it for granted that he or she is engaged in something nothing less than wicked—and naturally I don't want to know anything about it!

> Ibid., "Smoke: A Monologue"

5 O beautiful Earth! alive, aglow,
With your million things that grow,
I would lay my head on your ample knee. . . .

> "Songs of Earth," I, St. 1, Nenuphar
> 1911

6 Earth rules all her children by the solar clock;—
Should they dare to mock,
Running loose before she gives them leave,
They assuredly will grieve.

> Ibid., II, St. 2

7 For passion has come to the verge and leaps
Headlong to the blind abyss,
Yet gathers thereby the strength of deeps,
And eddies a moment and swirls and sweeps
Till peril is one with bliss!

> Ibid., "Songs of Water," IV, St. 4

8 O sensitive Air who are one with Thought,
To my seeking soul you have brought
(On wings of silence or breeze or gale,)
Your manifold messages. . . .

> Ibid., "Songs of Air," X, St. 1

9 "There is no fear for those who truly see
What is, or will be, springs from all that was,—
How all that happens fitly has to be,
And what ye name 'effect' and 'cause'
Make up but one decree."

> Ibid., "Songs of Fire," IX, St. 7

## 587.  Lina Eckenstein

### (fl. 1890s–1931)

1 The contributions of nuns to literature, as well as incidental remarks, show that the curriculum of study in the nunnery was as liberal as that accepted by the monks, and embraced all available writing whether by Christian or profane authors.

> Women Under Monasticism
> 1896

## 588. Anita Owen

(fl. 1890s)

1 And in these eyes the love-light lies
And lies—and lies and lies!
      "Dreamy Eyes"       *c.1894*

2 . . . Daisies won't tell.
      "Sweet Bunch of Daisies"       *1894*

## 589. Hattie Starr

(fl. 1890s)

1 Nobody loves me, well do I know,
Don't all the cold world tell me so?
      "Nobody Loves Me"       *1893*

2 Somebody loves me; How do I know?
Somebody's eyes have told me so!
      "Somebody Loves Me"       *1893*

## 590. Daisy Ashford

(1890?–1972)

1 I am parshial [sic] to ladies if they are nice.
I suppose it is my nature. I am not quite a
gentleman but you would hardly notice it.
      *The Young Visitors,** Ch. 1       *1919*

2 You look rather rash my dear your colours
don't quite match your face.       Ibid., Ch. 2

3 Here I am tied down to this life he said. . . .
Being royal has many painful drawbacks.
      Ibid., Ch. 6

4 My life will be sour grapes and ashes without
you.       Ibid., Ch. 8

## 591. Elizabeth Gurley Flynn

(1890–1964)

1 He was *an agitator*, born of the first national
awakening of American labor. The shame of
servitude and the glory of struggle were em-
blazoned in the mind of every worker who
heard [Eugene V.] Debs.
      "Eugene V. Debs," *Debs, Haywood,*
      *Ruthenberg*       *1939*

2 We study their lives to understand better the
past, as lessons for the present and inspiration
for the future. The past is the background, the
struggle part. . . .       Ibid., Conclusion

* Written when the author was nine years old.

3 Time was, when the ACLU was young, they
were Anarchists, Socialists, Christian pacifists,
trade unionists, I.W.W., Quaker, Irish Republican and Communist! Today, they are no longer
heretics, non-conformists, radicals—they are
respectable.
      "I Am Expelled from Civil Liberties!,"
      *Sunday Worker*       *March 17, 1940*

4 History has a long-range perspective. It ultimately passes stern judgment on tyrants and
vindicates those who fought, suffered, were imprisoned, and died for human freedom, against
political oppression and economic slavery. Pioneers who were reviled, persecuted, ridiculed,
and abused when they fought for free public
schools, woman's suffrage against chattel slavery, for labor unions, are honored and revered
today.       *Labor's Own: William Z. Foster*
      *1949*

5 We know that the solid foundation of a Communist Party are the workers and that our
Party must be rooted in their struggle. . . . A
study of the inner workings of capitalism with
all its failures and contradictions, its excesses
and abuses, will convince them that capitalism's days are numbered; it has been tried and
found wanting; it hampers progress. . . .
Negro and white workers, young workers,
women workers—will come to understand the
need of being a member of the Communist
Party. . . .       Ibid.

6 We hated the rich, the trusts they owned, the
violence they caused, the oppression they represented.       *The Rebel Girl*, Pt. I       *1955*

7 I said then and am still convinced that the full
opportunity for women to become free and
equal citizens with access to all spheres of
human endeavor cannot come under capitalism, although many demands have been won
by organized struggle.       Ibid.

8 "What freedom?" we asked again. To be wage-
slaves, hired and fired at the will of a soulless
corporation, paid low wages for long hours,
driven by the speed of a machine? What freedom? To be clubbed, jailed, shot down—and
while we spoke, the hoofs of the troopers'
horses clattered by on the street.
      Ibid., Pt. III

9 So confident was he [Nicola Sacco] of his
innocence that sunny afternoon that he had no
fear. He was sure when he told his story in
court he would go free. He did not know that
he was approaching the valley of the shadow
of death. He feared no evil because the truth
was with him. But greed, corruption, prejudice,
fear and hatred of radical foreign-born work-
ingmen were weaving a net around him.
      Ibid., Pt. VII

10 I was a convict, a prisoner without rights, writing a censored letter. But my head was unbowed. Come what may, *I was a political prisoner* and proud of it, at one with some of the noblest of humanity who had suffered for conscience's sake. I felt no shame, no humiliation, no consciousness of guilt. To me my number 11710 was a badge of honor.
*The Alderson Story,\* Ch. 3    1963*

11 One of my correspondents asked me: "What do you think are the main differences between a women's prison and a men's prison?" I replied: "You would never see diapers hung on a line at a men's prison or hear babies crying in the hospital on a quiet Sunday afternoon." The physiological differences—menstruation, menopause, and pregnancy—create intense emotional problems among many women in prison.    *Ibid., Ch. 13*

12 A popular saying in Alderson went as follows: "They work us like a horse, feed us like a bird, treat us like a child, dress us like a man—and then expect us to act like a lady."
*Ibid., Ch. 25*

13 We who are members of the Communist Party repudiate the exclusive identification of democracy with capitalism. We declare that democracy can be widened, take on new aspects, become truly a rule of the people, only when it is extended to the economic life of the people, as in the Soviet Union. As far as women are concerned, the U.S.S.R. is a trailblazer for equal rights and equal opportunities.
*Defense Speech (May 7, 1940), The Trial of Elizabeth Gurley Flynn by the American Civil Liberties Union,* Corliss Lamont, ed.    *1968*

## 592. Frances Noyes Hart
(1890–1943)

1 "I cried at first . . . and then, it was such a beautiful day, that I forgot to be unhappy."
"Green Garden," *Scribner's Magazine* *1921*

## 593. Hedda Hopper
(1890–1966)

1 At one time I thought he wanted to be an actor. He had certain qualifications, including no money and a total lack of responsibility.
*From Under My Hat    1952*

\* The Federal Reformatory for Women at Alderson, West Virginia.

2 I decided that [Arthur] Brisbane was a member of the 7-H club—Holy howling hell, how he hates himself.    Ibid.

3 His footprints\* were never asked for, yet no one has ever filled his shoes.    Ibid.

4 In Hollywood gratitude is Public Enemy Number One.    Ibid.

## 594. Rose Fitzgerald Kennedy
(1890–   )

1 The secret of the Kennedy successes in politics was not money but meticulous planning and organization, tremendous effort and the enthusiasm and devotion of family and friends.
*Times to Remember    1974*

2 Sedentary people are apt to have sluggish minds. A sluggish mind is apt to be reflected in flabbiness of body and in a dullness of expression that invites no interest and gets none.    Ibid.

3 Birds sing after a storm; why shouldn't people feel as free to delight in whatever remains to them?    Ibid.

4 We cannot always understand the ways of Almighty God—the crosses which He sends us, the sacrifices which He demands of us. . . . But we accept with faith and resignation His holy will with no looking back to what might have been, and we are at peace.
Ibid., Television Broadcast After Robert Kennedy's Death (1968)

## 595. Beatrice Llewellyn-Thomas
(1890–?)
\* \* \*

1 O We have a desperate need of laughter! Give us laughter, Puck!
"To Puck"

## 596. Mariia, Grand Duchess of Russia
(1890–1958)

1 . . . death, the mysterious disillusion and disappearance, of a human being.
*Education of a Princess,* Ch. 1 *1930*

\* Referring to D.W. Griffith and Grauman's Theatre in Hollywood.

2 Girls' games never had any interest for me; I hated dolls; the congealed expression on their porcelain faces provoked me. It was with lead soldiers that we played, without ever growing tired. Ibid., Ch. 3

3 Russia still writhed and stumbled. The wave of revolts and uprisings, the constant agitations, the incessant inflammatory orations of men possessed of little political competence, had by this time cowed the emperor and the ruling class into bewildered and sullen inertia.
Ibid., Ch. 8

4 The mouthpieces of the so-called public opinion; those men, who by high-sounding formulas had so impressed the densely ignorant masses. . . . They had neither sufficient moral force nor experience necessary to build up a new system. Their mental store was limited to theories, often excellent but inapplicable to reality. Ibid.

## 597. Aimee Semple McPherson
### (1890–1944)

1 O Hope! dazzling, radiant Hope!—What a change thou bringest to the hopeless; brightening the darkened paths, and cheering the lonely way. *This Is That*, Pt. I, Ch. 1 1923

2 We are all making a crown for Jesus out of these daily lives of ours, either a crown of golden, divine love, studded with gems of sacrifice and adoration, or a thorny crown, filled with the cruel briars of unbelief, or selfishness, and sin, and placing it upon His brow.
Ibid., Pt. II, "What Shall I Do with Jesus"

3 Right here let us make it plain, that each individual is either a sinner or a saint. It is impossible to be both; it is impossible to be neutral; there is no half-way business in God. Either you are the child of the Lord or you are serving the devil—there is no middle territory. Ibid., "The Two Houses"

4 "Pit-a-pat! Pit-a-pat!"—say the hundreds and thousands of feet, surging by the church doors of our land. "Pat! Pat! Pit-a-pat!"—hurrying multitudes, on business and pleasure bent.
Ibid., "Is Jesus Christ the Great 'I Am' or Is He the Great 'I Was'?"

## 598. Katherine Anne Porter
### (1890–   )

1 She had sat down and read the letter over again; but there were phrases that insisted on being read many times, they had a life of their own separate from the others. . . .
"Theft," *Flowering Judas and Other Stories* 1930

2 In this moment she felt that she had been robbed of an enormous number of valuable things, whether material or intangible: things lost or broken by her own fault, things she had forgotten and left in houses when she moved: books borrowed from her and not returned, journeys she had planned and had not made, words she had waited to hear spoken to her and had not heard, and the words she meant to answer with. . . . Ibid.

3 . . . all that she had had, and all that she had missed, were lost together, and were twice lost in this landslide of remembered losses. Ibid.

4 She laid the purse on the table and sat down with the cup of chilled coffee, and thought: I was right not to be afraid of any thief but myself, who will end by leaving me nothing.
Ibid.

5 "*What* could you buy with a hundred dollars?" she asked fretfully.
"Nothing, nothing at all," said their father, "a hundred dollars is just something you put in the bank." *Old Mortality*, Pt. II 1936

6 "It don't *look* right," was his final reason for not doing anything he did not wish to do.
*Noon Wine* 1937

7 "I don't see no reason to hold it against a man because he went loony once or twice in his lifetime and so I don't expect to take no steps about it. Not a step. I've got nothin' against the man, he's always treated me fair. They's things and people," he went on, "'nough to drive any man loony. The wonder to me is, more men don't wind up in straitjackets, the way things are going these days and times."
Ibid.

8 Nothing is mine, I have only nothing but it is enough, it is beautiful and it is all mine. Do I even walk about in my own skin or is it something I have borrowed to spare my modesty?
*Pale Horse, Pale Rider* 1939

9 After working for three years on a morning newspaper she had an illusion of maturity and experience; but it was fatigue merely. . . .
Ibid.

10 "Adam," she said, "the worst of war is the fear and suspicion and the awful expression in all the eyes you meet . . . as if they had pulled down the shutters over their minds and their hearts and were peering out at you, ready

to leap if you make one gesture or say one word they do not understand instantly."
> Ibid.

11 "The mind and the heart sometimes get another chance, but if anything happens to the poor old human frame, why, it's just out of luck, that's all."
> Ibid.

12 No more war, no more plague, only the dazed silence that follows the ceasing of the heavy guns; noiseless houses with the shades drawn, empty streets, the dead cold light of tomorrow. Now there would be time for everything.
> Ibid.

13 All believed they were bound for a place for some reason more desirable than the place they were leaving, but it was necessary to make the change with the least possible delay and expense. Delay and expense had been their common portion at the hands of an army of professional tip-seekers, fee-collectors, half-asleep consular clerks and bored migration officials who were not in the least concerned whether the travelers gained their ship or dropped dead in their tracks.    *Ship of Fools*, Pt. I    *1962*

14 "People on a boat, Mary, can't seem to find any middle ground between stiffness, distrust, total rejection, or a kind of evasive, gnawing curiosity. Sometimes it's a friendly enough curiosity, sometimes sly and malicious, but you feel as if you were being eaten alive by fishes."
> Ibid., Pt. II

15 Miracles are instantaneous, they cannot be summoned, but come of themselves, usually at unlikely moments and to those who least expect them.
> Ibid., Pt. III

16 They exchanged one or two universal if minor truths—pleasure was so often more exhausting than the hardest work; they had both noticed that a life of dissipation sometimes gave to a face the look of gaunt suffering spirituality that a life of asceticism was supposed to give and quite often did not.
> Ibid.

17 "The real sin against life is to abuse and destroy beauty, even one's own—even more, one's own, for that had been put in our care and we are responsible for its well-being. . . ."
> Ibid.

18 Such ignorance. All the boys were in military schools and all the girls were in the convent, and that's all you need to say about it.
> Quoted in "Lioness of Literature
> Looks Back" by Henry Allen,
> *Los Angeles Times*    *July 7, 1974*

19 It is disaster to have a man fall in love with me. They aren't content to take what I can give; they want everything from me.    Ibid.

20 Evil puts up a terrible fight. And it always wins in the end. I do not understand the world, but I watch its progress. I am not reconciled. I will not forgive it.    Ibid.

21 No man can be explained by his personal history, least of all a poet.    Ibid.

22 My grandmother, when she heard that Mr. Lincoln had abolished slavery and the Negroes were free, was heard to say "I hope it works both ways," and lived to realize that it did not.
> "Notes on the Texas I Remember,"
> *The Atlantic*    March, 1975

## 599. Rachel
### (1890–1931)

1 Like a bird in the butcher's palm you flutter in my hand, insolent pride.
> "Revolt," *Poems from the Hebrew*,
> Robert Mezey, ed.    *1973p*

2 This is a bond nothing can ever loosen. What I have lost: what I possess forever.
> Ibid., "My Dead"

## 600. Ellen West
### (1890?–1923?)

1 I am twenty-one years old and am supposed to be silent and grin like a puppet.
> Diary Entry (c.1911), Quoted in
> *Women and Madness* by
> Phyllis Chesler    *1972p*

## 601. Margaret Culkin Banning
### (1891– )

1 I get a little angry about this highhanded scrapping of the looks of things. What else have we to go by? How else can the average person form an opinion of a girl's sense of values or even of her chastity except by the looks of her conduct?    *Letters to Susan*    *1936*

2 You wouldn't be caught wearing cheap perfume, would you? Then why do you want to wear cheap perfume on your conduct?    Ibid.

3 Did it ever occur to you that there's something almost crooked in the way decent girls nowadays use the shelter of their established respectability to make things awkward for men?    Ibid.

4 It isn't easy to be the person who sometimes has to try to preserve your happiness at the expense of your fun.        Ibid.

5 The women's magazines are advertising mediums as well as publishers of fiction and articles on current subjects. They are fashion and marketing experts, instructors in home economics.        Ibid.

## 602. Fanny Brice
### (1891–1951)

1 Your audience gives you everything you need. They tell you. There is no director who can direct you like an audience.
       Quoted in *The Fabulous Fanny*, Ch. 6,
       by Norman Katkov    *1952p*

2 Being a funny person does an awful lot of things to you. You feel that you mustn't get serious with people. They don't expect it from you, and they don't want to see it. You're not entitled to be serious, you're a clown, and they only want you to make them laugh.
       Ibid., Ch. 9

3 After the emotion is ended in your life, I found I got great joy from just being myself and relaxing. When love is out of your life, you're through in a way. Because while it is there it's like a motor that's going, you have such vitality to do things, big things, because love is goosing you all the time. I found, after the love, that I needed help to keep going.
       Ibid., Ch. 19

4 Let the world know you as you are, not as you think you should be, because sooner or later, if you are posing, you will forget the pose, and then where are you?    Ibid., Ch. 24

## 603. Agatha Christie
### (1891–1975)

1 Curious things, habits. People themselves never knew they had them.
       *Witness for the Prosecution*    *1924*

2 "My friend—I had to save him. The evidence of a woman devoted to him would not have been enough—you hinted as much yourself. But I know something of the psychology of crowds. Let my evidence be wrung from me, as an admission, damning me in the eyes of the law, and a reaction in favor of the prisoner would immediately set in."    Ibid.

3 It is completely unimportant. That is why it is so interesting.    *The Murder of Roger*
       *Ackroyd*    *1926*

4 LADY ANGKATELL. People are quite right when they say nature in the mild is seldom raw.
       *The Hollow*, Act I    *1952*

5 LADY ANGKATELL. Tradespeople are just like gardeners. They take advantage of your not knowing.        Ibid.

6 GUDGEON. The trouble is there are no proper *employers* nowadays.        Ibid.

7 HENRIETTA. I say the word, you know, over and over again to myself. Dead-dead-dead-dead —and soon it hasn't any meaning, it hasn't any meaning at all. Just a funny little word like the breaking of a rotten branch. Dead-dead-dead-dead-dead.      Ibid., Act II, Sc. 2

8 CLARISSA. Oh dear, I never realized what a terrible lot of explaining one has to do in a murder!    *Spider's Web*, Act II, Sc. 1
       *1956*

9 SIR ROWLAND. You must know better than I do, Inspector, how very rarely two people's account of the same thing agrees. In fact, if three people were to agree exactly, I should regard it as suspicious. Very suspicious, indeed.
       Ibid., Sc. 2

10 TREVES. If one sticks too rigidly to one's principles one would hardly see anybody.
       *Toward's Zero*, Act I    *1957*

11 TREVES. In my experience, pride is a word often on women's lips—but they display little sign of it where love affairs are concerned.    Ibid.

12 Is there ever any particular spot where one can put one's finger and say, "It all began that day, at such a time and such a place, with such an incident?"    *Endless Night*, Bk. I, Ch. 1
       *1967*

13 . . . money isn't so hot, after all. What with incipient heart attacks, lots of bottles of little pills you have to take all the time, and losing your temper over the food or the service in hotels. Most of the rich people I've known have been fairly miserable.    Ibid., Ch. 3

14 I didn't want to work. It was as simple as that. I distrusted work, disliked it. I thought it was a very bad thing that the human race had unfortunately invented for itself.    Ibid.

15 One of the oddest things in life, I think, is the things one remembers.    Ibid.

16 "Look here," I said, "people like to collect disasters."        Ibid., Ch. 5

17 To put it quite crudely . . . the poor don't really know how the rich live, and the rich don't know how the poor live, and to find out is really enchanting to both of them.
*Ibid., Bk. II, Ch. 9*

18 "Doctors can do almost anything nowadays, can't they, unless they kill you first while they're trying to cure you." *Ibid., Ch. 11*

19 Every Night and every Morn
Some to Misery are born.
Every Morn and every Night
Some are born to Sweet Delight,
Some are born to Endless Night.
*Ibid., Ch. 14*

20 One doesn't recognize in one's life the really important moments—not until it's too late.
*Ibid.*

21 It's astonishing in this world how things don't turn out at all the way you expect them to!
*Ibid., Ch. 15*

22 Where large sums of money are concerned, it is advisable to trust nobody. *Ibid.*

## 604.  Laura Gilpin
(1891–      )

1 A river seems a magic thing. A magic, moving, living part of the very earth itself—for it is from the soil, both from its depth and from its surface, that a river has its beginning.
*The Rio Grande*, Introduction      *1949*

2 . . . much earnest philosophical thought is born of the life which springs from close association with nature.     *Ibid., "The Source"*

3 Since the earliest-known existence of human life in the Western World, all manner of men have trod the river's banks. With his progressing knowledge and experience, man has turned these life-giving waters upon the soil, magically evoking an increasing bounty from the arid land. But through misuse of its vast drainage areas—the denuding of forest lands and the destruction of soil-binding grasses—the volume of the river has been diminished, as once generous tributaries have become parched *arroyos*. Will present and future generations have the vision and wisdom to correct these abuses, protect this heritage, and permit a mighty river to fulfill its highest destiny?
*Ibid., "The Delta"*

## 605.  Vivian Yeiser Laramore
(1891–?)

* * *

1 I've shut the door on yesterday
And thrown the key away—
To-morrow holds no fears for me,
Since I have found to-day.
"To-day"

2 Talk to me tenderly, tell me lies;
I am a woman and time flies.
"Talk to Me Tenderly"

## 606.  Irene Rutherford McLeod
(1891–1964?)

1 I'm a lean dog, a keen dog, a wild dog, and alone.
"Lone Dog," *Songs to Save a Soul*
*1919*

## 607.  Anne Nichols
(1891–1966)

1 MRS. COHEN. How early it iss of late!
*Abie's Irish Rose*, Act I      *1922*

2 FATHER WHALEN. Shure, we're all trying to get to the same place when we pass on. We're just going by different routes. We can't all go on the same train.

RABBI. And just because you are not riding on my train, why should I say your train won't get there?     *Ibid., Act II*

## 608.  Victoria Ocampo
(1891–      )

1 Some regions of the earth, which are not rich or picturesque, attract us because of a mysterious relationship we have with them.
"A Man of the Desert," *338171TE*
*(Lawrence of Arabia)      1947*

2 He [T. E. Lawrence] was of the same stuff as the saints, and like them he had to find perfection in himself, and not like a great artist in the work he had conceived and executed.
*Ibid., "Childhood"*

3 In literature homosexuality is always the occasion for detailed grandiloquent justifications and scientific reflections, or of obscure unclean explanation mixed up with a sense of guilt, or a weakness which turns to be bragging. You apologize and then preen yourself upon it.
Ibid., "Homosexuality"

4 Sadism, masochism, neuroses, suppressed desires, complexes, all those things which psychoanalysis invents in order to debunk the scruples and ardent aspirations of mankind and their rebirth in secular disguises, are not sufficient to explain them. Ibid., "The Flesh"

5 . . . there is a touch of optimism in every worry about one's own moral cleanliness.
Ibid., "Scruples and Ambitions"

6 Moral, like physical, cleanliness is not acquired once and for all: it can only be kept and renewed by a habit of constant watchfulness and discipline. Ibid.

7 This eagerness to seek hidden but necessary connections, connections that revealed a close relationship between the world where I was born in the flesh and the other worlds where I was reborn, has been the enterprise of my whole life.
Speech, American Academy of Arts and Letters, New York *1973*

## 609. Ruth Law Oliver
### (1891?–1970)

1 I had a great desire to take off and go somewhere in flight, never having done it.
Quoted in *The American Heritage History of Flight*, Ch. 4 *1962*

## 610. Marie Rambert
### (1891– )

1 We want to create an atmosphere in which creation is possible.
Quoted in "Ballet Rambert: The Company That Changed Its Mind" by John Percival, *Dancemagazine February, 1973*

2 I don't do cartwheels any more, but I still do a *barre* to keep supple.
Ibid., "Old School Tights" by Beryl Hilary Ostlere

## 611. Nelly Sachs
### (1891–1970)

1 O you chimneys,
O you fingers
And Israel's body as smoke through the air!
"O the Chimneys," St. 4, *O the Chimneys* *1967*

2 When sleep leaves the body like smoke
and man, sated with secrets,
drives the overworked nag of quarrel
out of its stall,
then the fire-breathing union begins anew. . . .
Ibid., "When Sleep Enters the Body Like Smoke," St. 3

3 Peoples of the earth,
leave the words at their source,
for it is they that can nudge
the horizons into the true heaven. . . .
Ibid., "People of the Earth," St. 4

4 You, the inexperienced, who learn nothing in the nights.
Many angels are given you
But you do not see them.
"Chorus of Clouds," *The Seeker and Other Poems* *1970*

5 Are graves breath-space for longing?
Ibid., "Are Graves Breath-Space for Longing?"

6 But how shall time be drawn
from the golden threads of the sun?
Wound
for the cocoon of the silken butterfly
night?
Ibid., "Hunter"

## 612. Mary Ambrose
### (1892– )

1 The true vocation [of a nun is] settled on the day the girl looks around her and sees a young woman her own age in pretty clothes wheeling a baby carriage by the convent. Then her heart takes an awful flop and she knows what it is God really is asking of her.
Quoted in *Life* *March 15, 1963*

## 613. Djuna Barnes
### (1892– )

1 She knew what was troubling him, thwarted instincts, common beautiful instincts that he was being robbed of.
"A Night Among the Horses," *The Little Review* *1918*

2 No man needs curing of his individual sickness; his universal malady is what he should look to.
*Nightwood*     1937

3 No, I am not a neurasthenic; I haven't that much respect for people—the basis, by the way, of all neurasthenia.     Ibid.

## 614. Stella Benson

(1892–1933)

1 Call no man foe, but never love a stranger.
Build up no plan, nor any star pursue.
Go forth in crowds, in loneliness is danger.
Thus nothing fate can send,
And nothing fate can do
Shall pierce your peace, my friend.
"To the Unborn," St. 3,
*This Is the End*     1917

2 Family jokes, though rightly cursed by strangers, are the bond that keeps most families alive.
*Pipers and a Dancer*, Ch. 9     1924

## 615. Pearl S. Buck

(1892–1973)

1 It is better to be first with an ugly woman than the hundredth with a beauty.
*The Good Earth*, Ch. 1     1931

2 "We will eat meat that we can buy or beg, but not that which we steal. Beggars we may be but thieves we are not."     Ibid., Ch. 12

3 "Hunger makes a thief of any man."     Ibid., Ch. 15

4 "I do not need to tell you that there are no honorable rulers, and the people cry out under the cruelties and oppression of those who ought to treat them as fathers treat their sons."
*Sons*     1932

5 "Now we revolutionists are against every sort of god; our own or foreign, we are against them all and someday we will tear down temples, we will tear down gods. But if men in their ignorance must believe for a while in some god, let it be their own and not a foreign superstition such as these preach."
*The Young Revolutionist*, Ch. 6     1932

6 "Men do not take good iron to make nails nor good men to make soldiers."     Ibid., Ch. 8

7 "There was an old abbot in one temple and he said something of which I think often and it was this, that when men destroy their old gods they will find new ones to take their place."
Ibid., Ch. 15

8 "A woman must learn to obey. We must not ask why. We cannot help our birth. We must accept it and do the duty that is ours in this lifetime."     "The First Wife," *First Wife and Other Stories*     1933

9 Man was lost if he went to a usurer, for the interest ran faster than a tiger upon him. . . .
Ibid., "The Frill"

10 "But that land—it is one thing that will still be there when I come back—land is always there. . . ."     *A House Divided*, Ch. 1     1935

11 They were all trying so hard to live as they felt it beautiful to live, and their houses were so small—too small and too close, so that they had constantly to hush the crying of their children and their own laughter or anger or weeping as well. They had only silence to keep them private from each other. And they needed privacy, since they were not ignorant people and since decency was a necessity to them. They could make a joke of poverty and did.
*This Proud Heart*, Ch. 1     1938

12 Travel, the casual come and go of strange faces, people for whom she cared nothing and who did not care for her, these were not her life. She had to live not in that passing world but in her own deeps.     Ibid., Ch. 2

13 I feel no need for any other faith than my faith in human beings.     *I Believe*     1939

14 There were many ways of breaking a heart. Stories were full of hearts broken by love, but what really broke a heart was taking away its dream—whatever that dream might be.
*The Patriot*, Pt. II     1939

15     "We shall fight until all anti-Japanese feeling is stamped out and the Chinese are ready to co-operate with us."
I-wan stared at him, not believing what he heard.
"You mean," he repeated, "you will kill us and bomb our cities—and—and—rape our women—until we learn to love you?"     Ibid.

16 When hope is taken away from the people moral degeneration follows swiftly after.
Letter to the Editor,
*The New York Times*
November 14, 1941

17 . . . the basic discovery about any people is the discovery of the relationship between its men and women.     *Of Men and Women*, Ch. 1     1941

18 It is worse than folly . . . not to recognize the truth, for in it lies the tinder for tomorrow.
"Tinder for Tomorrow," *Asia*
*March, 1942*

19 For our democracy has been marred by imperialism, and it has been enlightened only by individual and sporadic efforts at freedom.
Speech, "Freedom for All," New York
*March 14, 1942*

20 I remember as a child hearing my impatient missionary father . . . [as] he explained to an elderly Chinese gentleman, "Does it mean nothing to you that if you reject Christ you will burn in hell?"
The Chinese gentleman smiled as he replied; "If, as you say, my ancestors are all in hell at this moment, it would be unfilial of me not to be willing to suffer with them."
Speech, "The Chinese Mind and India," Boston *April 28, 1942*

21 One faces the future with one's past. . . .
Lecture, "China Faces the Future,"
New York *October 13, 1942*

22 There is no one way of dividing us. We are different races, and that is a division. We are of different nations, and that is a division. Religion is a division, and wealth is a division, and education is a division. Climate and geography and food have their dividing effects, and so has history. But war is the great simplifier.
"The Spirit Behind the Weapon,"
*Survey Graphics November, 1942*

23 Fate proceeds inexorably . . . only upon the passive individual, the passive people. . . . Fate may be foreseen unacknowledged.
Address to Nobel Prize Winners,
New York *December 10, 1942*

24 Every era of renaissance has come out of new freedoms for peoples. The coming renaissance will be greater than any in human history, for this time all the peoples of the earth will share in it. *What America Means to Me,*
Introduction *1942*

25 Every great mistake has a halfway moment, a split second when it can be recalled and perhaps remedied. Ibid., Ch. 10

26 But when you remember the suffering, which you have not deserved, do not think of vengeance, as the small man does. Remember, rather, as the great remember, that which they have unjustly suffered, and determine only that such suffering shall not be possible again for any human being anywhere.
"A Letter to Colored Americans,"
*American Unity and Asia 1942*

27 "Who knows what you'll tell?" Wang Ma said severely.
"I never tell anything I know," Peony said demurely.
Wang Ma put down the bowl. "What do you know?" she inquired.
"Now you want me to tell," Peony said, smiling. *The Bondsmaid*, Ch. 1 *1949*

28 "Believing in gods always causes confusion."
Ibid.

29 She had always been too wise to tell him all she thought and felt, knowing by some intuition of her own womanhood that no man wants to know everything of any woman.
Ibid., Ch. 4

30 Self-expression must pass into communication for its fulfillment. . . .
"In Search of Readers," *The Writer's Book*, Helen Hull, ed. *1950*

31 The average person, fool that he often is, interests and amuses me more than the rare and extraordinary individual. The ways of common people are enchanting and funny and profound.
Ibid.

32 There are persons who honestly do not see the use of books in the home, either for information—have they not radio and even television? —or for decoration—is there not the wallpaper? Ibid.

33 Introversion, at least if extreme, is a sign of mental and spiritual immaturity. Ibid.

34 Endurance can be a harsh and bitter root in one's life, bearing poisonous and gloomy fruit, destroying other lives. Endurance is only the beginning. There must be acceptance and the knowledge that sorrow fully accepted brings its own gifts. For there is an alchemy in sorrow. It can be transmuted into wisdom. . . .
*The Child Who Never Grew*, Ch. 1
*1950*

35 Americans are all too soft. I am not soft. It is better to be hard, so that you can know what to do. Ibid.

36 Euthanasia is a long, smooth-sounding word, and it conceals its danger as long, smooth words do, but the danger is there, nevertheless.
Ibid., Ch. 2

37 Ours is an individualistic society, indeed, and the state must do for the individual what the family does for the older civilizations. Ibid.

38 Children who never grow are human beings, and suffer as human beings, inarticulately but deeply nevertheless. The human creature is always more than an animal.　　Ibid., Ch. 3

39 We had no police and needed none, because the family was responsible for all its members. . . . The child in Asia is loved not only for its own sake but as a symbol of hope for the future of both family and nation.
　　　　　*Children for Adoption,* Ch. 1
　　　　　　　　　　　　　　　1964

40 The American woman, when she is an unmarried mother, simply disappears for a while from her community and then comes back, childless, her secret hidden for life.　　Ibid.

41 What is a neglected child? He is a child not planned for, not wanted. Neglect begins, therefore, before he is born.　　Ibid., Ch. 3

42 The community must assume responsibility for each child within its confines. Not one must be neglected whatever his condition. The community must see that every child gets the advantages and opportunities which are due him as a citizen and as a human being.　　Ibid., Ch. 4

43 The problem of the mixed-race child, born displaced in the world community, must be faced in its entirety. It can be no credit to the United States to have half-American children running about as beggars and potential criminals in the streets of Asian cities and on the islands of the Pacific.　　Ibid., Ch. 7

44 If our American way of life fails the child, it fails us all.　　Ibid., Ch. 9

45 It is indeed exasperating to have a memory that begins too young and continues too long. I know, because this is my memory. It goes back too far, it holds everything too fast, it does not forget anything—a relentless, merciless, disobedient memory, for there are some things I would like to forget. But I never forget.　　*China, Past and Present,* Ch. 1
　　　　　　　　　　　　　　　1972

46 Nothing and no one can destroy the Chinese people. They are relentless survivors. They are the oldest civilized people on earth. Their civilization passes through phases but its basic characteristics remain the same. They yield, they bend to the wind, but they never break.　　　　Ibid.

47 Ah well, perhaps one has to be very old before one learns how to be amused rather than shocked.　　Ibid., Ch. 6

48 No one really understood music unless he was a scientist, her father had declared, and not just a scientist, either, oh, no, only the real ones, the theoreticians, whose language was mathematics. She had not understood mathematics until he had explained to her that it was the symbolic language of relationships. "And relationships," he had told her, "contained the essential meaning of life."
　　　　　*The Goddess Abides,* Pt. I　1972

49 I contemplate death as though I were continuing after its arrival. I, therefore, survive since I can contemplate myself afterward as well as before.　　Ibid.

50 "A hand is not only an implement, it's a sense organ. It's the eye of a blind man, it's the tone of those who cannot speak."　　Ibid., Pt. II

* * *

51 Be born anywhere, little embryo novelist, but do not be born under the shadow of a great creed, not under the burden of original sin, not under the doom of salvation.
　　　　　"Advice to Unborn Novelists"

52 Go out and be born among gypsies or thieves or among happy workaday people who live with the sun and do not think about their souls.
　　　　　　　　　　　　　　　Ibid.

## 616. Ivy Compton-Burnett
(1892–1969)

1 "But a gentlewoman is not able to spin gold out of straw; it required a full princess to do that."　　*A House and Its Head,* Ch. 1
　　　　　　　　　　　　　　　1935

2 "We do not discuss the members of our family to their faces. . . ."　　Ibid., Ch. 11

3 "It is no good to think that other people are out to serve our interests."
　　　　　*Elders and Betters,* Ch. 1　1944

4 "It is a lonely business, waiting to be translated to another sphere."　　Ibid., Ch. 7

5 "The relationship is only a shadow, but a shadow is not always easy to elude."
　　　　　*Two Worlds and Their Ways,* Ch. 3
　　　　　　　　　　　　　　　1949

6 "I do like approving of things. It is disapproving of them that is disturbing."　　Ibid., Ch. 4

7 "Parents have too little respect for their children, just as the children have too much for the parents. . . ."　　Ibid., Ch. 5

8 "We will let the dead past bury its dead, and go back to the old days and the old ways and the old happiness." Ibid.

9 "We can build upon foundations anywhere, if they are well and truly laid." Ibid., Ch. 7

10 "We are all children up to a point in our own homes. I expect it is the same with all of you. And we shall have plenty of time to be grown-up."
"If I were not a child with my parents, they would be more unloving towards me," said Gwendolen. Ibid.

11 "My youth is escaping without giving me anything it owes me."
*A Heritage and Its History*, Ch. 1
*1959*

12 "There is no change. That is your trouble. You want me to be altered by my father's death. And I have not been, and shall not be. I am what I am." Ibid., Ch. 3

13 "Civilised life exacts its toll." Ibid., Ch. 9

14 "There is no need to act on a truth that might never have emerged. It would not have in most cases, should not have, to my mind. Many must lie unsaid. We can put it from us and go forward." Ibid., Ch. 10

15 "A thing is not nothing, when it is all there is." Ibid.

16 "She should be thinking of higher things."
"Nothing could be higher than food," said Leah. *The Mighty and Their Fall*, Ch. 1
*1961*

17 "Destiny is over all of us, high or low." Ibid., Ch. 2

18 "They must release each other in time for their lives to grow." Ibid., Ch. 3

19 "Fancy daring to ask so much for yourself!" said Hugo.
"The more we ask, the more we have. And it is fair enough: asking is not always easy."
"And it is said to be hard to accept," said Lavinia. "So no wonder we have so little."
" 'Nothing venture, nothing have' is a heartless saying," said Egbert. "Fancy recognising that we may have nothing!"
"And we are to value things more when they don't come easily. There is no limit to the heartlessness." Ibid., Ch. 6

20 "You and Ninian will have each other," said Hugo. "That foolish thing that is said, when that is all people have. As if they did not know it! It is the whole trouble."

"It is not only trouble," said Ninian, smiling at Teresa. "Or it is trouble shared and therefore less." Ibid., Ch. 13

21 I have had such an uneventful life that there is little to say. *A Family and a Fortune*
*1962*

22 When an age is ended you see it as it is.
Quoted in *The Life of Ivy Compton-Burnett* by Elizabeth Sprigge
*1973p*

23 Life makes great demands on people's characters, and gives them great opportunities to serve their own ends by the sacrifice of other people. Such ill doing may meet with little retribution, may indeed be hardly recognized, and I cannot feel so surprised if people yield to it. Ibid.

## 617. Diana Cooper
### (1892– )

1 Naturally good until now, I had never lied, for nothing tempted me to lie except fear of wounding and I had nothing to fear. But now with the advent of the young men—benign serpents —came the apple . . . and many little lies to save her [mother's] disappointment in me. I felt that it was for happiness, and the only difficulties of the untruths were the crimson blushes and fears of detection. Childhood was over. *The Rainbow Comes and Goes*, Ch. 5 *1958*

2 In astrology there is room for precaution and obstruction; the disaster is not inevitable. One can dodge the stars in their courses.
*Trumpets from the Steep* *1960*

3 Childhood is stamped on the fair face of one's uncluttered memory as clearly as morning, and a heart beating with love, enterprise and procreancy seemed recordable, but when I come to armies clashing in the dark, to destruction, to the rulers and their strength, shortcomings or ambivalence . . . I am lost in a rabble of stampeding thoughts that can never be rounded up. Ibid., Ch. 2

4 It helped me in the air to keep my small mind contained in earthly human limits, not lost in vertiginous space and elements unknown.
Ibid., Ch. 5

5 I'll write no more memories. They would get too sad, tender as they are. Age wins and one must learn to grow old. As I learnt with the loss of a nurse to put childish things behind me, as I learnt when the joys of dependence

were over to embrace with fear the isolation of independence, so now I must learn to walk this long unlovely wintry way, looking for spectacles, shunning the cruel looking-glass, laughing at my clumsiness before others mistakenly condole, not expecting gallantry yet disappointed to receive none, apprehending every ache of shaft of pain, alive to blinding flashes of mortality, unarmed, totally vulnerable.                                        *Ibid.*, Ch. 8

## 618. Janet Flanner
### (1892–    )

1 Never have nights been more beautiful than these nights of anxiety. In the sky have been shining in trinity the moon, Venus and Mars. Nature has been more splendid than man.
> "Letter from Paris," *The New Yorker*
> *September 10, 1939*

2 Paris is now the capital of limbo.
> "Paris Germany," *The New Yorker*
> *December 7, 1940*

3 The German passion for bureaucracy—for written and signed forms, for files, statistics, and lists, and for printed permissions to do this or that, to go here or there, to move about, to work, to exist—is like a steel pin pinning each French individual to a sheet of paper, the way an entymologist pins each specimen insect past struggling to his laboratory board.          *Ibid.*

4 In place of certainty there is only a vast, tangled ball of rumor. In place of sensible, humane procedure, now destroyed by wars, revenge, suspicion and power politics, petty official strictures have been built up against which the individual is as helpless as a caged animal.
> "The Escape of Mrs. Jeffries,"
> *The New Yorker*
> *May 22, May 29, and June 5, 1943*

## 619. Edna St. Vincent Millay
### (1892–1950)

1 For my omniscience paid I toll
In infinite remorse of soul.
> "Renascence," St. 2, *Renascence and*
> *Other Poems      1917*

2 A grave is such a quiet place.
> *Ibid.*, St. 4

3 God, I can push the grass apart
And lay my finger on Thy heart.
> *Ibid.*, St. 7

4 The soul can split the sky in two,
And let the face of God shine through.
> *Ibid.*, St. 8

5 The room is full of you!
> *Ibid.*, "Interim," St. 1

6      What is the need of Heaven
When earth can be so sweet?
> *Ibid.*, St. 7

7      Strange how few,
After all's said and done, the things that are
Of moment.
> *Ibid.*, St. 8

8 I think our heart-strings were, like warp and woof
In some firm fabric, woven in and out. . . .
> *Ibid.*, St. 12

9      Not Truth, but Faith, it is
That keeps the world alive.
> *Ibid.*, St. 15

10 "Lonely I came, and I depart alone. . . ."
> *Ibid.*, "The Suicide," St. 1

11      "Father, I beg of Thee a little task
To dignify my days,—'tis all I ask. . . ."
> *Ibid.*, St. 12

12 Who told me time would ease me of my pain!
> *Ibid.*, "Time does not bring relief"

13 Life goes on forever like the gnawing of a mouse.
> *Ibid.*, "Ashes of Life," St. 3

14 O world, I cannot hold thee close enough!
> *Ibid.*, "God's World," St. 1

15 COLUMBINE.   I cannot *live*
Without a macaroon!
> *Aria Da Capo*      1920

16 PIERROT.   You see, I am always wanting
A little more than what I have,—or else
A little less.
> *Ibid.*

17 PIERROT.   I am become a socialist. I love Humanity; but I hate people.
> *Ibid.*

18 CORYDON.   "Here is an hour,—in which to think
A mighty thought, and sing a trifling song,
And look at nothing."
> *Ibid.*

19 CORYDON.    *Your* sheep! You are mad, to call
           them
           Yours—mine—they are all one
           flock!
                             Ibid.

20 CORYDON.    We seem to be forgetting
           It's only a game. . . .
           But one of us has to take a risk,
           or else,
           Why, don't you see?—the game
           goes on forever!
                             Ibid.

21 PIERROT.    Your mind is made of crumbs. . . .
                             Ibid.

22 COLUMBINE.    If there's one thing I hate
           Above everything else,—even
           more than getting my feet
           wet—
           It's clutter!
                             Ibid.

23 I had a little Sorrow,
Born of a little Sin.
         "The Penitent," St. 1, *A Few Figs
                 from Thistles*     1920

24 My candle burns at both its ends;
It will not last the night;
But oh, my foes, and oh, my friends—
It gives a lovely light.
                Ibid., "First Fig"

25 Whether or not we find what we are seeking
Is idle, biologically speaking.
        Ibid., "I shall forget you presently"

26 We talk of taxes, and I call you friend.
                       Ibid.

27 After the feet of beauty fly my own.
      Ibid., "Oh, think not I am faithful"

28 The fabric of my faithful love
No power shall dim or ravel
Whilst I stay here,—but oh, my dear,
If I should ever travel!
      Ibid., "To the Not Impossible Him,"
                             St. 3

29 With him for a sire and her for a dam,
What should I be but just what I am?
      Ibid., "The Singing-Woman from the
                    Wood's Edge," St. 9

30 Was it for this I uttered prayers,
And sobbed and cursed and kicked the stairs,
That now, domestic as a plate,
I should retire at half-past eight?
               Ibid., "Grown-Up"

31 Cut if you will, with Sleep's dull knife,
    Each day to half its length, my friend,—
The years that time takes off my life,
    He'll take from off the other end!
              Ibid., "Midnight Oil"

32 You leave me much against my will.
          Ibid., "To S.M. (If He Should
                     Lie A-dying)"

33 Yet woman's ways are witless ways,
    As any sage will tell,—
And what am I, that I should love
    So wisely and so well?
         Ibid., "The Philosopher," St. 4

34 Life in itself
Is nothing,
An empty cup, a flight of uncarpeted stairs.
       "Spring," *Second April*     1921

35       All my life,
Following Care along the dusty road,
Have I looked back at loveliness and
    sighed. . . .
             Ibid., "Journey," St. 1

36 Spring will not ail nor autumn falter;
    Nothing will know that you are gone. . . .
      Ibid., "Elegy Before Death," St. 3

37 I make bean-stalks, I'm
A builder, like yourself.
         Ibid., "The Bean-Stalk," St. 4

38 Life is a quest and love a quarrel. . . .
           Ibid., "Weeds," St. 1

39 I am waylaid by Beauty.
         Ibid., "Assault," St. 2

40 *Down you mongrel, Death!
   Back into your kennel!*
      Ibid., "The Poet and His Book," St. 1

41 Read me, do not let me die!
Search the fading letters, finding
Steadfast in the broken binding
All that once was I!
               Ibid., St. 6

42 My heart is what it was before,
    A house where people come and go. . . .
             Ibid., "Alms," St. 1

43 Many a bard's untimely death
Lends unto his verses breath. . . .
      Ibid., "To a Poet That Died
                   Young," St. 3

44 Life must go on;
I forget just why.
            Ibid., "Lament"

45 Always I climbed the wave at morning,
   Shook the sand from my shoes at night,
   That now am caught beneath great buildings,
   Stricken with noise, confused with light.
                    Ibid., "Exiled," St. 4

46 And what did I see I had not seen before?
   Only a question less or a question more. . . .
                    Ibid., "Wild Swans"

47 Longing alone is singer to the lute. . . .
                    Ibid., "Into the golden vessel of
                                        great song"

48 I turn away reluctant from your light,
   And stand irresolute, a mind undone,
   A silly, dazzled thing deprived of sight
   From having looked too long upon the sun.
                    Ibid., "When I too long have looked
                                        upon your face"

49 Your body was a temple to Delight. . . .
                    Ibid., "As to some lovely temple,
                                        tenantless"

50 I drank at every vine.
   The last was like the first.
   I came upon no wine
   So wonderful as thirst.
                    "Feast," St. 1, The Harp-Weaver
                           and Other Poems     1923

51 I only know that summer sang in me
   A little while, that in me sings no more.
                    Ibid., "What lips my lips have kissed,
                                   and where, and why"

52 Pity me that the heart is slow to learn
   What the swift mind beholds at every turn.
                    Ibid., "Pity me not because the
                                        light of day"

53 I would blossom if I were a rose.
                    Ibid., "Three Songs from the
                           Lamp and the Bell," I, St. 1

54 The heart grows weary after a little
   Of what it loved for a little while.
                    Ibid., II, St. 1

55 If ever I said, in grief or pride,
   I tired of honest things, I lied. . . .
                    Ibid., "The Goose-Girl"

56 He laughed at all I dared to praise,
   And broke my heart, in little ways.
                    Ibid., "The Spring and the Fall," St. 2

57 (Love, by whom I was beguiled,
   Grant I may not bear a child.)
                    Ibid., "Humoresque," St. 1

58 He that would eat of love must eat it where it
   hangs.
                    Ibid., "Never May the Fruit
                                        Be Plucked"

59 That Love at length should find me out. . . .
                    Ibid., "That love at length should find
                                   me out and bring"

60        Well I know
   What is this beauty men are babbling of;
   I wonder only why they prize it so.
                    Ibid., "Love is not blind. I see with
                                        single eye"

61 I know I am but summer to your heart,
   And not the full four seasons of the year. . . .
                    Ibid., "I know I am but summer
                                        to your heart"

62 Oh, oh, you will be sorry for that word!
   Give back my book and take my kiss instead.
   Was it my enemy or my friend I heard,
   "What a big book for such a little head!"
                    Ibid., "Oh, oh, you will be sorry
                                        for that word!"

63 She said at length, feeling the doctor's eyes,
   "I don't know what you do exactly when a
   person dies."
                    Ibid., "Sonnets from an Ungrafted
                                        Tree," XVI

64 Sweet sounds, oh, beautiful music, do not cease!
   Reject me not into the world again.
                    "On Hearing a Symphony of
                    Beethoven," St. 1, The Buck
                           in the Snow     1928

65 Music my rampart, and my only one.
                    Ibid.

66 I am not resigned to the shutting away of
       loving hearts in the hard ground
   So it is, and so it will be, for so it has been,
       time out of mind:
   Into the darkness they go, the wise and the
       lovely. Crowned
   With lilies and with laurel they go; but I am
       not resigned.
                    Ibid., "Dirge Without Music," St. 1

67 April is upon us, pitiless and young and harsh.
                    Ibid., "Northern April," St. 2

68 The anguish of the world is on my tongue.
   My bowl is filled to the brim with it; there is
       more than I can eat.
   Happy are the toothless old and the toothless
       young,
   That cannot rend this meat.
                    Ibid., "The Anguish," St. 2

69 Not for you was the pen bitten,
And the mind wrung, and the song written.
Ibid., "To Those Without Pity"

70 Night is my sister. . . .
"Fatal Interview," VII
*Fatal Interview*    1931

71 Life has no friend. . . .
Ibid., VIII

72 Unnatural night, the shortest of the year,
Farewell! 'Tis dawn. The longest day is here.
Ibid., XIII

73 Time, and to spare, for patience by and by,
Time to be cold and time to sleep alone. . . .
Ibid., XXII

74 I know the face of Falsehood and her tongue
Honeyed with unction, plausible with guile. . . .
Ibid., XXIII

75 Youth, have no pity; leave no farthing here
For age to invest in compromise and fear.
Ibid., XXIX

76 Desolate dreams pursue me out of sleep;
Weeping I wake; waking, I weep, I weep.
Ibid., XXXIII

77 My kisses now are sand against your mouth,
Teeth in your palm and pennies on your eyes.
Ibid., XXXIX

78 The heart once broken is a heart no more,
And is absolved from all a heart must be;
All that it signed or chartered heretofore
Is cancelled now, the bankrupt heart is free. . . .
Ibid., L

79 All skins are shed at length, remorse, even
shame.
*Wine from These Grapes*, "Time, that
renews the tissues of this frame"
*1934*

80 I dread no more the first white in my hair,
Or even age itself, the easy shoe,
The cane, the wrinkled hands, the special chair:
Time, doing this to me, may alter too
My anguish, into something I can bear.
Ibid.

81 There it was I saw what I shall never forget
And never retrieve.
Ibid., "The Fawn," St. 1

82 Childhood is the Kingdom Where Nobody
Dies.
Ibid., "Childhood Is the Kingdom
Where Nobody Dies," III

83 To be grown up is to sit at the table with people
who have died, who neither listen nor
speak. . . .
Ibid., St. 6

84 Soar, eat ether, see what has never been seen;
depart, be lost,
But climb.
Ibid., "On Thought in Harness," St. 3

85 Breed, crowd, encroach, expand, expunge your-
self, die out,
*Homo* called *sapiens.*
Ibid., "Apostrophe to Man"

86 I shall die, but that is all that I shall do for
Death; I am not on his pay-roll.
Ibid., "Conscientious Objector," St. 3

87 Am I a spy in the land of the living, that I
should deliver men to Death?
Ibid., St. 4

88        . . . what frosty fate's in store
For the warm blood of man,—man, out of ooze
But lately crawled, and climbing up the shore?
Ibid., "Epitaph for the
Race of Man," III

89 Man, with his singular laughter, his droll tears,
His engines and his conscience and his art,
Made but a simple sound upon your ears. . . .
Ibid., "O Earth, unhappy planet
born to die," IV

90 Ease has demoralized us, nearly so; we know
Nothing of the rigours of winter. . . .
"Underground System," St. 2,
*Huntsman, What Quarry?*    1939

91 Heart, do not stain my skin
With bruises; go about
Your simple function. Mind,
Sleep now; do not intrude;
And do not spy; be kind.

Sweet blindness, now begin.
Ibid., "Theme and Variations,"
II, Sts. 5–6

92 Even the bored, insulated heart,
That signed so long and tight a lease,
Can break its contract, slump in peace.
Ibid., IV, St. 6

93 Infinite Space lies curved within the scope
Of the hand's cradle.
Ibid., "Truce for a Moment," St. 2

94 . . . I shall love you always.
No matter what party is in power;
No matter what temporarily expedient com-
bination of allied interests wins the war;
Shall love you always.
Ibid., "Modern Declaration," St. 2

95      . . . my heart is set
On living—I have heroes to beget
Before I die. . . .
> Ibid., "Thou famished grave, I will
> not fill thee yet"

96 No, no, not love, not love. Call it by name,
Now that it's over, now that it is gone and
cannot hear us.

It was an honest thing. Not noble. Yet no
shame.
> Ibid., "What Savage Blossom," Sts. 3–4

97 Night falls fast.
Today is in the past.
> Ibid., "Not So Far as the
> Forest," I, St. 3

98 O Life, my little day, at what cost
Have you been purchased!
> Ibid., "Be sure my coming was a
> sharp offense"

99 Parrots, tortoises and redwoods
Live a longer life than men do,
Men a longer life than dogs do,
Dogs a longer life than love does.
> Ibid., "Pretty Love I Must Outlive You"

100 See how these masses mill and swarm
And troop and muster and assail:
God! we could keep this planet warm
By friction, if the sun should fail.
> Ibid., "Three Sonnets in
> Tetrameter," I

101 Love does not help to understand
The logic of the bursting shell.
> Ibid., III

102 The oils and herbs of mercy are so few;
Honour's for sale; allegiance has its price;
The barking of a fox has bought us all;
We save our skins a craven hour or two. . . .
> Ibid., "Czecho-Slovakia"

103 You think we build a world; I think we leave
Only these tools, wherewith to strain and
grieve.
> Ibid., "Count them unclean, these
> tears that turn no mill"

104 Wisdom enough to leech us of our ill
Is daily spun; but there exists no loom
To weave it into fabric. . . .
> Ibid., "Upon this age, that never
> speaks its mind"

105 It's not true that life is one damn thing after
another—it's one damn thing over and over.
> Letters of Edna St. Vincent Millay,
> Allen R. Macdougall, ed.    1952p

106 A person who publishes a book willfully appears before the populace with his pants
down. . . .                                   Ibid.

## 620. Vita Sackville-West
### (1892–1962)

1 So prodigal was I of youth,
Forgetting I was young;
I worshipped dead men for their strength,
Forgetting I was strong.
> "MCMXIII," St. 1, Poems of
> West and East    1917

2 We have tasted space and freedom, frontiers
falling as we went,
Now with narrow bonds and limits, never could
we be content,
For we have abolished boundaries, straitened
borders had we rent,
And a house no more confines us than the roving nomads' tent.
> Ibid., "Nomads," St. 6

3 Travel is the most private of pleasures. There
is no greater bore than the travel bore. We do
not in the least want to hear what he has seen
in Hong-Kong.
> Passenger to Teheran, Ch. 1    1926

4 For observe, that to hope for Paradise is to live
in Paradise, a very different thing from actually
getting there.                                Ibid.

5 This question of horizon, however; how important it is; how it alters the shape of the mind;
how it expresses, essentially, one's ultimate
sense of country! That is what can never be
told in words: the exact size, proportion, con-
tour; the new standard to which the mind must
adjust itself.                           Ibid., Ch. 4

6 If you are wise you will not look upon the long
period of time thus occupied in actual movement as the mere gulf dividing you from the
end of your journey, but rather as one of those
rare and plastic seasons of your life from
which, perhaps, in after times, you may love to
date the moulding of your character—that is,
your very identity. Once feel this, and you
will soon grow happy and contented in your
saddle home.                             Ibid., Ch. 6

7 . . . besides, the fingers which had once grown
accustomed to a pen soon itch to hold one
again: it is necessary to write, if the days are
not to slip emptily by. How else, indeed, to
clap the net over the butterfly of the moment?
for the moment passes, it is forgotten; the mood
is gone; life itself is gone. That is where the
writer scores over his fellows: he catches the
changes of his mind on the hop. Growth is
exciting; growth is dynamic and alarming.
Growth of the soul, growth of the mind. . . .
> Twelve Days, Ch. 1    1928

8 Those who have never dwelt in tents have no idea either of the charm or of the discomfort of a nomadic existence. The charm is purely romantic, and consequently very soon proves to be fallacious. Ibid., Ch. 6

9 Perhaps it would be better to go the whole hog and cut oneself off entirely from the outside world. A merely negative form of protest, I fear, against conditions one does not like; for resentment is vain unless one has an alternative to offer. Flight is no alternative; it is only a personal solution. But as a personal experiment it certainly offers material for reflection to the curious. Ibid., Ch. 15

10 Among the many problems which beset the novelist, not the least weighty is the choice of the moment at which to begin his novel.
*The Edwardians*, Ch. 1 *1930*

11 If this is Society, thought Anguetil, God help us, for surely no fraud has ever equalled it. Ibid.

12 For a young man to start his career with a love affair with an older woman was quite *de rigueur*. . . . Of course, it must not go on too long. Ibid., Ch. 3

13 All the world of feminine voluptuousness seemed to be gathered up and released in that one divine curving of the loosened lips. There was no humour in it, but there was an indescribable caress. Ibid.

14 The inner knowledge that he was behaving not only badly but histrionically increased his obstinacy. He was acutely ashamed of himself, since, for the first time in his life, he saw himself through other eyes; and saw his selfishness, his self-indulgence, his arrogance, his futile philandering, for what they were worth. Still he would not give way. Ibid., Ch. 4

15 Click, clack, click, clack, went their conversation, like so many knitting-needles, purl, plain, purl plain, achieving a complex pattern of references, cross-references, Christian names, nicknames, and fleeting allusions. . . .
Ibid., Ch. 6

16 And as her legal authority shrivelled, so did her personal authority turn suddenly into a thing which had never enjoyed any real existence.
Ibid., Ch. 7

17 Men do kill women. Most women enjoy being killed; so I'm told. *All Passion Spent 1931*

18 Now to my little death the pestering clock Beckons,—but who would sleep when he might wake?
"Solitude" *1938*

19 I suppose the pleasure of country life lies really in the eternally renewed evidences of the determination to live. That is a truism when said, but anything but a truism when daily observed. Nothing shows up the difference between the thing said or read, so much as the daily experience of it. *Country Notes 1940*

20 It is very necessary to have makers of beauty left in a world seemingly bent on making the most evil ugliness. Ibid.

21 I have grown wise, after many years of gardening, and no longer order recklessly from wildly alluring descriptions which make every annual sound easy to grow and as brilliant as a film star. I now know that gardening is not like that.
"January," *In Your Garden Again 1953*

22 I have come to the conclusion, after many years of sometimes sad experience, that you cannot come to any conclusion at all.
Ibid., "May"

23 "It is lucky for some people," I say to Laura, "that they can live behind their own faces."
*No Signposts in the Sea 1961*

24 Ambition, old as mankind, the immemorial weakness of the strong. Ibid.

25 When, and how, and at what stage of our development did spirituality and our strange notions of religion arise? the need for worship which is nothing more than our frightened refuge into propitiation of a Creator we do not understand? A detective story, the supreme Who-done-it, written in undecipherable hieroglyphics, no Rosetta stone supplied, by the consummate mystifier to tease us poor fumbling unravellers of his plot. Ibid.

26 My whole curse has been a duality with which I was too weak and too self-indulgent to struggle. Quoted in *Portrait of a Marriage* by Nigel Nicolson *1973p*

27 Women, like men, ought to have their youth so glutted with freedom they hate the very idea of freedom. Ibid., Letter to Harold Nicolson (June 1, 1919)

28 You have met and understood me on every point. It is this which binds me to you through every storm, and makes you so unalterably the one person whom I trust and love.
Ibid. (November 1, 1919)

29 I advance, therefore, the perfectly accepted theory that cases of dual personality do exist, in which the feminine and masculine elements alternately preponderate. I advance this in an impersonal and scientific spirit, and claim that

I am qualified to speak with the intimacy a professional scientist could acquire only after years of study and indirect information, because I have the object of study always at hand, in my own heart.      Ibid., "Autobiography" (September 27, 1920)

30 . . . I hold the conviction that as centuries go on, and the sexes become more nearly merged on account of their increasing resemblances, I hold the conviction that such connections will to a very large extent cease to be regarded as merely unnatural, and will be understood far better, at least in their *intellectual* if not in their physical aspect.      Ibid.

31 Since "unnatural" means "removed from nature," only the most civilized, because the least natural, class of society can be expected to tolerate such a product of civilization.      Ibid.

32 Things were not tragic for us then, because although we cared passionately we didn't care deeply.      Ibid. (September 29, 1920)

33 Of course I wish now that I had never made these discoveries. One doesn't miss what one doesn't know, and now life is made wretched by privations. I often long for ignorance and innocence.      Ibid.

## 621. Alfonsina Storni
### (1892–1938)

1 I gutted your belly as I would a doll's
Examining its artifice of cogs
And buried deep within its golden pulleys
I found a trap bearing this label: sex.
          "To Eros," *Mask and Trefoil*
                                    *c.1930*

2 . . . Ah, one favor:
If he telephones again,
Tell him it's no use, that I've gone out. . . .
          "I Shall Sleep,"* *La Nacion*
          (Buenos Aires newspaper)      *1938p*
                    * * *

3 I was in your cage, little man
Little man, what a cage you have given me,
I say little because you do not understand me;
You will never understand me.
                    "Dear Little Man"

4 To tell you, my love, that I desired you
With no instinctive hypocritic blush,
I was incapable, as tightly bound as Prometheus,
Until one day I burst my bonds.
                    "Twenty Centuries"

* Sent to *La Nacion* the day before she drowned herself.

5 You want me to be white
(God forgive you)
You want me to be chaste
(God forgive you)
You want me to be immaculate!
                    "You Want Me White"

## 622. Ruth Suckow
### (1892–1960)

1 To have someone tell his boys to do this and that! To take away his help on the farm just when he needed it most! To have somebody just step in and tell him where they had to go! Was that what happened in this country? Why had his people left the old country, then, if things were going to be just the same?
          *Country People*, Pt. II, Ch. 4      *1924*

2 All women were that way—except his mother and sister and aunt, whom he unconsciously excluded (since they need not count in the way of desire) and did not place under the head of "Woman." He scorned, so he thought, all that had to do with them, and declared only "men's books" worth reading—adventure, travel; scorned "Woman" for not having brains, and despised the ones who had.
          *The Odyssey of a Nice Girl*,
          Pt. IV, Ch. 2      *1925*

3 To most of the people it [World War I] had seemed far away, something that could never come close. Some resented it, others seized upon it now to help break up the long monotony of everyday living—more terribly thrilling than a fire in the business district, a drowning in the river, or the discovery that the cashier of the Farmers' Bank had been embezzling. Something had come, it seemed, to shake up that placid, solid, comfortable life of home, changing things around, shifting values that had seemed to be fixed.      Ibid., Ch. 3

4 Exercises, songs and recitations—pieces by children whose mothers would be offended if they were left off the program: good or bad, the audience clapped.
          "Eminence," *Children and Other*
          *People*      *1931*

5 That would be the most terrible thing of all, if she began to forget. Then her heart would have to close. Yes, but if she kept it open, to feel the happiness, then she would have to feel the rest, too. . . . She would have to feel again, like blows on her open heart, every cruel detail of Harold's suffering, and the awful blank fact of his death.      Ibid., "Experience"

## 623. Mae West

### (1892–    )

1 "You're a fine woman, Lou. One of the finest women that ever walked the streets."
*She Done Him Wrong*    *1932*

2 TIRA. She's the kind of girl who climbed the ladder of success, wrong by wrong.
*I'm No Angel*    *1933*

3 FRISCO DOLL. Between two evils, I always pick the one I never tried before.
*Klondike Annie*    *1936*

4 FLOWER BELLE LEE. I generally avoid temptation unless I can't resist it.
*My Little Chickadee*    *1940*

5 I believe in the single standard for men and women.
*The Wit and Wisdom of Mae West,*
Joseph Weintraub, ed.    *1967*

6 It's hard to be funny when you have to be clean.    Ibid.

7 It is better to be looked over than overlooked.
Ibid.

8 It's not the men in my life that counts—it's the life in my men.    Ibid.

9 Too much of a good thing can be wonderful.
Ibid.

10 I used to be Snow White . . . but I drifted.
Ibid.

11 The best way to hold a man is in your arms.
Ibid.

12 He who hesitates is last.    Ibid.

13 When women go wrong, men go right after them.    Ibid.

## 624. Rebecca West

### (1892–    )

1 Literature must be an analysis of experience and a synthesis of the findings into a unity.
*Ending in Earnest*    *1931*

2 When a book of great literary merit is denounced the first line of defence always is to point out that that kind of book, which conscientiously analyzes a human experience and gives its findings honestly, cannot do those who read it any harm, since it adds to the knowledge of reality by which man lives.
Ibid., "Concerning the Censorship"

3 Yes, if an age would deal fairly well with its children and let them do what they can!
Ibid., *"Manibus Date Lilia Plenis"*

4 It is not that they have any faith in Marxian or any other kind of Socialism, so much as that they believe a Labour government would scrap tradition and make a fresh start.
Ibid., "Feminist Revolt, Old and New"

5 Infantilism is not a happy state. The childhood of the individual and the race is full of fears, and panic-stricken attempts to avert what is feared by placating the gods with painful sacrifices.    Ibid., "Journey's End"

6 Most works of art, like most wines, ought to be consumed in the district of their fabrication.
Ibid., " 'Journey's End' Again"

7 It was true that her avarice operated continuously, collecting from him jewels and furs over and above her regular allowance at regular periods, but as at the beginning it was always as nicely calculated in relation to his means as if she had a highly-paid statistician working for her.    *The Abiding Vision*    *1935*

8 "We're on a permanent plateau of prosperity. There's never been anything like it before. It's America."    Ibid.

9 "That's what's wrong with us!" he exclaimed, getting up and walking about the room. "We can't talk. Nobody but writers know how to put things into words, and everybody goes around stuffed up with things they want to say and can't." It seemed to him that he had put his finger on the secret of all human sorrow.
*Life Sentence*    *1935*

10 There is no such thing as conversation. It is an illusion. There are intersecting monologues, that is all.
*There Is No Conversation*, Ch. 1
*1935*

11 It is queer how it is always one's virtues and not one's vices that precipitate one into disaster.    Ibid.

12 It appears that even the different parts of the same person do not converse among themselves, do not succeed in learning from each other what are their desires and their intentions.
Ibid., Ch. 2

13    "But then what did you want me to forgive you for?"
"I wanted you to forgive me for being mean," he said, "and having to be what I am, and do what I have done." A smile passed over his lips. "Just as you might ask me to forgive you for being you."
*The Salt of the Earth,*
Ch. 2    *1935*

14 "Why must you always try to be omnipotent, and shove things about? Tragic things happen sometimes that we just have to submit to."
                                                    Ibid.

15 "The point is that nobody likes having salt rubbed into their wounds, even if it is the salt of the earth."                        Ibid.

16 All the world over, the most good-natured find enjoyment in those who miss trains or sit down on frozen pavements.
                    "A Day in the Town," *The New Yorker*        *January 25, 1941*

17 For power claims to know what life is going to be about and what prescription to offer, and authority claims to be able to enforce that prescription. But the Slav knows . . . that life . . . is in essence unpredictable, that she often produces events for which there is no apt prescription, and that she can be as slippery as an eel when wise men attempt to control her; and they know that it is life, not power or authority, that gives us joy, and this often when she is least predictable.
                    "Dalmatia," *Black Lamb and Grey Falcon*        *1941*

18 But there are other things than dissipation that thicken the features. Tears, for example.
                                            Ibid., "Serbia"

19 There is . . . the mystic who went into the desert because his head was so full of ideas about the spiritual world that everyday talk was in his ears as a barrel-organ playing outside a concert-hall is to a musician, the mystic who does not want to eat or drink or sleep with women because that is to take time off from the ecstatic pleasure of pursuing the ramifications of good and evil through his bosom and through the universe. . . . If a naked woman appeared before him she would not be a temptation but an offence, offending as a person in a library who begins chatting to a student who has found a long-sought reference a few minutes before closing time. Life is not long enough for these men to enjoy the richness of their own perceptions, to transmute them into wisdom.        Ibid., "Old Serbia"

20 Now different races and nationalities cherish different ideals of society that stink in each other's nostrils with an offensiveness beyond the power of any but the most monstrous private deed.                        Ibid., Epilogue

21 The intellectual world is largely of English creation, yet our authors write of ideas as if they were things to pick and choose, even though the choice might be pushed to the extremity of martyrdom, as if they could be left alone, as if they came into play only as they were picked and chosen. But that ideas are the symbols of relationships among real forces that make people late for breakfast, that take away their breakfast, that makes them beat each other across the breakfast-table, is something which the English do not like to realize. Lazy, bone-lazy, they wish to believe that life is lived simply by living.                        Ibid.

22 . . . any authentic work of art must start an argument between the artist and his audience.
                    *The Court and the Castle,*
                    Pt. I, Ch. 1        *1957*

23 But humanity is never more sphinxlike than when it is expressing itself.
                                    Ibid., Pt. II, Ch. 1

24 It is so difficult to become a specialist that the mediocre man has been very eager to cry wolf to the specialist, often before it was actually necessary.        Speech, "McLuhan and the Future of Literature"        *1969*

## 625.  Margaret Anderson
### (1893–1973)

1 I have never been able to accept the two great laws of humanity—that you're always being suppressed if you're inspired and always being pushed into a corner if you're exceptional. I won't be cornered and I won't stay suppressed.
                    *My Thirty Years' War*        *1930*

2 My unreality is chiefly this: I have never felt much like a human being. It's a splendid feeling.                        Ibid.

3 I didn't know what to do about life—so I did a nervous breakdown that lasted many months.
                                            Ibid.

4 I have always had something to live besides a private life.                        Ibid.

5 In real love you want the other person's good. In romantic love you want the other person.
                    *The Fiery Fountains*        *1969*

## 626.  Faith Baldwin
### (1893–    )

1 The kiss was so much a part of the routine that it embarrassed him to withhold it.
                    *Alimony*, Ch. 2        *1928*

2 "Compromises aren't enough."
   "But," he protested, stupidly, "they're life, aren't they?"
   "If they are, then life isn't enough either!"
                                        Ibid., Ch. 8

3 He made more money than he could spend. His tastes were sound, not extravagant. There was no one dependent on him. He had a few close friends among his colleagues and a thousand pleasant acquaintances. Women had been kind to him and he had so arranged his life that he had been able to enjoy their generosity with discretion. He had recreations. . . . He liked to travel. . . . He liked his work. In short, the world with a fence around it was his.
*Medical Center*, Pt. I, Ch. 3     *1938*

4 Sometimes entering the ward he felt himself a god, with the gifts of life, of hope, of alleviation, of promise in his hands.
Ibid., Pt. V, Ch. 28

5 . . . it is hard to convince editors . . . that people of—or past—forty are not senile, and might even have problems, emotions and—*mirabile dictu*—romances, licit and illicit.
"Writing for the Women's Magazines,"
*The Writer's Book*, Helen Hull, ed.
*1950*

6 Oh well, one must adopt a New England attitude, saying not yea, nor nay, but perhaps, maybe, and sometimes.     Ibid.

7 The shadow of fear and uncertainty lies over most of us; for us the future seems far from being as clear and open as we believed it would be.     Ibid.

8 Gratitude is a humble emotion. It expresses itself in a thousand ways, from a sincere thank you to friend or stranger, to the mute, upreaching acknowledgement to God—not for the gifts of this day only, but for the day itself; not for what we believe will be ours in the future, but for the bounty of the past.
"December," *Harvest of Hope*     *1962*

9 One thing I know about March—whether it storms or shines, it is the key to spring. It can be a sun-warmed key, or a wet one, or a cold; but a key just the same.     Ibid., "March"

10 Men's private self-worlds are rather like our geographical world's seasons, storm, and sun, deserts, oases, mountains and abysses, the endless-seeming plateaus, darkness and light, and always the sowing and the reaping.
Ibid., "April"

11 Character builds slowly, but it can be torn down with incredible swiftness.     Ibid., "July"

12 . . . my temperament's temperature does not rise and fall with thermometers or barometers.
Ibid., "September"

\*  \*  \*

13 I think that life has spared these mortals much—
And cheated them of more—who have not kept
A breathless vigil by the little bed
Of some beloved child.
"Vigil"

## 627.  Bessie Breuer
(1893–     )

1 The habit of worry had settled so firmly into her mother's being that her worries were her aspects of love. . . .     *The Actress*, Ch. 1
*1955*

2 Hollywood . . . scripts . . . a medium where both syntax and the language itself were subjected to horrid mutilation by young men who thought of themselves as writers and who proved it by the enormous salaries they received from those higher up who were even less knowledgeable of the mother tongue.     Ibid., Ch. 15

3 When they first brought the baby in to her . . . she stared, inert, and thought, This is the author of my pain.     Ibid., Ch. 21

4 But why, she begged the doctor. "We must stimulate those secretions . . . or else . . ." and he walked away. Why did he always walk away with these half-explanations floating after him?     Ibid.

5 Did I stay with him the very next night because I, way deep down, thought I would learn the secret of acting by sleeping with him; was that it—the way women are always snatching at poets and composers and writers to bedizen themselves with a rag, a knuckle, a toe, the sacred toe of art?     Ibid., Ch. 32

6 Lust, this muscular dilation and contraction, this in itself, was that it—the *ding an sich,* memory of a college course?     Ibid., Ch. 36

## 628.  Vera Brittain
(1893–1970)

1 I thought that spring must last forevermore,
For I was young and loved, and it was May.
"May Morning," St. 4 (May, 1916),
*Poems of the War and After*     *1934*

2 Hope has forsaken me, by death removed,
And love that seemed so strong and gay has proved
A poor crushed thing, the toy of cruel chance.
Ibid., St. 7

3 Have I so changed, since sorrow set her seal
  On my lost youth, and left me solitary. . . .
                Ibid., "After Three Years," St. 2
                              (December, 1918)

4 I found in you a holy place apart,
  Sublime endurance, God in man revealed,
  Where mending broken bodies slowly healed
  My broken heart.
                Ibid., "Epitaph on My Days in
                              Hospital" (1919)

5 He was of those whose vanity untold
  Builds up complacency to shut out loss,
  Who, snatching after dross, believe in gold,
  And throw away unvalued gold as dross.
                Ibid., "The Fool," St. 1 (1920)

6 Meek wifehood is no part of my profession;
  I am your friend, but never your possession.
                Ibid., "Married Love" (1926)

7 For the courage of greatness is adventurous and
      knows not withdrawing,
  But grasps the nettle, danger, with resolute
      hands,
  And ever again
  Gathers security from the sting of pain.
                Ibid., "Evening in Yorkshire," St. 4
                              (December, 1932)

8 For though I must die, youth itself is immortal;
  its star begins to ascend the heaven of the
  future as mine sinks below the brief zenith of
  my generation.
                England's Hour, Ch. 24    1941

9 The idea that it is necessary to go to a university in order to become a successful writer,
  or even a man or woman of letters (which is
  by no means the same thing), is one of those
  phantasies that surround authorship.
                On Being an Author, Ch. 2    1948

10 His secret realisation of his physical cowardice
  led him to underrate his exceptional moral
  courage. . . .
                Born, Pt. I, Ch. 1    1949

11 He had never been afraid of death, which was
  still unreal to him, but he dreaded the end of
  the world.
                Ibid., Ch. 6

12 "There is a spiritual fellowship in suffering
  which unites men and women as nothing else
  can. Perhaps it will be by the world-wide members of this fellowship, in which those whom
  we call our enemies share, that the temple of
  civilisation will be rebuilt when peace returns."
                Ibid., Pt. II, Ch. 8

13 The history of men and women in the past
  fifty years suggests that the old conflict between
  male and female will ultimately reach reconciliation in a new synthesis which is already in
  sight. The organic type of human being which
  will emerge from that synthesis may well be
  the constructive achievement of the next half-
  century.    Lady into Woman, Ch. 1    1953

14 It is probably true to say that the largest scope
  for change still lies in men's attitude to women,
  and in women's attitude to themselves.
                Ibid., Ch. 15

15 Politics are usually the executive expression of
  human immaturity.    The Rebel Passion,
                              Ch. 1    1964

16 At no previous period has mankind been faced
  by a half-century which so paradoxically united
  violence and progress. Its greater and lesser
  wars and long series of major assassinations
  have been strangely combined with the liberation of more societies and individuals than ever
  before in history, and by the transformation of
  millions of second-class citizens—women, workers, and the members of subject races—to a
  stage at which first-rate achievement is no
  longer inhibited even if opportunities are not
  yet complete.    Ibid., Ch. 12

17 Nuclear weapons immediately vitiated cam-
  paigning methods of the secular pacifist society,
  since the individual renunciation of war, while
  retaining its moral authority, had lost its political validity. Wars would not now cease if the
  common man refused to fight when governments possessed weapons which were capable
  of annihilating both the enemy and his oppo-
  nent.    Ibid.

18 The pacifists' task today is to find a method of
  helping and healing which provides a revolutionary constructive substitute for war.    Ibid.

## 629. Elizabeth Coatsworth

(1893–    )

*    *    *

1 To a life that seizes
    Upon content,
  Locality seems
    But accident.
                "To Daughters, Growing Up," St. 1

## 630. Elizabeth Cotten

(1893–    )

1 But I didn't know people could takes songs
  from you.            Quoted by Stephen March
                              in Southern Voices
                              August/September, 1974

*    *    *

2 Freight train, freight train, goin' so fast. . . .
                         "Freight Train"

3 This life I been livin' is very hard.
  Work all the week, honey
  and I give it all to you.
  Honey, baby, what more can I do?
                   "Babe, It Ain't No Lie"

## 631. Lillian Day
### (1893–?)

1 A lady is one who never shows her underwear
unintentionally.        *Kiss and Tell*     *1931*

## 632. Marie Gilchrist
### (1893– )

1 But the life of poetry lies in fresh relationships between words, in the spontaneous fusion
of hitherto unrelated words.     *Writing Poetry,*
                                *Ch. 1*     *1932*

2 All American Indian poems are songs, and an
Indian was once asked which came first, the
words or the music. "They come together," he
replied.                    *Ibid., Ch. 3*

3 Nouns and verbs are almost pure metal; adjectives are cheaper ore.
            Quoted in "On the Teaching of
            Poetry" by Leonora Speyer, *The*
            *Saturday Review of Literature*
                                 *1946*

## 633. Helen Hathaway
### (1893–1932)
\*   \*   \*

1 More tears have been shed over men's lack of
manners than their lack of morals.
                        *Manners for Men*

## 634. Margery Eldredge Howell
### (1893–?)
\*   \*   \*

1 There's dignity in suffering—
Nobility in pain—
But failure is a salted wound
That burns and burns again.
                        "Wormwood"

## 635. Emily Beatrix Jones
### (1893–?)
\*   \*   \*

1 The pools of art and memory keep
Reflections of our fallen towers,
And every princess there asleep,
Whom once we kissed, is always ours.
                        "Middle-Age"

## 636. Suzanne LaFollette
### (1893– )

1 There is nothing more innately human than the
tendency to transmute what has become customary into what has been divinely ordained.
          "The Beginnings of Emancipation,"
                  *Concerning Women*     *1926*

2 The revolutionists did not succeed in establishing human freedom; they poured the new wine
of belief in equal rights for all men into the
old bottle of privilege for some; and it soured.
                                   *Ibid.*

3 . . . most people, no doubt, when they espouse
human rights, make their own mental reserva-
tions about the proper application of the word
"human."                        *Ibid.*

4 . . . where divorce is allowed at all . . . society
demands a specific grievance of one party
against the other. . . . The fact that marriage
may be a failure spiritually is seldom taken
into account.                     *Ibid.*

5 . . . laws are felt only when the individual
comes into conflict with them.        *Ibid.*

6 For the wage-earner gets his living on sufferance: while he continues to please his employer
he may earn a living. . . .          *Ibid.*

7 . . . the economic conditions brought about by
the State operate to make marriage the State's
strongest bulwark. . . .           *Ibid.*

8 It is a commonplace in this century that women
form the leisure class; and this leisure class of
women, like leisured classes everywhere, has its
leisure at the expense of other people, who in
this case are the husbands.         *Ibid.*

9 If responsibility for the upbringing of children
is to continue to be vested in the family, then
the rights of children will be secured only when
parents are able to make a living with so little difficulty that they may
give their best thought and energy to the child's
development. . . .             *Ibid.*

10 . . . where is the society which does not struggle along under a dead-weight of tradition and law inherited from its grandfathers?　　　　Ibid.

11 All political and religious systems have their root and their strength in the innate conservatism of the human mind, and its intense fear of autonomy.　　　　Ibid.

12 . . . people never move towards revolution; they are pushed towards it by intolerable injustices in the economic and social order under which they live.　　　　Ibid.

13 For man, marriage is regarded as a station; for women, as a vocation.
　　　　Ibid., "Women and Marriage"

14 . . . nothing could be more grotesquely unjust than a code of morals, reinforced by laws, which relieves men from responsibility for irregular sexual acts, and for the same acts drives women to abortion, infanticide, prostitution and self-destruction.　　　　Ibid.

15 The claim for alimony . . . implies the assumption that a woman is economically helpless. . . .
　　　　Ibid.

16 . . . when one hears the argument that marriage should be indissoluble for the sake of children, one cannot help wondering whether the protagonist is really such a firm friend of childhood. . . .　　　　Ibid.

17 . . . to institutionalize means in great degree to mechanize.　　　　Ibid.

18 It is necessary to grow accustomed to freedom before one may walk in it sure-footedly.
　　　　Ibid.

19 It is impossible for a sex or a class to have economic freedom until everybody has it, and until economic freedom is attained for everybody, there can be no real freedom for anybody.　　　　Ibid., "What Is to Be Done"

20 Rights that depend on the sufferance of the State are of uncertain tenure. . . .　　　　Ibid.

21 No system of government can hope long to survive the cynical disregard of both law and principle which government in America regularly exhibits.　　　　Ibid.

22 . . . the automobile had not yet come in and the family had not yet gone out.
　　　　Letter to Alice Rossi (July, 1971),
　　　　*The Feminist Papers*, Alice Rossi, ed.
　　　　*1973*

23 No one . . . who has not known that inestimable privilege can possibly realize what good fortune it is to grow up in a home where there are grandparents.　　　　Ibid.

24 I . . . watch with growing concern the disintegration of the Western World—above all our own country—and the steady growth of totalitarian influence and power. . . .　　　　Ibid.

## 637. Margaret Leech
### (1893– )

1 England was the friend whose policy stood like a bulwark against Continental animosity to the ambitions of the American republic.
　　　　*In the Days of McKinley*, Ch. 11
　　　　*1959*

2 Charity stood ready to atone for the heartlessness of the War Department.　　　　Ibid., Ch. 13

3 The colonial fever was mildly infectious in Washington. Some of the President's closest friends and counselors came down with it.
　　　　Ibid., Ch. 17

4 Never in history had the Union of the States been joined in such universal sorrow. North and South, East and West, the people mourned [William McKinley] a father and a friend, and the fervent strains of "Nearer, My God, to Thee"* floated, like a prayer and a leavetaking, above the half-masted flags in every city and town.　　　　Ibid., Ch. 26

5 Yet, for a space, Americans turned from the challenge and the strangeness of the future. Entranced and regretful, they remembered McKinley's firm, unquestioning faith; his kindly, frock-coated dignity; his accessibility and dedication to the people: the federal simplicity that would not be seen again in Washington.
　　　　Ibid.

6 The nation felt another leadership, nervous, aggressive, and strong. Under command of a bold young captain [Theodore Roosevelt], America set sail on the stormy voyage of the twentieth century.　　　　Ibid., Epilogue

## 638. Hesper Le Gallienne
### (1893–?)
*　*　*

1 The loose foot of the wanderer
　Is curst as well as blest!
It urges ever, ever on
　And never gives him rest.
　　　　"The Wanderer"

* McKinley's favorite hymn and last words.

## 639. Anita Loos

(1893–    )

1 "She always believed in the old adage: 'Leave them while you're looking good.'"
*Gentlemen Prefer Blondes*, Ch. 1
*1925*

2 "I really think that American gentlemen are the best after all, because . . . kissing your hand may make you feel very, very good, but a diamond and sapphire bracelet lasts forever."
Ibid., Ch. 4

3 So this gentleman said, "A girl with brains ought to do something else with them besides think." Ibid.

4 . . . I always say that a girl never really looks as well as she does on board a steamship, or even a yacht. Ibid.

5 JUDGE. Always go to a solitary drinker for the truth! *Happy Birthday*, Act I *1947*

6 ADDIE. I've always been my own best company, Mr. Bishop. Ibid.

7 ADDIE. Why, Benjamin Franklin says a man without a woman is like a half a pair of scissors. Ibid., Act II

8 ADDIE. I was making love to a man, a man I hardly even know. He was kissing the face off me and I was kissing the face off him. And I found it highly satisfactory. Ibid.

9 Of course, everybody knows that the greatest thing about Motherhood is the "Sacrifices," but it is quite a shock to find out that they begin so far ahead of time. *A Mouse Is Born,*
Ch. 1 *1951*

10 So after a Star has received five or six million of those Fan letters, you begin to realize you must be wonderful without having to read all those monitinous [sic] letters. Ibid.

11 For the most outstanding shock that Tourists ever get is to find out that "Hollywood" is meerly [sic] one of unnumerable other spots, which we Citizens term "Hollywood" as a "cover-up" for the whole accumilation [sic].
Ibid., Ch. 6

12 So I am beginning to wonder if maybe girls wouldn't be happier if we stopped demanding so much respeckt for ourselves and developped [sic] a little more respeckt for husbands.
Ibid., Ch. 19

13 "Why, with a mental equipment which allows me to tell the difference between hot and cold, I stand out in this community like a modern-day Cicero. Dropped into any other city of the world, I'd rate as a possibly adequate night watchman. And let's be fair, old pal, you yourself, a leader of public thought in Hollywood, wouldn't have sufficient mental acumen anywhere else to hold down a place in a bread line!" *No Mother to Guide Her*, Ch. 3
*1961*

14 "Childish" is the word with which the intelligentsia once branded Hollywood. And yet, those movies, which depicted Life as life can never be, were fairy tales for the adult. Today there are no fairy tales for us to believe in, and this is possibly a reason for the universal prevalence of mental crack-up. Yes, if we were childish in the past, I wish we could be children once again. Ibid., Ch. 10

15 . . . the Welsh are a very peculiar breed, poetic, unpredictable, remote, and fiercely independent. For such a man [D. W. Griffith] to be in love must be terribly frustrating, because his deepest instinct is to be a loner. *A Girl Like I*
*1966*

16 . . . memory is more indelible than ink.
*Kiss Hollywood Goodby*, Ch. 1
*1974*

17 That our popular art forms become so obsessed with sex has turned the U.S.A. into a nation of hobbledehoys; as if grown people don't have more vital concerns, such as taxes, inflation, dirty politics, earning a living, getting an education, or keeping out of jail. It's true that the French have a certain obsession with sex, but it's a particularly adult obsession. France is the thriftiest of all nations; to a Frenchman sex provides the most economical way to have fun. The French are a logical race. Ibid., Ch. 21

18 There's nothing colder than chemistry. Ibid.

## 640. Dorothy Parker

(1893–1967)

1 The affair between Margot Asquith and Margot Asquith will live as one of the prettiest love stories in all literature.
Book Review, *The New Yorker*
*1922*

2 (All your life you wait around for some damn man!)
"Chant for Dark Hours,"
*Enough Rope* *1927*

3 By the time you swear you're his,
Shivering and sighing,
And he vows his passion is
Infinite, undying—
Lady, make a note of this:
One of you is lying.
Ibid., "Unfortunate Coincidence"

4 Four be the things I am wiser to know:
Idleness, sorrow, a friend, and a foe.

Four be the things I'd be better without:
Love, curiosity, freckles, and doubt.
Ibid., "Inventory," Sts. 1–2

5 . . . the heart is bold
That pain has made incapable of pain.
Ibid.

6 Inertia rides and riddles me;
The which is called Philosophy.
Ibid., "The Veteran"

7 Lilacs blossom just as sweet
Now my heart is shattered.
If I bowled it down the street,
Who's to say it mattered?
Ibid., "Threnody," St. 1

8 Men seldom make passes
At girls who wear glasses.
Ibid., "News Item"

9 My soul is crushed, my spirit sore;
I do not like me any more.
I cavil, quarrel, grumble, grouse.
I ponder on the narrow house.
I shudder at the thought of men . . .
I'm due to fall in love again.
Ibid., "Symptom-Recital"

10 Oh, life is a glorious cycle of song,
A medley of extemporanea;
And love is a thing that can never go wrong;
And I am Marie of Roumania.
Ibid., "Comment"

11 Razors pain you
Rivers are damp;
Acids stain you;
And drugs cause cramp.
Guns aren't lawful;
Nooses give;
Gas smells awful;
You might as well live.
Ibid., "Resumé"

12 Scratch a lover, and find a foe.
Ibid., "Ballade of a Great Weariness,"
St. 1

13      This is what I know:
Lover's oaths are thin as rain;
Love's a harbinger of pain—
Would it were not so!
Ibid., "Somebody's Song," St. 3

14 Travel, trouble, music, art,
A kiss, a frock, a rhyme—
I never said they feed my heart,
But still they pass my time.
Ibid., "Faute de Mieux"

15 Where's the man could ease a heart
Like a satin gown?
Ibid., "The Satin Dress," St. 1

16 Authors and actors and artists and such
Never know nothing, and never know much.
"Bohemia," Sunset Gun     1928

17 But ever does experience
Deny me wisdom, calm, and sense!
Ibid., "A Fairly Sad Tale"

18 Byron and Shelley and Keats
Were a trio of lyrical treats.
Ibid., "A Pig's-Eye View of
Literature"

19 What time the gifted lady took
Away from paper, pen, and book,
She spent in amorous dalliance
(They do those things so well in France).
Ibid., "George Sand"

20 Her mind lives tidily, apart
From cold and noise and pain,
And bolts the door against her heart,
Out wailing in the rain.
Ibid., "Interior," St. 3

21 It costs me never a stab nor squirm
To tread by chance upon a worm.
"Aha, my little dear," I say,
"Your clan will pay me back one day."
Ibid., "Thought for a Sunshiny
Morning"

22 The love that sets you daft and dazed
Is every love that ever blazed;
The happier, I, to fathom this:
A kiss is every other kiss.
Ibid., "Incurable"

23 They sicken of the calm, who knew the storm.
Ibid., "Fair Weather," St. 1

24 They that have roses
Never need bread.
Ibid., "There Was One," St. 4

25 This living, this living, this living
Was never a project of mine.
Ibid., "Coda"

26 Popularity seemed to her to be worth all the
work that had to be put into its achievement.
"Big Blonde," Pt. I, Laments for the
Living     1929

27 She could not laugh at his whimsicalities, she
was so tensely counting his indulgences. And
she was unable to keep back her remon-
strances. . . .      Ibid.

28 There was nothing separate about her days. Like drops upon a window-pane, they ran together and trickled away.      Ibid.

29 They resumed friendly relations only in the brief magnanimity caused by liquor, before more liquor drew them into new battles.      Ibid.

30 She commenced drinking alone, short drinks all through the day. . . . It blurred sharp things for her. She lived in a haze of it. Her life took on a dream-like quality. Nothing was astonishing.      Ibid.

31 She was always pleased to have him come and never sorry to see him go.      Ibid., Pt. II

32 The thought of death came and stayed with her and lent her a sort of drowsy cheer. It would be nice, nice and restful, to be dead.      Ibid.

33 She had spent the golden time in grudging its going.      Ibid., "The Lovely Leave"    1929

34 Drink and dance and laugh and lie,
   Love, the reeling midnight through,
For tomorrow we shall die!
   (But, alas, we never do.)
           "The Flaw in Paganism,"
           *Death and Taxes*    1931

35   Here's my bitterness:
Would I knew a little more,
   Or very much less!
           Ibid., "Summary"

36 Kings are shaped as other men.
       Ibid., "Salome's Dancing-Lesson," St. 2

37 Death's the rarest prize of all!
           Ibid.

38 Scratch a king and find a fool!
           Ibid., St. 3

39 He lies below, correct in cypress wood,
And entertains the most exclusive worms.
           Ibid., "III. The Very Rich Man"

40 Poets alone should kiss and tell.
        Ibid., "Ballade of a Talked-Off Ear,"
                St. 3

41 The bird that feeds from off my palm
Is sleek, affectionate, and calm,
But double, to me, is worth the thrush
A-flickering in the elder-bush.
         Ibid., "Ornithology for Beginners"

42 There was nothing more fun than a man!
         Ibid., "The Little Old Lady
           in Lavendar Silk," St. 3

43 Women and elephants never forget.
        Ibid., "Ballade of Unfortunate
           Mammals," St. 1

44 Brevity is the soul of lingerie.
       Quoted in *While Rome Burns*
       by Alexander Woollcott    1934

45 Constant use had not worn ragged the fabric of their friendship.    *The Standard of Living*
                       1944

46 Wit has truth in it; wisecracking is simply calisthenics with words.
          Quoted in *Paris Review*
              *Summer, 1956*

47 As artists [lady novelists] they're rot, but as providers they're oil wells—they gush.
        Quoted in *The Years with Ross*
         by James Thurber    1959

48 She [Katharine Hepburn] runs the gamut of emotions from A to B.
       Quoted in *Publisher's Weekly*
            *June 19, 1967p*

49 The only "ism" she believes in is plagiarism.
           Ibid.

50 I was following in the exquisite footsteps of Miss Edna St. Vincent Millay, unhappily in my own horrible sneakers.      Ibid.

51 I heard someone say, and so I said it too, that ridicule is the most effective weapon. Well, now I know. I know that there are things that never have been funny, and never will be. And I know that ridicule may be a shield, but it is not a weapon.
       Quoted in *You Might as Well Live*
         by John Keats    1970p

\*    \*    \*

52 Excuse my dust.
           "Epitaph"

53 Accursed from their birth they be
Who seek to find monogamy,
Pursuing it from bed to bed—
I think they would be better dead.
           "Reuben's Children"

54 . . . art is a form of catharsis. . . .
           "Art"

# 641. Mary Pickford
## (1893–    )

1 I was forced to live far beyond my years when just a child, now I have reversed the order and I intend to remain young indefinitely.
     Quoted in "How Mary Pickford Stays
       Young" by Athene Farnsworth,
     *Everybody's Magazine*    May, 1926

2 I left the screen because I didn't want what happened to Chaplin to happen to me. When he discarded the little tramp, the little tramp turned around and killed him.
> Quoted in "America's Sweetheart Lives" by Aljean Harmetz,
> *The New York Times*
> *March 28, 1971*

## 642. Dorothy L. Sayers
### (1893–1957)

1 "A man goes and fights for his country, gets his inside gassed out, and loses his job, and all they give him is the privilege of marching past the Cenotaph once a year and paying four shillings in the pound income-tax."
> *The Unpleasantness at the Bellona Club*, Ch. 1    1928

2 The planet's tyrant, dotard Death, had held his gray mirror before them for a moment and shown them the image of things to come.
> *Ibid.*, Ch. 2

3 "I'm determined never to be a parent. Modern manners and the break-up of the fine old traditions have simply ruined the business. I shall devote my life and fortune to the endowment of research on the best method of producing human beings decorously and unobtrusively from eggs. All parental responsibility to devolve upon the incubator."    *Ibid.*, Ch. 3

4 "Very dangerous things, theories."
> *Ibid.*, Ch. 4

5 "But I don't believe women ever get sensible, not even through prolonged association with their husbands."    *Ibid.*, Ch. 8

6 "And a continued atmosphere of hectic passion is very trying if you haven't got any of your own."    *Ibid.*, Ch. 10

7 Death seems to provide the minds of the Anglo-Saxon race with a greater fund of amusement than any other single subject. . . .
> *The Third Omnibus of Crime,*
> Introduction    1935

8 "If you want to set up your everlasting rest, you are far more likely to find it in the life of the mind than the life of the heart."
> *Gaudy Night*    1936

9 "A desire to have all the fun," he says, "is nine-tenths of the law of chivalry."    *Ibid.*

10 "People who make some other person their job are dangerous."    *Ibid.*

11 "Once lay down the rule that the job comes first, and you throw that job open to every individual . . . who is able to do that job better than the rest of the world."    *Ibid.*

12 "There is perhaps one human being in a thousand who is passionately interested in his job for the job's sake. The difference is that if that one person in a thousand is a man, we say, simply, that he is passionately keen on his job; if she is a woman, we say she is a freak."
> *Ibid.*

13 ". . . of all devils let loose in the world there [is] no devil like devoted love. . . ."    *Ibid.*

14 ". . . love's a nervous, awkward, overmastering brute; if you can't rein him, it's best to have no truck with him."    *Ibid.*

15 "The only sin passion can commit is to be joyless."    *Busman's Honeymoon*    1947

16 ". . . a human being must have occupation if he or she is not to become a nuisance to the world."    *Ibid.*

17 "Many words have no legal meaning. Others have a legal meaning very unlike their ordinary meaning. For example, the word 'daffy-down-dilly.' It is a criminal libel to call a lawyer a 'daffy-down-dilly.' Ha! Yes, I advise you never to do such a thing. No, I certainly advise you *never* to do it."    *Unnatural Death*, Ch. 14
> *1955*

18 "Contrast," philosophized Lord Peter sleepily, "is life. . . ."    *Clouds of Witness*, Ch. 1
> *1956*

19 ". . . What? Sunday morning in an English family and no sausages? God bless my soul, what's the world coming to, eh . . . ?"
> *Ibid.*, Ch. 2

20 "Lawyers enjoy a little mystery, you know. Why, if everybody came forward and told the truth, the whole truth, and nothing but the truth straight out, we should all retire to the workhouse."    *Ibid.*, Ch. 3

21 "She always says, my lord, that facts are like cows. If you look them in the face hard enough they generally run away."    *Ibid.*, Ch. 4

22    "But after all, what's money?"
"Nothing, of course," said Peter. "But if you've been brought up to havin' it, it's a bit awkward to drop it suddenly. Like baths, you know."    *Ibid.*, Ch. 7

23 "Well-bred English people never have imagination. . . ."    *Ibid.*, Ch. 11

24 ". . . And the w'y they speak—that took some gettin' used to. Call that English, I useter say, give me the Frenchies in the Chantycleer Restaurong, I ses."      Ibid.

25 "Time and trouble will tame an advanced young woman, but an advanced old woman is uncontrollable by any earthly force."      Ibid., Ch. 16

\*   \*   \*

26 The keeping of an idle woman is a badge of superior social status.      Essay

## 643. Evelyn Scott
### (1893–1963)

1 If I could only *feel* the child! I imagine the moment of its quickening as a sudden awakening of my own being which has never before had life. I want to *live* with the child, and I am as heavy as a stone.     *Escapade*    *1913*

2 Inwardly shrinking and cold with an obscure fear, I make it a point to look very directly at all the men who speak to me. I want to shame them by the straightforwardness of my gaze.      Ibid.

3 I realized a long time ago that a belief which does not spring from a conviction in the emotions is no belief at all.      Ibid.

4 Yes, I want to be an outcast in order to realize fully what human beings are capable of. Now I know that fear and cruelty underlie all of society's protestations in favor of honesty and moral worth.      Ibid.

5 To have one's individuality completely ignored is like being pushed quite out of life. Like being blown out as one blows out a light.      Ibid.

6 Anything which is entirely beyond my control fascinates me and seems to me to have some awful and particular significance. . . . It is impossible to control creation.      Ibid.

7 If nobody recognizes me, then it is a sign that I have ceased to exist.      Ibid.

8 People think that in order to give up financial security one must be intoxicated.      Ibid.

9 . . . pain is timeless, absolute. It has removed itself from space. It always has been and always will be for it exists independent of relations.      Ibid.

10 He was too young to want milk but I held his face against my breast. In all my desire for him I was conscious of a heavy sensuality, a massiveness of appreciation.      Ibid.

## 644. Madame Sun Yat-sen
### (1893–    )

1 Liberty and equality, those two inalienable rights of the individual . . . but there is still Fraternity to be acquired. . . . And it may be for China, the oldest of nations, to point the way to this Fraternity.      Quoted in *The Wesleyan April, 1912*

2 In the last analysis, all revolutions must be social revolutions, based upon fundamental changes in society; otherwise it is not revolution, but merely a change of government. . . .      Article in the *People's Tribune July 14, 1927*

3 . . . I want especially to say to our young people . . . learn from Sun Yat-sen! Imbibe his continuous zeal, study his demand for constant progress, emulate his lack of subjectiveness, his humbleness and his closeness to the people. Make these characteristics part of your own makeup. With these you can surely go forward to build a great socialist China.      "The Chinese Women's Fight for Freedom," *Asia July-August, 1956*

4 Let us exert every ounce of man's energy and everything produced by him to ensure that everywhere the common people of the world get their due from life. This is to say that our task does not end until every hovel has been rebuilt into a decent house, until the products of the earth are within easy reach of all, until the profits from the factories are returned in equal amount to the effort exerted, until the family can have complete medical care from the cradle to the grave.      Ibid., Address (September 21, 1949)

5 Civil war cannot bring unity, liberation or livelihood. . . . The peasants will support the Communists, who give them land and lower taxes. . . . Why then do the reactionaries inflame a war which *they cannot win?*      Public Statement (1947), Quoted in *Women in Modern China* by Helen Foster Snow    *1967*

## 645. Clara Thompson
### (1893–1958)

1 Although this is a special group within the culture [the upper classes], it is an important group because, on the whole, it is a thinking group, nonconformist, and seeking to bring about changes in the cultural situation.      "The Role of Women in This Culture," *Psychiatry*, Vol. IV    *1941*

2 The question of her inferiority scarcely troubles her when her life is happily fulfilled, even though she lives in relative slavery.      Ibid.

3 Industry has been taken out of the home.      Ibid.

4 The women of past generations had no choice but to bear children. Since their lives were organized around this concept of duty, they seldom became aware of dislike of the situation, but there must have been many unwanted children then. Nowadays, when women have a choice, the illusion is to the effect that unwanted children are less common, but women still from neurotic compulsion bear children they cannot love.      Ibid.

5 Sexual freedom [for women] can be an excellent instrument for the expression of neurotic drives arising outside the strictly sexual sphere, especially drives expressive of hostility to men, or of the desire to be a man. Thus promiscuity may mean the collecting of scalps with the hope of hurting men, frustrating them, or taking away their importance, or in another case it may mean to the woman that she is herself a man.      Ibid.

6 The question that is raised in any study of change, whether by evolution or revolution, takes the form: Can one say that people are more benefited or harmed?      Ibid.

7 People who have a low self-esteem . . . have a tendency to cling to their own sex because it is less frightening.
      "Changing Concepts of Homosexuality in Psychoanalysis," *A Study of Interpersonal Relations, New Contributions to Psychiatry,* Patrick Mullahy, ed.      *1949*

8 The fact that one is married by no means proves that one is a mature person.      Ibid.

## 646. Sylvia Townsend Warner
(1893–    )

1 Blest fertile Dullness! mothering surmise, rumor, report, as stagnant water, flies, whose happy votaries, stung by every hatch, divinely itch, and more divinely scratch!
      *Opus Seven      1931*

2 "PANSY. *Pheonix pheonixissima formosissima arabiana.* This rare and fabulous bird is UNIQUE. The World's Old Bachelor. Has no mate and doesn't want one. When old, sets fire to itself

and emerges miraculously reborn. Specially imported from the East."      "The Phoenix," *The Cat's Cradle-Book      1940*

3 It was the ambiguous interval of winter nightfall when one seems to be wading through darkness as through knee-high water while there is still light overhead.
      "A Stranger with a Bag," *Swans on an Autumn River      1966*

4 But no one would possibly listen to her. No one ever listened to one unless one said the wrong thing.      Ibid., "Fenella"

5 . . . somewhere out to sea . . . was a bell buoy, rocking and ringing. It seemed as though a heart were beating—a serene, impersonal heart that rocked on a tide of salt water.
      Ibid., "Heathy Landscape with Dormouse"

6 You are only young once. At the time it seems endless, and is gone in a flash; and then for a very long time you are old.
      Ibid., "Swans on an Autumn River"

7 . . . Audrey carried in *The Daily Telegraph.* Mother turned with avidity to the Deaths. When other helpers fail and comforts flee, when the senses decay and the mind moves in a narrower and narrower circle, when the grasshopper is a burden and the postman brings no letters, and even the Royal Family is no longer quite what it was, an obituary column stands fast.      Ibid., "Their Quiet Lives"

8 There are some women, Meg was one of them, in whom conscience is so strongly developed that it leaves little room for anything else. Love is scarcely felt before duty rushes to encase it, anger impossible because one must always be calm and see both sides, pity evaporates in expedients, even grief is felt as a sort of bruised sense of injury, a resentment that one should have grief forced upon one when one has always acted for the best.      Ibid., "Total Loss"

9 Efficient people are always sending needless telegrams.      Ibid., "The View of Rome"

## 647. Katherine Bowditch
(1894–1933)
* * *

1 And what am I but love of you made flesh,
Quickened by every longing love may bring,
A pilgrim fire, homeless and wandering.
      "Reincarnation"

## 648. Rachel Lyman Field
(1894–1942)

1 You won't know why, and you can't say now
Such a change upon you came,
But—once you have slept on an island
You'll never be quite the same!
"If Once You Have Slept on an
Island," *Taxis and Toadstools*
*1926*

\* \* \*

2 Doorbells are like a magic game,
Or the grab-bag at a fair—
You never know when you hear one ring
Who may be waiting there.
"Doorbells"

## 649. Esther Forbes
(1894–1967)

1 Women have almost a genius for anti-climaxes.
*O Genteel Lady!* *1926*

2 Most American heroes of the Revolutionary
period are by now two men, the actual man
and the romantic image. Some are even three
men—the actual man, the image, and the de-
bunked remains. *Paul Revere* *1942*

## 650. Martha Graham
(1894–    )

1 Nothing is more revealing than movement.
"The American Dance," *Modern
Dance*, Virginia Stewart, ed. *1935*

2 America does not concern itself now with Im-
pressionism. We own no involved philosophy.
The psyche of the land is to be found in its
movement. It is to be felt as a dramatic force
of energy and vitality. We move; we do not
stand still. We have not yet arrived at the
stock-taking stage. *Ibid.*

3 We look at the dance to impart the sensation
of living in an affirmation of life, to energize
the spectator into keener awareness of the vigor,
the mystery, the humor, the variety, and the
wonder of life. This is the function of the
American dance. *Ibid.*

## 651. Agnes Kendrick Gray
(1894–?)

\* \* \*

1 Sure, 'tis God's ways is very quare,
An' far beyond my ken,
How o' the selfsame clay he makes
Poets an' useful men.
"The Shepherd to the Poet," St. 4

## 652. Osa Johnson
(1894–1953)

1 "A woman that's too soft and sweet is like
tapioca pudding—fine for them as likes it."
*I Married Adventure*, Ch. 10 *1940*

2 Theirs, it might be said, was a Utopian existence, for they [pygmies] showed neither hate,
greed, vanity, nor any other of the dominatingly
unpleasant emotions of our so-called civilized
world. Each dusky hop-o'-my-thumb plays his
pleasant game of life with no desire to interfere with, and caring little about, the conduct
of his fellows. *Ibid.*, Ch. 27

3 When I was most tired, particularly after a hot
safari in the dry, dusty plains, I always found
relaxation and refreshment in my garden. It
was my shop window of loveliness, and Nature
changed it regularly that I might feast my hungry eyes upon it. Lone female that I was, this
was my special world of beauty: these were
my changing styles and my fashion parade.
*Ibid.*, Ch. 9

4 "We must string him up in the presence of the
chief and the villagers. . . . We have to break
this murder madness on the island; we must
make a show of force that they will remember
every time they want to go on a rampage and
give them a picture of retribution they can't
doubt and will not forget."
*Bride in the Solomons*, Ch. 1 *1944*

5 "Animals and primitive people are alike in one
thing," he said. "They know when you are
friendly, they can sense it. . . . They can even
smell fear." *Ibid.*, Ch. 18

## 653. Jean Rhys
(1894–    )

1 . . . Miss Bruce, passing by a shop, with the
perpetual hunger to be beautiful and that thirst
to be loved which is the real curse of Eve.
. . . Then must have begun the search for *the*
dress, the perfect Dress, beautiful, beautifying,
possible to be worn. And lastly, the search for
illusion—a craving, almost a vice, the stolen
waters and the bread eaten in secret of Miss
Bruce's life. "Illusion," *The Left Bank*
*1927*

2 "I don't get any *kick* out of Anglo-Saxons,"
she said out loud. "They don't . . . they *don't*
stimulate my imagination!"
*Ibid.*, "Tout Montparnasse and Lady"

3 She respected Americans: they were not like
the English, who, under a surface of annoying

moroseness of manner, were notoriously timid and easy to turn round your finger.

        *Ibid.*, "Mannequin"

4 "But I do not wish to sell my pictures. And, as I do not wish to sell them, exhibiting is useless. My pictures are precious to me. They are precious, most probably, to no one else."

        *Ibid.*, "Tea with an Artist"

5 For the first time she had dimly realized that only the hopeless are starkly sincere and that only the unhappy can either give or take sympathy—even some of the bitter and dangerous voluptuousness of misery.

        *Ibid.*, "In the Rue de l'Arrivée"

6 Saved, rescued, fished-up, half-drowned, out of the deep, dark river, dry clothes, hair shampooed and set. Nobody would know I had ever been in it. Except, of course, that there always remains something. Yes, there always remains something. . . . Never mind, here I am, sane and dry, with my place to hide in. What more do I want?    *Good Morning, Midnight*, Pt. I
        *1939*

7 We can't all be happy, we can't all be rich, we can't all be lucky—and it would be so much less fun if we were. Isn't it so, Mr. Blank? There must be the dark background to show off the bright colours. Some must cry so that others may be able to laugh the more heartily. Sacrifices are necessary. . . . Let's say you have this mystical right to cut my legs off. But the right to ridicule me afterwards because I am a cripple —no, that I think you haven't got.    *Ibid.*

8 Next week, or next month, or next year I'll kill myself. But I might as well last out my month's rent, which has been paid up, and my credit for breakfast in the morning.

        *Ibid.*, Pt. II

9 "I often want to cry. That is the only advantage women have over men—at least they can cry."          *Ibid.*

## 654. Dora Russell
### (1894–?)

1 Marriage, laws, the police, armies and navies are the mark of human incompetence.
        *The Right to Be Happy*      *1927*

## 655. Adela Rogers St. Johns
### (1894– )

1 The modern woman is the curse of the universe. A disaster, that's what. She thinks that

before her arrival on the scene no woman ever did anything worthwhile before, no woman was ever liberated until her time, no woman really ever amounted to anything. . . .

    Quoted in "Some Are Born Great"
        by Mert Guswiler, *Los Angeles*
    *Herald-Examiner*     *October 13, 1974*

2 About twenty-five years ago . . . I made three resolutions of what I would never do again. They were: to put on a girdle, to wear high heels, and to go out to dinner.      *Ibid.*

3 I think every woman's entitled to a middle husband she can forget.

    Quoted in "She's Had the Last Word
        for Sixty Years" by Joyce Haber,
    *Los Angeles Times*     *October 13, 1974*

4 Roosevelt had great class. He not only handled them [the press], he used them. F.D.R. would send for reporters and pick their brains. . . . He adored Eleanor. He had mistresses, but let's face facts. If more people would face facts, there'd be fewer broken marriages.      *Ibid.*

5 I've often thought with Nixon that if he'd made the football team, his life would have been different.          *Ibid.*

6 Why keep the [Watergate] tapes around? It's like you left the corpse in the bullring.      *Ibid.*

7 Mrs. [Margaret] Sanger said the best birth control is to make your husband sleep on the roof.
        *Some Are Born Great*     *1974*

8 People don't think the only American saint is a woman [Mother Cabrini]. I knew her and didn't know she was a saint. She didn't know, either. She built the first school and first hospital in every town.          *Ibid.*

## 656. Genevieve Taggard
### . (1894–1948)
*     *     *

1 Try tropic for your balm,
Try storm,
And after storm, calm.
Try snow of heaven, heavy, soft and slow,
Brilliant and warm.
Nothing will help, and nothing do much harm.
    "Of the Properties of Nature for
        Healing an Illness," St. 1

## 657. Dorothy Thompson
### (1894–1961)

1 But I do not think that Communism as a belief, apart from overt and illegal actions, can be

successfully combatted by police methods, persecution, war or a mere anti spirit. The only force that can overcome an idea and a faith is another and better idea and faith, positively and fearlessly upheld.

> Quoted in the *Ladies' Home Journal*
> *October, 1954*

2 The United States is the only great and populous nation-state and world power whose people are not cemented by ties of blood, race or original language. It is the only world power which recognizes but one nationality of its citizens—American. . . . How can such a union be maintained except through some idea which involves loyalty? Ibid.

3 Of all forms of government and society, those of free men and women are in many respects the most brittle. They give the fullest freedom for activities of private persons and groups who often identify their own interests, essentially selfish, with the general welfare.
> *On the Record     May, 1958*

4 It is not the fact of liberty but the way in which liberty is exercised that ultimately determines whether liberty itself survives. Ibid.

5 They have not wanted *Peace* at all; they have wanted to be spared war—as though the absence of war was the same as peace. Ibid.

## 658. Babette Deutsch
### (1895–     )

1 But the poet's job is, after all, to translate God's poem (or is it the Fiend's?) into words.
> "Poetry at the Mid-Century,"
> *The Writer's Book,*
> Helen Hull, ed.     *1950*

2 The poets were among the first to realize the hollowness of a world in which love is made to seem as standardized as plumbing, and death is actually a mechanized industry. . . . Ibid.

3 . . . the poet . . . like the lover . . . is a person unable to reconcile what he knows with what he feels. His peculiarity is that he is under a certain compulsion to do so. Ibid.

\* \* \*

4 Their memories: a heap of tumbling stones,
Once builded stronger than a city wall.
> "Old Women"

5 You, also, laughing one,
Tosser of balls in the sun,
Will pillow your bright head
By the incurious dead.
> "A Girl"

## 659. Juana de Ibarbourou
### (1895–     )

1 I give you my naked soul
Like a statue unveiled.
> "The Hour," *Diamond Tongues*
> *1919*

2 For if I am so rich, if I have so much,
If they see me surrounded by every luxury,
It is because of my noble lineage
That builds castles on my pillow.
> Ibid., "Small Woman"

## 660. Dolores Ibarruri
### (1895–     )

1 It is better to die on your feet than to live on your knees!     Radio Speech
> *July 18, 1936*

2 It is better to be the widow of a hero than the wife of a coward.     Speech, Valencia
> *1936*

3 . . . the working people of the whole world know that if fascism were to triumph in Spain, every democratic country in the world would be confronted with the fascist danger.
> *Speeches and Articles, 1936–1938*
> *1938*

4 Wherever they pass they [the fascists] sow death and desolation. Ibid.

5 We shall very soon achieve victory and return to our children. . . . Ibid.

6 Women have always played a prominent part, supporting the men in the struggle for liberty and showing them by their example that it is better to die than to bow to the butchers and oppressors of the people. Ibid.

7 We dip our colours in honour of you, dear women comrades, who march into battle together with the men. Ibid.

8 Never shall we see you again, yet we feel your closeness. Ibid.

9 They lost their way and found themselves in the enemy's lines. They were surrounded and defended themselves until the bullets in their revolvers were exhausted. Lena kept the last bullet for herself. She committed suicide so as not to fall into the hands of the enemy. Ibid.

## 661. Bessie Rowland James
### (1895–?)
\*   \*   \*

1 No matter how lofty you are in your department, the responsibility for what your lowliest assistant is doing is yours.    *Adlai's Almanac*

## 662. Dorothea Lange
### (1895–1965)

1 These [country women] are women of the American soil. They are a hardy stock. They are the roots of our country. . . . They are not our well-advertised women of beauty and fashion. . . . These women represent a different mode of life. They are of *themselves* a very great American style. They live with courage and purpose, a part of our tradition.
*Quoted in The Woman's Eye
by Anne Tucker   1973p*

## 663. Susanne K. Langer
### (1895– )

1 Feeling, in the broad sense of whatever is felt in any way, as sensory stimulus or inward tension, pain, emotion or intent, is the mark of mentality.    *Mind, An Essay on Human Feeling*, Vol. I, Pt. I, Ch. 1
*1967*

2 The secret of the "fusion" is the fact that the artist's eye sees in nature . . . an inexhaustible wealth of tension, rhythms, continuities and contrasts which can be rendered in line and color; and those are the "internal forms" which the "external forms"—paintings, musical or poetic compositions or any other works of art —express for us.    Ibid., Pt. II, Ch. 4

3 Art is the objectification of feeling. . . .    Ibid.

4 Every artistic form reflects the dynamism that is constantly building up the life of feeling. It is this same dynamism that records itself in organic forms; growth is its most characteristic process, and is the source of almost all familiar living shape. Hence the kinship between organic and artistic forms, though the latter need not be modeled on any natural object at all. If a work of art is a projection of feeling, that kinship with organic nature will emerge, no matter through how many transformations, logically and inevitably.    Ibid., Ch. 7

5 "Consciousness" is not an entity at all, let alone a special cybernetic mechanism. It is a condition built up out of mental acts of a particular life episode. . . .    Ibid., Ch. 11

## 664. Monica Baldwin
### (1896–?)

1 . . . all the magic of the countryside which is ordained from the healing of the soul.
*I Leap Over the Wall   1950*

2 You might have been standing in the heart of an iceberg, so strange it was, so silent, so austere.    Ibid.

## 665. Ruth Gordon
### (1896– )

1 MAX. I *always* get seventy-eight. No more, no less. It's nerve-wracking. I'd almost rather flunk once in a while.    *Over Twenty-One*, Act I
*1943*

2 POLLY. People like us and people born to be soldiers are kind of getting to be one and the same.

GOW. They are not—they're just all dressing alike. A uniform doesn't make a soldier. It takes aptitude, just like anything else.
   Ibid., Act II

3 MAX. Say, is it too early for a drink?

POLLY. What's early about it? It's tomorrow in Europe and yesterday in China.
   Ibid., Act III

4 POLLY. Do you realize you've come damn close to breaking a man's spirit?

GOW. Well, it was his spirit or my bank account.
   Ibid.

5 JOE. You hit it! The truth's no good to me, Polly! History just isn't practical. . . . We can't stick to history. History's unbelievable! And it's up to us to make it seem real.

POLLY. Honest to God, Joe, you must have a brain of solid popcorn.    Ibid.

6 CLYDE. Nothing dates one so dreadfully as to think someplace is uptown. . . . At our age one must be watchful of these conversational gray hairs.    *The Leading Lady*, Act I
*1948*

7 CLYDE. I'm sure the way to be happy is to live well beyond your means!    Ibid.

8 CLYDE. The best impromptu speeches are the ones written well in advance.    Ibid.

9 GAY. So easy to fall into a rut, isn't it? Why should ruts be so comfortable and so unpopular?    Ibid., Act II

10 BENJY. The kiss. There are all sorts of kisses, lad, from the sticky confection to the kiss of death. Of them all, the kiss of an actress is the most unnerving. How can we tell if she means it or if she's just practicing?    Ibid.

11 MRS. GILSON. The circle comes around for everyone. It dips, but it comes round. Seven lean years and seven fat ones. And seven lean and seven fat. It doesn't always have to be seven, but some number! Never knew anyone didn't have the balloon go up and down.
    Ibid., Act III

12 MRS. GILSON. Up and the world is your oyster! This time you can't miss! Whack comes down the old shillaly and you're down again bitin' the dust! Can't face it! Screeching into your pillow nights! Put back your smile in the morning, trampin' to managers' offices! Home again in the evenin' ready to give up the ghost. Somebody comes by, to tell you: "Go see Frohman nine-thirty sharp!" Luck's turned, you're on the trolley again! Curl up your ostrich feathers! Sponge off the train of your skirt! Because it's all aboard tomorrow. . . .    Ibid.

13 At seventy-four I look better than seventy-three. If you make it through seventy-four years, can it be that things shape up?
    "Myself Among Others,"
    *Myself Among Others*    1970

14 To get it right, be born with luck or else make it. *Never* give up. Get the knack of getting people to help you and also pitch in yourself. A little money helps, but what *really* gets it right is to *never*—I repeat—*never* under any condition face the facts.    Ibid.

15 "The good that men do lives after them." That's a quote from myself. I know the correct one, but I don't think so. I think the *good* lives after. The evil gets accepted or forgotten. Or becomes hearsay. The *good* lives on and does us all some good.    Ibid., "The Good That Men Do"

## 666.  Vivien Kellems
(1896–1975)

1 Our tax law is a 1,598-page hydra-headed monster and I'm going to attack and attack and attack until I have ironed out every fault in it.
    Quoted in "Vivien Kellems, Crusader
    Against IRS" by Narda Z. Trout,
    *Los Angeles Times*
    *January 26, 1975*

2 Of course I'm a publicity hound. Aren't all crusaders? How can you accomplish anything unless people know what you're trying to do?
    Quoted in "Unforgettable Vivien
    Kellems" by Gloria Swanson,
    *Reader's Digest*    October, 1975p

3 Men always try to keep women out of business so they won't find out how much fun it really is.
    Ibid.

4 . . . the IRS has stolen from me over the past 20 years because I am single. It is unconstitutional to impose a penalty tax of 40 percent on me because I have no husband.
    Ibid. (c.1969)

## 667.  Martha Martin
(1896–1959)

1 I killed a sea otter today. I actually did kill a sea otter. I killed him with the ax, dragged him home, and skinned him.
    *O Rugged Land of Gold*    1952

2 This awful deep snow and hard cold is going to kill off much of our wild life. Poor creatures, what a pity they can't all be like bears and sleep the winter through.    Ibid.

3 I have never seen a child born. I always felt inadequate to help and was too modest to want to be a spectator. I have never seen anything born—not even a cat. . . . I am no longer afraid, yet I do wish someone were with me to help me take care of the child. . . .    Ibid.

4 My darling little girl-child, after such a long and troublesome waiting I now have you in my arms. I am alone no more. I have my baby.
    Ibid.

5 I told her the deer are our helpers and our friends, our subjects and our comfort, and they will give us food and clothing according to our needs. I told her of the birds. . . . Told her of the fishes. . . . Told her of the mink and the otter, and the great brown bear with his funny, furry cub. Told her of the forest and of the things it will give us . . . of the majestic mountain uprising behind us with a vein of gold-bearing ore coming straight from its heart. Told her that all these things were ours to have and to rule over and care for.    Ibid.

6 The Indians have come, good, good Indians. Shy, fat, smelly, friendly, kindhearted Indians.
    Ibid.

## 668. Beata Rank
### (1896–1967)

1 . . . examine the personality of the mother, who is the medium through which the primitive infant transforms himself into a socialized human being.
> "Adaptation of the Psychoanalytical Technique . . . ," *American Journal of Orthopsychiatry*    *January, 1949*

2 Because she is so barren of spontaneous manifestations of maternal feelings, she studies vigilantly all the new methods of upbringing and reads treatises about physical and mental hygiene.      *Ibid.*

## 669. Marjorie Kinnan Rawlings
### (1896–1953)

1 There was something about the most fertile field that was beyond control. A man could work himself to skin and bones, so that there was no flesh left on him to make sweat in the sun, and a crop would get away from him. There was something about all living that was uncertain.    *South Moon Under*, Ch. 3    *1933*

2 Sorrow was like the wind. It came in gusts, shaking the woman. She braced herself.
> Ibid., Ch. 9

3 You can't change a man, no-ways. By the time his mummy turns him loose and he takes up with some innocent woman and marries her, he's what he is.    "Benny and the Bird Dogs"    *1938*

4 It seemed a strange thing to him, when earth was earth and rain was rain, that scrawny pines should grow in the scrub, while by every branch and lake and river there grew magnolias. Dogs were the same everywhere, and oxen and mules and horses. But trees were different in different places.    *The Yearling*, Ch. 1    *1938*

5 The game seemed for him to be two different animals. On the chase, it was the quarry. He wanted only to see it fall. . . . When it lay dead and bleeding, he was sickened and sorry. . . . Then when it was cut into portions . . . his mouth watered at its goodness. He wondered by what alchemy it was changed, so that what sickened him one hour, maddened him with hunger the next. It seemed as though there were either two different animals or two different boys.    Ibid., Ch. 8

6 "A woman has got to love a bad man once or twice in her life, to be thankful for a good one."    Ibid., Ch. 12

7 Living was no longer the grief behind him, but the anxiety ahead.    Ibid., Ch. 33

8 "You figgered I went back on you. Now there's a thing ever' man has got to know. Mebbe you know it a'ready. 'Twa'n't only me. 'Twa'n't only your yearlin' deer havin' to be destroyed. Boy, life goes back on you."    *Ibid.*

9 "Ever' man wants life to be a fine thing, and a easy. 'Tis fine, boy, powerful fine, but 'tain't easy. Life knocks a man down and he gits up and it knocks him down agin. I've been uneasy all my life."    *Ibid.*

10 He was the delight of fine cooks, who took his absent-minded capacity for appreciation.    *The Sojourner*, Ch. 1    *1953*

11 He found himself denying this so-called force of gravity. It could not be what tied men to earth. It was a heavy weight, an unendurable pressure from the outer-land, and if a man could once break through it, soar high like a bird, he would be free, would meet, would join, something greater than he, and be complete at last.    Ibid., Ch. 15

12 They were all too tightly bound together, men and women, creatures wild and tame, flowers, fruits and leaves, to ask that any one be spared. As long as the whole continued, the earth could go about its business.    Ibid., Ch. 20

## 670. Betty Smith
### (1896–1972)

1 There's a tree that grows in Brooklyn. Some people call it the Tree of Heaven. No matter where its seed falls, it makes a tree which struggles to reach the sky. It grows in boarded-up plots and out of neglected rubbish heaps. It grows up out of cellar gratings. It is the only tree that grows out of cement. It grows lushly . . . survives without sun, water, and seemingly without earth. It would be considered beautiful except that there are too many of it.
> *A Tree Grows in Brooklyn*    *1943*

2 "If it makes her feel better to throw it away rather than to drink it, all right. *I* think it's good that people like us can waste something once in a while and get the feeling of how it would be to have lots of money and not have to worry about scrounging."    Ibid., Ch. 1

3 "My Francie wears no hair bow but her hair is long and shiny. Can money buy things like that? That means there must be something bigger than money."    Ibid., Ch. 27

4 Miss Gardner had nothing in all the world excepting a sureness about how right she was.    Ibid., Ch. 42

5 "The difference between rich and poor," said Francie, "is that the poor do everything with their own hands and the rich hire hands to do things."    Ibid., Ch. 45

6 "Is it not so that a son what is bad to his mother," he said, "is bad to his wife?"    *Maggie—Now*, Ch. 1    *1958*

7 She felt, vaguely, that she had given away her childhood that night. She had given it to him or he had taken it from her, and made it into something wonderful. In a way, her life was his now.    Ibid., Ch. 23

8 ". . . I can never give a 'yes' or a 'no.' I don't believe everything in life can be settled by a monosyllable."    Ibid., Ch. 39

## 671.  Dodie Smith
(1896–    )

1 I have found that sitting in a place where you have never sat before can be inspiring.    *I Capture the Castle*    *1948*

2 Noble deeds and hot baths are the best cures for depression.    Ibid., Ch. 3

3 . . . miserable people cannot afford to dislike each other. Cruel blows of fate call for extreme kindness in the family circle.    Ibid., Ch. 6

4 Oh, it was the most glorious morning! I suppose the best kind of spring morning is the best weather God has to offer. It certainly helps one to believe in Him.    Ibid.

5 ". . . she happens to belong to a type [of American woman] I frequently met—it goes to lectures. And entertains afterwards. . . . Amazing, their energy," he went on. "They're perfectly capable of having three or four children, running a house, keeping abreast of art, literature and music—superficially of course, but good lord, that's something—and holding down a job into the bargain. Some of them get through two or three husbands as well, just to avoid stagnation."    Ibid., Ch. 7

6 What a difference there is between wearing even the skimpiest bathing-suit and wearing nothing! After a few minutes I seemed to live

in every inch of my body as fully as I usually do in my head and my hands and my heart. I had the fascinating feeling that I could think as easily with my limbs as with my brain. . . .    Ibid., Ch. 12

7 Perhaps the effect wears off in time, or perhaps you don't notice it if you are born to it, but it does seem to me that the climate of richness must always be a little dulling to the senses. Perhaps it takes the edge off joy as well as off sorrow.    Ibid., Ch. 14

8 ". . . I don't like the sound of all those lists he's making—it's like taking too many notes at school; you feel you've achieved something when you haven't."    Ibid., Ch. 15

## 672.  Charlotte Whitton
(1896–1975?)

1 Whatever women do they must do twice as well as men to be thought half as good. Luckily, this is not difficult.    Quoted in *Canada Month*    *June, 1963*

## 673.  Dixie Willson
(1896–?)

\* \* \*

1 He may look just the same to you,
And he may be just as fine,
But the next-door dog is the next-door dog,
And mine—is—mine!
    "Next-Door Dog"

## 674.  Wallis Simpson Windsor
(1896–    )

1 I don't remember any love affairs. One must keep love affairs quiet.    Quoted in the *Los Angeles Times*    *April 11, 1974*

## 675.  Elizabeth Asquith Bibesco
(1897–1945)

1 I have made a great discovery.
    What I love belongs to me. Not the chairs and
tables in my house, but the masterpieces of the world.
    It is only a question of loving them enough.
    "Balloons"    *1922*

2 Being in a hurry is one of the tributes he pays to life.
Ibid.

3 It is sometimes the man who opens the door who is the last to enter the room.
*The Fir and the Palm*, Ch. 13
1924

4 You are such a wonderful Baedeker to life. All the stars are in the right places.
Ibid.

5 It is never any good dwelling on good-byes. It is not the being together that it prolongs, it is the parting.
Ibid., Ch. 15

## 676. Catherine Drinker Bowen
(1897–　)

1 I know what these people want; I have seen them pick up my violin and turn it over in their hands. They may not know it themselves, but they want music, not by the ticketful, the purseful, but music as it should be had, music at home, a part of daily life, a thing as necessary, as satisfying, as the midday meal. They want to *play*. And they are kept back by the absurd, the mistaken, the wicked notion that in order to play an instrument one must be possessed by that bogey called Talent. . . .
*Friends and Fiddlers*, Ch. 2　　1934

2 "We don't want her to take music too seriously." Real concern came into her voice. "We don't want her to become intense over something, and warped and queer. Such women are unhappy in later life. They don't," she rang the bell for more tea, "they don't make good wives."
Ibid., Ch. 4

3 Many a man who has known himself at ten forgets himself utterly between ten and thirty. . . .
Ibid., Ch. 9

4 The professors laugh at themselves, they laugh at life; they long ago abjured the bitch-goddess Success, and the best of them will fight for his scholastic ideals with a courage and persistence that would shame a soldier. The professor is not afraid of words like *truth*; in fact he is not afraid of words at all.
*Adventures of a Biographer*, Ch. 5
1946

5 For your born writer, nothing is so healing as the realization that he has come upon the right word.
Ibid., Ch. 11

6 There is a marvelous turn and trick to British arrogance; its apparent unconsciousness makes it twice as effectual.
Ibid., Ch. 14

7 In writing biography, fact and fiction shouldn't be mixed. And if they are, the fictional points should be printed in red ink, the facts printed in black ink.
Quoted in *Publisher's Weekly*
March 24, 1958

8 People who carry a musical soul about them are, I think, more receptive than others. They smile more readily. One feels in them a pleasing propensity toward the lesser sins, a pleasing readiness also to admit the possibility that on occasion they may be in the wrong—they may be mistaken.
Speech, "The Nature of the Artist," Scripps College
April 27, 1961

9 I have noted that, barring accidents, artists whose powers wear best and last longest are those who have trained themselves to work under adversity. . . . Great artists treasure their time with a bitter and snarling miserliness.
Ibid.

10 Your great artist looks on his talent as a responsibility laid on him by God, or perhaps a curse set on him by the devil. Whichever way he looks at it, while he is writing that book or composing that symphony, DOOM hangs over him. He is afraid something will interfere to stop him. . . . Artists often think they are going to die before their time. They seem to possess a heightened sense of the passing of the hours. . . . I think . . . artists dread death because they love life. Artists, even at their gloomiest, seem to maintain a constant love affair with life, marked by all the ups and downs, the depressions and ecstasies of infatuation. Artists have so much to do, and so little time to do it!
Ibid.

11 The things we believe in and want done will not be done until women are in elective office.
Quoted in *National Business Week*
September, 1974

## 677. Catherine Cate Coblentz
(1897–　)
* * *

1 Life is an archer, fashioning an arrow
With anxious care, for in it life must trust;
A single flash across the earthly spaces
Straight to the throat of death—one conquering thrust!
"Life"

## 678. Dorothy Day

(1897– )

1 Tradition! We scarcely know the word any more. We are afraid to be either proud of our ancestors or ashamed of them. We scorn nobility in name and in fact. We cling to a bourgeois mediocrity which would make it appear we are all Americans, made in the image and likeness of George Washington, all of a pattern, all prospering if we are good, and going down in the world if we are bad.

*The Long Loneliness,* Pt. I   *1952*

2 . . . who were the mad and who the sane? . . . People sold themselves for jobs, for the pay check, and if they only received a high enough price, they were honored. If their cheating, their theft, their lies, were of colossal proportions, if it were successful, they met with praise, not blame.   Ibid.

3 In our disobedience we were trying to obey God rather than men, trying to follow a higher obedience. We did not wish to act in a spirit of defiance and rebellion.

*Loaves and Fishes,* Ch. 16   *1963*

4 One of the greatest evils of the day among those outside of prison is their sense of futility. Young people say, What is the sense of our small effort? They cannot see that we must lay one brick at a time, take one step at a time; we can be responsible only for the one action of the present moment. But we can beg for an increase of love in our hearts that will vitalize and transform all our individual actions, and know that God will take them and multiply them, as Jesus multiplied the loaves and fishes.   Ibid.

5 Much of the world has changed to a new society where collective and communal ownership is being emphasized to handle the matter of man and his work. But these changes have been brought about by violence and coercion, at the expense of man's freedom. The greatest challenge of the day is: how to bring about a revolution of the heart, a revolution which has to start with each one of us? When we begin to take the lowest place, to wash the feet of others, to love our brothers with that burning love, that passion, which led to the Cross, then we can truly say, "Now I have begun."

Ibid., Ch. 19

## 679. Hermione Gingold

(1897– )

1 My father dealt in stocks and shares and my mother also had a lot of time on her hands.
*The World Is Square,* Pt. I   *1945*

2 To call him a dog hardly seems to do him justice, though inasmuch as he had four legs, a tail, and barked, I admit he was, to all outward appearances. But to those of us who knew him well, he was a perfect gentleman.

Ibid., Pt. II

3 This isn't a recipe for soup, although it can land you right in the *potage* if you aren't careful.
"I Make Summer Stock,"
*Sirens Should Be Seen and Not Heard*   *1963*

4 "Have you anything to back up your theory?"
"I cannot truthfully say I have," Mr. Smith replied. "I just believe implicitly."
"Well," I said, "I suppose it's like believing in the creation. There is much less to back up that theory these scientific days, and yet in spite of everything people still believe."
Ibid., "The Bomb That Had Mr. Smith's Name on It"

## 680. Iréne Joliot-Curie

(1897–1956)

1 That one must do some work seriously and must be independent and not merely amuse oneself in life—this our mother [Marie Curie] has told us always, but never that science was the only career worth following.
Quoted in *A Long Way from Missouri,*
Ch. 10, by Mary Margaret McBride
*1959p*

## 681. Caroline Lejeune

(1897–1973)

1 Nothing is said that can be regretted. Nothing is said that can even be remembered.
"Dietrich as an Angel,"
*The Observer* (London)   *1936*

2 Not the least remarkable thing about this remarkable picture is its apparent power of dormant development.
Ibid., "The Truth About Balaklava,"
*1937*

3 In a world as ravaged as ours there is still room for joy over the maturing of a great talent.   Ibid., "The Little Man Grows Up,"
*1940*

4 . . . for a good book has this quality, that it is not merely a petrifaction of its author, but that once it has been tossed behind, like Deucalion's little stone, it acquires a separate and vivid life of its own.
*Chestnuts in Her Lap, 1936–1946,*
Introduction   *1947*

5 It's odd how large a part food plays in memories of childhood. There are grown men and women who still shudder at the sight of spinach, or turn away with loathing from stewed prunes and tapioca. . . . Luckily, however, it's the good tastes one remembers best.
*Thank You for Having Me*, Ch. 1
*1964*

6 Sometimes it seems to me as if the only quality admired in modern writing, or play-making, or film-making, is truth-and-ugliness. This, for some reason, is described as realism; as if nothing could be real that is not sordid, disagreeable or violent.　　Ibid., Ch. 21

7 I learned a lesson about retirement that was certainly true for me, and might be a help to many other people. When you finish with a job it is wiser to make the break completely. Cut off the old life, clean and sharp. If your mind is tired, that is the only way. If your mind is lively you will soon find other interests.
Ibid., Ch. 22

## 682. Ruth Pitter

### (1897–    )

\* \* \*

1 I go about, but cannot find
The blood-relations of the mind.
"The Lost Tribe," St. 1

2 Though our world burn, the small dim words
Stand here in steadfast grace,
And sing, like the indifferent birds
About a ruined place.
"On an Old Poem," St. 2

## 683. Lillian Smith

### (1897–1966)

1 Faith and doubt both are needed—not as antagonists but working side by side—to take us around the unknown curve.
*The Journey*　1954

2 To believe in something not yet proved and to underwrite it with our lives: it is the only way we can leave the future open. Man, surrounded by facts, permitting himself no surprise, no intuitive flash, no great hypothesis, no risk, is in a locked cell. Ignorance cannot seal the mind and imagination more securely.
Ibid.

3 . . . I am caught again in those revolving doors of childhood.　　*Killers of the Dream* (Rev. Ed.), Foreword　*1961*

4 *Segregation* . . . a word full of meaning for every person on earth. A word that is both symbol and symptom of our modern, fragmented world. We, the earth people, have shattered our dreams, yes; we have shattered our own lives, too, and our world.　　Ibid.

5 Man is a broken creature, yes; it is his nature as a human being to be so; but it is also his nature to create relationships that can span the brokenness. This is his first responsibility; when he fails, he is inevitably destroyed.
Ibid.

6 The human heart dares not stay away too long from that which hurt it most. There is a return journey to anguish that few of us are released from making.　　Ibid., Pt. I, Ch. 1

7 I knew, though I would not for years confess it aloud, that in trying to shut the Negro race away from us, we have shut ourselves away from so many good, creative, honest, deeply human things in life. I began to understand slowly at first but more clearly as the years passed, that the warped, distorted frame we have put around every Negro child from birth is around every white child also. Each is on a different side of the frame but each is pinioned there. And I knew that what cruelly shapes and cripples the personality of one is as cruelly shaping and crippling the personality of the other.　　Ibid.

8 When . . . [people] unite in common worship and common fear of one idea we know it has come to hold deep and secret meanings for each of them, as different as are the people themselves. We know it has woven itself around fantasies at levels difficult for the mind to touch, until it is a part of each man's internal defense system, embedded like steel in his psychic fortifications. And, like the little dirty rag or doll that an unhappy child sleeps with, it has acquired inflated values. . . .
Ibid., Ch. 4

9 Sometimes we blame Mom too much for all that is wrong with her sons and daughters. After all, we might well ask, who started the grim mess? Who long ago made Mom and her sex "inferior" and stripped her of her economic and political and sexual rights? . . . Man, born of woman, has found it a hard thing to forgive her for giving him birth. The patriarchal protest against the ancient matriarch has borne strange fruit through the years. . . .
Ibid., Pt. II, Ch. 4

10 It is a man's dreams that make him human or inhuman and a man who knows few words to dream with, who has never heard, in words said aloud, other men's dreams of human dig-

nity and freedom and tender love, and brother-hood, who has never heard of man the creator of truth and beauty, who has never even seen man-made beauty, but has heard only of man the killer, and words about sex and "race" which fill him with anger and fear and lust, and words about himself that make him feel degraded, or blow him up crazily into paranoid "superiority"—how can he know the meaning of *human*! How can he know that?

Ibid., Pt. III, Ch. 1

11 Education is a private matter between the person and the world of knowledge and experience, and has little to do with school or college. . . .

"Bridges to Other People," *Redbook*
*September, 1969p*

12 When you stop learning, stop listening, stop looking and asking questions, always new questions, then it is time to die. . . . Ibid.

## 684. Margaret Chase Smith
### (1897–    )

1 I believe that in our constant search for security we can never gain any peace of mind until we secure our own soul. And this I do believe above all, especially in my times of greater discouragement, *that I must believe*—that I must believe in my fellow men—that I must believe in myself—that I must believe in God—if life is to have any meaning.

Essay in *This I Believe,*
Raymond Swing, ed. *1952*

2 My creed is that public service must be more than doing a job efficiently and honestly. It must be a complete dedication to the people and to the nation with full recognition that every human being is entitled to courtesy and consideration, that constructive criticism is not only to be expected but sought, that smears are not only to be expected but fought, that honor is to be earned but not bought.

"My Creed," *Quick*
*November 11, 1953*

3 In these perilous hours, I fear that the American people are ahead of their leaders in realism and courage—but behind them in knowledge of the facts because the facts have not been given to them. Address, U.S. Senate
*September 21, 1961*

4 Strength, the American way, is not manifested by threats of criminal prosecution or police state methods. Leadership is not manifested by coercion, even against the resented. Greatness is not manifested by unlimited pragmatism,

which places such a high premium on the end justifying *any* means and *any* methods.

Address, National Republican
Women's Conference Banquet
*April 16, 1962*

5 In today's growing, but tragic, emphasis on materialism, we find a perversion of the values of things in life as we once knew them. For example, the creed once taught children as they grew up was that the most important thing was not in whether you won or lost the game but rather in "how you played the game." That high level attitude that stresses the moral side no longer predominates in this age of pragmatic materialism that increasingly worships the opposite creed that "the end justifies the means" or the attitude of get what you can in any way, manner, or means that you can.

RCA Victor Recording *1964*

6 We are rapidly approaching a day when the United States will be subject to all sorts of diplomatic blackmail and a strategy of terror waged by the Soviet Union.

"It's Time to Speak Up for National
Defense," *Reader's Digest*
*March, 1972*

7 We are sick to death of war, defense spending and all things military. We are disgusted with and weary of the vilification that has been heaped upon us, at home as well as abroad, for our attempts to block communist enslavement in Southeast Asia. We yearn to turn away from foreign entanglements and to begin making our own house a better place to live in.

Ibid.

8 The key to security is public information.

Ibid.

9 There are enough mistakes of the Democrats for the Republicans to criticize constructively without resorting to political smears. . . . Freedom of speech is not what it used to be in America. ˙ *Declaration of Conscience*
*1972*

10 Before you can become a statesman you first have to get elected, and to get elected you have to be a politician pledging support for what the voters want.

Ibid., "Nuclear Test Ban Treaty"

## 685. Berenice Abbott
### (1898–    )

1 Photography can never grow up if it imitates some other medium. It has to walk alone; it has to be itself.

"It Has to Walk Alone,"
*Infinity* (magazine) *1951*

2 If a medium is represented by nature of the realistic image formed by a lens, I see no reason why we should stand on our heads to distort that function. On the contrary, we should take hold of that very quality, make use of it, and explore it to the fullest.       Ibid.

## 686.  Judith Anderson

### (1898–    )

1 There is nothing enduring in the life of a woman except what she builds in a man's heart.
News Item       March 8, 1931

## 687.  Louise Bogan

### (1898–1970)

1 The art of one period cannot be approached through the attitudes (emotional or intellectual) of another.
"Reading Contemporary Poetry,"<br>College English       February, 1953

2 The simile has been superseded by the metaphor and the metaphor is often reduced to the image or the symbol.       Ibid.

3 There is no way of reading as one runs, or looking as one runs, when we come to the examination of any highly developed art.
Ibid.

4 True revolutions in art restore more than they destroy.       Ibid.

5 Fear kept for thirty-five years poured through his mane,
and retribution equally old, or nearly, breathed through his nose.
"The Dream," Collected Poems<br>(1923–1953)       1954

6 The terrible beast, that no one may understand,
Came to my side, and put down his head in love.
Ibid.

7 Now, innocent, within the deep
Night of all things you turn the key,
Unloosing what we know in sleep.
Ibid., "M., Singing"

8 The good novelist is distinguished from the bad one chiefly by a gift of choice. Choice, itself a talent, as taste is a talent, is not, however, enough. Only extreme sanity and balance of selection can give to prose fiction the dignity and excitement inherent in more rigid forms of writing: drama, poetry, and the expositions of ideas.       "Colette," Selected Criticism
(1930)       1955

9 It is a dangerous lot, that of the charming, romantic public poet, especially if it falls to a woman. . . . it is almost impossible for the poetess, once laurelled, to take off the crown for good or to reject values and taste of those who tender it.*       Ibid., "Unofficial Feminine
Laurate" (1939)

10 But is there any reason to believe that a woman's spiritual fibre is less sturdy than a man's? Is it not possible for a woman to come to terms with herself if not with the world; to withdraw more and more, as time goes on, her own personality from her productions; to stop childish fears of death and eschew charming rebellions against facts?       Ibid.

11 But childhood prolonged, cannot remain a fairyland. It becomes a hell.†
Ibid., "Childhood's False Eden"<br>(1940)

12 The reiterated insinuation that formal art is fraudulent because it is difficult to understand and makes no effort to appeal to the majority —that it is, in fact, somehow treasonable to mankind's higher purposes and aims—is a typical bourgeois notion that has been around for a long time.
Ibid., "Some Notes on Popular and<br>Unpopular Art" (1943)

13 The intellectual is a middle-class product; if he is not born into the class he must soon insert himself into it, in order to exist. He is the fine nervous flower of the bourgeoisie.       Ibid.

14 Because language is the carrier of ideas, it is easy to believe that it should be very little else than such a carrier.
"A Revolution in European Poetry"<br>(1941), A Poet's Alphabet       1970

15 Once form has been smashed, it has been smashed for good, and once a forbidden subject has been released it has been released for good.
Ibid., "Experimentalists of A New<br>Generation" (1957)

16 The verbal arts, which forty years or so ago were supposed to be spiralling upward toward an ultimately expressive richness and freedom, at present, according to one gloomy set of prophets, are gyrating downward toward silence. It must be remarked, however, that they are being excessively noisy on their downward way.
Ibid., "Pro-Tem" (1967)

* Referring to Edna St. Vincent Millay.
† Referring to Katherine Mansfield.

17 How fortunate the rich and/or married, who have servants and *wives* to expedite matters.
*What the Woman Lived: Selected Letters 1920–1970*, Ruth Limmer, ed.
*1974p*

18 I don't like quintessential certitude.
Ibid., Letter to Rolfe Humphries

19 . . . I wish there was something between love and friendship that I could tender him [William Maxwell]; and some gesture, not quite a caress, I could give him. A sort of smoothing. . . . I simply love him like a brother.     Ibid.

20 The reason I get so mad at the comrades is that they always sound as though they had discovered everything yesterday. . . .     Ibid.

21 What we suffer, what we endure, what we muff, what we kill, what we miss, what we are guilty of, is done by us, as individuals, in private.     Ibid.

22 A second blooming and the bough can scarcely bear it.     Ibid.

23 Wifehood is too damned full of hero-husband-worship for one of my age and disabusedness.
Ibid.

24 I cannot believe that the inscrutable universe turns on an axis of suffering; surely the strange beauty of the world must somewhere rest on pure joy!     Ibid., Letter to John Hall Wheelock

25 How good life is! How complicated! . . . I love and revere life; and intend to keep on being vulgarly alive just as long as possible.
Ibid.

\* \* \*

26 I'll lie here and learn How, over their ground, Trees make a long shadow And a light sound.
"Knowledge"

27 Men loved wholly beyond wisdom Have the staff without the banner.
"Men Loved Wholly"

28 Women have no wilderness in them, They are provident instead, Content in the tight hot cell of their hearts To eat dusty bread.
"Women"

## 688.  Madame Chiang Kai-shek
(1898–     )

1 Of all the inventions that have helped to unify China perhaps the airplane is the most outstanding. Its ability to annihilate distance has been in direct proportion to its achievements in assisting to annihilate suspicion and misunderstanding among provincial officials far removed from one another or from the officials at the seat of government.
"Wings Over China," *Shanghai Evening Post     March 12, 1937*

2 There is no shadow of protection to be had by sheltering behind the slender stockades of visionary speculation, or by hiding behind the wagon-wheels of pacific theories.
Quoted in the *New York Herald Tribune     March 21, 1938*

3 This changing world is rolling towards the abyss of self-destruction with a breath-taking rapidity.     Speech, International Women's Conference, Sydney, Australia (February, 1938), *War Messages and Other Selections     1938*

4 My friends, the world situation is so grave that we can no longer afford to congratulate each other upon the splendid success that we have achieved internationally. It is imperative that we be frank, honest, and effective. As a first step, I propose that we recognize our failure mercilessly, even at the expense of our personal pride. We are guilty, every one of us. Let us say *"mea culpa"* and not blame the rest of the world for what is happening around us.     Ibid.

5 Machinery should be used to make necessities which hands cannot make, but there it should stop.     Ibid., Letter to a Friend (May 14, 1938)

6 No nation that descends to murder, rape and rapine can expect to prosper or be respected.
Ibid., Article in the *Birmingham Post*, England (May, 1938)

7 The faults of a government can be removed by the citizens, but the citizens must first remove their own faults, and learn in full what self-sacrifice really means. They must be self-reliant, and have self-respect.     Ibid. (1938)

8 Out of the ashes which the Japanese are spreading over our country will arise a phoenix of great national worth.
Ibid., "People's Spiritual Mobilization" (March 18, 1939)

9 Hammered out on the anvil of experience are four cardinal principles of life, as we Chinese understand life: 1. The way in which human beings behave one toward another. 2. Justice for all classes within our social framework. 3.

Honesty in public administration and in business. 4. Self-respect, and a profound sense of the value of personality.
*This Is Our China*, Sec. I, Ch. 1
*1940*

10 I am convinced that we must train not only the head, but the heart and hand as well.
Ibid., Sec. II

11 If one task is more outstandingly important than any other in connection with the reform and rehabilitation of our country it must be the eradication of the criminal stagnation that has for so many generations stifled the natural development of our economic life and stood upon our horizon like a grim spectre of predestined rule.     *China Shall Rise Again*
Pt. I, Ch. 6     *1941*

12 Cliques seem to hold sway in many places. They are like dry rot in the administration. They stifle enterprise and initiative. They operate to oust honesty and efficiency by preventing a patriotic "outsider," or a stranger to the clique, from gaining a position, no matter how capable he may be. And they eject, or try to, any one of any independence of character or mind who may happen to be near them but not of them. Every clique is a refuge for incompetence. It fosters corruption and disloyalty, it begets cowardice, and consequently is a burden upon and a drawback to the progress of the country. Its instincts and actions are those of the pack.
Ibid., Ch. 8

13 They [the Chinese people] will remember never to believe in international promises or professions—no matter how well-intentioned they may appear to be; no matter how many imposing-looking seals may adorn the documents. To be sure this new wisdom of theirs has been dearly paid for; it will have to be paid for over and over again in more loss of blood and life. But, then I suppose they will have to learn the lesson of life that where there are no pains, there can be no real gains.
Ibid., Pt. III, Ch. 23

14 America is not only the cauldron of democracy, but the incubator of democratic principles.
Speech, U.S. House of Representatives
*February 18, 1943*

15 The universal tendency of the world as represented by the United Nations is as patent and inexorable as the enormous sheets of ice which float down the Hudson in winter. The swift and mighty tide is universal justice and freedom.
Speech, Madison Square Garden
*March 3, 1943*

16 For is it not true that human progress is but a mighty growing pattern woven together by the tenuous single threads united in a common effort?     Speech, Wellesley College
*March 7, 1943*

17 . . . is it not true that faith is the substance of things hoped for, the evidence of things not seen?     Speech, Chicago
*March 22, 1943*

18 China's struggle now is the initial phase of a gigantic conflict between good and evil, between liberty and communism.
Radio Address, New York
*January 9, 1950*

19 Truth requires that each people live according to its own traditions in a climate of human liberty and dignity. That has been the soul of Chinese civilization.     Ibid.

## 689.  Amelia Earhart
(1898–1937)

1 Courage is the price that Life exacts for granting peace.     *Courage*     1927

2 There are two kinds of stones, as everyone knows, one of which rolls.
*20 Hours: 40 Minutes—Our Flight in the Friendship*, Ch. 1     1928

3 There is so much that must be done in a civilized barbarism like war.     Ibid.

4 In soloing—as in other activities—it is far easier to start something than it is to finish it.
Ibid., Ch. 2

5 Of course I realized there was a measure of danger. Obviously I faced the possibility of not returning when first I considered going. Once faced and settled there really wasn't any good reason to refer to it [the "Friendship" flight] again.     Ibid., Ch. 5

## 690.  Gracie Fields
(1898–    )

1 You can get good fish and chips at the Savoy; and you can put up with fancy people once you understand that you don't have to be like them.     *Sing as We Go*, Ch. 4     1960

2 Now sometimes it can be a very dangerous thing to go in search of a dream for the reality does not always match it. . . .     Ibid.

## 691. Cecily R. Hallack

(1898–1938)

1 Make me a saint by getting meals, and washing up the plates!
"The Divine Office of the Kitchen,"
St. 1    *c.1928*

## 692. Beatrice Lillie

(1898–    )

1 I'll simply say here that I was born Beatrice Gladys Lillie at an extremely tender age because my mother needed a fourth at meals.
*Every Other Inch a Lady*, Ch. 1
*1927*

2 In my experience, anyone can paint if he doesn't have to. . . . During my apprentice days I felt encouraged by the advice of Winston Churchill, who used to say, "Don't be afraid of the canvas." I have now reached the point where the canvas is afraid of me.
Ibid., Ch. 15

3 I took up knitting from time to time as a relaxation, but I always put it down again before going out to buy a rocking chair.    Ibid.

4 The vows one makes privately are more binding than any ceremony or even a Shubert contract.    Ibid.

## 693. Golda Meir

(1898–    )

1 Can we today measure devotion to husband and children by our indifference to everything else? Is it not often true that the woman who has given up all the external world for her husband and her children has done it not out of a sense of duty, out of devotion and love, but out of incapacity, because the soul is not able to take into itself the many-sidedness of life, with its sufferings but also with its joys?
*The Plough Woman*    *c.1930*

2 I can honestly say that I was never affected by the question of the success of an undertaking. If I felt it was the right thing to do, I was for it regardless of the possible outcome.
Quoted in *Golda Meir: Woman with a Cause* by Marie Syrkin    *1964*

3 . . . sitting in America and talking about hard work is easier than doing the work. To deny oneself various comforts is also easier in talk than in deed.    Ibid., Letter to Her Brother-in-Law (August 24, 1921)

4 There is only one way: he who is a Zionist, he who cannot rest in the *Galuth\** must come here, but he must be ready for anything.
Ibid.

5 I ask only one thing, that I be understood and believed. My social activities are not an accidental thing; they are an absolute necessity for me.    Ibid., Letter to Her Sister Shana (1929)

6 There are not enough prisons and concentration camps in Palestine to hold all the Jews who are ready to defend their lives and property.
Ibid., Speech (May 2, 1940)

7 If a Jew or Jewess who uses firearms to defend himself against firearms is a criminal, then many new prisons will be needed.
Ibid., Sirkin-Richlin Arms Trials (September, 1943)

8 We only want that which is given naturally to all peoples of the world, to be masters of our own fate, only of *our* fate, not of others, and in cooperation and friendship with others.
Ibid., Address, Anglo-American Committee of Inquiry (March 25, 1946)

9 Hebrew is our language, just as English is your language, just as French is the language of the French and Chinese the language of China. None of these probably would be questioned as to why they spoke their language.    Ibid.

10 The spirit is there. This spirit alone cannot face rifles and machine guns. Rifles and machine guns without spirit are not worth very much. But spirit without these in time can be broken with the body.    Ibid., Address, Council of Jewish Federation (January 21, 1949)

11 We are not a better breed; we are not the best Jews of the Jewish people. It so happened that we are there and you are here. I am certain that if you were there and we were here, you would be doing what we are doing there, and you would ask us who are here to do what you will have to do.    Ibid.

12 Religious families have sons as well as daughters. If army life is degrading why are they not concerned for the morals of their sons?
Ibid., Address (1953)

13 There is no Zionism except the rescue of Jews.
Quoted in *As Good as Golda* (1943), Israel and Mary Shenker, eds.    *1970*

14 A leader who doesn't hesitate before he sends his nation into battle is not fit to be a leader.
Ibid. (1967)

\* Forced exile.

15 I want to be able to live without a crowded calendar. I want to be able to read a book without feeling guilty, or go to a concert when I like. . . . But I do not intend to retire to a political nunnery. Ibid., Comment on Resignation (1968)

16 We intend to remain alive. Our neighbors want to see us dead. This is not a question that leaves much room for compromise.
Quoted in "The Indestructible Golda Meir" by David Reed, *Reader's Digest* July, 1971

17 Being seventy is not a sin. Ibid.

18 Women's Liberation is just a lot of foolishness. It's the men who are discriminated against. They can't bear children. And no one's likely to do anything about that.
Quoted in *Newsweek* October 23, 1972

19 I believe there are a couple of gross injustices in the world: against African blacks and against Jews. Moreover, I think these two instances of injustice can only be remedied by Socialist principles. Quoted by Oriana Fallaci in *L'Europeo* 1973

20 How can one accept crazy creatures who deem it a misfortune to get pregnant and a disaster to give birth to children? When it's the greatest privilege we women have compared with men!
Ibid.

21 At work, you think of the children you've left at home. At home, you think of the work you've left unfinished. Such a struggle is unleashed within yourself: your heart is rent.
Ibid.

22 Those who do not know how to weep with their whole heart don't know how to laugh either. Ibid.

23 Show me the sensible person who likes himself or herself! I know myself too well to like what I see. I know but too well that I'm not what I'd like to be. Ibid.

24 If you knew how often I say to myself: to hell with everything, to hell with everybody, I've done my share, let the others do theirs now, enough, enough, enough! Ibid.

25 I must govern the clock, not be governed by it. Ibid.

26 . . . old age is like a plane flying through a storm. Once you're aboard, there's nothing you can do. You can't stop the plane, you can't stop the storm, you can't stop time. So one might as well accept it calmly, wisely. Ibid.

27 I hate fashion, I've always hated it. Fashion is an imposition, a rein on freedom. Ibid.

28 . . . there's no difference between one's killing and making decisions that will send others to kill. It's exactly the same thing, or even worse.
Ibid.

29 I have had enough.
Statement upon Resignation as Prime Minister of Israel *April 11, 1974*

30 For me party discipline is a sacred matter, not just lust for power as some people claim: I was brought up that way all my life. Ibid.

31 Once in a Cabinet we had to deal with the fact that there had been an outbreak of assaults on women at night. One minister suggested a curfew: women should stay home after dark. I said, "But it's the men who are attacking the women. If there's to be a curfew, let the men stay home, not the women."
Quoted in *Against Rape*, Andra Medea and Kathleen Thompson, eds. *1974*

## 694. Bessie Smith
### (1898–1937)

1 I woke up this mornin', can't even get out of my do',
There's enough trouble to make a poor girl wonder where she wanna go.
"Back Water Blues" *1927*

2 No time to marry, no time to settle down;
I'm a young woman, and I ain't done runnin' aroun'.
"Young Woman's Blues" *1927*

3 While you're living in your mansion, you don't know what hard times mean.
Poor working man's wife is starving; your wife is living like a queen.
"Poor Man's Blues" *1930*

4 It's a long old road, but I know I'm gonna find the end.
"Long Old Road" *1931*

## 695. Dorothy Speare
### (1898–1951)

1 The intoxication of rouge is an insidious vintage known to more girls than mere man can ever believe. *Dancers in the Dark* *1922*

## 696. Elizabeth Bowen
(1899–1973)

1 "The best type of man is no companion."
*The Hotel*    *1928*

2 "I have a horror, I think, of not being, and of my friends not being, quite perfectly balanced."
Ibid.

3 "There being nothing was what you were frightened of all the time, eh? Yes."
*The Little Girls*    *1963*

4 "Did you exchange embraces of any kind?" "No. She was always in a hurry."
*Eva Trout*    *1968*

## 697. Indra Devi
(1899– )

1 Like an ugly bird of prey, tension hovers over the heads of millions of people, ready to swoop down on its victims at any time and in any place. More and more men, women, and even children are caught up in its cold grip and held for years, sometimes for the whole of their lives. Tension, in fact, is probably one of the greatest menaces the civilized world must face these days.    *Renewing Your Life Through Yoga*, Ch. 1    *1963*

2 Tranquilizers do not change our environment, nor do they change our personalities. They merely reduce our responsiveness to stimuli. They dull the keen edge of the angers, fears, or anxiety with which we might otherwise react to the problems of living. Once the response has been dulled, the irritating surface noise of living muted or eliminated, the spark and brilliance are also gone.    Ibid.

3 Like water which can clearly mirror the sky and the trees only so long as its surface is undisturbed, the mind can only reflect the true image of the Self when it is tranquil and wholly relaxed. A ghost of wind—and the rippling waters will distort the reflection; a storm—and the reflection disappears altogether. . . . It therefore becomes necessary to learn how to clear the mind of all clouds, to free it of all useless ballast and debris by dismissing the burden of too much concern with material things.    Ibid.

4 Our body is a magnificently devised, living, breathing mechanism, yet we do almost nothing to insure its optimal development and use. . . . We must begin at the beginning, just as the gardener who wants beautiful flowers in summer must start by cultivating the soil and properly nourishing the seedlings that come up in the early spring. The human organism needs an ample supply of good building material to repair the effects of daily wear and tear.
Ibid., Ch. 2

5 Yoga is not a religion, nor is it a magic formula or some form of calisthenics. In the country of its origin it is called a science—the science of living a healthy, meaningful, and purposeful life—a method of realizing the true self when the body, mind, and spirit blend into one harmonious whole. The system of Yoga, as developed by the ancient Indian philosophers and sages, has no temples, religious creed, or rites. . . . Yoga is a philosophy, a way of life, and organized religion forms no part of it. . . . The word Yoga symbolizes the unity of body, mind and spirit. It is derived from the Sanskrit word *yuj* which means a joining, a union, a reintegration. This actually is the aim of Yoga—to achieve union between man who is finite and the Spirit which is infinite.
Ibid., Ch. 10

## 698. Marguerite Harris
(1899– )

1 In tidy terminal homes,
agape at the stalking Rorschach
shapes that menace our cosmos,
pawns now, we itch and surmise.
"The Chosen," St. 1, *The East Side Scene*, Allen de Loach, ed.    *1968*

## 699. Emily Kimbrough
(1899– )

Co-author of *Our Hearts Were Young and Gay* with Cornelia Otis Skinner. See 744:4.

## 700. Eva Le Gallienne
(1899– )

1 . . . no mechanical device can ever, it seems to me, quite take the place of that mysterious communication between players and public, that sense of an experience directly shared, which gives to the living theatre its unique appeal.
*The Mystic in the Theatre: Eleanora Duse*, Ch. 1    *1965*

2 Innovators are inevitably controversial.    Ibid.

3 People who are born even-tempered, placid and untroubled—secure from violent passions or temptations to evil—those who have never

needed to struggle all night with the Angel to emerge lame but victorious at dawn, never become great saints.                    Ibid., Ch. 2

4 But the breathtaking part of it all was not so much the planning as the fantastic skill with which the planning was concealed.
Ibid., Ch. 5

5 There can be no generalizations as far as the art of acting is concerned. There can be no over-all "method"—above all no short cuts. Each actor must find his own way for himself.
Ibid., Ch. 6

## 701. Mary Margaret McBride
(1899–    )

1 Yes, we have a good many poor tired people here already, but we have plenty of mountains, rivers, woods, lots of sunshine and air, for tired people to rest in. We have Kansas wheat and Iowa corn and Wisconsin cheese for them to eat, Texas cotton for them to wear. So give us as many as come—we can take it, and take care of them.
America for Me, Ch. 1      1941

2 It takes time to straighten these things out, but the big item is. that we're still moving. This country began with people moving, and we've been moving ever since. . . . As long as we keep at that I guess we'll be all right.
Ibid., Ch. 2

3 "Terrible things happen to young girls in New York City. . . ."
A Long Way from Missouri, Ch. 1
1959

## 702. Helen Hill Miller
(1899–    )

1 France prides itself on being very old, on being not only the first-born among modern nations but the heir of the ancient world, the transmitter to the West of Mediterranean civilization.      Pamphlet, "The Spirit of Modern France"      1934

2 Logical clarity is the genius of the French language.                    Ibid.

3 Then, the word tyrant did not carry the pejorative meaning it conveys today. Tyrants seized and held their power by force, exercised it subject to no restraint, and perpetrated notorious cruelties. But many of them were great generals who fought wide-sweeping wars, lavish patrons of the arts, public figures who brought

their cities riches and renown. The times combined civilization and savagery.
Sicily and the Western Colonies of Greece      1965

4 "It isn't very often that a person who has been at the very center of one period in the life of a political party has the forward-lookingness and the resilience to note the transition to a new time, much less to bring it forcefully to the attention to the current members of the party."
Letter to Eleanor Roosevelt (1956), Quoted in Eleanor: The Years Alone by Joseph P. Lash      1972

## 703. Gloria Swanson
(1899–    )

1 When I die, my epitaph should read: She Paid the Bills. That's the story of my private life.
Quoted in "Gloria Swanson Comes Back" by S. Frank, Saturday Evening Post      July 22, 1950

## 704. Lena Guilbert Ford
(fl. early 1900s–1916?)

1 Keep the home fires burning,
While your hearts are yearning,
Though your lads are far away
They dream of home.
There's a silver lining
Through the dark cloud shining:
Turn the dark cloud inside out,
Till the boys come home.
"Keep the Homes Fires Burning"
1915

## 705. Eva Lathbury
(fl. early 1900s)

1 The fall, like the serpent, was mythical: the apple was sound and Eve hysterical.
Mr. Meyer's Pupil      1907

2 I can't help it . . . that's what we all say when we don't want to exert ourselves.      Ibid.

## 706. Moira O'Neill
(fl. early 1900s)

1 Youth's for an hour,
Beauty's a flower,
But love is the jewel that wins the world.
"Beauty's a Flower," Songs of the Glens of Antrim      1901

2 The memory's fairly spoilt on me
Wid mindin' to forget.
Ibid., "Forgettin'," St. 5

### 707. Lady Troubridge
(fl. early 1900s–1946)

1 A bad woman always has something she regards as a curse—a real bit of goodness hidden away somewhere.     *The Millionaire*   1907

2 If I had had a pistol I would have shot him—either that or fallen at his feet. There is no middle way when one loves.     Ibid.

3 It is far easier to love a woman in picturesque rags than in the common place garments of respectability.     Ibid.

4 A girl can't analyze marriage, and a woman—daren't.     Ibid.

### 708. Grace Adams
(1900–  )

1 Whenever serious intellectuals, psychologists, sociologists, practicing physicians, Nobel prize novelists take time off from their normal pursuits to scrutinize and appraise the Modern American Woman, they turn in unanimously dreary reports.     "American Women Are Coming Along," *Harper's*   1939

### 709. Polly Adler
(1900–1962)

1 Too many cooks spoil the brothel.
*A House Is Not a Home*   1953

2 . . . I am one of those people who just can't help getting a kick out of life—even when it's a kick in the teeth.     Ibid., Ch. 1

3 The degree to which a pimp, if he's clever, can confuse and delude a prostitute is very nearly unlimited.     Ibid., Ch. 4

4 "My home is in whatever town I'm booked."
Ibid., Ch. 9

5 What it comes down to is this: the grocer, the butcher, the baker, the merchant, the landlord, the druggist, the liquor dealer, the policeman, the doctor, the city father and the politician—these are the people who make money out of prostitution, these are the real reapers of the wages of sin.     Ibid.

6 The women who take husbands not out of love but out of greed, to get their bills paid, to get a fine house and clothes and jewels; the women who marry to get out of a tiresome job, or to get away from disagreeable relatives, or to avoid being called an old maid—these are whores in everything but name. The only difference between them and my girls is that my girls gave a man his money's worth.
Ibid., Ch. 10

### 710. Dorothy Arzner
(1900–  )

1 It is my theory that if you have authority, know your business and know you have authority, you have the authority.
Quoted in *The New York Times*
*June 15, 1972*

2 I was led by the grace of God to the movies. I would like the industry to be more aware of what they're doing to influence people. . . .
Quoted in *Popcorn Venus*
by Marjorie Rosen   1973

### 711. Taylor Caldwell
(1900–  )

1 "Honest men live on charity in their age; the almhouses are full of men who never stole a copper penny. Honest men are the fools and the saints, and you and I are neither."
*Dynasty of Death*, Bk. I, Ch. 12
*1938*

2 ". . . I knew you would not betray us. Not because of—honor. But profit. And profits are not bedfellows of honor.     Ibid.

3 "Protestantism forgets that men are men, and that there are appetites that it is better to wink at, provided that certain duties are observed. We don't strain at a gnat and swallow a camel, nor swim in an ocean and drown in a puddle."
Ibid., Bk. II, Ch. 70

4 Men who retain irony are not to be trusted, thought Ernest. They can't always resist an impulse to tickle themselves.     Ibid., Ch. 78

5 "He that hath no rule over his own spirit is like a city that is broken down and without walls."
*This Side of Innocence*, Pt. I, Ch. 5
*1946*

6 A civilization based purely on agriculture was a civilization which never went hungry. But a raucous and ruthless civilization, dependent on the churning of the "devil machines" within brick walls, was vulnerable to every sensitive wind that blew from Wall Street.
*Ibid., Pt. III, Ch. 43*

7 Despair, Philip thought, is sometimes the great energizer of the mind, though sometimes its flowering may be sterile. *Ibid., Ch. 45*

8 Why, hadn't Pa often told him that no one could understand a person who had a gift? They lived in a world of their own, beyond criticism, beyond the knowing of other men. . . . "In Germany we understand these things, these geniuses," Mr. Enger had often told Edward dolefully. "But not in America. America has no soul." *The Sound of Thunder, Pt. I, Ch. 1 1957*

9 "Learning," he would say, "should be a joy and full of excitement. It is life's greatest adventure; it is an illustrated excursion into the mind's noble and learned men, not a conducted tour through a jail. So its surroundings should be as gracious as possible, to complement it." *Ibid., Ch. 9*

10 "Shakespeare speaks of 'lean and hungry men,' but he never seemed to notice that a lot of women are lean and hungry, too, and much more vulturous than many men." *The Late Clara Beame, Ch. 16 1963*

11 "It never pays to complicate a woman's mind too much." *Ibid.*

12 But what was a body? Dust, dung, urine, itches. It was the light within which was important, and it was not significant if that light endured after death, or if the soul was blinded eternally in the endless night of the suspired flesh. *Great Lion of God, Pt. I, Ch. 1 1970*

13 One, if one is sensible, blames government, not the servers of the government, not those entangled in their governments. *Ibid., Ch. 10*

14 Every object . . . burned with a blinding radiance as if each were being consumed by the sun. A very holocaust of flaming scintillation hovered over all things, appeared to emanate even from the pebbles of the paths. And the heat mounted. *Ibid., Pt. II, Ch. 24*

15 ". . . it is not always wise to appear singular." *Ibid., Pt. III, Ch. 35* *Ibid., Ch. 43*

16 Is it not deplorable that a few heedless zealots can bring calamity to their law-abiding fellows?

17 The old [Roman] gods understood that life was reasonable and favors were exchanged for favors, and that is how it should be. *Ibid., Ch. 53*

18 At the end—and as usual—God had betrayed the innocent and had left them comfortless. *Captains and the Kings, Pt. I, Ch. 1 1972*

19 It was business, and none of them had allegiances or attachments or involvements with any nation, not even their own. . . . Joseph immediately called them "the gray and deadly men," and did not know why he detested them, or why he found them the most dangerous of all among the human species. *Ibid., Ch. 21*

20 "Once power is concentrated in Washington—admittedly not an immediate prospect—America will take her place as an empire and calculate and instigate wars, for the advantage of all concerned. We all know, from long experience, that progress depends on war." *Ibid.*

21 "Mankind is the most selfish species this world has ever spewed up from hell, and it demands, constantly, that neighbors and politicians be 'unselfish,' and allow themselves to be plundered —for its benefit. Nobody howls more against 'public selfishness,' or even private selfishness, as much as a miser, just as whores are the strongest supporters of public morality, and robbers of the people extol philanthropy. I've lived a long time, but my fellow man baffles me more and more, which no doubt is naïve of me." *Ibid., Pt. II, Ch. 13*

## 712. Helen Gahagan Douglas
### (1900– )

1 The Eleanor Roosevelt I shall always remember was a woman of tenderness and deep sympathy, a woman with the most exquisite manners of anyone I have known—one who did what she was called upon to do with complete devotion and rare charm. *The Eleanor Roosevelt We Remember 1963*

2 Would Eleanor Roosevelt have had to struggle to overcome this tortuous shyness if she had grown up secure in the knowledge that she was a beautiful girl? If she hadn't struggled so earnestly, would she have been so sensitive to the struggles of others? Would a beautiful Eleanor Roosevelt have escaped from the confinements of the mid-Victorian drawing room

society in which she was reared? Would a beautiful Eleanor Roosevelt have wanted to escape? Would a beautiful Eleanor Roosevelt have had the same need to be, to do?          Ibid.

3 I know the force women can exert in directing the course of events.          Ibid.

4 If the national security is involved, *anything goes.* There are no rules. There are people so lacking in roots about what is proper and what is improper that they don't know there's anything wrong in breaking into the headquarters of the opposition party.
> Quoted in "Helen Gahagan Douglas"
> by Lee Israel, *Ms.*          *October, 1973*

5 . . . the first step toward liberation for *any* group is to use the power in hand. . . . And the power in hand is the vote.          Ibid.

6 If I go to Congress, it won't be to spar with anybody, man or woman. I'm not a wit. I'm not a fencer. I don't enjoy that kind of thing. It's all nonsense and an insult to the intelligence of the American people.
> Ibid., News Item (1944)

7 Such pip-squeaks as Nixon and McCarthy are trying to get us so frightened of Communism that we'll be afraid to turn out the lights at night.          Ibid., Speech (1950)

## 713.  Queen Elizabeth
### (1900–    )

1 The children will not leave unless I do. I shall not leave unless their father does, and the King will not leave the country in any circumstances whatever.          Attributed          *1940*

2 I'm glad we've been bombed [Buckingham Palace]. It makes me feel I can look the East End in the face.          Attributed          *1940*

## 714.  Joanna Field
### (1900–    )

1 I used to trouble about what life was for— now being alive seems sufficient reason.
> *A Life of One's Own* (June 8)
> *1934*

2 I feel we have picked each other from the crowd as fellow-travellers, for neither of us is to the other's personality the end-all and the be-all.          Ibid. (September 20)

3 . . . as soon as you are happy enjoying yourself, something hunts you on—the hounds of heaven—you think you'll be lost—damned, if you are caught. . . .          Ibid. (October 10)

4 I came to the conclusion then that "continual mindfulness" . . . must mean, not a sergeant-major-like drilling of thoughts, but a continual readiness to look and readiness to accept whatever came.          Ibid.

5 I began to suspect that thought, which I had always before looked on as a cart-horse to be driven, whipped and plodding between shafts, might be really a Pegasus, so suddenly did it alight beside me from places I had no knowledge of.          Ibid.

6 . . . the growth of understanding follows an ascending spiral rather than a straight line.
> Ibid. (Undated)

## 715.  Zelda Fitzgerald
### (1900–1948)

1 Women, despite the fact that nine out of ten of them go through life with a death-bed air either of snatching-the-last-moment or with martyr-resignation, do not die tomorrow—or the next day. They have to live on to any one of many bitter ends.
> "Eulogy on the Flapper," *Metropolitan*
> *Magazine*          *June, 1922*

2 Most people hew the battlements of life from compromise, erecting their impregnable keeps from judicious submissions, fabricating their philosophical drawbridges from emotional retractions and scalding marauders in the boiling oil of sour grapes.
> *Save Me the Waltz*, Ch. 1          *1932*

3 Possessing a rapacious, engulfing ego, their particular genius swallowed their world in its swift undertow and washed its cadavers out to sea. New York is a good place to be on the up-grade.          Ibid., Ch. 2

4 Women sometimes seem to share a quiet, unalterable dogma of persecution that endows even the most sophisticated of them with the inarticulate poignancy of the peasant.          Ibid.

5 "Lives aren't as hard as professions," she gasped.          Ibid., Ch. 3

6 Wasn't any art the expression of the inexpressible? And isn't the inexpressible always the same, though variable—like the *Time* in physics?
> Ibid.

7 "Oh, the secret life of man and woman— dreaming how much better we would be than we are if we were somebody else or even ourselves, and feeling that our estate has been unexploited to its fullest. I have reached the point where I can only express the inarticulate,

taste food without taste, smell whiffs of the past, read statistical books, and sleep in uncomfortable positions." *Ibid.*, Ch. 4

8 "By the time a person has achieved years adequate for choosing a direction, the die is cast and the moment has long since passed which determined the future." *Ibid.*

9 ". . . We grew up founding our dreams on the infinite promise of American advertising. I *still* believe that one can learn to play the piano by mail and that mud will give you a perfect complexion." *Ibid.*

10 "It's very expressive of myself. I just lump everything in a great heap which I have labelled 'the past,' and, having thus emptied this deep reservoir that was once myself, I am ready to continue." *Ibid.*, Ch. 4

11 . . . I don't want to live—I want to love first, and live incidentally. . . .
Letter to F. Scott Fitzgerald (1919),
Quoted in *Zelda* by Nancy Milford
*1970p*

12 Don't you think I was made for you? I feel like you had me ordered—and I was delivered to you—to be worn—I want you to wear me, like a watch-charm or a button hole boquet [sic]—to the world. *Ibid.*

13 Home is the place to do the things you want to do. Here we eat just when we want to. Breakfast and luncheon are extremely moveable feasts. It's terrible to allow conventional habits to gain a hold on a whole household; to eat, sleep and live by clock ticks.
*Ibid.*, Interview in the *Baltimore Sun* (1923)

14 I don't seem to know anything appropriate for a person of thirty. . . .
*Ibid.*, Letter to F. Scott Fitzgerald (1930)

15 Your entire life will soon be accounted for by the toils we have so assiduously woven—your leisure is eaten up by habits of leisure, your money by habitual extravagance, your hope by cynicism and mine by frustration, your ambition by too much compromise.
*Ibid.* (Undated)

16 A vacuum can only exist, I imagine, by the things which enclose it.
*Ibid.*, Journal (1932)

17 . . . I have often told you that I am that little fish who swims about under a shark and, I believe, lives indelicately on its offal. Anyway, that is the way I am. Life moves over me in a vast black shadow and I swallow whatever it

drops with relish, having learned in a very hard school that one cannot be both a parasite and enjoy self-nourishment without moving in worlds too fantastic for even my disordered imagination to people with meaning.
*Ibid.*, Letter to F. Scott Fitzgerald (1932)

18 I wish I could write a beautiful book to break those hearts that are soon to cease to exist: a book of faith and small neat worlds and of people who live by the philosophies of popular songs. . . . *Ibid.*, Letter to Dr. Rennie (May, 1934)

19 I take a sun bath and listen to the hours, formulating, and disintegrating under the pines, and smell the resiny hardi-hood of the high noon hours. The world is lost in a blue haze of distances, and the immediate sleeps in a thin and finite sun. *Ibid.*, Journal (1938)

## 716. Lisa Gardiner
(1900–1956)

1 And remember, expect nothing and life will be velvet. Quoted in *Don't Fall Off the Mountain* by Shirley MacLaine
*1970p*

## 717. Elizabeth Goudge
(1900–   )

1 Her birthdays were always important to her; for being a born lover of life, she would always keep the day of her entrance into it as a very great festival indeed. . . .
*Green Dolphin Street*, Bk. I,
Pt. II, Ch. 1    1944

2 His hatred of his wife horrified him. It was the first hatred of his life, it was growing in bitterness and intensity day by day, and he had no idea what to do about it.
*Ibid.*, Bk. II, Pt. III, Ch. 1

3 The elements were "seeking" each other in rage and confusion, and in the fury of the conflict boastful man was utterly humiliated, sucked down, drowned. *Ibid.*, Ch. 2

4 She had a deep sense of justice and sometimes this made her feel as uncomfortable in her spirit if she deserved a whipping and did not get it as she felt in her body if she did get it, and of the two she preferred to suffer in body.
*The Child from the Sea*,
Bk. I, Ch. 1    1970

5 Peace, she supposed, was contingent upon a certain disposition of the soul, a disposition to receive the gift that only detachment from self made possible.                    Ibid., Ch. 7

6 . . . the butterflies. . . . Yet not quite birds, as they were not quite flowers, mysterious and fascinating as are all indeterminate creatures.
                    Ibid., Pt. II, Ch. 1

7 ". . . The travail of creation of course exaggerates the importance of our work while we are engaged in it; we know better when the opus is finished and the lion is perceived to be only a broken-backed mouse. . . ."
                    Ibid., Pt. III, Ch. 2

8 "All true glory, while it remains true, holds it. It is the maintaining of truth that is so hard."
                    Ibid.

9 "All we are asked to bear we can bear. That is a law of the spiritual life. The only hindrance to the working of this law, as of all benign laws, is fear."                    Ibid., Ch. 17

## 718.  Helen Hayes
(1900–    )

1 An actress's life is so transitory—suddenly you're a building.*                    News Item
                    *November, 1955*

2 One has to grow up with good talk in order to form the habit of it.
                    *A Gift of Joy*, with Lewis Funke,
                    Introduction    *1965*

3 We rely upon the poets, the philosophers, and the playwrights to articulate what most of us can only feel, in joy or sorrow. They illuminate the thoughts for which we only grope; they give us the strength and balm we cannot find in ourselves. Whenever I feel my courage wavering I rush to them. They give me the wisdom of acceptance, the will and resilience to push on.
                    Ibid.

4 Actors cannot choose the manner in which they are born. Consequently, it is the one gesture in their lives completely devoid of self-consciousness.                    *On Reflection*, with
                    Sandford Dody, Ch. 1    *1968*

5 When I was very young, I half believed one could find within the pages of these [biographical] memoirs the key to greatness. It's rather like trying to find the soul in the map of the human body. But it is enlightening—and it does solve some of the mysteries.
                    Ibid., Ch. 6

* Referring to a New York theater named for her.

6 Yes, I have doubted. I have wandered off the path. I have been lost. But I always returned. It is beyond the logic I seek. It is intuitive—an intrinsic, built-in sense of direction. I seem always to find my way home. My faith has wavered but has saved me.                    Ibid., Ch. 15

## 719.  Laura Z. Hobson
(1900–    )

1 It was the rhythm of all living, apparently, and for most people. Happiness, and then pain. Perhaps then happiness again, but now, with it, the awareness of its own mortality.
                    *Gentlemen's Agreement*, Ch. 1
                    *1946*

2 Did it never occur to one of them to write about a fine guy who was Jewish? Did each one feel some savage necessity to pick a Jew who was a swine in the wholesale business, a Jew who was a swine in the movies, a Jew who was a swine in bed?                    Ibid., Ch. 3

3 Where did ideas come from, anyway? This one had leaped at him when he'd been exhausted, AWOL from his search.                    Ibid., Ch. 4

4 We are born in innocence. . . . Corruption comes later. The first fear is a corruption, the first reaching for a something that defies us. The first nuance of difference, the first need to feel better than the different one, more loved, stronger, richer, more blessed—these are corruptions.                    Ibid., Ch. 6

5 The anti-Semite offered the effrontery—and then the world was ready with harsh yardsticks to measure the self-control and dignity with which you met it. You were insensitive or too sensitive; you were too timid or too bellicose; they gave you at once the wound and the burden of proper behavior toward it.
                    Ibid., Ch. 8

6 What trouble it was to be young! At sixty you grieved for the world; in youth you grieved for one unique creature.                    Ibid., Ch. 13

7 What was it, this being "a good father"? To love one's sons and daughters was not enough; to carry in one's bone and blood a pride in them, a longing for their growth and development—this was not enough. One had to be a ready companion to games and jokes and outings, to earn from the world this accolade. The devil with it.    *The First Papers*, Pt. I,
                    Ch. 2    *1964*

8 If she began to imagine that he would be grateful for any understanding she gave him, she would launch herself on the long stony road of disappointment.    *Consenting Adult* 1975

9 She forced herself to stop thinking. . . . She was disciplined enough to do this nonthinking for short stretches, during the daytime at least. She had done it in other crises of her life; at times it was the only way to manage.    Ibid.

10 Why didn't children ever see that they could damage and harm their parents as much as parents could damage and harm children? Ibid.

11 It was all happening in a great, swooping free fall, irreversible, free of decision, in the full pull of gravity toward whatever was to be. Ibid.

12 "Dear Mama. . . . I have something to tell you that I guess I better not put off any longer . . . you see, I am a homosexual. I have fought it off for months and maybe years, but it just grows truer. . . ."    Ibid.

## 720. Kathryn Hulme

(1900– )

1 I saw more of them [concentration-camp brands] on that first day. I saw so many that I was sure my memory was branded forever and that never again would I be able to think of mankind with that certain friendly ease which characterizes Americans like a birthright.
*The Wild Place*, Ch. 2    1953

2 Interior silence, she repeated silently. That would be her Waterloo. How without brain surgery could you quell the rabble of memories? Even as she asked herself the question, she heard her psychology professor saying quite clearly across a space of years, "No one, not even a saint, can say an *Ave* straight through without some association creeping in; this is a known thing."    *The Nun's Story*, Ch. 1 1956

3 "You must never lose the awareness that in yourself you are nothing, you are only an instrument. An instrument is nothing until it is lifted."    Ibid., Ch. 8

4 Her defeat had so many facets, she could not define it all at once, but only her scorching shame for being a hypocrite in the religious life, for wearing the garb of obedience while flaunting the Holy Rule, and the Cross of Christ above a heart filled with hate.
Ibid., Ch. 18

5 "I believe, Father," she said, "that even the smallest gesture of charity made in the world, with joy, would be ten times more pleasing to God than all the work I do here under the Holy Rule I only pretend to obey."    Ibid.

6 Then there had been the inspection of their child from head to toe as he watched Annie undress the baby before bedtime. The tiny perfect fingernails and toenails astonished him the most. They were like the small pink shells you scuffed up in the sands of tropical beaches, he whispered, counting them. And, for the twentieth time, he exclaimed, "I don't know *how* you did it all alone!" His admiration for her bravery sent a glow of happiness through her. It was a new kind of tribute from him. It was a payment in full for all the terrors of her lonely ordeal.    *Annie's Captain*, Ch. 9 1961

7 Their fright seemed to turn them into children.
Ibid., Ch. 18

8 Annie clung to life like a shipwrecked soul on a slender spar adrift in an ocean of pain. She denied the pains but the doctor guessed them when she began refusing all medicines for fear he would slip in the morphine he had promised not to give until she herself asked. Her fortitude surpassed anything he had ever encountered and it turned him into a cursing madman every time he came downstairs. "She'd go through hell to keep her wits clear until *he* comes," he groaned. "God damn that bloody old scow!"    Ibid.

## 721. Loran Hurnscot

(1900?–1970)

1 There are times when I feel I can no longer bear that grey room where I go once a week or fortnight in order to discover (presumably) how to turn from one sort of person into another sort of person.
*A Prison, a Paradise*, Vol. II    1959

2 It came over me, blindingly, for the first time in my life, that suicide was a wrong act, was indeed "mortal sin." In that moment, God stopped me. I did not want my life, but I knew I was suddenly forbidden by something outside myself to let it go.    Ibid. (July 9, 1939)

3 It had always been pride that had held me off from Him. Now it was broken the obstacle was gone. One is never simple enough, while things go well.    Ibid.

4 And suddenly I was swept out of myself—knowing, knowing, knowing. Feeling the love

of God burning through creation, and an ecstasy of bliss pouring through my spirit and down into every nerve.

Ibid. (October 4, 1939)

## 722. Guion Griffis Johnson

(1900– )

1 Government existed for the best people—the intelligent, educated and wealthy. In a society where all are equally free and share alike in political privileges, there are some more fit for the exercise of good government than others.

"Southern Paternalism Toward
Negroes After Emancipation,"
*The Journal of Southern History*
*November, 1957*

2 It was always the responsibility of the strong, so ran the benevolent paternalist's argument, to bear the burden of the weak. The strong race by virtue of its superior intelligence, culture, and wealth was the national protector of the Negro.                                      Ibid.

3 The argument against mixing in the schools stresses again the concept of superior and inferior races and the obligation of the superior to give the inferior equal but separate facilities so that the Negro may have the opportunity to rise within his own social system. In this way, God's plan will be carried out, for He separated the races and it is a violation of His will for blacks and whites to be mixed in educational facilities.                        Ibid.

## 723. Wilhelmina Kemp Johnstone

(1900– )

1 But how glad I am, how very glad and grateful for that window looking out upon the sea!

"My Window," *Bahamian Jottings*
*1973*

2 Pride, we are told, my children, "goeth before a fall," and oh, the pride was there and so the fall was not far away!

Ibid., "The Old Ship's Story"

3 The dawn artist was already out, tipping the clouds with glory, and transforming the sky into a glow of wonder.

Ibid., "Our Trip to Green Cay"

## 724. Meridel Le Sueur

(1900– )

1 In the mid-centre of America a man can go blank for a long, long time. There is no community to give him life; so he can go lost as

if he were in a jungle. No one will pay any attention. He can simply be as lost as if he had gone into the heart of an empty continent. A sensitive child can be lost too amidst all the emptiness and ghostliness. I am filled with terror when I think of the emptiness and ghostliness of mid-America. The rigors of conquest have made us spiritually insulated against human values. No fund of instinct and experience has been accumulated, and each generation seems to be more impoverished than the last.

"Corn Village" (1930),
*Salute to Spring    1940*

2 "I put my hand where you lie so silently. I hope you will come glistening with life power, with it shining upon you as upon the feathers of birds. I hope you will be a warrior and fierce for change, so all can live."

Ibid., "Annunciation"

3 Every generation must go further than the last or what's the use in it? A baker's son must bake better bread—a miner's son—each generation a mite further.

Ibid., "The Dead in Steel"

4 "They can kill the bodies of Sacco and Vanzetti but they can't kill what they stand for—the working class. It is bound to live. As certainly as this system of things, this exploitation of man by man, will remain, there will always be this fight, today and always until . . ."                      Ibid., "Farewell"

5 Hard times ain't quit and we ain't quit.

Ibid., "Salute to Spring"

6 Now I have always cried to these forebears and cried to them for answers, for compasses, and seen their deeds, their actions, solid and muscular. . . . Now, in a moment of crisis and cold, they point out where the warm ash of the old fires can give you warmth, where strength is cached. I can even catch their heraldic voices in the wind of struggle.    *Crusaders*
*1955*

7 . . . there is only one force that creates value and that is labor, and one manner of expropriation of wealth, the exploitation of labor and the natural resources.             Ibid.

8 . . . the history of an oppressed people is hidden in the lies and the agreed-upon myth of its conquerors.                      Ibid., Ch. 3

9 . . . for there is no cruelty like that of the oppressor who fells his loss of the bit on those it has been his gain to oppress.         Ibid.

10 Security seemed to be something you had more of by being true to your beliefs. A house was

only a house—it was nothing you gave your life to have, or sacrificed an idea to protect; the same with a job.      Ibid., Ch. 5

11 Memory in America suffers amnesia.
     Ibid., Ch. 6

12 The funeral has long been an instrument also of conveying history that has become hidden, of subtly informing the young, and of mining and blowing the mineral of collective poetry and courage.      Ibid.

13 For none shall die who have the future in them.
     Ibid.

14 Money is only money, beans tonight and steak tomorrow. So long as you can look yourself in the eye.      Ibid., Ch. 7

## 725. Margaret Mitchell
### (1900–1949)

1 "I'm tired of everlastingly being unnatural and never doing anything I want to do. I'm tired of acting like I don't eat more than a bird, and walking when I want to run and saying I feel faint after a waltz, when I could dance for two days and never get tired. I'm tired of saying, 'How wonderful you are!' to fool men who haven't got one-half the sense I've got and I'm tired of pretending I don't know anything, so men can tell me things and feel important while they're doing it. . . ."
     *Gone with the Wind*, Pt. I, Ch. 5
     *1936*

2 "Until you've lost your reputation, you never realize what a burden it was or what freedom really is."      Ibid., Pt. II, Ch. 9

3 "What most people don't seem to realize is that there is just as much money to be made out of the wreckage of a civilization as from the up-building of one."      Ibid.

4 "Fighting is like champagne. It goes to the heads of cowards as quickly as of heroes. Any fool can be brave on a battle field when it's be brave or else be killed."      Ibid., Pt. IV, Ch. 31

5 "Southerners can never resist a losing cause."
     Ibid., Ch. 34

6 "The Irish . . . are the damnedest race. They put so much emphasis on so many wrong things."      Ibid.

7 Now he disliked talking business with her as much as he had enjoyed it before they were married. Now he saw that she understood entirely too well and he felt the usual masculine

indignation at the duplicity of women. Added to it was the usual masculine disillusionment in discovering that a woman has a brain.
     Ibid., Ch. 36

8 If! If! If! There were so many ifs in life, never any certainty of anything, never any sense of security, always the dread of losing everything and being cold and hungry again.
     Ibid., Ch. 38

9 "Death and taxes and childbirth! There's never any convenient time for any of them!"
     Ibid.

10 "Everybody's mainspring is different. And I want to say this—folks whose mainsprings are busted are better dead."      Ibid., Ch. 40

11 "You kin polish a mule's feets an' shine his hide an' put brass all over his harness an' hitch him ter a fine cah'ige. But he a mule jes' de same. He doan fool nobody."      Ibid., Ch. 48

12 "My pet, the world can forgive practically anything except people who mind their own business."      Ibid.

13 "Life's under no obligation to give us what we expect. We take what we get and are thankful it's no worse than it is."
     Ibid., Pt. V, Ch. 53

14 "I won't think of it now. I can't stand it if I do. I'll think of it tomorrow at Tara. Tomorrow's another day."      Ibid., Ch. 57

15 "You're so brutal to those who love you, Scarlett. You take their love and hold it over their heads like a whip."      Ibid., Ch. 63

16 "What is broken is broken—and I'd rather remember it as it was at its best than mend it and see the broken places as long as I lived."
     Ibid.

## 726. Barbara Morgan
### (1900– )

1 The Navajo and Pueblo Indian tribes who danced the rituals . . . as partners in the cosmic process, attuned me to the universally primal—rather than to either the "primitive" or the "civilized."      Quoted in *The Woman's Eye* by Anne Tucker      *1973*

2 . . . as the life style of the Space Age grows more inter-disciplinary, it will be harder for the "one-track" mind to survive. . . . I see simultaneous intake, multiple-awareness, and synthesized comprehension as inevitable, long before the year 2000 A.D.      Ibid.

## 727. Louise Nevelson

(1900–    )

1 The freer that women become, the freer will men be. Because when you enslave someone— you *are* enslaved.     Quoted in *AFTRA Summer, 1974*

## 728. Martha Ostenso

(1900–1963)

1 Fire overhead sounded a voluminous prolonged cry, like a great trumpet call. Wild geese flying still farther north, to a region beyond human warmth . . . beyond even human isolation.     *Wild Geese*, Ch. 1    *1925*

2 The garden cost Amelia no end of work and worry; she tended the delicate tomato vines as though they were new born infants, and suffered momentary sinking of the heart whenever she detected signs of weakness in any of the hardier vegetables. She was grateful for the toil in which she could dwell as a sort of refuge from deeper thought.     Ibid., Ch. 7

3 Wherever the wind was bound, Elsa thought, there the whole world seemed to be going.     *The Mad Carews*, Ch. 4    *1927*

4 Some clear intuition bade her fight the emotions which his coming stirred within her. It was a fight against that irresistible force which sought ever to turn back to the earth that which was the earth's; a struggle to evade the trap which would close her forever within Elder's Hollow.     Ibid., Ch. 6

5 She was especially happy in the violence, the stride of the great, obstreperous city [Chicago], the fierce roar of the wind that was its voice, the white-green tumult of the waves breaking on the shore of Lake Michigan, its soul.     Ibid., Ch. 21

6 "You have stirred the soil with your plow, my friend. It will never be the same again."     *O River, Remember*, Ch. 4    *1943*

7 It came to him sharply then that his mother had gradually discarded every vestige of her immigrant past, while his father was still— well, what *was* his father? Surely an American now, but with the best, the most vigorous and honest and spiritually simple qualities of the old land giving something to the new.     Ibid., Ch. 8

\* \* \*

8 Pity the Unicorn,
Pity the Hippogriff,
Souls that were never born
Out of the land of If!
    "The Unicorn and the Hippogriff," St. 1

## 729. Vijaya Lakshmi Pandit

(1900–    )

1 I feel torn in two between my duty to the children and the other duties of serving the country which, in our case, has come to mean long months of imprisonment.     *Prison Days* (March 17, 1943) *1946*

2 It [political imprisonment] is a slow daily sacrifice which can be so much more deadly than some big heroic gesture made in a moment of emotional upheaval. . . .     Ibid. (May 3, 1943)

3 When my public activities are reported it is very annoying to read how I looked, if I smiled, if a particular reporter liked my hair style.     Quoted in *The Scotsman* (Glasgow) *August 29, 1955*

4 You know, what happens to anybody who has been in these two places [Moscow and Washington, D.C.] and looked at them objectively, is the horrifying thought—if I may use that word in quotes—that they are so similar. . . . Take that passion for science—they're both absolutely dedicated to the machine, they are both extroverts, they both function in much the same way. . . .     Ibid.

5 It has simply been taken for granted that men and women are equal [in India] and even though some centuries separated the period when woman functioned as a free citizen in her own right and her re-emergence after India's independence, the theoretical acceptance of equality has always remained.     "The Second Sex," *Punch May 16, 1962*

6 Difficulties, opposition, criticism—these things are meant to be overcome, and there is a special joy in facing them and in coming out on top. It is only when there is nothing but praise that life loses its charm and I begin to wonder what I should do about it.     Quoted in *The Envoy Extraordinary* by Vera Brittain    *1965*

7 The Indian temperament exceeds in emotionally worded epistles, which keep one in suspense as to what the aim of the writer is, until one has waded through a sea of beautiful metaphors to the final paragraph.    Ibid. (c.1963)

8 Freedom is not for the timid. If one wishes to be in politics, one must be ready to face all eventualities.    Ibid. (c.1964)

## 730. Malvina Reynolds
(1900– )

1 Where are you going, my little one, little one,
Where are you going, my baby, my own?
Turn around and you're two,
Turn around and you're four,
Turn around and you're a young girl going out
    of my door.
    "Turn Around"    1958

2 Everybody thinks my head's full of nothing,
Wants to put his special stuff in,
Fill the space with candy wrappers,
Keep out sex and revolution,
But there's no hole in my head,
Too bad.
    "No Hole in My Head"    1965

3 While that baby is a child it will suffer from
    neglect,
Be picked upon and pecked, run over and
    wrecked,
And its head will be crowned with the thorn,
But while it's inside her it must remain intact,
And it cannot be murdered till it's born.
    "Rosie Jane"    1973

## 731. Christina Stead
(1900?– )

1 "I know your breed; all your fine officials debauch the young girls who are afraid to lose their jobs: that's as old as Washington."
    *The Man Who Loved Children*, Ch. 4
    *1940*

2 "There are so many ways to kill yourself, they're just old-fashioned with their permanganate: do you think I'd take permanganate? I wouldn't want to burn my insides out and live to tell the tale as well; idiots! It's simple. I'd drown myself. . . . Why be in misery at the last?"    Ibid., Ch. 5

3 "Anyone would think a thin stick like me, weak and miserable, would go down with everything: do you think I get more than my old cough every winter? I bet I live till ninety, with all

my aches and pains. To think that's fifty more years of the Great I-Am."    Ibid.

4 "I do not want to go to heaven; I want my children, forever children, and other children, stalwart adults, and a good, happy wife, that is all I ask, but not paradise; earth is enough for me: it is because I believe earth is heaven, Naden, that I can overcome all my troubles and face down my enemies."    Ibid., Ch. 7

5 "A mother! What are we worth really? They all grow up whether you look after them or not. That poor miserable brat of his is growing up, and I certainly licked the hide off her; and she's seen marriage at its worst, and now she's dreaming about 'supermen' and 'great men.' What is the good of doing anything for them?"    Ibid., Ch. 10

6 A cat and dog life it was; we didn't think we'd be able to stick it out. Eh, what a bloody egotist, love. . . .    *Dark Places of the Heart*
    *1966*

7 "It's all bourgeois waste and caprice anyway. Someone taking the ideas of some Frenchman, great blocks of flats with angles and courtyards, a brick prison, it won't suit England; no fireplaces, no chimney and everything laid on from a center. . . . With this Corbusier there'll be no relaxing and no dreaming; only a soulless measured-off engineer's world with no place for us."    Ibid.

8 "Ye want to tell the plain truth all your life, woman, and speak straight and see straight; otherwise ye get to seein' double."    Ibid.

9 "Loneliness is a terrible blindness."    Ibid.

## 732. Violet Alleyn Storey
(1900– )
\* \* \*

1 I have a small-town soul.
It makes me want to know
Wee, unimportant things
About the folks that go
Past on swift journeys.
    "Ironical"

## 733. Opal Whiteley
(1900?– )

1 The mamma where I love
says I am a new sance.
I think it is something grown-ups
don't like to have around.
    *The Story of Opal*\*    *1920*

\* Written between the ages of five and twelve.

2 It is such a comfort to have a friend
 near.
 when lonesome feels do come.
 Ibid.

3 Potatoes are very interesting folks
 I think they must see a lot
 of what is going on in the earth
 They have so many eyes.
 Ibid.

4 And this I have learned
 grown-ups do not know the language
 of shadows.
 Ibid.

5 Some days are long.
 Some days are short.
 The days that I have to stay in the
 house
 are the most long days of all.
 Ibid.

### 734. Frances Winwar
(1900–    )

1 In her [Eleonora Duse] intellectual acquisitiveness she selected people as a bee chooses its flowers, for what they had to offer. Her lack of formal education made her the eternal disciple. *Wingless Victory*, Ch. 14
 *1956*

### 735. Yocheved Bat-Miriam
(1901–    )

1 Singing like a hope, shining like a tear,
 Silent, the echo of what will befall.
 "Parting," St. 1, *Poems from the
 Hebrew*, Robert Mezey, ed. *1973*

2 I shall put on my dead face with a silence free
 Of joy and of pain forevermore,
 And dawn will trail like a child after me
 To play with shells on the shore.
 Ibid., St. 5

3 Not to be, to be gone—I pray for this
 At the gates of infinity, like a fey child.
 Ibid., "Distance Spills Itself," St. 5

### 736. Miriam Beard
(1901–    )

1 "Haven't you some small article I could send her, very attractive—typically American?" The sales expert looked depressed. . . . "American, you say? . . . Why, my dee-ur, *we*

don't carry those *Colonial* goods. All *our* things are *imported*."
 *Realism in Romantic Japan*, Ch. 1
 *1930*

2 A country honeycombed with agitation and a life made vivid by unending clash and controversy—that is what the traveler finds in Japan to-day. Ibid., Ch. 5

### 737. Doris Fleeson
(1901–1970)

1 It is occasionally possible to charge Hell with a bucket of water but against stupidity the gods themselves struggle in vain.
 Newspaper Column
 *February 17, 1964*

### 738. Elinor Hays
(1901?–    )

1 It was not only childbearing that wore away women's lives. There were slower erosions.
 *Morning Star*, Pt. I, Ch. 1 *1961*

2 Those most dedicated to the future are not always the best prophets.
 Ibid., Pt. IV, Ch. 29

### 739. Gertrude Lawrence
(1901–1952)

1 In London I had been by terms poor and rich, hopeful and despondent, successful and down-and-out, utterly miserable and ecstatically dizzily happy. I belonged to London as each of us can belong to only one place on this earth. And, in the same way, London belonged to me.
 *A Star Danced*, Ch. 1 *1945*

2 "So this is America!" I exclaimed. "Look at that bath, will you? Feel that delicious warmth. Central heating, my girl. No wonder they call this the most luxurious country on earth."
 Ibid., Ch. 11

3 Perhaps you have to be born an Englishwoman to realize how much attention American men shower on women and how tremendously considerate all the nice ones among them are of a woman's wishes. Ibid., Ch. 12

## 740. Margaret Mead
### (1901–　　)

1 The negative cautions of science are never popular. If the experimentalist would not commit himself, the social philosopher, the preacher, and the pedagogue try the harder to give a short-cut answer.
*Coming of Age in Samoa*, Ch. 1
*1928*

2 The Samoan background which makes growing up so easy, so simple a matter, is the general casualness of the whole society. For Samoa is a place where no one plays for very high stakes, no one pays very heavy prices, no one suffers for his convictions or fights to the death for special ends. . . . No one is hurried along in life or punished harshly for slowness of development. Instead the gifted, the precocious, are held back, until the slowest among them have caught the pace. And in personal relations, caring is as slight.　　Ibid., Ch. 13

3 A society which is clamouring for choice, which is filled with many articulate groups, each urging its own brand of salvation, its own variety of economic philosophy, will give each new generation no peace until all have chosen or gone under, unable to bear the conditions of choice. The stress is in our civilization. . . .
Ibid., Ch. 14

4 And while every culture has in some way institutionalized the roles of men and women, it has not necessarily been in terms of contrast between the prescribed personalities of the two sexes, nor in terms of dominance or submission.　　*Sex and Temperament in Three Primitive Societies　　1935*

5 The knowledge that the personalities of the two sexes are socially produced is congenial to every programme that looks forward towards a planned order of society. It is a two-edged sword. . . .　　Ibid.

6 Just as the difference in height between males is no longer a realistic issue, now that lawsuits have been substituted for hand-to-hand encounters, so the difference in strength between men and women is no longer worth elaboration in cultural institutions.　　Ibid.

7 To insist that there are no sex-differences in a society that has always believed in them and depended upon them may be as subtle a form of standardizing personality as to insist that there are many sex-differences.　　Ibid.

8 The insistence . . . that the woman as a mother prevails over the woman as a citizen at least puts a slight drag upon agitation for war. . . .
Ibid.

9 The removal of all legal and economic barriers against women's participating in the world on an equal footing with men may be in itself a standardizing move towards the wholesale stamping-out of the diversity of attitudes that is such a dearly bought product of civilization.
Ibid.

10 Just as a festive occasion is the gayer and more charming if the two sexes are dressed differently, so it is in less material matters.
Ibid.

11 An occupation that has no basis in sex-determined gifts can now recruit its ranks from twice as many potential artists.　　Ibid.

12 If we are to achieve a richer culture, rich in contrasting values, we must recognize the whole gamut of human potentialities, and so weave a less arbitrary social fabric, one in which each diverse human gift will find a fitting place.
Ibid.

13 . . . we may say that many, if not all, of the personality traits which we have called masculine or feminine are as lightly linked to sex as are the clothing, the manners, and the form of headdress that a society at a given period assigns to either sex.　　Ibid.

14 We must recognize that beneath the superficial classifications of sex and race the same potentialities exist, recurring generation after generation, only to perish because society has no place for them.　　*From the South Seas 1939*

15 We know of no culture that has said, articulately, that there is no difference between men and women except in the way they contribute to the creation of the next generation. . . .
*Male and Female　　1948*

16 If little boys have to meet and assimilate the early shock of knowing that they can never create a baby with the sureness and incontrovertibility that is a woman's birthright, how does that make them more creatively ambitious, as well as more dependent upon achievement?
Ibid.

17 Living in the modern world, clothed and muffled, forced to convey our sense of our bodies in terms of remote symbols like walking sticks and umbrellas and handbags, it is easy to lose sight of the immediacy of the human body plan.　　Ibid.

18 Furthermore, the little girl learns that she will have a baby not because she is strong or energetic or initiating, not because she works and struggles and tries, and in the end succeeds, but

simply because she is a girl and not a boy, and girls turn into women, and in the end—if they protect their femininity—have babies.     Ibid.

19 Man's role is uncertain, undefined, and perhaps unnecessary. By a great effort man has hit upon a method of compensating himself for his basic inferiority.     Ibid.

20 Women, it is true, make human beings, but only men can make men.     Ibid.

21 It is of very doubtful value to enlist the gifts of women if bringing women into fields that have been defined as male frightens the men, unsexes the women, muffles and distorts the contribution women could make. . . .     Ibid.

22 When we stopped short of treating women as people after providing them with all the paraphernalia of education and rights, we set up a condition whereby men also became less than full human beings and more narrowly domestic.
"American Man in a Woman's World,"
*The New York Times Magazine*
*February 10, 1957*

23 Women want mediocre men, and men are working to be as mediocre as possible.
Quoted in *Quote Magazine*
*May 15, 1958*

24 Early domesticity has always been characteristic of most savages, of most peasants and of the urban poor.
Quoted in "New Look at Early Marriages," *U.S. News & World Report*     *June 6, 1960*

25 Why have we returned, despite our advances in technology, to the Stone Age picture? . . . In this retreat into fecundity, it is not the individual woman who is to blame. It is the climate of opinion that developed in this country.     "American Women: The Changing Image," *Saturday Evening Post*
*March 3, 1962*

26 A tribal people will be jealous of their women, or will offer them to male visitors in ways that are hard to resist, but tribal women do not fear that a woman anthropologist will take their men.     *Field Work in the Pacific Islands, 1925–1967     1967*

27 . . . most people prefer to carry out the kinds of experiments that allow the scientist to feel that he is in full control of the situation rather than surrendering himself to the situation, as one must in studying human beings as they actually live.     *Blackberry Winter     1972*

28 She was unquestionably female—small and dainty and pretty and wholly without masculine protest or feminist aggrievement.     Ibid.

29 . . . I had no reason to doubt that brains were suitable for a woman. And as I had my father's kind of mind—which was also his mother's— I learned that the mind is not sex-typed.
Ibid.

30 We are living beyond our means. As a people we have developed a life-style that is draining the earth of its priceless and irreplaceable resources without regard for the future of our children and people all around the world.
"The Energy Crises—Why Our World Will Never Again Be the Same,"
*Redbook     April, 1974*

31 The contempt for law and the contempt for the human consequences of lawbreaking go from the bottom to the top of American society.
Ibid., Quoted in "Impeachment?" by Claire Safran

## 741. Grace Moore
(1901–1947)

1 There, in repressed defiance, lies the natural instinct to tell the world where to get off: an instinct, alas, that too often takes itself out in the tardy retort framed *sotto voce*, or the year-in, year-out threat mumbled to oneself, "Just wait till I write that book!"
*You're Only Human Once*, Ch. 1
*1944*

2 I think that to get under the surface and really appreciate the beauty of any country, one has to go there poor.     Ibid., Ch. 4

## 742. Ruth Rowland Nichols
(1901–1961)

1 Many newspaper articles . . . discussed the supposed rivalry between Amelia Earhart and me. I have no hesitation in stating that they were exaggerated or slanted or untrue. . . . We were united by common bond of interest. We spoke each other's language—and that was the language of pioneer women of the air.
*Wings for Life     1957*

2 It was a great source of concern, to put it mildly, when I finally had reached my altitude peak and discovered that I was down to my last five gallons of gasoline.
Quoted in *The American Heritage History of Flight*, Ch. 7     *1960*

## 743. Laura Riding

(1901–    )

1 We must distinguish better
Between ourselves and strangers.
There is much that we are not.
There is much that is not.
There is much that we have not to be.
"The Why of the Wind,"
*Collected Poems*    1938

2 I met God.
"What," he said, "you already?"
"What," I said, "you still?"
Ibid., "Then Follows"

3 You have pretended to be seeing.
I have pretended that you saw.
Ibid., "Benedictory"

4 Conversation succeeds conversation,
Until there's nothing left to talk about
Except truth, the perennial monologue,
And no talker to dispute it but itself.
Ibid., "The Talking World"

5 The mercy of truth—it is to be truth.
Ibid., "The Last Covenant"

6 I do not doubt you.
I know you love me.
It is a fact of your indoor face. . . .
Ibid., "In Due Form"

7 In our unwilling ignorance we hurry to listen
to stories of old human life, new human life,
fancied human life, avid of something to while
away the time of unanswered curiosity.
"The Telling," *The Telling*    1967

8 Until the missing story of ourselves is told,
nothing besides told can suffice us: we shall go
on quietly craving it.    Ibid.

9 May our Mayness become All-embracing. May
we see in one another the All that was once
All-one rebecome One.    Ibid.

10 There can be no literary equivalent to truth.
Ibid., "Extracts from
Communications"

11 To a poet the mere making of a poem can seem
to solve the problem of truth. . . . but only a
problem of art is solved in poetry.
*Selected Poems: In Five Sets,*
Preface    1975

12 Art, whose honesty must work through artifice,
cannot avoid cheating truth.    Ibid.

## 744. Cornelia Otis Skinner

(1901–    )

1 I can enjoy flowers quite happily without translating them into Latin. I can even pick them with success and pleasure. What, frankly, I can't do is arrange them.
"Floral Piece," *Dithers and Jitters*
1937

2 There are compensations for growing older. One is the realization that to be sporting isn't at all necessary. It is a great relief to reach this stage of wisdom.
Ibid., "Bonnie Boating Weather"

3 It's not that I don't want to be a beauty, that I don't yearn to be dripping with glamor. It's just that I can't see how any woman can find time to do to herself all the things that must apparently be done to make herself beautiful and, having once done them, how anyone without the strength of mind of a foreign missionary can keep up such a regime.
Ibid., "The Skin-Game"

4 We were young enough still to harbor the glad illusion that organized forms of get-together were commendable.
*Our Hearts Were Young and Gay,*
with Emily Kimbrough    1942

5 One of the most incongruous facets of the nature of *homo* not so *sapien* is the delight with which he wallows in temporary orgies of utter misery.    "Crying in the Dark,"
*Bottoms Up!*    1950

6 That food has always been, and will continue to be, the basis for one of our greater snobbisms does not explain the fact that the attitude toward the food choice of others is becoming more and more heatedly exclusive until it may well turn into one of those forms of bigotry against which gallant little committees are constantly planning campaigns in the cause of justice and decency.
Ibid., "Your Very Good Health"

7 It is disturbing to discover in oneself these curious revelations of the validity of the Darwinian theory. If it is true that we have sprung from the ape, there are occasions when my own spring appears not to have been very far.
"The Ape in Me,"
*The Ape in Me*    1959

8 Courtesy is fine and heaven knows we need more and more of it in a rude and frenetic world, but mechanized courtesy is as pallid as Pablum . . . in fact, it isn't even courtesy. One can put up with "Service with a Smile" if the

smile is genuine and not mere compulsory tooth-baring. And while I am hardly advocating "Service with a Snarl," I find myself occasionally wishing for "Service with a Deadpan," or just plain Service, executed with efficiency and minus all the Charm School garnish.

Ibid., "Production-Line Courtesy"

9 . . . that amenity which the French have developed into a great art . . . conversation.
*Elegant Wits and Grand Horizontals,*
Ch. 4     *1962*

10 These were clever and beautiful women, often of good background, who through some breach of the moral code or the scandal of divorce had been socially ostracized but had managed to turn the ostracism into profitable account. Cultivated, endowed with civilized graces, they were frankly—kept women, but kept by one man only, or, at any rate, by one man at a time.      Ibid., Ch. 8

\* \* \*

11 Woman's virtue is man's greatest invention.
Quoted in *Paris '90*

## 745. Edith Mendel Stern

(1901–   )

1 The role of the housewife is, therefore, analogous to that of the president of a corporation who would not only determine policies and make over-all plans but also spend the major part of his time and energy in such activities as sweeping the plant and oiling the machines. . . . For a woman to get a rewarding sense of total creation by way of the multiple monotonous chores that are her daily lot would be as irrational as for an assembly line worker to rejoice that he had created an automobile because he tightened a bolt.

"Women Are Household Slaves,"
*American Mercury*     January, 1949

## 746. Jan Struther

(1901–1953)

1 It took me forty years on earth
    To reach this sure conclusion:
There is no Heaven but clarity,
    No Hell except confusion.
"All Clear," *The Glass Blower and
Other Poems*     *1940*

2 She saw every personal religion as a pair of intersecting circles. . . . Probably perfection is

reached when the area of the two outer crescents, added together, is exactly equal to that of the leaf-shaped piece in the middle. On paper there must be some neat mathematical formula for arriving at this; in life, none.
*Mrs. Miniver*     *1940*

## 747. Edith Summerskill

(1901–   )

1 The breach of promise . . . I can think of no action more basically insincere than one conducted with the maximum publicity, for damages for a broken heart by a young woman who must already loathe the man who has rejected her.      *A Woman's World*, Ch. 4
*1967*

2 I learned that economics was not an exact science and that the most erudite men would analyze the economic ills of the world and derive a totally different conclusion. . . . [Yet] governments still pin their faith to some new economic nostrum which is produced periodically by some bright young man. Only time proves that his alleged magic touch is illusory.
Ibid., Ch. 5

3 Prize-fighting is still accepted as a display worthy of a civilized people despite the fact that all those connected with it are fully aware it caters to the latent sadistic instincts.
Ibid., Ch. 12

4 The practice of abortion is as old as pregnancy itself. . . . [But] historically the opposition to abortion and birth control, like the laws of Moses, which were concerned with elementary hygiene and the safe preparation of food, stemmed from the urgency of the need to decrease the mortality and morbidity rates and to increase the population. . . . Today, literate people of the space age, in well-populated countries, are not prepared to accept taboos without question; and in the matter of abortion the human rights of the mother with her family must take precedence over the survival of a few weeks' old foetus without sense or sensibility.
Ibid., Ch. 19

5 There are those who believe that a divorce is better than subjecting a child to frequent scenes and quarrels but I am not among them. According to the report of some Judges sitting in custody, it is at the moment of the break-up of the home that the child shows signs of serious deterioration in bad behaviour and speech defects.      Ibid., Ch. 20

## 748. Marian Anderson

(1902–    )

1 Now I understand, if the good Lord doesn't like to behold the misery on the earth, He takes the clouds and covers it from His sight; but where human beings dwell there is always a dark shadow.    Quoted in *Marian Anderson, a Portrait* by Kosti Vehanen
*1941*

2 Where there is money, there is fighting.
Ibid.

3 As long as you keep a person down, some part of you has to be down there to hold him down, so it means you cannot soar as you otherwise might.    Interview on CBS-TV
*December 30, 1957*

4 I had gone to Europe . . . to reach for a place as a serious artist, but I never doubted that I must return. I was—and am—an American.
Quoted in "Marian Anderson,"
*Famous American Women*
by Hope Stoddard    *1970*

5 I could see that my significance as an individual was small. . . . I had become, whether I liked it or not, a symbol, representing my people. I had to appear. . . . I could not run away from this situation.    Ibid.

## 749. Barbara Cartland

(1902?–    )

1 What did we in our teens realize of war? Only that we were unsatisfied after our meals, bored, in the selfishness of youth, with mourning and weeping, sick of being told plaintively that the world would "never be the same again."
*The Isthmus Years*, Ch. 1    *1942*

2 I have always found women difficult. I don't really understand them. To begin with, few women tell the truth. I always say what I think and feel—it's got me into a lot of trouble but only with women. I've never had a cross word with a man for speaking frankly but women don't like it—I can't think why, unless it's natural love of subterfuge and intrigue.    Ibid., Ch. 8

3 Only through freedom will man find salvation, only through freedom can civilization survive and progress. We shall win, I am as sure of that as I am that England with all her faults, her mistakes, her snobbery and her social injustices is worth any individual sacrifice—this England which means far more in the sum

total of human existence than a small green island surrounded by blue seas.
Ibid., Epilogue

## 750. Stella Gibbons

(1902–    )

1 Graceless, Pointless, Feckless and Aimless waited their turn to be milked.
*Conference at Cold Comfort Farm*,
Ch. 3    *1932*

2 Something nasty in the woodshed.
Ibid., Ch. 8

## 751. Madeline Gray

(1902–    )

1 Sex, as I said, can be summed up in three P's: procreation, pleasure, and pride. From the long-range point of view, which we must always consider, procreation is by far the most important, since without procreation there could be no continuation of the race. . . . So female orgasm is simply a nervous climax to sex relations . . . and as such it is a comparative luxury from nature's point of view. It may be thought of as a sort of pleasure-prize like a prize that comes with a box of cereal. It is all to the good if the prize is there, but the cereal is valuable and nourishing if it is not.
*The Normal Woman*    *1967*

## 752. Elsa Lanchester

(1902–    )

1 If I can't be a good artist without too much pain, then I'm damned if I'll be an artist at all.
*Charles Laughton and I*    *1938*

2 Comedians on the stage are invariably suicidal when they get home.    Ibid.

3 Every artist should be allowed a few failures.
Ibid.

4 Perhaps the beginning of our interest in each other was first shown by the fact that although we are both the kind of people who can usually express ourselves and our ideas with great ease in conversation, we were practically dumb when we were alone together. . . .
Ibid., Ch. 3

5 One has to let slimmers act of their own free will. If you wag a finger and say: "Now, now, you must not eat cake," it is quite enough to make anyone immediately eat a cake.
Ibid., Ch. 11

6 To complain too bitterly of the load of mischief that notoriety brings with it would mean that you are unsuited to the position you have made for yourself. Ibid., Ch. 20

7 As the film actor is seen by thousands of people simultaneously all over the world he is, compared to the stage actor, relatively independent of the critics. His fame depends upon something much less secure than the opinion of one man or the approval of one town; it depends on his capacity to keep up with public taste. Ibid., Ch. 21

## 753. Iris Origo

(1902–    )

1 But one resource is still left to man: a brotherly love and solidarity, a fearless recognition of the truth, untainted by praise or blame, which alone will render him capable of facing the insensibility of nature. *Leopardi*, Ch. 13
1935

2 It is only comparatively seldom that the so-called "turning points" in a country's history—so convenient to the historian—are actually observable by those present at the time.
*War in Val d'Orcia* (February 2, 1943)
1947

3 We are being governed by the dregs of the nation—and their brutality is so capricious that no one can feel certain that he will be safe tomorrow. Ibid. (November 28, 1943)

4 It is odd how used one can become to uncertainty for the future, to a complete planlessness, even in one's most private mind. What we shall do and be, and whether we shall, in a few months' time, have any home or possessions, or indeed our lives, is so clearly dependent on events outside our own control as to be almost restful.
Ibid. (February 9, 1944)

5 What fraction of even that small part of us of which we are fully aware have we ever succeeded in communicating to any other human being? *A Measure of Love*, Introduction
1957

6 A life-sentence can be pronounced in many ways; and there are as many ways of meeting it. What is common to all who have received it—the consumptive, the paralyzed, the deaf, the blind—is the absence of a fixed point on the mind's horizon. Ibid.

7 All of my past life that has not faded into mist has passed through the filter, not of my mind, but of my affections. *Images and Shadows*
1970

8 It is the extreme concreteness of a child's imagination which enables him, not only to take from each book exactly what he requires —people, or genii, or tables and chairs—but literally to furnish his world with them.
Ibid., Pt. II, Ch. 6

9 I write because, exacting as it may be to do so, it is still more difficult to refrain, and because —however conscious of one's limitations one may be—there is always at the back of one's mind an irrational hope that this next book will be different: it will be the rounded achievement, the complete fulfillment. It never has been: yet I am still writing. Ibid., Ch. 8

## 754. Leni Riefenstahl

(1902–    )

1 I only know how happy it makes me when I meet good men, simple men. But it repulses me so much to find myself faced with false men that it is a thing to which I have never been able to give artistic form.
Quoted by Michel Delahaye in
*Cahiers du Cinema*, No. 5    1966

2 I state precisely: it is *film-verité*. It reflects the truth that was then, in 1934, history. It is therefore a documentary. Not a propaganda film. Oh! I know very well what propaganda is. That consists of recreating certain events in order to illustrate a thesis or, in the face of certain events, to let one thing go in order to accentuate another. Ibid.

3 There must be movement. Controlled movement of successive highlight and retreat, in both the architecture of the things filmed and in that of the film. Ibid.

4 Whatever is purely realistic, slice-of-life, what is average, quotidian, doesn't interest me. Only the unusual, the specific, excites me. Ibid.

5 Little by little, I discovered that the constraints imposed at times by the event could often serve me as a guide. The whole thing lay in knowing when and how to respect or violate those constraints. Ibid.

6 My life became a tissue of rumors and accusations through which I had to beat a path. . . .
Ibid.

## 755. Marya Zaturenska

(1902–    )

* * *

1 Once they were flowers, and flame, and living
bread;
Now they are old and brown and all but dead.
"Spinners at Willowsleigh"

## 756. Bettina Ballard

(1903–1961)

1 Steichen had a talent for making people drop
their affectations and pretensions so that what
came through on his film were true portraits,
whether that was what the sitter wanted or not.
Steichen himself was incapable of pretense.
*In My Fashion*, Ch. 1    *1960*

2 None of the people I wrote about were as exciting in reality as I imagined them to be.
Ibid., Ch. 3

3 The feeling about time and what to do with it
has changed. What has become of those long
hours when we brushed our hair, fooled with
our nails, tried for the most effective place of
a beauty spot? Fashion is one of the great
sacrifices of the jet age—there just isn't time to
play at it.    Ibid., Ch. 21

4 Fashion is sold by loud-voiced barkers who
claim magic claims for their wares; the super-
latives mount to a higher pitch with each season. There is no privacy to fashion—no exclu-
sivity.    Ibid.

5 Fashions are born and they die too quickly
for anyone to learn to love them.    Ibid.

## 757. Tallulah Bankhead

(1903–1968)

1 I have three phobias which, could I mute them,
would make my life as slick as a sonnet, but
as dull as ditch water: I hate to go to bed,
I hate to get up, and I hate to be alone.
*Tallulah*, Ch. 1    *1952*

2 It's one of the tragic ironies of the theatre that
only one man in it can count on steady work—
the night watchman.    Ibid.

3 I'm the foe of moderation, the champion of
excess. If I may lift a line from a die-hard
whose identity is lost in the shuffle, "I'd rather
be strongly wrong than weakly right."
Ibid., Ch. 4

4 Here's a rule I recommend. Never practice two
vices at once.    Ibid.

5 I've been called many things, but never an
intellectual.    Ibid., Ch. 15

## 758. Dorothy Dow

(1903–    )

1 Shall I tremble at a gray hair. . . .
"Unbeliever," *Time and Love*    *1942*

2 Things that are lovely
Can tear my heart in two—
Moonlight on still pools,
You.

Ibid., "Things"

## 759. Barbara Hepworth

(1903–    )

1 . . . I rarely draw what I see. I draw what I
feel in my body.
Quoted by A. M. Hammersmith in the
*World of Art* Series    *1968*

## 760. Clare Boothe Luce

(1903–    )

1 MRS. MOREHEAD. Time comes when every man's
got to feel something new—when he's got to
feel young again, just because he's growing old.
. . . A man has only one escape from his old
self: to see a different self—in the mirror of
some woman's eyes.    *The Women*, Act I
*1936*

2 JANE. Why does she get so mad every time he
says they've got to consider the child? If children ain't the point of being married what is?
Ibid., Act II

3 MAGGIE. Marriage is a business of taking care
of a man and rearing his children. . . . It ain't
meant to be no perpetual honeymoon.    Ibid.

4 MISS WATTS. I relieve him of a thousand foolish
details. I remind him of things he forgets,
including, very often these days, his good
opinion of himself. I never cry and I don't nag.
I guess I *am* the office-wife. And a lot better
off than Mrs. Haines. He'll never divorce me!
Ibid.

5 MIRIAM. Two kinds of women, Sylvia, owls and
ostriches. To the feathered sisterhood.    Ibid.

6 MARY. Reno's full of women who all have their pride.                                    Ibid.

7 MARY. Love has pride in nothing—but its own humility.                                   Ibid.

8 LITTLE MARY. You know, that's the only good thing about divorce; you get to sleep with your mother.                                    Ibid., Act III

9 EDITH. Always remember, Peggy, it's matrimonial suicide to be jealous when you have a really good reason.                             Ibid.

10 If "poor Germany" with eight million unemployed, ringed around with a wall of steel, could physically conquer half of Europe and rock the other half with her pagan, immoral, revolutionary ideas . . . what could we not do with our greater brains and greater initiative and all the raw materials and the greatest productive plants in the world out of which, as you have already announced, we are determined to create the greatest army on earth? I ask again what shall we do with that army? *Quo vadis?*          *Europe in the Spring*, Ch. 12
                                        *1940*

11 You see few people here in America who really care very much about living a Christian life in a democratic world.                       Ibid.

12 Much of what Mr. [Vice-President Henry] Wallace calls his global thinking is, no matter how you slice it, still Globaloney.
            Speech, U.S. House of Representatives
                                *February 9, 1943*

13 To put a woman on the ticket would challenge the loyalty of women everywhere to their sex, because it would be made to seem that the defeat of the ticket meant the defeat for a hundred years of women's chance to be truly equal with men in politics.
                Quoted in *New York World-
                Telegram*     *June 28, 1948*

14 I am for lifting everyone off the social bottom. In fact, I am for doing away with the social bottom altogether.          Quoted in *Time
                                February 14, 1964*

15 BLACK WOMAN'S VOICE. There's no human being a man can buy anymore—except a woman.
                *Slam the Door Softly*     *1970*

16 NORA. But if God had wanted us to think with our wombs, why did He give us a brain?
                                          Ibid.

17 NORA. When a man can't explain a woman's actions, the first thing he thinks about is the condition of her uterus.               Ibid.

18 NORA. Know what Freud wrote in his diary when he was 77? "What do women want? My God, what do they want?" Fifty years this giant brain spends analyzing women. And he still can't find out what they want. So this makes him the world's greatest expert on female psychology?                             Ibid.

19 In our free-enterprise system, the resources of the nation . . . all turn the wheels of industry. But public confidence greases the axles. And the lack of confidence is the sand that can temporarily stall the machinery.
            "A Call to Women," *Ladies' Home
                Journal     March, 1974*

20 . . . the American woman is the key—the utterly essential key—to consumer confidence. . . . Confidence, like charity, begins at home . . . begins with women.                     Ibid.

21 The American Republic is now almost 200 years old, and in the eyes of the law women are still not equal with men. The special legislation which will remedy that situation is the Equal Rights Amendment. Its language is short and simple: *Equality of rights under the law shall not be abridged in the United States or by any state on account of sex.*
            Quoted in the *Bulletin of the Baldwin
                School*, Pennsylvania
                    *September, 1974*

22 Childhood is a blissful time of play and fantasizing, of uninhibited sensual delight.    Ibid.

23 Endless commercials and television programs show the lovable woman as a cuddly, soft, yielding girl-child sex object, with hair that bounces, lips that invite deep kisses, a body that smells like heavenly spring.         Ibid.

24 A man's home may seem to be his castle on the outside; inside, it is more often his nursery.
                                          Ibid.

25 To be a liberated woman is to renounce the desire of being a sex object or a baby girl. It is to acknowledge that the Cinderella-Prince Charming story is a child's fairy tale.    Ibid.

26 In politics women . . . type the letters, lick the stamps, distribute the pamphlets and get out the vote. Men get elected.
                Quoted in *Saturday Review/World
                    September 15, 1974*

27 Male supremacy has kept woman down. It has not knocked her out.              ·         Ibid.

28 The oppressed never free themselves—they do not have the necessary strengths.       Ibid.

29 Women can't have an honest exchange in front of men without having it called a cat fight.
    *Television Interview*
*April 1, 1975*

## 761. Virginia Moore

### (1903–    )

* * *

1 Suspicion is the badge of base-born minds,
And calculation never understands.
    "Tragic Conclusions"

## 762. Empress Nagako

### (1903–    )

1 We have always been trained in the past to a life of service and I am afraid that as these new changes come about there may be a loss of real values.     Meeting with Eleanor Roosevelt (1953), Quoted in *Eleanor: The Years Alone* by Joseph P. Lash     *1972*

## 763. Anaïs Nin

### (1903–1977)

1 Mystical geometry. The arithmetic of the unconscious which impelled this balancing of events.     *Winter of Artifice*     *1945*

2 The imagination is far better at inventing tortures than life because the imagination is a demon within us and it knows where to strike, where it hurts. It knows the vulnerable spot, and life does not, our friends and lovers do not, because seldom do they have the imagination equal to the task.     *Ibid.*

3 . . . all elegant women have acquired a technique of weeping which has no . . . fatal effect on the make-up.     *Ibid.*

4 She could not believe in that which she wanted others to believe in—in a world made as one wanted it, an ideal world.     *Ibid.*

5 He wove a veritable spider web about himself. No man was ever more completely installed in the realm of possessions. . . . He had prepared a fortress against need, war and change.     *Ibid.*

6 He had a mania for washing and disinfecting himself. . . . For him the only danger came from the microbes which attacked the body. He had not studied the microbe of conscience which eats into the soul.     *Ibid.*

7 This enthusiasm which must be held in check was a great burden for a child's soul. . . . to restrain meant to kill, to bury.     *Ibid.*

8 Ice and Silence. Then I heard voices, first talking too fast for me to understand. A curtain was parted, the voices still tripped over each other, falling fast like a waterfall, with sparks, and cutting into my ears.
    "Birth," *Under a Glass Bell*     *1948*

9 He wants to interfere with his instruments, while I struggle with nature, with myself, with my child and with the meaning I put into it all, with my desire to give and to hold, to keep and to lose, to live and to die.     *Ibid.*

10 There is blood in my eyes. A tunnel. I push into this tunnel, I bite my lips and push. There is a fire and flesh ripping and no air. Out of the tunnel! All my blood is spilling out. Push! Push! Push! It is coming! It is coming! I feel the slipperiness, the sudden deliverance, the weight is gone.     *Ibid.*

11 She hated him because she could not remain detached. . . .     *Ibid.*

12 I thought we were above questions of good and evil. I am not saying you are bad. That does not concern me. I am saying only that you are *false* with me.     *Ibid.*

13 I stopped loving my father a long time ago. What remained was the slavery to a pattern.     *Ibid.*

14 When one is pretending the entire body revolts.     *Ibid.*

15 Certain gestures made in childhood seem to have eternal repercussions.     *Ibid.*

16 No need to hate. No need to punish. . . . The little girl in her was dead. . . . The woman was saved. And with the little girl died the need of a father.     *Ibid.*

17 She* is bizarre, fantastic, nervous, like someone in a high fever. Her beauty drowned me. . . . I feel she does not know what to do when confronted with these legends which are born around her face and body; she feels unequal to them.     *The Diary of Anaïs Nin*, Vol. I (December 30, 1931)     *1966*

18 She lacks confidence, she craves admiration insatiably. She lives on the reflections of herself in the eyes of others. She does not dare to be herself.     *Ibid.*

* Referring to Henry Miller's wife, June.

19 I want the firsthand knowledge of everything, not fiction, intimate experience only. . . . I don't care for films, newspapers, "reportages," the radio. I only want to be involved while it is being lived.      Ibid.

20 I worship that courage to hurt which she has, and I am willing to be sacrificed.      Ibid.

21 I was so filled with love for her I did not notice my effect on her.      Ibid.

22 Too much awareness, without accompanying experience, is a skeleton without the flesh of life.      *The Diary of Anaïs Nin*, Vol. II (February, 1937)    *1967*

23 Analysis does not take into account the creative products of neurotic desires.      Ibid.

24 Perhaps a child, like a cat, is so much inside of himself that he does not see himself in the mirror.      Ibid. (March, 1937)

25 I can remember what I did but not the reflection of what I did.      Ibid.

26 The face is masklike. It does not smile. It does not want to charm the mirror, or deceive the mirror, or flirt with it and gain a false answer. . . . You can never catch the face alive, laughing or loving.      Ibid.

27 To make history or psychology alive I personify it. . . . Myself . . . is an instrument to connect life and the myth.      Ibid. (August, 1937)

28 I am not interested in fiction. I want faithfulness.      Ibid.

29 Woman does not forget she needs the fecundator, she does not forget that everything that is born of her is planted in her.      Ibid.

30 The art of woman must be born in the womb-cells of the mind. She must be the link between synthetic products of man's mind and the elements.      Ibid.

31 For the womb has dreams. It is not as simple as the good earth.      Ibid.

32 The crowd is a malleable thing, it can be dominated, dazzled, it's a public, it is faceless. This is the opposite of relationship.      Ibid. (October, 1937)

33 Electric flesh-arrows . . . traversing the body. A rainbow of color strikes the eyelids. A foam of music falls over the ears. It is the gong of the orgasm.      Ibid.

34 Inner chaos, like those secret volcanoes which suddenly lift the neat furrows of a peacefully plowed field, awaited behind all disorders of face, hair and costume, for a fissure through which to explode.
     *A Spy in the House of Love*    *1968*

35 Secrets. Need to disguise. The novel was born of this.    *The Diary of Anaïs Nin*, Vol. III (January, 1943)    *1969*

36 Those who live for the world . . . always lose their personal, intimate life.      Ibid.

37 What I consider my weaknesses are feminine traits: incapacity to destroy, ineffectualness in battle.      Ibid.

38 What I cannot love, I overlook. Is that real friendship?    "San Francisco," *The Diary of Anaïs Nin*, Vol. V    *1974*

39 Illusion. First there is the illusion of perfect accord, then revelation by experience of the many differences, and then I come upon a crossroad, and unless there is a definite betrayal, I finally accept the complete person.      Ibid.

40 . . . we cannot cure the evils of politics with politics. . . . Fifty years ago if we had gone the way of Freud (to study and tackle hostility within ourselves) instead of Marx, we might be closer to peace than we are.
     Ibid., Letter to Geismar

41 A trite word is an overused word which has lost its identity like an old coat in a second-hand shop. The familiar grows dull and we no longer see, hear, or taste it.      Ibid.

42 Memory is a great betrayer.      Ibid.

43 If we are unable to make passion a relationship of duration, surviving the destruction and erosions of daily life, it still does not divest passion of its power to transform, transfigure, transmute a human being from a rather limited, petty, fearful creature to a magnificent figure reaching at moments the status of a myth.      Ibid.

44 How wrong it is for women to expect the man to build the world she wants, rather than set out to create it herself.      Ibid.

45 Anxiety is love's greatest killer, because it is like the strangle hold of the drowning.      Ibid.

46 The alchemy of fiction is, for me, an act of embalming.      Ibid., "Sierra Madre"

47 I will not be just a tourist in the world of images, just watching images passing by which I cannot live in, make love to, possess as permanent sources of joy and ecstasy.   Ibid.

48 The drugs, instead of bringing fertile images which in turn can be shared with the world . . . have instead become a solitary vice, a passive dreaming which alienates the dreamer from the whole world, isolates him, ultimately destroys him.   Ibid.

49 This year I finally achieved objectivity, very difficult for a romantic.
   Ibid., Letter to Geismar

50 I don't need to be published. I only need to continue my personal life . . . and to do my major work. . . . I merely forgot for a few years what I had set out to do.   Ibid.

51 When you make a world tolerable for yourself you make a world tolerable for others.
   Ibid.

52 One handles truths like dynamite. Literature is one vast hypocrisy, a giant deception, treachery. All writers have concealed more than they revealed.   Ibid.

53 The role of the writer is not to say what we can all say but what we are unable to say.
   Ibid.

## 764.  Nelly Ptaschkina
### (1903-1920)

1 Youth does not know how to concentrate, and, on the other hand, does not want to confide in others. Hence the diary. The old work out everything in themselves.
   *The Diary of Nelly Ptaschkina*
   (January 23, 1918)   *1923p*

2 I am mentally short-sighted because, after all, I am but a child. . . .
   Ibid. (January 25, 1918)

3 Whatever I neglect now I shall have to pay for later.   Ibid. (January 26, 1918)

4 It seems to me that man at birth does not represent a lump of clay, which can be shaped at will: for instance, either he is born intelligent or he is born stupid. Goodness can, on the other hand, be acquired.   Ibid.

5 I shall drive away my thoughts as soon as they touch upon dangerous ground. I . . . I shall *deceive myself.*   Ibid. (March 5, 1918)

6 Give women scope and opportunity, and they will be no worse than men.
   Ibid. (October 1, 1918)

7 Marriage is slavery. . . . Human personality must develop quite freely. Marriage impedes this development; even more than that, it often drives one to "moral crimes," not only because forbidden fruit is sweet, but because the new love, which could be perfectly legitimate, becomes a crime.   Ibid. (October 25, 1918)

8 . . . love must and can only be an appendix to life, it certainly must not form its substance.
   Ibid. (April 21, 1919)

9 Yes, one must renounce that which is too emotional. There is no need for these moods, this longing, these *attendrissements.* . . . Work is waiting for us.   Ibid. (May 27, 1919)

## 765.  Teng Ying-Ch'ao
### (1903-   )

1 . . . in order to fight the Japanese we must study Japanese!
   Quoted in *Women in Modern China*
   by Helen Foster Snow   *1967*

## 766.  Thyra Samter Winslow
### (1903-1961)

1 Platonic love is love from the neck up.
   Quoted by James Simpson in
   *Interview*   *August 19, 1952*

## 767.  Marguerite Yourcenar
### (1903-   )

1 The worst examples of savage ferocity only harden the auditor that much more, and since the human heart has about as much softness as a stone anyhow I see no need for going further in that direction. Our men were certainly not lacking in invention either, but so far as I was concerned I preferred to deal out death without embellishment, as a rule. Cruelty is the luxury of those who have nothing to do, like drugs or racing stables. In the matter of love, too, I hold for perfection unadorned.
   *Coup de Grâce*   *1939*

2 There is so little basic difference between total innocence and complete degradation. . . .
   Ibid.

3 The successive phases of love follow a monotonous course; what they still seem to me to resemble the most are the endless but sublime repetitions and returns in Beethoven's Quartets.
Ibid.

4 This morning it occurred to me for the first time that my body, my faithful companion and friend, truly better known to me than my own soul, may be after all only a sly beast who will end by devouring his master.
"Animula Vagula Blandula,"
*Memoirs of Hadrian*    1954

5 I have often thought that men who care passionately for women attach themselves at least as much to the temple and to the accessories of the cult as to their goddess herself. . . . I should have desired more: to see the human creature unadorned, alone with herself as she indeed must have been at least sometimes, in illness or after the death of a first-born child, or when a wrinkle began to show in her mirror. A man who reads, reflects, or plans belongs to his species rather than to his sex; in his best moments he rises above the human.    Ibid.,
"Varius Multiplex Multi Formis"

6 I have done much rebuilding. To reconstruct is to collaborate with time gone by, penetrating or modifying its spirit, and carrying it toward a longer future. Thus beneath the stones we find the secret of the springs.
Ibid., "Tellus Stabilita"

7 The memory of most men is an abandoned cemetery where lie, unsung and unhonored, the dead whom they have ceased to cherish. Any lasting grief is reproof to their forgetfulness.
Ibid., "Saeculum Aureum"

8 Nothing seemed simpler: a man has the right to decide how long he may usefully live. . . . [But] sickness disgusts us with death, and we wish to get well, which is a way of wishing to live. But weakness and suffering, with manifold bodily woes, soon discourage the invalid from trying to regain ground: he tires of those respites which are but snares, of that faltering strength, those ardors cut short, and that perpetual lying in wait for the next attack.
Ibid., "Patientia"

## 768. Margery Allingham
### (1904–1966)

1 Lying, they say, is a new modern art of the enemy's, but telling the truth is not easy.
*The Oaken Heart*, Preface    1941

2 We—he and thee and the parson and all the other lads of the village—constitute the public, and the politicians are our servants. They apply for the job (often rather obsequiously, we notice with instant suspicion), we give it to them, we pay them in honours or cash, and we judge them solely by results.    Ibid., Ch. 1

3 "Do you know it occurred to me when I was listening to him that both in a past and in a future age this tremendous insistence of ours upon the nice importance of manners and breeding may well have seemed and still seem again to be absurd."
. . . "Fashion!" he repeated, as if the word had annoyed him. "I'll wager it goes far deeper than fashion."
"Few things go deeper than fashion," objected Castor.    Ibid., Ch. 8

4 It is always difficult to escape from youth; its hopefulness, its optimistic belief in the privileges of desire, its despair, and its sense of outrage and injustice at disappointment, all these spring on a man inflicting indelicate agony when he is no longer prepared.
Ibid., Ch. 21

5 Normally he was the happiest of men. He asked so little of life that its frugal bounty amazed and delighted him. . . . He believed in miracles and frequently observed them, and nothing astonished him. His imagination was as wild as a small boy's and his faith ultimate. In ordinary life he was, quite frankly, hardly safe out.
*The Tiger in the Smoke*, Ch. 2
1952

6 Chemists employed by the police can do remarkable things with blood. They can find it in shreds of cloth, in the interstices of floor boards, on the iron of a heel, and can measure it and swear to it and weave it into a rope to hang a man.    Ibid., Ch. 9

7 "Because nobody wants a prosaic explanation of fraud and greed."
*The Villa Marie Celeste*    1960

## 769. Elaine Frances Burton
### (1904–  )

1 A woman in authority is often unpopular, only because she is efficient.
*What of the Women?*    1941

2 If you get a good woman, you get the finest thing on earth.    Ibid.

## 770. Ève Curie

(1904–    )

1 Let's face it: however old-fashioned and out of date and devaluated the word is, we like the way of living provided by democracy.
*Address, American Booksellers Association, New York*
*April 9, 1940*

2 We discovered that peace at any price is no peace at all. . . . We discovered that life at any price has no value whatever; that life is nothing without the privileges, the prides, the rights, the joys which make it worth living, and also worth giving. And we also discovered that there is something more hideous, more atrocious than war or than death; and that is to live in fear.    Ibid.

3 Public opinion waged the war. Statesmen, diplomats, government officials waged the war. To beat the Axis, it was not enough to win battle in the field, to kill millions of men. We also had to kill ideas that knew no frontiers and spread like disease.
*Journey Among Warriors*, Pt. V, Ch. 26
*1943*

## 771. Lilly Daché

(1904–    )

1 When I was six I made my mother a little hat —out of her new blouse.
*Newspaper Interview*
*December 3, 1954*

2 Glamour is what makes a man ask for your telephone number. But it also is what makes a woman ask for the name of your dressmaker.
*Quoted in Woman's Home Companion    July, 1955*

## 772. Adelle Davis

(1904–1974)

1 Nutrition is a young subject; it has been kicked around like a puppy that cannot take care of itself. Food faddists and crackpots have kicked it pretty cruelly. . . . They seem to believe that unless food tastes like Socratic hemlock, it cannot build heath. Frankly, I often wonder what such persons plan to do with good health in case they acquire it.
*Let's Eat Right to Keep Fit*, Ch. 1
*1954*

2 When the blood sugar is extremely low, the resulting irritability, nervous tension, and mental depression are such that a person can easily go berserk. . . . Add a few guns, gas jets, or razor blades, and you have the stuff murders and suicides are made of. The American diet has become dangerous in many more ways than one.    Ibid., Ch. 2

3 Thousands upon thousands of persons have studied disease. Almost no one has studied health.    Ibid., Ch. 29

4 If this country is to survive, the best-fed-nation myth had better be recognized for what it is: propaganda designed to produce wealth but not health.    Ibid., Ch. 30

5 You can't eat well and keep fit if you don't shop well.    Quoted in "The Great Adelle Davis Controversy" by Daniel Yergin, *The New York Times Magazine    May 20, 1973*

6 Nutritional research, like a modern star of Bethlehem, brings hope that sickness need not be a part of life.    Ibid.

7 People in nutrition get the idea that they are going to live to be a hundred and fifty. And they never do.    Ibid.

## 773. Marlene Dietrich

(1904–    )

1 The average man is more interested in a woman who is interested in him than he is in a woman —any woman—with beautiful legs.
*News Item    December 13, 1954*

2 Latins are tenderly enthusiastic. In Brazil they throw flowers at you. In Argentina they throw themselves.    Quoted in *Newsweek*
*August 24, 1959*

## 774. Margaret Fishback

(1904–    )

* * *

1 The same old charitable lie
Repeated as the years scoot by
Perpetually makes a hit—
"You really haven't changed a bit!"
"The Lie of the Land"

## 775. Marya Mannes

(1904–　　)

1 "I think funerals are barbaric and miserable. Everything connected with them—the black, the casket, the shiny hearse, the sepulchral tones of the preacher—is destructive to true memory." "The First Days," *Message from a Stranger*    1948

2 Promiscuous. . . . That was a word I had never applied to myself. Possibly no one ever does, for it is a sordid word, reducing many valuable moments to nothing more than dog-like copulation.    Ibid., "The Second Month"

3 They had no serenity, for true serenity comes after knowledge of pain. They had only the stillness of spiritual inertia. They were half alive.    Ibid., "The Seventh Month"

4 Who's kidding whom? What's the difference between Giant and Jumbo? Quart and *full* quart? Two-ounce and *big* two-ounce? What does Extra Long mean? What's a *tall* 24-inches? And what busy shopper can tell?
"New Bites by a Girl Gadfly," *Life*    June 12, 1964

5 The art of flirtation is dying. A man and woman are either in love these days or just friends. In the realm of love, reticence and sophistication should go hand in hand, for one of the joys of life is discovery.    Ibid.

6 What I call the destructive anxieties are not the growth of women's minds and powers, but quite the contrary: the pressures of society and the mass media to make woman conform to the classic and traditional images in men's eyes. "The Roots of Anxiety in Modern Women," *Journal of Neuropsychiatry*    May, 1964

7 The real demon is success—the anxieties engendered by this quest are relentless, degrading, corroding. What is worse, there is no end to this escalation of desire. . . .    Ibid.

8 Affluent as it was for the majority, the society we had produced was not admirable. It might be better than others, but it was nowhere near what it should have been. It was, in fact, going rotten. The private gain had for so long triumphed over the public need that the cities had become unlivable, the country desecrated, the arteries choked, and pollution—of air, of water, yes, of spirit too—a daily, oppressive, fact. And who else but our generation (if not ourselves) had made it so?    *Them*    1968

9 "Well, my theory has always been," said Lev, "that if each of our senses—sight, hearing, touch, smell, taste—was developed to its utmost capacity we would then have attained not only total physical awareness, as in animals, but total spiritual development, as in man. Ideal man. Everything," pursued Lev, "atrophies without use."    Ibid.

10 Timing and arrogance are decisive factors in the successful use of talent. The first is a matter of instinct, the second part carapace and part self-hypnosis; the shell that protects, the ego that assumes, without question, that the talent possessed is not only unique but important, the particular vision demanding to be shared.    *Out of My Time*, Preface    1971

11 While the young fight the official barbarism of unsentient power—the insanities of war and the ruinous priorities imposed by leaders and organizations in the *name* of reason, perhaps our last duty is to fight for the civilization *of* reason.    Ibid., Ch. 9

12 The barbarian weapon is fission: the splitting asunder. It has been perfected for death. Our only weapon is fusion: an imperfect process still, though designed for life.    Ibid.

## 776. Nancy Mitford

(1904–1973)

1 "I simply don't see the point of getting up at six all the time you are young and working eighteen hours a day in order to be a millionaire, and then when you are a millionaire still getting up at six and working eighteen hours a day. . . . What does it all mean?"    *Pigeon Pie*, Ch. 1    1940

2 "Always remember, children, that marriage is a very intimate relationship. It's not just sitting and chatting to a person; there are other things, you know."    *Love in a Cold Climate*, Pt. I, Ch. 14    1949

3 An aristocracy in a republic is like a chicken whose head has been cut off: it may run about in a lively way, but in fact it is dead.    *Noblesse Oblige*    1956

4 Americans relate all effort, all work, and all of life itself to the dollar. Their talk is of nothing but dollars. The English seldom sit happily chatting for hours on end about pounds. In England, public business is its own reward, nobody would go into Parliament in order to become rich, neither do riches bring public appointments.    Ibid.

5 All the heat there was seemed to concentrate in the Hons' cupboard, which was always stifling. Here we would sit, huddled up on the slatted shelves, and talk for hours about life and death. *The Pursuit of Love*, Ch. 2
1957

## 777. Virgilia Peterson
(1904–1966)

1 Before Eve did bite into the apple, she had first to be alone with Adam under the tree where the apple grew.
*A Matter of Life and Death* 1961

2 In Reno, there is always a bull market, never a bear market, for the stocks and bonds of happiness. Ibid.

3 Perhaps it is the expediency in the political eye that blinds it. Ibid.

4 A lady, that is an enlightened, cultivated, liberal lady—the only kind to be in a time of increasing classlessness—could espouse any cause: wayward girls, social diseases, unmarried mothers, and/or birth control with impunity. But never by so much as the shadow of a look should she acknowledge her own experience with the Facts of Life. Ibid.

5 European society . . . automatically assumes its superiority to Americans whether they have money or not, but money tends to blur the sharpness of the distinction. Ibid.

## 778. Anne Roe
(1904–   )

1 Nothing in science has any value to society if it is not communicated. . . .
*The Making of a Scientist*, Ch. 1
1952

2 Freedom breeds freedom. Nothing else does.
Ibid., Ch. 16

## 779. Sally Stanford
(1904–   )

1 No, no one sets out to be a madam; but madams answer the call of a well-recognized and very basic human need. Their responsibilities are thrust upon them by the fundamental nitwittedness and economic shortsightedness of most hustling broads. And they become tempered and sharpened and polished to the highest degree of professional awareness by constant intercourse with men devoutly dedicated to the policy of getting something for nothing. *The Lady of the House*, Prologue
1966

2 Well, there's a Book that says we're all sinners and I at least chose a sin that's made quite a few people happier than they were before they met me, a sin that's left me with very little time to consider other extremely popular moral misdemeanors, like usury, intolerance, bearing false tales, extortion, racial bigotry, and the casting of that first stone. And, I might add, a hell of a lot worse. Ibid., Ch. 4

3 No man can be held throughout the day by what happens throughout the night.
Ibid., Ch. 13

4 Romance without finance is a nuisance. Few men value free merchandise. Let the chippies fall where they may. Ibid.

## 780. Charlotte Wolff
(1904–   )

1 I have no doubt that lesbianism makes a woman virile and open to *any* sexual stimulation, and that she is more often than not a more adequate and lively partner in bed than a "normal" woman. *Love Between Women* 1972

2 A niggling feeling of discomfort and unease follows masturbation, even in those who do not feel guilty about it. Ibid.

## 781. Jane Ace
(1905–1974)

1 I'm a ragged individualist.
Quoted in *The Fine Art of Hypochondria* by Goodman Ace 1966

2 Well, time wounds all heels.
Ibid.

## 782. Shulamit Aloni
(1905–   )

1 Thus the Israeli woman, like her American counterpart, pushes aside all youthful enthusiasm and ambition to develop an active personality and instead copies the model with which she is presented—an agreeable beautiful doll and cheap servant. One day, when the children have grown up, she comes face to face with the emptiness and looks for fulfill-

ment in language courses, ceramics and art circles, volunteer work and charity, wrapped around a cup of coffee watching a fashion show.      Article in *Israel Magazine* *April, 1971*

2 According to civil law, women are equal to men. But I have to go to a religious court as far as personal affairs are concerned. Only men are allowed to be judges there—men who pray every morning to thank God He did not make them women. You meet prejudice before you open your mouth. And because they believe women belong in the home, you are doubly discriminated against if you work.

Quoted in "Women in Israel" (November, 1973), *Crazy Salad* by Nora Ephron    *1975*

## 783. Ilka Chase
(1905– )

1 She thought of all foreign lands as lands of promise, and with the same yearning that so many Europeans had for America.
*I Love Miss Tilli Bean*, Ch. 1    *1946*

2 She knew that no human being is immune to sorrow and she wanted me to be tough, the way a green branch is tough, and to be independent, so that if anything happened to her I would be able to take hold of my own life and make a go of it. Besides, she had a lot of respect for the human spirit; she never thought one person owned another.    Ibid., Ch. 6

3 People are subject to moods, to temptations and fears, lethargy and aberration and ignorance, and the staunchest qualities shift under the stresses and strains of daily life. Like liberty, they are not secured for all time. They are not inevitable.    *Free Admission*, Ch. 1    *1948*

4 There are various theories as to what characteristics, what combination of traits, what qualities in our men won the war. The democratic heritage is highly thought of; the instinctive mechanical know-how of thousands of our young men is frequently cited; the church and Coca-Cola, baseball, and the movies all come in for their share of credit; but, speaking from my own observation of our armed forces, I should say the war was won on coffee.
   Ibid., Ch. 10

5 The very fact that we make such a to-do over golden weddings indicates our amazement at human endurance. The celebration is more in the nature of a reward for stamina. . . .
   Ibid., Ch. 15

## 784. Viña Delmar
(1905– )

1 It must be true that whenever a sensational murder is committed there are people who—though they are, quite properly, of no interest to law enforcers, attorneys, or newspaper reporters—weep, lie sleepless, and realize at last that their lives have been changed by a crime in which they played no part.
   *The Becker Scandal*    *1968*

2 "We have strict orders on how to teach. There are certain methods that must be employed. Your way is easier to learn, but it hasn't been approved by the school board for use in the classroom."    Ibid.

3 . . . her plumpness was so neat and firm that she was rather like one of the better apples that are purchased for fruit-bowl display.    Ibid.

## 785. Frances Frost
(1905–1959)

1 I am the keeper of wall and sill,
I kneel on the hearth to a tempered fire:
(Flesh that was wild can learn to be still,
But what of a heart that was born to briar?)
   "Capture," St. 4, *Hemlock Wall* *1929*

2 But the trees that lost their apples
In the early windy year—
Hard-cheeked little apples,
Round and green and clear,—
They have nothing more to lose
And nothing more to fear.
   Ibid., "Loss," St. 2

3 Grow, white boy! Drink deep of living,
Deeper yet of mirth,
For there is nothing better than laughter
Anywhere on earth!
   Ibid., "White Boy," St. 3

## 786. Greta Garbo
(1905– )

1 There are many things in your heart you can never tell to another person. They are you, your private joys and sorrows, and you can never tell them. You cheapen yourself, the inside of yourself, when you tell them.
Quoted in *The Story of Greta Garbo* by Bruce Biery    *1928*

2 I never said, "I want to be alone." I only said, "I want to be *left* alone." There is all the difference. Quoted in *Garbo* by John Bainbridge      *1955*

3 Why can't we avoid being followed and examined? It is cruel to bother people who want to be left in peace. This kills beauty for me. Ibid., Newspaper Interview, Naples (1938)

## 787. Ethel Jacobson
(1905?–      )

1 Behind every man who achieves success
Stand a mother, a wife and the IRS. Quoted in *Reader's Digest* *April, 1973*

## 788. Adelaide Johnson
(1905–1960)

1 The neurotic needs of the parent . . . are vicariously gratified by the behavior of the child.      "The Genesis of Antisocial Acting Out in Children and Adults," *Psychoanalytic Quarterly*, Vol. 21 *1952*

2 Firmness bespeaks a parent who has learned . . . how all of his major goals may be reached in some creative course of action. . . .      Ibid.

## 789. Maggie Kuhn
(1905–      )

1 We want to give old folks a new sense of power and worth. We've been brainwashed by the youth cult to keep up youthful appearances, and to be ashamed of our age. Quoted in "Profile of a Gray Panther" by Carol Offen, *Retirement Living* *December, 1972*

2 Ageism is any discrimination against people on the basis of chronological age—whether old or young. It's responsible for an enormous neglect of social resources.      Ibid.

3 Our [old people's] citizenship is not served when we take ourselves out of the mainstream of society and consign ourselves to a life of play. . . . Arbitrary retirement at a fixed age ought to be negotiated and decided according to the wishes of the people involved. Mandatory retirement ought to be illegal.      Ibid.

4 One reason our society has become such a mess is that we're isolated from each other. The old are isolated by government policy. So we have all sorts of stereotypes floating around about blacks, old people, and women. Quoted in "How to Forget Age Bias," *Ms.      June, 1975*

5 Power should not be concentrated in the hands of so few, and powerlessness in the hands of so many.      Ibid.

## 790. Erika Mann
(1905–      )

1 "I want the child to become a human being, a good and decent man who knows the difference between lies and truth, aware of liberty and dignity and true reason, not the opportunistic reason 'dictated by policy' which turns black white if it's useful at the moment. I want the boy to become a decent human being—a man and not a Nazi!"      *School for Barbarians*, Prologue      *1938*

2 But the Hitler Youth organization, that third circle around the child, is the most expansive, most important, and by far the most comprehensive of his influences. Ibid., "The State Youth"

3 "There's absolutely no discipline in the democracies. The other day our propaganda minister said that the democracies strike him as being a collection of comical old fogies. But I've got to say it myself; they're rotten and corrupt to the marrow." "The City," *The Lights Go Down* *1940*

4 Music, the theatre, the beauty of men and things, a fine day, a child, an attractive animal —from all these he [Thomas Mann] drew much pleasure, provided he was getting on with his work. Without work—that is, without active hope—he would not have known how to live. *The Last Year of Thomas Mann, a Revealing Memoir by His Daughter* *1958*

5 The nightmare dreamer is delivered up to the horror he himself has created, and derives not the slightest relief from the neutral world, such as would be granted by feeling that it is hot or windy, that other people are present, or that the day or the night is coming to an end. The dreamer knows and perceives nothing but the horror of his dream.      Ibid.

## 791. Phyllis McGinley
### (1905– )

1 Oh, shun, lad, the life of an author.
　It's nothing but worry and waste.
Avoid that utensil,
The laboring pencil,
　And pick up the scissors and paste.
　　　　　"A Ballad of Anthologies,"
　　　　*A Ballad of Anthologies* 　1941

2 　Mere wealth, I am above it.
　It is the reputation wide,
The playwright's pomp, the poet's pride
　That eagerly I covet.
　　　　　　　　　　　　*Ibid.*

3 Forever that Ode on the Urn, sir,
　Has headed the publisher's list.
But the name isn't Keats
On the royalty sheets
　That go out to the anthologist,
My lad,
The sedulous anthologist.
　　　　　　　　　　　　*Ibid.*

4 Compromise? Of course we compromise. But compromise, if not the spice of life, is its solidity. It is what makes nations great and marriages happy and Spruce Manor the pleasant place it is. 　　"Suburbia, of Thee I Sing,"
　　　　*The Province of the Heart* 　1959

5 It's this no-nonsense side of women that is pleasant to deal with. They are the real sportsmen. They don't have to be constantly building up frail egos by large public performances like over-tipping the hat-check girl, speaking fluent French to the Hungarian waiter, and sending back the wine to be recooled.
　　　Ibid., "Some of My Best Friends . . ."

6 Nothing fails like success; nothing is so defeated as yesterday's triumphant Cause.
　　　Ibid., "How to Get Along with Men"

7 Sin . . . has been made not only ugly but passé. People are no longer sinful, they are only immature or under privileged or frightened or, more particularly, sick.
　　　　　　Ibid., "In Defense of Sin"

8 We have not owned our freedom long enough to know exactly how it should be used.
　　　Ibid., "The Honor of Being a Woman"

9 Yet who could deny that privacy is a jewel? It has always been the mark of privilege, the distinguishing feature of a truly urbane culture.
　　　　　　Ibid., "A Lost Privilege"

10 Buffet, ball, banquet, quilting bee,
　Wherever conversation's flowing,
Why must I feel it falls on me
　To keep things going?
　　　　　　　"Reflections at Dawn," St. 3,
　　　　　*Times Three: 1932–1960* 　1960

11 　. . . "I am he
Who champions total liberty—
Intolerance being, ma'am, a state
No tolerant man can tolerate.
　　　　　Ibid., "The Angry Man," St. 2

12 I'm a middle-bracket person with a middle-bracket spouse
And we live together gaily in a middle-bracket house.
We've a fair-to-middlin' family; we take the middle view;
So we're manna sent from heaven to internal revenue.
　　　　Ibid., "The Chosen Peoples," St. 1

13 Oh! *do* you remember Paper Books
　When paper books were thrilling,
When something to read
Was seldom Gide
Or Proust or Peacock
Or Margaret Mead
　And seldom Lionel Trilling?
　　　　　Ibid., "Dirge for an Era," St. 4

14 Pressed for rules and verities,
All I recollect are these:
Feed a cold to starve a fever.
Argue with no true believer.
Think too-long is never-act.
Scratch a myth and find a fact.
　　　　Ibid., "A Garland of Precepts," St. 2

15 Senor Dali,
　Born delirious,
Considers it folly
　To be serious. . . .
　　　　　　Ibid., "Spectators' Guide to
　　　　　　　Contemporary Art," St. 3

16 The thing to remember about fathers is, they're men.
　　　　　　Ibid., "Girls-Eye View of
　　　　　　　　　　Relatives," St. 3

17 These are my daughters, I suppose.
　But where in the world did the children vanish?
　　　　　Ibid., "Ballade of Lost Objects"

18 Time is the thief you cannot banish.
　　　　　　　　　　　Ibid., St. 4

19 Though doubtless now our shrewd machines
Can blow the world to smithereens
　More tidily and so on,
Let's give our ancestors their due.

Their ways were coarse, their weapons few.
But ah! how wondrously they slew
With what they had to go on.
Ibid., "The Conquerors," St. 5

20 We might as well give up the fiction
That we can argue any view.
For what in me is pure Conviction
Is simple Prejudice in you.
Ibid., "Note to My Neighbor"

21 When blithe to argument I come,
Though armed with facts, and merry,
May Providence protect me from
The fool as adversary,
Whose mind to him a kingdom is
Where reason lacks dominion,
Who calls conviction prejudice
And prejudice opinion.
Ibid., "Moody Reflections," St. 1

22 For the wonderful thing about saints is that
they were *human*. They lost their tempers, got
hungry, scolded God, were egotistical or testy
or impatient in their turns, made mistakes and
regretted them. Still they went on doggedly
blundering toward heaven.
"Running to Paradise,"
*Saint-Watching*  1969

23 History must always be taken with a grain of
salt. It is, after all, not a science but an art. . . .
Ibid., "Aspects of Sanctity"

24 We live in the century of the Appeal. . . . One
applauds the industry of professional philanthropy. But it has its dangers. After a while
the private heart begins to harden. We fling
letters into the wastebasket, are abrupt to telephone solicitations. Charity withers in the
incessant gale. Ibid.

25 Wit is not the prerogative of the unjust, and
there is truly laughter in holy places. Ibid.

* * *

26 Always on Monday morning the press reports
God as revealed to his vicars in various dis-
guises—
Benevolent, stormy, patient, or out of sorts.
God knows which God is the God God
recognizes.
"The Day After Sunday"

27 Few friends he has that please his mind.
His marriage failed when it began,
Who worked unceasingly for mankind
But loathed his fellowman.
"The Old Reformer"

28 Meek-eyed parents hasten down the ramps
To greet their offspring, terrible from camps.
"Ode to the End of Summer"

29 We never sit down to our pottage,
We never go calm to our rest,
But lo! at the door of our cottage,
The knock of the guest.
"Elegy of a Country Dooryard," St. 3

## 792. Eileen O'Casey

(1905?–    )

1 I was liberated but not too liberated. I was
Catholic, you see, and my conscience always
bothered me. Quoted in "Eileen O'Casey
Remembers" by Lee Grant,
*Los Angeles Times*
*November 13, 1974*

2 Unless it's right next door, people don't notice
killing and bloodshed. We take it in like the
sun shines and the rain falls. Ibid.

3 I feel very sorry commercialism has gone so
far. Ibid.

## 793. Gretta Brooker Palmer

(1905–1953)

* * *

1 Happiness is a by-product of an effort to make
someone else happy. *Permanent Marriage*

## 794. Ivy Baker Priest

(1905–1975)

1 We women ought to put first things first. Why
should we mind if men have their faces on the
money, as long as we get our hands on it?
*Green Grows Ivy*, Ch. 1    1958

2 My father had always said that there are four
things a child needs—plenty of love, nourishing
food, regular sleep, and lots of soap and water
—and after those, what he needs most is some
intelligent neglect. Ibid., Ch. 11

3 We seldom stop to think how many peoples'
lives are entwined with our own. It is a form
of selfishness to imagine that every individual
can operate on his own or can pull out of the
general stream and not be missed.
Ibid., Ch. 18

## 795. Ayn Rand

(1905–    )

1 You came as a solemn army to bring a new
life to men. You tore that life you knew nothing about, out of their guts—and you told

them what it had to be. You took their every hour, every minute, every nerve, every thought in the farthest corners of their souls—and you told them what it had to be. You came and you forbade life to the living.

*We the Living* 1936

2 "Civilization is the progress toward a society of privacy. The savage's whole existence is public, ruled by the laws of his tribe. Civilization is the process of setting man free from men." *The Fountainhead* 1943

3 "Creation comes before distribution—or there will be nothing to distribute." Ibid.

4 "We praise an act of charity. We shrug at an act of achievement." Ibid.

5 Every form of happiness is private. Our greatest moments are personal, self motivated, not to be touched. The things which are sacred or precious to us are the things we withdraw from promiscuous sharing. Ibid.

6 "Every major horror of history was committed in the name of an altruistic motive. Has any act of selfishness ever equalled the carnage perpetrated by disciples of altruism?" Ibid.

7 Great men can't be ruled. Ibid.

8 He didn't want to be great, but to be thought great. He didn't want to build, but to be admired as a builder. He borrowed from others in order to make an impression on others.
Ibid.

9 If you learn how to rule one single man's soul, you can get the rest of mankind. Ibid.

10 "Independence is the only gauge of human virtue and value. What a man is and makes of himself; not what he has or hasn't done for others. There is no substitute for personal dignity. There is no standard of personal dignity except independence." Ibid.

11 Kill reverence and you've killed the hero in man. Ibid.

12 "The world is perishing from an orgy of self-sacrificing." Ibid.

13 "Throughout the centuries there were men who took first steps down new roads armed with nothing but their own vision. Their goals differed, but they all had this in common: that the step was first, the road new, the vision unborrowed, and the response they received—hatred. The great creators—the thinkers, the artists, the scientists, the inventors—stood alone against the men of their time." Ibid.

14 We can divide a meal among many men. We cannot digest it in a collective stomach.
Ibid.

15 "We are one in all and all in one.
There are no men but only the great WE,
One, indivisible and forever."

*Anthem*, Ch. 1 1946

16 It is forbidden, not to be happy. For, as it has been explained to us, men are free and the earth belongs to them; and all things on earth belong to all men; and the will of all men together is good for all; and so all men must be happy. Ibid., Ch. 2

17 My happiness is not the means to any end. It is the end. It is its own goal. It is its own purpose. Neither am I the means to any end others may wish to accomplish. I am not a tool for their use. I am not a servant of their needs. I am not a bandage for their wounds. I am not a sacrifice on their altars.
Ibid., Ch. 9

18 The word which can never die on this earth, for it is the heart of it and the meaning and the glory. The sacred word: EGO.
Ibid., Ch. 12

19 It was an immense betrayal—the more terrible because he could not grasp what it was that had been betrayed.
*Atlas Shrugged*, Pt. I, Ch. 1 1957

20 "Disunity, that's the trouble. It's my absolute opinion that in our complex industrial society, no business enterprise can succeed without sharing the burden of the problems of other enterprises." Ibid., Ch. 3

21 He could not stop the thing in his mind that went on throwing words at him; it was like trying to plug a broken hydrant with his bare hands. Ibid., Ch. 6

22 "What you think you think is an illusion created by your glands, your emotions and, in the last analysis, by the content of your stomach. . . . That gray matter you're so proud of is like a mirror in an amusement park which transmits to you nothing but distorted signals from a reality forever beyond your grasp."
Ibid., Pt. II, Ch. 1

23 "The entire history of science is a progression of exploded fallacies, not of achievements."
Ibid.

24 "That which you see is the first thing to disbelieve." Ibid.

25 "To demand 'sense' is the hallmark of nonsense. Nature does not make sense. Nothing makes sense." *Ibid.*

26 Questions of right have no bearing on human existence. *Ibid., Ch. 4*

27 The day of the hero is past. *Ibid.*

28 "People don't look for *kinds* of work any more, ma'am," he answered impassively. "They just look for work." *Ibid., Ch. 10*

29 "If my fellow men believe that the force of the combined tonnage of their muscles is a practical means to rule me—let them learn the outcome of a contest in which there's nothing but brute force on one side, and force ruled by a mind, on the other." *Ibid., Pt. III, Ch. 2*

30 "It has long been conceded by all progressive thinkers that there are no entities, only actions —and no values, only consequences." *Ibid., Ch. 3*

31 They did not know . . . that the same force that had made him tolerant, was now the force that made him ruthless—that the justice which would forgive miles of innocent errors of knowledge, would not forgive a single step taken in conscious evil. *Ibid., Ch. 6*

32 The modern mystics of muscle who offer you the fraudulent alternative of "human rights" versus "property rights," as if one could exist without the other, are making a last, grotesque attempt to revive the doctrine of soul versus body. Only a ghost can exist without material property; only a slave can work with no right to the product of his effort. *Ibid., Ch. 7*

33 . . . those ages when . . . a sunset put an end to human activity. *Ibid., Ch. 10*

34 . . . "society" may do anything it pleases, since "the good" is whatever it chooses to do *because* it chooses to do it. And—since there is no such entity as "society," since society is only a number of individual men . . . *some* men (the majority or any gang that claims to be its spokesman) are ethically entitled to pursue any whim (or any atrocities) they desire to pursue, while *other* men are ethically obliged to spend their lives in the service of that gang's desires.
Speech, "Ethics in Our Time,"
University of Wisconsin
*February 9, 1961*

35 If we ask our intellectual leaders what *are* the ideals we should fight for, their answer is such a sticky puddle of stale syrup—of benevolent bromides and apologetic generalities about

brotherlove, global progress and universal prosperity at America's expense—that a fly would not die *for* it or *in* it.
*For the New Intellectual    1961*

36 Man's unique reward, however, is that while animals survive by adjusting themselves to their background, man survives by adjusting his background to himself. *Ibid.*

37 Morality is a code of values to guide man's choices and actions; when it is set to oppose his own life and mind, it makes him turn against himself and blindly act as the tool of its own destruction. *Ibid.*

38 Professional intellectuals are the voice of a culture and are, therefore, its leaders, its integrators and its bodyguards. *Ibid.*

39 Integrity does not consist of loyalty to one's subjective whims, but of loyalty to rational principles. A "compromise" (in the unprincipled sense of that word) is not a breach of one's comfort, but a breach of one's convictions. A "compromise" does not consist of doing something one dislikes, but of doing something one knows to be evil.
"Doesn't Life Require Compromise?"
(July, 1962), *The Virtue of
Selfishness    1964*

40 Love and friendship are profoundly personal, selfish values: love is an expression and assertion of self-esteem, a response to one's own values in the person of another. One gains a profoundly personal, selfish joy from the mere existence of the person one loves. It is one's own personal, selfish happiness that one seeks, earns and derives from love.
*Ibid.,* "The Ethics of Emergencies"
(1963)

41 Ever since Kant divorced reason from reality, his intellectual descendants have been diligently widening the breach.
"The Cashing-In: The Student
'Rebellion,' " *The New Left    1968*

42 If a dramatist had the power to convert philosophical ideas into real, flesh-and-blood people and attempted to create the walking embodiment of modern philosophy—the result would be the Berkeley rebels. *Ibid.*

43 The hippies were taught by their parents, their neighbors, their tabloids and their college professors that faith, instinct and emotion are superior to reason—and they obeyed. They were taught that material concerns are evil, that the State or the Lord will provide, that the Lilies of the Field do not toil—and they obeyed. They were taught that love, indiscrimi-

nate love, for one's fellow-men is the highest virtue—and they obeyed. They were taught that the merging of one's self with a herd, a tribe or a community is the noblest way for men to live—and they obeyed. There isn't a single basic principle of the Establishment which they do not share—there isn't a belief which they have not accepted.     Ibid., "Apollo and Dionysus"

## 796. Mary Renault

(1905–    )

1 Miss Searle had always considered boredom an intellectual defeat.     *North Face*, Ch. 1
*1948*

2 It was pleasant to talk of these things again: but, as he reminded himself, to her it was all a kind of keepsake, like the flower her grandmother might have pressed in a book. Exchanging ideas with women was always an illusion; they tagged everything on to some emotion, they were all incapable of the thing in itself.
Ibid., Ch. 5

3 Which of youth's pleasures can compare with the making ready for one's first big war?
*The King Must Die*, Bk. II, Ch. 3
*1958*

4 Man born of woman cannot outrun his fate. Better then not to question the Immortals, nor when they have spoken to grieve one's heart in vain. A bound is set to our knowing, and wisdom is not to search beyond it. Men are only men.     Ibid., Bk. V, Ch. 2

5 "Go with your fate, but not beyond. Beyond leads to dark places."
"Marathon," *The Bull from the Sea*
*1962*

6 I thought of my life, the good and evil days; of the gods, and fate; how much of a man's life and of his soul they make for him, how much he makes for himself. . . . Fate and will, will and fate, like earth and sky bringing forth the grain together; and which the bread tastes of, no man knows.     Ibid., "Skyros"

## 797. Anna F. Trevisan

(1905–    )

1 MRS. BRENTA. When they're grown up, you might just as well not have them. They come home and they go out. This is like a railroad station and a restaurant.     *Easter Eve*
*1946*

2 ELZA. Some things are very important and some are very unimportant. To know the difference is what we are given life to find out. . . .
Ibid.

3 ELZA. The mother! She is what keeps the family intact. . . . It is proved. A fact. Time and time again. The father, no matter how good . . . a father cannot keep the family intact.

MRS. BRENTA. They scatter when the mother dies.

ELZA. True. In almost every instance.
Ibid.

4 ANNIE. How was they to know the ould war would take them so soon and last so long?
*In the Valley of the Shadow*    *1946*

5 ANNIE. Give me first the courage and the strength to bear my lot. And all the mothers the world over, who have sons acrost the seas.
Ibid.

6 BARRY. He'll be ruined tied to yer apron and yer teachin's. Pamperin' and pettin', pettin' and pamperin'.     Ibid.

7 MRS. GRISWOLD. The world is exhausted.
Ibid.

## 798. Margaret Webster

(1905–    )

1 When an actor says a line, he makes his point and his thought moves on to the next; but a singer has to repeat the same words over a dozen times, the emotional shading varying with the music, the thought progressing only in terms of sound.    *Don't Put Your Daughter on the Stage*    *1972*

2 Revivals at the Met are unmitigated torture for the stage director and an almost total waste from his point of view.     Ibid.

## 799. Hannah Arendt

(1906–1975)

1 Against the egalitarian order of persuasion stands the authoritarian order, which is always hierarchical. If authority is to be defined at all, then, it must be in contradistinction to both coercion by force and persuasion through arguments.    *Nomos I: Authority*,
Carl J. Frederich, ed.    *1958*

2 With the loss of tradition we have lost the thread which safely guided us through the vast realms of the past, but this thread was also the

chain fettering each successive generation to a predetermined aspect of the past. It could be that only now will the past open up to us with unexpected freshness and tell us things that no one as yet had ears to hear.               Ibid.

3 Culture relates to objects and is a phenomenon of the world; entertainment relates to people and is a phenomenon of life. An object is cultural to the extent that it can endure; its durability is the very opposite of functionality, which is the quality which makes it disappear again from the phenomenal world by being used and used up. The great user and consumer of objects is life itself, the life of the individual and the life of society as a whole. Life is indifferent to the thingness of an object; it insists that everything must be functional, fulfill some needs.               *Daedalus     1960*

4 Our tradition of political thought had its definite beginning in the teachings of Plato and Aristotle. I believe it came to a no less definite end in the theories of Karl Marx.
               *Between Past and Future*, Ch. 1
                                        *1961*

5 Only beginning and end are, so to speak, pure or unmodulated; and the fundamental chord therefore never strikes its listeners more forcefully and more beautifully than when it first sends its harmonizing sound into the world and never more irritatingly and jarringly than when it still continues to be heard in a world whose sounds—and thought—it can no longer bring into harmony.               Ibid.

6 Immortality is what nature possesses without effort and without anybody's assistance, and immortality is what the mortals must therefore try to achieve if they want to live up to the world into which they were born, to live up to the things which surround them and to whose company they are admitted for a short while.
               Ibid., Ch. 2

7 Eichmann, much less intelligent and without any education to speak of, at least dimly realized that it was not an order but a law which had turned them all into criminals. The distinction between an order and the Führer's word was that the latter's validity was not limited in time and space, which is the outstanding characteristic of the former.
               *Eichmann in Jerusalem*, Ch. 8     *1963*

8 It is true that totalitarian domination tried to establish these holes of oblivion into which all deeds, good and evil, would disappear, but . . . holes of oblivion do not exist. . . . One man will always be left alive to tell the story. . . . For the lesson of such stories is simple and

within everybody's grasp. Politically speaking, it is that under conditions of terror most people will comply but *some people will not. . . .* Humanly speaking, no more is required, and no more can reasonably be asked, for this planet to remain a place fit for human habitation.               Ibid., Ch. 14

9 It is quite gratifying to feel guilty if you haven't done anything wrong: how noble! Whereas it is rather hard and certainly depressing to admit guilt and to repent.               Ibid., Ch. 15

10 It is in the very nature of things human that every act that has once made its appearance and has been recorded in the history of mankind stays with mankind as a potentiality long after its actuality has become a thing of the past. No punishment has ever possessed enough power of deterrence to prevent the commission of crimes. On the contrary, whatever the punishment, once a specific crime has appeared for the first time, its reappearance is more likely than its initial emergence could ever have been.
               Ibid., Epilogue

11 The trouble with Eichmann was precisely that so many were like him, and that the many were neither perverted nor sadistic, that they were, and still are, terribly and terrifyingly normal. From the viewpoint of our legal institutions and of our moral standards of judgment, this normality was much more terrifying than all the atrocities put together, for it implied— as had been said at Nuremberg over and over again by the defendants and their counsels— that this new type of criminal, who is in actual fact *hostis generis humani*, commits his crimes under circumstances that make it well-nigh impossible for him to know or to feel that he is doing wrong.               Ibid.

12 Wars and revolutions . . . have outlived all their ideological justifications. . . . No cause is left but the most ancient of all, the one, in fact, that from the beginning of our history has determined the very existence of politics, the cause of freedom versus tyranny.
               *On Revolution*, Introduction     *1963*

13 It may be a truism to say that liberation and freedom are not the same; that liberation may be the condition of freedom but by no means leads automatically to it; that the notion of liberty implied in liberation can only be negative, and hence that even the intention of liberating is not identical with the desire for freedom. Yet if these truisms are frequently forgotten, it is because liberty has always loomed large and the foundation of freedom has always been uncertain, if not altogether futile.
               Ibid., Ch. 1

14 From this he [Marx] concluded that freedom and poverty were incompatible. His most explosive and indeed most original contribution to the cause of revolution was that he interpreted the compelling needs of mass poverty in political terms as an uprising, not for the sake of bread or wealth, but for the sake of freedom as well. Ibid., Ch. 2

15 . . . without the presence of misfortune, pity could not exist, and it therefore has just as much vested interest in the existence of the unhappy as thirst for power has a vested interest in the existence of the weak. Moreover, by virtue of being a sentiment, pity can be enjoyed for its own sake, and this will almost automatically lead to a glorification of its cause, which is the suffering of others. Ibid.

16 Why should the vice that covered up vices become the vice of vices? Is hypocrisy then such a monster? . . . What makes it so plausible to assume that hypocrisy is the vice of vices is that integrity can indeed exist under the cover of all other vices except this one. Only crime and the criminal, it is true, confront us with the perplexity of radical evil; but only the hypocrite is really rotten to the core. Ibid.

17 . . . [America's] own failure to remember that a revolution gave birth to the United States and that the republic was brought into existence by no "historical necessity" and no organic development, but by a deliberate act: the foundation of freedom. . . . When we were told that by freedom we understood free enterprise, we did very little to dispel this monstrous falsehood. . . . Wealth and economic well-being, we have asserted, are the fruits of freedom, while we should have been the first to know that this kind of "happiness" . . . has been an unmixed blessing only in this country, and it is a minor blessing compared with the truly political freedoms, such as freedom of speech and thought, of assembly and association, even under the best conditions. Economic growth may one day turn out to be a curse rather than a good, and under no conditions can it either lead into freedom or constitute a proof for its existence.
Ibid., Ch. 6

18 In this system the opinions of the people are indeed unascertainable for the simple reason that they are nonexistent. Opinions are formed in a process of open discussion and public debate, and where no opportunity for the forming of opinions exists, there may be moods—moods of the masses and moods of individuals, the latter no less fickle and unreliable than the former—but no opinion. Ibid.

19 Secrecy—what diplomatically is called "discretion," as well as the *arcana imperii*, the mysteries of government—and deception, the deliberate falsehood and the outright lie used as legitimate means to achieve political ends, have been with us since the beginning of recorded history. Truthfulness has never been counted among the political virtues, and lies have always been regarded as justifiable tools in political dealings. "Lying in Politics," *Crises of the Republic* 1972

20 For the trouble with lying and deceiving is that their efficiency depends entirely upon a clear notion of the truth that the liar and deceiver wishes to hide. In this sense, truth, even if it does not prevail in public, possesses an ineradicable primacy over all falsehoods. Ibid.

21 Disobedience to the law, civil and criminal, has become a mass phenomenon in recent years, not only in America, but also in a great many other parts of the world. The defiance of established authority, religious and secular, social and political, as a world-wide phenomenon may well one day be accounted the outstanding event of the last decade.
Ibid., "Civil Disobedience"

22 There is all the difference in the world between the criminal's avoiding the public eye and the civil disobedient's taking the law into his own hands in open defiance. This distinction between an open violation of the law, performed in public, and a clandestine one is so glaringly obvious that it can be neglected only by prejudice or ill will. Ibid.

23 Man's urge for change and his need for stability have always balanced and checked each other, and our current vocabulary, which distinguishes between two factions, the progressives and the conservatives, indicates a state of affairs in which this balance has been thrown out of order. No civilization—the man-made artifact to house successive generations—would ever have been possible without a framework of stability, to provide the wherein for the flux of change. Foremost among the stabilizing factors, more enduring than customs, manners and traditions, are the legal systems that regulate our life in the world and our daily affairs with each other. Ibid.

24 Promises are the uniquely human way of ordering the future, making it predictable and reliable to the extent that this is humanly possible. Ibid.

25 The ceaseless, senseless demand for original scholarship in a number of fields, where only erudition is now possible, has led either to

sheer irrelevancy, the famous knowing of more and more about less and less, or to the development of a pseudo-scholarship which actually destroys its object. Ibid., "On Violence"

26 Power and violence are opposites; where the one rules absolutely, the other is absent. Violence appears where power is in jeopardy, but left to its own course it ends in power's disappearance. Ibid.

## 800. Margaret Bourke-White
### (1906–1971)

1 Usually I object when someone makes overmuch of men's work versus women's work, for I think it is the excellence of the results which counts. *Portrait of Myself* 1963

2 . . . war correspondents . . . see a great deal of the world. Our obligation is to pass it on to others. Quoted in *The Woman's Eye* by Anne Tucker 1973p

3 . . . to understand another human being you must gain some insight into the conditions which made him what he is. Ibid.

4 What makes Soviet Russia the new land of the machine are the new social relationships of the men and women around the machine. The new man . . . and with him, on an equal footing, the new woman—operating drill presses, studying medicine and engineering—are integral parts of a people working collectively toward a common goal. Ibid.

## 801. Jacqueline Cochran
### (1906?– )

1 I can cure your men of walking off the program. Let's put on the girls. Quoted in *The American Heritage History of Flight*, Ch. 8 1962

## 802. Catherine Cookson
### (1906– )

1 "Catholic, be damned! They tell 'em to have bairns, but do they bloody well keep them?" *The Fifteen Streets*, Ch. 1 1952

2 God knew there was no happiness came out of a mixed marriage. With a Church of England one it would be bad enough, but with a Spiritualist! . . . And yet . . . what was the obstacle of religion compared with the obstacle of class? Ibid., Ch. 7

3 "It's no good saying one thing and thinking another." Ibid., Ch. 8

## 803. Anna Roosevelt Halsted
### (1906–1975)

1 There are so many indignities to being sick and helpless. . . .
Letter to David Gray (November 1, 1962), Quoted in *Eleanor: The Years Alone* by Joseph P. Lash 1972

## 804. Lillian Hellman
### (1906– )

1 MRS. MORTAR. But the cinema is a shallow art. It has no—no—no fourth dimension. *The Children's Hour*, Act I 1934

2 MRS. TILFORD. I have seen too many people, out of pride, act on that pride. In the end they punish themselves. Ibid., Act II, Sc. 1

3 MARTHA. I look forward all day to that bath. It's my last touch with the full life. It makes me feel important to know that there's one thing ahead of me, one thing I've *got* to do. Ibid., Act III

4 CARDIN. Karen, there are a lot of people in this world who have had bad trouble in their lives. We're three of those people. We could sit around the rest of our lives and exist on that trouble, until in the end we had nothing else and we'd want nothing else. Ibid.

5 KAREN. So you've come here to relieve your conscience? Well, I won't be your confessor. It's choking you, is it? And you want to stop the choking, don't you? You've done a wrong and you have to right that wrong or you can't rest your head again. You want to be "just," don't you, and you wanted us to help you be just? Ibid.

6 HANNAH. Lucy, there were people made to think and people made to listen. I ain't sure either you or Lundee were made to do either. *Days to Come*, Act I 1936

7 EASTER. When you got nothin' to do, we can't do it for you. Ibid., Act II, Sc. 1

8 ANDREW. Lonely. I always thought loneliness meant alone, without people. It means something else.

JULIE. That's a late discovery. You're lucky.

ANDREW. Why do people always think it's lucky to find out the simple things long after one should have known them?

JULIE. Because each year you can put off knowing about them gives you one more year of peace.

ANDREW. I don't think so. Unless you can put it off forever. Ibid.

9 WHALEN. Didn't anybody ever tell you that Christians aren't supposed to act like Christians?     Ibid., Sc. 2

10 WHALEN. When you don't feel yourself anything, I mean any part of anything, that's when you get scared.     Ibid.

11 WHALEN. Do you think you can love the smell that comes from dirty skin, or the scum on dishes, or the holes in the floor with the bugs coming through—or the meanness and the cowardice that comes with poverty? I hate the poor, Mrs. Rodman. But I love what they could be.     Ibid.

12 WILKIE. You're a noble lady, and I am frightened of noble ladies. They usually land the men they know in cemeteries.     Ibid., Sc. 3

13 ANDREW. Polite and blind, we lived.
    Ibid., Act III

14 ANDREW. Murder is worse than lost love. Murder is worse than a broken heart.     Ibid.

15 Cynicism is an unpleasant way of saying the truth.     *The Little Foxes*, Act I     *1939*

16 God forgives those who invent what they need.
    Ibid.

17 Fashions in sin change.
    *Watch on the Rhine*
    *1941*

18 It doesn't pay well to fight for what we believe in.     Ibid., Act I

19 Years ago I heard somebody say that being a Roumanian was not a nationality, but a profession.     Ibid., Act III

20 KARP. But I will tell you this: when the end is on its way, no amount of noise will help. If you act noisy, you lose face with yourself.
    *The North Star*     *1943*

21 KURIN. A famous doctor comes back to his village. To write. To write a history of our village. Who cares about our village? What has ever happened here-? Wars, revolutions—that's in everybody's life. It would be better if you wrote a nice cookbook. History people make themselves; cooking they have to learn.
    Ibid.

22 RODION. It is not modest to think one has the key to everything.     Ibid.

23 GRISHA. Those who are clumsy in the body are often clumsy in the head.     Ibid.

24 KOLYA. The brightest of women are not bright.
    Ibid.

25 KOLYA. You are what you are. It is my opinion the trouble in the world comes from people who do not know what they are, and pretend to be something they're not.     Ibid.

26 VON HARDEN. If you wish to be a warrior, Doctor Richter, you must take chances with your life.     Ibid.

27 KURIN. The civilized men who are sorry . . . to me *you* are the real filth. Men who do the work of Fascists and pretend to themselves they are better than those for whom they work. Men who do murder while they laugh at those who order them to do it.     Ibid.

28 MARCUS. Carry in your own valise, son. It is not seemly for a man to load his goods on other men, black or white.
    *Another Part of the Forest*, Act I
    *1946*

29 PENNIMAN. The judgement of music, like the inspiration for it, must come slow and measured, if it comes with truth.     Ibid., Act II

30 MARCUS. Your people deserved to lose their war* and their world. It was a backward world, getting in the way of history. Appalling that you still don't realize it. Really, people should read more books.     Ibid.

31 BIRDIE. You lose your manners when you're poor.     Ibid.

32 MARCUS. A dead man, a foolish man, an empty man from an idiot world. A man who wants nothing but war, any war, just a war. A man who believes in nothing, and never will. A man in space. . . .     Ibid.

33 LAVINIA. Imagine taking money for other people's misery.     Ibid., Act III

34 LAVINIA. But maybe half a lie is worse than a real lie.     Ibid.

35 LAVINIA. I'm not going to have any Bibles in my school. That surprise you all? It's the only book in the world but it's just for grown people, after you know it don't mean what it says.
    Ibid.

36 I am not willing, now or in the future, to bring bad trouble to people who, in my past association with them, were completely innocent of any talk or any action that was disloyal or subversive. . . . I cannot and will not cut my conscience to fit this year's fashions, even though I long ago came to the conclusion that I was not a political person and could have no comfortable place in any political group.     Letter to the House Committee on Un-American Activities, *The Nation* *May 31, 1952*

* Referring to the Civil War.

37 CARRIE. Not like the country. My. I never heard anybody say a thing like that before. It takes courage to just up and say you don't like the country. Everybody likes the country.
*Toys in the Attic*, Act I     *1959*

38 JULIAN. . . . success isn't everything but it makes a man stand straight. . . .     Ibid.

39 LILY. Because I must ask truth, and speak truth, and act with truth, now and forever.

ALBERTINE. Do you think this is the proper climate? So hot and damp. Puts mildew on the truth.     Ibid., Act II

40 LILY. I don't want to be wise, ever, Mama, ever. I'm in love.     Ibid.

41 ALBERTINE. People don't want other people to guess they never knew what they wanted in the first place.     Ibid.

42 ALBERTINE. You do too much. Go and do nothing for a while. Nothing.     Ibid.

43 CARRIE. I read in a French book that there was nothing 'so abandoned as a respectable young girl.     Ibid.

44 ANNA. The leaf came in the spring, stayed nice on the branch in the autumn until the winter winds would blow it in the snow. Mama said that in that little time of holding on, a woman had to make ready for the winter ground where she would lie the rest of her life.
Ibid., Act III

45 CARRIE. There are lives that are shut and should stay shut. . . .     Ibid.

46 ANNA. Well, people change and forget to tell each other. Too bad—causes so many mistakes.
Ibid.

47 . . . he was a man of great force, given, as she was given, to breaking the spirit of people for the pleasure of exercise.
*An Unfinished Woman*     *1969*

48 I didn't know what she was saying when she moved her lips in a Baptist church or a Catholic cathedral or, less often, in a synagogue, but it was obvious that God could be found anywhere. . . .     Ibid.

49 Mama seemed to do only what my father wanted, and yet we lived the way my mother wanted us to live.     Ibid.

50 I was taught, also, that if you gave, you did it without piety and didn't boast about it.     Ibid.

51 . . . the first sexual stirrings of little girls, so masked, so complex, so foolish as compared with the sex of little boys.     Ibid.

52 My father was often angry when I was most like him.     Ibid.

53 . . . if you are willing to take the punishment, you are halfway through the battle. That the issue may be trivial, the battle ugly, is another point.     Ibid.

54 By the time I grew up, the fight for the emancipation of women, their rights under the law, in the office, in bed, was stale stuff.     Ibid.

55 Dashiell Hammett used to say I had the meanest jealousy of all. I had no jealousy of work, no jealousy of money. I was just jealous of women who took advantage of men, because I didn't know how to do it.
Quoted in "A Star Is Born," *Crazy Salad* by Nora Ephron     *1973*

## 805. Mirra Komarovsky

### (1906– )

1 It is possible, of course, that the only effect of . . . sheltering is to create in women a generalized dependency which will then be transferred to the husband and which will enable her all the more readily to accept the role of wife in a family which still has many patriarchal features.
"Functional Analysis of Sex Roles," *American Sociological Review* *August, 1950*

2 What are we educating women for? To raise this question is to face the whole problem of women's role in society. We are uncertain about the end of women's education precisely because the status of women in our society is fraught with contradictions and confusion.
*Women in the Modern World*     *1953*

3 Today the survival of some . . . stereotypes is a psychological strait jacket for both sexes.
Ibid.

4 What is important to a relationship is a harmony of emotional roles and not too great a disparity in the general level of intelligence.
Ibid.

5 A social order can function only because the vast majority have somehow adjusted themselves to their place in society and perform the functions expected of them.     Ibid.

6 With new and old patterns both in the air, it is all too human for each partner to reach out for the double dose of privileges, those of the old and those of the new role, leaving to the mate the double dose of obligation.
Ibid., Ch. 3

7 For an interest to be rewarding, one must pay in discipline and dedication, especially through the difficult or boring stages which are inevitably encountered.      *Ibid.*, Ch. 4

8 Were our knowledge of human relationships a hundredfold more reliable than it is now, it would still be foolish to seek ready-made solutions for problems of living in the index of a book.      *Ibid.*, Ch. 6

9 The most elusive knowledge of all is self-knowledge and it is usually acquired laboriously through experience outside the classroom.      *Ibid.*

10 The price of concentration on home-making involves the sacrifice of other instruction.      *Ibid.*, Ch. 7

11 The greatest danger of traditional education is that learning may remain purely verbal. Words are learned and placed in dead storage in one part of the mind while life is lived unilluminated and unguided by this learning. Such a danger is inherent in the very nature of education.      *Ibid.*

12 Controversy both within and between disciplines is an inevitable feature of scientific development. . . . But not all intellectual controversy is equally beneficial. Pseudo-issues produced by verbal or logical ambiguities are much too frequent and waste our resources. They are usually occasioned by the failure to discern the tacit assumption of the contending positions.      *Common Frontiers of the Social Sciences*, Introduction      *1957*

# 806. Dilys Laing
## (1906–1960)

1 Proud inclination of the flesh,
most upright tendency, salute
in honor of the secret wish.
     "Villanelle," St. 1, *Collected Poems*
     *1967p*

2 . . . memory is a storm I can't repel.
     *Ibid.*, "Venus Petrified," St. 3

3 The woman took a train
away away from herself.
     *Ibid.*, "The Double Goer," St. 1

4      and I
grow younger as I leave
my me behind.
     *Ibid.*, St. 2

5 She faced the crowd and cried:
I love you all but one:
the one who wears my face.
She is the one I fled from.
     *Ibid.*, St. 6

6 I was a child who clutched the amulet
of childhood in a terror of time. I saw
archangels, worshipped trees, expected God.
     *Ibid.*, "The Little Girls," St. 2

7 Time is illumined with inverted light:
the past all whole, the present weird with fault.
     *Ibid.*, "Lot's Daughter," St. 3

8 Vague, submarine, my giant twin
swims under me, a girl of shade
who mimics me.
     *Ibid.*, "Ego"

9 Women receive
the insults of men
with tolerance,
having been bitten
in the nipple
by their toothless gums.
     *Ibid.*, "Veterans"

10 The end will be, perhaps, the end of me,
which will, I humbly guess, be his beginning.
     *Ibid.*, "Private Entry in the Diary of a Female Parent"

11      To be a woman and a writer
is double mischief, for
the world will slight her
who slights "the servile house," and who would rather
make odes than beds.
     *Ibid.*, "Sonnet to a Sister in Error," St. 2

# 807. Anne Morrow Lindbergh
## (1906–     )

1 Travelers are always discoverers, especially those who travel by air. There are no signposts in the sky to show a man has passed that way before. There are no channels marked. The flier breaks each second into new uncharted seas.      *North to the Orient*, Ch. 1      *1935*

2 Rivers perhaps are the only physical features of the world that are at their best from the air.      *Ibid.*, Ch. 17

3 One can never pay in gratitude; one can only pay "in kind" somewhere else in life. . . .      *Ibid.*, Ch. 19

4 . . . the fundamental magic of flying, a miracle that has nothing to do with any of its practical purposes—purposes of speed, accessibility, and convenience—and will not change as they change.      *Ibid.*, Ch. 23

5 The wave of the future is coming and there is no fighting it.      *The Wave of the Future*
*1940*

6 Somehow the leaders in Germany, Italy and Russia have discovered how to use new economic forces. . . . They have felt the wave of the future and they have leapt upon it.
*Ibid.*

7 Lost time was like a run in a stocking. It always got worse.      *The Steep Ascent*, Ch. 3
*1944*

8 There is no harvest for the heart alone;
The seed of love must be
Eternally
Resown.
     "Second Sowing," St. 4, *The Unicorn*
*and Other Poems*      *1948*

9 Perhaps middle-age is, or should be, a period of shedding shells; the shell of ambition, the shell of material accumulations and possessions, the shell of the ego.      *Gift from the Sea*
*1955*

10 One cannot collect all the beautiful shells on the beach.      *Ibid.*

11 It isn't for the moment you are struck that you need courage, but for the long uphill climb back to sanity and faith and security.
     *Hours of Gold, Hours of Lead*
*1973*

12 Ideally, both members of a couple in love free each other to new and different worlds.
     *Ibid.*, Introduction

13 But total freedom is never what one imagines and, in fact, hardly exists. It comes as a shock in life to learn that we usually only exchange one set of restrictions for another. The second set, however, is self-chosen, and therefore easier to accept.      *Ibid.*

14 The loneliness you get by the sea is personal and alive. It doesn't subdue you and make you feel abject. It's a stimulating loneliness.
     *Ibid.*, Letter to Charles Lindbergh
(March 17, 1929)

15 Fog is very terrible. It comes about you before you realize and you are suddenly blind and dumb and cold. It really does seem like death. . . .
     *Ibid.*, Letter to Mother, Mrs. Charles
Long Cutty (September 7, 1929)

16 Is there *anything* as horrible as *starting* on a trip? Once you're off, that's all right, but the last moments are earthquake and convulsion, and the feeling that you are a snail being pulled off your rock.      *Ibid.* (January 2, 1930)

17 For miles out in the China Sea you see mud from the Yangtze river, then suddenly you are on China, and you gasp at the flat fields stretching as far as you can see, the great flat river. . . . There is something magnificent about it. A feeling of its grandeur and age. . . .
     *Ibid.* (September 26, 1931)

18 . . . suffering . . . no matter how multiplied . . . is always individual.
     Quoted by Dorothea Lange in
*The Woman's Eye* by Anne Tucker
*1973*

19 Love is a force. . . . It is not a result; it is a cause. It is not a product; it produces. It is a power, like money, or steam or electricity. It is valueless unless you can give something else by means of it.
     *Locked Rooms and Open Doors*
*1974*

20 People talk about love as though it were something you could give, like an armful of flowers.
     *Ibid.*

## 808. Maria Goeppert Mayer
### (1906–1972)

1 No one has ever seen, nor probably ever will see, an atom, but that does not deter the physicist from trying to draw a plan of it, with the aid of such clues to its structure as he has.      "The Structure of the Nucleus,"
*Scientific American*      March, 1951

2 Of course my father always said I should have been a boy. He said, Don't grow up to be a woman, and what he meant by that was, a housewife . . . without any interests.
     Quoted in "Maria Goeppert-Mayer,"
*A Life of One's Own*
by Joan Dash      *1973p*

3 Mathematics began to seem too much like puzzle solving. Physics is puzzle solving, too, but of puzzles created by nature, not by the mind of man.      *Ibid.*

## 809. Rita Boumy Pappas
### (1906–    )

1 I did not let them nail my soul
as they do butterflies.
     "Roxane M."      *1975*

2 My fine days? Oh, a few fleeting birds,
I had no other treasure than my tears.
That is why none of those who tortured me
have seen me weep.

           Ibid.

## 810. Ting Ling
### (1906– )

1 In the Chinese family system, there is superficial quiet and calmness and quarreling is frowned upon, but in reality all is in conflict.

     Quoted in *Women in Modern China*
     by Helen Foster Snow     *1967*

2 I wanted to escape from love but didn't know how.       Ibid.

3 The Red Army soldiers are a totally new type that cannot be found anywhere else in China. They have never known anything but revolution. Because they originally lived in the Sovietized areas, they have no ideology of private property and no domestic ideas. No unhappiness ever comes to mind. They think only of how to overcome the difficulties of their work and never of their troubles.      Ibid.

## 811. Dorothy Baker
### (1907–1968)

1 In the first place maybe he shouldn't have got himself mixed up with Negroes. It gave him a funny slant on things and he never got over it. It gave him a feeling for undisciplined expression, a hot, direct approach, a full-throated ease that never did him any final good in his later dealings with those of his race, those whom civilization has whipped into shape, those who can contain themselves and play what's written.     *Young Man with a Horn*, Bk. I,
                           Ch. 1     *1938*

2 It left him a little fluttery in the stomach, things like that are so close. You're thrown out for insubordination or else you aren't, and where the actual line of demarcation stands out clear, God Himself only can know. . . . All he knew was that recognition, that sweet thing, had been given to him because he had been doing some good playing. It's a simple formula: do your best and somebody might like it.

      Ibid., Bk. III, Ch. 2

3 Fortune, in its workings, has something in common with the slot-machine. There are those who can bait it forever and never get more than an odd assortment of lemons for their pains; but once in a while there will come a

man for whom all the grooves will line up, and when that happens there's no end to the showering down.      Ibid., Bk. IV, Ch. 2

4 "Now, the easy thing to say is that they wrote great poetry because they had these weaknesses. . . . It's much too easy. We could make a grand tour of all the jails right now, and find a thousand drug addicts and homosexuals who never wrote a line of poetry in their lives and never will. It isn't because of these things that her poems were great, it's in spite of them."

          *Trio*    *1945*

5 And you've tried to make me believe we were something we weren't and that we lived on a higher plane and saw everything clearer and freer than anybody else. . . . Well, I've been through it all now. I've learned everything you wanted me to learn. . . . I know what higher morality's like, and no decent person would be caught dead with me.      Ibid.

6 "She wastes herself, she drifts, all she wants to do with her life is lose it somewhere."

     *Cassandra at the Wedding*    *1962*

7 "Same thing everywhere I'd looked. Large amounts of safety, very few risks. Let nothing endanger the proper marriage, the fashionable career, the nonirritating thesis that says nothing new and nothing true."      Ibid.

## 812. Rachel Carson
### (1907–1964)

1 The ocean is a place of paradoxes.

     "Under Sea," *Atlantic Monthly*
                *September, 1937*

2 All the people of a country have a direct interest in conservation. . . . Wildlife, water, forests, grasslands—all are part of man's essential environment; the conservation and effective use of one is impossible except as the others are also conserved.

      "Guarding Our Wildlife Refuge,"
      *Conservation in Action*    *1946*

3 Like the resource it seeks to protect, wildlife conservation must be dynamic, changing as conditions change, seeking always to become more effective.      Ibid.

4 Beginnings are apt to be shadowy and so it is the beginnings of that great mother of life, the sea.     *The Sea Around Us*, Pt. I, Ch. 1
                                *1951*

5 Spring moves over the temperate lands of our Northern Hemisphere in a tide of new life, of pushing green shoots and unfolding buds, all

its mysteries and meanings symbolized in the northward migration of the birds, the awakening of sluggish amphibian life as the chorus of frogs rises again from the wet lands, the different sound of the wind which stirs the young leaves where a month ago it rattled the bare branches. Ibid., Ch. 3

6 For the sea lies all about us. . . . In its mysterious past it encompasses all the dim origins of life and receives in the end, after, it may be, many transmutations, the dead husks of that same life. For all at last return to the sea —to Oceanus, the ocean river, like the ever-flowing stream of time, the beginning and the end. Ibid., Pt. III, Ch. 14

7 Always the edge of the sea remains an elusive and indefinable boundary. The shore has a dual nature, changing with the swing of the tides, belonging now to the land, now to the sea. "The Marginal World," *The Edge of the Sea* 1955

8 The rested waters, the cold wet breath of the fog, are of a world in which man is an uneasy trespasser; he punctuates the night with the complaining groan and grunt of a foghorn, sensing the power and menace of the sea. Ibid., "The Enduring Sea"

9 The discipline of the writer is to learn to be still and listen to what his subject has to tell him. Speech, American Association of University Women *June 22, 1956*

10 In every outthrust headland, in every curving beach, in every grain of sand there is a story of the earth. "Our Ever-Changing Shore," *Holiday July, 1958*

11 As cruel a weapon as the cave man's club, the chemical barrage has been hurled against the fabric of life. *The Silent Spring* 1962

12 No witchcraft, no enemy action had silenced the rebirth of new life in this stricken world. The people had done it themselves. Ibid., Ch. 1

13 For the first time in the history of the world, every human being is now subjected to contact with dangerous chemicals, from the moment of conception until death. Ibid., Ch. 3

14 If we are going to live so intimately with these chemicals—eating and drinking them, taking them into the very marrow of our bones—we had better know something about their nature and their power. Ibid.

15 In an age when man has forgotten his origins and is blind even to his most essential needs

for survival, water along with other resources has become the victim of his indifference. Ibid., Ch. 4

16 Our attitude toward plants is a singularly narrow one. If we see any immediate utility in a plant we foster it. If for any reason we find its presence undesirable or merely a matter of indifference, we may condemn it to destruction forthwith. Ibid., Ch. 6

17 Under the philosophy that now seems to guide our destinies, nothing must get in the way of the man with the spray gun. Ibid., Ch. 7

18 Over increasingly large areas of the United States, spring now comes unheralded by the return of the birds, and the early mornings are strangely silent where once they were filled with the beauty of bird song. Ibid., Ch. 8

19 Who has decided . . . that the supreme value is a world without insects, even though it be also a sterile world ungraced by the curving wing of a bird in flight? The decision is that of the authoritarian temporarily entrusted with power. . . . Ibid.

20 The battle of living things against cancer began so long ago that its origin is lost in time. But . . . man, alone of all forms of life, can *create* cancer producing substances. . . . Ibid., Ch. 14

21 If Darwin were alive today the insect world would delight and astound him with its impressive verification of his theories of the survival of the fittest. Under the stress of intensive chemical spraying the weaker members of the insect populations are being weeded out. . . . Only the strong and fit remain to defy our efforts to control them. Ibid., Ch. 16

22 The "control of nature" is a phrase conceived in arrogance, born of the Neanderthal age of biology and the convenience of man. Ibid., Ch. 17

## 813. Daphne Du Maurier
### (1907– )

1 These things were permanent, they could not be dissolved. They were memories that cannot hurt. All this I resolved in my dream, while the clouds lay across the face of the moon, for like most sleepers I knew that I dreamed. *Rebecca*, Ch. 1 1938

2 We can never go back again, that much is certain. The past is still too close to us. The things we have tried to forget and put behind us would stir again, and that sense of fear, of

furtive unrest . . . might in some manner un-foreseen become a living companion, as it had been before.　　　　　　　*Ibid., Ch. 2*

3 We were like two performers in a play, but we were divided, we were not acting with one another. We had to endure it alone, we had to put up this show, this miserable, sham perform-ance for the sake of all these people I did not know and did not want to see again.
　　　　　　　　　　　　　　*Ibid., Ch. 17*

4 Forgotten the lies, the deceit, the sudden bursts of temper. Forgotten the wild extravagance, the absurd generosity, the vitriolic tongue. Only the warmth remained, and the love of living.
　　　　*Mary Anne, Pt. I, Ch. 1　　1954*

5 She could not separate success from peace of mind. The two must go together; her observa-tion pointed to this truth. Failure meant pov-erty, poverty meant squalor, squalor led, in the final stages, to the smells and stagnation of Bowling Inn Alley.　　　　　*Ibid., Ch. 10*

6 One second's hesitation. Tears, or laughter? Tears would be an admission of guilt, so laughter was best.　　　　*Ibid., Pt. II, Ch. 7*

7 "Corruption continues with us beyond the grave," she said, "and then plays merry hell with all ideals. . . ."　　　　　*Ibid., Ch. 11*

8 All courtiers gossip madly, it's part of their business.　　　　　　*Ibid., Pt. III, Ch. 5*

9 The pair were playing a game that defied inter-vention, they were matched like reel and rod and there was no unwinding. They juggled in jargon, dabbled in *double-entendres*, wallowed in each other's witticisms, and all at the ex-pense of the Defendant.　　*Ibid., Pt. IV, Ch. 2*

10 How replace the life of a loved lost child with a dream?　　　　　*Don't Look Now　　1970*

11 . . . the little festive atmosphere of strange-ness, of excitement, that only a holiday bed-room brings. This is ours for the moment, but no more. While we are in it we bring it life. When we have gone it no longer exists, it fades into anonymity.　　　　　　　　　　*Ibid.*

12 "The trouble is," said Laura, "walking in Venice becomes compulsive once you start. Just over the next bridge, you say, and then the next one beckons."　　　　　　　*Ibid.*

## 814. Edith Head
### (1907–　　)

1 The subjective actress thinks of clothes only as they apply to her; the objective actress

thinks of them only as they affect others, as a tool for the job.　　　*The Dress Doctor, with Jane Kesner Ardmore　　1959*

## 815. Zora Neale Hurston
### (1907–1960)

1 Ships at a distance have every man's wish on board. For some they come in with the tide. For others they sail forever on the horizon, never out of sight, never landing, until the Watcher turns his eyes away in resignation, his dreams mocked to death by Time. That is the life of men. Now, women forget all those things they don't want to remember, and re-member everything they don't want to forget. The dream is the truth. Then they act and do things accordingly.　　　　　　*Their Eyes Were Watching God, Ch. 1　　1937*

2 She had the misfortune to be too good-looking and too available for women to take to her, but not pretty enough for any man to excuse her generosity and want to protect her. Nor had she the avarice nor the hardness to turn her position to profit.
　　　　*Seraph on the Suwanee, Ch. 15
　　　　　　　　　　　　　　　　1948*

3 "I'll bet you when you get down on them rusty knees and get to worrying God, He goes in His privy-house and slams the door. That's what he thinks about *you* and *your* prayers."
　　　　　　　　　　　　　　　　*Ibid.*

4 "You love like a coward. Don't take no steps at all. Just stand around and hope for things to happen outright. Unthankful and unknow-ing like a hog under an acorn tree. Eating and grunting with your ears hanging over your eyes, and never even looking up to see where the acorns are coming from."　　　*Ibid., Ch. 23*

5 "Don't you realize that the sea is the home of water? All water is off on a journey unlessen it's in the sea, and it's homesick, and bound to make its way home someday."　*Ibid., Ch. 27*

## 816. Violette Leduc
### (1907–1972)

1 I was and I always shall be hampered by what I think other people will say.　　*La Bâtarde
　　　　　　　　　　　　　　　　1965*

2 "She is killing me and there's nothing I can accuse her of."　　　　　　　　*Ibid.*

3 The pearl wanted what I wanted. I was discovering the little male organ we all of us have. A eunuch taking heart again.
*Therese and Isabelle* 1968

4 To give oneself, one must annihilate oneself.
Ibid.

5 To write is to inform against others.
*Mad in Pursuit* 1971

6 "Will you sell your sex for the sake of your pen? . . . I would sell everything for greater exactness."
Ibid.

7 "I desire, am only able to desire, myself."
Ibid.

8 "I walk without flinching through the burning cathedral of the summer. My bank of wild grass is majestic and full of music. It is a fire that solitude presses against my lips."
Ibid.

## 817. Elsa Schiaparelli
### (1907?– )

1 So fashion is born by small facts, trends, or even politics, never by trying to make little pleats and furbelows, by trinkets, by clothes easy to copy, or by the shortening or lengthening of a skirt.
*Shocking Life,* Ch. 9 1954

2 Courtesans used to know more about the soul of men than any philosopher. The art is lost in the fog of snobbism and false respectability.
Ibid., Ch. 21

3 A good cook is like a sorceress who dispenses happiness.
Ibid.

4 The moment that people stop copying you, it means that you are no longer any good, and that you have ceased to be news.
Ibid.

5 Eating is not merely a material pleasure. Eating well gives a spectacular joy to life and contributes immensely to goodwill and happy companionship. It is of great importance to the morale.
Ibid.

## 818. Helen Foster Snow
### (1907– )

1 To be a Marxist does not mean that one becomes a Communist party member. There are as many varieties of Marxists as there are of Protestants.
"Women and Kuomintang,"
*Women in Modern China* 1967

2 The war between the artist and writer and government or orthodoxy is one of the tragedies of humankind. One chief enemy is stupidity and failure to understand anything about the creative mind. For a bureaucratic politician to presume to tell any artist or writer how to get his mind functioning is the ultimate in asininity. The artist is no more able to control his mind than is any outsider. Freedom to think requires not only freedom of expression but also freedom from the threat of orthodoxy and being outcast and ostracized.
Ibid.

3 . . . one can judge a civilization by the way it treats its women.
Ibid., "Bound Feet and Straw Sandals"

## 819. Barbara Stanwyck
### (1907– )

1 Sponsors obviously care more about a ninety-second commercial and *want* to pay you more than any guest star gets for a ninety-minute *acting* performance.
Quoted in *McCall's*
*March, 1965*

2 There is a point in portraying surface vulgarity where tragedy and comedy are very close.
Quoted in *Starring Miss Barbara Stanwyck* by Ella Smith 1974

3 They don't seem to write . . . comedy anymore —just a series of gags.
Ibid., Interview with Hedda Hopper (1953)

4 My only problem is finding a way to play my fortieth fallen female in a different way from my thirty-ninth.
Ibid.

5 I marvelled at the pioneers. The real people who went into the wilderness with little other than their courage.
Ibid., *New York Journal-American* (1965)

## 820. Jessamyn West
### (1907– )

1 "No human would enjoy my singing . . . only maybe an old house that can't be choosy."
"Lead Her Like a Pigeon,"
*The Friendly Persuasion* 1945

2 "After a good heart," she said, "the least a woman can do is pick a face she fancies. Men's so much alike and many so sorry, that's the very least. If a man's face pleasures thee, that doesn't change. That is something to bank on."
Ibid.

3 She intended to forgive. Not to do so would be un-Christian; but she did not intend to do so soon, nor forget how much she had to forgive.
Ibid., "The Buried Leaf"

4 . . . but time for a woman was no such pliable commodity as it was for a man; time for a woman was rigid, and marked with names of duties.      Ibid., "A Likely Exchange"

5 "Men ain't got any heart for courting a girl they can't pass—let alone catch up with."
Ibid.

6 Eliza's face got pink. She'd never learned to take a compliment—and she'd had two a day for forty years. They made her feel uneasy— as if she weren't taken for granted like sun and moon.      Ibid., "The Illumination"

7 Old fool, Jess thought. Why's the old got to ladle out their past to the young? Got to say, I's a frolicsome sprout if ever there was one? If youngness is what we want here it is under our noses, not second-hand, not warmed over. Live in that. The young's got no time to travel back seventy-five years, watch thee sashay in and out of duck ponds, Jess Birdwell.
Ibid., "Homer and the Lilies"

8 "It's better to learn to say good-by early than late. . . ."      "Learn to Say Good-by,"
*Love, Death, and the Ladies'*
*Drill Team*     1955

9 She had been conscious throughout her girlhood of the eyes of all the potential lovers and husbands upon her, approving, disapproving. From those eyes, not knowing a thing about either lovers or husbands. . . . She had lived a hypothetical life. Nothing real, and the unreality she had conjured up was not really suitable, as it turned out, for the life she had been imagining.     Ibid., "Foot-Shaped Shoes"

10 Writing is so difficult that I often feel that writers, having had their hell on earth, will escape all punishment hereafter.
*To See the Dream*, Ch. 1     1956

11 My upbringing was such that I cannot easily converse with men as though they were normal human beings. They are too special for that. God knows how much knowledge and insight and sense and nonsense I've missed because of this.      Ibid., Ch. 2

12 Being consistent meant not departing from convictions already formulated; being a leader meant making other persons accept these convictions. It was a narrow track, and one-way, but a person might travel a considerable distance on it. A number of dictators have.
Ibid., Ch. 7

13 She thought God could put up with a married couple's making love—after all, it was His own idea for providing babies—but she supposed He considered worship one thing and love-making another. She did, certainly. Nevertheless, she was continually getting them mixed up.
*South of the Angels*, Bk. I, Ch. 2
*1960*

14 Continence is a habit more compelling than tomcatting. Enough tomcatting sooner or later acts as its own cure. Continence does not cure continence. There are more reformed rakes than reformed celibates.    Ibid., Bk. II, Ch. 5

15 The thoughtful California rain, which had fallen intermittently during the night, eased off toward daylight, and by ten had stopped altogether. The rain was also thoughtful enough not to scare people into thinking, when so much more was needed, that it had finished for good.
Ibid., Bk. IV, Ch. 2

16 March days, ending at six-thirty, with apricot skies and a soft wind off the ocean, a little blade-sized blower with only strength enough to move the grass at your feet, provided exactly as much day as a human being could stand.
Ibid., Ch. 4

17 We want the facts to fit the preconceptions. When they don't, it is easier to ignore the facts than to change the preconceptions.
*The Quaker Reader*, Introduction
*1962*

18 Friends [Quakers] refused to take legal oaths, since by doing so they acquiesced in the assumption that, unless under oath, one was not obliged to tell the truth.      Ibid.

19 It is particularly important, it seems to me, in an era of ever increasing departmentalization and specialization, to make the attempt occasionally to see wholes and to understand what lies behind the exterior manifestations.
Ibid.

20 A religious awakening which does not awaken the sleeper to love has roused him in vain.
Ibid.

21 Fiction reveals truths that reality obscures.
Quoted in *Reader's Digest*
*April, 1973*

22 "He should have put his wife to work. That's the way doctors and lawyers pay for their education nowadays."     *Hide and Seek*, Ch. 1
*1973*

23 Visitors to Los Angeles, then and now, were put out because the residents of Los Angeles had the inhospitable idea of building a city comfortable to live in, rather than a monument to astonish the eye of jaded travelers.
Ibid., Ch. 22

## 821. Anne Anastasi

(1908– )

1 . . . it is apparent that we cannot speak of inferiority and superiority, but only of specific differences in aptitudes and personality between the sexes. These differences are largely the result of cultural and other experiential factors. . . .    *Differential Psychology*   *1937*

## 822. Harriette Arnow

(1908– )

1 "If a religion is unpatriotic, it ain't right."
   *The Dollmaker*, Ch. 4   *1954*

2 "I've been readen th Bible an a hunten God fer a long while—off an on—but it ain't so easy as picken up a nickel off th floor."
   Ibid., Ch. 15

3 "Who inu hell," I said to myself, "wants to try to make pies like Mother makes when it's so much simpler to let Mother make um inu first place?"   Ibid., Ch. 28

4 "You never did see them ads an signs an letters beggen all th people back home to come up here an save democracy fer you all. They done it ina last war, too. Now you can git along without us, so's you cain't git shet a us quick enough. Want us to go back home an raise another crop a youngens at no cost to you an Detroit, so's they'll be all ready to save you when you start another war—huh?"
   Ibid., Ch. 33

5 There was something frantic in their blooming, as if they knew that frost was near and then the bitter cold. They'd lived through all the heat and noise and stench of summertime, and now each widely opened flower was like a triumphant cry, "We will, we will make seed before we die."   Ibid., Ch. 34

6 Christ had had no money, just his life. Life and money: could a body separate the two? What had Judas done for his money? Whispered a little, kept still as she did now.
   Ibid., Ch. 37

7 "Supposen the rebels lose. They'll try again. Supposen they win? How can they ever stick together in one nation? They'll be jarren and fighten around over slavery, trade and a lot of other things. Right now the East don't want the West, and the North is a different world from the South. And they've got Spain on their doorstep. But supposen they do clean out Spain, kill every Indian, plow up every acre a ground from the Atlantic to the Pacific? They'll still have their wars."   *The Kentucky Trace*
   *1974*

## 823. Sylvia Ashton-Warner

(1908– )

1 When I teach people, I marry them.
   *Teacher*   *1963*

2 Love interferes with fidelities.   Ibid.

3 When love turns away, now, I don't follow it. I sit and suffer, unprotesting, until I feel the tread of another step.   Ibid.

4 Ah, the simple rapture of fulfillment at my work being understood that cold morning. What unutterable reward for my labor.   Ibid.

5 I've got to relearn what I was supposed to have learned.   *Myself* (February, 1941)
   *1967*

6 I'm not one of these people who were born for nothing.   Ibid.

7 I'll follow them into their own minds and fraternize there. . . .   Ibid.

8 I flung my tongue round like a cat-o'-nine-tails so that my pleasant peaceful infant room became little less than a German concentration camp as I took out on the children what life should have got.   Ibid. (August, 1941)

9 I am my own Universe, I my own Professor.
   Ibid.

10 "The intellect is the tool to find the truth. It's a matter of sharpening it."
   Ibid. (March 22, 1942)

11 "Your work means more to me than my own does to me because your work involves your contentment and that comes before my work with me."   Ibid.

12 "The *need* to study, to do, to make, to think, *arises* from being married. I need to be married to work."   Ibid.

13 Love has the quality of informing almost everything—even one's work.
   Ibid. (November 12, 1942)

14 In mind I lay a hand on his arm but only in mind. That would be revealing a feeling, an offense against London.   *Three*   *1970*

15 As the blackness of the night recedes so does the nadir of yesterday. The child I am forgets so quickly.   Ibid.

16 I'm happy, not because I'm coming home to welcome and warmth but because I'm not. I have no home and am better off without one.
   Ibid.

17 "Women are so illogical. They find their baking
going wrong and blame the baking powder but
they haven't read the directions. They can't see
a thing objectively. They react subjectively.
They don't act, they react."     Ibid.

18 "God, the illogic! The impossibility of communication in this house. The sheer operation
alone of getting something through to somebody."     Ibid.

19 "Quite nice women suddenly have to wear this
title with the stigma on it and a crown of
thorns. We're so frightened of it that we change
our nature to avoid it and in so doing we end
up the classical mother-in-law we feared in the
first place; so gravely have we twisted ourselves."     Ibid.

20 What can be heavier in wealth than freedom?
     Ibid.

## 824. Simone de Beauvoir
### (1908–   )

1 But between the past which no longer is and
the future which is not yet, this moment when
he exists is nothing.
     *The Ethics of Ambiguity*, Ch. 1
     *1948*

2 Existence asserts itself as an absolute which
must seek its justification within itself and not
suppress itself, even though it may be lost by
preserving itself. To attain his truth, man must
not attempt to dispel the ambiguity of his being
but, on the contrary, accept the task of realizing it. He rejoins himself only to the extent
that he agrees to remain at a distance from
himself.     Ibid.

3 In the face of an obstacle which it is impossible to overcome, stubbornness is stupid.
     Ibid.

4 In order for the artist to have a world to express he must first be situated in this world,
oppressed or oppressing, resigned or rebellious,
a man among men.     Ibid., Ch. 3

5 And, furthermore, technic itself is not objectively justified; if it sets up as absolute goals
the saving of time and work which it enables
us to realize and the comfort and luxury which
it enables us to have access to, then it appears
useless and absurd, for the time that one gains
can not be accumulated in a storehouse; it is
contradictory to want to save up existence,
which, the fact is, exists only by being spent,
and there is a good case for showing that airplanes, machines, the telephone, and the radio
do not make men of today happier than those
of former times. But actually it is not a question of giving men time and happiness, it is
not a question of stopping the movement of
life; it is a question of fulfilling it.     Ibid.

6 A man would never get the notion of writing
a book on the peculiar situation of the human
male.     *The Second Sex     1953*

7 For him she is sex—absolute sex, no less. She
is defined and differentiated with reference to
man and not he with reference to her; she is
the incidental, the inessential as opposed to the
essential. He is the Subject, he is the Absolute
—she is the Other.     Ibid.

8 The couple is a fundamental unity with its two
halves riveted together, and the cleavage of
society along the line of sex is impossible.
     Ibid.

9 . . . the present enshrines the past. . . .
     Ibid.

10 How is it that this world has always belonged
to the men . . . ?     Ibid.

11 . . . no one is more arrogant toward women,
more aggressive or scornful, than the man who
is anxious about his virility.     Ibid.

12 But it is doubtless impossible to approach any
human problem with a mind free from bias.
     Ibid.

13 . . . the only public good is that which assures
the private good of the citizens. . . .     Ibid.

14 It is not clear just what the word *happy* really
means and still less what true values it may
mask. . . . In particular those who are condemned to stagnation are often pronounced
happy on the pretext that happiness consists in
being at rest.     Ibid.

15 There is no justification for present existence
other than its expansion into an indefinitely
open future.     Ibid.

16 Alain said that magic is spirit drooping down
among things; an action is magical when, instead of being produced by an agent, it emanates from something passive.     Ibid.

17 Refusal to make herself the object is not always what turns women to homosexuality; most
lesbians, on the contrary, seek to cultivate the
treasures of their femininity. . . .     Ibid.

18 Between women love is contemplative. . . .
There is no struggle, no victory, no defeat; in
exact reciprocity each is at once subject and
object, sovereign and slave; duality becomes
mutuality.     Ibid.

19 Anger or revolt that does not get into the muscles remains a figment of the imagination.     Ibid.

20 . . . humanity is something more than a mere species: it is a historical development.     Ibid.

21 Society, being codified by man, decrees that woman is inferior: she can do away with this inferiority only by destroying the male's superiority.     Ibid.

22 All oppression creates a state of war.     Ibid.

23 . . . what man and woman loathe in each other is the shattering frustration of each one's own bad faith and baseness.     Ibid.

24 What time and strength he squanders in liquidating, sublimating, transferring complexes, in talking about women, in seducing them, in fearing them! He would be liberated himself in their liberation.     Ibid.

25 Woman has to learn that exchanges—it is a fundamental law of political economy—are based on the value the merchandise offered has for the buyer, and not for the seller: she has been deceived in being persuaded that her worth is priceless.     Ibid.

26 . . . justice can never be done in the midst of injustice.     Ibid.

27 . . . the effort to inhibit all sex curiosity and pleasure in the child is quite useless; one succeeds only in creating repressions, obsessions, neuroses.     Ibid.

28 . . . those interested in perpetuating present conditions are always in tears about the marvelous past that is about to disappear, without having so much as a smile for the young future.     Ibid.

29 Let us not forget that our lack of imagination always depopulates the future; for us it is only an abstraction; each one of us secretly deplores the absence there of the one who was himself.     Ibid.

30 I fail to see . . . that liberty ever creates uniformity. . . . It is institutions that create uniformity.     Ibid.

31 . . . when we abolish the slavery of half of humanity, together with the whole system of hypocrisy that it implies, then the "division" of humanity will reveal its genuine significance and the human couple will find its true form.     Ibid.

32 "Ah! if only there were two of me," she thought, one who spoke and the other who listened, one who lived and the other who

watched, how I would love myself! I'd envy no one."     *All Men Are Mortal*, Ch. 1, Prologue    *1955*

33 "Once I was able to hold my breath for sixty years. But as soon as someone tapped me on the shoulder . . ."
"Sixty years!"
"Sixty seconds, if you like," he said. "What's the difference? There are moments when time stands still." He looked at his hands for what seemed a long while. "Moments when you're beyond life and yet still see. And then time begins flowing again, your heart beats, you stretch out your arms, you take a step forward. You still know, but you no longer see."     Ibid.

34 This stale taste of my life will never change. Always the same past, the same feelings, the same rational thoughts, the same boredom. For thousands of years! Never will I escape from myself!     Ibid., Bk. III

35 It was for them to decide. Why live, if living is merely not dying? But to die in order to save one's life, is not that the greatest dupery of all?     Ibid., Bk. V

36 We would walk the streets, talking about our lives and about Life; adventure, unseen but ever-present, rubbed shoulders with us everywhere.     *Memoirs of a Dutiful Daughter*, Pt. III    *1959*

37 She was trying to get rid of a religious hangover.     Ibid., Pt. IV

38 "Never talk about what you are not familiar with," said Mlle. Houchet. But in that case you would never open your mouth.     *Les Belles Images*, Ch. 1    *1966*

39 "There won't be a war. The gap between the capitalist and socialist countries will soon be done away with. Because now we're in the great twentieth-century revolution: producing is more important than possessing."     Ibid.

40 Whatever the country, capitalist or socialist, man was everywhere crushed by technology, made a stranger to his own work, imprisoned, forced into stupidity. The evil all arose from the fact that he had increased his needs rather than limited them; instead of aiming at an abundance that did not and perhaps never would exist, he should have confined himself to the essential minimum, as certain very poor communities still do. . . . As long as fresh needs continued to be created, so new frustrations would come into being. When had the decline begun? The day knowledge was preferred to wisdom and mere usefulness to

beauty. . . . Only a moral revolution—not a social or a political or a technical revolution—only a moral revolution would lead man back to his lost truth.      Ibid., Ch. 3

41 It's frightening to think that you mark your children merely by being yourself. . . . It seems unfair. You can't assume the responsibility for everything you do—or don't do.      Ibid.

42 I find it absurd to assume that all coitus is rape. By saying that, one agrees to the masculine myth that a man's sex is a sword, a weapon.
Quoted in "The Radicalization of Simone de Beauvoir" by Alice Schwarzer, *The First Ms. Reader*, Francine Klagsbrun, ed.    *1972*

43 Abolishing capitalism will not mean abolishing the patriarchal tradition as long as the family is preserved.      Ibid.

44 Since it is the Other within us who is old, it is natural that the revelation of our age should come to us from outside—from others. We do not accept it willingly.
*The Coming of Age*, Pt. II, Ch. 5 *1972*

45 For human reality, existing means existing in time: in the present we look towards the future by means of plans that go beyond our past, in which our activities fall lifeless, frozen and loaded with passive demands. Age changes our relationship with time: as the years go by our future shortens, while our past grows heavier.
     Ibid., Ch. 6

46 . . . it is old age, rather than death, that is to be contrasted with life. Old age is life's parody, whereas death transforms life into a destiny: in a way it preserves it by giving it the absolute dimension—"As into himself eternity changes him at last." Death does away with time.      Ibid., Conclusion

47 One is not born a genius, one becomes a genius.      Quoted in *The Woman's Eye* by Anne Tucker    *1973*

48 I tore myself away from the safe comfort of certainties through my love for truth; and truth rewarded me.    *All Said and Done*    *1974*

49 He was not ready to receive what I had to bring.      Ibid.

50 . . . the torment that so many young women know, bound hand and foot by love and motherhood without having forgotten their former dreams.      Ibid.

# 825. Bette Davis
(1908–  )

1 I have always been driven by some distant music—a battle hymn no doubt—for I have been at war from the beginning. I've never looked back before. I've never had the time and it has always seemed so dangerous. To look back is to relax one's vigil.
*The Lonely Life*, Ch. 1    *1962*

2 The male ego with few exceptions is elephantine to start with.      Ibid., Ch. 9

3 The sweetness of first love. It still clings like ivy to the stone walls of this institution called Bette Davis. Stonewall Davis! Alma Mater! You can't mortar bricks with treacle but I tried.      Ibid.

4 Discipline is a symbol of caring to a child. He needs guidance. If there is love, there is no such thing as being too tough with a child. A parent must also not be afraid to hang himself. If you have never been hated by your child, you have never been a parent.
     Ibid., Ch. 19

5 Love is not enough. It must be the foundation, the cornerstone—but not the complete structure. It is much too pliable, too yielding.
     Ibid.

6 I was always eager to salt a good stew. The trouble was that I was expected to supply the meat and potatoes as well.    Ibid., Ch. 20

7 The act of sex, gratifying as it may be, is God's joke on humanity. It is man's last desperate stand at superintendency.      Ibid.

8 The weak are the most treacherous of us all. They come to the strong and drain them. They are bottomless. They are insatiable. They are always parched and always bitter. They are everyone's concern and like vampires they suck our life's blood.      Ibid.

9 But my biggest problem all my life was men. I never met one yet who could compete with the image the public made out of Bette Davis.
Quoted in "Bette Davis," *Conversations in the Raw* by Rex Reed    *1969*

10 This became a credo of mine . . . attempt the impossible in order to improve your work.
*Mother Goddamn*, Ch. 10    *1974*

\* \* \*

11 I am a woman meant for a man, but I never found a man who could compete.
     Newspaper Interview

## 826. Agnes De Mille
(1908–    )

1 I learned three important things in college—
to use a library, to memorize quickly and
visually, to drop asleep at any time given a
horizontal surface and fifteen minutes. What I
could not learn was to think creatively on
schedule.    *Dance to the Piper    1952*

2 With the smell of iris and budding acacia coming through the windows, the sound of scholas-
ticism filling my dreams with a reassuring hum,
I sank deeper and deeper into a kind of cere-
bral miasma as I postponed all vital decisions.
*Ibid.*

3 There was no use in apologizing for the way
I looked. Nobody looked the way I did who
expected to be seen by anyone else.    *Ibid.*

4 No trumpets sound when the important decisions of our life are made. Destiny is made
known silently.    *Ibid.*

5 Dancing is not taught as an art in any university. There it is still in the gymnasium.
*Ibid.*

6 A good education is usually harmful to a
dancer. A good calf is better than a good head.
*News Item    February 1, 1954*

7 Theater people are always pining and agoniz-
ing because they're afraid that they'll be for-
gotten. And in America they're quite right.
They will be.
Quoted in "The Grande Dame of
Dance" by Jane Howard, *Life
November 15, 1963*

8 The truest expression of a people is in its dances
and its music. Bodies never lie.
"Do I Hear a Waltz?," *The New York
Times Magazine    May 11, 1975*

## 827. Sheilah Graham
(1908?–    )

1 I think people still want to marry rich. Girls
especially. . . . [It's] simple. Don't date poor
boys. Go where the rich are. . . . You don't
have to be rich to go where they go.
Quoted in "Sheilah Graham:
Still Upwardly, Verbally
Mobile" by Kathleen Hendrix,
*Los Angeles Times
October 13, 1974*

2 . . . you have to really drink a lot to enjoy
parties.    *Ibid.*

3 You just never know when you're going into
eternity.    *Ibid.*

## 828. Nancy Hale
(1908–    )

1 "Your father used to say, 'Never give away
your work. People don't value what they don't
have to pay for.'"
"Eyes or No Eyes, or The Art of
Seeing," *The Life in the Studio
1957*

2 She could never get used to the idea that most
people don't use their eyes except to keep from
running into things.    *Ibid.*

3 After my mother's death I began to see her as
she had really been. . . . It was less like losing someone than discovering someone.
*Ibid., "A Good Light"*

4 Like all real artists', her objective had been to
create riches with modest means; squandering
seemed to her a kind of stupidity. Since she
never had but one standard, perfection—which
in the nature of things fits art better than life—
she often gave a misleading impression of
Yankee parsimony.    *Ibid.*

5 . . . this mysterious thing, artistic talent; the
key to so much freedom, the escape from so
much suffering.
*Mary Cassatt: A Biography of the
Great American Painter*, Pt. I, Ch. 4
*1975*

6 . . . the cynicism of the young about society is
as nothing to the cynicism of young artists for
the art establishment.    *Ibid.*

7 An artist's originality is balanced by a corresponding conservatism, a superstitiousness,
about it; which might be boiled down to
"What worked before will work again."
*Ibid.*, Pt. II, Ch. 6

8 The best work of artists in any age is the work
of innocence liberated by technical knowledge.
The laboratory experiments that led to the
theory of pure color equipped the impression-
ists to paint nature as if it had only just been
created.    *Ibid.*, Ch. 7

9 I had wanted to say then to the young man,
"Painting one picture—even a mediocre picture
—is more important than collecting a hundred."
I'd wanted to say, "You couldn't have any col-
lections at all unless you first had pictures."
*Ibid.*, Epilogue

## 829. Amy Johnson
(1908?–1941)

1 Had I been a man I might have explored the
Poles or climbed Mount Everest, but as it was
my spirit found outlet in the air. . . .
Essay in *Myself When Young*,
Margot Asquith, ed.    *1938*

## 830. Madeline Mason-Manheim
(1908–    )

1 How shall you speak of parting?
How shall the bands be loosened
That Friendship fastened round you?
        "Parting," St. 3, *Hill Fragments*
                        1925

2 I share the heart-ache of the traveler
Who would retrace his steps
And find the way he came.
        Ibid., "Aspiration"

3       Know you Silence, my friend?
It is the dumbness of the tongue when the
   heart would be heard;
It is the muteness of the lips when the spirit
   speaks loudest.
It is the uttering of the unutterable.
        Ibid., "Silence," St. 1

4 My heart sings while I weep.
My heart knows
That Sorrow is a trail of dreams
To farther worlds.
        Ibid., "Compensation," St. 3

5 Your destiny, O River,
It is even as the destiny of man.
O, ye are brethren,
Souls unharboured,
Seeking to regain the Sea.
        Ibid., "The River"

6 Sleep, companion of Silence, walks in her
   garden;
Walks 'midst her deathless poppies and gathers
   them to her breast.
        Ibid., "Sleep"

7 They call you barren
Who, unseeing, gaze upon you.
Yet Time's most secret thoughts,
The jewels of the ages
Are buried in your breast
As in your loneliness you lie
Beneath the everlasting heights.
        Ibid., "The Desert," St. 1

8 Yours the voice
Sounding ever in my ears.
        Ibid., "To My Mother," St. 1

## 831. Alice Neel
(1908–    )

1 But we are all creatures in a way, aren't we?
And both men and women are wretched.
      Quoted in "Alice Neel: Portraits of
      Four Decades" by Cindy Nemser, *Ms.*
               *October, 1973*

2 You can't leave humanity out. If you didn't
have humanity, you wouldn't have anything.
                Ibid.

## 832. Ann Ronell
(1908–    )

1 Who's afraid of the big bad wolf?
    "Who's Afraid of the Big Bad Wolf?"
    from Walt Disney's *Three Little Pigs*
                       1933

## 833. Amy Vanderbilt
(1908–1974)

1 Ceremony is really a protection, too, in times
of emotional involvement, particularly at death.
If we have a social formula to guide us and
do not have to extemporize, we feel better able
to handle life. If we ignore ceremony entirely,
we are not normal, warm human beings. Con-
versely, if we never relax it, if we "stand on
ceremony" in all things, we are rigid. We must
learn which ceremonies may be breached occasionally at our convenience and which ones
may never be if we are to live pleasantly with
our fellow man.
      *New Complete Book of Etiquette,*
      Pt. I, Introduction    *1963*

2 Good manners have much to do with the emotions. To make them ring true, one must feel
them, not merely exhibit them.
        Ibid., Pt. II, Introduction

3 One face to the world, another at home makes
for misery.     Ibid., Pt. VI, Introduction

4 The civilian once under the mantle of official-
dom, wherever it may be, is subject to the
rules governing civilian behavior under official
circumstances.    Ibid., Pt. VIII, Introduction

## 834. Yang Ping
(1908–    )

1 That I should think, even now, of wanting to
continue to exist only as the vessel of a
chemical experimentation heartlessly, inexorably formulating itself within me! And against
my will! . . . And yet I love this little life!
With all the pain of it, I long for the wonderful thing to happen, for a tiny human creature
to spring from between my limbs bravely out
into the world. I need it, just as a true poet
*needs* to create a great undying work.
      "Fragment from a Lost Diary,"
      *Fragment from a Lost Diary and*
      *Other Stories*, Naomi Katz and
      Nancy Milton, eds.    *1973*

2 Only when the beat of life is lifted to this pitch, this fury, and this danger, only when destiny (here in my case it is but a wayward sperm carrying its implacable microscopic chromosomes, but nevertheless it is a form of destiny!) poses the choice between irreconcilable desires at a given moment, only when a human being feels the necessity of ignoring personal feeling in the decision taken—only then can one talk of a revolutionary awakening!      Ibid.

3 Women and revolution! What tragic, unsung epics of courage lie silent in the world's history!      Ibid.

## 835. Amalia Fleming
### (1909?– )

1 So much sorrow should certainly not come to a man who has given so much of value to humanity.      Letter to Ben May (November 5, 1949), Quoted in *The Life of Sir Alexander Fleming* by André Maurois *1959*

2 Alec is very well. I think he has a good wife! . . . I am working on a problem which fascinates me but I keep failing to do what I try. Still there is an end even to failures.
     Ibid. (December, 1954)

3 He, too, I thought, possesses, like Pasteur, and in the highest degree, the art of choosing the crucial experiment and of grasping the capital importance of a chance observation. . . . But . . . for Fleming there was a wide world lying beyond the confines of his lab. The appearance of a new flower in his garden was as interesting to him as the work he might be engaged on. . . . [He] felt himself to be an infinitesimal part of nature, and from that feeling was born his refusal to indulge in self-importance and his dislike of big words. It was almost possible to say that he was a genius in spite of himself, and reluctantly.      Ibid., Ch. 16

4 I respect every ideology, including communism, provided they are not trying to impose their will through force. I am against any totalitarian regime.      Quoted in *Newsweek* *October 11, 1971*

5 The innocent people who have nothing to say are tortured the most because when a prisoner admits something, the torture stops.
     Quoted in "Greece: Survival of the Shrewdest" by Susan Margolis, *Ms.* *October, 1973*

## 836. Anne Fremantle
### (1909– )

1 Among the most truly responsible for all people are artists and revolutionaries, for they most of all are prepared to pay with their lives.      Introduction to *Woman as Revolutionary*, Fred. C. Giffin, ed. *1973*

2 The revolutionary attempts a secular denial of mortality, the artist a spiritual one.      Ibid.

## 837. Katharine Hepburn
### (1909– )

1 I can remember walking as a child. It was not customary to say you were fatigued. It was customary to complete the goal of the expedition.      Quoted in "Hepburn: She Is the Best," *Los Angeles Times* *November 24, 1974*

2 It's such a cuckoo business. And it's a business you go into because you're egocentric. It's a very embarrassing profession.      Ibid.

3 Television, which sank the picture industry, has turned the Academy Awards into a big television show. I think it should be an intimate honor.      Ibid.

4 To keep your character intact you cannot stoop to filthy acts. It makes it easier to stoop the next time.      Ibid.

5 Trying to be fascinating is an asinine position to be in.      Dick Cavett Show, ABC-TV *April 2, 1975*

6 Without discipline, there's no life at all.
     Ibid.      *April 4, 1975*

7 You never feel that you have fame. It's always in back of you.      Ibid.

8 To be loved is very demoralizing.      Ibid.

9 As for me, prizes mean nothing. My prize is my work.      Quoted in *Kate* by Charles Higham      *1975*

10 I always wear slacks because of the brambles and maybe the snakes. And see this basket? I keep everything in it. So I look ghastly, do I? I don't care—so long as I'm comfortable.
     Ibid.

11 . . . plain women know more about men than beautiful ones do.      Ibid.

## 838. Queen Juliana
(1909–  )

1 You people of the United States of America have the wonderfully farseeing conception of being Democracy's material and spiritual arsenal, to save the world's highest values from annihilation. Radio Address, NBC
. *April 13, 1941*

2 I want to emphasize that for a queen the task of being a mother is just as important as it is for every other Netherlands woman.
Inauguration Address, Amsterdam
*September 6, 1948*

3 Though previous generations were also inspired by the fervent will to improve the world, they failed because they did not call a final halt to the forces of destruction. To do this is precisely the task of the present generation. . . .
Address, University of Paris
*May 25, 1950*

## 839. Gabrielle Roy
(1909–  )

1 The city was made for couples, not for four or five silly girls with their arms interlaced, strolling up St. Catherine Street, stopping at every shop-window to admire things they would never own. *The Tin Flute*, Ch. 1 *1947*

2 When there was enough money for their needs, the ties between them had been strong, but once the money was lacking, what a strain was put on their love! Ibid., Ch. 32

3 The Christian Scientists held that it was not God Who wanted sicknesses, but man who puts himself in the way of suffering. If this were the case, though, wouldn't we all die in perfect health? *The Cashier*, Ch. 3 *1955*

4 How clearly he realized that men did not like what they called love. That most embarrassing of subjects between men they approached with half-utterances, with false carelessness, or else with a vulgar leer, never easily and comfortably. Ibid., Ch. 8

5 Oh! The matchless release of the man asleep! Who has not realized through experience that sleep tells the truth about us? In sleep a human being is finally brought back to himself, having sloughed off everything else. Bound hand and foot, fettered with fatigue, he at last drifts toward the cavern of the unknown. Some men have returned therefrom with poems fully written, or with equations solved.
Ibid., Ch. 12

## 840. Eudora Welty
(1909–  )

1 He did not like illness, he distrusted it, as he distrusted the road without signposts.
"Death of a Travelling Salesman,"
*A Curtain of Green and Other
Stories 1936*

2 This time, when his heart leapt, something—his soul—seemed to leap too, like a little colt invited out of a pen. Ibid.

3 I have been sick and I found out, only then, how lonely I am. Is it too late? Ibid.

4 Come and stand in my heart, whoever you are, and a whole river would cover your feet and rise higher and take your knees in whirlpools, and draw you down to itself, your whole body, your heart too. Ibid.

5 These people cherished something here that he could not see, they withheld some ancient promise of food and warmth and light. Between them they had a conspiracy. Ibid.

6 How intensified, magnified, really vain all attempt at expression becomes in the afflicted!
Ibid., "The Key"

7 Radio, sewing machine, book ends, ironing board and that great big piano lamp—peace, that's what I like. Butterbean vines planted all along the front where the strings are.
Ibid., "Why I Live at the P.O."

8 "No, babe, it ain't the truth. . . . Truth is something worse, I ain't said what, yet. It's something hasn't come to me, but I ain't sayin' it won't." Ibid., "Powerhouse"

9 His memory could work like the slinging of a noose to catch a wild pony.
"First Love," *The Wide Net and
Other Stories 1943*

10 "We're walking along in the changing-time," said Doc. "Any day now the change will come. It's going to turn from hot to cold. . . . Old Jack Frost will be pinching things up. Old Mr. Winter will be standing in the door. Hickory tree there will be yellow. Sweet-gum red, hickory yellow, dogwood red, sycamore yellow. . . . Persimmons will all git fit to eat, and the nut will be dropping like rain all through the woods here. And run, little quail, run, for we'll be after you too." Ibid., "The Wide Net"

11 "I rather a man be anything, than a woman be mean." Ibid., "Livvie"

12 She was calm the way a child is calm, with never the calmness of a spirit. But like distant lightning that silently bathes a whole shimmering sky, one awareness was always trembling about her: one day she would be free to come and go. . . . Ibid., "At the Landing"

13 There was a need in all dreams for something to stay far, far away, never to torment with the rest, and the bright moon now was that. Ibid.

14 Haven't you noticed it prevail, in the world in general? Beware of a man with manners.
*The Golden Apples*, Ch. 1    *1949*

15 She yearned for her heart to twist. But it didn't, not in time. Ibid., Ch. 4

16 He spoke with no sign of pain. Just that edge of competition was in his voice. He was ever the most ambitious fool. To me ambition's always been a mystery. . . . Ibid., Ch. 5

17 Attrition was their wisdom. Ibid., Ch. 7

18 He loved being happy! He loved happiness like I love tea. *The Ponder Heart*    *1954*

19 She was dead as a doornail. And she'd died laughing. I could have shaken her for it. She'd never laughed for Uncle Daniel before in her life. And even if she had, that's not the same thing as smiling; you may think it is, but I don't. Ibid.

20 "Never think you've seen the last of anything. . . ." *The Optimist's Daughter*,
Pt. I, Ch. 1    *1969*

21 "I'm afraid my [minister] husband's running a little late. You know people like *this* don't die every day in the week. He's sitting home in his bathrobe now, tearing his hair, trying to do him justice." Ibid., Pt. II, Ch. 2

22 All they could see was sky, water, birds, light and confluence. It was the whole morning world. And they themselves were a part of the confluence. Their own joint act of faith had brought them here at the very moment and matched its occurrence, and proceeded as it proceeded. Direction itself was made beautiful, momentous. They were riding as one with it, right up front. Ibid., Pt. IV

## 841. Gale Wilhelm
(1909–    )

1 "I'm going to turn on the light and we'll be two people in a room looking at each other and wondering why on earth they were afraid of the dark." *We Too Are Drifting*    *1935*

## 842. Bertha Adams Backus
(fl. 1910s)

1 Build for yourself a strong-box,
Fashion each part with care;
When it's strong as your hand can make it,
Put all your troubles there.
"Then Laugh," St. 1    *1911*

## 843. Janet Begbie
(fl. 1910s)

* * *

1 Carry on, carry on, for the men and boys are gone,
But the furrow shan't lie fallow while the women carry on.
"Carry On"

## 844. Esther Lilian Duff
(fl. 1910s)

1 Some of the roofs are plum-color,
Some of the roofs are gray,
Some of the roofs are silverstone,
And some are made of clay;
But under every gabled close
There's a secret hid away.
"Not Three, But One,"
*Bohemian Glass*    *1916*

## 845. Hsiang Chin-yu
(fl. 1910s–1927)

1 . . . the emancipation of women can only come with a change in the social structure which frees men and women alike.
Quoted in *Women in Modern China*
by Helen Foster Snow    *1967p*

## 846. Annie Kenney
(fl. 1910s)

1 I was once told that the lesson I had to learn in life was patience. If that is true, I can only say I began life very badly indeed!
*Memoirs of a Militant*    *1924*

2 . . . Paradise would be there once the vote was won! I honestly believed every word I said. I had yet to learn that Nature's works are very slow but very sure. Experience is indeed the best though the sternest teacher. Ibid.

3 Prison. It was not prison for me. Hunger-strikes. They had no fears for me. Cat and

Mouse Act. I could have laughed. A prison cell was quiet—no telephone, no paper, no speeches, no sea sickness, no sleepless nights. I could lie on my plank bed all day and all night and return once more to my day dreams.      Ibid.

## 847. Myrtie Lillian Barker
### (1910– )

1 The idea of strictly minding our own business is moldy rubbish. Who could be so selfish?
*I Am Only One*    1963

## 848. Mary Ingraham Bunting
### (1910– )

1 When her last child is off to school, we don't want the talented woman wasting her time in work far below her capacity. We want her to come out running.      Quoted in *Life*
*January 13, 1961*

## 849. Hilda Conkling
### (1910– )
### * * *

1 Poems come like boats
With sails for wings;
Crossing the sky swiftly
They slip under tall bridges
Of cloud.
     "Poems"

2 The hills are going somewhere;
They have been on the way a long time.
They are like camels in a line
But they move more slowly.
     "Hills"

3 The world turns softly
Not to spill its lakes and rivers.
     "Water"

## 850. Margaret Halsey
### (1910– )

1 . . . she blushed like a well-trained sunrise.
*With Malice Toward Some*    1938

2 These people . . . talk simply because they think sound is more manageable than silence.
     Ibid.

3 The boneless quality of English conversation, . . . so far as I have heard it, is all form and no content. Listening to Britons dining out is like watching people play first-class tennis with imaginary balls.      Ibid.

4 . . . it takes a great deal to produce ennui in an Englishman and if you do, he only takes it as convincing proof that you are well-bred.
     Ibid.

5 The attitude of the English . . . toward English history reminds one a good deal of the attitude of a Hollywood director toward love.
     Ibid.

6 Living in England, provincial England, must be like being married to a stupid but exquisitely beautiful wife.      Ibid.

7 American interiors tend to have no happy medium between execrable taste and what is called "good taste" and is worn like a wart.
     Ibid.

8 Humility is not my forte, and whenever I dwell for any length of time on my own shortcomings, they gradually begin to seem mild, harmless, rather engaging little things, not at all like the staring defects in other people's characters.
     Ibid.

9 Such leaping to foot, such opening of doors, such lightning flourishes with matches and cigarettes—it is all so heroic, I never quite get over the feeling that someone has just said, "To the lifeboats!"      Ibid.

10 . . . the English think of an opinion as something which a decent person, if he has the misfortune to have one, does all he can to hide.
     Ibid.

11 All of Stratford, in fact, suggests powdered history—add hot water and stir and you have a delicious, nourishing Shakespeare.      Ibid.

12 . . . in England, having had money . . . is just as acceptable as having it, since the upper-class mannerisms persist, even after the bankroll has disappeared. But never having had money is unforgivable, and can only be atoned for by never trying to get any.      Ibid.

13 Father is also, in our country, The Boy We Left Behind Us.      *The Folks at Home*
*1952*

14 The whole flavor and quality of the American representative government turns to ashes on the tongue, if one regards the government as simply an inferior and rather second-rate sort of corporation.      Ibid.

15 . . . there is not enough loving-kindness afloat in the continental United States to see a crippled old lady across an Indian trail.      Ibid.

16 What I know about money, I learned the hard way—by having had it.      Ibid.

17 The role of a do-gooder is not what actors call a fat part.      Ibid.

## 851. Jacquetta Hawkes
(1910–　　)

1 . . . we do in fact maintain our fragile lives on a wafer balanced between a hellish morass and unlimited space. *A Land*　1952

2 The young are now kinder than they were and are more tender towards old age, more aware perhaps with the growth of self-consciousness that it will come also to them. *Ibid.*

3 We live in a world made seemingly secure by the four walls of our houses, the artificiality of our cities, and by the four walls of habit. Volcanoes speak of insecurity, of our participation in process. They are openings not any longer into a properly appointed hell, but into an equally alarming abysm of thought. *Ibid.*

4 . . . the universe is substantially homogeneous, and shooting stars are chips from globes very much like our own. They are, as the label in the Geological Museum soberly states, "fragments of former worlds." *Ibid.*

## 852. Mary Keyserling
(1910–　　)

1 Occupationally women are relatively more disadvantaged today than they were twenty-five years ago. . . . This deterioration has occurred despite the increase in women's share of total employment over the same period and the rising number of women who enroll in and graduate from institutions of higher education. *Windows on Day Care*　1972

2 There shouldn't be a single little child in America left alone to fend for himself. *Ibid.*, Ch. 2

3 Our ultimate goal as a nation should be to make available comprehensive, developmental child-care services to all families that wish to use them. *Ibid.*, Ch. 9

## 853. Alicia Markova
(1910–　　)

1 . . . glorious bouquets and storms of applause. . . . These are the trimmings which every artist naturally enjoys. But to *move* an audience in such a role, to hear in the applause that unmistakable note which breaks through good theatre manners and comes from the heart, is to feel that you have won through to life itself. Such pleasure does not vanish with the fall of the curtain, but becomes part of one's own life. *Giselle and I*, Ch. 18　1960

## 854. Mother Teresa
(1910–　　)

1 . . . the poor are our brothers and sisters. . . . [They are the] people in the world who need love, who need care, who have to be wanted. Quoted in "Saints Among Us," *Time December 29, 1975*

2 Our work brings people face to face with love. *Ibid.*

3 Loneliness and the feeling of being unwanted is the most terrible poverty. *Ibid.*

4 Our intellect and other gifts have been given to be used for God's greater glory, but sometimes they become the very god for us. That is the saddest part: we are losing our balance when this happens. We must free ourselves to be filled by God. Even God cannot fill what is full. *Ibid.*

5 To keep a lamp burning we have to keep putting oil in it. *Ibid.*

## 855. Simone Weil
(1910–1943)

1 Just as a person who is always asserting that he is too good-natured is the very one from whom to expect, on some occasion, the coldest and most unconcerned cruelty, so when any group sees itself as the bearer of civilization this very belief will betray it into behaving barbarously at the first opportunity. "Hitler and Roman Foreign Policy," *Nouveaux Cahiers*　January 1, 1940

2 I would suggest that barbarism be considered as a permanent and universal human characteristic which becomes more or less pronounced according to the play of circumstances. *Ibid.*

3 There is something else which has the power to awaken us to the truth. It is the works of writers of genius. . . . They give us, in the guise of fiction, something equivalent to the actual density of the real, that density which life offers us every day but which we are unable to grasp because we are amusing ourselves with lies. "Morality and Literature," *Cahiers du Sud*　January, 1944p

4 If I ever was afraid, it was then. I can still feel the way it was in the metal shop, the presses, the ten-hour-day, and the brutal foremen, and the missing fingers, and the heat, and the headaches, and. . . . *La Condition Ouvrière*　1951p

5 Obvious and inexorable oppression that cannot be overcome does not give rise to revolt but to submission.       *Ibid.*

6 You take the risk of becoming the arbiter of another human existence. My conclusion (which I offer only as a suggestion) is not that it is necessary to flee from love, but that one should not go looking for it, especially not when one is very young.    *Ibid., Letter to a Girl Student*

7 The human soul never ceases to be modified by its encounter with might, swept on, blinded by that which it believes itself able to handle, bowed beneath the power of that which it suffers. . . . Might is that which makes a thing of anybody who comes under its sway.
*La Source Grecque     1952p*

8 The vocation of each of the peoples of antiquity: a view of divine things (all but the Romans). Israel: God in one person. India: assimilation of the soul with God in mystical union. China: God's own method of operation, fullness of action which seems inaction, fullness of presence which seems absence, emptiness and silence. Egypt: immortality, salvation of the virtuous soul after death by assimilation with a suffering God, dead and resurrected, Charity toward one's neighbour. Greece (which greatly felt the influence of Egypt): the wretchedness of man, the distance and transcendence of God.      *Ibid.*

9 A right is not effectual by itself, but only in relation to the obligation to which it corresponds. . . . An obligation which goes unrecognized by anybody loses none of the full force of its existence. A right which goes unrecognized by anybody is not worth very much.
"L'Enracinement," Pt. I (1949),
*The Need for Roots     1952p*

10 One of the indispensable foods of the human soul is liberty. Liberty, taking the word in its concrete sense, consists in the ability to choose.      *Ibid.*

11 Punishment must be an honour. It must not only wipe out the stigma of the crime, but must be regarded as a supplementary form of education, compelling a higher devotion to the public good. The severity of the punishment must also be in keeping with the kind of obligation which has been violated, and not with the interests of public security.     *Ibid.*

12 Money destroys human roots wherever it is able to penetrate, by turning desire for gain into the sole motive. It easily manages to outweigh all other motives, because the effort it demands of the mind is so very much less. Nothing is *so* clear *and so* simple as a row of figures.      *Ibid., Pt. II*

13 Propaganda is not directed towards creating an inspiration: it closes, seals up all the openings through which an inspiration might pass; it fills the whole spirit with fanaticism.
*Ibid., Pt. III*

14 Evil becomes an operative motive far more easily than good; but once pure good has become an operative motive in the mind, it forms there the fount of a uniform and inexhaustible impulsion, which is never so in the case of evil.      *Ibid.*

15 Death and labour are things of necessity and not of choice.      *Ibid.*

16 The idea of a snare set for man by God is also the meaning of the myth of the labyrinth . . . that path where man, from the moment he enters upon it, loses his way and finds himself equally powerless, at the end of a certain time, to return upon his steps or to direct himself anywhere. He errs without knowing where, and finally arrives at the place where God waits to devour him.    *Intimations of Christianity,*
Elisabeth Chase Geissbuhler, ed.
*1957p*

17 If we want to traverse this somber age in manly fashion, we shall refrain, like the Ajax of Sophocles, from letting empty hopes set us afire.      "Revolution Proletarienne"
(August 25, 1933),
*Oppression and Liberty     1958p*

18 But not even Marx is more precious to us than the truth.      *Ibid.*

19 War, which perpetuates itself under the form of preparation for war, has once and for all given the State an important role in production.      *Ibid.*

20 Technical progress seems to have gone bankrupt, since instead of happiness it has only brought the masses that physical and moral wretchedness in which we see them floundering. . . .    *Ibid.,* "Reflections Concerning the Causes of Liberty and Social Oppression" (1934)

21 The word "revolution" is a word for which you kill, for which you die, for which you send the labouring masses to their death, but which does not possess any content.     *Ibid.*

22 . . . the time has come to give up dreaming of liberty, and to make up one's mind to conceive it.      *Ibid.*

23 . . . man alone can enslave man.     *Ibid.*

24 The inversion of the relation between means and end—an inversion which is to a certain

extent the law of every oppressive society—here becomes total or nearly so, and extends to nearly everything. The scientist does not use science in order to manage to see more clearly into his own thinking, but aims at discovering results that will go to swell the present volume of scientific knowledge. Machines do not run in order to enable men to live, but we resign ourselves to feeding men in order that they may serve the machines. Money does not provide a convenient method for exchanging products; it is the sale of goods which is a means for keeping money in circulation. Lastly, organization is not a means for exercising a collective activity, but the activity of a group, whatever it may be, is a means for strengthening organization. Ibid.

25 The majority of human beings do not question the truth of an idea without which they would literally be unable to live.
Ibid., "Is There a Marxist Doctrine?" (1943)

26 He [Marx] labelled this dream "dialectical materialism." This was sufficient to shroud it in mystery. These two words are of an almost impenetrable emptiness. A very amusing game —though rather a cruel one—is to ask a Marxist what they mean. Ibid.

27 The payment of debts is necessary for social order. The non-payment is quite equally necessary for social order. For centuries humanity has oscillated, serenely unaware, between these two contradictory necessities.
"On Bankruptcy" (1937), Selected Essays: 1934–1953 1962p

28 Imagination is always the fabric of social life and the dynamic of history. The influence of real needs and compulsions, of real interests and materials, is indirect because the crowd is never conscious of it.
Ibid., "A Note on Social Democracy" (1937)

29 . . . when a man's life is destroyed or damaged by some wound or privation of soul or body, which is due to other men's actions or negligence, it is not only his sensibility that suffers but also his aspiration toward the good. Therefore there has been sacrilege towards that which is sacred in him.
Ibid., "Draft for a Statement of Human Obligation" (1943)

30 The needs of a human being are sacred. Their satisfaction cannot be subordinated either to reasons of state, or to any consideration of money, nationality, race, or colour, or to the moral or other value attributed to the human being in question, or to any consideration whatsoever. Ibid.

31 At the bottom of the heart of every human being from earliest infancy until the tomb, there is something that goes on indomitably expecting, in the teeth of all experience of crimes committed, suffered, and witnessed, that good and not evil will be done to him. It is this above all that is sacred in every human being. Ibid., "Human Personality" (1943)

32 To us, men of the West, a very strange thing happened at the turn of the century; without noticing it, we lost science, or at least the thing that had been called by that name for the last four centuries. What we now have in place of it is something different, radically different, and we don't know what it is. Nobody knows what it is. "Classical Science and After" (1941), On Science, Necessity, and the Love of God, Richard Rees, ed. 1968p

33 The future is made of the same stuff as the present. Ibid., "Some Thoughts on the Love of God" (October, 1940– May, 1942)

34 . . . if we are suffering illness, poverty, or misfortune, we think we shall be satisfied on the day it ceases. But there too, we know it is false; so soon as one has got used to not suffering one wants something else. Ibid.

35 Evil is neither suffering nor sin; it is both at the same time, it is something common to them both. For they are linked together; sin makes us suffer and suffering makes us evil, and this indissoluble complex of suffering and sin is the evil in which we are submerged against our will, and to our horror. Ibid.

36 How could we search for God, since He is above, in a dimension not open to us? . . . We must only wait and call out.
Ibid., "Some Reflections on the Love of God" (October 1940–May, 1942)

37 Physical love and labour.
labour: to feel with one's whole self the existence of the world
love: to feel with one's whole self the existence of another being?
"The Pre-War Notebook," First and Last Notebooks, Richard Rees, ed. 1970p

38 Life does not need to mutilate itself in order to be pure. Ibid.

39 Lesson of the work of art: it is forbidden to touch things of beauty. The artist's inspiration is always *Platonic*. Thus art is the symbol of the two noblest human efforts: to construct (work), and to refrain from destruction (love overcome). For all love is naturally sadistic; and modesty, respect, reserve, are the mark of the human. Not to seize possession of what one loves . . . not to change it in any way . . . refuse power. . . . Ibid.

40 Learn to reject friendship, or rather the dream of friendship. To want friendship is a great fault. Friendship ought to be a gratuitous joy, like the joys afforded by art, or life (like aesthetic joys). I must refuse it in order to be worthy to receive it. . . . Ibid.

41 Evil being the root of mystery, pain is the root of knowledge. Ibid., "The New York Notebook" (1942)

42 To get power over is to defile. To possess is to defile. Ibid.

43 Charity. To love human beings in so far as they are nothing. That is to love them as God does. Ibid.

44 Nothing can have as its destination anything other than its origin. The contrary idea, the idea of progress, is poison. Ibid.

45 Truth is not discovered by proofs but by exploration. It is always experimental. But necessity also is an object of exploration. Ibid.

46 Joy fixes us to eternity and pain fixes us to time. But desire and fear hold us in bondage to time, and detachment breaks the bond. Ibid.

47 The proper method of philosophy consists in clearly conceiving the insoluble problems in all their insolubility and then in simply contemplating them, fixedly and tirelessly, year after year, without any hope, patiently waiting. Ibid., "London Notebook" (1943)

48 There is very profound truth in the Greek sophisms proving that it is impossible to learn. We understand little and badly. We need to be taught by those who understand more and better than ourselves. For example, by Christ. But since we do not understand anything, we do not understand them either. How could we know that they are right? How could we pay them the proper amount of attention, to begin with, which is necessary before they can begin to teach us? That is why miracles are needed. Ibid.

49 Why is it that reality, when set down untransposed in a book, sounds false? Ibid.

## 856. Virginia Mae Axline
(1911– )

1 Out again into the night where the dulled light obscures the decisive lines of reality and casts over the immediate world a kindly vagueness. . . . The darkened sky gives growing room for softened judgments, for suspended indictments, for emotional hospitality. What *is*, seen in such light, seems to have so many possibilities that definitiveness becomes ambiguous.
*Dibs: In Search of Self*, Ch. 2
*1965*

2 "So much to say. And so much not to say! Some things are better left unsaid. But so many unsaid things can become a burden."
Ibid., Ch. 8

3 Asking questions in therapy would be so helpful if anyone ever answered them accurately. But no one ever does. Ibid., Ch. 12

## 857. Lucille Ball
(1911– )

1 Luck? I don't know anything about luck. I've never banked on it, and I'm afraid of people who do. Luck to me is something else: hard work—and realizing what is opportunity and what isn't.
Quoted in *The Real Story of Lucille Ball*, by Eleanor Harris, Ch. 1   *1954*

2 I think knowing what you can *not* do is more important than knowing what you can do. In fact, that's good taste. Ibid., Ch. 7

## 858. Elizabeth Bishop
(1911– )

1 It is like what we imagine knowledge to be:
dark, salt, clear, moving, utterly free,
drawn from the cold hard mouth
of the world, derived from the rocky breast
forever, flowing and drawn, and since
our knowledge is historical, flowing, and flow.
"At the Fishhouses," *A Cold Spring*
*1955*

2 The Seven Wonders of the World are tired
and a touch familiar, but the other scenes,
innumerable, though equally sad and still, are
foreign.
Ibid., "Over 2000 Illustrations and a Complete Concordance"

3 Icebergs behoove the soul
  (Both being self-made from elements least
  visible)
  to see themselves: fleshed, fair, erected indivisible.
                    "The Imaginary Iceberg," *North
                          and South*    1955

4 Time is an *Etoile*; the hours diverge
  so much that days are journeys round the
  suburbs,
  circles surrounding stars, overlapping circles.
                    Ibid., "Paris, 7 A.M."

5 We stand as still as stones to watch
  the leaves and ripples
  while light and nervous water hold
  their interview.
                    Ibid., "Quai d'Orleans"

6 Brazilians are very quick, both emotionally and
  physically. Like the heroes of Homer, men can
  show their emotions without disgrace.
                    *Brazil*, Ch. 1    1962

7 The masses of poor people in the big cities, and
  the poor and not-so-poor of the "backlands,"
  love their children and kill them with kindness
  by the thousands. The wrong foods, spoiled
  foods, warm medicines, sleeping syrups—all
  exact a terrible toll. . . .    Ibid.

8 Democracy in the contemporary world demands, among other things, an educated and
  informed people. Up until now, Brazil has not
  had one. Illiteracy, slow communication, and
  a consequent lack of awareness among the
  people have made it possible for determined
  groups of men to control the affairs of the
  country without the general consent—even the
  knowledge—of the Brazilian people as a whole.
                    Ibid., Ch. 9

## 859. Hortense Calisher

(1911–    )

1 A happy childhood can't be cured. Mine'll hang
  around my neck like a rainbow, that's all, instead of a noose.    *Queenie*, Pt. I    1971

2 Every sixteen-year-old is a pornographer, Miss
  Piranesi. We had to know what was open to us.
                    Ibid.

3 On dirt—as Mrs. O. bitchily points out—there
  are still divisions among us between the ones
  who wash under their armpits and in all the
  private places presumably, no matter how
  fiercely street-stained their feet are—"and the
  ones who stink all through for the sake of
  whatever revolution is for today." Like any
  stool pigeon, she's half right.    Ibid.

4 But now, even to be anything anti-anti, you
  still have to do it with the body; anything
  purely mental is insincere. And I agree, oh, I
  agree—but why can I only do it mentally?
                    Ibid.

5 . . . the circulation of money is different from
  the circulation of the blood. Some eras obscure
  that; now it was nakedly appearing. I began to
  understand why the banker had jumped. A
  circulatory failure.    *Herself*, Pt. I    1972

6 An *oeuvre* is a body of work which, like a true
  body, interacts with itself, and with its own
  growth. We here in America are not allowed
  the sweet sense of growing them while in life;
  even after death, the obituary quickly picks
  over the works for "what will last." Yet if a
  writer's work has a shape to it—and most have
  a repetition like a heartbeat—the *oeuvre* will
  begin to construct him.    Ibid., Pt. II

7 She [Colette] is no more essentially feminine
  as a writer than any man is essentially masculine as a writer—certain notable attempts at
  the latter notwithstanding. She uses the psychological and concrete dossier in her possession
  as a woman, not only without embarrassment
  but with the most natural sense of its value,
  and without any confusion as to whether the
  sexual balance of her sensitivity need affect the
  virility of her expression when she wants virility
  there. Reading her, one is reminded that art—
  whether managed as a small report on a wide
  canvas, or vice versa—is a narrow thing in
  more senses than one, and that the woman
  writer, like any other, does her best to accept
  her part in the human condition, and go on
  from there.    Ibid.

8 Every art is a church without communicants,
  presided over by a parish of the respectable.
  An artist is born kneeling; he fights to stand.
  A critic, by nature of the judgment seat, is
  born sitting.    Ibid., Pt. IV

9 When anything gets freed, a zest goes round
  the world. What is most evident is that the old
  dictionary distinction between "license" and
  "freedom" doesn't do any more. As the Jew
  had come to know—and the blacks and the
  queers are now showing us, inside literature
  and out—"Freedom" is what you are given—
  and its iron hand often remains on your
  shoulder. "License" is what you *take*.    Ibid.

10 When you come to the end of the past—no
   more peroration. Tolerate life—a poem which
   annoys when it falls into grandeur. The past
   will come round again.    Ibid., Pt. V

## 860. Leah Goldberg
### (1911–1970)

1 There is a law of life in her hands milking,
For quiet seamen hold a rope like her.
> "Of Bloom," Pt. II, St. 2
> *Poems from the Hebrew,*
> Robert Mezey, ed.    *1973p*

2 Land of low clouds, I belong to you.
I carry in my heart your every drop of rain.
> Ibid., "Song of the Strange Woman,"
> Pt. III, St. 1

## 861. Mahalia Jackson
### (1911–1972)

1 It's easy to be independent when you've got
money. But to be independent when you
haven't got a thing—that's the Lord's test.
> *Movin' On Up,* with Evan McLoud
> Wylie, Ch. 1    *1966*

2 Gospel music in those days of the early 1930s
was really taking wing. It was the kind of music
colored people had left behind them down
south and they liked it because it was just like
a letter from home.    Ibid., Ch. 5

3 Blues are the songs of despair, but gospel songs
are the songs of hope.    Ibid., Ch. 6

4 Someday the sun is going to shine down on me
in some faraway place.
> Quoted in "Unforgettable Mahalia
> Jackson" by Mildred Falls, *Reader's
> Digest*    March, *1973p*

5 The grass is still green. The lawns are as neat
as ever. The same birds are still in the trees.
I guess it didn't occur to them to leave just
because we moved in.    Ibid.

## 862. Ruth McKenney
### (1911– )

1 If modern civilization had any meaning it was
displayed in the fight against Fascism.
> Letter to George Seldes, *The Great
> Quotations*, George Seldes, ed.
> *1960*

2 Man has no nobler function than to defend
the truth.    Ibid.

## 863. Josephine Miles
### (1911– )

1 All our footsteps, set to make
Metric advance,
Lapse into arcs in deference
To circumstance.
> "On Inhabiting an Orange," St. 2,
> *Poems, 1930–1960*    *1960*

2 This weight of knowledge dark on the brain is
never
To be burnt out like fever,

But slowly, with speech to tell the way and
ease it,
Will sink into the blood, and warm, and slowly
Move in the veins, and murmur, and come at
length
To the tongue's tip and the finger's tip most
lowly
And will belong to the body wholly.
> Ibid., "Physiologus," Sts. 2–3

3 Where is the world? not about.
The world is in the heart
And the heart is clogged in the sea lanes out of
port.
> Ibid., "Merchant Marine," St. 1

4 I chewed on a straw hoping it would get
sweeter.
It got drier and drier
And gradually caught on fire.
> Ibid., "Loser," St. 2

5 How conduct in its pride
Maintains a place and sits
At the head of the table at the head of the hall
At the head of the hosts and guests.
> Ibid., "Conduct," St. 1

6 My pride should affect your escape,
It carries every key.
Its own trusty, and a good chiseling trusty,
It can at its own price set everybody free.
> Ibid., "Pride," St. 1

7 Little things make Germany a lovely place. . . .
> "Germany," *House and Home*    *1961*

8 Accustomed as we are to change, or unaccustomed, we think of a change of heart, of
clothes, of life, with some uncertainty. We put
off the old, put on the new, yet say that the
more it changes the more it remains the same.
Every age is an age of transition.
> *Poetry and Change*, Introduction
> *1974*

9 True, translation may use the value terms of
its own tongue in its own time; but it cannot
force these on a truly alien text.
> Ibid., Ch. 12

## 864. Anna Russell

(1911–　　)

1 The reason that there are so few women comics is that so few women can bear being laughed at. Quoted in the *Sunday Times* (London) *August 25, 1957*

## 865. Rosalind Russell

(1911–1976)

1 . . . taste. You cannot buy such a rare and wonderful thing. You can't send away for it in a catalogue. And I'm afraid it's becoming obsolete.
Quoted in "Rosalind Russell: Screen's Career Career Girl," *Los Angeles Times* *March 31, 1974*

2 The sex symbol always remains, but the sophisticated woman has become old hat. Ibid.

3 Sex for sex's sake on the screen seems childish to me, but it's violence that really bothers me. I think it's degrading. It breeds something cancerous in our young people. We have a great responsibility to the future in what we're communicating. Ibid.

## 866. Viola Spolin

(1911?–　　)

1 We learn through experience and experiencing, and no one teaches anyone anything. This is as true for the infant moving from kicking to crawling to walking as it is for the scientist with his equations. If the environment permits it, anyone can learn whatever he chooses to learn; and if the individual permits it, the environment will teach him everything it has to teach. *Improvisation for the Theater*, Ch. 1 *1963*

2 In a culture where approval/disapproval has become the predominant regulator of effort and position, and often the substitute for love, our personal freedoms are dissipated. Ibid.

3 It stands to reason that if we direct all our efforts towards reaching a goal, we stand in grave danger of losing everything on which we have based our daily activities. For when a goal is superimposed on an activity instead of evolving out of it, we often feel cheated when we reach it. Ibid.

4 The audience is the most revered member of the theater. Without an audience there is no theater. . . . They are our guests, our evaluators, and the last spoke in the wheel which can then begin to roll. They make the performance meaningful. Ibid.

5 It is the avant-garde teachers who . . . have come to realize that body release, not body control, is what is needed for natural grace to emerge, as opposed to artificial movement. Ibid., Ch. 5

6 There are few places outside of his own play where a child can contribute to the world in which he finds himself. His world: dominated by adults who tell him what to do and when to do it—benevolent tyrants who dispense gifts to their "good" subjects and punishment to their "bad" ones, who are amused at the "cleverness" of children and annoyed by their "stupidities." Ibid., Ch. 13

7 Through spontaneity we are reformed into ourselves. Freed from handed-down frames of reference, spontaneity becomes the moment of personal freedom when we are faced with a reality, explore it, and act accordingly. It is the time of discovery, of experiencing, of creative expression.
Quoted in "Spolin Game Plan for Improvisational Theater" by Barry Hyams, *Los Angeles Times* *May 26, 1974*

8 First teach a person to develop to the point of his limitations and then—pfft!—break the limitation. Ibid.

9 One must be chary of words because they turn into cages. Ibid.

10 The physical is the known; through it we may find our way to the unknown, the intuitive, and perhaps beyond that to man's spirit itself. Ibid.

## 867. Madeleine Bingham

(1912–　　)

1 In every country the organization of society is like a section of a rock face, with new layers and old layers built one upon the other. The decay of old ways of behaving and old laws does not take place within a few years; it is a gradual process of erosion.
*Scotland Under Mary Stuart*, Ch. 2 *1971*

2 Once the fervour has gone out of it, a revolution can turn out to be dull work for the ordinary people. Ibid., Ch. 7

3 A country which is engaged in constant war, both internal and external, does not provide good ground in which the arts may flourish.
Ibid., Ch. 12

\* \* \*

4 Too many cooks may spoil the broth, but it only takes one to burn it.
*The Bad Cook's Guide*

5 There may be as many good fish in the sea as ever came out of it, but cooking them is even more difficult than catching them.    Ibid.

## 868. Julia Child
(1912–    )

1 Sometimes . . . it takes me an entire day to write a recipe, to communicate it correctly. It's really like writing a little short story. . . .
Quoted in "The Making of a Masterpiece" by Patricia Simon,
*McCall's*    October, 1970

2 Learn how to cook! That's the way to save money. You don't save it buying hamburger helpers, and prepared foods; you save it buying fresh foods in season or in large supply, when they are cheapest and usually best, and you prepare them from scratch at home. Why pay for someone else's work, when if you know how to do it, you can save all that money for yourself?    *Julia Child's Kitchen,*
Introduction    1975

## 869. Lucille Fletcher
(1912–    )

1 Such amazing things happened to the female sex on an ocean cruise. The sea air acted like an aphrodisiac. Or maybe it was the motion. Or the carnival atmosphere. Whatever it was, and he had never seen it otherwise, the ladies, married or single, young or old, simply went to pieces aboard the *S.S. Columbia*. They toppled like tenpins—into bed.
*The Girl in Cabin B54*, Ch. 2    1968

2 "The brain, of course, is still an unknown country in many respects—like outer space. And as a psychologist, I myself can believe that certain people, extraordinarily sensitive people, may possess special mental equipment which can tune in, as it were, certain waves, vibrations, even imagery, which other people cannot sense at all."    Ibid., Ch. 8

## 870. Virginia Graham
(1912–    )

1 It will be the firm intention of your hosts to take you, as soon as possible, *away* from their homes. Remember, they do not know what on earth to do with you and have been arguing about it for weeks, so do not be difficult and announce that all you want to do is sit still and look at the view. They are irrevocably determined you should be entertained, and it is a matter of little importance whether you wish to be or whether you don't.
*Say Please*, Ch. 1    1949

2 As hunting takes place in the open air and is ever so English and ever so traditional, the word bitch can be frequently employed without offence, and indeed is a rare pleasure for a lady to be able to look fearlessly into the eyes of another lady, even though she be on four legs, and say loudly and clearly, "Bitch!"
Ibid., Ch. 3

3 Good shot, bad luck and hell are the five basic words to be used in a game of tennis, though these, of course, can be slightly amplified.
Ibid., Ch. 8

4 Words, like fashions, disappear and recur throughout English history, and one generation's phraseology, while it may seem abominably second-rate to the next, becomes first-rate to the third. . . .    Ibid., Ch. 14

5 In society it is etiquette for ladies to have the best chairs and get handed things. In the home the reverse is the case. That is why ladies are more sociable than gentlemen.    Ibid.

6 Be blind. Be stupid. Be British. Be careful.
Ibid., Ch. 25

## 871. Lady Bird Johnson
(1912–    )

1 Lyndon [Johnson] acts like there was never going to be a tomorrow.
Quoted in *The New York Times Magazine*    November 29, 1964

2 It all began so beautifully. After a drizzle in the morning, the sun came out bright and clear. We were driving into Dallas. In the lead car were President and Mrs. Kennedy. . . .
*A White House Diary* (November 22, 1963)    1970

3 As I record this several days later, I must say that being with President Truman those days has been one of the biggest pluses of this period of my life. It has been an insight into history for me, a joy to see a man who has lived through so much public rancor and condemnation and has emerged philosophic, salty, completely unembittered, a happy man—and vindicated by history on most of his major decisions.
Ibid. (March 12, 1964)

4 It's odd that you can get so anesthetized by your own pain or your own problem that you don't quite fully share the hell of someone close to you.     Ibid. (February 8, 1965)

5 This was one of those terrific, pummeling White House days that can stretch and grind and use you—even I, who only live on the periphery. So what must it be like for Lyndon!
Ibid. (March 14, 1968)

## 872. Dena Justin
(1912-   )

1 The earth as Mother, the womb from which all living things are born and to which all return at death, was perhaps the earliest representation of the divine in protohistoric religions.
"From Mother Goddess to Dishwasher,"
*Natural History*    February, 1973

2 It is remarkable how many legends survive among preliterate cultures of an earlier matriarchal period and a violent uprising by men in which they usurped female authority.    Ibid.

3 Mythologically speaking, the ancients scooped our modern-day biologists by unknown thousands of years in their recognition of the female principle as the primal creative force. And they too buried the truth, restructuring the myths to accommodate male ideology.    Ibid.

4 Although the witch, incarnate or in surrogate mother disguise, remains a universal bogey, pejorative aspects of the wizard, her masculine counterpart, have vanished over the patriarchal centuries. The term *wizard* has acquired reverential status—wizard of finance, wizard of diplomacy, wizard of science.    Ibid.

## 873. Mary Lavin
(1912-   )

1 Her theme was happiness: what it was, what it was not; where we might find it, where not; and how, if found, it must be guarded. Never must we confound it with pleasure. Nor think sorrow its exact opposite.
"Happiness," *The New Yorker*
*December 14, 1968*

2 "Take my own father! You know what he said in his last moments? On his deathbed, he defied me to name a man who had enjoyed a better life. In spite of the dreadful pain, his face *radiated* happiness!" said Mother, nodding her head comfortably. "Happiness drives out pain, as fire burns out fire."    Ibid.

3 Our father, while he lived, had cast a magic over everything, for us as well as for her. He held his love up over us like an umbrella and kept off the troubles that afterward came down on us, pouring cats and dogs!    Ibid.

4 "Life is a vale of tears," they said. "You are privileged to find it out so young!" Ugh! After I staggered onto my feet and began to take hold of life once more, they fell back defeated. And the first day I gave a laugh—pouf, they were blown out like candles. They weren't living in a real world at all; they belonged to a ghostly world where life was easy: all one had to do was sit and weep. It takes effort to push back the stone from the mouth of the tomb.    Ibid.

5 . . . a new noise started in her head; the noise of a nameless panic that did not always roar, but never altogether died down.
"Via Violetta," *A Memory and Other Stories*    1972

## 874. Mary McCarthy
(1912-   )

1 The American, if he has a spark of national feeling, will be humiliated by the very prospect of a foreigner's visit to Congress—these, for the most part, illiterate hacks whose fancy vests are spotted with gravy, and whose speeches, hypocritical, unctuous, and slovenly, are spotted also with the gravy of political patronage, these persons are a reflection on the democratic process rather than of it; they expose it in its underwear.    "America the Beautiful,"
*Commentary*    September, 1947

2 . . . freedom to criticize is held to compensate for the freedom to err—this is the American system. . . . One is assured, gently, that one has the freedom to criticize, as though this freedom, *in itself*, as it attaches to a single individual, counterbalanced the unjust law on the books. This sacred right of criticism is always invoked whenever abuses are mentioned, just as the free circulation of ideas and works of art is offered as evidence of a basic cultural freedom.    "No News, or What Killed the Dog," *The Reporter*    July, 1952

3 Liberty, as it is conceived by current opinion, has nothing inherent about it; it is a sort of gift or trust bestowed on the individual by the state pending *good behavior.*
Speech, "The Contagion of Ideas"
*Summer, 1952*

4 . . . Elinor was always firmly convinced of other people's hypocrisy since she could not believe that they noticed less than she did.
*The Group*, Ch. 1     1954

5 "You mustn't force sex to do the work of love or love to do the work of sex."     Ibid., Ch. 2

6 Despite the fact that she had had no sexual experience, she had a very clear idea of the male member, and she could not help forming a picture of Put's as pale and lifeless, in the coffin of his trousers, a veritable *nature morte.*
Ibid., Ch. 6

7 "Medicine seems to be all cycles," continued Mrs. Hartshorn. "That's the bone I pick with Sloan. Like what's his name's new theory of history. First we nursed our babies; then science told us not to. Now it tells us we were right in the first place. Or were we wrong then but would be right now? Reminds me of relativity, if I understand Mr. Einstein."     Ibid., Ch. 10

8 She had tried to bind him with possessions, but he slipped away like Houdini.
Ibid., Ch. 13

9 Sometimes she felt that he was postponing being a success till he could wear out her patience; as soon as she gave up and left him, his name would mock her in lights.     Ibid.

10 Labor is work that leaves no trace behind it when it is finished, or if it does, as in the case of the tilled field, this product of human activity requires still more labor, incessant, tireless labor, to maintain its identity as a "work" of man.     "The *Vita Activa*," *The New Yorker*     *October 18, 1958*

11 There are no new truths, but only truths that have not been recognized by those who have perceived them without noticing.     Ibid.

12 . . . bureaucracy, the rule of no one, has become the modern form of despotism.     Ibid.

13 When an American heiress wants to buy a man, she at once crosses the Atlantic.
*On the Contrary*     1961

14 . . . Americans do not dissemble what they are up to. They do not seem to feel the need, except through verbiage; *e.g.*, napalm has become "Incinderjell," which makes it sound like Jell-O. And defoliants are referred to as weed-killers—something you use in your driveway. The resort to euphemism denotes, no doubt, a guilty conscience or—the same thing nowadays —a twinge in the public-relations nerve.
"The Home Program," *Vietnam*
*1967*

15 In politics, it seems, retreat is honorable if dictated by military considerations and shameful if even *suggested* for ethical reasons. . . .
Ibid., "Solutions"

16 One is against Communism because one *knows* that Communists massacre whoever is against them.     *Hanoi*, Foreword     1968

17 Anyway, it has to be acknowledged that in capitalist society, with its herds of hippies, originality has become a sort of fringe benefit, a *mere* convention, accepted obsolescence, the Beatnik model being turned in for the Hippie model, as though strangely obedient to capitalist laws of marketing.     Ibid., "Language"

18 In the Stalinist days, we used to detest a vocabulary that had to be read in terms of antonyms—"volunteers," denoting conscripts, "democracy," tyranny, and so on. Insensibly, in Vietnam, starting with the little word "advisors," we have adopted this slippery Aesopian language ourselves. . . .     Ibid.

19 He had never outgrown the feeling that a quest for information was a series of maneuvers in a game of espionage.
"Winter Visitors," *Birds of America*
*1965*

20 Maybe any action becomes cowardly once you stop to reason about it. Conscience doth make cowards of us all, eh, *mamma mia*? If you start an argument with yourself, that makes two people at least, and when you have two people, one of them starts appeasing the other.
Ibid., "Epistle from Mother Carey's Chicken"

21 Being abroad makes you conscious of the whole imitative side of human behavior. The ape in man.     Ibid.

## 875. Pat Nixon

(1912–     )

1 I have sacrificed everything in my life that I consider precious in order to advance the political career of my husband.
Quoted in *Women at Work*
by Betty Medsger     1975

## 876. Ann Petry
(1912–    )

1 It took me quite a while to realize that there were fashions in literary criticism and that they shifted and changed much like the fashions in women's hats.
*"The Novel as Social Criticism," The Writer's Book,* Helen Hull, ed. *1950*

2 It seems to me that all truly great art is propaganda. . . .     Ibid.

3 Time, that enemy of labels. . . .     Ibid.

## 877. May Sarton
(1912–    )

1 The college was not founded to give society what it wants. Quite the contrary.
*The Small Room*     *1961*

2 Excellence cost a great deal.     Ibid.

3 "There was such a thing as women's work and it consisted chiefly, Hilary sometimes thought, in being able to stand constant interruption and keep your temper. . . ."
*Mrs. Stevens Hears the Mermaids Singing*     *1965*

4 It's hard to be growing up in this climate where sex at its most crude and cold is O.K. but feeling is somehow indecent.     Ibid.

5 The Lord is not my shepherd. I shall want.     Ibid.

6 We are all monsters, if it comes to that, we women who have chosen to be something more and something less than women.     Ibid.

7 Women's work is always toward wholeness.     Ibid.

8 Women have moved and shaken me, but I have been nourished by men.     Ibid.

9 We have to expiate for this cursed talent someone handed out to us, by mistake, in the black mystery of genetics.     Ibid.

10 True feeling justifies, whatever it may cost.     Ibid.

11 My faults too have been those of excess; I too have made emotional demands, without being aware of what I was asking; I too have imagined that I was giving when I was battering at someone for attention.
*Journal of a Solitude*     *1973*

12 I would predicate that in all great works of genius masculine and feminine elements in the personality find expression, whether this androgynous nature is played out sexually or not.     Ibid.

13 The strange effect of all these "lovers" is to make me feel not richer, but impoverished and mean.     Ibid.

## 878. Barbara Tuchman
(1912–    )

1 Publicly his [the Kaiser's] performance was perfect; privately he could not resist the opportunity for fresh scheming.
*The Guns of August,* Ch. 1     *1962*

2 The Russian colossus exercised a spell upon Europe. On the chessboard of military planning, Russia's size and weight of numbers represented the largest piece . . . the Russian "steam roller." . . . Although the defects of the Russian Army were notorious, although the Russian winter, not the Russian Army, had turned Napoleon back from Moscow, . . . a myth of its invincibility prevailed.     Ibid., Ch. 5

3 Alone in Europe Britain had no conscription. In war she would be dependent on voluntary enlistment. . . . [Therefore] it was a prime necessity for Britain to enter war with a united government.     Ibid.. Ch. 7

4 Honor wears different coats to different eyes. . . .     Ibid.

5 The will to defend the country outran the means. . . . The army marched in a chaos of improvisation. It marched also, or was borne along, on a crest of enthusiasm, haloed by a mist of illusion.     Ibid., Ch. 11

6 . . . out of the excited fancy produced by the fears and exhaustion and panic and violence of a great battle a legend grew. . . .     Ibid.

7 For one August in its history Paris was French —and silent.     Ibid., Ch. 20

8 So close had the Germans come to victory, so near the French to disaster, so great, in the preceding days, had been the astonished dismay of the world as it watched the relentless advance of the Germans and the retreat of the Allies on Paris, that the battle that turned the tide came to be known as the Miracle of the Marne.     Ibid., Afterword

9 Men could not sustain a war of such magnitude and pain without hope—the hope that its very enormity would ensure that it could never

happen again and the hope that when somehow it had been fought through to a resolution, the foundations of a better-ordered world would have been laid. . . . When every autumn people said it could not last through the winter, and when every spring there was still no end in sight, only the hope that out of it all some good would accrue to mankind kept men and nations fighting. When at last it was over, the war had many diverse results and one dominant one transcending all others: disillusion.
Ibid.

10 We're being made to look like Lolitas and lion tamers. Quoted in *The Beautiful People* by Marilyn Bender 1968

11 The core of the military profession is discipline and the essence of discipline is obedience. Since this does not come naturally to men of independent and rational mind, they must train themselves in the habit of obedience on which lives and the fortunes of battle may someday depend. Reasonable orders are easy enough to obey; it is capricious, bureaucratic or plain idiotic demands that form the habit of discipline. *Stilwell and the American Experience in China: 1911–1945*, Pt. I, Ch. 1 1970

12 Through all changing circumstances and conditions in the coming period this remained the purpose of American aid and it retained the original flaw: the American purpose was not the Chinese purpose. Ibid., Pt. II, Ch. 9

13 China was a problem from which there was no American solution. The American effort to sustain the status quo could not supply an outworn government with strength and stability or popular support. It could not hold up a husk nor long delay the cyclical passage of the mandate of heaven. In the end China went her own way as if the Americans had never come.
Ibid., Ch. 20

14 . . . the deep-seated American distrust that still prevailed of diplomacy and diplomats. . . . Diplomacy means all the wicked devices of the Old World, spheres of influence, balances of power, secret treaties, triple alliances, and, during the interwar period, appeasement of Fascism. "If Mao Had Come to Washington in 1945," *Foreign Affairs* October, 1972

15 Friendship of a kind that cannot easily be reversed tomorrow must have its roots in common interests and shared beliefs, and even between nations, in some personal feeling.
"Friendship with Foreign Devils," *Harper's* December, 1972

16 In a country where misery and want were the foundation of the social structure, famine was periodic, death from starvation common, disease pervasive, thievery normal, and graft and corruption taken for granted, the elimination of these conditions in Communist China is so striking that negative aspects of the new rule fade in relative importance.
*Notes from China*, Ch. 1 1972

17 The farmer is the eternal China.
Ibid., Ch. 3

## 879. Charleszetta Waddles
(1912– )

1 You can't give people pride, but you can provide the kind of understanding that makes people look to their inner strengths and find their own sense of pride.
Quoted in "Mother Waddles: Black Angel of the Poor" by Lee Edson, *Reader's Digest* October, 1972

2 God knows no distance. Ibid.

## 880. Eleanor Clark
(1913– )

1 ". . . we've achieved what no nation ever has before in the world. *Saturation* ugliness! and all that goes with it, in the way of mental crack-up. Now we can sleep a while, and dream our pastures new."
*Baldur's Gate*, Pt. II, Ch. 2 1955

2 "He was the kind of man, if a mule kicked somebody down the street, he'd work till he gut it on his conscience."
Ibid., Pt. III, Ch. 2

3 "You can hang the wash without a line."
Ibid., Ch. 3

4 "We Occidentals have a congenital, it may even be a fatal, need for good manners, or you might say ceremony, in our approach to meaning, I suppose to make up for our crudeness in living." Ibid.

## 881. Nathalia Crane
(1913– )

* * *

1 But my heart is all aflutter like the washing on the line.
"The Flathouse Roof," St. 1

2 Crumpling a pyramid, humbling a rose,
The dust has its reasons wherever it goes.
"The Dust"

3 Every gaudy color
Is a bit of truth.
"The Vestal," St. 5

4 Great is the rose
That challenges the crypt,
And quotes millenniums
Against the grave.
"Song from Tadmor"

5 He showed me like a master
That one rose makes a gown;
That looking up to Heaven
Is merely looking down.
"My Husbands"

6 He wooed the daunted odalisques,
He kissed each downcast nude;
He whispered that an angel's robe
Is mostly attitude.
"The First Reformer"

7 In the darkness, who would answer for the
color of a rose,
Or the vestments of the May moth and the pilgrimage it goes?
"The Blind Girl," St. 1

8 The little *and*, the tiny *if*,
The ardent *ahs* and *ohs*,
They haunt the lane of poesy,
The boulevards of prose.
"Alliances"

9 There is a glory
In a great mistake.
"Imperfection"

10 You cannot choose your battlefield,
The gods do that for you,
But you can plant a standard
Where a standard never flew.
"The Colors"

## 882. Elizabeth Janeway

(1913–    )

1 Such simplicity cannot be taught. But it can be
denied and lost.    *The Writer's Book*, Ch. 1,
Helen Hull, ed.    *1950*

2 For there is always this to be said for the literary profession—like life itself, it provides its
own revenges and antidotes.    Ibid., Ch. 24

3 . . . it is through the ghost [writer] that the
great gift of knowledge which the inarticulate
have for the world can be made available.
Ibid., Ch. 29

4 In this nadir of poetic repute, when the only
verse that most people read from one year's
end to the next is what appears on greeting
cards, it is well for us to stop and consider our
poets. . . . Poets are the leaven in the lump of
civilization.    Ibid., Ch. 30

5 As long as mixed grills and combination salads
are popular, anthologies will undoubtedly continue in favor.    Ibid., Ch. 32

6 After all, every circle has a point for a center.
The size of the circle is determined by the
energy with which it is expanded, not by the
magnificence of what it may or may not take
off from.    Ibid., Ch. 40

7 After the city, where we had always lived,
those country years were startling. . . . The surprise of animals . . . in and out, cats and dogs
and a milk goat and chickens and guinea
hens, all taken for granted, as if man was intended to live on terms of friendly intercourse
with the rest of creation instead of huddling in
isolation on the fourteenth floor of an apartment house in a city where animals occurred
behind bars in the zoo.
"Steven Benedict," *Accident*    1964

8 The Goddamn human race deserves itself, and
as far as I'm concerned it can have it.
Ibid., "Charles Benedict"

9 I admire people who are suited to the contemplative life, but I am not one of them. They
can sit inside themselves like honey in a jar
and just be. It's wonderful to have someone
like that around, you always feel you can count
on them. You can go away and come back,
you can change your mind and your hairdo and
your politics, and when you get through doing
all these upsetting things, you look around and
there they are, just the way they were, just
being.    Ibid., "Elizabeth Jowett"

10 American women are not the only people in
the world who manage to lose track of themselves, but we do seem to mislay the past in
a singularly absent-minded fashion.
"Reflections on the History of Women,"
*Women: Their Changing Roles*
*1973*

11 Like their personal lives, women's history is
fragmented, interrupted; a shadow history of
human beings whose existence has been shaped
by the efforts and the demands of others.
Ibid.

12 If every nation gets the government it deserves,
every generation writes the history which corresponds with its view of the world.    Ibid.

13 Perhaps it is just a hangover from the past, but even those writers who declare that the importance of sex is its sheer pleasure do so with an evangelical zeal that is directive rather than permissive.
*Between Myth and Morning*    1974

14 . . . reaction isn't action—that is, it isn't truly creative.      *Ibid.*

15 We have to see, I think, that questioning the value of old rules is different from simply breaking them.      *Ibid.*

16 When dealing with adultery becomes a matter of private choice instead of public rules, middle-class morality, that bastion of social stability, has ceased to function.   *Ibid.*

17 Confronted with the possibility of public catastrophe, every tyrant will opt to let permissiveness rule in private. Besides, will not such permissiveness turn the attention of the people away from public problems to private pleasures? One can image a modern Machiavelli suggesting to his prince that sex would make a very good opiate for the people.   *Ibid.*

18 Young or old, skepticism about conventional wisdom can give way all too early to a relapse into credulity before the allurements of new certainties.      *Ibid.*

19 With the old rules for masculine superiority fading in the public sphere, how can men face the feminine superiority they have posited in the private world?      *Ibid.*

20 Poor engineer, hoist with his own petard!
     *Ibid.*

21 Love between women is seen as a paradigm of love between equals, and that is perhaps its greatest attraction.      *Ibid.*

22 Sexual freedom? Nonsense! These are directions for the greedy use of freedom in old, manipulative ways in order to gain the traditional feminine "catch-a-man" goal.   *Ibid.*

23 Sex cannot be contained within a definition of physical pleasure, it cannot be understood as merely itself for it has stood for too long as a symbol of profound connection between human beings.      *Ibid.*

\* \* \*

24 . . . it is almost shockingly delightful to read a book which could have been written by absolutely no one else in the world than the great and important figure whose name is signed to it. . . .      *"This I Remember"*

25 Unable to dedicate herself to her husband—why, we shall never be sure—she ended by dedicating herself to his work. . . . On the basis of an unusual if not unsatisfactory marriage was built an edifice of cooperation, of mutual aid and respect which was of immeasurable influence.      *Ibid.*

## 883. Margo Jones
(1913–1955)

1 Everything in life is theatre.
*Quoted in The New York Times*
*July 26, 1955p*

2 The theatre has given me a chance not only to live my own life but a million others. In every play there is a chance for one great moment, experience or understanding.      *Ibid.*

3 With imagination and a tremendous willingness for hard work, it is possible to create a great theatre, a vigorous and vital theatre, in the second half of the twentieth century.
*"Theatre '50: A Dream Come True,"*
*Ten Talents in the American Theatre,*
David H. Stevens, ed.    *1957p*

4 There are two kinds of theatre, good and bad. Much as I should like to see theatre in America, I would rather have no theatre than bad theatre. What we must strive for is perfection and come as close to it as is humanly possible.
     *Ibid.*

5 We have seen too much defeatism, too much pessimism, too much of a negative approach. The answer is simple: if you want something very badly, you can achieve it. It may take patience, very hard work, a real struggle, and a long time; but it can be done. That much faith is a prerequisite of any undertaking, artistic or otherwise.      *Ibid.*

## 884. Dorothy Kilgallen
(1913–1965)

1 I am off on a race around the world—a race against time and two men. I know I can beat time. I hope I can beat the men.
*Girl Around the World*    1936

2 The chief product of Baghdad is dates . . . and sheiks.      *Ibid.*

3 The world is grand, awfully big and astonishingly beautiful, frequently thrilling. But I love New York.      *Ibid.*

## 885. Vivien Leigh

(1913–1967)

1 In Britain, an attractive woman is somehow
suspect. If there is talent as well it is overshadowed. Beauty and brains just can't be
entertained; someone has been too extravagant.
          Quoted by Robert Ottaway in
          *Light of a Star* by Gwen Robyns
          *1968p*

2 I swing between happiness and misery and I
cry easily. I'm a mixture of my mother's determination and my father's optimism. I'm part
prude and part non-conformist and I must say
what I think and I don't dissemble. I'm a mixture of French, Irish and Yorkshire, and perhaps that's what it all is.           Ibid.

## 886. Tillie Olsen

(1913– )

1 And when is there time to remember, to sift,
to weigh, to estimate, to total?
          "I Stand Here Ironing" (1954),
          *Tell Me a Riddle*    1960

2 Now suddenly she was Somebody, and as imprisoned in her difference as she had been in
her anonymity.           Ibid.

3 My wisdom came too late.           Ibid.

4 It is destroying, dissolving him utterly, this
helpless warmth against him, this feel of a
child. . . .
          Ibid., "Hey Sailor, What Ship?"
          (1955)

5 That's what I want to be when I grow up, just
a peaceful wreck holding hands with other
peaceful wrecks. . . .           Ibid.

6 There are worse words than cuss words, there
are words that hurt.           Ibid.

7 In the beginning there had been youth and the
joy of raising hell. . . . And later there were
memories to forget, dreams to be stifled, hopes
to be murdered.           Ibid.

8 . . . the Law and the Wall: only so far shall
you go and no further, uptown forbidden, not
your language, not your people, not your
country.           Ibid.

9 "Not everybody feel religion the same way.
Some it's in their mouth, but some it's like a
hope in their blood, their bones."
          Ibid., "O Yes" (1956)

10 It is a long baptism into the seas of humankind, my daughter. Better immersion than to
live untouched. . . .           Ibid.

11 For forty-seven years they had been married.
How deep back the stubborn, gnarled roots of
the quarrel reached, no one could say—but
only now, when tending to the needs of others
no longer shackled them together, the roots
swelled up visible, split the earth between them,
and the tearing shook even the children, long
since grown.
          Ibid., "Tell Me a Riddle," Ch. 1
          (1960)

12 He could not, could not turn away from this
desire: to have the troubling of responsibility,
the fretting with money, over and done with;
to be free, to *be* care*free* where success was
not measured by accumulation. . . .      Ibid.

13 The television is shadows. Mrs. Enlightened!
Mrs. Cultured! A world comes into your
house—and it is shadows. People you would
never meet in a million lifetimes. Wonders.
          Ibid.

14 Like the hide of a drum shall you be, beaten
in life, beaten in death.           Ibid.

15 "Vinegar he poured on me all his life; I am
well marinated; how can I be honey now?"
          Ibid.

16 Heritage. How have we come from the savages,
now no longer to be savages—this to teach.
To look back and learn what humanizes man
—this to teach. To smash all ghettos that divide us—not to go back, not to go back—this
to teach.           Ibid., Ch. 2

17 "Remember your advice, easy to keep your
head above water, empty things float. Float."
          Ibid., Ch. 3

18 ". . . life may be hated or wearied of, but never
despised."           Ibid., Ch. 4

19 Always roused by the writing, always denied.
. . . My work died.
          *Silences: When Writers Don't Write*
          *1965*

20 The mute inglorious Miltons: those whose waking hours are all struggle for existence; the
barely educated; the illiterate; women—their
silence the silence of centuries as to how life
was, is, for most of humanity.        Ibid.

21 . . . the circumstances for sustained creation
are almost impossible.           Ibid.

22 More than in any other human relationship, overwhelmingly more, motherhood means being instantly interruptible, responsive, responsible. . . .      Ibid.

23 It is distraction, not meditation, that becomes habitual; interruption, not continuity; spasmodic, not constant toil.      Ibid.

24 Time granted does not necessarily coincide with time that can be most fully used.      Ibid.

## 887. Rosa Parks
### (1913– )

1 My only concern was to get home after a hard day's work.*      Quoted in *Time*
*December 15, 1975*

## 888. Sylvia Porter
### (1913– )

1 We are into an "era of aspirations" in our economy. In this era, most of us will spend a shrinking share of our income on the traditional necessities of food, clothing, shelter, and transportation while we spend a steadily increasing share of our income for goods and services which reflect our hopes and wants.
*Sylvia Porter's Money Book*, Ch. 1
*1975*

2 The average family exists only on paper and its average budget is a fiction, invented by statisticians for the convenience of statisticians. . . . There is no sense in attempting to fit into a ready-to-wear financial pattern which ignores your own personal wants and desires.
Ibid.

3 Money never remains just coins and pieces of paper. It is constantly changing into the comforts of daily life. Money can be translated into the beauty of living, a support in misfortune, an education, or future security. It also can be translated into a source of bitterness.
Ibid.

4 For millions, the retirement dream is in reality an economic nightmare. For millions, growing old today means growing poor, being sick, living in substandard housing, and having to scrimp merely to subsist. And this is the prospect not only for the one out of every ten

---

* Referring to her refusal to give up her seat on a bus in Montgomery, Alabama, in 1955 to a white who was standing. From her act of defiance grew the Montgomery bus boycott and the leadership of Martin Luther King, Jr.

Americans now over sixty-five . . . but also for the sixty-five million who will reach retirement age within the next thirty-three years.
Ibid., Ch. 19

## 889. Nancy Reeves
### (1913– )

1 Today the hemisphere of the public has been assigned to the male and the hemisphere of the private to the female. Each sex has become a symbol for its territory. The conflict between them can then be seen as a reflection of the longing of each to be part of the other's sphere, to link the public with the private in our schizoid world, to embrace the whole of life.
*Womankind Beyond the Stereotypes*
*1971*

## 890. Muriel Rukeyser
### (1913– )

1 Women and poets see the truth arrive,
Then it is acted out,
The lives are lost, and all the newsboys shout.
"Letter to the Front,"
*Beast in View*    1944

2 Women in drudgery knew
They must be one of four:
Whores, artists, saints, and wives.
Ibid., "Wreath of Women"

3 However confused the scene of our life appears,
however torn we may be who now do face that scene,
it can be faced, and we can go on to be whole.
*The Life of Poetry*    1949

4      . . . on second cry I woke
fully and gave to feed and fed on feeding.
"Night Feeding," St. 2,
*Selected Poems*    1951

5 The spies who wait for the spy at the deserted crossing,
a little dead since they are going to kill.
"Ann Burlak," St. 4, *Waterlily Fire: 1935–1962*    1962

6 Those women who stitch their lives to their machines
and daughters at the symmetry of looms.
Ibid.

7 Years when the enemy is in our state,
and liberty, safe in the people's hands,
is never safe and peace is never safe.
Ibid.

8    . . . the seeking marvelous look
Of those who lose and use and know their lives.
*Ibid.*, "Nine Poems for the
Unborn Child," II

9  The strength, the grossness, spirit and gall of choice.
*Ibid.*, VI, St. 1

10  You will enter the world which eats itself
Naming faith, reason, naming love, truth, fact.
*Ibid.*, VII, St. 1

11  I have forgotten what it was
that I have been trying to remember.
"Woman as Market,"
*The Speed of Darkness*   1968

12  my lifetime
listens to yours.
*Ibid.*, "Käthe Kollwitz," I, St. 1

13  the revolutionary look
that says    I am in the world
to change the world.
*Ibid.*, St. 2

14  A theme may seem to have been put aside,
but it keeps returning—
the same thing modulated,
somewhat changed in form.
*Ibid.*, II, St. 2

15  I believe
that bisexuality
is almost    a necessary factor
in artistic production. . . .
*Ibid.*, St. 6

16  What would happen if one woman told the truth about her life?
The world would split open
*Ibid.*, III, St. 4

17  No more masks! No more mythologies!
*Ibid.*, "The Poem as Mask," St. 3

18  Overtaken by silence

But this same silence is become speech
With the speed of darkness.
*Ibid.*, "The Speed of Darkness," II

19  The universe is made of stories,
not of atoms.
*Ibid.*, IX, St. 2

20  Whatever we stand against
We will stand feeding and seeding.
"Wherever," St. 3, *Breaking Open*
1973

21  Escape the birthplace; walk into the world
Refusing to be either slave or slaveholder.
*Ibid.*, "Secrets of American
Civilization," St. 3

22  The collective unconscience is the living history
brought to the present in consciousness.
Quoted in "Rare Battered She-Poet"
by Louise Bernikow, *Ms.*
*April, 1974*

## 891. Honor Tracy
### (1913–    )

1  He was a member of the eccentric race of fiscophobes, Englishmen who would do anything and live anywhere, no matter how bored and miserable they might be, rather than stay at home and pay English taxes.
*The Butterflies of the Province,*
Ch. 1    1970

2  "Early upbringing," David moaned. "One struggles against it in vain."    *Ibid.*, Ch. 5

## 892. Julia de Burgos
### (1914–1953)

1    You are the bloodless doll of social lies
And I the virile spark of human truth. . . .
"To Julia de Burgos," *The Nation*
*1972p*

2    You curl your hair and paint your face.
Not I:
I am curled by the wind, painted by the sun.
*Ibid.*

## 893. Agnes "Sis" Cunningham
### (1914–    )

1  We . . . were young radicals who felt that by singing ideas straightforwardly we could get more said in five minutes than in hours, or days, of talking.    "Songs of Hard Years," with
Madeline B. Rose, *Ms.*
*March, 1974*

\* \* \*

2  Oh, it's good to be living and working
when we know the land's our own
To know that we have got a right to
all the crops we've grown.
"When We Know the Land's Our Own"

## 894. Gypsy Rose Lee
### (1914–1970)

1 Mother, in a feminine way, was ruthless. She was, in her own words, a jungle mother, and she knew too well that in a jungle it doesn't pay to be nice. "God will protect us," she often said to June and me. "But to make sure," she would add, "carry a heavy club."
*Gypsy*, Ch. 1     *1957*

2 [He] often said I was the greatest no-talent star in the business.     Ibid.

## 895. Catherine Marshall
### (1914–   )

1 Often God has to shut a door in our face, so that He can subsequently open the door through which He wants us to go.
*A Man Called Peter*, Ch. 2     *1951*

2 . . . truth could never be wholly contained in words. All of us know it: At the same moment the mouth is speaking one thing, the heart is saying another. . . .     *Christy*, Prologue
*1967*

3 So once I shut down my privilege of disliking anyone I chose and holding myself aloof if I could manage it, greater understanding, growing compassion came to me. . . .
Ibid., Ch. 12

4 Usually passion wants to grab and to yank.
Ibid., Ch. 33

5 . . . in rejecting secrecy I had also rejected the road to cynicism.     Ibid.

6 . . . I learned that true forgiveness includes total acceptance. And out of acceptance wounds are healed and happiness is possible again.
Ibid.

## 896. Hazel Brannon Smith
### (1914–   )

1 I've always been too interested in what is happening in the present and what is going to happen to be much concerned about the past.
Quoted in "The 11-Year Siege of Mississippi's Lady Editor" by T. George Harris, *Look* *November 16, 1965*

2 I ain't no lady. I'm a newspaperwoman.
Ibid.

3 A crusading editor is one who goes out and looks for the wrongs of the world. I just try to take care of things as they come up. I try to make them a little better.     Ibid.

4 I can't think of but one thing that's worse than being called a nigger-lover. And that's a nigger-hater!     Ibid.

## 897. Barbara Ward
### (1914–   )

1 All archaic societies feel themselves bound to a "melancholy wheel" of endless recurrence. . . . No vision of reality as progressing forward to new possibilities, no sense of the future as better and fuller than the present, tempered the underlying fatalism of ancient civilization. It is only in the Jewish and Christian faith that a Messianic hope first breaks upon mankind.
*The Rich Nations and the Poor Nations*, Ch. 1     *1962*

2 It is very much easier for a rich man to invest and grow richer than for the poor man to begin investing at all. And this is also true of nations.     Ibid.

3 . . . there is no human failure greater than to launch a profoundly important endeavour and then leave it half done. This is what the West has done with its colonial system. It shook all the societies in the world loose from their old moorings. But it seems indifferent whether or not they reach safe harbour in the end.
Ibid., Ch. 2

4 To me, one of the most vivid proofs that there is a moral governance in the universe is the fact that when men or governments work intelligently and far-sightedly for the good of others, they achieve their own prosperity too.
Ibid., Ch. 6

5 It is only when people begin to shake loose from their preconceptions, from the ideas that have dominated them, that we begin to receive a sense of opening, a sense of vision. . . . That is the sort of time we live in now. We . . . live in an epoch in which the solid ground of our preconceived ideas shakes daily under our uncertain feet.
"Only One Earth," *Who Speaks for Earth?*, Maurice F. Strong, ed.
*1973*

6 . . . mankind must go beyond the limits of purely national government and begin to find out what the "post-national community" is like. . . . [But] it cannot, must not, mean a suppression of all variety and a civilization so standardized that we all end up hideously the same.     Ibid.

7 We can all cheat on morals. . . . But today the morals of respect and care and modesty come to us in a form that we cannot evade. We cannot cheat on DNA. We cannot get round photosynthesis. We cannot say I am not going to give a damn about phytoplankton. All these tiny mechanisms provide the preconditions of our planetary life. To say we do not care is to say in the most literal sense that "we choose death."  Ibid.

## 898. Babe Didrikson Zaharias
### (1914–1956)

1 All my life I've always had the urge to do things better than anybody else. Even in school, if it was something like making up a current events booklet, I'd want mine to be the best in the class.
Quoted in " 'Babe' Didrikson Zaharias," *Famous American Women* by Hope Stoddard 1970p

2 Boy, don't you men wish you could hit a ball like that!  Ibid.

3 All my life I've been competing—and competing to win. I came to realize that in its way, this cancer was the toughest competition I'd faced yet. I made up my mind that I was going to lick it all the way. I not only wasn't going to let it kill me, I wasn't even going to let it put me on the shelf.  Ibid.

## 899. Ingrid Bergman
### (1915–  )

1 . . . I saw my wrinkles in their wrinkles. You know, one looks at herself in the mirror every morning, and she doesn't see the difference, she doesn't realize that she is aging. But then she finds a friend who was young with her, and the friend isn't young anymore, and all of a sudden, like a slap on her eyes, she remembers that she, too, isn't young anymore.
Quoted in "Ingrid Bergman," *The Egotists* by Oriana Fallaci 1963

2 Things came to me asking to be done, and I did them—spontaneously, without asking whether it was wise or not. And the day after, I could say, "Maybe I shouldn't have done it." But years later, I always realized I was right in doing them.  Ibid.

3 I've never sought success in order to get fame and money; it's the talent and the passion that count in success.  Ibid.

## 900. Caroline Bird
### (1915–  )

1 The contraceptive pill may reduce the importance of sex not only as a basis for the division of labor, but as a guideline in developing talents and interests.
*Born Female*, Foreword 1968

2 We are destroying talent. The price of occupational success is made so high for women that barring exceptional luck only the unusually talented or frankly neurotic can afford to succeed. Girls size up the bargain early and turn it down.  Ibid.

3 A career woman who has survived the hurdle of marriage and maternity encounters a new obstacle: the hostility of men.  Ibid., Ch. 3

4 Secretaries may be specially prized, and the top secretaries exceptionally well paid, because they give men who can afford to pay well the subservient, watchful and admiring attention that Victorian wives used to give their husbands.  Ibid., Ch. 4

5 Equity speaks softly and wins in the end. But it is expedience, with its loud voice, that sets the time of victory.  Ibid., Ch. 10

6 Femininity appears to be one of those pivotal qualities that is so important no one can define it.  Ibid., Ch. 11

7 Are young women staying single because they have been influenced by women's liberation? Maybe. But I'm inclined to think that the causal relationship is the other way around. . . . Feminism has never been deader than it was during the 1950s, when the marriage rate hit a new high, the age of marriage a new low, and the ideal of universal, compulsory marriage boomed marriage counseling, psychiatric therapy and romantic portrayals of married life.  "The Case Against Marriage," *New Woman* September, 1971

8 Predictable demography has caught up with the university empire builders. . . . To keep their mammoth plants financially solvent, many institutions have begun to use hard-sell, Madison-Avenue techniques to attract students. They sell college like soap. . . .
*The Case Against College* 1975

9 . . . just as society had systematically damaged women by insisting that their proper place was in the home, so we may be systematically damaging 18-year-olds by insisting that their proper place is in college.  Ibid.

10 Equalizing opportunity through universal higher education subjects the whole population to the intellectual mode natural only to a few. It violates the fundamental egalitarian principle of respect for the differences between people.      Ibid.

11 The big advantage of getting your college money in cash now is that you can invest it in something that has a higher return than a diploma.      Ibid.

12 In fact there is no real evidence that the higher income of college graduates is due to college. College may simply attract people who are slated to earn more money anyway: those with higher IQs, better family backgrounds, a more enterprising temperament.      Ibid.

13 A liberal-arts education is supposed to provide you with a value system, a standard, a set of ideas, not a job. . . . The fact is, of course, that the liberal arts are a religion in every sense of that term. . . . [And if] the liberal arts are a religious faith, the professors are its priests.      Ibid.

14 College, then, may be a good place for those few young people who are really drawn to academic work, who would rather read than eat, but it has become too expensive, in money, time, and intellectual effort, to serve as a holding pen for large numbers of our young. We ought to make it possible for those reluctant, unhappy students to find alternative ways of growing up, and more realistic preparation for the years ahead.      Ibid.

## 901. Janet Harris
### (1915– )

1 . . . with the beginnings of the middle years, we face an identity crisis for which nothing in our past has prepared us.
     *The Prime of Ms. America*    1975

2 We were brought up with the value that as we sow, so shall we reap. We discarded the idea that anything we did was its own reward.      Ibid.

3 Reared as we were in a youth- and beauty-oriented society, we measured ourselves by our ornamental value.      Ibid.

4 I'm the ultimate in the throwaway society, the disposable woman.      Ibid.

5 . . . one searches the magazines in vain for women past their first youth. The middleaged face apparently sells neither perfume nor floor wax. The role of the mature woman in the media is almost entirely negative.      Ibid.

6 We are anonymous—graphed but not acknowledged, a shadowy presence—hinted at, but never defined.      Ibid.

7 At its most basic root, the death or disintegration of one's parents is a harsh reminder of one's own mortality.      Ibid.

8 We were born in an era in which it was a disgrace for women to be sexually responsible. We matured in an era in which it was an obligation.      Ibid.

9 Quite a few women told me, one way or another, that they thought it was sex, not youth, that's wasted on the young. . . .      Ibid.

## 902. Billie Holiday
### (1915–1959)

1 Mama may have
Papa may have
But God bless the child that's got his own
That's got his own.
     "God Bless the Child"    1941

2 And when you're poor, you grow up fast.
     *Lady Sings the Blues*, with William
     Dufty, Ch. 1    1956

3 You can be up to your boobies in white satin, with gardenias in your hair and no sugar cane for miles, but you can still be working on a plantation.      Ibid., Ch. 11

4 People don't understand the kind of fight it takes to record what you want to record the way you want to record it.    Ibid., Ch. 13

5 Sometimes it's worse to win a fight than to lose.      Ibid.

## 903. Ethel Rosenberg
### (1915–1953)

1 Together we hunted down the answers to all the seemingly insoluble riddles which a complex and callous society presented. . . . And yet for the sake of these answers, for the sake of American democracy, justice and brotherhood, for the sake of peace and bread and roses, and children's laughter, we shall continue to sit here [in prison] in dignity and in pride—in the deep abiding knowledge of our innocence before God and man, until the truth becomes a clarion call to all decent humanity.
     Letter to Julie Rosenberg, Sing Sing
     (May 27, 1951), *Death House Letters*
     *of Ethel and Julius Rosenberg*
     *1953p*

2 Work and build, my sons, and build
  a monument to love and joy,
  to human worth, to faith we kept
  for you, my sons, for you.
                   Ibid., "If We Die" (January 24, 1953)

3 . . . suffice it to say that my husband and I
shall die innocent before we lower ourselves
to live guilty! And nobody, not even you, whom
we continue to love as our own true brother,
can dictate terms to the Rosenbergs, who follow
only the dictates of heart and soul, truth and
conscience, and the God-blessed love we bear
our fellows!      Ibid., Letter to Emanuel H.
                   Bloch, Defense Attorney
                   (January 30, 1953)

## 904. Natalie Shainess

(1915–  )

1 In the generally progressive alienation of our
times, we are back to the laws of the jungle,
but without the gratification of biologic fulfillment.          "A Psychiatrist's View: Images of
             Woman—Past and Present, Overt
             and Obscured," *American Journal*
             *of Psychotherapy*     *January, 1969*

2 At a recent meeting devoted to the theme of
dissent, a Negro analyst pointed to the analyst's
blind spot, in studying only the dissenters, but
not the people or ideas dissented against. How
valid a perception!              Ibid.

3 It seems that the rewards of an affluent society
turn bitter as gall in the mouth.      Ibid.

4 As we have become a thing-oriented, impulse-
ridden, narcissistically self-preoccupied people,
we are increasingly dedicated to the acquisition of things, and cultivate little else.    Ibid.

## 905. Margaret Walker

(1915–  )

1 For my people thronging 47th Street in Chicago
  and Lenox
  Avenue in New York and Rampart Street
  in New
  Orleans, lost disinherited dispossessed and
  happy
  people filling the cabarets and taverns and
  other
  people's pockets. . . .
                 "For My People," St. 6,
                 *For My People*    *1942*

2 Let a new earth rise. Let another world be
  born. Let a bloody
  peace be written in the sky. Let a second
  generation
  full of courage issue forth;
  let a people loving freedom come to growth.
                      Ibid., St. 10

3 There were bizarre beginnings in old lands for
  the making
  of me.
              Ibid., "Dark Blood," St. 1

4 Now this here gal warn't always tough
  Nobody dreamed she'd turn out rough.
              Ibid., "Kissie Lee," St. 2

5 Old women working by an age-old plan
  to make their bread in ways as best they can.
              Ibid., "Whores," St. 1

6 Hurry up, Lucille, Hurry up
  We're Going to Miss Our Chance to go to Jail.
            "Street Demonstration," St. 2,
            *Prophets for a New Day*    *1970*

7 I like it fine in Jail
  And I don't want no Bail.
           Ibid., "Girl Held Without Bail," St. 2

8          . . . the filthy
  privies marked "For Colored Only"
  and the drinking-soda-fountains
  tasting dismal and disgusting
  with a dry and dusty flavor
  of the deep humiliation. . . .
                  Ibid., "Now"

9 Time to wipe away the slime.
  Time to end this bloody crime.
                       Ibid.

10 Everything I have ever written or hoped to
write is dedicated . . . to our hope of peace
and dignity and freedom in the world, not just
as black people, or as Negroes, but as free
human beings in a world community.
            Quoted in *By a Woman Writt,*
            Joan Goulianos, ed.    *1974*

## 906. Helen Yglesias

(1915–  )

1 They never ask the patient. The patient is
anesthetized on the operating table, cut open.
They call in the husband. "We think it best to
remove this precancerous breast. Since this is
your hunk of meat, do we have your permission, husband?"          *How She Died,* Ch. 1
                            *1972*

2 "Life is too short to understand God altogether, especially nowadays." Ibid.

3 I wanted to pull him toward me and comfort him with my body as I had when he was a child, but that time was over. We could only be to each other what any two human beings might be, close or far, quick or dull, yielding or hard. Ibid., Ch. 11

4 "I like to beat people at chess, and get better marks, and be elected to everything. It's disgusting to want those things. A person like that could do anything." Ibid.

5 Listening was a three times a day ritual with her, the news made even more nightmarish in the repetition: the war, the official statements, the enemy's denial, the traffic deaths, conspiracy charges, abortion reform fights, kidnappings, terrorism, peace talks, negotiations of all kinds, hijackings, charges and countercharges of anti-Semitism, Panther trials, civilian massacre trials, murder trials, riots, demonstrations, flaring wars between nations in corners of the world that didn't seem to really exist, the nonsense item they always found to end each broadcast with—and then the weather, reported as if every dip of the wind was a judgment day warning. Ibid., Ch. 16

## 907.  Dorothy Salisbury Davis
(1916–    )

1 There are seasons in Washington when it is even more difficult than usual to find out what is going on in the government. Possibly it is because nothing is going on, although a great many people seem to be working at it.
*Old Sinners Never Die*, Ch. 1     1959

2 We are all at the mercy of God as well as of one another. And for that we can be grateful, He has so much more of it than we have.
*Black Sheep Among White Lamb*, Ch. 7     1963

3 She listened with the remote and somewhat smug solicitude that one bestows on other people's tragedies. . . .
"The Purple Is Everything," *Ellery Queen's Mystery Magazine*     1964

4 She dressed more severely than was her fashion, needing herringbone for backbone. . . .
Ibid.

5 "The business of this street is business," the [police] sergeant said, "and that's my business."
Ibid.

6 A curator perhaps, but she would not have called him a connoisseur. One with his face and disposition would always taste and spit out. . . . Ibid.

7 But the discovery of the flaw does not in itself effect a cure; often it aggravates the condition. Ibid.

8 The law is above the law, you know.
*The Little Brothers*, Ch. 8     1973

9 You know what truth is, gentlemen? Truth is self-justification. That is everybody's truth. . . .
Ibid.

## 908.  Betty Furness
(1916–    )

1 You fellows have got to get this [phosphate-pollution problem] straightened out, because the laundry's piling up.
Quoted in *Bella!*, Mel Ziegler, ed.
1972

## 909.  Natalia Ginzburg
(1916–    )

1 I haven't managed to become learned about anything, even the things I've loved most in life: in me they remain scattered images, which admittedly feed my life of memories and feelings, but fail to fill my empty cultural wasteland.     "He and I" (1963), *Italian Writing Today*, Raleigh Trevelyan, ed.
1967

2 . . . it hurts me not to love music, because I feel my spirit is hurt by not loving it. But there's nothing to be done about it; I shall never understand music, and never love it. If I occasionally hear music I like, I can't remember it; so how could I love a thing I can't remember? Ibid.

3 My tidiness, and my untidiness, are full of regret and remorse and complex feelings.
Ibid.

4 He says they're all play-acting; and maybe he's right. Because, in the midst of my tears and his rages, I am completely calm. Over my real sorrows I never weep. Ibid.

5 . . . sometimes I wonder if we were those two people nearly twenty years ago along via Nazionale; two people who talked so politely, so urbanely, in the sunset; who chatted about everything, and nothing; two pleasant talkers,

two young intellectuals out for a walk; so young, so polite, so distracted, so ready to judge each other with absent kindliness, so ready to say goodbye for ever, in that sunset, on that street corner.                                     Ibid.

## 910. Françoise Giroud
### (1916–      )

1 Are there still virgins? One is tempted to answer no. There are only girls who have not yet crossed the line, because they want to preserve their market value. . . . Call them virgins if you wish, these travelers in transit.
*Quoted in Coronet
November, 1960*

2 Childhood is something so close, so special. . . . It's something you ought to keep to yourself. The way you keep back tears.
*I Give You My Word          1974*

3 To live several lives, you have to die several deaths.                                     Ibid.

4 Nothing is more difficult than competing with a myth.                                     Ibid.

5 As soon as a woman crosses the border into male territory, the nature of professional combat changes.                                     Ibid.

6 . . . the present evolution of women . . . is to my mind the most profound revolution that highly developed societies will have to contend with. . . .                                     Ibid.

7 As though femininity is something you can lose the way you lose your pocketbook: hmm, where in the world did I put my femininity?
Ibid.

8 . . . I don't for one moment believe that over the centuries some universal plot has been hatched by men to keep women in a state of servitude.                                     Ibid.

9 . . . the history of humanity is a very long one, during which the division of labor between men and women was, like many other things, dictated by profound necessity. . . .          Ibid.

10 When mores are no longer founded on the law of civilization but on habit, then comes the revolt.                                     Ibid.

11 One sometimes has the impression that American women have a kind of dishwashing fixation.                                     Ibid.

12 All missionaries are my enemies, even when their cause is good.                     Ibid.

13 To hold a man, or several men, was for her the epitome of female gamesmanship, the only thing that made life meaningful. What war is to men.                               Ibid.

14 The more subversive ideas are, the more moderate the language ought to be in expressing them. . . . If you look closely at most of the ideas expressed with violence, you begin to see that, once you've scraped away the terminology, you're usually left with the worst platitudes.                               Ibid.

15 When you are carrying on a struggle, you have to accept the notion that you will have enemies.
Ibid.

## 911. Elizabeth Hardwick
### (1916–      )

1 The curious modernity of the plot [*Hedda Gabler*] is that the workings of destiny have shrunk to yawning boredom.
*Seduction and Betrayal: Women in
Literature          1974*

2 Hedda [Gabler], rather than Nora [of *A Doll's House*], was the real prophecy.          Ibid.

3 Women, wronged in one way or another, are given the overwhelming beauty of endurance, the capacity for high or low suffering, for violent feeling absorbed, finally tranquilized, for the radiance of humility, for silence, secrecy, impressive acceptance. Heroines are, then, heroic.                               Ibid.

4 You cannot seduce anyone when innocence is not a value. Technology annihilates consequence. Heroism hurts and no one easily consents to be under its rule.          Ibid.

5 Stoicism . . . cannot be without its remaining uses in life and love; but if we read contemporary fiction we learn that improvisation is better.                               Ibid.

6 The raging productivity of the Victorians, shattered nerves and punctured stomachs, but it was a thing noble, glorious, awesome in itself.
Ibid.

7 They [the F. Scott Fitzgeralds] had created themselves together, and they always saw themselves, their youth, their love, their lost youth and lost love, their failures and memories, as a sort of living fiction.          Ibid.

## 912.  Jane Jacobs

(1916–    )

1 But look what we have built . . . low-income projects that become worse centers of delinquency, vandalism and general social hopelessness than the slums they were supposed to replace. . . . Cultural centers that are unable to support a good bookstore. Civic centers that are avoided by everyone but bums. . . . Promenades that go from no place to nowhere and have no promenaders. Expressways that eviscerate great cities. This is not the rebuilding of cities. This is the sacking of cities.
*The Death and Life of Great American*
*Cities*, Introduction     *1961*

2 There is a quality even meaner than outright ugliness or disorder, and this meaner quality is the dishonest mask of pretended order, achieved by ignoring or suppressing the real order that is struggling to exist and to be served.     Ibid.

3 Streets and their sidewalks, the main public places of a city, are its most vital organs. . . . If a city's streets are safe from barbarism and fear, the city is thereby tolerably safe from barbarism and fear. . . . To keep the city safe is a fundamental task of a city's streets and its sidewalks.     Ibid., Pt. I, Ch. 2

4 Conventionally, neighborhood parks or parklike open spaces are considered boons conferred on the deprived populations of cities. Let us turn this thought around, and consider city parks deprived places that need the boon of life and appreciation conferred on *them*.     Ibid., Ch. 5

5 The main responsibility of city planning and design should be to develop—insofar as public policy and action can do so—cities that are congenial places for . . . [a] great range of unofficial plans, ideas and opportunities to flourish, along with the flourishing of . . . public enterprises.     Ibid., Pt. III, Ch. 13

6 Innovating economies expand and develop. Economies that do not add new kinds of goods and services, but continue only to repeat old work, do not expand much nor do they, by definition, develop.
*The Economy of Cities*, Ch. 2
*1969*

7 A city that is large for its time is always an impractical settlement because size greatly intensifies whatever serious practical problems exist in an economy at a given time.
Ibid., Ch. 3

8 The only possible way to keep open the economic opportunities for new activities is for a "third force" to protect their weak and still incipient interests. Only governments can play this economic role. And sometimes, for pitifully brief intervals, they do. But because development subverts the status quo, the status quo soon subverts governments.     Ibid., Ch. 8

9 The bureaucratized, simplified cities, so dear to present-day city planners and urban designers, and familiar also to readers of science fiction and utopian proposals, run counter to the processes of city growth and economic development. Conformity and monotony, even when they are embellished with a froth of novelty, are not attributes of developing and economically vigorous cities. They are attributes of stagnant settlements.     Ibid.

## 913.  Florynce R. Kennedy

(1916–    )

1 . . . there can be no really pervasive system of oppression, such as that in the United States, without the consent of the oppressed.
"Institutionalized Oppression vs. the
Female," *Sisterhood Is Powerful*,
Robin Morgan, ed.     *1970*

2 Oppressed people are frequently very oppressive when liberated.     Ibid.

3 Women are dirt searchers; their greatest worth is eradicating rings on collars and tables. Never mind real-estate boards' corruption and racism, here's your soapsuds. Everything she is doing is peripheral, expendable, crucial, and non-negotiable. Cleanliness is next to godliness.
Ibid.

4 Every form of bigotry can be found in ample supply in the legal system of our country. It would seem that Justice (usually depicted as a woman) is indeed blind to racism, sexism, war and poverty.     Ibid.

5 Being a mother is a noble status, right? Right. So why does it change when you put "unwed" or "welfare" in front of it?
Quoted in "The Verbal Karate of
Florynce R. Kennedy, Esq." by
Gloria Steinem, *Ms.*
*March, 1973*

6 Niggerization is the result of oppression—and it doesn't just apply to black people. Old people, poor people, and students can also get niggerized.     Ibid.

7 The biggest sin is sitting on your ass.     Ibid.

8 Don't agonize. Organize.     Ibid.

9 If men could get pregnant, abortion would be a sacrament. Ibid.

10 My parents gave us a fantastic sense of security and worth. By the time the bigots got around to telling us we were nobody, we already *knew* we were somebody. Ibid.

11 There are very few jobs that actually require a penis or vagina. All other jobs should be open to everybody.
Quoted in "Freelancer with No Time to Write" by John Brady, *Writer's Digest     February, 1974*

12 If you have a child, you know that when he gets quiet, that's when you start to worry. That's why the Establishment should be worried about the antiestablishmentarians—the women, the Blacks, the youth, the aged, all the people who have no full part in the system, those I call the "niggers" of this country. They are planning campaigns in each legislative district. They are moving out of the streets and into the executive suites.
Quoted in "Impeachment?" by Claire Safran, *Redbook     April, 1974*

### 914.  Patricia McLaughlin
(1916–    )

1 Discoveries have reverberations. A new idea about oneself or some aspect of one's relations to others unsettles all one's other ideas, even the superficially related ones. No matter how slightly, it shifts one's entire orientation. And somewhere along the line of consequences, it changes one's behavior.
Quoted in *American Scholar Autumn, 1972*

### 915.  Cicely Saunders
(1916–    )

1 It makes a difference as a very frightened lady drops into unconsciousness that I believe in a religion which speaks of a God who dies, and rises.
Quoted in "Saints Among Us," *Time December 29, 1975*

### 916.  Anya Seton
(1916–    )

1 People in England seemed to think nothing of false teeth, even when they got them from the National Health.
*Green Darkness*, Pt. I, Ch. 1     *1972*

2 "As I grew up I got cynical. I'd see Mother enthusiastic and involved with charlatans. Numerologists and astrologers who charged five hundred dollars for a 'reading' which was so vague you could twist the meaning any way you wanted. And faith healers who couldn't seem to heal themselves, and a Yogi in California who preached purity, sublimity and continence, and then tried to seduce me one day while Mother was out." Ibid., Ch. 2

3 "Truth is naturally universal," said Akananda, "and shines into many different windows, though some of them are clouded."
Ibid., Pt. III, Ch. 19

### 917.  Frances Silverberg
(1916–    )

1 It was better not to speak, nor let your face or eyes show what you were feeling, because if people didn't know how you felt about them, or things, or maybe thought you had no feelings at all, they couldn't hurt you as much, only a little.     "Rebecca by Any Other Name," *American Scene: New Voices,* Don Wolfe, ed.     *1963*

### 918.  Annie Skau
(1916?–    )

1 The old Christian who has lived and walked with the Lord for many years is living in a treasure chamber.
Quoted in "Saints Among Us," *Time December 29, 1975*

### 919.  Hiltgunt Zassenhaus
(1916–    )

1 If they bomb my home in Hamburg, all I have left is what I can carry with me. . . . [But] there was something no suitcase could hold. It was intangible and the prisoners hungered for it. Only our minds and hearts could give truth and hope.
*Walls: Resisting the Third Reich— One Woman's Story     1974*

### 920.  Maeve Brennan
(1917–    )

1 She had found that the more the child demanded of her, the more she had to give. Strength came up in waves that had their source in a sea of calm and unconquerable

devotion. The child's holy trust made her open her eyes, and she took stock of herself and found that everything was all right, and that she could meet what challenges arose and meet them well, and that she had nothing to apologize for—on the contrary, she had every reason to rejoice.

"The Eldest Child," *The New Yorker* *June 23, 1968*

2 She . . . enjoyed the illusion that life had nothing to teach her. Ibid.

3 He wished they could go back to the beginning and start all over again, but the place where they had stood together, where they had been happy, was all trampled over and so spoiled that it seemed impossible ever to make it smooth again. Ibid.

## 921. Gwendolyn Brooks

(1917–    )

1 Abortions will not let you forget.
You remember the children you got that you did not get. . . .
"The Mother," St. 1,
*A Street in Bronzeville*    1945

2 To whatever you incline, your final choice here must be handling
Occasional sweet clichés with a dishonesty of deft tact.
For these people are stricken, they want none of your long-range messages,
Only the sweet clichés, to pamper them, modify fright.
Ibid., "The Funeral," St. 1

3 I hold my honey and I store my bread
In little jars and cabinets of my will.
I label clearly, and each latch and lid
I bid, Be firm till I return from hell.
I am very hungry. I am incomplete.
And none can tell when I may dine again.
Ibid., "My dreams, my works, must wait till after hell"

4 People like definite decisions,
Tidy answers, all the little ravellings
Snipped off, the lint removed, they
Hop happily among their roughs
Calling what they can't clutch insanity
Or saintliness.
"Memorial to Ed Blanc," St. 3,
*Annie Allen*    1949

5 Maxie Allen always taught her
Stipendiary little daughter
To thank her Lord and lucky star
For eye that let her see so far,
For throat enabling her to eat
Her Quaker Oats and Cream-of-Wheat,

For tongue to tantrum for the penny,
For ear to hear the haven't-any,
For arm to toss
For leg to chance,
For heart to hanker for romance.
Ibid., "Maxie Allen," St. 1

6 "Do not be afraid of no,
Who has so far, so very far to go". . . .
Ibid., "Do not be afraid of no," St. 1

7 It is brave to be involved,
To be fearful to be unresolved.
Ibid., St. 9

8 We do not want them to have less.
But it is only natural that we should think we have not enough.
We drive on, we drive on.
When we speak to each other our voices are a little gruff.
Ibid., "Beverly Hills, Chicago," St. 8

9 To be cherished was the dearest wish of the heart of Maude Martha Brown, and sometimes when she was not looking at dandelions . . . it was hard to believe that a thing of only ordinary allurements—if the allurements of any flower could be said to be ordinary—was as easy to love as a thing of heart-catching beauty.
*Maude Martha*, Ch. 1    1953

10 What she wanted was to donate to the world a good Maude Martha. That was the offering, the bit of art, that could not come from any other. She would polish and hone that.
Ibid., Ch. 6

11 But if the root was sour what business did she have up there hacking at a leaf?
Ibid., Ch. 19

12 She had a tremendous impatience with other people's ideas—unless those happened to be exactly like hers; even then, often as not, she gave hurried, almost angry, affirmative, and flew on to emphatic illumination of her own.
Ibid., Ch. 23

13 I am scarcely healthy-hearted or human.
What can I teach my cheated Woman?
"My Little 'Bout-Town Gal," St. 2,
*The Bean Eaters*    1960

14 We real cool. We
Left school. We

Lurk late. We
Strike straight. We

Sing sin. We
Thin gin. We

Jazz June. We
Die soon.
Ibid., "We Real Cool"

15 I wonder if the elephant
   Is lonely in his stall
   When all the boys and girls are gone
   And there's no shout at all,
   And there's no one to stamp before,
   No one to note his might.
   Does he hunch up, as I do,
   Against the dark of night?
                           Ibid., "Pete at the Zoo"

16 The man whose height his fear improved he
   arranged to fear no further.
                           "Medgar Evers," St. 1,
                           *In the Mecca*    1968

17 He opened us—
   who was a key,

   who was a man.
                           Ibid., "Malcolm X," Sts. 4–5

18 Does man love Art? Man visits Art, but
   squirms.
   Art hurts. Art urges voyages—
   and it is easier to stay at home,
   the nice beer ready.
                           Ibid., "The Chicago Picasso," St. 1

## 922. Barbara Deming
### (1917–    )

1 It is particularly hard on us as pacifists, of
  course, to face our own anger. It is particularly painful for us—hard on our pride, too—
  to have to discover in ourselves murderers.
                           "On Anger," *We Cannot Live
                           Without Our Lives*    1974

2 . . . not a bullying power, not the power to
  make people afraid. The power to make them
  see new things as possible.          Ibid.

3 If men put from them in fear all that is
  "womanish" in them, then long, of course, for
  that missing part in their natures, so seek to
  possess it by possessing us; and because they
  have feared it in their own souls seek, too, to
  dominate it in us—seek even to slay it—well,
  we're where we are now, aren't we?
                           Ibid., "Two Perspectives on
                           Women's Struggles"

## 923. Phyllis Diller
### (1917–    )

1 Cleaning your house while your kids are still
  growing
  Is like shoveling the walk before it stops snowing.
                           *Phyllis Diller's Housekeeping Hints*
                           1966

2 Never go to bed mad. Stay up and fight.
                           Ibid.

## 924. Indira Gandhi
### (1917–    )

1 Peace we want because there is another war
  to fight against poverty, disease and ignorance.
  We have promises to keep to our people of
  work, food, clothing, and shelter, health and
  education.
                           Radio Broadcast (January 26, 1966),
                           Quoted in *Indira Gandhi*
                           by Mithrapuram K. Alexander
                           1968

2 The young people of India must recognize that
  they will get from their country tomorrow what
  they give her today.              Ibid.

3 You cannot shake hands with a clenched fist.
                           Press Conference, New Delhi
                           (October 19, 1971), Quoted in
                           *Indira Speaks* by Dhiren Mullick
                           1972

4 Martyrdom does not end something; it is only
  the beginning.
                           Ibid., Address to Parliament,
                           New Delhi (August 12, 1971)

5 One cannot but be perturbed when fire breaks
  out in a neighbour's house.
                           Ibid., Address in Kremlin,
                           Moscow (September 28, 1971)

6 To natural calamities of drought, flood and
  cyclone has been added the man-made tragedy
  of vast proportions. I am haunted by tormented
  faces in our overcrowded refugee camps reflecting grim events, which have compelled
  exodus of these millions from East Bengal.
                           Ibid., Meeting with Richard Nixon,
                           Washington, D.C. (November 4, 1971)

7 No Government, no Head of Goverment can
  last if the people feel that this Government is
  not going to defend the security of the country.
                           Ibid., Address, Columbia University
                           (November 7, 1971)

8 The times have passed when any nation sitting
  three or four thousand miles away could give
  orders to Indians on the basis of their colour
  superiority to do as they wished. India has
  changed and she is no more a country of natives.            Ibid., Address, Workers' Congress,
                           New Delhi (December 2, 1971)

9 We know the true value of democracy, peace
  and freedom, since it was denied us for so
  long. . . . We have been slaves and will not
  allow others to make slaves of us again.
                           Ibid., Address, New Delhi
                           (December 12, 1971)

10 There are moments in history when brooding tragedy and its dark shadows can be lightened by recalling great moments of the past.
Ibid., Letter to Richard Nixon
(December 16, 1971)

11 There are many kinds of wars. One war has just ended but I do not know if peace has come.     Ibid., Address, Ambala
(December 24, 1971)

12 You must learn to be still in the midst of activity and to be vibrantly alive in repose.
Quoted in "The Embattled Woman"
by James Shepherd, *People*
*June 30, 1975*

13 Is it possible, was it ever possible, to keep alive in India the beautiful dream of parliamentarian democracy the British imported along with five o'clock tea?     Quoted in "Indira's Coup" by
Oriana Fallaci, *New York
Review of Books
September 18, 1975*

14 My father [Pandit Jawaharlal Nehru] was a statesman, I'm a political woman. My father was a saint. I'm not.     Ibid.

15 There exists no politician in India daring enough to attempt to explain to the masses that cows can be eaten.     Ibid.

16 To bear many children is considered not only a religious blessing but also an investment. The greater their number, some Indians reason, the more alms they can beg.     Ibid.

17 In a traditional society like India's, scandals are unavoidable. There is, in fact, the first consequence of the most ancient of social diseases: corruption.     Ibid.

18 As for Western women, it seems to me that they have often had to struggle to obtain their own rights. That did not leave them much time to prove their abilities. The time will come.
Quoted in "Conversation with
Indira Gandhi" by José-Luis de
Vilallonga, *Oui*     1975

19 I think that the highly industrialized Western world has neglected to the utmost degree to leave room for man. The infernal production-consumption cycle has completely dehumanized life. The individual has become a tool. He hardly has any contact with nature anymore. That is, with himself. He has lost his soul and is not even trying to find it again.     Ibid.

## 925. Katharine Graham
(1917–    )

1 Common humor is very basic, isn't it? At both the [Washington] *Post* and *Newsweek* there's a rather great, healthy irreverance that makes working a lot of fun.
Quoted in "The Power That Didn't
Corrupt" by Jane Howard, *Ms.
October, 1974*

2 If one is rich and one's a woman, one can be quite misunderstood.     Ibid.

3 Bromidic though it may sound, some questions *don't* have answers, which is a terribly difficult lesson to learn.     Ibid.

4 So few grown women like their lives.     Ibid.

5 To love what you do and feel that it matters—how could anything be more fun?     Ibid.

## 926. Fay Kanin
(1917?–    )

1 It's my feeling that the highest aspiration of the [screen] writer is to be a writer-executive in the sense that he goes on to control his material in one further aspect by producing or directing it. I believe every writer who can should try to accomplish that. Because it's the best way he can get his work done well.
Quoted in "Fay Kanin," *The Screen-
writer Looks at the Screenwriter*
by William Froug     *1972*

2 While other crafts have to sit around chewing their fingernails waiting for a movie to be put together, writers have one great strength. They can sit down and generate their own employment and determine their own fate to a great extent by the degree of their disciplines, their guts, and their talents.     Ibid.

3 For myself, I think the word auteur has been used, misused, paraded, fought over, intellectualized, and interpreted to the point of boredom. As I understand from my French, auteur means author. And I cannot see how someone is an author who, having a concept for a film, does not at some point sit down and write it. . . .     Ibid.

4 Only an insatiable ego or an intolerable sense of inferiority could lead a director to ignore the basic creativity of the man or woman who thought it up, sweated it out, and delivered those precious pages into his hands.     Ibid.

5 But in terms of the studio system, as I see it today, and as I knew it, it's as different as day and night. I see frightened people, unwilling to make a decision. Certainly not enjoying the making of the film because the end result is so perilous, so in question.     Ibid.

6 But, in the end, I believe that to be a creative person and not to be able to express it in your own terms is difficult, and eventually intolerable, for any human being anywhere.     Ibid.

## 927. Carson McCullers
### (1917–1967)

1 "There are those who know and those who don't know. And for every ten thousand who don't know there's only one who knows. That's the miracle of all time—that these millions know so much but don't know this."
*The Heart Is a Lonely Hunter,*
Pt. I, Ch. 2     *1940*

2 The inside room was a very private place. She could be in the middle of a house full of people and still feel like she was locked up by herself.     Ibid., Pt. II, Ch. 5

3 "Say a man died and left his mule to his four sons. The sons would not wish to cut up the mule into four parts and each take his share. They would own and work the mule together. That is the way Marx says all of the natural resources should be owned—not by one group of rich people but by all the workers of the world as a whole."     Ibid., Ch. 6

4 "Today we are not put up on the platforms and sold at the courthouse square. But we are forced to sell our strength, our time, our souls during almost every hour that we live. We have been freed from one kind of slavery only to be delivered into another."     Ibid.

5 An army post in peacetime is a dull place. Things happen, but then they happen over and over again. . . . But perhaps the dullness of a post is caused most of all by insularity and by a surfeit of leisure and safety, for once a man enters the army he is expected only to follow the heels ahead of him.
*Reflections in a Golden Eye,* Ch. 1
*1941*

6 Three words were in the captain's heart. He shaped them soundlessly with his trembling lips, as he had not breath to spare for a whisper: "I am lost." And having given up life, the Captain suddenly began to live.     Ibid., Ch. 3

7 His preoccupation with the soldier grew in him like a disease. As in cancer, when the cells unaccountably rebel and begin the insidious self-multiplication that will ultimately destroy the body, so in his mind did the thoughts of the soldier grow out of all proportion to their normal sphere.     Ibid., Ch. 4

8 This was the summer when for a long time she had not been a member. She belonged to no club and was a member of nothing in the world. Frankie had become an unjoined person who hung around in the doorways, and she was afraid.
*The Member of the Wedding,* Pt. I
*1946*

9 This August she was twelve and five-sixths years old. She was five feet and three-quarter inches tall, and she wore a Number 7 shoe. . . . If she reached her height on her eighteenth birthday, she had five and one-sixth growing years ahead of her. Therefore, according to mathematics and unless she could somehow stop herself, she would grow to be over nine feet tall. And what would be a lady who was over nine feet high? She would be a Freak.     Ibid.

10 "I see a green tree. And to me it is green. And you would call the tree green also. And we would agree on this. But is the colour you see as green the same colour I see as green? Or say we both call a colour black. But how do we know that what you see as black is the same colour I see as black?"     Ibid., Pt. II, Ch. 2

11 "We all of us somehow caught. We born this way or that way and we don't know why. But we caught anyhow. . . . And maybe we wants to widen and bust free. But no matter what we do we still caught. Me is me and you is you and he is he. We each one of us somehow caught all by ourself."     Ibid.

12 F. Jasmine did not want to go upstairs, but she did not know how to refuse. It was like going into a fair booth, or fair ride, that once having entered you cannot leave until the exhibition or the ride is finished. Now it was the same with this soldier, this date. She could not leave until it ended.     Ibid., Ch. 3

13 . . . the anodyne of time. . . .
"The Sojourner," *The Ballad of
the Sad Cafe*     *1951*

14 Sweet, casual intimacy, the soft-fleshed loveliness indisputably possessed.     Ibid.

15 His own life seemed so solitary, a fragile column supporting nothing amidst the wreckage
of the years.     Ibid.

16 Was it indeed true that at one time he had
called this stranger, Elizabeth, Little Butter-
duck during nights of love, that they had lived
together, shared perhaps a thousand days and
nights and—finally—endured in the misery of
sudden solitude the fiber by fiber (jealousy,
alcohol and money quarrels) destruction of the
fabric of married love.     Ibid.

17 The prelude was as gaily iridescent as a prism
in a morning room.     Ibid.

18 *"L'improvisation de la vie humaine,"* he said.
"There's nothing that makes you so aware of
the improvisation of human existence as a
song unfinished. Or an old address book."     Ibid.

19 Ferris glimpsed the disorder of his life: the
succession of cities, of transitory loves; and
time, the sinister glissando of the years, time
always.     Ibid.

## 928. Jessica Mitford

### (1917– )

1 Easier would it be, I thought, to recognize the
individual faces of sheep on an Australian
ranch than to match names and faces among
this monotonous sea of seemingly unvaried
human beings.     *Sons and Rebels,* Ch. 11
    *1960*

2 Things on the whole are much faster in America; people don't *stand for election,* they *run
for office.* If a person say he's *sick,* it doesn't
mean regurgitating; it means *ill. Mad* means
angry, not *insane.* Don't ask for the left-
luggage; it's called a check-room. A nice joint
means a good pub, not roast meat.     Ibid.

3 O death where is thy sting? O grave where is
thy victory? Where, indeed? Many a badly
stung survivor, faced with the aftermath of
some relative's funeral, has ruefully conceded
that the victory has been won hands down by
a funeral establishment—in disastrously unequal battle.     *The American Way of Death*
    *1963*

4 No doubt prison administrators sense that to
permit the media and the public access to their
domain would result in stripping away a major
justification for their existence: that they are
confining depraved, brutal creatures.
    *Kind and Unusual Punishment,* Ch. 1
    *1971*

5 What of homosexuality, recognized by everyone in Corrections as an inevitable consequence
of long-term segregation of the sexes? Having
driven them to it, why punish for it?
    Ibid., Ch. 2

6 When is conduct a crime, and when is a crime
not a crime? When Somebody Up There—a
monarch, a dictator, a Pope, a legislator—so
decrees.     Ibid., Ch. 5

7 One of the nicest American scientists I know
was heard to say, "Criminals in our peniten-
tiary are fine experimental material—much
cheaper than chimpanzees." I hope the chimpanzees don't come to hear of this.
    Ibid., Ch. 9

8 No doubt like schools, old-age homes, mental
hospitals, and other closed institutions that
house the powerless, prisons afford a very special opportunity to employees at all levels for
various kinds of graft and thievery.
    Ibid., Ch. 10

9 Radical and revolutionary ideologies are seep-
ing into the prisons. Whereas formerly convicts
tended to regard themselves as unfortunates
whose accident of birth at the bottom of the
heap was largely responsible for their plight,
today many are questioning the validity of the
heap.     Ibid., Ch. 13

10 Those of us on the outside [of prisons] do not
like to think of wardens and guards as our
servants. Yet they are, and they are intimately
locked in a deadly embrace with their human
captives behind the prison walls. By extension
so are we. A terrible double meaning is thus
imparted to the original question of human
ethics: Am I my brother's keeper?
    Ibid., Ch. 15

## 929. Estelle R. Ramey

### (1917– )

1 . . . what is human and the same about the
males and females classified as *Homo sapiens*
is much greater than the differences.
    "Men's Monthly Cycles (They Have
    Them Too, You Know)," *The First
    Ms. Reader,* Francine Klagsbrun, ed.
    *1972*

2 In man, the shedding of blood is always associated with injury, disease, or death. Only the
female half of humanity was seen to have the
magical ability to bleed profusely and still rise
phoenix-like each month from the gore.
    Ibid.

3 Women's chains have been forged by men, not by anatomy. Ibid.

4 I don't mind . . . the fun and games of being treated like a fragile flower. But as a physiologist working with the unromantic scientific facts of life, I find it hard to delude myself about feminine frailty.
Quoted in *The Prime of Ms. America* by Janet Harris　　1975

## 930. Christiane Rochefort
(1917–　　)

1 CELINE. It's not only that you are killing grass and trees. . . . You are killing LIFE.
*Les Stances à Sophie*　　1970

2 JULIA. Never argue with them. You're always forgetting you're a woman. They never listen to what you're saying, they just want to listen to the music of your voice. Ibid.

3 CELINE. Don't you read the paper? Don't you know that men don't hit their wives any more? Ibid.

4 . . . when someone tells you that you're paranoic in a situation that is not socialized yet, you feel you are.
Quoted in "Les Stances à Sophie" by Annette Levy, *Women and Film* (Vol. I, Nos. 3 and 4)　　1973

5 You can go to the hospital. If you don't go to the hospital, you can go to marriage. And if you don't go to marriage you can go to the women's movement. Ibid.

## 931. Han Suyin
(1917–　　)

1 What we loved best about England was the grass—the short, clean, incredibly green grass with its underlying tough, springy turf, three hundred years growing.
*Destination Chungking*, Ch. 2　　1942

2 The city hums with noise and work and hope. This is Chungking, not dead Pompeii—five hundred thousand Chinese with a will to withstand, to endure and build again. Next year, next spring, the planes will lay it waste again. Next autumn we shall be building. . . .
Ibid., Ch. 12

3 "Your laws are ineffective," Wen declared. "Why? Because no system of control will work as long as most of those administering the law against an evil have more than a finger dipped into it themselves." Ibid., Ch. 13

4 "I'd sell my love for food any day. The rice bowl is to me the most valid reason in the world for doing anything. A piece of one's soul to the multitudes in return for rice and wine does not seem to me a sacrilege."
*A Many-Splendoured Thing*, Preface　　1950

5 Our feelings are very much governed by commonplace associations, and often influenced by that sort of short-term logic which renders steady thinking superfluous.
Ibid., Pt. II, Ch. 1

6 "For sages and wise men have been mute for many centuries, and their names are forgotten. But drunkards leave a resounding echo after them." Ibid., Ch. 7

7 Foolish, mad, invulnerable in lunacy, having forgotten what I knew the winter before; that no one is invulnerable to repeated suggestion; that I was no different, no stronger, no more able to withstand reiteration than others. . . .
Ibid., Pt. III, Ch. 8

8 Afterwards, as happens when a man is safely dead, they sang his praise. Ibid., Pt. IV

9 This is Malaya. Everything takes a long, a very long time, in Malaya. Things get done, occasionally, but more often they don't, and the more in a hurry you are, the quicker you break down. *And the Rain My Drink*, Ch. 2
1956

10 Barbed wire fences the clearings where man survives, and outside it is the grey-green toppling surge, all-engulfing, of the jungle.
Ibid., Ch. 8

11 "I'm nicely dead," she told Leo, and it was his turn to find nothing to say.
*The Mountain Is Young*, Pt. I, Ch. 1　　1958

12 She was plunged in this new consciousness where vision and hearing was all, in which there was total forgetting of self, the body moving without knowing itself in movement, wholly transported in this same ecstasy, the trance concentration which here made her one with all the thousands gathered.
Ibid., Pt. II, Ch. 13

13 . . . all humans are frightened of their own solitude. Yet only in solitude can man learn to know himself, learn to handle his own eternity of aloneness. And love from one being to another can only be that two solitudes come nearer, recognize and protect and comfort each other. Ibid., Pt. V, Ch. 1

14 How few of us really try to find out what we're like, really, inside?     *Winter Love*
    *1962*

15 The world needs the artist who records, with dispassionate compassion, more than the missionary who proclaims with virulence unreal crusades against reality, especially those who want to put the clock back to an ideal past that never was.     *The Crippled Tree,*
    Pt. I, Ch. 1     *1965*

16 For exploitation and oppression is not a matter of *race*. It is the system, the apparatus of world-wide brigandage called imperialism, which made the Powers behave the way they did. I have no illusions on this score, nor do I believe that any Asian nation or African nation, in the same state of dominance, and with the same system of colonial profit-amassing and plunder, would have behaved otherwise.
    Ibid., Ch. 9

17 These ways to make people buy were strange and new to us, and many bought for the sheer pleasure at first of holding in the hand and talking of something new. And once this was done, it was like opium, we could no longer do without this new bauble, and thus, though we hated the foreigners and though we knew they were ruining us, we bought their goods. Thus I learned the art of the foreigners, the art of creating in the human heart restlessness, disquiet, hunger for new things, and these new desires became their best helpers.
    Ibid., Ch. 15

18 A country is not truly betrayed to the enemy outside its gates unless there are also traitors within. For money, for power, these can be found.     Ibid., Ch. 17

19 Looking back now, with the hindsight of history, I can understand it so much better. But understanding is also effacement, a vagueness, which explains, but explains away the minute agonies, the grief that warps a life, which accepts, as a tree, crippled at its root by some voracious stabbing insect and for ever after bearing the mark of the beast upon its unfolding, is accepted in the landscape.
    Ibid., Pt. II, Ch. 18

20 "Goldfish are flowers," said Papa, "flowers that move."     Ibid., Ch. 26

21 Pain occupies its verbal niche in a construction of words, building a life after it has been lived, for what is lived is encountered in a retrospect of sentences made to fit what happened shaped by what was.     Ibid., Ch. 30

22 On the railway. . . . beneficent dragons champing docile impatience on the iron tracks, insides of fire so still, hooting melody of the night proclaiming life, life roaring, life waiting to pounce.
    Ibid.

## 932. Pearl Bailey

(1918–   )

1 When you're young, the silliest notions seem the greatest achievements.
    *The Raw Pearl*, Ch. 1     *1968*

2 Vaudeville is a marvelous stepping stone to legit and movies. You learn to touch the audience, yet leave them alone, which no other part of the business teaches you so well. Sometimes a performer can become so much a part of the show business world that he loses touch with the people, the audiences, outside. It's good to be, as the Bible says, in the world but not of it.
    Ibid., Ch. 5

3 What is really sad is when a legend starts to fade. I think about the cowboys who carved notches in their guns for every man they killed. Everything the person has done is right there. You can see the experience in them. But sometimes, though the gun still has bullets and the aim is still good, the world stops the carving of the notches. It is so sad to see a legendary performer cut off from his audiences, even though the basic talent is still there, seasoned by experience. Who throws away a beautiful old bottle of wine?     Ibid., Ch. 6

4 There's a period of life when we swallow a knowledge of ourselves and it becomes either good or sour inside.     Ibid., Ch. 13

5 The fact is that it takes more than ingredients and technique to cook a good meal. A good cook puts something of *himself* into the preparation—he cooks with enjoyment, anticipation, spontaneity, and he is willing to experiment.
    *Pearl's Kitchen*, Preface     *1973*

6 My kitchen is a mystical place, a kind of temple for me. It is a place where the surfaces seem to have significance, where the sounds and odors carry meaning that transfers from the past and bridges to the future.
    Ibid., "Sanctuary"

7 I cannot understand how we can put together all those programs for sending food across the oceans when at home we have people who are slowly starving to death. We could use less foreign aid and more home aid.
    Ibid., Epilogue

8 Hungry people cannot be good at learning or producing anything, except perhaps violence.
*Ibid.*

### 933. Peg Bracken

(1918–   )

1 . . . unnecessary dieting is because everything from television to fashion ads have made it seem wicked to cast a shadow. This wild, emaciated look appeals to some women, though not to many men, who are seldom seen pinning up a *Vogue* illustration in a machine shop.
*The I Hate to Cook Book      1960*

### 934. Gertrude Louise Cheney

(1918–   )

1 All people are made alike.
They are made of bone, flesh and dinners.
Only the dinners are different.
"People"      *1927*

### 935. Betty Ford

(1918–   )

1 . . . I wouldn't be surprised [if her daughter had an affair]. I think she's a perfectly normal human being like all young girls. If she wanted to continue, I would certainly counsel and advise her on the subject. And I'd want to know pretty much about the young man . . . whether it was a worthwhile encounter. . . . She's pretty young to start affairs, [but] she's a big girl.     Interview, "60 Minutes,"
CBS-TV    *August 10, 1975*

### 936. Corita Kent

(1918–   )

1 There are so many hungry people that God cannot appear to them except in the form of bread.     "Enriched Bread" (silkscreen)
*1965*

2 One of the things Jesus did was to step aside from the organized religion of his time because it had become corrupt and bogged down with rules. Rules became more important than feeding the hungry.
Quoted in "A Time of Transition for Corita Kent" by Lucie Kay Scheuer, *Los Angeles Times      July 11, 1974*

3 Women's liberation is the liberation of the feminine in the man and the masculine in the woman.     *Ibid.*

\* \* \*

4 The real circus
with acrobats, jugglers
and bareback riders =
also an empty field
transformed, and
in the tent artists and
freaks, children and
pilgrims and animals
are gathered in com-
munion = us
Poster, New York Urban Coalition, Inc.

### 937. Ann Landers

(1918–   )

1 Women complain about sex more often than men. Their gripes fall into two major categories: (1) Not enough. (2) Too much.
*Ann Landers Says Truth Is Stranger . . . , Ch. 2      1968*

2 What the vast majority of American children needs is to stop being pampered, stop being indulged, stop being chauffeured, stop being catered to. In the final analysis it is not what you do for your children but what you have taught them to do for themselves that will make them successful human beings.
*Ibid., Ch. 3*

3 All married couples should learn the art of battle as they should learn the art of making love. Good battle is objective and honest— never vicious or cruel. Good battle is healthy and constructive, and brings to a marriage the principle of equal partnership.    *Ibid., Ch. 11*

### 938. Ida Lupino

(1918–   )

1 And believe me, *Bring it in on time* is such a major factor in television that I'd sometimes get absolutely sick to my stomach days beforehand. . . . So any ladies who want to take over men's jobs—if that's what they really want—had better have strong stomachs.
Quoted in *Popcorn Venus* by Marjorie Rosen      *1973*

### 939. Anna Magnani

(1918–1973)

1 Great passions, my dear, don't exist: they're liars' fantasies. What do exist are little loves that may last for a short or a longer while.
Quoted in "Anna Magnani," *The Egotists* by Oriana Fallaci      *1963*

2 . . . I might use foul language, but I do hate bad breeding.       Ibid.

3 Movies, today, are made up of festivals, cannibalism, the idiocy they call lack of communication, intellectuals who always make out that they're teaching something and undervalue the public, forgetting that the public is composed —all right—of insecure individuals, but, put together, these insecure individuals become a miracle of intelligence. And intelligence won't put up with being led by the nose by imbeciles who preach from the pulpit.       Ibid.

4 Children are like puppies: you have to keep them near you and look after them if you want to have their affection.       Ibid.

## 940. Martha Mitchell
### (1918–1976)

1 I'm not certain that we should have Democrats in the Cabinet.
Interview, "Today Show," NBC-TV
*February 11, 1971*

2 I've never said I was against integration. It should have started right after the Civil War. But why single out the South? The South has been imposed on long enough. It's the orphan of the nation.
Quoted in *Martha: The Mouth That Roared* by Charles Ashman and Sheldon Engelmayer    *1973*

## 941. Penelope Mortimer
### (1918– )

1 In all the years of her marriage, a long war in which attack, if not happening, was always imminent, she had learned an expert cunning. The way to avoid being hurt, to dodge unhappiness, was to run away. Feelings of guilt and cowardice presented no problems that couldn't be overcome by dreams, by games, by the gentle sound of her own voice advising and rebuking her as she went about the house.
*Daddy's Gone A-Hunting*, Ch. 1
*1958*

2 "There is an obsessive tenderness and passion, an eating out of one's heart, a sense of longing, an affliction, which remains buried and unchanged from childhood, this is what is called falling in love. The longing is for reciprocation, the affliction is in knowing that reciprocation is forbidden."    Ibid., Ch. 5

3 "I thought I was supposed to lie on a couch and you wouldn't say a word. It's like the Inquisition or something. Are you trying to make me feel I'm wrong? Because I do that for myself."    *The Pumpkin Eater*, Ch. 1
*1962*

4 . . . some of my innocence, trust, stupidity, idealism has been stripped away from me like skins. I was smaller, uglier, more powerful than I had been before, and I felt bewitched by fear.       Ibid., Ch. 5

5 It was intensely boring, but they all made a great fuss over me and I began to think that perhaps it was better to be bored and admired than interested and miserable.
Ibid., Ch. 10

6 "What do your patients do while you're away? Commit suicide, murder their wives, or do they just sit and cry and take pills and think about what they told you last time? . . . If I'm sane enough to be left alone with my *thoughts* for two weeks then I'm too sane to need these futile, boring conversations—because my God, they bore me—at six guineas a time."
Ibid., Ch. 11

7    "I have arguments with myself."
"About what?"
"Between the part of me that believes in things, and the part that doesn't."
"And which wins?"
"Sometimes one. Sometimes the other."
"Then stop arguing."    Ibid., Ch. 23

8 I was, and still am, running away from the person to whom . . . I had addressed my life.
*Long Distance*    *1974*

9 Grief is a very antisocial state. . . .    Ibid.

## 942. Muriel Spark
### (1918– )

1 "Being over seventy is like being engaged in a war. All our friends are going or gone and we survive amongst the dead and the dying as on a battlefield."    *Memento Mori*, Ch. 4
*1959*

2 "If I had my life over again I should form the habit of nightly composing myself to thoughts of death. I would practise, as it were, the remembrance of death. There is no other practise which so intensifies life. Death, when it approaches, ought not to take one by surprise. It should be part of the full expectancy of life."
Ibid., Ch. 11

3 There was altogether too much candour in married life; it was an indelicate modern idea, and frequently led to upsets in a household, if not divorce.      Ibid., Ch. 12

4 "Give me a girl at an impressionable age, and she is mine for life."
*The Prime of Miss Jean Brodie*, Ch. 1
*1961*

5 "One's prime is elusive. You little girls, when you grow up, must be on the alert to recognize your prime at whatever time of your life it may occur. You must then live it to the full."
Ibid.

6 "Art and religion first; then philosophy; lastly science. That is the order of the great subjects of life, that's their order of importance."
Ibid., Ch. 2

7 "To me education is a leading out of what is already there in the pupil's soul. To Miss Mackay it is a putting in of something that is not there, and that is not what I call education, I call it intrusion. . . ."      Ibid.

8 It is not to be supposed that Miss Brodie was unique. . . . There were legions of her kind during the nineteen-thirties, women from the age of thirty and upward who crowded their war-bereaved spinsterhood with voyages of discovery into new ideas and energetic practices in art or social welfare, education or religion.
Ibid., Ch. 3

9 Miss Brodie said: "Pavlova contemplates her swans in order to perfect her swan dance, she studies them. That is true dedication. You must all grow up to be dedicated women as I have dedicated myself to you."      Ibid.

10 "It is impossible to persuade a man who does not disagree, but smiles."      Ibid., Ch. 4

11 "Nothing infuriates people more than their own lack of spiritual insight, Sandy, that is why the Moslems are so placid, they are full of spiritual insight."      Ibid.

12 A house in which there are no people—but with all the signs of tenancy—can be a most tranquil good place.
"The Portobello Road," *Collected Stories: 1*    *1968*

13 Kathleen, speaking from that Catholic point of view which takes some getting used to, said, "She was at Confession only the day before she died—wasn't she lucky?"      Ibid.

14 For some years she had been thinking she was not much inclined towards sex. . . . It is not

merely a lack of pleasure in sex, it is dislike of the excitement. And it is not merely dislike, it is worse, it is boredom.
Ibid., "Bang-Bang You're Dead"

15 She did not know then that the price of allowing false opinions was the gradual loss of one's capacity for forming true ones.      Ibid.

16 Oh, the trifles, the people, that get on your nerves when you have a neurosis!
Ibid., "Come Along, Marjorie"

17 Now I realised the distinction between neurosis and madness, and in my agitation I half-envied the woman beyond my bedroom wall, the sheer cool sanity of her behaviour within the limits of her impracticable mania.      Ibid.

18 New York, home of the vivisectors of the mind, and of the mentally vivisected still to be reassembled, of those who live intact, habitually wondering about their states of sanity, and home of those whose minds have been dead, bearing the scars of resurrection. . . .
*The Hothouse by the East River*,
Ch. 1    *1973*

19 "Sex," she says, "is a subject like any other subject. Every bit as interesting as agriculture."
Ibid., Ch. 4

## 943. Abigail Van Buren

(1918– )

1 People who fight fire with fire usually end up with ashes.
"Dear Abby" Newspaper Column
*March 7, 1974*

2 Some people are more turned on by money than they are by love. . . . In one respect they're alike. They're both wonderful as long as they last.      Ibid.
*April 26, 1974*

3 Religion, like water, may be free, but when they pipe it to you, you've got to help pay for the piping. And the piper!      Ibid.
*April 28, 1974*

4 The best index to a person's character is (a) how he treats people who can't do him any good, and (b) how he treats people who can't fight back.      Ibid.    *May 16, 1974*

5 Psychotherapy, unlike castor oil, which will work no matter how you get it down, is useless when forced on an uncooperative patient.
Ibid.    *July 11, 1974*

## 944. Ella Grasso
(1919– )

1 I'm opposed to abortion because I happen to believe that life deserves the protection of society. Quoted in "Ella Grasso of Connecticut" by Joseph B. Treaster, *Ms.*
*October, 1974*

2 I would not be President because I do not aspire to be President. But I'm sure that a woman will be President. When? I don't know. It depends. I don't think the woods are full of candidates today. Quoted in *Newsweek*
*November 4, 1974*

3 In Connecticut I'm just an old shoe.
Quoted in *Time*
*November 18, 1974*

4 I keep my campaign promises, but I never promised to wear stockings. Ibid.

## 945. Uta Hagen
(1919– )

1 More than in the other performing arts the lack of respect for acting seems to spring from the fact that every layman considers himself a valid critic. *Respect for Acting*, Pt. I,
Introduction *1973*

2 The American theatre poses endless problems for any actor who wants to call himself an artist, who wants to be part of an art form.
Ibid.

3 Talent is an amalgam of high sensitivity; easy vulnerability; high sensory equipment (seeing, hearing, touching, smelling, tasting—*intensely*); a vivid imagination as well as a grip on reality; the desire to communicate one's own experience and sensations, to make one's self heard and seen. Ibid., Ch. I

4 Rebellion or revolt does not necessarily .find its expression in violence. A gentle, lyric stroke may be just as powerful a means of expression.
Ibid.

5 To maintain one's ideals in ignorance is easy. . . . Ibid.

6 We must overcome the notion that we must be *regular*. . . . It robs you of the chance to be extraordinary and leads you to the mediocre. Ibid., Ch. 2

7 A great danger is to take the five senses for granted. Most people do. Once you become aware that the sources which move in on you when you truly touch, taste, smell, see and hear

are endless, you must also realize that self-involvement deadens the senses, and vanity slaughters them until you end up playing alone—and meaninglessly. Ibid., Ch. 6

## 946. Pauline Kael
(1919– )

1 Movies have been doing so much of the same thing—in slightly different ways—for so long that few of the possibilities of this great hybrid art have yet been explored.
"Movies as Opera,"
*Going Steady*, Pt. I *1968*

2 Good movies make you care, make you believe in possibilities again. Ibid., Pt. II, Ch. 1

3 Technique is hardly worth talking about unless it's used for something worth doing. . . .
Ibid., Ch. 2

4 The new tribalism in the age of the media is not necessarily the enemy of commercialism; it is a direct outgrowth of commercialism and its ally, perhaps even its instrument.
Ibid., Ch. 4

5 Unsupervised enjoyment is probably not the only kind there is but it may feel like the only kind. Irresponsibility is part of the pleasure of all art, it is the part the schools cannot recognize. Ibid., Ch. 5

6 Art is still what teachers and ladies and foundations believe in, it's civilized and refined, cultivated and serious, cultural, beautiful, European, Oriental: it's what America isn't, and it's especially what American movies are not.
Ibid.

7 Trash has given us an appetite for art. Ibid.

8 The lowest action trash is preferable to wholesome family entertainment. When you clean them up, when you make movies respectable, you kill them. The wellspring of their *art*, their greatness, is in not being respectable.
Ibid., Ch. 6

9 If big film directors are to get credit for doing badly what others have been doing brilliantly for years with no money, just because they've put it on a big screen, then businessmen are greater than poets and theft is art.
Ibid., Ch. 8

10 The words "Kiss Kiss Bang Bang," which I saw on an Italian movie poster, are perhaps the briefest statement imaginable of the basic appeal of movies.
*Kiss Kiss Bang Bang*, Title Note
*1968*

11 What they think is creativity is simply the excitement of success, the exhilaration of power.
*Ibid., Pt. I*

12 . . . banality and luxuriant wastefulness . . . are so often called the superior "craftsmanship" of Hollywood. *Ibid.*

13 It seems likely that many of the young who don't wait for others to call them artists, but simply announce that they are, don't have the patience to make art. *Ibid.*

14 Good liberal parents didn't want to push their kids in academic subjects but oohed and aahed with false delight when their children presented them with a baked ashtray or a woven doily. Did anyone guess or foresee what narcissistic confidence this generation would develop in banal "creativity"? Now we're surrounded, inundated by artists. *Ibid.*

15 We try to protect ourselves as women by betraying other women. And, of course, women who *are* good writers succeed in betrayal but fail to save themselves. *Ibid., Pt. II*

16 . . . advertising determines what is accepted as art. *Ibid., Pt. III*

17 What makes movies a great popular art form is that certain artists can, at moments in their lives, reach out and unify the audience—educated and uneducated—in a shared response. The tragedy in the history of movies is that those who have this capacity are usually prevented from doing so. *Ibid.*

18 We may be reaching the end of the era in which individual movies meant something to people. In the new era, movies may just mean a barrage of images. *Ibid., Pt. V*

## 947. Elizabeth Duncan Koontz

(1919– )

1 . . . like steel that has been passed through fire, the century will be stronger for having been tested. Quoted in "Impeachment?" by Claire Safran, *Redbook April, 1974*

## 948. Isobel Lennart

(1919?– )

1 FANNY. Look—suppose all you ever had for breakfast was onion rolls. All of a sudden one morning, in walks a bagel. You'd say, "Ugh! What's that?" Until you tried it. *That's* my trouble. I'm a bagel on a plate full of onion rolls! *Funny Girl*, Act I, Sc. 3 *1964*

2 NICK. Success is something to enjoy—to flaunt! Otherwise, why work so hard to get it? *Ibid., Sc. 10*

3 NICK. Fanny, would you say you were a woman of—wide experience? . . .

FANNY. . . . I've been too busy. What about you? *Hundreds* of girls, huh?

NICK. The count is in mere dozens. Of very minor entanglements. I like to feel free.

FANNY. You can get lonesome—being that free.

NICK. You can get lonesome—being that busy. *Ibid., Sc. 11*

4 FANNY. It's wonderful to hear an audience applaud, but you can't take an audience home with you! *Ibid., Sc. 14*

## 949. Doris Lessing

(1919– )

1 . . . he went on to remark gently that some women seemed to imagine birth control was a sort of magic; if they bought what was necessary and left it lying in a corner of a drawer, nothing more was needed. To this attitude of mind, he said, was due a number of births every year which would astound the public. *A Proper Marriage*, Pt. I, Ch. 1 *1952*

2 Love had brought her here, to lie beside this young man; love was the key to every good; love lay like a mirage through the golden gates of sex. *Ibid.*

3 "Is there any evidence whatsoever that a person educated in one way rather than another will have different qualities, different abilities? And is there any evidence that the mass of human beings are better than brutes!" *Ibid.*

4 There is something in the word "meeting" which arouses an instinctive and profound distrust in the bosoms of British people at this late hour of their history. *Ibid., Pt. IV, Ch. 2*

5 "If people dug up the remains of this civilization a thousand years hence, and found Epstein's statues and that man Ellis, they would think we were just savages." *Martha Quest*, Pt. I, Ch. 1 *1952*

6 "Died of gas from the war, she says. Pity those War Office blokes never understood that people could be ill because of the war, and it only showed afterwards. He got no compensation, she says. Damned unfair." *Ibid., Pt. II, Ch. 2*

7 "In university they don't tell you that the greater part of the law is learning to tolerate fools." Ibid., Pt. III, Ch. 2

8 . . . she envied her lost capacity for making the most of time—that was how she put it, as if time were a kind of glass measure which one could fill or not. Ibid., Pt. IV, Ch. 1

9 What of October, that ambiguous month, the month of tension, the unendurable month? Ibid.

10 "Sometimes I look at a young man in the States who has a certain resemblance, and I ask myself: Perhaps he is my son? Yes, yes, my friend, this is a question that every man must ask himself, sometimes, is it not?" *The Habit of Loving,* Ch. 3    1957

11 The smell of manure, of sun on foliage, of evaporating water, rose to my head; two steps farther, and I could look down into the vegetable garden enclosed within its tall pale of reeds—rich chocolate earth studded emerald green, frothed with the white of cauliflowers, jewelled with the purple globes of eggplant and the scarlet wealth of tomatoes. Ibid., Ch. 9

12 Effort, after days of laziness, seemed impossible. Ibid., Ch. 15

13 Pleasure resorts are like film stars and royalty who—or so one hopes—must be embarrassed by the figures they cut in the fantasies of people who have never met them. Ibid., Ch. 17

14 . . . he hated her for his ineptitude. "One Off the Short List," *A Man and Two Women*    1958

15 . . . the rifle, justified by utility. . . . Ibid.

16 "Small things amuse small minds. . . ." Ibid., "A Woman on a Roof"

17 "Don't you think there's something awful in two grown people stuck together all the time like Siamese twins?" Ibid., "A Man and Two Women"

18 Bed is the best place for reading, thinking, or doing nothing. Ibid., "A Room"

19 "There's nothing in sight, not one object or building anywhere, that is beautiful. Everything is so ugly and mean and graceless that it should be bulldozed into the earth and out of the memory of man." Ibid., "England Versus England"

20 . . . she was thirty-nine. . . . No, she did not envy her eighteen-year-old self at all. But she did envy, envied every day more bitterly, that young girl's genuine independence, largeness, scope, and courage. Ibid., "Between Men"

21 . . . the satisfied fervour of one who has at last pinned a label on a rare specimen: "She is, of course, one of your typical English spinsters." . . . "I suppose she has given up?" "Given up what?" I asked. . . . Ibid, "Our Friend Judith"

22 They separated gently, but the movements both used . . . were more like a fitting together. Ibid., "Each Other"

23 Above all, intelligence forbids tears. Ibid., "To Room 19"

24 A high price has to be paid for the happy marriage with the four healthy children in the large white gardened house. Ibid.

25 Some people had to live with crippled arms, or stammers, or being deaf. She would have to live knowing she was subject to a state of mind she could not own. Ibid.

26 It seems to me like this. It's not a terrible thing —I mean it may be terrible, but it's not damaging, it's not poisoning to do without something one really wants. . . . What's terrible is to pretend that the second-rate is first-rate. To pretend that you don't need love when you do; or you like your work when you know quite well you're capable of better. *The Golden Notebook*    1962

27 After a certain age—and for some of us that can be very young—there are no new people, beasts, dreams, faces, events: it has all happened before . . . and everything is an echo and a repetition; and there is no grief even that it is not a recurrence of something long out of memory. *Particularly Cats,* Ch. 2    1967

28 If a fish is the movement of water embodied, given shape, then cat is a diagram and pattern of subtle air. Ibid.

29 Oh cat; I'd say, or pray: be-*ooo*tiful cat! Delicious cat! Exquisite cat! Satiny cat! Cat like a soft owl, cat with paws like moths, jewelled cat, miraculous cat! Cat, cat, cat, cat. Ibid.

30 What is charm then? The free giving of a grace, the spending of something given by nature in her role of spendthrift. . . . Charm is something extra, superfluous, unnecessary, essentially a power thrown away—given. Ibid., Ch. 9

31 ". . . that is what learning is. You suddenly understand something you've understood all your life, but in a new way."
　　　　*The Four-Gated City*　　1969

32 Thinking? She would not have said so. She was trying to catch hold of something, or to lay it bare so she could look and define; for some time now she had been "trying on" ideas like so many dresses off a rack.
　　　　*The Summer Before the Dark*　　1973

33 Laughter is by definition healthy.　　Ibid.

34 "The way to learn a language is to breathe it in. Soak it up! Live it!"　　Ibid.

35 And what authority even the creases in a suit can convey. . . .　　Ibid.

36 Nonsense, it was all nonsense: this whole damned outfit, with its committees, its conferences, its eternal talk, talk, talk, was a great con trick; it was a mechanism to earn a few hundred men and women incredible sums of money.　　Ibid.

37 This was a happy and satisfactory marriage because both she and Michael had understood, and very early on, that the core of discontent, or of hunger, if you like, which is unfailingly part of every modern marriage . . . was fed and heightened by what people were educated to expect of marriage, which was a very great deal because the texture of ordinary life . . . was thin and unsatisfactory. Marriage had had a load heaped on it which it could not sustain.
　　　　Ibid.

38 . . . older woman, younger man! Popular wisdom claims that this particular class of love affair is the most poignant, tender, poetic, exquisite one there is, altogether the choicest on the menu.　　Ibid.

39 . . . should one judge people by the attitudes expected of them by virtue of the years they had lived, their phase or stage as mammals, or as items in society? Well, that is how most people have to be judged; only a few people are more than that.　　Ibid.

40 There was nothing to prevent one or all of us becoming victims at any moment.
　　　　*The Memoirs of a Survivor*　　1975

## 950. Iris Murdoch
(1919–　　)

1　"What are you famous *for*?"
　"For nothing. I am just famous."
　　　　*The Flight from the Enchanter*　　1955

2 "We can only learn to love by loving. . . ."
　　　　*The Bell*　　1958

3 "Only lies and evil come from letting people off. . . ."　　*A Severed Head*　　1961

4 "You cannot have both civilization and truth. . . ."　　Ibid.

5 "To be a complete victim may be another source of power."　　*The Unicorn*　　1963

6 Munching the substance of one's life as if it were a fruit with a thin soft furry exterior and a firm sweet fleshy inside.
　　　　*The Nice and the Good*　　1968

7 One's most ordinary everyday mode of consciousness being busy and lively and unconcerned with self.　　Ibid.

8 Love can't always do work. Sometimes it just has to look into the darkness.　　Ibid.

9 In its own element, in its own silence, indubitably physical, indubitably present, and yet Other.　　Ibid.

10. He led a double life. Did that make him a liar? He did not feel a liar. He was a man of two truths.
　　　　*The Sacred and Profane Love Machine*
　　　　1974

## 951. Françoise Parturier
(1919–　　)

1 To tell a woman using her mind that she is thinking with a man's brain means telling her that she can't think with her own brain; it demonstrates your ineradicable belief in her intellectual inadequacy.
　　　　*Open Letter to Men*　　1968

2 In general all curvaceousness strikes men as incompatible with the life of the mind.
　　　　Ibid.

3 You men can't stand the truth, sir, as soon as it embarrasses your interests or your pleasure. . . .　　Ibid.

4 And the more deodorants there are in the drugstores, the worse [woman] smells in literature.
　　　　Ibid.

5 That the most intelligent, discerning and learned men, men of talent and feeling, should finally put all their pride in their crotch, as awed as they are uneasy at the few inches sticking out in front of them, proves how normal it is for the world to be crazy. . . .　　Ibid.

6 . . . we've never been in a democracy; we've always been in a phallocracy!    Ibid.

7 A real woman is a young, pretty, sexy, tender woman who is no taller than five feet six who adores you.    Ibid.

8 You say being a housewife is the noblest call-in the world. . . . You remind me of those company executives who . . . praise the "little guys" of their organization in their speeches. . . .    Ibid.

## 952. Eva Perón
### (1919–1952)

1 Our President [General Juan Perón] has declared that the only privileged person in our country are the children.
> Speech, "My Labour in the Field of Social Aid," American Congress of Industrial Medicine
> *December 5, 1949*

2 Almsgiving tends to perpetuate poverty; aid does away with it once and for all. Almsgiving leaves a man just where he was before. Aid restores him to society as an individual worthy of all respect and not as a man with a grievance. Almsgiving is the generosity of the rich; social aid levels up social inequalities. Charity separates the rich from the poor; aid raises the needy and sets him on the same level with the rich.    Ibid.

## 953. Mary Carolyn Davies
### (fl. 1920s)
* * *

1 As oft as on the earth I've lain
I've died and come to life again.
> "Out of the Earth"

2 A trap's a very useful thing:
Nature in our path sets Spring.
It is a trap to catch us two,
It is planned for me and you.
> "Traps"

3 If I had known what trouble you were bearing;
What griefs were in the silence of your face;
I would have been more gentle, and more caring,
And tried to give you gladness for a space.
> "If I Had Known"

4 Iron, left in the rain
And fog and dew,
With rust is covered. —Pain
Rusts into beauty too.
> "Rust"

5 May I forget
What ought to be forgotten; and recall
Unfailing, all
That ought to be recalled, each kindly thing,
Forgetting what might sting.
> "A Prayer for Every Day"

6 Let me be joy, be hope! Let my life sing!
> Ibid.

7 Men are the devil—they all bring woe.
In winter it's easy to say just "No."
Men are the devil, that's one sure thing,
*But what are you going to do in spring?*
> "Men Are the Devil"

8 The talking oak
To the ancient spoke.
But any tree
Will talk to me.
> "Be Different to Trees"

9 Three can laugh and doom a king,
Three can make the planets sing.
> "Three"

10 Women are doormats and have been,
The years these mats applaud—
They keep the men from going in
With muddy feet to God.
> "Door-Mats"

## 954. Mary J. Elmendorf
### (fl. 1920s)
* * *

1 Beauty's the thing that counts
In women; red lips
And black eyes are better than brains.
> "Beauty's the Thing"

## 955. Charlotte Hardin
### (fl. 1920s)

1 I found many who were continually wishing for beauty. I went to them with a sunset and a spray of mist, but they had already contented themselves in a shop with little painted candlesticks.    *Coins and Medals    1921*

## 956. Edith Summers Kelley
### (fl. 1920s–1956)

1 . . . the barnyard was an expression of something that was real, vital, and fluid, that . . . was of natural and spontaneous growth, that . . . turned with its surroundings, that . . . was a part of the life that offered itself to her.
> *Weeds    1923*

2 The only break in what would seem to an out-sider an intolerable stretch of tedium was the dinner. This usually consisted of salt hog meat, fried or boiled potatoes and some other vege-table, followed by a heavy-crusted apple pie or a soggy boiled pudding. *Ibid.*

## 957. Elizabeth Shane

(fl. 1920s)

\* \* \*

1 But every road is rough to me
That has no friend to cheer it.
"Sheskinbeg"

## 958. Margaret Turnbull

(fl. 1920s–1942)

1 No man is responsible for his father. That is entirely his mother's affair. *Alabaster Lamps 1925*

2 When a man confronts catastrophe on the road, he looks in his purse—but a woman looks in her mirror. *The Left Lady 1926*

## 959. Bella Abzug

(1920– )

1 I am not elevating women to sainthood, nor am I suggesting that all women share the same views, or that all women are good and all men bad. Women have screamed for war. Women, like men, have stoned black children going to integrated schools. Women have been and are prejudiced, narrowminded, reactionary, even violent. *Some* women. They, of course, have a right to vote and a right to run for office. I will defend that right, but I will not support them or vote for them.
Speech, National Women's Political
Caucus, Washington, D.C.
*July 10, 1971*

2 I've been described as a tough and noisy woman, a prize fighter, a man-hater, you name it. They call me Battling Bella, Mother Cour-age, and a Jewish mother with more com-plaints than Portnoy. There are those who say I'm impatient, impetuous, uppity, rude, pro-fane, brash, and overbearing. Whether I'm any of those things, or all of them, you can decide for yourself. But whatever I am—and this ought to be made very clear at the outset—I am a *very* serious woman.
*Bella!*, Mel Ziegler, ed., Introduction
*1972*

3 Liberals! They're not leaders! If they were real leaders they'd understand that their style of politicking and self-aggrandizement is what's destroying the capacity of any of us to get anywhere. *Ibid.* (January 19, 1971)

4 But the establishment is made up of little men, very frightened. *Ibid.* (May 5, 1971)

5 In Britain the government has to come down in front of Parliament every day to explain its actions, but here the President never answers directly to Congress. *Ibid.* (June 17, 1971)

6 One thing that crystallized for me like nothing else this year is that Congress is a very *un-representative* institution. . . . These men in Congress . . . represent their *own* point of view—by reason of their sex, background, and class. *Ibid.*, Epilogue

7 She [a woman politician] will be challenging a system that is still wedded to militarism and that saves billions of dollars a year by under-paying women and using them as a reserve cheap labor supply.
"Bella's-Eye View of Her Party's
Future," *Ms. April, 1974*

8 A thoughtful husband, the [candidate's] man-ual said, should squelch any rumors that his wife is running for office because their mar-riage is on the skids. (Why else would a woman want to be in Congress?) *Ibid.*

9 You can't have a Congress that responds to the needs of the workingman when there are practically no people here who represent him. And you're not going to have a society that understands its humanity if you don't have more women in government.
Quoted in "Impeachment?" by Claire
Safran, *Redbook April, 1974*

10 If we get a government that reflects more of what this country is really about, we can turn the century—and the economy—around.
*Ibid.*

11 . . . our time has come. We will no longer con-tent ourselves with leavings and bits and pieces of the rights enjoyed by men . . . we want our equal rights, nothing more but nothing less. We want an equal share of political and eco-nomic power. Quoted in *Gullible's Travels* by Jill Johnston *1974*

## 960. Rosemary Brown

(1920?– )

1 I'm not committed to welfare measures. I don't think they get at the root of the problem. I'm

committed to the eradication of all poverty, to its being wiped out. I'm not hung up on guaranteed incomes and that kind of thing, because I don't think that's the solution. We've got to change the system and make it impossible to be poor.

> Quoted in "The Radical Tradition of Rosemary Brown" by Sharon Batt, *Branching Out*　　July/August, 1975

2　We cannot swing our vote. We have to swing our party.　　　　　　　　*Ibid.*

3　The feeling is that until men are comfortable working in some of these fields that are traditionally considered to be female . . . women end up doing two jobs, and the men are still doing just one.　　　　　　　　*Ibid.*

4　The whole idea of the feminist struggle being a peripheral kind of thing that you do in your spare time is something that has to be changed.　　　　　　　　*Ibid.*

## 961.　Rosalind Franklin
### (1920–1958)

1　This was my first continental holiday by car . . . and I confirmed my impression that cars are undesirable. . . . Travelling around in a little tin box isolates one from the people and the atmosphere of the place in a way that I have never experienced before. I found myself eyeing with envy all rucksacks and tents.

> Quoted in *Rosalind Franklin and DNA* by Anne Sayre　　1975p

## 962.　Barbara Guest
### (1920–　　)

1　I wonder if this new reality is going to destroy me.

> "The Hero Leaves His Ship," St. 1, *The Location of Things*　　1962

2　I am talking to you
With what is left of me written off,
On the cuff, ancestral and vague,
As a monkey walks through the many fires
Of the jungle while the village breathes in its sleep.

> *Ibid.*, "Sunday Evening," St. 3

3　Then you took my hand. You told me that love was a sudden disturbance of the nerve ends that startled the fibers and made them new again.

> *Ibid.*, "Sadness," St. 3

4　Where goes this wandering blue,
This horizon that covers us without a murmur?
Let old lands speak their speech,
Let tarnished canopies protect us.

> *Ibid.*, "In the Alps," St. 1

## 963.　Shirley Jackson
### (1920–1965)

1　School was recently over for the summer, and the feeling of liberty sat uneasily on most of them. . . .　　　　"The Lottery"　　1948

2　"Listening to the young folks, nothing's good enough for *them*. Next thing you know, they'll be wanting to go back to living in caves, nobody work any more, live *that* way for a while."　　　　　　　　*Ibid.*

3　I believe that all women, but especially housewives, tend to think in lists. . . . The idea of a series of items, following one another docilely, forms the only possible reasonable approach to life if you have to live it with a home and a husband and children, none of whom would dream of following one another docilely.　　*Life Among the Savages*, Pt. II　　1953

4　"Cocoa," she said. "Cocoa. Damn miserable puny stuff, fit for kittens and unwashed boys. Did *Shakespeare* drink cocoa?"　　　　　　*The Bird's Nest*, Pt. I　　1954

5　. . . I saw that Beth now, looking about her and drawing herself together, was endeavoring to *form* herself, as it were; let my reader who is puzzled by my awkward explanations close his eyes for no more than two minutes, and see if he does not find himself suddenly not a compact human being at all, but only a consciousness on a sea of sound and touch; it is only with the eyes open that a corporeal form returns, and assembles itself firmly around the hard core of sight.　　*Ibid.*, Pt. IV

6　Her manner of dress, of speech, of doing her hair, of spending her time, had not changed since it first became apparent to a far younger Morgen that in all her life to come no one was, in all probability, going to care in the slightest how she looked, or what she did, and the minor wrench of leaving humanity behind was more than compensated for by her complacent freedom from a thousand small irritations.　　　　　　　　*Ibid.*, Pt. V

7　. . . February, when the days of winter seem endless and no amount of wistful recollecting can bring back any air of summer. . . .　　　　*Raising Demons*, Pt. II　　1956

8 It has long been my belief that in times of great stress, such as a four-day vacation, the thin veneer of family unity wears off almost at once, and we are revealed in our true personalities. . . .     *Ibid., Pt. IV*

9 She looked out the window . . . savoring the extreme pleasure of being on a moving train with nothing to do for six hours but read and nap and go into the dining-car, going farther and farther every minute from the children, from the kitchen floor, with even the hills being incredibly left behind, changing into fields and trees too far away from home to be daily.    "Pillar of Salt," *The Magic of Shirley Jackson*, Stanley Edgar Hyman, ed. *1966p*

10 She walked quickly around her one-room apartment. . . . After more than four years in this one home she knew all its possibilities, how it could put on a sham appearance of warmth and welcome when she needed a place to hide in, how it stood over her in the night when she woke suddenly, how it could relax itself into a disagreeable unmade, badly-put-together state, mornings like this, anxious to drive her out and go back to sleep.
    *Ibid.,* "Elizabeth"

## 964. Gerda Lerner
### (1920– )

1 Black people cannot and will not become integrated into American society on any terms but those of self-determination and autonomy.
    *Black Women in White America,* Preface    *1972*

2 . . . black women . . . are trained from childhood to become workers, and expect to be financially self-supporting for most of their lives. They know they will have to work, whether they are married or single; work to them, unlike to white women, is not a liberating goal, but rather an imposed lifelong necessity.     *Ibid.*

## 965. Mary McGrory
### (1920?– )

1 But he [Richard M. Nixon] was like a kamikaze pilot who keeps apologizing for the attack.
    Syndicated Newspaper Column *November 8, 1962*

2 Somehow it sounded as though his [Richard M. Nixon's] zeal in providing a generation of peace rather than his efforts to cover up a generation of corruption had gotten him into trouble.     *Ibid.*    *August 9, 1974*

\* \* \*

3 He [John F. Kennedy] came on, composed as a prince of the blood, chestnut thatch carefully brushed, facts straight, voice steady. "Look at him," breathed the proud Irishman next to me in the audience. "He's a thoroughbred."
    *Ibid.*

## 966. Elaine Morgan
### (1920– )

1 The trouble with specialists is that they tend to think in grooves.
    *The Descent of Woman,* Ch. 1 *1972*

2 We had taken the first step along the tortuous road that led to the sex war, sado-masochism, and ultimately to the whole contemporary snarl-up, to prostitution, prudery, Casanova, John Knox, Marie Stopes, white slavery, women's liberation, *Playboy* magazine, *crimes passionels,* censorship, strip clubs, alimony, pornography, and a dozen different brands of mania. This was the Fall. It had nothing to do with apples.
    *Ibid.,* Ch. 4

3 . . . everyone knows that you can't relieve an itch by stroking it gently.     *Ibid.,* Ch. 5

4 Housewives and mothers seldom find it practicable to come out on strike. They have no union, anyway. But the rumblings of women's liberation are only one pointer to the fact that you already have a discontented work force. And if conditions continue to lag so far behind the industrial norm and the discomfort increases, you will find . . . that you will end up with an inferior product.     *Ibid.,* Ch. 11

## 967. Eleanor Perry
### (1920?– )

1 "We've all known each other so long there's not even anyone to flirt with."
    *The Swimmer* (screenplay)    *1967*

2 "That's your hang-up, Neddy-boy. You're afraid the sky will fall down if everybody doesn't love you. You'll lose the popularity contest, you won't be elected Head Boy—as if the whole world's a prep school!"     *Ibid.*

3 Rape has become a kind of favor done to the female—a fairly commonplace male fantasy.
    Quoted in "Rebirth" by Kay Loveland and Estelle Changas, *The Hollywood Screenwriters,* Richard Corliss, ed. *1972*

4 . . . so long as a woman is dependent on a man for her self-image or her self-esteem she will remain without any sense of her own worth—can never be a fully realized human being.      Ibid.

5 I believe that "the unexamined life is not worth living"—and what a glorious medium film is on which to conduct our examinations!      Ibid.

6 Given a skillful cinematographer and technical staff almost any creative person can direct a film.      Ibid.

## 968. Hazel Scott

(1920–    )

1 If you reach for something and find out it's the wrong thing, you change your program and move on.      Quoted in "Great (Hazel) Scott!" by Margo Jefferson, *Ms. November, 1974*

2 There's only one free person in this society, and he is white and male.      Ibid.

3 Who ever walked behind anyone to freedom? If we can't go hand in hand, I don't want to go.      Ibid.

4 There's a time when you have to explain to your children why they're born, and it's a marvelous thing if you know the reason by then.      Ibid.

## 969. Dinah Shore

(1920–    )

1 I earn and pay my own way as a great many women do today. Why should unmarried women be discriminated against—unmarried men are not.      Quoted in "Dinah," *Los Angeles Times April 16, 1974*

2 I have never thought of participating in sports just for the sake of doing it for exercise or as a means to lose weight. And I've never taken up a sport just because it was a social fad. I really enjoy playing. It is a vital part of my life.      Ibid.

## 970. Harriet Van Horne

(1920–    )

1 Cooking is like love. It should be entered into with abandon or not at all.      Quoted in *Vogue October, 1956*

## 971. Betty Friedan

(1921–    )

1 Over and over women heard in voices of tradition and Freudian sophistication that they could desire no greater destiny than to glory in their own femininity [and] to pity the neurotic, unfeminine, unhappy women who wanted to be poets or physicians or presidents.      *The Feminine Mystique*, Ch. 1    *1963*

2 It can be less painful for a woman not to hear the strange, dissatisfied voice stirring within her.      Ibid.

3 And strange new problems are being reported in the growing generations of children whose mothers were always there, driving them around, helping them with their homework—an inability to endure pain or discipline or pursue any self-sustained goal of any sort, a devastating boredom with life.      Ibid.

4 American women no longer know who they are.      Ibid., Ch. 3

5 How did Chinese women, after having their feet bound for many generations, finally discover they could run?      Ibid., Ch. 4

6 The most powerful influence on modern women, in terms of both functionalism and the feminine protest, was Margaret Mead. . . . She was, and still is, the symbol of the woman thinker in America.      Ibid., Ch. 6

7 Anthropologists today are less inclined to see in primitive civilization a laboratory for the observation of our own civilization, a scale model with all the irrelevancies blotted out; civilization is just not that irrelevant.      Ibid.

8 Female biology, women's "biological career-line," may be changeless . . . but the nature of the human relationship to biology *has* changed.      Ibid.

9 For, of course, the natural childbirth-breast-feeding movement Margaret Mead helped to inspire was not at all a return to primitive earth-mother maternity. It appealed to the independent, educated, spirited . . . woman . . . because it enabled her to experience childbirth not as a mindless female animal, an object manipulated by the obstetrician, but as a whole person, able to control her own body with her aware mind.      Ibid.

10 There is little or no intellectual challenge or discipline involved in merely learning to adjust.      Ibid., Ch. 7

11 A mystique does not compel its own acceptance.      Ibid., Ch. 8

12 How to put the libido back, restore the lost spontaneity, drive, love of life, the individuality, that sex in America seems to lack?
Ibid., Ch. 9

13 The glorification of the "woman's role," then, seems to be in proportion to society's reluctance to treat women as complete human beings; for the less real function that role has, the more it is decorated with meaningless details to conceal its emptiness.          Ibid., Ch. 10

14 Instead of fulfilling the promise of infinite orgastic bliss, sex in the America of the feminine mystique is becoming a strangely joyless national compulsion, if not a contemptuous mockery.          Ibid., Ch. 11

15 It is easier to live through someone else than to become complete yourself.          Ibid., Ch. 14

16 The problem that has no name—which is simply the fact that American women are kept from growing to their full human capacities—is taking a far greater toll on the physical and mental health of our country than any known disease.          Ibid.

17 It is better for a woman to compete impersonally in society, as men do, than to compete for dominance in her own home with her husband, compete with her neighbors for empty status, and so smother her son that he cannot compete at all.          Ibid., Ch. 18

18 That we have not made any respectable attempt to meet the special educational needs of women in the past is the clearest possible evidence of the fact that our educational objectives have been geared exclusively to the vocational patterns of men.          Ibid., Ch. 11

19 Women, because they are not generally the principal breadwinners, can be perhaps most useful as the trail blazers, working along the bypaths, doing the unusual job that men cannot afford to gamble on.          Ibid.

20 If divorce has increased one thousand percent, don't blame the woman's movement. Blame our obsolete sex roles on which our marriages were based.          Speech          January 20, 1974

## 972. Zsa Zsa Gabor
### (1921?–     )

1 Husbands are like fires. They go out when unattended.          Quoted in Newsweek
March 28, 1960

2 A man in love is incomplete until he has married. Then he's finished.          Ibid.

## 973. Sybil Leek
### (1921?–     )

1 As for the Devil, I never met him myself, but I am gregarious enough to be polite to most people; so if I meet a man with little horns on his head and a peculiar taste in footwear, I'm not going to worry. You can't be sure who the Devil is these days. He might be a TV or movie producer in disguise.
Diary of a Witch, Ch. 1          1968

2 Perhaps telepathy will remain a mystery for many more years but it has always been within the power of a few people in every generation to transmit and receive thoughts. People in love often claim this power. Maybe we are being forced to realize that love is in itself a magical power and that awareness may be instrumental in preventing our own destruction.
Ibid., Ch. 6

3 We are about to move into the Aquarian age of clearer thinking. Astrology and witchcraft both have a contribution to make to the new age, and it behooves the practitioners of both to realize their responsibilities and obligations to the science and the religion.          Ibid., Ch. 11

4 Reincarnation is nothing more than the law of evolution applied to the consciousness of the individual. As in the material evolution of the birth, growth, and death of man, so there is a beginning, growth, and maturity in the consciousness. But there is not an end. The spirit is our only link with the Godhead, the divine force of life, and it is the indestructible part of ourselves.          Ibid., Ch. 12

5 We have to look at the broad spectrum of ESP, which can sometimes be a simple hunch, a flash of intuition, or an awareness outside the realm of the physical but not totally detached from it any more than the mind is detached from the organ of the brain.
ESP—The Magic Within You, Ch. 1
1971

6 We seem to be trapped by a civilization that has accelerated many physical aspects of evolution but has forgotten that other vital part of man—his mind and his psyche.
Ibid., Ch. 13

## 974. Eeva-Liisa Manner
### (1921–     )

1 MAIJA. Artfulness is a kind of capital.
Snow in May, Act I, Sc. 1          1966

2 PAAVO. Modesty makes women insincere.
Ibid.

3 LASSI. Women are awful—they know everything. Though they don't understand anything.
Ibid., Sc. 2

4 LASSI. Love makes *intelligent* beings depressed and flat. Only women, ostriches and monkeys are made happy by love. Oh yes, and parrots.
Ibid., Act II, Sc. 1

5 LASSI. The female is designed on the same principle as the starfish. Those creatures that the woman doesn't swallow she melts outside her body until the soft parts dissolve and only the shell remains.      Ibid.

6 LASSI. I love uncertain things . . . things that are certain bore me, make me depressed, like everlasting rain. And reliable and safe people are as boring as textbooks. Incalculable people are lovable, although they cause suffering too.
Ibid.

7 PAAVO. Illusions! Illusions. Illusion of innocent love. Illusion of the heart's goodness, illusion of the sacredness of the pure life. But your virtuousness is only love of comfort, bourgeois self-satisfaction. Give up what you hold so dear: your illusions, and you can return to reality and become your real self.
Ibid., Sc. 2

8 HELENA. If hope shows the depth of sorrow, then hopelessness must cure sorrow.      Ibid.

9 PAAVO. Great men are born in stable straw and they are put in a basket of reeds for the river to carry away. They are allowed to form their own souls—God looks after their bodies. They're not fed with warm milk, they must drink from the streams of the world, they do dirty work; the polisher of the mirror has dirty hands.      Ibid., Sc. 3

10 LASSI. Nothing is ever voluntary. Even when a person thinks he's doing something of his own free will, he's being compelled to do it. Only the dead are free, the chain is broken . . . but perhaps they miss their chains?
Ibid., Act III, Sc. 1

11 LASSI. Women! There isn't anything so bad that they don't soon start to enjoy it. Even if they lived in a barrel of shit they'd start making a home out of it, with everything nice and cozy.      Ibid.

12 The whole intelligence of a poem is in futility. . . .
"Untitled Poems," *The Other Voices*, Carol Cosman, ed.
*1975*

13 sleep builds stepping stones.
Ibid.

## 975. Del Martin
(1921– )

1 At a time when women, the forgotten sex, are voicing their rage and demanding their personhood, it is fitting that we [lesbians] emerge from the shadows.
*Lesbian/Woman*, with Phyllis Lyon
*1972*

2 To understand the lesbian as a sexual being, one must understand woman as a sexual being.
Ibid.

3 It is only when she can denounce the idiocy of religious scriptures and legal strictures that bind her and can affirm her Lesbian nature as but a single facet of her whole personality that she can become fully human.      Ibid.

4 There is nothing mysterious or magical about lesbian lovemaking. . . . The mystery and the magic come from the person with whom you are making love.      Ibid.

5 Much polarity between men and women has centered around procreation. But the sex act itself is neither male nor female: it is a human being reaching out for the ultimate in communication with another human being.      Ibid.

6 Most human sexual behavior is *learned*. It is only in the lower animals that it is totally instinctive. The higher on the evolutionary scale you are, the less instinctive are your sexual relations. So our life experiences "teach" us our sexuality, which may turn out to be hetero, homo, or bi.      Ibid.

7 As leaders . . . we could not display fear. In the process we overcame our own fears.
Ibid.

## 976. Donna Reed
(1921– )

1 If nuclear power plants are safe, let the commercial insurance industry insure them. Until these most expert judges of risk are willing to gamble with their money, I'm not willing to gamble with the health and safety of my family.      Quoted in the *Los Angeles Times*
*March 12, 1974*

## 977. Hannah Senesh
(1921–1944)

1 One needs something to believe in, something for which one can have whole-hearted enthusiasm. One needs to feel that one's life has meaning, that one is needed in this world.
*Hannah Senesh: Her Life and Diary*
(1938)      *1966p*

2 I dream and plan as if there was nothing happening in the world, as if there was no war, no destruction, as if thousands upon thousands were not being killed daily. . . .
    *Ibid.* (November 2, 1940)

3 There are events without which one's life becomes unimportant, a worthless toy; and there are times when one is commanded to do something, even at the price of one's life.
    *Ibid.* (December 25, 1943)

## 978. Alison Wyrley Birch
### (1922– )

1 There are sounds to seasons. There are sounds to places, and there are sounds to every time in one's life.  Quoted in *The Christian Science Monitor January 23, 1974*

## 979. Helen Gurley Brown
### (1922– )

1 You may marry or you may not. In today's world that is no longer the big question for women. Those who glom on to men so that they can collapse with relief, spend the rest of their days shining up their status symbol and figure they never have to reach, stretch, learn, grow, face dragons or make a living again are the ones to be pitied. They, in my opinion, are the unfulfilled ones.
    *Sex and the Single Girl* 1963

## 980. Judith Crist
### (1922– )

1 I am of the post-nickelodian pre-television generation, the children of Loew's Paradise. . . . Movies were our secret life. . . . There was somehow a perpetual edge of guilt . . . from the conviction held (and instilled) by parent and educator that time was better spent in developing the mind and body anywhere but in a moviehouse.
    *The Private Eye, the Cowboy and the Very Naked Girl,* Introduction
    *1968*

2 Movies suddenly became "film" and "cinema" and "art form" and terribly terribly chic. And the impossible dream came true overnight for those facile enough to latch on to a good and going thing, and film criticism became the means whereby a stream of young intellectuals could go straight from the campus film society into the professionals' screening room without managing to get a glimpse of the real world in between.    *Ibid.*

3 The critics who love are the severe ones . . . we know our relationship must be based on honesty.    *Ibid.*

4 In this lovely land of corrugated cartons and plastic bags, we want our entertainment packaged as neatly as the rest of our consumer goods: an attractive label on the outside, a complete and accurate detailing of contents there or on the inside, no loose ends, no odd parts, nothing left out.
    *Ibid., "Hud:* Unpackaged Reality"
    (June 2, 1963)

5 A moviegoer's version of not judging books by their covers might well be an adage about not judging films by their directors' statements of intent.   *Ibid.,* "Two Men in a House"
    (March 22, 1964)

6 In this era of affluence and of permissiveness, we have, in all but cultural areas, bred a nation of overprivileged youngsters, saturated with vitamins, television and plastic toys. But they are nurtured from infancy on a Dick-and-Jane literary and artistic level; and the cultural drought, as far as entertainment is concerned, sets in when they are between six and eight.
    *Ibid.,* "Forgotten Audience: American Children" (May 2, 1965)

7 Moviemaking, we are told, is a cooperative activity; hardy and rare and usually nonexistent is the individual who can take full credit for much more than a moment and super-perceptive and equally rare is the critic who can tell at a glance just where the credit lies. It's really no easier in the blame department.
    *Ibid.,* "Only in Hollywood—The Oscar" (March 13, 1966)

8 Happiness is too many things these days for anyone to wish it on anyone lightly. So let's just wish each other a bileless New Year and leave it at that. . . .
    *Ibid.,* "1966 at Its Worst: The Dishonor Roll" (January 1, 1967)

9 . . . the outcry against the current spate of sadism and violence in films is . . . more than justified by the indecencies that we are being subjected to on the big screen (and more and more on the little one at home), by the puddles of blood and piles of guts pouring forth from the quivering flesh that is being lashed and smashed, by the bouncing of breast and grinding of groin, by the brutalizing of men and desecration of women being fed to us by the hour for no possible social, moral or intellec-

tual purpose beyond our erotic edification and sensual delight and, above all, the almighty box-office return.

Ibid., "Against the Groin"
(December, 1967)

## 981. Mavis Gallant

(1922–  )

1   Flor looked at his closed fist. "Why do people keep things?" she said.
"I don't know," said George. "I guess it proves you were somewhere."

*Green Water, Green Sky*, Ch. 1
*1959*

2 Success can only be measured in terms of distance traveled. . . .     Ibid.

3 I was always putting myself in my sister's place, adopting her credulousness, and even her memories, I saw, could be made mine. It was Isobel I imagined as the eternal heroine— never myself. I substituted her feelings for my own, and her face for any face described. Whatever the author's intentions, the heroine was my sister.     *Its Image on the Mirror*
*1964*

4 No people are ever as divided as those of the same blood. . . .     Ibid.

5 Until the time of my own marriage I had sworn I would settle for nothing less than a certain kind of love. However, I had become convinced, after listening to my mother and to others as well, that a union of that sort was too fantastic to exist; nor was it desirable. The reason for its undesirability was never plain. It was one of the definite statements of rejection young persons must learn to make; "Perfect love cannot last" is as good a beginning as any.     Ibid.

6 We admitted we loved her—we who dread the word. We would rather say we adore: it is so exaggerated it can't be true. Adore equals like, but love is compromising, eternal.     Ibid.

7 The Knights had been married nearly sixteen years. They considered themselves solidly united. Like many people no longer in love, they cemented their relationship with opinions, pet prejudices, secret meanings, a private vocabulary that enabled them to exchange amused glances over a dinner table and made them feel a shade superior to the world outside the house.     "Bernadette," *My Heart Is Broken*
*1964*

8 The world drew into itself, became smaller and smaller, was limited to her room, her table in the dining room, her own eyes in the mirror, her own hand curved around a glass. Dreams as thick as walls rose about her bed and sheltered her sleep. . . .

Ibid., "The Moabitess"

9 They were young and ambitious and frightened; and they were French, so that their learned behavior was all smoothness. There was no crevice where an emotion could hold.

Ibid., "The Cost of Living"

10   "What is the appeal about cats?" he said kindly. "I've always wanted to know." . . .
"They don't care if you like them. They haven't the slightest notion of gratitude, and they never pretend. They take what you have to offer, and away they go. . . . It would be interesting to see what role the cat fancier *is* trying on," said Walter. . . . "He says he likes cats because they don't like anyone. I suppose he is proving he is so tough he can exist without affection."

Ibid., "An Unmarried Man's Summer"

11 "Don't cry whilst writing letters. The person receiving the letter is apt to take it as a reproach. Undefined misery is no use to anyone. Be clear, or, better still, be silent. If you must tell the world about your personal affairs, give examples. Don't just sob in the pillow hoping someone will overhear."

*A Fairly Good Time*, Ch. 1     *1970*

12 She had the loaded handbag of someone who camps out and seldom goes home, or who imagines life must be full of emergencies.

Ibid., Ch. 5

13 Swedish films had given her the impression that conversation in an unknown tongue consisted of nothing except "Where is God?" and "Should one have children?" although, in reality, everyone in those foreign countries was probably saying "How much does it cost?" and "Pass the salt."     Ibid.

14 [They] had been in a war they had not believed in and that was not officially a war at all. They were not veterans and not entitled to pensions. Privilege, a token income . . . were allowed for veterans of both world wars, the survivors of Indo-China, the old soldiers of the Resistance. But the combatants of Algeria seemed like bad weather. They were not a useful memory.     Ibid., Ch. 8

15 Good profession, good family, no money, foul temper—oh, the best of husbands.

Ibid., Ch. 9

16 Nobody in movies ever runs out of cigarettes or has to look for parking space.
Ibid., Ch. 12

17 The worst punishment I can imagine must be solitary confinement with nothing for entertainment except news of the world. Ibid.

18 She had gone into captivity believing in virtue and learned she could steal. Went in loving the poor, came out afraid of them; went in generous, came out grudging; went in with God, came out alone.
"The Pegnitz Junction," *The Pegnitz Junction* 1973

19 Now that he was rich he was not thought ignorant any more, but simply eccentric.
Ibid.

20 Everyone is lying; he will invent his own truth. Is it important if one-tenth of a lie is true? Is there a horror in a memory if it was only a dream? Ibid., "Ernst in Civilian Clothes"

## 982. Judy Garland
(1922–1969)

1 . . . they [MGM] had us working days and nights on end. They'd give us pep-up pills to keep us on our feet long after we were exhausted. Then they'd take us to the studio hospital and knock us cold with sleeping pills— Mickey [Rooney] sprawled out on one bed and me on another. Then after four hours they'd wake us up and give us the pep-up pills again so we could work another seventy-two hours in a row. Half of the time we were hanging from the ceiling, but it became a way of life for us. Quoted in *Judy Garland* by Anne Edwards, Ch. 11 1975p

2 Before every free conscience in America is subpoenaed, please speak up!
Ibid., Ch. 19 (c.1947)

3 How strange when an illusion dies
It's as though you've lost a child. . . .
Ibid., "An Illusion"

4 We cast away priceless time in dreams,
Born of imagination, fed upon illusion, and put to death by reality.
Ibid., "Imagination"

5 For 'twas not into my ear you whispered but into my heart.
'Twas not my lips you kissed, but my soul.
Ibid., "My Love Is Lost"

## 983. Grace Hartigan
(1922– )

1 . . . the face the world puts on to sell itself to the world.
Quoted by Cindy Nemser in *Art Talk* (magazine) 1975

2 I'd like to think that there are some things that . . . can't be analyzed to the point where they're finished off, either. Ibid.

3 . . . I don't mind being miserable as long as I'm painting well. Ibid.

4 There's a time when what you're creating and the environment you're creating it in come together. Ibid.

## 984. Gladys Heldman
(1922– )

1 It's a mental attitude you have about winning, about dying before you're willing to lose.
Quoted in "Queen of the Long-Way Babies" by Dan Rosen, *Signature* August, 1974

2 Players are always in the foreground, and they should be . . . anything else would be like Sol Hurok thinking that *he* was the star when it is really the ballet. Ibid.

## 985. Eda J. Le Shan
(1922– )

1 . . . most of us carry into marriage not only our childlike illusions, but we bring to it as well the demand that it *has* to be wonderful, because it's *supposed* to be. Of course the biggest illusion of all is that we are going to do the job of parenthood so well: it will all be fun and always deeply satisfying.
*How to Survive Parenthood*, Ch. 2 1965

2 We are learning that there are no longer any simple patterns or easy definitions. Each of us has to discover who and what we are, and our own special qualities; what makes us feel womanly. Passivity and weakness do not describe the feminine woman; devotion to kitchen or nursery serves us no better as a definition— where and what is the indefinable something our feminist grandmothers were so eager to give up and we are so anxious to recapture?
Ibid., Ch. 8

3 Psychotherapy can be one of the greatest and most rewarding adventures, it can bring with it the deepest feelings of personal worth, of purpose and richness in living. It doesn't mean that one's life situation will change dramatically or suddenly. . . . It does mean that one can develop new capacities and strengths with which to meet the natural vicissitudes of living; that one may gain a sense of inner peace through greater self-acceptance, through a more realistic perspective on one's relationships and experiences.           Ibid., Ch. 11

4 . . . in all our efforts to provide "advantages" we have actually produced the busiest, most competitive, highly pressured and over-organized generation of youngsters in our history—and possibly the unhappiest. We seem hell-bent on eliminating much of childhood.
              *The Conspiracy Against Childhood,*
                    Ch. 1       1967

5 The reason the young child learns [to talk] so well and so fast is that *his* way of learning is his own best way. When he is allowed this freedom to explore the world of language, he pursues his own interest and curiosity. . . . He comes at things from many directions and is therefore more likely to see the way they fit together and relate to one another. . . . He learns not to please others, but to please himself.                    Ibid., Ch. 2

6 Babies are necessary to grown-ups. A new baby is like the beginning of all things—wonder, hope, a dream of possibilities. In a world that is cutting down its trees to build highways, losing its earth to concrete . . . babies are almost the only remaining link with nature, with the natural world of living things from which we spring.            Ibid.

7 Because Maria Montessori was herself a creative thinker, I cannot believe that she would be at all happy about what is being done in her name. The passionate fervor of today's Montessori proponents, their single-minded dependence on a narrow formulation and program despite all that has been learned about children and education since Dr. Montessori was alive, does not represent an objective or thoughtful pooling of all the resources at our disposal. . . .            Ibid., Ch. 3

8 If, when we provide "enrichment" programs, our aim is merely to put pressure on children for accelerated mental development, we may be adding to their feelings of unworthiness rather than relieving those they already have. . . . Instead of focusing our attention on developing readiness for academic achievement

promulgating middle-class standards and behavior, we ought to be spending our time and our money on ways in which to help every child to feel that he is a person, that he is lovable and that he can contribute something of value to others.            Ibid., Ch. 4

9 We are not asking our children to do their own best but to be *the* best. Education is in danger of becoming a religion based on fear; its doctrine is to compete. The majority of our children are being led to believe that they are doomed to failure in a world which has room only for those at the top.
                         Ibid., Ch. 5

10 Excellence in life seems to me to be the way in which each human being makes the most of the adventure of living and becomes most truly and deeply himself, fulfilling his own nature in the context of a good life with other people. . . . What he knows and what he feels have equal importance in his life. . . .
                         Ibid., Ch. 9

11 We have kept our children so busy with "useful" and "improving" activities that we are in danger of raising a generation of young people who are terrified of silence, of being alone with their own thoughts. . . .
                         Ibid., Ch. 11

## 986. Grace Paley
### (1922–    )

1 He had had a habit throughout the twenty-seven years of making a narrow remark which, like a plumber's snake, could work its way through the ear down the throat, halfway to my heart. He would then disappear, leaving me choking with equipment.
         *Enormous Changes at the Last Minute*
                              1960

2 They were busy as bees in a ladies' murmur about life and lives. They worked. They took vital facts from one another and looked as dedicated as a kibbutz.            Ibid.

3 . . . a very large family. Four brothers and three sisters, they wouldn't touch birth control with a basement beam. Orthodox. Constructive fucking. Builders, baby.            Ibid.

4 I have always required a man to be dependent on, even when it appeared that I had one already. I own two small boys whose dependence on me takes up my lumpen time and my bourgeois feelings.            Ibid.

5 I don't believe civilization can do a lot more than educate a person's senses. If it's truth and honor you want to refine, I think the Jews have some insight. Make no images, imitate no God. After all, in His field, the graphic arts, He is pre-eminent. Then let that One who made the tan deserts and the blue Van Allen belt and the green mountains of New England be in charge of Beauty, which He obviously understands, and let man, who was full of forgiveness at Jerusalem, and full of survival at Troy, let man be in charge of Good.
         Ibid.

6 The man has the burden of the money. It's needed day after day. More and more of it. For ordinary things and for life. That's why holidays are a hard time for him. Another hard time is the weekend, when he's not making money or furthering himself.      Ibid.

7 Rosiness is not a worse windowpane than gloomy gray when viewing the world.
         Ibid.

8 I was a fantastic student until ten, and then my mind began to wander.
     Quoted in Grace Paley: "Art Is on the Side of the Underdog" by Harriet Shapiro, *Ms.*     *March, 1974*

9 There isn't a story written that isn't about blood and money. People and their relationship to each other is the blood, the family. And how they live, the money of it.      Ibid.

10 . . . I think art, literature, fiction, poetry, whatever it is, makes justice in the world. That's why it almost always has to be on the side of the underdog.      Ibid.

11 If you live an autonomous life you never really are repressed.      Ibid.

## 987. Vera Randal

(1922– )

1 . . . I opened my eyes to the nightmare from which I knew, with a knowledge deeper and surer than words, I would not wake.
     "Alice Blaine," *The Inner Room*
         *1964*

2 Fury gathered until I was swollen with it.
         Ibid.

3 Time, dough in a bowl, rose, doubling, trebling in bulk, and I was in the middle of the swelling, yeasty mass—lost.      Ibid.

4 ". . . If this is July, what, precisely, happened to June, and a sizable slice of May?"    Ibid.

5 Christ, even a murderer was electrocuted only once.      Ibid.

6 "John is dead."
"Yes."
"I am also dead," I said numbly.
"You're not dead. You're very far from dead."
"I feel dead."
"That's different."
"Is it?" I said. "Is it really?"
"It is. Really."      Ibid.

7 "I believe in people, which I suppose is a way of believing in God."      Ibid.

8 "There are many ways of crying."
"Yes." My tears were hidden behind my grinning mask face. "Yes, there are."      Ibid.

## 988. Alice Rossi

(1922– )

1 The emancipation or liberation of women involves more than political participation and the change of any number of laws. Liberation is equally important in areas other than politics; economics, reproduction, household, sexual and cultural emancipation are relevant.
     *The Feminist Papers,* Preface
         *1973*

2 A really radical break from the confinement of sex roles might lie in women's search for mates from very different social and intellectual circles, men who are not vain, self-centered and ambitious but tenderly devoted to home and children and the living of life.
     Ibid., Pt. I, "The Making of a Cosmopolitan Humanist"

3 Scholars all too often move in a world as restricted as that in which their subjects lived or from which they escaped.      Ibid.

4 As economic affluence increased with the growth of the new industrialism and expansion of trade, women's worth declined as producers and increased as consumers.
     Ibid., Pt. II, Introduction

5 While social class rests on economic factors of income and power, social status rests on less tangible cultural factors of life styles.
         Ibid.

6 Alcohol was a threat to women, for it released men from the moral control they had learned from a diet of preaching and scolding from ministers and mothers alike.      Ibid.

7 Students of women's lives have sometimes claimed that spinsterhood and childlessness are the price such women paid for the unusual career paths they pursued.
Ibid., "The Blackwell Clan"

8 The focus on heaven can be a lifetime pursuit, and there is no way to test whether the goal was worth the effort. . . .      Ibid.

9 It is curious that it may be the help of a housekeeper and a friend that facilitates a woman's life's work, while the closest analogy . . . one would find from the pen of a man is typically a tribute to his wife.
Ibid., "A Feminist Friendship"

10 Equal pay for equal work continues to be seen as applying to equal pay for men and women in the same occupation, while the larger point of continuing relevance in our day is that some occupations have depressed wages because women are the chief employees. The former is a pattern of sex discrimination, the latter of institutionalized sexism.      Ibid.

11 The single most impressive fact about the attempt by American women to obtain the right to vote is how long it took.
Ibid., "Along the Suffrage Trail"

12 Without the means to prevent, and to control the timing of conception, economic and political rights have limited meaning for women. If women cannot plan their pregnancies, they can plan little else in their lives. . . .
Ibid., "The Right to One's Body"

13 It has become more "reasonable" to argue that Adam was made from Eve than vice versa.
Ibid., "The 'Militant Madonna' "

14 The drum-beating martial mood of wartime is often followed by a pot-stirring and baby-rocking domestic ethos in its aftermath.
Ibid., Pt. IV, Introduction

15 For every war widow there may be several dozen wives who cope with the physical and emotional damage inflicted by war on their husbands and sons.      Ibid.

16 . . . sons forget what grandsons wish to remember. . . .      Ibid.

17 "Understanding" . . . is not a foundation for action if the terms in which a problem is "understood" tend toward acceptance of the status quo. . . .      Ibid.

18 Abridgement of any published book or essay is an assault, a cutting or pruning by one mind of the work of another.
Ibid., "Guineas and Locks"

19 Understanding through mastery and control versus understanding through empathetic projection and the absorption of the views of others . . . may be a comparison that frequently differentiates the sexes. . . .
Ibid., "Cultural Stretch"

## 989. Renee Winegarten
### (1922–    )

1 Extremist movements . . . have played skillfully and successfully upon panic terrors and cultural decay and decadence.
"The Idea of Decadence," *Commentary*
*September, 1974*

2 The book of the faults and complexities of the present cannot be closed like that containing the difficulties and errors of the past. . . .
Ibid.

3 What lies behind the concept of decadence to render it so appealing to the imagination?
Ibid.

4 The mighty are fallen and we shall not look upon their like again.      Ibid.

5 We still tend to share the idea that civilization must be either growing and pressing ever onward and upward, or else disintegrating into nothingness, instead of going on, variously developing and changing in a multitude of different areas, in ways not always perceptible to the human eye.      Ibid.

6 If epochs can grow old and die, what is to prevent them from becoming subject to disease?      Ibid.

7 . . . the quest for origin and end, zenith and nadir, growth and decline, rise and fall, florescence and decadence. Where would writers be without these essential props for their narrative?      Ibid.

8 The sad, dim shades of twilight seemed so much more moving than the clarity of day.
Ibid.

9 Old age cannot be cured. An epoch or a civilization cannot be prevented from breathing its last. A natural process that happens to all flesh and all human manifestations cannot be arrested. You can only wring your hands and utter a beautiful swan song.      Ibid.

## 990. Shelley Winters
### (1922–    )

1 It was so cold I almost got married.
Quoted in *The New York Times*
*April 29, 1956*

## 991. Diane Arbus

(1923–1971)

1 It's important to get out of your skin into somebody else's . . . that somebody else's tragedy is not the same as your own.

*Diane Arbus     1972p*

2 I really believe there are things nobody would see if I didn't photograph them.     Ibid.

3 Most people go through life dreading they'll have a traumatic experience. Freaks are born with their trauma. They've already passed it. They're aristocrats.     Ibid.

4 My favorite thing is to go where I've never been.     Ibid.

5 The world seemed to me to belong to the world. I could learn things but they never seemed to be my own experience.     Ibid.

## 992. Ursula Reilly Curtiss

(1923– )

1 It was the old principle of getting back on the horse that had thrown you (although why, Kate had always wondered? Why not just take up some other sport?) but sometimes, like a number of laudable things, it was wearing.

*The Wasp, Ch. 1     1963*

2 After a second's astonishment, Kate let the lie stand. Like most lies it was much easier than the truth, and to contradict it might turn out to be a very wearying affair.

Ibid., Ch. 3

3 This was not love; it was exactly what Georgia had said: ownership. If you owned a race horse, you got the winner's stakes. If you owned a play, you got the royalties. If you owned a son. . . .     Ibid., Ch. 17

4 If you were healed of a dreadful wound, you did not want to keep the bandage.

Ibid., Ch. 18

## 993. Nadine Gordimer

(1923– )

1 That was one of the things she held against the missionaries: how they stressed Christ's submission to humiliation, and so had conditioned the people of Africa to humiliation by the white man.

"Not for Publication," *Not for Publication and Other Stories*
*1965*

2 He was a Nyasa with a face so black that the blackness was an inverted dazzle—you couldn't see what he was thinking.     Ibid., "The Pet"

3 It had proved impossible to anthropomorphize him into a handsome, dignified, well-behaved bully-boy; and somewhere along the unsuccessful process, he had lost the instincts of a dog, into the bargain.     Ibid.

4 I'm forty-nine but I could be twenty-five except for my face and my legs.

Ibid., "Good Climate, Friendly Inhabitants"

5 These [teenage] girls had dropped childhood, with its bond of physical dependency on parents, behind them. They had forgotten what they had been, and they did not know that they would become what their parents were. For the brief hiatus they occupied themselves with preparations for a state of being very different—a world that would never exist.

Ibid., "Vital Statistics"

6 The two women gazed out of the slumped and sagging bodies that had accumulated around them.     Ibid.

7 Time is change; we measure its passage by how much things alter.

*The Late Bourgeois World     1966*

8 Why am I idiotically timid before such people, while at the same time so critical of their limitations?     Ibid.

9 Oh we bathed and perfumed and depilated white ladies, in whose wombs the sanctity of the white race is entombed! What concoction of musk and boiled petals can disguise the dirt done in the name of that sanctity?     Ibid.

10 "There's nothing moral about beauty."     Ibid.

11 It is in opposition (the disputed territory of the argument, the battle for self-definition that goes on beneath the words) . . . that intimacy takes place.

*The Conservationist     1975*

12 She filled her house with blacks, and white parsons who went around preaching Jesus was a revolutionary, and then when the police walked in she was surprised.     Ibid.

13 To keep anything the way you like it for yourself, you have to have the stomach to ignore—dead and hidden—whatever intrudes. . . .

Ibid.

14 Come to think of it all the earth is a graveyard, you never know when you're walking over heads—particularly this continent [Africa], cradle of man, prehistoric bones and the bits of shaped stone . . . that were weapons and utensils.     Ibid.

## 994. Carolina Maria de Jesus
(1923?–    )

1 Actually we are slaves to the cost of living.
*Child of the Dark: The Diary of Carolina Maria de Jesus*
(July 15, 1955)    *1962*

2 I don't look for defects in children . . . neither in mine nor in others. I know that a child is not born with sense.    Ibid. (July 18, 1955)

3 The only thing that does not exist in the *favela** is friendship.    Ibid.

4 The book is man's best invention so far.
Ibid. (July 21, 1955)

5 I classify Sao Paulo this way: The Governor's Palace is the living room. The mayor's office is the dining room and the city is the garden. And the *favela* is the back yard where they throw the garbage.    Ibid. (May 15, 1958)

6 "You had faith, and now you don't have it any more?"
"No, my son, democracy is losing its followers. In our country everything is weakening. The money is weak. Democracy is weak and the politicians are very weak. Everything that is weak dies one day."
Ibid. (May 20, 1958)

7 She neglects children and collects men.
Ibid. (June 1, 1958)

8 A child is the root of the heart.    Ibid.

9 I read the masculine names of the defenders of the country, then I said to my mother: "Why don't you make me become a man?"
She replied: "If you walk under a rainbow, you'll become a man."
When a rainbow appeared I went running in its direction. But the rainbow was always a long way off. Just as the politicians are far from the people. . . . I returned and told my mother: "The rainbow ran away from me."
Ibid. (June 7, 1958)

10 Actually, the world is the way the whites want it. I'm not white, so I don't have anything to do with this disorganized world.
Ibid. (June 23, 1958)

11 I started thinking about the unfortunate children who, even being tiny, complain about their condition in the world. They say that Princess Margaret of England doesn't like being a Princess. Those are the breaks in life.
Ibid. (July 30, 1958)

* Barrio or ghetto.

## 995. Shirley Kaufman
(1923–    )

1 Through every night we hate,
preparing the next day's
war. . . .

"Mothers, Daughters,"
*The Floor Keeps Turning*    *1970*

## 996. Jean Kerr
(1923–    )

1 I'm tired of all this nonsense about beauty being only skin-deep. That's deep enough. What do you want—an adorable pancreas?
"Mirror, Mirror, on the Wall,"
*The Snake Has All the Lines*
*1958*

2 I feel about airplanes the way I feel about diets. It seems to me that they are wonderful things for other people to go on.    Ibid.

3 Marrying a man is like buying something you've been admiring for a long time in a shop window. You may love it when you get it home, but it doesn't always go with everything else in the house.
Ibid., "The Ten Worst Things About a Man"

4 TIFFANY. Practically everybody Daddy knows is divorced. It's not that they're worse than other people, they're just richer.
*Mary, Mary*, Act I    *1960*

5 MARY. Well, being divorced is like being hit by a Mack truck. If you live through it, you start looking very carefully to the right and to the left.    Ibid.

6 BOB. I think success has no rules, but you can learn a great deal from failure.    Ibid.

7 MARY. . . . if you were absolutely convinced that you had no feeling in your hand, you'd be relieved to burn your fingers.
Ibid., Act II

8 MARY. It was hard to communicate with you. You were always communicating with yourself The line was busy.    Ibid.

9 SYDNEY. You don't seem to realize that a poor person who is unhappy is in a better position than a rich person who is unhappy. Because the poor person has hope. He thinks money would help.    *Poor Richard*, Act I
*1963*

10 SYDNEY. Even though a number of people have tried, no one has yet found a way to drink for a living. Ibid.

11 SYDNEY. Our generation isn't looking for love. We're looking for desperation. We think it isn't real unless we have a fever of 103.
Ibid., Act III

12 RICHARD. See, I believe in words. I think when they're put together they should mean something. They have an exact meaning, a precise meaning. There is more precision in one good sonnet than there is in an Atlas missile.
Ibid.

13 JEFF. Man is the only animal that learns by being hypocritical. He pretends to be polite and then, eventually, he *becomes* polite.
*Finishing Touches*, Act I    1973

14 KATY. If there is a fifty-fifty chance of immortality, why not play it with the believers? . . . I think you should impose standards and disciplines on yourself so that you might just possibly slip into eternity with Thomas More instead of going to hell with Hitler.
Ibid., Act II

15 FELICIA. Hope is the feeling you have that the feeling you have isn't permanent.
Ibid., Act III

## 997.  Denise Levertov
### (1923–    )

1 two by two in the ark of
the ache of it.
"The Ache of Marriage,"
*O Taste and See*    1963

2 "Life after life after life goes by

without poetry,
without seemliness,
without love."
"The Mutes," *The Sorrow Dance*
1966

## 998.  Inge Trachtenberg
### (1923?–    )

1 . . . my tenth year is marked as the year in which Adolf Hitler came to power in Germany. . . . Yet, when that event took place, Father wasn't sure that it was such a bad thing for Germany. Adolf Hitler had promised bread and order; Father was in favor of bread and order. . . . I, for one, had no premonition of bad things to come.
*So Slow the Dawning*, Ch. 4    1973

2 Decent was more than moral, decent was also being a good sport, a good friend, having a sense of humor, being tough.    Ibid., Ch. 14

3 I did a lot of writing that winter. . . . Putting things down lent them a sense of permanence, it seemed to stem the feeling of rushing time which was suddenly so compelling that I fancied hearing its sound.    Ibid., Ch. 16

## 999.  Sarah Caldwell
### (1924–    )

1 If you approach an opera as though it were something that always went a certain way, that's what you get. I approach an opera as though I didn't know it.
Quoted in "Sarah Caldwell: The Flamboyant of the Opera" by Jane Scovell Appleton, *Ms.*    May, 1975

2 The conductor and director must create the atmosphere, but a situation must exist where the singers can think and use their own remarkable faculties. It's like bringing up a gifted child.    Ibid.

3 We must continuously discipline ourselves to remember how it felt the first moment.
Ibid.

4 It [Tanglewood, summer home of the Boston Symphony Orchestra] was a place where gods strode the earth.
Quoted in "Music's Wonder Woman,"
*Time*    November 10, 1975

## 1000.  Shirley Chisholm
### (1924–    )

1 I was well on the way to forming my present attitude toward politics as it is practiced in the United States; it is a beautiful fraud that has been imposed on the people for years, whose practitioners exchange gilded promises for the most valuable thing their victims own, their votes. And who benefits most? The lawyers.    *Unbought and Unbossed*,
Pt. I, Ch. 4    1970

2 The seniority system keeps a handful of old men, many of them southern whites hostile to every progressive trend, in control of the Congress. These old men stand implacably across the paths that could lead us toward a better future. But worse than they, I think, are the majority of members of both Houses who continue to submit to the senility system. Apparently, they hope they, too, will grow to be old.    Ibid., Pt. II, Ch. 8

3 The difference between *de jure* and *de facto* segregation is the difference between open, forthright bigotry and the shamefaced kind that works through unwritten agreements between real estate dealers, school officials, and local politicians.     Ibid., Pt. IV, Ch. 14

4 I am a candidate for the Presidency of the United States. I make that statement proudly, in the full knowledge that, as a black person and as a female person, I do not have a chance of actually gaining that office in this election year.     Speech    *June 4, 1972*

5 We must get the message out that on these issues, child care, abortion and women in the labor force, white women must get in line behind us. The issue is survival.
    Speech, Eastern Regional Conference
    on Black Feminism
    *November 30, 1973*

6 I ran because someone had to do it first. In this country everyone is supposed to be able to run for President, but that's never been really true. I ran *because* most people think the country isn't ready for a black candidate, not ready for a woman candidate. Someday. . . .    *The Good Fight*, Ch. 1    *1973*

7 Richard M. Nixon . . . has a deeper concern for his place in history than for the people he governs. And history will not fail to note that fact.     Ibid., Ch. 11

8 We Americans have a chance to become someday a nation in which all racial stocks and classes can exist in their own selfhoods, but meet on a basis of respect and equality and live together, socially, economically, and politically. We can become a dynamic equilibrium, a harmony of many different elements, in which the whole will be greater than all its parts and greater than any society the world has seen before. It can still happen.
    Ibid., Ch. 14

## 1001. Carol Emshwiller
### (1924?–   )

1 As a mother I have served longer than I expected.    "Autobiography," *Joy in Our Cause*
    *1974*

2 For a long time I was powerless to resist: my father's opinions, marriage, and having three children, the lure of music.     Ibid.

3 Mother wants me to write something nice she can show to her friends.     Ibid.

## 1002. Janet Frame
### (1924–   )

1 Every morning I woke in dread, waiting for the day nurse to go on her rounds and announce from the list of names in her hand whether or not I was for shock treatment, the new and fashionable means of quieting people and of making them realize that orders are to be obeyed and floors are to be polished without anyone protesting and faces are made to be fixed into smiles and weeping is a crime.
    *Faces in the Water*, Ch. 1    *1961*

2 For in spite of the snapdragons and the dusty millers and the cherry blossoms, it was always winter.     Ibid., Ch. 2

3 Electricity, the peril the wind sings to in the wires on a gray day.     Ibid.

4. . . . very often the law of extremity demands an attention to irrelevance. . . .
    Ibid., Ch. 3

5 "For your own good" is a persuasive argument that will eventually make man agree to his own destruction.     Ibid., Ch. 4

## 1003. Cloris Leachman
### (1924–   )

1 Why can't we build orphanages next to homes for the elderly? If someone's sitting in a rocker, it won't be long before a kid will be in his lap.
    Quoted in "I Love My Career and
    I Love My Children . . ." by Jane
    Wilkie, *Good Housekeeping*
    *October, 1973*

## 1004. Phyllis Lyon
### (1924–   )

Co-author with Del Martin. See 975: 1–7.

## 1005. Bess Myerson
### (1924–   )

1 . . . the accomplice to the crime of corruption is frequently our own indifference.
    Quoted in "Impeachment?"
    by Claire Safran, *Redbook*
    *April, 1974*

2 It's always time for a change for the better, and for a good fight for the full human rights of every individual.
    Quoted in *AFTRA Magazine*
    *Summer, 1974*

## 1006. Alma Routsong

(1924–  )

1 Time enough later to teach her that it's better to be a real woman than an imitation man, and that when someone chooses a woman to go away with it's because a woman is what's preferred.     *A Place for Us*    1969

2 [I] wonder if what makes men walk lordlike and speak so masterfully is having the love of women.     Ibid.

## 1007. Phyllis Schlafly

(1924–  )

1 The advance planning and sense stimuli employed to capture a $10 million cigarette or soap market are nothing compared to the brainwashing and propaganda blitzes used to ensure control of the largest cash market in the world: the Executive Branch of the United States Government.
*A Choice Not an Echo*, Ch. 1
*1964*

2 The moral sickness of the Federal Government becomes more apparent every day. Public officials are caught in a giant web of payoffs, bribes, perversion, and conflicts of interest, so that few dare speak out against the establishment.     *Safe—Not Sorry*, Ch. 1    *1967*

3 America is waiting for an Attorney General who will enforce the law—and a President with the courage to demand that he do so.
Ibid., Ch. 8

4 The urgent need today is to develop and support leaders on every level of government who are independent of the bossism of every political machine—the big-city machine, the liberal Democrat machine, and the Republican kingmaker machine.     Ibid., Ch. 9

5 The left wing forces—both obvious and hidden —which have been running our country for the last seven years understand and appreciate the importance of *political action*. Their long tentacles reach out in many fields: to "orchestrate" propaganda through the communications media, to indoctrinate youth in our schools and universities, to create a Socialist intellectual climate through tax-exempt foundations, and to bend business into line with Government contracts.     Ibid., Ch. 12

6 One of the favorite slogans of the liberals is "U for Unity must precede V for Victory." Those who play this game forget that U and V are both preceded by P for Principle.
Ibid., Ch. 13

7 The claim that American women are downtrodden and unfairly treated is the fraud of the century.
Quoted by Lisa Cronin Wohl in *Ms.*
*March, 1974*

## 1008. Sally Weinraub

(1924–  )

1 Architects believed less and less in doors these days, so that houses were becoming like beehives, arches leading into chambers and more arches. It was lucky that Americans were still puritan in their habits. You could be alone in the bathroom.
"Knifed with a Black Shadow,"
*American Scene: New Voices*,
Don Wolfe, ed.    *1963*

## 1009. Shana Alexander

(1925–  )

1 Tadpole into frog, sketch into statue, tribe into stage—evolution is fascinating to watch. To me it is most interesting when one can observe the evolution of a single man.
"Evolution of a Rebel Priest" (April, 1966), *The Feminine Eye*    *1970*

2 Faithful horoscope-watching, practiced daily, provides just the sort of small but warm and infinitely reassuring fillip that gets matters off to a spirited start.
Ibid., "A Delicious Appeal to
Unreason" (May, 1966)

3 The sad truth is that excellence makes people nervous.
Ibid., "Neglected Kids—the Bright
Ones" (June, 1966)

4 A plane, if ,you're traveling alone, is also a good place to be melancholy. . . . A plane is a bad place for an all-out sleep, but a good place to begin rest and recovery from the trip to the faraway places you've been, a decompression chamber between Here and There. Though a plane is not the ideal place really to think, to reassess or reevaluate things, it is a great place to have the illusion of doing so, and often the illusion will suffice.
Ibid., "Overcuddle and Megalull"
(February, 1967)

5 Mankind still has monsters, of course. The trouble is that they are no longer mythological. Rather, they are the terrifying things man creates with his technology and then cannot control—things like Peenemünde; things like smog,

that foul thousand-mile blob visible from any jet; things like the cataclysmic, coiling, deadly dragon that is Vietnam.

> Ibid., "More Monsters, Please!"
> (December, 1967)

6 Roughly speaking, the President of the United States knows what his job is. Constitution and custom spell it out, for him as well as for us. His wife has no such luck. The First Lady has no rules; rather, each new woman must make her own.    Ibid., "The Best First Lady" (December, 1968)

7 . . . when two people marry they become in the eyes of the law one person, and that one person is the husband!

> *State-by-State Guide to Women's*
> *Legal Rights*, Introduction    1975

8 But certainly I knew that what all women's magazines were giving women to read was largely illusion, fantasy, and too often cruel deception. . . . I wanted to feed them reality, and clothe them with armor against the exploitation of women's needs and dreams which I knew abounded in the closed, essentially fake world of ladies' magazines.    Ibid.

9 The law changes and flows like water, and . . . the stream of women's rights law has become a sudden rushing torrent.    Ibid.

10 The [quail] females are so dowdy, drab, dun-colored, and diligent in their pecking, so hopelessly plodding compared to the handsome high-stepping ring-neck males, that for an atavistic moment I wonder anew whether and how the human female will ever transcend the lower, more dependent, less rights-ful station to which her reproductive nature has until the last-minute invention of The Pill confined her.

> Ibid.

## 1010. Dede Allen

(1925–    )

1 Editing [film] is really a creative art. Any editor needs to know certain techniques, but the real decisions are made in her or his head.

> Quoted in "The Power Behind the
> Screen" by Geraldine Febrikant, *Ms.*
> *February, 1974*

2 You know, when you're young and curious, people love to teach you.    Ibid.

## 1011. Svetlana Allilueva

(1925–    )

1 I think that before the marriage, it should be love. So if I will love this country and this country will love me, then the marriage will be settled.    Quoted in *Newsweek* *May 8, 1967*

2 Moscow, breathing fire like a human volcano with its smoldering lava of passion, ambition and politics, its hurly-burly of meetings and entertainment. . . . Moscow seethes and bubbles and gasps for air. It's always thirsting for something new, the newest events, the latest sensation. Everyone wants to be the first to know. It's the rhythm of life today.

> *Twenty Letters to a Friend*,
> Introduction (July 16, 1963)
> *1967*

3 He [her father, Stalin] is gone, but his shadow still stands over all of us. It still dictates to us and we, very often, obey.    Ibid., Ch. 2

4 Russia is immense, you cannot please everyone. "Brajesh Singh in Moscow," *Only One Year*    1969

5 . . . as a result of half a century of Soviet rule people have been weaned from a belief in human kindness.    Ibid., "The Journey's End"

## 1012. Marilyn Bender

(1925–    )

1 Female clothing has been disappearing literally and philosophically.

> *The Beautiful People*, Ch. 1    1967

2 To whip up desire for something that people don't really need, at least not in endless quantity, glamorous idols are essential. If desire begets need, then envy begets desire. The stimulation of envy or a longing to imitate is the function of the idol. The fashion industry, through its press agents and an eagerly cooperative, self-serving press, had to manufacture new goddesses.    Ibid., Ch. 3

3 What caused this . . . renaissance of the dandy in an era of technology? Pessimists attributed it to male decline. As women became more aggressive, invaded masculine professions and usurped male prerogatives, men fell back on being peacocks, they reasoned. With clothes, men were reconstructing their diminished manhood.    Ibid., Ch. 10

4 Any survey of what businessmen are reading runs smack into the open secret that most businessmen aren't. Reading books, that is.
"The Business of Reading About Business," *Saturday Review of the Society* *April, 1973*

5 Just as the court flunky tasted the king's food to screen it for poison, so today the corporate sovereign has his literary fare digested and presented in capsule form or laced into his speeches by his ghost writer. *Ibid.*

## 1013. Joyce Brothers
(1925?–    )

1 Marriage is not just spiritual communion and passionate embraces; marriage is also three-meals-a-day and remembering to carry out the trash. "When Your Husband's Affection Cools," *Good Housekeeping May, 1972*

2 Anger repressed can poison a relationship as surely as the cruelest words. *Ibid.*

## 1014. Kathryn Clarenbach
(1925?–    )

1 Liberation means having a voice in the significant decisions which affect one's own life and the wider society, . . . having access to whatever avenue or pathway one's commitment and bent may lead. It means the assumption of independent responsibility for the utilization of potential and opportunities.
Quoted in *NOW Accomplishments 1973*

2 The overemphasis on protecting girls from strain or injury and underemphasis on developing skills and experiencing teamwork fits neatly into the pattern of the second sex. . . . Girls are the spectators and the cheerleaders. . . . Perfect preparation for the adult role of woman —to stand decoratively on the sidelines of history and cheer on the men who make the decisions. . . .
*Sex Role Stereotyping in the Schools 1973*

3 Women who have had the regular experience of performing before others, of learning to win and lose, of cooperating in team efforts, will be far less fearful of running for office, better able to take public positions on issues in the face of public opposition. By working toward some balance in physical activity, we

may begin to achieve a more wholesome, democratic balance in all phases of our lives.
Quoted in "Old School System Curbed Sportswomen," *Los Angeles Times April 24, 1974*

## 1015. Elizabeth Gould Davis
(1925–1974)

1 The deeper the archeologists dig, the further back go the origins of man and society—and the less sure we are that civilization has followed the steady upward course so thoroughly believed in by the Victorians. It is more likely that the greatest civilizations of the past have yet to be discovered.
*The First Sex,* Prologue *1971*

2 Maleness remains a recessive genetic trait like color-blindness and hemophilia, with which it is linked. The suspicion that maleness is abnormal and that the Y chromosome is an accidental mutation boding no good for the race is strongly supported by the recent discovery by geneticists that congenital killers and criminals are possessed of not one but *two* Y chromosomes, bearing a double dose, as it were, of genetically undesirable maleness.
*Ibid.,* Pt. I, Ch. 1

3 It is . . . possible that the women of the old gynocracies brought on their own downfall by selecting the phallic wild men over the more civilized men of their own pacific and gentle world. *Ibid.,* Ch. 5

4 When man substituted God for the Great Goddess he at the same time substituted authoritarian for humanistic values. *Ibid.,* Ch. 7

5 In the Judeo-Christian creed the male body is the temple of God, while the female body is an object made for man's exploitation.
*Ibid.,* Pt. II, Ch. 9

6 The status of Western women has steadily declined since the advent of Christianity—and is still declining. . . . The Semitic myth of male supremacy was first preached in Europe to a pagan people to whom it came as a radical and astonishing novelty. *Ibid.,* Pt. IV, Ch. 14

7 They [nineteenth-century women] were a special kind of property, not quite like houses or beasts of burden, yet not quite people. . . . Her place in the scheme of things, if she was fortunate, was that of a household pet.
*Ibid.,* Ch. 20

8 It is men, not women, who have promoted the cult of brutal masculinity; and because men admire muscle and physical force, they assume that women do too. Ibid., Ch. 21

9 The innately logical mind of woman, her unique sense of balance, orderliness, and reason, rebels at the terrible realization that justice has been an empty word, that she has been forced for nearly two millennia to worship false gods and to prostrate herself at their empty shrines. Ibid.

10 If the human race is unhappy today, as all modern philosophers agree that it is, it is only because it is uncomfortable in the mirror image society man has made—the topsy-turvy world in which nature's supporting pillar is forced to serve as the cornice of the architrave, while the cornice struggles to support the building. The fact is that men need women more than women need men; and so, aware of this fact, man has sought to keep woman dependent upon him economically as the only method open to him of making himself necessary to her. Ibid., Ch. 22

## 1016. Flannery O'Connor
### (1925–1964)

1 The old man would point to his grandson, Haze. He had a particular disrespect for him because his own face was repeated almost exactly in the child's and seemed to mock him. *Wise Blood*, Ch. 1 1949

2 "I'm going to preach there was no Fall because there was nothing to fall from and no Redemption because there was no Fall and no Judgment because there wasn't the first two. Nothing matters but that Jesus was a liar." Ibid., Ch. 6

3 She felt justified in getting anything at all back that she could, money or anything else, as if she had once owned the earth and been dispossessed of it. She couldn't look at anything steadily without wanting it, and what provoked her most was the thought that there might be something valuable hidden near her, something she couldn't see. Ibid., Ch. 14

4 "I call myself The Misfit," he said, "because I can't make what all I done wrong fit what all I gone through in punishment." "A Good Man Is Hard to Find," *A Good Man Is Hard to Find* 1955

5 "Lady, a man is divided into two parts, body and spirit. . . . A body and a spirit," he repeated. "The body, lady, is like a house it don't go anywhere; but the spirit, lady, is like a automobile: always on the move, always. . . ." Ibid., "The Life You Save May Be Your Own"

6 Mr. Head stood very still and felt the action of mercy touch him again but this time he knew that there were no words in the world that could name it. He understood that it grew out of agony, which is not denied to any man and which is given in strange ways to children. He understood it was all a man could carry into death to give his Maker and he suddenly burned with shame that he had so little of it to take with him. He stood appalled, judging himself with the thoroughness of God, while the action of mercy covered his pride like a flame and consumed it. Ibid., "The Artificial Nigger"

7 Living had got to be such a habit with him that he couldn't conceive of any other condition. Ibid., "A Late Encounter with the Enemy"

8 He had schooled him in the evils that befall prophets; in those that come from the world, which are trifling, and those that come from the Lord and burn the prophet clean; for he himself had been burned clean and burned clean again. He had learned by fire. *The Violent Bear It Away*, Pt. I, Ch. 1 1955

9 Then the revelation came, silent, implacable, direct as a bullet. He did not look into the eyes of any fiery beast or see a burning bush. Ibid., Ch. 3

10 Once or twice I have been asked what the peacock is "good for"—a question which gets no answer from me because it deserves none. "Peacocks Are a Puzzle," *Mystery and Manners* 1957

11 "Knowing who you are is good for one generation only." "Everything That Rises Must Converge," *Everything That Rises Must Converge* 1965p

12 She was a good Christian woman with a large respect for religion, though she did not, of course, believe any of it was true. Ibid., "Greenleaf"

13 He would have hastened his end but suicide would not have been a victory. Death was coming to him legitimately, as a justification, as a gift from life. That was his greatest triumph. Ibid., "The Enduring Chill"

14 He had stuffed his own emptiness with good
work like a glutton.
Ibid., "The Lame Shall Enter First"

## 1017. Naomi Streshinsky

(1925–  )

1 The danger of a gift is an intriguing concept.
Primitive man may have believed that the gift
contained the spirit of the donor and therein
lay its potential harm. The belief in the donor's
spirit dissolved from modern man but the
danger is still very much present.
*Welfare Rights Organizations*, Ch. 2
1970

2 Political acceptability of social welfare can be
translated to mean what the general public will
permit to be granted, out of its tax money to
poor people, just because they are in need and
with no strings attached. Attitudes of hostility
toward and derogation of the assisted poor puts
serious obstacles in the way of future programs
and are precisely the ones which contribute to
the present bind.      Ibid., Ch. 6

## 1018. Toni Carabillo

(1926–  )

1 But powerlessness is still each woman's most
critical problem, whether or not she is a social
activist. It is at the root of most of her psycho-
logical disorders.
Address, "Power Is the Name of the
Game," California NOW State
Conference, San Diego
*October 28, 1973*

2 The sudden acquisition of power by those who
have never had it before can be intoxicating,
and we run the risk of becoming absorbed in
petty power games with our organization
[NOW] that in the last analysis can only be
self-defeating.      Ibid.

3 For the one equality women all over the world
have already achieved is the *Equality of Consequences*. No inventory of the major challenges
and crises of our times discloses any from
whose effects women will be exempt by virtue
of our sex.
Address, "Sharing the Power, the
Glory—and the Pain," NOW Western
Regional Conference, Long Beach,
California    *November 24, 1974*

4 We know that poverty in this country is primarily the problem of *all* women—that most
women are only a husband away from welfare.
Ibid.

5 . . . we must learn that we can disagree with
each other on issues, without becoming deadly
enemies, and without totally devastating our
opposition. We can in fact continue to acknowledge and admire the skills and dedication,
the genuine accomplishments and contributions
of those with whom we are otherwise in dissent.      Ibid.

6 . . . we have learned from the experience of
the first feminist movement that to stop short
of the basic reordering of society, as it is reflected in sex role stereotypes, is too small a
victory.      Address, "Womanpower and the
Media," National Association of
Broadcasters    1974

7 Rock music consistently degrades women and
makes it clear her place in this man's world is
limited to the kitchen and bedroom. Rock
music has been rightly characterized, in our
view, as a "frenzied celebration of masculine
supremacy."      Ibid.

8 . . . women are not a special interest group in
the usual sense of the term. We are half the
population. When the image of women presented in the media is offensive, it is offensive
to women of all social classes, races, religions
and ethnic origins.      Ibid.

9 Not only the CIA, but the FBI, as well as
many state and community police departments,
have devoted vast resources to monitoring the
activities of concerned citizens working in
concert to make social changes within our system. The "flatfoot mentality" insists that any
individual or organization that wants to change
*anything* in our present system is somehow
subversive of "the American way," and should
be under continuous surveillance—a task that
appears to absorb most of our resources for
fighting genuine crime.
"The 'Flatfoot Mentality,' " *Hollywood
NOW News*    *August, 1975*

## 1019. Elizabeth Douvan

(1926–  )

\*   \*   \*

1 The dream of college apparently serves as a
substitute for more direct preoccupation with
marriage: girls who do not plan to go to college are more explicit in their desire to marry,
and have a more developed sense of their own
sex role.      "Motivational Factors in College
Entrance," *The American College*,
with Carol Kaye

2 College and travel are alternatives to a more
open interest in sexuality.      Ibid.

## 1020. Rosalyn Drexler

(1926– )

1 Working with women is a new adventure; it is exciting. We are pioneering, beginning again. There is a feeling of conspiracy, that we are going to forge ahead.
> Quoted in *AFTRA Magazine*
> *Summer, 1974*

2 "I'm just a dog. Look, no opposable thumb."
> *The Cosmopolitan Girl*    1975

3 He visited the Museum of Modern Art, and was standing near the pool looking at his dark reflection when a curator of the museum noticed him. "My, my, what a fine work of art that is!" the curator said to himself. "I must have it installed immediately."    Ibid.

4 We reject the notion that the work that brings in more money is not more valuable. The ability to earn money, or the fact that one already has it, should carry more weight in a relationship.    Ibid.

## 1021. Marie Edwards

(1926?– )

1 Books, magazines, counselors, therapists sell one message to unmarrieds: "Shape up, go where other singles are, entertain more, raise your sex quotient, get involved, get closer, be more open, more honest, more intimate, above all, find Mr. Right or Miss Wonderful and *get married.*"
> *The Challenge of Being Single,*
> with Eleanor Hoover    1975

2 ". . . an intense, one-to-one involvement is as socially conditioned as a hamburger and malt. . . ."    Ibid.

## 1022. Elizabeth II

(1926– )

1 My whole life, whether it be long or short, shall be devoted to your [the public's] service and the service of our great imperial family to which we all belong. But I shall not have strength to carry out this resolution alone unless you join in it with me.
> Radio Broadcast    *April 21, 1947*

## 1023. Cissy Farenthold

(1926– )

1 I am working for the time when unqualified blacks, browns and women join the unqualified men in running our government.
> Quoted in the *Los Angeles Times*
> *September 18, 1974*

## 1024. Wilma Scott Heide

(1926– )

1 The only jobs for which no man is qualified are human incubator and wet nurse. Likewise, the only job for which no woman is or can be qualified is sperm donor.
> Quoted in *NOW Official Biography*
> *1971*

2 . . . we whose hands have rocked the cradle, are now using our heads to rock the boat. . . .
> Ibid.

3 . . . we will no longer be led only by that half of the population whose socialization, through toys, games, values and expectations, sanctions violence as the final assertion of manhood, synonymous with nationhood.    Ibid.

4 The pedestal is immobilizing and subtly insulting whether or not some women yet realize it. We must move up from the pedestal.    Ibid.

5 The path to freedom for women *or* men does *not* lie *down* the bunny trail!    Ibid.

6 To date, we have taught men to be brave and women to care. Now we must enlarge our concepts of bravery and caring. Men must be *brave enough to care* sensitively, compassionately and contrary to the masculine mystique about the quality and equality of our society. Women must *care enough* about their families and all families to *bravely assert* their voices and intellects to every aspect of every institution, whatever the feminine mystique. Every social trait labelled masculine or feminine is in truth a human trait. It is our human right to develop and contribute our talents whatever our race, sex, religion, ancestry, age. Human rights are indivisible!    Ibid.

7 As your president [of NOW] . . . I am one of thousands of us privileged to experience the joy, the risks, the gratifications, bone weariness, tragedies and triumphs of activist feminism. There are women and men and children in our lives and whose lives we touch who may never know how profoundly we care about ourselves and them and the quality of the world we must share and make liveable for all. We are self-helpers with the courage of our commitment.    Quoted in *NOW Accomplishments*
> *1973*

8 Now that we've organized [NOW] . . . all over the United States and initiated an international movement and actions, it must be apparent that feminism is no passing fad but indeed a profound, universal behavior revolution.
> Quoted in "About Women,"
> *Los Angeles Times*
> *May 12, 1974*

## 1025. Carolyn Heilbrun

(1926–   )

1 Ideas move fast when their time comes.
*Toward a Recognition of Androgyny*
*1973*

2 Androgyny suggests a spirit of reconciliation between the sexes; it suggests, further, a full range of experience open to individuals who may as women be aggressive, as men, tender; it suggests a spectrum upon which human beings choose their places without regard to propriety to custom.    Ibid., Introduction

3 Most of us nowadays regard the Victorian age as part of the very remote past. . . . Yet in the matter of sexual polarization and the rejection of androgyny we still accept the convictions of Victorianism; we view everything, from our study of animal habits to our reading of literature, through the paternalistic eyes of the Victorian era.             Ibid.

4 What is important now is that we free ourselves from the prison of gender and, before it is too late, deliver the world from the almost exclusive control of the masculine impulse.
            Ibid.

5 Great periods of civilization, however much they may have owed their beginnings to the aggressive dominance of the male principle, have always been marked by some sort of rise in the status of women. This in its turn is a manifestation of something more profound: the recognition of the importance of the "feminine" principle, not as other, but as necessary to wholeness.        Ibid., Pt. I

6 Today's shocks are tomorrow's conventions.
            Ibid., Pt. II

7 Routine, disposable novels, able to provide relief or distraction but not in themselves valuable—like the smoked cigarette, the used whore, the quick drink—are exactly suited to the conventions of their consumers.    Ibid.

8 . . . ardent, intelligent, sweet, sensitive, cultivated, erudite. These are the adjectives of praise in an androgynous world. Those who consider them epithets of shame or folly ought not to be trusted with leadership, for they will be men hot for power and revenge, certain of right and wrong.         Ibid., Pt. III

9 Queens may rule either as monarchs or as nationalized angels in the house.        Ibid.

10 From the critics of the past I have learned the futility of concerning oneself with the present.
           Ibid., Afterword

11 The genuine solitaries of life fear intimacy more than loneliness. The married are those who have taken the terrible risk of intimacy and, having taken it, know life without intimacy to be impossible.
      "Marriage Is the Message," *Ms.*
*August, 1974*

12 Only a marriage with partners strong enough to risk divorce is strong enough to avoid it. . . .
            Ibid.

13 Marriage today must . . . be concerned not with the inviolable commitment of constancy and unending passion, but with the changing patterns of liberty and discovery.     Ibid.

## 1026. Aileen Clarke Hernandez

(1926–   )

1 My comments to the thousands of persons at the peace march [the 1971 Another Mother for Peace march in Los Angeles] were directed not just against the Vietnam War, but against *all* war, against the masculine mystique which glorifies violence as a solution to problems, and against the vast diverting of American energies and resources from socially needed programs into socially destructive wars.
     Letter to Eve Norman, Quoted in
the NOW Newsletter
*April 29, 1971*

2 This movement . . . is the last stage of the drive for equality for women. We are determined that our daughters and granddaughters will live as free human beings, secure in their personhood, and dedicated to making this nation and the world a humane place in which to live.      Address, National Conference of
NOW, Los Angeles
*September 3–6, 1971*

3 There are no such things as women's issues! All issues are women's issues. The difference that we bring to existing issues of our society, the issues of war and peace; the issues of poverty; the issues of child care; the issues of political power—the difference that we bring is that we are going to bring the full, loud, clear determined voice of women into deciding how those issues are going to be addressed.
            Ibid.

4 We need to get about the business of becoming persons. We need to get about the business of addressing the major issues of society as full-fledged human beings in a society that puts humanity at the head of its list, rather than masculinity at the head of its list.    Ibid.

## 1027. Sue Kaufman
(1926–   )

1 Now Accounts is really a very good word. Accounts in its reportorial not calculative sense. Account, accounting—an account of what is going on. Better than journal or diary by far. *Diary* makes me think of those girls at camp. . . . *Journal* makes me think of all those college Lit courses. . . . Anyway, *Accounts* is good. Accounts is best. Yes, Accounts does very well indeed.   "Friday, September 12," *Diary of a Mad Housewife* 1967

2 I was afraid that if I opened my mouth, like Gerald McBoing-Boing, terrible inhuman sounds would come out—brakes screeching, metal clashing, tires skidding, trains roaring past in the night.   Ibid., "Saturday, October 7"

3 People. Along with doormen, elevator men and headwaiters, the opinions of People matter greatly to Jonathan these days. And who are People? His great secret public—strangers, anybody he doesn't know.   Ibid., "Monday, October 30"

4 "Make yourself a nice hut tuddy, and while you sip it, read Proust. Proust is the only thing when you're sick." . . . I skipped the hut tuddy, but by God it worked. Saved me. Was the antibiotic which wouldn't "touch" the Thing I had. Marvelous crazy poet. Marvelous Proust.   Ibid., "Friday, November 17"

5 "I'm sure he'd be delighted to meet you at long last—the model husband for the cured analysand. . . . You must give him your views of what both working roles in a successful marriage should be—he'll be thrilled by the brilliant simplicity of it all. You know—the Forceful Dominant Male, the Submissive Woman? The Breadwinner who has every right to expect the Obedient Wife to carry out all his orders? He'll lap it up."   Ibid., "Thursday, December 7"

6 Ever since she had gotten out of hospital, her eye kept seeking out and fastening on the cruel, the ugly, the sordid—trying to turn every nasty little incident or detail into some sort of concrete proof of just how rotten the world had become.   *Falling Bodies* 1974

7 "In violent and chaotic times such as these, our only chance for survival lies in creating our own little islands of sanity and order, in making little havens of our homes."   Ibid.

8 Burt told her that he loved her, she told him that she loved him. She thought she didn't mean it. She thought she was being very advanced, very pre-liberated, shattering the damned double standard and lying while she did it, if that's what was required.   Ibid.

9 "I loved my mother. And she died a horrible death. In unspeakable agony."
"She was *not* in agony when she died. . . . And you didn't love her. You wanted to love her and tried to love her, though God only knows why—but you *hated* her. With damned good reason. She was a castrating bitch, who cut your poor father's nuts off and finally drove him to drink himself to death. . . . It makes my blood run cold just imagining what that poor guy must've gone through, and what you must've gone through as a child. I've always felt it was proof of your terrific strength that you'd managed to come out of that relatively unscathed. But now she's finally gotten at you anyway. Finally did it by dying, the bitch—and screw that business about not speaking ill of the dead: she was a *bitch*."   Ibid.

## 1028. Gertrude Lemp Kerbis
(1926–   )

1 It was hell for women architects then. They didn't want us in school or in the profession. . . . One thing I've never understood about this prejudice is that it's so strange in view of the fact that the drive to build has always been in women.   Quoted in *Women at Work* by Betty Medsger 1975

## 1029. Margaret Laurence
(1926–   )

1 Each day dies with sleep.   *A Jest of God* (later known as *Rachel, Rachel*), Ch. 3 1966

2 Holidays are enticing only for the first week or so. After that, it is no longer such a novelty to rise late and have little to do.   Ibid., Ch. 4

3 "Presentation is all—that's what I believe. Everybody knows a product has to be attractively packaged—it's the first rule of sales—isn't that so?"   Ibid., Ch. 7

4 "The prime purpose of a funeral director is not all this beautician deal which some members of the profession go in for so much. No. It's this—to take over. Reassure people."   Ibid.

5  "Death's unmentionable?"
   "Not exactly unmentionable, but let's face
   it, most of us could get along without it."
   "I don't see how."                    Ibid.

6  How strange to have to keep on retreating to
   the only existing privacy, the only place one is
   permitted to be unquestionably alone, the lavatory.                            Ibid., Ch. 9

7  I was always afraid that I might become a
   fool. Yet I could almost smile with some grotesque lightheadedness at that fool of a fear,
   that poor fear of fools, now that I really am
   one.                            Ibid., Ch. 10

8  "You are out of danger," he said. I laughed,
   I guess, and said, "How can I be—I don't feel
   dead yet."                       Ibid., Ch. 11

9  God's mercy on reluctant jesters. God's grace
   on fools. God's pity on God.      Ibid., Ch. 12

## 1030. Harper Lee
### (1926–    )

1  A day was twenty-four hours long but seemed
   longer. There was no hurry, for there was
   nowhere to go, nothing to buy and no money
   to buy it with, nothing to see outside the
   boundaries of Maycomb County. But it was a
   time of vague optimism for some of the people: Maycomb County had recently been told
   that it had nothing to fear but fear itself.
                          *To Kill a Mockingbird*,
                          Pt. I, Ch. 1     *1960*

2  Until I feared I would lose it, I never loved
   to read. One does not love breathing.
                                    Ibid., Ch. 2

3  "People in their right minds never take pride
   in talents," said Miss Maudie.   Ibid., Ch. 10

4  "The one thing that doesn't abide by majority
   rule is a person's conscience."  Ibid., Ch. 11

5  Never, never, never, on cross-examination ask
   a witness a question you don't already know
   the answer to, was a tenet I absorbed with
   my baby-food. Do it, and you'll often get an
   answer you don't want, an answer that might
   wreck your case.                 Ibid., Ch. 17

6  "Our courts have their faults, as does any
   human institution, but in this country our
   courts are the great levelers, and in our courts
   all men are created equal. I'm no idealist to
   believe firmly in the integrity of our courts and
   in the jury system—that is no ideal to me, it
   is a living, working reality. Gentlemen, a court

is no better than each man of you sitting before
me on this jury. A court is only as sound as its
jury, and a jury is only as sound as the men
who make it up."              Ibid., Ch. 20

7  "As you grow older, you'll see white men cheat
   black men every day of your life, but let me
   tell you something and don't you forget it—
   whenever a white man does that to a black
   man, no matter who he is, how rich he is, or
   how fine a family he comes from, that white
   man is trash."                  Ibid., Ch. 23

## 1031. Pat Loud
### (1926–    )

1  A miserable marriage can wobble along for
   years until something comes along and pushes
   one of the people over the brink. It's usually
   another man or woman. For me, it was a
   whole production staff and camera crew.
                     *Pat Loud: A Woman's Story*, with
                           Nora Johnson     *1974*

2  College for women was a refinement whose
   main purpose was to better prepare you for
   your ultimate destiny . . . to make you a more
   desirable product.                    Ibid.

3  Life was diapers and little jars of puréed apri-
   cots and bottles and playpens and rectal thermometers, and all those small dirty faces and
   all those questions.                  Ibid.

4  Housework isn't bad in itself—the trouble with
   it is that it's inhumanely lonely.    Ibid.

## 1032. Marilyn Monroe
### (1926–1962)

1  I've been on a calendar, but never on time.
          Quoted in *Look*     *January 16, 1962*

2  A career is born in public—talent in privacy.
          Quoted in "Marilyn: The Woman Who
          Died Too Soon" by Gloria Steinem,
          *The First Ms. Reader*, Francine
          Klagsbrun, ed.     *1972p*

3  I have too many fantasies to be a housewife.
   . . . I guess I *am* a fantasy.       Ibid.

4  I don't want to make money. I just want to
   be wonderful.                        Ibid.

5  I hope at some future time to make a glowing
   report on the wonders that psychiatrists can
   do for you.                          Ibid.

6  I am always running into peoples' unconscious.
          Quoted in *Marilyn* by Norman Mailer
                                        *1973p*

## 1033. Jan Morris
(1926–    )

1 I was loved and I was loving, brought up kindly and sensibly, spoiled to a comfortable degree, weaned at an early age on Huck Finn and Alice in Wonderland, taught to cherish my animals, say grace, think well of myself, and wash my hands before tea.
*Conundrum*, Ch. 1    1974

2 To me gender is not physical at all, but is altogether insubstantial. It is soul, perhaps, it is talent, it is taste, it is environment, it is how one feels, it is light and shade, it is inner music. . . .    Ibid., Ch. 3

3 I had reached the conclusion myself that sex was not a division but a continuum, that almost nobody was altogether of one sex or another, and that the infinite subtlety of the shading from one extreme to the other was one of the most beautiful of nature's phenomena. Sex was like a biological pointer, but the gauge upon which it flickered was that very different device, gender.    Ibid., Ch. 5

4 Intercourse seemed to me a tool, a reproductive device, and at the same time, in its symbolical fusion of bodies, a kind of pledge or surrender, not to be lightly given, still less thrown away in masquerade.    Ibid., Ch. 6

5 But I have come to see within the mystery of the African genius, veiled as it is by superstition, fear, and resentment, something of the magic of the earth itself.    Ibid., Ch. 11

6 Englishmen . . . found the ambiguity in itself beguiling. . . . Frenchmen were curious, and tended to engage me in inquisitive conversation. . . . Italians, frankly unable to conceive the meaning of such a phenomenon, simply stared boorishly, or nudged each other in piazzas. Greeks were vastly entertained. Arabs asked me to go for walks with them. Scots looked shocked. Germans looked worried. Japanese did not notice.    Ibid., Ch. 12

7 We are told that the social gap between the sexes is narrowing, but I can only report that having, in the second half of the twentieth century, experienced life in both roles, there seems to me no aspect of existence, no moment of the day, no contact, no arrangement, no response, which is not different for men and for women.    Ibid., Ch. 17

## 1034. Charlotte Painter
(1926–    )

1 We are looking for some way to live in a world gone mad. We have left America the beautiful. But not because we know a better place.
*Confession from the Malaga Madhouse*    1971

2 If a thing is absolutely true, how can it not also be a lie? An absolute must contain its opposite.    Ibid.

3 Not persuaded enough against violence to go to jail for it. Not persuaded he can kill either. Not interested in that Army, that War, sure enough of himself only to know that he doesn't yet know the Way. . . .    Ibid.

4 The wars that always go on. You know, they don't have to. If everybody played war instead of really, really doing it.    Ibid.

5 The passion for destruction, glorious destruction. Must we seek grace in violence, more than any other way?    Ibid.

6 I don't know where in this shrunken world to take you, son, to let you grow to manhood.    Ibid.

7 To a lover of literature, life tends to will o' wisp on either side of the poem, the story, the play.    *Revelations: Diaries of Women,* with Mary Jane Moffat, Afterword    1974

8 We need only discover within ourselves how and when to call upon either of the functions we need—a task that may, like the *via longissima* of the alchemists, take more lives than one.    Ibid.

9 If we can distinguish between specialized art, as designed for an intellectual, educated group, and primitive art, as created through a group's unconscious symbols, then perhaps we can talk about some diaries as primitive.    Ibid.

10 . . . perhaps we have not fully understood that anger is a secondary emotional cover for hurt. (Righteous indignation feels good; hurts do not.)    Ibid.

11 . . . as awareness increases, the need for personal secrecy almost proportionately decreases.    Ibid.

12 Habits do not like to be abandoned, and besides they have the virtue of being tools.    Ibid.

13 Psychic bisexuality is a de-conditioning process, which can eventually eliminate sexist limitations for both men and women.    Ibid.

## 1035. Cynthia Propper Seton

(1926–　　)

1 To Angela her grandmother was old but had not grown older and was never younger. This is a usual way with grandmothers. She had the very shape of the old: vaguely conical, shortish, roundish; and was fortified by a carapace of corset under which it would have been shocking to surmise a live, warm, woman's body. *The Sea Change of Angela Lewes,* Ch. 1　*1971*

2 Well, banality is a terribly likely consequence of the underuse of a good mind. That is why in particular it is a female affliction. Ibid., Ch. 9

3 "It sometimes looks to me," said Angela, "that a middle-class marriage is a careful mismatching of two innocents—and the game is called Making the Best of It, while in actual fact each one does a terrible thing to the spirit of the other. . . . And you wonder why they endure each other, why they stand for it? And the explanation is that they really answer each other's needs, unconscious needs, and are in fact often admirably suited to each other, and that, unbelievable as it might seem from the outside, they do really *love* each other." Ibid., Ch. 12

4 Angela was spinning off, and Charlie was letting her. The shift in their marital relationship was remarkable for the absence of tension, of conflict—a peaceful *de*-consummation devoutly to be wished in the generality of aging marriages. Angela was becoming her own person, her own woman, and was alternately exhilarated and complacent. . . . Ibid., Ch. 18

5 To pursue yourself is an interesting and absorbing thing to do. Once you have caught the scent of a hidden being, your own hidden being, you won't readily be deflected from the tracking down of it. Ibid., Ch. 25

6 "Holding hands is a very intimate thing to do," she found herself whispering. "Even to hold a child's hand. It's very touching." Ibid.

7 She had trouble defining herself independently of her husband, tried to talk to him about it, but he said nonsense, he had no trouble defining her at all. *The Half-Sisters*　*1974*

## 1036. Joan Sutherland

(1926–　　)

1 I know I'm not exactly a bombshell, but one has to make the best of what one's got. Quoted in "Joan Sutherland," *Divas: Impressions of Six Opera Superstars* by Winthrop Sargeant　*1959*

2 If I weren't reasonably placid, I don't think I could cope with this sort of life. To be a diva, you've got to be absolutely like a horse. Ibid.

3 But I think Australians have a sort of independence, and I think that, rightly or wrongly, they tend to make their own decisions as to how a thing has gone. Pioneers are apt to be like that. I think that it's not a bad idea. You can listen to what everybody says, but the fact remains that you've got to get out there and do the thing yourself. Ibid.

## 1037. Johnnie Tillmon

(1926–　　)

1 I'm a woman. I'm a black woman. I'm a poor woman. I'm a fat woman. I'm a middle-aged woman. And I'm on welfare. In this country, if you're any one of those things, you count less as a person. If you're *all* those things, you just don't count, except as a statistic. I am a statistic. "Welfare Is a Woman's Issue," *The First Ms. Reader,* Francine Klagsbrun, ed.　*1972*

2 Welfare is like a traffic accident. It can happen to anybody, but especially it happens to women. Ibid.

3 Women aren't supposed to work. They're supposed to be married. Ibid.

4 Wages are the measure of dignity that society puts on a job. Ibid.

## 1038. Lynn Caine

(1927?–　　)

1 After my husband died, I felt like one of those spiraled shells washed up on the beach . . . no flesh, no life. . . . We add ourselves to our men, we exist in their reflection. And then? If they die? *Widow*　*1974*

2 Since every death diminishes us a little, we grieve—not so much for the death as for ourselves. Ibid.

3 "Widow" is a harsh and hurtful word. It comes from the Sanskrit and it means "empty." I have been empty too long. Ibid.

4 One of the chores of grief involves going over and over in one's mind the circumstances that led to the death, the details of the death itself. Ibid.

## 1039. Midge Decter

(1927–    )

1 Shifts in prejudice can work both ways.
*The Liberated Woman and Other Americans*, Pt. I, Ch. 3    1971

2 Ideas are powerful things, requiring not a studious contemplation but an action, even if it is only an inner action. Their acquisition obligates each man in some way to change his life, even if it is only his inner life. They demand to be stood for. They dictate where a man must concentrate his vision. They determine his moral and intellectual priorities. They provide him with allies and make him enemies. In short, ideas impose an interest in their ultimate fate which goes far beyond the realm of the merely reasonable.    Ibid., Pt. II, Ch. 2

3 . . . because I am a New Yorker, my experience is the more truly, the more typically, American one. It is my America that is moving in on them [Middle America]. God is about to bless them with an opportunity, and may He also save them from it, but there is no turning back now.    Ibid., Pt. III, Ch. 6

4 The hatred of the youth culture for adult society is not a disinterested judgment but a terror-ridden refusal to be hooked into the, if you will, ecological chain of breathing, growing, and dying. It is the demand, in other words, to remain children.
*The New Chastity and Other Arguments Against Women's Liberation*, Ch. 1    1972

5 Women's Liberation calls it enslavement but the real truth about the sexual revolution is that it has made of sex an almost chaotically limitless and therefore unmanageable realm in the life of women.    Ibid., Ch. 2

6 The fundamental impulse of the movement is neither masturbatory nor concretely lesbian—although it of course offers warm houseroom to both these possibilities; it is an impulse to maidenhood—to that condition in which a woman might pretend a false fear or loathing of the penis in order to escape from any responsibility for the pleasure and well-being of the man who possesses it.    Ibid.

7 Consciousness-raising groups are of a piece with a whole cultural pattern that has been growing up. This pattern begins with the term "rapping"—which is a process in which people in groups pretend that they are not simply self-absorbed because they are talking to each other.    Speech, Women's National Book Association, Quoted in "On Consciousness-Raising," *Crazy Salad* by Nora Ephron    1973

8 It might sound a paradoxical thing to say—for surely never has a generation of children occupied more sheer hours of parental time—but the truth is that we neglected you. We allowed you a charade of trivial freedoms in order to avoid making those impositions on you that are in the end both the training ground and proving ground for true independence. We pronounced you strong when you were still weak in order to avoid the struggles with you that would have fed your true strength. We proclaimed you sound when you were foolish in order to avoid taking part in the long, slow, slogging effort that is the only route to genuine maturity of mind and feeling. Thus, it was no small anomaly of your growing up that while you were the most indulged generation, you were also in many ways the most abandoned to your own meager devices by those into whose safe-keeping you had been given.
*Liberal Parents/Radical Children*, Ch. 1    1975

9 All they wished for her was that she should turn herself into a little replica of them.    Ibid., Ch. 3

## 1040. Anne Edwards

(1927–    )

1 What a difficult swallowing of ego and pride she [Judy Garland] must have suffered with each pill—what a frightening loss of self.
*Judy Garland*    1975

2 That was, of course, the problem—she *begged*, not demanded. She wanted a happy world and everyone in it happy, but she was at a loss as to how to accomplish this.    Ibid.

## 1041. Althea Gibson

(1927–    )

1 I always wanted to be somebody. I guess that's why I kept running away from home when I was a kid even though I took some terrible whippings for it.    *I Always Wanted to Be Somebody*, Ch. 1    1958

2 I was excited. I was confident, too. I don't mean that I wasn't nervous, because I was. But I was nervous and confident at the same time, nervous about going out there in front of all those people, with so much at stake, and confident that I was going to go out there and win.    Ibid., Ch. 8

3 I don't want to be put on a pedestal. I just want to be reasonably successful and live a normal life with all the conveniences to make it so. I think I've already got the main thing I've always wanted, which is to be somebody, to have identity. I'm Althea Gibson, the tennis champion. I hope it makes me happy.
*Ibid.*, Ch. 9

## 1042. Ruth Prawer Jhabvala
### (1927–　)

1 ". . . what she wants is a live guru—someone to inspire her . . . snatch her up and out of herself—simultaneously destroy and create her." *Travelers* 1973

2 These diseases that people get in India, they're not physical, they're purely psychic. We only get them because we try to resist India— because we shut ourselves up in our little Western egos and don't want to give ourselves. But once we learn to yield, then they must fall away. *Ibid.*

3 "Take me, make what you will of me, I have joy in my submission." *Ibid.*

4 "It is only," he says, "when you have given up all enjoyment that it is no longer enjoyment, it is only then that you can have these things back again." *Ibid.*

5 "India . . . is not a place that one can pick up and put down again as if nothing had happened. In a way it's not so much a country as an experience, and whether it turns out to be a good or a bad one depends, I suppose, on oneself." *Ibid.*

## 1043. Beverly Jones
### (1927–　)

1 Automation and unions have led to a continuously shortened day for men but the work day of housewives with children has remained constant. "The Dynamics of Marriage and Motherhood," *The Florida Paper on Women's Liberation* 1970

2 Now, as always, the most automated appliance in a household is the mother. *Ibid.*

3 If enforced wakefulness is the handmaiden and necessary precursor to serious brainwashing, a mother—after her first child—is ready for her final demise. *Ibid.*

4 Romance, like the rabbit at the dog track, is the illusive, fake, and never-attained reward which for the benefit and amusement of our masters keeps us running and thinking in safe circles. *Ibid.*

5 We who have been raised on pap must develop a passion for honest appraisal. *Ibid.*

## 1044. Coretta Scott King
### (1927–　)

1 There is a spirit and a need and a man at the beginning of every great human advance. Each of these must be right for that particular moment of history, or nothing happens.
*My Life with Martin Luther King, Jr.*,
Ch. 6　1969

2 My husband often told the children that if a man had nothing that was worth dying for, then he was not fit to live.
*Ibid.*, Press Conference
(April, 1968)

3 We are concerned not only about the Negro poor, but the poor all over America and all over the world. Every man deserves a right to a job or an income so that he can pursue liberty, life, and happiness. Our great nation, as he often said, has the resources, but his question was: Do we have the will?
*Ibid.*, Speech, Memphis City Hall
(April 8, 1968)

4 The more visible signs of protest are gone, but I think there is a realization that the tactics of the late sixties are not sufficient to meet the challenges of the seventies.
Speech, Quoted in the *Los Angeles Times*　May 14, 1974

## 1045. Leontyne Price
### (1927–　)

1 I think that recording is in a way much more personal than stage performance. In a theater the audience sees and hears you. So the costumes and the general *mise en scène* help you do the job, because they can see. In recording, you have to see and hear for them with the voice—which makes it much more personal.
Quoted in "Leontyne Price," *Divas: Impressions of Six Opera Superstars* by Winthrop Sargeant　1959

2 I feel that you have to rest the voice and avoid pressure for considerable periods. You have to reflect, too. I've been singing less and less everywhere. You cannot keep up that kind of pressure for considerable periods. I'm asked to be booked more and more, but look, I'd like to find out who I am. If I do have some success, I'd like to try to enjoy it, for heaven's sake! What is the point of having it otherwise? Everybody else gets excited, but *you're* the one who's always tired. That's not life. That's not living. Ibid.

3 All token blacks have the same experience. I have been pointed at as a solution to things that have not *begun* to be solved, because pointing at us token blacks eases the conscience of millions, and I think this is dreadfully wrong. Ibid.

## 1046. Lillian Ross
### (1927–    )

1 Good will was stamped on the faces of all, but there was no indication as to whom or what it was directed toward. As they entered, the guests exchanged quick glances, as though they were assuring each other and themselves that they were there. *Picture*, Ch. 1
1952

2 His name was not engraved on a brass plate on his door; it was typed on a white card placed in a slot, from which it could easily be removed. Ibid., Ch. 3

## 1047. Una Stannard
### (1927–    )

1 Woman's mask of beauty is the face of the child, a revelation of the tragic sexual immaturity of both sexes in our culture.
"The Mask of Beauty," *Woman in Sexist Society*, Vivian Gornick and Barbara Moran, eds. 1971

## 1048. Maya Angelou
### (1928–    )

1 All of childhood's unanswered questions must finally be passed back to [one's hometown] and answered there. Heroes and bogey men, values and dislikes, are first encountered and labeled in that early environment. In later years they change faces, places and maybe races, tactics, intensities and goals, but beneath those penetrable masks they wear forever the stocking-capped faces of childhood.
*I Know Why the Caged Bird Sings*, Ch. 4 1969

2 She said that I must always be intolerant of ignorance but understanding of illiteracy. That some people, unable to go to school, were more educated and even more intelligent than college professors. She encouraged me to listen carefully to what country people called mother wit. That in those homely sayings was couched the collective wisdom of generations.
Ibid., Ch. 15

3 Children's talent to endure stems from their ignorance of alternatives. Ibid., Ch. 17

4 The quality of strength lined with tenderness is an unbeatable combination, as are intelligence and necessity when unblunted by formal education. Ibid., Ch. 29

5 At fifteen life had taught me undeniably that surrender, in its place, was as honorable as resistance, especially if one had no choice.
Ibid., Ch. 31

6 The fact that the adult American Negro female emerges a formidable character is often met with amazement, distaste and even belligerence. It is seldom accepted as an inevitable outcome of the struggle won by survivors, and deserves respect if not enthusiastic acceptance.
Ibid., Ch. 34

7 I believe most plain girls are virtuous because of the scarcity of opportunity to be otherwise. They shield themselves with an aura of unavailableness (for which after a time they begin to take credit) largely as a defense tactic.
Ibid., Ch. 35

8 My life has been one great big joke,
A dance that's walked
A song that's spoke,
I laugh so hard I almost choke
When I think about myself.
"When I Think About Myself,"
*Just Give Me a Cool Drink of Water 'fore I Diiie* 1971

9 For Africa to me . . . is more than a glamorous fact. It is a historical truth. No man can know where he is going unless he knows exactly where he has been and exactly how he arrived at his present place.
Quoted in *The New York Times April 16, 1972*

10 One would say of my life—born loser—had
to be: from a broken family, raped at eight,
unwed mother at sixteen. . . . It's a fact but
not the truth. In the black community, however bad it looks, there's a lot of love and so
much humor.     Quoted by Jane Julianelli in
*Harper's Bazaar*     November, 1972

11 I speak to the black experience, but I am
always talking about the human condition—
about what we can endure, dream, fail at, and
still survive.     Quoted in *Current Biographies*
1974

12 A textured guilt was my familiar, my bed
mate to whom I had turned my back. My
daily companion whose hand I would not hold.
The Christian teaching dinned into my ears. . . .
*Gather Together in My Name*, Preface
1974

13 "I probably couldn't learn to cook creole
food, anyway. It's too complicated."
"Sheeit. Ain't nothing but onions, green peppers and garlic. Put that in everything and you
got creole food."     Ibid., Ch. 3

14 "You a cherry, ain't you?"
"Yes." Lying would get me nothing.
"Well, that's a thirty-second business. When
you turn the first trick, you'll be a 'ho. A stone
'ho. I mean for life. . . . I'm a damn good
one. I'm a mud kicker. In the streets I make
more money by accident than most bitches
make on purpose."     Ibid., Ch. 27

15 Separate from my boundaries, I had not known
before that he had and would have a life beyond being my son, my pretty baby, my cute
doll, my charge. In the plowed farmyard near
Bakersfield, I began to understand the uniqueness of the person. He was three and I was nineteen, and never again would I think of him
as a beautiful appendage of myself.
Ibid., Ch. 29

## 1049.  Shirley Temple Black
(1928–    )

1 Nonsense, all of it. Sunnybrook Farm is now
a parking lot; the petticoats are in the garbage
can, where they belong in this modern world;
and I *detest* censorship.
Quoted in *McCall's*     January, 1967

2 Won't the new "Suggested for Mature Audience" protect our youngsters from such films?
I don't believe so. I know many forty-five-year-
old men with the mentalities of six-year-olds,
and my feeling is that they should not see such
pictures, either.     Ibid.

3 Our whole way of life today is dedicated to
the *removal of risk*. Cradle to grave we are
supported, insulated, and isolated from the
risks of life—and if we fall, our government
stands ready with Bandaids of every size.
Speech, Kiwanis International
Convention, Texas (June, 1967),
Quoted in *The Sinking of The Lollipop*
by Rodney G. Minott     1968

## 1050.  Mary Daly
(1928–    )

1 The becoming of androgynous human persons
implies a radical change in the fabric of human consciousness and in styles of human behavior.     *Beyond God the Father*, Ch. 1
1973

2 . . . tokenism does not change stereotypes of
social systems but works to preserve them,
since it dulls the revolutionary impulse.
Ibid.

3 Courage to be is the key to the revelatory
power of the feminist revolution.     Ibid.

4 It is the creative potential itself in human
beings that is the image of God.     Ibid.

5 . . . "God's plan" is often a front for men's
plans and a cover for inadequacy, ignorance
and evil.     Ibid.

6 I have already suggested that if God is male,
then male is God. The divine patriarch cas-
trates women as long as he is allowed to live
on in the human imagination.     Ibid.

7 People attempt to overcome the threat of nonbeing by denying the self. The outcome of
this is ironic: that which is dreaded triumphs,
for we are caught in the self-contradictory bind
of shrinking our being to avoid nonbeing.
Ibid.

8 It is not good enough to talk about evil ab-
stractly while lending implicit support to traditional images that legitimate specific social
evils.     Ibid., Ch. 2

9 Why indeed must "God" be a noun? Why not
a verb—the most active and dynamic of all.
Ibid.

10 The image of Mary as Virgin, moreover, has
an (unintended) aspect of pointing to independence for women. This aspect of the symbol is of course generally unnoticed by theo-
logians.     Ibid., Ch. 3

11 Sexist society maintains its grasp over the psyche by keeping it divided against itself.
Ibid., Ch. 4

12 . . . we will look upon the earth and her sister planets as being *with* us, not *for* us. One does not rape a sister.
Ibid., Ch. 6

13 I had explained that a woman's asking for equality in the church would be comparable to a black person's demanding equality in the Ku Klux Klan.
"New Autobiographical Preface"
(1968), *The Church and the Second Sex*    1975

14 The liberation of language is rooted in the liberation of ourselves.
Ibid.

## 1051. Muriel Fox
(1928–    )

1 While you don't need a formal written contract before you get married, I think it's important for both partners to spell out what they expect from each other. . . . . There are always plenty of surprises—and lots of give and take—once you're married.
Quoted in "Wait Late to Marry"
by Barbara Jordan Moore,
*New Woman*    October, 1971

2 I realize that what happened to my mother was very wrong. She got pigeonholed in the wrong job. That job was housewife. She hated it and was a tragically inefficient housekeeper. There was no valid reason why she should have got stuck in that job when she could have filled many others with distinction.
Ibid.

3 Women and men have to fight together to change society—and both will benefit. We [her husband and herself] are strongly pro-marriage. I think it is a grave mistake for young girls to think that it has to be a career versus marriage, equality versus love. Partnership, not dependence, is the real romance in marriage.
Ibid.

4 Total commitment to family and total commitment to career is possible, but fatiguing.
Ibid.

## 1052. Thea Musgrave
(1928–    )

1 Music is a human art, not a sexual one. Sex is no more important than eye color.
Quoted in "A Matter of Art, Not Sex,"
*Time*    November 10, 1975

## 1053. Beah Richards
(1928?–    )

1 Having grown up in a racist culture where two and two are not five, I have found life to be incredibly theatrical and theatre to be profoundly lifeless.    *A Black Woman Speaks and Other Poems*, Preface    1974

2 . . . nature is neither reasonable nor just. Nature is exact.
Ibid.

3 Heaven and earth!
How is it that bodies join
but never meet?
Ibid., "It's Time for Love," St. 2

4 Lord,
there is no death,
no numb, no glacial sorrow
like the love of loveless love,
a tender grunting, sweating horror of obscenity.
Ibid., "Love Is Cause It Has to Be,"
St. 6

5 If I cannot with my blind eyes see
that to betray or deny my brother
is but to diminish me
then you may pity me. . . .
Ibid., "The Liberal," St. 11

## 1054. Anne Sexton
(1928–1974)

1 love your self's self where it lives.
"The Double Image,"
*To Bedlam and Partway Back*    1960

2 . . . I gather
guilt like a young intern
his symptoms, his certain evidence.
Ibid.

3      You, Dr. Martin, walk
from breakfast to madness.
Ibid., "You, Dr. Martin," St. 1

4      I am queen of all my sins
forgotten. Am I still lost?
Ibid., Last St.

5 Today life opened inside me like an egg. . . .
"Live," *Live or Die*    1966

6 lovers sprouting in the yard
like celery stalks. . . .
Ibid.

7 I say *Live, Live* because of the sun,
the dream, the excitable gift.
Ibid.

8  The trouble with being a woman,
      Skeezis,
   is being a little girl
   in the first place.
                "Hurry Up Please It's Time,"
                *The Death Notebooks*    1974

9  What is death, I ask: What is life, you ask.
                                        Ibid.

10  Even without wars, life is dangerous.
                                        Ibid.

11  I would have taken care of daisies, giving them
    an aspirin every hour and cutting their stems
    properly, but with roses I'm reckless. When
    they arrive in their long white box, they're
    already in the death house.
                "A Small Journal" (November 6,
                    1971), *The Poet's Story*,
                Howard Moss, ed.         1974

12  I took the radio, my vigil keeper, and played
    it for my waking, sleeping ever since. In me-
    moriam. It goes everywhere with me like a
    dog on a leash.     Ibid. (November 8, 1971)

13  Generally speaking, mental hospitals are lonely
    places, they are full of televisions and medica-
    tions.                                Ibid.

14  The sea is mother-death and she is a mighty
    female, the one who wins, the one who sucks
    us all up.          Ibid. (November 19, 1971)

15  It doesn't matter who my father was; it matters
    who I remember he was.
                Ibid. (January 1, 1972, 12:30 A.M.)

16  God owns heaven
    but He craves the earth.
                "The Earth," St. 2, *The Awful
                Rowing Toward God*      1975p

17  The eyes, opening and shutting like cameras
    and never forgetting, recording by thou-

    sands. . . .              Ibid., St. 3

18  The tongue, the Chinese say,
    is like a sharp knife:
    it kills
    without drawing blood.
                Ibid., "The Dead Heart," St. 3

## 1055. Muriel Siebert

### (1928?–     )

1  I know a twenty-eight-year-old woman, a recent graduate of Harvard Business School. She
   asked me the other day if I wasn't afraid of
   what people will say if I associate with the
   women's movement. What she doesn't under-

stand is that it's because of the movement and
people like me that it's now not as difficult for
her to make it.        Quoted in *Women at Work*
                        by Betty Medsger     1975

## 1056. Agnes Varda

### (1928–     )

1  You ask me, is it difficult to be a woman
   director? I'd say that it's difficult to be a director, period! It's difficult to be free; it's
   difficult not to be drowned in the system. It's
   difficult for women, and it's difficult for men,
   the same way.
                Quoted in "An Interview with
                Agnes Varda" by Barbara Confino,
                *Saturday Review*    *August 12, 1972*

2  The image of woman is crucial, and in the . . .
   movies that image is always switching between
   the nun and the whore, the mama and the
   bitch. We have put up with that for years,
   and it has to be changed. It is the image that
   is important, not so much who is making the
   film.                                 Ibid.

3  Humor is such a strong weapon, such a strong
   answer. Women have to make jokes about
   themselves, laugh about themselves, because
   they have nothing to lose.            Ibid.

## 1057. Anne Frank

### (1929–1945)

1  I soothe my conscience now with the thought
   that it is better for hard words to be on paper
   than that Mummy should carry them in her
   heart.           *The Diary of a Young Girl*
                    (January 2, 1944)       1952p

2  Mummy herself has told us that she looked
   upon us more as her friends than her daughters. Now that is all very fine, but still, a
   friend can't take a mother's place. I need my
   mother as an example which I can follow,
   I want to be able to respect her.
                    Ibid. (January 15, 1944)

3  I think what is happening to me is so wonderful, and not only what can be seen on my
   body, but all that is taking place inside. I
   never discuss myself or any of these things
   with anybody; that is why I have to talk to
   myself about them.                    Ibid.

4  We all live with the objective of being happy;
   our lives are all different and yet the same.
                    Ibid. (July 6, 1944)

5  Laziness may *appear* attractive, but work *gives*
   satisfaction.                         Ibid.

6 Parents can only give good advice or put them on the right paths, but the final forming of a person's character lies in their own hands. . . .
Ibid. (July 15, 1944)

7 I'm awfully scared that everyone who knows me as I always am will discover that I have another side, a finer and better side. I'm afraid they'll laugh at me, think I'm ridiculous and sentimental, not take me seriously. . . .
Ibid. (August 1, 1944)

## 1058. Linda Goodman
(1929?–　　　)

1 It seems to be quite a leap from the . . . lost continent of Atlantis to the jet-propelled twentieth century. But how far is it really? Perhaps only a dream or two.
*Linda Goodman's Sun Signs,*
Afterword　*1968*

2 Alone among the sciences, astrology has spanned the centuries and made the journey intact. We shouldn't be surprised that it remains with us, unchanged by time—because astrology is truth—and truth is eternal.
Ibid.

3 Astrological language is a golden cord that binds us to a dim past while it prepares us for an exciting future of planetary explorations.
Ibid.

## 1059. Shirley Ann Grau
(1929–　　　)

1 I know that I shall hurt as much as I have been hurt. I shall destroy as much as I have lost. It's a way to live, you know. It's a way to keep your heart ticking under the sheltering arches of your ribs. And that's enough for now.
"Abigail," *The Keepers of the House*
*1964*

2 She thought of all the distance between the two parts of her, the white and the black. And it seemed to her that those two halves would pull away and separate and leave her there in the open, popped out like a kernel from its husk.　　　　Ibid., "Margaret"

3 Why does it take so much trouble to keep your stomach full and quiet?　　　Ibid.

4 And isn't it funny, she thought, that it takes two generations to kill off a man? . . . First him, and then his memory. . . .　　Ibid.

5 There's only one night like that—ever—where you're filled with wonder and excitement for no other reason but the earth is beautiful and mysterious and your body is young and strong. . . . We hadn't really been friends before. It just sort of happened that we found ourselves together. It wasn't anything personal. It would have been the same with any man. . . . It happens like that and it's not the less precious. It's the thing you value and not the man. It happened that way with me.
Ibid.

6 Me? What am I? Nothing. The legs on which dinner comes to the table, the arms by which cocktails enter the living room, the hands that drive cars. I am the eyes that see nothing, the ears that don't hear. I'm invisible too. They look and don't see me. When they move, I have to guess their direction and get myself out of the way. If they were to walk into me— all six feet of black skin and white bone— they'd never again be able to pretend that I wasn't there. And I'd be looking for another job.　　　"Stanley," *The Condor Passes*
*1971*

7 He had to humor his body occasionally so that the rest of the time it obeyed his will.
Ibid., "The Old Man"

8 Why, she thought, do I always get angry at my mother? For not leaving me a memory, for being so vague and gentle and so busy with her job of procreating that she hardly noticed her children once they left her womb. . . .
Ibid., "Anna"

9 Took as much skill to get rid of a girl as to get one. He was learning how to do both.
Ibid., "Robert"

10 Her Father was waiting. When she saw him, she felt the usual shift in her feelings. A lift, a jump, a tug. Pleasure, but not totally. Love, but not completely. Dependence. Fear, familiarity, identification. That's part of me there, walking along. Tree from which I sprang. His spasm produced me. Shake of his body and here I am. . . .　　　Ibid., "Margaret"

11 To hell with love, Margaret thought. It's an ache in my stomach, it's a terrible feeling in my head, it's a skin-crawling fear that I've done something wrong. I've forgotten the password. And the frog isn't going to change into Prince Charming, the secret door isn't going to open. And the world is going to end any minute.　　　　　　　Ibid.

12 "You forget places you've been and you forget women you've had, but you don't forget fighting."
"Homecoming," *The Wind Shifting*
*West*　*1973*

13 Before, I used to like it [the highway], especially the sounds: the tires whistling and singing on the wet, and hissing on the dry. The soft growling sound—kind of like a sigh—when some trucker tested his air brakes. The way horns echo way off in the distance. The thin little screech of car brakes, too, almost like a laugh. And something else—a steady even whisper. Day and night, no difference. It ran like electric wires singing. Or maybe kind of like breathing. . . . But I didn't like the highway any more. . . . Like Joe would say, the highway brought everything to us, and took it away too.

> Ibid., "The Last Gas Station"

14 It hurts to worry this much, she thought. It really hurts like a cut, or a broken bone. It hurts more than my broken arm when I fell off the climbing bars in the third grade. A lot more than that. It hurts so much that it can't hurt any more.

> Ibid., "Sea Change"

15 Later on things did stop and time ended, and she perched on a single spot, weightless and empty in herself. Quite detached from her body, her mind stole out, prowling like a cat in the shadows, searching. And it found that there was nothing on any side of her, that she hung like a point, like a star in the empty sky.

> Ibid.

16 "Haven't you ever noticed how highways always get beautiful near the state capital?"

> Ibid., "The Way Back"

17 Trees come out of acorns, no matter how unlikely that seems. An acorn is just a tree's way back into the ground. For another try. Another trip through. One life or another. And what came out of sex now. Love maybe. But that wasn't as sure as a tree. Or maybe a tree was as unsure as Love. One capsule life or another.

> Ibid.

18 Women's lib is one of those great amorphous things. I don't think that you can characterize it as a single movement. It's really rather strange. . . . [But] you can't legislate equality. Until the basic feelings of people are changed, the facts won't change.

> Quoted in "Profile . . . Shirley Ann Grau" by Louis Gallo, *New Orleans February, 1974*

19 Women use children as excuses not to do anything.

> Ibid.

20 A lot more people can write than do. I think writers are only *born* in a small sense. You're born with a feeling for words and writers deliberately set out to develop this innate feeling. If you are born with or acquire this feeling for words, then you can become a writer.

> Ibid.

21 One of my current pet theories is that the writer is a kind of evangelist, more subtle than Billy Graham, of course, but of the same stuff.

> Ibid.

22 Nothing in life has bells ringing or choruses singing. I've long ago stopped looking for glamour and drama. Life isn't like that. As a matter of fact, it's the search for instant gratification that is so harmful to young writers. . . . The realization that something is good material for a story is no big bang. No need to dignify it with an explosion. Instant bangs never happen. No writer I know talks about it in those terms. Nonwriters tend to think of it that way, but writing is day to day grubby hard work. It's isolated and time consuming.

> Ibid.

## 1060. Matina Horner

(1929?–    )

1 Unusual excellence in women was clearly associated for them with the loss of femininity, social rejection, personal or societal destruction or some combination of the above.

> *Women and Success: The Anatomy of Achievement*   1964

## 1061. Jill Johnston

(1929–    )

1 I have a case of the most exquisite paranoia. It's a wonderful feeling. For a female lesbian bastard writer mental case I'm doing awfully well.    *Lesbian Nation: The Feminist Solution*   1973

2 It's necessary in order to attract attention, to dazzle at all costs, to be disapproved of by serious people and quoted by the foolish.

> Ibid.

3 I had the correct instinct to fuck things up but no political philosophy to clarify a course of action.     Ibid.

4 I never said I was a dyke even to a dyke because there wasn't a dyke in the land who thought she should be a dyke or even thought she was a dyke so how could we talk about it.

> Ibid.

5 Bisexuality is not so much a copout as a fearful compromise.     Ibid.

6 . . . we as womenfolk can't as i see it be all that smug and satisfied about where we're at anyhow until the ascending female principle is better established at large.
*Gullible's Travels* 1974

7 . . . i want these women in office who're in touch with their feelings and who know perfectly well when they're bullshitting and who don't have to displace their concealed feelings by dropping bombs on people who live thousands of miles away. . . . Ibid.

## 1062. Ursula K. Le Guin
### (1929– )

1 When action grows unprofitable, gather information; when information grows unprofitable, sleep. *The Left Hand of Darkness*, Ch. 3 1969

2 Legends of prediction are common throughout the whole Household of Man. Gods speak, spirits speak, computers speak. Oracular ambiguity or statistical probability provides loopholes, and discrepancies are expunged by Faith. Ibid., Ch. 4

3 A man wants his virility regarded, a woman wants her femininity appreciated, however indirect and subtle the indications of regard and appreciation. On [the planet] Winter they will not exist. One is respected and judged only as a human being. It is an appalling experience. Ibid., Ch. 7

4 . . . primitiveness and civilization are degrees of the same thing. If civilization has an opposite, it is war. Of those two things, you have either one, or the other. Not both. Ibid., Ch. 8

5 To oppose something is to maintain it. Ibid., Ch. 11

6 It is a terrible thing, this kindness that human beings do not lose. Terrible because when we are finally naked in the dark and cold, it is all we have. We who are so rich, so full of strength, wind up with that small change. We have nothing else to give. Ibid., Ch. 13

7 What is more arrogant than honesty? Ibid., Ch. 15

8 It is good to have an end to journey towards; but it is the journey that matters, in the end. Ibid.

9 I certainly wasn't happy. Happiness has to do with reason, and only reason earns it. What I was given was the thing you can't earn, and can't keep, and often don't even recognize at the time; I mean joy. Ibid., Ch. 18

10 He could also, now he was listening, hear doors, typewriters, voices, toilets flushing, in offices all up and down the hall and above him and underneath him. The real trick was to learn how not to hear them. The only solid partitions left were inside the head.
*The Lathe of Heaven*, Ch. 2 1971

11 "What the brain does by itself is infinitely more fascinating and complex than any response it can make to chemical stimulation. . . ." Ibid., Ch. 3

12 He was not interested in detached knowledge, science for science's sake: there was no use learning anything if it was of no use. Relevance was his touchstone. Ibid., Ch. 5

13 A person is defined solely by the extent of his influence over other people, by the sphere of his interrelationships; and morality is an utterly meaningless term unless defined as the good one does to others, the fulfilling of one's function in the sociopolitical whole. Ibid.

14 He had grown up in a country run by politicians who sent the pilots to man the bombers to kill the babies to make the world safe for children to grow up in. Ibid., Ch. 6

15 A person who believes, as she did, that things fit: that there is a whole of which one is a part, and that in being a part one is whole: such a person has no desire whatever, at any time, to play God. Only those who have denied their being yearn to play at it. Ibid., Ch. 7

16 The quality of the will to power is, precisely, growth. Achievement is its cancellation. To be, the will to power must increase with each fulfillment, making the fulfillment only a step to a further one. The vaster the power gained the vaster the appetite for more. Ibid., Ch. 9

17 He knew that in so far as one denies what is, one is possessed by what is not, the compulsions, the fantasies, the terrors that flock to fill the void. Ibid., Ch. 10

18 Love doesn't just sit there, like a stone, it has to be made, like bread; re-made all the time, made new. Ibid.

19 Outside the locked room is the landscape of time, in which the spirit may, with luck and courage, construct the fragile, makeshift, improbable roads and cities of fidelity: a landscape inhabitable by human beings.
*The Dispossessed* 1975

## 1063. Melina Mercouri

(1929–     )

1 When you are born and they tell you "what a pity that you are so clever, so intelligent, so beautiful but you are not a man," you are ashamed of your condition as a woman. I wanted to act like a man because the man was the master.          Quoted in "Greece: Survival of the Shrewdest" by Susan Margolis, *Ms.*          *October, 1973*

## 1064. Jeanne Moreau

(1929–     )

1 I have always liked things that are difficult, I have always had the urge to open forbidden doors, with a curiosity and an obstinacy that verge on masochism.
          Quoted in "Jeanne Moreau," *The Egotists* by Oriana Fallaci          *1963*

2 Success is like a liberation or the first phase of a love story. . . .          *Ibid.*

3 I don't think success is harmful, as so many people say. Rather, I believe it indispensable to talent, if for nothing else than to increase the talent.          *Ibid.*

4 For me it's not possible to forget, and I don't understand people who, when the love is ended, can bury the other person in hatred or oblivion. For me, a man I have loved becomes a kind of brother.          *Ibid.*

## 1065. Jacqueline Kennedy Onassis

(1929–     )

1 Can anyone understand how it is to have lived in the White House, and then, suddenly, to be living alone as the President's widow?
          Quoted by Billy Baldwin in *McCall's*          *December, 1974*

## 1066. Adrienne Rich

(1929–     )

1  Facts could be kept separate
by a convention; that was what
made childhood possible. Now knowledge finds
    me out;
in all its risible untidiness. . . .
          "From Morning-Glory to Petersburg" (1954), *Snapshots of a Daughter-in-Law*          *1963*

2 We who were loved will never
unlive that crippling fever.
          Ibid., "After a Sentence in 'Malte Laurids Brigge,' " (1958)

3 A thinking woman sleeps with monsters.
          Ibid., "Snapshots of a Daughter-in-Law," Pt. III, St. 1 (1958–1960)

4 Bemused by gallantry, we hear
our mediocrity over-praised,
indolence read as abnegation,
slattern thought styled intuition,
every lapse forgiven, our crime
only to cast too bold a shadow
or smash the mould straight off.
          Ibid., Pt. IX, St. 2

5 Nothing changes. The bones of the mammoths
are still in the earth.
          Ibid., "End of an Era," St. 4 (1961)

6 Only to have a grief
equal to all these tears!
          Ibid., "Peeling Onions," St. 1 (1961)

7 I'd call it love if love
didn't take so many years
but lust too is a jewel
a sweet flower. . . .
          "Two Songs," Pt. I (1964), *Necessities of Life*          *1966*

8 The future reconnoiters in dirty boots
along the cranberry-dark horizon.
          Ibid., "Autumn Sequence," Pt. III, St. 4 (1964)

9 The mind's passion is all for singling out.
Obscurity has another tale to tell.
          Ibid., "Focus," St. 7 (1965)

10 Desire. Desire. The nebula
opens in space, unseen
your heart utters its great beats
in solitude. . . .
          "The Demon Lover," *Leaflets*          *1969*

11 Posterity trembles like a leaf
and we go on making heirs and heirlooms.
          Ibid.

12 Only where there is language is there world.
          Ibid.

13 5. . . . A language is a map of our failures.
          "The Burning of Paper Instead of Children" (1968), *The Will to Change*          *1971*

14 Humans lived here once; it became sacred only when they went away.
          Ibid., "Shooting Script Part I," Pt. IV, St. 9 (November, 1969– February, 1970)

15      I am an instrument in the shape
of a woman trying to translate pulsations
into images     for the relief of the body
and the reconstruction of the mind.
>Ibid., "Planetarium," St. 14 (1968)

16 The victory carried like a corpse
from town to town
begins to crawl in the casket.
>Ibid., "Letters: March 1969: 1"
>(1969)

17 the moment of change is the only poem. . . .
>Ibid., "Images for Godard,"
>Pt. V, St. 7 (1970)

18 Finality broods upon the things that pass. . . .
>"A Walk by the Charles" (1950s),
>*Poems: Selected and New, 1950–1974*
>*1975*

19 The friend I can trust is the one who will let
me have my death.
The rest are actors who want me to stay and
further the plot.
>Ibid., Untitled (1960s)

20 . . . Love, our subject:
we've trained it like ivy to our walls
baked it like bread in our ovens
worn it like lead on our ankles
>Ibid., Untitled (1970s)

## 1067. Beverly Sills
### (1929– )

1 I don't want to be an exhibitionistic coloratura
who merely sings notes. I'm interested in the
*character.*
>Quoted in "Beverly Sills," *Divas:*
>*Impressions of Six Opera Superstars*
>by Winthrop Sargeant   *1959*

2 In a way, retarded children are satisfying.
Everything is a triumph. Even getting Bucky to
manage to get a spoon to his mouth was a
triumph. God compensates.   Ibid.

3 I would willingly give up my whole career if
I could have just one normal child. . . .
>Ibid.

4 A happy woman is one who has no cares at
all; a cheerful woman is one who has cares but
doesn't let them get her down.
>Interview, "60 Minutes," CBS-TV
>*1975*

5 There is something in me—I just can't stand
to admit defeat.   Ibid.

6 My singing is very therapeutic. For three hours
I have no troubles—I know how it's all going
to come out.   Ibid.

## 1068. Alisa Wells
### (1929– )

1 I understood not a word he spoke that first
night, and little in the endless ones following;
but his words, gestures, challenges were speaking to something, someone deep within me.
>Quoted in *The Woman's Eye*
>by Anne Tucker   *1973*

2 Now the real beginnings of the "freedom"
which we have discussed for many years—and
a heady freedom it is, coming after so many
years of reaching outward for it—to finally
discover all I had to do was reach inward, and
it was there waiting all the time for me!
>Ibid.

## 1069. Maria Castellani
### (fl. 1930s)

1 Fascism recognizes women as a part of the life
force of the country, laying down a division
of duties between the two sexes, without putting
obstacles in the way of those women who by
their intellectual gifts reach the highest positions.   *Italian Women, Past and Present*
>*1937*

## 1070. Elisabeth Craigin
### (fl. 1930s)

1 A so-called Lesbian alliance can be of the most
rarefied purity, and those who do not believe
it are merely judging in ignorance of the facts.
>*Either Is Love*   *1937*

## 1071. Lydia Gottschewski
### (fl. 1930s)

1 It is a curious fact that pacifism . . . is a mark
of an age weak in faith, whereas the people
of religious times have honored war as God's
rod of chastisement. . . . Only the age of
enlightenment has wished to decide the great
questions of world history at the table of
diplomats.   *Women in the New State*
>*1934*

## 1072. Jane Screven Heyward

(fl. 1930s–1939)

\* \* \*

1 More brightly must my spirit shine
Since grace of Beauty is not mine.
"The Spirit's Grace"

2 The dear old ladies whose cheeks are pink
In spite of the years of winter's chill,
Are like the Autumn leaves, I think,
A little crumpled, but lovely still.
"Autumn Leaves"

## 1073. Esther Lape

(fl. 1930s)

1 We have no illusions about the flexibility of
the Nobel Committee. Its statements reflect a
rigidity *extraordinaire.*
Letter to A. David Gurewitsch
(December 30, 1964), Quoted in
*Eleanor: The Years Alone*
by Joseph P. Lash　　*1972*

## 1074. Frances Newton

(fl. 1930s)

1 There, in that manufactured park with its
ghoulish artificiality, with its interminable
monuments to bad taste, wealth and social position, we were planning to place the body of
a beautiful and dignified old man who had
lived generously and loved beauty.
*Light, Like the Sun*　　*1937*

2 I can stand what I know. It's what I don't know
that frightens me.　　Ibid.

## 1075. Alice M. Shepard

(fl. 1930s)

\* \* \*

1 They shall not pass, tho' battleline
May bend, and foe with foe combine,
Tho' death rain on them from the sky
Till every fighting man shall die,
France shall not yield to German Rhine.
"They Shall Not Pass"

## 1076. Mabel Elsworth Todd

(fl. 1930s)

1 In the expiratory phase lies renewal of vigor
through some hidden form of muscular release. . . .　　*The Balancing of Forces in the
Human Body*　　*1929*

2 Emotion constantly finds expression in bodily
position. . . .　　Ibid.

## 1077. Bertye Young Williams

(fl. 1930s–1951)

\* \* \*

1 He who follows Beauty
Breaks his foolish heart.
"Song Against Beauty"

## 1078. Nguyen Thi Binh

(1930–　)

1 I was tortured [in the 1950s] by the Vietnamese,
with the French directing, just as now it is
with the Americans directing.
Quoted in "Madame Binh" by Becca
Wilson, *New York Review of Books
June 25, 1975*

2 We were moving from one place to another,
always moving . . . we lived underground
often, never coming into the air except at night.
1957 through 1959: those were the black years.
By 1960 the people could not bear it any
longer. They demanded the right to fight and
protect themselves.　　Ibid.

3 We tell our children that the bombs cannot kill
everyone, that they must not be afraid. . . . We
know our sacrifice is necessary. If the bombs
do not fall on you, they fall on friends. We
accept fate. We are calm. It is useless to be a
pessimist. Some day we will win a beautiful
life, if not for ourselves, then for our children.
Ibid.

## 1079. Julie Anne Bovasso

(1930–　)

1 BEBE. I want to know you. And I want you to
know me and understand me. What good is
love without understanding? How can we love
each other if we don't know each other and
understand each other? How can we understand each other if we don't know each other?
And how can we know each other if we don't
love each other?　　*Schubert's Last Serenade
1972*

## 1080. Lee Grant

(1930?–　)

1 The more stringent the conditions are, the
more the actor uses them—like hurdlers, or
emotional stuntmen.
"Selling Out to Hollywood, or Home,"
*The New York Times
August 12, 1973*

2 This is a period of great *angst*. The impermanence and flimsiness of houses built on faults, subject to landslides, add to a former apartment dweller's sense of insecurity. The stage-set quality of the streets, the green and blue spotlights illuminating every sallow palm in front of Hollywood court apartments, the 40-foot neon cross overlooking the freeway.     Ibid.

3 One's art adjusts to economic necessity if your metabolism does.     Ibid.

4 As more of us [actresses] are moving into producing and directing, the level of creativity among women has become very high, and therefore our relationships have changed—have themselves become more creative.
"Art Catches Up to Life," *Ms.*
*November, 1975*

5 . . . art always seems to be catching up to life.     Ibid.

## 1081. Lorraine Hansberry
(1930–1965)

1 WALTER. Baby, don't *nothing* happen for you in this world 'less you pay *somebody* off!
*A Raisin in the Sun*, Act I, Sc. 1
*1958*

2 BENEATHA. Why do you give money at church for the missionary work?

MAMA. Well, that's to help save people.

BENEATHA. You mean save them from *heathenism* . . . I'm afraid they need more salvation from the British and the French.     Ibid., Sc. 2

3 LINDNER. And at the moment the overwhelming majority of our people out there feel that people get along better, take more of a common interest in the life of the community, when they share a common background. I want you to believe me when I tell you that race prejudice simply doesn't enter into it.
Ibid., Act II, Sc. 3

4 ASAGAI. Ah, I like the look of packing crates! A household in preparation for a journey! . . . Something full of the flow of life. . . . Movement, progress. . . .     Ibid., Act III

5 BENEATHA. While I was sleeping in my bed in there, things were happening in this world that directly concerned me—and nobody asked me, consulted me—they just went out and did things—and changed my life.     Ibid.

6 BENEATHA. Don't you see there isn't any real progress, Asagai, there is only one large circle that we march in, around and around, each of us with our own little picture—in front of us—our own little mirage that we think is the future.     Ibid.

## 1082. Maureen Howard
(1930–    )

1 I started that book but something happened, my brother's children, my mother's gall bladder, something happened so I never finished.
*Bridgeport Bus*     *1966*

2 When I go home my mother and I play a cannibal game; we eat each other over the years, tender morsel by morsel, until there is nothing left but dry bone and wig.     Ibid.

3 . . . the ivy remembered another season, though I suppose it was the future that I really admired in them, because I had none.     Ibid.

4 I have a world now, about the size of a circle of light thrown by a desk lamp, that is mine and safe from my mother and the zipper company and my brother's children.     Ibid.

5 . . . they spoke to me. That happens now and again, even when you become a sophisticated reader with all kinds of critical impedimenta: you read something that is so direct, so pertinent to exactly where you are—the way you feel and your precise frame of mind.     Ibid.

6 . . . my mother is soothed at last by her television, watching lives much more professional than ours.     Ibid.

7 She was a survivor, frail, helpless, but a survivor: the past was one prop, the bottle another.     "Three Cheers for Mr. Spears,"
*Before My Time*     *1974*

8 "The process of losing my faith was so gradual," said Mr. Spears, "I didn't seem to notice it. I've thought since that it was a counterpart of attaining my physical growth, which I never noticed either. One day it was complete—my height and my loss of faith—and it was easy, painless. I wish that I had suffered."
Ibid.

## 1083. Dolores Huerta
(1930–    )

1 How do I stop eleven million people from buying the grape?
Quoted in "Stopping Traffic: One Woman's Cause" by Barbara L. Baer,
*The Progressive*     *September, 1975*

2 . . . if you haven't forgiven yourself something, how can you forgive others? Ibid.

3 Walk the street with us into history. Get off the sidewalk. Stop being vegetables. Work for justice. *Viva* the boycott! Ibid.

## 1084. Carol Kaye
(1930?–    )

Co-author with Elizabeth Douvan. See 1019: 1–2.

## 1085. Abbey Lincoln
(1930–    )

1 The fact that white people readily and proudly call themselves "white," glorify all that is white, and whitewash all that is glorified, becomes unnatural and bigoted in its intent only when these same whites deny persons of African heritage who are Black the natural and inalienable right to readily—proudly—call themselves "black," glorify all that is black, and blackwash all that is glorified.
"Who Will Revere the Black Woman?,"
*Negro Digest* September, 1966

2 Black womanhood is outraged and humiliated. Black womanhood cries for dignity and restitution and salvation. Black womanhood wants and needs protection, and keeping and holding. Who will assuage her indignation? Who will keep her precious and pure? Who will glorify and proclaim her beautiful image? To whom will she cry rape? Ibid.

## 1086. Gay Gaer Luce
(1930–    )

1 Swept along in the concepts of their business-oriented culture, many people berate themselves if they are not as consistent and productive as machines. *Body Time*, Preface
1971

2 Even as small children we are trained not to listen to our bodies or trust our sensations.
"Trust Your Body Rhythms,"
*Psychology Today* April, 1975

3 Our harmony is maintained by nature, since we are not closed systems, but are part of the turning earth, the sun, moon and cosmos beyond. In contradiction with our inner clockwork, our urban culture bids us to forget our sources of health and harmony and live by artificial clocks. Ibid.

4 . . . people are beginning to resist the rhythm of the machine and suspect that the path of inner harmony and health demands an inward attention. Ibid.

## 1087. Loretta Lynn
(1930?–    )

1 A woman's two cents worth is worth two cents in the music business.
Quoted in "Sexism Seen But Not Heard" by Tracy Hotchner,
*Los Angeles Times* May 26, 1974

## 1088. Ann McGovern
(1930–    )

1 Dumb. Dumb. Tiny drum beats. Dumb. Dumb. Her sister's favorite word. She called her dumb more than she called her Jane.
"Wonder Is Not Precisely Knowing,"
*American Scene: New Voices*,
Don Wolfe, ed. 1963

2 She shared much with her sister—the absence of a father, the presence of a shadowy unhappy mother. They had one bike and one sled between them, and had learned long ago that these possessions were not worth the fights. Ibid.

3 In those days, people did not think it was important for girls to read. Some people thought too much reading gave girls brain fever.
*The Secret Soldier* 1975

## 1089. Dory Previn
(1930–    )

1 men wander,
women weep
women worry
while men are asleep
"Men Wander" 1971

2 I said
your words
till my throat
closed up
and I had
no voice
and I had
no choice
but to do your song
I was you baby
I was you too long
"I Was You" 1971

3 Would you care to stay till sunrise
it's completely your decision
it's just the night cuts through me like a knife
would you care to stay awhile and save my
life?
"The Lady with the Braid"    *1971*

4 What most of us want is to be heard, to communicate—which gets back to the origins of
music, which are in the ballads of the wandering minstrel.
Quoted in "Sexism Seen But Not
Heard" by Tracy Hotchner,
*Los Angeles Times*    *May 26, 1974*

5 The infiltration of women writers into film will
bring new life to it because "the male idea"
is in a state of terminal perfection. . . . Films
by and about women will now answer the questions raised by male films and then there will
be a cycle when men will answer back.
Ibid.

## 1090. Dorothy Semenow
### (1930–    )

1 I share with the client how I arrive at my
responses. In so doing, I demonstrate that
analytic methods are knowable and imply that
the client too can master them. This demystifies
my utterances and punctures the myth often
held over from childhood by the client (and
by many of the rest of us too) that *big people,*
originally *her parents* and now *the analyst,*
can read her mind and heart with their powerful x-ray vision and thus know her sins *and*
her destiny.
Address, "Principles of Feminist
Psychoanalysis," Cedars-Sinai
Hospital, Los Angeles    *May, 1975*

2 As early as possible in our analytic journey we
try to sketch what kind of treasures the client
wants to build into her life. True, she often
comes to analysis caught up and spilling over
with what is wrong. But buried in the suffering
of those wrongs is some notion of stunted
rights. We uncover those rights lost in the
client's yesterdays and add to them her hopes
for her tomorrow.    Ibid.

## 1091. June L. Tapp
### (1930–    )

1 If I had to describe something as divine it
would be what happens between people when
they really get it together. There is a kind of
spark that makes it all worthwhile. When you

feel that spark, you get a good deep feeling
in your gut.
Quoted in "By Law Possessed"
by Carol Tavris, *Psychology Today*
*May, 1975*

2 . . . I cannot accept the idea of law as merely
repressive or punitive. It can be expressive
and conducive to the development of social
values.
Quoted in "The Notion of Conspiracy
Is Not Tasty to Americans" by
Gordon Bermant, *Psychology Today*
*May, 1975*

3 Now about the totalitarian liberal. . . . What
I found . . . were groups who in principle or
on paper were committed to religious values
that looked liberal, but who held these views
with a ferocity that would not, could not,
allow for a truly democratic interpretation of
the rights of others. Their liberality was more
apparent than real.    Ibid.

4 The liberal view, it seems to me, encourages
a diversity of views and open confrontation
among them. The belief is that conflict or
"dissensus," if properly harnessed, leads eventually to the most stable form of consensus.
What is important in all this is the *process* by
which the changes occur. The due process of
law as we use it, I believe, rests squarely on
the liberal idea of conflict and resolution.
Ibid.

5 Public participation—as in the jury trial—is
the cornerstone in the administration of justice
and vital to our system of law.    Ibid.

## 1092. Hilma Wolitzer
### (1930–    )

1 There is something terrific about not knowing
your father because it opens up possibilities. . . .
"Waiting for Daddy," *Esquire*
*July, 1971*

2 Their kitchen was full of piecework and vague
hope.    Ibid.

3 I was drawn into the back seat of his father's
green Pontiac and the pattern of those seat
covers stays in my head forever.    Ibid.

4 It seemed strange that I could do all those
things with him, discover all those sensations
and odors and that new voice that came from
the dark pit of my throat (*Don't—oh, yes, oh
God*) and that my mother and grandmother
didn't know.    Ibid.

## 1093. Patricia Carbine

(1931– )

1 We're seeing women organize together . . . with the realization that collective or organized action is much more important than individual change.     Quoted in *AFTRA Magazine* *Summer, 1974*

## 1094. Sally Gearhart

(1931– )

1 I look forward with great anticipation to the death of the church. The sooner it dies, the sooner we can be about the business of living the gospel.
"The Lesbian and God-the-Father or All the Church Needs Is a Good Lay—on Its Side"    *1972*

## 1095. Shirley Hazzard

(1931– )

1 How long women take to leave a room, Tancredi thought. They can't simply get up and walk out—all this shambling and turning back on their tracks, chattering and embracing. . . .
*The Evening of the Holiday*, Ch. 1 *1965*

2 When we are young, she thought, we worship romantic love for the wrong reasons . . . and, because of that, subsequently repudiate it. Only later, and for quite other reasons, we discover its true importance. And by then it has become tiring even to observe.     Ibid., Ch. 2

3 One would always want to think of oneself as being on the side of love, ready to recognize it and wish it well—but, when confronted with it in others, one so often resented it, questioned its true nature, secretly dismissed the particular instance as folly or promiscuity. Was it merely jealousy, or a reluctance to admit so noble and enviable a sentiment in anyone but oneself?
Ibid., Ch. 9

4 "Sometimes, surely, truth is closer to imagination—or to intelligence, to love—than to fact? To be accurate is not to be right."
Ibid., Ch. 11

5 "Perhaps if we lived with less physical beauty we would develop our true natures more."
Ibid., Ch. 13

6 "Do you ever notice," asked Luisa, "how easy it is to forgive a person any number of faults for one endearing characteristic, for a certain

style, or some commitment to life—while someone with many good qualities is insupportable for a single defect if it happens to be a boring one?"     Ibid.

7 When someone dies a long-expected death, the waiting goes on for a while—the waiting for what has already taken place but cannot yet be properly comprehended or decently acted upon.     Ibid., Ch. 15

8 Mr. Bekkus frequently misused the word "hopefully." He also made a point of saying locate instead of find, utilize instead of use, and never lost an opportunity to indicate or communicate; and would slip in a "basically" when he felt unsure of his ground.
"Nothing in Excess," *People in Glass Houses*    *1967*

9 Algie was collecting contradictions in terms: to a nucleus of "military intelligence" and "competent authorities" he had added such discoveries as the soul of efficiency, easy virtue, enlightened self-interest, Bankers Trust, and Christian Scientist.     Ibid.

10 Pylos' first official act was to name his new department. The interim titles that had been used—"Economic Relief of Under Privileged Territories" and "Mission for Under-Developed Lands"—were well enough in their way, but they combined a note of condescension with initials which, when contracted, proved somewhat unfortunate.
Ibid., "The Story of Miss Sadie Graine"

11 Nothing, Izmet thought, makes a more fanatical official than a Latin. Organization is alien to their natures, but once they get the taste for it they take to it like drink.
Ibid., "Official Life"

12 When I was a child . . . I would think it must be marvellous to issue those proclamations of experience—"It was at least ten years ago" or "I hadn't seen him for twenty years." But chronological prestige is tenacious: once attained, it can't be shed; it increases moment by moment, day by day, pressing its honours on you until you are lavishly, overly endowed with them. Until you literally sink under them.
*The Bay of Noon*, Ch. 1    *1970*

13 Had I been accompanied, I might have laughed out loud . . . but solitude, which is held to be a cause of eccentricity, in fact imposes excessive normality, at least in public. . . .
Ibid.

14 . . . children . . . seldom have a proper sense of their own tragedy, discounting and keeping hidden the true horrors of their short lives,

humbly imagining real calamity to be some prestigious drama of the grown-up world.
Ibid.

15 Words would have been as presumptuous as an embrace: yet the inadequacy of silence was painful.      Ibid., Ch. 6

16 Like many men who are compulsively cruel to their womenfolk, he also shed tears at the cinema, and showed a disproportionate concern for insects.      Ibid., Ch. 7

17 "People resort to violence," she said . . . . "not to relieve their feelings, but their thoughts. The demand for comprehension becomes too great, one would rather strike somebody than have to go on wondering about them."
Ibid., Ch. 8

18 The ultimate impression they made was of innocence—the novelty of passions not yet turned to slogans, of gifts not deployed for gain, of goodwill not turned to self-importance.
Ibid., Ch. 9

19 He himself had strengthened this impression by the defences . . . he had constructed; had become their victim, like those heavily fortified towns that invite their own downfall by suggesting that there is something within to be assaulted.      Ibid., Ch. 13

20 Although I wished I hadn't come, it did not occur to me to go back. In matters of importance there is no such thing as "best avoided"— avoidance is only a vacuum that something else must fill. Everything is the inevitable.
Ibid., Ch. 15

## 1096. Margaret O'Shaughnessy Heckler

(1931– )

1 When you undermine faith in a system, your child may not necessarily see the difference between the politician who is no longer respected and the policeman, the teacher, the parent.      Quoted in "Impeachment?" by Claire Safran, *Redbook* *April, 1974*

2 Once you start to separate public service from the enormous influence of the fat cats of society, you rob the vested interests of their most powerful weapons.      Ibid.

## 1097. Kristin Hunter

(1931– )

1 "How does a person become an outlaw, DuBois?" Elgar inquired mildly. . . .
"One is born to the calling," DuBois answered. "Many are called, but few choose. You see, society decides which of its segments are going to be outside its borders. Society says, 'These are the legitimate channels to my rewards. They are closed to you forever.' So then the outlawed segments must seek rewards through illegitimate channels. In other words, once my Great White Father declared me illegitimate, I had to be a bastard."
"Is Uncle Sam your Great White Father?"
"Exactly. The white society is my father and, in a figurative sense, every Negro's father. Our mother being Africa."      *The Landlord* *1966*

2 "A landlord is supposed to be brutal, stingy, insulting, and arrogant. Like the police, like the magistrates, like all the authority-figures of white society. That's what we're used to. That's what we understand. We're accustomed to our enemies, we know how to deal with them. A landlord who tries to be a friend only confuses us."      Ibid.

3 Phosdicker was as honest as the day was long. He was an old-fashioned, dedicated civil servant; a fine, upright, honorable old man, Elgar thought. God help us all. A monster.     Ibid.

4 Borden [the psychiatrist], his one stable reference point in reality. The way sailors needed the North Star to guide them through black seas, Elgar needed Borden to help him find his way out of the gathering chaos.      Ibid.

5 "First it is necessary to stand on your own two feet. But the minute a man finds himself in that position, the next thing he should do is reach out his arms."      Ibid.

6 The most amazing thing about little children, Elgar decided . . . was their fantastic adaptability.      Ibid.

7 "Love can't last around poverty. Neither can a woman's looks."      Ibid.

8 "But generally speaking I've always been too confused about who I was to decide who I was better than."      Ibid.

9 Life was both simpler and more complicated than he had imagined. One did not, after all, change one's skin or one's society. One was given both, along with one's identity, at birth.

And all things ossified as one grew older. But within the rigid framework were loopholes of possibility, spaces in which small miracles might occur.                                                    Ibid.

## 1098. Adrienne Kennedy
### (1931–    )

1 SARAH. As for myself I long to become even a more pallid Negro than I am now; pallid like Negroes on the covers of American Negro magazines; soulless, educated and irrelevant. I want to possess no moral value, particularly value as to my being. I want not to be. I ask nothing except anonymity.
*Funnyhouse of a Negro*    1964

2 SARAH. For, like all educated Negroes—out of life and death essential—I find it necessary to maintain a stark fortress versus recognition of myself. My white friends like myself will be shrewd, intellectual and anxious for death. Anyone's death.                              Ibid.

3 SARAH. I find there are no places only my *funnyhouse*.                                   Ibid.

4 SARAH. . . . for relationships was one of my last religions.                                 Ibid.

5 SARAH. I wanted to live in Genesis in the midst of golden savannas, nim and white frankopenny trees and white stallions roaming under a blue sky. I wanted to walk with a white dove. I wanted to be a Christian.                     Ibid.

## 1099. Toni Morrison
### (1931–    )

1 "Which you want? A whipping and no turnips or turnips and no whipping?"
*The Bluest Eye*    1961

2 . . . she lived out her days exploring her own thoughts and emotions, giving them full reign, feeling no obligation to please anybody unless their pleasure pleased her. . . .    *Sula*    1974

3 And like any artist with no art form, she became dangerous.                            Ibid.

4 "I don't know everything, I just do everything."                                          Ibid.

5     "I know what every colored woman in this country is doing."
"What's that?"
"Dying."                                        Ibid.

6    "I sure did live in this world."
"Really? What have you got to show for it?"
"Show? To who? Girl, I got my mind. And what goes on in it. Which is to say, I got me."
"Lonely, ain't it?"
"Yes. But my lonely is *mine*. Now your lonely is somebody else's. Made by somebody else and handed to you. Ain't that something? A secondhand lonely."                  Ibid.

## 1100. Alice Munro
### (1931–    )

1 Lovers. Not a soft word, as people thought, but cruel and tearing.
"Something I've Been Meaning to Tell You," *Something I've Been Meaning to Tell You*    1974

2 If they had been married, people would have said they were very happy.              Ibid.

3 But I never cleaned thoroughly enough, my reorganization proved to be haphazard, the disgraces came unfailingly to light, and it was clear how we failed, how disastrously we fell short of that ideal of order and cleanliness, household decency which I as much as anybody else believed in.          Ibid., "Winter World"

## 1101. Cynthia Ozick
### (1931–    )

1 He had once demonstrated that, since God had made the world, and since there was no God, the world in all logic could not exist.
*Trust*, Pt. I, Ch. 1    1966

2 It is true that money attracts; but much money repels.                          Ibid., Ch. 7

3 "He knows nothing about Literature—most great writers don't: all they know is life."
Ibid., Pt. III, Ch. 1

4 "Superfluity, excess of custom, and superstition would climb like a choking vine on the Fence of the Law if skepticism did not continually hack them away to make freedom for purity."
"The Pagan Rabbi" (1966), *The Pagan Rabbi and Other Stories*    1971

5 ". . . Paradise is only for those who have already been there."
Ibid., "Envy; or, Yiddish in America" (1969)

6 It was the old recurrent groan of life. It was the sound of nature turning on its hinge. Everyone had a story to tell him. What resentments, what hatreds, what bitterness, how little good will!    Ibid., "The Doctor's Wife" (1971)

7 Moral: In saying what is obvious, never choose cunning. Yelling works better.
"We Are the Crazy Lady and Other Feisty Feminist Fables," *The First Ms. Reader*, Francine Klagsbrun, ed. *1972*

8 Language makes culture, and we make a rotten culture when we abuse words.    Ibid.

9 I'm not afraid of facts, I welcome facts *but a congeries of facts is not equivalent to an idea.* This is the essential fallacy of the so-called "scientific" mind. People who mistake facts for ideas are incomplete thinkers; they are gossips.    Ibid.

10 Wondrous hole! Magical hole! Dazzlingly influential hole! Noble and effulgent hole! From this hole everything follows logically: first the baby, then the placenta, then, for years and years and years until death, a way of life. It is all logic, and she who lives by the hole will live also by its logic. It is, appropriately, logic with a hole in it.
Ibid., "The Hole/Birth Catalog"

11 The engineering is secondary to the vision.    Ibid.

12 If the fish had stuck to its gills there would have been no movement up to the land.    Ibid.

13 Judaism has no dying god, no embalming of dead bodies, above all no slightest version of death-instinct—"Choose life."    Ibid.

14 The usefulness of madmen is famous: they demonstrate society's logic flagrantly carried out down to its last scrimshaw scrap.    Ibid.

## 1102.  Amanda Row
(1931–    )

1 Jocelyn's childhood stood on the bookcase: *Pollyanna, The Bobbsey Twins, Now We Are Six, Black Beauty,* and *The Little Minister* beside *Heidi.*    *Where No Sea Runs    1963*

## 1103.  Jane Rule
(1931–    )

1 I didn't want to be a boy, ever, but I was outraged that his height and intelligence were graces for him and gaucheries for me.
*Lesbian Images*, Introduction    *1975*

2 I had never been as resigned to ready-made ideas as I was to ready-made clothes, perhaps because, although I couldn't sew, I could think.    Ibid.

3 Cleaving is an activity which should be left to snails for cleaning ponds and aquariums.    Ibid.

4 Morality, like language, is an invented structure for conserving and communicating order. And morality is learned, like language, by mimicking and remembering.
Ibid., "Myth and Morality, Sources of Law and Prejudice"

## 1104.  Barbara Walters
(1931–    )

1 . . . I happen to disagree with the well-entrenched theory that the art of conversation is merely the art of being a good listener. Such advice invites people to be cynical with one another and full of fake; when a conversation becomes a monologue, poked along with tiny cattle-prod questions, it isn't a conversation any more.
*How to Talk with Practically Anybody About Practically Anything    1970*

2 Celebrities used to be found in clusters, like oysters—and with much the same defensive mechanisms.    Ibid., Ch. 1

3 Don't confuse being stimulating with being blunt. . . .    Ibid., Ch. 2

4 If we could harness the destructive energy of disagreements over politics, we wouldn't need the bomb.    Ibid., Ch. 3

5 Parents of young children should realize that few people, and maybe no one, will find their children as enchanting as they do.
Ibid., Ch. 4

6 Most old people . . . are disheartened to be living in the ailing house of their bodies, to be limited physically and economically, to feel an encumbrance to others—guests who didn't have the good manners to leave when the party was over.    Ibid.

7 It's a fact that it is much more comfortable to be in the position of the person who has been offended than to be the unfortunate cause of it.                    Ibid., Ch. 6

8 A great many people think that polysyllables are a sign of intelligence. . . .    Ibid., Ch. 8

9 The origin of a modern party is anthropological: humans meet and share food to lower hostility between them and indicate friendship.
                    Ibid., Ch. 9

10 Success can make you go one of two ways. It can make you a prima donna, or it can smooth the edges, take away the insecurities, let the nice things come out.
        Quoted in "Barbara Walters—Star of
        the Morning," *Newsweek*
        *May 6, 1974*

## 1105.  Olga Connolly
### (1932–    )

1 Society feels that sport must be justified, and we have gotten away from the Greek concept of mind and body. That is a failure of the physical education process.
        Quoted in "Women in Sports: The
        Movement Is Real," *Los Angeles
        Times      April 23, 1974*

2 Women must be accepted as human beings, and it can't be done until women are physically strong enough to stand on their own feet.
                    Ibid.

## 1106.  Eva Figes
### (1932–    )

1 When modern woman discovered the orgasm it was (combined with modern birth control) perhaps the biggest single nail in the coffin of male dominance.
        Quoted in *The Descent of Woman* by
        Elaine Morgan      *1972*

2 Either one goes on gradually liberating the divorce laws, until marriage stands exposed as a hollow sham in which no one would wish to engage, or one takes a short cut and abolishes marriage altogether. . . .
        *Patriarchal Attitudes      1972*

3 Providing for one's family as a good husband and father is a water-tight excuse for making money hand over fist. Greed may be a sin, exploitation of other people might, on the face

of it, look rather nasty, but who can blame a man for "doing the best" for his children?
        "A View of My Own," *Nova
        January, 1973*

4 The law of individualism and private enterprise is that God helps those who help themselves; what is more, He is actually on their side, since it is a sin not to make use of the talents God gave you. So poverty definitely implies not only laziness but a fall from grace: God disapproves of paupers.                    Ibid.

5 . . . unless society recognises that its responsibility extends far beyond the provision of free schooling, the money spent on state education is largely wasted. School becomes just another way of institutionalising the poor.    Ibid.

## 1107.  Penelope Gilliatt
### (1932–    )

1 The reason why her face was unlined was perhaps that no expression ever passed through it, the owner having developed a reputation for herself as a sort of Delphic presence simply by a habit of nonparticipation that had begun as a defence against the efforts of a boisterous English nanny to boot her into vivacity.
        *A State of Change*, Pt. I, Ch. 3
        *1967*

2   "Why is it that beautiful women never seem to have any curiosity?"
    "Is it because they know they're classical? With classical things the Lord finished the job. Ordinary ugly people know they're deficient and they go on looking for the pieces."
                    Ibid., Pt. II, Ch. 8

3 ALEX. I can't see why having an affair with someone on and off is any worse than being married for a course or two at mealtimes.
        "Monday," *Sunday Bloody Sunday
        1971*

4 MRS. GREVILLE. Darling, you keep throwing in your hand because you haven't got the whole thing. There *is* no whole thing. One has to make it work.                    Ibid.

5 ALEX. I've had this business that anything is better than nothing. There are times when nothing has to be better than anything.
                    Ibid., "Saturday"

6 I do wish people wouldn't call English people eccentric!
        Quoted in "Rebirth?" by James Childs,
        *The Hollywood Screenwriters,*
        Richard Corliss, ed.      *1972*

7 Critics are probably more prone to clichés than fiction writers who pluck things out of the air. Ibid.

8 The odd thing is, whatever you've been stingy about is something you never use anyway. It's like life itself . . . spend it—spend it because you have it. Ibid.

9 Gossip columnists at it again. What a lousy job, thriving on invented rows. Ibid.

10 It would be difficult for a woman to be, I should think, the production head of a studio or a manager without being called a bull-dyke. Ibid.

11 Woman's past place in film history has been more significant in countries that aren't as prick-proud as England, America, Japan. . . . Ibid.

## 1108. Hannah Green
### (1932–     )

1 "On my surface . . . there must be no sign showing, no seam—a perfect surface." *I Never Promised You a Rose Garden,* Ch. 1     *1964*

2 A child's independence is too big a risk for the shaky balance of some parents. Ibid., Ch. 5

3 She had opened her mind to the words the way an eye used to darkness, veiled with its lashes, opens cautiously to the light, and, finding it even a little blinding, closes itself too late. The light had come, and come invincibly, even after the eye had renounced it. It was too late to unsee. Ibid., Ch. 8

4 "Look here," Furii said. "I never promised you a rose garden. I never promised you perfect justice. . . ." Ibid., Ch. 13

5 When she was this great soaring creature it seemed as if it was the earth ones who were damned and wrong, not she, who was so complete in beauty and anger. It seemed to her that they slept and were blind. Ibid., Ch. 16

6 "I had known all those years and years how sick I was, and nobody else would admit it."
"You were asked to mistrust even the reality to which you were closest and which you could discern as clearly as daylight. Small wonder that mental patients have so low a tolerance for lies." Ibid., Ch. 17

7 "If I can teach you something, it may mean that I can count at least somewhere." Ibid.

8 Later, they began to explore the secret idea that Deborah shared with all the ill—that she had infinitely more power than the ordinary person and was at the same time also his inferior. Ibid.

9 Outside the doors of study . . . an angel waits. Ibid., Ch. 20

10 "And if I fight, then for *what*?"
"For nothing easy or sweet, and I told you that last year and the year before that. For your own challenge, for your own mistakes and the punishment for them, for your own definition of love and of sanity—a good strong self with which to begin to live." Ibid., Ch. 21

11 "Besides, I like an anger that is not fearful and guilty and can come out in a good and vigorous England." Ibid.

12 Now that she held this tremulous but growing conviction that she was alive, she began to be in love with the new world. Ibid., Ch. 23

13 The girl . . . was a gentle, generous veteran of mechanical psychiatry in a dozen other hospitals. Her memory had been ravaged, but her sickness was still intact. Ibid., Ch. 27

14 "The senses are not discreet!" Ibid., Ch. 28

## 1109. Jacquelyne Jackson
### (1932–     )

1 Those black males who try to hold women down are expressing in sexist terms the same kinds of expressions in racist terms which they would deny. . . . Speech, First National Conference on Black Women     *March, 1974*

## 1110. Edna O'Brien
### (1932–     )

1 "Any news?" she said suddenly. When she said this I always felt obliged to entertain her, even if I had to tell lies. *The Country Girls,* Ch. 3     *1960*

2 "Are you fast?" Baba asked bluntly.
"What's fast?" I interrupted. The word puzzled me.
"It's a woman who has a baby quicker than another woman," Baba said quickly, impatiently. Ibid., Ch. 9

3 He had what I call a very religious smile. An inner smile that came on and off, governed as it were by his private joy in what he heard or saw. . . .     *The Love Object*    1963

4 I did not sleep. I never do when I am over-happy, over-unhappy, or in bed with a strange man.      Ibid.

5 When something has been perfect . . . there is a tendency to try hard to repeat it.    Ibid.

6 Bad moments, like good ones, tend to be grouped together. . . .      Ibid.

7 It is impossible to insist that bad news delivered in a certain manner and at a certain time will have a less awful effect.      Ibid.

8 There is something about holding on to things that I find therapeutic.      Ibid.

9 "I am committing suicide through lack of intelligence, and through not knowing, not learning to know, how to live."      Ibid.

10 . . . it is a shocking fact that although absence does not make love less it cools down our physical need for the ones we love.    Ibid.

11 I would mend and with vengeance.      Ibid.

12 That was the first time it occurred to me that all my life I had feared imprisonment, the nun's cell, the hospital bed, the places where one faced the self without distraction, without the crutches of other people. . . .     Ibid.

13 . . . a nothing is a dreadful thing to hold on to.      Ibid.

14 Later she came in the house and sat in front of the telephone, staring at it, waiting for it to come to life, hoping, beseeching, lifting it from time to time to make sure it was not out of order, then, relieved at its regular purr, she would drop it suddenly in case he should be dialing at that very moment, which he wasn't.     *August Is a Wicked Month*, Ch. 3    1965

15 . . . she longed for him as she stood in the street and thought the wickedest thing he had done was to come like that and give her false hope, and renew her life for an evening when she had resigned herself to being almost dead.      Ibid.

16 "After the rich, the most obnoxious people in the world are those who serve the rich."      Ibid., Ch. 8

17 Kindness. The most unkindest thing of all.      Ibid., Ch. 11

18 There are times when the thing we are seeing changes before our very eyes, and if it is a landscape we praise nature, and if it is a spectre, we shudder or cross ourselves, but if it is a loved one that defects, we excuse ourselves and say we have to be somewhere, and are already late for our next appointment.     "A Scandalous Woman," *A Scandalous Woman*    1974

19 Do you know what I hate about myself, I have never done a brave thing, I have never risked death.      Ibid., "Over"

20 . . . at heart she was quite willful and rebellious. . . . She had developed these traits of niceness and agreeableness simply to get away from people—to keep them from pestering her.      Ibid., "Honeymoon"

21 She thought of the bigness and wonder of destiny, meeting him in a packed train had been a fluke, and this now was a fluke, and things would either convene to shut that door, or open it a little, or open and close it alternately, and they would be together, or not be together as life the gaffer thought fit.      Ibid., "A Journey"

22 But it is not good to repudiate the dead because they do not leave you alone, they are like dogs that bark intermittently at night.     Ibid., "Love-Child"

## 1111. Sylvia Plath
### (1932-1963)

1 . . . they all wanted to adopt me in some way, and, for the price of their care and influence, have me resemble them.     *The Bell Jar*    1963p

2 I pushed myself into a flight I knew I couldn't stop by skill or any belated access of will.      Ibid.

3 "What does a woman see in a woman that she can't see in a man?" Doctor Nolan paused. Then she said, "Tenderness."      Ibid.

4 . . . I guess I feel about a hot bath the way those religious people feel about holy water. . . . The longer I lay there in the clear hot water the purer I felt, and when I stepped out at last and wrapped myself in one of the big, soft, white, hotel bath-towels I felt pure and sweet as a new baby.      Ibid., Ch. 2

5  "Do you know what a poem is, Esther?"
"No, what?" I would say.
"A piece of dust."
Then just as he was smiling and starting to look proud, I would say, "So are the cadavers you cut up. So are the people you think you're curing. They're dust as dust as dust. I reckon a good poem lasts a whole lot longer than a hundred of those people put together."
Ibid., Ch. 5

6  I never wanted to get married. The last thing I wanted was infinite security, and to be the place an arrow shoots off from. I wanted change and excitement and to shoot off in all directions myself, like the colored arrows from a Fourth of July rocket.    Ibid., Ch. 7

7  "If neurotic is wanting two mutually exclusive things at one and the same time, then I'm neurotic as hell. I'll be flying back and forth between one mutually exclusive thing and another for the rest of my days."    Ibid., Ch. 8

8  . . . I had followed the green, luminous course of the second hand and the minute hand and the hour hand of the bedside clock through their circles and semi-circles, every night for seven nights, without missing a second, or a minute, or an hour.    Ibid., Ch. 11

9  They understood things of the spirit in Japan. They disemboweled themselves when anything went wrong. . . . It must take a lot of courage to die like that.    Ibid.

10  I stored the fact . . . in the corner of my mind the way a squirrel stores a nut.    Ibid., Ch. 15

11  I lay, rapt and naked, on Irwin's ruffled blanket, waiting for the miraculous change to make itself felt. But all I felt was a sharp, startlingly bad pain.    Ibid., Ch. 19

12  Sunday—the doctor's paradise! Doctors at country clubs, doctors at the seaside, doctors with mistresses, doctors with wives, doctors in church, doctors in yachts, doctors everywhere resolutely being people, not doctors.    Ibid.

13  I took a deep breath and listened to the old brag of my heart. I am, I am, I am.
Ibid., Ch. 20

14  A living doll, everywhere you look.
It can sew, it can cook,
It can talk, talk, talk.

It works, there is nothing wrong with it.
You have a hole, it's a poultice.
You have an eye, it's an image.
My boy, it's your last resort.
Will you marry it, marry it, marry it.
"The Applicant," *Ariel*    *1966p*

15  Out of the ash
I rise with my red hair
and I eat men like air.
Ibid., "Lady Lazarus"

16  Viciousness in the kitchen!
Ibid., "Lesbos"

17  And your first gift is making stone out of everything.
I wake to a mausoleum; you are here,
Ticking your fingers on the marble table, looking for cigarettes,
Spiteful as a woman, but not so nervous,
And dying to say something answerable.
Ibid., "The Rival"

18  How long can I be a wall around my green property?
How long can my hands
Be a bandage to his hurt, and my words
Bright birds in the sky, consoling? consoling?
It is a terrible thing
To be so open: it is as if my heart
Put on a face and walked into the world. . . .
"A Poem for Three Voices"    *1968p*

19       What would the dark
Do without fevers to eat?
What would the light
Do without eyes to knife. . . .
"The Jailor," *Encounter*    *1969p*

20  Widow. The word consumes itself. . . .
"Widow," *Crossing the Water*    *1971p*
     *   *   *

21  I am no drudge
Though for years I have eaten dust
and dried plates with my dense hair.
"The Babysitters"

22  Spiderlike, I spin mirrors,
Loyal to my own image,
Uttering nothing but blood.
"Childless Woman"

23  Is there no way out of the mind?
"Apprehensions"

# 1112. Harriet Rosenstein
(1932?–    )

1  . . . violent outrage and equally violent despair seem inevitable responses to our era. All the horrors committed in the name of national honor or the sanctity of the family or individual integrity have caught up with us.
"Reconsidering Sylvia Plath," *The First Ms. Reader*, Francine Klagsbrun, ed.    *1972*

2 . . . the novel . . . traditionally, at least, has depended on the pretense of objectivity to lend it the status of truth: a little world seen full and clear. Ibid.

3 Destiny is something men select; women achieve it only by default or stupendous suffering. Quoted in *Ms.* *July, 1974*

4 Fiction, it seems, even living fiction, excuses just about anything. Ibid.

### 1113. Alix Kates Shulman
(1932–　)

1 Why was everything nice he did for me a bribe or a favor, while my kindnesses to him were my duty? *Memoirs of an Ex-Prom Queen*, Ch. 1 *1972*

2 If, as the girls always said, it's never too early to think about whom to marry, then it could certainly not be too early to think about who to be. Being somebody had to come first, because, of course, somebody could get a much better husband than nobody. Ibid., Ch. 2

3 In Columbia [University] waters I had to swim carefully to avoid being caught in the net laid for nonconforming traffickers in capitalism. Ibid., Ch. 6

### 1114. Elizabeth Taylor
(1932–　)

1 When people say: she's got everything, I've only one answer: I haven't had tomorrow. *Elizabeth Taylor* *1965*

2 My God, I was on a merry-go-round for so long. Now I've stopped spinning. I'm not afraid of myself. I'm no longer afraid of what I will do. I have absolute faith in our future. Richard [Burton] has given me all this. Ibid.

3 I want to be known as an actress. I'm not royalty. Interview in *The New York Times* (1964), Quoted in *Elizabeth* by Dick Sheppard *1974*

### 1115. Megan Terry
(1932–　)

1 CHESTER. My God, the human baby! A few weeks after birth, any other animal can fend for itself. But *you!* A basket case till you're twenty-one. *The Magic Realist* *1968*

2 CHESTER. Fourteen mewling brats and not a business brain in a bucketful. Ibid.

3 CHESTER. Tighten the belt. Tough it out, fellow Americans, tough it out! Ibid.

### 1116. Robin Worthington
(1932–　)

1 Mental health, like dandruff, crops up when you least expect it. *Thinking About Marriage* *1971*

2 The battle to keep up appearances unnecessarily, the mask—whatever name you give creeping perfectionism—robs us of our energies. Ibid.

### 1117. Maureen Duffy
(1933–　)

1 We all have to rise in the end, not just one or two who were smart enough, had will enough for their own salvation, but all the halt, the maimed and the blind of us which is most of us. *The Microcosm* *1966*

2 All reduction of people to objects, all imposition of labels and patterns to which they must conform, all segregation can lead only to destruction. *Rites* *1969*

3 The pain of love is the pain of being alive. It's a perpetual wound. *Wounds* *1969*

4 Love is the only effective counter to death. Ibid.

5 You will be wondering, putative reader, why I have reported all this. The answer is quite simple: it interests me, and you, forgive me, don't. I am not trying to tell you anything; I am at my childlike, priestlike task of creation. *Love Child* *1971*

6 I think basically I just think I want everyone and don't really want anybody. Ibid.

### 1118. Cynthia Fuchs Epstein
(1933–　)

1 During World War II, for instance, when the young men were off at war, dating did not consume the time of the college co-ed and she redirected her energies to study. . . . Work became an alternative even for those who did marry. Once engaged in an occupation, many had so firm a foothold they were loath to give it up. *Woman's Place* *1970*

## 1119. Pozzi Escot

(1933– )

1 In our [Peruvian] schools we teach Bach, Beethoven and Brahms but nothing that has been composed in the past 70 years.
Quoted in "A Matter of Art, Not Sex,"
*Time*    November 10, 1975

## 1120. Barbara C. Gelpi

(1933– )

1 . . . the masculine and feminine principles are not simply arbitrary manila folders for filing certain qualities; they are transcendent functions, spiritual realities which must be taken into account in the psychological makeup of every human being.
"The Androgyne," *Women and Analysis*, Jean Strouse, ed.    1974

2 Consciousness, as we tend to conceive of it, brings humanity into being—and that is good —but has certain negative consequences as well. Though it is man's triumph, it is divisive, separating him from the natural rhythms of life by virtue of the fact that he can observe those rhythms, looking forward and backward. He becomes then subject to the peculiarly human fear of death and the human affliction of boredom. He becomes also aware of his separateness, his individuality—and that is an achievement—but at the same time becomes competitive, suffering all the endless human misery which competition involves.    Ibid.

3 If women could help society to throw off the heavy yoke of the Fathers they might eventually move humanity forward. . . .    Ibid.

4 With myths, dreams, visions, poems, stories, conversations we must imagine a race in which both mind and soul are of equal importance and may be equally fulfilled for both sexes.    Ibid.

## 1121. Ruth Bader Ginsberg

(1933– )

1 In commercial law, the person duped was too often a woman. In a section on land tenure, one 1968 textbook explains that "land, like women, was meant to be possessed."
Quoted in "Portia Faces Life—The Trials of Law School" by Susan Edmiston, *Ms.*    April, 1974

2 The emphasis must be not on the right to abortion but on the right to privacy and reproductive control.    Ibid.

## 1122. Yoko Ono

(1933– )

1 I wonder why men can get serious at all. They have this delicate long thing hanging outside their bodies, which goes up and down by its own will. . . . If I were a man I would always be laughing at myself.
"On Film No. 4," (1967),
*Grapefruit*    1970

\* \* \*

2 Don't be too clever or we'll scratch your goodies out . . . or we'll blow your sillies off.
"Catman"

3 I'm a sphinx
Stamped on the Hilton poster
Hoping to see the desert. . . .
"A Thousand Times Yes"

4 The no that was hanging over the buildings
Faded like the moon at dawn.
Ibid.

5 I have a woman inside my soul.
"I Have a Woman Inside My Soul"

6 Keep your intentions in a clear bottle
and leave it on the shelf when you rap.
"Peter the Dealer"

7 On a windy day let's go flying
There may be no trees to rest on
There may be no clouds to ride
But we'll have our wings and the wind will be with us
That's enough for me, that's enough for me.
"Song for John"

8 The bed is shining like an old scripture
That's never been opened before.
"Winter Song"

9 What a bastard the world is.
"What a Bastard the World Is"

## 1123. Suzy Parker

(1933– )

1 I thank God for high cheekbones every time I look in the mirror in the morning.
Quoted in *This Fabulous Century:
1950–1960*    1970

## 1124. Jill Robinson

(1933?– )

1 Somewhere there was a gentle man with a cock that wore a jaunty grin and stayed long enough for you to get to know him.
*Bed/Time/Story*, Pt. I    1974

2 The fame fraud is so complete that all the Hollywood kids think everyone else has money. It is the suburban delusion. But then, suburbia was invented by Hollywood. Ibid.

3 I could hear the lovely, tiny swallowing gulps —you cover all ages in the sex-play cycle, from nursing infant to death in one terrifying swoop of the sexual plot. Ibid.

4 We have to get where we are going. In New York the getting is the thing. Ibid., Pt. II

5 And grownups have to act as if they know. That's how they show they love you, by knowing more stuff; it makes you feel secure. Ibid.

6 The transcontinental jet flight is a condensed metaphor of the escapist's Geographical Change. One starts out with the gorgeous hope that the self one abhors can be left behind. Three thousand miles is a powerful distance; such speed, such height should get you away before that self can catch up. Ibid.

7 "Ambition is destruction, only competence matters. . . ." Ibid.

8 "Everyone's parent is only a fantasy finally, neither as magical as, forgive me, you are, nor as prosaic. It is the image one has created in the head that one is fighting. Not the real parent at all." Ibid.

9 "It's a big risk—to stop drinking, going straight. Who knows? What you've got in mind could be very boring." Ibid.

## 1125. Miriam Schneir
### (1933– )

1 The decline of feminism after the First World War is attributable at least in part to the eventual concentration of the women's movements on the single narrow issue of suffrage— which was won. Other factors which have been cited are the postwar economic depression; the growing influence of anti-feminist Freudianism; and the development in Germany and the Soviet Union of authoritarian governments which tended to foster male supremacist values.
*Feminism: The Essential Historical Writings*, Introduction    1972

2 . . . centuries of slavery do not provide a fertile soil for intellectual development or expression. Ibid.

## 1126. Susan Sontag
### (1933– )

1 Ambition if it feeds at all, does so on the ambition of others.
*The Benefactor*, Ch. 1    1963

2 I was not looking for my dreams to interpret my life, but rather for my life to interpret my dreams. Ibid., Ch. 4

3 The love of the famous, like all strong passions, is quite abstract. Its intensity can be measured mathematically, and it is independent of persons. Ibid., Ch. 9

4 Persons who merely have-a-life customarily move in a dense fluid. That's how they're able to conduct their lives at all. Their living depends on not seeing. But when this fluid evaporates, an uncensored, fetid, appalling underlife is disclosed. Lost continents are brought to view, bearing the ruins of doomed cities, the sparsely fleshed skeletons of ancient creatures immobilized in their death throws, a landscape of unparalleled savagery. One can redeem skeletons and abandoned cities as human. But not a lost, dehumanized nature.
*Death Kit*    1967

5 How does an inexpressive face age? More slowly, one would suppose. Ibid.

6 Wiser and wiser. The scrim was raised. The gauzy light became, suddenly, knife-sharp. Almost gouged out his heart. Wiser. And suffering, for the first time. But not truly wise, wise enough to transcend suffering; and never likely to be. Ibid.

## 1127. Rosalie Sorrels
### (1933– )

1 Foreigners extol the American "energy," attributing to it both our unparalleled economic prosperity and the splendid vivacity of our arts and entertainments. But surely this is energy bad at its source and for which we pay too high a price, a hypernatural and humanly disproportionate dynamism that flays everyone's nerves raw. "What's Happening in America" (1966), *Styles of Radical Will* 1969

2 This is a doomed country, it seems to me; I only pray that, when America founders, it doesn't drag the rest of the planet down, too. But one should notice that, during its long elephantine agony, America is also producing its subtlest minority generation of the decent and sensitive, young people who are alienated *as* Americans. Ibid.

3 Though no longer a confession, art is more than ever a deliverance, an exercise in asceticism. Through it, the artist becomes purified—of himself and, eventually, of his art.
Ibid., "The Aesthetics of Silence" (1967)

4 The characteristic aim of modern art, to be *unacceptable* to its audience, inversely states the unacceptability to the artist of the very presence of an audience—audience in the modern sense, an assembly of voyeuristic spectators. Ibid.

5 Experiences aren't pornographic; only images and representations—structures of the imagination—are. Ibid., "The Pornographic Imagination" (1967)

6 Human sexuality is, quite apart from Christian repressions, a highly questionable phenomenon, and belongs, at least potentially, among the extreme rather than the ordinary experiences of humanity. Tamed as it may be, sexuality remains one of the demonic forces in human consciousness—pushing us at intervals close to taboo and dangerous desires, which range from the impulse to commit sudden arbitrary violence upon another person to the voluptuous yearning for the extinction of one's consciousness, for death itself. Even on the level of simply physical sensation and mood, making love surely resembles having an epileptic fit at least as much, if not more, than it does eating a meal or conversing with someone.
Ibid.

7 Let her discover all the things that she can do.
Sooner or later she's gonna discover
She can do without you.
"She Can Do Without You" 1974

8 There's no more rooms to retire to,
I've got to move, there's no place to stay.
I've nothing that's mine but my shadow,
If you need one, I'll give that away.
"Travelin' Lady" 1974

9 What can I say, but that it's not easy?
I cannot lift the stones out of your way,
And I can't cry your bitter tears for you.
I would if I could, what can I say?
"Apple of My Eye" 1974

10 I like to sing for my friends; I don't want to sing in fucking stadiums. I like to be able to see who I'm singing to, look them right in the eye and talk to them. . . . I can't get into that thing where you keep swelling up bigger and bigger, publicity, super-hype, higher prices, more equipment. . . . If you come around with a seven-piece band, three roadies, a manager

and groupies . . . you lose your mobility and miss all the *good* times.
Quoted in "Rosalie Sorrels" by Amie Hill, *Rolling Stone January 28, 1975*

## 1128. Helen Vendler
(1933–    )

1 It is a crushing burden . . . to reinterpret in a personal, and personally acceptable, way every conventional liturgical and religious act; to make devotion always singular, never simply communal . . . to particularize, not to merge; to individuate, not to accede.
*The Poetry of George Herbert*, Introduction 1975

## 1129. Nina Voronel
(1933–    )

1 In Russia today, anything new is dangerous.
Quoted in "Russia: No Exit for These Four Women" by Ruth Gruber, *Ms. April, 1974*

2 . . . I believe devoutly in the Word. The Word can save all, destroy all, stop the inevitable, and express the inexpressible. Ibid.

3 The echoes of pogroms sob in my verses
Making contact with history.
Ibid., "I Am a Jew"

## 1130. Freda Adler
(1934–    )

1 The phenomenon of female criminality is but one wave in this rising tide of female assertiveness—a wave which has not yet crested and may even be seeking its level uncomfortably close to the high-water mark set by male violence. *Sisters in Crime*, Prologue 1975

2 The type of fig leaf which each culture employs to cover its social taboos offers a twofold description of its morality. It reveals that certain unacknowledged behavior exists and it suggests the form that such behavior takes.
Ibid., Ch. 3

3 Euphemisms, like fashions, have their day and pass, perhaps to return at another time. Like the guests at a masquerade ball, they enjoy social approval only so long as they retain the capacity for deception. Ibid.

4 But there is another side to chivalry. If it dispenses leniency, it may with equal justification invoke control.      *Ibid.*, Ch. 4

5 Of all the tyrannies which have usurped power over humanity, few have been able to enslave the mind and body as imperiously as drug addiction.      *Ibid.*, Ch. 5

6 Man is not only an animal with a body and a being with a brain but also a social creature who is so ineluctably interconnected with his social group that he is hardly comprehensible outside it. . . .      *Ibid.*

7 Stripped of ethical rationalizations and philosophical pretensions, a crime is anything that a group in power chooses to prohibit.      *Ibid.*, Ch. 7

8 That man is a creature who needs order yet yearns for change is the creative contradiction at the heart of the laws which structure his conformity and define his deviancy.      *Ibid.*, Ch. 8

9 Woman throughout the ages has been mistress to the law, as man has been its master. . . . The controversy between rule of law and rule of men was never relevant to women—because, along with juveniles, imbeciles, and other classes of legal nonpersons, they had no access to law except through men.      *Ibid.*, Ch. 9

10 It is little wonder that rape is one of the least-reported crimes. Perhaps it is the only crime in which the victim becomes the accused and, in reality, it is she who must prove her good reputation, her mental soundness, and her impeccable propriety.      *Ibid.*

11 The Rubicons which women must cross, the sex barriers which they must breach, are ultimately those that exist in their own minds. . . . Like a distant planet, it [equality] has moved within their ken but will forever elude their grasp. It will remain for another generation of women. . . .      *Ibid.*, Epilogue

## 1131. Brigitte Bardot
### (1934– )

1 I leave before being left. I decide.
     Quoted in *Newsweek*
     *March 5, 1973*

## 1132. Arlene Croce
### (1934?– )

\* \* \*

1 At least some of the men who write sex books admit that they really don't understand female sexuality. Freud was one. Masters is another—that was why he got Johnson.
     Quoted in *Commentary*

## 1133. Diane Di Prima
### (1934– )

1 When the radio told me there was dancing in the streets,
I knew we had engineered another coup;
Bought off another army.
     "Goodbye Nkrumah," St. 1,
     *Intrepid #VI*    1966

2 We buy the arms and the armed men, we have placed them
on all the thrones of South America
we are burning the jungles, the beasts will rise up against us
     *Ibid.*, St. 4

3 Had you lived longer than your twenty-six years
You, too, wd have come up against it like a wall—
That the Beauty you saw was bought
At too great a price
Even in those days. . . .
     "Ode to Keats," St. 1, *The East Side Scene*, Allen De Loach, ed.    1968

## 1134. Oriana Fallaci
### (1934?– )

1 Listening to someone talk isn't at all like listening to their words played over on a machine. What you hear when you have a face before you is never what you hear when you have before you a winding tape.
     *The Egotists*, Foreword    1963

2 If I were to give human semblance to the America of today, this hated and often misunderstood country, I would choose Norman Mailer to be the model. . . . One tries to catch America—Mailer's stare—and one doesn't know which eye to choose, which eye to respond to. As a result one cannot reach a moral decision about him. But the practical dilemma remains: Should one be his friend or his enemy? Most people consider him an enemy; to be his friend is anything but easy.
     *Ibid.*, "Norman Mailer"

3 He [Nguyen Cao Ky] is the most famous man in South Vietnam and also the most hated. Reactionaries hate him because he is the most hostile enemy of the reactionaries; liberals hate him because he is the most hostile enemy of the liberals; Americans hate him because he is the most hostile enemy of the Americans.
*Ibid.,* "Nguyen Cao Ky"

4 We are all going to become Swedish, and we do not understand these Americans who, like adolescents, always speak of sex, and who, like adolescents, all of a sudden have discovered that sex is good not only for procreating children. *Ibid.,* "Hugh Hefner"

5 Glory is a heavy burden, a murdering poison, and to bear it is an art. And to have that art is rare. *Ibid.,* "Federico Fellini"

6 Every time she passed a mirror she was unable to resist the temptation of looking at the one thing that interested her most in the world—herself. And every time she was a bit disappointed—almost as if the girl facing her was some other person.
*Penelope at War,* Ch. 1    1966

7 But, with the optimism of those beings who will not give up even in the face of obvious defeat and who blindly raise their heads again after defeat thinking that it might have been worse and all is not lost, Giovanna did not want to understand—far less withdraw in good order. *Ibid.,* Ch. 5

8 I'm going to show you the real New York—witty, smart, and international—like any metropolis. Tell me this—where in Europe can you find old Hungary, old Russia, old France, old Italy? In Europe you're trying to copy America, you're almost American. But here you'll find Europeans who immigrated a hundred years ago—and we haven't spoiled them. Oh, Gio! You must see why I love New York. Because the whole world's in New York. . . .
*Ibid.,* Ch. 8

9 "You know that everyone else is at home—with his beer, his wife, his children, those children dressed like elves, in yellow, red, that well-dressed wife looking at the TV, that cool beer, that family, that is safe because they listen to the transistor radio, because they believe in business and civil religion, because they conform in a country where conformity means salvation. . . . Lastly, you understand why the rule of God and of America is the rule of selection, why it's a man-made law, why spiritual values are earthly values, why America is God equals America equals Business equals America equals God. And there's no alternative: you

have to be on the side of God equals America equals Business equals America equals God, or else you're alone. Alone and damned like me, understand?" *Ibid.,* Ch. 10

10 "America's a hard school, I know, but hard schools make excellent graduates."
*Ibid.,* Ch. 16

11 "I think when men die they do what the trees do in winter when they go dry, but then spring comes and they're reborn. So life must be something else." *Nothing, and So Be It,* Ch. 1
1972

12 But here's what I learned in this war, in this country, in this city: to love the miracle of having been born. *Ibid.,* Ch. 3

13 Have you ever thought that war is a madhouse and that everyone in the war is a patient? Tell me, how can a normal man get up in the morning knowing that in an hour or a minute he may no longer be there? How can he walk through heaps of decomposing corpses and then sit down at the table and calmly eat a roll? How can he defy nightmare-like risks and then be ashamed of panicking for a moment?
*Ibid.,* Ch. 6

## 1135. Marilyn Horne
### (1934– )

1 Ninety percent of what's wrong with singers today is that they don't breathe right.
Quoted in "Marilyn Horne," *Divas: Impressions of Six Opera Superstars* by Winthrop Sargeant    1959

2 You have to know exactly what you want out of your career. If you want to be a star, you don't bother with other things. *Ibid.*

3 The thing to do [for insomnia] is to get an opera score and read *that*. That will bore you to death. *Ibid.*

## 1136. Louise Kapp Howe
### (1934– )

1 Despite the focus in the media on the affluent and the poor, the average man is neither. Despite the concentration in TV commercials on the blond, blue-eyed WASP, the real American prototype is of Italian or Irish or Polish or Greek or Lithuanian or German or Hungarian or Russian or any of the still amazing number of national origins represented in this country —a "white ethnic," sociologists somberly call him. *The White Majority,* Introduction
1970

2 . . . if the error of the sixties was that the people of the white majority were never given a concrete personal reason for social advance, the clear and present danger of the seventies is that they won't be warned in time against the threat of social repression being waged in their name.      Ibid., Afterword

3 We all know what the American family is supposed to look like. We can't help it. The picture has been imprinted on our brains since we were tiny, through children's books, schools, radio, television, movies, newspapers, the lectures if not the examples of many of our parents, the speeches if not the examples of many of our politicians. . . . Now, the striking point about our model family is not simply the compete-compete, consume-consume style of life it urges us to follow. . . . The striking point, in the face of all the propaganda, is how few Americans actually live this way.

> *The Future of the Family,*
> Introduction     1972

4 . . . the assumption of a male-breadwinner society . . . ends up determining the lives of everyone within a family, whether a male breadwinner is present or not, whether one is living by the rules in suburbia or trying to break them on a commune:      Ibid.

5 While politicians carry on about the sanctity of the American family, we learn . . . that in the scale of national priorities our children and families really come last. After freeways. After pork subsidies. After the billions spent on munitions in the name of national defense. It is now time . . . to reverse the usual procedure. It is time to *change the economy* to meet the needs of American families.      Ibid.

## 1137. Diane Johnson
### (1934–    )

1 Waiting to be murdered has given me you might say something to live for.
> *The Shadow Knows*     1974

2 We are surrounded by the enraged.      Ibid.

## 1138. Audre Lorde
### (1934–    )

1 Since Naturally Black is Naturally Beautiful
I must be proud
And, naturally,
Black and
Beautiful

Who always was a trifle
Yellow
And plain though proud
Before.
> "Naturally," St. 1, *Cables to Rage*
> 1970

2 There are so many roots to the
  tree of anger
that sometimes the branches
  shatter
before they bear.
> "From a Land Where Other People
> Live," *From a Land Where*
> *Other People Live*    1975

3 . . . which me will survive all these liberations.      Ibid.

## 1139. Shirley MacLaine
### (1934–    )

1 The pain of leaving those you grow to love is only the prelude to understanding yourself and others.     *Don't Fall Off the Mountain*
> 1970

2 I asked, "Why, because a tree's arm got sick, did they have to cut down the whole body?" And they told me the tree doctor had said it was the right thing to do.      Ibid., Ch. 1

3 For if the talent or individuality is there, it should be expressed. If it doesn't find its way out into the air, it can turn inward and gnaw like the fox at the Spartan boy's belly.
> Ibid., Ch. 4

4 In Japan, courtesy had an esthetic value far greater than good manners in the West. A negative truth is frequently subordinate to the virtue of courtesy. Courtesy, therefore, is more of a virtue than honesty.      Ibid., Ch. 5

5 The more I traveled the more I realized that fear makes strangers of people who should be friends.      Ibid., Ch. 13

6 It was a circus without a tent; without brass bands and popcorn. The animals leaped with what looked like unfounded joy to me but to them was simply the way they always felt. . . . Africa seemed the harmonious voice of creation. Everything alive was inextricably intertwined until death. And even death was part of the life harmony.      Ibid., Ch. 13

7 India is a paradox, passionate, pulsating, even humorous in her poverty. And in her villages the subhuman drama plays itself out against a backdrop of such beauty that it seems grotesque mockery.      Ibid., Ch. 14

8 Freedom, with her front windows open and unlocked, with breezes and challenges blowing in. I wished that she [MacLaine's daughter, Sasha] would know herself through freedom. I wished that underneath she would understand that there is no such thing as being safe—that there are no safe havens for anyone who wants to know the TRUTH, *whatever* it is, about himself or others. Ibid., Ch. 19

9 If you attach yourself to one person, you ultimately end up having an unhealthy relationship. Quoted in "The Odyssey of Shirley MacLaine" by Arthur Bell, *Viva October, 1974*

10 The notion of good and evil being fought outside the confines of our responsibility is anathema to me. Good and evil is in us. Good and evil is what we decide it should be. I have more faith in human beings than that. We can figure out what we're doing. We don't have to shove it off on God and the fucking devil. Ibid.

11 Hollywood always had a streak of the totalitarian in just about everything it did. *You Can Get There from Here*, Ch. 2 *1975*

12 . . . the more I became involved in "big time" politics the more I realized how vicious the in-fighting could get in the desire to "make things better." Ibid., Ch. 11

13 I hoped that the trip would be the best of all journeys: a journey into ourselves. Ibid., Ch. 15

14 I stood in one nursery, watching the children, and I realized that an exaggerated sense of competition was being educated out of China's New Society through its children. . . . It made me wonder if the sense of competition was innate in human nature at all, and because the children seemed so happy and secure I wondered whether mothers and fathers were necessary to children in the same way we believed when their environment was healthy and happy otherwise. Ibid., Ch. 18

15 China was proud now—of herself and of her potential. She had pulled herself to dignity and unity and that spirit literally pervaded the communes, the backbone of China. The Chinese countryside was where the revolution was won and the countryside was the secret of China's future. Ibid., Ch. 20

16 In some ways, America had grown up to be a masterpiece of self-concern. Ibid., Epilogue

17 Perhaps Western values, for the past five hundred years, had been a human distortion, perhaps competition was simply not compatible with harmony, not conducive to human happiness, perhaps the competitive urge came only from the exaggerated emphasis on the individual. Maybe the individual was simply not as important as the group. Ibid.

18 I realized that if what we call human nature can be changed, then absolutely *anything* is possible. And from that moment, my life changed. Ibid.

19 I was not a soldier or a philosopher or a politician; I could cure no disease, solve no economic problems, or lead any revolution. But, I could dance, I could sing. I could make people laugh. I could make people cry. Ibid.

## 1140. Kate Millett
### (1934– )

1 . . . it is the threadbare tactic of justifying social and temperamental differences by biological ones. *Sexual Politics* *1969*

2 The care of children, even from the period when their cognitive powers first emerge, is infinitely better left to the best-trained practitioners of both sexes who have chosen it as a vocation, rather than to harried and all too frequently unhappy persons with little time or taste for the work of educating minds however young or beloved. . . . The family, as that term is presently understood, must go. Ibid.

3 Many women do not recognize themselves as discriminated against; no better proof could be found of the totality of their conditioning. Ibid.

4 Sexual congress in a Mailer novel is always a matter of strenuous endeavor, rather like mountain climbing—a matter of straining after achievement. Ibid.

5 Perhaps nothing is so depressing an index of the inhumanity of the male supremacist mentality as the fact that the more genial human traits are assigned to the underclass: affection, response to sympathy, kindness, cheerfulness. Ibid.

6 . . . I see the function of true Erotica (writing which is pro-, not antisexual) as one not only permissible but worthy of encouragement and social approval, as its laudable and legitimate function is to increase sexual appetite just as culinary prose encourages other appetites. Ibid.

7 For our highly repressive and Puritan tradition has almost hopelessly confused sexuality with sadism, cruelty, and that which is in general inhumane and antisocial. This is a deplorable state of affairs. *Ibid.*

8 . . . the female is rendered innocuous by her socialization. Before assault she is almost universally defenseless both by her physical and emotional training. *Ibid.*

9 Isn't privacy about keeping taboos in their place? Speech, Women's Writer's Conference, Los Angeles *March 22, 1975*

10 Aren't women prudes if they don't and prostitutes if they do? *Ibid.*

## 1141. Patricia Simon

(1934– )

1 An old French farm built on levels up and down a hillside near Grasse—overlooking, in the middle distance, the quiet cluster of the town and, in the further distance, hills, and beyond them other hills, and other hills, in a gentle, fertile, dreamlike landscape that continued forever—the Alpes-Maritimes.
"The Making of a Masterpiece," *McCall's October, 1970*

2 Flowers and sunlight, air and silence—*"luxe, calme et volupté."* *Ibid.*

## 1142. Gloria Steinem

(1934– )

1 The first problem for all of us, men and women, is not to learn, but to unlearn.
"A New Egalitarian Life Style," *The New York Times August 26, 1971*

2 It's clear that most American children suffer too much mother and too little father. *Ibid.*

3 We [women] are not more moral, we are only less corrupted by power. *Ibid.*

4 . . . no man can call himself liberal, or radical, or even a conservative advocate of fair play, if his work depends in any way on the unpaid or underpaid labor of women at home, or in the office. *Ibid.*

5 We are human beings first, with minor differences from men that apply largely to the act of reproduction. We share the dreams, capabilities, and weaknesses of all human beings, but our occasional pregnancies and other visible differences have been used—even more pervasively, if less brutally, than radical differences have been used—to mark us for an elaborate division of labor that may once have been practical but has since become cruel and false. The division is continued for clear reason, consciously or not: the economic and social profit of men as a group.
"Sisterhood," *The First Ms. Reader,* Francine Klagsbrun, ed. *1972*

6 God knows (*she* knows) that women try. *Ibid.*

7 As for logic, it's in the eye of the logician. *Ibid.*

8 The status quo protects itself by punishing all challengers. *Ibid.*

9 I have met brave women who are exploring the outer edge of human possibility, with no history to guide them, and with a courage to make themselves vulnerable that I find moving beyond words. *Ibid.*

10 She [Marilyn Monroe] was an actress, a person on whom no one's fate depended, and yet her energy and terrible openness to life had made some connection with strangers.
*Ibid.,* "Marilyn: The Woman Who Died Too Soon"

11 The long history of antiobscenity laws makes it very clear that such laws are most often invoked against political and life-style dissidents.
"Gazette News: Obscene?," *Ms. October, 1973*

12 The definition of woman's work is shitwork.
Quoted in "Freelancer with No Time to Write" by John Brady, *Writer's Digest February, 1974*

13 . . . intelligence at the service of poor instinct is really dangerous. . . . *Ibid.*

14 Ten years from now, as I see it, either the movements for change will be totally annihilated, dispirited or ground down—or they will really have entered the main stream and created major changes. It has come to the point of maximum push.
Quoted in "Impeachment?" by Claire Safran, *Redbook April, 1974*

15 . . . the new women in politics seem to be saying that we already know how to lose, thank you very much. Now we want to learn how to win. "Victory with Honor," *Ms. April, 1974*

16 A government's responsibility to its young citizens does not magically begin at the age of six. It makes more sense to extend the free universal school system downward—with the necessary reforms and community control that child care should have from the start.     Ibid.

## 1143. Susan Brownmiller

(1935– )

1 Man's discovery that his genitalia could serve as a weapon to generate fear must rank as one of the most important discoveries of prehistoric times, along with the use of fire and the first crude stone axe. From prehistoric times to the present, I believe, rape has played a critical function. It is nothing more or less than a conscious process of intimidation by which all men keep all women in a state of fear.     *Against Our Will: Men, Women, and Rape*    1975

2 "Hero" is the surprising word that men employ when they speak of Jack the Ripper.     Ibid.

3 . . . the incidence of actual rape combined with the looming spectre of the black man as rapist, to which the black man in the name of his manhood now contributes, must be understood as a control mechanism against the freedom, mobility and aspirations of all women, white and black. The crossroads of racism and sexism had to be a violent meeting place. There is no use pretending it doesn't exist.     Ibid.

4 It has been argued that, when killing is viewed as not only permissible but heroic behavior sanctioned by one's government or cause, the fine distinction between taking a human life and other forms of impermissible violence gets lost, and rape becomes an unfortunate but inevitable by-product of the necessary game called war.     Ibid.

5 Fighting back. On a multiplicity of levels, that is the activity we must engage in. . . .     Ibid.

6 My purpose in this book has been to give rape its history. Now we must deny it a future.     Ibid.

## 1144. Joan Didion

(1935– )

1 New York is full of people on this kind of leave of absence, of people with a feeling for the tangential adventure, the risk adventure, the interlude that's not likely to end in any double-ring ceremony.
"New York: The Great Reprieve,"
*Mademoiselle*     February, 1961

2 Was there ever in anyone's life span a point free in time, devoid of memory, a night when choice was any more than the sum of all the choices gone before?     *Run River*, Ch. 4
1963

3 "I think nobody owns land until their dead are in it. . . ."     Ibid., Ch. 8

4 She *knew* clocks weren't supposed to stop, don't be silly. She knew they needed a clock. But she could not work with it going every second. When it was going every second that way she could not seem to take her eyes off it, and because it made no noise she found herself making the noise for it in her mind.     Ibid., Ch. 18

5 . . . the day that I did not make Phi Beta Kappa nonetheless marked the end of something, and innocence may well be the word for it. I lost the conviction that lights would always turn green for me . . . lost a certain touching faith in the totem power of good manners, clean hair, and proven competence on the Stanford-Binet scale. To such doubtful amulets had my self-respect been pinned, and I faced myself that day with the nonplussed apprehension of someone who has come across a vampire and has no crucifix at hand.
"On Self-Respect" (1961), *Slouching Towards Bethlehem*     1968

6 As an adjective, the very word "Hollywood" has long been pejorative and suggestive of something referred to as "the System." . . . The System not only strangles talent but poisons the soul, a fact supported by rich webs of lore.
Ibid., "I Can't Get That Monster Out of My Mind" (1964)

7 Because when we start deceiving ourselves into thinking not that we want something or need something, not that it is a pragmatic necessity for us to have it, but that it is a *moral imperative* that we have it, then is when we join the fashionable madmen, and then is when the thin whine of hysteria is heard in the land, and then is when we are in bad trouble. And I suspect we are already there.
Ibid., "On Morality" (1965)

8 There has always been that divergence between our official and our unofficial heroes. It is impossible to think of Howard Hughes without seeing the apparently bottomless gulf between what we say we want and what we do want, between what we officially admire and secretly desire, between, in the largest sense, the people we marry and the people we love.
Ibid., "7000 Romaine, Los Angeles 38" (1967)

9 In the absence of a natural disaster we are left again to our own uneasy devices.
"A Problem of Making Connections,"
*Life*     December 5, 1969

10 Acquaintances read the New York *Times* and try to tell me the news of the world. I listen to call-in shows.     Ibid.

11 "I am what I am. To look for 'reasons' is beside the point."     *Play It As It Lays* 1970

12 Whether or not Carter could afford the rent, whether it was a month like this one when he was making a lot of money or a month when the lawyers were talking about bankruptcy, the boy came twice a week to vacuum the pool and the man came four days a week to work on the roses and the water in the pool was 85 degrees.     Ibid., Ch. 4

13 Each believed the other a murderer of time, a destroyer of life itself.     Ibid.

14 . . . they would exchange the addresses of new astrologers and the tag lines of old jokes.
Ibid., Ch. 10

15 The way he looked was the problem. He looked exactly the same. He looked untouched, and she did not.     Ibid.

16 "Hear that scraping, Maria?" the doctor said. "That should be the sound of music to you. . . ."     Ibid., Ch. 25

17 She had to have a telephone. There was no one to whom she wanted to talk but she had to have a telephone.     Ibid., Ch. 35

18 "I'm sorry."
"I know you're sorry. I'm sorry."
"We could try," one or the other would say after a while.
"We've already tried," the other would say.
Ibid., Ch. 37

19 Maria could never keep up her end of the dialogue with hairdressers.     Ibid., Ch. 45

20 She had watched them in supermarkets and she knew the signs. At 7:00 on a Saturday evening they would be standing in the checkout line reading the horoscope in *Harper's Bazaar* and in their carts would be a single lamb chop and maybe two cans of cat food and the Sunday morning paper, the early edition with the comics wrapped outside.     Ibid., Ch. 46

21 . . . she had deliberately not counted the months but she must have been counting them unawares, must have been keeping a relentless count somewhere, because this was the day, the day the baby would have been born.
Ibid., Ch. 54

22 She did not much like him but she liked his not knowing her.     Ibid., Ch. 60

23 To hear someone's voice she looked in the telephone book and dialed a few prayers. . . .
Ibid., Ch. 64

24 By the end of a week she was thinking constantly about where her body stopped and the air began, about the exact point in space and time that was the difference between *Maria* and *other*.     Ibid., Ch. 65

25 I am not much engaged by the problems of what you might call our day but I am burdened by the particular. . . .     Ibid., Ch. 68

26 Some nights he said that he was tired, and some nights she said that she wanted to read, and other nights no one said anything.
Ibid., Ch. 69

27 My father advised me that life itself was a crap game: it was one of the two lessons I learned as a child. The other was that overturning a rock was apt to reveal a rattlesnake. As lessons go those two seem to hold up, but not to apply.
Ibid., Ch. 74

28 I know something about dread myself, and appreciate the elaborate systems with which some people manage to fill the void, appreciate all the opiates of the people.
Quoted in *Ms.*     January, 1973


# 1145. Lois Gould

(1935?–     )

1 Danny Mack got past the nurses at two-fifteen by impersonating a doctor. All he did was clip four ballpoint pens on his vest pocket and march in looking preoccupied.
*Such Good Friends*     1970

2 "Hogamous, Higamous, men are polygamous, Higamous, Hogamous, women monogamous."
Ibid.

3 . . . you can't . . . sneak around trying to correct the conjugal imbalance sheet: doing unto others what I did last night. The sheer symmetry of it scares people; how can they tell the victims from the perpetrators? In the dark they are all to blame.     Ibid.

4 Life is the only sentence which doesn't end with a period.     Ibid.

5 ". . . the city *requires* a funeral. . . . All the ordinances are designed with your friendly funeral directors in mind—not to mention the cemeteries and coffin makers and gravestone cutters."    Ibid.

6 *Things* have squatter's rights; why else do we call them *belongings*?    Ibid.

7 What it is, I guess, is that I don't really miss *him*; I miss something that must have been *us*. Because we *were* something, in spite of each other, weren't we?    Ibid.

8 Amos Lowen taught his daughters carefully that poor was a curse word, and that if money couldn't buy happiness—a point he never conceded—there were still plenty of other selections.    *Necessary Objects*    1972

9 She hated the powdered oil smell they put on the baby. Rubbing away all his natural sourness and anointing him with foreign substances that were all ironically labeled *Baby*. So that he would never recognize his own body in the dark, the way she could recognize hers now. Small victory, discovering your acrid identity after eighteen years. Buried alive under thousands of layers of powdered oil.    Ibid.

10 "We are selling elegance. The idea of elegance. Throwaway chic, we are the last *word* in throwaway chic. . . . We have an image. I have. Either we can afford to be subtle, either we live *up* to the image, or we're just another tacky dress shop. I mean, if we've got it, I say we don't *have* to flaunt it."    Ibid.

11 Making love as if it were something one could make, as if it were making do or making believe. Hating her own hands, hating the thin desperate clinging body that responded by heart to echoes of old movements, like a mechanical toy. . . . Its working was an unbearable affront; it accused her. It made her admit the truth. I don't care if it still works, I hate it—*I don't want it any more*.    Ibid.

12 One of the new computers in the billing department had gone berserk, possibly from the strain of replacing five elderly bookkeepers, and a hundred thousand dollars' worth of credit had been erroneously issued to delinquent charge-account customers before anyone caught it.    Ibid.

13 "Why the hell don't women ever make a scene? Men are *always* making scenes, yelling in the halls. Why can't *you* yell in the halls?"
"Because," she sighed, "women don't get away with yelling in the halls. They call you a hysterical bitch if you yell in the halls."
"Also," Sophy noted wryly, "they fire you. It's *their* halls."    *Final Analysis*    1974

14 She burst into tears. Just like a woman. Tears of rage: the ultimate toy weapon.    Ibid.

15 "Women always run away," she said. "That's why women never get to run anything else. They can't stand the heat, so they get *back* in the kitchen."    Ibid.

16 Make up. Meaning invent. Make up something more acceptable, because that face you have on right there will not do.    Ibid.

17 The only reason I hated him was that I had needed him so much. That's when I found out about need. It goes much better with hate than with love.    Ibid.

## 1146. Jane Howard

### (1935–    )

1 An encounter group is a gathering, for a few hours or a few days, of twelve or eighteen personable, responsible, certifiably normal and temporarily smelly people. Their destination is intimacy, trust and awareness of why they behave as they do in groups; their vehicle is candor.    "Whatever Possessed Me,"    *Please Touch*    1970

2 The genealogy of the human potential movement is as hard to trace as a foundling baby's. Foundlings have no known ancestors, but the movement is alleged to have preposterously many.    Ibid., "Notes Toward History"

3 The re-entry from encounter groups to reality, and the business of keeping alive the elusive benefits of sensitivity training, are problems that preoccupy every student of the human potential movement.    Ibid., "Back Home"

4 Group philosophy—wise group philosophy, anyway—does not prescribe that you run to inform your old landlord that everyone secretly thinks he's effeminate, or your boss that you have always thought he was a stupid tyrant. The aim is first to know, in your head and below it, what you think and feel, and then to reflect on newly unearthed alternatives to your accustomed ways of being. Once it is unlocked, the door between your feelings and the cosmos need not be kept yawning open. It can be left ajar.    Ibid.

5 Parents, however old they and we may grow to be, serve among other things to shield us from a sense of our doom. As long as they are around, we can avoid the fact of our mortality; we can still be innocent children.    *A Different Woman*    1973

6 New links must be forged as old ones rust.
Ibid., Ch. 1

7 I wish women in the gay liberation movement
God-speed, although I take issue with their
premise that all men, without exception, are
intruding vandals bent only on the oppression
of womankind. I submit that some of them
can be welcome guests.     Ibid., Ch. 9

8 Wholesomeness is exotic to me. I pretended to
like the era of strobe lights and deafening acid
rock in discotheques but a lot of that sixties
frenzy really just made me nervous. More and
more I am drawn toward stillness.
Ibid., Ch. 34

## 1147. Anne Richardson Roiphe
(1935–    )

1 But how to burn it out—to purify one's mind
of worms and grubs and frights of strangers,
and a fear of the black Walpurgisnacht, when
all the demons will run loose over the suburban lawns saying "You must now be slaves.
Take your turn. It's only fair. The master must
grovel in the dirt." I mean to say that despite
my concern for civil liberties, for equality, for
justice in Mississippi—I am blond, and blond is
still beautiful, and if I have one life to lead it
will be as a white, and I am a mass of internal
contradictions, all of which cause me to finally
attempt some rite which will bring salvation,
save me from a system I despise but still carry
within me like any other of my vital organs.
"Out of Week One," *Up the Sandbox!*
*1970*

2   "What the world needs," he said, "is not a
Joan of Arc, the kind of woman who allows
herself to be burned on the cross. That's just
a bourgeois invention meant to frighten little
girls into staying home. What we require is a
real female military social leader."
"But that"—I smiled at him—"is just impossible. Women are tied to husband and children. Women are constructed to be penetrated;
a sword or a gun in their hands is a joke or a
mistake. They are open holes in which things
are poured. Occasionally, it's true, a woman
can become a volcano, but that's about it."
Ibid., "Out of Week Two"

3 What I'm doing in this car flying down these
screaming highways is getting my tail to Juarez
so I can legally rid myself of the crummy son-
of-a-bitch who promised me a tomorrow like a
yummy fruitcake and delivered instead wilted
lettuce, rotted cucumber, a garbage of a life.
*Long Division     1972*

4 She tried to be respectable because respectability kept away the chaos that sometimes overwhelmed her, causing her to call out in her
sleep, screaming wild sounds, a warning to the
future, a mourning for the past.     Ibid.

## 1148. Judith Rossner
(1935–    )

1 A nightmare is terrifying because it can never
be undone. . . . While in the beautiful well-
ordered lie of our everyday lives there was
almost nothing we could not do.
*Nine Months in the Life of an Old
Maid*, Pt. I     *1969*

2 "Being a witch is like royalty," I said calmly.
"You have to inherit it from someone."
Ibid.

3 As Lily had lost me years before from not
caring, you lost me that day from caring but
not nearly enough.     Ibid.

4 Identity is a bag and a gag. Yet it exists for me
with all the force of a fatal disease. Obviously
I am here, a mind and a body. To say there's
no proof my body exists would be arty and
specious and if my mind were more ephemeral,
less provable, the solution of being a writer
with solid (touchable, tearable, burnable) books
is as close as anyone has come to a perfect
answer. The obvious reason that every asshole
in the world wants to write.     Ibid., Pt. II

5 It is easier to betray than to remain loyal. It
takes far less courage to kill yourself than it
takes to make yourself wake up one more time.
It's harder to stay where you are than to get
out. (For everyone but you, that is.)     Ibid.

6 Love is the direct opposite of hate. By *definition* it's something you can't feel for more than
a few minutes at a time, so what's all this
bullshit about loving somebody for the rest of
your life?     Ibid.

7 So often I heard people paying blind obeisance
to change—as though it had some virtue of its
own. Change or we will die. Change or we will
stagnate. Evergreens don't stagnate. The per-
ennials that year after year die down for winter
then come up the following summer neither
die nor stagnate, and if they change at all it is
usually for the worse.     Ibid.

8 "I've been accused of selling out so often that
it's made me realize what extraordinary resources people saw in me in the first place. It's
why I can afford to sell out my ideas; I know
something new'll spring up to replace the ones
I'm unloading."     Ibid.

9 What was she to say now to her father, who thought change was the only serious mistake that could be made in a life?
*Any Minute I Can Split*    1972

10 "That's the New York thing, isn't it. People who seem absolutely crazy going around telling you how crazy they used to be before they had therapy."     Ibid.

11 "Self-government is a form of self-control, self-limitation. It goes against our whole grain. We're [Americans] supposed to go after what we want, not question whether we really need it."     Ibid.

12 "But I've been miserable ever since I came back. From Puerto Rico, that's where I had it [the abortion], it was like a vacation. It's almost like—it's not supposed to be that easy. It's too big a sin to get off that lightly."
*Looking for Mr. Goodbar*    1975

13 He always said she was smart, but their conversations were a mined field in which at any moment she might make the wrong verbal move and find her ignorance exploding in her face.     Ibid.

14 Sometimes she thought that the TV wasn't so much an escape as a filter through which he saw and heard everything but was kept from being affected by it too much.     Ibid.

15 A lie was something that hadn't happened but might just as well have.     Ibid.

16 "The point is," Evelyn said, "we're taught that we have to be perfect. Like objects in a museum, not people. People don't have to be perfect, only objects do."     Ibid.

## 1149. Françoise Sagan
(1935–    )

1 It is healthier to see the good points of others than to analyze our own bad ones.
*A Certain Smile*, Pt. I, Ch. 5    1956

2 We had the same gait, the same habits and lived in the same rhythm; our bodies suited each other, and all was well. I had no right to regret his failure to make the tremendous effort required of love, the effort to know and shatter the solitude of another.    Ibid., Pt. II, Ch. 2

3 "Look here, why don't you love me? I should feel so much more peaceful. Why not put up that pane of glass called passion between us? It may distort things at times, but it's wonderfully convenient." But no, we were two of a kind, allies and accomplices. In terms of gram-

mar, I could not become the object, or he the subject. He had neither the capacity nor the desire to define our roles in any such way.     Ibid.

## 1150. Audrey Thomas
(1935–    )

1 How could I tell her that she was wrong about things when essentially she was right? Life was cruel, people hurt and betrayed one another, grew old and died alone.
*Songs My Mother Taught Me*
1973

2 . . . cats everywhere asleep on the shelves like motorized bookends.     Ibid.

## 1151. Judith Viorst
(1935?–    )

1 The honeymoon is over
And we find that dining by candlelight makes us squint,
And that all the time
I was letting him borrow my comb and hang up his wet raincoat in my closet,
I was really waiting
To stop letting him.
"The Honeymoon Is Over," *It's Hard to Be Hip Over Thirty and Other Tragedies of Married Life*    1968

2 With four walk-in closets to walk in,
Three bushes, two shrubs, and one tree,
The suburbs are good for the children,
But no place for grown-ups to be.
Ibid., "The Suburbs Are Good for the Children"

3 But it's hard to be hip over thirty
When everyone else is nineteen,
When the last dance we learned was the Lindy,
And the last we heard, girls who looked like Barbara Streisand
Were trying to do something about it.
Ibid., "It's Hard to Be Hip Over Thirty"

4 Love is much nicer to be in than an automobile accident, a tight girdle, a higher tax bracket or a holding pattern over Philadelphia.
"What IS This Thing Called Love?,"
*Redbook*    February, 1975

5 Brevity may be the soul of wit, but not when someone's saying, "I love you."     Ibid.

## 1152. Sandy Boucher
(1936–    )

1 My father's voice says, Watch out for little men. They are more aggressive, meaner, nastier, trickier, more combative. A big man is secure in his strength, so he doesn't push it. A little man is always proving something. The same goes for little dogs versus big dogs.
"Mountain Radio," *Assaults and Rituals*    1975

2 Thus we were equally, though differently, sophisticated, and our game was the same: not to *care*—to arrive at each other without being there.    Ibid.

3 The reality it took me ten hard years to discover is that a dyke is a flaming threat to some of the most cherished institutions of this society, and it is for this reason that Lenora was viewed with hatred and treated with cruelty.
Ibid.

## 1153. Natalya Gorbanevskaya
(1936–    )

1 Opening the window, I open myself.
Untitled Poem, *Poems, the Trial, Prison*    1972

2 I am awaiting the birth of my child quite calmly, and neither my pregnancy nor the birth will prevent me from doing what I wish— which includes participating in every protest against any act of tyranny.
*Red Square at Noon*    1972

## 1154. Sandra Hochman
(1936–    )

1 What I wanted
Was to be myself again.
"The Inheritance," *Love Letters from Asia*    1967

## 1155. Xaviera Hollander
(1936?–    )

1 *Mundus vult decipi decipiatur ergo.* The world wants to be cheated, so cheat.
*The Happy Hooker*, with Robin Moore and Yvonne Dunleavy, Ch. 1    1972

2 For me the madam life has become a big ego trip. I enjoy the independence and what's more, for me prostitution is not just a way to make a living, but a real calling, which I enjoy.
Ibid., Ch. 10

3 There is only one other profession that out-ranks bankers as dedicated clients, and that is the stockbroker. . . . When the stocks go up, the cocks go up!    Ibid., Ch. 11

4 Actually, if my business was legitimate, I would deduct a substantial percentage for depreciation of my body.    Ibid., Ch. 14

5 . . . if my business could be made legal . . . I and women like me could make a big contribution to what Mayor Lindsay calls "Fun City," and the city and state could derive the money in taxes and licensing fees that I pay off to crooked cops and political figures.
Ibid.

## 1156. Barbara Jordan
(1936–    )

1 I never intended to become a run-of-the-mill person.    Quoted in *Newsweek* November 4, 1974

2 Politicians don't talk about "wielding power." That's so crass. The only thing I can hope is that I will continue to be able to influence the Congress by . . . persuasion. . . . Nothing heavy-handed. Just openness and good relations.
Quoted in "Barbara Jordan" by Charles L. Sanders, *Ebony* February, 1975

3 . . . if I have anything special that makes me "influential" I simply don't know how to define it. If I knew the ingredients I would bottle them, package them and sell them, because I want everyone to be able to work together in a spirit of cooperation and compromise and accommodation without, you know, any caving in or anyone being woefully violated personally or in terms of his principles.    Ibid.

4 If you're going to play the game properly you'd better know every rule.    Ibid.

## 1157. June Jordan
(1936–    )

1 There was no loneliness in the living room. So it was a good part, and maybe the best part, of the house.    *New Life, New Room* 1975

2 "But what's more important. Building a bridge or taking care of a baby?"    Ibid.

## 1158. Dacia Maraini

(1936–    )

1 He talked and talked because he didn't know what to say.    *The Holiday*, Ch. 1    *1962*

2 "Our strength is like the sea," Pompei announced, lifting his chin up proudly. "Nothing can divert it. Elastic and mobile, strong. That's the main thing. Strong with an immense strength."    Ibid., Ch. 8

3 the disgust with myself, weak and weary throughout my intestines
I couldn't stop it nor vomit it. . . .
"His Foot on the Sand,"
*Crudelta all Aria' Aperia*    *1966*

4 the nausea of being the thing I was
leapt from my throat like sobbing. . . .
Ibid.

\* \* \*

5 A woman who writes poetry and knows
she is woman, has no choice but to hang on tight
to contents because the sophistication
of forms is something that belongs to power
and the power that woman has is always an
un-power, a scorching inheritance never entirely
hers.

Her voice may be hard and earthen
but it is the voice of a lioness that has been
reared too long a sensible sheep. . . .
"Woman's Poetry," *Donne Mie*

## 1159. Rochelle Owens

(1936–    )

1 CY. And I have no hate for anybody, but wanting to love the animals the way I do. *They*, mean folks, hate my face.    *Futz*, Sc. 1
*1961*

2 CY. I don't want no sow with two feet but with four! Them repeats true things with their grunts not like you human-daughter.    Ibid.

3 CY. I wasn't near people. They came to me and looked under my trousers all the way up to their dirty hearts. They minded my *own* life.
Ibid., Sc. 2

4 KATKA. Depression is often a sign of worthy pleasure.    Ibid., Sc. 5

5 ALICE. Hypocrites, what hypocrites! Jerusalem is always a pretext for getting to Constantinople!    *Istanbul*, Sc. 2    *1965*

6 BECLCH. Your lesson to your son is a hangnail to us—we don't need it.
*Beclch*, Act I, Sc. 1    *1966*

7 BECLCH. No, sweet Jose . . . a cock fight is not cruel . . . for me . . . us to see . . . it's simply an evil reality . . . that's all. . . .
Ibid., Sc. 2

8 BECLCH. Persecution is a fact of the condition of being a monarch!    Ibid., Act II, Sc. 2

9 MARX. Labor! Sucking Capital! Capital! The exploiting class! The milking class—the ruling class!    *The Karl Marx Play*    *1971*

10 MARX. . . . the bourgeoisie, the fat enemy will get their reactionary asses *schtupped* up with horseshit and whipped cream! A new era will dawn.    Ibid.

11 MARX. Little rolls with butter is good! Viennese torte is good! And a revolution is good!
Ibid.

12 MARX. Beware the eternal, unredeemed Jew, the everlasting bargainers! They are hot for buying and selling, they would kill my beautiful revolution!    Ibid.

13 MARX. Machinery sweeps away every moral and material restriction, in its blind unrestrainable passion, its werewolf hunger.    Ibid.

14 MARX. Economics is not only a cause. But the *only* cause for all human rancor. All human exploitation.    Ibid.

## 1160. Marge Piercy

(1936–    )

1 Reflecting the values of the larger capitalistic society, there is, no prestige whatsoever attached to actually working. Workers are invisible.
"The Grand Coolie Damn,"
*Sisterhood Is Powerful*,
Robin Morgan, ed.    *1970*

2 In an elitist world, it's always "women and children last."    Ibid.

3 One trouble: to be a professional anything in the United States is to think of oneself as an expert and one's ideas as semi-sacred, and to treat others in a certain way—professionally.
Ibid.

4 The ruling class isn't dissatisfied: they are healthy, well-fed, live in beauty, enjoy their own importance: fun-loving cannibals.    Ibid.

5 There are lies that glow so brightly we consent
to give a finger and then an arm
to let them burn.
> Ibid., "Song of the Fucked Duck"
> (1969)

6 The will to be totally rational
is the will to be made out of glass and steel:
and to use others as if they were glass and
steel.
> Ibid.

7 The manipulator liberates only
the mad bulldozers of the ego to level the
ground.
> Ibid.

8 "You're not pretty, Miriam-mine, so you better
be smart. But not too smart."
> *Small Changes*    1973

9 "All women hustle. Women watch faces, voices,
gestures, moods. The person who has to survive
through cunning."
> Ibid.

10 "You and I both have livers, large and small
intestines, kidneys, spines, blood vessels, nerves,
spleens, stomachs, hearts and, I had thought,
brains in common. What conclusions do you
draw from anatomy? That I am about to take
you to the cleaners?"
> Ibid.

## 1161. Gail Sheehy
### (1936?–    )

1 For there is no more defiant denial of one
man's ability to possess one woman exclusively
than the prostitute who refuses to be redeemed.
> *Hustling*, Ch. 1    1971

2 Into this anonymous pit they climb—a fumbling, frightened, pathetic man and a cold, contemptuous, violated woman—prepared to exchange for twenty dollars no more than ten
minutes of animal sex, untouched by a stroke
of their common humanity.    Ibid., Ch. 3

3 It is a silly question to ask a prostitute why
she does it. . . . These are the highest-paid
"professional" women in America.
> Ibid., Ch. 4

4 The prostitutes continue to take all the arrests,
the police to suffer frustration, the lawyers to
mine gold, the operators to laugh, the landowners to insist they have no responsibility, the
mayor to issue press releases. The nature of
the beast is, in a word, greed.    Ibid., Ch. 5

5 . . . the upper East Side of Manhattan. This is
the province of Let's Pretend located in the
state of Anomie.    Ibid.

6 The difference between the call girl and the
courtesan . . . comes down to one word.
Discipline.    Ibid., Ch. 9

7 The best way to attract money, she had discovered, was to give the appearance of having
it.    Ibid.

## 1162. Lily Tomlin
### (1936–    )

1 If you have a psychotic fixation and you go to
the doctor and you want these two fingers
amputated, he will not cut them off. But he *will*
remove your genitals. I have more trouble
getting a prescription for Valium than I do
having my uterus lowered and made into a
penis.    Quoted by David Felton in
> *Rolling Stone*    October 24, 1974

2 Thanks to medical technology, major break-
throughs in psychiatric care, I'm no longer a
woman obsessed with an unnatural craving. Just
another normal . . . very socially acceptable
. . . alcoholic.    Ibid., "Rubber Freak"*

3 If you can't be direct, why be?
> Ibid., "Mary Jean"*

4 Once poor, always wantin'. Rich is just a way
of wantin' bigger.    Ibid., "Wanda V."*

5 Lady . . . lady, I do not make up things. That
is lies. Lies is not true. But the truth could be
made up if you know how. And that's the truth.
> Ibid., "Edith Ann"*

## 1163. Sidney Abbott
### (1937–    )

1 Lesbianism is far more than a sexual prefer-
ence: it is a political stance.
> *Sappho Was a Right-On Woman,*
> with Barbara J. Love    1972

2 . . . a woman who wants a woman usually
wants a woman.    Ibid.

3 There is no political gain in silence and submission.    Ibid.

4 Multiple relationships made it possible to comprehend people, not acquire them or own them.
> Ibid.

* Characters created by Lily Tomlin.

## 1164. Margaret Lowe Benston
### (1937– )

1 In sheer quantity, household labor, including child care, constitutes a huge amount of socially necessary production. Nevertheless, in a society based on commodity production, it is not usually considered as "real work" since it is outside of trade and the marketplace. . . . In a society in which money determines value, women are a group who work outside the money economy.        "The Political Economy of Women's Lib," *Monthly Review September, 1969*

2 Industrialization is, in itself, a great force for human good; exploitation and dehumanization go with capitalism and not necessarily with industrialization.        Ibid.

3 Once women are freed from private production in the home, it will probably be very difficult to maintain for any long period of time a rigid definition of jobs by sex.        Ibid.

4 . . . possible alternatives—cooperatives, the kibbutz, etc. . . . show that psychic needs for community and warmth can in fact be better satisfied if other structures are substituted for the nuclear family.        Ibid.

## 1165. Sallie Bingham
### (1937– )

1 The clock would never let him forget the amount of time he was wasting. . . .
        "Winter Term," *Mademoiselle July, 1958*

2 . . . he wondered again, how much of her desire was passion and how much grasping: girls used sex to get a hold on you, he knew—it was so easy for them to pretend to be excited.        Ibid.

## 1166. Toni Cade
### (1937?– )

1 Personally, Freud's "anatomy is destiny" has always horrified me. *Kirche, Kusse, Kuche, Kinde* made me sick. Career woman versus wife-mother has always struck me as a false dichotomy. The-pill'll-make-you-gals-run-wild a lot of male chauvinist anxiety. Dump-the-pill a truncated statement. I think most women have pondered, those who have the heart to ponder at all, the oppressive nature of pregnancy, the tyranny of the child burden, the stupidity of male-female divisions, the obscene nature of employment discrimination. And day-care and nurseries being what they are, paid maternity leaves being rare, the whole memory of wham bam thank you ma'am and the Big Getaway a horrible nightmare, poverty so ugly, the family unit being the last word in socializing institutions to prepare us all for the ultimate rip-off and perpetuate the status quo, and abortion fatalities being what they are—of course the pill.        "The Pill," *Onyx        August, 1969*

2 We are involved in a struggle for liberation: liberation from the exploitive and dehumanizing system of racism, from the manipulative control of a corporate society; liberation from the constrictive norms of "mainstream" culture, from the synthetic myths that encourage us to fashion ourselves rashly from without (reaction) rather than from within (creation).
        *The Black Woman*, Preface        1970

3 The genocidal bloodbath of centuries and centuries of witch hunts sheds some light on the hysterical attitude white men have regarding their women.
        Ibid., Lecture, "The Scattered Sopranoes," Livingston College Black Women's Seminar (December, 1969)

4 Revolution begins with the self, in the self. The individual, the basic revolutionary unit, must be purged of poison and lies that assault the ego and threaten the heart, that hazard the next larger unit—the couple or pair, that jeopardize the still larger unit—the family or cell, that put the entire movement in peril.
        Ibid.

5 Not all speed is movement. . . . Ain't no such animal as an instant guerilla.        Ibid.

## 1167. Marian Wright Edelman
### (1937– )

1 Just because a child's parents are poor or uneducated is no reason to deprive the child of basic human rights to health care, education, proper nutrition. Clearly we ignore the needs of black children, poor children, and handicapped children in the country.
        Quoted in "Society's Pushed-Out Children" by Margie Casady, *Psychology Today        June, 1975*

2 Some school officials have forgotten the reason they are there. Expediency and efficiency in administration have somehow become more important than educating children.        Ibid.

3 Parents have become so convinced that educators know what is best for children that they forget that they themselves are really the experts.        Ibid.

4 I've been struck by the upside-down priorities of the juvenile-justice system. We are willing to spend the least amount of money to keep a kid at home, more to put him in a foster home, and the most to institutionalize him.    Ibid.

## 1168. Jane Fonda
(1937–   )

1 I don't care about the Oscar. I make movies to support the causes I believe in, not for any honors. I couldn't care less whether I win an Oscar or not.
> Quoted in *Jane: An Intimate Biography of Jane Fonda* by Thomas Kiernan, Prologue    *1973*

2 I didn't like what I saw the acting profession do to people who went into the theater. All the young actresses I've met are obsessed with the theater. They think and talk only about one thing. Nothing else matters to them. It's terribly unhealthy to sacrifice everything—family, children—for a goal. I hope I never get that way. I don't believe in concentrating your life in terms of one profession, no matter what it is.
> Ibid., Pt. II, Ch. 8 (c.1958)

3 Before I went into analysis, I told everyone lies—but when you spend all that money, you tell the truth. I learned that I had grown up in an atmosphere where nobody told the truth. Everyone was so concerned with appearances that life was just one big lie. Now all I want to do is live a life of truth. Analysis has also taught me that you should know who to love and who to hate and who to just plain like, and it's important to know the difference.
> Ibid., Ch. 13 (c.1962)

4 You can do one of two things: just shut up, which is something I don't find easy, or learn an awful lot very fast, which is what I tried to do.    Ibid., Pt. IV, Ch. 22

5 Prostitutes are the inevitable product of a society that places ultimate importance on money, possessions and competition.
> Ibid., Ch. 24 (c.1970)

6 All I can say is that through the people I've met, the experiences I've had, the reading I've done, I realize the American system must be changed. I see an alternative to the usual way of living and relating to people. And this alternative is a total change of our structures and institutions—through Socialism. Of course I am a Socialist. But without a theory, without an ideology.    Ibid., Ch. 26 (c.1971)

## 1169. Kathleen Fraser
(1937–   )

1 He is all of him urge.
> Untitled Poem, *What I Want*    *1974*

2 I think you have many shelves
but never put love there.
> Ibid., Untitled Poem

3 "Personal things is all I care about."
> Ibid., Untitled Poem

## 1170. Gail Godwin
(1937–   )

1 "The only reason people forget is because they want to. If we were all clear, with no aberrations, we could remember everything, before we were born, even."
> *The Perfectionists*, Ch. 1    *1970*

2 Anchored by the heavy bright heat, she closed her eyes and ears and let it press her down. *Let* the sun bake her senseless in the hottest part of the day. Let it broil her brain free of all complexities. Let it burn her back into the same earth which held the bones of ancient peasants and the decayed petals of bygone flowers. She did not wish to compete, or to understand or to participate anymore. . . . She felt tight in the head, like something was growing—a flower someone planted in a pot too small.    Ibid., Ch. 2

3 "You sort of glitter rather than glow. Small talk comes easy to you. You dress well. You are all crisp, sharp edges. You look like one of those young career women on the go."
> Ibid., Ch. 8

4 "With a husband you have to keep up appearances. I don't care who says not. They have their aura, we have ours. They are eternally different auras."    Ibid., Ch. 12

5 . . . life is a disease. . . .
> *The Odd Woman*    *1974*

6 . . . trying to organize the loneliness and the weather and the long night into something of abiding shape and beauty.    Ibid.

7 . . . though all came to horrible ends, they kept track of themselves so beautifully along the way.    Ibid.

8 "Good teaching is one-fourth preparation and three-fourths theatre. . . ."    Ibid.

9 I turn into an anachronism every time I come home, she thought angrily. I start measuring myself by standards thirty, fifty, a hundred years old.    Ibid.

## 1171. Bessie Head

(1937–　　)

1 But in a society like this, which man cared to be owned and possessed when there were so many women freely available? And even all the excessive love-making was purposeless, aimless, just like tipping everything into an awful cesspit where no one really cared to take a second look.　　*When Rain Clouds Gather*, Ch. 8
*1968*

2 He wanted a flower garden of yellow daisies because they were the only flower which resembled the face of his wife and the sun of his love.　　　　　　　　*Maru*, Pt. I　　*1971*

3 And if the white man thought that Asians were a low, filthy nation, Asians could still smile with relief—at least, they were not Africans. And if the white man thought that Africans were a low, filthy nation, Africans in southern Africa could still smile—at least, they were not bushmen. They all have their monsters.
Ibid.

4 Love is mutually feeding each other, not one living on another like a ghoul.
*A Question of Power*　　*1973*

## 1172. Barbara J. Love

(1937–　　)

Co-author with Sidney Abbot. See 1163: 1–4.

## 1173. Liane Norman

(1937–　　)

1 If conscience is regarded as imperative, then compliance with its dictates commends a society not to forgive, but to celebrate, its conscientious citizens.
"Selective Conscientious Objection,"
*The Center Magazine*
*May/June, 1972*

2 To kill implies that the claims of some men to life are better than others. . . .　　　Ibid.

3 While the State may respectfully require obedience on many matters, it cannot violate the moral nature of a man, convert him into a serviceable criminal, and expect his loyalty and devotion.　　　　　　　　　　　　Ibid.

4 . . . if the Indochina war proves anything at all, it is the susceptibility of government to self-deluded error.　　　　　　　　Ibid.

5 Whenever government's interests become by definition more substantial than the humanity of its citizens, the drift toward government by divine right gathers momentum.　　　Ibid.

## 1174. Eleanor Holmes Norton

(1937–　　)

1 Racial oppression of black people in America has done what neither class oppression nor sexual oppression, with all their perniciousness, has ever done: destroyed an entire people and their culture.　　　"For Sadie and Maude,"
*Sisterhood Is Powerful,*
Robin Morgan, ed.　　*1970*

2 There is no reason to repeat bad history.
Ibid.

3 On the road to equality there is no better place for blacks to detour around American values than in forgoing its example in the treatment of its women and the organization of its family life.　　　　　　　　　　　　Ibid.

4 With children no longer the universally accepted reason for marriage, marriages are going to have to exist on their own merits.　　Ibid.

5 There are not many males, black or white, who wish to get involved with a woman who's committed to her own development.
Quoted in "The Black Family and Feminism" by C. Ware, *The First Ms. Reader*, Francine Klagsbrun, ed.
*1972*

## 1175. Jill Ruckelshaus

(1937?–　　)

1 Women's rights in essence is really a movement for freedom, a movement for equality, for the dignity of all women, for those who work outside the home and those who dedicate themselves with more altruism than any profession I know to being wives and mothers, cooks and chauffeurs, decorators and child psychologists and loving human beings.
Quoted in "Jill Ruckelshaus: Lady of Liberty" by Frederic A. Birmingham,
*Saturday Evening Post*
*March 3, 1973*

2 I have no hostility towards men. Some of my best friends are men. I married a man, and my father was a man.　　　　　　　　Ibid.

3 What the emergence of woman as a political force means is that we are quite ready now to take on responsibilities as equals, not protected partners.　　　　　　　　　　　　Ibid.

4 The best way to win an argument is to begin by being right. . . .        *Ibid.*

5 The family is the building block for whatever solidarity there is in society.        *Ibid.*

6 It occurred to me when I was thirteen and wearing white gloves and Mary Janes and going to dancing school, that no one should have to dance backward all their lives.
       Speech      *1973*

7 The Equal Rights Amendment is designed to establish in our Constitution the clear moral value judgment that all Americans, women and men, stand equal under the law. . . . It will give woman's role in the home new status, recognizing that the homemaker's role in a marriage has economic value. . . . Critics say ERA will open the draft to women. At the moment, the United States has an oversubscribed volunteer army, many of whom are women. ERA means that women who serve will get equal benefits.
       Quoted in "Forum," *Ladies' Home Journal*      *August, 1975*

## 1176. Diane B. Schulder

(1937–   )

1 Law is a reflection and a source of prejudice. It both enforces and suggests forms of bias.
       "Does the Law Oppress Women?," *Sisterhood Is Powerful,* Robin Morgan, ed.      *1970*

2 Legislation and case law still exist in some parts of the United States permitting the "passion shooting" by a husband of a wife; the reverse, of course, is known as homicide.
       *Ibid.*

3 . . . prejudice (the mythology of class oppression) is enshrined in laws. Laws lead to enforcement of practices. Practices reinforce and lead to prejudice. The cycle continues. . . .
       *Ibid.*

## 1177. Diane Wakoski

(1937–   )

1   thinking how cage life drove an animal into
   mazes of him-
     self,
his cage mates chosen for him his life circumscribed and focused
on eating, his play watched by it-doesn't-matter-
   whom, just
watched, always watched.
       "The Birds of Paradise Being Very Plain Birds," St. 5, *The East Side Scene,* Allen De Loach, ed.      *1968*

2     It happens all the time, I told her,
some of us have bad vision, are crippled, have
   defects, and
our reality is a different one, not the
correct and ascertainable one,
and sometimes it makes us dotty and lonely
but also it makes us poets.
       *Ibid.,* St. 9

3 My face
that my friends tell me is so full of character;
my face
I have hated for so many years;
my face
I have made an angry contract to live with
though no one could love it
       "I Have Had to Learn to Live with My Face," St. 2, *The Motorcycle Betrayal Poems*      *1971*

4 I wonder how we learn to live
with out faces?
They must hide so much pain,
so many deep trenches of blood,
so much that would terrorize and drive others
   away, if they
could see it. The struggle to control it
articulates the face
       *Ibid.,* St. 12

## 1178. Renata Adler

(1938–   )

1 I . . . doubt that film can ever argue effectively against its own material: that a genuine anti-war film, say, can be made on the basis of even the ugliest battle scenes. . . . No matter what filmmakers intend, film always argues yes. People have been modeling their lives after films for years, but the medium is somehow unsuited to moral lessons, cautionary tales or polemics of any kind. If you want to make a pacifist film, you must make an exemplary film about peaceful men.
       "The Movies Make Heroes of Them All" (January 7, 1968), *A Year in the Dark*      *1969*

2 Everyone dances, and sings and draws and acts, or knows to a degree what these involve. It is precisely because so few people make films that they belong more or less equally to everyone— are put arbitrarily before people for equal comment, within limitations of taste and experience, like a passing day.
       *Ibid.,* "Time, Old Movies, and Exhausting Life" (August 4, 1968)

3 Though films become more daring sexually, they are probably less sexy than they ever were. There haven't been any convincing love

scenes or romances in the movies in a while. (Nobody even seems to neck in theaters any more.) . . . When the mechanics and sadism quotients go up, the movie love interest goes dead, and the film just lies there, giving a certain amount of offense.
Ibid., "Temper, Misogyny, and<br>Couples in Theaters"<br>(October 13, 1968)

4 The writer has a grudge against society, which he documents with accounts of unsatisfying sex, unrealized ambition, unmitigated loneliness, and a sense of local and global distress. The square, overpopulation, the bourgeois, the bomb and the cocktail party are variously identified as sources of the grudge. There follows a little obscenity here, a dash of philosophy there, considerable whining overall, and a modern satirical novel is born.
"Salt into Old Scars" (June 22, 1963),<br>*Toward a Radical Middle*    1971

5 When a society becomes so benevolent that there can be no legitimate confusion between personal insufficiencies and social grievances, the armed rebel has simply lost his cause to the good citizen, and his arms to the sick man of violence, in exile or in crime.
Ibid., "Sartre, Saint Genet, and the<br>Bureaucrat" (November 9, 1963)

6 If anything has characterized the [peace] movement, from its beginning and in all its parts, it has been a spirit of decentralization, local autonomy, personal choice, and freedom from dogma.    Ibid., "Early Radicalism: The Price
of Peace Is Confusion"<br>(December 11, 1965)

7 . . . nothing defines the quality of life in a community more clearly than people who regard themselves, or whom the consensus chooses to regard, as mentally unwell.
Ibid., "The Thursday Group"<br>(April 15, 1967)

## 1179. Ti-Grace Atkinson
(1938?–    )

1 Love is the victim's response to the rapist.
Quoted in "Rebellion" by Irma Kurtz,<br>*Sunday Times Magazine* (London)<br>*September 14, 1969*

## 1180. Rona Barrett
(1938–    )

1 It's ironic, but until you can free those final monsters within the jungle of yourself, your life, your soul is up for grabs.
*Miss Rona: An Autobiography,*<br>Prologue    *1974*

2 . . . the *healthy*, the *strong* individual, is the one who asks for help when he needs it. Whether he's got an abscess on his knee or in his soul.    Ibid., Ch. 15

## 1181. Vivian Gornick
(1938–    )

1 Behind the "passive" exterior of many women there lies a growing anger over lost energies and confused lives, an anger so sharp in its fury but so diffuse in its focus that one can only describe it as the price society must pay for creating a patriarchal system in the first place, and for now refusing to let it go. And make no mistake, it is not letting go.
"Why Women Fear Success,"<br>*The First Ms. Reader,*<br>Francine Klagsbrun, ed.    *1972*

2 She takes daily walks on the land that was once the bottom of the sea, marking and classifying, sifting through her thoughts the meaning of the jagged edges of discontent that have begun to make inroads anew inside her.
"Stillness at the Center," *Ms.*<br>*October, 1973*

3 There is a desperate lack of variety to the poverty here [Egypt], a kind of stupor of simplicity, an aimlessness that covers the people in a thick expressionless haze. . . .
*In Search of Ali-Mahmoud*    *1973*

4 If the word for London is decency and the word for New York is violence, then, beyond doubt, the word for Cairo is tenderness. Tenderness is what pervades the air here.
Ibid., Pt. I

5 I lived once in the American desert. The solitude opens up. It becomes an enormous surrounding comfort. But the solitude in the city is a confusing and painful thing.
Ibid., Pt. II

6 Suddenly, I see that the diffused love, which is the deepest lesson of the East, has within it the seeds of nonpossessive love. And with a surprised weariness I remember my own country. For God knows, those clutched, nonseparating marriages of the West don't indicate love.    Ibid., Pt. IV

## 1182. Barbara Howar
(1938?–    )

1 . . . the cocktail party remains a vital Washington institution, the official intelligence system.    *Laughing All the Way,* Ch. 5    *1973*

2 In our long history of shooting politicians . . .
I have come to feel that Washington politicians
look upon these events as little more than temporary setbacks in the continuing process of
government.        Ibid., Ch. 12

3 Eventually most television stations around the
country achieved their minority quota by hir-
ing "twofers," which is a trade expression meaning a "black, female, on-air personality," two
television unthinkables, at one salary—a salary,
I might add, that generally falls short of the
"equal pay for equal work" cliché.
        Ibid., Ch. 15

4 Kissinger likes intrigue rather than confrontation. . . . [He] believes all power begins in the
White House. It is his firm belief that he and
the President know what is best; the rest of
us are to be patient and they will announce
our destiny.        Ibid., Ch. 16

5 Those complicated people that make Washington the mysterious jungle it is, those famous
men and women who to the rest of the world
are glamorous and powerful, even ruthless,
public figures, have in them a specialness that
is inconsistent with the city's official image—a
combination of worldly involvement and personal commitment that makes Washington
genuine despite its reach for power.
        Ibid., Ch. 21

## 1183. Jane Kramer
### (1938?– )

1 Prophecy today is hardly the romantic business
that it used to be. The old tools of the trade,
like the sword, the hair shirt, and the long fast
in the wilderness, have given way to more contemporary, mundane instruments of doom—the
book, the picket and the petition, the sit-in . . .
at City Hall.
        "The Ranks and Rungs of Mrs. Jacobs'
        Ladder," *Off Washington Square*
        *1963*

2 Dawia maintained that the Europeans were . . .
favored by Allah because Allah liked automo-
biles and was hoping that the Europeans would
bring their cars to Heaven with them. Omar,
however, said no, that Allah loved the Europeans because the Europeans always got to
their appointments on time.
        *Honor to the Bride*, Pt. I    *1973*

3 "It is a burden to have daughters," Dawia
said, sighing. "My husband looks at Jmaa now
and he says, 'What can I expect from her?

More of the same problems I have suffered
with the first two.' "
    "He has a point," Musa remarked. "Having
daughters is not profitable."    Ibid., Pt. II

## 1184. Mary Jane Moffat
### (1938?– )

1 Why do women keep diaries? . . . The form
has been an important outlet for women partly
because it is an analogue to their lives: emotional, fragmentary, interrupted, modest, not
to be taken seriously, private, restricted, daily,
trivial, formless, concerned with self, as endless
as their tasks.
        *Revelations: Diaries of Women*, with
        Charlotte Painter, Foreword    *1974*

## 1185. Joyce Carol Oates
### (1938– )

1 "Personal relationships start off so cleanly but
then become too involved."
        "Norman and the Killer," *Upon the
        Sweeping Flood and Other Stories*
        *1965*

2 "Nothing can be right and balanced again
until justice is won—the injured party has to
have justice. Do you understand that? Nothing
can be right, for years, for lifetimes, until that
first crime is punished. Or else we'd all be
animals."        Ibid.

3 Anger always excited and pleased them; it was
sacred.      *A Garden of Earthly Delights,*
        Pt. I, Ch. 1    *1967*

4 The only trouble was that here an odor of
harsh antiseptic was everywhere, floating
everywhere . . . it seemed to be eating its
way into your lungs to get you clean even if
it killed you.        Ibid., Ch. 8

5 She felt like a plant of some kind, like a
flower on a stalk that only looked slender but
was really tough, tough as steel, like the
flowers in fields that could be blown down flat
by the wind but yet rose again slowly coming
back to life.        Ibid., Pt. II, Ch. 6

6 Whoever was stupid was beneath worry or
thought; you did not have to figure them out.
This eliminated hundreds of people. In this life
you had time only for a certain amount of
thinking, and there was no need to waste any
of it on people who were not threatening.
        Ibid., Pt. III, Ch. 7

7 Swan smiled. He did not know what his smile meant: just the reaction of witnessing rituals, ceremonies that have been repeated many times.
Ibid., Ch. 9

8 This is a work of history in fictional form—that is, in personal perspective, which is the only kind of history that exists.
*Them*, Author's Note     *1969*

9 Shakily he thought of the future: that night, and the next day, and the real future. The future was important, not the present. These minutes spent around the supper table, these ten or fifteen minutes he had to get through, were not important except as they were part of a process leading to the future, a future that would be a good surprise, he felt sure.
Ibid., Pt. I, Ch. 9

10 She ransacked her mind but there was nothing in it.        Ibid., Ch. 15

11 "I admit that I have no fixed income like your friend, and I have no desire for it," he said to Faye. "I like adventure. I don't dare prophesy where my liking for adventure will lead."
Ibid., Pt. II, Ch. 2

12 ". . . women don't understand these things. They only understand money when they can see it. They're very crude essentially. They don't understand where money comes from or what it means or how a man can be worth money though he hasn't any at the moment. But a man understands all that."     Ibid.

13 She would have a baby with her husband, to make up for the absence of love, to locate love, to fix herself in a certain place, but she would not really love him.
Ibid., Pt. III, Ch. 1

14 . . . it is a fever, this racing, this constant thought.
"What Is the Connection Between Men and Women?," *Mademoiselle*
*February, 1970*

15 Old women snore violently. They are like bodies into which bizarre animals have crept at night; the animals are vicious, bawdy, noisy. How they snore! There is no shame to their snoring. Old women turn into old men.    Ibid.

16 In love there are two things: bodies and words.
Ibid.

17 In the catatonic state small wars are waged in the body, acted out, memorized, rehearsed, unleashed, begun again, repeated.     Ibid.

18 Her mind churns so that she can't hear, she can't think.           Ibid.

19 He hated her for the selfishness of her death and for her having eclipsed him forever, obliterated him as if she had smashed an insect under her shoe.
"The Wheel of Love," (1967), *The Wheel of Love and Other Stories*
*1970*

20 "Loneliness is dangerous. It's bad for you to be alone, to be lonely, because if aloneness does not lead to God, it leads to the devil. It leads to the self."     Ibid., "Shame" (1968)

21 Night comes to the desert all at once, as if someone turned off a light.
Ibid., "Interior Monologue" (1969)

22 When a marriage ends, who is left to understand it?     Ibid., "Unmailed, Unwritten Letters" (1969)

23 Minutes pass in silence, mysteriously. It is those few minutes that pass after we make love that are most mysterious to me, uncanny.
Ibid.

24 . . . the necessity for patience had aged her magically; she was content in her age.
Ibid., "Bodies" (1970)

25 The ringing of a telephone is always louder in an empty house.     Ibid., "I Was in Love"
(1970)

26 Before falling in love, I was defined. Now I am undefined, weeds are growing between my ribs.           Ibid.

27 "We're off! Another week come and gone! Month in, month out! Even, odd—black, white—life, death—father, son. The cycles continue!"
Ibid., "Wild Saturday" (1970)

28 Premeditated crime: the longer the meditating, the dreaming, the more triumphant the execution!     *Do with Me What You Will*,
Pt. I, Ch. 1     *1970*

29 "I don't think that California is a healthy place. . . . Things disintegrate there."
Ibid., Ch. 8

30 The plaque at the front of the courtroom, high on the wall, was permanent and yet its words were new each time Jack read them, read them half against his will, his eyes moving restlessly forward and up to them while testimony droned on: *Conscience Speaks the Truth.*
Ibid., Pt. II, Ch. 6

31 The worst cynicism: a belief in luck.
Ibid., Ch. 15

32 . . . he believed in the justice of his using any legal methods he could improvise to force the other side into compromise or into dismissals of charges, or to lead a jury into the verdict he wanted. Why not? He was a defense lawyer, not a judge or a juror or a policeman or a legislator or a theoretician or an anarchist or a murderer.        Ibid.

33 . . . like all virtuous people he imagines he must speak the truth. . . .        Ibid.

34 Light love draws us up into the galaxy . . . but heavy love drags us down into the mud of self and the great mud of wars. . . . Down in the mud we fight one another, compete from birth till death; in the galaxy we are free of that tragic struggle.        Ibid., Ch. 10

35 You're such a virgin, a sweet perpetual virgin. You're so perfect that you turn other people hard as ice. . . .        Ibid., Ch. 15

36 Nothing is accidental in the universe—this is one of my Laws of Physics—except the entire universe itself, which is Pure Accident, pure divinity.        Ibid., "The Summing Up: Meredith Dawe"

37 What relationship had a dagger to the human hand, that it must be invented, imagined out of the shape of the hand?—where did the sharpness come from, was it from the soul and its unstoppable imaginings?—because the hand in itself was so defenseless, so vulnerable in its flesh.        Ibid., "Elena"

## 1186.  Diane Ravitch
### (1938–    )

1 The ladder was there, "from the gutter to the university," and for those stalwart enough to ascend it, the schools were a boon and a path out of poverty.        *The Great School Wars*
        *1974*

## 1187.  Maria Isabel Barreno
### (1939–    )

1 . . . all friendship between women has a uterine air about it, the air of a slow, bloody, cruel, incomplete exchange, of an original situation being repeated all over again.
        *New Portuguese Letters*, with Maria Fatima Velho da Costa and Maria Teresa Horta    *1972*

2 The time of discipline began. Each of us the pupil of whichever one of us could best teach what each of us needed to learn.        Ibid.

3 . . . we are still the property of men, the spoils today of warriors who pretend to be our comrades in the struggle, but who merely seek to mount us. . . .        Ibid.

4 One lives and endures one's life with others, within matrices, but it is only alone, truly alone that one bursts apart, springs forth.        Ibid.

5 Let no one tell me that silence gives consent, because whoever is silent dissents.        Ibid.

## 1188.  Judy Chicago
### (1939–    )

1 We have made a space to house our spirit, to give form to our dreams. . . .
        "Let Sisterhood Be Powerful,"
    *Womanspace*    *February/March, 1973*

2 . . . I suddenly knew that I was alone forever, that I could lose the people I loved any time, any moment, and that the only thing I had in this life was myself.
        *Through the Flower: My Struggle as a Woman Artist*, Ch. 1    *1975*

3 I did not understand that wanting doesn't always lead to action.        Ibid., Ch. 4

4 The acceptance of women as authority figures or as role models is an important step in female education. . . . It is this process of identification, respect, and then self-respect that promotes growth.        Ibid., Ch. 5

5 We were wedded together on the basis of mutual work and goals.        Ibid., Ch. 9

## 1189.  Judy Collins
### (1939–    )

1 I look in the mirror through the eyes of the child that was me.
        "Secret Gardens of the Heart"
        *1972*

2 Secret gardens of the heart where the old stay young forever. . . .        Ibid.

## 1190.  Yaël Dayan
### (1939–    )

1 Within me I would be the mistress; outside, if necessary, a slave. I would knit my world together, make contact with the outside world, write the right kind of letters, and be as I thought appropriate to different people.
        *New Face in the Mirror*    *1959*

2 High society is, of course, mainly habit. . . .
       Ibid.

3 My father, I remembered, had no fears at all. In that he differed greatly from me. But he could not be called a courageous man because he had no fears to overcome.      Ibid.

4 He picked up some earth and poured it into the boy's palm. "Grasp it, feel it, taste it. There is your God. If you want to pray, boy, pray to the sky to bring rain to our land and not virtue to your souls."
     *Envy the Frightened*, Ch. 4    *1960*

5 It is very difficult to analyze the deed, to know how much of it was a result of youthful stupidity, what part the physical attraction of the mountain and snow played in it, what part looking for danger. Or perhaps it was an unconscious will to encounter fear, an element within him stronger than himself.
       Ibid., Ch. 16

6 It wasn't a battle really, as it wasn't a war. Nor was it a game, not when you heard the poisonous shrieking of the bullets—confused, scattered, searching above your heads—there was no feeling of deep revenge or hatred. It was almost as quiet as a day's work, only moments seemed eternal and seconds endless. . . . Not a war, or a battle, but a fight.
       Ibid., Ch. 18

7   "Do you think he is a brave man?" . . .
   "Either too much of a coward to face it—or the bravest, facing it in solitude, not sharing the fear. Perhaps we'll never find out."
     *Death Had Two Sons*, Ch. 1    *1967*

8 She was friendless and yet a friend to others and the same intensity with which she ignored the future marked her passionate attitude to the past.      Ibid., Ch. 8

9 How long it takes us to gather the component parts of our memory—the problems, self-appraisals, the self-analysis, our little daily dilemmas, petty quests for comfort. And how quickly they all can disappear.
     *Israel Journal: June, 1967*    *1967*

10 People in politics are not very kind to each other.      Quoted in the *Los Angeles Times*
       *March 7, 1974*

## 1191. Shelagh Delaney
### (1939–    )

1 HELEN. The only consolation I can find in your immediate presence is your ultimate absence.
     *A Taste of Honey*, Act I, Sc. 1
       *1959*

2 BOY. Women never have young minds. They are born three thousand years old.
       Ibid., Sc. 2

3 JO. In this country [England] there are only two seasons, winter and winter.    Ibid.

4 HELEN. Why don't you learn from my mistakes? It takes half your life to learn from your own.      Ibid.

5 JO. We don't ask for life, we have it thrust upon us.      Ibid., Act II, Sc. 2

6 GEOF. You need somebody to love you while you're looking for someone to love.    Ibid.

7 I am here and I am safe and I am sick of it.
   "Sweetly Sings the Donkey," *Sweetly*
     *Sings the Donkey*    *1963*

8 "He was very ugly but people can't help the faces they're born with."      Ibid.

9 According to her, only a revolution will ever bring true democracy to this country and the sooner revolution comes (she said) the better and even though hundreds of innocents will be slaughtered they will die in a good cause and men must be willing to sacrifice themselves. But that depends I suppose on which men you're thinking of. . . .      Ibid.

10 He didn't play with his food anymore till it got cold; instead, down it went like fuel into a furnace keeping the ovens hot, and the energy at boiling point, as Tom hurtled through his life catching up with himself at last.
       Ibid., "Tom Riley"

11 We teach you the pleasure of physical exercise —the team-spirit of games, too, for when you leave school finally you will find that life is a game, sometimes serious, sometimes fun, but a game that must be played with true team-spirit—there is no room for the outsider in life.      Ibid., "The Teacher"

12 "There aren't enough secrets to go round anymore. Some spies are having to invent secrets in order to earn a living. . . . I can't help wondering what will happen when redundant spies join the ranks of the unemployed."
     Ibid., "My Uncle, the Spy"

13 . . . Poles seem to be as much condemned to a diet of caviar, vodka and the Polka as the English are to rare old port and pheasant.
     Ibid., "Vodka and Small
       Pieces of Gold"

## 1192. Colette Dowling

(1939?–     )

1 . . . the fifties . . . was a time of fevered fantasies—dreams of freedom and adulthood.
"A Woman Sounds Off on Those Sexy Magazines," *Redbook*
*April, 1974*

2 I tell you, the great divide is still with us, the awful split, the Us and Them. Like a rubber band tautened to the snapping point, the polarization of the sexes continues, because we lack the courage to face our likenesses and admit to our real need.     Ibid.

## 1193. Margaret Drabble

(1939–     )

1 It appalled him, the complacency with which such friends would describe the advantages of living in a mixed area. As though they licensed seedy old ladies and black men to walk their streets, teaching their children of poverty and despair, as their pet hamsters and guinea pigs taught them of sex and death.
*The Needle's Eye*, Pt. I     *1972*

2 . . . affluence was, quite simply, a question of texture. . . . The threadbare carpets of infancy, the coconut matting, the ill-laid linoleum, the utility furniture, the curious upholstery . . . had all spoken of a life too near the bones of subsistence, too little padded, too severely worn.     Ibid.

3 Rose . . . had the sense that there was something unpleasant that she had promised herself that she would do. While she gave the children their breakfast and drank a cup of tea, she tried to work out what it could be—unearthing accidentally, as she did so, a whole heaped cupboard-full of nasty obligations, such as shoe-buying and glazier-visiting, and of nagging guilts, about people she should have rung back and hadn't, people she should have written to and hadn't, birthday presents unbought and promises unfulfilled.     Ibid.

4 . . . she used to pray . . . and she still prayed, occasionally, not incessantly as she had done through childhood, but every now and then a natural or man-made calamity would push her imperiously to her knees, a massacre, an earthquake, a drowning, and she would implore justice, mercy, intercession, explanation, not praying any more for herself, as she had once so futilely done . . . wondering even as she knelt whether there were any use in such genuflections, and yet pushed down as certainly as

if a hand had descended on her head to thrust her from above, crushing her hair and weighing on her skull.     Ibid., Pt. II

5 How easy it was to underestimate what had been endured.     Ibid.

6 . . . if I'd known twenty years ago. . . . A pity, really, that one couldn't have had that particular thrill then—the thrill of knowing. It wasn't worth much now.
"A Success Story," *Spare Rib*
*Magazine     1972*

7 People like admiration more than anything. Whatever can one do about it?     Ibid.

8 We seek a utopia in the past, a possible if not ideal society. We seek golden worlds from which we are banished, they recede infinitely, for there never was a golden world, there was never anything but toil and subsistence, cruelty and dullness.     *The Realms of Gold     1975*

9 "Much have I travelled in the realms of gold."     Ibid.

10 "To hear him talk of tradition and the individual talent was to enter into a world where old labels had meanings."     Ibid.

11 She taught herself, over the years, to see his death as a healing of some kind, the end of a long illness, a sacrifice. Taken from them for their better health.     Ibid.

12 . . . the human mind can bear plenty of reality but not too much unintermittent gloom.     Ibid.

13 As a geologist, he took a long view of time: even longer than Frances Wingate, archaeologist, and very much longer than Karel Schmidt, historian.     Ibid.

## 1194. Roxanne Dunbar

(1939–     )

1 Man, in conquering nature, conquered the female, who had worked with nature, not against it, to produce food and to reproduce the human race.
"Feminine Liberation as the Basis for
Social Revolution," *Sisterhood Is*
*Powerful*, Robin Morgan, ed.     *1970*

2 We live under an international caste system, at the top of which is the Western white male ruling class, and at the very bottom of which is the female of the nonwhite colonized world.     Ibid.

3 In reality, the family has fallen apart. Nearly half of all marriages end in divorce, and the family unit is a decadent, energy-absorbing, destructive, wasteful institution for everyone except the ruling class for which the institution was created.　　　　　　Ibid.

## 1195.　Terry Garthwaite
(1939–　　)

1 from bessie to bebe to billie to boz
there's a lot more power than the wizard of oz
"Rock and Roller"　　*1975*

## 1196.　Joan Goulianos
(1939–　　)

1 . . . these . . . women . . . wrote in a world which was controlled by men, a world in which women's revelations, if they were anything but conventional, might not be welcomed, might not be recognized, and they wrote nevertheless.
*By a Woman Writt*, Introduction
(February, 1972)　　*1973*

2 But, overall, it was men who were the critics, the publishers, the professors, the sources of support. It was men who had the power to praise women's works, to bring them to public attention, or to ridicule them, to doom them . . . to obscurity.　　　　　　Ibid.

## 1197.　Germaine Greer
(1939–　　)

1 The consequences of militancy do not disappear when the need for militancy is over. Freedom is fragile and must be protected. To sacrifice it, even as a temporary measure, is to betray it.　　　　　　*The Female Eunuch,*
Introduction　　*1971*

2 If marriage and family depend upon the castration of women let them change or disappear.
Ibid., "The Psychological Sell"

3 What is the arms race and the cold war but the continuation of male competitiveness and aggression into the inhuman sphere of computer-run institutions? If women are to cease producing cannon fodder for the final holocaust they must rescue men from the perversities of their own polarization.　　　　　　Ibid.

4 Womanpower means the self-determination of women, and that means that all the baggage of paternalistic society will have to be thrown overboard.　　　　　Ibid., "Womanpower"

5 Every time a man unburdens his heart to a stranger he reaffirms the love that unites humanity.　　　　　　Ibid., "The Ideal"

6 The only causes of regret are laziness, outbursts of temper, hurting others, prejudice, jealousy and envy.　　　　　　Ibid.

7 Our life-style contains more *Thanatos* than *Eros*, for egotism, exploitation, deception, obsession and addiction have more place in us than eroticism, joy, generosity and spontaneity.　　　　　　Ibid.

8 As soon as we find ourselves working at being indispensable, rigging up a pattern of vulnerability in our loved ones, we ought to know that our love has taken the socially sanctioned form of egotism.　　　　Ibid., "Egotism"

9 Love, love, love—all the wretched cant of it, masking egotism, lust, masochism, fantasy under a mythology of sentimental postures.
Ibid., "Obsession"

10 Shared but secret behavior will cement any group into a conspiracy. . . . Changing partners is such a thoroughly unspontaneous activity, so divorced from the vagaries of genuine sexual desire—no more than a variant on the square dance. In such a transaction sex is the sufferer: passion becomes lechery.　　　Ibid., "Family"

11 There is no such thing as security. There never has been.　　　　　　Ibid., "Security"

12 Although security is not in the nature of things, we invent strategies for outwitting fortune, and call them after their guiding deity—insurance, assurance, social security.　　　　　　Ibid.

13 Security is when everything is settled, when nothing can happen to you; security is the denial of life. Human beings are better equipped to cope with disaster and hardship than they are with unvarying security, but as long as security is the highest value in a community they can have little opportunity to decide this for themselves.　　　　　　Ibid.

14 Loneliness is never more cruel than when it is felt in close propinquity with someone who has ceased to communicate.　　　　　　Ibid.

15 Women have very little idea of how much men hate them.　　　Ibid., "Loathing and Disgust"

## 1198.　Maria Teresa Horta
(1939–　　)

Co-author with Maria Isabel Barreno and Maria Fatima Velho da Costa. See 1187: 1–5.

## 1199. Barbara Kolb

(1939– )

1 . . . composing a piece of music is very feminine. It is sensitive, emotional, contemplative. By comparison, doing housework is positively masculine.

Quoted in "A Matter of Art, Not Sex,"
*Time*    *November 10, 1975*

## 1200. Letty Cottin Pogrebin

(1939– )

1 . . . lifestyles and sex roles are passed from parents to children as inexorably as blue eyes or small feet.

"Down with Sexist Upbringing,"
*The First Ms. Reader*, Francine
Klagsbrun, ed.    *1972*

2 In school books, the Dick and Jane syndrome reinforced our emerging attitudes. The arithmetic books posed appropriate conundrums: "Ann has three pies . . . Dan has three rockets. . . ." We read the nuances between the lines: Ann keeps her eye on the oven; Dan sets his sights on the moon.    Ibid.

3 Boys don't make passes at female smart-asses.
Ibid.

4 . . . children's liberation is the next item on our civil rights shopping list.    Ibid.

## 1201. Joan Rivers

(1939– )

1 The psychic scars caused by believing that you are ugly leave a permanent mark on your personality.    Quoted in "An Ugly Duckling Complex" by Lydia Lane, *Los Angeles Times* *May 10, 1974*

2 There is not one female comic who was beautiful as a little girl.    Ibid.

3 Diets, like clothes, should be tailored to you.
Ibid.

## 1202. Susan Sherman

(1939– )

1 Analysis. Cross-reference analysis. The age of analysis.
Psychological, philosophical, poetic analysis. Not the
event, but the picturing of the event.

"The Fourth Wall," St. 2, *El Corno Emplumado*    *1966*

## 1203. Joan Silver

(1939?– )

1 Standing erect, like overgrown bookends on either side of Mr. MacAfee's desk, were two Air Force officers.

*Limbo*, Ch. 1, with Linda Gottlieb
*1972*

2 Just as war bound together the men under fire, Mary Kaye thought, it united the women left behind back home.    Ibid., Ch. 5

3 The mother of an eighteen-year-old boy who had had to secure his mother's consent for enlisting in the Army, she now cried at the slightest provocation. "How could I tell him not to go?" she once asked Fay Clausen, the tears brimming in her eyes. "He always loved guns—from the time he was just a little boy he would play with toy guns, BB guns—you know, pretended he was in the marines and things. I once got him that big illustrated history of the Second World War—it cost seventeen dollars—from American Heritage, and he read it over and over again."    Ibid., Ch. 8

4 Red Fortner felt an unaccustomed clutch in his throat. Those savages over there! We ought to bomb the hell out of them, blast them from the face of the earth! He wished some of his dove colleagues at the office could hear this girl, so young, so pretty, so brave, without even a father for her child! They'd change their tune all right.    Ibid., Ch. 22

## 1204. Naomi Weisstein

(1939– )

1 . . . there isn't the tiniest shred of evidence that . . . fantasies of servitude and childish dependence have anything to do with woman's true potential. . . .

Address, " 'Kinder, Kuche, Kirche' as
Scientific Law: Psychology Constructs
the Female," American Studies
Association, California
*October 26, 1968*

2 To summarize: the first reason for psychology's failure to understand what people are and how they act is that clinicians and psychiatrists, who are generally the theoreticians on these matters, have essentially made up myths without any evidence to support these myths; the second reason for psychology's failure is that personality theory has looked for inner traits when it should have been looking at social context.
Ibid.

3 . . . in order to understand why people do what they do, and certainly in order to change what people do, psychologists must turn away from the theory of the causal nature of the inner dynamic and look at the social context within which individuals live.      Ibid.

4 Until psychologists realize that it is they who are limiting discovery of human potential . . . by their assumption that people move in a context-free ether, with only their innate dispositions and their individual traits determining what they will do, then psychology will have nothing of substance to offer in this task.      Ibid.

5 Psychology has nothing to say about what women are really like, what they need and what they want, for the simple reason that psychology does not know. Yet psychologists will hold forth endlessly on the true nature of woman, with dismaying enthusiasm and disquieting certitude.
     "Woman as Nigger," *Psychology Today*      *October, 1969*

6 The problem with insight, sensitivity and intuition is that they tend to confirm our biases. At one time people were convinced of their ability to identify witches. All it required was sensitivity to the workings of the devil. Clinical experience is not the same thing as empirical evidence.      Ibid.

7 . . . a typical minority-group stereotype—woman as nigger—if she knows her place (home), she is really a quite lovable, loving creature, happy and childlike.      Ibid.

8 Except for their genitals, I don't know what immutable differences exist between men and women. Perhaps there are some other unchangeable differences; probably there are a number of irrelevant differences. But it is clear that until social expectations for men and women are equal, until we provide equal respect for both sexes, answers to this question will simply reflect our prejudices.      Ibid.

9 Why have they been telling us women lately that we have no sense of humor—when we are always laughing? . . . And when we're not laughing, we're smiling.
     Introduction to *All She Needs*      by Ellen Levine      *1973*

10 Humor as a weapon in the social arsenal constructed to maintain caste, class, race, and sex inequalities is a very common thing.      Ibid.

## 1205. Louise Bernikow
(1940–   )

1 Pep is what happened in American history before *vigah*, but it only applied to females. Pep was cheerfulness. It mysteriously resided in the Ipana smile.      "Confessions of an Ex-Cheerleader," *Ms.*      *October, 1973*

2 Everytime I say "sure" when I mean "no," every time I smile brightly when I'm exploding with rage, every time I imagine my man's achievement is my own, I know the cheerleader never really died. I feel her shaking her ass inside me and I hear her breathless, girlish voice mutter "T-E-A-M, Yea, Team."      Ibid.

3 The question arises as to whether it is possible *not* to live in the world of men and still to live in the world. The answer arises nearly as quickly that this can only happen if men are not thought of as "the world."
     *The World Split Open*, Introduction      *1974*

## 1206. Isabel do Carmo
(1940–   )

1 The movement [in Spain] must be accompanied by force. . . . There must be an armed insurrection.
     Quoted in *Time*      *October 30, 1975*

2 There can be no halfway solutions, no half measures. That won't work. We must have either pure socialism or we will go back to fascism.      Ibid.

3 In our party, being a woman is no problem. After all, it is a revolutionary party.      Ibid.

## 1207. Phyllis Chesler
(1940–   )

1 At this moment in history only women can (if they will) support the entry or re-entry of women into the human race.
     *Women and Madness*      *1972*

2 There is a double standard of mental health—one for men, another for women—existing among most clinicians. . . . For a woman to be healthy, she must "adjust" to and accept the behavioral norms for her sex—passivity, acquiescence, self-sacrifice, and lack of ambition—even though these kinds of "loser" behaviors are generally regarded as socially undesirable (i.e., nonmasculine).      Ibid.

3 While [women] live longer than ever before, and longer than men, there is less and less use for them in the only place they have been given—within the family. Many newly useless women are emerging more publicly and visibly into insanity and institutions.      Ibid.

4 In addition, asylum life resembles traditional family treatment of the female adolescent in its official imposition of celibacy and its institutional responses to sexuality and aggression—fear, scorn, and punishment.      Ibid.

## 1208. Frances Fitzgerald
### (1940–    )

1 By intervening in the Vietnamese struggle the United States was attempting to fit its global strategies into a world of hillocks and hamlets, to reduce its majestic concerns for the containment of Communism and the security of the Free World to a dimension where governments rose and fell as a result of arguments between two colonels' wives.
*Fire in the Lake*, Pt. I, Ch. 1      *1972*

2 Americans see history as a straight line and themselves standing at the cutting edge of it as representatives for all mankind. They believe in the future as if it were a religion; they believe that there is nothing they cannot accomplish, that solutions wait somewhere for all problems, like brides.      Ibid.

3 In a sense, the design of the Confucian world resembled that of a Japanese garden where every rock, opaque and indifferent in itself, takes on significance from its relation to the surrounding objects.      Ibid.

4 For most Americans, Southeast Asia came to look like the most complicated place in the world. And naturally enough, for the American official effort to fit the new evidence into the old official assumptions was something like the effort of the seventeenth-century astronomers to fit their observations of the planets into the Ptolemaic theory of the universe.      Ibid., Ch. 2

5 The Americans began by underestimating the Vietnamese guerrillas, but in the end they made them larger than life. During the invasion of Cambodia in 1970, American officials spoke of plans to capture the enemy's command headquarters for the south as if there existed a reverse Pentagon in the jungle. . . . Paradoxically, the exaggeration diminished them, for in the dimension of mythology all things are fabulous and unaccountable. By turning their enemy into a mirror image of themselves, the Americans obscured the nature of the Vietnamese accomplishment.      Ibid., Ch. 4

6 Quite consciously, Ho Chi Minh forswore the grand patriarchal tradition of the Confucian emperors. Consciously he created an "image" of himself as "Uncle Ho"—the gentle, bachelor relative who has only disinterested affection for the children who are *not* his own sons. As a warrior and a politician he acted ruthlessly upon occasion, but in public and as head of state he took pains to promote that family feeling which Vietnamese have often had for their leaders, and which he felt was the proper relationship between the people and their government.      Ibid.

7 . . . [Lyndon B.] Johnson condemned his officials who worked on Vietnam to the excruciating mental task of holding reality and the official version of reality together as they moved farther and farther apart.
     Ibid., Pt. II, Ch. 13

8 . . . the Americans were once again embarked upon a heroic and (for themselves) almost painless conquest of an inferior race. . . . [They] were white men in Asia, and they could not conceive that they might fail in their enterprise, could not conceive that they could be morally wrong.      Ibid.

9 . . . the American government did not want to face the consequences of peace. It was, after all, one thing to wish for an end to the war and quite another to confront the issues upon which the war had begun. President Johnson had wanted to end the war; so, too, had President Kennedy. But to end the war and not to lose it: the distinction was crucial, and particularly crucial after all the American lives that had been spent and all the political rhetoric expended.      Ibid., Pt. III, Ch. 17

10 Personally, socially, politically, the disorder of the cities is a highly unstable condition—a vacuum that craves the oxygen of organized society. The Americans might force the Vietnamese to accept the disorder for years, but behind the dam of American troops and American money the pressure is building towards one of those sudden historical shifts when "individualism" and its attendant corruption gives way to the discipline of the revolutionary community.      Ibid.

## 1209. Judy Grahn
### (1940–    )

1 a woman is talking to death. . . .
     "A Woman Is Talking to Death"
     *1974*

2 . . . I looked into the mirror and nobody was there to testify.
     Ibid.

## 1210. Joan Haggerty

(1940–    )

1 It was the novelty of the attraction that capti-
vated her as much as the woman herself.
*Daughters of the Moon*     *1971*

2 Afterwards, you know, afterwards, I often feel
like being fucked by a man too. . . . You *tune*
me, d'you see, and then I want a man to
counter me, but we together, we just keep
traveling to strung out space. We can't comfort
each other.     Ibid.

## 1211. Molly Haskell

(1940–    )

1 One of the definitions of the loss of innocence
is perhaps the fragmenting of that united self
—a split that is different, and emblematic, not
only for each sex, but also for each era.
*From Reverence to Rape*     *1973*

2 . . . the propaganda arm of the American
Dream machine, Hollywood. . . .     Ibid.

3 If there has been a falling off in feminine eroticism on the screen, it is from the *loss* of humor,
or that aspect of humor that gives distance and
perspective, rather than from an excess of it.
    Ibid.

4 But one of the attributes of love, like art, is
to bring harmony and order out of chaos, to
introduce meaning and affect where before
there was none, to give rhythmic variations,
highs and lows to a landscape that was pre-
viously flat.     Ibid.

5 . . . Chaplin and Keaton developed wit and
ingenuity the way other men develop muscles.
    Ibid.

6 The mammary fixation is the most infantile—
and most American—of the sex fetishes. . . .
    Ibid.

7 Our sexual emancipators and evangelists sometimes miss half of the truth: that if puritanism
is the source of our greatest hypocrisies and
most crippling illusions it is, as the primal
anxiety whose therapy is civilization itself, the
source of much, perhaps most, of our achievement.     Ibid.

8 There have been very few heroines in literature
who defined their lives morally rather than
romantically and likewise but a handful in
film. . . .     Ibid.

9 Politics remains the most heavily—and jealously
—masculine area. . . .     Ibid.

10 The idea that acting is quintessentially "feminine" carries with it a barely perceptible sneer,
a suggestion that it is not the noblest or most
dignified of professions. Acting is role-playing,
role-playing is lying, and lying is a woman's
game.     Ibid.

11 . . . her [Marilyn Monroe's] suicide, as suicides
do, casts a retrospective light on her life. Her
"ending" gives her a beginning and middle,
turns her into a work of art with a message
and a meaning.     Ibid.

12 We have ample evidence of the fakery that
went into creating the stars' facades, of the
misery that went on behind these, and of the
tyranny of studio despots who insisted on the
image at the expense of the human being underneath. All of which inevitably raises the question whether it is possible to be both a star
and a human being. If it isn't, how many would
have traded stardom for pale humanity?
    Ibid.

## 1212. Arlie Hochschild

(1940–    )

1 It has become a sad commonplace to associate
being old with being alone. We call isolation a
punishment for the prisoner, but perhaps a
majority of American old people are in some
degree isolated or soon will be.
"Communal Living in Old Age," *The
Future of the Family*, Louise Kapp
Howe, ed.     *1972*

2 . . . the decline of the extended family creates
the need for a new social shelter, another pool
of friendships, another bond with society apart
from family.     Ibid.

## 1213. Juliet Mitchell

(1940–    )

1 Socialism should properly mean not the abolition of the family, but the diversification of
the socially acknowledged relationships which
are today forcibly and rigidly compressed. This
would mean a plural . . . range of institutions
which matched the free invention and variety
of men and women.
"Women—The Longest Revolution,"
*New Left Review*
*November/December, 1966*

2 Circumstantial accounts of the future are ideal-
istic and, worse, static.     Ibid.

3 A fixed image of the future is in the worst
sense ahistorical. . . .     Ibid.

4 Anatomy may, at its point of hypothetical normality, give us two opposite but equal sexes (with the atrophied sex organs of the other present in each), but Freudian psychoanalytic theory does not.
> "On Freud and the Distinction Between the Sexes," *Women and Analysis*, Jean Strouse, ed.      *1974*

5 It seems to me that in Freud's psychoanalytical schema, here, as elsewhere, we have at least the beginnings of an analysis of the way in which a patriarchal society bequeaths its structures to each of us . . . and which, unless patriarchy is demolished, we will pass on willy-nilly to our children and our children's children. Individual experimentation with communes and so forth can do no more than register protest. . . . Present or absent, "the father" always has his place.      Ibid.

## 1214. Valerie Solanis
### (1940–     )

1 Life in this society being, at best, an utter bore and no aspect of society being at all relevant to women, there remains to civic-minded, responsible, thrill-seeking females only to overthrow the government, eliminate the money system, institute complete automation and destroy the male sex.      SCUM Manifesto*
> *1967–1968*

2 Dropping out gives control to those few who don't drop out; dropping out is exactly what the establishment leaders want; it plays into the hands of the enemy; it strengthens the system instead of undermining it, since it is based entirely on non-participation, passivity, apathy and non-involvement. . . .      Ibid.

3 To be sure he's a "Man," the male must see to it that the female be clearly a "Woman," the opposite of a "Man," that is, the female must act like a faggot.      Ibid.

## 1215. Maria Fatima Velho da Costa
### (1940?–     )

Co-author with Maria Isabel Barreno and Maria Teresa Horta. See 1187: 1–5.

---

* SCUM is an acronym for Society for Cutting Up Men.

## 1216. Joan Baez
### (1941–     )

1 Only you and I can help the sun rise each coming morning.
If we don't, it may drench itself out in sorrow.
> "Farewell Angelina"      *1965*

2 Jesus, gold and silver—you have no boots on, and you have no helmet or gun—no briefcase.
Powerful Jesus gold and silver with young, hundred-year-old eyes.
You look around and you know you must have failed somewhere.      Ibid.

3 . . . hypothetical questions get hypothetical answers.      *Daybreak*      *1966*

4 . . . you don't get to choose how you're going to die. Or when. You can only decide how you're going to live. Now.      Ibid.

5 War was going on long before anybody dreamed up Communism. It's just the latest justification for self-righteousness.      Ibid.

6 There's a consensus out that it's OK to kill when your government decides who to kill. If you kill inside the country you get in trouble. If you kill outside the country, right time, right season, latest enemy, you get a medal.      Ibid.

7 If it's natural to kill why do men have to go into training to learn how?      Ibid.

8 That's all nonviolence is—organized love.      Ibid.

9 "Don't you believe in self-defense?"
"No, that's how the Mafia got started."      Ibid.

10 The point of nonviolence is to build a floor, a strong new floor, beneath which we can no longer sink. A platform which stands a few feet above napalm, torture, exploitation, poison gas, A and H bombs, the works. Give man a decent place to stand.      Ibid.

11 By the middle of the twentieth century men had reached a peak of insanity. They grouped together in primitive nation-states, each nation-state condoning organized murder as the way to deal with international differences. . . .      Ibid.

12 Instead of getting hard ourselves and trying to compete, women should try and give their best

qualities to men—bring them softness, teach them how to cry.
Quoted in "Sexism Seen But Not Heard" by Tracy Hotchner, *Los Angeles Times* May 26, 1974

13 And if you're offering me diamonds and rust I've already paid.
"Diamonds and Rust"     1975

14 Unguarded fantasies flying too far
Memories tumbling like sweets from a jar. . . .
"Winds of the Old Days"     1975

## 1217. Bridget Rose Dugdale
(1941–   )

1 For how long you sentence me is of no relevance; I regard it with the contempt it deserves. I am guilty and proudly so if guilty has come to describe one who takes up arms to defend the people of Ireland against the English tyrant.    Quoted in "Englishwoman Trips on Revolutionary Road" by Tom Lambert, *Los Angeles Times* June 26, 1974

## 1218. Nora Ephron
(1941–   )

1 We have lived through the era when happiness was a warm puppy, and the era when happiness was a dry martini, and now we have come to the era when happiness is "knowing what your uterus looks like."
"Vaginal Politics" (December, 1972), *Crazy Salad*    1975

2 . . . I cannot understand any woman's wanting to be the first woman to do anything. . . . It is a devastating burden and I could not take it, could not be a pioneer, a Symbol of Something Greater.
Ibid., "Bernice Gera, First Lady Umpire" (January, 1973)

3 Consciousness-raising is at the very least supposed to bring about an intimacy, but what it seems instead to bring about are the trappings of intimacy, the illusion of intimacy, a semblance of intimacy.
Ibid., "On Consciousness-Raising" (March, 1973)

4 I am not sure that even with a leader, encounter therapy works; without a leader, it is dangerous.     Ibid.

5 I am uncomfortable flirting, it requires a great deal of energy and ego, and I manage to do it only a couple of times a year, and not with interview subjects.    Ibid., "A Star Is Born" (October, 1973)

6 She [Rose Mary Woods] has often said that she was very much impressed by him [Nixon] before she even knew him, because he kept such neat expense accounts.
Ibid., "Rose Mary Woods—The Lady or the Tiger?" (March, 1974)

## 1219. Linda Gottlieb
(1941?–   )

Co-author with Joan Silver. See 1203: 1–4.

## 1220. Barbara Grizzuti Harrison
(1941–   )

1 Profoundly ignorant, we were obliged to invent.
"Talking Dirty," *Ms.* October, 1973

2 Fantasies are more than substitutes for unpleasant reality; they are also dress rehearsals, plans. All acts performed in the world begin in the imagination.     Ibid.

3 To offer the complexities of life as an excuse for not addressing oneself to the simpler, more manageable (trivial) aspects of daily existence is a perversity often indulged in by artists, husbands, intellectuals—and critics of the Women's Movement.    *Unlearning the Lie: Sexism in School*, Introduction    1973

4 True revolutionaries are like God—they create the world in their own image. Our awesome responsibility to ourselves, to our children, and to the future is to create ourselves in the image of goodness, because the future depends on the nobility of our imaginings.    Ibid., Ch. 9

5 Women's propensity to share confidences is universal. We confirm our reality by sharing.
"Secrets Women Tell Each Other," *McCall's*     August, 1975

6 I refuse to believe that trading recipes is silly. Tuna-fish casserole is at least as real as corporate stock.     Ibid.

7 . . . to have a crisis, and act upon it, is one thing. To dwell in perpetual crisis is another.     Ibid.

8 Kindness and intelligence don't always deliver us from the pitfalls and traps: there are always failures of love, of will, of imagination. There is no way to take the danger out of human relationships.     Ibid.

## 1221. Marie Herbert

(1941–     )

1 The Eskimos described everyone other than themselves as Kasdlunas. They called themselves the Inuit—which simply means "the people." For centuries, since they never saw anyone else, they believed they were the only human beings in the world.
*The Snow People*, Ch. 5     1973

2 Unlike children in other countries, the Eskimos played no games of war. They played with imaginary rifles and harpoons, but these were never directed against people but against the formidable beasts that haunted the vast wastes of their land.          Ibid.

## 1222. Shirbey Johnson

(1941–     )

1 . . . women are carrying a new attitude. They've cast aside the old stereotypes. They don't believe you have to be ugly or have big muscles to play sports.
Quoted in "Women in Sports: The Movement Is Real," *Los Angeles Times*     April 23, 1974

2 As coaches and facilities are slowly upgraded, as girls get interested at earlier ages, they become integrated into the sports system more naturally.          Ibid.

## 1223. Carole King

(1941–     )

1 When my soul was in the lost-and-found
You came along to claim it.
"A Natural Woman"     1967

2 You've got to get up every morning with a smile on your face
And show the world all the love in your heart
Then people gonna treat you better
You're gonna find, yes you will
That you're beautiful as you feel.
"Beautiful"     1971

3 Doesn't anybody stay in one place any more?
"So Far Away"     1971

4 My life has been a tapestry of rich and royal hue.
An everlasting vision of the everchanging view.
"Tapestry"     1971

5 Winter, spring, summer or fall
All you have to do is call
And I'll be there,
You've got a friend.
"You've Got a Friend"     1971

## 1224. Robin Morgan

(1941–     )

1 . . . it isn't until you begin to fight in your own cause that you (a) become really committed to winning, and (b) become a genuine ally of other people struggling for their freedom.
*Sisterhood Is Powerful*, Introduction     1970

2 . . . although every organized patriarchal religion works overtime to contribute its own brand of mysogyny to the myth of woman-hate, woman-fear, and woman-evil, the Roman Catholic Church also carries the immense power of very directly affecting women's lives everywhere by its stand against birth control and abortion, and by its use of skillful and wealthy lobbies to prevent legislative change. It is an obscenity—an all-male hierarchy, celibate or not, that presumes to rule on the lives and bodies of millions of women.          Ibid.

3 There's something contagious about demanding freedom.          Ibid.

4 Anthropologists continue to turn up examples which prove that competitive, aggressive, warlike cultures are those in which sexual stereotypes arc most polarized, while those social structures allowing for an overlap of roles and functions between men and women (in tasks, childrearing, decision-making, etc.) tend to be collectivist, cooperative and peaceful.          Ibid.

5     poetry can be quite dangerous propaganda,
especially since all worthwhile propaganda
ought to move its readers like a poem.
Graffiti do that; so do some songs,
and rarely, poems on a page.
Ibid., "Letter to a Sister Underground"

6          the Conquerors.
They're always watching,
invisibly electroded in our brains,
to be certain we implode our rage against each other
and not explode it against them.
Ibid.

7 Don't accept rides from strange men,
and remember that all men are strange as hell.
Ibid.

8 And I will speak less and less to you
And more and more in crazy gibberish you cannot understand:
witches' incantations, poetry, old women's mutterings. . . .
"Monster," *Monster*    1972

9 Some have named this space where we are rooted
a place of death.
We fix them with our callous eyes
and call it, rather, a terrain of resurrection.
Ibid., "Easter Island, I: Embarcation"

10 Meanwhile, for now, this must suffice:
that murder and resurrection are the levers of change,
that creation and complexity are one,
that miracle is contradiction.
Ibid., "II: Arrival"

11 All the secretaries hunch at their IBM's,
snickering at keys.
What they know could bring down the government.
"On the Watergate Women," St. 7    1974

12 This quality of grief
could bring down
mankind.
Ibid., St. 20

## 1225. Gail Parent
(1941?– )

1 Do you want to live in a world where a man lies about calories?
"The Facts," *Sheila Levine Is Dead and Living in New York*    1972

2 Don't we realize we're a business, we single girls are? There are magazines for us, special departments in stores for us. Every building that goes up in Manhattan has more than fifty percent efficiency apartments . . . for the one million girls who have very little use for them.
Ibid., "On Jobs and Apartments"

3 *Fact*: Girls who are having a good sex thing stay in New York. The rest want to spend their summer vacations in Europe.
Ibid., "Europe"

4 What happened to the good old days of homemade ice cream and Trojans? . . . When did it become the woman's chore?
Ibid., "The Second Year"

5 . . . volleyball is a Jewish sport. It's fun, and nobody can get hurt.    Ibid., "Fire Island"

6 Thank you, Agatha, for the lovely bracelet, but I still haven't changed my mind. I have no desire to touch you in places that I already own. Sincerely, Sheila Levine."
Ibid., "Enough Already"

7 Do you realize the planning that goes into a death? Probably even more than goes into a marriage. This, after all, really is for eternity.
Ibid.

8 Actually, I have only two things to worry about now: afterlife and reincarnation.
Ibid., "The End"

## 1226. Judith Rascoe
(1941– )

1 "There are more important rights than the so-called right to know. That is not the right that is being violated nowadays. People have the right to know *something*. They have the right to know that something is being done. That is more important than the right to know. They have the right to know how long they will have to wait until something is done. That is more important than the right to know. I know you would rather know that I am doing something than know what I am doing."
"Evening's Down Under," *Yours and Mine*    1973

2 . . . the grandmother opens the envelope with the letter-opener that Helen's first husband gave her and finds a colored photograph of Helen's second husband and his new wife, Myrna, surrounded by Myrna's children from her first marriage: "Season's Greetings from the Hannibals!"
Ibid., "Yours and Mine"

## 1227. Helen Reddy
(1941– )

1 I am Woman, hear me roar
In numbers too big to ignore,
And I know too much
To go back and pretend.
"I Am Woman"    1972

2 But I'm still an embryo
With a long, long way to go.
Ibid.

3 Yes, I am wise, but it's wisdom full of pain
Yes, I've paid the price, but look how much
   I've gained
I am wise, I am invincible, I am Woman.
                                           Ibid.

4 Women temper men. We have a good influence
on them.              Interview on ABC-TV
                                March 1, 1974

5 Glamour to me is being spotlessly clean and
courteous at all times.
              Quoted in the *Los Angeles Times*
                              April 23, 1974

6 Gentleness is not a quality exclusive to women.
                                           Ibid.

7 The most exciting thing about women's liberation is that this century will be able to take
advantage of talent and potential genius that
have been wasted because of taboos.     Ibid.

## 1228. Buffy Sainte-Marie
### (1941–   )

1 We'll make a space in the lives that we
planned
And here I'll stay until it's time for you to go.
          "Until It's Time for You to Go"
                                        1965

2 And yet where in your history books is the tale
of the genocide basic to this country's birth?
of the preachers who lied?
how the Bill of Rights failed.
          "My Country 'Tis of Thy People
             You're Dying"        1966

3 You have to sniff out joy, keep your nose to
the joy-trail.
          Quoted by Susan Braudy in *Ms.*
                              March, 1975

4 Music has been my playmate, my lover, and
my crying towel. It gets me off like nothing
else.                                      Ibid.

5 The white man wants everyone who isn't white
to think white.                            Ibid.

6 . . . red, I mean, *white* tape. . . .    Ibid.

7 Here the melting pot stands open—if you're
willing to get bleached first.             Ibid.

## 1229. Susan Fromberg Schaeffer
### (1941–   )

1 The sky is reduced,
A narrow blue ribbon banding the lake.
Someone is wrapping things up.
          "Post Mortem," St. 1, *The Witch and
             the Weather Report*       1972

2 What can be wrong
That some days I hug this house
Around me like a shawl, and feel
Each window like a tatter in its skin,
Or worse, bright eyes I must not look through?
          Ibid., "Housewife," St. 1

3 The assistants, relying on the proverbial competition among pre-meds, had assumed there
would be no help among the gladiators, no
risks taken which might raise the curve. It
seemed to Elizabeth that higher mathematics
were useless to them in real life; the students
did not care how high the curve spiraled, provided they were on top, climbing the bean-
stalk, collecting the golden eggs, the medical
acceptances, the gallstones in jars.
          *Falling*, Ch. 1        1973

4 In her drugged state, she felt only a euphoria,
as if all the pain of her life had become a vast
salty water, buoying up, where she floated on
the great blue waves of a vast, melodramatic
sea.                                       Ibid.

5 "Time is only a force; it is neither good nor
evil, only necessary."          Ibid., Ch. 6

## 1230. Judy Wenning
### (1941?–   )

1 Women are freer to express their competitiveness now. Women's competitiveness in the past
has been limited to competing for men, but
those days are over. It's no longer a totally
negative thing.
          Quoted in "Women in Sports: The
             Movement Is Real," *Los Angeles
             Times*      April 23, 1974

## 1231. Ama Ata Aidoo
### (1942–   )

1 "Sissie, men are like that."
"They are selfish."
"No, it's just that women allow them to behave the way they do instead of seizing some
freedom themselves."          *No Sweetness Here*
                                        1970

2 People are worms, and even the God who created them is immensely bored with their antics.
                                           Ibid.

3 . . . tears . . . one of the most potent weapons
in woman's bitchy and inexhaustible arsenal.
                                           Ibid.

4 Eternal death has worked like a warrior rat, with a diabolical sense of duty, to gnaw at my bottom.    "The Message," *Fragment from a Lost Diary and Other Stories,* Naomi Katz and Nancy Milton, eds.
*1973*

5 It's a sad moment, really, when parents first become a bit frightened of their children.
Ibid.

6 "She's a natural for the part of the Great Earth Mother. But I rather resent being viewed in such an agricultural light."    Ibid.

7 The fact is that women . . . have inherited, through bitter centuries, a ruthless sense of self-preservation. . . . That cool, subtle determination to find her security and hang on to it, that all's-fair attitude—not in love, which she discounted, but in war, for it *was* war, the gaining or losing of a kingdom. . . . As it was, victory, conquest, success, call it what you will, was the only virtue. And, of course, the really absurd thing was that nobody would have been more appalled . . . if you had called her a feminist.    Ibid.

## 1232.  Alta
### (1942–    )

1 [Of] course, if you think only terrible people go to prison, that solves that problem.
Untitled Poem    *1972*

2 if you come in me
a child is likely to
come back out.
my name is alta.
i am a woman.
Untitled Poem    *1969–1973*

3 I want to say the words that take you
back there. . . .
there, where
you would like to be again.
Untitled Poem    *1969–1973*

## 1233.  Eve Babitz
### (1942?–    )

1 Culturally, Los Angeles has always been a humid jungle alive with seething L.A. projects that I guess people from other places can't see. It takes a certain kind of innocence to like L.A., anyway. . . . When people are not happy, they fight against L.A. and say it's a "wasteland," and other helpful descriptions.
"Daughters of the Wasteland," *Eve's Hollywood*    *1974*

2 When they reach the age of *fifteen* and their beauty arrives, it's very exciting—like coming into an inheritance. . . .    Ibid., "The Sheik"

3 Packaging is all heaven is.
Ibid., "Rosewood Casket"

4 It's the frames which make some things important and some things forgotten. It's all only frames from which the content rises.    Ibid.

5 We made the smell of Banana in Chemistry once, and I nearly cried because it actually smelled like Bananas and was so simple and so fake.    Ibid., "The Answer"

6 But by the time I'd grown up, I naturally supposed that I'd grown up.
Ibid., "The Academy"

## 1234.  Charlotte Bingham
### (1942–    )

1 I was thinking in bed the other night I must have been out with nearly three hundred men, and I still haven't found a Superman. I don't know what a Superman is, but I know there must be one somewhere.
*Coronet Among the Weeds,* Ch. 1    *1963*

2 I think it must have been quite fun when women were rather mysterious and men didn't know all about them. Look at the end product of women being free. I mean, go on, look at it. It's a poor old career girl sitting in her digs wondering whether she ought to ring up her boyfriend or not.    Ibid.

3 Beatniks were too conventional anyway. I mean they thought they were getting away from it, which is pretty corny. You never do. You just change one thing for another.
Ibid., Ch. 5

4 An isolated outbreak of virginity like Lucinda's is a rash on the face of society. It arouses only pity from the married, and embarrassment from the single.    *Lucinda,* Ch. 1    *1966*

5 "And the only way to avoid playing the game is never to belong to a club, class, set, or trade union. As soon as you do, you're accepting someone else's rules, and as soon as you do that, you start looking down on the other chap with different rules."    Ibid., Ch. 3

6 "I'm glad you understand, Mr. Flint, I'm the last person in the world who would wish to ruin my life by inheriting a fortune. There are quite enough evils in it, without complicating the issues with money."    Ibid., Ch. 8

## 1235. Susan Castro

(1942–     )

1 All children are musicians; all children are artists. Everything they do at this age [two and a-half to five] is new. Play is work for them that constantly extends their limits—it is a most vital creative function. If we can make it rich, the best that is human will flourish within the child.

Quoted in "A New Era in Day Care"
by Mildred Hamilton, *San Francisco
Chronicle      December 19, 1971*

2 I am opposed to the custodial idea of day care. That is a mistake. Enrichment is what we are after.                                              Ibid.

3 The merits of good child care for all who need it or want it are many. The health and well-being of our society depends on it. Those unconvinced are people who have no need of high quality public programs, and who choose not to see the children and parents who suffer from lack of them.

"The Impediments to Public Day Care
Programs in San Francisco"      *1974*

4 At all levels of government, the question is one of priorities and money. The contradiction between what consumers (the bulk of whom are low-income) pay out in taxes and what they receive in goods and services is simply sharper the closer it is to home.                        Ibid.

5 Some of us would like to ignore the institutions and the money problems. I do not see how that is possible. The provision of child care on even a moderate scale requires the use of institutional money, public money. I have no trouble with using public money. Child care and other services [are] exactly what it should be used for.

Address, University of California
Conference on Child Care, Berkeley
*April, 1975*

## 1236. Carol Glassman

(1942?–     )

1 For its recipients, the welfare system carried with it most of the hazards of "housewife and mother," and a few of the rewards. Domination by a husband was replaced with control over every aspect of a woman's life by the welfare agency. Strangers could knock at any hour to pass judgment on her performance as mother, housekeeper, and cook—as well as her fidelity to the welfare board. The welfare board, like

a jealous husband, doesn't want to see any men around who might threaten its place as provider and authority.

"Women and the Welfare System,"
*Sisterhood Is Powerful,*
Robin Morgan, ed.      *1970*

2 Throughout the welfare department one finds the combined view that poverty is due to individual *fault* and that *something is wrong with women who don't have men.*                 Ibid.

3 It is the woman who is ultimately held responsible for pregnancy. While not being allowed to have control over her body, she is nevertheless held responsible for its products.
Ibid.

## 1237. Marilyn Hacker

(1942–     )

1 The child of wonder, deep in his
gut, knows how long forever is,
and, like a haunted anarchist,
hears a repeated order hissed
not to exist.

"Chanson de L'Enfant Prodigue,"
*Presentation Piece      1974*

2 I am in exile in my own land.
Ibid., "Exiles," St. 1

3 Between us on our wide bed we cuddle an
incubus
whom we have filled with voyages. We wake
more apart than before, with open hands.
Ibid., "The Navigators, I," St. 1

4      "Have you done
flaunting your cunt and your pen in her face
when she's not looking? high above your bed,
like a lamppost with eyes, stern as a pay toilet,
she stands, waiting to be told off
and tolled out."
Ibid., "For Elektra," St. 2

5 I wish I had a lover instead of letters
from strangers. The arrival of the mail
is the only time that someone hands
me movement. Nothing real is going to happen
yet, except this dessicated ritual.
Ibid., "Waiting," St. 5

## 1238. Flora Purim

(1942–     )

1 Clear days, feel so good and free
So light as a feather can be. . . .
"Light as a Feather"      *1973*

## 1239. Sally Quinn

(1942?– )

1 Washington is . . . a company town. Most of the interesting people in Washington either work for the government or write about it.
*We're Going to Make You a Star*
*1975*

2 . . . there has been such a mythology built up around the supposed glamour of television life that it's hard for the average person to imagine turning down anything on TV.     Ibid.

## 1240. Marjorie Rosen

(1942– )

1 Does art reflect life? In movies, yes. Because more than any other art form, films have been a mirror held up to society's porous face.
*Popcorn Venus*, Preface    *1973*

2 Movies have always been a form of popular culture that altered the way women looked at the world and reflected how men intended to keep it.     Ibid.

3 Which is strongest—the reality out of which the illusion is created, the celluloid illusion itself, or the need for illusion? Do we hold the mirror up and dive in? And if we do, what are the consequences? And what are the responsibilities of the illusion makers?    Ibid., Pt. I, Ch. 2

4 Women were the sacrificial lambs of the Depression, but amid the collective pain of the nation's empty bellies, they scarcely felt the knife.     Ibid., Pt. III, Ch. 8

5 It's unfortunate that Hollywood could not visualize a woman of mental acumen unless she was fixing up a mess her man/boss had made, covering a scoop to prove herself to a man, or deftly forging a life of dishonesty.   Ibid.

6 Hollywood expediently ignored reality.    Ibid.

7 If proof were needed of the power of woman's film image on women in life, the number of platinum heads tells the story.    Ibid., Ch. 9

8 Studios, purporting to ease the anguish of Depression reality, transformed movies into the politics of fantasy, the great black-and-white opiate of the masses.     Ibid.

9 On December 7, 1941, the Japanese bombed hell out of Pearl Harbor. Johnny got his gun. America mobilized. And social roles shifted with a speed that would have sent Wonder Woman into paroxysms of power pride.
Ibid., Pt. IV, Ch. 12

10 The forties, since dubbed the era of "women's pictures." . . . Women, neither as bored, listless, nor depressed as they had been a decade earlier, were not as malleable either; hence, where the screen had not long before created a reality for them, now the females created their own. The Hollywood product mirrored—and altered—it.     Ibid.

11 Women's films [in the fifties] became "how-to's" on catching and keeping a man. Veneer. Appearance. Sex Appeal. Hollywood descended into mammary madness.
Ibid., Pt. V, Ch. 17

12 Still, we chiefly remember the fifties, not for the horror of civil defense drills or witchhunts, but for kitschy fads like hoola hoops and poodle cuts and crinolines. For Lucy and Miltie and Howdy and Kukla. . . . One of the few constants during the decade was the direction women were heading: backward.    Ibid.

13 Sex, drugs, rapping, a passion for total independence to "do their thing" forced renunciation of traditional values—the popular artifice of clothing, purchasing power, education, employment. Looking "natural," they created costumes out of odds and ends and nodded off in the name of peace and love. They were flower children.     Ibid., Pt. VI, Ch. 21

14 Once upon a time sex was romance. . . . Today, however, to be clinical is to be in.
Ibid., Ch. 22

15 It is ironic that sixties' and seventies' women have seized on a more productive lifestyle than ever before, but the [film] industry has turned its back on reflecting it in any constructive or analytical way.     Ibid.

## 1241. Susan C. Ross

·(1942– )

1 The court will even make up or accept a spurious purpose for the law in order to justify differential treatment.
*The Rights of Women*, Ch. 1    *1973*

2 No one can ever be sure how courts will interpret any new law or amendment.    Ibid.

3 The brutal fact is that convicted women . . . have not yet won the right to equal treatment in the criminal and juvenile justice system.
Ibid., Ch. 5

4 . . . alimony is one way of compensating women for those financial disabilities aggravated, or caused, by marriage: unequal educational opportunities; unequal employment op-

portunities; and an unequal division of family responsibilities, with no compensation for the spouse who works in the home. . . . Thus, women should not be cowed into believing that to ask for alimony is to be unliberated, or that their husbands provide alimony out of the largesse of their noble hearts.    *Ibid., Ch. 7*

5 For many persons, law appears to be black magic—an obscure domain that can be fathomed only by the professional initiated into its mysteries.    *Ibid., Ch. 10*

6 The concept of *enforcing* a right gives meaning to the concept of the right itself.    *Ibid.*

7 Law then is not a preordained set of doctrines, applied rigidly and unswervingly in every situation. Rather, law is molded from the arguments and decisions of thousands of persons. It is very much a human process, a game of trying to convince others . . . that your view of what the law requires is correct.    *Ibid.*

## 1242. Sally E. Shaywitz
(1942– )

1 . . . just as breast milk cannot be duplicated, neither can a mother.
"Catch 22 for Mothers," *The New York Times Magazine March 4, 1973*

2 It is misleading and unfair to imply that an intelligent woman must "rise above" her maternal instincts and return to work when many intelligent, sensitive women have found that the reverse is better for them.    *Ibid.*

3 To be somebody, a woman does not have to be more like a man, but has to be more of a woman.    *Ibid.*

## 1243. Barbra Streisand
(1942– )

1 Success to me is having ten honeydew melons and eating only the top half of each one.
*Quoted in Life September 20, 1963*

## 1244. Charlotte Bonny Cohen
(1943– )

1 For the Chinese Communists, ideology is always ahead of practice.
"Chung-kuo Fu Nu (Women of China)," *Sisterhood Is Powerful*, Robin Morgan, ed.    *1970*

2 There is a great difference between the top and the bottom of the Chinese power pyramid.    *Ibid.*

3 The commune was a sudden attempt to overcome past failures. For women this meant resolving the contradiction between the desire to work and the necessity of being a housewife.    *Ibid.*

4 China is not our model. . . . But Mao and the Chinese Communists do show us that society is changed by changing people's daily lives. Working side by side with men partially liberates women. Freedom—however you want it —comes from new ways of living together.    *Ibid.*

## 1245. Nikki Giovanni
(1943– )

1 Why, LBJ has made it
quite clear to me
He doesn't give a
Good goddamn what I think
(else why would he continue to *masterbate* in public?)
"A Historical Footnote to Consider Only When All Else Fails," St. 2, *Black Feeling/Black Talk/Black Judgement   1970*

2 A nigger can die
We ain't got to prove we can die
We got to prove we can kill
*Ibid.*, "The True Import of Present Dialogue, Black vs. Negro"

3 But we can't be Black
And not be crazy
*Ibid.*, "A Short Essay of Affirmation Explaining Why," St. 7

4     But on the other hand the whole point
of points is pointless when its boiled all the way down
to the least common denominator. But I was never one
to deal with fractions when there are so many wholes
that cannot be dissected—at least these poor hands
lack both skill and tool and perhaps this poor heart
lacks even the inclination to try because emotion is
of itself a wasteful thing because it lacks the power
to fulfill itself.
*Ibid.*, "Letter to a Bourgeois Friend Whom Once I Loved (And Maybe Still Do If Love Is Valid)"

5 Mistakes are a fact of life
It is the response to error that counts
Ibid., "Of Liberation," St. 16

6 There is a new game I must tell you of
It's called Catch The Leader Lying
(And knowing your sense of the absurd
you will enjoy this)
Ibid., "Poem for Black Boys," St. 5

7 And you will understand all too soon
That you, my children of battle, are your heroes
You must invent your own games and teach us
old ones
how to play
Ibid., St. 8

8 His headstone said
FREE AT LAST, FREE AT LAST
But death is a slave's freedom
We seek the freedom of free men
And the construction of a world
Where Martin Luther King could have lived
and preached non-violence
Ibid., "The Funeral of
Martin Luther King, Jr."

9 In the name of peace
They waged the wars
ain't they got no shame
Ibid., "The Great Pax Whitie," St. 3

10 and nothing is worse
than a
dream deferred
Ibid., "From a Logical Point of
View," St. 1

11 You could say we've lost our innocence. That's
a little worse than losing the nickel to put in
Sunday school, though not quite as bad as
losing the dime for ice cream afterward.
*Spin a Soft Black Song,*
Introduction     1971

12 You can have Jesus but give me the world. I'll
take it even though it's losing twenty-five percent of its energy every one hundred years or
something ridiculous.
*James Baldwin—Nikki Giovanni:
A Dialogue*     1973

13 I think one of the nicest things that we created
as a generation was just the fact that we could
say, Hey, I don't like white people.     Ibid.

14 Everybody's dead.     Ibid.

15 You have to decide who you are going to smile
at. Job or no job. Future or no future. 'Cause
all those reasons you give me for your actions
don't make sense if I can't enjoy you. I think

men are very different from women. But I think
men build their standards on false rationales.
The question is: What makes a man? The question is: Can you be a man wherever you are
and whatever the circumstances?     Ibid.

## 1246. Susan Griffin

(1943–     )

1 In no state can a man be accused of raping
his wife. How can any man steal what already
belongs to him?     Quoted in *Ramparts*
*September, 1971*

2 "do you know why
we di-
vorced? . . .
We would go to the movies
your father and I."
I nodded at her.
"And I'd come out
being Carol Lombard,
only he refused
to be Humphrey Bogart."
"Grenadine," *Dear Sky*     1973

3 I've been inside institutions,
my family,
kindergarten,
grammar school, high
school, college and then
marriage, waiting
to be
grown up, graduated, & divorced,
but before I
turned around,
here I am
back in as the
jailor, a
mother and a
teacher.
Ibid., "Letter to the Outside"

4 sleep leads to dreaming
waking to imagination and to
imagine what we
could be, o,
what we could be.
Ibid., "To Gather Ourselves"

*   *   *

5 because tiredness at least
you
have always been
faithful.
"Tiredness Cycle"

## 1247. Erica Jong

(1943?–    )

1 I am thinking of the onion again,
  . . . Not self-righteous
like the proletarian potato, nor a siren like the
  apple. No
show-off like the banana. But a modest, self-
  effacing
vegetable, questioning, introspective, peeling
  itself away,
or merely radiating halos like lake ripples.
    "Fruits and Vegetables,"
    *Fruits and Vegetables    1971*

2 Everyone has talent. What is rare is the courage
to follow the talent to the dark place where it
leads.    "The Artist as Housewife: The
    Housewife as Artist," *The First
    Ms. Reader*, Francine
    Klagsbrun, ed.    *1972*

3 If sex and creativity are often seen by dictators as subversive activities, it's because they
lead to the knowledge that you own your own
body (and with it your own voice), and that's
the most revolutionary insight of all.    Ibid.

4 Perhaps all artists were, in a sense, housewives:
tenders of the earth household.    Ibid.

5 I can live without it all—
love with its blood pump,
sex with its messy hungers,
men with their peacock strutting,
their silly sexual baggage,
their wet tongues in my ear
and their words like little sugar suckers
with sour centers.
    "Becoming a Nun," *About Women*,
    Stephen Berg and S. J. Marks, eds.
    *1973*

6 . . . he never regarded himself as crazy. The
world was.    *Fear of Flying    1973*

7 Q: Why does a Jew always answer a question
with a question?
A: And why should a Jew *not* answer a question with a question?
    Ibid., Ch. 1

8 Growing up female in America. What a liabil-
ity! You grew up with your ears full of cosmetic
ads, love songs, advice columns, whoreoscopes,
Hollywood gossip, and moral dilemmas on the
level of TV soap operas. What litanies the
advertisers of the good life chanted at you!
What curious catechisms!    Ibid.

9 Solitude is un-American.    Ibid.

10 Phallocentric, someone once said of Freud. He
thought the sun revolved around the penis. And
the daughter, too.    Ibid., Ch. 2

11 Throughout all of history, books were written
with sperm, not menstrual blood.    Ibid.

12 Europe is dusty plush,
First-class carriages
with first-class dust.
    Ibid., "The 8:29 to Frankfurt," Ch. 4

13 Men have always detested women's gossip because they suspect the truth: their measure-
ments are being taken and compared.
    Ibid., Ch. 6

14 Gossip is the opiate of the oppressed.    Ibid.

15 There is nothing fiercer than a failed artist.
The energy remains, but, having no outlet, it
implodes in a great black fart of rage which
smokes up all the inner windows of the soul.
    Ibid., Ch. 9

16 Coupling doesn't always have to do with sex.
. . . Two people holding each other up like
flying buttresses. Two people depending on each
other and babying each other and defending
each other against the world outside. Sometimes it was worth all the disadvantages of
marriage just to have that: one friend in an
indifferent world.    Ibid., Ch. 10

17 The idea of the future is our greatest entertainment, amusement, and time-killer. Take it away
and there is only the past—and a windshield
spattered with dead bugs.    Ibid., Ch. 11

18 The cure for starvation in India *and* the cure
for overpopulation—both in one big swallow!
    Ibid., Ch. 17

19 It was easy enough to kill yourself in a fit of
despair. It was easy enough to play the martyr.
It was harder to do nothing. To endure your
life. To wait.    Ibid.

20 Surviving meant being born over and over.
    Ibid., Ch. 19

21 Each month
the blood sheets down
like good red rain.

I am the gardener.
Nothing grows without me.
    "Gardener," *Half-Lives    1973*

22 It is a sad paradox that when male authors
impersonate women, they are said to be dealing
with "cosmic, major concerns"—but when we
impersonate *ourselves* we are said to be writing
"women's fiction" or "women's poetry."
    "Colette: The Difficulty of Loving,"
    *Ms.    April, 1974*

## 1248. Janis Joplin
(1943–1970)

1 They ain't never gonna love you any better,
babe
And they're nee-eever gonna love you ri-ight
So you better dig it right now, right now.
"Kozmic Blues"    *1969*

2 Don't compromise yourself. You are all you've
got.    Quoted in *Reader's Digest*
*April, 1973p*

\* \* \*

3 You got to get it while you can. . . .
"Get It While You Can"

4 Oh Lord won't you buy me a night on the
town?
"Oh Lord Won't You Buy Me a
Mercedes-Benz"

## 1249. Sally Kempton
(1943?–    )

1 I became a feminist as an alternative to be-
coming a masochist.
"Cutting Loose," *Esquire*
*July, 1970*

2 All children are potential victims, dependent
upon the world's good will.    Ibid.

3 Men have laid down the rules and definitions
by which the world is run, and one of the objects of their definitions is woman.    Ibid.

4 Men define intelligence, men define usefulness,
men tell us what is beautiful, men even tell us
what is womanly.    Ibid.

5 Constance Chatterley was a male invention;
Lawrence invented her, I used to think, specifically to make me feel guilty because I didn't
have the right kind of orgasms.    Ibid.

6 Self-love depressed becomes self-loathing.
Ibid.

7 And yet wherever there exists the display of
power there is politics, and in women's relations with men there is a continual transfer of
power, there is, continually, politics.    Ibid.

8 Women are natural guerrillas. Scheming, we
nestle into the enemy's bed, avoiding open warfare, watching the options, playing the odds.
Ibid.

9 . . . women are the true maintenance class.
Society is built upon their acquiescence, and
upon their small and necessary labors.    Ibid.

10 When men imagine a female uprising they
imagine a world in which women rule men as
men have ruled women: their guilt, which is
the guilt of every ruling class, will allow them
to see no middle ground.    Ibid.

11 To discover that something has been wrong is
not necessarily to make it right.    Ibid.

12 It is hard to fight an enemy who has outposts
in your head.    Ibid.

## 1250. Billie Jean King
(1943–    )

1 I've always wanted to equalize things for us.
. . . Women can be great athletes. And I think
we'll find in the next decade that women
athletes will finally get the attention they deserve.    Interview    *September, 1973*

2 I'm not sure if it's the environment in which
you live or if it's innate, because I've always
played better under pressure, even when I was
a youngster.    Quoted by Marlene Jensen in
*The Sportswoman*
*November/December 1973*

3 I think self-awareness is probably the most important thing towards being a champion.
Ibid.

## 1251. Susan Lydon
(1943?–    )

1 The Victorians had needed to repress sexuality
for the success of Western industrialized society; in particular, the total repression of
woman's sexuality was crucial to ensure her
subjugation. So the Victorian, . . . supported by
Freud, passed on to us the heritage of the
double standard.    "The Politics of Orgasm,"
*Ramparts    December, 1968*

2 Our society treats sex as a sport, with its
record-breakers, its judges, its rules and its
spectators.    Ibid.

## 1252. Joni Mitchell
(1943–    )

1 Moons and Junes and Ferris wheels
The dizzy dancing way you feel
As every fairy tale comes real
I've looked at love that way
"Both Sides, Now"    *1969*

2 I've looked at life from both sides now
From up and down, and still somehow
It's life's illusions I recall
I really don't know life at all
                         *Ibid.*

3 Woke up, it was a Chelsea morning, and the
   first thing that I knew
There was milk and toast and honey and a bowl
   of oranges, too
And the sun poured in like butterscotch and
   stuck to all my senses

Oh, won't you stay
We'll put on the day
And we'll talk in present tenses
           "Chelsea Morning"     *1969*

4 if you're feeling contempt
well then you tell it
if you're tired of the silent night
Jesus, well then you yell it
      "Judgement of the Moon and Stars"
                           *1972*

5 Mama thinks she spoilt me
Papa knows somehow he set me free
Mama thinks she spoilt me rotten
She blames herself
But Papa he blesses me
      "Let the Wind Carry Me"     *1972*

6 Golden in time
Cities under sand
Power, ideals and beauty
Fading in everyone's hands.
      "The Hissing of Summer Lawns"
                           *1975*

7 Critics of all express
Judges in black and white
Saying it's wrong
Saying it's right
Compelled by standards
Of some ideals we fight
                         *Ibid.*

8 Sweet bird you are
Brighter than a falling star
All these vain promises on beauty jars
Somewhere in your wings on time
You might be laughing. . . .
           "Sweet Bird"     *1975*

9 We are stardust, we are golden.
           "Woodstock"     *1975*

## 1253. Gail Thain Parker
### (1943–  )

1 . . . Quaker meetings [were] the first enclaves
in American society in which women were en-

couraged to speak out in public . . . [with] the
faith . . . that each individual, regardless of
sex, had to act according to his inner lights. . . .
     *The Oven Birds*, Introduction, Pt. I
                         *1972*

2 Literature was a great factor in the socialization
of women, and without novels (and poems)
which portrayed women on an heroic scale,
whole generations of nascent feminists might be
stunted in their development.       *Ibid.*

3 Sentimentalism restructured the Calvinist model
of salvation, making the capacity to feel, and
above all to weep, in itself evidence of redemption.                      *Ibid.*

4 In the process of getting ahead in the world,
of becoming smart and up-to-date, they have
lost the ability to really feel.     *Ibid.*, Pt. II

5 What this country needs is a *good* impeachment. In itself impeachment is not evil or
divisive, unless it is done cheaply. If it is done
admirably and it tears the country apart, then
the country is so fragile that anything could
tear it apart.      Quoted in "Impeachment?"
         by Claire Safran, *Redbook*
                     *April, 1974*

## 1254. Susan Shnall
### (1943–  )

1 The professed purpose of the United States
military is to maintain the peace, but its
methods toward this goal are destructive and
have resulted in the promotion of suffering
and death of foreign peoples, as well as of its
own.           "Women in the Military,"
          *Sisterhood Is Powerful,*
     Robin Morgan, ed.     *1970*

2 Because I wore a peace symbol, I had to have
an extra interview to determine my suitability
as a member of the military.       *Ibid.*

## 1255. Viva
### (1943–  )

1 I think that he exercised a lot of restraint,
limiting his kicks to the wall and a painting.
I only wish that the heads of governments had
the same instincts.     *The Baby*     *1975*

2 Like marriage, nursing was turning out to be
one of those painful addictions; damned if you
do, damned if you don't.       *Ibid.*

3 If Mother had let us go to bed whenever we
wanted, not forced us to go to church, allowed

us to masturbate, go to bars at night, see any movie we wanted, eat whenever we felt like it, sleep with her and Daddy, then I'm sure we'd now be exactly the way she had hoped us to be.      Ibid.

## 1256. Ingrid Bengis
(1944?–   )

1 No amount of evidence is ever sufficient to compensate for the deviousness with which human beings manage to conceal themselves. . . .
     "Monroe According to Mailer," *Ms.*
     *October, 1973*

2 Imagination has always had powers of resurrection that no science can match.      Ibid.

3 The form that our bodies take, particularly with women, dictates more often than we wish it would the form that a portion of our lives will take.      Ibid.

4 Psychic starvation is a desperate business: one does not wait around for Baked Alaska.
     Ibid.

5 The real trap of fame is its irresistibility.
     Ibid.

6 Once I had abandoned the search for everyone else's truth, I quickly discovered that the job of defining my own truth was far more complex than I had anticipated.
     *Combat in the Erogenous Zone,*
     Introduction      *1973*

7 The real questions are the ones that obtrude upon your consciousness whether you like it or not, the ones that make your mind start vibrating like a jackhammer, the ones that you "come to terms with" only to discover that they are still there. The real questions refuse to be placated. They barge into your life at the times when it seems most important for them to stay away. They are the questions asked most frequently and answered most inadequately, the ones that reveal their true natures slowly, reluctantly, most often against your will.
     Ibid., "Man-Hating"

8 One of these days I'm going to put bandaids across my mouth so that smiling will become less of a reflex in uncomfortable situations.
     Ibid.

9 For me words still possess their primitive, mystical, incantatory healing powers. I am inclined to use them as part of an attempt to make my own reality more real for others, as part of an effort to transcend emotional damage.

For me, words are a form of action, capable of influencing change. Their articulation represents a complete, lived experience.      Ibid.

10 Let me off this idiot merry-go-round. My psyche is not an ideological playground. My inner feelings, at their most genuine, are not ruled by social decree.      Ibid., "Love"

11 When all of the remedies and all of the rhetorical armor have been dropped, the absence of love in our lives is what makes them seem raw and unfinished.      Ibid.

12 What about the fact that everything ever constructed by civilization seems to be a dam against disintegration.      Ibid.

## 1257. Rita Mae Brown
(1944–   )

1 One doesn't get liberated by hiding. One doesn't possess integrity by passing for "white."
     Untitled Essay      *March, 1970*

2 To love without role, without power plays, is revolution.      Ibid.

3 I do not want to be separate from any woman . . . [but] until heterosexuals will treat lesbians as full human beings and fight the enormity of male supremacy with us, I have no option but to be separate from them, just as they have no option but to be separate from men until men begin to change their own sexism.
     Untitled Essay      *May, 1970*

4 I move in the shadow of the great guillotine
That rhythmically does its work
On heads remaining unbowed.
     "The Self Affirms Herself" (1966)
     *The Hand That Cradles the Rock*
     *1971*

5 I've come through a land
You'll never know.
     Ibid., "The Bourgeois Question"
     (1967)

6 An army of lovers shall not fail.
     Ibid., "Sappho's Reply" (1970)

## 1258. Angela Davis
(1944–   )

1 Domestic labor was the only meaningful labor for the slave community.
     "Reflections on the Black Woman's
     Role in the Community of Slaves,"
     *The Black Scholar*
     *December, 1971*

2 In order to function as slave, the black woman had to be annulled as woman, that is, as woman in her historical stance of wardship under the entire male hierarchy. The sheer force of things rendered her equal to her man.
Ibid.

3 Expending indispensable labor for the enrichment of her [the black woman's] oppressor, she could attain a practical awareness of the oppressor's utter dependence on her—for the master needs the slave far more than the slave needs the master.
Ibid.

4 The master subjected her to the most elemental form of terrorism distinctly suited to the female: rape.
Ibid.

5 In fact, the intense levels of resistance historically maintained by black people—and thus the historical function of the Black Liberation Struggle as harbinger of change throughout society—are due in part to the greater *objective* equality between the black man and woman.
Ibid.

6 We, the black women of today, must accept the full weight of a legacy wrought in blood by our mothers in chains. As heirs to a tradition of perseverance and heroic resistance, we must hasten to take our place wherever our people are forging toward freedom.
Ibid.

7 . . . the brother . . . had painted a night sky on the ceiling of his cell, because it had been years since he had seen the moon and stars.
*An Autobiography* 1974

8 When the iron door was opened, sounds peculiar to jails and prisons poured into my ears—the screams, the metallic clanging, officers' keys clinking.
Ibid.

9 Trapped in this wasteland inhabited by the sick, the drugged and their indifferent keepers. . . .
Ibid.

10 But before my thoughts led me further in the direction of self-pity, I brought them to a halt, reminding myself that this was precisely what solitary confinement was supposed to evoke.
Ibid.

11 Jails and prisons are designed to break human beings, to convert the population into specimens in a zoo—obedient to our keepers, but dangerous to each other.
Ibid.

12 I was bewildered and awed by the way in which the vast majority of the jail population had neatly organized itself into generations of families: mothers/wives, fathers/husbands, sons and daughters, even aunts, uncles, grandmothers and grandfathers.
Ibid.

13 Many of them—both the butches and the femmes—had obviously decided to take up homosexuality during their jail terms in order to make that time a little more exciting, in order to forget the squalor and degradation around them.
Ibid.

14 Many people are unaware of the fact that jail and prison are two entirely different institutions. People in prison have already been convicted. Jails are primarily for pretrial confinement, holding places until prisoners are either convicted or found innocent. More than half of the jail population have never been convicted of anything, yet they languish in those cells.
Ibid.

15 Racism, in the first place, is a weapon used by the wealthy to increase the profits they bring in by paying Black workers less for their work.
Ibid.

## 1259. Claudia Dreifus
(1944–    )

1 We spent a winter learning the feminist basics from the textbook of each other's lives. . . .
*Woman's Fate*, Introduction 1973

2 . . . girls enforce the cultural code that men invent. Ibid., "The Adolescent Experience"

## 1260. Marcia Gillespie
(1944–    )

1 We have been looking at it [feminism] warily. Black women need economic equality but it doesn't apply for me to call a black man a male chauvinist pig. Our anger is not at our men. I don't think they have been the enemy.
Quoted in "About Women," *Los Angeles Times* May 12, 1974

## 1261. Julia Phillips
(1944?–    )

1 Here's how I define the role of producer: the producer is there long before the shooting starts, and way after the shooting stops.
Quoted in *American Film Magazine* December, 1975

2 As a director you become the focal point, and if you look tired your crew will feel tired. But I'm not worried about stamina. I've found that women . . . generate more energy than anyone else on a [film] set. And as a producer, I've

had to build up twice as much creative energy because half of it was drained just getting a picture off the ground.      Ibid.

3 It [filmmaking] has to be in your blood because three times a day you ask yourself why are you doing this. Especially when you've done it before and you know up front it's going to be pure torture. But if you love the screenplay, and the director and cast amplify it, then it's magic—and the rewards are fantastic.      Ibid.

## 1262. Arlene Raven

(1944–    )

1 In my view, the content of feminist art, and its deepest meaning, is consciousness: a woman's full awareness of herself as an entity, including her sensations, her emotions, and her thoughts —mind in its broadest sense.
> "Woman's Art: The Development of a Theoretical Perspective," *Womanspace* *February/March, 1973*

2 . . . if art is about consciousness grounded in reality, good art is about high consciousness— a real world view about the real world.
> Ibid.

3 Historical consciousness is in no way separate from self-consciousness. The way in which we think of ourselves has everything to do with how our world sees us and how we can see ourselves successfully acknowledged by that world.      Ibid.

4 The artist who shows us his/her world without this essential sense of optimism is without hope and without power: We can empathize with that art, but it cannot inspire in us the high level of human aspiration that we need to enrich ourselves, to grow, and to change.
> Ibid.

5 Animals which are traditionally referred to as female include the cow, sow, bitch and cat— all derogatory words in our language when they are applied to human beings. English does not use gender extensively, but its linguistic sexism is intact because sexism is intact.
> Ibid.

## 1263. Alice Walker

(1944–    )

1 The sight of a Black nun strikes their sentimentality; and, as I am unalterably rooted in native ground they consider me a work of primitive art, housed in a magical color; the

incarnation of civilized, anti-heathenism, and the fruit of a triumphing idea.
> "The Diary of an African Nun," *Freedomways*      *Summer, 1968*

2 How teach a barren world to dance? It is a contradiction that divides the world.      Ibid.

3 She wants to live for once. But doesn't know quite what that means. Wonders if she has ever done it. If she ever will.
> "Roselily," *In Love and Trouble: Stories of Black Women*      *1973*

4 I wait, beautiful and perfect in every limb, cooking supper as if my life depended on it. Lying unresisting on his bed like a drowned body washed to shore. But he is not happy. For he knows now that I intend to do nothing but say yes until he is completely exhausted.
> Ibid., "Really, *Doesn't* Crime Pay?"

5 A slight, pretty flower that grows on any ground, and flowers pledge no allegiance to banners of any man.
> Ibid., "The Child Who Favored Daughter"

6 They stumbled blindly through their lives: creatures so abused and mutilated in body, so dimmed and confused by pain, that they considered themselves unworthy even of hope . . . exquisite butterflies trapped in an evil honey, toiling away their lives in an era, a century, that did not acknowledge them, except as "the *mule* of the world."
> "In Search of Our Mother's Gardens," *Ms.*      *May, 1974*

7 In search of my mother's garden I found my own.      Ibid.

## 1264. Victoria Billings

(1945–    )

1 Sexual liberation, as a slogan, turns out to be another kind of bondage. For a woman it offers orgasm as her ultimate and major fulfillment; it's better than motherhood.
> "What Is Individuality?," *The Womansbook*      *1974*

2 Whether he admits it or not, a man has been brought up to look at money as a sign of his virility, a symbol of his power, a bigger phallic symbol than a Porsche.
> Ibid., "Getting It Together"

3 The best thing that could happen to motherhood already has. Fewer women are going into it.      Ibid., "Meeting Your Personal Needs"

4 Physicians tend to take women's complaints less seriously so you're more apt to pay for a sympathic smile than a diagnosis. You're also more apt to be tranquilized instead of being treated.    Ibid.

5 Constant togetherness is fine—but only for Siamese twins.    Ibid., "A Love to Believe In"

6 Rape is a culturally fostered means of suppressing women. Legally we say we deplore it, but mythically we romanticize and perpetuate it, and privately we excuse and overlook it. . . .
Ibid., "Sex: We Need Another Revolution"

## 1265. Annie Dillard
### (1945–    )

1 We wake, if we ever wake at all, to mystery, rumors of death, beauty, violence.
*Pilgrim at Tinker Creek*, Ch. 1
1974

2 Every live thing is a survivor on a kind of extended emergency bivouac.    Ibid.

3 Cruelty is a mystery, and the waste of pain.
Ibid.

4 I am an explorer, then, and I am also a stalker, or the instrument of the hunt itself.    Ibid.

5 The world's spiritual geniuses seem to discover universally that the mind's muddy river, this ceaseless flow of trivia and trash, cannot be dammed, and that trying to dam it is a waste of effort that might lead to madness.
Ibid., Ch. 2

6 The secret of seeing is to sail on solar wind. Hone and spread your spirit till you yourself are a sail, whetted, translucent, broadside to the merest puff.    Ibid.

7 It is ironic that the one thing that all religions recognize as separating us from our creator—our very self-consciousness—is also the one thing that divides us from our fellow creatures. It was a bitter birthday present from evolution. . . .    Ibid., Ch. 6

8 No; we have been as usual asking the wrong question. It does not matter a hoot what the mockingbird on the chimney is singing. . . . The real and proper question is: Why is it beautiful?    Ibid., Ch. 7

9 Somewhere, and I can't find where, I read about an Eskimo hunter who asked the local missionary priest, "If I did not know about God and sin, would I go to hell?" "No," said the priest, "not if you did not know." "Then why," asked the Eskimo earnestly, "did you tell me?"    Ibid.

10 I don't know what it is about fecundity that so appalls. I suppose it is the teeming evidence that birth and growth, which we value, are ubiquitous and blind, that life itself is so astonishingly cheap, that nature is as careless as it is bountiful, and that with extravagance goes a crushing waste that will one day include our own cheap lives. . . .    Ibid., Ch. 10

11 The world has signed a pact with the devil; it had to. . . . The terms are clear: if you want to live, you have to die; you cannot have mountains and creeks without space, and space is a beauty married to a blind man. The blind man is Freedom, or Time, and he does not go anywhere without his great dog Death. The world came into being with the signing of the contract.    Ibid.

12 I am a frayed and nibbled survivor in a fallen world and I am getting along. I am aging and eaten and have done my share of eating too.
Ibid., Ch. 13

13 The universe was not made in jest but in solemn incomprehensible earnest. By a power that is unfathomably secret, and holy, and fleet. There is nothing to be done about it, but ignore it, or see. And then you walk fearlessly, eating what you must, growing wherever you can. . . .    Ibid., Ch. 15

## 1266. Shulamith Firestone
### (1945–    )

1 Perhaps it is true that a presentation of only the female side of things . . . is limited. But . . . is it any more limited than the prevailing male view of things, which—when not taken as absolute truth—is at least seen as "serious," relevant and important.
*The Dialectic of Sex*    1970

2 A man is allowed to blaspheme the world because it belongs to him to damn.    Ibid.

3 I submit that women's history has been hushed up for the same reason that black history has been hushed up . . . and that is that a feminist movement poses a direct threat to the establishment. From the beginning it exposed the hypocrisy of the male power structure.
Ibid., Ch. 2

4 I conclude that, contrary to what most historians would have us believe, women's rights were never won. The Women's Rights Movement did not fold because it accomplished its objectives, but because it was defeated. *Seeming* freedoms appear to have been won. Ibid.

5 The bar is the male kingdom. For centuries it was the bastion of male privilege, the gathering place for men away from their women, a place where men could go to freely indulge in The Bull Session . . . a serious political function: the release of the guilty anxiety of the oppressor class. "The Bar as Microcosm," *Voices from Women's Liberation*, Leslie B. Tanner, ed. *1970*

## 1267. Ruth Iskin
### (1945– )

1 In the dealer-critic system, galleries exist primarily for sale purposes and it is the critic's role to promote the art product by establishing its value and providing a justification for its importance.
"A Space of Our Own, Its Meaning and Implications," *Womanspace February/March, 1973*

2 The star system: the focus on the artist and his/her entire career, which was a by-product of the sale orientation developed in the dealer-critic system, replaced the older emphasis on individual paintings and schools of painters, which prevailed in the academy. Ibid.

## 1268. Kathy Kahn
### (1945– )

1 There is still a natural tendency for the people of one class to look down on people who they think are lower class—as if they are less than human. Quoted in "Kathy Kahn: Voice of Poor White Women" by Meridee Merzer, *Viva April, 1974*

2 In places like the textile mills, where superhuman production rates are set, the people have to take speed (amphetamines) in order to keep up production. . . . Virtually every factory in this country is run on speed, grass, or some other kind of upper. Ibid.

3 I do not believe in being paid for organizing . . . because a revolution is a revolution. And nobody—*nobody*—gets paid for making a revolution. Ibid.

## 1269. Paula Nelson
### (1945– )

1 Women's battle for financial equality has barely been joined, much less won. Society still traditionally assigns to woman the role of money-handler rather than money-maker, and our assigned specialty is far more likely to be home economics than financial economics.
*The Joy of Money*, Ch. 1 *1975*

2 The making of money simply is not a sex-linked skill. Women can and are turning it all around. We are discovering for ourselves the challenge —and the joy—of money. Ibid.

3 A good rule to follow here is that a credit card —and I speak from sad experience—should never be used unless you already have the money in the bank or can clearly identify where the money will come from, and when. . . . A credit card is a money tool, *not* a supplement to money. The failure to make this distinction has "supplemented" many a poor soul right into bankruptcy. Ibid., Ch. 4

4 . . . launching your own business is like writing your own personal declaration of independence from the corporate beehive, where you sell bits of your life in forty-hour (or longer) chunks in return for a paycheck. . . . Going into business for yourself, becoming an entrepeneur, is the modern-day equivalent of pioneering on the old frontier. Ibid., Ch. 6

5 Americans want action for their money. They are fascinated by its self-reproducing qualities if it's put to work. . . . Gold-hoarding goes against the American grain; it fits in better with European pessimism than with America's traditional optimism. Ibid., Ch. 15

## 1270. Karin Sheldon
### (1945– )

1 Environment, in all its forms and relations, sustains us. We depend upon it. I truly believe that the fundamental principles of ecology govern our lives, wherever we live, and that we must wake up to this fact or be lost.
Quoted in "Found Women: Defusing the Atomic Establishment" by Anna Mayo, *Ms. October, 1973*

## 1271. Anne Tucker
### (1945– )

1 Society's double behavioral standard for women and for men is, in fact, a more effective deterrent than economic discrimination because

it is more insidious, less tangible. Economic disadvantages involve ascertainable amounts, but the very nature of societal value judgments makes them harder to define, their effects harder to relate.          *The Woman's Eye,*
                              Introduction    *1973*

2 All art requires courage.          Ibid.

3 Exploration, whether of jungles or minds, is considered unfeminine.          Ibid.

4 For centuries men have defined themselves in terms of other men, but women have been defined by and in terms of men. . . . The ubiquitous nature of masculine images of Woman has contributed significantly to the struggles of woman artists because that which is publicly acceptable art does not conform with their own needs and experiences, and their own art does not conform with popular standards.          Ibid.

## 1272.  Candice Bergen
### (1946–      )

1 Hollywood is like Picasso's bathroom.
              Quoted by Sheila Graham in the
      *New York Post*    *February 14, 1967*

2 THE MAN. You've been renovated, my sweet, like an urban renewal project!
                        *The Freezer*    *1968*

3 THE MAN. Can't they realize that mankind was founded on two basic principles? *Religion and Death?* The one motivates the other. *Both* motivate the man!          Ibid.

4 THE MAN. Man has always been under death's dictatorship, always questioned it, always challenged it.          Ibid.

## 1273.  Jacqueline Bisset
### (1946–      )

1 Character contributes to beauty. It fortifies a woman as her youth fades. A mode of conduct, a standard of courage, discipline, fortitude and integrity can do a great deal to make a woman beautiful.
                  Quoted by Lydia Lane in the
      *Los Angeles Times*    *May 16, 1974*

## 1274.  Carter Heyward
### (1946–      )

1 I'm a priest, not a priestess. . . . "Priestess" implies mumbo jumbo and all sorts of pagan goings-on. Those who oppose us would love to call us priestesses. They can call us all the names in the world—it's better than being invisible.          Quoted in "Who's Afraid of Women Priests?" by Malcolm Boyd,
                      *Ms.    December, 1974*

2 It's obvious throughout secular and church history that significant legislation follows only after dramatic action.          Ibid.

## 1275.  Mary McCaslin
### (1946?–      )

1 Bury me out on the lone prairie
Near the mountains I could never see

The speakers, they all gasp to clear their lungs
    for their luncheon speeches
This year's new campaign is save the canyons
    and the beaches
                  "The Dealers"    *1975*

## 1276.  Honor Moore
### (1946–      )

1 I have thought the cancer was in my control. If I decide she will recover, it will go away. . . .
              *Mourning Pictures* (verse play)
                                        *1974*

2 A ring or two.
Her turquoise beads
The green-striped chair
What will she leave me
Except alone. . . .
        Ibid., "What Will She Leave Me?"

## 1277.  Laura Nyro
### (1946–      )

1 And when I die
and when I'm gone
there'll be one child born
and a world to carry on. . . .
              "And When I Die"    *1966*

2 I was born from love
and my poor mother worked the mines
I was raised on the good book Jesus
till I read between the lines. . . .
                  "Stoney End"    *1966*

3 Nothing cures like time and love. . . .
              "Time and Love"    *1970*

4 I've got a lot of patience, baby
And that's a lot of patience to lose.
              "When I Was a Freeport"    *1971*

5 money money money
do you feel like a pawn
in your own world?
you found the system
and you lost the pearl. . . .
         "Money"     *1975*

## 1278. Judee Sill
(1946?–   )

1 The great storm raged and the power kept
    growin',
Dragons rose from the land below
And even now I wonder where I'm goin'
Ever since a long time ago,
I've tried to let my feelin's show.
         "The Phoenix"     *1969*

## 1279. Barbara Smith
(1946–   )

1 Then there was the magazine called LIFE
which promised more about the Deaths.
    "Poem for My Sister (One) Birmingham
    Sunday, 1963," *Southern Voices*
         *August/September, 1974*

## 1280. Bernadette Devlin
(1947–   )

1 To gain that which is worth having, it may be
necessary to lose everything else.
       *The Price of My Soul,*
       Preface     *1969*

## 1281. Melanie
(1947–   )

1 don't hold the sprout against the seed
don't hold this need against me. . . .
    "Gather on a Hill of Wildflowers"
         *1975*

## 1282. Sally Priesand
(1947–   )

1 Clergy are father figures to many women, and
sometimes they are threatened by another
woman accomplishing what they see as strictly
male goals. But I can see them replacing that
feeling with a sense of pride that women can
have that role.    Quoted in *Women at Work*
      by Betty Medsger     *1975*

## 1283. Victoria Bond
(1949–   )

1 The conductor traditionally has been anything
but a mother figure. The conductor is much
more like a general than a mother or teacher.
It's a kind of enforced leadership, the kind of
leadership more likely to be expected of men
than women. A woman conductor, because of
those traditions, must rely completely on being
able to transmit authority purely on the grounds
of her musical ability.
      Quoted in *Women at Work*
      by Betty Medsger     *1975*

## 1284. Gayl Jones
(1949–   )

1 "My great-grandmama told my grandmama the
part she lived through that my grandmama
didn't live through and my grandmama told my
mama what they both lived through and my
mama told me what they all lived through and
we were suppose to pass it down like that from
generation to generation so we'd never forget."
         *Corregidora*     *1975*

2 It was as if the words were helping her, as if
the words repeated again and again could be
a substitute for memory, were somehow more
than the memory.           Ibid.

## 1285. Alicia Bay Laurel
(1949–   )

1 When we depend less on industrially produced
consumer goods, we can live in quiet places.
Our bodies become vigorous; we discover the
serenity of living with the rhythms of the
earth. We cease oppressing one another.
      *Living on the Earth*     *1971*

2 Let's all go out into the sunshine, take off our
clothes, dance and sing and make love and get
enlightened.
      Quoted in *Contemporary Authors*
         *1974*

## 1286. Holly Near
(1949–   )

1 First he'll want to talk about it
Then he'll want to fight
Then he'll want to make love to me all night
My man's been laid off got, trouble, got
    trouble. . . .
         "Laid Off"     *1973*

2 Get off me baby, get off and leave me alone
I'm lonely when you're gone but I'm lonelier
    when you're home. . . .
                    "Get Off Me Baby"    1973

3 Well if you think traveling three is a drag
Pack up loner
I've got my own bag full of dreams for this
    little child of wonder
And you can only stay if you start to under-
    stand. . . .
                    "Started Out Fine"    1973

## 1287. Theodora Van Runkle
(1949?–    )

1 Death is very sophisticated. It's like a Noel
Coward comedy. You light a cigarette and wait
for it in the library.
            Quoted in "People You Should Know"
            by Mary Reinholz, Viva    April, 1974

2 Just at a time when women are becoming free
and buoyant, and developing sexually and in a
feeling way, they're dressing to look like huge,
tottering objects, like courtesans during the
Renaissance period.                    Ibid.

## 1288. Gigliola Pierobon
(1950?–    )

1 It is horrible to listen to men in black togas
[in court] having discussions about your morals,
your cystitis, your feelings, your womb, the
way you straddled your legs.
                "Gazette News: Abortion in
                Italy," Ms.    October, 1973

## 1289. Arianna Stassinopoulos
(1950–    )

1 Whether we regard the Women's Liberation
movement as a serious threat, a passing convulsion, or a fashionable idiocy, it is a movement that mounts an attack on practically
everything that women value today and intro-
duces the language and sentiments of political
confrontation into the area of personal relationships. . . .
                "The Emancipated Woman," The
                Female Woman    1973

2 It would be futile to attempt to fit women into
a masculine pattern of attitudes, skills and
abilities and disastrous to force them to suppress their specifically female characteristics
and abilities by keeping up the pretense that
there are no differences between the sexes.
                Ibid., "The Natural Woman"

3 Emancipation means equal status for different
roles. . . . Liberation . . . is a demand for the
abolition of wife and mother, the dissolution
of the family. . . .
                Ibid., "The Family Woman"

4 Our current obsession with creativity is the
result of our continued striving for immortality
in an era when most people no longer believe
in an after-life.
                Ibid., "The Working Woman"

5 Not only is it harder to be a man, it is also
harder to become one.
                Ibid., "The Male Man"

6 Liberation is an evershifting horizon, a total
ideology that can never fulfill its promises.
. . . It has the therapeutic quality of providing
emotionally charged rituals of solidarity in
hatred—it is the amphetamine of its believers.
                Ibid., "The Liberated Woman? . . .
                and Her Liberators"

## 1290. Barbara Holland
(1951–    )

1 Speech that is but percussion under melody
is bones to music. I do not understand
a word you say, and yet you tell me in your
    rhythms,
your harmonies, and richness of their structure.
                "Translation," St. 1,
                The East Side Scene,
                Allen De Loach, ed.    1968

## 1291. Janis Ian
(1951–    )

1    How do you do
    would you like
    to be friends?
No I just want a bed for the night
Someone to tell me they care.
You can fake it, that's all right
In the morning I won't be here.
                "The Come On"    1974

## 1292. Phoebe Snow
(1951–    )

1 Sometimes this face looks so funny
That I hide it behind a book
Sometimes this face has so much class
That I have to sneak a second look.
                "Either or Both"    1973

2 It must be Sunday
Everybody's telling the truth. . . .
                "It Must Be Sunday"    1973

## 1293. Denise M. Boudrot
(1952–    )

1 I don't ride to beat the boys, just to win.
                Quoted in Women at Work
                by Betty Medsger    1975

## 1294. Isidora Aguirre

1 CAROLINA. Besides, when I say "nothing," what I mean is: everything.
> *Express for Santiago*     1960

2 CARLOS. Remember: don't start conversations with strangers on a trip. No way of getting rid of them later!     Ibid.

3 CAROLINA. It's awful to be the wife of a lawyer.
> Ibid.

## 1295. Dora Alonso

1 The shadow, the color of the man, and the kind of living, all are the same; black in one hundred tones, either so light as to be cinnamon flesh or as dark as black coffee, it carries the sign of subjection.
> "Time Gone By," *Fragment from a Lost Diary and Other Stories*, Naomi Katz and Nancy Milton, eds.     1973

2 Life goes on, buried in pain for those who wait; swollen with haughtiness and arrogance for those who fear.     Ibid.

3 There's no higher right than might, and I am mighty.     Ibid.

4 Her body broke down like the collapse of forked poles which could no longer bear the weight of an entire life dedicated to obedience, without a single pillar of rebellion to hold up the structure.     Ibid.

## 1296. Geneviève Antoine-Dariaux

1 [Habit]
is the chloroform of love.
is the cement that unites married couples.
is getting stuck in the mud of daily routine.
is the fog that masks the most beautiful scenery.
is the end of everything.
> "The Men in Your Life"     1968

2 A stranger loses half his charm the day he is no longer a stranger.     Ibid.

3 She began to think about her friends' happy tranquillity, of their affection, of their two non-problem children: the boy wasn't on drugs; the girl wasn't a nymphomaniac; they weren't even quarrelsome. The kind of children nobody had any more.     *The Fall Collection*, Ch. 1
> 1973

4 Make ready-to-wear clothing like everybody else? Of course, after all, there is not much difference between the two. The creation is the same. It becomes haute couture if it's made to order with three fittings, or boutique if it's made in advance in standard sizes.     Ibid.

5 Elegance has become so rare today that a well-cut black jersey cape makes heads turn. It isn't chic to be chic any more!
> Ibid., Ch. 3

6 The general rule should be respected without favoritism in business and there is no reason why the best workers should earn ten centimes more than the less good ones. Workers shouldn't depend on one boss' good will any more than they should be the victims of the ill will of the bad one.     Ibid., Ch. 7

## 1297. Frances M. Beal

1 The advertising media in this country continuously informs the American male of his need for indispensable signs of his virility. . . .
> "Double Jeopardy: To Be Black and Female" (1969), *Sisterhood Is Powerful*, Robin Morgan, ed.
> 1970

2 Let me state here and now that the black woman in America can justly be described as a "slave of a slave."     Ibid.

3 Men may be cruelly exploited and subjected to all sorts of dehumanizing tactics on the part of the ruling class, but they have someone who is below them—at least they're not women.
> Ibid.

4 Any white women's group that does not have an anti-imperialist and antiracist ideology has absolutely nothing in common with the black woman's struggle.     Ibid.

5 To die for the revolution is a one-shot deal; to live for the revolution means taking on the more difficult commitment of changing our day-to-day life patterns.     Ibid.

## 1298. Christine Billson

1 I am admired because I do things well. I cook, sew, knit, talk, work and make love very well. So I am a valuable item. Without me he would suffer. With him I am alone. I am as solitary as eternity and sometimes as stupid as clotted cream. Ha ha ha! Don't think! Act as if all the bills are paid     *You Can Touch Me*
> 1961

## 1299. Rosellen Brown

1 "Do you think there could be something like victims without crimes?"
"A Letter to Ismael in the Grave,"
*Street Games*    1974

2 "I wish you were alive, I wish, I wish, so I could hate you and get on with it."    Ibid.

3 I know how he dreams me. I know because I dream his dreams.    Ibid., "How to Win"

4 . . . I remember sort of half dreaming as if I had dozed for a few unlikely minutes down by the bay and some sea animal had crawled up, slimy, from below the pilings, had bit me painfully between the legs, and had retreated to its secret life, invisible under the water, covered with blood like something wounded. For an initiation, I assume it was about average.    Ibid., "Street Games"

## 1300. Phila Henrietta Case

1 Oh! why does the wind blow upon me so wild? Is it because I'm nobody's child?
"Nobody's Child"    1954

## 1301. Loma Chandler

1 Sometimes asylums are just what they should be—a resting place for people who get lost in life.    "They're Expecting Us," *Reader's Digest*    October, 1973

2 A smile appeared upon her face as if she'd taken it directly from her handbag and pinned it there.    Ibid.

## 1302. Mildred Clingerman

1 Nobody really looks at a bartender. . . . Even the bar philosophers (the dreariest customers of all) prefer to study their own faces in the back-bar mirror. And however they accept their reflected images, whether shudderingly or with secret love, it is to this aloof image that they impart their whisky-wisdom, not to the bartender.    *Stair Trick*    1952

2 She faced him as if he were Judgment and she standing up pleading for mankind.    Ibid.

## 1303. Beatrice Conrad

1 Their lives had intertwined into a comfortable dependency, like the gnarled wisteria on their front porch, still twisted around the frail support which long ago it had outgrown.
"The Night of the Falling Star,"
*American Scene: New Voices,*
Don Wolfe, ed.    1963

2 We are poor helpless creatures on an undistinguished planet in an obscure corner of a small and fading universe.    Ibid.

## 1304. Jeane Dixon

1 The rare and beautiful experiences of divine revelation are moments of special gifts. Each of us, however, lives each day with special gifts which are a part of our very being, and life is a process of discovering and developing these God-given gifts within each one of us.
*My Life and Prophecies*, with Rene Noorbergen, Ch. 4    1969

## 1305. Helen Dudar

1 Contrary to the folklore of abortion as lifelong trauma, it is not necessarily a profoundly scarring one either.
"Abortion for the Asking," *Saturday Review of the Society*    April, 1973

2 In this era of radicalized and politicized clergy, it is no longer even surprising when a woman shows up at [an abortion] clinic with the blessing of her priest.    Ibid.

## 1306. Alice Embree

1 Shortly after the turn of the century, America marshalled her resources, contracted painfully, and gave birth to the New Technology. The father was a Corporation, and the New Technology grew up in the Corporate image.
"Media Images I: Madison Avenue Brainwashing—The Facts,"
*Sisterhood Is Powerful,*
Robin Morgan, ed.    1970

2 Humans must breathe, but corporations must make money.    Ibid.

3 Women are the neglected orphans of the technological age.                                    Ibid.

4 The message of the media is the commercial.
                                                  Ibid.

5 America's technology has turned in upon itself; its corporate form makes it the servant of profits, not the servant of human needs.    Ibid.

## 1307. Joan Fleming

1 "It's the money," Molly said clumsily, "if you've once had no money, and I mean no money at all, it means something always ever afterwards."
                  *The Chill and the Kill*, Ch. 7    *1964*

2 "Folk love being told things about themselves they already know."                    Ibid.

3 His despondent mood led to unusual frankness when he told Molly that, when he grew up, a murder at the end of a party was the regular thing but you didn't expect it of gentry; it made you lose heart, really it did.          Ibid.

## 1308. Mary Anne Guitar

1 We have to stop being so teacher-centered, and become student-centered. It's not what you think they need, but what they think they need. That's the functional approach.
                  "College Marriage Courses—Fun or
                           Fraud?," *Mademoiselle*
                                  *February, 1961*

## 1309. Eleanor Hoover

Co-author with Marie Edwards. See 1021: 1–2.

## 1310. Helen Hudson

1 A white casket with silver handles, she thought. Not a soft bed with a pink quilt but four sides and a lid that closes. To be shipped like a shoe in a box from this world to the next.
                  "Sunday Morning," *American Scene:
                  New Voices*, Don Wolfe, ed.    *1963*

2 As he worked, putting the mask of sleep over the faces of death, he felt a vague excitement, as though he were, indeed, reviving her, as

though the eyes he had closed so carefully might open again and see him, without reproach: a kindly man who knew his trade and did it well.                          Ibid.

## 1311. Mary Hyde

1 The art of managing men has to be learned from birth. . . . It depends to some extent on one's distribution of curves, a developed instinct, and a large degree of sheer feline cunning.          *How to Manage Men*    *1955*

## 1312. Susan Jacoby

1 Political détente notwithstanding, the Soviet Union is still a nation with a deeply ingrained suspicion of foreign influence.
                  *Inside Soviet Schools*    *1974*

2 A Russian child on a collective farm faces educational inequities as grave as those confronting a black American child in a city slum.    Ibid.

3 Educational opportunity for all citizens is as much an article of social faith in the Soviet Union as it is in the United States. Everyone believes in education: Party leaders, intellectuals, factory workers, farm laborers. The Soviets have much more faith than Americans in the ability of public institutions to transform their lives; schools—not Marxist-Leninist theory —are seen by parents as the key to a better future for their children.          Ibid.

4 . . . all foreigners regard other societies through the prisms of their own value systems.
                                                  Ibid.

5 I have always regarded the development of the individual as the only legitimate goal of education. . . .                          Ibid.

6 Soviet schools are extraordinarily good at squeezing the fight out of the individuals they process.                          Ibid.

## 1313. Lena Jeger

1 . . . no legislation can compel anybody to give the unmarried mother what she usually most needs—friendship, understanding and companionship in what is almost inevitably a lonely and deeply traumatic experience.
                  *Illegitimate Children and Their
                  Parents*, Foreword    *1951*

2 The child is different, not because he is illegitimate, but because he is fatherless and he is going to miss a father in the same way that any child who loses his father early, through death or separation, misses him.                     *Ibid.*

3 . . . we feel that there is often too little concern with the unmarried father. In our social records he is an elusive figure, often anonymous, alternately reviled, beloved or blackmailed. . . . Often he needs as much help as the mother to regain a mental and emotional equilibrium and so to make subsequently a good husband to somebody, if not to the mother of his first child.                     *Ibid.*

## 1314.  Rosabeth Moss Kanter

1 The [commune] movement is part of a reawakening of belief in the possibilities for utopia that existed in the nineteenth century and exist again today, a belief that by creating the right social institution, human satisfaction and growth can be achieved.
"Getting It All Together: Communes Past, Present, Future," *The Future of the Family*, Louise Kapp Howe, ed.
*1972*

## 1315.  Marjorie Karmel

1 It is a great pity that a man should stand back, helpless and inadequate, *de trop*, while his wife alone knows the profound experience of the birth of the child they have created together.
*Thank You, Dr. Lamaze*, Ch. 3
*1959*

2 Who ever said that doctors are truthful or even intelligent? You're getting a. lot if they know their profession. Don't ask any more from them. They're only human after all—which is to say, you can't expect much."
*Ibid.*, Ch. 7

3 "One-way first-name calling always means inequality—witness servants, children and dogs."
*Ibid.*

## 1316.  Helen Lawrenson

1 They are a curious mixture of Spanish tradition, American imitation, and insular limitation.

This explains why they never catch on to themselves.                     "Latins Are Lousy Lovers,"
*Esquire        October, 1939*

2 Any definition of sophistication must include the word "worldliness"; and how can people be worldly who seem to have no inkling of what's going on in the world?
"A Farewell to Yesterday," *Latins Are Still Lousy Lovers        1968*

3 Most of today's film actresses are typical of a mass-production age: living dolls who look as if they came off an assembly line and whose uniformity of appearance is frequently a triumph of modern science, thanks to which they can be equipped with identical noses, breasts, teeth, eyelashes, and hair.
*Ibid.*, "Where Did It Go?"

4 A skirt is no obstacle to extemporaneous sex, but it is physically impossible to make love to a girl while she is wearing trousers.
*Ibid.*, "Androgyne, You're a Funny Valentine"

## 1317.  Enriqueta Longauex y Vasquez

1 A woman who has no way of expressing herself and of realizing herself as a full human has nothing else to turn to but the owning of material things.
"The Mexican-American Woman," *Sisterhood Is Powerful*,
Robin Morgan, ed.        *1970*

2 The Anglo woman is always there with her superiority complex. The Chicana woman will be looked upon as having to prove herself even in the smallest task.                     *Ibid.*

3 When a family is involved in a human rights movement, as is the Mexican-American family, there is little room for a woman's liberation movement alone.                     *Ibid.*

## 1318.  Norma Meacock

1 . . . in all my life I have never found reasoning satisfactory as a means of progress.
*Thinking Girl        1968*

2 If the texture of our daily life gets any thinner, it'll disappear up its own arsehole.        *Ibid.*

3 Being human, we should bear all we can.
*Ibid.*

## 1319. Susanna Millar

1 The term "play" has long been a linguistic wastepaper basket for behaviour which looks voluntary, but seems to have no obvious biological or social use.
*The Psychology of Play*, Foreword
*1968*

2 If animals play, this is because play is useful in the struggle for survival; because play practises and so perfects the skills needed in adult life.    Ibid., Ch. 1

3 For the healthy, a monotonous environment eventually produces discomfort, irritation and attempts to vary it.    Ibid., Ch. 4

4 The social life of a child starts when he is born.    Ibid., Ch. 7

5 It is the business of psychologists to be puzzled by every action, but if the questions are formulated so that they require answers in terms of special motives, they soon become unsatisfactory.    Ibid., Ch. 10

## 1320. Jane O'Reilly

1 . . . the click! of recognition, that parenthesis of truth around a little thing that completes the puzzle of reality in women's minds—the moment that brings a gleam to our eyes and means the revolution has begun.
"The Housewife's Moment of Truth,"
*The First Ms. Reader*, Francine
Klagsbrun, ed.    *1972*

2 Parables are unnecessary for recognizing the blatant absurdity of everyday life. Reality is lesson enough.    Ibid.

3 . . . housewives, the natural people to turn to when there is something unpleasant, inconvenient or inconclusive to be done.    Ibid.

4 Men will always opt for things that get finished and stay that way—putting up screens, but not planning menus.    Ibid.

## 1321. Anna Maria Ortese

1 It was the easiest and at the same time the most sinister thing possible that was happening to me: when one thing recalls another, and so on, till your present vanishes, and everything before you is purely past, the echo of a life that was more real than this one.
"The Lights of Genoa," *Italian
Writing Today*, Raleigh Trevelyan,
ed.    *1967*

2 History is something that, like the rest of Italy, it [Genoa] no longer has: but what it has is the present.    Ibid.

3 I was searching for a piece of luggage that seemed to have been mislaid, as my own life had for some time seem slightly mislaid. . . .
Ibid.

4 I felt desolate at the thought of the inevitable rudeness or raucousness that, in Rome or to some extent anywhere else, greets anyone who is lost and stops someone to ask the way.
Ibid.

5 People were alone, and at the same time never alone, at least not in the terrible way you are in Milan and in Rome, where, if you aren't socially eminent or rich or important, others simply don't notice you, and if you're ill you could be thrown out with the rubbish. . . .
Ibid.

6 . . . in order to feel anything you need strength. . . .    Ibid.

## 1322. Carol Polowy

1 Educational institutions mirror the stereotypes of the larger society. The fact that education has become known as a "woman's field" stems at least in part from the identification of childcare and child-rearing as woman's work. Men frequently view teaching as a stepping stone to educational administration while women look to careers as classroom teachers.
Address, "Sex Discrimination: The
Legal Obligations of Educational
Institutions," *Vital Speeches
February 1, 1975*

2 When textbooks are examined in terms of their presentation and reinforcement of a social order, women and minority groups are dissatisfied with the lack of reality in the presentation.
Ibid.

## 1323. Aurelia Potor

1 Middle-aged rabbits don't have a paunch, do have their own teeth and haven't lost their romantic appeal.
Quoted in *The New York Times
September 22, 1956*

## 1324. Muriel Resnik

1 JOHN. . . . that's nothing but a tax dodge! . . . This is what the Internal Revenue Service expects. It's all part of the game. They play their part, we have to play ours. It's our duty as American citizens!     *Any Wednesday,*
Act I, Sc. 1    *1963*

2 ELLEN. . . . it's só horrible to be—oh God— *thirty.* . . . Today is a turning point in my life, the beginning of the end. It's pushing forty—and menopause out there waiting to spring—and before you can even turn around you're a senior citizen.     Ibid.

3 JOHN. But she doesn't *know* I'm hurting her, so I'm not. Is that a happy woman? Is she? You see? We're not hurting her, we're not taking anything away from her. In point of fact, having you in my life makes me happy, a happy husband for Dorothy! Far from hurting her, pet, we're *helping* her.

ELLEN. We are?

JOHN. Of course! If I didn't have you, Dorothy would be *miserable!*     Ibid., Act II, Sc. 1

4 JOHN. I happen to feel that suburbia is as much of a blight as billboards on country roads.
    Ibid., Sc. 2

5 JOHN. I'll tell you about babies. Whenever I see one, I want to give it a cigar and discuss the Common Market.     Ibid.

## 1325. Virginie des Rieux

1 "Gentlemen, in life, there is one thing that fascinates everybody, and that's rear ends. Talk about backsides and only backsides, and you will have friends everywhere always."
    *La Satyre,* Ch. 1    *1967*

\* \* \*

2 Marriage is a lottery in which men stake their liberty and women their happiness.     Epigram

## 1326. Gabriela Roepke

1 AMANDA. I just can't seem to go on—without a good morning in a big baritone voice.
    *A White Butterfly*    *1960*

2 SMITH. You lose an umbrella. You can also lose time.     Ibid.

3 SMITH. . . . the reflection in my shaving mirror tells me things nobody else ever would.     Ibid.

4 OLD LADY. The best thing others can do for us is to tell us lies.     Ibid.

## 1327. Betty Rollin

1 . . . biological *possibility* and desire are not the same as biological *need.* Women have childbearing equipment. For them to choose not to use the equipment is no more blocking what is instinctive than it is for a man who, muscles or no, chooses not to be a weightlifter.
    "Motherhood: Who Needs It?," *Look*
*May 16, 1971*

2 How can birth-control programs really be effective as long as the concept of glorious motherhood remains unchanged? (Even poor old Planned Parenthood has to euphemize—why not Planned Unparenthood?)     Ibid.

3 Motherhood affords an instant identity. First, through wifehood, you are somebody's wife; then you are somebody's mother. Both give not only identity and activity, but status and stardom of a kind.     Ibid.

## 1328. Sonya Rudikoff

1 . . . the idea has gained currency that women have often been handicapped not only by a fear of failure—not unknown to men either— but by a fear of success as well.
    "Women and Success," *Commentary*
*October, 1974*

2 Although there are countless alumni of the school of hard knocks, there has not yet been a move to accredit that institution.     Ibid.

3 History provides abundant examples of . . . women whose greatest gift was in redeeming, inspiring, liberating, and nurturing the gifts of others.     Ibid.

4 The embattled gates to equal rights have indeed opened up for modern women, but I sometimes think to myself: "That is not what I meant by freedom—it is only 'social progress.' "     Ibid.

5 There are surely lives which display very few of the signs of success until very late, or after life is over. There are lives of great significance which go unrecognized by peers for a very long time, there are those who achieve nothing for

themselves but leave a legacy for others who come after, there are lives sacrificed for causes.
Ibid.

6 Should we, perhaps, see the development of the commune movement in another light, as a less expensive form of summer camp for a growing population—post-adolescent, post-industrial, post-Christian and unemployed?
Article in *Commentary*          *1974*

## 1329. Merle Shain

1 We tend to think of the rational as a higher order, but it is the emotional that marks our lives. One often learns more from ten days of agony than from ten years of contentment. . . .
*Some Men are More Perfect Than Others*, Pt. I, Ch. 1          *1973*

2 Most women would rather have someone whisper their name at optimum moments than rocket with contractions to the moon. . . .
Ibid., Ch. 3

3 So mistresses tend to get a steady diet of whipped cream, but no meat and potatoes, and wives often get the reverse, when both would like a bit of each.          Ibid., Pt. II, Ch. 4

## 1330. Mary Jane Sherfey

1 There is a great difference between satisfaction and satiation.
"A Theory on Female Sexuality,"
*Journal of the American Psycho-analytical Association*          *1966*

2 The nature of female sexuality as here presented makes it clear that . . . woman's inordinate orgasmic capacity did not evolve for monogamous, sedentary cultures.          Ibid.

3 The strength of the drive determines the force required to suppress it.          Ibid.

4 There is no such thing as a vaginal orgasm distinct from a clitoral orgasm. The nature of the orgasm is the same regardless of the erotogenic zone stimulated to produce it.          Ibid.

## 1331. Margaret Sloan

1 We feel that there can't be liberation for less than half a race. We want *all* black people in this country to be free.
Manifesto, National Black Feminist Organization          *1975*

2 It has been hard for black women to emerge from the myriad of distorted images that have portrayed us as grinning Beulahs, castrating Sapphires, and pancake-box Jemimahs.          Ibid.

## 1332. Evelyn E. Smith

1 It turned out that all the scientists had been doing the same thing, making a lot of hoopla about inventing stuff—atom bombs, jet planes, television—when actually they did it all with witchcraft. Seems all the magicians had gone underground since the Age of Enlightenment and had been passing off their feats as science —except for a few unreconstructed gypsies.
*The Martian and the Magician*          *1952*

2 Enemies whispered that he had bewitched the voting machines, but that wasn't true; he'd won fair and square through mass hypnosis.
Ibid.

3 That's always the way when you discover something new; everybody thinks you're crazy.
Ibid.

## 1333. Judy Syfers

1 The problems of an American wife stem from the fact that we live in a society which is structured in such a way as to profit only a few at the expense of the many. As long as we women tolerate such a capitalist system, all but a privileged few of us must necessarily be exploited as workers and as wives.
"I Want a Wife," *The First Ms. Reader*, Francine Klagsbrun, ed.          *1972*

2 My God, who *wouldn't* want a wife?          Ibid.

## 1334. Octavia Waldo

1 The rain fell like a cascade of pine needles over Rome. Rain—thirty days of it. It marked the interlude between winter and spring, and spring was late in coming. There was nothing to do about it but wait. There is nothing to do about most things that are late in Rome, whether it be an appointment, or a bus, or a promise. Or even hope.
    "Roman Spring," *American Scene: New Voices,* Don Wolfe, ed.     *1963*

2 ". . . Adam Maxwell, age twenty-four, husband to Ruth. A boy who wants to go to the top. As if the world had a top!"          Ibid.

3 "Living," he had said, "like studying, needs a little practice."          Ibid.

4 But sleep had been taking a vacation from her; as if she were a pariah, it visited her too infrequently, and then only out of unavoidable duty.          Ibid., Ch. 2

5 The lazy pattern of living had reinstated itself, had returned an assuagement made of compromises and complacency. It had made things safe again between them.          Ibid.

6 "The war has caved the very heart out of modesty and has left her rather bare."          Ibid.

# Biographical Index

# Biographical Index

NOTES TO BIOGRAPHICAL INDEX

Every contributor is listed alphabetically and her contributor number given (these numbers will be found in page headings throughout the Quotations section). If a woman is well known by a name other than the one used at the heading of her entry in the Quotations section, that name is cross-indexed here. All co-authors are listed here except "as told to" authors.

Brief biographical information is given for each woman: her full name (those parts of her name not used at the heading of her quotations are in brackets), and any hereditary or honorary title she is known to hold; her nationality, and—if different— her country of residence (i.e., Am./It. indicates a woman was born in the United States but has lived most of her life in Italy); her profession; her family relationship to other well-known persons; any major awards or honors she is known to have received; any "firsts" or outstanding achievements for which she is responsible; any other names by which she is known.

Abbreviations (other than nationality) are: m.–married name; w.–wife of; d.–daughter of; s.–sister of; pseud.–fictitious name used specifically in her work; aka (also know as)—nicknames, aliases, and any other names by which she was known.

The term educator encompasses teachers, professors—whether full, associate or assistant—and other instructors; college administrators are specifically designated. The term composer is used in reference to classical music; composers of popular music are designated as songwriters.

The term (cont./no date) denotes contemporary/no date. This was utilized in the case of women who are alive but for whom no birth date could be found.

Dargan, Olive (1869–1968)     348
  Am. poet, writer; née Tilford; pseud.
  Fielding Burke
Davies, Mary Carolyn (fl. 1920s)     953
  Am. poet, songwriter, playwright, editor
Davis, Adelle (1904–1974)     772
  Am. nutritionist, writer; pseud. Jane Dun-
  lap
Davis, Angela [Yvonne] (1944–   )     1258
  Am. educator, political activist, writer
Davis, Bette (1908–   )     825
  Am. actress; Academy Award, 1935, 1938
Davis, Dorothy Salisbury (1916–   )     907
  Am. writer
Davis, Elizabeth Gould (1925?–1974)     1015
  Am. librarian, writer
Davis, Rebecca Harding (1831–1910)     127
  Am. writer, social critic
Day, Dorothy (1897–   )     678
  Am. religious leader, writer
Day, Lillian (1893–   )     631
  Am. writer
Dayan, Yaël (1939–   )     1190
  Isr. writer, war correspondent; d. Moshe
  Dayan
DeBary, Anna Bunston (1869–?)     349
  Eng. poet
Decter, Midge (1927–   )     1039
  Am. writer, editor, social critic; née Rosen-
  thal
Delaney, Shelagh (1939–   )     1191
  Eng. playwright
Delmar, Viña (1905–   )     784
  Am. playwright; née Croter
Demarest, Mary Lee (1857–1888)     254
  Ir. poet
De Mille, Agnes (1908–   )     826
  Am. choreographer, dancer, writer; d.
  Cecil B. De Mille; Antoinette Perry
  Award, 1947, 1962
Deming, Barbara (1917–   )     922
  Am. pacifist, feminist, writer
Deroine, Jeanne-Françoise (1805–1894)     17
  Fr. feminist
Detourbey, Jeanne (1837–1908)     155
  Fr. hostess, writer; aka Comtesse de Loy-
  nes; mistress of Prince Napoleon, Dumas
  fils, Flaubert
Deutsch, Babette (1895–   )     658
  Am. writer, educator, poet, translator,
  editor; m. Yarmolinsky
Deutsch, Helene (1884–   )     520
  Am. psychiatrist, writer
Devi, Indra (1899–   )     697
  Russ./Am. yogini, writer; née Petersen; m.
  Knauer
Devlin, [Josephine] Bernadette (1947–   )     1280
  Ir. politician

De Wolfe, Elsie (1865–1950)     317
  Eng. actress, hostess, writer; m. Lady
  Mendel
Dickinson, Emily [Elizabeth] (1830–1886)     117
  Am. poet
Didion, Joan (1935–   )     1144
  Am. journalist, writer, scenarist; w. John
  Gregory Dunne
Didrikson, Babe (see Zaharias, Babe Didrik-
  son)
Diehl, Guida (1868–?)     341
  Ger. political activist
Dietrich, Marlene (1904–   )     773
  Ger./Am. actress, singer
Dillard, Annie (1945–   )     1265
  Am. writer, poet; née Doak; w. Richard
  Henry Wilde Dillard; Pulitzer Prize, 1975
Diller, Phyllis (1917–   )     923
  Am. comedienne, writer
Dinesen, Isak (1885–1962)     535
  Dan. writer; née [Baroness] Karen Blixen
Di Prima, Diane (1934–   )     1133
  Am. poet, writer, editor, playwright
Dix, Dorothea [Lynde] (1802–1887)     6
  Am. humanitarian, reformer
Dix, Dorothy (1861–1951)     291
  Am. journalist, columnist; née Elizabeth
  Meriwether; m. Gilmer
Dixon, Jeane (cont./n.d.)     1304
  Am. psychic, writer
Dobree, Henrietta [Octavia de Lisle] (1831–
  1894)     128
  Hymnist
Dodge, Mabel (1879–1962)     466
  Am. writer, patron of arts; née Ganson;
  m. Luhan
Dodge, Mary Abigail (see Hamilton, Gail)
Dodge, Mary [Elizabeth] Mapes (1838?–
  1905)     156
  Am. writer, editor
Dolliver, Clara (fl. 1870s)     358
  Am. poet
Doolittle, Hilda (1886–1961)     550
  Am. poet; pseud. H. D.; m. Aldington
Dorr, Julia [Caroline] (1825–1913)     96
  Am. writer, poet; née Ripley
Dorset, F. H. (see Llewellyn-Thomas, Bea-
  trice)
Dostoevsky, Anna (1846–1918)     201
  Russ. diarist; w. Feodor Dostoevsky
Doten, Elizabeth (1829–?)     113
  Am. poet
Doudney, Sarah (1843–1926)     180
  Eng. writer, poet
Douglas, Lady Alford (see Custance, Olive)
Douglas, Helen Gahagan (1900–   )     712
  Am. writer, lecturer, congresswoman, ac-
  tress; w. Melvyn Douglas; U.S. delegate
  to United Nations, 1946

Hibbard, [Helen] Grace (1870?–1911) 363
Am. writer, poet; née Porter
Hickey, Emily [Henrietta] (1845–1924) 198
Ir. poet
Higginson, Ella [Reeves] (1862–1940) 302
Am. poet, writer, historian
Hinkle, Beatrice [Mores] (1874–1953) 405
Am. psychiatrist, writer, translator; née Van Geisen; developed first psychotherapeutic clinic in U.S. at Cornell Medical College, 1908
Hinkson, Katharine Tynan (1861–1931) 295
Ir. poet, writer
Hobbes, John Oliver (see Craigie, Pearl M. T.)
Hobson, Laura Z. (1900– ) 719
Am. writer, publicist, journalist
Hochman, Sandra (1936– ) 1154
Am. poet; m. Leve
Hochschild, Arlie [Russell] (1940– ) 1212
Am. educator, writer
Hoffman, Malvina (1885–1966) 536
Am. sculptor; m. Grimson
Holiday, Billie (1915–1959) 902
Am. singer; née Eleanora Fagan
Holland, Barbara (1951– ) 1290
Am. poet
Holland, Norah M. (1876–1925) 434
Am. poet
Hollander, Xaviera (1936?– ) 1155
Dutch/Am. madam; née de Vries
Holley, Marietta (1836?–1926) 152
Am. writer, humorist; pseud. Josiah Allen's Wife
Holmes, Mary Jane [Hawes] (1828–1907) 111
Am. writer
Hooper, Ellen Sturgis (1816–1841) 50
Am. poet
Hoover, Eleanor (cont./n.d.) 1309
Am. writer
Hope, Laurence (1865–1904) 320
Eng. poet; aka Adela Florence Nicolson
Hopkins, Jane Ellice (1836–1904) 153
Eng. social reformer, writer
Hopper, Hedda (1890–1966) 593
Am. columnist, writer
Horne, Marilyn (1934– ) 1135
Am. opera singer
Horner, Matina (1929?– ) 1060
Am. psychiatrist, educator, college administrator, writer
Horney, Karen (1885–1952) 537
Ger./Am. psychiatrist, writer, educator; née Danielson
Horta, Maria Teresa (1939– ) 1198
Port. writer, poet
Howar, Barbara (1938?– ) 1182
Am. socialite, writer
Howard, Jane [Temple] (1935– ) 1146
Am. writer

Howard, Maureen [Keans] (1930– ) 1082
Am. writer
Howarth, Ellen [Clementine Doran] (1827–1899) 108
Am. poet; pseud. Clementine
Howe, Julia Ward (1819–1910) 65
Am. writer, lecturer, social reformer, civil and woman's rights activist, suffragist, poet
Howe, Louise Kapp (1934– ) 1136
Am. writer, editor
Howell, Margery Eldredge (1893– ) 634
Am. poet
Howells, Mildred (1872–1966) 381
Am. painter, poet; d. William Dean Howells
Howland, Mrs. Robert Shaw (see Woolsey, Mary)
Hoyt, Helen (1887– ) 562
Am. poet; m. Lyman
Hsiang Chin-yu (fl. 1910s–1927) 845
Chin. militant
Hubbard, Alice (1861–1915) 296
Am. writer; née Moore
Hudson, Helen (cont./n.d.) 1310
Am. writer
Huerta, Dolores (1930– ) 1083
Am. union organizer; née Hernandez; vice president of United Farm Workers of America
Hulme, Kathryn (1900– ) 720
Am. writer
Hungerford, Margaret Wolfe (1855?–1897) 244
Ir. writer; née Hamilton; pseud. The Duchess
Hunt, Helen Fiske (see Jackson, Helen Fiske Hunt)
Hunter, Kristin (1931– ) 1097
Am. writer
Huntington, Helen (1875?–1950) 424
Eng. writer, translator; née Gates; w. Harley Granville-Barker; pseud. H. H. Lynde
Hurnscot, Loran (1900?–1970) 721
Eng. writer; pseud. Gay Stuart Taylor
Hurst, Fannie (1889–1968) 580
Am. writer; m. Danielson
Hurston, Zora Neale (1907–1960) 815
Am. writer, folklorist, anthropologist
Hutchinson, Ellen [MacKay] (fl. 1880s–1933) 478
Am. writer, journalist, editor, poet; m. Cortissoz
Hutten, Baroness Bettina von (1874–1957) 406
Am./Eng. writer; née Riddle
Huxley, Mrs. Thomas Henry (see Heathorn, Henrietta)
Hyde, Mary (cont./n.d.) 1311
Am. writer

## I

Ian, Janis (1951– ) 1291
Am. composer, singer

Lenéru, Marie (1875–1940) 425
  Fr. writer, playwright; deaf and blind
Lennart, Isobel (1919?– ) 948
  Am. playwright, scenarist
Lerner, Gerda (1920– ) 964
  Aus./Am. educator, writer, lecturer, scenarist; née Kronstein
Le Row, Caroline Bigelow (1843–?) 183
  Am. editor, poet
LeShan, Eda J. (1922– ) 985
  Am. educator, family counselor, writer
Leslie, Amy (1860–1939) 282
  Am. drama critic, actress; aka Lillie West Brown Buck
Lessing, Doris (1919– ) 949
  Eng. writer, playwright
Le Sueur, Marian (1877–1954) 448
  Am. lawyer, political activist; mother of Meridel Le Sueur
Le Sueur, Meridel (1900– ) 724
  Am. writer, historian, poet; d. Marian Le Sueur
Letts, Winifred [Mary] (1882– ) 502
  Ir. poet, writer; m. Verschoyle
Leveridge, Lilian (1879–1953) 471
  Can. poet
Leverson, Ada [Beddington] (1862–1933) 303
  Eng. writer
Levertov, Denise (1923– ) 997
  Eng./Am. poet, educator
Lewis, Edith (1880?–1955?) 482
  Am. biographer
Liddell, Catherine [Fraser Tytler] (1848–?) 211
  Eng. writer, poet
Liliuokalani, Lydia Kamekeha (1838–1917) 158
  Queen of the Hawaiian Islands, 1891–1893; songwriter
Lillie, Beatrice (1898– ) 692
  Eng. actress, comedienne; m. Lady Peel
Lin, Frank (see Atherton, Gertrude)
Lincoln, Abbey (1930– ) 1085
  Am. singer, actress; née Anna Marie Wooldridge
Lincoln, Mary Todd (1818–1882) 60
  Am. First Lady, public figure; w. Abraham Lincoln
Lind, Jenny (1820–1887) 75
  Swed. opera singer; m. Goldschmidt; aka "The Swedish Nightingale"
Lindbergh, Anne [Spencer] Morrow 1906– ) 807
  Am. writer, poet, aviator; w. Charles Lindbergh; d. Elizabeth Reeve Morrow
Livermore, Mary [Ashton] (1820?–1905) 76
  Am. social reformer, lecturer, writer; née Rice
Livingstone, Belle (1875–1957) 426
  Am. actress, hostess

Llewellyn-Thomas, Beatrice [Caroline] (1890– ) 595
  Eng. writer, poet; pseud. F. H. Dorset
Lloyd, Marie (1870–1922) 365
  Eng. entertainer; née Mathilda Alice Victoria Wood
Locke, Una (see Bailey, Urania Locke)
Lockwood, Belva [Ann] (1830–1917) 121
  Am. lawyer, feminist; née Bennett
Long, Gabrielle Margaret Vere (see Bowen, Marjorie)
Longauex y Vasquez, Enriqueta (cont./n.d.) 1317
  Am. civil rights activist
Longworth, Alice Roosevelt (1884– ) 525
  Am. hostess; d. Theodore Roosevelt
Loos, Anita (1893– ) 639
  Am. writer, playwright, humorist, scenarist; m. Emerson
Lorde, Audre [Geraldine] (1934– ) 1138
  Am. educator, poet
Lothrop, Amy (see Warner, Anna B.)
Lothrop, Harriet Mulford (see Sidney, Margaret)
Loud, Pat (1926– ) 1031
  Am. writer, television personality
Love, Barbara J. (1937– ) 1172
  Am. writer, editor
Lovell, Marie [Anne Lacy] (1803–1877) 10
  Eng. actress, playwright
Low, Juliette (1860–1927) 283
  Eng./Am. humanitarian; née Gordon; founder of Girl Scouts of America, 1912
Lowell, Amy (1874–1925) 408
  Am. poet, literary critic; Pulitzer Prize, 1926
Loynes, Comtess le (see Detourbey, Jeanne)
Lucas, Mrs. F. L. (see Jones, E. B. C.)
Luce, Clare Boothe (1903– ) 760
  Am. diplomat, congresswoman, writer, playwright, government official; w. Henry Robinson Luce; U.S. Ambassador to Italy
Luce, Gay Gaer (1930– ) 1086
  Am. writer, researcher
Ludendorff, Mathilde Spiess (see Kemnitz, Mathilda von)
Luhan, Mabel Dodge (see Dodge, Mabel)
Lupino, Ida (1918– ) 938
  Eng./Am. actress, film director and producer; ex-w. Howard Duff
Luxemburg, Rosa (1870–1919) 366
  Pol./Ger. revolutionary, writer, Socialist
Lyall, Edna (1857–1903) 257
  Eng. writer; née Ada Ellen Bayly
Lydon, Susan (1943?– ) 1251
  Am. writer, political activist, feminist
Lyman, Mrs. W. W. (see Hoyt, Helen)
Lynn, Loretta [Webb] (1930?– ) 1087
  Am. singer

Am. writer, poet; née Cutter; m. Whitney; mother of Anne Morrow Lindbergh

Mortimer, Penelope (1918–    )    941
Eng. writer; née Fletcher

Moses, Grandma (1860–1961)    285
Am. painter; née Anna Mary Robertson

Motoni, Nomura (1806–1867)    24
Jap. political activist, poet

Moulton, Louise (1835–1908)    147
Am. writer, poet; née Chandler

Mumford, Ethel Watts (1878–1940)    461
Am. writer, playwright, humorist; m. Grant

Munro, Alice (1931–    )    1100
Can. writer

Murdoch, Iris (1919–    )    950
Ir. writer; m. Bayley

Murray, Ada Foster (*see* Alden, Ada)

Murry, Kathleen Beauchamp (*see* Mansfield, Katherine)

Musgrave, Thea (1928–    )    1052
Eng. composer

Myerson, Bess (1924–    )    1005
Am. government official, television personality, columnist; Miss America, 1948

### N

Nagako, Empress (1903–    )    762
Jap. empress; w. Hirohito

Naidu, Sarojini [Chattopadhyay] (1879–1949)    472
Ind. poet

Nation, Carry [Amelia] (1846–1911)    204
Am. prohibitionist; née Moore

Near, Holly (1949?–    )    1286
Am. singer, songwriter

Neel, Alice (1908–    )    831
Am. painter

Nelson, Paula (1945–    )    1269
Am. economist, business executive; founder of Joy of Money, Inc.

Nesbit, Edith (1858–1924)    264
Eng. writer, poet; w. Hubert Bland; one of the founders of the Fabian Society

Nevelson, Louise (1900–    )    727
Russ./Am. sculptor, feminist

Nevill, Lady Dorothy (1826–1913)    104
Eng. writer, hostess

Newbold, Frances (*see* Hart, Frances Noyes)

Newman, Frances (1883?–1928)    514
Am. writer, librarian

Newton, Frances (fl. 1930s)    1074
Am. writer

Nichols, Anne (1891–1966)    607
Am. playwright

Nichols, Ruth Rowland (1901–1960)    742
Am. aviator; first woman to pilot a passenger airplane; set woman's world altitude, speed, and long-distance records

Nicolson, Adela Florence (*see* Hope, Laurence)

Nightingale, Florence (1820–1910)    78

Eng. nurse, writer; aka "The Lady with the Lamp"; founder of nursing profession; first woman to receive British Order of Merit

Nin, Anaïs (1903–1977)    763
Fr./Am. writer, lecturer

Nixon, [Thelma Catherine] Pat (1912–    )    875
Am. First Lady, public figure; née Ryan; w. Richard M. Nixon

Norman, Liane (1937–    )    1173
Am. educator

Norris, Kathleen (1880–1966)    483
Am. writer; née Thompson

Norton, Caroline [Elizabeth Sarah] (1808–1877)    29
Eng. writer, poet; née Sheridan; granddaughter of William Brinsley Sheridan

Norton, Eleanor Holmes (1937–    )    1174
Am. lawyer, civil rights activist

Norton, Grace Fallow (1876–1926)    437
Am. poet

Novis, Emile (*see* Weil, Simone)

Nyro, Laura (1946–    )    1277
Am. singer, songwriter

### O

Oakley, Annie (1860–1926)    286
Am. markswoman, entertainer; née Phoebe Ann Mozee; w. Frank Butler

Oates, Joyce Carol (1938–    )    1185
Am. writer

O'Brien, Edna (1932–    )    1110
Ir./Eng. writer, pacifist

Ocampo, Victoria (1891–    )    608
Argen. writer

O'Casey, Eileen (1905?–    )    792
Ir./Eng. actress, writer; née Carey; w. Sean O'Casey

O'Connor, Flannery (1925–1964)    1016
Am. writer

O'Keeffe, Georgia (1887–    )    565
Am. painter; m. Stieglitz

Oliphant, Margaret (1828–1897)    112
Eng. writer, historian; m. Wilson

Oliver, Ruth Law (1891?–1970)    609
Am. aviator; set altitude and long-distance records

Olsen, Tillie (1913–    )    886
Am. writer

Onassis, Jacqueline Kennedy (1929–    )    1065
Am. First Lady, public figure; née Bouvier; widow of John F. Kennedy and Aristotle Onassis

O'Neill, Carlotta Monterey (1888–1970)    575
Sp./Am. actress; w. Eugene O'Neill

O'Neill, Moira (fl. early 1900s)    706
Ir. poet; née Agnes Higginson Skrine

O'Neill, Rose [Cecil] (1874–1944)    414
Am. writer, poet, illustrator; created the Kewpie Doll

Reed, Donna (1921– ) 976
Am. actress, civil rights leader, pacifist; Academy Award, 1954; co-founder of Another Mother for Peace

Reese, Lizette [Woodworth] (1856–1935) 249
Am. poet, writer

Reeves, Nancy (1913– ) 889
Am. lawyer, writer, educator; née Goldhaber

Renault, Mary (1905– ) 796
Eng. writer; pseud. Challans

Repplier, Agnes (1858–1950) 266
Am. writer, social critic

Resnik, Muriel (cont./n.d.) 1324
Am. playwright

Reynolds, Malvina (1900– ) 730
Am. folksinger, songwriter

Rhys, Jean (1894– ) 653
W. Ind./Eng. writer, dancer

Rice, Alice Caldwell [Hegan] (1870–1942) 369
Am. writer, humorist

Rice, Ruth Mason (1884–1927) 527
Am. poet

Rich, Adrienne [Cecile] (1929– ) 1066
Am. poet, educator

Richards, Beah (1928?– ) 1053
Am. actress, poet, playwright

Richards, Laura [Elizabeth] Howe (1850–1943) 225
Am. writer; d. Julia Ward Howe; Pulitzer Prize, 1917

Richardson, Dorothy Miller (1873–1957) 395
Eng. writer

Ricker, Marilla (1840–1920) 168
Am. lawyer, civil rights activist, humanitarian; aka "The Prisoner's Friend"

Riding, Laura (1901– ) 743
Am. poet, writer; née Gottchalk; aka Laura (Riding) Jackson

Riefenstahl, Leni (1902– ) 754
Ger. filmmaker, actress, scenarist

Rieux, Virginie des (cont./n.d.) 1325
Fr. writer

Rinehart, Mary Roberts (1876–1958) 438
Am. writer, playwright, journalist

Rittenhouse, Jessie [Belle] (1869–1948) 354
Am. poet, editor, writer, literary critic; founder of Poetry Society of America

Rivers, Joan (1939– ) 1201
Am. comedienne, television personality; m. Rosenberg

Roarke, Constance [Mayfield] (1885–1941) 542
Am. writer

Robertson, Anna Mary (see Moses, Grandma)

Robinson, Agnes Mary [Frances] (1857–1944) 258
Eng./Fr. poet; m. Darmesteter and Duclaux

Robinson, Corinne Roosevelt (1861–1933) 298
Am. poet; s. Theodore Roosevelt

Robinson, Harriet [Hanson] (1825–1911) 99
Am. suffragist, mill worker, writer

Robinson, Jill (1933?– ) 1124
Am. writer; d. Dore Schary

Robinson, Mabel Louise (1883?–1962) 515
Am. writer, educator

Rochefort, Christiane (1917– ) 930
Fr. scenarist, filmmaker, writer

Roe, Anne (1904– ) 778
Am. psychologist, writer

Roepke, Gabriela (cont./n.d.) 1326
Chilean playwright, educator, founder of El Teatro de Ensayo, Santiago

Roiphe, Anne Richardson (1935– ) 1147
Am. writer

Roland, Pauline (fl. 1850s) 218
Fr. feminist

Rollin, Betty (cont./n.d.) 1327
Am. writer, editor, actress

Ronell, Ann (1908– ) 832
Am. songwriter, orchestra conductor; first woman to conduct and compose for film

Roosevelt, Eleanor (1884–1962) 528
Am. First Lady, government official, writer, humanitarian, lecturer; w. Franklin D. Roosevelt; U.S. delegate to United Nations, 1945–1953, 1961

Rose, Ernestine [Potowski] (1810–1892) 33
Pol./Am. abolitionist, feminist, socialist

Rosen, Marjorie (1942– ) 1240
Am. writer, film critic

Rosenberg, Ethel (1915–1953) 903
Am. public figure; née Greenglass; w. Julius Rosenberg; she and her husband were the only U.S. citizens to be executed for treason

Rosenstein, Harriet (1932?– ) 1112
Am. writer

Ross, Lillian (1927– ) 1046
Am. writer, journalist

Ross, Susan C. (1942– ) 1241
Am. lawyer, educator, civil rights activist, writer

Rossetti, Christina [Georgina] (1830–1894) 123
Eng. poet, writer; pseud. Ellen Alleyne; s. Dante Gabriel Rossetti

Rossi, Alice (1922– ) 988
Am. educator, scholar, editor

Rossner, Judith (1935– ) 1148
Am. writer

Routsong, Alma (1924– ) 1006
Am. writer, feminist; pseud. Isabel Miller

Row, Amanda (1931– ) 1102
Am. writer, educator

Rowland, Helen (1876–1950) 439
Am. writer, journalist, humorist

Roy, Gabrielle (1909– ) 839
Fr./Can. writer

# Subject Index

# Subject Index

The numbers preceding the colons are contributor numbers; guides to these numbers are found at the top of each page in the Quotations section. The numbers following the colons refer to the specific quotations.

Entries are in the form of nouns, present participles, or proper names. Because of the amorphous nature of the English language, however, where the use of a noun might be confusing, "the" has been added for clarification (e.g., the obvious), or a noun is given in its plural form to clarify the author's use of the word (e.g., appearance has a different connotation than appearances, speech than speeches).

In subentries the symbol ~ is used to replace the main word; it is placed either before or after the subentry, whichever makes a whole phrase. For example, overpopulation is listed under population as over~, while marriage laws are listed under marriage as ~ laws.

Where there are two words in a main entry with a slash between them, the broader term appears first (e.g., barbarism/barbarian; nursing/nurse). This has been done when there were too few quotations under one or the other of such related subjects to warrant a separate listing.

For a statement on the purpose and style of the Subject Index, please see the Author's Preface.

711:18; 767:2; 909:5; 911:4; 1095:18; 1159:1; loss of ∼, 501:1; 1144:5; 1211:1; 1245:11
innovator, 700:2; 795:13
insect, 95:6; 812:19
insecticide, 812:17, 21
insecurity, 547:8; 967:2; emotional ∼, 473:2; 520:5; 763:18; 1057:7
insight (*also see* perceptiveness), 578:3; 824:33; 942:11; 949:31
insignificance, 112:3; 553:6
insomnia, 1110:4; 1111:8; 1135:3; 1334:4
inspiration, 31:19; 154:13; 310:12; 348:1; 469:6; 481:2; 547:13; 584:3; 718:3; 1068:1; 1101:11
instinct, 31:19; 83:2; 95:16, 17; 580:6; 613:1; 899:2; 1169:1; fighting ∼, 728:4; maternal ∼, 45:62; 281:26, 41
institution (*also see* mental institution), 824:30; 1246:3
integration, racial, 563:7; 811:1; 861:5
integrity (*also see* principle), 19:57; 270:3; 386:39; 684:5; 795:39; 837:4; 1257:1
intellectualism/intellectual, 336:3; 687:13; 757:5; 795:38; 805:12; anti-∼, 615:52
intelligence (*also see* the mind), 15:31; 18:5; 425:3, 6; 438:6; 555:6; 578:1; 619:21; 639:13; 795:22, 29; 823:10; 854:4; 949:23; 1066:9; 1104:8; 1142:13; native ∼, 1048:2
intensity, 36:45
interaction, social, 1046:1; 1110:1
interdependence, 223:5; 266:7; 486:5; 669:12; 794:3; 1188:5
interior decorating, 387:89; 850:7
interrogation, 1030:5
interruption, 1082:1
intimacy, 840:5; 927:14; 993:11; 1025:11; 1034:6; 1091:1; 1218:3; 1237:1
introspection, 88:2; 1099:2; 1247:1
invention/inventor, 477:1; 480:16; 804:16; 1220:1
invincibility, 386:26
Ireland, 27:2; 129:2; 380:1; ∼ in relation to England, 1217:1
Irish, the, 5:11; 31:42; 274:11; 393:7; 564:10; 725:6
irony, 266:30; 711:4
irrelevance, 554:10; 561:23; 1245:4
irresponsibility, 946:5; 950:3; 994:7
irritability, 36:36; 274:13; 624:15
island, 392:2; 648:1
isolation, 31:22; 425:4; 619:10; 789:4; 804:10; 927:15; 1110:12
isolationism, 528:42
Israel/Israelis, 217:4; 528:50, 54, 63; 693:8; 782:2; 860:2; sexism in ∼, 782:2; women in ∼, 782:1
Italy/Italians, 19:47; 107:2; 240:9; 251:1; 503:3, 4; 807:6; history of ∼, 1321:2
itch, 966:3
James, Henry, 306:16
Janus, 22:1

Japan/Japanese, 24:1; 558:9, 10; 736:2; 765:1; 1111:9; 1139:4
jealousy (*also see* envy), 21:2; 64:15, 21; 124:12; 287:21; 387:26; 740:26; 760:9; 804:55
Jerusalem, 1159:5
Jesus (*see* Christ, Jesus)
Jew (*see* Judaism)
jewelry, 387:84; 639:2
Jewishness, 1225:5
Johnson, Andrew, 88:13
Johnson, Lyndon B., 871:1; 1208:7; 1245:1
journalist (*also see* writer), 161:4; 800:2; 896:2
journey (*see* travel)
joy (*also see* happiness), 98:2, 10; 124:9; 223:4; 298:2; 319:2; 337:9; 386:27; 387:37; 529:2, 3; 543:3; 564:8; 594:3; 687:24; 953:6; 1062:9; 1228:3
Joyce, James, 564:20
Judaism/Jew, 45:74; 64:47; 217:3; 528:54, 63; 568:5; 693:6, 7, 11, 13, 19; 1101:13; 1159:12; 1247:7; persecution of ∼, 611:1; 1129:3; image of ∼, 719:2
Judas, 822:6
judge (*also see* the judiciary), 270:3; 350:31; 578:16
judgment (*also see* opinion), 47:12, 15; 263:1; 320:5; 601:1; 620:22; 1117:1; value ∼, 1252:7; pass ∼, 949:39; 993:8
Judgment Day, 164:1
judiciary, the (*also see* judge; jury), 578:15; 913:4; 1030:6; 1185:32; sexism in ∼, 1241:3
June, 103:8; 242:2; 295:2
jungle, 931:10
jury (*also see* the judiciary), 1030:6
justice, 5:18; 60:2, 6; 127:4; 181:3; 265:3; 271:5; 386:25; 528:18; 533:4; 824:26; 900:5; 913:4; 1185:2, 32; juvenile ∼, 1167:4; international ∼, 215:37; 504:8; 688:15

K

Kansas, 45:41
Kant, Emmanuel, 795:41
karma, 125:7; 517:8; 1185:2
Keaton, Buster, 1211:5
Keats, John, 640:18; 1133:3
Kennedy, John F., 528:75; 965:3; assassination of ∼, 871:2
Kennedy family, the, 594:1
killing (*also see* murder), 414:1; 500:7; 619:86, 87; 693:28; 1173:2; 1216:6, 7
kindness, 19:5; 47:4; 87:2; 300:2; 345:4; 387:86, 97; 416:44; 497:4; 578:21; 1062:6; 1110:17; 1113:1
King, Martin Luther, 1044:3; 1054:3; 1245:8
*King Lear*, 278:3
kiss, 64:36; 72:3; 131:3; 291:10; 374:2; 387:59; 439:7; 529:11; 583:2; 585:1; 626:1; 639:8; 640:22; 665:10

740:20; 760:24; 815:1; 824:10; 858:6; 953:7; 972:2; 1122:1; 1175:2; 1224:7; 1289:5; aging ～, 386:12; 439:16; 760:1; competition and ～, 1197:3; creativity of ～, 537:3; image of ～, 1297:1; ～ in relation to women (*also see* relationships, between men and women), 15:10; 36:14; 45:17; 124:7; 132:29; 191:1; 240:5; 246:21; 252:4; 286:1; 287:10; 291:8; 323:8; 439:13, 14, 18, 20, 25; 441:6; 466:2; 501:6; 506:1; 508:18, 30; 532:8; 615:29; 620:17; 623:13; 739:3; 744:11; 760:1, 17; 767:5; 773:1; 820:5; 1006:2; 1015:10; 1059:14; 1142:4; 1166:3; 1174:5; 1247:13; 1249:4, 7; physical size of ～, 1152:1; power of ～, 1196:2; 1249:3, 4; 1266:2; responsibilities of ～, 986:6; role of ～, 360:1; 740:19; 1194:1

menstruation, 929:2; 1247:21

mental health, 513:8; 1116:1

mental illness (*also see* madness), 6:1, 4; 598:7; 942:17; 987:6; 1002:1; 1108:6, 8, 13; 1178:7; 1185:17; 1207:3; 1247:6; 1301:1

mental institution, 1054:13; 1207:4; 1301:1

mental retardedness, 615:38; 1067:2

mental telepathy, 973:2

merchandising (*also see* advertising; publicity), 1029:3

mercy, 19:5; 64:12, 24; 124:6; 619:102; 907:2; 1016:6; 1302:2

mermaid, 180:4

metaphor, 687:2

Mexican-Americans, 561:22; 1317:3; women ～, 1317:2

middle age (*see* age, middle)

middle class (*see* bourgeoisie; classes, middle)

middle of the road, 546:8; 626:6

militancy, 265:9; 484:2; 1197:1

militarism, 121:5; 215:35; 350:27; 366:8; 480:9; 516:10; 684:7; opposition to ～, 441:4

military, the (*see* armed forces)

Millay, Edna St. Vincent, 687:9

mime, 387:9

mind, the (*also see* intelligence; reason), 61:7; 117:25; 336:4, 5; 500:2; 642:8; 682:1; 697:3; 740:29; 1191:2; 1265:5; cultivated ～, 259:7, 8; empty ～, 1185:10; flexibility of ～, 368:14; limitations of ～, 1111:23; military ～, 804:32; state of ～, 417:1; 949:25

miracle, 386:29; 537:7; 598:15; 855:48; 1224:10

mirror, 763:24, 26; 1209:2

mischief, 9:6; 395:3; 771:1

misery, 64:31; 292:1; 470:4; 603:19; 671:3; 744:5; 748:1; 941:5; 981:11; 983:3

mishap, 624:16

misogyny, 154:14; 572:6; 622:2; 1095:16; 1224:2

missionary, 615:20; 910:12; 931:15; 993:1; 1081:2; 1265:9

mistake, 84:10, 18; 98:6; 152:2; 318:1; 408:25; 528:75; 615:25; 881:9; 907:7; 1104:7; 1191:4; 1245:5

mistress, 426:4; 624:7; 642:26; 1329:3

moderation, 75:2; 576:12; 603:4; 757:3

modernity, 156:11

modesty, 8:6; 132:9; 240:19; 273:4; 887:1; 974:2; 1334:6

monarchy, 25:1; 1159:8

money, 14:1; 57:11; 127:9; 132:13, 17; 145:1; 186:10; 208:2; 228:5; 274:1; 305:1; 306:4; 386:17; 404:10; 416:21; 425:7; 454:1; 489:4; 578:5; 598:5; 603:13, 22; 642:22; 670:3; 724:14; 725:3; 776:4; 839:2; 850:16; 855:12, 24; 859:5; 888:2; 943:2; 986:6; 996:9; 1020:4; 1101:2; 1145:8; 1161:7; 1164:1; 1185:12; 1234:6; 1264:2; 1277:5; acquisition of ～, 228:7; 897:2; Americans and ～, 1269:5; evil of ～, 748:2; saving ～, 528:77; women and ～, 794:1; 1269:1, 2

monogamy, 95:21; 447:1; 532:11; 640:53; 1145:2; 1330:2

Monroe, Marilyn, 1142:10; 1211:11

monster, 1009:5

Montessori, Maria, 985:7

moon, 74:4; 101:20; 408:20

morale, 693:10

morality, 12:10; 18:11, 15; 20:2; 125:5; 148:1; 240:14; 265:9, 20; 278:4, 12; 350:3; 416:3; 450:1; 453:1; 468:8; 526:1; 563:15; 586:3, 5; 608:6; 633:1; 684:5; 795:26, 37; 811:5; 1062:13; 1103:4; 1130:2; 1144:7; 1173:3; middle-class ～, 882:16

morning, 198:1; 1252:3

mortality, 91:10; 719:1; 901:7

Moscow, 729:4; 1011:2

motherhood/mother (*also see* parents), 19:31; 36:25; 45:42, 46, 58, 73; 75:3; 88:3; 95:6, 11, 12; 132:32; 193:7; 215:3, 27, 29; 243:1; 246:17; 281:23, 25, 32, 35; 291:6; 324:3; 343:3; 384:4; 387:13, 22, 23, 34, 43; 441:9; 459:11; 467:4; 514:1; 516:13, 19, 23; 517:2; 518:2; 551:2; 570:6; 581:4; 583:4; 639:9; 667:4; 668:1, 2; 683:9; 731:5; 797:3, 5; 822:3; 824:50; 830:8; 838:2; 886:20; 992:3; 1001:1; 1031:3; 1043:2, 3; 1057:2; 1059:13; 1082:2; 1242:1, 2; 1252:5; 1264:3; 1327:3; glorification of ～, 281:26; 1327:2; inadequaiies of ～, 281:24, 46; ～-in-law, 823:19; ～ in relation to children, 228:14; 439:6; 553:7; 906:3; 1111:18; overbearing ～, 559:1; 1027:9; overprotective ～, 228:2; rights of ～, 459:9; stage ～, 894:1; unwed ～, 387:35; 615:40; 913:5; 1313:1; welfare ～, 913:5; working ～, 215:30; 281:33; 441:1

mountain (*also see* hill), 348:2; 436:4; 457:4

mourning (*also see* grief), 12:7; 29:5; 36:39; 55:2; 500:5; 566:12; 637:4

movement, physical, 650:1, 2

movement, social (*also see* specific *movements*), 989:1; 1142:14

movie (*see* film)

mulatto, 1059:7

murder (*also see* killing), 309:1; 603:8; 652:4; 784:1; 804:14; 1307:3
Museum of Modern Art, New York, 1020:3
music (*also see* opera; singing; song; symphony), 15:22; 31:32; 98:7; 242:6; 263:6; 322:2; 385:6; 386:14; 459:8; 469:1, 2, 5; 481:3; 615:48; 619:64, 65; 676:1; 893:1; 909:2; 927:17; 1052:1; 1089:4; 1228:4; American ~, 459:15; blues, 861:3; composing ~, 1199:1; gospel ~, 861:2, 3; ~ lover, 676:8; ~ lyrics, 573:1; recording of ~, 1045:1; rock ~, 1018:7; women in ~, 1283:1
musical instruments, 355:3
music business, 902:4; 1087:1; sexism in ~, 1087:1
musician, 31:32; 263:6; 811:1; 999:4
muteness, 425:1
mysticism, 78:5
mystique, 971:11
mythology, 22:1; 230:3; 872:3; 890:17; 910:4; Roman ~, 711:17

N

nagging, 306:11
naïveté, 32:6; 270:2; 386:24; 472:7; 687:20; 715:9; 768:5; 874:4
name, 45:78
Naples, Italy, 408:17
Napoleon, 19:4
Napoleonic Wars, 878:2
narcissism, 31:38; 640:1; 816:7; 824:32; 946:14
narrow-mindedness, 246:5; 459:3; 554:8; 683:2; 949:16; 955:1
nation, 19:53; 246:36, 37; 688:6; 855:1; 1216:11; confidence in ~, 528:48; 760:19; differences between ~, 624:20; 1033:6; hypocrisy of ~, 215:33; relations among ~, 760:12; 878:15; 924:5
national defense, 688:2; 878:5; 1075:1
nationalism (*also see* patriotism), 376:1; 451:1; 563:10; 1011:1
National Organization of Women, 1018:2; 1024:8
national security, 684:8; 712:4; 924:7
natives, 416:18; 535:11
naturalness, 5:15; 61:1; 892:2
nature (*see* human nature)
Nature, 11:1; 12:6; 15:11, 27, 28; 31:16; 36:50; 45:16; 61:9; 85:4; 95:10, 22; 103:5; 117:9; 127:10; 156:15; 246:30; 269:1; 294:1; 308:3; 335:2; 349:1; 368:2; 384:4, 7; 385:13; 387:109; 413:2, 528:5; 566:14; 574:18; 586:5; 603:4; 604:2; 618:1; 619:3; 643:6; 667:5; 669:12; 715:19; 717:3; 753:1; 795:33; 812:10, 22; 849:3; 858:5; 881:5; 930:1; 956:1; 985:6; 1053:2; 1141:2; 1265:10; 1285:1
Nazi, 538:2; 790:1, 2; Hitler Youth Organization, 790:2
nearness, 230:1; 306:14
neatness (*see* orderliness)

necessity, 15:1; 44:1; 246:23; 266:20; 346:3; 619:15; 855:45
needs, 388:1; 855:30; 1145:17; 1281:1
negativity, 921:6; 1197:7
negligence, 55:21; 615:41; 764:3
Negro (*see* blacks)
Nehru, Pandit Jawaharlal, 924:14
neighborhood, mixed, 1193:1
nervousness, 416:38; 445:2
Netherlands, the (*see* Holland)
neurosis, 537:8; 571:1; 613:3; 763:23; 942:16; 1111:7
New England (*also see* United States), 214:2; 408:28; 626:6; slavery in ~, 36:23
news, 906:5; 981:17; 1279:1; bad ~, 1110:7; unexpected ~, 36:19
newspaper, 161:5; 484:8; ~ editor, 896:3; exaggeration in ~, 333:10; 742:1; sensationalism in ~, 310:7
newspapermen (*see* journalist)
New Year, 137:2; 980:8
New York City, 281:54; 468:6; 527:3; 701:3; 715:3; 884:3; 942:18; 1134:8; 1144:1; 1148:10; 1161:5; 1181:4
night, 13:1; 139:1; 147:1; 618:1; 619:70, 72; 856:1; 1185:21
nightmare, 790:5; 987:1; 1148:1
Nixon, Richard M., 528:36, 69, 74; 655:5; 965:1, 2; 1000:7; 1218:6
Nobel Prize Committee, 1073:1
nonconformity, 228:11; 453:1; 494:3; 711:15; 1257:4
nonviolence, 1216:8, 10
normalcy, 416:14; 1067:3
North, the/Northerners, U.S. (*also see* United States), 11:4; 88:7
nose, 12:2
nosiness, 232:3; 274:2; 315:2; 561:23; 725:12; 732:1; 786:3; 847:1; 1159:3
nostalgia, 256:3; 824:28
nothing, 616:15; 696:3; 804:42; 1107:5; 1110:13
novel (*also see* fiction; writing), 620:10; 1025:7; 1112:2
novelist (*see* writer)
November, 132:12
NOW (*see* National Organization of Women)
nuclear power, use of, 976:1
nudity, 109:1; 553:5; 671:6
nuisance, 733:1
nun, 83:6; 219:3, 5; 612:1; 720:4, 5; black ~, 1263:1; education of ~, 587:1
Nuremberg Trials, 799:11
nursing/nurse, 45:61; 78:2; 438:5; 491:1; 554:1; 628:4
nutrition, 255:2; 772:1, 2, 4, 5, 6, 7

O

oath, legal, 820:18
obedience, 219:2, 3; 333:1; 720:5; 878:11; 1002:1; blind ~, 1295:4

sexes, the *(also see* men; relationships between men and women; women), conflict between ∼, 441:6; 628:13; 889:1; differences between ∼, 31:39; 47:26; 68:8; 95:2; 196:2; 215:25; 224:3; 247:13; 279:6; 281:58; 287:19; 291:3, 11; 394:4; 439:7; 501:2; 620:30; 642:12; 740:6, 7, 10,15, 20, 26, 29; 820:4; 821:1; 824:31; 929:1, 2; 958:2; 975:5; 988:19; 1009:10; 1015:4; 1024:1; 1033:7; 1052:1; 1089:1; 1112:3; 1140:1; 1142:5; 1145:13; 1160:10; 1185:12; 1192:2; 1204:8; 1213:4; 1224:4; 1245:15; 1266:1; 1289:2; 1320:4; mistrust between ∼, 824:23; roles of ∼, 95:8; 281:10; 350:16; 508:34; 740:4, 21; 805:6; 889:1; 960:3; 971:20; 988:2; 1157:2; 1320:4

sexism *(also see* male supremacy; prejudice), 8:26; 45:1, 5, 66, 74; 63:4, 9; 265:9, 13; 619:62; 666:3; 672:1; 740:14, 22; 782:2; 872:4; 910:8; 951:2; 969:1; 988:10; 1018:7, 8; 1034:13; 1050:11; 1063:1; 1120:4; 1140:1; 1142:5; 1143:3; 1166:1; 1175:6; 1194:2; 1214:1; 1224:6; 1257:3; 1259:2; 1266:1; 1271:1

sex manual, 1132:1

sex symbol, 865:2

shade, 403:6

Shakespeare, William, 19:16; 167:5; 212:4; 215:18; 278:3; 850:11

shame, 372:1; 643:2

sharing, 487:5; 616:20; 1088:2; 1220:5

Shaw, George Bernard, 315:3

Shelley, Percy Bysshe, 640:18

ship, 124:16; 435:1; 598:14; 815:1

shopping, 772:5; window ∼, 839:1

shortcoming, 850:8; 877:11

shortsightedness, 152:2; 279:7; 764:2

show business *(also see* entertainment; theater; vaudeville), 530:1; 837:2

shyness *(see* timidity)

sibling *(also see* sister), 8:30

sight, 828:2; 1265:6

significance, 446:2; 603:3; 619:7; 797:2

silence, 19:21; 64:41; 96:6; 101:13; 130:3; 151:3; 247:19; 362:1; 387:9, 12; 458:3; 511:10; 615:11; 830:3; 850:2; 886:20; 890:18; 985:11; 1095:15; 1163:3; 1187:5; inner ∼, 720:2

simplicity, 132:3; 266:4; 317:3; 715:18; 721:3; 767:1; 882:1

sin/sinner, 84:6, 13; 163:1; 190:1; 323:3; 597:3; 598:17; 619:23; 642:15; 779:2; 791:7; 804:17; 855:35; 913:7; 1054:4

singing/singer *(also see* music; opera), 225:4; 1067:6; 1135:1; bad ∼, 282:4; 820:1

singleness *(also see* bachelor), 8:31; 15:20; 63:10; 132:37; 350:10; 439:9, 15; 900:7; 942:8; 949:21; 969:1; 979:1; 988:7; 1021:1; 1225:2; discrimination toward ∼, 666:4

sister *(also see* sibling), 123:14; 132:18; 981:3; 1088:1, 2

skepticism, 118:16; 882:18; 1101:4

sky, 103:11; 117:25; 565:5

slander, 253:4; 684:9; 754:6; 880:3

Slav, 624:17

slave, 30:2; 46:3; 196:6; 1258:1, 3; achievements of ∼, 46:3; woman ∼, 356:1

slavery, 18:10; 20:7; 30:4; 36:2, 18; 46:1, 2, 4; 88:7, 8; 196:4; 246:31; 516:4; 727:1; 855:2; 902:3; 924:9; 927:4; 1125:2

sleep, 62:1; 96:3; 103:1; 119:4; 131:2; 134:1; 146:1; 147:1; 207:10; 289:3; 343:1; 346:8; 387:61, 63; 472:3; 554:4; 619:31; 620:18; 757:1; 830:6; 839:5; 974:13; 1029:1

sleepiness, 287:7

smile, 189:2; 247:3; 287:20; 387:15; 467:8; 620:13; 840:19; 1110:3; 1185:7; 1256:8; 1301:2

snail, 519:1

snobbery/snob, 32:2; 68:6; 391:2; 404:7; 461:4; 514:2; 548:2; 688:12; 736:1; 1315:3; food ∼, 744:6

snow, 123:29

social intercourse, 55:12; 83:1; 744:4

socialism/socialist, 281:55; 504:5; 619:17; 644:4; 693:19; 1168:6; 1206:2; 1213:1

social welfare, 952:2; 960:1; 1017:1, 2; 1037:2; 1236:1, 2

society *(also see* civilization), 19:46; 31:22; 368:4; 528:20; 615:37; 643:4; 740:3; 795:34; 805:5; 824:40; 867:1; 1178:5; 1249:9; fashionable ∼, 4:12; 104:2; 118:1; 162:8; 240:1; 620:11; 777:5; 1190:2; ideals of ∼, 624:20; 1000:8; oppressive ∼, 855:23; 1197:7; primitive ∼, 740:25; 971:7

Socrates, 336:13, 14

soldier *(also see* veteran), 29:4; 106:1; 216:1; 272:3; 350:28; 386:24; 471:2; 502:2; 615:6; 619:87; 665:2; 704:1; 797:4, 5; 822:4; 1203:1; mother of ∼, 553:7; wife of ∼, 988:15

solidarity, 17:2; 399:2

solitude *(also see* aloneness), 12:6; 132:43; 142:1; 186:14; 234:2; 289:2; 386:32; 443:1; 456:4; 511:5; 816:8; 931:13; 1095:13; 1181:5; 1187:4; 1247:9

solution *(also see* answer), 86:1; 554:2; 805:8

son, 101:26; 320:8; 439:6; 583:1, 3; 670:6; 988:16; 1034:6; 1048:15

song *(also see* music), 162:5; 632:2

sophistication, 68:3; 365:2; 404:7; 574:10; 598:9; 1144:10; 1152:2; pseudo ∼, 1316:2

sophistry, 760:12

sorrow *(also see* grief), 98:2; 119:5; 124:3, 9; 132:30; 151:3; 197:3; 214:12; 247:1; 263:2; 333:8; 529:2, 4; 543:3; 570:1; 615:34; 619:23; 669:2; 783:2; 830:4; 835:1; 909:3; 1193:12

soul *(also see* the spirit) 15:30; 19:36; 31:6; 40:12, 43:3; 45:45; 47:17; 57:4; 117:29; 124:14; 221:9; 246:5; 247:14; 413:3; 466:3, 4; 508:6; 529:5; 619:1, 4; 664:1; 711:12; 743:6; 809:1; 1223:1

sounds, 978:1

wholeness, 489:6; 820:19

wholesomeness, 1146:8

wickedness (*also see* evil), 36:3, 7; 124:6; 586:4

widow/widower, 103:9; 321:2; 576:17; 660:2; 988:15; 1038:1, 3; 1065:1; 1111:20; 1145:7

wife, 5:14; 31:2; 88:3; 124:4; 196:1; 281:34; 306:5; 323:10; 477:1; 547:6; 628:6; 636:8; 687:17, 23; 693:1; 882:25; 988:9; 1329:3; 1333:2; American ~, 1333:1; ~ beating, 930:3; role of ~, 229:5; 575:4; 1051:2; working ~, 820:22

wilderness, 103:7; 206:2; 931:10

wildlife (*also see* animal), 225:7; 294:2; 384:2, 9; 535:5, 6; 667:2; 812:3; 832:1

wiles, 387:80; 511:1

Wilhelm II, Kaiser, 878:1

Wilson, Woodrow, 251:2; 269:5

wind, 123:30; 340:4; 728:3; 1002:3

windfall, 156:8; 228:5

wine, 12:11

winning (*also see* victory), 118:8; 984:1

winter, 30:8; 117:11; 386:11; 483:9; 566:26; 667:2; 840:10; 1002:2; 1191:3

wisdom (*also see* knowledge), 15:57; 84:5; 246:9; 320:1; 408:19; 439:19; 493:2; 534:1; 582:1; 619:104; 640:4; 796:4; 799:25; 886:3; 927:1; 1126:6

wisecrack, 640:46

wistfulness, 1193:6

wit, 266:13, 29; 287:10; 306:16; 414:4; 508:37; 640:46; 791:25; 1211:5

witchcraft/witch, 276:1; 872:4; 973:3; 1148:2; 1332:1

withdrawal, 117:26; 416:9; 546:2; 981:8; 1059:20; 1214:2

wizard, 872:4

wolf, 832:1

womanliness, 224:3; 1006:1; 1242:3

womb, 760:16; 763:21

women (*also see* the sexes), 15:5; 55; 45:23, 27, 84; 47:11; 61:4; 63:2; 64:13; 70:11, 12; 76:4; 83:9; 95:13, 16; 124:7; 154:21; 162:1; 246:7, 21, 38; 247:9; 252:3; 263:4; 278:6; 281:9; 306:8; 310:11; 334:2; 340:1; 342:1; 355:8; 387:65; 395:2, 4; 404:15; 405:2; 406:1; 417:2; 418:7; 439:1; 468:8; 489:9; 501:3; 508:26; 516:19; 520:1; 532:9; 535:2, 3; 538:1; 571:2; 578:30; 642:5, 25; 649:1; 652:1; 660:6; 687:10, 28; 711:10, 11; 715:1; 740:20; 760:5; 763:29, 30; 791:5; 796:2; 815:1, 2; 824:6; 840:11; 865:2; 869:1; 877:6; 890:16; 913:3; 959:1, 2; 974:2, 3, 5, 11; 1015:9, 10; 1024:2; 1056:3; 1066:3, 15; 1095:1; 1101:10; 1111:14, 15; 1120:3; 1122:5; 1142:6; 1191:2; 1204:9; 1207:1; 1209:1; 1227:3; 1249:8; accomplishments of ~, 132:35; 229:1, 2, 4; aging ~, 64:55; 351:7; 372:8; 387:4, 21; 578:10; 605:2; 642:25; 1185:15; alternatives for ~, 930:5; 1242:2; appearance of ~, 587:7; 837:11; 885:1; 1107:2; capabilities of ~, 31:14; 36:52; 45:18;

70:7; 250:1; 671:5; 672:1; 764:6; 769:1; 924:18; 1026:3; 1105:2; 1204:1; 1227:1; career ~, 229:3; 693:21; 900:2, 3; 988:7; 1028:1; competition and ~, 971:17; 1230:1; conditioning of ~ (*also see* girl, conditioning of; women, image of), 95:15; 971:1; 1054:8; 1140:3, 8; country ~, 662:1; dependent ~, 763:44; 805:1; 922:3; 929:3; 967:4; dissatisfactions of ~, 925:4; duplicity of ~, 355:11; 725:7; 749:2; 1160:9; equality of ~, 17:2; 18:19; 31:4; 45:7, 33, 34, 35, 36, 41; 261:2; 265:21; 413:6; 520:9; 591:7; 760:21; 1018:3; 1105:2; 1130:11; exceptional ~, 45:4; 769:2; 804:12; 1142:9; exploitation of ~, 15:10; 825:6; 1142:4, 5; 1249:9; 1333:1; growth of ~, 910:6; 1227:2; 1240:12; history of ~, 36:25; 558:20; 882:11; 1266:3; 1328:3; idealized ~, 215:16; 323:8; 744:11; 993:9; image of ~, 708:1; 760:23; 782:1; 878:10; 911:3; 951:4; 1018:8; 1056:2; 1240:5, 11, 15; 1271:4; independent ~, 45:50, 73, 85; 350:6; 395:10; 485:3; inferiority of ~, 31:3; 350:18; influence of ~, 18:1; 20:1; 712:3; 1025:5; ~ in relation to men (*also see* relationships, between men and women), 15:52; 36:14, 47; 45:14; 54:3; 70:3; 132:35; 171:1; 246:7, 27; 286:1; 287:22; 291:8; 350:9; 439:12; 501:6; 508:18; 532:11; 601:3; 615:29; 623:11; 640:2; 645:5; 686:1; 760:29; 779:3; 806:9; 808:2; 820:11; 825:9; 837:11; 877:8; 882:22; 884:1; 898:2; 930:2; 953:7, 10; 986:4; 988:2; 1089:2; 1111:3; 1187:3; 1197:3; 1205:3; 1216:12; 1227:4; 1231:1; 1234:1; 1249:7; 1298:1; 1311:1; ~ in relation to women (*also see* friendship, among women), 18:13; 34:1; 132:33; 467:3; 877:8; 946:15; 1006:1; intellectual ~, 118:3; 520:2; 639:3; 1160:8; intelligence of ~, 246:12; 501:2; 804:24; 951:1; 1200:3; limitations of ~, 45:22; 560:5; 823:17; 1018:1; 1145:15; 1204:7; 1246:3; militant ~, 265:6, 22; 1147:2; modern ~, 246:33; 350:2; 506:2; 655:1; morality of ~, 508:28; 561:31; 1142:3; needs of ~, 31:21; 319:3; 530:2; objectification of ~, 195:3; 729:3; 954:1; 1231:6; 1298:1; older ~, 326:3; 620:12; oppressed ~, 8:7, 28; 15:52; 17:1; 18:12; 45:8; 56:1; 70:17; 88:1; 196:1; 395:6; 430:10; 537:4; 683:9; 715:4; 760:15; 910:8; 1007:7; 1015:7; 1037:1; passive ~, 51:2; 55:7; 1140:8; power of ~, 20:2; 1158:5; 1195:1; progress of ~, 121:3; 246:8, 33; 571:3; repressed ~, 31:43; 45:67; 70:2; 1111:16; 1181:1; reproductive function of ~, 498:2, 3; 1247:21; responsibilities of ~, 20:1; 95:20; 350:29; 516:6; 1236:3; revolution and ~, 122:1; 834:3; role of ~ (*also see* housewife), 1:1; 30:7; 36:28; 45:70; 64:20; 70:3; 95:7; 157:1; 195:4; 215:26; 302:1; 350:28; 360:1; 386:31; 407:1; 508:22; 516:5; 558:16; 615:8; 693:1; 740:8, 9, 25; 775:6; 805:2; 890:2; 910:5, 13; 971:13; 1019:1; 1024:4; 1038:1; 1147:2; 1188:4; 1194:1; 1207:2, 3;